Key to Hardiness Zones

This map shows eleven geographical zones based on the average annual minimum temperatures recorded for the years 1974 to 1986. The zone numbers accompanying the plants in this book indicate their lower limits of winter cold hardiness. Extreme summer heat and humidity also play a part in a plant's adaptability; many plants hardy in colder zones grow poorly in warmer, wetter ones.

Zone	Temperature
1	below –50°F below –46°C
2	–50° to –40°F –46° to –40°C
3	–40° to –30°F –40° to –34°C
4	–30° to –20°F –34° to –29°C
5	–20° to –10°F –29° to –23°C
6	–10° to 0°F –23° to –18°C
7	0° to 10°F –18° to –12°C
8	10° to 20°F –12° to –7°C
9	20° to 30°F –7° to –1°C
10	30° to 40°F –1° to 4°C
11	above 40°F above 4°C

THE HERB SOCIETY OF AMERICA

ENCYCLOPEDIA of HERBS & THEIR USES

"...and what I have been preparing to say is, that in Wildness is the preservation of the World. Every tree sends its fibers forth in search of the Wild. The cities import it at any price. Men plow and sail for it. From the forest and wilderness come the tonics and barks which brace mankind..."

Henry David Thoreau, Walden, or Life in the Woods, *1854*

THE HERB SOCIETY OF AMERICA

ENCYCLOPEDIA of HERBS & THEIR USES

DENI BOWN

DK

DORLING KINDERSLEY

LONDON • NEW YORK • STUTTGART • MOSCOW

A Dorling Kindersley Book

To PJ, who understands the sense in which this is a life's work, and to our daughters, Anna and Dani, and sons, Will, Robin, and Ben

Project Editor Laura Langley
Editor Claire Folkard
US Editor Ray Rogers
Additional editorial assistance Maureen Rissik

US Consultant Holly H. Shimizu

Project Art Editor Rachel Gibson
Designer Julian Holland
Additional design assistance Gillian Andrews, Ursula Dawson, Sasha Kennedy, Rachael Parfitt
DTP Designer Chris Clark

Managing Editor Francis Ritter
Managing Art Editor Gillian Allan

Photographers Deni Bown, Andrew de Lory, Christine Douglas, Neil Fletcher, Nancy Gardiner, Tony Rodd, Matthew Ward, Steven Wooster
Illustrators Karen Cochrane, Martine Collings, Valerie Hill
Production Hilary Stephens, Ruth Charlton
Picture Research Anna Lord

IMPORTANT NOTICE
The author and the publishers can accept no liability for any harm, damage, or illness arising from the misuse of the plants described in this book.

First American Edition 1995
2 4 6 8 10 9 7 5 3 1

Published in the United States by Dorling Kindersley Publishing Inc., 95 Madison Avenue, New York, New York 10016

Published in Great Britain by Dorling Kindersley Limited
Distributed by Houghton Mifflin Company, Boston

Library of Congress Cataloging-in-Publication Data
Bown, Deni.
Encyclopedia of Herbs and their uses by Deni Bown – 1st American ed.
p. cm
Includes index.
ISBN 0-7894-0184-3
1. Herbs–Encyclopedias. 2. Herbs–Pictorial works. 3. Herb Gardening. I. Title.
SB351 .H5B645 1995
581.6'3'03–dc20 95–8171
CIP

Text film output by Graphical Innovations, London
Color reproduction by GRB Editrice, Italy
Printed and bound in Italy by A. Mondadori Editore, Verona

CONTENTS

PREFACE 6
AUTHOR'S INTRODUCTION 7
HOW TO USE THIS BOOK 8

Plant Classification and Legal Restrictions 10
Herb Culture Through the Ages 12
Herbs in Myth and Legend 14
Herbs that Changed the World 16
Herbal Books 18

DESIGNING AN HERB GARDEN 20
FORMAL GARDEN DESIGNS 22
Geometric Garden 22
A Knot Garden 24
Color Wheel Raised Beds 25
DESIGNS FOR A PURPOSE 26
Potpourri Herb Bed 26
Repeating Border Pattern 28
An Island Bed of Culinary Herbs 29
INFORMAL GARDEN DESIGNS 30
Individual Garden Areas 30
Mediterranean Herb Bed 32
Woodland Herb Garden 33

HERBS AMONG THE FLOWERS 34
White Bed with Herbs 34
A Mixed Border with Herbs 36
Herbs in a Rose Garden 37

A VEGETABLE POTAGER 38
A Garden of Variety 38

HERBS IN CONTAINERS 40
A Culinary Windowbox 40
A Planter of Home Remedies 41
Colorful Urn of Herbs 41

USING HERBS 42
Culinary Uses of Herbs 44
Medicinal Uses of Herbs 46
Cosmetic Uses of Herbs 48

HERBS IN THE WILD 50
North America 52
Central and South America 54
Europe 56
Africa 58
The Middle East 60
The Indian Subcontinent 62
China and its Neighbors 64
Australasia 66
Southeast Asia 67

THE HERB CATALOG 68
Including features on:
Allium 80
Artemisia 88
Capsicum 100
Lavandula 148
Mentha 158
Ocimum 166
Origanum 168
Pelargonium 172
Prunus 184
Rosmarinus 192
Salvia 196
Tanacetum 208
Thymus 212

THE HERB DICTIONARY 224

CULTIVATING HERBS 374
Style and Site 376
Choosing and Planting Herbs 378
Herbs in Containers 380
Growing under Cover 382
Routine Garden Care 384
Methods of Propagation 386
Vegetative Propagation 388
Harvesting Your Crop 390
Processing and Storing 392

GLOSSARY OF TERMS 394
INDEX 400
HERB GARDENS TO VISIT 423
BOOKS FOR FURTHER READING 423
ACKNOWLEDGMENTS 424

Preface

The mission of The Herb Society of America is to promote the knowledge, use, and delight of herbs through educational programs, research, and sharing the experience of its members with the community. It is committed to protecting our global environment for the health and well-being of humankind and all growing things, and also encourages gardeners to practice environmentally sound horticulture.

The Herb Society of America Encyclopedia of Herbs and Their Uses supports this mission and will enlighten its readers about the rich world of herbs – reconfirming their ability to enhance the quality of life and bring delight to any garden. This book provides comprehensive information on herb cultivation and growth in the wild, along with extensive coverage of contemporary and historic herb usage. It also distinguishes itself by combining many diverse elements, clearly and concisely, for easier understanding of the relevance of herbs in today's world. This encyclopedia advocates an ecological approach to herb use and cultivation, and it is sensitive to the conservation efforts that need to go hand in hand with herb culture and harvest. The presentation of herbal traditions around the world offers a global view on the importance of herbs in many aspects of people's lives.

Plant descriptions and detailed photographs provide the reader with a thorough knowledge and appreciation of this fascinating and wide-ranging subject. Creative and innovative herb garden designs will inspire many themes and layouts, and the book's original approach to the world of herbs suggests new ways of looking at and considering new herbal combinations, particularly in food and medicine.

By linking practical garden information with historical insight, current research findings, and creative garden designs, *The Herb Society of America Encyclopedia of Herbs and Their Uses* offers a holistic, fresh approach that is truly inspiring.

Holly H. Shimizu
Former National Chairman
of Botany & Horticulture
The Herb Society of America
Washington, DC, Summer, 1995

Author's Introduction

When my interest in herbs began 30 years ago, few kitchens had more than a packet of dried mixed herbs. I have vivid memories of discovering herbs as a student: on my first visit to an Indian restaurant, finding what appeared to be a dead leaf in the curry (*ecce*, bay!), and handling basil seedlings for the first time, scenting my fingers and the air with an exhilarating aroma.

As so often happens, an interest in herbs for cooking soon progressed to cosmetic and medicinal herbs, growing herbs, and also a fascination for how people around the world use herbs. My "bible" was *A Modern Herbal* by Mrs. Grieve, published in 1931, which began in response to a critical shortage of crude drug imports during World War I. Though only sparsely illustrated with black and white drawings, and the content inevitably no longer "modern," it has remained until now the most comprehensive herbal available.

Since the 1960s, interest in herbs has grown dramatically through increased travel and communication, and greater concern for health and the environment. As a result, the subject is becoming more specialized – ginkgo, for example, means quite different things to a gardener, a botanist, a pharmacologist, and a herbalist. New uses for traditional herbs, and even new herbs, have been discovered, which were all unknown to Mrs. Grieve. Hers was largely a war effort; our main battles are AIDS and stress in ourselves, loss of habitats, and rapid extinction of species in the plant world. Mrs. Grieve also lived in an era when herbs were imported with little concern for their origins or for their survival. We belong now to a multicultural society with trading partners, and are more aware of how and where herbs are produced, whether it is traditional saffron harvesting in Spain or the collection of medicinal plants from rainforests.

Herbs play a far greater part in our everyday lives than most of us realize. Both horticulture and botany began with the study of herbs: the earliest gardens were herb gardens, and the first botanic gardens started as physic gardens to educate medical students about drug plants. Herbs have changed the course of history, and in economic terms are nowadays of even greater importance as ingredients in food, medicine, perfumery, and cosmetics, as well as garden plants. I like to think that the gardener who plants a peony for its beauty will enjoy learning that it is also an ancient Chinese medicinal herb, now adopted by Western medicine to treat eczema in children.

All herbals build on earlier knowledge, while reflecting the practices and interests of the time. This book is no exception. Its aim is to draw strands of knowledge together, providing a reference source for the millenium that in turn will accommodate new information and perspectives. I hope, too, that it may stimulate the curiosity and imagination of its readers.

How to Use this Book

The Herb Society of America Encyclopedia of Herbs and Their Uses is a comprehensive encyclopedia of plants that provide a huge range of herbal uses. As well as containing an extensive illustrated Herb Catalog and Herb Dictionary, this encyclopedia includes features on many different aspects of herb cultivation and uses.

The Herb Catalog (pp.68–223)

Arranged in alphabetical order, each entry has an introductory description of the genus, together with information on distribution, other relevant species, and name derivations. A botanical description is given for every species or cultivar illustrated under the genus heading. Symbols refer to information given in the Dictionary, and to the hardiness of the plant. A select list of common names appears at the foot of each page.

The Herb Dictionary (pp.224–373)

The Dictionary contains entries for every genus listed in the encyclopedia, including a number not illustrated in the Catalog. This section discusses research into the genus, historical uses, and associations with legend or folklore. The parts of the plant used are listed, with their properties, and the uses to which the herb may be put (see also *Using Herbs*, pp.42–49). Concise information (in a box after each genus entry) on how the herbs grow and are harvested is expanded in the feature section *Cultivating Herbs* (pp.374–393).

Feature Sections

Feature sections appear throughout the book: on designing a herb garden in a variety of styles; on many uses of herbs, past and present, in the kitchen, for medicines, and in cosmetics and perfumery; a survey of herbs in their native habitats worldwide; and a comprehensive section on growing and propagating herbs.

The Herb Catalog

Symbols

Parts of the Plant that are Used

- Whole plant
- Leaves
- Stems
- Bark or wood
- Rhizomes, bulbs, corms, roots
- Flowers
- Fruit, pods
- Seeds
- Oil, sap, resin, gum, latex

Uses of the part of the plant

- Medicinal
- Culinary
- Economic
- Aromatic

Plant's Level of Hardiness

In this book, the ability of a plant to withstand winter temperatures is designated by the USDA hardiness zone numbers given in the Catalog entries, alongside the symbols under the plant descriptions. The temperature ranges indicated by these numbers are shown on the endpaper map in this book. Plants that do not tolerate any frost are described as tender, indicated by the letter T or this symbol:

Growing temperatures for tender plants are shown in the Growth and Harvest box that follows each entry in the Herb Dictionary, pp.224–373, within the following ranges:

1) Warm – minimum 65°F (18°C)
2) Intermediate – minimum 55°F (13°C)
3) Cool – minimum 50°F (10°C)

The letter A instead of a hardiness zone number indicates that the plant is an annual. Zone numbers are not given for annuals in this book, because most annuals are grown for only one season and then die, though some will seed and others may be restarted from cuttings.

Climatic Zones

The climates of the world are divided into four main zones and two intermediate zones. The growth and development of plants are influenced to a large extent by the climatic zone that they inhabit.

TROPICAL	High temperatures, high humidity, and heavy rainfall throughout the year.
DESERT	Daytime temperatures exceeding 100°F (38°C), cold nights, and annual rainfall of less than 10in (25cm).
TEMPERATE	Temperature and rainfall more evenly distributed throughout the year, but changeable from day to day, and varying greatly in local conditions.
POLAR	Extreme cold, high winds, and low precipitation.
SUBTROPICAL	High temperatures throughout the year, but marked seasonal rainfall.
MEDITERRANEAN	Hot, dry summers and mild, moist winters.

Climate also changes with altitude. Within all these zones, temperature drops by 11°F (6°C) for every 3250ft (1km) of increase in altitude.

1 Genus introduction
Gives the number of species in the genus, with their distributions. Suitability for garden planting is indicated. The name derivation of the genus is given in many cases. The family to which the genus belongs is shown in the Dictionary entry for that genus.

2 Plant portrait
Color photographs show every species or variety listed. A cultivar or variety illustration will follow that of its species.

3 Species name
The full botanical name is given for each plant. Any synonym will be found in the Dictionary entry for the genus.

4 Common names
Up to three common names are listed for each species. Generic common names appear with the genus entry in the Dictionary.

5 Plant description
Describes the species shown and the part of the plant used. Approximate height (H) and spread (S) when fully grown are given at the end of each caption. However, climatic and soil conditions of your site should be taken into account, since these may affect the ultimate size of the plant.

6 Symbols
Symbols below the plant description indicate the part of the herb used, the category of use, whether it is an annual, and the hardiness zones. A key to these symbols will be found in the box on this page.

ERYNGIUM

1

ERYNGIUM
A large genus of some 230 biennials and perennials, occurring in temperate and subtropical regions, especially in S America. *E. foetidum* is found in seasonally dry grassland in the West Indies, C America, and Florida; *E. maritimum* in coastal sand and pebble in Europe, northern Africa, and southwestern Asia. Many species are grown for their handsome foliage and long-lasting flowers, which often dry well. The metallic appearance of some species contrasts well with lime green or bronze foliage.

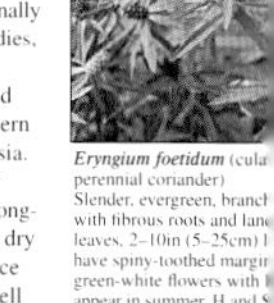

Eryngium maritimum (sea holly, eryngo)
Spiny perennial with very large, fleshy roots and leathery, blue-green, rounded leaves, 2–5in (5–12cm) across. Umbels of powder blue flowers, surrounded by spiny, leaflike bracts appear in summer. H and S 12–18in (30–45cm)
6–9

ERYTHROXYLUM
A genus of some 250 species of tropical trees and shrubs found mainly in the Americas and Madagascar. *E. coca* is native to high altitudes in the eastern Andes. Coca extracts provided the

2

3 *Eryngium foetidum* (culantro, fitweed,
4 false coriander)
5 Slender, evergreen, branched perennial with fibrous roots and lanceolate leaves, 2–10in (5–25cm) long, which have spiny-toothed margins. Numerous, green-white flowers with leafy bracts appear in summer. H and S 24in (60cm).
6

THE HERB DICTIONARY

The Herb Dictionary contains information on the development of the uses of herbal plants, the parts of the plant used, with their properties, and brief notes on growing and harvesting the species described.

WARNINGS AND LEGAL RESTRICTIONS

Warnings on the medicinal use of any herb are given under its entry in the Herb Dictionary, in the form of a WARNING appearing in the note on Medicinal Uses. Restrictions that may apply on the cultivation of any species are indicated by a WARNING in the Growth and Harvest box following each genus entry. There is also advice on the safe usage of herbs in the Introduction to *Using Herbs* (pp.42–43).

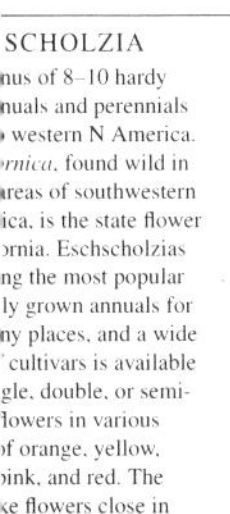

Eschscholzia californica (California poppy)

…lzia californica, Ballerina

7 ERYNGO, see *Eryngium maritimum*, above
ESERE BEAN, see *Physostigma venenosum*, p.327

7 FOOTNOTES
A select list of common names, following the order of the entries on the page above, is cross-referenced to the Herb Catalog or Dictionary entries. All names are indexed.

1 GENUS NAME
Full name, with family name, and generic common name, if any.

2 GENUS ENTRY
This discusses historical uses of relevant or related species, occurrence in legend or folklore, and development and research into modern applications.

3 SPECIES NAME
Synonyms and up to three common names are included, with a cross-reference to its entry in the Herb Catalog.

PLANT DESCRIPTION
Botanical description of any species not listed in the Herb Catalog.

4 PARTS USED
Listing the parts of the plant used, or material extracted, corresponding to the symbols shown in the Herb Catalog.

5 PROPERTIES
The herb's properties, for healing or other purposes.

6 USES OF THE HERB
How the herb is put to use, under four categories: Culinary, Aromatic, Medicinal, and Economic. Medicinal compounds with other herbs are indicated. Warnings are given of legal restrictions on the therapeutic use of the herb in any country.

CROSS-REFERENCE
Cross-references between genera are given throughout the Herb Dictionary. Cross-references to individual species are shown within the genus concerned.

7 VARIANT
The page number refers to the variant or cultivar's description and illustration in the Herb Catalog. If not illustrated in the Herb Catalog, the description will appear in the Herb Dictionary. The properties and uses of a variant are the same as those of the species unless otherwise shown.

8 GROWTH AND HARVEST
Gives cultivation category, followed by brief outline of how species described grows and is harvested, and how the parts used are processed. Legal restrictions on cultivation, if any, and warnings of toxicity or possible allergies. Advice on cultivation, invasive plants, companion planting, and pest and disease problems are included. Information may not apply to species not covered by this book.

CULTIVATION CATEGORIES
Every species is placed in one of three categories of cultivation and use, shown at the beginning of the Growth and Harvest box. These are as follows:
Ornamental – Herbs that are widely grown as ornamentals, as well as for use, and that make good garden plants.
Crop – Herbs that are mainly grown as crops for culinary, medicinal, and other uses. Some are common in herb nurseries and herb gardens, but are grown as plants for use, rather than as ornamentals.
Wild-collected – Herbs that are mainly harvested from the wild, and generally seldom cultivated. This group includes species that are difficult to cultivate, such as mosses, lichens, fungi, and seaweeds. It also includes species from countries where policies of conservation and cultivation are poorly developed.

1 CYTISUS Broom
(Leguminosae/Papilionaceae)

2 *C. scoparius* contains alkaloids, notably sparteine, which affect the heart and nerves in similar ways to curare (see *Chondrodendron* species, p.260, and *Strychnos* species, p.357). Its medicinal uses are listed in all the early European herbals under *Planta genista*, from which the British royal house of Plantagenet took its name.

3 ***C. scoparius***, syn. *Sarothamnus scoparius* (broom, Scotch broom) p.116

4 PARTS USED Whole plant.
5 PROPERTIES A bitter, narcotic herb that depresses respiration, regulates heart action, and has diuretic and purgative effects.
6 USES OF THE HERB
MEDICINAL Internally, mainly for heart complaints, especially with *Convallaria majalis* (see p.266) in heart failure. Excess causes respiratory collapse. Not given to pregnant women or patients with high blood pressure. For use by qualified practitioners only. WARNING This herb is subject to legal restrictions in some countries.
7 VARIANT
C. s. var. ***prostratus***, p.116.

8 GROWTH AND HARVEST
GROWTH Ornamental. Well-drained soil in sun. Propagate by seed sown under cover in spring or autumn, or by semiripe cuttings in summer. Germination is erratic. Cut back shoots by two-thirds after flowering. Cytisus does not transplant well. Subject to statutory control as a weed in some countries, notably in parts of Australia.
HARVEST Tops of shoots are cut as flowering begins and dried for use in decoctions, infusions, liquid extracts, and tinctures; stocks are renewed annually.
WARNING Toxic if eaten.

PLANT CLASSIFICATION AND LEGAL RESTRICTIONS

All plants are classified according to their relationships, much as we have a family tree to trace our origins. Relationships are established by shared characteristics, especially of reproductive parts. The binomial system we use today gives each plant a name in two Latinized words: the first is the name of the genus, and the second denotes the species. This system of classification was largely the work of the Swedish botanist Carl Linnaeus, and though later amended, is still accepted worldwide to identify plants.

UPPSALA UNIVERSITY
The Orangery in the gardens at Uppsala University, near Stockholm, Sweden. Carl Linnaeus was here from 1741 as a professor of medicine and later of botany. While at Uppsala he established his system of plant classification in several books, including Species Plantarum *(1753), and replanted the physic garden, which had been founded in 1655, accordingly.*

Traditionally, the plant kingdom consists of six divisions, given below, though more recent systems classify fungi as a kingdom separate from plants and animals. Further subdivisions separate the groups into classes and orders, and then into families, genera, and species.
1 Flowering plants (angiosperms) – herbaceous perennials, annuals, biennials, and many trees and shrubs.
2 Naked-seeded plants (gymnosperms) – conifers and related groups, such as cycads and ginkgo.
3 Ferns, clubmosses, and horsetails (pteridophytes).
4 Mosses and liverworts (bryophytes).
5 Fungi and lichens.
6 Algae (including seaweeds).

WHAT IS AN HERB?

The term "herb" also has more than one definition. Botanists describe an herb as a small, seed-bearing plant with fleshy, rather than woody, parts (from which we get the term "herbaceous"). In this book, it refers to a far wider range of plants. In addition to herbaceous perennials, herbs include trees, shrubs, annuals, vines, and more primitive plants, such as ferns, mosses, algae, lichens, and fungi. They are valued for their flavor, fragrance, medicinal and healthful qualities, economic and industrial uses, pesticidal properties, and coloring materials (dyes). Many people are skeptical about the effectiveness of herbal remedies, but there is no doubt that herbs contain ingredients that have a measurable effect on the body. Related herbs may have similar chemistry, but each herb, regardless of the family it belongs to, or which part is used, has unique constituents that are as individual as a fingerprint, though the proportions

CARL LINNAEUS (1707–78)
The great Swedish botanist, from Robert Thornton's The Temple of Flora *(1797–1807). Above his head is* Linnaea borealis, *a plant species named after him.*

PLANT CLASSIFICATION

Plants are further classified into smaller groups, to describe finer differences:
1 *Family* (group of related genera): e.g. Boraginaceae.
2 *Genus* (group of related species, indicated by the first part of the Latin name): e.g. *Borago*, *Symphytum*.
3 *Species* (individuals that are alike and naturally breed with each other, denoted by the second part of the Latin name): e.g. *Symphytum asperum*, *Symphytum officinale*.
4 *Hybrid* (cross between two species, which may happen in the wild, but more usually occurs accidentally or artificially in cultivation). A hybrid is given a different name from either parent: e.g. *Symphytum* x *uplandicum*, Russian comfrey (cross between *S. asperum* x *S. officinale*).
5 *Variety* (var.), subspecies (subsp.), and form (forma, f.) are subdivisions within a species or natural hybrid, that differ consistently in small but distinct ways from the type, e.g. *Symphytum officinale* var. *ochroleucum* (white-flowered comfrey). These natural variants are often rare in the wild but common in cultivation, having attractive differences in habit and/or color.
6 *Cultivar* (a variant, produced and maintained by cultivation, that has desirable characteristics of habit, color, flavor, etc.), e.g. *Symphytum* x *uplandicum* 'Variegatum'.

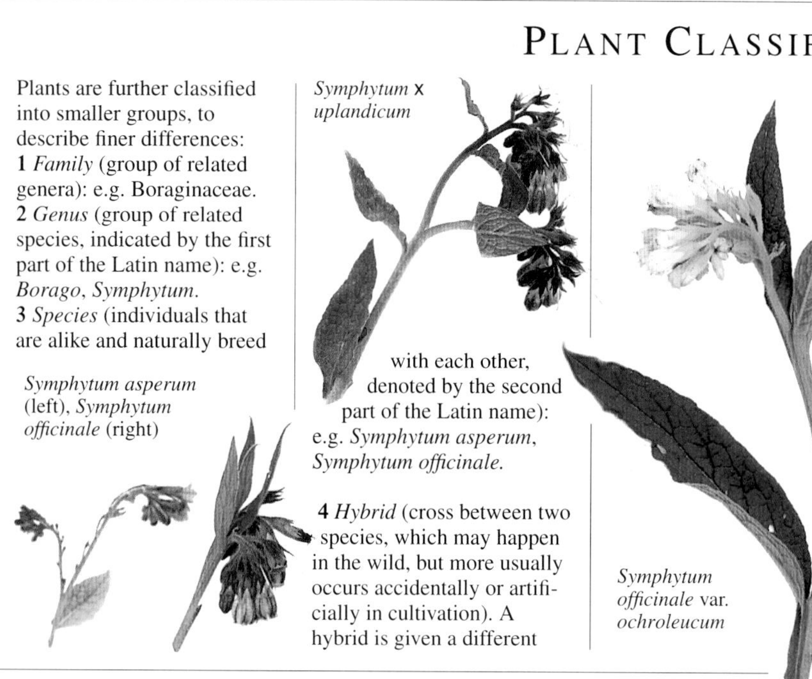

Symphytum x *uplandicum*

Symphytum asperum (left), *Symphytum officinale* (right)

Symphytum officinale var. *ochroleucum*

Symphytum x *uplandicum* 'Variegatum'

RHUBARB'S EARLY HISTORY
*Among the most important medicinal herbs is rhubarb root (*Rheum officinale *and* R. palmatum*), a laxative drug known in China as da huang. Records show that dried roots were exported from China along caravan routes to Europe as early as 114BC. Due to Chinese, and later Russian, monopolies, plants did not reach the West until the 1750s. Before this, great efforts were made to find suitable substitutes.* Rheum rhaponticum *was found in the Rhodope Mountains, Bulgaria, in about 1608, and was soon cultivated as a medicinal plant.*

of the constituents may fluctuate. The chemistry of most herbs is very complex – *Catharanthus roseus* is known to contain over 75 different alkaloids – and involves much research.

HOW PLANT INGREDIENTS WORK

Herbal medicines differ greatly from the compounds isolated or synthesized from them. The whole plant (and extracts derived from it) contains many ingredients that work together, and which may produce a quite different effect (known as a synergistic effect) from that of a constituent given on its own. An example is meadowsweet (*Filipendula ulmaria*), which contains salicylates (substances akin to aspirin). Meadowsweet contains healing ingredients, plus buffering substances that protect the mucous membranes from the corrosive effects of salicylates. The complex chemistry of the whole herb appears to lower the risk of side effects, whereas isolated compounds may be surprisingly toxic. This is especially true of volatile oils derived from herbs.

ACTIVE PLANT CONSTITUENTS

While the gardener and cook favor herbs rich in volatile oils, which give pleasurable aromas, those containing alkaloids and glycosides are of greater interest to pharmacologists. Some of the main active constituents found in herbs are:

ACIDS – these are sour, often antiseptic and cleansing, e.g. citric acid in *Citrus* species.
ALKALOIDS – bitter, often based on alkaline nitrogenous compounds; they affect the central nervous system, and many are very toxic and often addictive, e.g. *Papaver somniferum*.
ANTHRAQUINONES – these are bitter, irritant, and laxative, acting also as dyes, e.g. *Rheum palmatum*.
BITTERS – various compounds (mainly iridoids and sesquiterpenes) with a very bitter taste that increases appetite and improves digestion, e.g. *Gentiana lutea*.
COUMARINS – antibacterial and anticoagulant, with a smell of new-mown hay, e.g. *Melilotus officinalis*.
FLAVONES – these are bitter or sweet, often diuretic, antiseptic, antispasmodic, and anti-inflammatory. Typically yellow, and present in most plants, e.g. *Fagopyrum esculentum*.
GLYCOSIDES (four main kinds): cardiac – affecting heart contractions, e.g. *Digitalis lanata*; cyanogenic – bitter, antispasmodic, sedative, affecting heart rate and respiration, e.g. *Prunus serotina*; mustard oil – acrid, extremely irritant, e.g. *Sinapis alba*, and sulfur – acrid, stimulant, antibiotic, e.g. *Allium sativum*.
GUMS AND MUCILAGES – bland, sticky or slimy, soothing, and softening, e.g. marsh mallow (*Althaea officinalis*).
RESINS (often as oleoresins or oleogum resins) – acrid, astringent, antiseptic, healing, e.g. *Commiphora myrrha*.
SAPONINS – sweet, stimulant, hormonal; often anti-inflammatory or diuretic; soapy in water, e.g. *Saponaria officinalis*.
TANNINS – astringent, often antiseptic, checking bleeding and discharges, e.g. *Potentilla erecta*.
VOLATILE OILS – aromatic, antiseptic, fungicidal, irritant, and stimulant, e.g. *Thymus vulgaris*.

LEGAL RESTRICTIONS

A number of herbs discussed in this book are potentially dangerous. They are subject to legal restrictions regarding formulation, use, and sale, in three main categories:
- Poisonous therapeutic herbs
- Herbs that may be hazardous as garden plants
- Herbs that have become pernicious weeds outside their country of origin

RESTRICTIONS ON THERAPEUTIC USE
There are legal restrictions on the use, supply, and sale of many herbs intended for therapeutic use. They may apply to the whole herb, or to specific parts, preparations, or substances derived from it. Some herbs and their extracts are regarded as too toxic for general use and are subject to legislative control. These regulations differ from country to country, and are very complex. Restrictions also concern individuals permitted to prescribe, administer, supply, and sell certain herbs and preparations, and the permitted concentrations, doses, and preparations.

An indication of a restricted herb is shown in the Herb Dictionary (pp. 224-373) by the WARNING note in the entry concerned; detailed information may be obtained from the appropriate department of your government.

RESTRICTIONS ON CULTIVATION
A number of countries have legal restrictions on the cultivation of certain herbs. They concern those plants from which illegal drugs are produced, plus species that have been introduced and have spread widely, becoming weeds and threatening local flora and fauna. Laws and regulations governing dangerous drugs and plants are too complex to detail in this book. Readers are advised to obtain more information from the appropriate regulatory body on any herb that carries a WARNING in the Growth and Harvest box in the Herb Dictionary (pp. 224-373).

ANCIENT USES
*Meadowsweet (*Filipendula ulmaria*) is a herb with very ancient uses besides its medicinal applications. It was one of three herbs sacred in Druid worship, and because of its sweet smell was strewn on floors in the Middle Ages. Meadowsweet contains salicylates that relieve the pain of peptic ulcers, while other constituents protect and heal damaged tissues.*

HERB CULTURE THROUGH THE AGES

The history of herb culture is woven into the histories of peoples and civilizations. Wild plants depended upon from earliest times for food, medicine, fiber, and other raw materials were taken into cultivation, and were joined by others from farther afield as people traveled as a result of trade, warfare, or migration. Many medicinal herbs are also food, oil, and fiber plants, and have always been grown for a range of purposes. In most parts of the world herbs are still grown mainly as field crops, or on a small scale as odd crops among vegetables and ornamentals, as they were thousands of years ago.

EGYPTIAN GARDEN DESIGN
A formal, walled garden in ancient Egypt. Blue and white lotus flowers can be seen on the central pond.

▲ A SULTAN'S DIVAN
Islamic gardens were often enclosed, and contained a pool and scented flowers.

Some of the earliest herb gardens were planted about 4000 years ago in Egypt. Herb growing was often associated with temples, which required herbs and sacred flowers for daily worship and ritual. Olives (*Olea* spp.) and pomegranates (*Punica granatum*) were introduced to Egypt at a very early date; Queen Hatshepsut (c.1473–1458BC) had frankincense (*Boswellia sacra*) and myrrh (*Commiphora myrrha*). Cornflowers (*Centaurea cyanus*), poppies (*Papaver* spp.), mandrakes (*Mandragora* spp.), figs (*Ficus* spp.), and lotuses (*Nymphaea lotus*) appear in many wall paintings. Chamomile (*Chamaemelum nobile*) was identified by pollen analysis as the main herb constituent in the embalming oil used to mummify Rameses II, d.1224BC.

ISLAMIC AND CHRISTIAN GARDENS

The present-day concept of an herb garden (an open area with divisions for different kinds of herbs) has developed largely from ancient Egyptian, Christian, and Islamic religious traditions. Wherever cultivation is closely associated with buildings, it tends to be orderly, making economic use of space. In Islam, paradise is seen as an enclosed garden, with cool shade and water, and exquisite flowers and fruits. Islamic gardens contained roses (*Rosa* spp.), jasmine (*Jasminum* spp.), lilies (*Lilium* spp.), and trees such as apricots (*Prunus armeniaca*), pomegranates, and almonds (*Prunus dulcis*), often hedged with myrtle (*Myrtus communis*).

Early Christian monasteries resembled Roman villas in design. They also inherited Roman garden style, which was essentially geometric and formal. Favorite plants in Roman times included rosemary (*Rosmarinus officinalis*), bay (*Laurus nobilis*), and myrtle, together with hedges and topiary, grown as much for their scent and beauty as for their usefulness. Monastic gardening also owed much to Egyptian, Syrian, and Persian traditions, in which useful plants were grown in enclosures to protect them from animals, provide shade, and make the best use of water supplies in a dry climate.

SELF-SUFFICIENT MONASTERIES

The first Christian monastery was founded by St. Anthony in El Faiyum, northern Egypt, in 305AD. He made a small enclosed garden with a water supply to provide the basic necessities. Monastic cultivation became so firmly established that when St. Benedict founded the Benedictine order at Monte Cassino in Italy in 540AD, gardening was second only to prayer in the monastic regime. Expanding on St. Jerome's instructions a century earlier to "hoe your ground, set out cabbages…," he specified in the *Regula Monachorum* – the foundation of monastic rule to this day – that vegetables, fruit, grapes, herbs, dye plants, and aromatics for incense should be grown. A plan drawn up in the ninth century at St. Gall, a Swiss Benedictine monastery, shows a rectangular garden with 16 beds of "herbs both beautiful and health-giving," such as sage (*Salvia* spp.) and rosemary, and a larger garden with 18 beds of vegetables and herbs. Monasteries were largely self-

◄ MEDIEVAL GARDEN
In this illustration from Roman de la Rose *(c.1400), a doctor selects herbs for medicinal use. Herb gardens had a range of plants, which might include culinary and decorative species.*

sufficient in produce, placing special emphasis on herbs to heal the sick. They also made great use of herbs for flavoring a vegetarian diet, and were expert in the brewing and distillation of ale, wine, liqueurs such as Benedictine, and the cosmetic Carmelite water which was based on *Melissa officinalis*.

PHYSIC GARDENS

Herb gardening grew in popularity during the 13th century, often a result of instruction by infirmary sisters. Most large houses grew a wide variety of herbs for household use, while small properties were surrounded by a mixture of orchard, grass, and kitchen garden in which vegetables, herbs, and flowers were grown.

In the 16th century, herb gardens were planted by universities for teaching botany and medicine – subjects that were inextricably linked until separated by advances in science during the 18th century. The first of these "physic gardens" was at the University of Padua in 1545. By the end of the 17th century, there were physic gardens at universities throughout Europe. The demands of teaching influenced how the herbs were laid out – in Edinburgh, for example, medicinal herbs were grown in alphabetical order. As new species were brought back by colonial explorers and botanical knowledge expanded, physic gardens embraced a far wider range of plants and became the botanic gardens we know today.

DEVELOPMENT OF THE FORMAL GARDEN

The 17th and 18th centuries saw great changes in style. Some of the finest formal herb gardens in the world were created in France, at châteaux such as Villandry, where the reconstructed boxwood gardens and *potager* are unparalleled in grandeur. Landscape gardening, with an abhorrence of unnatural symmetry, became fashionable during the 18th century, and as the industrial revolution got under way, nostalgia for the cottage garden and rural idyll increased the popularity of informal style. Today we see an eclectic approach, choosing formal or informal as taste and situation permit. Both approaches have a long and fascinating history. Even the windowbox has its pedigree; it first appeared as a space-saving device in cramped Elizabethan London.

During the colonial era, Europeans settled in many parts of the world, taking seeds and cuttings of indispensable plants with them. Through trial and error, settlers learned which of their plants thrived. The Dutch, who were acknowledged as the finest gardeners in Europe at the time, were the first to plant boxwood (*Buxus sempervirens*, on Shelter Island, Long Island, New York, in 1652), but in New England, boxwood hedges failed to survive the severe winters and were replaced by the hardier wormwood (*Artemisia* spp.) and ornamental quince (*Chaenomeles speciosa*).

GARDENS AROUND THE WORLD

The story is similar in Canada, Australia, New Zealand, and South Africa, where the traditional European style of herb garden is also enduringly popular – so much so that the Plants Naturally Nursery of Victoria, Australia, created an herb garden at London's Chelsea Flower Show in 1987. In Cape Town, there are formal public gardens west of Government Avenue where the kitchen gardens of the Dutch East India Company were set out in the 17th century, and the first nonnative species were planted in southern Africa. Many of the herbs nurtured by colonists escaped into the wild and became pernicious weeds that threaten the survival of native plants and ecosystems. The Aztecs of Mexico used some 3000 herbs and had sophisticated systems of cultivation and botanical classification. The "floating gardens" of Xochimilco are of great antiquity, their irrigated plots dating back to the sixth century AD. Cortés wrote to Charles V of Spain in 1522 that Moctezuma's gardens at Huaxtepec (present-day Oaxtepec) were the finest he had seen; they boasted cacao (*Theobroma cacao*) and vanilla (*Vanilla* spp.), brought from the coastal tropics.

▲ THE KNOT GARDEN
Medieval rectangles and trellises became elaborate knot gardens and parterres.

HERB GROWING IN CHINA

Herb growing in China has belonged more to rural industry than to the noble art of gardening. Both Chinese medicine and Chinese gardens follow abstract concepts (the theory of the five elements, for example), the ultimate goal of both being to create harmony. Chinese, and also Japanese, gardens are stylized scenes from nature, with a disciplined use of plants, and they are never symmetrical.

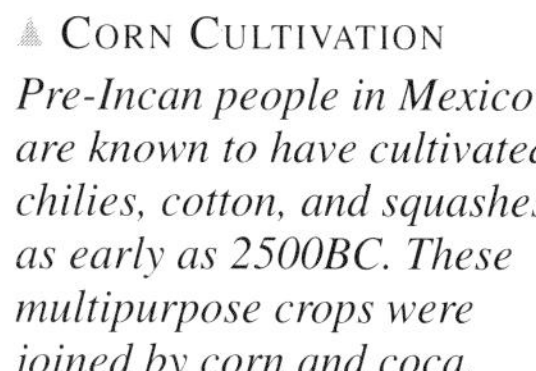

▲ CORN CULTIVATION
Pre-Incan people in Mexico are known to have cultivated chilies, cotton, and squashes as early as 2500BC. These multipurpose crops were joined by corn and coca.

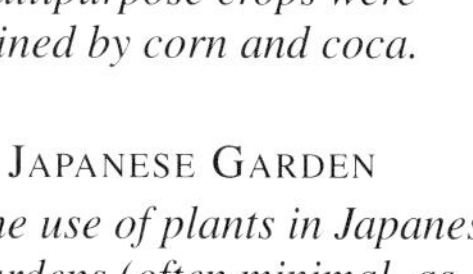

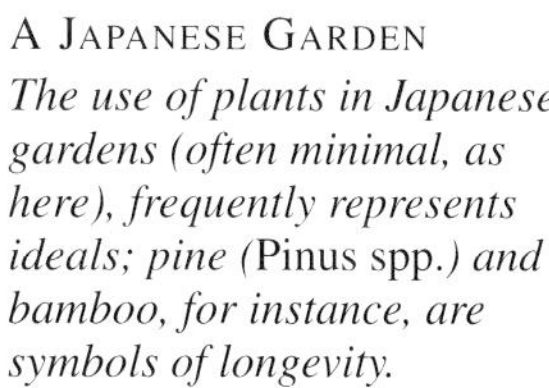

A JAPANESE GARDEN
*The use of plants in Japanese gardens (often minimal, as here), frequently represents ideals; pine (*Pinus *spp.) and bamboo, for instance, are symbols of longevity.*

HERBS IN MYTH AND LEGEND

Folk medicine has always been closely allied to ritual and magic. In most cultures, curing the sick, fumigating buildings with incense, and perfuming the body (or embalming it when dead) were once considered divine acts to be performed according to religious rituals. Plants of great beauty and fragrance came to be regarded as sacred for their importance in mediating between sickness and health, humanity and divinity, death and eternal life. Most of these plants had medicinal properties, too, since fragrance is usually due to volatile oils that have a wide range of curative effects.

SACRED CORN
*As a staple crop, corn (*Zea mays*) was synonymous with life to the ancient civilizations of Central and South America and was elevated to the status of deity. This vessel originated from the Mochica people, who lived on the coast of Peru AD100–800; their advanced agricultural system included irrigation.*

The use of incense has long been important in ritual; frankincense (*Boswellia sacra*) and myrrh (*Commiphora myrrha*) were burned in the temples of ancient Babylon, Egypt, Rome, Greece, India, and China, and were traded throughout these regions from Arabia. The trees were protected by legendary multicolored winged serpents, and their resins were held to be worth their weight in gold.

THE LOTUS AND THE ROSE

Scented blue and white lotus flowers (from *Nymphaea caerulea*, a narcotic in ancient Egypt, and the night-blooming *N. lotus*, respectively) were the favorite flowers offered 4000 years ago by Egyptians to their gods and used for garlands in funeral rites. The lotus was revered as symbol of the Nile, giver of life, and sacred to Isis, goddess of fertility. Egyptian lotuses are quite different from the sacred lotus (*Nelumbo nucifera*), which is Asian in origin and was not known in Egypt before 500BC. This species is sacred in Indian, Chinese, and Tibetan cultures. The lotus germinates in mud and unfolds its immaculate flowers in the sunlight; it is seen as analogous to the growth of consciousness, purity, and enlightenment.

Roses are to Islam what the sacred lotus is to Hinduism and Buddhism. The original sacred rose was the white, pink-budded damask rose, *Rosa damascena*. One legend gives its origin as drops of sweat, fallen from the prophet Mohammed as he ascended into heaven. Accounts of the creation of red and white roses are found in ancient Greek, Roman, and Christian legends. In one Roman myth, the goddess Venus, on her way to meet Adonis, pricked her foot on a thorn of a white rose, turning it red with her blood.

Inevitably, the rose also found favor in Christian imagery. The Virgin Mary is known as the *Rosa Mystica*, symbolized by a white rose, while the red rose represents the blood of Christ, its five petals denoting his wounds. In one legend, the Virgin lays her veil on a rosebush to dry, and the red roses beneath it turn white. *Rosa damascena* was closely associated with the Virgin Mary because of its coloring – the dark pink buds representing human flesh and blood, and its open white petals symbolizing the divine spirit.

THE LOTUS IN HINDUISM
In Hindu legend, the sacred lotus was created from the supreme being's navel. Inside the flower sat Brahma, who turned the lotus into a new world. In Buddhist mythology, Buddha first appeared floating on a lotus, and is depicted on a stylized lotus "throne," with the soles of his feet resting on his thighs – a posture known in yoga as the "lotus position."

SYMBOLISM OF THE LILY
The madonna lily is closely associated with the Virgin Mary as a symbol of purity. Early Christians believed that the life cycle of the lily symbolized the life of the soul.

CLASSICAL MYTHS

A number of pagan symbols and myths became absorbed into Christianity, and it may be no coincidence that the Romans dedicated the white madonna lily, *Lilium candidum*, to Juno, goddess of all that is essentially female, and that both she and the Virgin Mary were known as "queen of heaven." According to Greek myth, the lily originated in drops of milk, spilled from the breast of Hera, queen of the gods, as she suckled the infant Hercules – drops that also spread through the sky to form the Milky Way.

Myrtle (*Myrtus communis*) was dedicated to Venus, often depicted wearing a crown of myrtle, and who was on occasion worshipped as *Myrtilla*, from the Latin name of the plant. Venus is identified with the Greek goddess Aphrodite, and linked with Ishtar, the Babylonian and Assyrian goddess of love and fertility. To this day myrtle is carried in wedding bouquets. In ancient Greece, winning athletes in the Olympic games were crowned with bay (*Laurus nobilis*), as were victorious warriors and poets. Ancient Greeks hung a branch of bay over the door of a sick person to fend off evil and death. This led to the garlanding of newly qualified doctors with a bay wreath, the *bacca laureus*, which gave us "baccalaureate" (university degree).

RED AND WHITE ROSES
The garden roses in the Hours of the Duke of Burgundy (1454–55) invoked a blessing by their association with the Virgin Mary, and prefigured the Paradise garden.

HERBS IN WITCHCRAFT

Henbane (*Hyoscyamus niger*), deadly nightshade (*Atropa belladonna*), and mandrake (*Mandragora officinarum*) all feature in European witchcraft and sorcery. The image of witches on broomsticks has origins in the use of these plants which, when rubbed into the skin or inhaled, cause intoxicating sensations of flying. Mandrake was one of the most magical and feared plants in the world. The root was seen to resemble a man, and was uprooted by a tethered dog, lest its shrieking would cause death. Outbreaks of lycanthropy (supposed transformation of a human being into a wolf) have also been associated with ointments made from nightshades, aconite (*Aconitum napellus*), and narcotic herbs such as cannabis (*Cannabis sativa*) and opium (*Papaver somniferum*).

HERBS IN NORTHERN LEGEND

Elder (*Sambucus nigra*) is a magical plant in many cultures. It is sacred to the gypsies, and is planted in the courtyards of synagogues in the Israeli town of Safad, where it was probably associated with occult practices. According to German folklore, one's hat must be doffed whenever an elder tree is passed. In Denmark one should always ask permission of Hylde-Moer (elder mother) before harvesting the tree, and never make a cradle from elder wood, lest Hylde-Moer strangle the baby in revenge. The hawthorn, or may (*Crataegus laevigata* and *C. monogyna*), has been associated with fertility rites since earliest times. The customs of going "a-Maying," and of crowning the may queen with hawthorn, are pre-Christian. The white flowers are regarded in British folklore as omens of death or disaster if brought into the house – perhaps as a memory of the human sacrifices required as part of the May Day ritual. Mistletoe (*Viscum album*) was sacred to the Druids during pre-Christian times in Gaul, Britain, and Ireland. It could only be cut with a golden knife at a certain phase of the moon, and must not touch the ground. Branches (the original Golden Bough) were carried to announce the New Year. In Norse mythology, Balder, a gentle god, was killed by a dart of mistletoe; now it may grow only in tree tops, and those meeting under it kiss as a sign of love and peace. In German folklore, mistletoe bestows the power to see ghosts and make them speak.

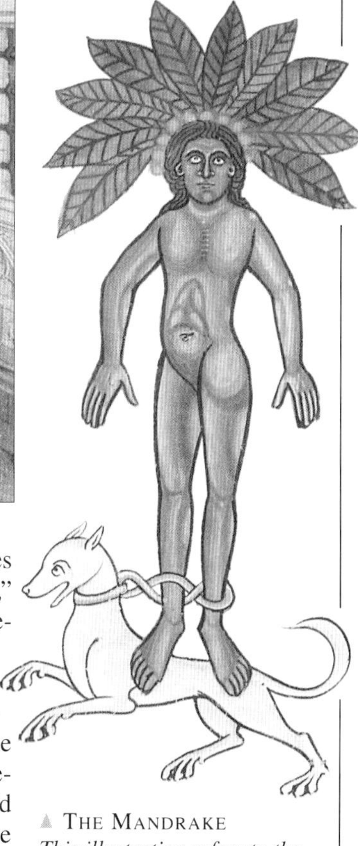

▲ THE MANDRAKE
This illustration refers to the superstition of tying a dog to the plant to avoid hearing its shrieks when uprooted.

▼ GOING A-MAYING
In ancient times the queen of the may was put to death to ensure a good harvest.

HERBS THAT CHANGED THE WORLD

The lives of people and plants are more entwined than is often realized. Some herbs have such power to change our physiological functioning that they have revolutionized medicine, created fortunes for those who grow, process, and trade them, and in certain cases have assumed social and religious significance. The foxglove (*Digitalis* species) is a wild flower and folk remedy that became a vital drug. Wars have been fought over opium, and conflict continues over both it and coca. Paracelsus (c.1493–1541) wrote that "All substances are poisons; there is none which is not a poison. The right dose differentiates a poison and a remedy."

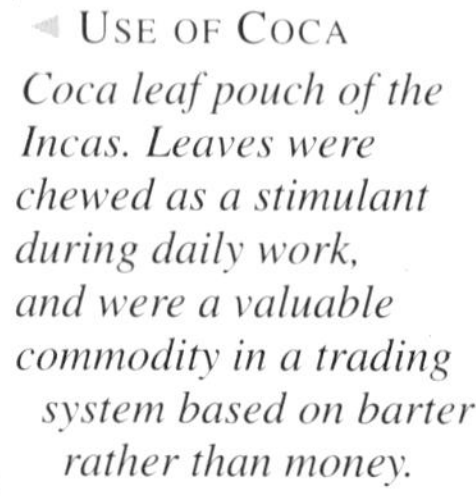

USE OF COCA
Coca leaf pouch of the Incas. Leaves were chewed as a stimulant during daily work, and were a valuable commodity in a trading system based on barter rather than money.

ERYTHROXYLUM COCA
Fresh leaves of the coca plant; these contain the powerful alkaloid, cocaine.

OPIUM PIPE
Introduced into China from Java in the 17th century, opium brought serious social problems.

AUTUMN CROCUS *(COLCHICUM AUTUMNALE)*

Cure for gout and key to genetic engineering

The poisonous properties of *Colchicum* species were probably known in ancient Egypt, and were used medicinally in ancient Greece to relieve the pain of gout, and as a poison. The extreme toxicity of the plant earned it names such as "vegetable arsenic." The active constituent is the toxic alkaloid colchicine. It remains a standard treatment for gout, and its effects on cells have revolutionized plant breeding. If applied to plant cells when they are dividing, chromosome numbers can be manipulated, rendering sterile hybrids fertile, and bringing improvements – such as increased size and vigor – in food plants and ornamentals.

COCA *(ERYTHROXYLUM COCA)*

Local anesthetic; origin of a famous soft drink

The chewing of coca leaves by the early peoples of Peru has been dated to at least 500AD; small bags of coca leaves have been found in the funeral urn of a mummified potentate from the pre-Inca Nazca period. The first detailed description of coca was given by Nicolas Monardes in 1565. The alkaloid cocaine was isolated in 1860, and was used as a local anesthetic in 1884 in the first painless cataract operation. Social use of cocaine and coca-leaf products was popular during the 19th century, and widely used in society. Coca wine became a craze, and many alcohol-free imitations appeared with the onset of Prohibition in the US. One of the most popular was made by John Pemberton, who in 1886 produced the "Intellectual Beverage and Temperance Drink," *Coca-Cola*. Only decocainized coca has been used to make it since the sale of cocaine was banned in 1902. Cocaine has also been largely replaced in surgery by synthetics such as procaine.

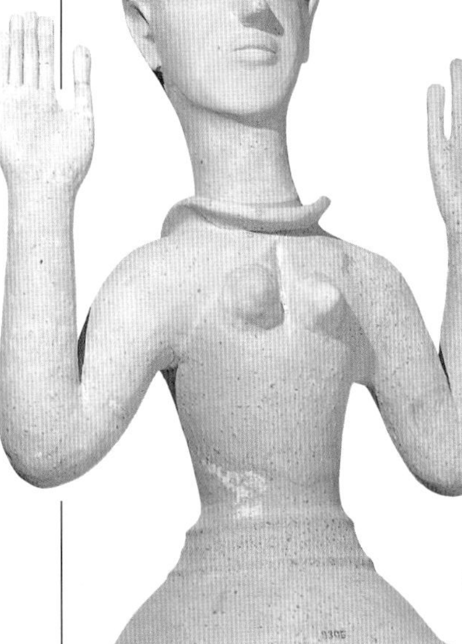

OPIUM GODDESS
Statue, crowned with poppy seed capsules, at Heraklion, Crete, dated 1400–1100BC. The Greeks dedicated the opium poppy to the gods of night, dreams, and death.

ERGOT *(CLAVICEPS PURPUREA)*

St. Anthony's fire, childbirth, and LSD

Outbreaks of ergotism, or St. Anthony's fire – poisoning by a fungus that affects rye – have been recorded throughout history. Medically significant alkaloids of ergot were isolated between 1906 and 1920, notably ergonovine and ergotamine; these drugs have greatly improved the management of labor, postpartum hemorrhage, and migraine. Another ergot derivative, lysergic acid diethylamide (LSD), was extracted in 1943 and attracted a great deal of attention in the 1970s as a potent hallucinogenic. Though not addictive, it is a common cause of psychosis, suicide, homicide, abortion, and congenital abnormalities.

KHELLA *(AMMI VISNAGA)*

The antiasthmatic

The aromatic fruits of *Ammi visnaga* have been used medicinally in Egypt since ancient times, mainly to treat kidney stones. They contain various chromones, including khellin, that relax smooth (visceral) muscle. This was first isolated in 1879, but in 1946 an Egyptian pharmacologist discovered that extracts of the herb also had a powerful effect on the bronchioles and coronary arteries, and gave a good control of asthmatic symptoms. Over 670 compounds were synthesized before the

DIOSCOREA
Leaves and (right) dried root of Dioscorea villosa, *one of several species of this genus from which saponins are extracted for conversion into steroid hormones.*

production of sodium cromoglycate, a bischromone that prevents release of the antiallergenic substances responsible for an asthmatic attack.

MADAGASCAR PERIWINKLE *(CATHARANTHUS ROSEUS)*

The fight against cancer

The Madagascar periwinkle is frequently cited as an example of a "wonder drug," and to demonstrate the importance of screening tropical plants for active constituents. The analysis of its alkaloids began in the 1920s; recent counts put the total at over 70. Of these, vincristine and vinblastine are now well established in the treatment of acute leukemia, Hodgkin's disease, and other cancers that were previously incurable.

MEADOWSWEET *(FILIPENDULA ULMARIA)*

Plant aspirin

The analgesic salicin was first isolated from meadowsweet leaves in 1827. Salicylic acid was made in 1838, and synthesized in 1859, but proved suitable only for the external treatment of skin conditions. It did, however, provide the basis for acetylsalicylic acid, which was first produced in 1899, and named aspirin after *Spiraea ulmaria*, the old name for *Filipendula ulmaria*. Aspirin is the world's most widely used drug, recommended for over 40 different complaints. The latest discovery is that aspirin may prevent heart attack and stroke in patients with a history of such disorders.

MEXICAN YAM *(DIOSCOREA SPECIES)*

Blueprint for the oral contraceptive

The discovery of hormones came very late in the history of medicine. It took until 1934 to isolate cortisone, after which plants were investigated for saponins that could be converted cheaply into steroids and other drugs. Mexican yams yield diosgenin, and in the early 1940s, in great secrecy, several kilograms were produced of a hormone whose market value would now be $36,000 per pound. Large-scale cultivation of yams for steroidal drugs – corticosteroids, oral contraceptives, anabolic agents, and sex hormones – became a major industry in Mexico, producing over 80 percent of the raw material required for steroidal drugs.

OPIUM POPPY *(PAPAVER SOMNIFERUM)*

The irreplaceable painkiller

Opium is as old as medicine itself, and there has never been a painkiller to equal it. Its uses were inscribed on clay tablets by Sumerians in the 4th millenium BC, and it was known to the ancient Greeks. Opium is the world's greatest painkiller and is still the drug of choice for serious accidents and terminal illnesses. It is also one of the most addictive substances known. By the 19th century, international trade in opium was of major economic importance. When China tried to tackle the social problems of addiction by banning imports, Britain declared war and defeated the Chinese in the Opium Wars of the 1840s, gaining Hong Kong in the process. Morphine is the principal alkaloid of the 20 or more in opium, and has potent analgesic, euphoric, and narcotic effects. It was the first alkaloid to be isolated in the history of chemistry, in 1806. Opioid alkaloids, which also include codeine and methadone, cannot be synthesized. Hence the growing and processing of opium for the pharmaceutical industry is still today of major importance in world trade.

QUININE CULTIVATION
Quinine (Cinchona *spp.) trees under cultivation in Java. Demand for the bark to combat malaria has led to many searches for alkaloid-rich species. Plantations have been established in many areas of SE Asia. Synthetic antimalarial drugs were developed after World War II, and the mosquito populations decimated by spraying with DDT, but resistance to synthetic drugs has since increased.*

RAUVOLFIA
Calming herb used in India and the Far East. Its chemistry was described in 1887 in Java.

PAREIRA *(CHONDRODENDRON TOMENTOSUM)*

Arrow poison and muscle relaxant

Extract from the stems of the large rainforest liana, *Chondrodendron tomentosum*, is one of the main toxic ingredients of curare, a black gum which causes instantaneous muscular paralysis. In many parts of S America native people hunt with darts tipped with curare, which does not taint the meat. Curare was first used as an adjunct to general anesthesia in 1942, and is now essential in all surgical procedures. It cannot be synthesized, however, and stocks must be wild-collected.

QUININE *(CINCHONA SPECIES)*

The first antimalarial drug

By the end of the 17th century, cinchona bark was in demand worldwide to cure malaria, and vast quantities were shipped from Peru and Bolivia. In 1820 the alkaloid quinine was isolated, and fierce competition followed to find high-yielding strains. *Cinchona ledgeriana* had the highest alkaloid content ever recorded, and ensured a world monopoly of quinine from Dutch plantations in Java.

RAUVOLFIA *(RAUVOLFIA SERPENTINA)*

The first tranquilizer

The earliest mention of rauvolfia is in *Charaka Samhita*, a weighty Hindu medical treatise that was written in 600BC, a time when rauvolfia was used for snakebite and "moon disease" (insanity). Its most important alkaloid, reserpine, was isolated in 1952, and the term "tranquilizer" was coined the year after, when the effects of reserpine on the central nervous system were described. Rauvolfia alkaloids have also revolutionized the management of psychotic patients and led to advances in antihypertensive drugs.

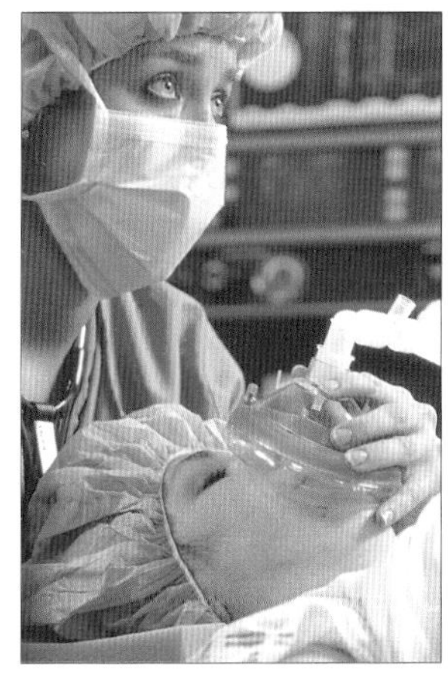

PAREIRA IN SURGERY
Before the use in surgery of tubocurarine, from pareira, muscle relaxation was obtained only by deep anesthesia, which carried considerable risk.

A WONDER DRUG
Catharanthus roseus *was screened in the 1960s as a cure for diabetes, but its effect on white blood cells has led to its use in treating cancers.*

HERBAL BOOKS

Knowledge of herbs has been handed down from generation to generation for thousands of years. In the 1970s a grave was found in northern Iraq, belonging to a Neanderthal man who, 60,000 years ago, was buried surrounded by flowers. The plant fragments were analyzed and found to be mostly herbs still used by local people; one of them was yarrow (*Achillea millefolium*). For much of human history, traditions of herbal use have thus been oral, often divulged only to the initiated, for ritual or healing purposes. In some cultures, such as those of Amazonian peoples, they remain so to this day.

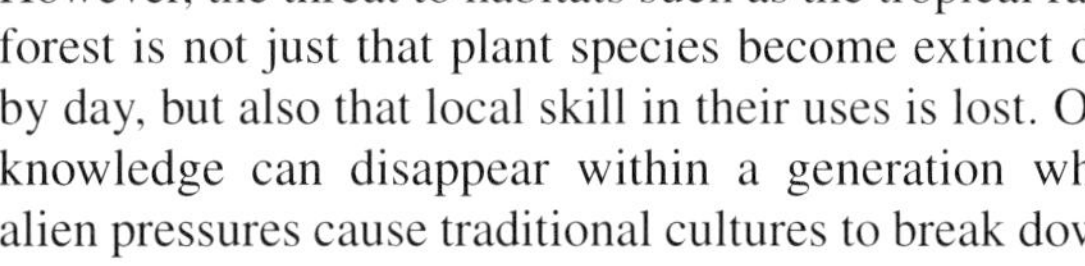

However, the threat to habitats such as the tropical rainforest is not just that plant species become extinct day by day, but also that local skill in their uses is lost. Oral knowledge can disappear within a generation when alien pressures cause traditional cultures to break down.

ANCIENT HERBAL RECORDS

Chinese herbalism is widely regarded as the oldest in the world, because it has the longest unbroken history of recorded knowledge; several ancient Chinese herbals are still in regular use today. Ayurvedic medicine is ancient and well recorded, too; herbs are mentioned in the *Rig Veda*, a sacred Hindu text dating from at least 2000BC. It is known that there were Chaldean herbalists c.5000BC, and Assyrian clay tablets from c.2500BC describe some 250 herbs. The ancient Egyptians undoubtedly had a sophisticated knowledge of herbs by 3000BC, but there is little written evidence to amplify archaeological finds, though herbs are illustrated in tomb wall paintings and carvings dating back to c.2000BC. The illustrations are more decorative and symbolic than an aid to identification, indicating familarity with herbs in everyday use. All that remains is the Ebers papyrus (c.1500BC), which records long usage of herbs such as elder and wormwood, and a few fragments from the second century AD, some of which were written in Greek. Egyptian herbal traditions passed to the Copts, who were early Christian descendants of the ancient Egyptians.

'HEALING HERBS'
From the Illustrated Family Library, *vii, Leipzig, 1901.*

HERBALS IN MANUSCRIPT

Before the invention of printing in 1440, herbals were written and illustrated by hand. They were often copied many times, giving rise to errors and different versions. Early herbals combine myth and magic with the descriptive and practical. They contain information that is in itself ancient, and often show foreign influences that were communicated via trade and travel. The *Leech Book of Bald* (c.900AD) includes, for example, a detailed knowledge of native plants and Syrian prescriptions sent to King Alfred from the Patriarch of Jerusalem, alongside magical charms that are common to many ancient cultures. A herbal written in the 13th century by the physicians of Myddfai, Wales, presents herbal knowledge that dates back to the Druids. The Druids, in their turn, were influenced by ancient Greek medicine and the works of Hippocrates. One of the best examples of early printed herb illustration is the *Herbarius zu Teusch*, printed at Mainz in 1485 and widely copied. The drawings by Leonhard Fuchs in *Neue Kreuterbuch* (1543) and *De historia Stirpium* (1545) were copied throughout Europe in the 16th century. In the late 17th century, herbals were joined by still-room books, which collated recipes, notes, and advice for the running of a large household. Much information concerned the use of herbs. Gardening books also began to appear, as new plants were introduced from the colonies. By the 18th century, botany and medicine were developing as sciences in their own right, requiring specialist textbooks. Separation of these various subject areas continued through the 19th century. This can clearly be seen in *The Universal Herbal* by Thomas Green (1816), which is subtitled "Botanical, Medical, and Agricultural Dictionary. Specifying the uses to which they are or may be applied, whether as Food, as Medicine, or in the Arts and Manufactures. Adapted to the use of the Farmer – the Gardener – the Husbandman – the Botanist – the Florist – and Country Housekeepers in General". The increase in knowledge in the 20th century has produced an era of specialization, with databases and scientific journals for the student of medical herbalism and ethnobotany, but the herbal still remains important as the easiest way to learn how to use plants.

KREÜTERBUCH (HERBAL)
The title-page of the Kreüterbuch of Pierandrea Mattioli, or Matthiolus (1501–77), physician to the Emperor Maximilian II. It was published in 1586, after Mattioli had died of the plague.

Major Herbal Books

Western herbals

c.300BC *Enquiry into Plants* (*Historia Plantarum*) and ***Growth of Plants*** (*De Causis Plantarum*) by Theophrastus. A total of 500 herbs, based on Aristotle's botanical writings, with his own observations.

AD77 *Natural History* (*Historia Naturalis*) by Pliny. 37 volumes of fact and fantasy, including medicinal uses of plants; origin of the Doctrine of Signatures.

▲ Dioscorides
A Greek physician, probably with the Roman army in the 1st century AD. The author of De Materia Medica.

1st century AD *De Materia Medica* by Dioscorides. The most influential Western herbal of all time, and a standard reference work for 1500 years. It describes some 600 herbs, many of which remain today in modern pharmacopoeias.

c.AD150 *De Simplicibus* by Galen, a Greek physician from the Middle East. His works, which codified existing medical knowledge and propounded the theory of humors, were standard medical texts in Europe and the Arab world until the Renaissance.

c.900 *Leech Book of Bald* Manual of a Saxon doctor, and the earliest European herbal written in the vernacular.

c.1000 *Canon of Medicine* by Avicenna, the great physician of the Islamic world. Based on Galen, written in Arabic, translated into Latin, it was a standard text until the 17th century.

c.1250 *De Proprietatibus Rerum* by Bartolomaeus Anglicus. 19 volumes of natural history, the 17th constituting the only original herbal written in England during the Middle Ages.

1525 *Banckes's Herbal*. The first printed English herbal. An anonymous compilation of earlier herbals, including the 10th century Aemilius Macer's herbal (*De Virtutibus Herbarum*), a poem on the virtues of 77 herbs, and the famous discourse on rosemary sent by the French Countess of Hainault to her daughter, Philippa, Edward I's queen.

1551–68 *A New Herball* (in three parts) by William Turner. The first English herbal with a scientific approach, illustrated with over 400 outstanding woodcuts, mostly reproduced from drawings by Leonhard Fuchs in Swiss herbals.

1570 *Herbal* by Paracelsus (Theophrastus Bombastus von Hohenheim), a Swiss physician and alchemist. It expounded the Doctrine of Signatures.

1597 *The Herball or Generall Historie of Plants* by John Gerard, an eminent Elizabethan herbalist and gardener. Based on Dodoens' *Cruÿdboeck* (1554), and extended by Thomas Johnson in 1633, it has delightful descriptions of plants from all over the world.

1629 *Paradisi in Sole Paradisus Terrestris*; 1640 *Theatrum Botanicum* by John Parkinson. The latter is the largest herbal in English. Less known than the former, which is more of a gardening book, describing 3800 herbs, divided into 17 groups, though one group consists of "straglers" the author had omitted to include elsewhere!

1652 *The English Physitian* by Nicholas Culpeper. One of the best-selling herbals of all time, containing astrological, often flippant, descriptions of 398 herbs. It promoted the Doctrine of Signatures and was castigated as "ignorant" by physicians of the day. *The English Physitian Enlarged* came out in 1653, followed by many later revisions.

1656 *The Art of Simpling* by William Coles. "An Introduction to the Knowledge and Gathering of Plants," including the first account of herbs for treating animals.

1710 *Botanologia. The English Herbal or History of Plants* by William Salmon. The last major herbal before the disciplines of botany and medicine parted company.

1838 *Flora Medica* by John Lindley. A worldwide survey of medicinal plants, written by an eminent botanist and horticulturist, typical of the new scientific approach.

1866 *A Botanic Guide to Health* by Albert Coffin. He brought Physiomedicalism from America to England, leading to the founding in 1864 of the National Institute of Medical Herbalists.

1931 *A Modern Herbal* by Mrs. M. Grieve. Second perhaps only to Culpeper's herbal in its popularity. It describes over 1000 herbs.

Chinese herbals

c.1000BC *Yellow Emperor's Classic of Internal Medicine* First treatise on principles of health, by Huang Di (Yellow Emperor), founding father of Chinese medicine, who lived c.2697–2595BC.

AD25-220 *Shen Nong Canon of Herbs* Attributed to Shen Nong, god of husbandry and legendary emperor, said to have lived c.3000BC. It lists 252 drugs from plants.

c.659 *Tang Materia Medica* by Su Ying. 54 volumes of Chinese plants. It was commissioned during the Tang dynasty by the government.

1590 *Compendium of Materia Medica* by Li Shi Zhen. 52 volumes describing nearly 2000 drugs, mainly of plant origin. This was revised in 1765 by Zhao Xue Min, who added a further 900.

1970 *The Atlas of Commonly Used Chinese Traditional Drugs* by the Chinese Academy of Sciences. A product of the Communist revival of traditional medicine after years of disrepute during the Kuomintang era.

▲ Paradisi in Sole
John Parkinson's herbal (1629); the title is a pun on his name (Park-in-sun).

American herbals

1569 *Joyfull Newes Out of the Newe Founde Worlde* by Nicolas Monardes, a Spanish doctor. The first American herbal, translated into English Latin, Italian, Flemish, and French to provide information on the herbs of the Americas.

1672 *New England's Rarities Discover'd* by John Josselyn. The first account of useful European plants that thrived in North America, written to help settlers garden in unfamiliar surroundings.

1672 *The American Physitian* by William Hughes. Famous for its account of chocolate.

1715 *The South-Sea Herbal* by James Petiver. The first account in English of herbs in Peru and Chile.

1835 *New Guide to Health, Or, Botanic Family Physician*; 1841 *The Thomsonian Materia Medica* by Samuel Thomson. Native American herbs and therapies formulated by him as Physiomedicalism.

▼ Pepper Plant
Illustration of Capsicum *species in an English 17th-century manuscript.*

Designing an Herb Garden

An herb garden can be almost any size or shape. It does not necessarily have to be in a sunny, open position; there are herbs that will thrive in shade, in heavy wet ground, and even in water. The most popular kind of herb garden is a small bed or border of culinary herbs within easy reach of the kitchen. You can, however, equally well devote your herb garden to plants for medicinal uses, or to those that come from different parts of the world. You may wish to specialize in a single genus of herbs to grow, or perhaps plants characteristic of an old medieval monastery garden. There is no limit to the possibilities. Part of the fun, too, of creating an herb garden lies in researching and tracking down the plants, which will make you quite an expert by the time that you have finished. In this section you will find ideas and suggestions for formal and informal plantings in town and country settings, and designs for containers and a potager.

A Raised Border
Natural stone is used to create an attractive raised herb bed.

A Neat Design
Designed as a low-allergen garden, this formal design makes good use of a restricted space. Different colors and textures make the geometric divisions more interesting, and there are containers, climbers, and tall, narrow plants to give height.

When planning a new garden, it is important to take in the practical considerations. Whatever your style and interests, don't get too carried away; instead, work on something you know you will be able to achieve in terms of space, time, energy, and money.

The section *Cultivating Herbs* at the end of this book (pages 374–393) will give you fuller information on all stages of planning and making an herb garden. Make the best use of available space, and keep within the bounds of your gardening experience. The best way to start is with a notebook and pen. Write down the factors that you will have to take into account in your plan: dimensions, soil type and conditions, existing contours, and the amount of sun and wind the garden is likely to receive at different times of day and during the year. Pinpoint the extreme positions – sunniest, windiest, shadiest, most sheltered, and so on, and problems, such as perennial weeds. Surrounding features are important, too – a tree could provide a support for hops and give shade for woodland herbs, but it should not overhang a planting site for thymes. Access and viewpoint are also important. If you want to pick herbs through the year, all-weather paths or stepping stones should be part of the plan, and you will not want the bed to be too far from the house door. Or maybe you are thinking more of a place to relax, in which case a sitting area, perhaps a fragrant arbor, might be more of a priority.

Formal or Informal Style?

Once these practical matters have been thought through, the next stage is to consider the style. The basic choice is between formal and informal designs, but you will need to consider how best to fit the style of the herb garden to the rest of your garden. Formal gardens are geometric, usually subdivided by paths or dwarf hedges into symmetrical compartments. They may be square, rectangular, circular, star-shaped, or triangular in outline, or may combine several shapes, but the overall aim is to make a pattern. It is an ideal way of filling space, be it the builder's rubble of a new garden, an unwanted area of grass, or a bare courtyard or patio. An informal herb garden is better suited to adapting space, such as an existing border, or to finding a niche for certain kinds of herbs – Mediterranean herbs on a dry, sunny bank, for example.

Formal Designs

On a large scale that involves bulk quantities of hedging herbs and/or paving materials, a formal herb garden can be a major undertaking and expense, especially if professional construction is needed.

A Classic Formal Herb Garden
*This garden has symmetrical beds, outlined with clipped boxwood hedges (*Buxus sempervirens*). The element of height is provided by the topiary, hedge and rose-hung trellis.*

However, formal gardens are fairly easily planted and maintained, and look interesting from the moment of completion, unlike informal borders that depend on plant growth for effect. A formal garden is more than just an esthetic exercise, though; the resulting small divisions provide a neat, practical basis for growing herbs. You can grow each kind of herb in its own compartment, or you can use the divisions to show different features: medicinal herbs arranged according to ailments (bronchial diseases, heart complaints, nervous disorders, digestive problems, and such); or traditional medicinal plants, using separate divisions for each region, as has been done in the Garden of World Medicine at the Chelsea Physic Garden in London. Alternatively, the pattern can be emphasized by restricting your choice of plants to certain colors. You can use the same herb in different colors – Gervase Markham (*The English Husbandman*, 1613) recommended blocks of white, "mingle-coloured," and blood-red carnation gillyflowers – or you might alternate differently colored herbs, such as gray-leaved artemisias with purple-leaved sage or perilla.

Informal Designs

An informal design may begin with a geometric outline, but it will not have the planned symmetry of the formal garden. It depends for esthetic effect on plant combinations and grouping. An informal herb garden can take on the look of a cottage garden, herbaceous border, or rock garden. This more relaxed arrangement gives scope for incorporating whatever plants and features you already have in the garden, whereas a formal herb garden requires much more of a start from scratch. There are interesting climbing herbs for existing walls and fences, such as variegated nightshade and akebia. Groundcover among trees and shrubs can be provided by spreading herbs. Both sweet woodruff and variegated goutweed combine well with spring-flowering bulbs, producing fresh new foliage as the leaves of the bulbs begin to look ragged. Where evergreen cover is preferred, ivy can be used either as a climber or to carpet the ground, even in heavy shade.

A French-style Potager
This vegetable patch is bright with rows of herbs and flowers. There are interesting combinations of colors and textures, and crops such as onions become features in their own right.

◄ Container Gardening
An entire herb garden can consist of containers, which may be interestingly arranged on steps or among other plants. Climbers can be most effective subjects for large pots when trained on a frame, as is this golden hops (Humulus lupulus *'Aureus'*).

▼ Herbs as Garden Plants
Herbs such as lavender make excellent garden plants in their own right, as well as having special properties. Here, the deep purple of Lavandula angustifolia *'Hidcote' is edging a border dominated by spiky, gray-blue eryngiums (sea holly).*

Herbs that are particular about growing conditions can be accommodated in special places to suit them – acid-loving wintergreen and witch hazel in a woodland situation, perhaps, or meadowsweet, sweet flag, and skunk cabbage, in rich mud beside a pool.

Herbs with Other Plants

Informal herb gardening gives scope for combining herbs with other kinds of plants altogether. Many herbs are good garden plants in their own right, having subtle colors that are easy to place among shrubs and other perennials. Examples of these include the late-flowering soapwort, cultivars of feverfew, which are excellent for cutting, and the range of various sages, lavenders, and foxgloves, whose colors and habits complement roses so well. White gardens catch the imagination of plant lovers for their calm, peaceful atmosphere; an example is given on pages 34–35. Many herbs are well suited to this color combination, having silver-gray foliage or white flowers: artemisia, Queen Anne's lace, myrtle, white-flowered sage, lavender, marjoram, hyssop, and thyme are all ideal, to give but a few examples. Other herbs, such as emerald green curly parsley and purple-black lettuce-leaved basil, have bold colors and striking textures that do not look out of place among beds and containers of summer bedding, and in addition provide a useful "catch-crop" in the process. In France, herbs are traditionally grown alongside fruit and vegetables in an ornamental garden known as a *potager*. This concept combines many aspects of convenience and good husbandry in a small space, tailor-made for today's average-sized garden. Ideas for these and other herb gardens, both formal and informal, are given on the following pages. Many more will occur to you as your enthusiasm for this intriguing and satisfying aspect of gardening develops.

Planting Plan Key

The key below shows the symbols and colors used to denote each type of plant shown in the planting plans for the garden designs on the following pages.

Tree

Shrub

Perennial

Annual/ Biennial

Bulb

Evergreen

Formal Garden Designs

A herb garden designed to a formal pattern allows you to grow plants in a pleasing and ordered way. It is easily managed and gives access to the herbs, while creating a haven of restful colors and scents. Choose herbs not only for their aroma or uses but also to make interesting combinations of color, texture, and habit: the soft pinks and blues of lavender (*Lavandula*), rosemary (*Rosmarinus*), rue (*Ruta graveolens*), and hyssop (*Hyssopus*), or the fresh, clean appeal of golden-variegated sage (*Salvia officinalis* 'Icterina'), marjoram (*Origanum onites*), and lemon balm (*Melissa officinalis* 'Aurea') with white double feverfew (*Tanacetum parthenium*).

***Salvia officinalis* 'Icterina' and *Tanacetum parthenium* 'Tom Thumb White Stars'**
The leaves of golden-variegated sage complement the white flowers and bright green foliage of dwarf double feverfew, and both reach about the same height.

Geometric Garden

The plants in the small beds are all chosen for their tidy habit of growth, to maintain the shape of the beds. It is best to plant tall herbs, such as the angelica (*Angelica archangelica*) and hemp agrimony (*Eupatorium cannabinum*), around the edge, rather than in the middle, since they may swamp other plants. The most self-contained tall herb is fennel (*Foeniculum vulgare*), with its feathery foliage and stiff, upright habit.

A Fragrant Collage

The rich mixture of color, texture, and fragrance that a herb garden can provide is almost unlimited. The combination of both aromatic and colorful plants seen here produces a delightful array of color and scent.

Plant List

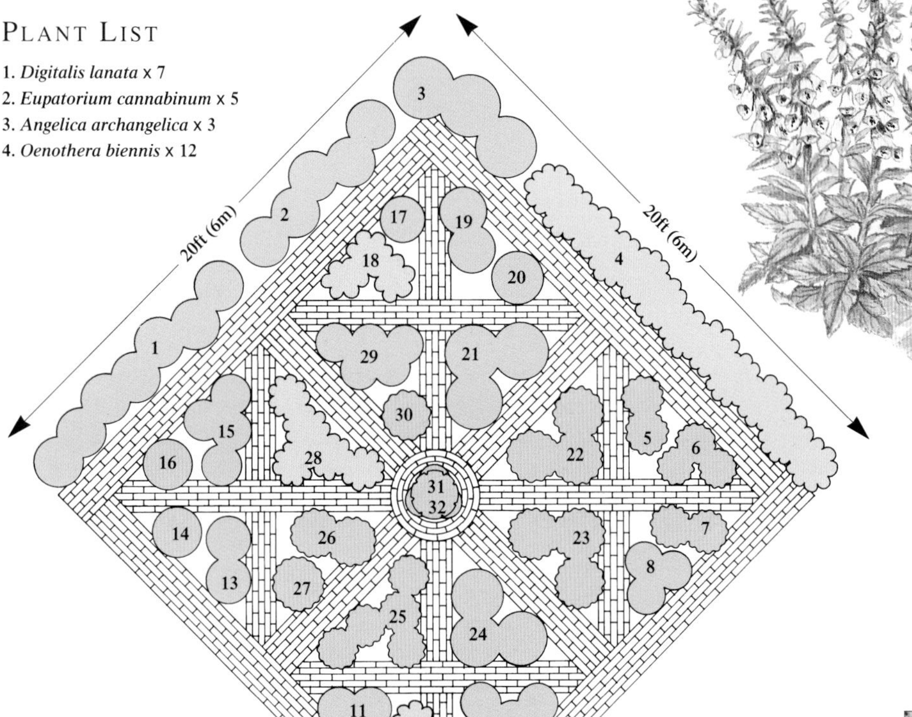

1. *Digitalis lanata* x 7
2. *Eupatorium cannabinum* x 5
3. *Angelica archangelica* x 3
4. *Oenothera biennis* x 12
5. *Lavandula angustifolia* 'Rosea' x 2
6. *Lavandula angustifolia* 'Hidcote' x 3
7. *Helichrysum italicum* x 2
8. *Allium schoenoprasum* x 3
9. *Artemisia pontica* x 3
10. *Salvia officinalis*, Purpurascens Group x 2
11. *Origanum vulgare* x 2
12. *Borago officinalis* x 3
13. *Monarda didyma* x 1
14. *Mentha spicata* x 2
15. *Mentha* x *piperita* x 4
16. *Allium cepa* Proliferum Group x 1
17. *Foeniculum vulgare* 'Purpureum' x 1
18. *Calendula officinalis* x 3
19. *Origanum onites* 'Aureum' x 2
20. *Melissa officinalis* 'Aurea' x 1
21. *Calamintha nepeta* x 3
22. *Rosmarinus officinalis* x 3
23. *Hyssopus officinalis* x 3
24. *Mentha suaveolens* 'Variegata' x 3
25. *Thymus serpyllum* 'Pink Chintz' x 5
26. *Thymus vulgaris* x 2
27. *Santolina chamaecyparissus* x 1
28. *Petroselinum crispum* x 5
29. *Tanacetum parthenium* 'Tom Thumb White Stars' x 5
30. *Salvia officinalis* 'Icterina' x 1
31. *Laurus nobilis* x 1
32. *Chamaemelum nobile* 'Flore Pleno' x 1

Quantities refer to the number of plants in each group planting

Borago officinalis* and *Origanum vulgare
Bright blue borage flowers intermingle with the pale pink flower heads of marjoram.

Origanum onites 'Aureum' and *Melissa officinalis* 'Aurea'
The new growth of golden-variegated pot marjoram and lemon balm shows up well early in the year.

Lavandula angustifolia 'Rosea' and 'Hidcote'
Growing the pink and deep purple lavenders together gives more visual interest while providing a choice of color for cutting.

Helichrysum italicum and *Allium schoenoprasum*
Chives are useful for edging, and their plain green foliage associates well with the silvery leaves of the curry plant.

Artemisia pontica and *Salvia officinalis*, Purpurascens Group
The filigree foliage of Roman wormwood contrasts well with the broad velvety leaves of purple sage.

A KNOT GARDEN

Knot gardens were the favorite style of Elizabethan England, expressing the confident, adventurous *joie de vivre* of the age. Composed of intricate geometric patterns, dwarf hedges of evergreen herbs and/or paths were laid out on a raised square. Two kinds were devised: closed knots, with no access and compartments containing colored sand or gravel; and open knots, with paths forming part of the pattern, and the compartments filled with sweet-smelling plants. They were not herb gardens as such, but most of the fragrant plants so beloved by Elizabethans happen to be what we now categorize as herbs: rosemary, hyssop, sage, and lavender made excellent small, fragrant hedges upon which the wash was spread out to dry.

DWARF BOXWOOD HEDGES

Boxwood was widely used too, though the unpleasant scent it produced when it was cut was considered a drawback. Knots were traditionally made in groups of four, which might be alike or different in pattern. One is sufficient for most gardeners today, bearing in mind the amount of very careful trimming that a dwarf hedge needs. The pattern can be as simple or complex as you like; the only limitation is that dwarf hedges reach 9–12in (23–30cm) wide, and paths need to be about 18in (45cm) across. The pattern you choose can also be symbolic; the initial letters of a name, for example.

INVESTING IN YOUR GARDEN

Boxwood is the best all-purpose dwarf hedge for knot gardens, as it is for any situation where compact low hedging is required. It is slower growing but longer-lived than any other, and usually more expensive. However, since it is grown mainly for hedging, it is often available at a discount for quantity. A boxwood hedge is for life, so it is best regarded as an investment. Choose also compact plants to grow inside the hedges, since tall herbs that lie on the hedge can damage or kill patches of it if they are left there too long.

OPEN KNOT GARDEN DESIGN
Here the color contrast of the gray of santolina (Santolina chamaecyparissus) *with the purple lavender* (Lavandula) *sections inside the hedges of boxwood* (Buxus sempervirens) *is an integral part of the design. Small paths allow for maintenance and trimming. Knot gardens are often best appreciated when the whole pattern can be seen from above.*

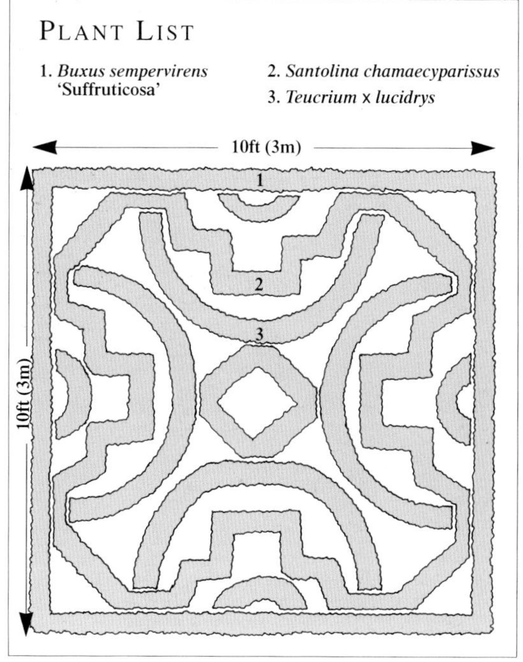

CONTRASTS IN HEDGING
Elements of the design, especially of a closed knot, can be emphasized by hedging in a different color. Three different types have been used in this design, which could have colored gravel or other material in the spaces between the hedges. The outer hedge of boxwood (Buxus sempervirens) *encloses repeating patterns in hedge germander* (Teucrium x lucidrys) *and silvery santolina. Take care to buy the correct species of germander, since the hedge type may be labeled as* T. chamaedrys, *the more spreading wall germander. Hedge germander has an upright habit and small glossy leaves.*

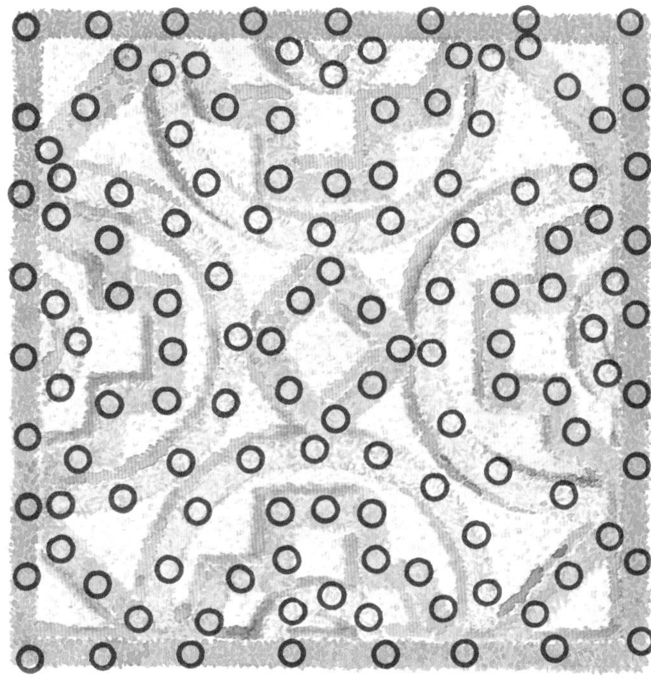

Color Wheel Raised Beds

Dividing a garden into geometric beds gives a sense of order, separates access from growing space, and simplifies planting and routine tasks. Raised beds were a feature of gardens during medieval and Renaissance times; in recent years they have undergone a revival as part of the organic movement, when it was discovered by experimentation that soil condition was greatly improved if left undisturbed. William Lawson (*The Countrie Housewife's Garden*, 1617) regarded raised beds as essential for plants other than trees, because they need drier conditions. His reasoning may be questionable, but raised beds do provide better drainage. This garden is a very simple example of something that can be made for the elderly and disabled in a confined space. There is ample room for seating in the central circular area, and paths are wide enough for wheelchair access. Gardeners with impaired vision might prefer a scheme chosen more for its range of aromas, with the added delight of texture too – the occasional silky marsh mallow or spiky houseleek among the sage and thyme. As an alternative to a tree, a central water feature could provide the relaxing sound of running water.

Plant List

Central Bed

1. *Tropaeolum majus* 'Empress of India' x 3
2. *Tagetes patula* x 3
3. *Tanacetum parthenium* 'Aureum' x 3
4. *Petroselinum crispum* 'Moss Curled' x 3
5. *Ruta graveolens* 'Jackman's Blue' x 3
6. *Salvia officinalis*, Purpurascens Group x 3

Triangular Beds

7. *Monarda didyma* x 5
8. *Tropaeolum majus* 'Empress of India' x 7
9. *Calendula officinalis* x 9
10. *Tagetes patula* x 7
11. *Melissa officinalis* 'Aurea' x 3
12. *Tanacetum parthenium* 'Aureum' x 5
13. *Rumex scutatus* x 5
14. *Petroselinum crispum* 'Moss Curled' x 5
15. *Hyssopus officinalis* x 5
16. *Ruta graveolens* 'Jackman's Blue' x 5
17. *Lavandula angustifolia* 'Imperial Gem' x 5
18. *Salvia officinalis*, Purpurascens Group x 5

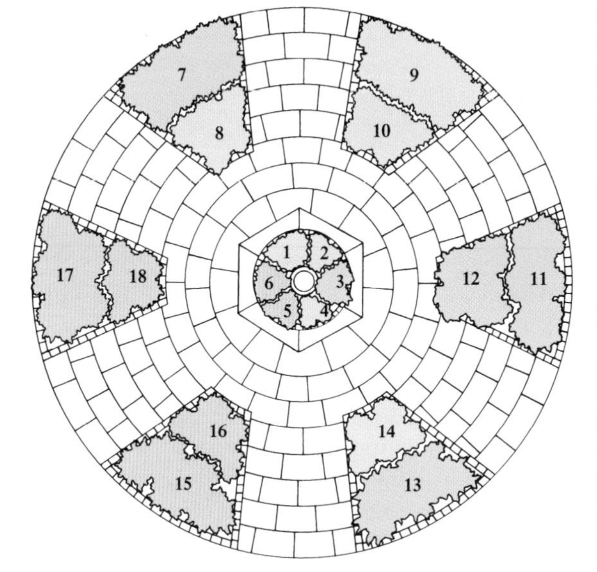

Diameter 35ft (11m)
Path width 4ft (1.2m)

Choosing Materials

The materials most suited to the garden are either precut lumber or precast edging, if the bed is up to about 12in (30cm) high, or a brick wall to hold greater quantities of soil within bounds. In theory, any shape is possible, but geometric shapes are easiest when a group of beds is designed as a unit.

Advantages of Height

Raising the beds clear of pathways makes it much easier to tend the herbs. A bed raised higher still, to a convenient working height, opens up the rewarding pastime of gardening to the elderly and disabled.

A Wheel of Color

Having fun with color appeals to gardeners of all ages; this particular planting plan is based mainly on short-lived, colorful herbs, so that changes can be made each year to provide interest and challenge.

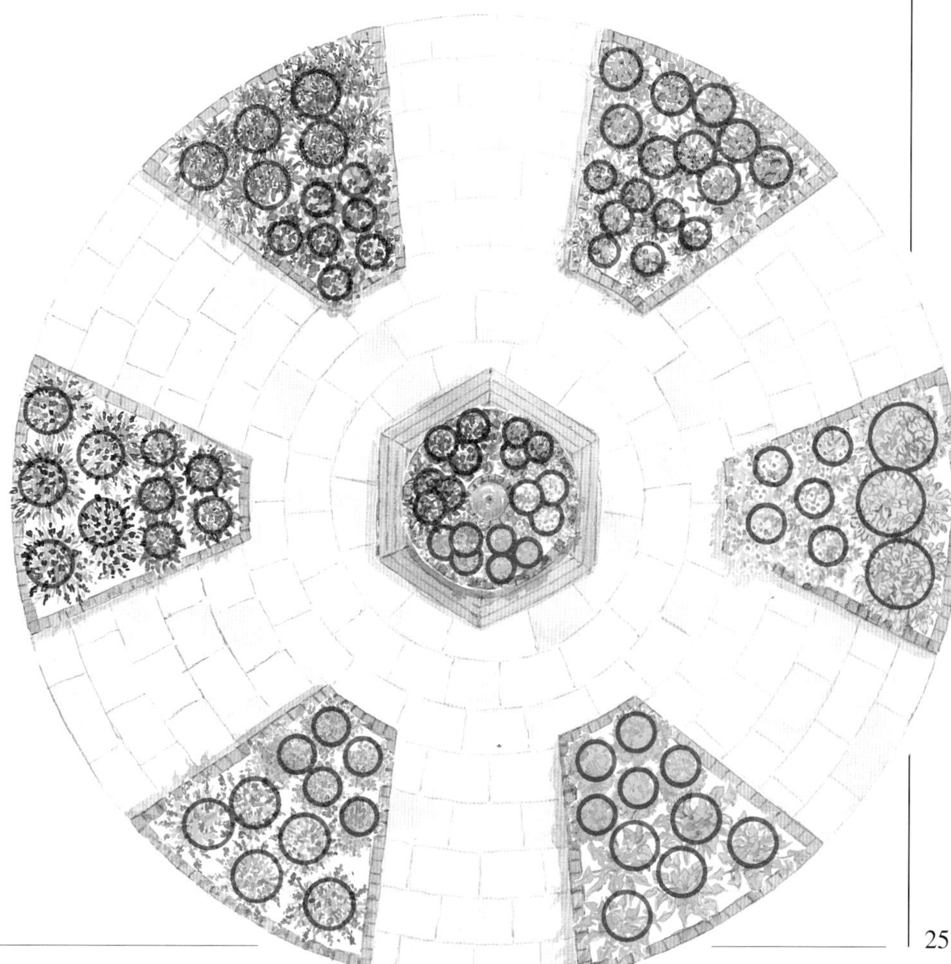

DESIGNS FOR A PURPOSE

These gardens show designs to suit various purposes. Plants for fragrance and potpourri are shown below, in a diagonal mirror-image plan; a design for color contrasts in a small, rectangular bed, perhaps under a house wall; and a circular island bed with a brick path, planted with a variety of culinary herbs to supply your kitchen all year round.

POTPOURRI HERB BED

The plants in this plan are only suggestions and can be changed as you wish – a peppermint geranium substituted for a rose-scented one, for example, or green-leaved instead of purple-leaved sage. You might choose the white button flowers of double chamomile (*Chamaemelum nobile* 'Flore Pleno') rather than those of *Tanacetum parthenium* 'Tom Thumb White Stars'. Different annuals may be grown each year: 'Dark Opal' basil, cornflowers, and nutmeg flowers (*Nigella sativa*), perhaps, with pansies for their beautiful colors. Essential potpourri ingredients include lavender and roses; almost any kind can be used, but *Lavandula angustifolia* 'Hidcote' has very deep purple, strongly scented flowers, and *Rosa gallica* var. *officinalis* is favored for its fragrant, deep red buds and petals. A lemon tree (or orange) is useful for its blossom and leaves, as well as for its fruits.

Coriandrum sativum* and *Agastache foeniculum
The seeds of coriander are easily grown as a perfume fixative. It has pretty white flowers, seen here with the purple spikes of anise hyssop, with its unusual scent of patchouli and mint.

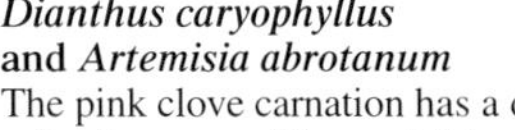

Dianthus caryophyllus* and *Artemisia abrotanum
The pink clove carnation has a delicious spicy fragrance. The upright artemisia provides background support; its leaves can be used in moth-repellant sachets.

A PLANTING WITH MANY POSSIBILITIES
This planting offers many combinations of scents and colors. The rich scents of the pink and red plants may be combined with those of the gray-leaved sage or thyme; sharp yellows and golds with the musky aromas of hops or coriander. Though attractive in its own right, Iris germanica *var.* florentina *is grown for its rhizomes. The powder, or orris, made from the dried root, produces one of the few aromatic fixatives that can be grown at home.*

Coriandrum sativum* and *Monarda didyma
The white-flowered coriander is pretty among the vibrant reds and pinks of bee balm in this bed. The soft pastel pinks of mallows (*Malva* spp.) have no scent, but can be dried as a color element of potpourri. Pot marigold (*Calendula officinalis*) flowers keep their vivid orange color well when dried, intensifying the warm yellows or golds of citrus potpourri blends.

PLANT LIST

1. *Rosa gallica* var. *officinalis* x 2
2. *Artemisia abrotanum* x 6
3. *Lavandula angustifolia* 'Hidcote' x 10
4. *Dianthus caryophyllus* x 7
5. *Salvia officinalis* Purpurascens Group x 5
6. *Rosmarinus officinalis* x 5
7. *Mentha suaveolens* 'Variegata' x 6
8. *Thymus vulgaris* 'Silver Posie' x 5
9. *Jasminum officinale* x 1
10. *Teucrium chamaedrys* x 16
11. *Tanacetum vulgare* x 2
12. *Humulus lupulus* 'Aureus' x 2
13. *Origanum vulgare* 'Aureum' x 5
14. *Tanacetum parthenium* 'Tom Thumb White Stars' x 5
15. *Iris germanica* var. *florentina* x 7
16. *Salvia sclarea* x 3
17. *Foeniculum vulgare* x 4
18. *Citrus limon* x 1
19. *Coriandrum sativum* x 5
20. *Calendula officinalis* x 3
21. *Agastache foeniculum* x 3
22. *Malva moschata* x 3
23. *Monarda didyma* x 3
24. *Pelargonium* 'Rober's Lemon Rose' x 1
25. *Aloysia triphylla* x 1

Tanacetum vulgare* and *Humulus lupulus

A fragrant mixture of sweetly scented golden marjoram (*Origanum vulgare* 'Aureum'), the dark green, pinnate leaves of tansy, the feathery foliage of aniseed-scented fennel (*Foeniculum vulgare*), and musky hops, with their golden trifoliate leaves.

***Salvia officinalis*, Purpurascens Group and *Thymus vulgaris* 'Silver Posie'**

These strongly scented herbs are useful for rich, piquant mixtures. The gray-purple leaves of the sage and the pink-flowered sprigs of silver thyme would be a perfect foil for deep red rose petals.

***Mentha suaveolens* 'Variegata' and *Lavandula angustifolia* 'Hidcote'**

Mints of all kinds can be dried for potpourri, but the soft, fruity fragrance of pineapple mint is more subtle than most. This lavender cultivar has fine spikes of purple flowers and is one of the best lavenders for scent.

REPEATING BORDER PATTERN

This design for a formal herb border has bold, simple shapes, in units that can be repeated, or half-repeated, as required. It uses colorful evergreen herbs, giving year-round interest and needing little maintenance. Borders such as this can be laid at the edge of a garden or along a house wall, and are useful for any awkward space. Alternatively, they can stand independently on either side of an entrance, or flank the sides of a knot garden. The use of standards, tall, clipped shrubs, or topiary has been a popular device since Elizabethan times to give height and an air of dignity to an otherwise uniformly low planting. In some situations, such as in front of house windows, standards may be unsuitable and smaller, perhaps globe-shaped, clipped shrubs may be preferable.

PREPARING AND CARING FOR YOUR BORDERS

When you are planning and constructing the borders, remember to allow enough space for the hedging plants. They may only be a few inches wide on arrival, but will reach 9–12in (23–30cm), depending on how closely you keep them trimmed. Maintenance consists of an annual mulch of compost in late spring; trimming the hedges with care and precision in spring and after flowering, or in the case of boxwood (*Buxus sempervirens*), two or three times during the growing season, and similarly cutting back the sages (*Salvia* species). Though perennial, sages tend to become woody after three or four years and may need replacing. This can be done by taking cuttings in summer or early autumn.

PLANTING WITH CONTRASTING COLORS
A formal border in Berkshire, England, planted with Lavandula angustifolia, *hedges of rich dark red* Berberis thunbergii *f.* atropurpurea, *and a centerpiece of* Thymus vulgaris *'Silver Posie', from which arise the standards of contrasting silver willow (*Salix alba *var.* sericea*). The green, silver, and purple color design works well, but many other combinations can be equally effective.*

BORDER WITH DIAMOND MOTIF

*If you are adapting an existing border that is narrower than the one in this plan, you could omit the inner hedge of lavender (*Lavandula angustifolia*). Bay trees (*Laurus nobilis*) could be replaced by boxwood (silver boxwood,* Buxus sempervirens *'Elegantissima', would be most effective), and the outer hedge of rock hyssop by dwarf white lavender (*L. x intermedia *'Alba'). Another good combination would be broad-leaved thyme (*Thymus pulegioides*) and the golden marjoram (*Origanum vulgare *'Aureum').*

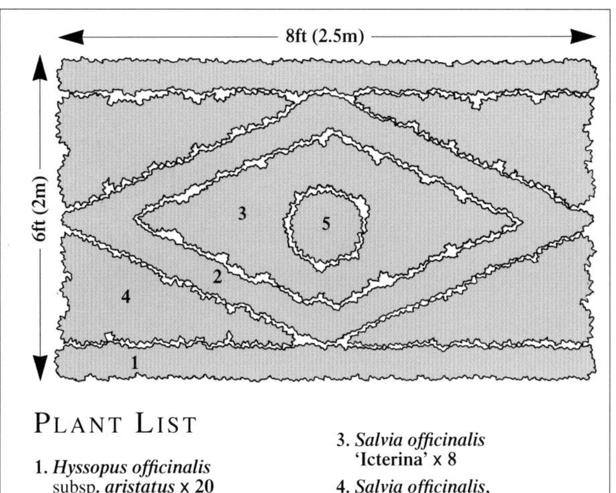

PLANT LIST

1. *Hyssopus officinalis* subsp. *aristatus* x 20
2. *Lavandula angustifolia* 'Hidcote' x 16
3. *Salvia officinalis* 'Icterina' x 8
4. *Salvia officinalis*, Purpurascens Group x 14
5. *Laurus nobilis* x 1

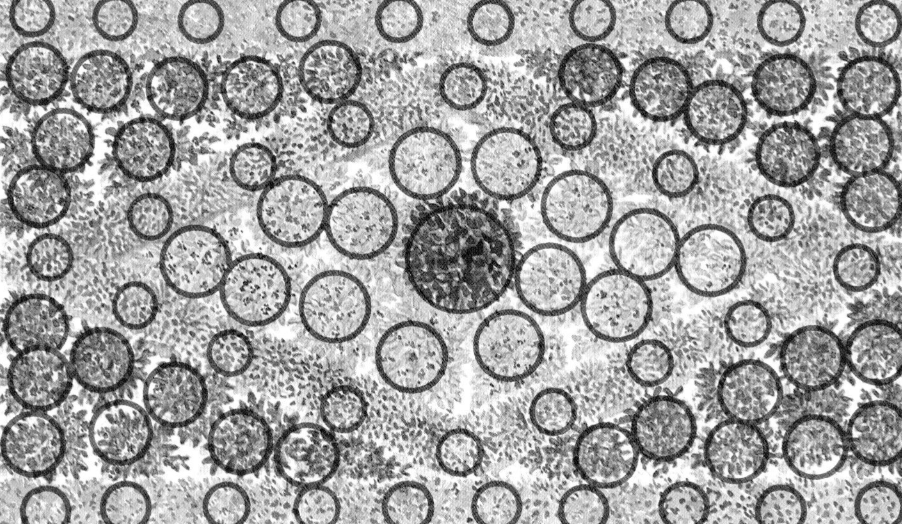

AN ISLAND BED OF CULINARY HERBS

Many of the popular culinary herbs take up little space and can be grown in quite a small area. A circular bed about 15ft (5m) across will provide an excellent range of fresh herbs for cooking and salads, with plenty to dry and freeze for winter use. It is advisable to start with more than one specimen of each herb, even though a single plant of the larger herbs, such as fennel (*Foeniculum vulgare*) and rosemary (*Rosmarinus officinalis*), would eventually be enough. Putting in several plants of the same kind helps avoid planting different herbs too close together, gives a mature look very quickly, and ensures plenty of harvestable herbs within a few weeks of planting. Coriander (*Coriandrum sativum*) and dill (*Anethum graveolens*) tend to have very short life cycles, which is fine if you are growing them for seed, but you will need two or three sowings a season to ensure a supply of young leaves. Although parsley (*Petroselinum crispum*) is biennial, it is best to make two plantings, in early spring and in late summer, for a year-round supply.

PLANT LIST

1. *Myrtus communis* x 1
2. *Petroselinum crispum* 'Moss Curled' x 5
3. *Artemisia dracunculus* x 5
4. *Thymus* x *citriodorus* x 6
5. *Borago officinalis* x 5
6. *Coriandrum sativum* x 9
7. *Rosmarinus officinalis* x 1
8. *Mentha spicata* x 3
9. *Thymus vulgaris* x 7
10. *Salvia officinalis* x 1
11. *Origanum vulgare* 'Compactum' x 7
12. *Ocimum basilicum* x 3
13. *Anethum graveolens* x 5
14. *Rumex acetosa* x 7
15. *Foeniculum vulgare* x 1
16. *Allium schoenoprasum* x 5
17. *Satureja montana* x 4

DIAMETER 15FT (5M)
PATH WIDTH 3FT (1M)

GRADUATED PAVING
A series of stepping stones, or a flagged path, as here, enable the planting to have different levels, and your herbs will still be easy to reach, even in wet weather.

AN INFORMAL CULINARY BED
This culinary herb bed in a country setting has a relaxed feel in the evening sun. There is also space to add additional ornamental plants.

A DECORATIVE AND USEFUL PLANTING
*Many of the herbs in this plan are hardy. One exception is basil (*Ocimum basilicum*), which in cold areas can only be grown outdoors during the summer. Also, myrtle (*Myrtus communis*) and tarragon (*Artemisia dracunculus*) need protection in hard winters, and rosemary (*Rosmarinus officinalis*) is susceptible to cold, wet conditions in heavy soils. The various thymes and compact marjoram (*Origanum vulgare *'Compactum') are planted in gaps between the paving stones.*

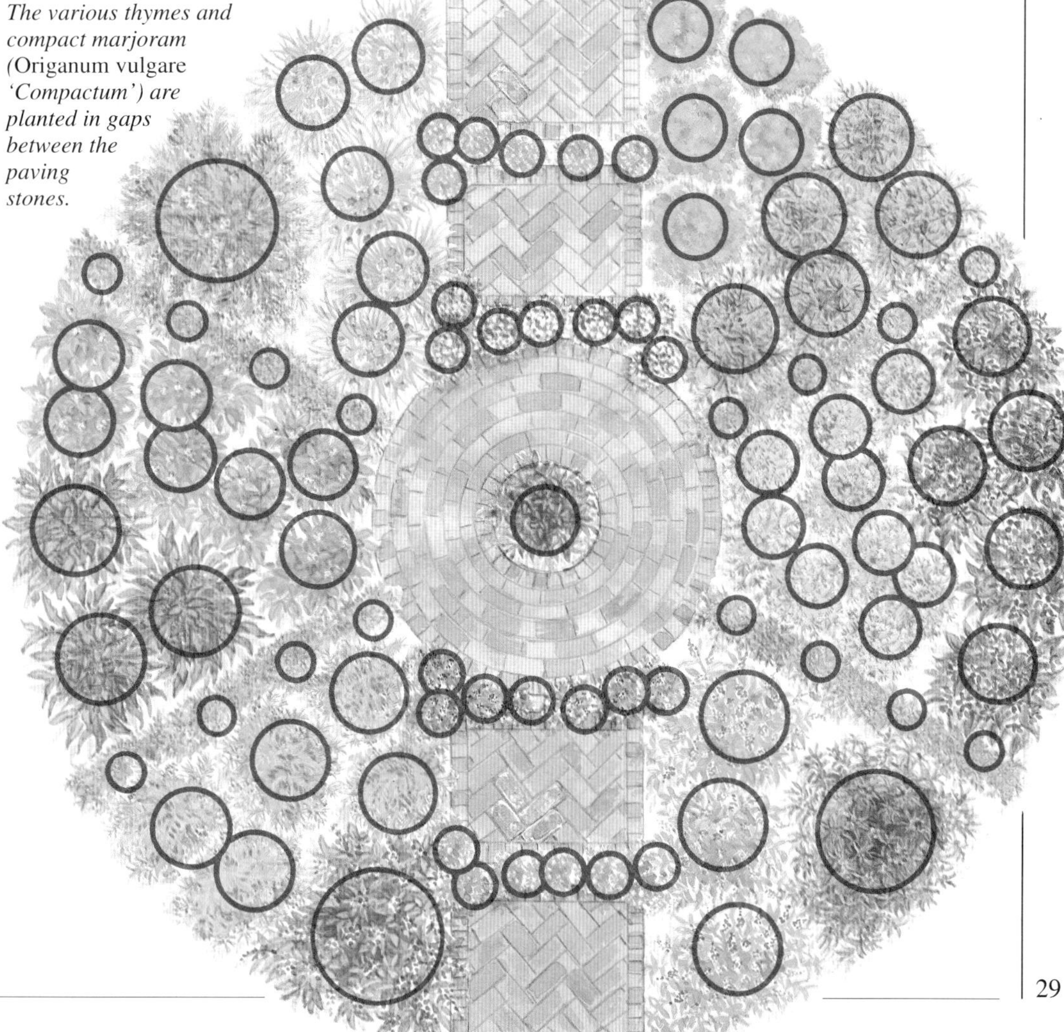

Informal Garden Designs

Informal herb gardens can be made in many styles, adapted to suit the conditions in your garden, and the next few pages offer some suggestions for these. The plan below is really several small herb gardens in one, including bog or water plants, ramblers, and creepers. On the following pages are contrasting gardens for sun and shade, suited to town or country conditions.

Individual Garden Areas

Each of the mini-gardens shown here has its own character. Groupings have been planned for scent, color, and culinary use. The ideal setting for this garden, which has seven separate areas, would be in paving or gravel, which need little maintenance, and give all-weather access. Stone also makes an attractive, warm, well-drained setting for the plants. Alternatively, the areas containing the creeping herbs, containers, and arbor could be paved or graveled, and the pool, bog garden, and borders surrounded by lawn.

A Place for Everything

Taller perennials and shrubs are planted against the boundary wall or hedge, which displays them to best advantage; moisture-loving herbs are amply supplied with rich mud and water in an aquatic environment. Tender herbs, invasive ones, or favorites for cutting are best in pots of their own, which can be moved and replanted according to need. A group of pots could also house a specialty collection, perhaps of scented geraniums.

Humulus lupulus **'Aureus' and *Lonicera japonica* 'Halliana'**
The golden hops and honeysuckle shown here are well suited to an arbor, and in combination provide both ample shade and a pleasant fragrance in summer, when the heavily scented honeysuckle comes into flower.

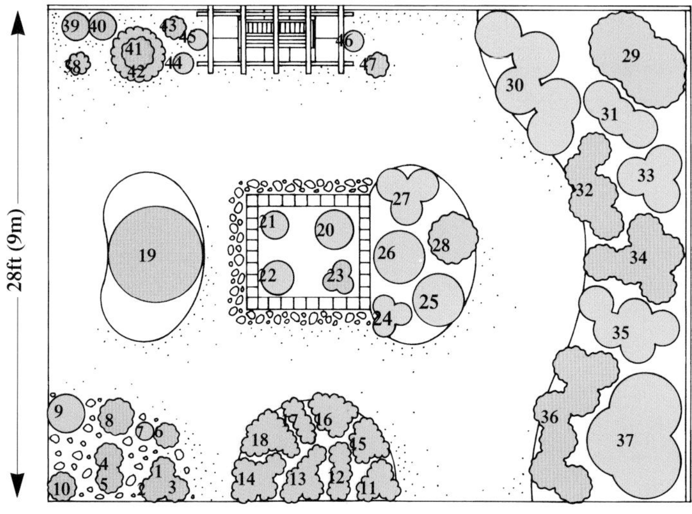

Plant List

1. *Thymus vulgaris* 'Aureus' x 1
2. *Thymus pseudolanuginosus* x 1
3. *Thymus serpyllum* var. *coccineus* x 1
4. *Thymus serpyllum* 'Russetings' x 1
5. *Thymus serpyllum* 'Snowdrift' x 1
6. *Thymus serpyllum* 'Pink Chintz' x 1
7. *Mentha requienii* x 3
8. *Satureja spicigera* x 1
9. *Mentha pulegium* x 1
10. *Thymus herba-barona* x 3
11. *Anethum graveolens* x 3
12. *Borago officinalis* x 3
13. *Papaver rhoeas* x 5
14. *Centaurea cyaneus* x 5
15. *Ocimum basilicum* x 9
16. *Calendula officinalis* x 5
17. *Coriandrum sativum* x 5
18. *Satureja hortensis* x 5
19. *Chamaemelum nobile* 'Treneague' (25 per sq yd)
20. *Typha latifolia* 'Variegata' x 1
21. *Menyanthes trifoliata* x 1
22. *Nymphaea alba* x 1
23. *Acorus gramineus* 'Variegatus' x 3
24. *Ranunculus ficaria* var. *flore pleno* x 3
25. *Symplocarpus foetidus* x 1
26. *Symphytum* x *uplandicum* 'Variegatum' x 1
27. *Filipendula ulmaria* 'Aurea' x 3
28. *Myrica gale* x 1
29. *Sambucus nigra* 'Guincho Purple' x 2
30. *Allium schoenoprasum* 'Forescate' x 3
31. *Saponaria officinalis* 'Rubra Plena' x 1
32. *Salvia officinalis* 'Tricolor' x 3
33. *Foeniculum vulgare* 'Purpureum' x 3
34. *Ruta graveolens* 'Jackman's Blue' x 5
35. *Salvia officinalis,* Purpurascens Group x 3
36. *Lavandula angustifolia* 'Hidcote' x 5
37. *Cynara scolymus* x 3
38. *Petroselinum crispum* 'Moss Curled' x 1
39. *Pelargonium* 'Graveolens' x 1
40. *Pelargonium crispum* 'Variegatum' x 1
41. *Laurus nobilis* x 1
42. *Perilla frutescens* var. *crispa* x 5
43. *Rosmarinus officinalis,* Prostratus Group x 1
44. *Mentha spicata* 'Crispa' x 1
45. *Humulus lupulus* 'Aureus' x 1
46. *Lonicera japonica* 'Halliana' x 1
47. *Myrtus communis* 'Variegata' x 1

Chamaemelum nobile **'Treneague'**
Establishing a chamomile lawn on a large scale is very difficult (which is why chamomile lawns are such a rarity), but the relatively small area suggested here is much more realistic – and bare patches that appear after winter can easily be replanted.

Papaver rhoeas and *Borago officinalis*
This planting is entirely devoted to annuals so that it can be cleared in winter and given a new look each spring, rearranging the different herbs or changing varieties. The blue borage and red poppies shown here could be followed by white borage and pastel poppies the next year.

Thymus 'Pink Chintz' and *Mentha requienii*
These creeping herbs are suited to an open, sunny area, where they are not in danger of being overgrown, and where their fragrance can be released by being crushed underfoot.

MEDITERRANEAN HERB BED

The wide range of herbal plants available to the gardener allows even the most extreme planting situations to be considered when planning a herb garden. The design illustrated here would suit a baking hot, very dry bed that is exposed to the sun all day. It is all a question of selecting the right plants for the conditions – in a sunny location (such as shown at right) you could create a predominantly silver herb garden, full of the aromas of the Mediterranean.

USING SILVER PLANTS

This hot weather garden would be best against a patio wall, where the aromatic scents would be close at hand. The containers are optional but add an even more exotic element, with tall, rustling eucalyptus, spiky agave, and velvet-leaved, tender lavender. Spiny foliage, silver-gray hairy leaves, and pungent aromas are common survival mechanisms in dry, bright environments, protecting the plants against high levels of ultraviolet light and desiccation. The planting is enlivened by the colors of California poppies (*Eschscholzia californica*), which flower all summer.

Lavandula angustifolia*, *Artemisia ludoviciana* 'Silver Queen', and *Tanacetum densum* subsp. *amani
This grouping of silver-leaved plants is a variation on the combinations suggested in the planting plan below. In the background, the brilliant purple of the lavender sets off the silver foliage of the artemisia, which will spread sideways very adaptably to fill extra space. Cascading over the wall in front are the bright yellow flowers and finely cut foliage of the tanacetum. As a contrast to these small-leaved plants, there are dramatic clumps of giant thistles at the back, and the broad, downy leaves of self-sown mullein (*Verbascum* species) in the foreground.

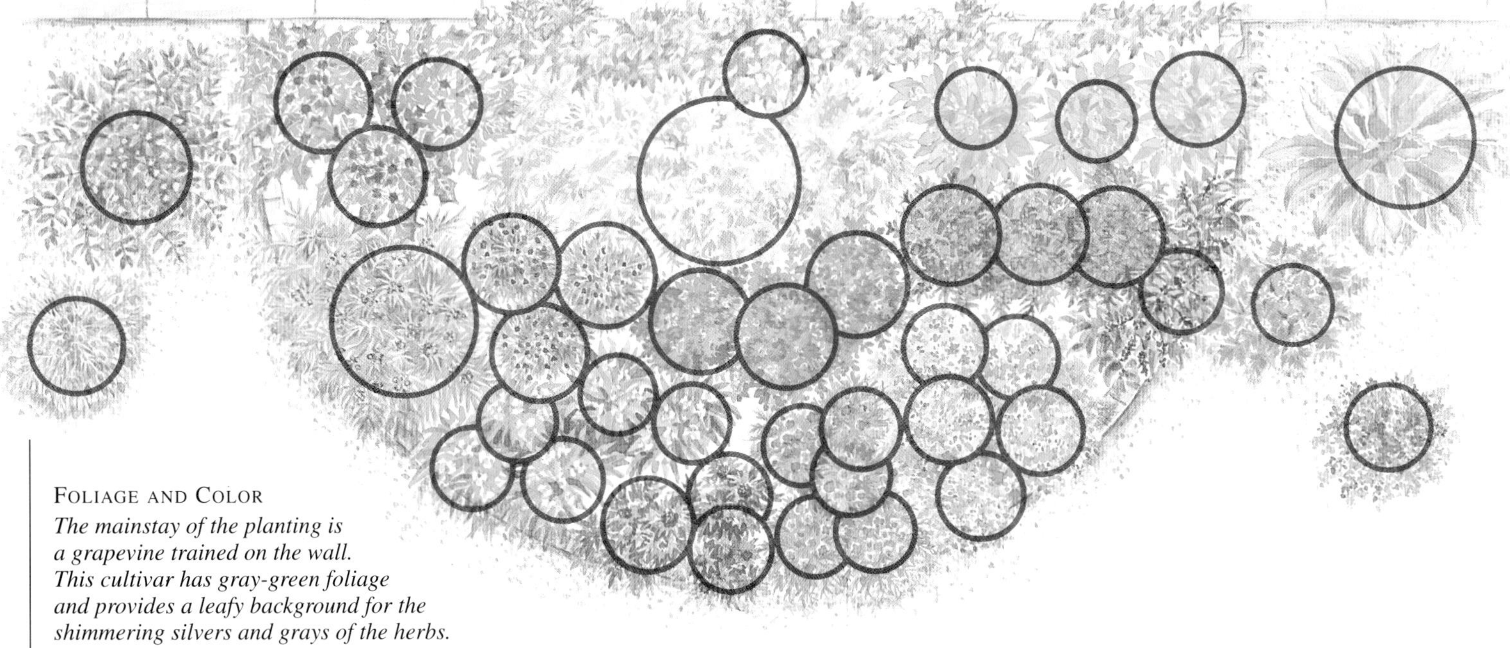

FOLIAGE AND COLOR

The mainstay of the planting is a grapevine trained on the wall. This cultivar has gray-green foliage and provides a leafy background for the shimmering silvers and grays of the herbs.

PLANT LIST

1. *Lavandula lanata* x 1
2. *Eucalyptus globulus* x 1
3. *Silybum marianum* x 3
4. *Vitis vinifera* 'Incana' x 1
5. *Artemisia absinthium* 'Lambrook Silver' x 1
6. *Tanacetum balsamita* var. *tomentosum* x 3
7. *Helichrysum italicum* x 1
8. *Lavandula stoechas* subsp. *pedunculata* x 3
9. *Ruta graveolens* x 3
10. *Rosmarinus officinalis* x 3
11. *Salvia officinalis* 'Berggarten' x 1
12. *Iris germanica* var. *florentina* x 5
13. *Eryngium maritimum* x 3
14. *Eschscholzia californica* x 5
15. *Thymus vulgaris* 'Silver Posie' x 5
16. *Agave americana* x 1
17. *Pelargonium* 'Mabel Grey' x 1
18. *Acinos arvensis* x 3

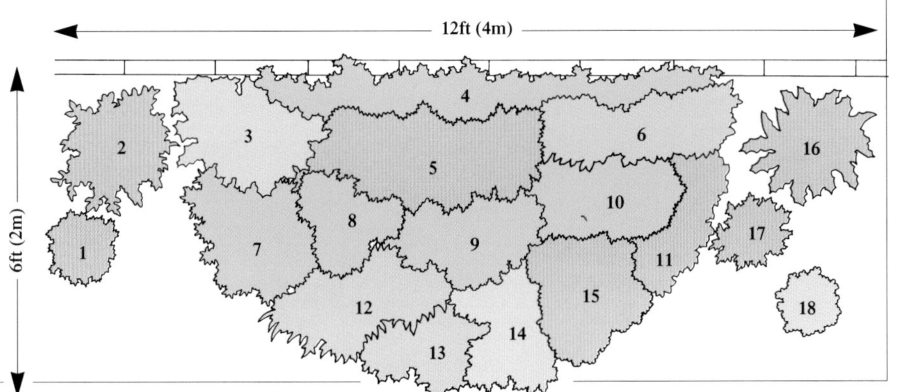

WOODLAND HERB GARDEN

Many interesting herbs that have medicinal properties, and are also very ornamental, originated in a woodland habitat. As a result, they thrive in moist, sheltered conditions, and tolerate shade. In such cool, humid conditions they evolved delicate, often fernlike leaves, or developed a carpeting habit to cover the humus-rich ground beneath trees. An exception to this pattern is the foxglove *(Digitalis)*, which is specially adapted to growing in woodland clearings. Foxglove seeds need light to germinate, and can remain dormant for years until a clearing appears in the trees, whereupon thousands of young plants come up one year and flower *en masse* in the next. This biennial pattern means that at first you need to replant foxgloves annually to supplement those that self-seed and to guarantee flowers each year. Herb Robert *(Geranium robertianum)* and sweet cicely *(Myrrhis odorata)* often self-seed prolifically, whereas periwinkle *(Vinca)* and woodruff *(Galium odoratum)* are rampant spreaders. Remember that, if your woodland is not to become a jungle, you will have to be ruthless about weeding out seedlings and runners.

PLANT LIST

1. *Sambucus nigra* 'Marginata' x 1
2. *Myrrhis odorata* x 3
3. *Mentha suaveolens* 'Variegata' x 3
4. *Vinca major* x 5
5. *Valeriana officinalis* x 1
6. *Aconitum napellus* x 1
7. *Trillium erectum* x 3
8. *Geranium robertianum* x 1
9. *Ajuga reptans* 'Atropurpurea' x 3
10. *Digitalis lanata* x 3
11. *Melissa officinalis* x 1
12. *Convallaria majalis* x 5
13. *Galium odoratum* x 1
14. *Polygonum bistorta* x 3
15. *Aegopodium podagraria* 'Variegatum' x 1

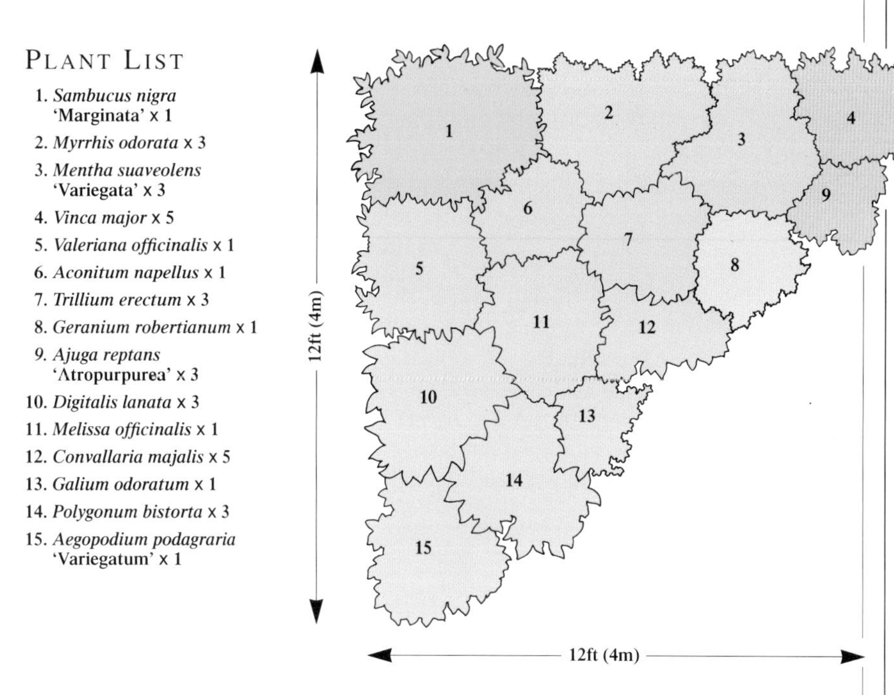

Sambucus nigra and Geranium robertianum
The variegated leaves of this elder (*Sambucus nigra* 'Marginata') are encouraged by cutting it back hard, before it leafs out in early spring. Pink herb Robert (*Geranium robertianum*) makes a delicate contrast.

Alchemilla mollis* and *Geranium robertianum
The rounded, lobed leaves of lady's mantle (*Alchemilla mollis*) complement the ferny, red-tinged foliage and pink flowers of herb Robert.

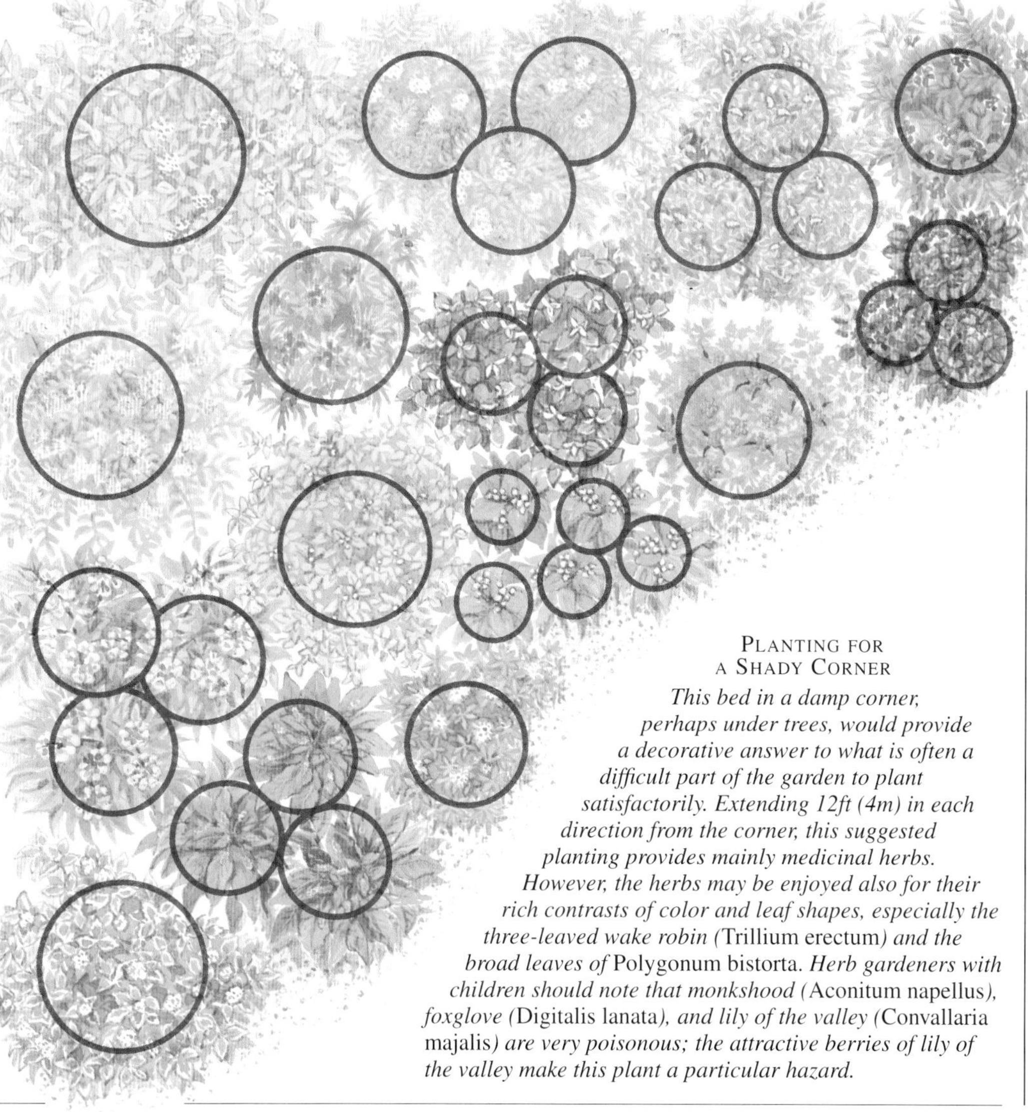

PLANTING FOR A SHADY CORNER

*This bed in a damp corner, perhaps under trees, would provide a decorative answer to what is often a difficult part of the garden to plant satisfactorily. Extending 12ft (4m) in each direction from the corner, this suggested planting provides mainly medicinal herbs. However, the herbs may be enjoyed also for their rich contrasts of color and leaf shapes, especially the three-leaved wake robin (*Trillium erectum*) and the broad leaves of* Polygonum bistorta. *Herb gardeners with children should note that monkshood (*Aconitum napellus*), foxglove (*Digitalis lanata*), and lily of the valley (*Convallaria majalis*) are very poisonous; the attractive berries of lily of the valley make this plant a particular hazard.*

HERBS AMONG THE FLOWERS

Combining herbs with flowers or other plants can give you the best of all worlds in your garden. The fragrant, white border shown below is wonderful on a warm summer evening; the rose garden blends scents and warm shades of color; the curved border allows plenty of choice and contrast, with herbs and flowers to last all year.

Rosa* x *alba* 'Semiplena' and *Crambe cordifolia
Clouds of tiny crambe flowers provide a contrasting background for the heavy, scented blooms of the white rose of York.

WHITE BED WITH HERBS

The best site for this kind of planting is against a dark green hedge, against which white flowers show up well. A number of herbs naturally have white flowers, such as orris (*Iris germanica* var. *florentina*) and madonna lilies (*Lilium candidum*), and many others have white-flowered cultivars. These include some of the most popular culinary herbs, such as sage (*Salvia officinalis*), which you will find in this plan; there are also white-flowered chives (*Allium schoenoprasum*), marjorams (*Origanum* spp.) and thymes (*Thymus* spp.).

A MIXED BORDER

The plants in this plan are perennials and shrubs, with the exception of Lavatera trimestris *'Mont Blanc' and* Nicotiana sylvestris, *which are grown as annuals, and* Lunaria annua *'Alba Variegata', a hardy biennial that usually comes true from seed and self-seeds, though the variegation may not be apparent in young plants.*

Gillenia trifoliata* and *Artemisia pontica
A filigree of artemisia leaves is effective beside the reddish stems and sprays of narrow-petaled white flowers of *Gillenia trifoliata*.

PLANT LIST

Taxus baccata – for hedge

1. *Galega officinalis* 'Alba' x 1
2. *Crambe cordifolia* x 1
3. *Rosa alba* 'Semiplena' x 1
4. *Nicotiana sylvestris* x 3
5. *Philadelphus* 'Belle Etoile' x 1
6. *Veronicastrum virginicum* f. *album* x 1
7. *Tanacetum parthenium* 'Aureum' x 3
8. *Gillenia trifoliata* x 3
9. *Agastache foeniculum* 'Alabaster' x 3
10. *Lavatera trimestris* 'Mont Blanc' x 7
11. *Artemisia* 'Powis Castle' x 1
12. *Lunaria annua* 'Alba Variegata' x 3
13. *Hosta* 'Royal Standard' x 1
14. *Lilium candidum* x 3
15. *Artemisia pontica* x 5
16. *Iris germanica* var. *florentina* x 3
17. *Aquilegia*, Music Series Hybrids (white) x 3
18. *Galium odoratum* x 1
19. *Ruta graveolens* 'Jackman's Blue' x 3
20. *Geranium dalmaticum* 'Album' x 3
21. *Lavandula* x intermedia 'Alba' x 5
22. *Dianthus* 'Mrs. Sinkins' x 3
23. *Viola cornuta* 'Alba' x 3
24. *Salvia officinalis* 'Albiflora' x 3
25. *Hyssopus officinalis* f. *albus* x 3

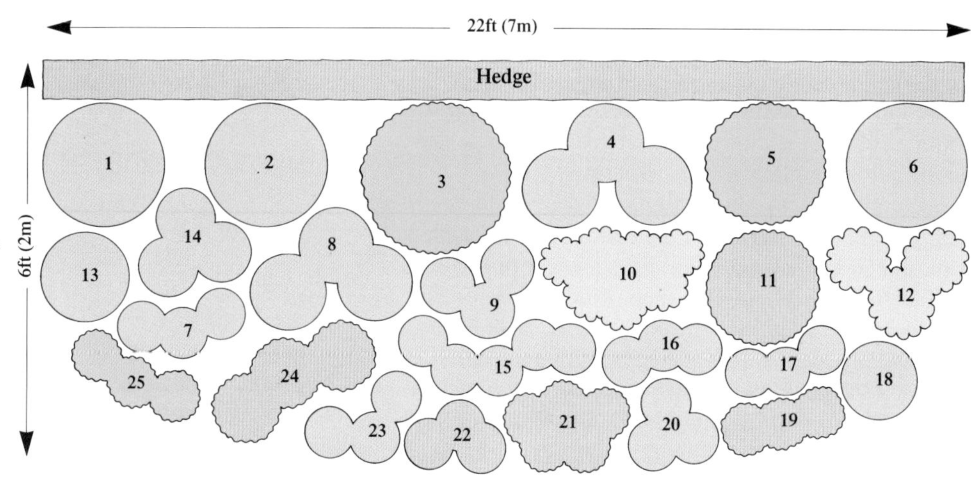

Artemisia 'Powis Castle' and *Lavatera trimestris* 'Mont Blanc'

Simple white mallow flowers are delightful among the finely cut silver leaves of this compact wormwood.

Ruta graveolens 'Jackman's Blue' and *Aquilegia, Music Series Hybrids*

The darting flowers of a white aquilegia overhang a neat blue-gray mound of rue.

A Mixed Border with Herbs

A specifically made herb garden is a great asset, but not essential – herbs grown alongside other plants in the garden will still smell as sweet! There are a number of things to consider when planting in this way. Height is obviously important, so make sure that any herbs you are adding are a suitable size for their companions. Low-growing savory (*Satureja spicigera*) and parsley (*Petroselinum crispum*) have been planted here as edging, backed by neat, compact dwarf dahlias that are unlikely to smother them. Consider color and texture, too; try putting lacy coriander (*Coriandrum sativum*) among the magenta spikes of field gladioli to give interesting plant associations. In late winter, pansies (*Viola* x *wittrockiana*) and chicory (*Cichorium intybus*) will brighten the border.

***Begonia semperflorens* 'Cocktail' and *Thymus* x *citriodorus* 'Archer's Gold'**
The greenish-gold foliage of this creeping thyme, excellent for both aromatic and culinary use, is a good foil for the bright mixed colors of the evergreen hybrid begonias.

UNUSUAL COMBINATIONS

Culinary herbs flourish in a mixed border of perennials and bedding plants. This choice of ornamentals includes some interesting plant associations, but other plants of your own preference could easily be substituted.

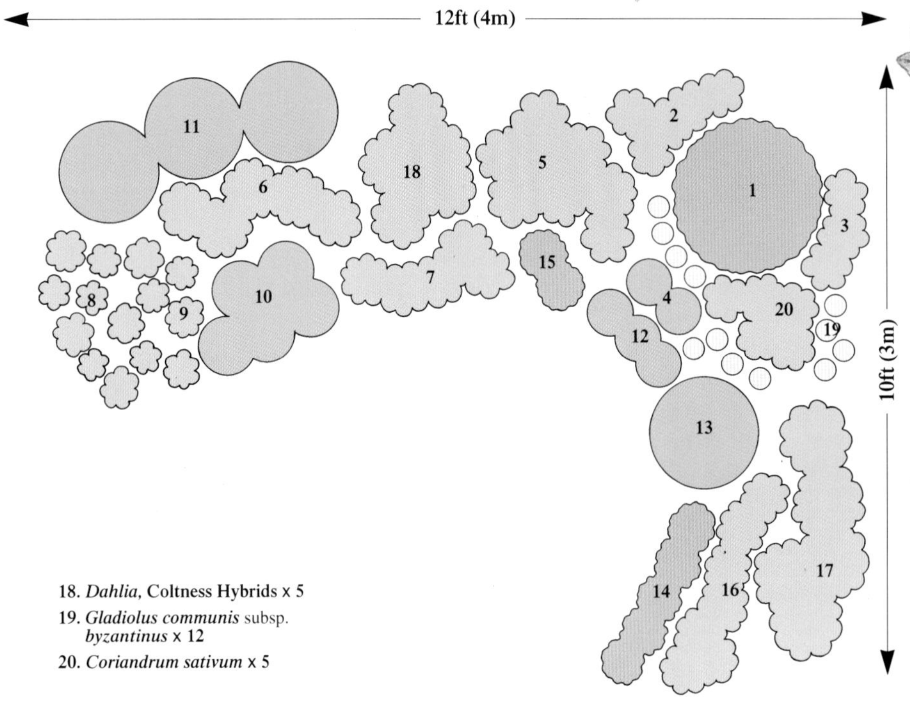

12ft (4m)

10ft (3m)

Plant List

1. *Phygelius capensis* x 1
2. *Anethum graveolens* x 5
3. *Borago officinalis* x 3
4. *Artemisia schmidtiana* 'Nana' x 2
5. *Ocimum basilicum* 'Dark Opal' x 7
6. *Dendranthema*, Suncharm Series x 5
7. *Petroselinum crispum* 'Moss Curled' x 5
8. *Viola* x *wittrockiana*, Universal Series x 7
9. *Cichorium intybus* 'Giulio' x 7
10. *Allium schoenoprasum* x 5
11. *Allium tuberosum* x 30
12. *Origanum vulgare* 'Compactum' x 3
13. *Rumex scutatus* 'Silver Shield' x 1
14. *Thymus* x *citriodorus* 'Archer's Gold' x 5
15. *Satureja spicigera* x 2
16. *Begonia semperflorens* 'Cocktail' x 7
17. *Portulaca oleracea* 'Golden' x 5
18. *Dahlia*, Coltness Hybrids x 5
19. *Gladiolus communis* subsp. *byzantinus* x 12
20. *Coriandrum sativum* x 5

HERBS IN A ROSE GARDEN

The rich colors and exquisite scents of roses are glorious highlights of summer, but the plants can present a rather uninspiring picture for the rest of the year. Adding a selection of aromatic herbs is an ideal solution to this problem; their finely cut, often velvety, grayish foliage provides a contrast to the primarily broad, dark green rose leaves, and their small, pastel-colored flowers complement rather than compete with the opulence of the roses. All the herbs in this planting are closely related to each other and their flowers range from white to pink and purple-blue. Their similarity in appearance contributes to the harmony of shapes and colors. Purple-leaved sage (*Salvia officinalis*, Purpurascens Group) is particularly effective with pale pink roses, whereas the white-flowered sage (*Salvia officinalis* 'Albiflora') is a better choice beside salmon-yellow.

PLANT LIST

1. *Rosa* 'Mme. Alfred Carrière' x 2
2. *Rosa gallica* 'Versicolor' x 1
3. *Rosa* x *centifolia* 'Muscosa' x 1
4. *Rosa* 'Mme. Isaac Pereire' x 1
5. *Rosa* 'Comte de Chambord' x 1
6. *Rosa* 'Complicata' x 1
7. *Teucrium chamaedrys* x 27
8. *Salvia officinalis* 'Albiflora' x 2
9. *Lavandula angustifolia* 'Folgate' x 3
10. *Hyssopus officinalis* f. *roseus* x 3
11. *Salvia officinalis*, Purpurascens Group x 3
12. *Dianthus caryophyllus* x 14
13. *Lavandula angustifolia* 'Rosea' x 3
14. *Salvia officinalis* 'Berggarten' x 3
15. *Origanum vulgare* x 3

20ft (6m)

28ft (9m)

CHOOSING EDGING

An excellent herb for the inner edging is wall germander (Teucrium chamaedrys). *However, obtaining the right plant can be difficult, since many nurseries confuse both the plant and the name of* Teucrium chamaedrys *with the hybrid hedge germander,* T. x lucidrys. *The true wall germander is better for edging, having a smaller, more spreading habit. If you plant the hybrid instead, it will need trimming in spring, and again after flowering.*

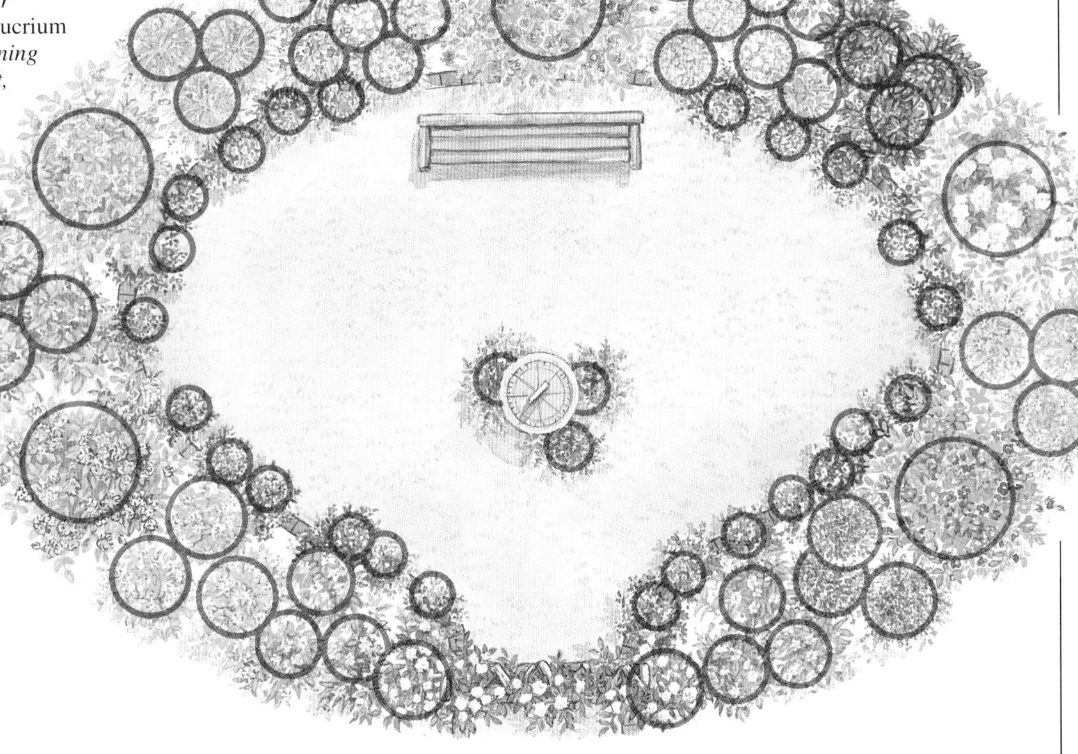

Rosa 'Mme. Isaac Pereire' and *Dianthus caryophyllus*
The brilliant blooms of the pink bourbon rose contrast with the deep red of the clove pink and the paler, red-centered *Dianthus chinensis* in the foreground.

Rosa gallica 'Versicolor' with *Lavandula angustifolia* 'Folgate' and *Digitalis* species
This fragrant pastel display is reminiscent of an old English cottage garden, with elegant spires of pink and white foxgloves (*Digitalis* species) waving over a profusion of pink roses and the compact, violet-flowered 'Folgate' lavender.

A VEGETABLE POTAGER

In gardens where space is at a premium, many people forego the pleasure of growing their own fresh produce. But shortage of space can be a challenge, as gardeners in France have shown by devising the *potager* – an ornamental, formal garden in which herbs mingle with fruit and vegetables.

***Tropaeolum majus* and *Allium porrum* 'Musselburgh'**
Choose a compact, bushy nasturtium (*Tropaeolum majus*), rather than a climbing one, for this kind of planting. If they spread into the bed, the bases of the leeks (*Allium porrum*) should blanch beautifully under cover of the nasturtium leaves.

A GARDEN OF VARIETY

The area is divided into neat little beds that can be at ground level, or raised up. Raised beds allow easy access for both cultivation and harvesting. Crop rotation will happen automatically, since you will almost certainly vary what you grow each year, just for the fun of trying out new planting combinations.

Brassica oleracea* 'Red Drumhead' and *Petroselinum crispum
Toward the end of the growing season, the red cabbages (*Brassica oleracea*) mature beneath the flowering stems of the parsley (*Petroselinum crispum*).

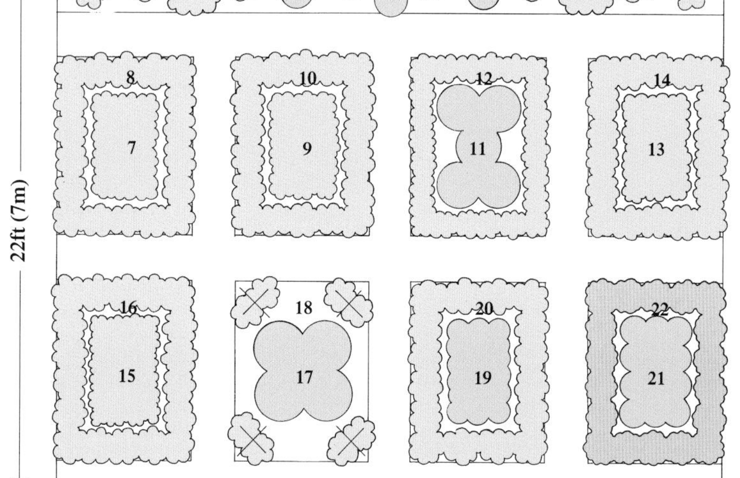

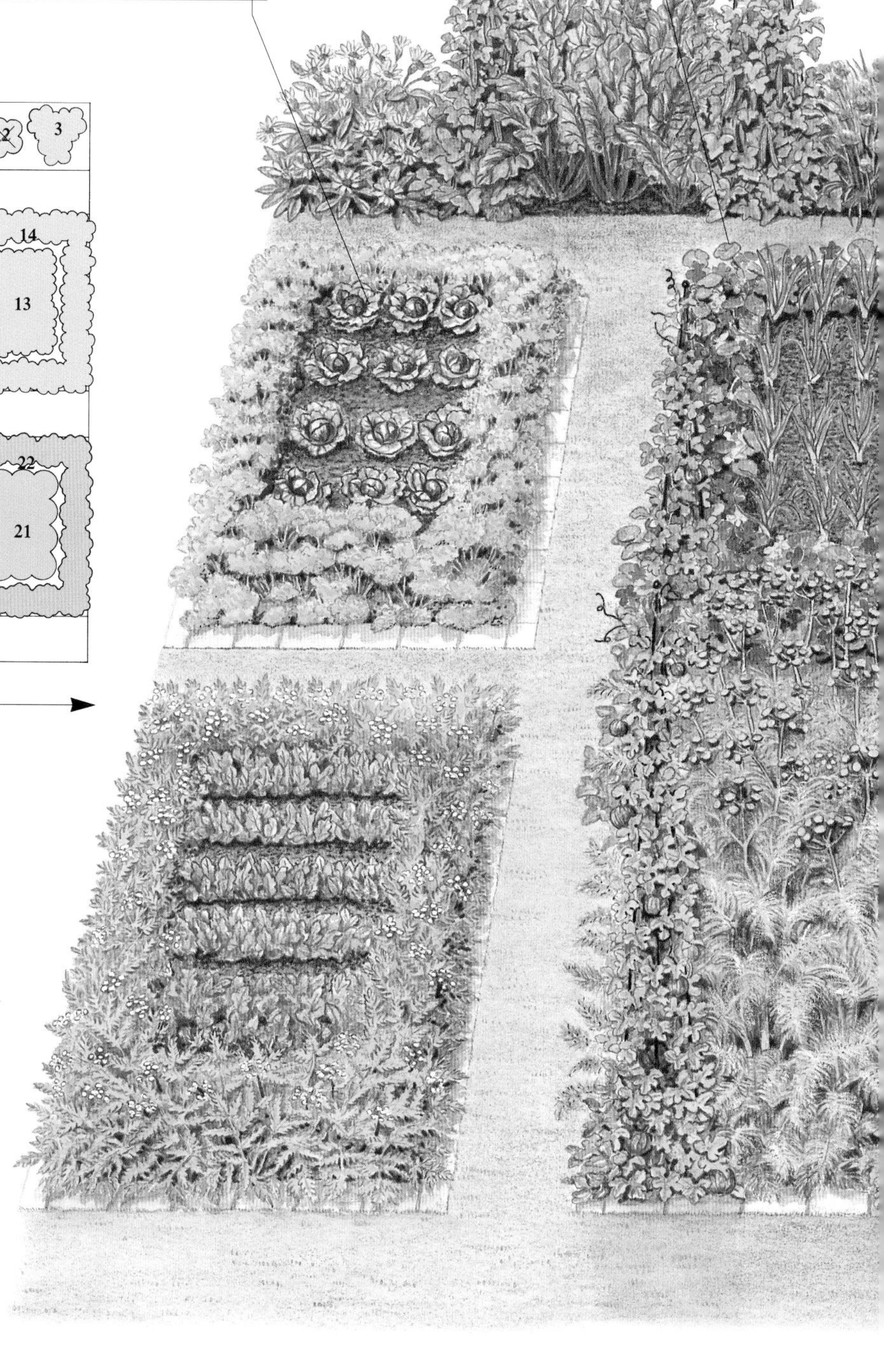

PLANT LIST

1. *Morus nigra* x 1
2. *Cucumis sativus* 'Telegraph Improved' x 4
3. *Calendula officinalis* x 6
4. *Beta vulgaris*, Cycla Group x 12
5. *Allium schoenoprasum* x 3
6. *Fragaria vesca* x 7
7. *Brassica oleracea* 'Red Drumhead' x 12
8. *Petroselinum crispum* x 18
9. *Allium porrum* 'Musselburgh' x 16
10. *Tropaeolum majus*, Whirlybird Series x 18
11. *Asparagus officinalis* x 5
12. *Tagetes patula* 'Sophia Mixed' x 24
13. *Atriplex hortensis* 'Rubra' x 12
14. *Phaseolus vulgaris* 'Purple Teepee' x 18
15. *Raphanus sativus* 'Cherry Belle' x 24
16. *Anthriscus cerefolium* x 18
17. *Foeniculum vulgare* x 4
18. *Cucurbita pepo* 'Butternut' x 8
19. *Lactuca sativa* 'Cocarde' x 16
20. *Origanum vulgare* 'Aureum' x 8
21. *Rumex acetosa* x 6
22. *Lavandula angustifolia* x 18

The Importance of Height

*The skillful use of height adds another dimension to simple geometric designs, which otherwise depend largely on colorful planting for visual interest. In this design, it is provided by a mulberry tree as a permanent feature, and by some climbing herbs and vegetables trained on tall supports such as teepees of stakes. The position of climbers can be changed annually, as can the kind of plant chosen. As an alternative to the cucumbers (*Cucumis sativus*) and miniature pumpkins (*Cucurbita pepo*) shown here, try climbing beans, vining nasturtiums, or a loofah gourd (*Luffa cylindrica*).*

Tagetes patula* and *Asparagus officinalis
Some plant combinations fulfill a practical purpose as well as being colorful. The golden French marigold (*Tagetes patula*) is used in companion planting to deter soil pests and whitefly from vegetables such as asparagus, as shown here.

Lavandula angustifolia* 'Munstead' and *Rumex acetosa
The broad, bright green leaves of sorrel are not especially ornamental in themselves, but the foliage makes a lush contrast to the purple spikes of the lavender bushes.

***Lactuca sativa* 'Cocarde' and *Origanum vulgare* 'Aureum'**
This red oakleaf lettuce 'Cocarde', has deeply cut, bronze leaves that are ornamental as well as edible. Grow them with a golden marjoram such as *Origanum vulgare* 'Aureum', an herb that is excellent both in flavor and effect as a garden plant.

Herbs in Containers

Planting herbs in containers is a practical and ornamental way of displaying your favorites, particularly if garden space is limited. They can be positioned close to hand for harvesting, and will look completely different from year to year if you replant them with a different selection of herbs.

Varied Containers

An interesting grouping of herbs in a variety of pots, using their different heights to advantage. If your domain includes a balcony or flight of steps, a collection of interesting containers can turn it into a very individual herbary. Hanging baskets can be used, too, and climbers trained on special trellises designed for pots.

A Culinary Windowbox

A windowbox is one of the best ways to grow culinary herbs, providing access to a supply of fresh leaves, and a sheltered site for the plants. Replant the windowbox when the plants become crowded; the bay (*Laurus nobilis*) and rosemary (*Rosmarinus officinalis* 'Severn Sea') will be worth saving either for larger containers or for planting out in the open ground, and the chives (*Allium schoenoprasum*) and marjoram (*Origanum vulgare* 'Gold Tip') can be divided for replanting.

Culinary Windowbox

1. *Allium schoenoprasum* x 1
2. *Petroselinum crispum* 'Moss Curled' x 1
3. *Laurus nobilis* x 1
4. *Salvia officinalis* x 1
5. *Satureja hortensis* x 1
6. *Rosmarinus officinalis* 'Severn Sea' x 1
7. *Origanum vulgare* 'Gold Tip' x 1

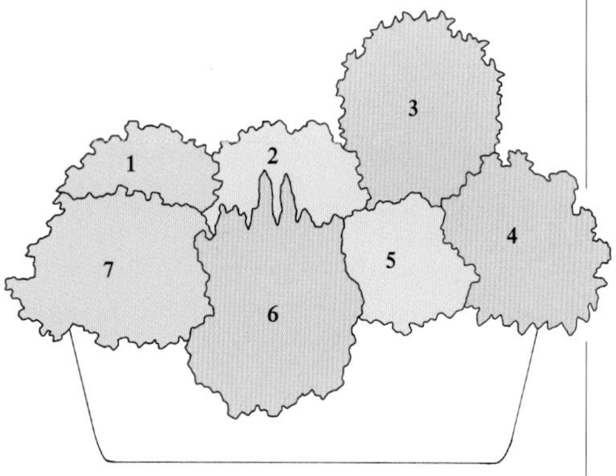

An Easy Culinary Selection

This example of herbs suitable for a windowbox includes seven of the most popular culinary herbs. Some are reasonably hardy, but this selection will perform best if brought into a cool room or greenhouse for winter in cold areas.

A Planter of Home Remedies

A pocketed herb planter – known as a strawberry jar from its original use – gives an interesting display. Filled with suitable plants, it would be an ideal "starter" for someone developing an interest in medicinal herbs, who would like to try making a few teas and simple remedies. Strawberry jars enable a number of herbs to be grown in a small space, though the large number of herbs growing in a relatively small amount of soil means that pots of this kind will soon become overcrowded. They need to be replanted every spring – especially if they contain mint, which during the year is likely to invade every pocket.

Care of the Planter

Strawberry jars dry out quickly, and are then difficult to water because the soil shrinks and the water merely runs out of the pockets. To make watering easier and more effective, stand the planter in a bowl and water from above and below.

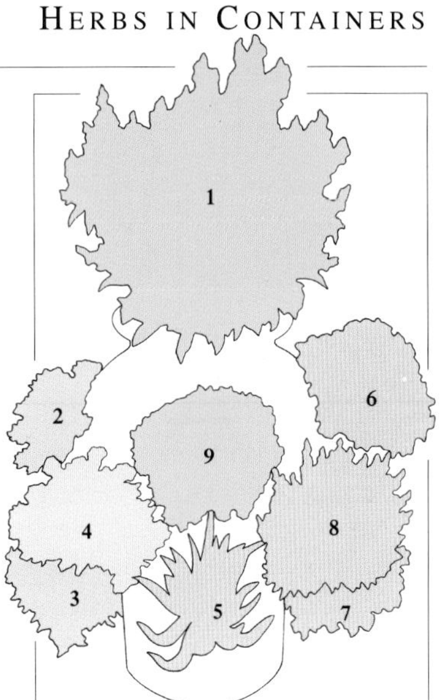

Strawberry Jar

1. *Aloysia triphylla* x 1
2. *Sempervivum tectorum* x 1
3. *Thymus vulgaris* x 1
4. *Calendula officinalis* x 1
5. *Aloe vera* x 1
6. *Tanacetum parthenium* x 1
7. *Chamaemelum nobile* 'Flore Pleno' x 1
8. *Hyssopus officinalis* x 1
9. *Mentha* x *piperita* x 1

Colorful Urn of Herbs

Though chosen for their ornamental merit, some of the herbs used in this container are also useful. Picking sprigs of basil (*Ocimum basilicum* 'Purple Ruffles') or sage (*Salvia officinalis* 'Tricolor') will help keep the plants bushy. The bright red nasturtium (*Tropaeolum majus* 'Alaska') flowers are edible, and there will also be plenty of leaves and flowers for salads. The medicinal herbs heartsease (*Viola tricolor*) and variegated ground ivy (*Glechoma hederacea* 'Variegata') are perfect subjects for containers: the heartsease produces a long succession of miniature pansies, and the ground ivy sends out chains of neat, scalloped leaves that trail to the ground.

Colorful Urn

1. *Salvia officinalis* 'Tricolor' x 1
2. *Pelargonium crispum* 'Variegatum' x 1
3. *Viola tricolor* x 1
4. *Ocimum basilicum* 'Purple Ruffles' x 1
5. *Tropaeolum majus* 'Alaska' x 1
6. *Glechoma hederacea* 'Variegata' x 1

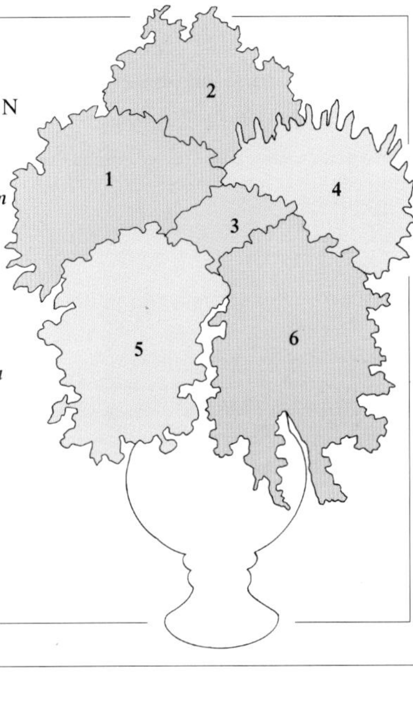

Bright Colors

These colorful, easily-grown herbs will brighten any small space. Although the plants are perennials, it is best to replace most of them each year.

Using Herbs

A common misapprehension is that herbs are small, green, leafy plants with a strong aroma. In both economic and medicinal terms they include an astonishing diversity of plants, from mighty rainforest trees to seaweeds and fungi. No less surprising is the range of parts used as well as some of the uses for which they are harvested. One part of an herb often has quite different properties from the others. In *Hibiscus sabdariffa*, for example, only the calyx of the flower provides the flavoring and the coloring, which is used in herb teas. Chinese medicine also has many examples of specific usages, such as that peels from the ripe and unripe fruits of *Citrus reticulata* are seen as producing quite different drugs. Methods of preparation and storage also affect the properties of an herb. Volatile oils evaporate easily when exposed to light or heat, and while certain herbs must be used fresh, others are used only when dried. This section looks at various uses of herbs, past and present, with some suggestions for modern adaptations.

Herbs for Use
Dried herbs and aromatic plants, ready for processing.

If you are planning to use any herb for culinary, medicinal, or any other purposes, it is essential that you make sure you have the right plant. Common names are often misleading, since the same common name may apply to different species. Do not be tempted to substitute with a similar herb, even if related, particularly for medicinal use; subspecies and varieties may differ in chemistry, although cultivars with minor variations from the species may not do so. Be sure to use *only* the part specified, and to harvest and process herbs only in the ways recommended in the Herb Dictionary (pp. 224-373).

Parts of the Herb

The Dictionary distinguishes which parts of each herb are used for specific purposes. The term *whole plant* usually refers to the parts above the ground (aerial parts). *Leaves* and *stems* (*stalks*) are the most commonly used parts. Green tissues are where photosynthesis occurs, and many compounds, such as volatile oils and alkaloids, are present. Leaves and stalks are at their best in late spring and summer.

In many plants the *flower* forms the reproductive part. The corolla (petals) is often colorful and fragrant to attract pollinators. Petals are protected by a ring of sepals, forming the calyx, which often has a strong aroma, different from the open flower. In the center are the female organ, the pistil, and/or the male part, or stamens. In many plants the *seeds*

Varied Uses
*Cobs of corn (*Zea mays*) are used for food and oil, but only the stigmas and styles, known as "cornsilk," are used medicinally, in remedies for urinary problems.*

Parts of the Plant
This herbal medicine stall in Kaili, western China, shows how specific parts are sold for use in traditional remedies. On sale are whole plants, fruits, bundles of leafy stems, dried bark, and underground parts, including bulbs, rhizomes, and tubers.

▲ Saffron Crocus
Saffron consists only of the scarlet stigma and styles (collectively known as the pistil) of Crocus sativus; *other parts of the flower are useless for coloring or medicinal purposes. The pistils of other kinds of crocus cannot be used as a substitute.*

are surrounded by a *fruit*, which protects them as they develop. The underground parts of a plant are storage organs of various types, usually rich in nutrients that are most concentrated when the plant is dormant. They include *roots*, *rhizomes* (often thickened stems bearing buds that produce shoots), *tubers* (thickened stems), *corms* (thickened stem bases), and *bulbs* (fleshy leaf bases). All types have an outer layer of peel or *bark*, which may often have different properties from the inner tissues, as well as from bark of parts above ground. Tree trunks and branches consist of heartwood in the center, surrounded by sapwood, which is protected by an outer layer of bark. The hard tissue contains lignin, a complex aromatic compound, rich in resins, gums, and oils. Removing sections of bark from a tree or shrub makes it very vulnerable to infection; if removed in a complete ring around the trunk, it will almost certainly cause the plant's death.

NUTRIENT STORAGE
Hamburg parsley (Petroselinum crispum *var.* tuberosum) *is an example of a plant whose main root swells into a tap root to store nutrients during dormancy in winter. Since the nutrients are most concentrated in the tap root during dormancy, harvesting is usually carried out in autumn or before new growth begins in spring.*

USING HERBS SAFELY

It is often said that herbal remedies are safe because they are natural. This is not necessarily the case. Any herb, whether used internally or externally, can cause unpleasant reactions in some people. All herbs are toxic in excess and can cause unpredictable reactions when mixed with other herbs or medications. The information in this book is for general interest only and should not be taken as a recommendation for use.

Self-medication with herbal remedies should only be used for minor complaints such as coughs and colds, stomach upsets, or cuts and bruises. Do not exceed the dose. Babies, pregnant women, and the elderly should not take any herbal remedies unless they have been prescribed by a qualified practitioner. Self-medication during pregnancy endangers the unborn child. Do not take herbal remedies in conjunction with other medications, whether bought over the counter or prescribed by your doctor, without checking with a qualified practitioner that it is safe to do so.

Take great care with inhalant remedies, which are rich in essential oils. These oils are concentrated – it takes the peel of 85 lemons to produce 1oz (30g) of lemon oil – and highly toxic, internally and externally. Essential oils are also widely available for use in food flavoring, potpourris, and aromatherapy. Avoid taking herbal remedies for conditions such as obesity, exhaustion, and nervous tension; these are often better treated with a change of lifestyle. Diet formulas, tonics, and sedatives based on herbs often contain potent ingredients.

Think of herbs in terms of improving health rather than curing ailments. Used regularly and in moderation as part of a balanced diet and lifestyle, herbs can boost immunity and give a sense of well-being. Grow them to use in cooking, salads, or teas, for skin and hair preparations, and to enjoy their colors and fragrance.

FRANKINCENSE RESIN
Frankincense (Boswellia sacra) *on sale in a Somali market. It is collected by shaving off plates of bark, and either scraping off the gum resin as it exudes, or allowing it to drip onto palm leaf mats, where it solidifies. Harvesting methods are the same today as in antiquity, but prices have changed; in Roman times, frankincense was as costly as gold.*

POISONOUS HERBS

Herbs vary greatly in toxicity, from food-cum-medicinal plants such as globe artichokes (*Cynara scolymus*) to deadly nightshade (*Atropa belladonna*), but it goes without saying that if they can do good, they must contain substances that in excess can poison. This is true even of everyday culinary herbs such as thyme, marjoram, rosemary, and mint – they all contain volatile oils that are extremely poisonous in large amounts. Although quite safe when used fresh or dried in the quantities given in recipes, they are potentially dangerous in the form of essential oils, which need very careful measuring and dosage, even for external use.

Many poisonous herbs are commonly grown as ornamentals. These include:

- Foxgloves (*Digitalis* spp.)
- Monkshoods (*Aconitum* spp.)
- Meadow saffron (*Colchicum* spp.)
- Lily of the valley (*Convallaria majalis*)

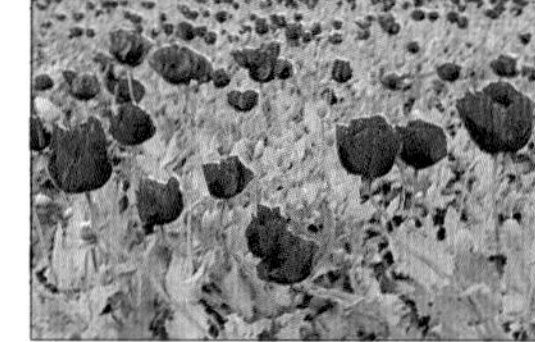

Papaver somniferum

- Opium poppies (*Papaver somniferum*)
- Pokeweeds (*Phytolacca* spp.)
- Madagascar periwinkle (*Catharanthus roseus*)
- Glory lilies (*Gloriosa* spp.)
- Castor bean (*Ricinus communis*)
- Variegated nightshade (*Solanum dulcamara* 'Variegatum')
- Daphnes (*Daphne* spp.)

The following may cause skin irritation when handled:

- Cowslip (*Primula veris*)
- Primrose (*Primula vulgaris*)
- Rue (*Ruta graveolens*)

Warning labels are provided in some countries to alert gardeners to these dangers, but anyone planting herbs should consider the safety of children and animals.

CULINARY USES OF HERBS

Herbs make all the difference to food; the cuisine of a region is characterized as much by the herbs it uses as by the staple foods. We tend to differentiate between herbs, spices, and flavorings, but the differences are small: "herbs" usually refers to aromatic leafy parts; "spices" to pungent seeds, roots, and bark; and "flavorings" to commodities that are often used in the same ways as herbs and spices but are foods in their own right, such as coffee, chocolate, nuts, citrus fruits, onion, garlic, and horseradish. Both the leaves and the seeds are used in some plants, such as fennel, dill, and coriander.

HERBS FOR FLAVOURING
A selection of fresh leafy herbs, such as parsley, bay, or rosemary, picked straight from the garden, adds appreciable amounts of vitamins to a meal, as well as giving flavor.

Another category is the salad herb, or potherb as it was once known. Though most commonly added to salads, salad herbs can also be used in soups and stews. They include watercress, sorrel, dandelion, rocket, and chicory. All herbs and spices have very distinctive aromas and flavors, but they undergo subtle changes according to the foods or other flavorings. Fragrant mixtures have come to characterize the cooking of certain regions – *bouquet garni* (parsley, thyme, bay leaf) in France, *garam masala* (cumin, coriander seeds, cardamom, cloves, mace, cinnamon, bay leaf, black pepper) in northern India, and five-spice powder (see opposite) in China. Mint, an uncompromising flavor, affects the taste buds very differently in Moroccan mint tea, mint sauce and jelly, mint julep (a sweet drink), *harissa* (a Tunisian paste made from mint, chilies, cumin, coriander, caraway seeds, and garlic), *tabbouleh* (a Middle Eastern salad of mint, parsley, and bulghur wheat), and *tzatziki* (mint, cucumber, and yogurt salad).

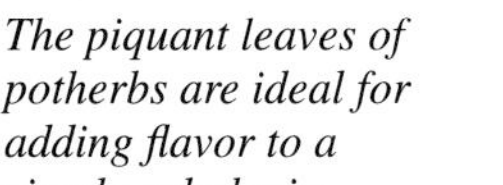

UNUSUAL SALAD MIXES
The piquant leaves of potherbs are ideal for adding flavor to a simple salad mix.

AIDING THE DIGESTION OF FOOD

Herbs add color as well as flavor. Soups made from pale ingredients are much more appetizing when green-flecked with finely chopped parsley or chives. Yellow is an especially appetizing color – most subtle in saffron, and brightest in turmeric. Though seldom seen in the form of seeds, annatto is a coloring in butter, margarine, and "red" cheeses, which would otherwise be cream-colored.

FIERY TUNISIAN PASTE
The Tunisian chili paste harissa *contains dried red chilies (top left), caraway seeds (top right), and dried mint leaves (bottom right), with ground cumin and coriander seeds. Salt and crushed garlic may be added. The dried chilies are soaked in warm water and then pounded or blended with the other ingredients. Fresh chilies are easily dried and then processed in a spice grinder for coarse or finely ground chili powder.*

A LOCAL FOOD SHOP
This Sri Lankan shop shows some of the diversity of food. One herb local to the region is Murraya koenigii, *or curry leaves. They are seldom found elsewhere since the leaves need to be used fresh.*

Paprika gives a glorious brick red color to dishes such as goulash. It is made from dried, powdered red peppers (*Capsicum annuum*), as is cayenne, but can be used in much larger quantities because it lacks cayenne's fiery alkaloid, capsaicin. There are also unseen benefits in adding herbs and spices to food. They increase the vitamin and mineral content, and improve digestion. Garlic is rich in germanium, which has beneficial effects on the circulation. The bitter element in herbs and spices serves to "prime" the digestive system, stimulating the liver and gall bladder, improving digestion, especially of fats, and helping to eliminate toxins. Aperitifs with a hint of bitterness, and raw foods in the form of salads and *crudités*, are traditionally eaten for this purpose.

COOKING WITH HERBS AND SPICES

Use the freshest possible herbs and spices, since essential oils (the main aromatic component) evaporate readily. For optimum flavor, grow your own herbs and buy spices whole, grinding them in small quantities as you need to use them.

Add herbs towards the end of cooking to give the best flavor and retain a fresh green color. A lovely aroma in the kitchen means that the volatile oils are in the air, not in the food! Garlic, spices, and tougher herbs, such as bay leaves, can be added at the beginning to give their flavors a chance to permeate.

Add herbs or spices to vinegars, oils, and mustard to give a subtle flavor to garnishes, dressings, and marinades. Prepare a quantity in advance to allow flavors to permeate (bottles of vinegar or oil with a sprig of herb added will keep up to a year; see *Cultivating Herbs*, p. 393, for method). This is a good way of using strongly flavored herbs, such as lavender, that are difficult to add directly to food (especially to salads).

Try adding potherbs, such as dandelion and nasturtium leaves, rocket, or sorrel to green salads, for their piquant flavour. Many of these also contain valuable vitamins, and watercress has high levels of iron, essential in a healthy diet.

COLLECTING SAFFRON
*Picking saffron flowers (*Crocus sativus*) in southern Europe. The pistils from each crocus are later separated by hand. Saffron has been used in cookery since the 10th century BC.*

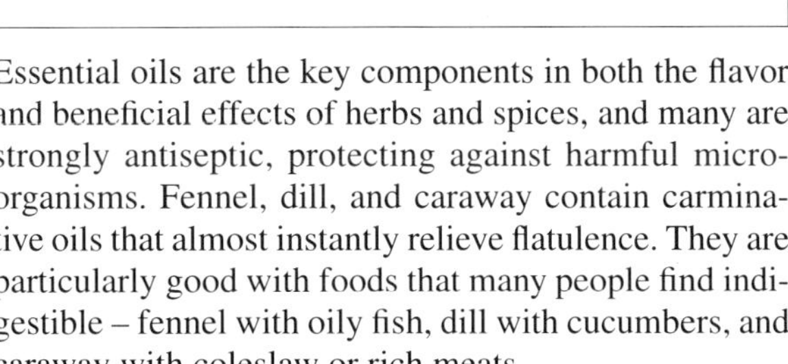

Essential oils are the key components in both the flavor and beneficial effects of herbs and spices, and many are strongly antiseptic, protecting against harmful micro-organisms. Fennel, dill, and caraway contain carminative oils that almost instantly relieve flatulence. They are particularly good with foods that many people find indigestible – fennel with oily fish, dill with cucumbers, and caraway with coleslaw or rich meats.

BENEFICIAL EFFECTS OF HERBS

Peppermint has a soothing, mildly anesthetic effect on the digestive tract, hence the popularity of after-dinner mints and peppermint tea. Perilla, which is used with raw fish dishes in Japan, contains antidotes to seafood poisoning. Garlic is an excellent gastric disinfectant, well worth taking in capsule form as well as in food, while traveling to prevent bouts of diarrhea and vomiting. The therapeutic side to culinary herbs was once more popular than it is today. Sloe gin originally contained pennyroyal and valerian to calm the fraught housewife, which gave it the name "mother's ruin." In the Middle Ages, a hot purgative porridge was made with rough grain, fat, and tansy, and nettle soup was consumed to "spring clean" the body of wastes accumulated in winter through lack of exercise and heavy food. Medicinal meals remain important in traditional Chinese and Ayurvedic practice. In warm countries, the effects of eating hot spices, such as chili, ginger, and pepper, are to raise the metabolic rate, increasing perspiration, effectively cooling the body, and speeding the excretion of toxins. Spices act as preservatives, too, of great importance in warm regions where food deteriorates rapidly. Some herbs and spices are almost universally popular. As well as pepper, ginger, cinnamon, nutmeg, and cloves, garlic is beloved in most cuisines. Chilies and cayenne were unknown outside S America before Columbus discovered the New World in 1492 but are now characteristic of north African, Indian, and Asian dishes, and important in temperate countries, too.

▼ PEPPER HARVEST
Pepper being gathered in the kingdom of Quilon, Kerala, India; an illustration from the French 15th-century Livre des Merveilles. *From very early times pepper, ginger, cinnamon, nutmeg, and cloves have been traded worldwide, causing intense competition between companies and nations.*

▲ FIVE-SPICE POWDER
The ingredients of five-spice powder: star anise, Sichuan pepper or fagara, cassia, fennel seeds, and cloves. This is found throughout China and Vietnam. The woody fruits of star anise open into these attractive star shapes when ripe.

MEDICINAL USES OF HERBS

Herbs have been an essential factor in health care throughout the ages and in all cultures. They are prepared in a number of ways to extract their active ingredients for internal and external use. Western herbalists today are trained in anatomy and physiology, as any doctor is, but they prescribe herbs to correct underlying imbalances, rather than to give temporary relief. Most prescriptions call for several herbs, which work together to greater effect, known as a "synergistic effect."

MEDIEVAL WESTERN MEDICAL PRACTICE
An anonymous French 18th-century painting illustrating the reception room of a master apothecary.

There are a number of different systems of herbal medicine, followed by practitioners in various parts of the world. In tribal cultures, herbal remedies are part of shamanism (spirit worship), in which illness is attributed to evil spirits. Early European herbals often attribute disease to malevolent goblins; Amazonian medicine men diagnose the magical cause of a complaint through hallucinogenic drugs and dancing. Herbs are used as talismans, as well as cures.

PLAINS INDIANS
This medicine bundle belonged to the native American Crow people. During ceremonial dances it was opened to gain supernatural powers, which would ensure the fertility and growth of the tribe.

CHINESE AND AYURVEDIC MEDICINE

Chinese herbalists see illness as a symptom of disharmony in the balance between opposite cosmic energies (*yin*: female, dark, cold; *yang*: male, light, hot), and elements (wood, fire, earth, metal, and water). Energy (*qi*) flows through channels known as meridians. Over 700 prescriptions are commonly used by Chinese herbalists, and the *materia medica* describes over 5500 herbs. Ayurvedic practitioners similarly view the patient as a microcosm of all-pervading forces: *prana* (breath/life), *agni* (spirit/fire), and *soma* (love/harmony), which interact with the elements of earth, water, fire, air, and ether, flowing through energy centers or *chakras*. The elements are combined into three humors, *vata* (wind), *pitta* (fire/bile), and *kapha* (phlegm), which make up the individual's health profile and determine the kind of herb and foods prescribed. Ayurveda ("science of living") uses some 500 herbs.

Western herbalism is essentially eclectic. Historically influenced by ancient Egyptian, Assyrian, and Indian practices, it was for many centuries dominated by early Greek theories of elements (fire, air, earth, water), humors (sanguine, choleric, melancholic, phlegmatic), and essential body fluids (blood, yellow bile, black bile, phlegm). Herbs and foods were categorized as hot, dry, cold, and damp, and prescribed to balance the body's systems. The medicine of Hippocrates (468–377BC) and Galen (second century AD) evolved this system, on which Unani (Islamic) medicine is still based. For several centuries European herbalism was influenced by the Doctrine of Signatures, developed by the Swiss alchemist and physician, Paracelsus (c.1493–1541), which taught that healing herbs were given a symbolic color or shape by God to indicate their use. In the 19th century came Samuel Thomson's Physiomedicalism, a system that combined aspects of native American medicine with traditional European healing of the late 18th century. Physiomedicalism emphasized warmth as a healing force, and aimed to restore vitality through herbs that stimulated or sedated the nervous system, and had astringent or relaxing effects on the tissues. Homeopathy is quite different from herbalism, using minute doses of an herb that in healthy people produces symptoms similar to those of the illness being treated. It is based on the theory that "like cures like," formulated by Samuel Hahnemann in 1796.

COLLECTING IN CHINA
Collecting the herbal material is the first step in preparing traditional remedies.

WILD INGREDIENTS
This medicine stall in São Paulo, Brazil, shows the enormous variety of goods made available after the wild plants are processed.

Herbal remedies are prepared in a number of ways. Some are taken internally, others applied to the skin.

INFUSIONS are prepared by pouring near-boiling water over the herb and covering for 5–10 minutes. This method is best for leaves and flowers. Standard quantities are 3oz (75g) of fresh herb or 1¼oz (30g) of dried herb to 17fl oz (500ml) of water. Infusions must be taken the same day.

DECOCTIONS are made by simmering the herb for at least 15 minutes and straining. Decoctions are best for tough parts, such as bark or roots. Standard quantities are 2½oz (60g) of fresh herb or 1¼oz (30g) of dried herb to 17fl oz (500ml) of water. Decoctions must be taken the same day.

MACERATIONS, preferred for herbs likely to lose some therapeutic value if heated, are made by steeping the herb in water at room temperature for 12 hours; strained or pressed, the mixture is used similarly to infusions and decoctions. Standard quantities are one part weight of herb to five parts volume of water; for example 1oz (25g) of dried herb to 17fl oz (500ml) of water.

TINCTURES are made in the same way as macerations, but using an alcohol/water mix, which preserves as well as extracts the constituents. Ethyl alcohol is used commercially, but diluted vodka is also suitable. Quantities are given in ratios of 1:4, i.e. a tincture uses one part herb to four parts liquid. They store well and are more concentrated than infusions and decoctions.

FLUID EXTRACTS are made according to pharmaceutical grades, giving a concentrated, preserved extract. Quantities are one part herb to one part alcohol.

TEAS (TISANES) are made as infusions, but with aromatic herbs, such as linden flowers (*Tilia* spp.), fennel (*Foeniculum vulgare*), or chamomile (*Chamaemelum nobile*). Herb teas may be sweetened but should not have milk added. Nettle is bland and nonaromatic, and can be added to Indian or China tea for its tonic effect.

JUICING is good for herbs that are best used fresh, such as goosegrass (*Galium aparine*). Use a juice extractor and consume fresh, or freeze. Yields are low, so large quantities of fresh herb are needed.

SYRUPS are concentrated sugar solutions that help preserve infusions and decoctions; they add a soothing element to herbs such as horehound (*Marrubium vulgare*) and make them more palatable. The liquid is heated before adding the sugar or honey. Standard quantities are 17fl oz (500 ml) of liquid to 18oz (500g) of sweetening agent.

POULTICES consist of a pulp or paste made by heating chopped fresh, dried, or powdered herbs with a little water, and are applied as shown below, and replaced as necessary. Research has shown that the healing constituents of comfrey (*Symphytum officinale*) penetrate deeply into the tissues when applied in this way. The simplest poultice is a dock leaf applied to a nettle sting!

A COMPRESS is an alternative to a poultice, made by soaking a clean cloth in a hot infusion, decoction, or diluted tincture, and applying to the part. May be preferred cold for headaches and minor fevers.

OILS are used for healing, skin and hair conditioning, and massage. Sunflower oil is suitable for the treatment of muscular aches and minor injuries, but almond oil is better for conditioning and relaxing. Medicated oils are made in three ways: by heating 9oz (250g) of dried herb or 27oz (750g) of fresh herb in 17fl oz (500ml) of oil in a bowl over boiling water for 2–3 hours – suitable for chickweed (*Stellaria media*), comfrey, and rosemary (*Rosmarinus officinalis*); by filling a jar with fresh herb, topping up with oil, covering and leaving for 2–3 weeks, renewing the herb for a further 2–3 weeks to increase the concentration – better for flowers such as St. John's wort (*Hypericum perforatum*) and pot marigolds (*Calendula officinalis*); or by adding 25–50 drops of essential oil to 100ml (5 tbs) oil for an immediate rubbing or massage oil.

OINTMENTS are made by heating herbs in petroleum jelly or other solid fat in a bowl over boiling water for about 2 hours, and straining while still hot into jars. Standard quantities are 2½oz (60g) of dried herb to 18oz (500g) of fat.

POWDERS consist of ground dried herbs and are used to make pills, capsules, or pastes. Powders may be taken with milk or water, or mixed with oil or honey.

▲ MODERN HERBALISM
Dried herbs and loofahs in a modern herbalist's shop.

MAKING A TINCTURE
The first stage in making a tincture. Pour near-boiling water onto the herb to prepare a tincture. Leave the mixture for two weeks, shaking it at intervals. It may be applied hot or cold.

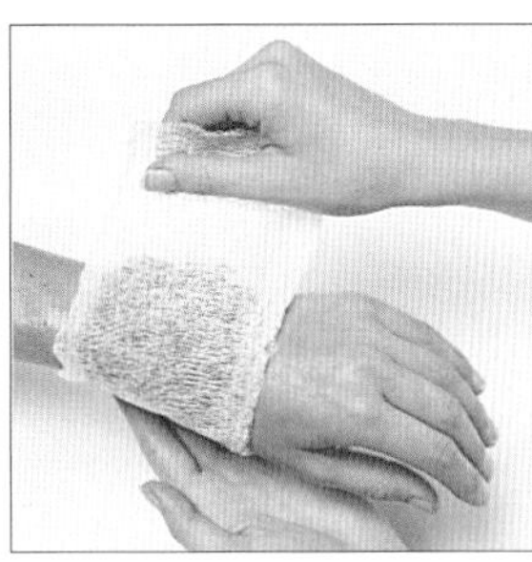

APPLYING A POULTICE
The herb paste is spread between two layers of gauze and applied as hot as bearable to the affected part.

TREATING YOURSELF WITH HERBAL REMEDIES

Using herbal remedies that you have made at home, or bought for the purpose, is fine for the occasional minor problem, but is not recommended for any persistent or serious complaint.

A SIMPLE HERBAL MEDICINE CHEST

- *chamomile or linden (limeflower) tea* for nervous tension and sleeplessness.
- *lemon balm (melissa) tea* for stress-related stomach upsets (especially in children).
- *chickweed ointment* for skin irritations.
- *comfrey ointment* for minor injuries.
- *distilled witch hazel* for bruises and sore eyes.
- *garlic capsules* for colds, influenza, excess mucus.
- *commercial herbal cough mixtures* for particular kinds of cough: chesty (productive or "wet"), or dry and irritant. (They need different remedies.)
- *commercial herbal decongestant* for colds.
- *ginger capsules* for travel sickness.
- *caraway seeds* (which are chewed) or *fennel tea* for indigestion.
- *lavender oil* for minor burns and scalds.
- *tea tree oil* for cold sores.
- *clove oil* for toothache while awaiting dental treatment.

Cosmetic Uses of Herbs

The ancient Egyptians valued cosmetics and perfumery so highly that they were buried with their beauty products, such as kohl and eye pencils, which were kept in ornate vases. Perfumes in the tomb of Tutankhamun were still faintly fragrant after more than 3000 years. The most common ingredients were frankincense and myrrh, which were mixed with sesame, almond, olive, or *balanos* oil. Gum resins such as myrrh were added for their aroma and as fixatives for elusive scents. In a recipe for lily oil, myrrh is added to cardamom, sweet flag, cinnamon, and the petals of 2000 lilies.

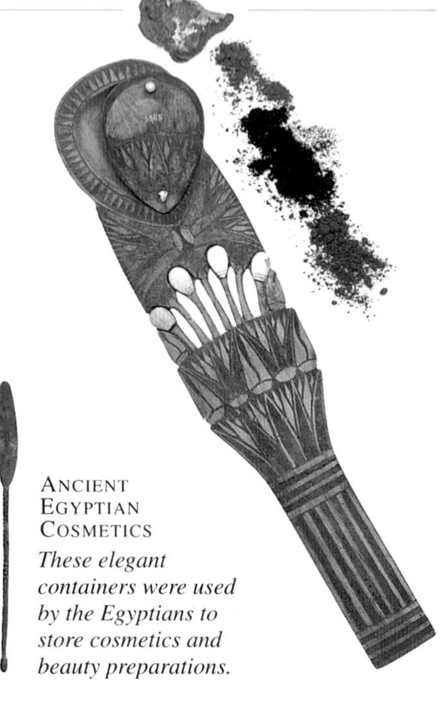

Ancient Egyptian Cosmetics

These elegant containers were used by the Egyptians to store cosmetics and beauty preparations.

Tussie-Mussie

Aromatic herbal posies were carried by the well-to-do to ward off infection and conceal unpleasant smells.

The earliest forms of perfumes were unguents, which were based on animal fat, heated with aromatic plant ingredients. When cold, they were either used as ointment or formed into cones that were worn on the head, so that they melted gradually, anointing the body and clothes with scented grease. The ancient Egyptians also had prototypes of most skin preparations that we use today: depilatories made from gum, cucumber, fig juice, and other ingredients; incense-based deodorants; cleansing creams of oil and lime; and hair tonics made from juniper berries, fir oil, or lettuce.

The Popularity of Bath Oils

Perfumed oils were known to the ancient civilizations of Egypt, Persia, and India. The ancient Greeks studied the art of perfumery and passed on their love of cosmetics and scents to the Romans, who in turn influenced most of Europe. The Romans developed different kinds of perfume: solid and liquid unguents, and powder perfumes. These were especially popular after bathing, which was a major social function in Roman times. Essential oils became available after techniques of distillation were perfected by the Arabs in the Middle Ages. Body oils to perfume and moisturize the skin after bathing are as popular today as in ancient times. Although bath preparations are now mostly made with synthetics, one of the few dispersable natural oils is Turkey red oil (sulfonated castor oil). To make your own natural bath oil, add 50 drops of essential oil to 50ml Turkey red oil (available from suppliers of essential oils). Try lemon (refreshing), lavender (sedative), geranium (relaxing), rosemary (stimulating), or clary sage (uplifting).

Ylang-ylang

The flowers of ylang-ylang, shown here freshly picked on the island of Mayotte, off Madagascar, are often used in perfumery.

The Development of Fragrances

Lavender, which scented the hot water of Roman public baths and was introduced to far corners of the empire, became closely associated with both personal and domestic cleanliness. The first recipe for lavender water dates from 1615. Lavender was soon widely used as a strewing herb and in bags to freshen the air, among fabrics to repel moths, and in wax to prevent woodworm in furniture. The unpleasant smell of soap, which until the 1800s was made by boiling animal fat with wood ash, was disguised by the addition of lavender oil.

The making of household fragrances and cleaning and hygiene preparations took a great deal of time before the days of mass production, and recipes for these items of domestic economy were handed down from mother to daughter. Large houses had a still-room in which herbs, spices, and other raw materials were concocted into powders, polishes, washballs, sachets ("sweet bags"), floral waters, and potpourri. Pomanders and nosegays or tussie-mussies of aromatic herbs were carried against infection, especially during epidemics of plague. Rue was often included because of its reputation for killing fleas.

The first toilet water was "Hungary water," made in the 14th century from rosemary macerated in alcohol. The sophisticated perfumes we know today were developed in France towards the end of the 18th century. *Eau de Cologne*, made from essential oils and alcohol, was first produced in Cologne in 1709. One of the earliest of floral scents was orange blossom water or neroli, introduced c.1725. From 1850 oriental fragrances came into popularity, such as vetiver, patchouli, vanilla, and benzoin. Synthetic essences were introduced at the end of the 19th century, but natural oils still predominate in quality perfumes. A perfume is made up of three main kinds of scent: top notes, derived from ingredients with fresher, sharper scents (lemon, lime, basil, bergamot, coriander, lavender, chamomile); middle or "heart" notes, from herbs and spices with pervasive perfumes (clary sage, clove, ginger, jasmine, lemon grass, rose, nutmeg, ylang-ylang); and base notes, mostly from woods, roots, resins, and gums, such as frankincense, myrrh, sandalwood, cinnamon, and cedarwood. The art of perfumery is to combine scents of differing intensity and duration. Formulas for famous fragrances are closely guarded secrets, but the main ingredients of some are known. *Chanel No. 5*, for example, has top notes of bergamot, lemon, and neroli, middle notes of rose, jasmine, and ylang-ylang, and base notes of cedarwood, vetiver, and vanilla.

BODY PAINTING AND MAKEUP

Ancient Britons painted their bodies with woad, a blue dye obtained by fermenting *Isatis tinctoria*, and native North Americans had a sophisticated repertoire of body pigments based on plant dyes, fats, and oils. Face painting as we know it came via the Romans from the ancient Egyptians and Persians. Red colorings were usually produced by red ochre, a natural mineral soil; today such colorants are mainly derived from annatto (*Bixa orellana*). Trends in makeup through the ages have been set by courts and upper classes; Mary Queen of Scots bathed in wine, and ladies of the Spanish court improved their complexions with almond paste and creams of vanilla and cacao. Beauty products became so popular and elaborate that in 1770 a bill was introduced to the English parliament to dissolve a marriage if the man was deceived into it by "scents, paints, cosmetic washes…," according to laws against witchcraft. A similar law was passed in Pennsylvania; cosmetics were frowned on in Puritan New England, but flourished in colonies of French origin. Body painting is still traditional among many tribal peoples.

FRANKINCENSE RESIN
Resin from Boswellia sacra *has been used in perfumery for thousands of years. The Egyptians used it in anti-wrinkle cream, for which purpose it is still used today. It is also used as a base note in many perfumes.*

HENNA FOR DECORATION
*This Indian girl is using a henna (*Lawsonia inermis*) paste to decorate the hands of her friend for a special occasion, probably a religious ceremony such as a marriage.*

SOME PLANT INGREDIENTS USED IN COSMETICS AND PERFUMERY

Aloe vera
ALOE VERA
A "miracle" herb used for soothing and healing sunburn and to moisturize irritated or sensitive skin.

Calendula officinalis
POT MARIGOLD
An antiseptic, soothing, anti-inflammatory herb, very effective for healing very dry, sensitive skin, especially after sunburn.

***Citrus* species**
CITRUS FRUITS
Contain antioxidants and vitamin C to repair damaged skin, and AHAs (alpha-hydroxy acids) to peel away old tissues.

Chamaemelum nobile
CHAMOMILE
A healing, anti-inflammatory herb that also conditions the hair and lightens fair hair.

Cucumis sativus
CUCUMBER
A cooling herb that has an astringent, softening effect on the skin.

***Fucus* species**
SEAWEED
Contains extracts rich in minerals and vitamins to condition skin and hair.

Hamamelis virginiana
WITCH HAZEL
Perhaps the most widely used astringent, present in most toning lotions.

Krameria triandra
RHATANY ROOT
A powerful astringent that improves gum health.

Mentha* x *piperita
PEPPERMINT
Antiseptic, cooling, mildly anesthetic and deodorant essential oil, added to almost all oral hygiene preparations, and to face masks, foot lotions, shampoo, and conditioners.

Mentha spicata
SPEARMINT
Potent antiseptic and deodorant with a cooling, refreshing taste due to mild anesthetic effects. Used in almost all oral hygiene preparations, often in the form of menthol, a part of the essential oil.

Oenothera biennis
EVENING PRIMROSE
Oil is used to soften and replenish dry skin; seeds are ground for use in facial scrubs.

Prunus armeniaca
APRICOT
Skin-softening enzymes are found in the pulp, and extra-moisturizing oil containing vitamin B15, which speeds skin regeneration.

Prunus dulcis
SWEET ALMOND OIL
A fine, emollient oil, widely used in moisturizers and an ingredient of cold creams.

Fucus vesiculosus

***Rosa* species**
ROSE
Astringent, tonic, healing extracts are used in cold creams and skin preparations.

Rosmarinus officinalis
ROSEMARY
Circulatory stimulant that improves scalp and hair health.

Sambucus nigra
ELDERFLOWER
Soothes irritated and inflamed skin.

Sanguinaria canadensis
BLOODROOT
Antibacterial extracts added to oral hygiene preparations.

Simmondsia chinensis
JOJOBA
A recently discovered natural liquid wax, similar to the skin's own oils.

Symphytum officinale
COMFREY
One of the most effective healing agents, containing allantoin, which speeds the formation of new cells.

Theobroma cacao
COCOA BUTTER
Yields a rich, softening oil, used to moisturize the skin.

Thymus vulgaris
THYME
One of the strongest natural antiseptics, used mainly in the form of thymol in mouthwashes and toothpastes.

Herbs in the Wild

People all over the world have picked and uprooted herbs from the wild since ancient times. Some of the most commonly used culinary herbs, such as chili peppers (*Capsicum annuum* var. *annuum*) and basil (*Ocimum basilicum*), have such a long history of use and cultivation that truly wild plants have never been recorded; these presumably became extinct early on from overcollection. Medicinal herbs in particular have always been mainly collected from the wild, and the knowledge of where they grow, and the best time to gather them, has formed an important oral tradition among healers in many different cultures. These ancient traditions successfully balanced supply and demand, allowing plant stocks to regenerate seasonally. Due to the strong commercial pressures of the food and pharmaceutical industries of today, the balance has now been disrupted by unregulated gathering. Over 20,000 species of higher plants are used worldwide, nearly 10 percent of all those known.

Surinam Rainforest
Rich habitat for plant species with therapeutic properties.

Rainforest Medicine
Medicine being prepared from herbs in a village in Surinam, S America. Most rainforest people have ancient oral traditions; if their cultures break down, these are soon lost. The plants themselves are also threatened if rainforest ecosystems are disturbed and destroyed.

The early 20th century brought great optimism that science would conquer disease. In reality, most countries are too poor to benefit fully from medical advances, and they lack the basic infrastructure of reliable supplies of electricity and clean water that is necessary for modern medical services. Some 80 percent of the world's people still rely on traditional, plant-based medicine for primary health care. This reliance continues to a certain extent in developed countries as well; despite major advances in developing synthetic drugs, plant extracts are still present in a high proportion of Western drugs. Research takes its quota of plants, too, as pharmaceutical companies turn to them in the search for new compounds to treat incurable conditions and diseases caused by drug-resistant organisms.

Changes in Attitudes to Herbal Medicine

The most noticeable change in developed countries this century has, however, been in the interest shown by the ordinary person. From being regarded as "old-fashioned" and distrusted, herbs such as ginseng and guaranà are now hailed as wonder drugs. Change began in the 1960s, when the "hippie" movement advocated a return to more natural living, initiating "alternative" medicine and therapies. The growth of the conservation movement and the founding of companies using mainly natural products in an environmentally friendly way were also major factors. As a result, an increasingly wide range of herbs is now available fresh, dried, and as ingredients of cosmetics, perfumes, and over-the-counter medicines. Jojoba oil (from *Simmondsia chinensis*) was unheard of 20 years ago; it was promoted as a substitute for sperm whale oil in industrial high-performance lubricants as part of the campaign to save whales, and went on to become a revolutionary new emollient in skin- and hair-care products. Fortunately, the jojoba plant has been micropropagated, but many others are now perilously close to extinction, or so reduced in the wild that only a narrow genetic base remains for regeneration.

Saving the Plants that Save Lives

Protecting herbs from overexploitation requires international cooperation and a pooling of expertise. Ecologists, horticulturists and plant breeders, traditional healers and health professionals, and policy makers and communicators must all explain the importance of conservation if the message is to reach the public.

Cultivation of Ginseng
The American species, Panax quinquefolius, *being grown commercially in S Korea. This species was introduced in the 18th century to supplement the depleted native* P. ginseng.

Protection of plants in the wild may take one or more forms, in which the individual contribution is as important as the commercial or national one.

- Conservation may be *in situ*: that is, reserves and national parks are established in the regions where species are at risk. Collecting of wild herbs can be strictly controlled, and depleted species reintroduced.
- Other forms of conservation may include seed banks, where seed is stored against shortages; cryopreservation (a new technique for low-temperature storage of tissues for cell culture); or the establishment of collections of living plants for study and propagation.
- The cultivation of herbs, whether in the garden or on a commercial scale, reduces pressure on wild populations. On a commercial level it encourages plant breeders to improve vigor and quality, and develop techniques for propagation, harvesting, and processing.

SIMMONDSIA CHINENSIS
The jojoba plant, native to the Mexican desert, is now micropropagated on a large scale for commercial production of emollients for cosmetic preparations.

PROTECTING WILD HERBS FOR THE FUTURE

Many herbs are protected under one of the following categories:

RARE – species with very restricted distribution and/or a very small population.

VULNERABLE – seriously depleted or under threat from overcollection and/or habitat destruction.

ENDANGERED – in danger of extinction, because remaining populations are too small to breed successfully or to survive further losses.

EXTINCT – no longer known to exist in the wild.

There are protected plant species in these categories in most countries. Details are available from conservation organizations, botanic gardens, and appropriate government departments. Species protected at international level are monitored by the IUCN (International Union for the Conservation of Nature) and are listed in CITES (Convention on International Trade in Endangered Species of Wild Fauna and Flora). CITES is enforced by customs controls, and by compulsory documentation of imports and exports. It is further monitored by TRAFFIC (Trade Records Analysis of Flora and Fauna in Commerce) which was established in 1976 to support legislation. The IUCN publishes "Red Data Books" that list and describe the rarest species in particular areas.

RECORDING THE FLORA
This herbarium (dried plant collection) is owned by a mining company in Linhares Forest Reserve, Brazil. There is pressure on industries to show concern for their environment.

OBSERVE THE LAW

- Do not pick or uproot protected species. In some countries it is illegal to pick or uproot any wild plant without the landowner's permission, or at all.
- Do not bring plants or seeds into the country without first checking whether it is legal to do so. Most countries have strict quarantine regulations and plant controls to prevent the spread of pests, diseases, and weeds.

COLLECTING HERBS

Collecting from the wild has a varying impact on plant populations, according to the type of plant sought and the part harvested. Weed species are least at risk, and harvesting a few leaves, flowers, fruits, and seeds from common herbs has a low impact on populations.

CHARACTERISTICS OF HERBS AT RISK:
- slow-growing
- low reproduction rate
- naturally few leaves and flowers
- endemic species, with localized distribution

CAUSES OF DAMAGING EFFECTS:
- whole plant is taken or (in the case of trees especially) cut down for harvesting of any parts
- stripped for bark (bark-ringing usually kills a tree)
- dug up for tubers, rhizomes, or roots

NORTH AMERICA

There is an extraordinary range of environments in this huge land mass, from arctic tundra, various kinds of forest and extensive prairies, to semidesert and subtropical swamps, with the Rocky Mountains and Appalachians running through the west and east respectively. Many of the characteristic landscapes, habitats, and plants of the United States are preserved in an outstanding system of National Parks that was originated by John Muir (1838–1914), an explorer, naturalist, and visionary conservationist who presented the case for saving wilderness areas to Theodore Roosevelt in 1903.

MOUNT RAINIER NATIONAL PARK
Rich forests and alpine meadows are characteristic of the Cascade Range in the Pacific Northwest.

HYDRANGEA ARBORESCENS
The wild hydrangea has long been used in traditional North American medicine as a remedy for kidney disorders. The roots are used, however, so the plant is killed to obtain them.

Despite widespread active conservation campaigning and legislation, the United States and Canada are battling against the odds to save their native plants. Here, as elsewhere in the world, urbanization is a major cause of habitat loss; leisure industries and removal of wild plants for the herb trade are others. There is also the psychological barrier; both the United States and Canada have a strong pioneering tradition of exploiting natural resources in a land that at first seemed infinitely bounteous.

Nearly all of the most important medicinal North American herbs are woodland species, and were originally native American remedies. Indigenous uses had little impact on wild populations, involving very small amounts for local use, and careful use of the resource. As settlers adopted these remedies, commercial collecting increased with little regard to the consequences. Demand for native American herbs increased greatly through Samuel Thomson's Physiomedical movement, which was based largely on indigenous medicine. In 1838 Physiomedicalism was taken to Britain by Dr. Albert Isaiah Coffin, where the movement eventually gained some three million followers.

Trees and shrubs account for a high proportion of the plants used in native American medicine and its derivatives, including birches (*Betula* species), pines (*Pinus* species), red cedar (*Juniperus virginiana*), cascara sagrada (*Rhamnus purshiana*), sassafras (*Sassafras albidum*), sweet gum (*Liquidambar styraciflua*), seven barks (*Hydrangea arborescens*), and arborvitae (*Thuja occidentalis*). In many cases, the bark is harvested, often causing terminal damage to the plant. Species with a limited distribution, such as *Rhamnus purshiana*, are even more vulnerable. A herb marketing guide, published in 1977, stated that "the end of the cascara business in the Northwest is in sight, because every tree stripped is killed...The demand for this bark since 1903 has been a boon to many small farmers and homesteaders in Oregon and Washington."

NORTH AMERICAN MEDICINE BAG
This medicine bag of the early 1900s contains herbs for a range of ailments. The packaging prevents the herbs from mixing with each other and drying out, and also maintains the air of mystique that surrounds the power of the healer.

THREATENED FOREST SPECIES

Plants of the forest floor include some of the most important remedies used both in North America and by herbalists abroad, such as birthroot (*Trillium erectum*), goldenseal (*Hydrastis canadensis*), and black cohosh (*Cimicifuga racemosa*). Trilliums are in especially great demand, being collected for both the horticultural and herb trades. In most cases it is the roots that are used, so again, many plants are entirely destroyed during collection. Slow-growing, uncommon species, such as American ginseng (*Panax quinquefolius*), are especially threatened by uprooting. This species was discovered near Montreal in 1716 after a search initiated by Jesuit missionaries who knew the value of ginseng in China. A thriving export trade quickly developed. However, in 1752 a huge quantity of roots was collected out of season and carelessly dried, with the result that the Chinese rejected the consignment and ceased trading. American traders took advantage of the Canadian disaster, and by

Major Herbs of the Region

Aletris farinosa
UNICORN ROOT
Rhizomes used as a digestive tonic; now endangered in Canada, largely because trail bikes have destroyed most of its sites.

Ceanothus americanus
NEW JERSEY TEA
Used in treating skin cancer by native Americans, and by settlers as a substitute for tea.

Chionanthus virginicus
FRINGE TREE
One of the best remedies for liver and gall bladder disorders.

Eschscholzia californica
CALIFORNIA POPPY
Popular garden annual and sedative herb.

Hamamelis virginiana
WITCH HAZEL
Astringent used in eye lotions, skin toners, and healing creams.

Hydrastis canadensis
GOLDENSEAL
A tonic herb used mainly for digestive and menstrual complaints. Antibacterial.

Ledum groenlandicum
LABRADOR TEA
Characteristic shrub of northern forests, used as a substitute for tea during the 18th century.

Lobelia inflata
LOBELIA
A respiratory stimulant and antiasthmatic, used in cough medicines and anti-smoking mixtures.

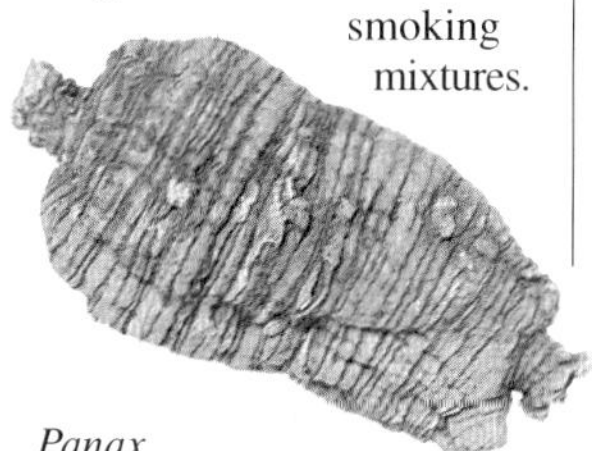

Panax quinquefolius – dried root

Panax quinquefolius
AMERICAN GINSENG
Considered more *yin* than *P. ginseng*; reduces respiratory and digestive heat.

Passiflora incarnata
PASSION FLOWER
One of the best known herbal tranquilizers.

Phytolacca americana
POKEBERRY
Native American remedy for rheumatism, now important to the pharmaceutical industry for antiviral compounds, and in the control of water snails that cause schistosomiasis.

Podophyllum peltatum
MAY APPLE
Source of anticancer drugs.

Rhamnus purshiana
CASCARA SAGRADA
Well-known laxative, used as food, medicine, and as a dye plant by native people.

Sanguinaria canadensis
BLOODROOT
Originally an expectorant. Now valued as a dental plaque inhibitor.

Sassafras albidum
SASSAFRAS
Probably the first American plant drug to reach Europe, c.1560.

Scutellaria lateriflora
VIRGINIA SKULLCAP
Important herbal sedative.

Senna marilandica
WILD SENNA
Native American laxative.

Serenoa repens
SAW PALMETTO
Used in treatment of prostate disorders.

Simmondsia chinensis
JOJOBA
Emollient oil, widely used in cosmetics, originally for use in lubricants.

Smilax glauca
WILD SARSAPARILLA
Tonic and flavoring for soft drinks.

Thuja occidentalis
ARBORVITAE
Made into antirheumatic tea by loggers, now used to treat mucus and cystitis.

Ulmus rubra
SLIPPERY ELM
Inner bark is a soothing remedy for serious digestive complaints, such as ulcers.

the 1890s there were such shortages that experiments in cultivation were started – though often of wild-collected roots. *P. quinquefolius* has been on CITES Appendix II since its inception in 1975. Exports of wild-collected plants have fallen greatly, but as recently as 1987 they still accounted for six percent of the total (some 100,000 lbs weight). Wild-collecting still goes on in the southern Appalachians, the Ozarks, and the Pacific Northwest, often of scarce species such as *Echinacea angustifolia*, *Sanguinaria canadensis*, *Hydrastis canadensis*, and *Rhamnus purshiana*. Even as far back as 1913 one herb trader reported that *Hydrastis* had long been scarce. Today, as in the past, collecting is mostly done by rural people working for wholesale distributors who pay very little; for example, *Caulophyllum thalictroides* fetches a mere fifty cents per pound weight. In some cases, wild-collecting threatens other related species that are taken as substitutes, a particular problem with *Echinacea* species, which are now becoming increasingly rare in the wild. Attempts have been made to regulate collection of wild plants; the National Forests in the US, for example, have lists of plants that may not be collected within their boundaries, and issue permits for others.

Cultivation as a Solution

Where regulation fails, cultivation will often succeed. *Echinacea purpurea* is cultivated successfully, but the hardy orchid lady's slipper (*Cypripedium parviflorum*) is more difficult. It does not transplant easily, and can be raised from seed only in laboratory conditions. Jojoba (*Simmondsia chinensis*) has also been problematic, though it is now successfully micropropagated. It takes three years from seed before male and female plants can be told apart. Only female plants yield the oil-rich seeds, and seven females to one male are needed for successful fruiting. North American plants cultivated in any quantity include *Panax quinquefolius*, *Passiflora incarnata*, *Lobelia inflata*, and *Echinacea purpurea*.

▲ TRADITIONAL CEREMONY
This 19th-century engraving shows a native American, with a pipe of peace on forked sticks, preparing for a peace ceremony. Herbs would be used on such occasions as much as in medicine.

▼ *ESCHSCHOLZIA CALIFORNICA*
The California poppy, shown here growing in a profusion of orange cup-shaped flowers in Antelope State Park, California, is named for that state and is the state's official flower.

Central and South America

Central and South America are unparalleled in the richness of their flora. Brazil alone has some 55,000 species of flowering plants, compared with about 20,000 in the US (excluding Hawaii), and less than 1450 in the UK. The Amazon region contains the world's largest area of tropical rainforest, renowned for its role in the global ecosystem. Here, it is often said, lies our greatest hope of finding new drugs to combat incurable diseases. In most parts of the world, the main concern is to protect specific plants, but in this vast and complex wilderness, where countless species are yet to be discovered, it is the unknown that needs as much conservation as the known.

▲ South American Rainforest
This forest in Serra dos Carajás, southeastern Pará State, in northern Brazil, is home to many different plant species.

Tropical forests of various kinds stretch from lowland Amazonia to the lower slopes of the Andes, the Guiana Highlands and the Caribbean, through central America to southern Mexico. Elsewhere there are temperate montane forests, high plateaus, dry woodlands, and grasslands, with a Mediterranean-type climate prevailing through most of Mexico and central Chile, and cool temperate conditions at the southern tip of the continent. Many familiar plants come from the drier regions, including Mexican marigolds (*Tagetes* species), sages (such as *Salvia hispanica* and *S. microphylla*), and corn (*Zea mays*). The region is also home to some of the world's most important edible and medicinal plants, such as peppers and squashes (*Capsicum* and *Cucurbita* species), and papayas (*Carica papaya*). Some southern South American species have odd affinities: the aromatic *Drimys winteri*, of Chile and western Argentina, is related to the Australian pepper tree (*Tasmannia lanceolata*), indicating that these widely separated regions were once a single land mass.

Sir Hans Sloane (1660–1753)
The English physician and naturalist is credited with the discovery of the medicinal properties of Guaiacum officinale *(lignum vitae), which was used as a cure for syphilis. It is one of the earliest examples of a protected species.*

The Discovery of Modern Drugs

Botanical discoveries in the New World have had a profound impact on world trade and culture. Amerigo Vespucci (c.1454–1512), a Florentine navigator after whom the two continents were named, came across Colombian tribes chewing coca leaves (*Erythroxylum coca*), a practice known from 2100BC. The alkaloid cocaine proved a valuable topical anesthetic, but also a disastrously addictive narcotic drug. It has been estimated that 1.7 million acres of rainforest in Peru alone have been destroyed for coca cultivation since

Curare Extraction
Pulping and drying the fruit of Strychnos nux-vomica *to extract the poisonous seeds; the traditional method for making curare. Alexander von Humboldt (1769–1859) gave the first detailed description of curare arrow poison, which kills by causing instantaneous muscular paralysis.*

▼ Native Amazonian
The blowpipe is used for shooting darts tipped with curare, which paralyzes and kills rapidly (even in tiny amounts) but does not contaminate the flesh.

the early 20th century. Curare, containing strychnine, from *Strychnos nux-vomica*, and ipecac (from *Cephaelis ipecacuanha*) were among other early finds, as was quinine (*Cinchona* species), a cure for malaria that, ironically, enabled Europeans to survive the alien conditions and conquer the people who taught them about it. *Chondrodendron tomentosum*, a rainforest liana, is a common ingredient of curare among tribes in Colombia, Peru, and Ecuador. It contains tubocurarine, a potent muscle relaxant that plays a vital role in modern surgery; it cannot be synthesized, so the pharmaceutical industry relies on wild-collected plants.

CONSERVATION OF THE RAINFORESTS

Research into the vegetation of Brazil, and its neighbors in the Amazon region, has a deservedly high profile, and there is international pressure to halt destruction of remaining rainforests. No less important is how forest people use the plants. Certain tribes use as many as 100 species for medicinal purposes and have a very sophisticated knowledge. Unfortunately, this knowledge forms part of an oral tradition and is fast disappearing as Western medicine is introduced to even the remotest areas, replacing the traditional culture. Statistics of rainforest destruction in this part of the world are especially depressing. On the positive side, painstaking work is being done by universities and botanical gardens, often in conjunction with medical institutes and conservation charities, to survey plant resources and set up protected areas and cultivation projects for vulnerable species. Costa Rica was among the first countries in the region to gain widespread support for national parks. Others, such as the Dominican Republic, find that ecological tourism can help make conservation pay. Even in 1701, demand for *Guaiacum officinale* had so reduced wild stocks that the republic of Martinique listed it as a protected species. Overcollection of the tree for its fine wood and medicinal resin during the last couple of centuries has resulted in vast depletion. However, the Dominican Republic, Guadeloupe, Colombia, Puerto Rico, Costa Rica, El Salvador, and Nicaragua now protect both it and *G. sanctum*. Research has shown that these slow-growing, long-lived trees are easily grown from seed and adapt readily to cultivation in many regions.

▲ *CARICA PAPAYA*
The papaya is thought to have originated in Peru. It is valued for its medicinal uses for digestive disorders, edible seeds and fruit, and the commercial uses of the papain extracted from the sap.

◄ *DIOSCOREA MACROSTACHYA*
Yams are a valuable source of food and contain hormonal substances. They are also used by the pharmaceutical industry in the production of steroids.

MAJOR HERBS OF THE REGION

Agave americana
CENTURY PLANT
An important fiber, food, and medicinal plant, whose leaf waste yields steroid drug precursors.

Anacardium occidentale
CASHEW
Native to Brazil and the Caribbean, but now a major crop throughout the tropics for food, medicinal, and industrial products; bark extracts used by Amazon tribes as a contraceptive.

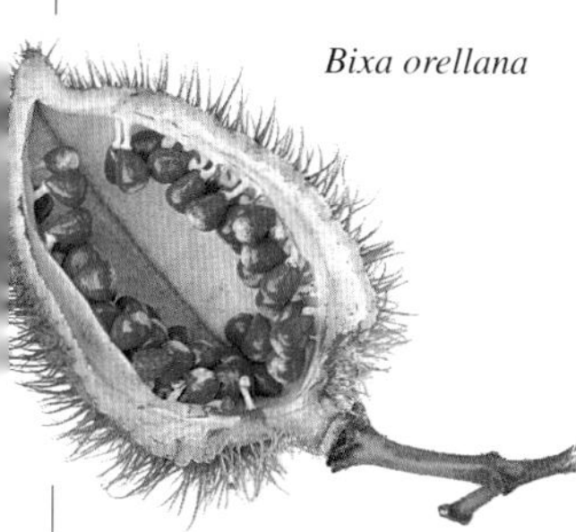

Bixa orellana

Bixa orellana
LIPSTICK TREE
Mexican culinary herb, used worldwide as a colorant for foods and cosmetics.

***Capsicum* species**
CHILI PEPPER
Of worldwide importance as a spice, and key remedy in 19th-century American Physiomedicalism.

Carica papaya
PAPAYA
Source of papain, an enzyme that tenderizes meat and helps digestion of proteins.

Cephaelis ipecacuanha
IPECAC
A potent emetic, which in the correct dose is an excellent expectorant, widely used in commercial cough remedies.

Chenopodium ambrosioides
WORMSEED
The Mexican herb *epazote*, which is an acquired taste, having its origin as a medicine to expel worms.

***Cinchona* species**
PERUVIAN BARK
Source of antimalarial quinine.

***Datura* species**
THORN APPLE
Rich in tropane alkaloids.

Dioscorea macrostachya
MEXICAN YAM
Source of hormone diosgenin for oral contraceptives until it was synthesized in 1970.

Erythroxylum coca
COCA
Leaves chewed to relieve fatigue and hunger in S America; alkaloid cocaine extracted for anesthetics by pharmaceutical industry and as an illegal narcotic by drug dealers.

Guaiacum officinale
LIGNUM VITAE
National flower of Jamaica, endangered species, and fine lumber tree, also famed as a cleansing, tonic herb.

Ilex paraguensis
MATÉ
Stimulant herb, mostly taken as an alternative to tea, now endangered in the wild.

Peumus boldus
BOLDO
An economically important Chilean tree, used medicinally for liver and gall bladder complaints, and often added to diet formulas.

Pfaffia paniculata
BRAZILIAN GINSENG
Tonic aphrodisiac, increasingly popular in the West.

***Pilocarpus* species**
JABORANDI
Source of pilocarpine, used to treat glaucoma.

Pimenta dioica
ALLSPICE
Clovelike spice, grown mainly in Jamaica.

Piscidia piscipula
JAMAICA DOGWOOD
Contains rotenone, a powerful insecticide, and pain-killing compounds, but used locally to stupefy fish, leaving them easy to catch yet safe to eat.

Strychnos nux-vomica
STRYCHNINE
Highly toxic seeds used in curare and rodent poisons, but with tonic properties in minute, accurately measured doses.

Theobroma cacao
CACAO
Used to make the Aztec beverage *chocolatl*; now a universal flavoring and food (cocoa solids); with rich emollient oils (cocoa butter).

Vanilla planifolia
VANILLA
Fermented pods provide alcoholic tinctures for perfumes, as well as one of the world's most popular flavorings.

Zea mays
CORN
Familiar as a staple food, but less well known for its medicinal flowers, which have a soothing, cooling effect that was described in Aztec herbals.

EUROPE

Europe stretches from Arctic regions in the Nordic countries to hot, dry regions bordering on the Mediterranean, and its central areas have a typical continental climate of hot, dry summers and cold winters. With the exception of the Low Countries (Netherlands, Belgium, and Luxembourg), mountains are a feature of almost every country in the region, with a distinctive flora that has evolved in response to their differences in topography and climate. Plants such as bearberry (*Arctostaphylos uva-ursi*) and juniper (*Juniperus communis*) are found both in Scandinavia and northern N America.

NATURAL WOODLAND
View of the still surviving natural woodland around the town of Vranov and the river Dyji, in Moravia, eastern Europe.

GENTIANA LUTEA
The great yellow gentian grows wild in lime-rich meadows above 2000ft (600m) in central and southern Europe. The rootstock contains bitter glycosides.

The northern and upland areas of Europe were once clad in evergreen and mixed forests. Large natural woodlands remain in eastern Europe, but elsewhere most of them have disappeared under the ax and the plow. The now bare landscape of Scotland was until the last few hundred years covered by Caledonian forest, dominated by pines (*Pinus sylvestris*). European woodland trees and shrubs include a number of important herbs, such as beech (*Fagus sylvatica*), oak (*Quercus robur*), alder buckthorn (*Rhamnus frangula*), and the small-leaved linden (*Tilia cordata*), which is now rare in the north of its range. There were mixed forests of evergreen oaks, pines, and mastic trees (*Pistacia lentiscus*) in Mediterranean countries before deforestation, erosion, and overgrazing reduced the region to thorny scrubland. Human activity has degraded the vegetation in the area, but the aromatic, drought-resistant scrub that now covers it is home to some of the most widely used herbs in the world – lavender, olive, sage, thyme, savory, oregano, rosemary, and bay.

TRADITIONAL EUROPEAN HERBS

European herbalism is eclectic, derived largely from ancient Greek and Roman traditions, which were in turn influenced by theories and practices from ancient Egypt, Assyria, India, and the Arab world. Herbs from the East therefore took their place long ago beside native European plants in the medicine of the region. Outstanding among European herbs are yellow gentian (*Gentiana lutea*) of alkaline alpine pastures; arnica (*Arnica montana*), an inhabitant of acidic alpine soils; the pasque flower (*Pulsatilla vulgaris*), which thrives on dry, calcareous hillsides; and dittany of Crete (*Origanum dictamnus*), found wild only in the mountains of Crete. All have specific cultivation requirements and have been overcollected for medicinal use or as ornamentals. Arnica is rare and protected in many areas, and especially difficult to grow at low altitudes. Pasque flowers are increasingly rare in the wild, due to both overcollection and loss of habitat; they have been greatly reduced in England due to the extensive plowing up of chalk downland for the commercial production of arable crops. Some herbs have become weeds in other parts of the world; many native European herbs are weeds in their own right and have been inadvertently introduced to other countries. These include chickweed (*Stellaria media*), dandelion (*Taraxacum officinale*), shepherd's purse (*Capsella bursa-pastoris*), goosegrass (*Galium aparine*), nettle (*Urtica dioica*), and greater plantain (*Plantago major*).

▼ RESIN COLLECTION
*This sticky aromatic substance from mastic trees (*Pistacia lentiscus*) was the original chewing gum, chewed to sweeten the breath. The industry is now centered on the Greek island of Chios.*

► ORIGANUM DICTAMNUS
This dittany is native to the mountains of Crete. It is also cultivated as a crop and is prized as an ornamental.

Major Herbs of the Region

Aconitum napellus
MONKSHOOD
Extremely poisonous herb, used in homeopathy for shock.

Aesculus hippocastanum
HORSE CHESTNUT
Familiar as an ingredient of shampoos for dark hair, and used medicinally for circulatory problems.

Alchemilla **species**
LADY'S MANTLE
Herbs used to alleviate disorders of the female reproductive system.

Arnica montana
ARNICA
Healing herb, popular in Germany for heart conditions.

Artemisia absinthium
WORMWOOD
Oil was once used to flavor alcoholic aperitifs, such as absinthe.

Atropa belladonna
DEADLY NIGHTSHADE
Source of tropane alkaloids, used in surgical procedures and to control travel sickness.

Borago officinalis
BORAGE
Cucumber-flavored leaves traditionally added to alcoholic summer drinks; seeds contain oil that helps regulate hormonal functions.

Calendula officinalis
POT MARIGOLD
Soothing, anti-inflammatory herb for digestive and skin problems.

Chamaemelum nobile
CHAMOMILE
Popular tisane, taken as a mild sedative and digestive, also used as a rinse for fair hair.

Crocus sativus
SAFFRON
The world's most expensive herb by weight; only the flower's pistils are used.

Digitalis **species**
FOXGLOVE
Source of cardiac glycosides.

Digitalis purpurea

Drimia maritima
SQUILL
Common ingredient of cough medicines.

Filipendula ulmaria
MEADOWSWEET
Contains pain-killing salicylates and antacids that help heal ulcers.

Foeniculum vulgare
FENNEL
Like the closely related dill (*Anethum graveolens*), a popular culinary herb that also relieves indigestion.

Gentiana lutea
YELLOW GENTIAN
A very bitter herb, unparalleled for treating gastrointestinal disorders.

Humulus lupulus
HOPS
Sedative medicinal herb, grown worldwide as a flavoring for beers.

Juniperus communis
JUNIPER
Flavoring for gin and useful remedy for cystitis and rheumatism.

Laurus nobilis
BAY
Important flavoring for sweet and savory foods; an ingredient of *bouquet garni*.

Lavandula **species**
LAVENDER
Oil used in perfumery, aromatherapy, and medicine.

Mentha spicata
SPEARMINT
Clean, refreshing flavor for sweet and savory foods and for oral hygiene preparations.

Oenothera biennis
EVENING PRIMROSE
Oil is used to help regulate hormonal functions and to relieve skin problems.

Origanum **species**
OREGANO
Warm, pungent flavor widely used in Italian and Greek cuisine.

Petroselinum crispum
PARSLEY
Leaves are used as a garnishing and culinary herb; seeds have diuretic effects.

Pimpinella anisum
ANISE
Favorite flavoring for alcoholic drinks in the Mediterranean region.

Rhamnus frangula
ALDER BUCKTHORN
Non-griping laxative.

Salvia officinalis
SAGE
Popular culinary herb, used medicinally for digestive problems and excessive perspiration.

Silybum marianum
MILK THISTLE
Contains silymarin, which detoxifies the liver.

Thymus vulgaris
THYME
Favorite culinary herb and source of thymol, a potent antiseptic used in oral hygiene preparations.

Valeriana officinalis
VALERIAN
Used worldwide as a sedative.

Vinca major
PERIWINKLE
Source of alkaloids that have hypotensive and vasodilatory effects.

▲ WILD HERBS IN SPAIN
*Holly oaks (*Quercus ilex*) with lavender (*Lavandula stoechas*), growing wild in Spain. Oil of lavender has many commercial uses.*

▼ *PLANTAGO MAJOR*
The greater plantain has spread worldwide from Europe. A common weed, it has also long been valued for antibacterial properties.

AFRICA

This vast continent ranges from Mediterranean coastal areas in the north, which were fertile agricultural areas in Roman times, through the harsh, desiccated Saharan and Kalahari deserts to "safari country" – dry savanna, grassland, and open woodland, with short, unreliable rainy seasons. In contrast, central Africa is dominated by equatorial rainforests that extend along the Congo Basin and fringe the coast from Cameroon to the Gambia. Tropical rainforest also occurs on the island of Madagascar, which has been cut off from the mainland so long that it has evolved unique plant and animal species.

CENTRAL AFRICAN LANDSCAPE
*Dry woodland covers vast areas of central Africa. Kiaat trees (*Pterocarpus angolensis*), important locally for lumber, occur in lowland forest, here in the Chote National Park, Namibia.*

TRADITIONAL COLLECTOR
The modern "witch doctor" (here in Zimbabwe, near the Victoria Falls) protects supplies of wild herbs for his medicines in the same way that his predecessors did. Traditional collecting is restricted by taboos that ensure plants have time to recover and reproduce to ensure future supplies.

In Cape Province, in the extreme south of the country, the prevailing pattern of hot, dry summers and winter rain supports one of the richest floras in the world. The Table Mountain massif rises abruptly from the south coast, creating innumerable ecological niches for plants. African rainforests are home to such important medicinal plants as *Catharanthus roseus*, *Physostigma venenosum*, *Rauvolfia vomitoria*, and various species of *Strophanthus* and *Voacanga*, but a surprising number of herbs come from Africa's drylands and montane woodlands, which are equally threatened by urbanization and poor land management. Much of the continent is arid, and dry regions are especially vulnerable to overgrazing, deforestation, and burning, which lead to the spread of deserts and famines. Africa has the highest rate of urbanization in the world, with urban populations doubling every 14 years and yet it is still dependent on wild plants for primary health care.

CULTURAL CHANGES IN TRADITIONAL MEDICINE

Collecting herbs was once a local activity, carried out by traditional practitioners and governed by age-old codes of practice – "taboos" – that served to balance resources and demand. Now it has become part of the cash economy, and wild herbs are regarded as "free for all." It has been estimated that 80 percent of African plants have medicinal uses, and a very high proportion of people in Africa – some 70–80 percent – rely on plants for their health care. There are, too, some 30 traditional practitioners for every qualified doctor. Whereas traditional herb gathering had little impact on populations of wild plants, commercial collecting can be compared to a swarm of locusts, which damages or kills every specimen in its path. An example is *Harpagophytum procumbens*, which is now traded worldwide; in 1984 commercial collectors harvested 66 percent of known plants in Botswana for their tubers, a

ROOIBOS TEA
Plantations of Aspalathus linearis, *the source of rooibos tea, growing in the arid Cedarberg Mountains, in the west of Cape Province. The rooibos tea industry expanded greatly during World War II, due to shortages of oriental tea, and also recently, following research in the 1980s into its beneficial properties.*

Major Herbs of the Region

***Agathosma* species**
BUCHU
Versatile herbs for blackcurrant flavoring, insect repellants, and diuretic tea.

Aloe vera
Source of purgative bitter aloes and healing skin care ingredients, used since ancient Egyptian times.

Artemisia afra
WILDE ALS, WILD WORMWOOD
A favorite African remedy for bronchial and skin complaints.

Aspalathus linearis
ROOIBOS
Desert shrub made into a tea by the Hottentots, now a major crop for caffeine-free beverages.

Catharanthus roseus
MADAGASCAR PERIWINKLE
Alkaloids for cancer chemotherapy, especially childhood leukemia.

Euphorbia tirucalli
MILK BUSH
Zimbabwean succulent with acrid latex that removes warts, repels mosquitoes, and also yields fuel hydrocarbons.

Gloriosa superba
GLORY LILY
Toxic roots contain colchicine, used in gout remedies and genetic engineering.

Harpagophytum procumbens

Harpagophytum procumbens
DEVIL'S CLAW
A veld plant, hailed as a remedy for arthritis and digestive problems.

Pausinystalia yohimbe
YOHIMBE
The bark of this West African tree contains yohimbine, used as aphrodisiac.

***Pelargonium* species**
Favorite ornamental and perfume plants.

Physostigma venenosum
CALABAR BEAN
Source of physostigmine, an alkaloid used in ophthalmology, but deadly seeds were used in Nigerian "ordeal by poison" to establish innocence or guilt of suspect.

Prunus africana
AFRICAN CHERRY
Multiple-use tree for local people, now internationally important for bark extracts to treat prostate disorders.

Ricinus communis
CASTOR BEAN
Originally from E Africa and best known as a purgative, this shrub is now grown worldwide for products in the paint, paper, and fiber industries.

***Strophanthus* species**
Traditionally used as arrow poison, important now as a source of cardiac glycosides.

Voacanga africana
Source of drugs used in cerebrovascular disorders.

▲ ALOE PLANT
Aloes are a common feature of African landscapes. There are hundreds of different species, and most have medicinal uses. The southern Cape area was once well known for Cape aloes, extracted from Aloe ferox, *first exported in 1761.*

rate that is obviously not sustainable. Local demand can be ruthless, too; *Warburgia salutaris*, a tree related to *Canella winterana*, is regarded in Africa as a cure-all, though it is almost unknown elsewhere. A warning of its decline through bark-ringing and the need for cultivation was made in 1946, but only in the last few years, with extinction looming, has any attempt been made to protect it.

Problems in Conservation

One problem in Africa is that conservation areas and botanical gardens suffer the same fate as wild places, with declining medicinal plants almost impossible to establish before being "harvested." As ever, slow-growing species exploited for bark, roots, and bulbs or tubers are most at risk, especially if they have a restricted distribution. Cultivation of herbs in Africa is also thwarted by low prices and poverty, which make it nearly impossible to cultivate them as cheaply as they can be collected. There is also a widespread belief that cultivated plants have no "power." As a result, most African herbs still come from the wild, and it is only *in extremis*, now that stocks are so depleted, that those concerned – collectors, users, administrators, and scientists – are discussing the problems and agreeing strategies to conserve through cultivation.

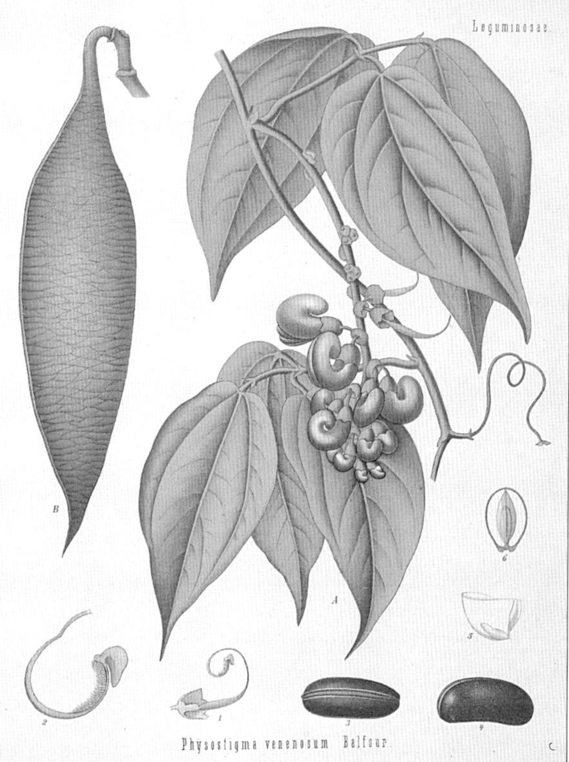

◄ CALABAR BEAN
A plate from Köhler's Medizinal-Pflanzen *of 1888–90, illustrating* Physostigma venenosum. *This tropical climber grows to 50ft (15m), and bears pink, pealike flowers, as shown here. The brownish black seeds, shown at the foot of this plate, contain valuable alkaloids.*

THE MIDDLE EAST

The Middle East is a region of extremes, with the Hindu Kush, Elburz, and Taurus Mountains to the north, and the arid Syrian Desert and Arabian Peninsula in the center and to the south. Cool uplands are home to several ancestors of garden roses: the damask rose (*Rosa damascena*) comes from this part of the world, and was long cultivated in Persia before its introduction to Europe by Crusaders returning from the Holy Land. Roses are of supreme importance in Islam; 10 tons of rose water are required to wash the walls of the holy city of Mecca during the annual *hajj* or pilgrimage.

HINDU KUSH MOUNTAINS, AFGHANISTAN
This Himalayan range extends over 500 miles (800km) from the Dasht-i-Margo (Desert of Death) to the Pamir Knot.

TURKISH PINE
Regarded as a cure-all in Turkish folk medicine, Pinus halepensis *subsp.* brutia *occurs from Turkey to Lebanon and the eastern Black Sea coast.*

Western areas of the Middle East (Israel, Lebanon, Syria, and southern Turkey) are similar in climate and vegetation to coastal zones of the Mediterranean in southern Europe and North Africa, with hot dry summers and winter rain. Characteristic shrubs include the olive (*Olea europaea*), fig (*Ficus carica*), myrtle (*Myrtus communis*), and oleander (*Nerium oleander*). Forests of oak and pine once covered much of this area, but thousands of years of deforestation and overgrazing have irrevocably changed the Middle Eastern landscape and flora. As long ago as 1907 only 50 cedars of Lebanon (*Cedrus libani*) still remained on Mount Lebanon, but the species is now protected in Lebanon and in nature reserves in Turkey.

Away from the coasts, the land is drier, and home to drought-resistant shrubs such as frankincense (*Boswellia sacra*), myrrh (*Commiphora myrrha*), the toothbrush tree (*Salvadora persica*), and gum arabic (*Acacia senegal*). Bulbous plants abound, surviving drought underground. Famous throughout the world is the madonna lily (*Lilium candidum*), which is native to the eastern Mediterranean. This lily has been used since ancient times for skin complaints, but it is now so scarce in the wild, and unreliable in cultivation, that it is seldom used today.

PROTECTING ENDANGERED SPECIES

Reforestation, and restrictions on trade in endangered bulbous species, are priorities for Middle Eastern countries. Israel has led the way in greening the desert, as part of a pledge made in 1948 when the state was created. Western Asia and adjoining Mediterranean regions constitute a so-called "Vavilov Center" – one of the several centers of botanical diversity that have given rise to almost all the world's major crops. Named after the Russian scientist and botanist N. I. Vavilov, who originated the theory in the 1920s, Vavilov Centers constitute only a quarter of the earth's arable land, but are extremely varied in topography and climate. These "evolutionary cradles" were home to ancient civilizations, such as Assyria (now Iraq) in the region of the Tigris and Euphrates rivers, that first brought edible and medicinal plants into cultivation. Nearly all the world's major crops have a very narrow genetic base, making them prone to epidemics.

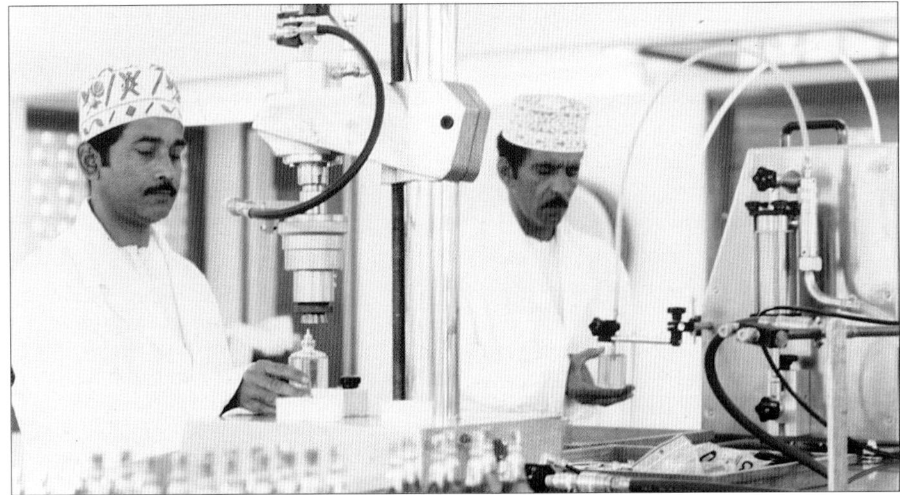

DISTILLATION OF ROSE OIL
The distillation process was an invention of early Arab scientists, and most of the world's rose water still comes mainly from Turkey and Iran.

PROGRESS IN CONSERVATION

The conservation of the habitats and plant species within Vavilov Centers is especially important, because the wild ancestors of crop plants contain genes that may prove vital in breeding plants to combat pests and diseases. Crops originating in the Middle East include oats, barley, flax, sesame, safflower, cabbages, onions, garlic, alfalfa, grapes, figs, olives, almonds, and pomegranates. All these have medicinal uses. A number of floras for Middle Eastern countries are currently in progress, notably *Flora Iranica* and *Flora of Arabia*, following completion of the *Flora of Turkey* in 1988. As a result of work in progress on the Arabian flora, the World Wide Fund for Nature has set up a project based at the Royal Botanic Garden Edinburgh to advise the Yemeni government on sustainable development that will safeguard Socotra's delicate dry tropical ecosystem. This island off the coast of Yemen has been so long isolated from the mainland that 216 of its 680 plant species are now endemic, and a high proportion of the whole number is endangered. In ancient times Socotra was of major importance as a source of aloes (from *Aloe perryi*) for medicine and embalming, and all *Aloe* species are listed on CITES Appendix II.

Major Herbs of the Region

Acacia senegal
GUM ARABIC
Resin is used in medicated lozenges and chewing gum, and as a food additive.

Allium cepa
ONION
Food and flavoring, with anti-infective compounds.

Allium sativum
GARLIC
Pungent flavoring and potent antibiotic.

Aloe perryi – sap collection

Aloe perryi
SOCOTRINE ALOE
Purgative, anti-inflammatory sap.

Ammi majus
QUEEN ANNE'S LACE
Has specific effects on skin pigmentation.

Anethum graveolens
DILL
Important culinary and medicinal herb in the Middle East since biblical times, improving digestion and relieving indigestion.

Astragalus gummifer
TRAGACANTH
Mucilaginous herb, used mainly as a stabilizing and thickening agent.

Avena sativa
OATS
Middle Eastern in origin, now a staple food of northern regions, with medicinal uses as a nerve restorative.

Boswellia sacra – resin

Boswellia sacra
FRANKINCENSE
Legendary perfume and incense with relaxant, antiseptic, and decongestant effects.

Brassica juncea* and *Sinapis alba
MUSTARD
Pungent spice and condiment, also used externally to stimulate the circulation.

Cannabis sativa
HEMP
Hallucinogenic herb and fiber plant with analgesic, anti-emetic, and sedative properties.

Carthamus tinctorius
SAFFLOWER
Circulatory stimulant and source of fine cooking oil and dyes; burned to make kohl.

Carum carvi
CARAWAY
Pungent digestive herb, popular in Jewish cuisine, named after Caria, an ancient region of SW Asia.

Catha edulis
QAT, KHAT
Leaves and stems chewed as a stimulant drug, used by Muslim communities worldwide.

Cedrus libani

***Cedrus* species**
CEDAR
Wood repels insects; oil used in perfumery and aromatherapy.

Commiphora myrrha
MYRRH
Potent antiseptic used in oral hygiene preparations.

Coriandrum sativum
CORIANDER
One of the oldest known herbs, cultivated for over 3000 years; leaves and seeds have quite different aromas.

Cuminum cyminum
CUMIN
Characteristic flavor in Middle Eastern dishes; used in Ayurvedic medicine to improve liver function.

Lawsonia inermis

Ferula assa-foetida
ASAFOETIDA
Unpleasant-smelling gum resin gives characteristic flavor to curries and Worcestershire sauce.

Ficus carica
FIG
Probably Arabian in origin, valued for its prolific, gently laxative fruits.

Lawsonia inermis
HENNA
Powdered henna yields a red dye for hair, skin, and nails.

Medicago sativa
ALFALFA
Detoxicant, diuretic herb, best known as sprouted seeds for salads.

Morus nigra
BLACK MULBERRY
Multipurpose tree with edible fruits, medicinal properties, and industrial uses.

Papaver somniferum
OPIUM POPPY
The world's most important painkiller.

Peganum harmala
SYRIAN RUE
Source of Turkey red dye for tarbooshes, and much-used in Arab medicine and ritual.

Prunus dulcis
ALMOND
Source of sweet, emollient, laxative oil, and bitter oil for food flavoring.

Punica granatum
POMEGRANATE
Fruits made into cordial (grenadine) and syrup for flavoring Middle Eastern dishes; medicinally used to expel tapeworms.

Rosa damascena
DAMASK ROSE
Oil and extracts used in perfumery, cosmetics, and food flavoring.

Salvadora persica
TOOTHBRUSH TREE
Roots used for dental hygiene; seeds are "mustard seeds" of the New Testament parable.

Sesamum indicum
SESAME
Source of oil, paste, and seeds, used especially in Middle Eastern dishes.

Trachyspermum ammi
AJOWAN
Bitter seeds with a thyme-like aroma, used in Middle Eastern cuisine (especially with breads and legumes).

Trigonella foenum-graecum
FENUGREEK
Important in Middle Eastern cuisine, spice mixes, and Ayurvedic medicine.

Vitis vinifera
GRAPE
Ancient culinary and medicinal uses.

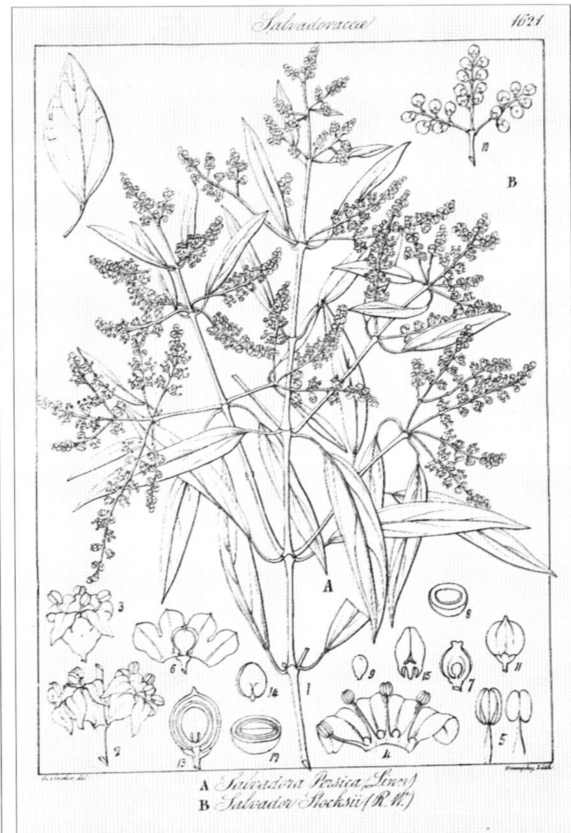

◄ *Salvadora persica* – root
▼ *Salvadora persica* – botanical drawing

THE INDIAN SUBCONTINENT
INDIA, NEPAL, BHUTAN, PAKISTAN, SRI LANKA

Mountainous regions are nearly always rich in plant life, being relatively inaccessible and providing an array of habitats as contours and altitude change. The Indian subcontinent has the world's highest mountain range, the Himalayas, home to some 9000 plant species, and tropical ranges, such as the Western Ghats in Maharashtra, with about 1500 endemic species. Rainforest and rugged mountains continue in Sri Lanka; 30 percent of species on the island are endemic, notably cinnamon (*Cinnamomum zeylanicum*).

HIMALAYAN FOOTHILLS IN NEPAL
Terracing hillsides allows easier food cultivation, and helps to prevent soil erosion in heavy rains.

CALUMBA WOOD IN THE SINHARAJA RESERVE
This is one of the last areas of virgin rainforest in Sri Lanka. Stems and roots of this woody climber contain alkaloids similar to those in Berberis *species, and a turmericlike dye.*

As in China, traditional medicine in the Indian subcontinent has an ancient history, with written texts dating from c.2500BC. The medicine is known as Ayurveda (literally, "life knowledge") and uses some 600 indigenous herbs. Unani and Siddha systems are similarly dependent on many local plants, as are India's hundreds of tribal groups. Some 200 species are in common use, many of them trees from the rich forests of the region: kino, or bastard teak (*Pterocarpus marsupium*); eaglewood (*Aquilaria malaccensis*); and various myrobalans (*Phyllanthus emblica*, *Terminalia bellirica* and *T. chebula*). Myrobalan fruits are particularly important as a rejuvenative tonic, known as the *triphala*, which is a recurrent combination in Tibetan medicine as well. *T. arjuna*, a heart tonic, is also commonly used, as is sandalwood (*Santalum album*). Though originally from SE Asia, sandalwood is naturalized in parts of India and Sri Lanka, and is central to Hindu practices and traditional medicine. It is the customary wood for funeral pyres.

ENDANGERED SPECIES

One of the region's most endangered herbs is *Saussurea lappa*, a thistlelike alpine, found in the Himalayas from Pakistan to Himachal Pradesh in India, and used in both Ayurvedic and Chinese medicine. Another is *Rauvolfia serpentina*, a small woodland shrub, well known in 1563, when a Portuguese account published in Goa described it as "the foremost and most praiseworthy Indian medicine." Rauvolfia provides reserpine, a major tranquilizing drug. The roots of both plants are used, so collecting wild plants means killing them. *Saussurea* is now so rare in the wild from overcollection that it is listed on CITES Appendix I. India has banned the export of both species. Shortages of *R. serpentina* have led to intensive efforts in many countries to cultivate it

▼ MEDICINAL PLANT NURSERY
This nursery at Haputale, Sri Lanka, is one of several run by the Royal Botanic Gardens, Peradeniya, to carry out research and propagate plants for sale to growers.

COLLECTING CARDAMOM ►
The capsules ripen during the dry season in autumn and winter. They are either sun-dried on mats, which takes about five days, and produces a superior, whiter product, or dried with hot-air machines in two days.

for the pharmaceutical industry, and inevitably also to the exploitation of at least four other *Rauvolfia* species, which may be threatened in their turn by overcollection.

Gloriosa superba, found in teak forest and savanna in many parts of tropical Asia and Africa, is rare in the wild, and considered endangered in Bangladesh. Its flamelike lilies were first seen in the West in 1690, since when it has been in great demand. The flowers vary in color from purple-red to scarlet, orange, and yellow; the most widely cultivated is the red and yellow *G. superba* 'Rothschildiana'. The tubers are toxic, and a traditional form of suicide in India. They contain colchicine, an alkaloid used in medicine and genetic engineering, and are grown in India and China.

WOODFORDIA FRUTICOSA
The flowers of Woodfordia *are an ingredient in many Ayurvedic remedies, especially for dysentery and liver diseases. This tropical shrub occurs mainly in India, Myanmar (Burma), and Sri Lanka.*

CONSERVATION AND CULTIVATION WORK

India, Bangladesh, and Sri Lanka now give priority to research programs concerning the distribution, abundance, uses, and efficacy of medicinal plants, and are aiming to increase conservation and cultivation. An all-India survey of its many hundreds of tribal groups is near completion, and monitoring units for medicinal plants are being set up in each state under the Ministry of Health and Family Welfare. India has over two million acres (800,000 ha) devoted to the cultivation of herbs for home use and export – the largest area of any country to date. Sri Lanka has an integrated health policy of traditional (Ayurvedic) and western medicine, and established a Ministry of Indigenous Medicine in 1980. Areas for conservation and cultivation are well advanced; botanic gardens in different climatic zones grow and propagate many of the 600 native medicinal plants; in addition, some 400 Forest Reserves and 50 Protected Areas have localized reservations for medicinal plants.

GRINDING MUSTARD SEEDS IN BHUTAN
*Indian mustard (*Brassica juncea*) is a common crop in the Indian subcontinent. It is the only mustard native to Asia.*

MAJOR HERBS OF THE REGION

Andrographis paniculata
Controls bacillary dysentery.

Berberis aristata*, *B. asiatica
BARBERRY
Main remedy for diarrhea and dysentery.

Centella asiatica
GOTU KOLA
Key rejuvenative herb in Ayurvedic medicine.

Cinnamomum zeylanicum
CINNAMON
Important culinary spice.

Commiphora mukul
GUGGULU
Source of myrrh, now exploited for cholesterol-lowering saponins.

Coptis teeta
Important detoxicant and antipyretic, often used as substitute for equally rare *C. chinensis*.

Coscinium fenestratum
CALUMBA WOOD
A bitter tonic in Ayurvedic medicine, and source of an antitetanus drug.

Dioscorea deltoidea
YAM
One of the main commercial sources of steroidal saponins.

Elettaria cardamomum
CARDAMOM
Seeds are characteristic of Indian desserts.

Gloriosa superba
FLAME LILY
Highly toxic roots contain colchicine, used to treat gout and in genetic engineering.

Jasminum sambac
ARABIAN JASMINE
Grown throughout the subcontinent for its perfume.

Gloriosa superba

Nelumbo nucifera
SACRED LOTUS
A tonic for heart energy in Ayurvedic medicine.

Phyllanthus emblica
AMALAKI
Astringent fruits used with those of *Terminalia bellirica* and *T. chebula* as a rejuvenative tonic, known as the *triphala*, in Ayurvedic and Tibetan medicine.

Piper nigrum
PEPPER
The world's most widely used spice.

Plantago indica
BLACK PSYLLIUM
One of several plantains used as a bulk laxative and to soothe inflammation.

Podophyllum hexandrum
INDIAN MANDRAKE
Himalayan woodland plant with valuable antitumor compounds.

Rauvolfia serpentina
INDIAN SNAKEROOT
Important as a tranquilizer and sedative; from India and Myanmar (Burma).

Santalum album
SANDALWOOD
Aromatic oil used in Ayurvedic medicine, aromatherapy, perfumery, and incense.

Saussurea lappa
COSTUS, *KUTH*
Thistlelike Himalayan plant, important in both Ayurvedic and Chinese traditional medicine.

Swertia chirata
CHIRETTA
Himalayan gentianlike plant with bitter, digestive properties.

***Terminalia* species**
MYROBALAN
Fruits of several species are used in Ayurvedic and Tibetan medicine for their rejuvenative properties.

Withania somnifera
ASHWAGANDHA
The "ginseng" of Ayurvedic medicine.

Woodfordia fruticosa
Flowers yield a liver remedy, a tragacanthlike gum, and dye.

CHINA AND ITS NEIGHBORS

The vastness of China is legendary; its sheer size is encapsulated in the phrase "for all the tea in China." One-fifth of the world's human population live there, and 10 percent of all known plant species are found in the country's wide range of habitats. These range from tundra, deserts, and grasslands to forests of every description – coniferous, bamboo, oak, rich deciduous woodlands, and tropical rainforest. Of the 35,000 species of plants growing in these varied habitats, some 5000 are used in traditional Chinese medicine, which yield 700,000 tons (634,900 tonnes) of raw materials annually, and provide 40 percent of all China's medication.

HERBS IN FOLKLORE
The Chinese goddess Ma-kou, with her basket of medicinal plants, from Henri Doré's Recherches sur les superstitions en Chine, *1918.*

Written records of medical knowledge in China began over 2000 years ago. In the early 20th century, as in most parts of the world, the wisdom of these ancient remedies was questioned as modern medicine gained favor. Advances in chemistry took place, and Chinese scientists began to analyze herbs to evaluate their efficacy. At first, they concentrated on isolating chemical components in a single herb, and in all the Chinese *materia medica* found only one new, exciting compound – ephedrine, from *Ephedra sinica*. In 1949 this approach changed; they started to compare the actual formulas with traditional concepts of a plant's uses, and found a remarkably positive correlation between the two approaches. Evidence gained in the 1950s convinced the authorities that to provide an effective health system for the entire population, China should combine Western medicine with traditional methods, which were cheaper and more readily available.

ONE OF CHINA'S SPECTACULAR HABITATS
An extraordinary landscape, at Yangshou in southern central China. Every variety of plant habitat can be found in China.

CULTIVATION OF MEDICINAL HERBS

Colleges of traditional Chinese medicine were established by Mao Tse-tung, training both graduates in Western medicine and paramedics ("barefoot doctors") to serve the rural population. Research now gives equal prominence to Chinese herbs and Western-style drugs; anisodine and anisodamine, important anticholinergic drugs that affect involuntary muscles, have recently been discovered in *Scopolia tangutica*, a species from northwest China. Integrating traditional with Western medicine had the effect of increasing the demand for herbs. In order to meet this demand, when in fact supplies were diminishing through loss of habitats and overcollection, China pioneered a national program of medicinal plant cultivation. Some 800,000 acres (324,000 ha) are now devoted to herbs, controlled by the Chinese Crude Drugs Company in each province. The greatest demand is for *Panax ginseng* and *P. notoginseng*, *Angelica polymorpha* var. *sinensis*, *Coptis chinensis*, *Rehmannia glutinosa*, *Paeonia suffruticosa*, *Cinnamomum cassia*, and *Atractylodes macrocephala*. The Chinese have also introduced into cultivation several herbs of foreign origin that they have long imported in large quantities. Notable among these is American ginseng (*Panax quinquefolius*), which has been reproduced using tissue culture. Some herbs are inherently more difficult to cultivate than others; fungi such as *Wolfiporia cocos* and the saprophytic orchid *Gastrodia elata,* presented an enormous challenge.

MARITIME HARVEST
*Seaweed (*Gelidium amansii*) being collected off the coast of Japan, to be dried for use in the pharmaceutical and food industries.*

THE GROWING DEMAND FOR GINSENG

The best-known Chinese herb is undoubtedly ginseng. This ancient Taoist tonic herb has featured in Chinese formulas for over 3000 years. It was known in Europe from the 9th century onward, notably when presented to Louis XIV (1638-1715) by the King of Siam, but only became widely used in the West as a result of Soviet research into "adaptogens" during the 1950s. *Panax ginseng*, a slow-growing woodland perennial with a very limited natural distribution, was near-extinct in the wild by the 19th century, and collection was forbidden during the reign of Tao Kuang (1821-51). Scarcity of Chinese ginseng prompted the discovery of American ginseng (*Panax quinquefolius*) in the 18th century, and

TRADITIONAL CHINESE MEDICINE
Weighing out remedies in Yunnan, China. Traditional procedures are combined with Western practices.

of Siberian ginseng (*Eleutherococcus senticosus*) in the 1950s. The latter was found as the result of a search by Soviet scientists for a ginseng substitute. They found that *Eleutherococcus* was surprisingly similar in its constituents; in addition to a wider distribution than *Panax* species (from northern China and southeastern Russia to Japan and Korea), it was a larger, more easily cultivated plant.

CHINESE HERBS BROUGHT TO THE WEST

Some Chinese herbs are popular garden plants, introduced to cultivation in the West by missionaries and explorers from the 18th century onward. The familiar forsythia is a Chinese medicinal herb. Forsythia fruits are an important remedy for acute infections, often combined with the flowers and stems of the common shrub, *Lonicera japonica*. Peonies soon became favorite garden plants when introduced from China, where they have been cultivated for 1000 years as favorite flowers of the emperors and also for their medicinal roots. When western plant collectors searched for tree peonies (*Paeonia suffruticosa*) in China at the beginning of this century, they found few remaining in the wild, the species having been overexploited even by then. Reginald Farrer found a single hillside with them in Kansu in 1914, but it was not until 1925 that more were found by Joseph Rock, who sent seed back to the Arnold Arboretum in Boston, which some years later returned seed to him in China so that he could reestablish them in the wild. One of China's rarest and most unusual species is *Ginkgo biloba*, the sole survivor of a large group of plants that was wiped out during the last ice age. Known in China as a sacred tree around Buddhist temples, it was introduced to the West in 1727, where it gained fame as a "living fossil." Recently, the first wild ginkgos have been found in two remote areas of China. Fortunately, it is very easily cultivated and is a common ornamental worldwide.

THE ASIAN RHUBARB TRADE

Purgation is regarded as an all-purpose cure in most cultures, and the borderlands between China and Russia are home to medicinal rhubarbs (*Rheum* species), which are used as laxatives. Dried rhubarb roots were traded overland across Asia and Europe since earliest times. Names were given to rhubarbs – Turkey, Russian, Chinese, East Indian – according to the route taken, rather than the species or origin of the roots. Live plants were unknown in the West until the 18th century, largely because the Chinese and Russians held trade monopolies. When seed was introduced to European botanic gardens c.1750, large acreages were devoted to its cultivation.

ORNAMENTALS IN THE WEST

Forsythia suspensa

Paeonia suffruticosa 'Reine Elizabeth'

Lonicera japonica 'Halliana'

These familiar garden plants all came from China originally. In China they are more often grown as farm crops for their medicinal properties than as ornamentals.

MAJOR HERBS OF THE REGION

Artemisia annua

Artemisia annua
QING HAO
New antimalarial drug.

Cinnamomum camphora
CAMPHOR
Used in moth repellants and liniments.

Dioscorea nipponica
YAM
Commercial source of steroidal compounds.

Eleutherococcus senticosus
SIBERIAN GINSENG
Substitute for rarer ginsengs.

Ephedra sinica, E. equisetina
EPHEDRA, *MA HUANG*
Source of ephedrine.

Ginkgo biloba
Leaves contain unique flavonoids.

Glycyrrhiza uralensis
LICORICE
Tonic, harmonizing herb, used in almost all Chinese formulas.

Mentha arvensis* var. *piperascens
JAPANESE PEPPERMINT
Major source of menthol.

Paeonia lactiflora
PEONY
Circulatory tonic, a new treatment for childhood eczema.

***Rheum* species**
RHUBARB
Important laxative herbs.

Panax ginseng
GINSENG
World-famous adaptogen.

ASTHMA REMEDY
The small yellow flowers of Ginkgo biloba *give way to these plum-like fruits. The brown seeds have traditionally been used to treat asthma sufferers.*

AUSTRALASIA

AUSTRALIA, NEW ZEALAND, OCEANIA

The plant life of Australasia owes its character to the region's ancient geological history, when part of the southern continental mass of Gondwanaland collided with the landmass of Laurasia to the north of it. This joined New Guinea and the islands to the north of Australia with a land bridge that permitted movement of plant and animal species. The area of interchange, known as Wallace's Line, runs between Borneo and Sulawesi in Southeast Asia, and explains some odd distributions in the plant life of these regions.

AUSTRALIAN BUSHFIRES
Plants have evolved high levels of resin and oil that encourage a fierce but short burn in order to speed the passage of a fire.

The rich variety of Australian plant life has provided food and healing plants for thousands of years. It is characterized by species that have adapted to increasing aridity; much of Australia is subject to bushfires, and many plants have developed oils and resins to encourage a rapid burning of aerial parts that leaves woody tissues and underground parts unharmed. Eucalyptus trees, whose oils and resins are of major importance in medicine and industry, are an example. Species of this genus in northern, tropical parts of Australia have lower oil and resin contents than those in the south.

ABORIGINES, MAORIS, AND POLYNESIANS

Aboriginal uses of native plants are poorly documented, since many oral traditions were lost before records could be made. It is known, however, that both native people and early settlers made extensive use of eucalypt gum, or kino, to control infections, bleeding, and diarrhea. Research into Maori uses shows that native species such as New Zealand flax (*Phormium tenax*) and manuka (*Leptospermum scoparium*), now familiar worldwide as ornamentals, were used in a wide range of remedies, including those for gunshot wounds. Herbal medicines were administered by the Tohunga, who was both doctor and spiritual leader. Rituals and vapor baths were an integral part of the healing process. New Zealand's plants have little in common with those of Australia (no eucalypts or melaleucas, for example); in northern parts they resemble those of Southeast Asia, while central regions are temperate, and the cool, wet southern zone has many unique alpine species.

The Polynesian islands were the last places on earth to be settled; migrants first came from Asia about 1000BC, reaching the Hawaiian Islands in about AD400. The most important plant sustaining these settlers was taro (*Colocasia esculenta*), of which there are over 1000 varieties. Migrations of people across the Pacific can be traced through the genetics of this ancient crop plant. It became the staple food on many islands and was used widely for medicinal purposes, treating everything from boils to heart complaints.

ARID LANDSCAPE
White gum trees and red rocks, Hamersley Ranges, Western Australia. This deceptively barren land supports a rich flora, including some 450 species of Eucalyptus.

CONTROLLING ALIEN SPECIES

What Australia and New Zealand do share in terms of their floras is the threat to native plants from the introduction of plants and animals from other parts of the world. Both countries have strict regulations governing the introduction of seeds and plants from abroad, as well as the control of established exotics. Nevertheless, in some areas native plants are dominated by alien species. Many of these are European herbs, such as fennel (*Foeniculum vulgare*), horehound (*Marrubium vulgare*), and pennyroyal (*Mentha pulegium*), presumably brought by settlers for household use.

MAJOR HERBS OF THE REGION

Acacia **species**
WATTLE
Floral emblem of Australia, source of tanbark, and traditional remedy for diarrhea.

Abrus precatorius
JEQUIRITY
Tropical northern species, used by Aborigines as body ornaments; and cure for trachoma (sandy blight).

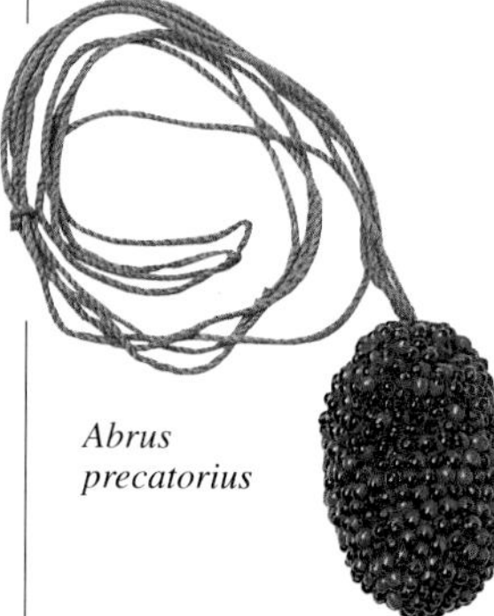

Abrus precatorius

Atriplex nummularia
OLD MAN SALTBUSH
Rich source of vitamin C, used by settlers to cure scurvy.

Colocasia esculenta
TARO
Staple food and all-purpose medicine of many Oceanic islands, notably in the Hawaiian group.

Dodonaea viscosa
STICKY HOP BUSH
Astringent leaves chewed for toothache and applied to stings.

Duboisia **species**
CORKWOOD
Known to Aborigines as *pituri*, a narcotic stimulant chewed on long journeys, now the main source of tropane alkaloids for the pharmaceutical industry.

Eucalyptus **species**
GUM TREE
Rich in resinous, tannin-rich kino, long used as a healing astringent, and aromatic oils now used worldwide in cough medicines, cold remedies, and liniments.

Melaleuca alternifolia
TEA TREE
Oil used as an antibacterial and antifungal treatment, and popular in aromatherapy.

Pandanus odoratissimus
SCREW PINE
A multipurpose plant on Pacific islands, providing food, medicine, and perfume, and materials for thatch and weaving.

Phormium tenax
NEW ZEALAND FLAX
Maori uses include decoctions for battle injuries, and as a binding for splints.

Prostanthera **species**
MINT BUSH
Rich in antibiotic, fungicidal oils, and popular as ornamental plants.

Santalum lanceolatum
PLUMBUSH
Important to Aborigines for edible fruits and medicinal leaves, bark, and roots.

Santalum spicatum
SANDALWOOD
Source of native Australian sandalwood oil.

SOUTHEAST ASIA

INDONESIA, MALAYSIA, SINGAPORE, PHILIPPINES, THAILAND, CAMBODIA, VIETNAM, BURMA, LAOS

Until recently, most of Southeast Asia was covered in dense tropical rainforests, rich in lumber trees, and source of some of the world's most important spice plants; both nutmeg and cloves originated in the Moluccas ("Spice Islands"). The creeping, aromatic rhizomes of the ginger family are common on the rainforest floor. A number of other plant families, important for their medicinal uses, have their greatest diversity of species in this region, including the Apocynaceae, a source of cardiac and tranquilizing alkaloids.

MYRISTICA FRAGRANS
Nutmeg and mace are two of the many popular spices that are native to the depleted rainforests of Southeast Asia.

The rate of trees being cut from rainforest is, however, by no means balanced by their natural regeneration, though species vary greatly in their vulnerability to harvesting. For example, research in Indonesia has shown that *Aquilaria malaccensis* is found only in primary forest and is nowhere abundant. It is felled for its resinous wood, but this varies considerably in quality, and of the great many trees that are felled in the process, some yield little or nothing, and stumps rarely resprout. Severe depletion of the species has occurred in many forests. In contrast, *Melaleuca leucadendron* grows in disturbed areas, forming dense stands, and is widely cultivated, resprouting readily when felled for oil extraction. Threatened trees such as *Aquilaria malaccensis* are an urgent priority for conservation.

RAINFOREST TREE PALMS
Irreplaceable tropical forests, like this one in Krabi, Thailand, are increasingly at risk from urban development.

PROTECTING THE ENVIRONMENT

Like many developing countries, Indonesia has a rising population, with a corresponding loss of habitats, especially of tropical rainforest, through urban development, agricultural expansion, and mining. As a result, there are serious shortages of herbs both for traditional medicine (known as *jamu*) and for an enlarging export market in pharmaceutical materials. The hundreds of widely scattered islands that make up Indonesia present a considerable challenge for programs of conservation, cultivation, and education. Various nature reserves and living collections of medicinal and industrial plants have been established, and the Department of Health is encouraging a nationwide "living pharmacy" – the cultivation of herbs in gardens for home use.

Thailand is endeavoring to make traditional remedies available throughout the country, especially in rural areas where medical services are limited. Drug cooperatives have been set up in 45,000 villages, with 1000 villages involved in cultivating about 50 of the most commonly used medicinal plants.

TRADITIONAL MEDICINE
This Javanese woman is selling jamu, traditional herbal medicine. Serious plant shortages in the region now threaten both traditional and pharmaceutical products.

MAJOR HERBS OF THE REGION

Cananga odorata

Alpinia galanga
GALANGAL
Gingerlike flavoring in SE Asian cooking.

Aquilaria malaccensis
EAGLEWOOD
Tonic herb and flavoring for Malaysian curries.

Cananga odorata
YLANG-YLANG
The "queen of perfumes."

Croton tiglium
PURGING CROTON
Drastic purgative.

Hydnocarpus kurzii
CHAULMOOGRA
Unique oil used for skin diseases, such as leprosy.

Melaleuca leucadendron
CAJUPUT
Antiseptic oil used in cough medicines, soaps, and aromatherapy.

Myristica fragrans
NUTMEG AND MACE
Both spices are used worldwide.

Strychnos nux-vomica
STRYCHNINE
Deadly poison; stimulant in minute amounts.

Styrax benzoin
BENZOIN
Ingredient of friar's balsam.

Syzygium aromaticum
CLOVES
Important spice, and cure for toothache.

THE HERB CATALOG

Full botanical descriptions and detailed plant portraits of a wide range of herbal plants, with a guide to their hardiness and uses

ABELMOSCHUS

This genus contains 15 species of bristly or downy, hibiscus-like annuals and perennials (formerly included in *Hibiscus*, see p.138), and is native to the tropics of Africa and Eurasia. *A. moschatus* is the only species used widely as an herb. It is a colorful, exotic perennial that can easily be raised from seed and grown as a half-hardy annual in cool climates. The name comes from the Arabic *abu-l-mosk*, "father of musk," because of the musk-scented seeds.

Abelmoschus moschatus (ambrette, musk seed, musk mallow)
Bushy perennial with palmate leaves; large, sulfur yellow, hibiscus-like flowers with maroon centers appear in summer. Hairy seed pods contain gray-brown seeds with a musklike aroma.
H 3–6ft (1–2m), S 18–36in (45–90cm).

9

***Abelmoschus moschatus* 'Mischief'**
This cultivar has cherry red, white-centered flowers, 2½–4in (6–10cm) across. H 15–18in (38–45cm), S 9–12in (23–30cm).

9

ABIES

A genus of about 50 species of large evergreen conifers, which is distributed throughout subalpine and temperate zones in the northern hemisphere and C America. *A. alba*, which is large and fast-growing, is found in mountain valleys of Europe, from the Pyrenees to the Balkans; the short-lived *A. balsamea*, with its conical crown and balsam-scented leaves, grows in northern N American woods. Both are too large for most gardens, but *A. b.* 'Hudsonia' is an attractive dwarf cultivar.

Abies alba (silver fir)
Conifer with symmetrical crown and bark that cracks to form squarish plates in older trees. Glossy, dark green needles, up to 1in (2.5cm) long, have 2 pale bands on the underside. Cones are 6in (15cm) long, with reflexed bracts. H 150ft (45m), S 70ft (20m).

3–7

Abies balsamea (balsam fir, balm of Gilead)
Conifer with dark gray bark, fissured in older trees. Flattened leaves have 2 grayish stripes on the underside. Erect cones are purple when young, brown when mature, up to 2–4in (5–10cm) long. H 45ft (15m), S 15ft (5m).

3–7

***Abies balsamea* 'Hudsonia'**
Slow-growing, rounded dwarf shrub with a flattish crown and short, dense needles. It is more lime-tolerant than the species. H and S 2–3ft (60cm–1m).

3–7

ABRUS

Seventeen species of tender, deciduous, semievergreen or evergreen twining shrubs make up this genus, found through the tropics in lowland forests. *A. precatorius*, native to India, has acquired numerous common names from its many uses. The name "jequirity" is from the Portuguese translation of the Tupi-Guarani *jekiriti*, "lucky bean." "Indian licorice" refers to the fact that this species, whose leaves taste of licorice, contains glycyrrhizin, a substance 50–60 times sweeter than sugar.

Abrus precatorius (jequirity, crab's eyes, Indian licorice)
Deciduous or semievergreen vine with pinnate leaves. Pink-purple flowers are produced in racemes, mainly in summer, followed by 2in (5cm) long pods, containing scarlet, black-tipped seeds.
H 3–12ft (1–4m), S indefinite.

SELECT LIST OF COMMON NAMES:

AARON'S ROD, see *Verbascum thapsus*, p.218
ABELE, see *Populus alba*, p.182
ABSCESS ROOT, see *Polemonium reptans*, p.180

ACACIA

This genus of 1,000 or more evergreen, semievergreen, or deciduous trees and shrubs is found throughout dry tropical to warm temperate regions, mainly in Africa and Australia. *A. catechu* is found in India, Myanmar (Burma), Sri Lanka, and tropical eastern Africa; *A. farnesiana* occurs in SE Asia and is naturalized in Australia. Wattles are popular as ornamentals for gardens in warmer regions, or make elegant indoor plants. They are generally fast-growing and flower when young.

Acacia catechu (black catechu)
Deciduous tree with a short trunk and divided, feathery leaves, 3–6in (7.5–15cm) long. The shoots bear hooked spines at the base. Pale yellow flowers appear in twos or threes, or in a short spike, in the axils in summer. H to 80ft (25m), S to 50ft (15m).

Acacia farnesiana (prickly Moses, cassie)
Large shrub or small tree with slender spines. Sparse, feathery leaves 3in (7.5cm) long are divided into 4–8 pairs of leaflets. Fragrant yellow flowers appear in the axils in summer.
H 10–22ft (3–7m), S 10–15ft (3–5m).

ACHILLEA

Over 85 species of hardy, often aromatic, commonly mat-forming perennials make up this genus, which occurs throughout northern temperate regions. *A. millefolium*, native to Europe and western Asia, is also widely naturalized in N America, Australia, and New Zealand. Yarrows make attractive plants for the border, with long-lived flowers that last well in water. *Achillea* was named after Achilles, who reputedly used it to heal his soldiers' wounds after the siege of Troy.

Achillea millefolium (yarrow, milfoil, soldier's woundwort)
Aromatic perennial with tough stems and feathery leaves 2–6in (5–15cm) long. Corymbs of grayish white to pink flowers appear from early summer to late autumn. H 2–12in (5–30cm), S 2–8in (5–20cm), variable in the wild.

3–10

***Achillea millefolium* 'Cerise Queen'**
Deep pink flowers are produced in midsummer. This cultivar is less invasive than the species. H and S 12–24in (30–60cm).

3–10

***Achillea millefolium* 'Lilac Beauty'**
This cultivar has bright lilac-pink flowers in midsummer and is less invasive than the species. H and S 24in (60cm).

3–10

ACAJOU, see *Anacardium occidentale*, p.83
ACHIOTE, see *Bixa orellana*, p.94

ACHYRANTHES

This genus of six variable, weedy perennials is found mostly in the subtropics and tropics of Eurasia, Australia, and Africa. *A. bidentata* occurs in east and SE Asia, and is also widely naturalized, notably in southern US. It is grown in China on a large scale for the herb trade, mainly in Henan Province. The rich soil there produces exceptionally large roots, the best reaching 3–4ft (1–1.2m) in length. A few species are used as food or medicinal plants, but are almost unknown outside their native lands.

Achyranthes bidentata (two-toothed amaranthus)
Slender perennial with stout roots and velvety, elliptic leaves up to 5in (12cm) long. In late summer, inconspicuous flowers open on spikes, accompanied by tiny spines. H 15–36in (38cm–1m), S 9–18in (23–45cm).

8–9

ACINOS

In this genus there are 10 species of hardy and half-hardy annuals or short-lived perennials, closely related to *Calamintha* (see p.97), and resembling thymes in appearance. *Acinos* species are found mainly on alkaline soils, in dry, sunny areas throughout Europe (*A. arvensis)*, the Mediterranean, and central Asia. One or two are grown as ornamentals, forming attractive, low-growing trailers for the rock garden.

Acinos arvensis (basil thyme)
Overwintering annual or short-lived perennial with weakly upright stems and small, lanceolate to ovate leaves. Whorls of light purple, white-centered flowers, usually in a cluster of 5 or more, appear in summer. H 6–8in (15–20cm), S 8–12in (20–30cm).

7–8

***Aconitum carmichaelii* 'Arendsii'**
This cultivar is larger all around than the species. It may need staking in windy or shady sites. H 5ft (1.5m), S 12in (30cm).

2–9

ACONITUM

This genus consists of about 100 species of poisonous, hardy tuberous perennials, which are found throughout northern temperate regions in woods, grassland, and near water. *A. carmichaelii* occurs in China, *A. napellus* in western and central Europe. Monkshoods were used in making arrow poisons, but they also make handsome border plants, with attractive spring foliage and delphinium-like flowers. The characteristic hooded shape of the flowers allows pollination only by bees.

Aconitum carmichaelii (azure monkshood, Sichuan aconite)
Tuberous perennial with glossy, dark green deeply cut leaves up to 6in (15cm) across. Racemes of deep blue flowers with 1½in (3.5cm) hoods appear in late summer and early autumn. H 36in (90cm), S 15in (38cm).

2–9

Aconitum napellus (monkshood, aconite, wolfsbane)
Tuberous perennial with upright stems and midgreen, divided leaves up to 6in (15cm) across. Spikes of deep blue flowers with hoods 1½in (3.5cm) long appear in late summer. H 4–5ft (1.2–1.5m), S 15in (38cm).

2–9

ACONITE, see *Aconitum napellus*, above

***Aconitum napellus* 'Carneum'**
Flesh pink flowers are borne from early to late summer. This cultivar needs cool, rich, moist soil for good color. H 36in (90cm), S 12–18in (30–45cm).

2–7

ACORUS

The two species of aquatic rhizomatous perennials in this genus are found wild in northern and eastern Asia (*A. gramineus*), and in N America. *A. calamus* is also naturalized in Europe. Sweet flag has been cultivated and traded for over 4,000 years. It probably reached eastern Europe from Mongolia and Siberia during the 13th century, spreading to western Europe in the 16th century. Variegated forms are popular ornamentals for waterside plantings and as pot plants.

Acorus calamus (sweet flag, calamus, myrtle flag)
Semievergreen rhizomatous perennial with lanceolate leaves and a tangerine scent. A solitary spadix with yellow-green flowers appears in summer. H 1–5ft (30cm–1.5m), S indefinite.

3–9

***Acorus calamus* 'Variegatus'**
This cultivar has cream-striped leaves. It is one of the finest ornamentals for wet situations. H 1–5ft (30cm–1.5m), S indefinite.

4–9

Acorus gramineus (rock sweet flag, grass-leaved sweet flag)
Very variable, semievergreen perennial with branched rhizomes and stiff, grasslike leaves. Minute greenish flowers are borne in a spadix, 2–4in (5–10cm) long, in summer. H 4–20in (10–50cm), S 4–9in (10–23cm).

7–10

***Acorus gramineus* 'Ogon'**
This cultivar has cream-striped leaves and is more colorful than the more common *A. g.*'Variegatus'. H 12in (30cm), S 15in (38cm).

7–10

***Acorus gramineus* 'Pusillus'**
One of the smallest variants, this has leaves only 3in (8cm) long. H 3in (8cm), S 5in (13cm).

7–10

ADENOPHORA

Closely related to *Campanula*, this genus contains 40 species of perennials, Eurasian in origin. *A. stricta* is found on hillsides in eastern Asia. They are elegant plants for the border, with bell-shaped, sometimes scented flowers, but few are well known or widely available in the West. The genus name *Adenophora* means "gland bearing," and refers to the cylindrical nectary at the base of the style, hence the common name of gland bellflower.

Adenophora stricta (fickle ladybell)
Tall perennial with a conical root, upright stems, and oval, toothed basal leaves clad in fine white hairs. Narrow racemes of pendulous, blue, bell-shaped flowers, also hairy, open in late summer and autumn. H 24–36in (60–90cm), S 12in (30cm).

3–8

ADIANTUM

In this genus there are over 200 species of hardy to tender ferns that are deciduous, semievergreen, or evergreen. The majority are native to tropical America, with a few species in northern temperate regions, including the European *A. capillus-veneris*. *A. aethiopicum* is one of several found in Australia. Several species are grown as ornamentals. *A. capillus-veneris* is a graceful fern for mild gardens or as a pot plant. The foliage is water-repellent.

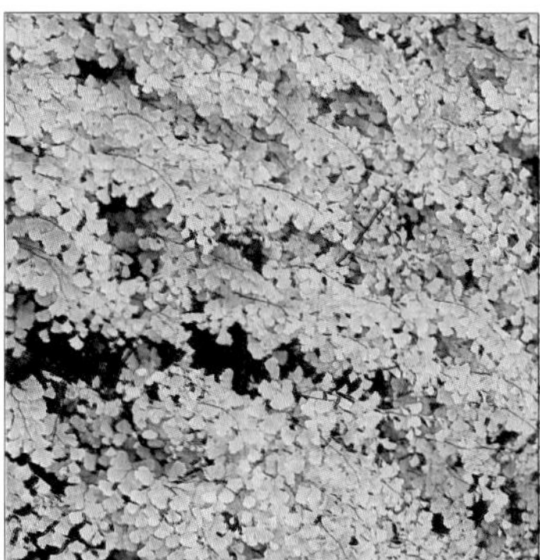

Adiantum capillus-veneris (maidenhair fern)
Evergreen or semievergreen rhizomatous fern with arching fronds, 18–24in (45–60cm) long, of lobed, fan-shaped leaflets. The undersides of mature leaflets carry red-brown sori. H 6–14in (15–35cm), S 12in (30cm).

ADONIS

About 20 species of annuals and herbaceous perennials make up this genus, which occurs in temperate Europe and Asia in a variety of habitats. *A. vernalis* is rare and protected in many areas. Several species are valued as ornamentals for their exquisite, early flowers. The genus is named after Adonis, the beautiful youth of Greek myth who was killed by a boar. The flowers that sprang from his blood as it touched the earth are planted in Greece to celebrate his return to life each spring.

Adonis vernalis (false hellebore, yellow pheasant's eye)
Clump-forming perennial with a stout rootstock and numerous, finely dissected leaves. Solitary yellow flowers resembling large buttercups appear in early spring. H 6–16in (15–40cm), S 12–18in (30–45cm).

4–7

AEGOPODIUM

There are five to seven species of creeping perennials in this genus. They are found in woodland and scrub and on waste ground through Europe and temperate Asia. *A. podagraria* is also naturalized in N America. Most species are invasive weeds. The name *Aegopodium* is derived from the Greek *aigos*, "goat," and *podos*, "foot." The specific epithet *podagraria* derives from the Latin *podagra*, "gout," and refers to the plant's medicinal uses.

Aegopodium podagraria (goutweed, ground elder)
Herbaceous perennial with a creeping, invasive rootstock and strong-smelling, long-stalked leaves 3–9in (8–23cm) long. Umbels of tiny white flowers appear in summer. H 12–36in (30–90cm), S indefinite.

4–8

***Aegopodium podagraria* 'Variegatum'**
Vigorous, less invasive, white-variegated cultivar that makes good groundcover under trees and shrubs. Umbels of white flowers are borne in summer. H 9–12in (23–30cm), S indefinite.

5–8

AESCULUS

This genus of 13 species of deciduous trees and shrubs occurs in southeastern Europe, eastern Asia, and N America; *A. hippocastanum* is found wild from the Balkans to the Himalayas. Introduced to Europe in the 16th century, horse chestnuts have handsome foliage that may turn rich brown in autumn. The seeds resemble edible chestnuts (*Castanea sativa*, see p.102); their resemblance to the eyes of deer gave rise to the common name of "buckeye."

Aesculus hippocastanum (common horse chestnut)
Large tree with sticky buds and palmate leaves. Erect spikes of white flowers appear in late spring. Globular, green-brown, spiny fruits contain 1–3 shiny, red-brown seeds ("conkers"). H 80–130ft (25–40m), S 15–25ft (5–8m).

3–7

***Aesculus hippocastanum* 'Baumannii'**
This cultivar has long-lasting double flowers that do not set seed. H 100ft (30m), S 50ft (15m).

3–7

AGASTACHE

The 30 species of aromatic perennials in this genus are native to central and eastern Asia, N America, and Mexico; *A. foeniculum* is found in N and C America, and *A. rugosa* in eastern Asia. *A. foeniculum* is an especially rich source of nectar, attracting bees during its long flowering period. It has a tidy habit and makes a good, long-flowering border plant. *Agastache* is from the Greek *agan*, "very much," and *stachys*, "ear of wheat," which describes the look of the flower spikes.

Agastache foeniculum (anise hyssop, blue giant hyssop, fennel giant hyssop)
Perennial with pointed, ovate leaves, which have pale undersides and a strong anise scent. Bold spikes of light purple flowers with conspicuous bracts appear in summer. H 24–36in (60–90cm), S 18in (45cm).

6–9

***Agastache foeniculum* 'Alabaster'**
This bears white flowers on a dense, bushy plant. H 18–24in (45–60cm), S 12in (30cm).

6–9

Agastache rugosa (Korean mint, wrinkled giant hyssop)
Short-lived, upright perennial with square stems and pointed leaves that have white, hairy undersides and a mintlike aroma. Small purple flowers are produced in spikes in late summer. H 3–4ft (1–1.2m), S 24in (60cm).

6–9

AGATHOSMA

Native to S Africa, this genus consists of about 135 species of small, tender evergreen shrubs. *A. crenulata* is found on heaths in south-western Cape Province. Most are intensely aromatic, filling the surrounding air with fragrance in areas where they are plentiful. Their attractive habit, aroma, and flowers, which are produced at an early age, make them popular as ornamentals in warmer parts of the world, or as garden-room and patio plants in temperate areas.

Agathosma crenulata (oval buchu)
Tender shrub with bright green, ovate leaves and conspicuous oil glands that release a strong, blackcurrant-like aroma. Five-petaled white flowers with purple anthers appear in spring. H 3–8ft (1–2.5m), S 3–6ft (1–2m).

AGAR-AGAR, see *Gelidium amansii*, p.287

AGAVE

This genus consists of about 300 species of perennial succulents, occurring in arid regions from southern US to S America. *A. americana* is also naturalized in parts of India, Africa, and southern Europe. Agaves vary greatly in size and can take 5–20 years to reach flowering size. Most are tender, but those with green or gray-green leaves are slightly frost hardy. They are widely grown as garden plants in warm countries, and for pots or summer bedding in temperate zones.

Agave americana (century plant)
Large perennial with stout roots and rosettes of thick, hard, gray-green, toothed leaves. Spikes of bell-shaped, white to creamy yellow flowers appear on about 10-year-old plants in summer. H 3–6ft (1–2m), up to 25ft (8m) at flowering, S 6–10ft (2–3m).

10

***Agave americana* 'Variegata'**
This cultivar has yellow leaf margins and produces offsets freely. As with the species, most plants bloom after about 10 years. H and S 6ft (2m).

AGLAIA

A genus of about 250 species of evergreen trees and shrubs native to Asia and the Pacific Islands. *A. odorata* is found in SE Asia and China. Its flowers have an exquisite perfume that lasts almost indefinitely when they are dried. It is often grown as a hedge in the tropics and may be planted alternately with *Murraya paniculata* (orange jasmine), which has very similar foliage in a darker shade of green. *Aglaia* is an ancient Greek word meaning "splendid."

Aglaia odorata (mock lime)
Elegant shrub or tree with divided leaves up to 6in (15cm) long, having 5–7 leaflets and panicles of tiny yellow, vanilla-scented flowers in spring. H 50ft (15m), S 30ft (10m).

AGRIMONIA

A genus of 15 species of rhizomatous perennials found in northern temperate regions and in S America. *A. eupatoria* is found widely in Europe, western Asia, and northern Africa. Agrimony adapts well to cultivation and may be grown in the border or wildflower meadow. *Agrimonia* may come from the Greek *arghemon*, an eye disease (albugo), which agrimony was reputed to cure, or from the Latin *agri moenia*, "defender of the fields," after the masses of agrimony found beside fields.

Agrimonia eupatoria (agrimony, sticklewort, cocklebur)
Perennial with upright, often hairy, stems and downy leaves with 3–5 pairs of leaflets. Racemes of faintly scented yellow flowers appear in summer, followed by bristly fruits. H 12–24in (30–60cm), S 8–12in (20–30cm).

6–9

AILANTHUS

Five species of handsome, fast-growing deciduous trees are included in this genus, which is found from eastern Asia to Australia. *A. altissima* is native to northern China and was introduced to Europe in 1751. Tolerant of atmospheric pollution, it is widely planted as a street tree. In France, it is cultivated as a substitute for *A. vilmoriniana*, on which silk moths are raised for the production of shantung silk. The name *Ailanthus* is from the Amboinese *ai lanto*, "tree of the gods."

Ailanthus altissima (tree of heaven, ailanto, Chinese sumac)
Spreading tree with ashlike leaves up to 3ft (1m) long in young specimens. Male and female flowers are borne on separate plants; female trees bear large clusters of dark red, winged fruits in autumn. H 80ft (25m), S 50ft (15m).

4–9

AGNUS CASTUS, see *Vitex agnus-castus*, p.221
AGRIMONY, see *Agrimonia eupatoria*, above
AILANTO, see *Ailanthus altissima*, above

AJUGA

This genus of 50 species of hardy annuals and perennials is found mainly in temperate parts of Eurasia, with some species in Australia and tropical Africa. *A. reptans* is found in Europe, north-western Africa, Turkey, Iran, and the Caucasus. Many bugles are evergreen or semievergreen and make neat, colorful groundcover. *A. reptans* is an excellent garden plant for moisture-retentive soil in sun or shade as groundcover, for borders, or for the wildflower garden.

Ajuga reptans (bugle)
Evergreen rhizomatous perennial with basal rosettes of obovate leaves. Spikes of deep blue, occasionally pink or white flowers are produced in spring and early summer. H 4–12in (10–30cm), S indefinite.

3–9

Ajuga chamaepitys (ground pine)
Low-growing annual with narrow, gray-green leaves that are deeply divided and toothed, yellow flowers in the axils from late spring to early autumn. The whole plant has a pine-like odor. H and S 6in (15cm).

A

***Ajuga reptans* 'Burgundy Glow'**
With its light bronze and pink foliage, this is among the most colorful of all evergreen groundcover plants. H 3–6in (8–15cm), S indefinite.

3–9

***Ajuga reptans* 'Atropurpurea'**
(bronze bugle)
This cultivar has dark, purple-brown leaves and is most effective when planted with white-variegated herbs, such as pineapple mint. H 4–12in (10–30cm), S indefinite.

3–9

***Ajuga reptans* 'Variegata'**
The light green foliage of this cultivar is irregularly variegated with gray-green and cream. It is less vigorous than the species and is well suited to the rock garden and containers. H 3–6in (8–15cm), S indefinite.

3–9

AJOWAN, AJWAIN, see *Trachyspermum ammi*, p.363

AKEBIA

Five evergreen or deciduous, twining perennial climbers are included in this genus, which is native to China, Japan, and Korea. Several are grown as garden ornamentals for their attractive, lobed leaves and small, often scented flowers. The conspicuous, edible fruits give added interest but are only produced in warm areas where several plants are grown together. *Akebia* is the Latinized version of *akebi*, the Japanese name for these plants.

Akebia trifoliata (akebia)
Deciduous, twining climber with trifoliate leaves, bronze when young, and racemes of maroon, 3-petaled flowers in spring. Sausage-shaped, pale violet fruits, produced in threes, are up to 5in (13cm) long and contain black seeds in a white pulp. H 30ft (10m).

7–9

Alcea rosea **'Chater's Double'**
This 19th-century cultivar is similar to the species, but has fully double, peony-like flowers in a variety of colors, including pink, maroon, yellow, and white. H 6–8ft (2–2.5m), S 18–24in (45–60cm).

2–9

ALBIZIA

There are some 150 species of deciduous, occasionally thorny trees, shrubs, and lianas in this genus, which occurs throughout the tropics, often on poor soils. *A. julibrissin*, native to warm parts of Asia, is a graceful tree that tolerates hot, dry conditions. It is popular as an ornamental, though susceptible to pests and diseases in urban situations. Due to its long history of cultivation, cultivars vary in hardiness, with the Korean *A. j.* 'Rosea' flowering in Zone 6.

Albizia julibrissin (mimosa, silk tree)
Small domed to flat-topped, spreading tree with smooth, gray-brown bark and doubly pinnate leaves to 8in (20cm) long. Clusters of pink flower heads, made up mostly of long stamens, are borne in summer. H 20–30ft (6–10m), S 30ft (10m).

6–10

ALCEA

In this genus are 60 species of biennials or short-lived perennials occurring from the Mediterranean to central Asia. Several species are grown for their showy flowers. *A. rosea* reached Europe in the 16th century (from either China or the Middle East, perhaps Turkey) and became a popular garden plant and medicinal herb. The name *Alcea* is derived from the Greek *alkaria*, "mallow," the common name from the 16th-century "holy hock" (*hoc* was the Old English word for "mallow").

Alcea rosea (hollyhock)
Tall biennial or short-lived, summer-flowering perennial with rounded lobed leaves and spikes of single or double, hibiscus-like flowers, which may be white, pink, purple, or occasionally pale yellow. H 4–8ft (1.2–2.5m), S 15–24in (38–60cm).

2–9

Alcea rosea **'Nigra'**
A hollyhock that resembles the species except for its very dark maroon, single flowers. H 5ft (1.5m), S 18in (45cm).

2–9

ALDER, see *Alnus*, p.81
ALDER BUCKTHORN, see *Rhamnus frangula*, p.189
ALECOST, see *TANACETUM*, pp.208–9
ALEHOOF, see *Glechoma hederacea*, p.134
ALEXANDERS, see *Smyrnium olusatrum*, p.204
ALEXANDRIAN SENNA, see *Senna alexandrina*, p.202
ALFALFA, see *Medicago sativa*, p.157
ALKANET, see *Alkanna*, p.79

ALCHEMILLA

In this genus there are 250 species of hardy perennials found throughout northern temperate regions and at high altitudes in the tropics. *A. alpina*, found in mountain grassland in northwestern and central Europe, and Greenland, is a handsome foliage plant for rock gardens. *A. xanthochlora*, a variable, aggregate species, occurs in northern Europe and mountainous parts of central and southern Europe. It resembles *A. mollis*, also known as lady's mantle, which is widely grown for its foliage.

Alchemilla alpina (alpine lady's mantle)
Perennial with creeping rootstock and long-stalked, round to kidney-shaped leaves, palmately lobed almost to the base. Leaf undersides are clad in silky hairs. Clusters of green flowers appear in summer. H and S 4–8in (10–20cm).

3–7

Alchemilla xanthochlora (lady's mantle, lion's foot)
Perennial with a woody rootstock, densely hairy stems, and finely toothed, kidney-shaped leaves with 7–11 lobes. Dense clusters of tiny green flowers appear from late spring to early autumn. H and S 20in (50cm).

4–8

ALISMA

This genus of 10 species of frost-hardy to fully hardy, marginal aquatic perennials occurs in northern temperate regions and in Australia. *A. plantago-aquatica*, found in shallow water in temperate Eurasia, is popular in garden ponds and lakes for its attractive flowers. It was once regarded as a cure for rabies, hence a common name, "mad dog weed." The specific epithet, *plantago-aquatica*, refers to its aquatic habitat and the similarity of its leaves to *Plantago major* (see p.179).

Alisma plantago-aquatica (water plantain)
Aquatic perennial with a stout, upright stem and long-stalked, ovate leaves 3–8in (8–20cm) long. Tall panicles of small, pale lilac flowers appear in summer, opening later in the day. H and S 12–36in (30–90cm).

5–8

ALKANNA

This genus consists of some 25–30 perennials, and occurs from southern Europe to Iran. *A. tinctoria* is native to limestone screes, pine forests, and coastal sands in eastern Mediterranean areas, and is a useful plant for very dry, sandy, or alkaline soils. Several species, known as "alkanets," are important as dye plants. The name *Alkanna* is from the Spanish *alcanna*, which in turn derives from the Arabic word for henna.

Alkanna tinctoria (dyer's bugloss, Spanish bugloss)
Perennial with a stout, purple-brown root and linear to lanceolate, hairy leaves up to 3in (8cm) long. Funnel-shaped, 5-petaled, blue flowers appear in late summer. H 4–12in (10–30cm), S 8–12in (20–30cm).

9

ALLIARIA

This genus of five species of hardy perennials or biennials is found throughout Europe and temperate Asia. *A. petiolata*, found in Europe, northern Africa, and western and central Asia, is the only species with any interest as a garden plant. It is a good subject for damp, shady places where few other herbs will survive, and is also popular in conservation gardening as a food plant (in Europe) for caterpillars of the orange-tip butterfly.

Alliaria petiolata (garlic mustard, hedge garlic, Jack-by-the-hedge)
Garlic-smelling biennial with an erect stem and bright green, kidney-shaped leaves. In spring and summer, small white flowers are followed by upright, cylindrical pods. H 1–4ft (30cm–1.2m), S 12–18in (30–45cm).

4–8

ALLIUM

Onions form a large genus of about 700 species of strong-smelling, bulbous or rhizomatous biennials and perennials native to the northern hemisphere, Ethiopia, southern Africa, and Mexico, varying in hardiness according to origin. Various alliums have been cultivated since the earliest times and are universally important as vegetables, flavorings, and medicinal plants. Their distinctive smell varies in pungency from species to species, and a few are almost odorless. There are hundreds of cultivars of *A. cepa* worldwide, adapted to latitude and climate and varying in size, color, and flavor. Egypt, Italy, Spain, Turkey, and the US are the main producers. *A. fistulosum* is the most important *Allium* species grown in China, Japan, and SE Asia.

▲ ***Allium cepa*** var. ***proliferum*** (tree onion, Catawissa onion, Egyptian onion)
An interesting and useful plant for the herb garden, producing (among the flowers) large bulbils that sprout leaves while still attached to the umbel.
H 3ft (1m), S 1ft (30cm).
4–9

◄ ***Allium fistulosum*** (Welsh onion, scallion, spring onion)
Biennial or perennial with cylindrical bulbs, pencil-thick stems, and hollow leaves. Bell-shaped, yellow-white flowers subtended by a large spathe are borne in umbels during summer. They may be entirely replaced by bulbils. H 3ft (1m), S 6–9in (15–23cm).
4–9

◄ ***Allium ampeloprasum*** var. ***ampeloprasum*** (elephant garlic, round-headed garlic)
Perennial with a 2-lobed bulb and axillary bulbs not enclosed in a papery membrane. Purple to pink-white flowers in a dense umbel appear in summer. H 1½–5¾ft (45cm–1.8m), S 2in (5cm).
4–9

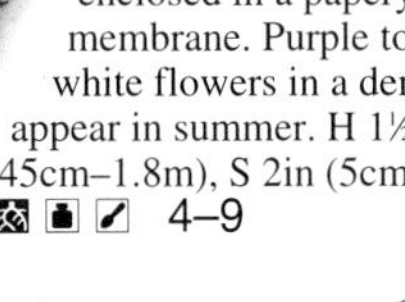

◄ ***Allium fistulosum*** **'White Lisbon'**
A white-skinned, mild-flavored cultivar that is very hardy and quick-growing. H 8–12in (20–30cm), S up to 6in (15cm).
4–9

◄ ***Allium sativum*** (garlic)
Perennial with a globose bulb of 5–15 bulblets (cloves), encased in a papery white, or mauve-tinged skin. Flat leaves are up to 2ft (60cm) long. An umbel of green-white to pink flowers, with a deciduous spathe, is borne in summer. H 12–36in (30cm–1m), S 9–12in (23–30cm).
4–9

► ***Allium cepa*** (onion)
Robust biennial with a bulb up to 4in (10cm) across, and hollow leaves, semicircular in cross-section,up to 16in (40cm) long. An umbel of star-shaped, green-white flowers is produced in summer. H 4ft (1.2m), S 6in (15cm).
4–9

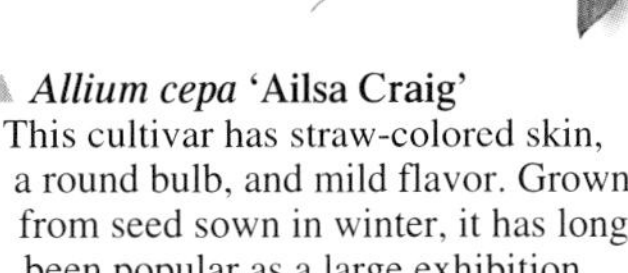

▲ ***Allium cepa*** **'Ailsa Craig'**
This cultivar has straw-colored skin, a round bulb, and mild flavor. Grown from seed sown in winter, it has long been popular as a large exhibition onion. H 12–18in (30–45cm), S to 12in (30cm).
4–9

► ***Allium cepa*** **'Sweet Sandwich'**
The large, globose, brown-skinned bulbs of this cultivar become exceptionally mild and sweet after about 2 months in storage. H 12–18in (30–45cm), S 6–12in (15–30cm).
4–9

▲ ***Allium cepa*** **'Noordhollandse Bloedrode'** ('North Holland Blood Red')
A mild-flavored cultivar with deep red skin and pink flesh. It is easily grown from seed and stores well. H 12–18in (30–45cm), S 6–12in (15–30cm).
4–9

▲ ***Allium schoenoprasum*** (chives)
Clump-forming perennial with slender bulbs, ½in (1cm) across, clustered on a rhizome, and cylindrical, hollow leaves. Pale purple to pink, rarely white, bell-shaped flowers are borne in umbels in summer. H 4–24in (10–60cm), S 12in (30cm).
3–9

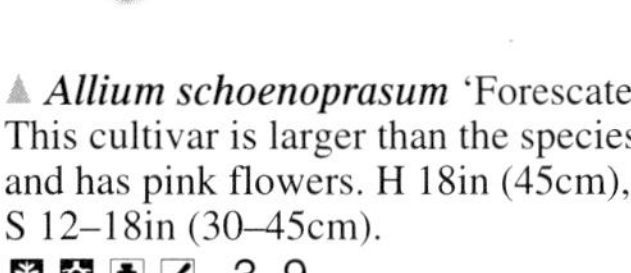

▲ ***Allium schoenoprasum*** **'Forescate'**
This cultivar is larger than the species and has pink flowers. H 18in (45cm), S 12–18in (30–45cm).
3–9

◄ ***Allium scorodoprasum*** (rocambole, sand leek)
Stiff perennial with flat, strap-shaped leaves and small, garlic-flavored bulbs. An inflorescence is borne in summer, consisting of purple bulbils and a few long-stalked, pink-purple flowers.
H 3ft (1m), S 2–3in (5–8cm).
3–9

◄ ***Allium tuberosum*** (Chinese chives, garlic chives, *cuchay*)
Perennial with a stout rhizome and flat, solid, keeled leaves, sheathed at the base to form cylindrical bulbs. Umbels of sweet-scented, white, star-shaped flowers appear in late summer. Reseeds prolifically.
H and S 20in (50cm).
3–9

▲ ***Allium ursinum*** (ramsons)
Carpeting perennial with a pervasive garlic smell, elliptic leaves up to 11in (28cm) long, and rounded clusters of white, starlike flowers borne above the foliage in late spring and early summer.
H 16in (40cm), S 12in (30cm).
4–9

ALNUS

This genus of 35 species of hardy deciduous trees and shrubs is found mainly in northern temperate regions. Alders are adaptable, easily grown, and excel in damp situations. *A. glutinosa*, found in Europe and Asia, is very hardy, and thrives in wet soils, making it a good choice for bog gardens and waterside places. The piles of wood upon which 16th-century Venice was built are reputedly made from alder, and it has been used for dishes, spoons, canoe paddles, cradles, clogs, and salmon smoking.

Alnus glutinosa (common alder, European alder, black alder)
Bushy tree with purple to gray-brown bark. Pendent twigs have obovate leaves, 1¼–3½in (3–9cm) long. Flowers appear in early spring; male catkins are 1–2½in (2.5–6cm) long, females shorter.
H 80ft (25m), S 30ft (10m).
3–9

***Alnus glutinosa* 'Imperialis'**
A graceful, slow-growing cultivar with deeply cut leaves.
H 30ft (10m), S 12ft (4m).
3–9

ALOE

Native to southern Africa, Arabia, and the Cape Verde Islands, this genus consists of about 325 species of tender evergreen perennials, shrubs, trees, and climbers, many of which are hard to tell apart. *A. vera* is native to southern and northern Africa. Aloes vary greatly in size, but all are architectural plants with thick, spiky foliage, often glaucous or patterned, and bold spikes of colorful flowers. Some larger species are grown in gardens in warm climates.

Aloe vera (Barbados aloe, Curaçao aloe)
Clump-forming perennial, freely suckering, with dense rosettes of thick, spiky, gray-green leaves, red-spotted only in young specimens. Tubular yellow flowers are borne in summer.
H 2–3ft (60–90cm), S indefinite.

ALLSPICE, see *Pimenta dioica*, p.328
ALMOND, see *PRUNUS*, pp.184-5
ALOE, see *Aloe vera*, above
ALOEWOOD, see *Aquilaria malaccensis*, p.86

ALOYSIA

There are 37 species of deciduous or evergreen aromatic shrubs in this genus, which is native to N and S America, and closely related to *Lippia*. *A. triphylla*, known in Victorian times simply as "the lemon plant," is found in fields and along roadsides in Argentina and Chile. It has been a favorite for garden rooms since its introduction from Chile in 1794. *Aloysia* was named after Maria Louisa, Princess of Parma, who died in 1819.

Aloysia triphylla (lemon verbena)
Deciduous shrub with lemon-scented, pointed, lanceolate leaves up to 4in (10cm) long, in whorls of 3–4. Tiny, pale lilac to white flowers are produced in terminal or axillary panicles in summer. H and S up to 10ft (3m).

9

ALTHAEA

A genus of about 12 species of annuals and perennials, closely resembling the genus *Malva* (see p.156), that occurs throughout western Europe to central Asia and north Africa. It once included hollyhock (formerly *Althaea rosea*, now *Alcea rosea*, see p.78). A few species are grown as border plants; *A. officinalis* is useful for waterlogged ground. The name *Althaea* comes from the Greek *altha*, "to cure," and refers to the healing properties of these plants.

Althaea officinalis (marsh mallow)
Robust perennial with fleshy taproot and upright, downy stems. Leaves are velvety, round to ovate, 1¼–3in (3–8cm) across. Pale pink flowers, ¾–1½in (2–4cm) across, appear in the axils in summer. H 3–4ft (1–1.2m), S 24–36in (60–90cm).

3–9

ALPINIA

This genus of about 200 species of ginger-scented, rhizomatous perennials is native to Asia and Australia. *A. galanga* is found in tropical rainforests in SE Asia. Lesser galingal (*A. officinarum*) is the most important species for culinary and medicinal uses; greater galingal (*A. galanga*) has less pungent rhizomes. These tropical galingals are not to be confused with the European galingal, or sweet galingale (*Cyperus longus*), which has violet-scented roots that are used in perfumery.

Alpinia galanga (galangal, greater galingal, Siamese ginger)
Perennial with ginger-scented rhizomes, reedlike stems, and lanceolate leaves up to 20in (50cm) long. Pale green, orchid-like flowers with a white lip appear all year. Fruit is a red, 3-valved, spherical capsule. H to 6ft (2m), S indefinite.

AMARANTHUS

This genus consists of 60 spinachlike annuals, found worldwide in both temperate and tropical regions; *A. hypochondriacus* occurs in southern US, Mexico, India, and China. Many are edible and have medicinal uses. A few species have ornamental foliage and colorful flowers, and are grown as pot plants or summer annuals. Amaranth is the magenta-red pigment found in some species. *Amaranthus* is from the Greek *amarantos*, "unfading," referring to the long-lasting flowers.

Amaranthus hypochondriacus
(prince's feather)
Tall, bushy annual with oblong to lanceolate, purple-green leaves up to 6in (15cm) long. In summer, minute, dark red flowers are followed by tiny, red-brown to black seeds. H 4–5ft (1.2–1.5m), S 18–24in (45–60cm).

A

ALSTONIA

A genus of about 43 species of evergreen trees and shrubs with milky sap, found in Africa, C America, and SE Asia, to the west Pacific and Australia. *A. scholaris* is found in SE Asian rainforests. Some species have been severely reduced by collection of bark for treating fevers. *A. boonei* is used both medicinally and to make domestic items in Ghana. It is called "sky god's tree," since a branch is put up to the sky god in each village. *Alstonia* is named after the Scots botanist Charles Alston (1716–60).

Alstonia scholaris (devil tree, dita bark, milky pine)
Evergreen tree with rough gray bark, whorls of leathery leaves 6–8in (15–20cm) long, and clusters of small, tubular, green-white flowers. The fruits are paired and elongated. H 40–60ft (12–18m), S 20–30ft (6–10m).

AMMI

Ten species of annuals and biennials, closely related to *Daucus* (see p.116), make up this genus, distributed through southwestern Asia to southern Europe and neighboring Atlantic islands. *A. majus* is found throughout, and widely distributed elsewhere. It is an attractive, white-flowered umbellifer, grown for the cut-flower trade and often as an ornamental, that combines well with tall, more colorful annuals. *A. visnaga* is native to the eastern Mediterranean, especially Egypt.

Ammi majus (bullwort, bishopsweed, Queen Anne's lace)
Tall annual with finely divided, glaucous foliage, and umbels with 9–40 rays of tiny white flowers borne in summer, followed by small, ridged, pale brown fruits (seeds). H 18–30in (45–75cm), S 18in (45cm).

5–9

ALPINE LADY'S MANTLE, see *Alchemilla alpina*, p.79
ALUMROOT, see *Geranium maculatum*, p.133; *Heuchera americana*, p.138
AMBRETTE, see *Abelmoschus moschatus*, p.70
AMBROSIA, see *Chenopodium ambrosioides*, p.106
AMERICAN CRANESBILL, see *Geranium maculatum*, p.133
AMERICAN GINSENG, see *Panax quinquefolius*, p.170
AMERICAN IPECAC, see *Gillenia trifoliata*, p.134
AMERICAN LAUREL, see *Kalmia*,

Ammi visnaga (khella)
Tall, stout annual or biennial with lobed, divided, aromatic leaves. Tiny yellow-white flowers appear in summer in long-stalked umbels with 30–150 rays that thicken and remain erect after flowering. Small seeds are oblong-ovoid. H 18–30in (45–75cm), S 18in (45cm).

5–9

ANAGALLIS

A genus of 20 species of annuals, biennials, and perennials found all over the world; *A. arvensis* is native to Europe, and a common weed of cultivated ground. The scarce, blue-flowered variety was once thought to be the female form of the scarlet pimpernel. The name *Anagallis* is from the Greek *anagelas*, "to laugh," from its use in treating depression. Several of the common names relate to weather forecasting, since flowers open and close with changing light and temperature.

Anagallis arvensis (scarlet pimpernel, poor man's weatherglass)
Prostrate annual or biennial with 4-angled stems, ovate to lanceolate leaves, and star-shaped, salmon-red flowers, often with purple centers, throughout summer. H 1–2in (2.5–5cm), S 6–12in (15–30cm).

7–10

Anagallis arvensis var. ***caerulea***
(blue pimpernel)
This variety differs from the species in having gentian-blue flowers. It is a prized plant for rock gardens and containers. H 1–2in (2.5–5cm), S 6–12in (15–30cm).

7–10

ANACARDIUM

Fifteen species of small to very tall, tender trees make up this genus native to tropical parts of S and C America and the W Indies, naturalized in the tropics. *A. occidentale*, found in dry areas, especially coastal regions in northeastern Brazil and the Caribbean, was introduced from Brazil as a crop to India and the Malay Archipelago during the 16th century, but did not reach Europe until 1699. The seeds became known as cashews, after the Portuguese *cajú*.

Anacardium occidentale (cashew, *marañon*, *acajou*)
Evergreen tree or shrub with ovate leaves up to 9in (22cm) long. Sweetly scented, pale green, red-striped flowers appear all year in terminal panicles. Fruit has kidney-shaped shelled nut at its base. H 40ft (12m), S 30ft (10m).

ANACYCLUS

This genus of nine species of annuals and perennials is native to the Mediterranean. Several of the species are cultivated for their finely cut foliage and daisylike flowers. *A. pyrethrum*, from Spain, Algeria, and Morocco, is rarely grown as an ornamental, but a prostrate variety, *A. p.* var. *depressus*, from the Atlas Mountains, is popular with rock-garden enthusiasts. Their attractive red buds open into brilliant white daisies with red undersides.

Anacyclus pyrethrum (pellitory, pellitory of Spain)
Low, rosette-forming perennial with finely divided leaves. Solitary daisy flowers are produced on 12in (30cm) stalks. They have yellow centers and white ray petals with a red stripe below. H 12in (30cm), S 10–12in (25–30cm).

6–10

ANETHUM

There is one species in this genus, widely distributed in warm parts of Eurasia; *A. graveolens* is found in Mediterranean regions and western Asia. Dill resembles fennel but is shorter, with a single, easily uprooted stem, slightly gray-green leaves, and matte, rather than shiny, appearance. Its leaves have a strong parsley–caraway smell. Indian dill was formerly classed as a separate species, *A. sowa*, but is now regarded as a subspecies of *A. graveolens*.

Anethum graveolens (dill)
Annual or biennial with usually only one upright, hollow stem, and glaucous foliage divided into threadlike segments. Umbels of yellow flowers are borne in summer, followed by ovoid, flattened, aromatic seeds. H 24–36in (60–90cm), S 6–12in (15–30cm).

A

p.146
AMERICAN LIVERWORT, see *Hepatica nobilis*, p.138
AMERICAN MANDRAKE, see *Podophyllum peltatum*, p.180
AMERICAN PENNYROYAL, see *Hedeoma pulegioides*, p.136
AMERICAN SANICLE, see *Heuchera americana*, p.138
AMERICAN SPIKENARD, see *Aralia racemosa*, p.86
AMERICAN VALERIAN, see *Cypripedium parviflorum* var. *pubescens*, p.115
AMMONIAC, see *Dorema ammonaicum*, p.275
AMUR CORK TREE, see

***Anethum graveolens* 'Mammoth'**
This cultivar has sparse foliage and quickly runs to seed, producing large seedheads. It is considered the best for pickling. H 24–36in (60–90cm), S 6–12in (15–30cm).

A

Angelica polymorpha* var. *sinensis
(Chinese angelica)
Perennial with a short rhizome, upright stems, and pinnately divided leaves. Greenish flowers are produced in umbels in late summer, followed by elliptic, notched seeds. H 2½–5ft (75cm–1.5m), S 15–36in (38–90cm).

9

ANGELICA

This genus of about 50 biennials and perennials is native to temperate parts of the northern hemisphere. *A. archangelica* is found in northern and eastern Europe, to Greenland and central Asia; *A. polymorpha* in eastern Asia. The name is from the medieval Latin *herba angelica*, "angelic herb," from a belief that it would protect against evil and cure all ills. Its connection with the Feast of the Annunciation and the Archangel Michael may indicate pagan origins, taken over into Christian customs.

Angelica archangelica
Robust, aromatic biennial or short-lived perennial with thick, hollow stems and long-stalked, deeply divided leaves. Umbels of tiny green-white flowers appear in early summer, followed by ovate, ridged seeds. H 3–8ft (1–2.5m), S 1½–3½ft (45cm–1.1m).

4–9

ANTENNARIA

Approximately 45 species of small, evergreen or semievergreen woolly perennials make up this genus, which is distributed throughout most temperate and warm regions except Africa. *A. dioica*, found in Europe, N America, and northern Asia, and its many cultivars are popular in rock gardens. The flowers dry well for floral arrangements. The name *Antennaria* is after the fluffy appendages on the seeds that resemble insects' antennae.

Antennaria dioica (pussy-toes, catsfoot, cat's ear)
Mat-forming, aromatic perennial with small, gray-green, spoon-shaped leaves and upright clusters of white to pale pink flowers in late spring and early summer. H 2–8in (5–20cm), S 10–18in (25–45cm).

3–8

ANGOSTURA, see *Galipea officinalis*, p.285
ANGULAR SOLOMON'S SEAL, see *Polygonatum odoratum*, p.181
ANISE, see *Pimpinella anisum*, p.176
ANISE HYSSOP, see *Agastache foeniculum*, p.75
ANISE TREE, see *Illicium*, p.296
ANISEED, see *Pimpinella anisum*, p.176
ANISILLO, see *Tagetes lucida*, p.207
ANNATTO, see *Bixa orellana*, p.94
APOTHECARY'S ROSE, see *Rosa gallica* var. *officinalis*, p.191
APPLE GERANIUM, see *PELARGONIUM*, pp.172–3

***Antennaria dioica* 'Rosea'**
This variant has deeper pink flowers than the species. H 4–6in (10–15cm), S 10in (25cm).

3–8

APHANES

This genus of 20 annuals is closely related to *Alchemilla* (see p.79) and is widely distributed in Europe, the Mediterranean, Ethiopia, central Asia, Australia, and N America. *A. arvensis*, found in Europe, northern Africa, and N America, may be grown as an edging for paths or borders. Its common names, "parsley piert" (from the French *perce-pierre*) and "breakstone parsley," probably arose from the plant's medical uses.

Aphanes arvensis (parsley piert, breakstone parsley)
Radiating, near-prostrate annual with hairy, fan-shaped, pale green leaves up to ½in (1cm) long. Clusters of minute green flowers are borne from spring to autumn. H 1in (2.5cm), S 8in (20cm).

A

ANTHOXANTHUM

A genus of 18 species of perennial grasses native to Europe, temperate Asia, and Africa. The S African *A. drogeanum* is fragrant while flowering, whereas the scent of *A. odoratum* intensifies when cut and dried. The flowers of *A. odoratum*, one of the first grasses to flower in Europe and temperate Asia, are distinguished from most other grasses by having two stamens (not three) and yellow, rather than purple, anthers. The name derives from the Greek *xanthos*, "yellow," and *anthos*, "flower."

Anthoxanthum odoratum
(sweet vernal grass)
Tufted perennial grass with aromatic, relatively short, narrowly lanceolate leaves and dense, compact, rather blunt flower spikes up to 1¼in (3cm) long, appearing from spring to summer. H 7–20in (18–50cm), S 5–12in (12–30cm).

3–9

APIUM

Perennials, annuals, and biennials are included in this genus of 20 species found wild in Europe, N America, temperate Asia, and Antarctic regions. *A. graveolens* occurs in Europe, southwestern Asia, and northern Africa. The name *Apium* is the Latinized form of the Celtic *apon*, "water," referring to the natural habitat of the genus; the specific epithet *graveolens* means "strong-smelling," since all parts have a characteristic strong smell of celery.

Apium graveolens
(wild celery, smallage)
Biennial with a bulbous, fleshy root, solid, grooved stems, and pinnately divided leaves. Umbels of tiny green-white flowers are followed by small gray-brown, ridged seeds. H 1–3ft (30cm–1m), S 6–12in (15–30cm).

7–9

ANTHRISCUS

Hardy annuals, biennials, and perennials make up this genus of 12 species native to Europe, Asia, and northern Africa. They are upright plants that resemble parsley in appearance. *A. cerefolium*, native to Europe and western Asia, is one of the best herbs for containers in a cool, shady position; it combines well with other shade-loving culinary herbs, such as pineapple mint (*Mentha suaveolens* 'Variegata', see p.159) and golden lemon balm (*Melissa officinalis* 'Aurea', see p.157).

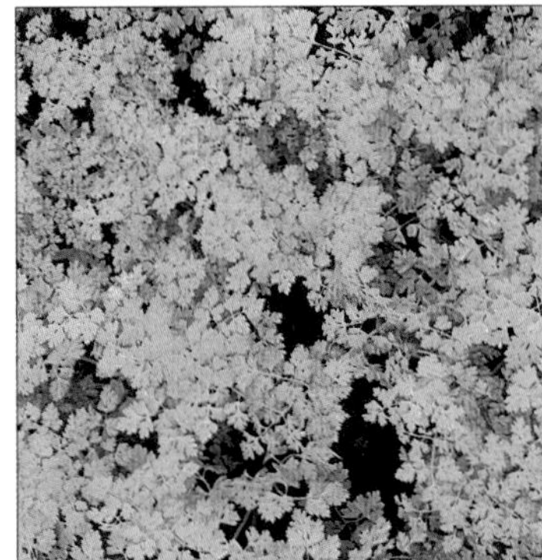

Anthriscus cerefolium (chervil)
Aromatic biennial often grown as an annual, with hollow, furrowed stems and bright green, divided leaves. Umbels of tiny white flowers are borne in the axils in early summer, followed by tiny narrow fruits. H 12–24in (30–60cm), S 9–12in (23–30cm).

3–8

APOCYNUM

Nine hardy, poisonous perennials with milky sap are included in this genus, which occurs in N America, eastern Europe, and Asia; *A. cannabinum* is found on sandy or gravelly soils, especially near water, in northeastern US and Canada. One or two species are occasionally grown for their striking forked fruits. The fruits of *A. cannabinum* are 4–8in (10–20cm) long and many-seeded; they are pollinated by monarch butterflies and are also a food plant for their caterpillars.

Apocynum cannabinum (dogbane, Canadian hemp, black Indian hemp)
Rhizomatous perennial with ovate to lanceolate, pointed leaves up to 6in (15cm) long. Small, green-white, bell-shaped flowers appear in terminal clusters in summer, followed by forked fruits. H and S 2–4ft (60cm–1.2m).

4–8

APPLE-BEARING SAGE, see *SALVIA*, pp.196–7
APPLEMINT, see *MENTHA*, pp.158–9

AQUILARIA

A genus of 15 species of tropical shrubs and trees native to India and Malaysia. *A. malaccensis*, found in primary forest at low and medium altitudes, is believed to be the aloe of the Bible. According to legend, all trees are descended from a single shoot of it taken by Adam from the garden of Eden. The heartwood, known as "agallochum," contains a dark resin (*chuwar*, or agar attar) with an odor similar to sandalwood.

Aquilaria malaccensis (eaglewood, aloewood)
Evergreen tree with a smooth, pale trunk and thin, leathery leaves. Umbels of insignificant, bell-shaped, green to dull yellow flowers are followed by capsules containing red, hairy seeds. H up to 130ft (40m), S 10–40ft (3–12m).

ARALIA

Deciduous or evergreen trees, shrubs, lianas, and rhizomatous perennials make up this genus of about 40 species distributed through southern and eastern Asia and N America. Several shrubby aralias are grown for their large, exotic-looking, compound leaves. *A. racemosa*, found throughout N America, is a handsome plant suited to woodland conditions, as is the less ornamental A. *nudicaulis*. *Aralia* is a Latinized version of *aralie*, an old French-Canadian name for these plants.

Aralia nudicaulis (wild sarsaparilla)
Rhizomatous perennial producing a single, pinnately divided leaf annually. Tiny green-white flowers are borne in umbels in late spring and early summer, followed by purple-black berries. H 6–16in (15–40cm), S 6–12in (15–30cm).

3–7

Aralia racemosa (American spikenard, life-of-man)
Rhizomatous perennial with aromatic rootstock and compound leaves up to 30in (75cm) long. Tiny green-white flowers are borne in umbels in summer, followed by purple to brown fruits. H 3–7ft (1–2.2m), S 2–6ft (60cm–2m).

3–7

ARCTIUM

Occurring widely in temperate Eurasia, this genus consists of about 10 species of upright biennials. *A. lappa*, found in Europe and western Asia, is an imposing plant for the wild garden. *Arctium* is from the Greek *arktos*, "a bear," after the rough-coated fruits. Burdock, the common name of *A. lappa*, refers to the fruits (burs) and the large, docklike leaves. The specific epithet *lappa*, from the Latin *lappare*, "to seize," arises from the burs clinging to passing animals.

Arctium lappa (burdock, lappa, beggar's buttons)
Robust biennial with stout taproots, and long-stalked, ovate leaves up to 20in (50cm) long. Purple, thistlelike flowers are followed by fruits covered in hooked spines, containing fawn seeds. H 5ft (1.5m), S 3ft (1m).

2–10

ARCTOSTAPHYLOS

About 50 species of hardy deciduous or evergreen shrubs and small trees make up this genus distributed mainly in western N America; *A. uva-ursi* is found on moorland heath and in rocky areas from northern Europe to northern Asia, Japan, and N America. Several species make good ornamentals for rock gardens. *A. uva-ursi* is a fast-growing shrublet, useful on banks to control erosion. The name is from the Greek *arkton staphyle*, "bear's grapes," since the fruits are an important food for bears.

Arctostaphylos uva-ursi (bearberry, mountain box, uva-ursi)
Mat-forming evergreen shrub with rooting branches and obovate, dark green leaves. Racemes of white, pink-tinged flowers appear from early spring, followed by glossy red fruits. H 4–6in (10–15cm), S 1–4ft (30cm–1.2m).

2–6

ARECA

Some 50–60 species of tall evergreen palms belong to this genus, which occurs in India and Malaysia, Australia, and the Solomon Islands. The seeds of *A. catechu* (betel palm), common in moist coastal regions of SE Asia, have been chewed as a stimulant in India, Pakistan, and SE Asia since ancient times; trees are widely cultivated for the purpose in all these areas. Chewing the seeds is now discouraged since it is thought to be a possible cause of oral cancer.

Areca catechu (betel palm, areca palm)
Slender palm tree with a gray-green trunk and pinnate leaves up to 6ft (2m) long. Pale yellow flowers are produced on trees aged 6 years or more, followed by yellow to orange or scarlet, egg-shaped fruits, containing one acorn-sized seed. H 70ft (20m), S 12ft (4m).

ARABIAN COFFEE, see *Coffea arabica*, p.110
ARBORVITAE, see *Thuja*, p.211
ARCHANGEL, see *Lamium album*, p.146
ARECA PALM, see *Areca catechu*, above
ARUGULA, see *Eruca vesicaria*, p.123

ARISAEMA

This genus contains about 150 species of tuberous or rhizomatous, tender or hardy perennials. Species are widely distributed in Asia, from arid regions to the tropics and the Himalayas; they also occur in N America and eastern Africa. *A. consanguineum* is found from the eastern Himalayas to northern Thailand, central China, and Taiwan. Dragon plants, with their handsome foliage and unusual blooms and fruits, make striking specimen plants for shady borders.

Arisaema consanguineum (dragon plant)
Perennial with a rounded tuber, mottled stalk, and a solitary, compound leaf. The inflorescence consists of a green hooded spathe and a green spadix, followed by a pendent cluster of scarlet fruits. H 3ft (1m), S 12in (30cm).
8–9

Arisaema triphyllum (Jack-in-the-pulpit, Indian turnip)
Perennial with globose tubers, blotched stalks, and 1–2 trifoliate leaves. A hooded, striped, green to purple spathe and spadix appear in spring, followed by red berries. H 1–2ft (30cm–1m), S 9–24in (23–60cm).
4–9

ARISTOLOCHIA

This genus consists of some 300 species of poisonous, tender, and hardy twining climbers, shrubs, scramblers, and herbaceous perennials, occurring mainly in warm and tropical parts of the Americas; *A. clematitis* is found in central and southern Europe. Many of the climbing species are grown for their attractive foliage and intriguing, foul-smelling flowers. The name *Aristolochia* is derived from the Greek *aristos*, "best," and *lokhia*, "childbirth," and refers to the main medicinal uses.

Aristolochia clematitis (birthwort, heartwort)
Perennial with a long creeping rhizome, upright stems, and heart-shaped leaves. Clusters of yellow-green flowers appear throughout summer, followed by pear-shaped capsules. All parts have a fetid smell. H and S 8–34in (20–85cm).
5–9

ARMORACIA

Three species of tall, tap-rooted, hardy perennials make up this genus found throughout Europe and Siberia. *A. rusticana*, native to western Asia and now naturalized in many parts of the world, appears to have entered cultivation relatively recently, perhaps less than 2,000 years ago. It was primarily a medicinal plant and did not become popular as a flavoring until the late 16th century. *Armoracia* is the original Latin name for the related wild radish.

Armoracia rusticana (horseradish)
Upright, stout perennial with a thick, branched taproot. Basal leaves are bright green, ovate to oblong, reaching 20in (50cm) long. Tiny white flowers are produced in terminal racemes in early summer. H 1–4ft (30cm–1.2m), S 24–36in (60–90cm).
3–10

***Armoracia rusticana* 'Variegata'**
The leaves of this cultivar have irregular white variegation, which sometimes extends over most of the blade. H 1–4ft (30cm–1.2m), S 24–36in (60–90cm).
3–10

ARNICA

About 30 species of rhizomatous perennials make up this genus found mostly in subalpine zones of the northern hemisphere. *A. montana*, a European species, is an attractive plant for the rock garden or peat bed. Being an alpine, it needs a cool climate and dislikes winter wet; these conditions may be met by growing it on ridges or in raised beds. *Arnica* is the ancient Greek name for this plant. It may be derived from *arnakis*, "lamb's skin," because of the soft texture of the leaves.

Arnica montana (arnica, leopard's bane, mountain tobacco)
Aromatic, rhizomatous perennial with a basal rosette of ovate, hairy leaves, 2–7in (5–17cm) long. Golden yellow, daisylike flowers, 2in (5cm) across, appear in summer. H 4–24in (10–60cm), S 6in (15cm).
6–9

ARTEMISIA

A genus of about 300 species of hardy and half-hardy annuals, biennials, perennials, or subshrubs, which grow wild in northern temperate regions, western S America, and southern Africa. A number of artemisias are grown as ornamentals for their finely cut, often silver foliage and interesting aromas. They are easily cultivated, even on poor, dry soils. Several are attractive border plants, especially for white gardens. *A. abrotanum*, *A. absinthium* 'Lambrook Silver', and *A. arborescens* may be grown as informal hedges. *A. annua* is a large but tidy plant with handsome, fragrant foliage, useful for filling gaps in the back of a border or providing contrast to smaller, more colorful plants; *A. caucasica* makes a low, spreading plant for walls and rock gardens. The leaves of many artemisias are attractive in floral arrangements. *A. vulgaris* is known as "mugwort," from the Anglo-Saxon *mucgwrt*, "midge plant," because of its use in repelling insects.

▲ ***Artemisia absinthium*** (wormwood)
Subshrub with gray-green, deeply dissected foliage with silky hairs on both sides. Insignificant, yellow, globose flowers are borne in panicles in summer. H 3ft (1m), S 24–36in (60–90cm).
3–9

▲ ***Artemisia absinthium* 'Lambrook Silver'**
This cultivar has luxuriant silver-gray foliage and long, graceful panicles of inconspicuous flowers in summer. H 18–32in (45–80cm), S 20in (50cm).
5–9

▲ ***Artemisia abrotanum*** (southernwood, lad's love, old man)
Semievergreen subshrub with gray-green, pinnately divided leaves, which have a pungent smell. Tiny, dull yellow flowers are borne in dense panicles in late summer; flowering does not occur in cool summers. H 3ft (1m), S 12–24in (30–60cm).
6–10

▲ ***Artemisia annua*** (sweet wormwood, sweet Annie)
Fast-growing, giant annual with upright, often red stems and bright green, pinnately divided, saw-toothed leaves. Tiny yellow flowers appear in loose panicles in summer. H 5–10ft (1.5–3m), S 3–5ft (1–1.5m).
A

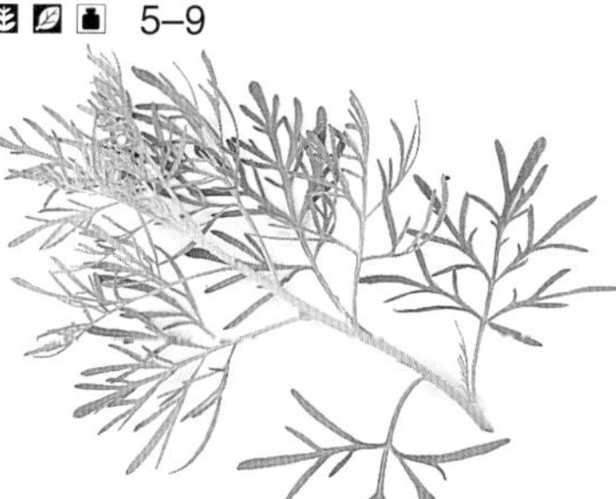

▲ ***Artemisia arborescens***
(tree artemisia, tree wormwood)
Aromatic, upright, evergreen or semi-evergreen subshrub with a rounded habit and finely divided, silver-gray foliage. Panicles of small yellow flowers appear in summer and early autumn. H and S 3½ft (1.1m).
8–9

► ***Artemisia* 'Powis Castle'**
This dwarf, non-flowering, silver-leaved artemisia is possibly a hybrid between *A. absinthium* and *A. arborescens*, from the garden of Powis Castle, Wales. It is more compact than *A. absinthium* 'Lambrook Silver'. H 24–36in (60–90cm), S 4ft (1.2m).
6–9

▲ ***Artemisia capillaris***
(fragrant wormwood)
A much-branched subshrub with purple stems and finely divided, aromatic, silky leaves. Panicles of minute, purple-brown flowers are borne from late summer. H and S 1–3ft (30cm–1m).
9

▲ ***Artemisia caucasica***
Tufted, mat-forming, evergreen or semievergreen, shrublet with silky, finely cut, fernlike, silver-green leaves. Loose panicles of tiny, globose, yellow flowers appear in summer. H and S 6–12in (15–30cm).
4–7

► ***Artemisia dracunculus* var. *sativa*** (tarragon, French tarragon, *estragon*)
Aromatic perennial with upright, branched stems and linear, smooth leaves 3–6cm (1¼–2½in) long, with a mint-anise flavor. The tiny green flowers do not open, and they do not produce viable seed in cool summers. H 1½–3ft (45cm–1m), S 12–15in (30–38cm).
4–7

Artemisia dracunculus subsp. ***dracunculoides*** (Russian tarragon) The subspecies is hardier and more vigorous than the species, with narrower, paler leaves. It sets seed and has a pungent, less pleasant flavor, which is said to improve in mature plants. H 5ft (1.5m), S 24in (60cm).
2–9

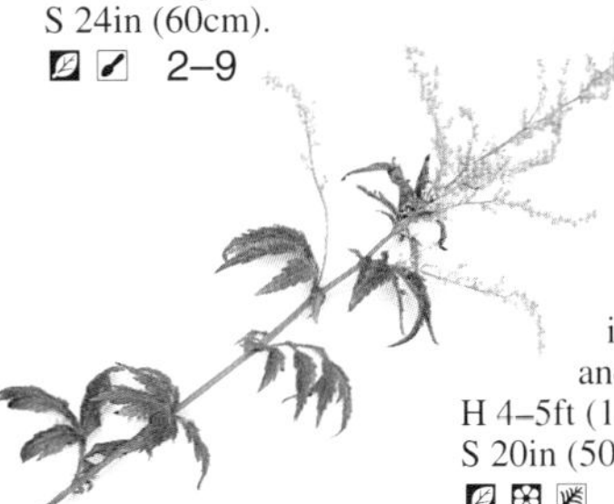

Artemisia lactiflora (white mugwort) Vigorous, upright perennial with pinnately divided, coarsely toothed, green leaves. Plumes of tiny off-white flowers are produced in late summer and autumn. H 4–5ft (1.2–1.5m), S 20in (50cm).
5–8

***Artemisia lactiflora*, Guizhou Group** This cultivar has dark maroon stems, which are an effective contrast to the cream flowers. H 4–5ft (1.2–1.5m), S 20in (50cm).
5–8

Artemisia ludoviciana (western mugwort, white sage, cudweed) Bushy, rhizomatous perennial with green to silver-green, linear to lanceolate leaves up to 4½in (11cm) long, which are toothed or divided lower down the stem. Tiny, creamy yellow flowers are borne in panicles in summer and autumn. H 2–4ft (60cm–1.2m), S indefinite.
4–9

***Artemisia ludoviciana* 'Silver Queen'** This cultivar has jagged silver leaves and plumes of yellow-gray flowers. H 30in (75cm), S indefinite.
5–9

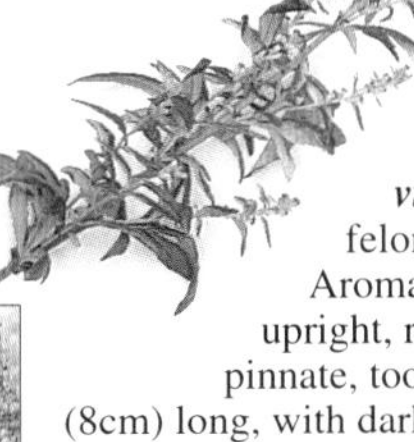

Artemisia vulgaris (mugwort, felon herb, Chinese *moxa*) Aromatic perennial with upright, red-purple stems and pinnate, toothed leaves, up to 3in (8cm) long, with dark green upper surfaces and downy, white undersides. Panicles of insignificant, red-brown flowers are borne from late summer. H 2–5½ft (60cm–1.7m), S 1–3ft (30–1m).
4–10

Artemisia pontica (Roman wormwood, small absinthe) Rhizomatous subshrub with upright, little-branched stems and finely cut, downy, silver-green leaves up to 1½in (4cm) long. Tiny, dull yellow flowers are produced in narrow panicles in summer. H 1½–4ft (45cm–1.2m), S 1–2ft (30–60cm).
5–9

***Artemisia vulgaris* 'Variegata'** This cultivar has white-flecked foliage. H 2–5½ft (60cm–1.7m), S 1–3ft (30cm–1m).
4–10

ASARUM

Found widely through northern temperate zones but centered on Japan, this genus consists of 70 or more deciduous or evergreen, rhizomatous, perennials. *A. canadense* is native to eastern N America. Wild ginger species are mostly woodland plants with a creeping habit and gingerlike smell. Their foliage resembles that of cyclamen, and it is mainly for this feature that several species are popular in rock gardens and grown as groundcover.

Asarum canadense (wild ginger) Evergreen, prostrate perennial with a slender rhizome smelling strongly of ginger, and dark green, hairy, heart-shaped leaves 2–8in (5–20cm) across. Urn-shaped, purple-brown flowers on short stalks are borne near ground level in spring. H 3in (8cm), S 24in (60cm).
3–8

ASCLEPIAS

This genus of about 120 species of tuberous annuals, perennials, shrubs, and subshrubs is found mainly in N America and Africa. *A. tuberosa* is found in eastern and southern US in dry, grassy places. Several species are grown as border plants for their colorful flowers, and pods that split open to show the silk-tufted seeds. They vary in hardiness according to origin and some are evergreen. *Asclepias* is named after Asklepios, the Greek god of medicine.

Asclepias tuberosa (butterfly weed, pleurisy root) Perennial with large, tuberous roots, erect, hairy stems, and linear leaves up to 4in (10cm) long. Orange flowers appear in summer, followed by slender seed pods, 6in (15cm) long. H 12–24in (30–60cm), S 9–18in (23–45cm).
4–9

ASPALATHUS

A large genus of 255 leguminous, mostly spiny shrubs found only in southern Africa. In the 19th century they were cultivated as greenhouse shrubs for their attractive flowers. *A. linearis*, native to the arid Cedarberg Mountains in the western Cape Province, is the source of rooibos tea, first recorded in 1772 by Carl Thunberg, a Swedish botanist, as a beverage drunk by the Hottentots. It is one of the few wild species to be developed as a crop in the 20th century.

Aspalathus linearis (rooibos) Variable upright to weeping shrub with red-tinged branches and linear, bright green leaves that turn red-brown when fallen. Tiny yellow pea flowers are borne in clusters during the summer. H and S to 6ft (2m).
9–10

ASAFOETIDA, see *Ferula assa-foetida*, p.127
ASH, see *Fraxinus*, p.129
ASH PUMPKIN, see *Benincasa hispida*, p.93
ASHWAGANDHA, see *Withania somnifera*, p.222
ASIAN PLANTAIN, see *Plantago asiatica*, p.178

ASPARAGUS

In this genus there are about 100 species distributed in temperate and subtropical parts of Eurasia. *A. officinalis* grows wild in coastal sands and cliffs in Europe; *A. racemosus* is found from Australia through West Africa to southern Asia. The genus includes hardy and tender, usually tuberous perennials, shrubs, and climbers, all with feathery foliage. *Asparagus* is from a Greek word, corrupted into such common names as "spearage" and "sparrow grass."

Asparagus officinalis (asparagus)
Perennial with creeping rhizomes and upright stems that appear in the spring as stout, fleshy shoots. Dense, soft foliage consists of cladodes. In summer, green-white, bell-shaped flowers are followed by red berries. H 3–5ft (1–1.5m), S 18in–36in (45–90cm).

2–9

Asparagus racemosus (*shatavari*)
Climbing rhizomatous perennial with leaves hardened at the base into spines, and foliage of pointed cladodes up to ½–1½in (1–3.5cm) long. Fragrant white flowers up to ¼in (5mm) across, appear in summer, followed by red berries. H 22ft (7m).

9

ASTRAGALUS

This large genus of about 2,000 species of annuals, perennials, and shrubs is distributed throughout northern temperate zones; *A. membranaceus* grows in dry, sandy soils in eastern Asia. Several species are used as food and fodder crops and as a source of gel-forming substances. Some accumulate minerals and are used as indicators in prospecting. Those toxic to livestock are known as "locoweeds." About 100 species are cultivated for their colorful spikes of flowers.

Astragalus membranaceus (milk vetch)
Perennial with grooved, hairy stems and leaves divided into 12–18 pairs of leaflets. Racemes of yellow pea flowers, ¾in (2cm) long, appear in early summer, followed by pendulous pods up to 6in (15cm) long. H and S 10–16in (25–40cm).

5–8

ATRACTYLODES

Seven species of rhizomatous perennials are included in this genus, which is eastern Asian in distribution. *A. macrocephala* is found wild in pasture and waste ground in China, Japan, and Korea, and is the most important species in this genus used in traditional Chinese medicine. The demand for it is so great that it is now grown on a large scale. Botanical gardens in China are also researching the cultivation requirements of other species used similarly, such as *A. lancea*.

Atractylodes macrocephala (Chinese thistle daisy)
Erect perennial with thick warty rhizomes and divided, pointed, toothed leaves. Purple, thistlelike flowers, 1½in (3.5cm) across, are produced in summer, followed by bristly seeds. H 12–24in (30–60cm), S 18in (45cm).

6–8

ATRIPLEX

About 100 species of evergreen and semi-evergreen annuals, perennials, and shrubs make up this genus, which occurs worldwide in both temperate and warm regions; *A. hortensis* is found widely in eastern Europe and Asia. Oraches are unusual in being mostly salt-tolerant, which gives them potential in reclaiming saline soil. The common name "orache" may be a corruption of the Latin *aurum*, "gold," because the plant was supposed to cure yellow jaundice.

Atriplex hortensis (orache)
Fast-growing annual with upright, often red-tinged stems and triangular to heart-shaped leaves. Insignificant yellow-green, red-flushed flowers appear in spikelike panicles in summer. H 2–4ft (60cm–1.2m), S 6–12in (15–30cm).

A

***Atriplex hortensis* 'Rubra'** (red orache, red mountain spinach)
This cultivar differs from the species in its beet red leaves and stems, and comes true from seed. H 2–4ft (60cm–1.2m), S 6–12in (15–30cm).

A

ASPARAGUS, see *Asparagus officinalis*, above
ASTHMA WEED, see *Euphorbia hirta*, p.126; *Lobelia inflata*, p.153
ATLAS CEDAR, see *Cedrus Libani*, p.103
AUSTRALIAN PENNYROYAL, see *MENTHA*, pp.158–9
AUSTRALIAN PEPPERMINT, see *Eucalyptus dives*, p.125
AUTUMN CROCUS, see *Colchicum autumnale*, p.110
AVENS, see *Geum urbanum*, p.134
AWL TREE, see *Morinda citrifolia*, p.161
AZORES THYME, see *THYMUS*, pp.212–3

ATROPA

Four species of tall perennials make up this genus occurring from western Europe to northern Africa and the Himalayas. *Atropa* comes from the Greek *Atropos*, one of the Three Fates who snips the thread of life, and refers to the poisonous nature of these plants. The common name "dwale" is from a Nordic word for something that causes stupor. Legends tell of the use of deadly nightshade to subdue invaders, notably the Danish army by Macbeth (Buchanan, *History of Scotland*, 1582).

Atropa belladonna (deadly nightshade, dwale)
Tall perennial with erect, branched stem and ovate leaves up to 8in (20cm) long. Purple-brown, bell-shaped flowers appear during summer, followed by shiny black berries with a persistent calyx. H 3–5ft (1–1.5m), S 24–36in (60–90cm).

6–9

AVENA

A genus of approximately 15 species of annual grasses found wild in Eurasia and northern Africa. The most important are *A. fatua* (wild oat), a southern European species that reached northern parts during the Iron Age and became the main subsistence crop of Scotland, and *A. sativa* (cultivated oat), which was developed from wild oats. *A. sativa* is widely grown in northern temperate regions, since it needs more water and humidity than wheat and dislikes dry weather in early summer.

Avena sativa (oat, groats)
Erect annual grass with flat leaves, smooth stems, and spreading panicles of large, pendulous spikelets in summer. Seeds are spindle-shaped and pale gold. H 1–3ft (30cm–1m), S 6–9in (15–23cm).

A

AZADIRACHTA

There are two species of gum-secreting trees in this genus, which occurs in the tropics of Eurasia and Africa. *A. indica*, probably native to Myanmar (Burma), is a fast-growing but long-lived tree that is popular in the tropics, where it is grown as an ornamental, for fuel, and for its workable but unpleasant-smelling lumber. It is closely related to, and often confused with, *Melia azederach* (see p.157), which has more northerly distribution. The name is from the Persian *azaddhirakt*, "noble tree."

Azadirachta indica (neem, *nimba*, *margosa*)
Evergreen tree with pinnate leaves up to 12in (30cm) long. Panicles of small, yellow-white, fragrant flowers appear from spring to early winter, with yellow to red-brown, berry-like fruits. H 40–50ft (12–15m), S 40ft (12m).

BALLOTA

Native to Europe, the Mediterranean region, and western Asia, this genus contains 35 species of hardy and near-hardy perennials and subshrubs. Most species are rather weedy in appearance, but a few have velvety foliage that makes them worth growing as foliage plants. *B. nigra*, though of little merit on its own, makes a good garden feature in a clump with other plants, and is very attractive to bees. *Ballota* was apparently named from the Greek *ballote*, "to reject," since livestock avoid the plants.

Ballota nigra (black horehound)
Hardy perennial with lanky habit and pungent smell. Leaves are round to ovate, and hairy, with toothed margins. Dense whorls of purple, rarely white, 2-lipped, tubular flowers are produced throughout the summer. H 16–36in (40cm–1m), S 10–24in (24–60cm).

4–9

Ballota nigra **'Archer's Variety'**
This cultivar has handsome, white-variegated foliage. H 16–36in (40cm–1m), S 10–24in (24–60cm).

4–9

BABCHI, see *Psoralea corylifolia*, p.336
BACHELOR'S BUTTONS, see *Centaurea cyanus*, p.104
BADIAN, see *Illicium verum*, p.296
BAIKAL SKULLCAP, see *Scutellaria baicalensis*, p.201
BALLOON FLOWER, see *Platycodon grandiflorus*, p.179
BALM, see *Melissa officinalis*, p.157
BALM OF GILEAD, see *Abies balsamea*, p.70; *Cedronella canariensis*, p.103; *Populus* x *candicans*, p.182
BALMONY, see *Chelone glabra*, p.106
BALSAM PEAR, see *Momordica charantia*, p.160
BÁLSAMO, see *Myroxylon*, p.162

BAPTISIA

A genus of 17 species of eastern N American, hardy perennials. Several are grown as border plants for their yellow, white, or blue lupinelike flowers. Charles Millspaugh (*Medicinal Plants*, 1892, republished as *American Medicinal Plants*, 1974) wrote of *B. tinctoria*, "young shoots of this plant resemble in form … those of asparagus, and are used, especially in New England, in lieu of that herb for pottage." The name is derived from the Greek *bapto*, "to dye," since some species yield dyes.

B. tinctoria (wild indigo, indigoweed, rattleweed)
Erect, much-branched perennial with small, cloverlike leaves and arching racemes, up to 4in (10cm) long, of small, yellow pea flowers in summer, followed by brown pods, ½in (1cm) long. H 4ft (1.2m), S 24in (60cm).
5–9

BELAMCANDA

Two species of hardy perennials make up this genus found in eastern Asia. *B. chinensis* is an unusual plant for the herb garden or border, somewhere between an iris and a lily in appearance. Its common names, blackberry lily or leopard lily, refer respectively to the shiny black seed clusters and to the spotted flowers that only last a day. It does best in areas with long, hot summers. The three-chambered fruits are a feature in autumn when they split open to reveal the seeds.

Belamcanda chinensis (blackberry lily, leopard lily)
Perennial with short rhizome, branched stems, and fan of sword-shaped leaves. Orange-red, dark-spotted flowers are borne in summer, followed by globular black seeds. H 2–4ft (60cm–1.2m), S 6–10in (15–25cm).
5–10

***Bellis perennis* 'Alba Plena'**
A variant of the English daisy, with double white flowers. It dates back to the 16th century. H 4in (10cm), S 3–5in (7–12cm).
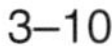
3–10

BELLIS

This genus consists of seven species of hardy annuals and perennials native to Europe and the Mediterranean. *B. perennis* is a variable species, abundant throughout Europe and western Asia in grassland, and with a long history as a healing herb. It has many named cultivars, which are well suited to rockeries and containers, or which may be treated as biennials for bedding. They are easily grown plants with a long flowering season. The name *Bellis* comes from the Latin *bellus*, "pretty."

Bellis perennis (English daisy)
Perennial with a basal rosette of obovate scalloped leaves. Numerous flowers, up to 1in (2.5cm) across, with bright yellow discs and white, often pink-flushed, female ray florets, appear from spring to autumn. H 1–6in (2.5–15cm), S 3–5in (7–12cm).
3–10

***Bellis perennis* 'Pomponette'**
A good cultivar for spring bedding or the rock garden, with double flowers up to 1½in (3.5cm) across in pink, cerise, or white. H and S 4–6in (10–15cm).
3–10

***Bellis perennis* 'Prolifera'**
(hen-and-chickens daisy)
This unusual variant, known in Elizabethan times as the "childing daisy," has double, white, often pink-flushed flowers that send out small ones from the main flower head. H 4in (10cm), S 3–5in (7–12cm).
3–10

BARBADOS ALOE, see *Aloe vera*, p.81
BARBERRY, see *Berberis*, p.93
BARLEY, see *Hordeum vulgare*, p.139
BASIL, see *OCIMUM*, pp.166–7
BASIL THYME, see *Acinos arvensis*, p.72
BASTARD CARDAMOM, see *Amomum xanthioides*, p.237
BAY, see *Laurus nobilis*, p.147
BAYBERRY, see *Myrica cerifera*, p.162
BEAD TREE, see *Melia azederach*, p.157
BEARBERRY, see *Arctostaphylos*, p.86
BEAVER TREE, see *Magnolia virginiana*, p.155
BEE BALM, see *Monarda didyma*, p.160
BEECH, see *Fagus*, p.127

BENINCASA

A genus consisting of a single species of tender, climbing or trailing, annual vine, similar in appearance to a number of members of the cucumber family. It is found in Asia and tropical Africa, and has become naturalized in many warm countries. Its growth averages 1in (2.5cm) per hour. Male and female flowers are borne separately on the same plant. They are bell-shaped and yellow: males are 2–7in (5–17cm) in length, on long stalks, and the females 1–1½in (2.5–4cm).

Benincasa hispida (wax gourd, white gourd, ash pumpkin)
Climbing annual with hairy stems, forked tendrils, and lobed, hairy leaves. Pollinated female flowers grow into dark green fruits, 10–16in (25–40cm) long, with white flesh. The skin is coated in wax, giving a white bloom. H 20ft (6m).

A

BERBERIS

Some 450 species of evergreen, semievergreen, and deciduous shrubs make up this genus, widely distributed in Eurasia, the Americas, and northern Africa; *B. vulgaris* is native to hedges and scrub throughout most of Europe. Many species are grown for their scented flowers, brightly colored fruits, and neat foliage, which, in the case of deciduous kinds, gives good autumn color. The dense, spiny habit makes barberries among the best shrubs for hedging or on steep banks.

Berberis vulgaris (common barberry)
Deciduous shrub with yellow roots, grooved, yellow-gray stems, 3-pronged spines, and obovate, toothed leaves. Yellow flowers are produced in pendent racemes, up to 2½in (6cm) long, in spring, followed by slender, oval, red fruits. H 6ft (2m), S 4ft (1.2m).

5–8

***Betula pendula* 'Laciniata'** (cutleaf birch)
An elegant, slender tree with deeply cut leaves; this variant was found in the wild in Sweden in 1767. H 20–28ft (6–9m), S 12–15ft (4–5m).

2–7

BETULA

A genus of about 60 species of hardy, deciduous, mostly fast-growing trees and shrubs distributed throughout the northern hemisphere. *B. pendula* is native to woodland margins and moorland from Siberia to western Asia and northern Africa. Birches are among the most common trees in most northern regions and are important in cultivation, being easily grown on most soils. They have a graceful habit, and the foliage of many species turns yellow in autumn.

Betula pendula (silver birch)
Deciduous tree with drooping branches and silver-white, peeling bark. Catkins of male and female flowers are borne in spring on the same tree before the leaves; males pendent, females short and erect, followed by winged nutlets. H 30–80ft (10–25m), S 12–30ft (4–10m).

2–6

***Betula pendula* 'Tristis'**
This cultivar is a tall, graceful tree with a narrow, symmetrical head and drooping branches. H 22ft (7m), S 22–25ft (7–8m).

2–7

***Betula pendula* 'Youngii'** (Young's weeping birch)
A small-growing tree, this cultivar has a mushroom-shaped crown and strongly weeping branches. H 22ft (7m), S 22–30ft (7–10m).

2–7

BEEFSTEAK PLANT, see *Perilla frutescens*, p.174
BEGGAR'S BUTTONS, see *Arctium lappa*, p.86
BELL PEPPER, see *CAPSICUM*, p.100
BEN, see *Moringa oleifera*, p.161
BENJAMIN, see *Lindera benzoin*, p.152
BENZOIN, see *Styrax benzoin*, p.357
BERGAMOT, see *Monarda didyma*, p.160
BERGAMOT ORANGE, see *Citrus bergamia*, p.262
BETEL, see *Piper betle*, p.178
BETEL PALM, see *Areca catechu*, p.86
BETONY, see *Stachys officinalis*, p.205
BHRINGARAJA, see *Eclipta prostrata*, p.122

BIDENS

A genus of about 200 species of cosmopolitan annuals, perennials, and shrubs; *B. tripartita* is found throughout temperate Eurasia. The best known species are *B. ferulifolia*, grown for its autumn display of golden daisies, and *B. atrosanguinea* (now *Cosmos atrosanguineus*), with its arching stems and deep maroon, chocolate-scented, solitary flowers. *Bidens* comes from the Latin *bis*, "twice," and *dens*, "tooth," and refers to the barbed fruits, which adhere to fur and clothing.

Bidens tripartita (trifid bur marigold, water agrimony)
Waterside annual with 4-angled, purple stems and toothed, lanceolate or divided leaves. Yellow-brown, buttonlike flowers, surrounded by leaflike bracts, appear in summer. H 6–24in (15–60cm), S 4–12in (10–30cm).

A

BIXA

This genus consists of one species of tender, evergreen, shrubby tree native to tropical America and the W Indies. *B. orellana* is found throughout tropical America on rich soil along forest margins. It is grown commercially in the tropics for its seeds, and is also planted for shade and hedges. The bright red, spiny capsules, 2in (5cm) long, are very decorative; the flowers are a rich source of nectar for honey bees. The name *Bixa* comes from *biche*, the S American name for the plant.

Bixa orellana (annatto, *achiote*, lipstick tree)
Small tree with pointed, broadly ovate leaves up to 8in (20cm) long. Panicles of pink or white flowers appear from late summer, followed by red, spiny capsules containing red seeds. H 22ft (7m), S 10–12ft (3–4m).

BLETILLA

A genus of nine species of terrestrial orchid, occurring in eastern Asia. Only one, *B. striata*, is widely cultivated in the West as an ornamental, and in the East grown largely as a medicinal plant. Native to China and Japan, it is an attractive plant for shady borders in mild areas, or for pots. More tender cultivars, such as variegated forms, need to be grown under cover in a greenhouse or cold frame. *Bletilla* is named after Don Louis Blet, a Spanish botanist.

Bletilla striata (bletilla)
Deciduous, terrestrial orchid with flattened, underground pseudobulbs and pleated leaves up to 20in (50cm) long. Loose spikes of magenta, occasionally white, flowers, 1¼in (3cm) across, appear in late spring. H 12–24in (30–60cm), S 8–12in (20–30cm).

6–9

BORAGO

Three species of hardy annuals and perennials make up this genus native to the Mediterranean region and western Asia. Two species, *B. officinalis* and *B. pygmaea*, are popular for their clear blue flowers. Though sometimes stocked by nurseries, *B. pygmaea* cannot be used as a substitute for culinary or medicinal uses of *B. officinalis*. Borago may be derived from the Latin *burra*, a hairy garment, alluding to the bristly foliage. It was called *Euphrosinum* by Pliny, because of its euphoric effect.

Borago officinalis (borage)
Hairy annual with upright, hollow stems and lanceolate leaves. Blue, 5-petaled flowers, ½in (1cm) across, appear in summer, followed by tiny brown-black seeds. Plants may appear with variegated foliage. H 1–3ft (30cm–1m), S 6–12in (15–30cm).

A

***Borago officinalis* 'Alba'**
This variety has the same bristly, cucumber-flavored leaves as the species, and pure white flowers. H 1–3ft (30cm–1m), S 6–12in (15–30cm).

A

BILBERRY, see *Vaccinium myrtillus*, p.217
BIRCH, see *Betula*, p.93
BITTER CRESS, see *Cardamine*, p.101
BLACK CUMIN, see *Nigella sativa*, p.165
BLACK HOREHOUND, see *Ballota nigra*, p.91
BLACK LOVAGE, see *Smyrnium olusatrum*, p.204
BLACK-TANG, see *Fucus vesiculosus*, p.130
BLACKBERRY, see *Rubus fruticosus*, p.194
BLACKCURRANT, see *Ribes nigrum*, p.190
BLADDERWRACK, see *Fucus vesiculosus*, p.130
BLAZING STAR, see *Liatris spicata*, p.151; *Chamaelirium luteum*, p.258

BOSWELLIA

A genus of 25 species of evergreen bushes or small trees native to tropical Asia and Africa; *B. sacra* is native to dry, mountainous regions in Arabia and the Horn of Africa. Frankincense, an oleo-gum resin, exudes from the bark of the trees. Exploited species include *B. papyrifera* and *B. sacra* from tropical north-eastern Africa, as well as *B. frereana* and *B. serrata*. In one myth, Adam was given gold, frankincense, and myrrh by God to console him for his expulsion from the garden of Eden.

Boswellia sacra (frankincense, olibanum, mastic tree)
Resinous evergreen tree with papery, peeling bark and clusters of pinnately divided leaves. Small, 5-petaled, white flowers appear in spring, followed by 3–5-angled, red-brown capsules.
H 6–15ft (2–5m), S 3–10ft (1–3m).

BRASSICA

A genus of about 30 species of hardy, mainly annual or biennial herbs distributed throughout Eurasia. The Romans mixed the ground seeds with grape juice; the word "mustard" derives from *mustum*, "grape must," and *ardens*, "burning." *B. juncea* has properties similar to other mustards but is used more for culinary than for medicinal purposes. It can be harvested mechanically, making it more commercially viable than *B. nigra*, though having only 70 percent of its pungency.

Brassica juncea (brown mustard, Indian mustard, Chinese mustard)
Annual with glaucous, irregularly lobed leaves, 6–12in (15–30cm) long. Racemes of pale yellow flowers appear in summer, followed by beaked pods containing dark red-brown seeds.
H 3–4ft (1–1.2m), S 12in (30cm).

A

Brassica nigra (black mustard)
Annual with a much-branched stem and lobed, roughly lyre-shaped leaves. Bright yellow flowers are produced all summer, followed by small, erect, 4-angled pods. Seeds are very dark brown. H 3–10ft (90cm–3m) or more, S 3–4ft (90cm–1.2m).

A

BRUCEA

Seven species of tender evergreen and deciduous shrubs make up this genus, which occurs in SE Asia. The berries of several species are used to treat dysentery. So well known are they for this purpose that one species was named *B. antidysenterica*. This species and *B. sumatrana* were listed in *The Illustrated Dictionary of Gardening* (ed. G. Nicholson, 1885), as "ornamental evergreen shrubs…clothed with rufescent down." They are seldom seen in cultivation today, even in botanic gardens.

Brucea javanica (kusam seeds)
Tall deciduous shrub with downy branches and pinnately divided leaves with 4–6 pairs of leaflets. Small, purple, 4-petaled flowers are produced in axillary panicles in summer; the black berries contain a single, flat seed.
H 10ft (3m), S 6–10ft (2–3m).

BRUNFELSIA

Some 40 species of evergreen shrubs and small trees belong to this tropical American genus; *B. uniflora* is found in cloud forests in Brazil and Venezuela. Several species are grown as ornamentals in warm regions or under glass for their large, often scented, five-lobed flowers, which in some species change color as they age, giving rise to such common names as "yesterday, today, and tomorrow." The genus is named after Otto Brunfels (1489–1534), a monk and physician.

Brunfelsia uniflora (*manaca, pohl*, vegetable mercury)
Shrub with pointed leaves up to 3in (8cm) long, and blue-violet, yellow-throated flowers, usually solitary but sometimes paired, measuring ¾–1¼in (2–3cm) across. H and S 20in (50cm).

BRYONIA

This genus of about 10 species of tuberous climbing perennials occurs in Eurasia, northern Africa, and the Canary Islands. The name *Bryonia* comes from the Greek *bryo*, "to sprout," and refers to the annual growth from the tuber. The specific epithet *dioica* means "dioecious"; that is, with male and female flowers on separate plants. *B. dioica* is an easy, fast-growing climber for the wild garden or to cover eyesores, flowering from late spring to late summer. The red berries are poisonous.

Bryonia dioica (white bryony, red bryony, English mandrake)
Climbing deciduous perennial with large tuber, wiry stems, and palmate leaves. The 5-petaled flowers are pale green; males long-stalked, females short-stalked, in umbels of two to five, followed by red berries. H 12ft (4m).

4–9

BLESSED THISTLE, see *Cnicus benedictus*, p.109
BLOODROOT, see *Potentilla erecta*, p.183; *Sanguinaria*, p.198
BONESET, see *Eupatorium perfoliatum*, p.126
BORAGE, see *Borago officinalis*, p.94
BOTTLEBRUSH, see *Equisetum arvense*, p.123
BOXWOOD, see *Buxus*, p.96
BRAMBLE, see *Rubus*, p.194
BROOM, see *Cytisus*, p.116; *Genista*, p.132
BUCKTHORN, see *Rhamnus catharticus*, p.189
BUGLE, see *Ajuga*, p.77

BUPLEURUM

There are about 100 species of hardy and frost-hardy annuals, perennials, and the occasional evergreen shrub in this genus distributed through Europe, temperate Asia, and N America. *B. falcatum* is found wild in southern, central, and eastern Europe, and in Asia. A few species are grown as ornamentals for their foliage and flowers. The common name thorow-wax is the Old English for "through grow," referring to the perfoliate leaves that are characteristic of many species.

Bupleurum falcatum (sickle-leaved hare's ear)
Slender perennial with a woody rootstock, hollow stems, obovate basal leaves, and narrow stem leaves. Umbels of tiny yellow flowers are borne from midsummer to autumn. H 1–3ft (30cm–1m), S 12–24in (30–60cm).

4–9

BUXUS

Found in western Europe, N and C America, eastern Asia, and the W Indies, this genus contains about 30 species of hardy and tender evergreen shrubs and small trees. The slow-growing, long-lived *B. sempervirens*, widely grown in Europe and N America, has been used for topiary since Classical times: Pliny (AD23–79) described a terrace "adorned with the representation of divers animals in box." The wood is very hard, and was often used to make boxes; hence the name.

Buxus sempervirens (boxwood)
Evergreen shrub or small tree with gray-brown bark and glossy, ovate to oblong leaves. Pale green, petal-less flowers with a honey scent appear in spring; 3-horned fruits contain black seeds. H 6–15ft (2–5m), occasionally 30ft (10m); S 4–6ft (1.2–2m) or more.

5–8

***Buxus sempervirens* 'Kingsville Dwarf'**
Growing only ½in (1cm) a year, this cultivar is slow to reach its maximum height and spread. It is often used as a bonsai specimen. H and S 3ft (1m).

6–8

***Buxus sempervirens* 'Elegantissima'** (silver boxwood)
This dense, slow-growing cultivar has smaller than average leaves, with irregularly white margins. Like the species, male and female flowers are produced separately on the same plant. H 6ft (2m), S 3–5ft (1–1.5m).

6–8

***Buxus sempervirens* 'Latifolia Maculata'**
This cultivar forms a dense, mound-shaped shrub with relatively large leaves that have irregular, dull yellow marbling. New growths are bright yellow when grown in a sunny position. H and S 3–6ft (1–2m).

6–8

***Buxus sempervirens* 'Suffruticosa'** (edging boxwood)
A dwarf cultivar with medium-sized, glossy, bright green foliage, this has long been cultivated for formal hedging and topiary. H and S after many years to 3–6ft (1–2m).

6–8

BUR MARIGOLD, see *Bidens*, p.94
BURDOCK, see *Arctium lappa*, p.86
BURNET SAXIFRAGE, see *Pimpinella saxifraga*, p.176
BURNING BUSH, see *Dictamnus albus*, p.118; *Euonymus atropurpureus*, p.125
BURWEED, see *Xanthium*, p.222
BUTCHER'S BROOM, see *Ruscus aculeatus*, p.195
BUTTER-AND-EGGS, see *Linaria vulgaris*, p.152
BUTTERCUP, see *Ranunculus*, p.188
BUTTERFLY WEED, see *Asclepias tuberosa*, p.89
BUTTON SNAKEROOT, see *Liatris spicata*, p.151

CALAMINTHA

Seven species are included in this genus ranging throughout Europe to central Asia. *C. nepeta*, a Eurasian species, found also in northern Africa, grows in grassy places, often near rivers. Several species are attractive, aromatic perennials for dry, sunny borders or containers. In addition to those described below, the pink *C. grandiflora* (large-flowered calamint) and its variegated cultivar, *C. grandiflora* "Variegata', are widely grown in herb gardens.

Calamintha nepeta (lesser calamint)
Bushy perennial with a long, creeping rhizome, upright, branched stems, and peppermint-scented small, ovate leaves. Loose clusters of tubular, pale lilac to white flowers, ¼in (6mm) long, appear in summer. H 8–30in (20–75cm), S 24–36in (60–90cm).

5–10

Calamintha nepeta subsp. ***nepeta***
This variant is larger in all its parts than the species, and is similarly scented. H 18–24in (45–60cm), S 24–36in (60–90cm).

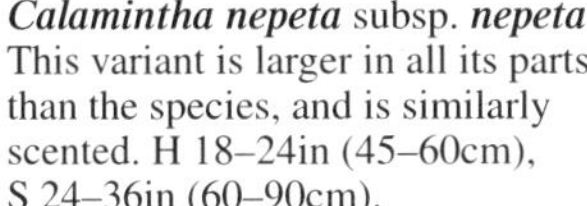

5–10

Calamintha sylvatica (common calamint)
Hardy, rhizomatous perennial with hairy, mint-scented, slightly toothed leaves. Pale lilac flowers, spotted darker, are produced from midsummer to early autumn. H and S 24in (60cm).

5–10

CALENDULA

Twenty or so species of hardy annuals, perennials, and evergreen subshrubs make up this genus distributed throughout Mediterranean regions. Only *C. officinalis* and its cultivars are common in cultivation as ornamentals and for culinary and medical uses. The name *Calendula* comes from the Latin *kalendae*, "first day of the month" in the Roman calendar, since they can be found in flower at the beginning of most months of the year. "Marigold" refers to its links with the Virgin Mary.

Calendula officinalis (pot marigold, calendula)
Bushy, aromatic, long-lived annual with branched stems and lanceolate leaves. Flowers are up to 3in (7cm) across, with yellow to orange ray florets, produced during summer and autumn. H and S 20–28in (50–70cm).

A

Calendula officinalis **'Prolifera'** (hen-and-chickens calendula)
This cultivar has been grown for centuries for its curious flowers, in which the main flower head produces several smaller ones from its base. H and S 16–20in (40–50cm).

A

CACAO, see *Theobroma cacao*, p.210
CAJUPUT, see *Melaleuca leucadendron*, p.157
CALABAR BEAN, see *Physostigma venenosum*, p.327
CALAMINT, see *Calamintha*, above
CALAMUS, see *Acorus calamus*, p.73
CALICO BUSH, see *Kalmia latifolia*, p.146
CALIFORNIA LAUREL, CALIFORNIA SASSAFRAS, see *Umbellularia californica*, p.217
CALIFORNIA LILAC, see *Ceanothus*, p.103
CALIFORNIA POPPY, see *Eschscholzia*, p.124

CALLUNA

This genus consists of a single species of evergreen shrublet that occurs in most of Europe, and is closely related to *Erica*. There are over 300 variants of *C. vulgaris* grown for their year-round interest. Flowering heather dries well, retaining its color for years, and white heather is considered lucky. *Calluna* comes from the Greek *kalluno*, "to sweep," since it was used in brooms. It was also gathered for fuel (the common name "ling" is from Anglo-Saxon *lig*, "fire"), and used in thatch.

Calluna vulgaris (heather, ling)
Dense evergreen shrublet with numerous tortuous, rooting branches, and very small, stalkless leaves. Loose racemes, 1¼–6in (3–15cm) long, of small, pink-purple, bell-shaped flowers appear from late summer. H 6–30in (15–75cm), S 3–18in (7–45cm).

4–7

***Calluna vulgaris* 'Alba Plena'**
A double, white-flowered cultivar, similar in other respects to the species. H and S 12–18in (30–45cm).

4–7

***Calluna vulgaris* 'Multicolor'**
A dwarf, pink-flowered cultivar grown for its colorful foliage, which has orange, bronze, yellow, and red tints all year. H 8in (20cm), S 9in (23cm).

4–7

***Calluna vulgaris* 'Darkness'**
This cultivar has deep rose-purple flowers and dark green foliage. H and S 12–18in (30–45cm).

4–7

***Calluna vulgaris* 'Silver Queen'**
This cultivar has silver-gray foliage and a spreading habit. H 10–16in (25–40cm), S to 24in (60cm).

4–7

CALUMBA, see *Jateorhiza palmata*, p.298
CAMPHOR PLANT, see *TANACETUM*, pp.208–9
CAMPHOR TREE, see *Cinnamomum camphora*, p.108
CANADIAN FLEABANE, see *Conyza canadensis*, p.112
CANADIAN HEMP, see *Apocynum cannabinum*, p.85
CANDLEBERRY, see *Myrica cerifera*, p.162
CANELLA, see *Canella winterana*, p.99
CAPE JASMINE, see *Gardenia augusta*, p.131
CAPER, see *Capparis spinosa*, p.99
CARA-CARA, see *Aniba roseaodora*, p.239
CARAWAY, see *Carum carvi*, p.101

CAMELLIA

Some 100–150 species of evergreen shrubs and trees make up this Asian genus. The most important species commercially is *C. sinensis* (tea), native to China, which is cultivated on a vast scale, and has over 350 cultivars. It was introduced to Europe in the 17th century. Many species are grown as ornamentals for their handsome, glossy foliage and fine flowers. *Camellia* is named after George Joseph Kamel (1661–1706), a Jesuit pharmacist who wrote a history of Philippine plants.

Camellia sinensis (tea)
Small, variable, evergreen shrub with leathery, elliptic leaves. White flowers, about 1in (2.5cm) across, with a boss of yellow stamens, are borne in the axils during winter, followed by capsules containing large, oily seeds. H 3–20ft (1–6m), S 2–12ft (60cm–4m).

7–9

CANNABIS

A genus containing a single species of tall, coarse annual native to central Asia, found on most soils, especially as a weed of nitrogen-rich soils near human habitation. The Scythians, who lived north of the Black Sea 3,000 years ago, produced intoxicating vapors by throwing cannabis onto hot stones. In Victorian gardening manuals it was listed as an elegant "dot plant" for summer borders. *Cannabis* is the Greek word for "hemp," from which the word "canvas" is derived, after the plant's fibrousness.

Cannabis sativa (hemp, marijuana, *hasheesh*)
Strong-smelling annual with a long tap-root, erect, branched stem, and palmate leaves. Panicles of small green flowers appear in summer, male and female on separate plants. H 3–15ft (90cm–5m), S 1–5ft (30cm–1.5m).

A

CANANGA

A genus of two species of tender evergreen trees native to tropical Asia and Australia. *C. odorata*, or ylang-ylang, a night-scented species, is native to lowland forests from India to northern Australia. In the tropics it is prized as an ornamental for the intense perfume of its pale flowers, which show up in the dark to attract pollinating moths. The use of ylang-ylang flowers in a coconut oil pomade in the Molucca Islands was recorded by Guibourt in *Natural History of Simple Drugs* (1866).

Cananga odorata (ylang-ylang, ilang-ilang)
Open-headed evergreen tree with drooping branches and ovate-oblong leaves. Intensely fragrant flowers with 6 narrow, yellow-green petals appear all year, followed by green fruits. H 88ft (27m) or more, S 30ft (10m).

CAPPARIS

This large genus of about 250 species of evergreen shrubs and small trees is native to tropical and subtropical regions. *C. spinosa* is common in the wild and popular as an ornamental in warm parts of the Mediterranean region. It was described in *The Illustrated Dictionary of Gardening* (ed. G. Nicholson, 1885) as "an excellent greenhouse shrub… perfectly hardy in the southern counties in England," though it is seldom seen now. The Greek name *kapparis* is from the Persian *kabar*, "caper."

Capparis spinosa (caper)
Prostrate shrub with trailing stems up to 5ft (1.5m) long, and ovate leaves, 2½in (6cm) long, with 2 spines at the base. Solitary, white to pink flowers with 4 petals and long, pink stamens open from early summer to autumn. H 3ft (1m), S 5ft (1.5m).

9

CANELLA

One species of evergreen shrubby tree constitutes this genus, which occurs in the W Indies and Florida Keys. The name is a diminutive of *canna*, "a reed," referring to the quills of bark (not to be confused with *Cinnamomum* species, see p.108) produced for the pharmaceutical and food industries. It was grown as a "stove" (warm greenhouse) evergreen during Victorian times, but is rarely seen today outside the tropics. The whole tree is aromatic, filling the air with fragrance when in flower.

Canella winterana (canella, white cinnamon, W Indian wild cinnamon)
Erect, evergreen shrub or tree with aromatic bark and laurel-scented leaves up to 4in (10cm) long. Fragrant violet to purple flowers in summer are followed by red to black berries. H 30–50ft (10–15m), S 22–30ft (7–10m).

T

CAPSELLA

A genus of five hardy annual or biennial herbs found throughout temperate and warm areas. The distinctive heart-shaped seed pods of *C. bursa-pastoris* have given rise to its specific name and various common names which refer to purses and pouches. This annual weed flourishes in a variety of situations, and became established in many countries during European colonization, notably the US. According to Mrs. Grieve (*A Modern Herbal*, 1931), the seeds were food for cage birds.

Capsella bursa-pastoris (shepherd's purse, witches' pouches, pick-pocket)
Annual or biennial with a rosette of entire to pinnate basal leaves and a branched stem with smaller leaves. Tiny white flowers appear all year, followed by heart-shaped seed pods. H 1¼–16in (3–40cm), S 1¼–6in (3–15cm).

A

Capsicum

About ten wild species and four or five domesticated species of shrubby annuals, biennials, and perennials are included in this tropical American genus. Numerous cultivars are grown in warm regions, and under cover in temperate parts, ranking second in importance to black pepper (*Piper nigrum*) among the world's spices. Capsicum peppers were first described in 1493 by Dr. Chauca, physician on Columbus's voyage, and were introduced from S America to India and Africa by the Portuguese. Fruiting plants are ornamental, and a number of compact, dwarf cultivars have been developed for the pot plant industry. Capsicum may derive from the Latin *capsa*, "box," on account of the hollow fruits which these plants yield.

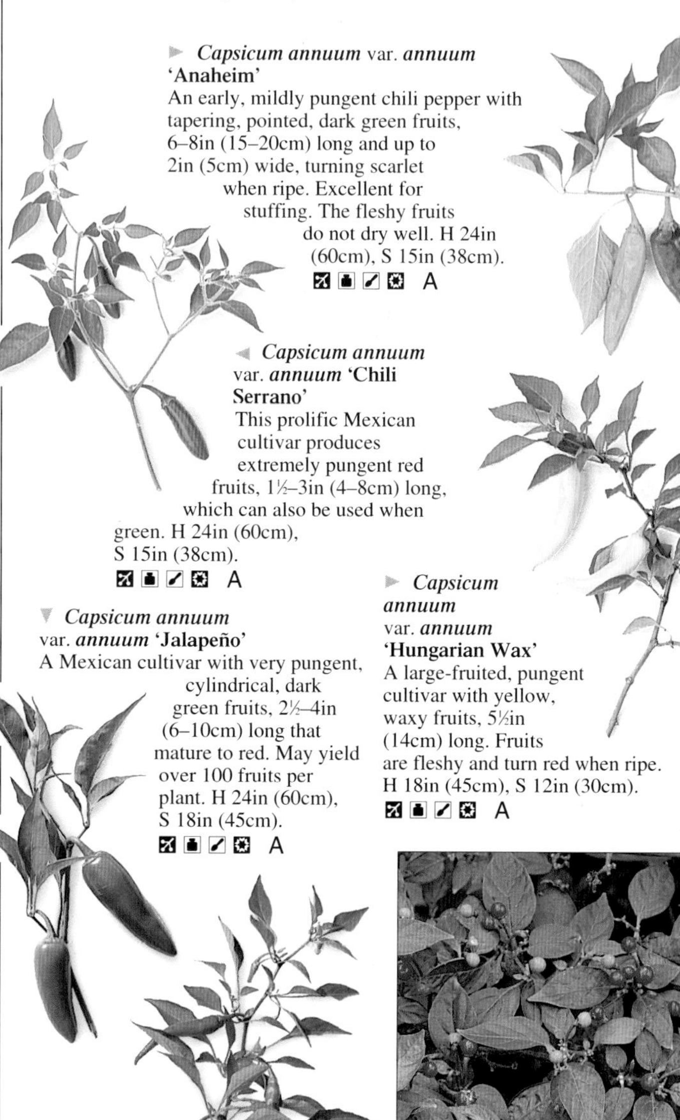

► ***Capsicum annuum*** var. ***annuum*** **'Anaheim'**
An early, mildly pungent chili pepper with tapering, pointed, dark green fruits, 6–8in (15–20cm) long and up to 2in (5cm) wide, turning scarlet when ripe. Excellent for stuffing. The fleshy fruits do not dry well. H 24in (60cm), S 15in (38cm).
A

◄ ***Capsicum annuum*** var. ***annuum*** **'Chili Serrano'**
This prolific Mexican cultivar produces extremely pungent red fruits, 1½–3in (4–8cm) long, which can also be used when green. H 24in (60cm), S 15in (38cm).
A

▼ ***Capsicum annuum*** var. ***annuum*** **'Jalapeño'**
A Mexican cultivar with very pungent, cylindrical, dark green fruits, 2½–4in (6–10cm) long that mature to red. May yield over 100 fruits per plant. H 24in (60cm), S 18in (45cm).
A

► ***Capsicum annuum*** var. ***annuum*** **'Hungarian Wax'**
A large-fruited, pungent cultivar with yellow, waxy fruits, 5½in (14cm) long. Fruits are fleshy and turn red when ripe. H 18in (45cm), S 12in (30cm).
A

▲ ***Capsicum annuum*** var. ***annuum*** **'Super Cayenne'**
This F1 hybrid is exceptionally vigorous and high-yielding, with slender, very hot, deep red fruits, 4in (9cm) long, which can be used ripe or unripe. It does well in containers.
H 24–30in (60–75cm), S 18in (45cm).
A

▲ ***Capsicum baccatum***
Spreading, shrubby perennial with white to yellow flowers about ½in (1cm) across, marked beige or green at the base and spotted yellow to tan. Small red fruits are held erect and contain cream to yellow seeds.
H 10ft (3m), S 5–6ft (1.5–2m).
A

► ***Capsicum chinense*** **'Habañero'**
A cultivar with orange-yellow, lantern-shaped fruits, 1–2in (2.5–5cm) long, which have a smoky flavor. Reputedly the hottest of all peppers. H 3–4ft (1–1.2m), S 24in (60cm).
A

▲ ***Capsicum frutescens*** **'Tabasco'**
A cultivar with small, upright, fiery, green fruits that ripen to red. Used for Tabasco, and Louisiana hot sauce.
H 3ft (1m), S 24in (60cm).
A

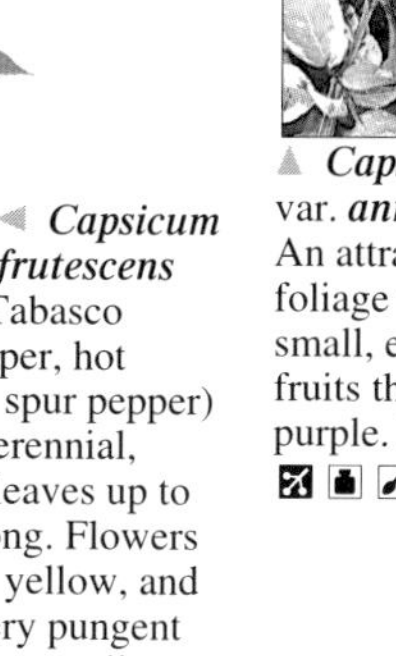

◄ ***Capsicum frutescens*** (Tabasco pepper, hot pepper, spur pepper)
Bushy perennial, with elliptic leaves up to 4in (10cm) long. Flowers are pale green to yellow, and followed by green, very pungent fruits which turn red, orange, or yellow.
H 1½–5ft (45cm–1.5m), S 24in (60cm).
A

▲ ***Capsicum annuum*** var. ***annuum*** 'Purple Tiger'
An attractive, compact cultivar with foliage variegated white and purple, and small, extremely pungent tear-shaped fruits that ripen through red to deep purple. H 28in (70cm), S 20in (50cm).
A

CARDAMINE

Some 130 annuals and perennials, found almost worldwide in temperate areas, comprise this genus. About a dozen species are grown as ornamentals in moist ground; *C. pratensis* is found in northern Asia, N America, and Europe, where it flowers as the cuckoos arrive; this association gave rise to its common name of cuckoo flower. *Cardamine* is from the Greek *kardamon*, "cress," since many resemble watercress in appearance and flavor.

Cardamine pratensis (cuckoo flower, lady's smock, meadow cress)
Slender, clump-forming perennial with a basal rosette of long-stalked, pinnate leaves. Small, lilac to white, 4-petaled flowers appear in late spring, followed by narrow, erect pods. H 6–24in (15–60cm), S up to 12in (30cm).

3–9

***Cardamine pratensis* 'Flore Pleno'**
This popular double-flowered cultivar was first recorded in the mid-17th century. H 18in (45cm), S 12in (30cm).

3–9

CARICA

This S American genus has 22 trees and shrubs, characteristically with thick, unbranched trunks. The best known is the papaya, *C. papaya*, found in lowland tropical forest, which is grown for its pear-shaped fruits and as an ornamental. It has been cultivated since pre-Columbian times, reaching Europe in 1690 and Asia in the 18th century. Both male and female trees are normally needed for fruiting, but there are now cultivars with male and female flowers on the same plant, such as *C. p.* 'Solo'.

Carica papaya (papaya, pawpaw)
Evergreen tree with 7-lobed, palmate leaves up to 28in (70cm) across. Fruits are pear-shaped, 18in (45cm) long, with a leathery, yellow-green skin, apricot-colored pulp, and a central cavity of round, black seeds. H 20ft (6m), S 10ft (3m), less in containers.

CARLINA

This genus of 28 species of annual, biennial, and perennial thistles is found in Europe and Mediterranean regions and western Asia. *C. acaulis* grows on grasslands in mountainous regions of central, southern, and eastern Europe. Its fruits are typical of thistles, with a plume to aid wind dispersal. Some species are grown for their flowers, which dry well. *Carlina* was named after Charlemagne, who had a vision that the plant would ward off the plague.

Carlina acaulis (stemless carline thistle)
Low-growing hardy biennial or perennial with a long taproot and a rosette of prickly leaves, 12in (30cm) long. Stemless, disc-shaped flowers surrounded by silvery bracts are produced in summer. H 2-4in (5–10cm), S 12–24in (30–60cm).

5–9

CARTHAMUS

A thistlelike genus of 14 annuals and a few perennials native to Asia and Mediterranean regions. *C. tinctorius* was introduced into Europe from Egypt in 1551. It is now cultivated mainly for its seeds in Australia, China, SE Asia, India, Africa, and the Mediterranean. The name *Carthamus* comes from the Arabic *qurtom* or the Hebrew *qarthami*, "to paint," because the flowers yield a pigment (carthamin) that is yellow in water and red in alcohol.

Carthamus tinctorius (safflower, saffron thistle, false saffron)
Tall annual with erect stem and spiny-toothed leaves. Deep yellow florets surrounded by leafy, spine-edged bracts appear in summer, followed by oblong white seeds, ¼in (6mm) long. H 3ft (1m), S 12–15in (30–38cm).

A

CARUM

Thirty species make up this genus of biennials and perennials, which is found in Europe, northern Africa, and temperate Asia. The most important herb in the genus is *C. carvi* (caraway), found in damp grassland and disturbed ground. It was used in the Middle East for 5,000 years before introduction to Europe in the 13th century. *Carum* is named after Caria, an ancient region of Asia Minor that corresponds to present-day southern Aydin and western Mugla in Turkey.

Carum carvi (caraway)
Erect biennial with a spindle-shaped taproot, hollow stems, and deeply divided, fernlike leaves. Umbels of tiny, white- to pink-rayed flowers ¾–1½in (2–4cm) across are followed by aromatic ellipsoid fruits. H 10–36in (25cm–1m), S 6–12in (15–30cm).

5–8

CARDAMOM, see *Elettaria cardamomum*, p.122
CARLINE THISTLE, see *Carlina acaulis*, above
CARNATION, see *Dianthus caryophyllus*, p.117
CAROLINA JESSAMINE, see *Gelsemium sempervirens*, p.132
CARRAGHEEN, see *Chondrus crispus*, p.260
CARROT, see *Daucus*, p.116
CARRIZO, see *Phragmites australis*, p.175
CASCARA SAGRADA, see *Rhamnus purshiana*, p.340
CASHEW, see *Anacardium occidentale*, p.83
CASSIA BARK, see *Cinnamomum cassia*, p.108
CASSIE, see *Acacia farnesiana*, p.xxx

CASTANEA

This genus includes about 12 species of deciduous trees and shrubs from warm temperate parts of the northern hemisphere. *C. sativa* has been planted as a nut tree and ornamental since Roman times. It flowers late, and in areas with cool summers rarely produces large, ripe nuts. *C. sativa* is probably native to the Balkans but is widely naturalized. Its prickly fruits contain one to three brown nuts with a pale basal scar. The genus is named after Castania in Greece, which was renowned for its chestnuts.

***Castanea sativa* 'Albomarginata'**
The leaves of this cultivar have creamy white margins. H 100ft (30m), S 50ft (15m).

6–8

Castanea sativa (sweet chestnut, Spanish chestnut)
Deciduous tree with furrowed bark and toothed leaves up to 10in (24cm) long. Tiny, yellow-green, musky-smelling flowers appear in late spring, followed by prickly fruits containing 1–3 brown nuts. H 100ft (30m), S 50ft (15m).

6–8

CASTANOSPERMUM

Native to northeastern Australia and New Caledonia, where it is found in forests and along watercourses, this is a genus of one species of evergreen tree. *C. australe* is a large, handsome tree with racemes of flowers in shades of yellow, aging to orange and red, that appear in summer. It is widely cultivated in the tropics as an ornamental specimen or shade tree. The name comes from the Greek *kastanon*, "chestnut," and *sperma*, "seed," referring to the chestnutlike seeds.

Castanospermum australe (Moreton Bay chestnut, black bean)
Vigorous, rounded tree with leathery, pinnate leaves about 7in (18cm) long, and yellow flowers followed by oblong, often curved, red-brown pods, 10–12in (25–30cm) long, containing poisonous seeds. H 70ft (20m), S 25ft (8m).

CATHARANTHUS

Eight species of Madagascan annuals and perennials are included in this genus. *C. roseus* has now become a pantropical weed, though it is grown in temperate regions as an indoor plant or summer bedding plant because of its neat habit and attractive flowers. Varieties with white flowers (*C. r.* var. *alba*) and pink-eyed, white flowers (*C. r.* var. *ocellatus*) are often seen. It contains over 75 alkaloids, toxic in isolation but with valuable uses in treating leukemia.

Catharanthus roseus (Madagascar periwinkle, rosy periwinkle, Cayenne jasmine)
Small, erect perennial with smooth, shiny, oval leaves up to 2in (5cm) long, and flat-petaled, pink flowers, 1½in (4cm) across, with darker pink centers. H 24in (60cm), S 12in (30cm).

10

***Catharanthus roseus*, Pacifica Series**
This large-flowered cultivar has a vigorous, compact, bushy habit, making it ideal for containers and summer bedding in warm areas. Colors include white with a red eye, rose-red with a deeper center, and a true red. H and S 12in (30cm).

10

CASTOR BEAN, see *Ricinus*, p.190
CATAWISSA ONION, see *ALLIUM*, pp.80–81
CATERPILLAR FUNGUS, CHINESE, see *Cordyceps sinensis*, p.267
CATMINT, CATNIP, see *Nepeta cataria*, p.165
CAT'S EAR, CATSFOOT, see *Antennaria dioica*, p.84
CATTAIL, see *Typha latifolia*, p.216
CAYENNE JASMINE, see *Catharanthus rosea*, above
CEDAR, see *Cedrus*, p.103
CEDRON, see *Simaba cedron*, p.353

CAULOPHYLLUM

Two species of rhizomatous perennials belong to this genus: one found in eastern Asia, and *C. thalictroides* in rich, moist woods in eastern N America. The name comes from the Greek *kaulon*, "stem," and *phyllon*, "leaf," referring to the way the stem of the plant forms a stalk for the solitary compound leaf, which divides into three deeply lobed leaflets. The flowers of *C. thalictroides* arise from the base of the uppermost leaflet in spring. The common name "cohosh" is of Algonquin origin.

Caulophyllum thalictroides (blue cohosh, squaw root, papoose root)
Rhizomatous perennial with a matted rootstock and compound leaf. Yellow-green, star-shaped flowers, ½in (1cm) across, appear before foliage is fully grown, followed by deep blue berries. H 12–30in (30–75cm), S indefinite.

3–9

CEANOTHUS

Some 50–60 species of evergreen and deciduous shrubs or small trees belong to this N American genus, which is mainly west coast in distribution. The blue-flowered species are among the most popular garden shrubs for warm situations. Less ornamental, but interesting for its medicinal properties, is *C. americanus*, which is found in eastern N America. It was used as a substitute for tea during the Revolutionary War and is a parent of many hybrids.

Ceanothus americanus (New Jersey tea, redroot)
Small deciduous shrub with dark red roots and ovate leaves up to 4in (10cm) long. Dense, long-stalked panicles of tiny off-white flowers appear in summer, followed by triangular seed pods. H 3ft (1m), S 18in (45cm).

4–8

CEDRONELLA

This genus contains a single species of perennial endemic to the Canary Islands. *C. canariensis* is an attractive, fragrant plant, which is often seen in herb gardens but has no known therapeutic uses. It may be grown in a large pot under cover, on the patio, or in a sunny position in the open garden in warm areas. *Cedronella* is a diminutive of *kedros*, "cedar," and refers to the cedarlike aroma given off by the plant's leaves.

Cedronella canariensis (balm of Gilead, Canary balm)
Shrubby semievergreen perennial with a square stem, aromatic, trifoliate leaves up to 4in (10cm) long, and spikes of pink-violet to lilac, tubular, 2-lipped flowers in summer. H 5ft (1.5m), S 3ft (1m).

T

CEDRUS

Four species of conifer are true cedars, quite different from the many other trees that share the same common name. Native to western Asia and northwestern Africa, they have large, spreading branches, which tend to form flat plates of foliage. *C. libani* subsp. *atlantica* is native to the Atlas Mountains of Morocco and Algeria. The fragrant, durable timber is prized for joinery and veneers. King Solomon is said to have felled most of the cedars on Mount Lebanon to build his temple.

Cedrus libani subsp. ***atlantica*** (Atlas cedar)
Large tree with ascending branches. Leaves are needlelike, in whorls of 30–40 and variable in color, from gray-green to blue-gray. Female cones disintegrate after 2–3 winters. H 50–80ft (15–25m), S 15–30ft (5–10m).

6–8

Cedrus libani subsp. ***atlantica*, Glauca Group** (blue cedar)
Like the species, male cones, up to 2in (5cm) long, are borne mainly on lower branches; female cones occur higher up, barrel-shaped and 3in (8cm) long when mature. H 50–80ft (15–25m), S 15–30ft (5–10m).

6–8

CEIBA

A genus of four species of large deciduous trees, often with buttressed trunks, native to tropical America and Africa. *C. pentandra* is widely cultivated and naturalized throughout the tropics for medicinal uses and kapok fiber. Probably the largest tree in Africa, it is found there and in moist forests of S America. It is venerated in Africa and in the W Indies as the home of spirits. All parts of the tree are used. The yellow, pink, or white five-petaled flowers, pollinated by bats, appear before the leaves.

Ceiba pentandra
(kapok, silk cotton tree)
Deciduous or semievergreen tree with a spiny trunk and buttresses, and wide-spreading branches with palmate leaves. Spiny fruits 4–12in (10–30cm) long contain seeds in silky, cream fiber. H and S 130ft (40m) or more.

CENTAUREA

There are some 450 species of annuals, biennials, perennials, and subshrubs in this genus, which occurs in Mediterranean regions, Eurasia, N America, and Australia; *C. cyanus* is found in cornfields and waste places in Europe and western Asia. Various species are grown as ornamentals for their brightly colored, thistle-like flowers. *Centaurea* is named after the legendary centaur, Chiron, known for his knowledge of herbs, who first revealed the healing properties of knapweed.

Centaurea cyanus (bachelor's buttons, cornflower, bluebottle)
Tall, slender annual, sometimes over-wintering, with gray-green, lanceolate leaves. Bright blue, occasionally white, pink, or purple, flowers are borne in summer. H 8–36in (20cm–1m), S 6–12in (15–30cm).

A

***Centaurea cyanus*, Florence Series**
This compact cultivar has flowers in shades of blue, pink, carmine, and white. H 15–18in (38–45cm), S 6–12in (15–30cm).

A

CENTAURIUM

A genus of about 40 species of annuals and biennials, occasionally perennials, found throughout temperate regions. *C. erythraea* is native to dunes and dry grassland in Europe and southwestern Asia, and naturalized in N America. In common with many members of the gentian family, it is extremely bitter, prompting Culpeper to comment in *The English Physitian Enlarged, or the Herbal* (1653) that "it is very wholesome, but not very toothsome."

Centaurium erythraea (centaury, feverwort)
Variable small biennial with a basal rosette and elliptic, veined leaves up to 2in (5cm) long. Five-petaled, pink flowers are borne in dense clusters on long, branched stalks in summer. H 6–10in (15–24cm), S 3–6in (7–15cm).

4–8

CENTELLA

About 20 species of low-growing perennials are included in this genus, which occurs in southern Africa and most parts of the tropics. Best known is *C. asiatica*, an outstandingly important medicinal herb, resembling the related European marsh pennywort (*Hydrocotyle vulgaris*) in appearance. It is a variable species, pantropical in distribution, which thrives in wet places, such as rice paddies, but also grows in rocky areas and on walls.

Centella asiatica (gotu kola, Indian pennywort, tiger grass)
Creeping perennial, rooting at nodes, with clusters of kidney-shaped leaves, up to 2in (5cm) across, with indented margins. Tiny pink flowers are borne beneath the foliage in summer. H 6–8in (5–20cm), S indefinite.

8–10

CEPHAELIS

Closely related to the genera *Psychotria* and *Palicourea*, the 180 or so species of *Cephaelis* are tender, mostly evergreen shrubs and small trees, which occur in various parts of the tropics. Many species are known to contain alkaloids, but only *C. ipecacuanha*, an understory shrub of Brazilian rainforests, is in large-scale production in Singapore and Malaysia, often grown under rubber trees. The terminal clusters of trumpet-shaped flowers are produced in the rainy season.

Cephaelis ipecacuanha
(ipecacuanha, ipecac)
Slender evergreen shrub with creeping rootstock and glossy, pointed, ovate leaves, 3–6in (8–16cm). White flowers, ½in (1cm) long, are followed by blue-purple berries with two seeds. H and S 12–20in (30–50cm).

CELANDINE, see *Chelidonium*, p.106
CENTAURY, see *Centaurium erythraea*, above
CENTURY PLANT, see *Agave americana*, p.76
CEYLON CINNAMON, see *Cinnamomum zeylanicum*, p.108
CHAMOMILE, see *Chamaemelum*, p.105
CHASTE TREE, see *Vitex agnus-castus*, p.221
CHAULMOOGRA, see *Hydnocarpus kurzii*, p.140
CHECKERBERRY, see *Gaultheria procumbens*, p.132
CHEESE RENNET, see *Galium verum*, p.131

CETRARIA

A genus of 40 species of lichens found worldwide, especially in Arctic regions. *C. islandica* forms tufts on heaths in hilly and montane regions of Europe, Arctic regions, and Australasia. It is ecologically important as a food for reindeer. Lichens have been used since earliest times for medicines, dyes, and perfumes. They are not cultivated, and are now rare in the wild due to pollution. Many herbalists now use lichen-based remedies in serious cases only.

Cetraria islandica (Iceland moss)
Lichen with leathery, crinkled, gray-green to dark brown branches, which are profusely forked and have minute, spiny projections along the margins. H ¾–2½in (2–6cm), S indefinite.

3–5

***Chaenomeles speciosa* 'Nivalis'**
This cultivar has large white flowers, and is particularly effective when grown against red brick walls. H 6–20ft (2–6m), S 4–10ft (1.2–3m).

4–8

CHAENOMELES

A genus of three species of hardy, deciduous, sometimes spiny shrubs and small trees native to eastern Asia. All are widely cultivated, both in the open and as wall shrubs. *C. speciosa*, a Chinese woodland species, has many cultivars, with a variety of habits and single or double flowers, ranging from white to pink and crimson. These are among the loveliest and most easily grown of early spring-flowering plants, with the added interest of edible fruits.

Chaenomeles speciosa (flowering quince, Japanese quince, japonica)
Deciduous shrub with dense, spiny twigs and ovate leaves. Scarlet, 5-petaled flowers, up to 2in (5cm) across, appear during late winter, followed by aromatic, speckled fruits. H 6–20ft (2–6m), S 4–10ft (1.2–3m).

4–8

***Chaenomeles speciosa* 'Moerloosii'**
In this cultivar the dense clusters of pink-flushed white flowers resemble apple blossoms. H 6–20ft (2–6m), S4–10ft (1.2–3m).

4–8

CHAMAEMELUM

Containing only four species of annuals and evergreen perennials, this small genus is native to Europe and Mediterranean regions and is closely related to *Anthemis*, *Chamomilla*, and *Matricaria*. The name of the genus comes from the Greek *chamaimelon*, which means "apple on the ground"; it refers to the strong apple scent of the foliage when stepped on. *C. nobile* is a prostrate plant with a delightful aroma that can be best appreciated when planted in paving, containers, or lawns.

Chamaemelum nobile (chamomile, Roman chamomile)
Mat-forming evergreen perennial with aromatic, finely divided leaves, up to 2in (5cm) long. Long-stalked, solitary flowers, with yellow discs and creamy white ray florets, appear in summer. H 6in (15cm), S 18in (45cm).

4–8

***Chamaemelum nobile* 'Flore Pleno'**
(double chamomile)
A charming cultivar with rather shaggy, creamy white, double flowers. H 6in (15cm), S 18in (45cm).

4–8

***Chamaemelum nobile* 'Treneague'**
(lawn chamomile)
A nonflowering cultivar that forms a mossy carpet. H 1in (2.5cm), S 18in (45cm).

4–8

CHELIDONIUM

A genus containing a single species of hardy perennial that in general appearance resembles the closely related Himalayan poppies (*Meconopsis* species). A native of temperate and subarctic Eurasia, *C. majus* is found along banks, hedgerows, and walls, usually on waste ground near human habitation; it is naturalized in N America. The four-petaled flowers, borne from early to midsummer, are followed by capsules 1¼–2in (3–5cm) long, containing black seeds with a white crest.

Chelidonium majus (greater celandine, swallow wort, tetterwort)
Perennial with a short rootstock and brittle stems that exude orange sap when damaged; divided leaves have oblong leaflets. Yellow flowers are followed by linear capsules. H 12–36in (30–90cm), S 8–18in (20–45cm).

4–8

***Chelidonium majus* 'Flore Pleno'**
This cultivar has double yellow flowers. H 12–36in (30–90cm), S 8–18in (20–45cm).

4–8

***Chelidonium majus* 'Laciniatum Flore Pleno'**
This cultivar is smaller than the species, with deeply cut leaves and small ragged flowers. It was first recorded at Heidelberg, Germany, c.1590. H 10–15in (25–38cm), S 6–15in (15–38cm).

4–8

CHELONE

This genus of N American perennials contains six species. *C. glabra*, found in wet woodland in eastern N America, is one of several species grown as border plants in damp situations for their snapdragon-like flowers. The genus is named *Chelone,* the Greek word for "tortoise," because the tubular flower, seen from the front, resembles a tortoise's head. This shape has also given rise to such common names for the plant as fishmouth, snakehead, and snakemouth, as well as turtlehead.

Chelone glabra (turtlehead, balmony)
Summer-flowering, upright perennial with lanceolate leaves up to 6in (15cm) long, and terminal clusters of white, sometimes pink-tinged flowers, in which the upper lip forms a hood over the bearded lower lip. H 24in (60cm), S 14in (35cm).

3–9

CHENOPODIUM

A cosmopolitan genus of some 150 species of annuals, perennials, and subshrubs. *C. ambrosioides*, a pungent, tropical American weed, is widely used in Mexican cooking, but almost unknown elsewhere. Several nonaromatic species have a long history of use as food plants. Seeds of *C. album* (fat hen, pigweed, lamb's quarters) were found in the stomach of Tollund man (100BC). It is still grown as a vegetable and pot herb, as is *C. bonus-henricus* (Good King Henry).

Chenopodium ambrosioides
(wormseed, Mexican tea, *epazote*)
Strong-smelling, upright annual or short-lived perennial, with oblanceolate leaves. Tiny green flowers appear in panicles in summer, followed by green-brown fruits, containing a single, black seed. H 4ft (1.2m), S 30in (75cm).

A

CHEROKEE ROSE, see *Rosa laevigata*, p.191
CHERRY, see *PRUNUS*, pp.184–5
CHERRY LAUREL, see *PRUNUS*, pp.184–5
CHERVIL, see *Anthriscus cerefolium*, p.85
CHESTNUT, see *Castanea*, p.102
CHICKWEED, see *Stellaria media*, p.205
CHICORY, see *Cichorium intybus*, p.107
CHILI PEPPER, see *CAPSICUM*, p.100
CHINA ROOT, see *Smilax china*, p.204
CHINESE CUCUMBER, see *Trichosanthes kirilowii*, p.214
CHINESE DATE, see *Ziziphus jujuba*, p.223
CHINESE FOXGLOVE, see *Rehmannia glutinosa*, p.189
CHINESE FOXNUT, see *Euryale ferox*, p.126
CHINESE GOLDTHREAD, see *Coptis*

CHIMAPHILA

Six species of shrubby evergreen perennials make up this genus, distributed throughout N America, Europe, and eastern Asia. *C. umbellata* is found in eastern N America, northern and central Europe, and Japan in acid woodland, often on sandy soils. Several species are occasionally grown in rock gardens and peat beds for their neat, ground-covering foliage and waxy flowers. The name *Chimaphila* comes from the Greek *cheima*, "winter," and *phileo*, "love," because the plants remain green in winter.

Chimaphila umbellata (pipsissewa, prince's pine, ground holly)
Shrubby perennial with a creeping rootstock, slender stems and whorls of glossy toothed leaves. Clusters of 3–10 white to pink flowers, ½in (1cm) across, are borne in summer. H 4–10in (10–24cm), S indefinite.

4–7

CHIONANTHUS

A genus of about 120 species of mostly tender deciduous trees and shrubs, found in tropical and subtropical eastern Asia, Australia, and eastern N America, with a few in Africa and Madagascar. There are just two hardy species, the better known being *C. virginicus*, a deciduous N American species, which is widely grown for its delightful display of white blossoms in early summer. The name *Chionanthus* comes from the Greek *chion*, "snow," and *anthos*, "flower."

Chionanthus virginicus (fringe tree)
Shrub or small tree with bright green, ovate leaves, 2–4in (5–10cm) long. Loose panicles, 4–8in (10–20cm) long, of fragrant white flowers are borne on second-year wood, followed by blue-purple berries. H 25ft (8m), S 15ft (5m).

4–8

CICHORIUM

A genus of eight species of perennials and annuals, occurring in Europe, temperate Asia, and Ethiopia. *C. intybus*, or chicory, found in Europe, western Asia, and northern Africa, is related to endive (*C. endivia*); the words *intybus* and endive both derive from the Arabic *hendibeh*. *Cichorium* is from an Egyptian word taken into many European languages, such as *chicorée* (French), and *cicoria* (Italian). Confusingly, in some countries curly endive is known as *chicorée* and Witloof chicory is called "endive."

Cichorium intybus (chicory, succory)
Tall perennial with a stout taproot and oblanceolate, toothed leaves, arranged spirally. Clusters of sky-blue flowers resembling dandelions, that may also be pink or white, appear in the upper axils throughout summer. H 1–5ft (30cm–1.5m), S 6–18in (15–45cm).

3–10

***Cichorium intybus* 'Red Devil'**
One of several radicchio-type cultivars that produce loose, deep red, cabbage-like heads, attractively veined with cream. The heads mature in autumn and withstand early frosts. H 6–8in (15–20cm), S 3–4in (7–10cm).

3–10

CIMICIFUGA

This genus of 15 species of hardy perennials is found in northern temperate regions. *C. foetida* occurs in Siberia and eastern Asia; *C. racemosa* is a N American species found in rich, open woodlands. Several species are grown in borders, especially in woodland settings, for their tall graceful spikes of flowers and elegantly cut leaves. The generic name *Cimicifuga* is derived from the Latin *cimex*, "bug," and *fugere*, "to run away," and, like the common names, refer to the use of these plants to repel insects.

Cimicifuga foetida (fetid bugbane)
Tall perennial with a woody rootstock and graceful spikes of star-shaped, green-white flowers in midsummer. The leaves are divided into ovate leaflets with toothed margins and a 3-lobed terminal leaflet. H 4–6ft (1.2–2m), S 24in (60cm).

4–8

Cimicifuga racemosa (black cohosh, cohosh bugbane, black snakeroot)
Tall perennial with a woody rootstock and broadly ovate leaves, divided into 3-lobed leaflets with toothed margins. Slender, bottlebrush spikes of fragrant white flowers are borne in midsummer. H 5ft (1.5m), S 24in (60cm).

3–9

chinensis, p.266
CHINESE LICORICE, see *Glycyrrhiza uralensis*, p.135
CHINESE LANTERN, see *Physalis alkekengi*, p.176
CHINESE SUMAC, see *Ailanthus altissima*, p.76
CHINESE THISTLE DAISY, see *Atractylodes macrocephala*, p.90
CHINESE YAM, see *Dioscorea opposita*, p.119
CHIVES, see *ALLIUM*, pp.80–1
CLARY SAGE, see *SALVIA*, pp.196–7
CHRYSANTHEMUM, see *Dendranthema*, p.117
CHURCH STEEPLES, see *Agrimonia eupatoria*, p.76

CINCHONA

This genus of about 40 species of tender evergreen trees and shrubs is found on warm, moist slopes of the Andes, mostly at 5,000–8,000ft (1,500–2,500m); *C. pubescens* is native to Ecuador. The species are difficult to tell apart; some authorities consider that there may be as few as 20. Cultivation of cinchona has been of global importance since the 17th century. Now grown in many tropical regions, some 8,000–10,000 tons of bark produce 400–500 tons of alkaloids (mainly quinine) annually.

Cinchona pubescens (red cinchona, Peruvian bark, Jesuit's bark)
Fast-growing evergreen tree with ovate leaves, sometimes flushed red on the undersides. Lilaclike panicles of small, tubular pink flowers are followed by 2-lobed capsules ¾in (2cm) long. H 80ft (25m), S variable.

Cinnamomum zeylanicum (cinnamon, Ceylon cinnamon)
Evergreen tree with light brown, papery bark and leathery leaves up to 7in (18cm) long. Small yellow-white flowers appear in clusters in summer, followed by ovoid, purple berries. H 30–60ft (10–18m), S 20–30ft (6–10m).

CINNAMOMUM

Some 250 species of evergreen trees and shrubs belong to this genus, occurring in eastern and SE Asia, and in Australia. *C. camphora* is found in forests from Japan to tropical Asia, while *C. cassia* is a native of lowland China. *C. zeylanicum*, from Sri Lanka and southern India, is a major spice. The Portuguese invaded Ceylon in 1536 to obtain a monopoly on cinnamon; the Dutch began to cultivate it in 1770, and the Dutch East India Company dominated world trade in it from 1796 to 1833.

Cinnamomum camphora (camphor)
Evergreen tree with pointed, glossy leaves up to 4in (10cm) long, which are red when young and camphor-scented. Pale, yellow-green flowers are produced in spring and summer, followed by black fruits. H 40–100ft (12–30m), S 40ft (12m).

Cinnamomum cassia (cassia bark, Chinese cinnamon)
Evergreen tree with thick, leathery leaves up to 8in (20cm) long. Yellow flowers appear in panicles 3–7in (8–18cm) long in summer, followed by single-seeded berries. H 40–70ft (12–20m), S 20–40ft (6–12m).

CISTUS

Native to southern Europe and northern Africa, this genus contains about 20 species of evergreen and semi-evergreen shrubs. Cistuses are attractive plants, popular in dry, warm borders and coastal gardens for their short-lived but showy flowers. The young stems and leaves of *C. ladanifer* exude a resin that becomes opaque in cold weather, giving the plant a leaden appearance. The name *Cistus* comes from the Greek *kiste*, "box," and refers to the shape of the capsules.

Cistus ladanifer (gum cistus)
Evergreen shrub with a stiff, upright habit and sticky, aromatic, linear-lanceolate leaves. Solitary, 5-petaled white flowers, about 3in (7cm) across, with a maroon basal blotch on each petal, appear from early to late summer. H and S 6–8ft (2–2.5m).

8–9

CITRUS

Some 16 species of small evergreen trees and shrubs comprise this genus, native to SE Asia and Pacific islands; *C. aurantiifolia* is native to humid tropics, mainly the W Indies. Most citruses have been cultivated for so long that their origins are obscure. The species are very closely related, with numerous hybrids and cultivars. The first to arrive in Europe was the bitter orange, *C. aurantium*, probably brought by the Portuguese from the East Indies; it was followed by *C. limon* in the 13th century.

Citrus aurantiifolia (lime)
Small tree with short, spiny branches and light green, ovate leaves. Clusters of 2–7 white flowers appear in lax racemes in spring and summer, followed by ovoid, green fruits up to 2½in (6cm) across, with a sour pulp. H 10–15ft (3–5m), S 6–10ft (2–3m).

10–11

CINCHONA, see *Cinchona pubescens*, above
CINNAMON, see *Cinnamomum zeylanicum*, above
CINQUEFOIL, see *Potentilla*, p.183
CLARY, CLEAREYE, see *SALVIA*, pp.196–7
CLEAVERS, see *Galium aparine*, p.131
CLEMENTINE, see *Citrus reticulata*, p.109
CLIMBING OLEANDER, see *Strophanthus gratus*, p.206
CLIVERS, see *Galium aparine*, p.131
CLOVE, see *Syzygium aromaticum*, p.206
CLOVE PINK, see *Dianthus caryophyllus*, p.117
CLOVER, see *Trifolium*, p.214
CLUBMOSS, see *Lycopodium*, p.154

Citrus aurantium (bitter orange, Seville orange)
Rounded tree with slender, blunt-spined branches and ovate leaves. Large white, very fragrant flowers are borne during spring and summer, followed by orange fruits with aromatic rind, and acidic pulp. H 30ft (10m), S 22ft (7m).

10–11

***Citrus limon* 'Variegata'**
An attractive cultivar for pot culture, with irregular yellow-margined leaves and immature fruits striped yellow and green. H 6–22ft (2–7m), S 3–10ft (1–3m).

10–11

Citrus reticulata (mandarin orange, tangerine, clementine)
Shrub or small spreading tree with lanceolate leaves. White flowers, less than 1in (2.5cm) across, appear in spring and summer. Fruits are yellow- to red-orange, with sweet pulp. H 6–25ft (2–8m), S 4–20ft (1.2–6m).

10–11

CLAVICEPS

This cosmopolitan genus contains 35 species of fungi, parasitic on grasses and rushes. Outbreaks of poisoning by *C. purpurea* have long been recorded. Rye flour contaminated with the fungus causes hallucinations, convulsions, and a burning sensation in the limbs, followed by gangrene as the blood supply is restricted. The syndrome is now known as "ergotism," but was once believed to be a punishment for sin, when it was called "St. Anthony's fire" or "holy fire."

Claviceps purpurea (ergot)
Poisonous fungus with pale pink to purple, drumstick-shaped fruiting bodies in spring and sclerotial (resting) stage in summer. Sclerotia are violet-black, spindle-shaped structures, up to ½in (1cm) long, formed in the inflorescences of grasses (notably rye).

CNICUS

A genus containing a single species of thistlelike annual, native to the Mediterranean region. Widely naturalized in most of Europe, having escaped from cultivation as a medicinal herb in the Middle Ages, it is now grown, mainly in central Europe, for the pharmaceutical industry. The name *Cnicus* comes from the Greek *knekos*, "thistle," which in turn may be derived from *chnizein*, "to injure," referring to the plant's extreme prickliness.

Cnicus benedictus (blessed thistle, holy thistle)
Spiny annual with a cylindrical taproot and branched, hairy stems. Leaves are gray-green, pinnately lobed or toothed. Solitary flowers, up to 1½in (4cm) across, have yellow florets and bristly bracts. H 26in (65cm), S 12in (30cm).

5–8

CODONOPSIS

Thirty species of perennial climbers belong to this genus, which is distributed through the Himalayas to Japan. *C. tangshen*, found in upland fields in China, is extensively cultivated there as a medicinal plant. Most of the species are in cultivation, often grown on banks and trained over supports or larger plants, so that the intricately patterned insides of the flowers can be appreciated. The name is from the Greek *kodon*, "bell," and *opsis*, "resemblance," because the flowers are bell-shaped.

Codonopsis tangshen (*dang shen*)
Twining climber with spindle-shaped root and small toothed leaves with a downy surface. Solitary, bell-shaped, yellow to olive green flowers, veined and spotted purple inside, appear in summer. H 6ft (2m).

5–9

COCA, see *Erythroxylum coca*, p.124
COCKLEBUR, see *Agrimonia eupatoria*, p.76; *Xanthium strumarium*, p.222
COCO GRASS, see *Cyperus rotundus*, p.115
COCOA, see *Theobroma cacao*, p.210

COFFEA

Forty or so species of mainly evergreen shrubs and small trees belong to this genus, which occurs in tropical Asia and Africa. *C. arabica*, native to northeastern Africa, is the most widely grown species; it suits containers under cover in cool climates, as does its compact variant *C. a.* 'Nana'. Coffee drinking was first noted by Leonhart Rauwolf, a German traveler to the Middle East, in 1573. Europeans acquired the taste in the 17th century; since then coffee has become a crop of global importance.

Coffea arabica (coffee, Arabian coffee)
Evergreen shrub with glossy leaves, up to 4in (10cm) long, and dense, axillary clusters of fragrant white flowers in late summer. Ripe fruits are red, ⅝in (1.5cm) long, with 2 seeds ("beans"). H 22ft (7m), S 4ft (1.2m).

COLCHICUM

There are 45 species of cormous perennials in this genus, distributed throughout Europe, northern Africa, and western Asia to western China. *C. autumnale* is found throughout Europe to Ukraine. Despite their toxicity, colchicums are popular garden plants, with large, colorful blooms in late summer and early autumn. They may be grown in borders, rock gardens, under trees, and in damp grassland. *Colchicum* is named after Colchis, an area of Georgia near the Black Sea, where these plants abound.

Colchicum autumnale (autumn crocus, meadow saffron, naked ladies)
Perennial with ovoid corm up to 2½in (6cm) long, and 3–5 linear to lanceolate leaves. Up to 6 pale purple goblet-shaped flowers are produced from late summer, followed by obovoid seed capsules. H 12in (30cm).

5–8

COIX

Six species of annual and perennial grasses make up this tropical Asian genus. *C. lacryma-jobi* is found in swampy places in SE Asia, and has been grown as an ornamental since antiquity. It is an interesting plant for summer bedding in cool areas or in pots under cover. Female flowers are enclosed in a hard, tear-shaped husk; green at first, it turns gray or gray-mauve in autumn; male flowers are borne in clusters at the end of the flower spike. Theophrastus gave the name *Coix* to a reedlike plant.

Coix lacryma-jobi (Job's tears)
Robust, upright annual grass, with linear leaves up to 24in (60cm) long and arching inflorescences in summer. Male flowers are carried at the ends of the spikes, females enclosed in a hard, beanlike case. H 5ft (1.5m), S 4–6in (10–15cm).

A

Colchicum autumnale var. ***album***
A variant with white flowers, which is particularly effective against a background of dark shrubs. H 12in (30cm).

5–8

***Colchicum autumnale* 'Pleniflorum'**
This cultivar is like the species, but produces double flowers with 15–30 narrow petals. Though longer-lasting, the flowers are heavier and less weather-resistant. H 12in (30cm).

5–8

COLA

A genus of about 125 species of tropical African evergreen trees. Cola has been used for centuries as a masticatory in Africa, being exported from the western tropics into arid regions via camel traders, who chewed the seeds to maintain alertness on long, monotonous journeys. Cola nuts are important in social ceremonies in Africa, S America, and Asia, and are often chewed before meals to aid digestion. The name *Cola* probably comes from *kolo*, the Mandingo name for the plant.

Cola nitida (cola, kola, *goora* nut)
Evergreen tree with glossy, obovate leaves up to 8in (20cm) long. Small cream flowers, usually with purple-red markings inside, are followed by large compound fruits, containing up to 10 seeds ("nuts"), 1½–2in (4–5cm) long. H 70ft (20m), S 30–55ft (10–17 m).

COLLINSONIA

This small genus consists of five species of perennials from eastern N America. It includes the important herb *C. canadensis*, which, like many herbs of the mint family, has strongly aromatic foliage. One of its common names is "stone root," which may refer to either its unusually hard roots or its use in treating kidney stones. The genus was named after Peter Collinson, an 18th-century English Quaker, who introduced many N American plants to Britain.

Collinsonia canadensis (horse balm, stone root, richweed)
Tall, lemon-scented perennial with thick, hard rhizomes, erect, ridged stems, and ovate leaves up to 6in (15cm) long. Pale yellow tubular flowers are borne in summer. H 2–4ft (60cm–1.2m), S 18–36in (45–90cm).

3–9

COFFEE, see *Coffea arabica*, above
COHOSH, see *Cimicifuga racemosa*, p.107
COLA, see *Cola nitida*, above
COLIC ROOT, see *Aletris farinosa*, p.232; *Dioscorea villosa*, p.273
COLORADO COUGH ROOT, see *Ligusticum porteri*, p.303
COLTSFOOT, see *Tussilago farfara*, p.216
COMFREY, see *Symphytum officinale*, p.206
COMPASS PLANT, see *Lactuca serriola*, p.146
CONDURANGO, see *Marsdenia cundurango*, p.309
CONEFLOWER, see *Echinacea*, p.121
CONEHEAD THYME, see *THYMUS*, pp.212–3

COMPTONIA

This genus consists of one species of deciduous shrub, native to eastern N America, found in scrub on poor, dry, acid soils, especially in coastal regions. The genus is closely related to *Myrica*. *C. peregrina* is a distinctive, aromatic plant for acid soils, but it is seldom seen in cultivation. Its scent is more noticeable in early morning and evening. *Comptonia* is named after Henry Compton (1632–1713), Bishop of London, who was an expert on trees and shrubs.

Comptonia peregrina (sweet fern)
Shrub with linear, pinnately toothed leaves up to 5in (12cm) long, clad in rust-colored hairs. In summer, male flowers are catkinlike; females smaller and spherical, followed by small, shiny, brown nutlets. H 3–5ft (1–1.5cm), S 2–4ft (60cm–1.2m).

2–7

CONIUM

Two species of biennials make up this genus, which occurs in northern temperate regions. *C. maculatum* is a common wayside plant in Europe and temperate Asia, and naturalized in parts of Australia. Both species are extremely poisonous. White-flowered umbellifers with parsleylike leaves are notoriously difficult to tell apart; some self-seed freely, so they should not be grown near culinary herbs or where children have access. *Conium* is from the Greek *koneion*, "hemlock."

Conium maculatum (hemlock, poison parsley)
Tall, fetid biennial with finely cut, ovate leaves, up to 12in (30cm) long. Stems are purple-spotted. In summer, umbels of small white flowers are followed by tiny, rounded fruits. H 5–10ft (1.5–3m), S 3–4ft (1–1.2m).

5–10

CONVALLARIA

There are three species of rhizomatous perennials in this genus, which occurs in northern temperate regions. The name comes from the Latin *convallis*, "valley," and refers to the plant's natural habitat, while *majalis* signifies the flowering time, May. *C. majalis* is more common in gardens than in the wild in many parts of Europe. In addition to the cultivars described below, lilies of the valley with pink (*C. m.* 'Rosea') and double (*C. m.* 'Prolificans') flowers are seen occasionally.

Convallaria majalis (lily of the valley, May lily)
Creeping perennial with pairs of ovate to elliptic leaves. Racemes of 5–13 white, fragrant, bell-shaped flowers, waxy in texture, appear in late spring, followed by globose, red berries. H 9–12in (23–30cm), S indefinite.

4–8

***Convallaria majalis* 'Albostriata'**
A handsome cultivar with golden-striped leaves. It tends to revert if grown in deep shade. H 9–12in (23–30cm), S indefinite.

4–8

***Convallaria majalis* 'Hardwick Hall'**
This cultivar differs from the species in having broader leaves with gold margins and an occasional gold band down the blade. It forces well. H 18in (45cm), S indefinite.

4–8

CONGA ROOT, see *Petiveria alliacea*, p.174

CONYZA

Fifty or so annuals and perennials comprise this N American genus, which is widely naturalized in Europe, Asia, Australia, and various Pacific islands. *C. canadensis* is a common weed, found in southern parts of Canada and throughout the US into tropical America. Recorded at the Botanic Garden in Blois (northern France) in 1653, it spread widely in 30 years, and appeared in England in 1690. Having no ornamental merit, it was presumably imported as a medicinal plant.

Conyza canadensis (horseweed, Canadian fleabane)
Tall annual with narrow, sometimes toothed leaves. Panicles of tiny thistle-like flowers, with green-white to pale mauve ray florets and yellow discs, appear in late summer and early autumn. H 4ft (1.2m), S 24in (60cm).

4–10

CORIANDRUM

Two species of slender, upright annuals belong to this genus, which is native to southwestern Asia and northern Africa. *C. sativum* (coriander) is a weed of cultivated and waste ground. One of the oldest known herbs, it has been cultivated for over 3,000 years. It is mentioned in Sanskrit, ancient Egyptian, Greek, and Latin texts, as well as in virtually all medieval herbals. *Coriandrum* comes from the Greek *koriannon*, a type of bedbug that is thought to smell like coriander leaves.

Coriandrum sativum (coriander, *cilantro*)
Erect annual with pungently aromatic, lobed to pinnately divided leaves. In summer, white to mauve flowers are followed by pale brown fruits that have a fruity scent when ripe. H 6–28in (15–70cm), S 4–12in (10–30cm).

A

CORNUS

Found mostly in temperate regions of the northern hemisphere, this is a genus of some 45 species of trees, shrubs, subshrubs, and perennials. *C. officinalis* is a native of China, Japan, and Korea. Most *cornus* are ornamental and are easily grown in mixed borders, or as specimen plants, for their flowers, fruits, often interesting bark, and good autumn color. The name *Cornus* comes from the Latin *cornu*, "horn," because the wood of some species is extremely hard.

Cornus officinalis (Japanese cornel, Japanese cornelian cherry)
Deciduous, large shrub or small tree with peeling bark and ovate leaves, richly colored in autumn. Tiny yellow flowers appear along the bare branches in late winter, followed by bright red fruits. H and S 30ft (10m).

4–8

CORYDALIS

About 300 species of annuals and perennials, commonly tuberous and often floppy in habit, make up this genus, widely distributed through the northern temperate zone and tropical montane regions. *C. solida* is found in woods in Europe and western Asia. Although related to poppies, *Corydalis* species are quite different in appearance, with fernlike leaves and spurred, tubular flowers. *C. solida* and *C. cava* have both been known in horticulture as *C. bulbosa*.

Corydalis solida (bulbous corydalis)
Tuberous perennial with upright stem, and segmented, ferny leaves. Terminal racemes of dull purple flowers with a long, nearly straight spur, appear in spring. H 4–8in (10–20cm), S 4–6in (10–15cm).

5–8

***Corydalis solida* 'George Baker'**
This cultivar has deep rose-pink flowers. H 4–8in (10–20cm), S 4–6in (10–15cm).

5–8

CRATAEGUS

A genus of about 280 deciduous, often thorny, shrubs and trees is found throughout northern temperate regions. *C. pinnatifida* is native to northern China. *C. laevigata*, found mainly in northern Europe, and *C. monogyna* are very similar, the latter differing mainly in having more deeply lobed leaves, and fruits with one stony seed rather than two. *C. monogyna* occurs throughout Europe as far as Afghanistan. Hybrids between *C. laevigata* and *C. monogyna*, known as *C.* x *media*, are common.

Crataegus laevigata (hawthorn, may, quickset)
Deciduous shrub or small tree, densely branched and spiny, with lobed, obovate leaves. Scented white flowers appear in late spring, followed by dark red, egg-shaped fruits. H 15–20ft (5–6m), S 15–18ft (5–5.5m).

4–7

COPAIBA, COPAIVA, see *Copaifera lansdorffii*, p.266
COPPER BEECH, see *Fagus sylvatica*, Purpurea Group, p.127
CORIANDER, see *Coriandrum sativum*, above
CORK TREE, CORKWOOD TREE, see *Duboisia myoporoides*, p.121; *Phellodendron amurense*, p.175
CORN, see *Zea mays*, p.223
CORN MINT, see *MENTHA*, pp.158–9
CORN POPPY, see *Papaver rhoeas*, p.171
CORNBIND, CHINESE, see *Polygonum multiflorum*, p.333
CORNFLOWER, see *Centaurea cyanus*, p.104
CORSICAN MINT, see *MENTHA*, pp.158–9

***Crataegus laevigata* 'Paul's Scarlet'**
This cultivar has double cerise flowers. It arose as a sport of *C. laevigata* 'Rosea Flore Pleno' (which has paler pink flowers) in a garden in Hertfordshire, England in 1858. H and S 20ft (6m).

4–7

***Crataegus laevigata* 'Rosea'**
This cultivar has single pink flowers. It is similar in all respects to the species, except that the flowers are pink. H and S 20ft (6m).

4–7

Crataegus pinnatifida (Chinese haw)
A hardy, deciduous small tree with short thorns and deeply lobed leaves. White flowers with pink anthers are borne in spring, followed by red fruits over ½in (1cm) across. H and S up to 20ft (6m).

4–7

***Crataegus laevigata* 'Plena'**
This cultivar has double white flowers. Though indistinguishable from the species at a distance, the blossom is most attractive at close quarters. It has been grown in gardens since c.1770. H and S 20ft (6m).

4–7

CRITHMUM

This genus contains a single species, found among rocks and cliffs of the Black Sea, the Mediterranean, the English Channel, and the Atlantic coasts of Europe. *Crithmum* is from the Greek *krithe*, "barley," and refers to the ribbed, ovate seeds. The common name "samphire" is derived from the French *sampière*, a contraction of *herbe de Saint Pierre* (St. Peter having been a fisherman). Also known as sea fennel, it bears little resemblance to true fennel (see *Foeniculum vulgare*, p.128).

Crithmum maritimum (samphire, rock samphire, sea fennel)
Fleshy, spreading perennial with branched, ridged stems and glaucous leaves with rounded, linear-lanceolate segments. Tiny yellow-green flowers are produced in umbels in summer. H and S 6–12in (15–30cm).

7–9

CROCUS

A genus of about 80 species of hardy, corm-forming perennials, which grow wild in the Mediterranean region, and north and east as far as western China. Almost every species is ornamental; many are grown as garden plants, or as specimens for the alpine house, for their show of flowers in autumn, winter, and spring. *C. sativus* is a sterile triploid not known in the wild. The name *Crocus* is derived from the Greek *krokas* "thread" and alludes to the stigmas.

Crocus sativus (saffron crocus)
Perennial with linear leaves, each with a white midrib, which appear in autumn with lilac-purple flowers. Flowers have purple filaments with yellow anthers, and a red style with branches up to 1¼in (3cm) long, followed by 3-valved capsules. H and S 4in (10cm).

4–8

COSTMARY, see *TANACETUM*, pp.208–9
COTTON, see *Gossypium herbaceum*, p.136
COTTONWEED, see *Gnaphalium uliginosum*, p.135
COUCH GRASS, see *Elymus repens*, p.122
COW PARSNIP, see *Heracleum sphondylium*, p.138
COWHAGE, COWITCH, see *Mucuna pruriens*, p.314
COWSLIP, see *Primula veris*, p.183
CRAB'S EYES, see *Abrus precatorius*, p.70
CRAMP BARK, see *Viburnum opulus*, p.219
CRANESBILL, see *Geranium*, p.133

CROTON

Some 750 shrubs, trees, and perennials are included in this genus, which is found worldwide in tropical and subtropical regions. *C. tiglium* is found in mixed forest from India to Malaysia. It is an unpleasant smelling, very poisonous plant. *Croton* is from the Greek *kroton*, "a tick," and refers to the appearance of the ovoid, light brown seeds. The ornamental foliage plants that are commonly known as "crotons" belong to the genus *Codiaeum* and do not have the same properties as *Croton*.

Croton tiglium (croton)
Evergreen tree, with pointed, metallic green to bronze leaves up to 7in (17cm) long. Racemes of tiny yellow-green flowers appear in spring, males at the top and females at the base, followed by fruits containing a single large seed. H 15–70ft (5–20m), S 40ft (12m).

CRYPTOTAENIA

A genus of four species of annuals and perennials occurs in northern temperate regions and montane, tropical Africa. *C. canadensis* is found in woodland ravines and on river banks from Manitoba to Texas and in parts of Vietnam, China, and Japan. Popular for its celery-like odor and flavor, it is widely distributed and cultivated as a vegetable and a pot herb, both in Japan and by Japanese communities in other parts of the world.

Cryptotaenia canadensis (honewort, Japanese wild chervil, *mitsuba*)
Upright, succulent perennial with creeping rootstock, hollow stalks, and trifoliate leaves with toothed leaflets. Minute white flowers appear in umbels in the summer. H 3ft (1m), S 12–36in (30–90cm).

4–9

CUCUMIS

A genus of about 30 climbing or scrambling annuals and perennials native to tropical Asia and Africa. *C. sativus*, native to India, has been cultivated there since earliest times and was known to ancient Greeks and Romans. There are numerous cucumber variants worldwide, from self-fertile, female cultivars to hardier ridge cucumbers and small-fruited gherkins. Most are picked when immature for use as vegetables, although ripe fruits contain seeds that are rich in edible oils.

Cucumis sativus (cucumber)
Trailing annual with triangular-ovate leaves up to 7in (18cm) long and across. Yellow, funnel-shaped flowers appear in spring: males in the axils; females, larger and usually solitary, are followed by ovoid to elongate fruits containing white ovate seeds. H 6ft (2m).

A

CUCURBITA

This genus includes 27 species of prostrate or climbing annuals and perennials, native to tropical and subtropical America. *C. maxima* was first grown in Peru and reached Europe after the Spanish conquest of 1532. *C. moschata*, also known as pumpkin or squash, may have originated in Mexico, but was known in S and N America 5,000 years ago. *C. pepo*, which is Mexican in origin, has been grown in southern N America for over 8,000 years.

Cucurbita maxima (pumpkin, winter squash)
Variable, trailing annual with 5-angled stems and toothed leaves. Yellow flowers in summer are followed by fleshy fruits that may be green, yellow, orange, or red when ripe, filled with white seeds. H 3ft (1m), S 6ft (2m).

A

CUMINUM

Found wild from the Mediterranean to the Sudan and central Asia, this genus contains two species of annuals. Cumin was a favorite condiment in ancient Greek times. In Greek culture cumin also symbolized avarice, and miserly people were said to have eaten it. The name *Cuminum* comes from a Greek word of Hebrew origin for a plant resembling *Carum carvi* (caraway, see p.101). Although similar, they have distinctive aromas and flavors and cannot be used interchangeably.

Cuminum cyminum (cumin, *comino*, *jeera*)
Slender annual with dark green leaves divided into linear or threadlike segments. Umbels of tiny white or pink flowers are followed by bristly, ovoid seeds. H 6–12in (15–30cm), S 3–4in (8–10cm).

A

CURCUMA

Forty species of perennials belong to this genus, found in tropical Asia and Australia. *C. aromatica* is a native of Indian teak forests; *C. longa* is found in seasonally dry forest in India. Many have large rhizomes or tubers used as spices, sources of starch, and dyes. *C. longa* is a source of orange and yellow dyes for silk and wool, traditional coloring for the robes of Buddhist monks. The name comes from *kurkum*, the Arabic name for these plants.

Curcuma aromatica (wild turmeric)
Perennial with a large rhizome, and pointed, oblong leaves up to 24in (60cm) long. Yellow-white, pink-tinged flowers emerge from pale green lower bracts and pink upper bracts of a dense inflorescence, borne on a separate stem in spring. H 3ft (1m), S indefinite.

CROTON, see *Croton tiglium*, above
CUBEB, see *Piper cubeba*, p.178
CUCHAY, see *ALLIUM*, pp.80–1
CUCKOO FLOWER, see *Cardamine pratensis*, p.101
CUCUMBER, see *Cucumis sativus*, above
CUDWEED, see *ARTEMISIA*, pp.88–9
CULANTRO, see *Eryngium foetidum*, p.124
CULVER'S ROOT, see *Veronicastrum virginicum*, p.218
CUMIN, see *Cuminum cyminum*, above
CURAÇAO ALOE, see *Aloe vera*, p.81
CURRANT, see *Ribes*, p.190
CURRY LEAF, see *Murraya koenigii*, p.161
CURRY PLANT, see *Helichrysum italicum*, p.137

Curcuma longa (turmeric, *haridra*)
Perennial with a large rhizome and pointed, oblong-elliptic leaves up to 20in (50cm) long. Yellow flowers accompanied by pale green lower bracts and pink upper bracts are borne in a dense inflorescence in summer. H 3ft (1m), S indefinite.

CYMBOPOGON

This genus of 56 species of perennial, occasionally annual, aromatic grasses occurs in the tropics and warm temperate regions of Eurasia. *C. citratus* is found on savanna in southern India and Sri Lanka. As well as *C. citratus*, several species are grown for their oils, which are important in perfumery, including *C. flexuosus* (east Indian lemon grass). The name is from the Greek *kymbe*, "boat," and *pogon*, "beard," referring to the appearance of the floral spikelets.

Cymbopogon citratus (lemon grass)
Clump-forming perennial with robust, often canelike stems, and lemon-scented, linear leaves up to 36in (90cm) long. Lax panicles of spikelets appear in summer, though rarely if in cultivation. H 5ft (1.5m), S 3ft (1m).

CYNARA

This genus includes 10 species of frost-hardy perennials native to the Mediterranean region and northern Africa. *C. cardunculus,* Scolymus Group, is an architectural plant, suited to the back of a large border or as a feature in the herb garden. Unknown in the wild, it was probably developed from *C. cardunculus* at a very early date. *Cynara* comes from the Greek *kuon*, "dog," referring to the supposed resemblance of the involucral (flower-head bracts) spines to dogs' teeth.

***Cynara cardunculus,* Scolymus Group** (globe artichoke)
Giant perennial, with downy, gray-green, deeply cut, leathery leaves, up to 32in (80cm) long and 16in (40cm) across. Large, thistlelike flowers with purple florets are produced in summer. H 6ft (2m), S 4ft (1.2m).

9

CYNOGLOSSUM

A genus of about 55 species of hardy biennials, with some annuals and perennials, is widely distributed in temperate regions. *C. officinale* is found in central Europe, southern and central Russia, and central Asia in dry grassy places, especially near coasts. The name *Cynoglossum* is derived from the Greek *kunoglosson*, "dog's tongue," after the shape and texture of the leaves. The common name "rats-and-mice" refers to the odor of the foliage.

Cynoglossum officinale (houndstongue, rats-and-mice)
Erect biennial with elliptic-oblong, hairy, gray-green leaves, 2–5in (5–12cm) long. Maroon flowers appear in summer, followed by fruits covered in fine hooked spines. H 32–36in (80cm–1m), S 12–24in (30–60cm).

4–9

CYPERUS

Some 600 species of rhizomatous, grasslike annuals and perennials belong to this genus, which occurs worldwide. It includes such plants as *C. involucratus* (umbrella grass), a popular house plant; *C. papyrus*, the Egyptian paper rush; and *C. esculentus* var. *sativus* (chufa or edible tiger nut). *C. rotundus* is a cosmopolitan plant of damp places, and is among the world's most invasive weeds. *Cyperus* is from the Greek word for sedge.

Cyperus rotundus (nut grass, sedge root, coco grass)
Perennial with a slender, scaly rhizome, and linear leaves, up to 24in (60cm) long and ½in (1cm) wide. An inflorescence of tiny flowers with red-brown husks in summer is followed by black, 3-angled nuts. H 4–24in (10–60cm), S indefinite.

3–10

CYPRIPEDIUM

A genus of 35 species of perennial, terrestrial orchids, found in C and N America, Europe, and Asia; *C. parviflorum* var. *pubescens* is found in N America. These choice plants for the rock garden or woodland border are slow growing and difficult. Collecting slipper orchids from the wild for horticultural and medicinal use has been a major factor in their increasing rarity in the wild. *Cypripedium* is from the Greek *Kypris*, "Venus," and *pedilon*, "slipper," from the inflated shape of the flower lip.

Cypripedium parviflorum var. ***pubescens*** (larger yellow lady's slipper, nerve root, American valerian)
Rhizomatous perennial with 3–4 ovate-oblong leaves. Solitary flowers, with twisted petals and a yellow lip, appear in early summer. H 12–24in (30–60cm), S 9–16in (23–40cm).

3–8

CUSCUS, see *Vetiveria zizanioides*, p.219
CUSPARIA BARK, see *Galipea officinalis*, p.285
CUTLEAF BIRCH, see *Betula pendula* 'Laciniata', p.93
CYPRESS OAK, see *Quercus robur* f. *fastigiata*, p.187
CYPRUS TURPENTINE, see *Pistacia terebinthus*, p.178

CYTISUS

More than 30 species of evergreen and deciduous shrubs and small trees belong to this genus, which occurs in northern Africa, western Asia, and Europe. *C. scoparius*, a native of heaths, waste ground, and woods in Europe, is a familiar plant in the wild and in cultivation. Most of the variants listed in catalogs are, in fact, hybrids, and are not suitable for medicinal use. The name *Cytisus* comes from the Greek *kytisos*, a term used in ancient times to describe various woody legumes.

Cytisus scoparius (broom, Scotch broom)
Erect shrub with green, 5-angled twigs and small, mostly trifoliate leaves, about ¾in (2cm) long. In summer, bright yellow pea flowers are followed by black pods, 1–1½in (2.5–4cm) long. H and S 2–6ft (60cm–2m).

5–8

Cytisus scoparius* var. *prostratus
This variety is low-growing, with arching, overlapping stems and gray-green foliage. H 8in (20cm), S 4–6ft (1.2–2m).

5–8

DAPHNE

Fifty or so species of deciduous and evergreen shrubs belong to this genus, occurring in Europe, northern Africa, and Asia. Daphnes are choice, small shrubs for borders and containers, though certain species, such as the Chinese *D. genkwa*, may be hard to grow. *Daphne* is the Greek word for laurel, perhaps so called because some species have laurel-like leaves; in legend, the nymph Daphne was saved from Apollo's advances by being changed into a laurel tree.

Daphne genkwa
Upright, sparsely branched, deciduous shrub with light green, lanceolate to ovate leaves, 1¼–2½in (3–6cm) long. Clusters of slightly fragrant, lilac flowers appear in the axils before the new leaves. H 3ft (1m), S 12–15in (30–38cm).

5–7

DATURA

There are only eight species of tropical annuals or short-lived perennials in this genus, since the shrubby species are now included among the *Brugmansia*. *D. stramonium* is native to N and S America. All thorn apples are poisonous but several are grown as ornamentals for their large, often scented, trumpet-shaped flowers. The name *Datura* derives from *dhât*, the Hindi word for these plants, which were used as a poison by the *thuggi*, bands of robbers and assassins in India.

Datura stramonium (jimson weed, thorn apple, devil's apple)
Bushy annual with unpleasant-smelling, elliptic to ovate leaves, up to 7in (18cm) long. White, funnel-shaped flowers appear in summer, followed by prickly, ovoid capsules containing black seeds. H 6ft (2m), S 4ft (1.2m).

A

DAUCUS

A genus of 22 species of hairy annuals and biennials, distributed through temperate regions in both hemispheres. Only *D. carota* is common in cultivation, being grown as a vegetable, medicinal herb, and fodder crop. It grows wild near the sea in Europe, temperate Asia, and northern Africa, and is widely naturalized in N America and elsewhere. It is one of the easier white-flowered umbellifers to identify in a notoriously difficult family, which contains many poisonous species.

Daucus carota (wild carrot, Queen Anne's lace)
Hardy biennial with fernlike leaves. Tiny white flowers appear in summer, in umbels up to 3in (7cm) across, with a single purple central flower. Ovoid fruits have spiny ridges. H 1–3ft (30cm–1m), S 6–24in (15–60cm).

3–10

DAISY, ENGLISH, see *Bellis*, p.92
DAMIANA, see *Turnera diffusa* var. *aphrodisiaca*, p.365
DANDELION, see *Taraxacum*, p.210
DAWYCK BEECH, see *Fagus sylvatica* 'Dawyck', p.127
DEADLY NIGHTSHADE, see *Atropa belladonna*, p.91
DEVIL'S APPLE, see *Datura stramonium*, above
DEVIL'S APPLES, see *Mandragora officinarum*, p.156
DEVIL'S BIT, see *Chamaelirium luteum*, p.258
DEVIL'S CLAW, see *Harpagophytum procumbens*, p.291

Daucus carota subsp. *sativus* (carrot)
The cultivated carrot is similar to the species except for its large, succulent, bright orange taproot. It is grown as a hardy annual for use as a vegetable and as a hardy biennial for medicinal use in the second year. H and S 12–15in (30–38cm).

3–10

DELPHINIUM

A genus of some 250 species of biennials and perennials, found in northern temperate regions and central African mountains; *D. staphisagria* is a Mediterranean species. Delphiniums are closely related to monkshoods (*Aconitum* species, see p.72). Both are poisonous, but widely grown for their fine blue flowers. The common name "stavesacre" is from *staphis*, "raisin," and *agria*, "wild." *Delphinium* is from the Greek *delphis*, "dolphin," which the flowers of some species resemble.

Delphinium staphisagria (stavesacre)
Hairy biennial with stout stems and glossy, downy, palmate leaves. Dense racemes of small, dusky purple-blue, short-spurred flowers appear in late spring and early summer. H 5ft (1.5m), S 18–30in (45–75cm).

9

DEVIL'S DUNG, see *Ferula assa-foetida*, p.127
DEWPLANT, see *Drosera rotundifolia*, p.120

DENDRANTHEMA

Formerly classified as *Chrysanthemum*, this genus consists of 20 species of aromatic, mainly frost-hardy perennials, which grow wild in Europe and central and eastern Asia. It includes the florists' chrysanthemum, *D.* x *grandiflorum*, a complex hybrid group of perennials raised in China before 500BC from *D. indicum* and other species. They bear clusters of large, single or double flowers, up to 12in (30cm) across with white, yellow, bronze, pink, or red ray florets.

Dendranthema* x *grandiflorum
(florists' chrysanthemum, mulberry-leaved chrysanthemum)
Perennial with branched erect, or spreading stems and strongly scented, pinnately lobed leaves up to 5in (12cm) long. Flowers appear from late summer. H 1–7ft (30cm–2.2m), S to 3ft (1m).

6–8

DENDROBIUM

Over 1,000 species of orchids belong to this genus, found through eastern Asia to Australia. Most are epiphytic or lithophytic (rarely terrestrial) perennials. *D. nobile* is found from northeastern India to China, Laos, and Thailand. It is grown worldwide for its lovely flowers, described as smelling of grass in the morning, honey at noon, and primroses in the evening. *Dendrobium* is from the Greek *dendron*, "tree," and *bios*, "life," referring to these orchids' tree-dwelling habit.

Dendrobium nobile
Evergreen, epiphytic perennial with erect pseudobulbs, 12–20in (30–50cm) tall, and oppositely arranged, ovate leaves. Mauve, scented flowers, 2½–3in (6–8cm) across with a maroon, yellow- to white-banded throat, appear in winter and early spring. H 12–24in (30–60cm), S 3ft (1m).

DIANTHUS

A genus of about 300 species of hardy and half-hardy, evergreen or semievergreen annuals, biennials, and perennials, found from Eurasia to S Africa; *D. caryophyllus* is native to southern Europe and northern Africa, *D. chinensis* to eastern Asia. Pinks have long been cultivated for their fragrant flowers. Cultivars of *D. chinensis* provide excellent bedding plants for dry, alkaline sites. The word "carnation" has the same origin as "coronation"; pinks were used for celebratory garlands in ancient Greece.

Dianthus caryophyllus (clove pink, carnation, gillyflower)
Evergreen perennial, with a woody base, and 4-angled stems with lanceolate, gray-green leaves. Small, deep pink to purple, clove-scented flowers appear in a lax cyme in summer. H 8–20in (20–50cm), S 4–10in (10–25cm).

5–8

Dianthus chinensis (rainbow pink, Chinese pink)
Bushy, slow-growing annual, biennial, or short-lived perennial. Leaves are pointed and light green. Red, pink, white, or spotted flowers with blue stamens appear in summer and early autumn. H and S 6–12in (15–30cm).

4–7

***Dianthus chinensis* 'Strawberry Parfait'**
A very compact plant, good for bedding and containers, especially with gray-leaved companions. White, pink-flushed flowers, 2in (5cm) across, with red centers, produce well all summer and into autumn. H and S 8in (20cm).

4–7

Dictamnus albus* var. *purpureus
This variety has pink flowers, striped in darker pink and is more commonly seen in cultivation than the species. H 16–32in (40–80cm), S 10–18in (24–45cm).

2–9

DICTAMNUS

Six species of perennials were formerly included in this genus, but it is now regarded as monotypic. *D. albus*, found in dry scrub and pine woods from eastern Asia to southwestern Europe, is an attractive, long-lived plant for borders. It is rich in volatile oils which can be ignited as they evaporate, leaving the plant undamaged. *Dictamnus* is named after the similarly-scented *Origanum dictamnus* (see pp.168–9), which, in turn, is probably named after Mount Dikte in Crete.

Dictamnus albus (gas plant, dittany, burning bush)
Aromatic perennial that has gland-dotted leaves with 3–6 pairs of leaflets. Racemes of white or pink flowers with long stamens appear in summer, followed by capsules containing black seeds. H 16–32in (40–80cm), S 10–18in (24–45cm).

2–9

DIGITALIS

This genus of about 20 species of biennials and perennials occurs in Europe, northern Africa, and western and central Asia; *D. lanata* is found in eastern Europe. Although very poisonous, foxgloves are popular for their elegant spires of flowers. Both *D. purpurea* and *D. lanata* are grown commercially, but the latter is favored as a source of digoxin for the pharmaceutical industry. *Digitalis* is from the Latin *digitus*, "finger," because the flowers fit neatly over the fingers.

Digitalis lanata (woolly foxglove)
Biennial or short-lived perennial with usually one stem only, and stalkless, lanceolate leaves up to 5in (12cm) long. A spike of cream to fawn, veined flowers is produced in summer, followed by many-seeded capsules. H 3ft (1m), S 10in (24cm).

4–10

DILL, see *Anethum graveolens*, p.83
DITTANY, see *Dictamnus albus*, above
DITTANY OF CRETE, see *Origanum dictamnus*, p.168

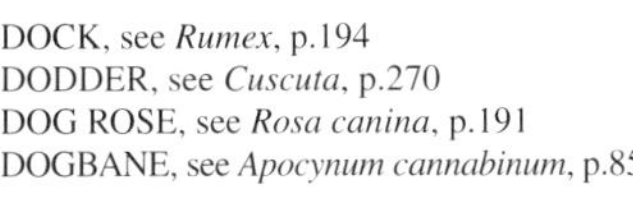

DOCK, see *Rumex*, p.194
DODDER, see *Cuscuta*, p.270
DOG ROSE, see *Rosa canina*, p.191
DOGBANE, see *Apocynum cannabinum*, p.85
DOGWOOD, see *Cornus*, p.112
DOKU-DAMI, see *Houttuynia cordata*, p.139
DOUBLE CHAMOMILE, see *Chamaemelum nobile* 'Flore Pleno', p.105
DRAGON PLANT, see *Arisaema consanguineum*, p.87

DIOSCOREA

About 600 species make up this large genus of tropical and subtropical twining climbers. The hardiest of the commercially cultivated yams is *D. opposita,* which thrives in northern parts of China and in Japan. A few are grown as ornamentals and many are cultivated as food crops in warm regions. Some of the edible yams produce very large tubers – those of *D. alata* (white yam) can reach 110lb (50kg). The common name "yam" is from the W African dialect word meaning "eat."

Dioscorea opposita (Chinese yam, cinnamon yam)
Perennial climber with vertical tubers up to 3ft (1m) long, and heart-shaped leaves. Tiny, white, cinnamon-scented flowers are produced in axillary spikes (male and female separate), followed by 3-angled capsules. H 10ft (3m).

10

DIOSPYROS

Nearly 500 species of evergreen and deciduous trees and shrubs belong to this mainly tropical genus, which occurs in southern Europe, N and S America, Africa, Asia, and Australia. The trees are best known as the source of valuable ebonies. A few are grown for their fruit. *D. kaki* normally requires both male and female trees for successful fruiting. Hermaphrodite and dwarf cultivars are suited to growing under cover. *D. lotus* (date plum) and *D. virginiana* (persimmon) are also attractive.

Diospyros kaki (Chinese persimmon, Japanese persimmon, kaki)
Deciduous tree with large, ovate leaves, orange-red in autumn. Yellow flowers appear in spring: males in groups of 2–5; females solitary; yellow to orange-red fruits are up to 3in (7.5cm) across. H 30–50ft (10–15m), S 30ft (10m).

6–9

DODONAEA

Some 50 species of evergreen trees and shrubs make up this genus, occurring in the tropics and subtropics. *D. viscosa,* found in rainforests in southern Africa, Australia, and Mexico, and *D. v.* 'Purpurea' are popular garden shrubs, making good hedges for windy sites and handsome foliage plants for containers. *Dodonaea* is named after Rembert Dodoens (1517–85), a Flemish royal physician and professor of medicine at Leiden, who published a herbal (*Cruÿdboeck*) in 1554 .

Dodonaea viscosa (sticky hop bush, native hops)
Dense, spreading shrub or small tree with sticky, yellow-green, elliptic leaves up to 5in (13cm) long. Green-yellow flowers appear in summer, followed by round, black seeds in 3-winged cases. H 10ft (3m), S 5ft (1.5m).

***Dodonaea viscosa* 'Purpurea'**
This variety has bronze-purple foliage and the seed capsules are purple-red. H 6ft (2m), S 5ft (1.5m).

DRIMIA

This genus consists of about 100 species of bulbous perennials, found throughout the Mediterranean region and Portugal; *D. maritima* is native to coastal sands and dry, rocky ground. Drimias are widely cultivated for commercial use but they are also grown as ornamental garden plants for their impressive flower spikes, rather like those of foxtail lilies (*Eremurus* species), in early autumn. Although easily grown in positions that dry out during summer, they are shy-flowering in northern regions.

Drimia maritima (squill, sea onion)
Robust perennial with a globose bulb up to 6in (15cm) across, and fleshy, glaucous leaves, up to 3ft (1m) long. Small star-shaped, white flowers are produced in a dense spike after the foliage has withered. H 5ft (1.5m), S 12–18in (30–45cm).

9

DRIMYS

This genus contains about 40 species of evergreen, aromatic trees and shrubs. It has an odd distribution, from Mexico to southern S America, and from the Malay Peninsula to New Guinea, Australia, and New Zealand; *D. winteri* is native to Chile and Argentina, and is the only species common in cultivation. The dwarf *D. w.* var. *andina* flowers when only 12in (30cm) high and is ideal for small gardens. Also grown is the closely related *Tasmannia lanceolata*, formerly classified as *D. lanceolata*.

Drimys winteri (Winter's bark)
Tall, conical, often shrubby tree, with elliptic to lanceolate, glossy, pointed leaves up to 6in (15cm) long, and loose clusters of fragrant, star-shaped, ivory-white flowers in late spring and early summer. 50ft (H 15m), S 25ft (8m).

9

DROSERA

About 100 species of evergreen, carnivorous perennials belong to this diverse genus, which occurs worldwide; *D. rotundifolia* is found in wetlands throughout temperate Eurasia and N America. Many sundews are grown by collectors of carnivorous plants and the more common species are sold as pot plants. The name comes from the Greek *drosos*, "dew," and refers to the sticky droplets of digestive enzymes on the leaf hairs, which trap and ingest insects.

Drosera rotundifolia (round-leaved sundew, *rosée du soleil*, dewplant)
Small perennial, occasionally annual, with a rosette of red-green, sticky, rounded leaves. Stems of 5-petaled, white flowers appear in summer, followed by capsules of winged seeds. H 4–6in (10–15cm), S 3in (8cm).

3–10

DRYOBALANOPS

Seven species of SE Asian rainforest trees belong to this genus. *D. aromatica*, found in Malaysia, Sumatra, and Borneo, has a long history of use in Eastern medicine. It was mentioned by Marco Polo as being exported from northern Sumatra and Johore to the Middle East since at least the sixth century AD. Its uses include embalming; organic matter has been found preserved in borneol after 2,000 years. The name, from the Greek *drys*, "tree," *balanos*, "acorn," and *opsis*, "look," refers to the fruits.

Dryobalanops aromatica (Borneo camphor, borneol)
Tall evergreen tree with flaking bark and broadly ovate, leathery leaves. Small white flowers appear during summer, every 3–4 years. Fruit is a 3-celled nut. H 130–160ft (40–50m), rarely to 200ft (60m), S 50ft (15m).

DRYOPTERIS

A cosmopolitan genus of deciduous or semi-evergreen, rhizomatous ferns containing some 150 species. *D. filix-mas* is common in Eurasia, N America, and S America, south to Argentina. Many species are grown for their often vase-shaped crowns of fine foliage. Some are demanding in requirements, but several species, including *D. filix-mas*, are easily grown as garden plants, being very hardy and drought-resistant. *D. filix-mas* is very variable in size, and in frond shape.

Dryopteris filix-mas (male fern)
Deciduous or semievergreen fern with thick rhizomes and crowns of broadly lanceolate fronds up to 36in (90cm) long. Spores are released from the undersides of the upper leaflets in summer. H and S 16–36in (40–90cm).

4–9

***Dryopteris filix-mas* 'Crispa Cristata'**
This cultivar differs from the species in being smaller growing and having the leaflets crisped and crested. H and S 12–15in (30–38cm).

4–9

DUKE OF ARGYLL'S TEA-TREE, see *Lycium barbarum*, p.154
DUSTY MILLER GRAPE, see *Vitis vinifera* 'Incana', p.221
DUTCH RUSH, see *Equisetum hyemale*, p.123
DWALE, see *Atropa belladonna*, p.91
DWARF MOUNTAIN PINE, see *Pinus mugo* var. *pumilio*, p.177
DYER'S BUGLOSS, see *Alkanna tinctoria*, p.79
DYER'S GREENWEED, see *Genista tinctoria*, p.132
EAGLE VINE, see *Marsdenia cundurango*, p.309
EAGLEWOOD, see *Aquilaria malaccensis*, p.86

***Dryopteris filix-mas* 'Linearis'**
A cultivar with more slender, graceful fronds than the species. H and S 16–36in (40–90cm).

4–9

DUBOISIA

Three species of trees and shrubs belong to this genus, which occurs in Australasia and New Guinea. *D. myoporoides* is found on sandy soils in open forest, rainforest margins, and coastal dunes in Queensland and New South Wales, Australia, and in New Caledonia and New Guinea. All parts of the plant are poisonous. *Duboisia* is named after Charles Du Bois (1656–1740), treasurer of the East India Company, who compiled a large herbarium.

Duboisia myoporoides (corkwood, cork tree, eyeplant)
Small tree or tall shrub, with soft, spoon-shaped leaves. Tiny white to pale lavender flowers appear from late winter to spring, followed by small, juicy, black berries containing 6–12 seeds. H 40ft (12m), S 6–15ft (2–5m).

ECBALLIUM

Only one species of trailing perennial is included in this genus, which occurs in semiarid and waste areas of the Mediterranean region and western Asia. *E. elaterium* is often recommended as a novelty plant for the border or for containers, because of its explosive fruits, which are gray-green, bristly, and ovoid, up to 2in (5cm) long. The fruits are poisonous and their acrid contents are ejected with considerable force to 6ft (2m) or more and may damage the eyes.

Ecballium elaterium (squirting cucumber)
Tuberous, bushy perennial with stout, hairy stems and gray-green, large, ovate-triangular leaves. Pale yellow flowers with 5 petals are produced in summer, males in a raceme and females solitary. H 12in (30cm), S 24in (60cm).

10

ECHINACEA

Nine species of hardy rhizomatous perennials make up this genus, which is native to eastern US. *E. purpurea* is one of several species, including *E. pallida* and *E. angustifolia*, used by native N Americans, mainly to treat wounds. Coneflowers give a colorful display in the border from midsummer to early autumn, and are excellent for cutting. The generic name *Echinacea* comes from the Greek *echinos*, "hedgehog," and refers to the prickly scales of the flowers' central cone.

Echinacea purpurea (purple coneflower, purple echinacea)
Tall rhizomatous perennial with ovate-lanceolate leaves. Purple, honey-scented, daisylike flowers with conical, orange-brown centers, are produced in summer and early autumn. H 4ft (1.2m), S 18in (45cm).

3–10

***Echinacea purpurea* 'Robert Bloom'**
A richly colored cultivar with brown centers and magenta-pink ray florets that open out wide; raised at Bressingham, England. H 4ft (1.2m), S 20in (50cm).

3–10

EARTH SMOKE, see *Fumaria officinalis*, p.130
EASTERN WHITE CEDAR, see *Thuja occidentalis*, p.211
EAU-DE-COLOGNE MINT, see *MENTHA*, pp.158–9

***Echinacea purpurea* 'White Swan'**
This cultivar makes a smaller plant than the species and has white ray florets. It comes true from seed and is similar to *E. p.* 'White Lustre', a cultivar with drooping ray florets.
H 18–24in (45–60cm), S 12in (30cm)

3–10

ECLIPTA

Four species of annuals and perennials are included in this genus native to warm parts of N and S America and now widely naturalized in Eurasia. Originally from wet and muddy areas of warm temperate and tropical America, *E. prostrata* spread as a weed into many parts of Asia and became important in Ayurvedic and traditional Chinese medicine. The Ayurvedic name, *bhringaraja*, means "ruler of the hair," and refers to its use as a hair restorative.

Eclipta prostrata (false daisy, *bhringaraja*)
Weedy annual with lanceolate, saw-toothed leaves up to 10in (25cm) long. Tiny white, daisylike flowers are borne in summer, followed by tiny fruits, each with a tuft of small teeth. H 4–24in (10–60cm), S 8–36in (20cm–1m).

A

ELETTARIA

About four species of rhizomatous perennials belong to this genus, which occurs in India, Sri Lanka, Sumatra, and Malaysia. *E. cardamomum*, from Indian rainforests, has been exported from the East to Europe via caravan routes since Classical times, mainly for use in perfumery. It can be grown under cover in temperate regions but will rarely flower or fruit. *Elettaria* is derived from *elettari*, the name given to the plant in southwestern India.

Elettaria cardamomum (cardamom)
Rhizomatous perennial with stems bearing lanceolate leaves up to 2ft (60cm) long. White flowers, each with a pink- to violet-striped lip, are borne in a loose spike. Fruits are pale green to fawn, 3-celled capsules, containing aromatic seeds. H 10ft (3m), S indefinite.

8–10

ELEUTHEROCOCCUS

Thirty or so species of deciduous, often prickly, shrubs and trees belong to this genus, which occurs in southern and eastern Asia. *E. senticosus*, from northeastern Asia, is fully hardy but seldom seen in Western herb gardens. It does not appear in traditional Russian medicine, but it was researched by the Russian scientists Brekhman and Dardymov from 1960 onward as part of an extensive study of adaptogenic herbs. Since then it has been widely publicized and marketed as a ginseng.

Eleutherococcus senticosus (Siberian ginseng, *eleuthero*)
Deciduous shrub with stout roots and dark green, palmately divided leaves. Umbels of tiny flowers appear in summer: males lilac to purple; females green, followed by blue-black berries.
H to 22ft (7m), S indefinite.

3–8

ELYMUS

About 100 species make up this genus of hardy perennial grasses, which is common in northern temperate regions. *E. repens* is a persistent weed throughout Europe, northern Africa, Siberia, and N America. Though pernicious to gardeners, it is an important medicinal plant that has appeared in herbals and pharmacopoeias since the time of Dioscorides (first century AD). The name *Elymus* comes from the Greek *elymos*, "a cereal."

Elymus repens (couch grass, twitch, quackgrass) Hardy perennial with far-reaching rhizomes up to ⅛in (3mm) across, and dull green leaves. Stiff, erect flower spikes, with spikelets arranged in zigzag formation, are produced on long stalks in summer.
H 12–36in (30cm–1m), S indefinite.

3–9

EPHEDRA

This genus of about 40 species of shrubs and climbers occurs in southern Europe, northern Africa, Asia, and subtropical America. *E. distachya* is found in southern and eastern Europe. Joint firs have green branches and scale-like, much-reduced leaves. Scientists find the genus of great interest as an evolutionary link between flowering plants and conifers. A few species are cultivated, mainly as ground-cover for dry situations. Male and female plants must be grown together for fruits to be produced.

Ephedra distachya (joint fir, *ma huang*, shrubby horsetail)
Dwarf shrub with upright to sprawling stems, and minute leaves, reduced to scales at the nodes. Male inflorescence is conelike; female is solitary, appearing in early summer, followed by fleshy red fruits. H and S 3ft (1m).

6–9

EDGING BOXWOOD, see *Buxus sempervirens* 'Suffruticosa", p.96
EGYPTIAN ONION, see *ALLIUM*, pp.80–81
EGYPTIAN PRIVET, see *Lawsonia inermis*, p.150
ELDER, see *Sambucus*, p.197
ELECAMPANE, see *Inula helenium*, p.143
ELM, see *Ulmus*, p.217
ENGLISH HOLLY, see *Ilex aquifolium*, p.142
ENGLISH IVY, see *Hedera helix*, p.136
ENGLISH MANDRAKE, see *Bryonia dioica*, p.95
ENGLISH OAK, see *Quercus robur*, p.187
ENGLISH SERPENTARY, see *Polygonum bistorta*, p.181

EPIGAEA

A genus of three species of creeping evergreen subshrubs native to N America and Japan. *E. repens*, from central and eastern N America, is a choice plant for lime-free soil in rock gardens, raised beds, and containers; it combines well with dwarf rhododendrons and conifers. It does not transplant successfully from the wild and is a protected plant in some states. *Epigaea* comes from the Greek *epi*, "upon," and *gaia*, "the earth"; *repens* is the Latin word for "creeping."

Epigaea repens (trailing arbutus, Mayflower)
Prostrate evergreen shrub with leathery, glossy leaves up to 3in (8cm) long. In spring, clusters of white or pink, spicily fragrant flowers are followed by globose capsules containing numerous seeds. H 4in (10cm), S 12–20in (30–50cm).

2–7

Equisetum hyemale (Dutch rush, rough horsetail)
Perennial with upright, glaucous, unbranched stems that remain green in winter. The swollen joints are banded and have tiny blunt teeth. The spore-producing "cones" ripen in summer. H 28–36in (70cm–1m), S indefinite.

3–11

EPIMEDIUM

About 25 species of semi-evergreen or evergreen perennials belong to this genus, which occurs in Mediterranean regions and western and eastern Asia. *E. sagittatum* is found in moist woodlands in central China, and is naturalized in Japan. Various species and hybrids are grown in shady borders, and with shrubs, mainly as groundcover. The name comes from the Greek *epimedion*, which was Dioscorides' name for these plants (literally "akin to a plant growing in Media").

Epimedium sagittatum (horny goat weed, barrenwort)
Rhizomatous perennial with trifoliate, leathery leaves and lanceolate-ovate leaflets to 2in (5cm) long, which have spiny-toothed margins. Tiny white flowers are borne in spring. H 10–20in (25–50cm), S 12–18in (30–45cm).

7–9

ERIOBOTRYA

This genus contains about 27 species of frost-hardy and tender evergreen shrubs and trees native to the Himalayas, eastern Asia, and Malaysia. *E. japonica* is found in woodland in China and Japan. One or two species are grown for their handsome foliage and edible fruits. *E. japonica* is widely grown in courtyards in warm regions, or against walls and in containers in cold areas as an ornamental. *Eriobotrya* is from the Greek *erion*, "wool," and *botrys*, "a bunch of grapes," referring to the flower clusters.

Eriobotrya japonica (loquat, Japanese medlar, *nispero*)
Tree with corrugated, obovate, pointed leaves, up to 10in (25cm) long. Upright clusters of fragrant, white flowers appear in winter, followed by globose, edible yellow fruits, 1½in (4cm) long. H and S 25ft (8m).

8–10

EQUISETUM

A genus of 29 species of hardy, spore-bearing perennials that occurs worldwide (except Australasia) in cool, damp places. *E. arvense* and *E. hyemale* are found in Europe, N America, and Asia. Horsetails have hardly changed since prehistoric times, when they formed a large part of the vegetation that decomposed to form coal seams. Some species are pernicious weeds. Once they have produced the conelike heads from which the spores are shed, the fertile stems die and are replaced by sterile ones.

Equisetum arvense (field horsetail, bottlebrush, shave grass)
Perennial with a hairy, tuberous rhizome. Upright, often branched, sterile stems have black-toothed sheaths and whorls of spreading, green branches. Spores ripen in spring. H 8–32in (20–80cm), S indefinite.

6–10

ERUCA

This genus includes five species of annuals and perennials, which occur in Mediterranean regions. *E. vesicaria* subsp. *sativa*, native to the Mediterranean and eastern Asia, is naturalized in parts of N America. It was a popular salad plant in Roman times, and is still sometimes referred to as Roman rocket. It has such a long history of cultivation that cultivated plants are now classified as a subspecies, being larger all around than wild plants, and bearing paler flowers.

Eruca vesicaria subsp. ***sativa*** (rocket, arugula, rucola)
Upright, mustardlike annual with asymmetric, toothed leaves. Cream, 4-petaled flowers, veined purple, appear from late winter to autumn, followed by slender, erect pods. H 24–36in (60cm–1m), S 6–8in (15–20cm).

A

ENGLISH WALNUT, see *Juglans regia*, p.145
EPAZOTE, see *Chenopodium ambrosioides*, p.106
ERGOT, see *Claviceps purpurea*, p.109

ERYNGIUM

A large genus of some 230 biennials and perennials, occurring in temperate and subtropical regions, especially in S America. *E. foetidum* is found in seasonally dry grassland in the West Indies, C America, and Florida; *E. maritimum* in coastal sand and pebble in Europe, northern Africa, and southwestern Asia. Many species are grown for their handsome foliage and long-lasting flowers, which often dry well. The metallic appearance of some species contrasts well with lime green or bronze foliage.

Eryngium foetidum (culantro, fitweed, perennial coriander)
Slender, evergreen, branched perennial with fibrous roots and lanceolate leaves, 2–10in (5–25cm) long, which have spiny-toothed margins. Numerous, green-white flowers with leafy bracts appear in summer. H and S 24in (60cm).

7–10

Eryngium maritimum (sea holly, eryngo)
Spiny perennial with very large, fleshy roots and leathery, blue-green, rounded leaves, 2–5in (5–12cm) across. Umbels of powder blue flowers, surrounded by spiny, leaflike bracts appear in summer. H and S 12–18in (30–45cm)

6–9

ERYTHROXYLUM

A genus of some 250 species of tropical trees and shrubs found mainly in the Americas and Madagascar. *E. coca* is native to high altitudes in the eastern Andes. Coca extracts provided the basis for Coca-Cola until 1902, when cocaine was banned in the US, and cocaine-free extracts were used instead. The name *Erythroxylum* derives from the Greek *erythros*, "red," and *xylon*, "wood." It is frequently, although incorrectly, spelled *Erythroxylon*.

Erythroxylum coca (coca)
Evergreen shrub with red-brown bark and spirally arranged, brown-green, elliptic leaves up to 3in (7cm) long. Clusters of small white flowers appear in the axils, followed by orange-red berries. H and S to 6ft (2m) in cultivation, 12–15ft (4–5m) in the wild.

ESCHSCHOLZIA

A genus of 8–10 hardy annuals and perennials native to western N America. *E. californica*, found wild in coastal areas of southwestern N America, is the state flower of California. Eschscholzias are among the most popular and easily grown annuals for dry, sunny places, and a wide range of cultivars is available with single, double, or semi double flowers in various shades of orange, yellow, cream, pink, and red. The poppylike flowers close in cloudy or wet weather.

Eschscholzia californica (California poppy)
Hardy annual or short-lived perennial, with finely cut, blue-green leaves. Yellow to orange flowers, 2–3in (5–7cm) across, are followed in summer by ribbed capsules, 3–4in (7–10cm) long. H 8–24in (20–60cm), S 6–12in (15–30cm).

A

***Eschscholzia californica*, Ballerina Series**
This cultivar has the same upright or spreading stems and finely cut, blue-green leaves of the species and double flowers with fluted petals in a range of colors. H and S 10in (24cm).

8–10

ERYNGO, see *Eryngium maritimum*, above
ESERE BEAN, see *Physostigma venenosum*, p.327
ESTRAGON, see *ARTEMISIA*, pp.88–9

EUCALYPTUS

Over 500 species of aromatic evergreen trees and shrubs belong to this genus, which is native to Australia. *E. camaldulensis* is found throughout Australia; *E. citriodora* on dry plateaus in Queensland; *E. dives* in woodland, and *E. globulus* in moist valleys in New South Wales and Victoria. Eucalyptus are among the world's fastest-growing and tallest trees, recorded at 326ft (99m). Many are grown for lumber and as ornamentals for their handsome foliage and patterned bark.

Eucalyptus camaldulensis (river red gum, Murray red gum, red gum)
Spreading riverside tree with smooth, white through brown to red bark. The lanceolate leaves lengthen and become more pointed in mature trees. Umbels of small cream flowers open in summer. H 70–150ft (20–45m), S 70ft (20m).

9–10

Eucalyptus dives (broad-leaved peppermint, Australian peppermint)
Short-trunked tree with stalkless, heart-shaped, blue-green juvenile leaves. Adult foliage is thick, shiny, and broadly lanceolate. Small white flowers appear in the axils in summer. H 80ft (25m), S 50–70ft (15–20m).

9–10

Eucalyptus globulus (blue gum, Tasmanian blue gum)
Large, spreading tree with smooth, creamy white, peeling bark and ovate, silver-blue juvenile foliage. The glossy adult leaves are sickle-shaped and up to 10in (25cm) long. H 100–150ft (30–45m), S 40ft (12m).

9–10

Eucalyptus citriodora (lemon-scented gum)
Slender tree with white (sometimes pink or red), powdery bark and rough, lanceolate juvenile leaves. The smooth adult foliage is narrower and longer. All parts are strongly lemon-scented.
H 80–160ft (25–50m), S to 80ft (25m).

9–10

EUONYMUS

A large and widespread genus of 177 species of deciduous and evergreen trees and shrubs found in N America, Eurasia, and Australia. Many are grown as ornamentals. Some deciduous species, such as *E. atropurpureus*, found in central and eastern N America, and *E. europaeus*, found in woods and scrub in Europe and western Asia, are quite spectacular in autumn, with pink to red tints and brilliantly colored, lobed fruits.

Euonymus atropurpureus (wahoo, burning bush, Indian arrow-wood)
Deciduous large, shrubby tree with oblong-ovate leaves, up to 5in (12cm) long that turn yellow in autumn. Tiny purple flowers are followed in summer by purple capsules, containing red seeds. H 6–25ft (2–8m), S 4–10ft (1.2–3m).

4–9

Euonymus europaeus (spindle tree)
Deciduous shrub or small tree with smooth, gray bark and ovate leaves, 1¼–5in (3–13cm) long that turn red in autumn. Small green flowers in axillary clusters are followed by 4-lobed, bright pink capsules, containing orange seeds. H 6–25ft (2–8m), S 4–10ft (1.2–3m).

3–8

***Euonymus europaeus* 'Red Cascade'**
This cultivar has richer autumn color than the species, and a heavier crop of rose-pink fruits. H 6–25ft (2–8m), S 4–10ft (1.2–3m).

3–8

EUPATORIUM

This genus of 38 species of hardy and half-hardy shrubs and perennials is native to Eurasia and the eastern US; *E. fortunei* is a riverside plant of Korea, China, and Japan. Both *E. perfoliatum* and *E. purpureum* are found in eastern US. Thoroughworts have rayless, long-stamened flowers; some are ornamental plants for damp garden conditions. *E. cannabinum* is an imposing plant, bettered only by its double-flowered cultivar, *E. c.* 'Flore Pleno', which bears showier, longer-lasting flowers.

Eupatorium cannabinum (thoroughwort)
Aromatic perennial with erect downy stems. Leaves are oppositely arranged and divided in 3–5 segments. Corymbs of mauve-pink flowers are borne from midsummer. H 1–4ft (30cm–1.2m), S 12–24in (30–60cm).

5–9

Eupatorium perfoliatum (boneset, thoroughwort, feverwort)
Tall, hardy perennial with erect stems and lanceolate, perfoliate leaves, up to 8in (20cm) long. Large corymbs of white, often purple-tinged, flowers open in late summer. H up to 5ft (1.5m), S 1–3ft (30cm–1m).

3–8

Eupatorium purpureum (Joe Pye weed, gravel root, queen of the meadow)
Very tall hardy perennial with upright stems and whorls of finely toothed, ovate leaves, vanilla-scented when crushed. Dense corymbs of pink flowers appear in late summer and autumn. H 4–10ft (1.2–3m), S 2–3ft (60cm–1m).

3–10

EUPHORBIA

A large, cosmopolitan genus of about 2,000 annuals, biennials, perennials, shrubs, and trees, many of which are succulent. *E. hirta* is native to tropical and subtropical regions. All contain white latex and most are poisonous. Many spurges are grown as ornamentals. They include such familiar plants as poinsettias (*E. pulcherrima*) and the caper spurge, or mole plant (*E. lathyrus*), often seen in herb gardens, but far too toxic for culinary or medicinal use.

Euphorbia hirta (asthma weed, pill-bearing spurge)
Annual weed with hairy stems and ovate leaves, up to 1½in (4cm) long. Insignificant flowers borne in dense, globose clusters are followed by 3-celled, red-green capsules. H 8–16in (20–40cm), S 8–12in (20–30cm).

A

EUPHRASIA

This cosmopolitan genus includes some 450 semi-parasitic species. Euphrasias are difficult to cultivate because of this habit of growth. *E. officinalis* is common in grassland throughout Europe, parasitic on *Trifolium pratense* (see p.214), *Plantago* species (see p.178), and grasses. The genus is generally considered to be a group of similar species, sometimes given separate species status, as in *E. rostkoviana* and *E. montana*. *Euphrasia* is a translation of the Greek, meaning "good cheer."

Euphrasia officinalis (eyebright)
Variable annual with upright stems and rounded, toothed leaves, usually less than ½in (1cm) long. Small white flowers, often purple-veined, with a yellow-marked throat and 3-lobed lower lip, appear in summer. H and S 2–12in (5–30cm).

A

EURYALE

A genus containing a single species of giant, tropical aquatic found in deep, still, and slow-moving fresh water in northern India, China, Japan, and Taiwan. *E. ferox* is grown as an ornamental in tropical pools, often as an annual. It has a stout rhizome and the common name, "foxnut," refers to the black, pea-sized seeds, contained in prickly, berrylike fruits, 3in (7cm) in diameter. *Euryale* is named after one of the Three Gorgons, who had monstrous, thorny hair.

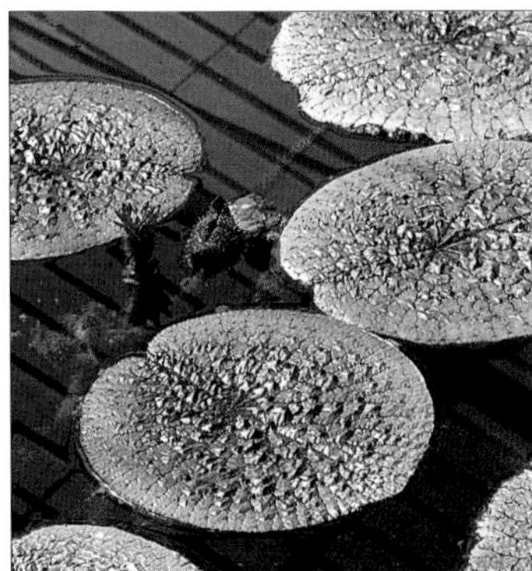

Euryale ferox (prickly waterlily, Chinese foxnut)
Perennial aquatic with circular peltate leaves up to 5ft (1.5m) across, puckered and spiny on the upper surface and purple-red beneath. Purple flowers are borne on or below the surface in summer. S 10ft (3m) or more.

7–10

EVERNIA

This cosmopolitan genus consists of about 10 species of lichens. Common in areas with an unpolluted atmosphere, *E. prunastri* is extremely slow-growing. It is an attractive lichen that often occurs naturally in gardens but is difficult to cultivate. It was imported from Greece and Cyprus to Egypt for packing embalmed mummies. Centuries later, in Europe, it was in great demand for powdering wigs and was described in the *Compendium Aromatorium* by Saladin of Askalon (1137–93).

Evernia prunastri (oak moss)
Lichen with soft, pendent, antler-shaped branches that are gray-green above and have white, cottony undersurfaces. Pink-brown, spore-producing discs are rare. H and S 2½in (6cm).

4–10

EVENING PRIMROSE, COMMON, see *Oenothera biennis*, p.167
EVERLASTING FLOWER, see *Helichrysum*, p.137
EYEBRIGHT, see *Euphrasia officinalis*, see above
EYEPLANT, see *Duboisia myoporoides*, p.121
FAGARA, see *Zanthoxylum piperitum*, see p.222

FAGOPYRUM

This genus includes about six species of annuals native to temperate Eurasia. Being fast-growing, even on poor, acid soils, *F. esculentum* provides grain for flour in areas of subsistence farming. The fruits mature over a long period, giving a relatively low yield when harvested. It is popular as a green manure among organic gardeners, since it attracts hoverflies, whose larvae eat large quantities of aphids. The nutlets vary in color according to the cultivar.

Fagopyrum esculentum (buckwheat)
Slender annual with an upright, often red-tinged stem and broadly triangular leaves, up to 3in (7cm) long. Clusters of scented, pink-white flowers are followed by brown nutlets, about ¼in (6mm) long. H 8–24in (20–60cm), S 4–9in (10–23cm).

A

***Fagus sylvatica,* Heterophylla Group**
(cut leaved beech, fern-leaved beech)
This group covers beeches from seed-raised plants whose leaves are variously cut and lobed. Outstanding seedlings have been given cultivar names, such as *F. s.* (Heterophylla Group) 'Asplenifolia'.
H 80–130ft (25–40m), S 50ft (15m).

4–7

***Fagus sylvatica,* Purpurea Group**
(copper beech)
This group covers purple-leaved beeches that arise from seed-raised plants. Outstanding seedlings have been given cultivar names, such as *F. s.* (Purpurea Group) 'Riversii'.
H 80–130ft (25–40m), S 50ft (15m).

4–7

FAGUS

There are about 10 species of deciduous trees in this genus, which occurs widely in northern temperate regions. *F. sylvatica* is the most adaptable species of beech in cultivation and has numerous cultivars, varying greatly in habit, leaf shape, and foliage color. It is one of the most successful large trees for alkaline soils but thrives just as well in acidic conditions. Many of the leaves remain throughout the winter, although they change color from green to brown.

Fagus sylvatica (European beech)
Large tree with smooth, gray bark and ovate, toothed leaves, up to 4in (10cm) long. Inconspicuous flowers are borne in spring, followed by brown, 4-valved, woody fruits, clad in blunt spines, that contain usually two shiny brown nuts.
H 80–130ft (25–40m), S 50ft (15m).

4–7

***Fagus sylvatica* 'Dawyck'** (Dawyck beech)
This conical form was first found as a seedling by Sir John Naesmyth on his estate at Dawyck, Peeblesshire, Scotland, c.1850. The neat, upright habit makes a good subject for urban planting. H 100ft (30m), S 22ft (7m).

4–7

FERULA

This genus consists of 172 species of robust perennials found from the Mediterranean to central Asia. *F. assa-foetida* is native to coastal regions and rocky areas of Iran. Although known as giant fennels because of their similarity to *Foeniculum* species (see p.128), many have an unpleasant smell. *F. assa-foetida* and *F. gummosa* have long been important for their gum resin: the former was subject to a tax in Alexandria during the second century AD, and the latter was mentioned as an ingredient in Moses' incense.

Ferula assa-foetida (asafoetida, devil's dung)
Giant perennial with a thick rootstock, and large, finely divided leaves that have an unpleasant, garliclike odor. Tiny yellow flowers, followed by small seeds, usually appear in the 5th year, after which the plant dies. H 6ft (2m), S 5ft (1.5m).

7–9

FICUS

A large genus of about 800 species of tropical and subtropical trees, shrubs, lianas, epiphytes, and semiepiphytes. *F. carica* is now common throughout the Mediterranean, having originated in south-western Asia. The flowers are completely hidden within a round to pear-shaped, fleshy receptacle, with a tiny opening to the outside that admits pollinating wasps. Most cultivars are self-fertile. The fig was sacred to the Romans, having sheltered the wolf that suckled Romulus and Remus.

Ficus carica (fig)
Deciduous small tree or spreading shrub with palmately lobed leaves, up to 8in (20cm) long, and pear-shaped fruits, 2–3in (5–8cm) long, which ripen green- to brown-purple. H 30ft (10m), S 15ft (5m).

7–10

FAIRY WAND, see *Chamaelirium luteum*, p.258
FALSE DAISY, see *Eclipta prostrata*, p.122
FALSE INDIGO, see *Baptisia*, p.92
FALSE JASMINE, see *Gelsemium sempervirens*, p.132
FALSE UNICORN ROOT, see *Chamaelirium luteum*, p.258
FELON HERB, see *ARTEMISIA*, p.88–9
FENNEL, see *Foeniculum vulgare*, p.128
FENUGREEK, see *Trigonella foenum-graecum*, p.214
FERN-LEAVED TANSY, see *TANACETUM*, pp.208–9
FEVERFEW, see *TANACETUM*, pp.208–9

Ficus carica **'Brown Turkey'**
An early, prolific cultivar, hardier than the species, with large, pear-shaped, brown fruits. In cold areas it does best against a wall or in pots that can be moved under cover in winter.
H 8–10ft (2.5–3m), S 12–15ft (4–5m).

7–10

Filipendula ulmaria **'Flore Pleno'**
This cultivar has long lasting double flowers that are a better value as a garden plant and cut flower. H 2–4ft (60cm–1.2m), S 18in (45cm).

3–9

Filipendula ulmaria **'Variegata'**
The leaves of this cultivar are irregularly splashed with bright yellow which fades to cream at the onset of flowering. H 24in (60cm), S 12in (30cm).

3–9

FILIPENDULA

A genus of 10 species of hardy spring- and summer-flowering perennials found in moist or boggy soils throughout Europe, N America, and temperate Asia. Several species are popular ornamentals, especially for waterside planting. *F. ulmaria* has an aromatic rootstock and the foliage yields an aroma of wintergreen when crushed. The common name derives from "meadwort," meaning a herb ("wort") used to flavor mead and beer, not from the plant's habitat in meadows.

Filipendula ulmaria (meadowsweet, queen of the meadow)
A hardy herbaceous perennial with irregularly pinnate leaves. Large heads of creamy white, almond-scented flowers are borne from midsummer to early autumn. H 2–4ft (60cm–1.2m), S 18in (45cm).

3–9

Filipendula ulmaria **'Aurea'**
This variety has yellow new foliage, turning pale golden-green in summer. It is less vigorous than the type and scorches in full sun. H 12–18in (30–45cm), S 12in (30cm).

3–9

FOENICULUM

The single species of hardy biennial or perennial in this genus is found in Mediterranean Europe and Asia on wasteland and in dry, sunny places, especially coastal areas. It is widely naturalized elsewhere, notably Australia. Fennel has been cultivated as a vegetable and an herb since Classical times. Under Charlemagne (742–814) it spread into northern and central Europe and was grown on the imperial farms. All its parts are aromatic, with an anise-like scent and flavor. It provides a focal point as an ornamental.

Foeniculum vulgare (fennel)
Tall, handsome biennial or perennial with erect, hollow stems and glossy, pinnate foliage divided into threadlike leaflets. Umbels of minute, dull yellow flowers are produced in summer, followed by gray-brown seeds. H 6ft (2m), S 18in (45cm).

4–10

Foeniculum vulgare var. ***azoricum***
(Florence fennel, sweet fennel, bulb fennel, finocchio)
The bulbous stalk bases of this variety are eaten as a vegetable. It is smaller than the species. H 24in (60cm), S 18in (45cm).

5–9

Foeniculum vulgare **'Purpureum'**
(bronze fennel)
This variety has bronze-purple foliage and is slightly hardier than the species. H 4–5ft (1.2–1.5m), S 18in (45cm).

4–9

FIELD HORSETAIL, see *Equisetum arvense*, p.123
FIELD POPPY, see *Papaver rhoeas*, p.171
FIG, see *Ficus carica*, p.127
FIGWORT, see *Scrophularia*, p.201
FISH POISON TREE, see *Piscidia piscipula*, p.330
FITWEED, see *Eryngium foetidum*, p.124
FLAX, see *Linum usitatissimum*, p.152
FLORENCE FENNEL, see *Foeniculum vulgare* var. *dulce*, above
FLOWERING QUINCE, see *Chaenomeles speciosa*, p.105
FLUELLEN, see *Veronica officinalis*, p.218
FETID BUGBANE, see *Cimicifuga foetida*, p.107

FORSYTHIA

Seven species of deciduous shrubs make up this genus, which occurs mainly in eastern Asia, with a single species in southeastern Europe. Forsythias were introduced to cultivation in the 19th century and gained rapid popularity for their spring display of yellow flowers. *F. suspensa* is both a familiar garden shrub and a Chinese medicinal herb. It is a parent of *F.* x *intermedia*, one of the most widely planted of all shrubs. Forsythia is named after William Forsyth (1737–1804), gardener at Kensington Palace, London.

Forsythia suspensa (weeping forsythia)
Deciduous, arching shrub with simple, sometimes trilobed or trifoliate toothed leaves, 2–4in (5–10cm) long. Bright yellow flowers in spring are followed by woody fruits. H and S 8–10ft (2.5–3.5m).

6–8

Forsythia suspensa **f. *atrocaulis***
This is a more striking plant than the species, with dark maroon young stems and larger, pale yellow flowers. *F. s.* 'Nymans' is a sport of this form, with larger, more open flowers. H and S 10ft (3.5m).

6–8

Fragaria vesca **'Fructu Albo'**
This cultivar has unusual creamy white, alpine strawberries that taste the same as red-fruited varieties. They are reputedly less attractive to birds. H 10in (25cm), S 8in (20cm).

4–8

Fragaria vesca **'Multiplex'**
An ornamental cultivar with double flowers and small, red fruits. H 10in (25cm), S 8in (20cm).

4–8

FRAGARIA

This genus contains about six species of low-growing perennials, widely distributed in northern temperate regions. Alpine strawberries are cultivars of *F. vesca*, found in woods and grassland in Europe, western Asia, and N America. They have smaller, more aromatic fruits on bushier plants than the species, and include *F. v.* 'Alexandria' and *F. v.* 'Baron Solemacher'. *F.* x *ananassa*, the cultivated strawberry, was developed during the 18th century by crossing the American species *F. chiloensis* and *F. virginiana*.

Fragaria vesca (wild strawberry)
Perennial with long runners, rooting at the nodes, and trifoliate leaves with ovate, toothed leaflets, up to 2½in (6cm) long. The 5-petaled, white flowers have yellow centers. Bright red, ovoid fruits have seeds embedded in the skin. H 10in (25cm), S 8in (20cm).

5–9

FRAXINUS

About 65 species of mostly hardy deciduous trees make up this genus, occurring throughout temperate parts of the northern hemisphere. *F. ornus* is found in woods in southern Europe and western Asia. Most ashes are fast-growing and tolerate a range of conditions. They have pinnate leaves and inconspicuous flowers, with the exception of the so-called "flowering ashes." These include a number of ornamental species, such as *F. ornus*, that produce panicles of showy white flowers.

Fraxinus ornus (manna ash)
Small, hardy, deciduous tree with a rounded crown and smooth gray bark. It has pinnately divided, dull green leaves and dense panicles of heavily scented, creamy white flowers in late spring. H 15–30ft (5–10m), S 10–15ft (3–5m).

6–9

FOXGLOVE, see *Digitalis*, p.118
FRANKINCENSE, see *Boswellia sacra*, p.95
FRENCH JUJUBE, see *Ziziphus jujuba*, p.223
FRENCH MARIGOLD, see *Tagetes patula*, p.207
FRENCH PARSLEY, see *Petroselinum crispum* 'Italian', p.174
FRENCH SORREL, see *Rumex scutatus*, p.194
FRENCH TARRAGON, see *ARTEMISIA*, pp.88–9
FRINGE TREE, see *Chionanthus virginicus*, p.107
FRINGED LAVENDER, see *LAVANDULA*, pp.148–9

FRITILLARIA

A genus of about 100 species of hardy and frost-hardy, bulbous perennials found throughout northern temperate zones. *F. verticillata* is native to woodland and meadows in central Asia and western Siberia. Most species flower in spring and become dormant during summer. They range in size from diminutive alpines to the rugged crown imperial (*F. imperialis*), which reaches 3ft (1m). *Fritillaria* derives from the Latin *fritillus*, "dice box," and refers to the squarish spotted markings.

Fritillaria verticillata
Hardy bulbous perennial with globose bulbs up to 1½in (4cm) in diameter, and whorled, narrowly lanceolate leaves with tendril-like tips. Bell-shaped, cream flowers, patterned green to brown, appear in spring. H 8–24in (20–60cm), S 3–4in (8–10cm).

7–9

FUCUS

This genus of six species of marine algae is found widely in shallow waters and on shores in the northern hemisphere, where it often forms a distinct zone. *F. vesiculosus,* found on coasts of the Atlantic, English Channel, North Sea, and Baltic, has conspicuous air bladders arranged in groups of two or three, along the fronds. The common name "wrack" is derived from the same source as "wreck," meaning something that has been washed ashore.

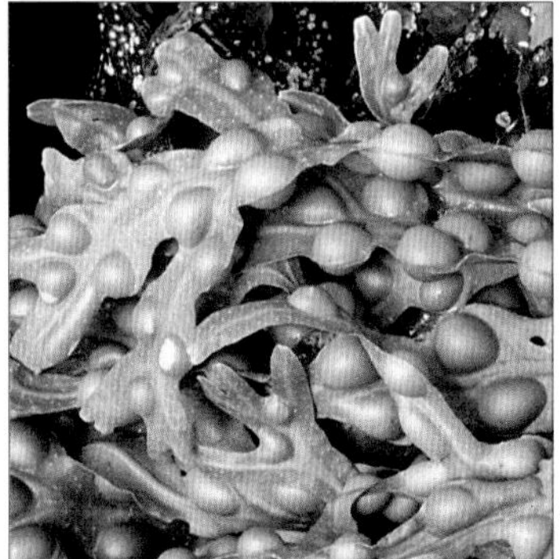

Fucus vesiculosus (bladderwrack, black-tang)
Leathery, olive-brown seaweed with branched, straplike fronds, which are forked at the tips, and have a thick midrib and smooth margins. H 6–36in (15cm–1m), S 3–20in (7.5–50cm).

FUMARIA

A genus of 55 annuals, usually climbing or scrambling, which occur throughout Europe to central Asia, and in eastern African highlands. *F. officinalis* is found throughout Europe to Iran and is naturalized in N America. Fumitories are closely related to poppies and similarly contain alkaloids, although in smaller amounts. *Fumaria* is from the Latin *fumus*, "smoke," referring either to a legend that the plant grew from earthly vapors, or to the irritating smoke it produces when it is burned.

Fumaria officinalis (fumitory, earth smoke, wax dolls)
Variable, self-fertile annual with climbing stem and small gray-green leaves. Fleshy, pinkish purple flowers, tipped dark maroon, are borne in racemes from midsummer to late autumn. H and S 6–12in (15–30cm).

A

GALEGA

About six species of perennials make up this genus, which occurs in central and southern Europe, western Asia (*G. officinalis*), and tropical eastern Africa. A few species are grown for their attractive, pinnate leaves and spikes of pea flowers. The common name "goat's rue" arises from the foul smell of the foliage when bruised. The name *Galega* comes from the Greek *gala*, "milk," because these plants have a reputation for increasing lactation.

Galega officinalis (goat's rue, French lilac)
Bushy perennial with pinnately divided leaves. Lavender to white flowers, with standards ½in (1cm) long, are borne in axillary racemes in summer, followed by pods up to 2in (5cm) long. H 3–5ft (1–1.5m), S 2–3ft (60cm–1m).

3–9

***Galega officinalis* 'Alba'**
A popular cultivar with pure white flowers. H 3–5ft (1–1.5m), S 24–36in (60cm–1m).

3–9

FRITILLARY, see *Fritillaria*, above
FRUIT-SCENTED SAGE, see *SALVIA*, pp.196–7
FUMITORY, see *Fumaria officinalis*, above
GALANGAL, see *Alpinia galanga*, p.82; *Alpinia officinarum*, p.235
GALBANUM, see *Ferula gummosa*, p.282
GARDEN HELIOTROPE, see *Valeriana officinalis*, p.217
GARDEN MYRRH, see *Myrrhis odorata*, p.162

GALIUM

This cosmopolitan genus includes about 400 species of annuals and perennials. *G. aparine* is a common weed throughout Europe and northern and western Asia. *G. odoratum*, found also in Siberia and northern Africa, is the best-known garden species. It makes good deciduous groundcover in shady areas. *G. verum* is widespread in grassland from western Asia to N America. The name *Galium* comes from the Greek *gala*, "milk," because several species are used to curdle milk in cheesemaking.

Galium aparine (goosegrass, cleavers, sticky Willie)
Scrambling annual, climbing by hooked bristles. It has whorls of 6–9 elliptic leaves, and tiny green-white flowers during spring and summer, followed by bristly, globose, green-purple fruits. H 4ft (1.2m), S to 10ft (3m).

A

Galium verum (lady's bedstraw, yellow bedstraw, cheese rennet)
Perennial with a slender, creeping rootstock, 4-angled stems, and whorls of 8–12 small linear leaves. Tiny, bright yellow honey-scented flowers are produced in panicles in summer. H 6–36in (15cm–1m), S indefinite.

3–8

Galium odoratum (sweet woodruff)
Rhizomatous, far-creeping perennial with 4-angled stems and whorls of lanceolate leaves up to 1½in (4cm) long. Fragrant, pure white, star-shaped flowers appear in cymes during early summer. H 20in (50cm), S indefinite.

3–9

GANODERMA

A genus of 50 species of saprophytic bracket fungi, which occur in most regions, especially the tropics. They obtain their nutrients from wood, growing either on dead trees or on living specimens, causing serious heart rot. Wood-decaying fungi play an important role in forest ecosystems. *G. lucidum* is widespread in warm and temperate regions, at the base of oaks and other deciduous trees. It is not considered edible, but is cultivated in China for the herb trade.

Ganoderma lucidum (lacquered bracket fungus, *reishi*)
Annual bracket fungus with a large, stalked, fan-shaped, fruiting body (toadstool). It has a shiny upper surface, zoned yellow to dark red. Rust-colored spores are released from the undersurface in summer. H and S 6–12in (15–30cm).

4–10

GARDENIA

Some 200 species of evergreen shrubs and trees are included in this genus, which occurs in tropical and warm regions of Africa and Eurasia. *G. augusta*, native to woodland in southern China, is widely grown for its handsome foliage and fragrant flowers. It is known as the "happiness herb" in the East; it improves liver function, which in turn releases blocked emotions. *Gardenia* is named after Dr. Alexander Garden (1730–91), a Scottish physician who corresponded with Linnaeus.

Gardenia augusta (gardenia, Cape jasmine)
Evergreen shrub with glossy, elliptic leaves and strongly fragrant, waxy white flowers, 3in (7cm) across, which appear in summer, followed by oblong fruits up to 1in (2.5cm) long. Rarely exceeds H 5ft (1.5m), S 4ft (1.2m) in cultivation.

8–10

Gardenia augusta **'Fortuniana'**
This is a common cultivar, with larger, double flowers than the species. It blooms mainly in summer, differing in this respect from *G. a. vetchiana*, which blooms in winter. H and S 2–4ft (60cm–1.2m) in containers.

8–10

GELSEMIUM

There are three species of evergreen, twining shrubs in this genus, which occurs in the Americas and SE Asia. *G. sempervirens*, found in woodland from the southern US to Guatemala, is widely grown as an ornamental in the open in warm regions, or under cover. It makes a fine specimen when trained against a wall or trellis; it is the state flower of South Carolina. *Gelsemium* is from the Italian *gelsomino*, "jessamine," and refers to the jasminelike flowers.

Gelsemium sempervirens (Carolina jessamine, false jasmine)
Evergreen climber with twining stems and shiny, lanceolate leaves. Fragrant, funnel-shaped, yellow flowers appear in summer, followed by 2-valved capsules that contain flattened seeds. H 10–20ft (3–6m).

7–9

GENISTA

This genus contains about 85 species of shrubs and differs from *Cytisus* only in minute anatomical detail. Brooms range through Europe, northern Africa, and western Asia, and are in many cases spiny. *G. tinctoria*, found in grassland in Europe and W Asia, was once grown as a dye plant for the yellow color yielded by its flowers. When mixed with woad (*Isatis tinctoria*, see p.144) it produces Kendal green, the color used to dye woollen cloth, and also Lincoln green, the color worn by Robin Hood.

Genista tinctoria (dyer's greenweed)
Variable, deciduous, nonspiny shrub with bright green, stalkless, lanceolate leaves to 1in (2.5cm) long. Yellow pea flowers, about ½in (1cm) long, appear in summer in leafy spikes at the ends of the branches. H and S 3ft (1m).

4–7

GAULTHERIA

This genus includes 150 species of dwarf shrubs, closely related to *Vaccinium* (see p.217), occuring mainly in the Andes but also in N America, eastern Asia, and Australasia, *G. procumbens* being found in dry woods in eastern N America. Many are grown for their neat habit, waxy flowers, and colorful fruits. A number are suitable for rock gardens and containers. *Gaultheria* was named after Jean François Gaulthier (1708–56), a physician and botanist who worked in Canada.

Gaultheria procumbens (wintergreen, checkerberry, teaberry)
Creeping shrublet with glossy, elliptic leaves, up to 2in (5cm) long and solitary, pendent, pink-white flowers in summer. Globose, red, aromatic fruits remain all winter. H 3–6in (7–15cm), S 3ft (1m) or more.

3–7

GENTIANA

A cosmopolitan genus of about 400 species of perennials, annuals, and biennials. *G. lutea* is native to European alpine pastures and woodland; *G. macrophylla* and *G. scabra* are found in northern and eastern Asia. Gentians of many kinds are grown for their funnel-shaped flowers, which in some species are bright blue and in others may be purple, yellow, or white. *Gentiana* was named after king Gentius of Illyria (c.500BC), who is credited with discovering the medicinal uses of *G. lutea*.

Gentiana lutea (great yellow gentian)
Robust perennial with stout, hollow stems and broadly ovate basal leaves up to 12in (30cm) long. Clusters of 3–10 short-tubed, yellow flowers appear in the axils in summer. H 3–6ft (1–2m), S 24in (60cm).

6–9

GARDENIA, see *Gardenia augusta*, p.131
GARLIC, see *ALLIUM*, pp.80–81
GARLIC MUSTARD, see *Alliaria petiolata*, p.79
GAS PLANT, see *Dictamnus albus*, p.118
GAY FEATHER, see *Liatris spicata*, p.151
GENTIAN, see *Gentiana*, above
GERANIUM, see *PELARGONIUM*, p. 172
GERMAN CHAMOMILE, see *Matricaria recutita*, p.156
GERMANDER, see *Teucrium*, p.210

Gentiana macrophylla
(large-leaved gentian)
Erect perennial with a stout rootstock and pale green, pointed, lanceolate leaves, 8–16in (20–40cm) long. Violet-blue flowers appear in dense clusters in the upper axils during summer.
H 16–28in (40–70cm), S 24in (60cm).
5–9

Gentiana scabra (Japanese gentian, *ryntem* root)
Perennial with leafy stems and paired, ovate to lanceolate, 3-veined leaves to 1½in (3.5cm) long. Deep blue, often spotted, flowers appear in terminal clusters or axillary pairs, from summer.
H 12in (30cm), S 8in (20cm).
5–9

GERANIUM

A genus of some 300 species of perennials, with a few annuals and subshrubs, widely distributed in temperate regions; *G. maculatum* is found in north-eastern US, *G. robertianum* is common in Europe, eastern US, northwestern Africa, and western Asia. Cranesbills are popular garden plants, with attractive leaves and small, delicately veined flowers borne over a long period. The related pelargoniums, also known as "geraniums" (see *Pelargonium*, pp.172–3), have different uses.

Geranium maculatum (American cranesbill, alumroot, spotted cranesbill)
Clump-forming perennial with a compact rootstock and deeply divided, palmate leaves, up to 8in (20cm) across. In summer, pink, saucer-shaped flowers are followed by 1in (2.5cm) beaked fruits.
H 30in (75cm), S 18in (45cm).
3–8

Geranium maculatum f. *albiflorum*
This cultivar is like the species, but has white flowers, 1–1½in (2.5–4cm) across, appearing from late spring to late summer. H 30in (75cm), S 18in (45cm).
3–9

Geranium robertianum (herb Robert)
Fetid annual or biennial with hairy red-tinged stems and palmate leaves to 4½in (11cm) wide. Deep pink flowers, ½in (1cm) across, are produced from early summer to late autumn. H and S 20in (50cm).
3–9

Geranium robertianum 'Celtic White'
This is a smaller-growing, more compact cultivar than *G. m.* 'Album'. It has smaller, pure white flowers and brighter green foliage with very little red-brown pigmentation. H 10in (25cm), S 20in (50cm).
3–9

GEUM

There are 65 species of perennials in this genus, which occurs in temperate and cold regions. Geums are easily grown in the front of borders or in rock gardens and have long-lasting flowers in shades of red through to yellow. *G. urbanum*, found in Europe, western Asia, and Mediterranean regions, was once known as *herba benedicta*, because its aromatic roots were thought to protect against evil and poisons: hence the common names "herb bennet" or "herb Benedict."

Geum urbanum (avens, wood avens, herb bennet)
Slender perennial with a clove-scented rhizome, upright stems, and pinnate leaves. Tiny yellow flowers appear in summer, followed by purple-tinged fruits covered in hooked bristles.
H and S 8–24in (20–60cm).

5–9

GILLENIA

Two very closely related species of rhizomatous perennials belong to this eastern N American genus. *G. trifoliata*, found in moist, rich woodland, is important as an herb and is widely grown as an garden plant. *G. stipulata*, similar in both properties and appearance, is found farther south in the wild. They are distinguished mainly by the number of leaflets: three in the case of *G. trifoliata* and five in the case of *G. stipulata* (the two extra ones are actually stipules).

Gillenia trifoliata (Indian physic, Bowman's root, American ipecac)
Perennial with red-green, wiry stalks and sprays of narrow-petaled, white or pink-tinged flowers, ½in (1cm) across in late spring and summer.
H 3–4ft (1–1.2m), S 24in (60cm).

4–8

***Ginkgo biloba* 'Pendula'**
This cultivar has a weeping habit. It makes an interesting and unusual centerpiece for a lawn, especially when the leaves turn yellow in autumn.
H 10ft (3m), S 15ft (5m).

3–9

GINKGO

A single species of deciduous tree makes up this genus, which is found wild in Zhejiang and Guizhou Provinces, central China, and which has no close relatives. *G. biloba* is rare in the wild but has long been grown as a sacred tree in China and Japan. Male and female flowers are borne on separate plants; fruiting occurs only when male and female trees are grown together, and in warm summers. The name *Ginkgo* comes from the Japanese words *gin*, "silver," and *kyo*, "apricot."

Ginkgo biloba (ginkgo, maidenhair tree)
Deciduous tree with a conical habit when young, and fan-shaped leaves up to 5in (12cm) across, which turn yellow in autumn. Tiny female flowers are sometimes followed by fetid, plum-like fruits, about 1in (2.5cm) long.
H 130ft (40m), S 70ft (20m).

3–9

GLECHOMA

About six species of Eurasian perennials make up this genus. *G. hederacea*, found in grassland and scrub in woods, is a common weed with a variegated cultivar that is sometimes seen in cultivation. *G. h.* 'Variegata' is attractive combined with bedding plants or as a trailing plant for tubs, windowboxes, and hanging baskets. It is equally useful as groundcover beneath shrubs and hedges. The name *Glechoma* comes from the Greek *glechon*, "mint-like plant."

Glechoma hederacea (ground ivy, alehoof)
Creeping perennial with aromatic, kidney-shaped leaves, often purple-tinged, which have scalloped margins. Tubular, 2-lipped, blue-mauve flowers are produced in spring and early summer. H 6in (15cm), S 24in (60cm).

4–9

GIANT FENNEL, see *Ferula*, p.127
GIANT HYSSOP, see *Agastache foeniculum*, p.75
GINGER, see *Zingiber officinale*, p.223
GINSENG, see *Panax ginseng*, p.170
GLAND BELLFLOWER, see *Adenophora*, p.74
GLOBE ARTICHOKE, see *Cynara scolymus*, p.115
GLORY LILY, see *Gloriosa superba*, p.135
GOAT'S RUE, see *Galega officinalis*, p.130
GOAT NUT, see *Simmondsia chinensis*, p.203
GOLDTHREAD, see *Coptis*, p.266
GOLDEN MARJORAM, see *ORIGANUM*, pp.168–9

***Glechoma hederacea* 'Variegata'**
(variegated ground ivy)
This cultivar has irregular white variegation. It is usually grown as a trailing plant but, if planted in the ground, will root at the nodes, forming a large clump. H 6in (15cm), S 24in (60cm).

5–9

GLYCYRRHIZA

A genus of 20 species of sticky, summer-flowering perennials found in Eurasia, Australia, and the Americas. *G. uralensis* occurs in central, Asia, China, and Japan. *G. glabra*, native to scrub in southwestern Asia and Mediterranean regions, was an important herb in ancient Egypt, Assyria, and China, reaching Europe in the 15th century. It was introduced by Dominican friars to Pontefract, Yorkshire, which became famous for Pontefract cakes, or pomfrets (licorice lozenges).

Glycyrrhiza glabra (licorice)
Variable perennial with stoloniferous roots, downy stems, and pinnate leaves, which have 9–17 often sticky leaflets. Pale blue to violet pea flowers are borne in loose spikes, followed by oblong pods up to 1¼in (3cm) long. H 5ft (1.5m), S 3ft (1m).

7–9

Glycyrrhiza uralensis (Chinese licorice, Manchurian licorice)
Erect perennial with extensive branched rhizomes and pinnate leaves up to 10in (25cm) long. Small violet flowers appear in dense, compact spikes, followed by curved, linear-oblong pods. H 16–36in (40cm–1m), S 12–24in (30–60cm).

9–10

GLORIOSA

There used to be several species of tuberous perennials in this genus, but recent classification has reduced them to variants of a single species occurring widely in tropical Africa and Asia. *G. superba*, native to savanna bush and teak forest, was introduced into cultivation in 1690 and became a favorite exotic ornamental. The flowers may be yellow, orange, dark red, or bicolored, with narrow, recurved petals up to 4in (10cm) long, which are usually waved along the margins.

Gloriosa superba (glory lily, Malabar glory lily, Mozambique lily)
Climber with brittle tubers and sparsely branched stems bearing glossy, ovate-lanceolate leaves up to 7in (18cm) long, which end in a tendril. Variable colored flowers are borne in leaf axils in summer. H 8ft (2.5m), S 12–18in (30–45cm).

11

GNAPHALIUM

About 150 species of annuals and perennials belong to this cosmopolitan genus, which is closely related to *Anaphalis*. *G. uliginosum* is found in damp ground in Europe, western Asia, and N America. Most have little to recommend them as garden plants, but a few of the New Zealand species are sought after by alpine enthusiasts. The name *Gnaphalium* comes from the Greek *gnaphalion*, "soft down," and refers to the woolly foliage of most species.

Gnaphalium uliginosum (marsh cudweed, low cudweed, cottonweed)
Woolly annual with spreading stems and silver-gray, stalkless leaves up to 2in (5cm) long. Tiny yellow-brown flowers are borne in dense, terminal clusters in summer. H 1½–8in (4–20cm), S 8in (20cm).

A

GOLDEN RAGWORT, see *Senecio aureus*, p.202
GOLDENROD, see *Solidago virgaurea*, p.204
GOLDENSEAL, see *Hydrastis canadensis*, p.141
GOORA NUT, See *Cola nitida*, p.110
GOOSEFOOT, see *Chenopodium*, p.106
GOOSEGRASS, see *Galium aparine*, p.131
GOUTWEED, see *Aegopodium podagraria*, p.74

GOSSYPIUM

There are 39 species of annuals, perennials, subshrubs, shrubs, and small trees in this genus, which is distributed throughout warm temperate and tropical regions. *Gossypium* is closely related to *Hibiscus* (see p.138) but is less ornamental. The seeds are covered with long hairs, which can be spun into thread and short hairs, which are suitable for felt. Although perennial, cotton plants are usually grown as annuals in order to minimize the incidence of pests and diseases.

Gossypium herbaceum (cotton, Levant cotton)
Short-lived shrubby perennial with lobed leaves, 6in (15cm) across, dotted with black oil glands. In summer, yellow flowers are followed by a brittle capsule, filled with lint-covered seeds. H 5ft (1.5m), S 3ft (1m).

9–10

GRATIOLA

About 25 species of perennials belong to this genus, which occurs throughout temperate regions. Few have any merit as garden plants, although *G. officinalis*, found in wet grassland in Europe, has attractive flowers. It is an extremely poisonous plant, and cannot be used for the same purposes as the culinary hyssops (*Hyssopus* species, p.141). The name *Gratiola* comes from the Latin *gratia*, "thanks," an old name for the plant, which was revered for its medicinal virtues.

Gratiola officinalis (hedge hyssop)
Perennial with white, scaly rhizomes and hollow stems, bearing lanceolate leaves. Small, solitary, yellow-white tubular flowers, veined purple-red, appear in summer, followed by 4-valved seed capsules. H 12–24in (30–60cm), S 8–15in (20–38cm).

5–8

GUAIACUM

Six species of evergreen shrubs and trees make up this genus, which occurs in the W Indies and warm parts of the Americas. *G. officinale*, native to dry coastal areas of southern C America and the Caribbean, is the national flower of Jamaica. It is an impressive tree when flowering but is now rare in the wild, having been intensively exploited for over four centuries. *Guaiacum* is from the Spanish *guayaco*, originally a Taino Indian word for the plants. The common name means "wood of life."

Guaiacum officinale (lignum vitae, guaiacum, guaiac)
Small tree with divided pinnate leaves about 3½in (9cm) long. Profuse clusters of deep blue flowers, up to 1in (2.5cm) across, are followed by orange-yellow capsules for much of the year. H 15–28ft (5–9m), S 22–25ft (7–8m).

11

HAMAMELIS

Five species of deciduous shrubs and small trees are included in this genus, which ranges across N America, Europe, and eastern Asia; *H. virginiana* is found in moist woods in the southeastern US. *Hamamelis* species and hybrids are among the hardiest and most weather-tolerant shrubs that flower between autumn and spring. The common name refers to the occult powers attributed to these plants, whose hazel-like branches were used as divining rods for water and gold.

Hamamelis virginiana (common witch hazel)
Shrub or small tree with obovate leaves, that turn yellow in autumn. Clusters of 2–4 scented flowers with crinkled linear, yellow petals, appear in autumn as the leaves fall, followed by dehiscent fruits. H 15ft (5m), S 10ft (3m).

4–9

HEDEOMA

There are 38 species of annuals and perennials in this N American genus. They have no great merit as garden plants but are often seen in herb gardens, due to their value in repelling insects. *H. pulegioides* is found in open woods in the eastern US, west to the Dakotas. Its aromatic foliage makes it especially suitable for planting near seats and entrances. The name *Hedeoma* comes from the Greek *hedys*, "sweet," and *osme*, "scent," referring to the fragrant foliage.

Hedeoma pulegioides (American pennyroyal, squaw mint)
Bushy annual with small, ovate leaves, which have a pungent, mintlike aroma. Tiny pale lilac flowers appear in the axils in summer. H 4–16in (10–40cm), S 3–10in (7–24cm).

A

HEDERA

This genus of eleven species of woody evergreen climbers and creepers occurs in Europe, Asia, and northern Africa; *H. helix* is common in woods and hedges throughout Europe and western Asia. Ivy was sacred to Dionysus (Bacchus), the god of wine; if bound to the brow, it was supposed to prevent intoxication. Wreaths of ivy symbolize fidelity and were part of the marriage ceremony in ancient Greece. They were banned by the early Christian church as a pagan custom.

Hedera helix (English ivy)
Climbing or carpet-forming evergreen with stems clad in adventitious roots and dark green leaves. Yellow-green flowers, rich in nectar, appear during autumn on mature plants, followed by globose, black berries. H 30–100ft (10–30m), S 15ft (5m).

4–9

GRAINS OF PARADISE, see *Afromomum melegueta*, p.230; *Amomum xanthioides*, p.237
GRAPE, see *Vitis vinifera*, p.221
GROMWELL, see *Lithospermum*, p.153
GROUND ELDER, see *Aegopodium podagraria*, p.74
GROUND IVY, see *Glechoma hederacea*, p.134
GROUNDSEL, see *Senecio*, p.202
GUARANÀ, see *Paullinia cupana*, p.171
GUELDER ROSE, see *Viburnum opulus*, p.219
GULFWEED, see *Sargassum fusiforme*, p.349
GUM ARABIC, see *Acacia senegal*, p.226
GUMPLANT, GUMWEED, see *Grindelia camporum*, p.290

***Hedera helix* 'Erecta'**
This is an upright, bushy, nonclimbing cultivar, similar to *H. h.* 'Congesta'. H 3ft (1m), S 4ft (1.2m).

6–9

***Hedera helix* 'Glacier'**
A cultivar that has small leaves, marbled silver-gray, with white margins. Less hardy than the species and ideal for containers. H 10ft (3m), S 6ft (2m).

6–9

***Hedera helix* 'Goldheart'**
An outstanding climbing cultivar with dark green leaves that have bright yellow centers. H 20ft (6m), S 10ft (3m).

6–9

HELIANTHUS

A genus of 67 species of tall annuals and perennials native to N and S America. *H. annuus* was grown by native peoples for 3,000 years before its introduction to Spain in 1514. Cultivation as an oilseed crop began in Germany and Russia in the 18th century and spread into central Europe and the Mediterranean. Sunflower seeds, numbering about 1,000 per head, are arranged in concentric, hyperbolic spirals and are usually striped black and white.

Helianthus annuus (sunflower)
Giant, summer-flowering annual with erect stems and large, drooping flower heads, up to 12in (30cm) across, with brown disc florets and yellow ray florets. H to 10ft (3m) or more, S 12–18in (30–45cm).

A

***Helianthus annuus* 'Italian White'**
This cultivar has small, black-centered cream flowers on branched plants. H 4ft (1.2m), S 24in (60cm).

A

***Helianthus annuus* 'Teddy Bear'**
A dwarf cultivar with fully double blooms, smaller growing than *H. a.* 'Flore Pleno'. H 24in (60cm), S 12–15in (30–45cm).

A

HELICHRYSUM

This large genus of about 500 species of annuals, perennials, shrubs, and subshrubs is distributed in Eurasia, southern Africa, and Australasia; *H. italicum* is from southern Europe. Many species have aromatic, gray foliage and papery "everlasting" flowers. They are attractive plants for sunny borders; several are grown in herb gardens for their scent and appearance. *Helichrysum* comes from the Greek *helios*, "sun," and *chrysos*, "golden," and refers to the flower color.

Helichrysum italicum (curry plant)
Dense evergreen subshrub with linear, silver-gray leaves and clusters of yellow, buttonlike flowers in summer. The whole plant smells strongly of curry, especially after rain. H 24in (60cm), S 3ft (1m).

8–9

GUM TRAGACANTH, see *Astragalus gummifer*, p.245
GUM TREE, see *Eucalyptus*, p.125
HASHEESH, see *Cannabis sativa*, p.99
HAWTHORN, see *Crataegus laevigata*, p.112
HEARTSEASE, see *Viola tricolor*, p.220
HEATHER, see *Calluna vulgaris*, p.98
HEMLOCK, see *Conium maculatum*, p.111
HEMP, see *Apocynum cannabinum*, p.85; *Cannabis sativa*, p.99
HEMP AGRIMONY, see *Eupatorium cannabinum*, p.126
HENBANE, see *Hyoscyamus niger*, p.141
HENNA, see *Lawsonia inermis*, p.150
HENS AND CHICKS, see *Sempervivum tectorum*, p.202

HEPATICA

Ten species of small perennials belong to this genus, which occurs throughout northern temperate regions; *H. nobilis* is native to rich European woodlands. They are delightful plants for the rock garden or containers, with anemone-like flowers in early spring. The name *Hepatica* comes from the Greek *hepar*, "liver," and refers to the liverlike shape and color of the leaves, which, according to the Doctrine of Signatures, indicate its use for liver complaints.

Hepatica nobilis (European liverwort, liverleaf, kidneywort)
Variable, semievergreen perennial with a thick rhizome, 3-lobed leaves that have silky-hairy, often purple undersides, and blue-purple to pink or white flowers up to 1in (2.5cm) across. H 3in (8cm), S 4–5in (10–12cm).

4–8

***Hepatica nobilis* 'Rubra Plena'**
This cultivar has delicate, double pink flowers, which, like the species, appear as the new leaves emerge. It is less vigorous than the species and needs careful cultivation. H 3in (8cm), S 4–5in (10–12cm).

4–8

HERACLEUM

This genus of 70 species of annuals, biennials, and perennials is distributed in northern temperate regions and on tropical mountains; *H. sphondylium* is found in Europe, Asia, and northwestern Africa. In eastern Europe the foliage is fermented to make a beer, known as *Parst* or *Bartsch*. The leaf stalks are distilled alone or with bilberries, as a spirit. The name *Heracleum* comes from the Greek *herakleia*, "in honor of Hercules," and alludes to the great size of some species.

Heracleum sphondylium (hogweed, cow parsnip, keck)
Variable, stout biennial with hollow stems and rough, pinnate leaves up to 24in (60cm) long. White or pink flowers are produced in umbels up to 8in (20cm) across in summer, followed by pale brown fruits. H 6ft (2m), S 4ft (1.2m).

3–9

HEUCHERA

There are about 50 species of perennials in this genus, which is N American and Mexican in distribution. *H. americana*, native to central and eastern US, was introduced to Europe from N America in 1656. Several species are attractive enough to be grown as ornamentals, having broad, handsome leaves, and delicate flowers, which are effective *en masse*. *Heuchera* is named after Johann Heinrich von Heucher (1677–1747), once professor of medicine at Wittenberg.

Heuchera americana (alumroot, American sanicle)
Perennial with round to heart-shaped, toothed leaves, marbled brown in spring. Small purple-green flowers appear in tall panicles during late spring and summer. H 12–36in (30cm–1m), S 12–18in (30–45cm).

4–9

HIBISCUS

Some 220 species of annuals, perennials, subshrubs, shrubs, and trees belong to this genus, which occurs in warm temperate and tropical regions; *H. sabdariffa* is found on disturbed ground in tropical Africa and Eurasia. *H. rosa-sinensis* originated in China. Its distinctive flowers, with their projecting column of stamens and style, have become a symbol of exotic places, such as Hawaii, and are important in Hindu devotional ceremonies, being sacred to Ganesh, the elephant god.

Hibiscus rosa-sinensis (Chinese hibiscus)
Dense evergreen shrub with broadly ovate leaves about 3in (8cm) long, and numerous, short-lived, crimson flowers, 3–4in (7–10cm) across. H and S 5–10ft (1.5–3m).

9–11

***Hibiscus rosa-sinensis* 'Cooperi'**
This cultivar dates back to Victorian times. It has narrower leaves, which are variegated pink and white. H and S 5–10ft (1.5–3m).

9–11

HERB BENNET, see *Geum urbanum*, p.134
HERB OF GRACE, see *Ruta graveolens*, p.195
HERB ROBERT, see *Geranium robertianum*, p.133
HOGWEED, see *Heracleum sphondylium*, above
HOLLY, see *Ilex*, p.142
HOLLYHOCK, see *Alcea rosea*, p.78
HOLY GRASS, see *Hierochloë odorata*, p.139
HONEYSUCKLE, see *Lonicera japonica*, p.153
HOP, see *Humulus lupulus*, p.140
HOREHOUND, see *Marrubium vulgare*, p.156
HORNY GOAT WEED, see *Epimedium sagittatum*, p.123

Hibiscus sabdariffa (roselle, Jamaica sorrel, red sorrel)
Woody-based perennial with prickly stems and palmately lobed leaves up to 6in (15cm), and pale yellow, occasionally pink, flowers. The calyx turns bright red as the capsules develop. H 8ft (2.5m), S 6ft (2m).

9–11

HORDEUM

About 20 species of annual and perennial grasses belong to this genus, distributed in northern temperate regions and S America. *H. vulgare* is found wild usually only as an escape from cultivation. Pliny referred to barley as the "oldest among human foods," a staple of bread- and beermaking. It is one of the hardiest grain crops, succeeding in parts of Lapland, Siberia, Alaska, and notably in Tibet, where it is the staple food. It was first grown in Massachusetts in 1602.

Hordeum vulgare (barley)
Annual grass with pale green leaf blades and 6 rows of flowers in cylindrical spikes, up to 4in (10cm) tall. Seeds are covered in a scalelike, membranous bract. H 20–36in (50–90cm), S 12in (30cm).

A

HIERACIUM

This complex genus consists of 250–260 species, which are distributed throughout Europe, northern and western Asia, northwestern Africa, and N America. *H. pilosella* is native to dry, grassy places in Europe. In many cases the species are groups of micro-species, able to produce viable seed without fertilization. They are also highly variable. Most hawkweeds are weedy, but some are grown in rock gardens. *Hieracium* is from the Greek *hierakion*, a name given to various dandelion-like species.

Hieracium pilosella (mouse-ear hawkweed)
Rosette-forming, hairy perennial. Elliptic leaves about 3in (7cm) long, with white felted undersides. Solitary, lemon yellow flowers, 1¼in (3cm) across, appear from late spring to autumn. H 2–12in (5–30cm), S indefinite.

4–9

HOUTTUYNIA

This genus consists of a single species of perennial marginal aquatic native to China, Japan, Laos, and Vietnam. *H. cordata* is widely grown as an ornamental for wet soils, shallow water, and containers. It is invasive in ideal conditions, making excellent groundcover. The whole plant has an unusual orange-coriander aroma, which is especially strong in the rhizomes. *Houttuynia* is named after Maarten Houttuyn (1720–94), a celebrated Dutch physician and naturalist.

Houttuynia cordata (*doku-dami, giáp cá*)
Aromatic, rhizomatous perennial with erect, branched stems and pointed purple-green leaves. Insignificant flowers, surrounded by 4–8 white bracts, appear in conical heads in summer. H 6–24in (15–60cm), S indefinite.

6–10

HIEROCHLOË

A genus of 15 species of fragrant perennial grasses, occurring mainly in temperate regions. *H. odorata* is found in damp, grassy places in colder parts of both hemispheres. *Hierochloë* is closely related to the genus *Anthoxanthum* (see p.85), and shares the same characteristic scent of new-mown hay when dried. *Hierochloë* ("holy grass"), sacred to the Virgin, is burned in New Mexico by the Kiowa as incense and used to scent clothes laid at church doors during festivals in central Europe.

Hierochloë odorata (sweet grass, holy grass, vanilla grass, *zubrovka*)
Tuft-forming, vigorous, deciduous perennial with pointed, flat, linear leaves, ¼in (0.5cm) wide. Pyramidal panicles of ovate, brown spikelets appear in spring. H 10–20in (25–50cm), S 16–24in (40–60cm).

3–9

***Houttuynia cordata* 'Chameleon'**
A more colorful cultivar than *H. c.* 'Variegata', with leaves irregularly marked with yellow and bright pink. H 6–24in (15–60cm), S indefinite.

6–10

***Houttuynia cordata* 'Flore Pleno'**
This cultivar is like the species but has more numerous, white bracts in the flower heads. H 6–24in (15–60cm), S indefinite.

6–10

HORSE BALM, see *Collinsonia canadensis*, p.110
HORSE CHESTNUT, COMMON, see *Aesculus hippocastanum*, p.75
HORSEMINT, see *MENTHA*, pp.158–9; *Monarda*, p.160
HORSERADISH, see *Armoracia rusticana*, p.87
HORSETAIL, see *Equisetum arvense*, p.123
HOUNDSTONGUE, see *Cynoglossum officinale*, p.115
HOUSELEEK, see *Sempervivum*, p.202

HUMULUS

Two species of climbing perennials make up this genus, distributed in northern temperate regions; *H. lupulus* is found in Europe, western Asia, and N America. Male and female flowers are borne on separate plants. From the 9th century, the use of hops in brewing beer gained popularity due to their preservative qualities, replacing bitter herbs such as *Glechoma hederacea*. Regarded as an "unwholesome weed," it was banned in Britain by Henry VI (1422–61) and Henry VIII (1509–47).

Humulus lupulus (hop)
Twining, herbaceous climber with bristly stems and 3–5-lobed, coarsely toothed leaves up to 6in (15cm) long. Tiny male flowers are round, in branched clusters; larger females appear in strobili ("hops") beneath soft, pale green bracts. H 10–20ft (3–6m).

3–8

***Humulus lupulus* 'Aureus'**
This cultivar has yellow-green foliage and is among the finest golden-leaved climbers, with little or no tendency to scorch in sun. H 10–20ft (3–6m).

5–8

HYDNOCARPUS

This genus of some 35 species of medium to large evergreen trees occurs in the Indian subcontinent and Malaysia. It belongs to the Flacourtiaceae, a large tropical family containing about 1,250 species in all. *H. kurzii*, native to rainforest in SE Asia, is one of the few species of economic importance in the family. "Chaulmoogra," the Bengali word for the herb traditionally used to cure leprosy, is the common name also used for *H. wightiana* and *H. anthelmintica*.

Hydnocarpus kurzii (*chaulmoogra*)
Large tree with a trunk up to 4ft (1.2m) thick, and lanceolate leathery leaves about 9in (22cm) long. Male and female flowers are borne separately in summer, followed by round berries containing 12–18 seeds in an oily pulp. H 70–100ft (20–30m), S 50ft (15m).

HYDRANGEA

There are about 100 species of deciduous and evergreen shrubs, small trees, and root climbers in this genus, which occurs in China, Japan, the Himalayas, Indonesia, and both N and S America; *H. arborescens* is native to eastern US. Many hydrangeas are grown for their showy floral clusters. Most cultivars have a high proportion of sterile flowers, often with larger sepals. The name *Hydrangea* comes from the Greek *hydor*, "water," and *angos*, "jar," and refers to the cup-shaped fruits.

Hydrangea arborescens (wild hydrangea, seven barks)
Open, deciduous shrub with toothed leaves up to 7in (18cm) long. Off-white fertile flowers and creamy white sterile flowers are borne in corymbs 2–6in (5–15cm) across, in summer. H 3–10ft (1–3m), S 4–6ft (1.2–2m).

4–10

***Hydrangea arborescens* 'Annabelle'**
This cultivar has even larger flower heads than *H. a.* 'Grandiflora', reaching up to 12in (30cm) across. H 3–10ft (1–3m), S 4–6ft (1.2–2m).

4–10

HYSSOP, see *Hyssopus officinalis*, p.141

HYDRASTIS

Two species of rhizomatous perennials make up this genus, which occurs in northeastern N America (*H. canadensis*) and Japan. Goldenseal shares the same habitats as American ginseng (*Panax quinquefolius*, see p.170); "seng" diggers therefore increase profits by also collecting "seal" (goldenseal) plants. In 1909 "seal" fetched up to $1.50 per pound (.45kg), when the rate for common herbs was 2.5–5 cents. *H. canadensis* is difficult to cultivate.

Hydrastis canadensis (goldenseal, yellowroot, orangeroot)
Perennial with a thick yellow rhizome, and palmate, deeply toothed leaves. Insignificant flowers with green-white stamens appear in late spring, followed by red, inedible fruits. H 8–15in (20–38cm), S 6–12in (15–30cm) or more.

4–8

HYOSCYAMUS

There are 15 species of annuals, biennials, and perennials in this genus, which is distributed through western Europe, northern Africa, and central and southwestern Asia. *H. niger* is found in bare sandy soil, often near the sea. Some henbanes are occasionally seen in herb gardens. They make interesting plants for dry slopes or walls, but are seldom cultivated. *Hyoscyamus* is from the Greek *hys*, "pig," and *kyamos*, "bean," perhaps because pigs can eat henbane without being poisoned.

Hyoscyamus niger (henbane, hogbean)
Fetid annual or biennial with pale green, ovate leaves up to 12in (30cm) long, which are hairy and sticky. Purple-veined, cream flowers appear from spring to autumn, followed by capsules ½in (1cm) long. H 24–36in (60–90cm), S to 4ft (1.2m).

A

HYPERICUM

A genus of about 370 species of annuals, perennials, and deciduous, semievergreen, and evergreen subshrubs and shrubs found mainly in temperate regions. *H. perforatum* is native to woods in Europe and temperate Asia. This varied group provides many fine garden plants for most settings. *Hypericum* may derive from the Greek *hyper*, "above," and *eikon*, "picture," because the flowers were placed above religious images to keep away evil at the northern midsummer festival (June 24).

Hypericum perforatum (perforate St. John's wort, common St. John's wort)
Upright, rhizomatous perennial, woody at the base, with blunt, linear-ovate leaves. Yellow, 5-petaled, gland-dotted flowers, ¾in (2cm) across, appear in summer. H 12–24in (30–60cm), S 6–18in (15–45cm).

4–8

HYSSOPUS

Five species of aromatic perennials are included in this genus, which occurs from Mediterranean regions to central Asia. *H. officinalis*, native to central and southern Europe, western Asia, and northern Africa, is an excellent plant for attracting bees and butterflies. It may also be grown as a low hedge in knot gardens. Rock hyssop (*H. o.* subsp. *aristatus*) is a colorful, late-flowering subshrub. *Hyssopus* is the name used by Hippocrates, derived from the Hebrew *ezob*, "holy herb."

Hyssopus officinalis (hyssop)
Semievergreen perennial, woody at the base, with linear leaves, up to 1in (2.5cm) long, and dense spikes of tubular, 2-lipped, purple-blue flowers (rarely pink or white) in late summer. H 18–24in (45–60cm), S 24–36in (60–90cm).

3–9

Hyssopus officinalis f. ***albus*** (white hyssop)
This variant has pure white flowers. It makes a choice specimen plant or informal hedge for white gardens and borders. H 18–24in (45–60cm), S 24–36in (60–90cm).

3–9

Hyssopus officinalis subsp. ***aristatus*** (rock hyssop)
A compact variant with smaller spikes of flowers than those of the species, appearing rather later in the summer. H and S 12in (30cm).

3–9

Hyssopus officinalis f. ***roseus*** (pink hyssop)
An attractive pink form of hyssop, which combines well with gray-leaved herbs, such as artemisias. H 18–24in (45–60cm), S 24–36in (60–90cm).

3–9

ILEX

A genus of about 400 species of evergreen and deciduous trees and shrubs occurring worldwide, especially in tropical and temperate parts of Asia and N and S America. Many species are in cultivation; the most widely grown is *I. aquifolium*, a very variable species found in western and southern Europe, northern Africa, and western Asia. *I. paraguensis* is native to woods and scrubs in Paraguay, Brazil, and Argentina; *I. verticillata* occurs in swamps in N America.

Ilex aquifolium (English holly)
Small evergreen tree or shrub with shiny leathery leaves, which have undulating, spiny margins. In summer, small, off-white, scented flowers are borne on older wood, with male and female on separate plants. Females produce poisonous red berries. H 10–70ft (3–20m), S 20ft (6m).

7–9

***Ilex aquifolium* 'Ferox Argentea'** (silver hedgehog holly)
This cultivar is male, with purple twigs and small leaves, which have creamy white margins and spines over the entire upper surface. It is slower growing than the species. H 20ft (6m), S 12ft (4m).

7–9

ICELAND MOSS, see *Cetraria islandica*, p.105
ILANG-ILANG, see *Cananga odorata*, p.99
INDIAN BORAGE, see *Plectranthus amboinicus*, p.179
INDIAN BREAD, see *Wolfiporia cocos*, p.372
INDIAN CRESS, see *Tropaeolum majus*, p.215
INDIAN DATE, see *Tamarindus indica*, p.207
INDIAN LICORICE, see *Abrus precatorius*, p.70
INDIAN MADDER, see *Rubia cordifolia*, p.193
INDIAN MULBERRY, see *Morinda citrifolia*, p.161
INDIAN MUSTARD, see *Brassica juncea*, p.95

***Ilex aquifolium* 'Madame Briot'**
A female cultivar with purple-green twigs, scarlet berries, and large, stoutly spined leaves, which have irregular, bright yellow margins. H 30ft (10m), S 15ft (5m).

7–9

Ilex paraguensis (*maté, yerba maté,* Paraguay tea)
Evergreen tree with elliptic-ovate leaves to 5in (12cm) long, which have scalloped margins. Small, green-white flowers appear in the axils of younger branches, followed by clusters of small, deep red berries. H 50ft (15m), S 30ft (10m).

INULA

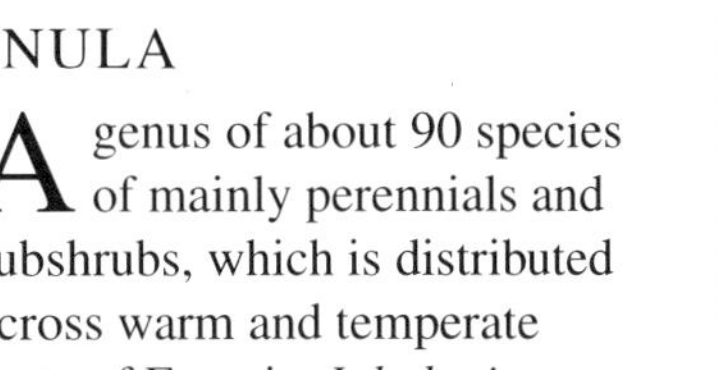

A genus of about 90 species of mainly perennials and subshrubs, which is distributed across warm and temperate parts of Eurasia. *I. helenium,* native to southern Europe and western Asia, is a giant, summer-flowering species, which provides a focal point in the herb garden. Many others are grown in rock gardens and borders for their showy daisy-like flowers. *Inula* is the Latin name used by Horace for the plant. It is thought to be a variant of *Helenium,* named after Helen of Troy.

Inula helenium (elecampane, scabwort)
Robust perennial with thick rhizomes, and stout, erect stems. Leaves are pointed, and toothed, up to 28in (70cm) long. Yellow daisylike flowers, up to 3in (7cm) across, appear from mid-summer to midautumn. H 10ft (3m), S 5ft (1.5m).

3–9

Ilex verticillata (black alder, winterberry)
Large, deciduous, suckering shrub with elliptic, toothed leaves, to 3in (7cm) long. In early summer, insignificant white flowers appear; female plants bear bright red, poisonous berries. H 6–15ft (2–5m), S 4–10ft (1.2–3m).

3–9

IRIS

This large genus consists of about 300 species of perennials, found mainly in northern temperate regions. *I. germanica* var. *florentina* is native to the eastern Mediterranean, *I. versicolor* to northeast N America. Most species are in cultivation, and range from rock-garden plants to aquatics. Iris flowers are the origin of the scepter and the fleur-de-lis; the three inner petals, or standards, represent faith, wisdom, and valor. *Iris* is named after the Greek goddess of the rainbow.

Iris versicolor (blue flag, wild iris)
Wetland perennial with a branched, creeping rhizome and sword-shaped leaves up to 3ft (1m) long. Purple, yellow-veined flowers are produced in groups of 4–6 in summer. H 20in–3½ft (50cm–1.1m), S indefinite.

3–8

IMPATIENS

There are some 500 species of frost-hardy to tender annuals, perennials, and subshrubs in this genus, which is widely distributed, especially in tropical and subtropical parts of Asia and Africa. *I. pallida,* found mainly in limestone regions in eastern N America, has more glaucous foliage and paler, less spotted flowers than the similar, more common *I. capensis.* Most jewelweeds have succulent stems, orchid-like flowers, and five-valved capsules that open explosively to release the seeds.

Impatiens pallida (pale touch-me-not, jewelweed)
Tall, hairless annual with succulent stems and gray-green, coarsely toothed leaves. Yellow pendent flowers, occasionally spotted red-brown, appear in summer. H 2–5ft (60cm–1.5m), S 12–24in (30–60cm).

A

Iris germanica var. ***florentina*** (orris)
Stout perennial with a rhizome to 2in (5cm) thick and narrow, sword-shaped leaves up to 18in (45cm) long. White, violet-tinged flowers appear on branched stems in early summer. H 2–4ft (60cm–1.2m), S indefinite.

4–10

INDIAN PENNYWORT, see *Centella asiatica*, p.104
INDIAN PHYSIC, see *Gillenia trifoliata*, p.134
INDIAN POKEBERRY, see *Phytolacca acinosa*, p.176
INDIAN SANDALWOOD, see *Santalum album*, p.198
INDIAN SNAKEROOT, see *Rauvolfia serpentina*, p.189
INDIAN TOBACCO, see *Lobelia inflata*, p.153
INDIGO WEED, see *Baptisia tinctoria*, p.92
IPÊ-ROXA, see *Tabebuia impetiginosa*, p.207
IPECAC, IPECACUANHA, see *Cephaelis ipecacuanha*, p.104

Iris versicolor 'Kermesina'
This cultivar has plum-colored flowers. Like the species, it has very long, sword-shaped leaves. H 20in–3½ft (50cm–1.1m), S indefinite.

3–8

ISATIS

About 30 species of annuals, biennials, and perennials belong to this genus, which occurs throughout Europe into central Asia. *I. tinctoria* (woad), found on chalky soil in central and southern Europe and western Asia, is widely grown as a dye and medicinal plant. It was a major crop in the Middle Ages, especially in southern France whence the expression "Land of Cockaigne" arose, after the earthenware cups (coques) in which the dye paste was sold.

Isatis tinctoria (woad)
Biennial or short-lived perennial with a stout taproot, branched stem, and lanceolate leaves, 1½–4in (4–10cm) long. Numerous yellow, 4-petaled flowers are borne in summer, followed by pendent, fiddle-shaped, black seeds. H 20in–4ft (50cm–1.2m), S 24in (60cm).

3–8

JASMINUM

A genus of about 350 species of deciduous and evergreen shrubs, climbers, and ramblers, distributed mainly in tropical Africa and Eurasia; *J. grandiflorum* and *J. officinale* are both native to the Himalayas. *J. sambac* is found widely in Asia, but probably originated in India. Several species of jasmine have a long history of use in perfumery, medicine, and flavoring tea. They are also popular as ornamentals for their exquisitely scented flowers. *Jasminum* is from a Latinized version of the Persian *yasmin*.

Jasminum grandiflorum (royal jasmine, Spanish jasmine, *jati*)
Evergreen rambler bearing pinnate leaves with 7 or 9 leaflets. Clusters of up to 50 scented, white, often pink-tinged, flowers appear in summer and autumn. H 15ft (5m).

9–11

Jasminum officinale (common jasmine, jessamine)
Vigorous, twining deciduous climber with green stems and pinnate leaves, which have 3–9 leaflets. Fragrant white flowers are borne throughout summer, followed by black berries. H 30ft (10m).

9–11

Jasminum officinale **'Aureum'**
This variant has fragrant white flowers but differs from the species in having yellow-variegated leaves. It is a most effective climber against dark surfaces. H 30ft (10m).

9–11

Jasminum officinale **f. *affine***
A form with larger flowers than the species and with pink-tinged buds. It should not be confused with the tender *J. grandiflorum*. H 30ft (10m).

9–11

IRISH MOSS, see *Chondrus crispus*, p.260
IVY, see *Hedera helix*, p.136
IVY BUSH, see *Kalmia latifolia*, p.146
JABORANDI, see *Pilocarpus microphyllus*, p.327
JACK-BY-THE-HEDGE, see *Alliaria petiolata*, p.79
JACK-IN-THE-PULPIT, see *Arisaema triphyllum*, p.87
JACOB'S LADDER, see *Polemonium caeruleum*, p.180
JALAP, see *Ipomoea purga*, p.297
JAMAICA DOGWOOD, see *Piscidia piscipula*, p.330
JAMAICA QUASSIA, see *Ceiba pentandra*, p.104

Jasminum sambac (Arabian jasmine)
Evergreen rambler with simple, ovate leaves up to 3in (8cm) long. Tight clusters of 3 or more fragrant, tubular, white flowers, aging to pink-purple, with 4–9 rounded lobes, are borne throughout the year, mainly at the tips of lateral shoots. H 30ft (10m).

9–10

***Jasminum sambac* 'Grand Duke of Tuscany'** (*kudda-mulla*, Tuscan jasmine)
This rare, slow-growing cultivar has leaves arranged in threes and solitary, exceptionally large, double flowers. It was imported from Goa to Pisa c.1691. H 6ft (2m).

9–10

JUGLANS

This genus consists of 21 species of deciduous trees distributed from Mediterranean regions to eastern Asia and through N America into the Andes. *J. regia* is found wild from southern Europe to southern China. Some walnuts are grown for their ashlike, often very large leaves that in some species turn yellow in autumn. Although often called "English" walnuts, trees in the British Isles rarely crop as well as those in warmer climates. *Juglans* comes from the Latin *Iupiter*, "Jupiter," and *glans*, "acorn."

Juglans regia (English walnut)
Deciduous tree with silver-gray bark, and divided, aromatic leaves. Dark yellow male catkins and spikes of female flowers appear in late spring to early summer, followed by dark green fruits, each containing a woody nut. H 120ft (35m), S 70ft (20m).

5–8

JOB'S TEARS, see *Coix lacryma-jobi*, p.110

***Juglans regia* 'Laciniata'** (cut-leaved walnut)
This cultivar has slightly pendent branches and deeply cut leaflets. H 120ft (35m), S 70ft (20m).

5–8

JUNIPERUS

About fifty species of coniferous trees and shrubs belong to this genus, which occurs throughout the northern hemisphere. *J. communis*, found on both acid and calcareous soils, is widely distributed and exceptionally variable. Many of its variants are propagated vegetatively from male plants and do not bear "berries." Junipers are popular ornamentals, with a great variety of size, habit, and color. Most have two kinds of foliage: scalelike adult leaves, and pointed juvenile leaves.

Juniperus communis (common juniper)
Upright, spreading, or prostrate shrub with red-brown, papery bark and spiny juvenile foliage only. Flowers are insignificant. Fruits are green at first, turning black with a gray bloom when ripe. H and S 6–12ft (2–4m), occasionally to 40ft (12m).

2–8

JUSTICIA

This large genus consists of about 420 species of evergreen perennials, subshrubs, and shrubs, occurring in tropical and subtropical parts of both hemispheres. *J. adhatoda*, common in India, is sometimes confused with the closely related, fragrant-flowered *J. adhatodoides*, commonly known as "snake bush." The genus includes some ornamentals, notably the famous shrimp plant, *Justicia brandegeana*. *Justicia* is named after James Justice, an 18th-century Scottish horticulturist.

Justicia adhatoda (Malabar nut, *vasak*)
Erect, evergreen, sparsely branched shrub with ovate to lanceolate, prominently veined leaves up to 6in (15cm) long. Dense, terminal spikes of tubular, white flowers, veined pink to purple, appear in summer. H 6–10ft (2–3m), S 3–6ft (1–2m).

KAEMPFERIA

A genus of about 70 species of rhizomatous, aromatic perennials found in tropical Africa and SE Asia; *K. galanga* ranges from India to China. A few species are grown as groundcover in the tropics or under cover in cold areas. They need high humidity and do well in pots alongside warm-growing orchids or in beds beneath greenhouse staging. *Kaempferia* is named after Engelbert Kaempfer (1651–1716), a German physician who described Japanese plant species.

Kaempferia galanga (resurrection lily)
Low perennial with 2–3 almost round, spreading leaves, 3–6in (8–15cm) across, and short-lived, 3-petaled, white flowers, up to 1in (2.5cm) in diameter, marked purple on the lip. H 12in (30cm), S 12–24in (30–60cm).

9–11

LACTUCA

This genus contains about 100 species of annuals and perennials, which occur worldwide, especially in northern temperate regions. *L. serriola* is a cosmopolitan weed, originally from Europe. It is more like a sow thistle (*Sonchus* species) than a garden lettuce (*L. sativa*) and has little to recommend it as an ornamental or culinary plant. *Lactuca* is from the Latin *lac*, "milk," and refers to the milky sap (latex), source of lactucarium, the "lettuce opium" of the 18th century.

Lactuca serriola (prickly lettuce, wild lettuce, compass plant)
Fetid, hairless annual or biennial with prickly stems and prickly, glaucous leaves up to 12in (30cm) long. Yellow flowers that resemble miniature dandelions appear in panicles in summer. H 3–5ft (1–1.5m), S 12–36in (30cm–1m).

A

KALMIA

A genus of six or seven species of evergreen shrubs and small trees, which occurs in N America and Cuba. All have poisonous foliage. *K. latifolia* is found in dry, rocky areas in eastern N America. Most species are cultivated for their clusters of exquisite, saucer-shaped, pink to red or white flowers. *K. latifolia* is the most spectacular of them when in flower, as a garden plant and in the wild. It is the state flower of Connecticut and Pennsylvania.

Kalmia latifolia (mountain laurel, calico bush, ivybush)
Shrub or small tree with downy young shoots and glossy, leathery, lanceolate leaves, up to 2in (5cm) long. Pink to white flowers are borne in late spring and early summer. H 10–30ft (3–10m), S 10ft (3m).

4–7

***Kalmia latifolia* 'Clementine Churchill'**
A fine cultivar with umbels of deep pink buds that open into two-tone flowers, dark pink inside and mauve-pink on the outside. H 10–30ft (3–10m), S 10ft (3m).

4–7

LAMIUM

A genus comprising about 40 species of annuals and perennials known as deadnettles. They resemble stinging nettles (*Urtica* species, see p.217) in appearance, and are distributed throughout Eurasia (*L. album*) and northern Africa. Deadnettles are so called because they do not sting. Only a few of the species are attractive enough for garden use. These include ornamental cultivars of several species, such as *L. album*, which are otherwise common weeds.

Lamium album (white deadnettle, archangel)
Hairy perennial with creeping rhizomes, 4-angled stems and ovate, coarsely-toothed leaves, 1¼–3in (3–7cm) long. Whorls of tubular, white, 2-lipped flowers appear from spring. H 6–24in (15–60cm), S 24–36in (60–90cm).

3–9

***Lamium album* 'Friday'**
This cultivar has gold-centered leaves in 2 shades of green, 1¼–3in (3–7cm) long. The colors are brightest in spring, fading as flowering progresses. H and S 18–24in (45–60cm).

3–9

KAVA KAVA, see *Piper methysticum*, p.329
KHAKI WEED, see *Tagetes minuta*, p.207
KHELLA, see *Ammi visnaga*, p.83
KIDNEYWORT, see *Hepatica nobilis*, p.138
KINO, see *Pterocarpus marsupium*, p.186
KNAPWEED, see *Centaurea*, p.104
KNITBONE, see *Symphytum officinale*, p.206
KNOTWEED, see *Polygonum*, p.181
KOREAN MINT, see *Agastache rugosa*, p.75
KUDZU, see *Pueraria lobata*, p.186
KUSAM SEEDS, see *Brucea javanica*, p.95
LABRADOR TEA, see *Ledum groenlandicum*, p.150
LACQUERED BRACKET FUNGUS, see *Ganoderma lucidum*, p.131

LARIX

Nine species of large, coniferous trees make up this genus, which abounds in cool parts of the northern hemisphere; *L. decidua* is native to the mountains of central Europe, and to northern Russia and Siberia. Larches resemble *Cedrus* species (see p.103), except that the cones mature in a single year and the foliage is deciduous. Widely grown for lumber, they are also popular as ornamentals. *L. decidua* is particularly attractive in spring and has fine autumn color.

Larix decidua (common larch, European larch)
Deciduous conifer with grayish-red bark, drooping branches and rosettes of soft, light green needles. Female cones are erect and pink (known as larch "roses"), ripening brown, 1–1½in (2.5–4cm) long. H 160ft (50m), S 50ft (15m).

2–6

***Larix decidua* 'Pendula'**
Though often rather irregular in habit, the weeping larch makes an attractive specimen when young. This cultivar dates back to c.1836. H 160ft (50m), S 50ft (15m).

2–6

***Laurus nobilis* 'Angustifolia'** (willow-leaf bay)
An unusual cultivar with narrow, wavy-edged, pale green leaves, 1¼–3in (3–7cm) long. It is hardier than the species. H 10–50ft (3–15m), S 30ft (10m).

8–10

LAURUS

There are only two species of evergreen shrubs or small trees in this genus, which occurs in southern Europe, the Canary Islands, and the Azores. *L. nobilis* is native to the Mediterranean region. Although both are grown as ornamentals, the popularity of *L. nobilis* as a culinary herb makes it far more common in cultivation than the more tender *L. azorica* (Canary Island laurel). *Laurus* is from the Latin *laus*, "praise," and refers to the crown of bay leaves worn by victorious Romans.

Laurus nobilis (bay, bay laurel, sweet bay)
Dense evergreen shrub or small tree with leathery, pointed leaves. Clusters of small, cream-yellow flowers with conspicuous stamens appear in spring, followed by dark purple berries. H 10–50ft (3–15m), S 30ft (10m).

8–10

***Laurus nobilis* 'Aurea'** (golden bay)
This cultivar has yellow-tinged leaves, which are at their best in winter and spring. It is slightly hardier than the species. H 10–50ft (3–15m), S 30ft (10m).

8–10

LAD'S LOVE, see *ARTEMISIA*, pp.88–9
LADY'S BEDSTRAW, see *Galium verum*, p.131
LADY'S MANTLE, see *Alchemilla xanthochlora*, p.79
LADY'S SLIPPER ORCHID, see *Cypripedium*, p.115
LADY'S SMOCK, see *Cardamine pratensis*, p.101
LAPPA, see *Arctium lappa*, p.86
LARCH, see *Larix decidua*, above
LAUREL, see *Prunus laurocerasus*, p.184
LAVENDER, LAVANDIN, see *LAVANDULA*, pp.148–9
LAVENDER COTTON, see *Santolina chamaecyparissus*, p.198

Lavandula

A genus of 21 aromatic evergreen perennials and shrubs that are found throughout Mediterranean regions, the Middle East, and India. Lavenders are among the most popular plants for herb gardens, having subtle coloring and delightful fragrance. The hardier kinds make attractive hedges, while tender variants may be grown under cover. Lavenders differ in habit, foliage, and flower color, which ranges from typical lavender-blue to various shades of purple and white. Due to their popularity and long history of cultivation, garden lavenders are mostly hybrids and cultivars. As a result, accurate identification is often difficult.

Lavandula angustifolia 'Hidcote'
A very popular cultivar for hedging, with a compact, erect habit, lanceolate, gray leaves, and strongly scented, deep violet flowers in dense spikes on stems 12–14in (30–35cm) long in early summer. H 12–24in (30–60cm), S 12in. (30cm).
5–8

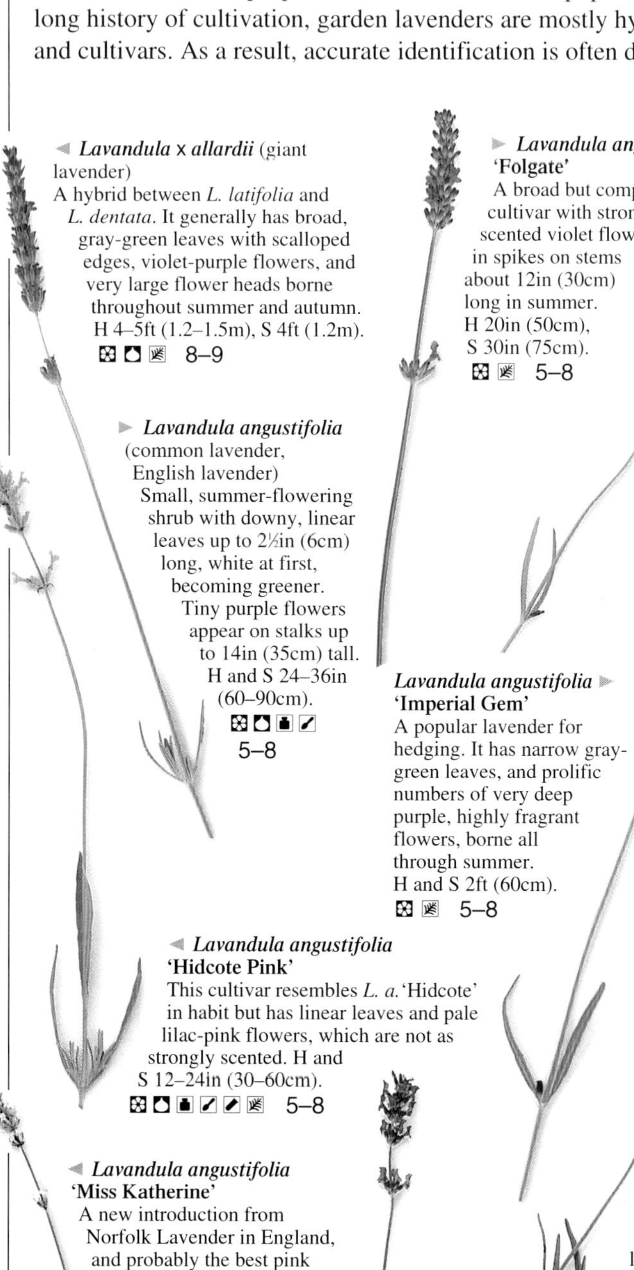

Lavandula* x *allardii (giant lavender)
A hybrid between *L. latifolia* and *L. dentata*. It generally has broad, gray-green leaves with scalloped edges, violet-purple flowers, and very large flower heads borne throughout summer and autumn. H 4–5ft (1.2–1.5m), S 4ft (1.2m).
8–9

***Lavandula angustifolia* 'Folgate'**
A broad but compact cultivar with strongly scented violet flowers in spikes on stems about 12in (30cm) long in summer. H 20in (50cm), S 30in (75cm).
5–8

Lavandula angustifolia (common lavender, English lavender)
Small, summer-flowering shrub with downy, linear leaves up to 2½in (6cm) long, white at first, becoming greener. Tiny purple flowers appear on stalks up to 14in (35cm) tall. H and S 24–36in (60–90cm).
5–8

***Lavandula angustifolia* 'Imperial Gem'**
A popular lavender for hedging. It has narrow gray-green leaves, and prolific numbers of very deep purple, highly fragrant flowers, borne all through summer. H and S 2ft (60cm).
5–8

***Lavandula angustifolia* 'Hidcote Pink'**
This cultivar resembles *L. a.*'Hidcote' in habit but has linear leaves and pale lilac-pink flowers, which are not as strongly scented. H and S 12–24in (30–60cm).
5–8

***Lavandula angustifolia* 'Royal Purple'**
A large cultivar that is good for hedging, with narrow, gray-green leaves, and long spikes of deep purple flowers, which retain their color well after drying. H and S 32in (80cm).
5–8

***Lavandula angustifolia* 'Miss Katherine'**
A new introduction from Norfolk Lavender in England, and probably the best pink lavender to date, with flowers of a deeper, more lasting pink than 'Hidcote Pink' or 'Rosea' and a fine fragrance. H and S 2½ft (75cm).
5–8

***Lavandula angustifolia* 'Rosea'**
The original pink lavender, with green, rather than gray-green leaves. H 9–18in (23–45cm), S 12–18in (30–45cm).
5–8

***Lavandula angustifolia* 'Munstead'**
A compact, early-flowering cultivar. It has small leaves and strongly scented, bright lavender-blue flowers in loose spikes on stems reaching 12in (30cm). H 12–18in (30–45cm), S 30in (75cm).
5–8

Lavandula lanata (woolly lavender)
Small shrub with linear to oblong-lanceolate, white-felted leaves and slender, long-stalked spikes of lilac flowers from mid-summer. H 2ft (60cm), S 20in (50cm).
8–9

***Lavandula angustifolia* 'Nana Alba'**
A dwarf, compact, erect cultivar introduced before 1938. It has linear silver-gray leaves 1in (2.5cm) long. It is ideal for containers, rock gardens, white borders, and edging. H 6–12in (15–30cm), S 6–18in (15–45cm).
5–8

◄ *Lavandula dentata* (fringed lavender)
Shrub with toothed, linear to lanceolate, gray-green leaves with woolly undersides. Dark purple flowers appear in dense spikes from mid- to late summer. H and S 2–3ft (60-90cm).
8–9

◄ *Lavandula dentata* var. ***candicans***
This variety is identical to the species, except for its gray-white foliage. H and S 2–3ft (60–90cm).
8–9

◄ *Lavandula multifida* (branched lavender)
A distinctive lavender with hairy stems and gray-green, feathery leaves. The flower heads are divided into several spikes of violet-blue flowers arranged in spirals. H 12–24in (30–60cm), S 24–30in (60–75cm).
8–9

◄ *Lavandula pinnata*
This delicate lavender has branched, hairy stems and divided, soft gray-green leaves about 3in (8cm) long. Lilac-blue flowers appear almost all year in a sheltered position. H 3ft (1m), S 24in (60cm).
9–10

► *Lavandula* **'Sawyers'**
A hybrid lavender between *L. angustifolia* and *L. lanata*. It has gray leaves and large lavender-blue flowers, which open purple. H 18 27in (45–68cm), S 3½ft (1.1m).
7–9

Lavandula x *intermedia* ► (lavandin)
Robust, variable hybrids between *L. angustifolia* and *L. latifolia*, with a rounded habit and long, gray-green to gray leaves. Long spikes of highly fragrant flowers, from dark violet to white, are borne from mid- to late summer. H and S very variable.
5–7

◄ *Lavandula* x *intermedia* **Dutch Group**
This group was introduced in the 1920s. It has a rounded habit, large gray leaves, and lavender-blue flowers. H 16–36in (40–90cm), S 16in (40cm).
5–7

◄ *Lavandula stoechas* (French lavender, Spanish lavender)
Dense, bushy shrub with narrowly lanceolate, light green leaves and dark purple flowers in spikes up to 1¼in (3cm), topped by purple-white bracts. Given a dry, sheltered position, it is often hardy in cold areas. H and S 12–36in (30–90cm).
8–9

◄ *Lavandula viridis* (green lavender)
This unusual lavender has broad, fresh green leaves and inconspicuous white flowers with green bracts. The plant has a pungent, lemony aroma. H and S 18–24in (45–60cm).
9–10

► *Lavandula* x *intermedia* **'Grosso'**
One of the finest commercial lavandin cultivars, discovered in Vaucluse, France c.1972. It has a wide-spreading habit, gray-green foliage, and large spikes of dark violet flowers. H 4ft (1.2m), S 3ft (1m).
5–9

▲ *Lavandula* x *intermedia* **'Grappenhall'**
A robust cultivar with rather broad, gray-green leaves and strong stems of lavender-blue flowers, often with smaller spikes on sideshoots, in midsummer. H 3–4ft (1–1.2m), S 5ft (1.5m).
5–9

► *Lavandula stoechas* subsp. ***pedunculata*** (Spanish lavender)
This subspecies has long, magenta-purple bracts and long flower stalks reaching 8–12in (20–30cm). H and S 30in (75cm).
8–9

▼ *Lavandula* x *intermedia* **'Twickel Purple'**
A broad, rather untidy bushy cultivar. The leaves tend to flush purple in winter, and it bears strongly scented, lavender-blue flowers in spikes up to 4½in (11cm) long. H 20–24in (50–60cm), S 24–36in (60–90cm).
5–9

▲ *Lavandula* x *intermedia* **'Provence'**
A French commercial cultivar with a bushy habit, long gray-green leaves, and dark violet flowers on stems 18in (45cm) long. H and S 1½–3ft (45–90cm).
5–9

▲ *Lavandula stoechas* f. ***leucantha***
A form with white flowers and bracts, which otherwise shares the same characteristics as the species. H and S 12–36in (30–90cm).
8–9

◄ *Lavandula* x *intermedia* **'Seal'**
A very vigorous cultivar with green foliage and strong stems of pale lavender flowers. It was introduced by The Herb Farm, Seal, Kent, England before 1935. H 5ft (1.5m), S 4ft (1.2m).
5–9

LAWSONIA

A single species of evergreen shrub makes up this genus, which occurs in northern Africa, southwestern Asia, Australia, and is naturalized in America. Found on plains, low hills, and river banks, the species was traditionally planted as a windbreak for vineyards. Referred to as "camphire" in the Bible, *L. inermis* is now more familiar as "henna," from the Arabic name. Its religious significance derived from its symbolization of fire and earth.

Lawsonia inermis (henna, mignonette tree, Egyptian privet)
Variable, thorny shrub with oblong leaves, to 2in (5cm). Small white to pink, highly scented flowers are borne in panicles up to 16in (40cm) long in summer, followed by capsular fruits. H 20ft (6m), S 15ft (5m).

LEDUM

There are four species of low-growing evergreen shrubs in this genus, occurring in wet moorland throughout cool northern temperate regions. *L. groenlandicum* is found wild throughout northern N America to Greenland. All ledums are in cultivation, and make neat, rhododendron-like plants for pool edges and peat gardens. The dried foliage of *L. groenlandicum* makes a passable substitute for tea and was used as such during the Revolutionary War.

Ledum groenlandicum (Labrador tea)
Upright, evergreen shrub with woolly twigs and aromatic leaves, ¾–2½(2–6cm) long, which have red-brown undersides. Small, scented, white flowers appear in rounded clusters in spring and early summer. H and S 3ft (1m).

2–6

Leonurus sibiricus (Chinese motherwort)
Erect biennial with branched stems, square in cross-section, bearing deeply veined leaves, up to 4in (10cm) long. In late summer, small, 2-lipped, pink to off-white flowers are followed by black nutlets. H 3ft (1m), S 24in (60cm).

4–8

LEONURUS

Four species of upright biennials and perennials make up this genus, which is distributed throughout temperate Eurasia. *L. cardiaca*, native to Europe, including southern and central Russia, and the similar *L. sibiricus*, native to Siberia, China, Korea, and Taiwan, are attractive in spring, when the divided, deeply veined foliage is at its best. They are widely grown in herb gardens, making an attractive background for herbs with undistinguished foliage.

Leonurus cardiaca (motherwort)
Strong-smelling perennial with purple stems and palmate, deeply lobed leaves up to 3in (7cm) long. Mauve-pink to white downy flowers with purple-spotted lips are produced in axillary whorls from midsummer to mid-autumn. H 4ft (1.2m), S 24in (60cm).

4–8

LEVISTICUM

A genus of a single species of perennial, occurring in the eastern Mediterranean region. *L. officinale* is useful since it produces new shoots in early spring when few other fresh herbs are available. In medieval texts, lovage appears as *luvesche* (Old French) and *loveache*, associating the plant with love potions and aphrodisiacs. Both *Levisticum* and "lovage" are corruptions of the Latin *ligusticum*, "Ligurian," because *L. officinale* was once abundant in Liguria, Italy.

Levisticum officinale (lovage, love parsley)
Large, celery-scented perennial with stout, fleshy roots, hollow stems and smooth, divided leaves up to 28in (70cm) long. Tiny yellow-green flowers are borne in summer, followed by tiny aromatic seeds. H 6ft (2m), S 3ft (1m).

5–8

LAWN CHAMOMILE, see *Chamaemelum nobile* 'Treneague', p.105
LEEK, see *ALLIUM*, pp.80–81
LEMON, see *Citrus limon*, p.108
LEMON BALM, see *Melissa officinalis*, p.157
LEMON GRASS, see *Cymbopogon citratus*, p.115
LEMON VERBENA, see *Aloysia triphylla*, p.82
LEMON-SCENTED GUM, see *Eucalyptus citriodora*, p.125
LEOPARD LILY, see *Belamcanda chinensis*, p.92
LEOPARD'S BANE, see *Arnica montana*, p.87
LESSER CELANDINE, see *Ranunculus*

LIATRIS

There are about 35 species of perennials in this genus, which occurs only in eastern N America. All grow from corms or flattened rootstocks. *L. spicata* (often called *L. callilepis* in horticulture) is found wild in damp places in rocky woodland, pine barrens, and grassland. It was introduced from N America to Europe in 1732, and now has a number of cultivars. All make outstanding, late-flowering plants for boggy ground beside streams and ponds.

Liatris spicata (blazing star, button snakeroot, gay feather)
Stiffly upright perennial with linear leaves up to 16in (40cm) long. Dense spikes of pink-purple, thistlelike flowers appear from late summer to late autumn. H 3ft (1m), S 24in (60cm).

4–9

***Liatris spicata* 'Alba'**
This cultivar is like the species, except for its white flowers.
H 3ft (1m), S 24in (60cm).

4–9

LIGUSTRUM

A genus of about 50 species of deciduous and evergreen trees and shrubs, which are widely distributed in Europe, northern Africa, eastern and SE Asia, and Australia. *L. lucidum* is found on hillsides and along roadsides in China and Korea. The flowers have a strong, often sickly odor. *Ligustrum* is the Latin word used by Pliny for privet, possibly derived from the Latin *ligare*, "to tie," referring to the use of the flexible twigs as cordage.

Ligustrum lucidum (glossy privet, Chinese privet)
Small evergreen tree or shrub with glossy, dark green, ovate leaves, 3–6in (7.5–15cm) long. From late summer, tiny, creamy white, fragrant flowers are followed by blue-black berries. H 50ft (15m), S 10ft (3m).

7–10

***Ligustrum lucidum* 'Excelsum Superbum'**
An outstanding variegated cultivar that has yellow-edged, bright green leaves with pale green markings.
H 50ft (15m), S 10ft (3m).

6–10

LIGUSTICUM

A genus of 25 species of perennials, occurring in northern temperate regions, closely related to *Levisticum officinale* (lovage, see p.150). *L. scoticum*, found in Europe, Greenland, and N America, is a celery-like plant, often grown as a pot herb. The Chinese *L. sinense* is widely cultivated in China for the herb trade, the most commonly grown being *L. sinense* 'Chuanxiong'. The name *Ligusticum* comes from the Greek *ligustikas*, describing a plant that grows in the Italian province of Liguria.

Ligusticum scoticum (Scots lovage, sea lovage)
Perennial with red-green stems and glossy leaves, divided into three broad, toothed leaflets. Green-white flowers are produced in summer, followed by tiny oblong to ovoid seeds. H 16–36in (5–90cm), S 4–24in (10–60cm).

5–8

LILIUM

This genus of about 100 species of bulbous perennials is found throughout temperate parts of the northern hemisphere. *L. candidum* is native to the eastern Mediterranean. Many lilies are grown as ornamentals. *L. candidum* can be unpredictable in cultivation, and will flower only when conditions are exactly right. It is a symbol of purity associated with the Virgin Mary; in pre-Christian times, it was sacred to Juno, consort of Jupiter and queen of heaven.

Lilium candidum (madonna lily)
Perennial with pale yellow, scaly bulbs, and dark maroon stems, bearing lanceolate leaves to 3in (7cm) long. Five to 20 pure white, fragrant flowers, yellow inside at the base, are borne in summer. H 3–5ft (1–1.5m), S 12–18in (30–45cm).

4–9

ficaria, p.188
LETTUCE, see *Lactuca*, p.146
LEVANT COTTON, see *Gossypium herbaceum*, p.136
LIFE EVERLASTING, see *Antennaria dioica*, p.84
LIFE-OF-MAN, see *Aralia racemosa*, p.86
LIFEROOT, see *Senecio aureus*, p.202
LIGNUM VITAE, see *Guaiacum officinale*, p.136
LILY, see *Lilium*, above
LILY OF THE VALLEY, see *Convallaria majalis*, p.111
LIME, see *Citrus aurantiifolia*, p.108

LINARIA

There are about 100 species of annuals and perennials in this genus, which is found in Europe and other northern temperate regions. *L. vulgaris*, found in grassland and hedgerows, is an easily grown, late-blooming plant. A peloric (monstrous) form occurs occasionally, which has five spurs instead of the normal one. The flowers then appear regular in shape, rather than having the usual irregular form. *Linaria* is from the Greek *linon*, "flax," and refers to the flaxlike leaves of the plant.

Linaria vulgaris (butter-and-eggs)
Slender, upright perennial with linear leaves. Yellow, snapdragon-like flowers, marked orange at the mouth with a ½in (1cm) long spur, are borne from summer to autumn. H 6–36in (15–90cm), S 4–18in (10–45cm).

6–9

LINDERA

This genus of about 80 species of deciduous and evergreen, often aromatic, trees and shrubs, is closely related to the bay tree (*Laurus nobilis*, see p.147). Most occur in southern and eastern Asia, with two species in N America; *L. benzoin* is native to damp areas in southeastern US. Some are grown as ornamentals for their aromatic foliage; the deciduous species are colorful in autumn. Male and female flowers are borne on separate plants, making it necessary to grow both for fruiting.

Lindera benzoin (spice bush, Benjamin, feverbush)
Aromatic, deciduous shrub with obovate leaves, which turn yellow in autumn. Dense clusters of small green-yellow flowers appear in spring, followed by bright red berries on female plants. H and S 15ft (5m).

4–9

LINUM

This large genus of some 200 species of annuals, biennials, perennials, and shrubs, is found in northern temperate regions. Some are grown as ornamentals, producing numerous, brightly colored flowers throughout the summer. *L. usitatissimum*, found only in cultivation, is also one of the world's oldest crop plants, grown as a source of flax since 5000BC. In the 8th century, the Emperor Charlemagne decreed that flax seeds should be consumed in order to maintain good health.

Linum usitatissimum (flax, linseed, flaxseed)
Erect annual with narrow, gray-green leaves, to 1in (2.5cm) long. Sky-blue flowers are borne in summer, followed by spherical capsules, which contain shiny, oval, flattened seeds. H 2½–4ft (80cm–1.2m), S 12–24in (30–60cm).

A

LIPPIA

About 200 species of tender and half-hardy shrubs and small trees belong to this genus, which occurs in tropical Africa and the Americas. *L. graveolens* is found in dry areas from Texas into C America. *Lippia* is closely related to *Aloysia*; *A. triphylla* (lemon verbena) was once classified as *Lippia citriodora*. A dozen or more species are wild-collected or cultivated in warmer parts of the world for their aromatic foliage, but are rarely seen in northern temperate regions.

Lippia graveolens (Mexican oregano)
Aromatic shrub with elliptic to oblong, downy, crinkled leaves to 2½in (6cm) long. Small yellow-white flowers, often with a yellow eye, are produced from spring to winter. H 6ft (2m), S 1–5ft (30cm–1.5m).

9–11

LIQUIDAMBAR

A genus of four species of deciduous trees found through N America and Eurasia into China. *L. orientalis* is found in damp places in western Asia; *L. styraciflua* in damp woodland from eastern US to Guatemala. They have handsome, maplelike leaves and spectacular autumn color. Species grown in cultivation reach only about half the height of wild specimens. *Liquidambar* is from the Latin *liquidus*, "liquid," and *ambar*, "amber," describing the fragrant resin produced by the tree.

Liquidambar orientalis (oriental sweet gum, storax)
Bushy, deciduous tree with mostly 5-lobed leaves, which have coarsely toothed margins. Inconspicuous flowers appear in spring, followed by small, spiny, ball-shaped fruits. H to 100ft (30m), S 15–70ft (5–20m).

7–9

Liquidambar styraciflua (sweet gum, American storax)
Large deciduous tree with glossy leaves that turn yellow and crimson in autumn. Inconspicuous flowers appear in spring as the fragrant, new leaves open, followed by globose, spiny fruits. H 100ft (30m), S 70ft (20m) in cultivation.

5–9

LINALOE, see *Bursera glabrifolia*, p.251
LINDEN, see *Tilia*, p.214
LING, see *Calluna vulgaris*, p.98
LINSEED, see *Linum usitatissimum*, above
LION'S FOOT, see *Alchemilla xanthochlora*, p.79
LIPSTICK TREE, see *Bixa orellana*, p.94
LICORICE, see *Glycyrrhiza glabra*, p.135
LIVERLEAF, see *Hepatica nobilis*, p.138
LONGLEAF PINE, see *Pinus palustris*, p.329
LOOFAH, see *Luffa cylindrica*, p.154
LOOSESTRIFE, see *Lythrum*, p.154
LOQUAT, see *Eriobotrya japonica*, p.123
LOTUS, see *Nelumbo*, p.164
LOVAGE, see *Levisticum*, p.150; *Ligusticum*, p.151

***Liquidambar styraciflua* 'Aurea'**
An American cultivar with leaves striped and marbled yellow. It does best in areas with warm summers. It is very similar to *L. s.* 'Variegata', which some authorities regard as a synonym. H and S are not determined because no plants of this cultivar are yet mature.

5–9

***Liquidambar styraciflua* 'Worplesdon'**
This cultivar has long, narrowly lobed leaves, which turn yellow and orange in autumn. As for *L. s.* 'Aurea', the H and S of this recently introduced cultivar are not yet determined because no plants are yet mature.

5–9

Lobelia inflata (Indian tobacco, asthma weed, pukeweed)
Spreading, downy annual, with ovate, toothed leaves, 2–3in (5–8cm) long. Light blue, often pink-tinged flowers in summer are followed by inflated, 2-valved capsules. H 8–24in (20–60cm), S 4–12in (10–30cm).

A

LITHOSPERMUM

A genus of 59 species of rhizomatous perennials, found in all temperate regions, except Australasia. *L. erythrorhizon* is found on sunny hillsides in eastern China, Korea, and Japan. Until recently this genus included several shrubby species, now known as *Lithodora*, which are widely grown in rock gardens. Few of the perennial species have any merit as ornamentals. *Lithospermum* is from the Greek *lithos*, "stone," and *spermum*, "seed," referring to the small, hard nutlets.

Lithospermum erythrorhizon (red-rooted gromwell)
Erect, coarsely hairy perennial with thick roots that turn purple when dried. It has lanceolate leaves and white flowers, borne in clusters in summer, followed by gray-white nutlets. H 16–28in (40–70cm), S 12in (30cm).

8–9

LOBELIA

This large genus consists of about 360 species of annuals, perennials, deciduous and evergreen shrubs, and small trees distributed throughout temperate and tropical zones, especially in the Americas; *L. chinensis* is native to eastern Asia; *L. inflata* is common in eastern and central N America. It provides a wide range of colorful, long-flowering plants for most sites, including damp soil and containers. *Lobelia* is named after Matthias de l'Obel (1538–1616), physician to James I of England.

Lobelia chinensis (Chinese lobelia)
Slender, creeping perennial rooting at nodes, with ascending branches and lanceolate leaves up to 10in (25cm) long. White to rose-purple flowers are produced singly or in pairs in summer. H 8in (20cm), S indefinite.

5–9

LONICERA

A genus of 180 species of deciduous, occasionally evergreen shrubs and climbers found throughout the northern hemisphere into Mexico, and in the Philippines; *L. japonica* is native to eastern Asia and naturalized in Australia and parts of the US. Many are grown as ornamentals, mainly for their flowers. One of the most popular is *L. japonica*, especially its long-flowering, very fragrant cultivar, *L. j.* 'Halliana'. This has escaped from cultivation in the US and is now a serious weed.

Lonicera japonica (Japanese honeysuckle)
Twining evergreen or semievergreen climber with hollow, hairy stems and ovate, downy leaves up to 4in (10cm) long. Fragrant white flowers appear in summer and autumn, followed by poisonous black berries. H to 30ft (10m).

4–9

***Lonicera japonica* 'Aureoreticulata'**
This is a cultivar of the purple-flushed *L. j.* var. *repens*. It has yellow veins and is especially good for covering unsightly features or growing alongside wall shrubs with sparse foliage. H to 30ft (10m).

4–10

LOVE PARSLEY, see *Levisticum officinale*, p.150
LOW CUDWEED, see *Gnaphalium uliginosum*, p.135

LUCERNE, see *Medicago sativa*, p.157

LUFFA

Six species of unpleasant-smelling, climbing annuals, related to cucumbers and melons, belong to this genus, which occurs throughout the tropics; *L. cylindrica* is found in tropical Africa and Asia. Their large fruits contain a network of fibers – the familar bathroom loofah – which persist long after the flesh has decayed, and is resistant to molds, even when regularly wetted. *L. cylindrica* may be grown outdoors in warm regions, or under cover in a cold climate.

Luffa cylindrica (loofah, sponge gourd, dishcloth gourd)
Annual, tendril climber with large, bristly leaves. Male and female flowers are both yellow and strongly veined: males have shorter stalks than females. Cylindrical green fruits up to 20in (50cm) long turn yellow when ripe. H 50ft (15m).

A

LYCOPODIUM

This large, cosmopolitan genus consists of about 450 species of evergreen perennial clubmosses, which may be terrestrial or epiphytic in habit; *L. clavatum* is found widely in temperate zones. They are primitive plants with small, scale- or needle-like leaves, reproducing by spores. Clubmoss spores are used in sound experiments, being so fine that they vibrate into patterns of sound waves, and also for stage effects and fireworks, since they are flammable.

Lycopodium clavatum (stag's horn clubmoss, ground pine)
Trailing perennial with erect, forked branches and upward-pointing, lanceolate, tapered leaves. Yellow spores are shed from upright, forked, club-shaped branches, which appear in summer. H 5in (12cm), S 3ft (1m).

2–8

LYCIUM

This genus of about 100 species of deciduous and evergreen, often spiny shrubs occurs in most temperate and subtropical regions. Although poisonous, *L. barbarum*, native to lowland China, is a useful, fast-growing shrub for hedging, especially in coastal sites or on unstable, sandy banks. The fruits are attractive in autumn. In cultivation, it is often labeled *L. europaeum*. *Lycium* comes from the Greek *lykion*, the name given by Dioscorides to a thorny shrub from Lycia, in Asia Minor.

Lycium barbarum (matrimony vine, Duke of Argyll's tea-tree, Chinese box thorn)
Deciduous, arching shrub, rarely spiny, with ovate leaves and small, funnel-shaped purple flowers that appear in summer, followed by ovoid, orange to scarlet berries. H 12ft (4m), S 10ft (3m).

5–9

LYCOPUS

A genus of four species of perennials, which occur in wet, lowland habitats throughout northern temperate regions; *L. virginicus* is native to southeastern US. They are similar to *Mentha* (see pp.158–9), with stoloniferous rootstocks and angled stems, but are only faintly mint-scented. None have ornamental value, although *L. virginicus* and *L. europaeus* are sometimes grown in damp situations. The name *Lycopus* comes from the Greek *lykos*, "wolf," and *pous*, "foot."

Lycopus virginicus (Virginia bugleweed)
Perennial with hairy stems and sharply toothed leaves, 2½–3½in (6–9cm) long, which have purple-felted undersides. Tiny white flowers, sometimes purple-marked, appear in late summer, followed by 3-angled nutlets. H 8–32in (20–80cm), S 20–24in (50–60cm).

5–9

LYCOPERDON

A cosmopolitan genus of about 50 species of saprophytic fungi. *L. perlatum* is common in woodland throughout temperate regions. All produce globose toadstools that release their spores in clouds when the ripe flesh is ruptured – hence the common name, "puffballs." The spores are very irritant to the lungs. Many *Lycoperdon* species are edible when young; however, the flesh changes texture and color (from white to brown) as the spores develop, and becomes unpalatable.

Lycoperdon perlatum (puffball)
Pear- to club-shaped fungus with a warted skin that is white at first, becoming yellow-brown. Skin becomes perforated at apex, releasing yellow-brown spores in autumn. H 1–3½in (2.5–9cm), S 1–2½in (2.5–6cm).

4–9

LYTHRUM

There are 38 species of purple- or pink-flowered annuals, perennials, and small shrubs in this cosmopolitan genus. *L. salicaria*, native to Europe, Asia, and northern Africa, is an adaptable, long-lived species with a range of brightly colored cultivars for damp, rich soil. It has escaped from cultivation into many wetlands, becoming a serious weed. The name *Lythrum* comes from the Greek *lythron*, "blood," which may refer to the plant's medicinal uses.

Lythrum salicaria (purple loosestrife)
Tall, upright perennial with 4-angled stems and willowlike leaves up to 3in (7cm) long. Bright pink-purple flowers are produced in whorled spikes from midsummer to midautumn. H 2–5ft (60cm–1.5m), S 1.5–4ft (45cm–1.2m).

4–9

LUNGWORT, see *Pulmonaria officinalis*, p.186
MAD DOG SKULLCAP, see *Scutellaria lateriflora*, p.201
MADAGASCAR PERIWINKLE, see *Catharanthus roseus*, p.102
MADDER, see *Rubia*, p.193
MADONNA LILY, see *Lilium candidum*, p.151
MAGNOLIA, see *Magnolia officinalis*, p.155
MAIDENHAIR FERN, see *Adiantum capillus-veneris*, p.74
MAIDENHAIR TREE, see *Ginkgo biloba*, p.134

MAGNOLIA

A genus consisting of about 125 species of deciduous and evergreen trees and shrubs, distributed through eastern N America to Venezuela, and from the Himalayas to eastern and SE Asia. *M. liliiflora* is found throughout China, *M. officinalis* in western and central China, and *M. virginiana* in the eastern US. Magnolias are among the most exotic of the flowering trees and shrubs that are sufficiently hardy for gardens in most temperate regions. Their solitary, fragrant blooms resemble water lilies.

Magnolia liliiflora (lily-flowered magnolia)
Spreading, deciduous shrub with elliptic to obovate leaves up to 8in (20cm) long. Fragrant, white, purple-flushed flowers appear with the new leaves in spring. H 10ft (3m), S 12ft (4m).

6–9

Magnolia officinalis (magnolia)
Deciduous tree with peeling, gray bark and obovate leaves, up to 16in (40cm) long, which have pale, downy undersides. Creamy white, strongly scented flowers appear in late spring and early summer. H 70–75ft (20–22m), S 30–50ft (10–15m).

6–9

Magnolia virginiana (sweet bay, beaver tree)
Semievergreen shrub or small tree with glossy, elliptic to obovate leaves, up to 5in (13cm) long, which have blue-white undersides. Fragrant, creamy white, globular flowers appear in summer. H 28ft (9m), S 20ft (6m).

***Magnolia liliiflora* 'Nigra'**
This cultivar is far more widely grown than the species; it has a compact habit and larger, more numerous deep purple flowers over a longer period. H and S 12ft (4m).

6–9

MAHONIA

Some 70 evergreen shrubs and small trees belong to this genus, which grows wild in N and C America and eastern Asia; *M. aquifolium* is native to northwestern US. It is closely related to *Berberis* (see p.93), differing mainly in its pinnate leaves and spineless stems. A number of mahonias have handsome foliage, scented, yellow flowers, and bloom-covered berries, providing a long period of interest. Smaller species, such as *M. aquifolium*, make excellent groundcover.

Mahonia aquifolium (Oregon grape, mountain grape)
Suckering shrub with spiny, glossy, dark green leaves turning purple-red in winter. Fragrant yellow flowers are borne in large, terminal clusters in spring, followed by blue-black berries. H 3–5ft (1–1.5m), S 5–6ft (1.5–2m).

5–8

***Mahonia aquifolium* 'Apollo'**
A vigorous cultivar with a low-growing, dense, spreading habit; red-stalked, brown-tinged leaves that turn bronze in winter; and large clusters of bright yellow flowers. H 24in (60cm), S 5–6ft (1.5–2m).

5–8

MALABAR GLORY LILY, see *Gloriosa superba*, p.135
MALABAR KINO, see *Pterocarpus marsupium*, p.186
MALABAR NUT, see *Justicia adhatoda* p.299
MALAGUETA, see *CAPSICUM*, p.100
MALAY TEA, see *Psoralea corylifolia*, p.336
MALE FERN, see *Dryopteris filix-mas*, p.120
MALLOW, see *Malva*, p.156

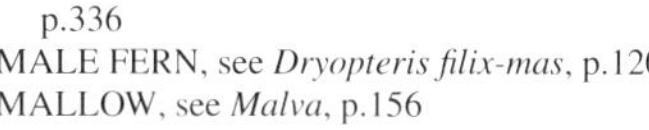

MALVA

A genus of about 30 species of annuals, biennials, perennials, and subshrubs distributed through Europe, Asia, and Africa, and widely naturalized in temperate and tropical regions. *M. sylvestris* is native to Europe, northern Africa, and southwestern Asia. A few species make attractive border plants that are easily grown, even in poor soils. The plant's names are derived from the old English *malwe*, "soft," and refers to the abundant mucilage in certain species, which softens the skin.

Malva sylvestris (common mallow, blue mallow, high mallow)
Robust, variable perennial with lobed leaves, each usually with a dark basal spot. Pale to purple-pink flowers with darker veining are borne from early summer to autumn. H 18–36in (45–90cm), S 24–36in (60–90cm).

4–9

***Malva sylvestris* 'Cottenham Blue'**
A handsome mallow with bluer flowers than the species. H 18–36in (45–90cm), S 24–36in (60–90cm).

4–9

Malva sylvestris subsp. ***mauritiana* 'Bibor Felho'**
An improved version of this tall, hollyhock-like subspecies with larger, glossy, magenta flowers, often semi-double, which have purple-black veining. H 3–6ft (1–2m), S 24–36in (60–90cm).

4–9

MANDRAGORA

Six species of short-stemmed, rosette-forming perennials belong to this genus, which is distributed through Mediterranean regions to the Himalayas. *M. officinarum* is found on rocky slopes in the Mediterranean region. It is occasionally grown in herb gardens as a curiosity. *Mandragora* is the ancient Greek name for the plant and may be a corruption of the Assyrian *nam tar ira*, "male drug of Namtar," since the plant was reputed to cure sterility.

Mandragora officinarum (mandrake, devil's apples)
Stemless perennial with a fleshy taproot and broadly ovate leaves. Small white to blue-white, bell-shaped flowers are borne at ground level in spring, followed by aromatic yellow fruits. H 2in (5cm), S 12in (30cm).

6–8

MARRUBIUM

This genus consists of 30 species of annuals and perennials ranging through Europe and Mediterranean regions; *M. vulgare* is native to dry areas throughout Eurasia and northern Africa. Their main attraction is the velvety or woolly foliage. *Marrubium* may be derived from *Maria urbs*, an ancient town in Italy, or from the Hebrew *marrob*, "bitter juice." (Horehound seems to have been one of the bitter herbs eaten during the first two meals, or Seders, of Passover.)

Marrubium vulgare (horehound, hoarhound, white horehound)
Aromatic woody perennial with downy stems and ovate, downy, gray-green leaves, up to 2in (5cm) long, which have toothed margins. Small, off-white, hairy flowers appear in summer. H and S 8–24in (20–60cm).

4–8

MATRICARIA

A genus of about five species of Eurasian annuals, which occasionally may live longer as biennials or short-lived perennials. The genus has undergone revision, and *M. recutita*, common in Europe and western Asia to India, is often listed under its synonyms in older literature. Easily raised from seed, it gives an attractive display of feathery foliage and daisylike flowers in summer. It is not suitable for chamomile lawns.

Matricaria recutita (German chamomile, scented mayweed)
Sweetly scented annual or biennial with much-branched stems and finely divided leaves. Daisylike flowers are produced from early summer to autumn. H 6–24in (15–60cm), S 4–15in (10–38cm).

A

MANDRAKE, see *Mandragora officinarum*, above
MANNA ASH, see *Fraxinus ornus*, p.129
MARIGOLD, see *Tagetes*, p.207
MARIJUANA, see *Cannabis sativa*, p.99
MARJORAM, see *ORIGANUM*, pp.168–9
MARSH CUDWEED, see *Gnaphalium uliginosum*, p.135
MARSH MALLOW, see *Althaea officinalis*, p.82
MARSH TREFOIL, see *Menyanthes trifoliata*, p.160
MARSH WOUNDWORT, see *Stachys palustris*, p.205
MASTIC TREE, see *Boswellia sacra*, p.95; *Pistacia lentiscus*, p.178

MEDICAGO

A genus of about 55 species of annuals, perennials, and small shrubs widely distributed in Europe, Mediterranean regions, Ethiopia, southern Africa, and Asia. The cultivated *M. sativa* is thought to have originated in central Asia. From there it was introduced to China 2,000 years ago, to Greece in the fifth century BC, and into northern Africa and Spain during the spread of the Ottoman Empire in the eighth century, where it became known by its Arabic name, *alfalfa*.

Medicago sativa (alfalfa, lucerne)
Bushy perennial with trifoliate leaves, which have ovate, toothed leaflets. Small purple to lilac pea flowers are produced in racemes in summer, followed by pods containing many shiny seeds. H 12–36in (30–90cm), S 6–24in (15–60cm).

4–8

MELALEUCA

This large genus of some 150 species of half-hardy to tender evergreen trees and shrubs is distributed mainly in Australia; *M. leucadendron* is native to wetland areas in northern Australia, southern New Guinea, and the Moluccas. Closely related to *Callistemon* (bottlebrushes), many species are cultivated for their spiky, often brightly colored flowers, though some are difficult to tell apart. The species may be grown outdoors in mild areas or under cover in cool temperate regions.

Melaleuca leucadendron (weeping tea tree, weeping paperbark, cajuput)
Large tree with pale, peeling bark, slender, drooping branches, and narrow, pointed leaves. Slender, creamy white flower spikes, 2½–6in (6–15cm) long, appear in summer and autumn. H 50–130ft (15–40m), S variable.

MELIA

Five species of deciduous and semievergreen trees and shrubs belong to this genus, which occurs in Eurasia, tropical Africa, and Australia. *M. azederach*, native to woodland in northern India and China, is widely grown for shade and as a street tree in warm parts of the world. It is a short-lived, fast-growing species resistant to drought, with ornamental foliage, scented flowers, and abundant golden fruits, which, although poisonous, are often used as beads.

Melia azederach (chinaberry, bead tree, Persian lilac)
Deciduous tree with elegant, doubly pinnate leaves up to 32in (80cm) long. Fragrant lilac flowers are borne in loose panicles in summer, followed by ovate yellow fruits about 2in (5cm) across. H 40–50ft (12–15m), S 40ft (12m).

7–10

MELILOTUS

Some 20 species of annuals, biennials, and short-lived perennials belong to this genus, which spans Eurasia, northern Africa, and Ethiopia. *M. officinalis*, found in fields and on waste ground, is widely cultivated for hay, silage, and green manure. It makes an attractive addition to the herb border and wildflower meadow. The name *Melilotus* comes from the Greek *meli*, "honey," and *lotos*, "fodder," or "clover," because these plants are important sources of nectar and animal fodder.

Melilotus officinalis (yellow sweet clover, yellow melilot, ribbed melilot)
Upright or spreading biennial with ribbed stems and trifoliate leaves. Yellow honey-scented flowers appear in slender racemes in summer, followed by brown, hairless pods. H 2–5ft (60cm–1.5m), S 8in–3ft (20–90cm).

3–8

MELISSA

A genus of three species of perennials, which occurs throughout Europe to central Asia. *M. officinalis*, native to southern Europe, western Asia, and northern Africa, has been cultivated for over 2,000 years. It was originally grown as a bee plant, which probably gave rise to its name, since *Melissa* is the Greek word for "honey-bee." Its therapeutic uses were promoted by Arab physicians in the 10th and 11th centuries. *M. officinalis* is still widely cultivated today for both its scent and its practical uses.

Melissa officinalis (lemon balm, balm, melissa)
Lemon-scented perennial with a 4-angled stem and ovate, toothed leaves, 1¼–3in (3–7cm) long. Insignificant pale yellow flowers are produced in axillary clusters in summer. H 12–32in (30–80cm), S 12–18in (30–45cm).

4–9

***Melissa officinalis* 'All Gold'**
This cultivar has bright yellow foliage ideal for brightening up damp, shady corners. It does best in good light, with midday shade, since it scorches in full sun. H 12–24in (30–60cm), S 12–18in (30–45cm).

4–9

***Melissa officinalis* 'Aurea'**
Very similar to the species, but with yellow-variegated leaves. The color fades in summer, but a new crop of young foliage is encouraged by cutting plants back after flowering. H 12–24in (30–60cm), S 12–18in (30–45cm).

4–9

MATÉ, see *Ilex paraguensis*, p.142
MATRIMONY VINE, see *Lycium barbarum*, p.154
MAY, see *Crataegus laevigata*, p.112
MAY LILY, see *Convallaria majalis*, p.111
MAYAPPLE, see *Podophyllum peltatum*, p.180
MEDICK, see *Medicago*, above
MEADOW SAFFRON, see *Colchicum autumnale*, p.110
MEADOWSWEET, see *Filipendula ulmaria*, p.128
MELEGUETA PEPPER, see *Aframomum melegueta*, p.230

*M*ENTHA

This genus consists of 25 often variable species of aromatic perennials and a few annuals, occurring in temperate regions of Eurasia and Africa. Most flower from summer to early autumn. Mints of various kinds have a place in most gardens. The bright green *M. spicata* has been the indispensable culinary mint since Roman times. Variegated mints can be grown in the border, provided that they have dense or vigorous neighbors. *M. aquatica* thrives beside pools, and the small-growing but strongly scented *M. pulegium*, *M. diemenica,* and *M. requienii* will grow between paving stones and at the edges of paths. *Mentha* is the original Latin name for these plants and is derived from the Greek *minthe*.

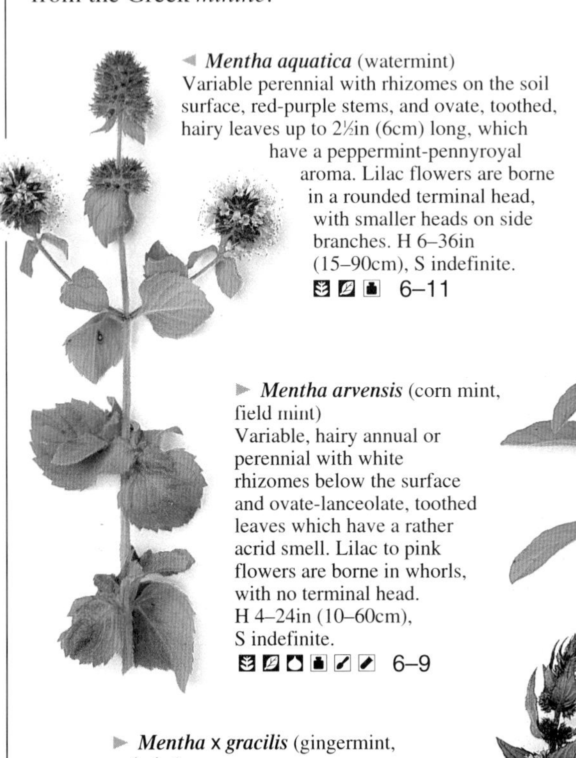

◄ ***Mentha aquatica*** (watermint)
Variable perennial with rhizomes on the soil surface, red-purple stems, and ovate, toothed, hairy leaves up to 2½in (6cm) long, which have a peppermint-pennyroyal aroma. Lilac flowers are borne in a rounded terminal head, with smaller heads on side branches. H 6–36in (15–90cm), S indefinite.
6–11

► ***Mentha arvensis*** (corn mint, field mint)
Variable, hairy annual or perennial with white rhizomes below the surface and ovate-lanceolate, toothed leaves which have a rather acrid smell. Lilac to pink flowers are borne in whorls, with no terminal head. H 4–24in (10–60cm), S indefinite.
6–9

▲ ***Mentha longifolia*** (horsemint)
Creeping, downy, peppermint-scented perennial with rhizomes below the surface and narrowly lanceolate, toothed, gray-green, stalkless leaves. Lilac, mauve, or white flowers are borne in tapering spikes. H 16in–48in (40cm–1.2m), S indefinite.
6–9

► ***Mentha* x *gracilis*** (gingermint, redmint)
Variable, sweetly scented perennial with erect, often red-tinged stems and ovate-lanceolate, more or less smooth, leaves, 1¼–3in (3–7cm) long. Lilac flowers are produced in distinct whorls. A hybrid between *M. arvensis* and *M. spicata*. H 12–36in (30–90cm), S indefinite.
7–9

► ***Mentha* x *piperita* 'Citrata'**
(lemon mint, eau-de-cologne mint, bergamot mint)
A cultivar with ovate, bronze-purple leaves, and a lavender-like aroma. H 12–36in (30–90cm), S indefinite.
4–9

◄ ***Mentha* x *gracilis* 'Variegata'** (gingermint)
Very like *M.* x *gracilis*, but with yellow-variegated, fruit-scented leaves. H 12–36in (30–90cm), S indefinite.
7–9

► ***Mentha* x *piperita***
(peppermint)
Vigorous, creeping, often purple-tinged perennial with smooth, lanceolate, toothed leaves up to 3in (8cm) long. Lilac-pink, sterile flowers are borne in oblong, terminal spikes. A hybrid between *M. aquatica* and *M. spicata*. H 12–36in (30–90cm), S indefinite.
4–9

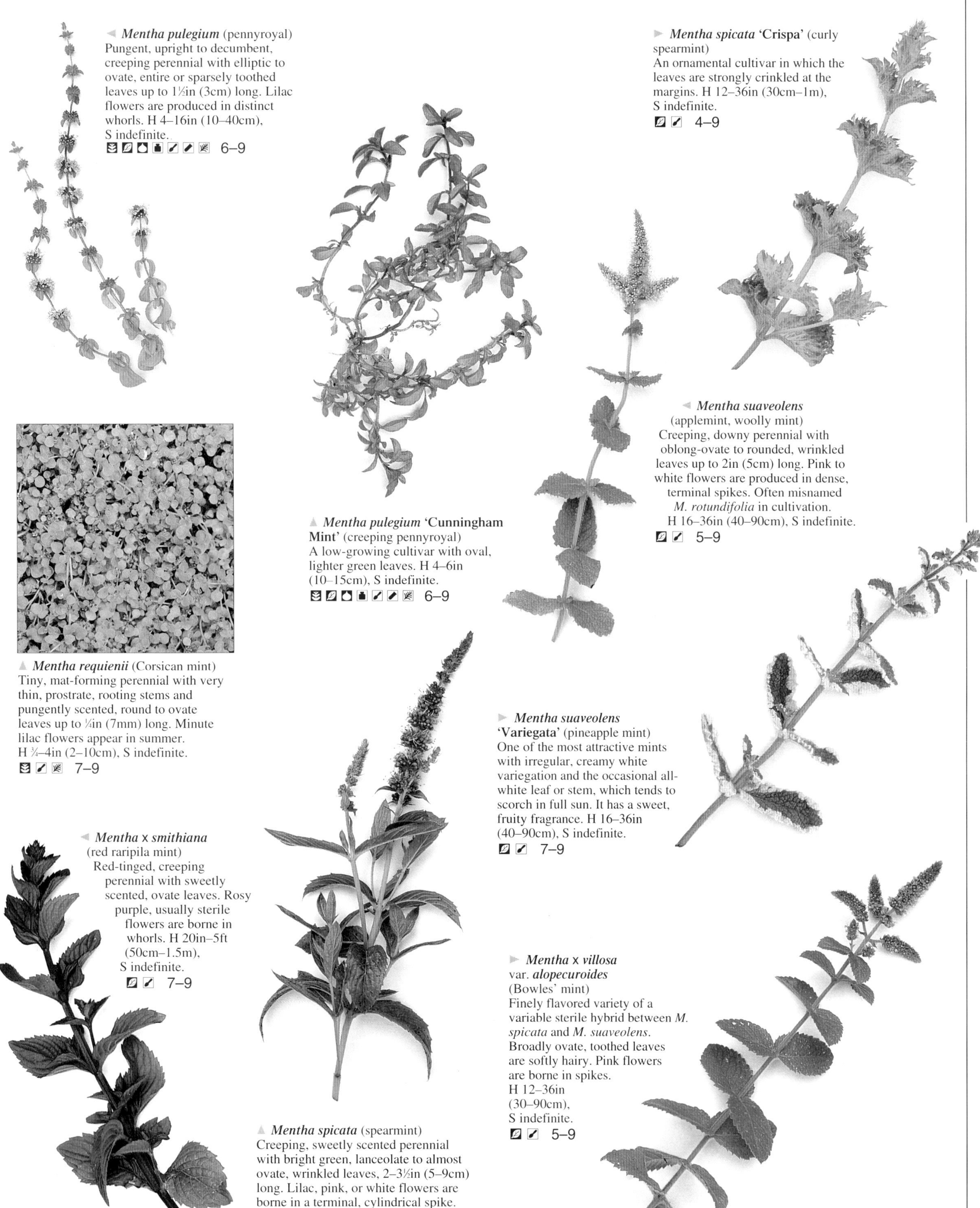

◄ ***Mentha pulegium*** (pennyroyal)
Pungent, upright to decumbent, creeping perennial with elliptic to ovate, entire or sparsely toothed leaves up to 1½in (3cm) long. Lilac flowers are produced in distinct whorls. H 4–16in (10–40cm), S indefinite.
6–9

▲ ***Mentha pulegium* 'Cunningham Mint'** (creeping pennyroyal)
A low-growing cultivar with oval, lighter green leaves. H 4–6in (10–15cm), S indefinite.
6–9

► ***Mentha spicata* 'Crispa'** (curly spearmint)
An ornamental cultivar in which the leaves are strongly crinkled at the margins. H 12–36in (30cm–1m), S indefinite.
4–9

◄ ***Mentha suaveolens*** (applemint, woolly mint)
Creeping, downy perennial with oblong-ovate to rounded, wrinkled leaves up to 2in (5cm) long. Pink to white flowers are produced in dense, terminal spikes. Often misnamed *M. rotundifolia* in cultivation. H 16–36in (40–90cm), S indefinite.
5–9

▲ ***Mentha requienii*** (Corsican mint)
Tiny, mat-forming perennial with very thin, prostrate, rooting stems and pungently scented, round to ovate leaves up to ¼in (7mm) long. Minute lilac flowers appear in summer. H ¾–4in (2–10cm), S indefinite.
7–9

► ***Mentha suaveolens* 'Variegata'** (pineapple mint)
One of the most attractive mints with irregular, creamy white variegation and the occasional all-white leaf or stem, which tends to scorch in full sun. It has a sweet, fruity fragrance. H 16–36in (40–90cm), S indefinite.
7–9

◄ ***Mentha* x *smithiana*** (red raripila mint)
Red-tinged, creeping perennial with sweetly scented, ovate leaves. Rosy purple, usually sterile flowers are borne in whorls. H 20in–5ft (50cm–1.5m), S indefinite.
7–9

► ***Mentha* x *villosa* var. *alopecuroides*** (Bowles' mint)
Finely flavored variety of a variable sterile hybrid between *M. spicata* and *M. suaveolens*. Broadly ovate, toothed leaves are softly hairy. Pink flowers are borne in spikes. H 12–36in (30–90cm), S indefinite.
5–9

▲ ***Mentha spicata*** (spearmint)
Creeping, sweetly scented perennial with bright green, lanceolate to almost ovate, wrinkled leaves, 2–3½in (5–9cm) long. Lilac, pink, or white flowers are borne in a terminal, cylindrical spike. H 12–36in (30–90cm), S indefinite.
4–9

MENYANTHES

A single species of creeping, deciduous aquatic or marginal aquatic perennial belongs to this genus, which is widely distributed in northern temperate regions. *M. trifoliata* has distinctive leaves resembling those of the broad bean, and delicately fringed flowers. It is a decorative plant for bog gardens and pool margins. The name *Menyanthes* comes from the Greek *menyanthos*, a name used by Theophrastus for a water plant.

Menyanthes trifoliata (bog bean, buckbean, marsh trefoil)
Upright perennial with a thick, horizontal rhizome and long-stalked, trifoliate leaves. White fringed flowers, flushed pink on the outside, are borne in long spikes from late spring to mid-summer. H 12in (30cm), S 3ft (1m).
4–9

MITCHELLA

Two species of trailing evergreen subshrubs make up this genus, which occurs in N America and in Japan. *M. repens*, native to eastern and central US, is a pretty plant for rock gardens and groundcover. It flowers in late spring and early summer. In Victorian times it was grown beneath specimen plants in ferneries. *Mitchella* is named after John Mitchell (1711–68) of Virginia, a botanist, physician, and early correspondent of Linnaeus, the Swedish botanist.

Mitchella repens (partridge berry, squaw vine, running box)
Mat-forming evergreen creeper with rooting stems and small, shiny, ovate leaves. Fragrant, tubular, white flowers, sometimes pink-tinged, are followed by scarlet edible berries. H 2–12in (5–30cm), S indefinite.
4–9

MOMORDICA

There are 45 species of scrambling annuals and perennials in this genus, which occurs in tropical Africa and Asia, and is naturalized in the Americas. *M. charantia*, native to savanna and bush in tropical Africa and Asia, was introduced to Europe in 1710 and recorded as a garden plant in France by Vilmorin in 1870. It may be grown under cover in cool areas for its intricate foliage and colorful, knobby fruits, which are highly decorative against a wall or trellis.

Momordica charantia (balsam pear, bitter gourd)
Annual climber with palmately lobed leaves. Solitary yellow flowers are produced in summer, followed by ovoid, warty, orange fruits, which split into 3 segments when ripe, revealing seeds with red arils. H 15ft (5m).
A

MONARDA

This N American genus contains 12 species of annuals, perennials, and shrubs. *M. didyma*, found in rich, moist woodland, and *M. fistulosa*, native to dry hillsides and rocky woods, make good border plants. Many excellent hybrids are available; a fine example is *M.* 'Cambridge Scarlet'. The brightly colored flowers attract butterflies and hummingbirds. Monardas are known as bergamots, because their aroma resembles that of the bergamot orange (*Citrus bergamia*, see p.262).

Monarda didyma (bee balm, oswego tea, bergamot)
Aromatic perennial with erect, 4-angled stems and ovate, toothed leaves. Bright red flowers with red-green bracts are produced in a terminal whorl in summer and autumn. H 16–48in (40cm–1.2m), S 12–24in (30–60cm).
4–10

Monarda fistulosa (wild bergamot, horsemint)
Pungent, hairy perennial with lanceolate, gray-green, tapering leaves. Lilac to pink flowers with pink-tinged bracts are produced in a terminal whorl from summer to autumn. H 4ft (1.2m), S 18in (45cm).
3–9

Monarda punctata (horsemint)
Aromatic perennial with lanceolate, toothed leaves about 2in (5cm) long. Yellow, purple-spotted flowers are produced in dense whorls in summer and autumn. H 12–36in (30–90cm), S 12–18in (30–45cm).
3–9

MEXICAN OREGANO, see *Lippia graveolens*, p.152
MILK VETCH, see *Astragalus membranaceus*, p.90
MILKWORT, see *Polygala*, p.332
MINT, see *MENTHA*, pp.158–9
MINT BUSH, see *Prostanthera*, p.183
MISTLETOE, see *Viscum album*, p.221
MOCK LIME, see *Aglaia odorata*, p.76
MONKSHOOD, see *Aconitum napellus*, p.72
MORETON BAY CHESTNUT, see *Castanospermum australe*, p.102
MORNING GLORY, see *Ipomoea*, p.297
MOTHERWORT, see *Leonurus cardiaca*, p.150
MOUNTAIN BOX, see *Arctostaphylos*

MORINDA

This genus includes some 50–80 species of deciduous small trees, shrubs, and woody climbers, most of which occur in tropical Africa, Asia, and Australia; *M. citrifolia* is found in tropical coastal regions from India and Sri Lanka, through SE Asia to Australia and Polynesia. Most species have white, often scented flowers, and the roots yield a yellow dye, known as morindin, once used in Javanese batik. Recommended for greenhouse culture in the 19th century, they are rarely seen today.

Morinda citrifolia (Indian mulberry, awl tree, cheesefruit)
Small tree with ovate, glossy leaves 6–8in (15–20cm) long. Clusters of fragrant, white, tubular flowers appear all year, followed by irregularly ovoid, fetid, cream fruits up to 3in (7.5cm) long. H 10ft (3m), S 6–8ft (2–2.5m).

MORINGA

A genus of 14 species of deciduous succulent trees, which occur in Africa, Madagascar, India, and Arabia. *M. oleifera*, native to forests in India and Arabia, is a fast-growing, decorative tree that resembles *Robinia* in appearance, and bears flowers and fruits all year. It is the most commonly grown species, with medicinal uses that date back to ancient Greek times. The edible roots are similar to horseradish, and the foliage is mustard-flavored.

Moringa oleifera (horseradish tree, ben)
Deciduous tree with a pale gray to copper-colored trunk, which stores water, and large, compound, pinnately divided leaves. Scented, yellow-white, 5-petaled flowers are followed by large, pendulous, beanlike capsules. H 25–50ft (8–15m), S 20–30ft (6–10m).

***Morus alba* 'Pendula'**
This cultivar makes a small, weeping tree with close-set branches. It is particularly attractive when laden with fruit, and in autumn, when the leaves turn yellow. H 10ft (3m), S 15ft (5m).

4–9

MORUS

Seven species of deciduous trees belong to this genus, which occurs in N and S America, Africa, and Asia, mainly in subtropical regions. Both *M. alba*, native to China, and *M. nigra* have been cultivated for centuries and have an attractive, often gnarled appearance, edible fruits, and medicinal properties. *Morus* is the original Latin name for mulberry. It comes from *demorari*, "to delay," and refers to the tree's habit of not expanding its buds until after the last frosts.

Morus alba (white mulberry)
Deciduous tree with dull green, orange-tinged bark and ovate, toothed leaves. Female flowers are borne in erect, cylindrical catkins, followed by white or purple fruits; male flowers are borne separately on the same plant.
H 70ft (20m), S 30ft (10m).

4–9

MURRAYA

A genus of four species of evergreen trees and shrubs that occurs in tropical Asia, Pacific islands, and tropical and subtropical parts of Australia; *M. koenigii* is native to India, Pakistan, Sri Lanka, and the Andaman Islands. The only species common in cultivation in the West is the orange jasmine, *M. paniculata*, grown as an indoor plant for its aromatic foliage, fragrant white flowers, and edible red berries. *M. koenigii* is known in southern India and Sri Lanka for its edible leaves.

Murraya koenigii (curry leaf)
Small evergreen shrub with large, pinnate leaves, which have a strong curry aroma when bruised. Clusters of small, fragrant, white flowers are produced in summer, followed by edible, peppery-tasting, black berries. H 20ft (6m), S 10–15ft (3–5m).

uva-ursi, p.86
MOUNTAIN LAUREL, see *Kalmia latifolia*, p.146
MOUNTAIN MINT, see *Pycnanthemum*, p.187
MOUSE-EAR HAWKWEED, see *Hieracium pilosella*, p.139
MUGWORT, see *ARTEMISIA*, pp.88–9
MULBERRY, see *Morus*, above
MULLEIN, see *Verbascum*, p.218
MUSK MALLOW, MUSK SEED, see *Abelmoschus moschatus*, p.70
MUSTARD, see *Brassica*, p.95; *Sinapis*, p.203

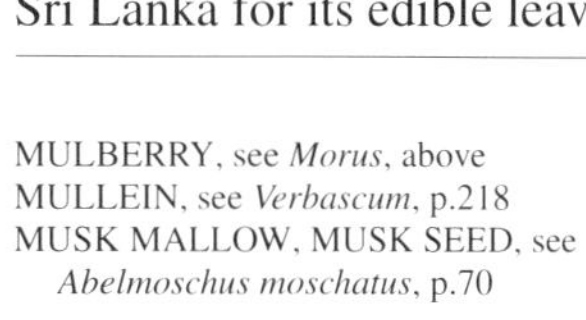

MYRICA

This cosmopolitan genus contains about 35 species of deciduous and evergreen shrubs and small trees. *M. cerifera* is found in coastal areas of the US, from New Jersey to Florida and Texas; *M. gale* in N America, and through Europe to Japan. Several species have aromatic foliage and are able to thrive in difficult situations. *M. cerifera* is especially adaptable, since it tolerates both poor, sandy soils and swamps. *M. pennsylvanica* (also known as bayberry) is similar, but hardier.

Myrica cerifera (bayberry, wax myrtle, candleberry)
Evergreen shrub or small tree with oblanceolate leaves up to 3½in (9cm) long. Male flowers are borne in scaly catkins, and females in an ovoid cluster, followed by globose, gray, waxy fruits. H 10–40ft (3–12m), S 10ft (3m).

8–9

Myrica gale (sweet gale, bog myrtle)
Deciduous, suckering shrub with red-brown twigs and narrow, oblanceolate leaves. Male and female catkins are borne on separate plants in spring before the new leaves, followed by tiny yellow-brown fruits. H 1–5ft (30cm–1.5m), S 9–36in (22cm–1m).

1–6

MYRISTICA

This genus of about 100 large evergreen trees ranges through Asia and Australia. *M. fragrans*, native to tropical rainforest in the Moluccas and the Banda Islands, is an important crop in Indonesia and Sri Lanka. The golden fruits split open when ripe to reveal a single seed (nutmeg) in a woody, brown shell, which in turn is clasped by a bright red aril (mace). Inferior fruits are obtained from *M. argentea*, *M. malabarica*, and *M. fatua*.

Myristica fragrans (nutmeg, jatiphala)
Bushy evergreen tree with oblong leaves up to 5in (12cm) long, covered in silvery, aromatic scales when young. Pale yellow flowers, produced in axillary clusters are followed by fleshy, yellow, globose to pear-shaped fruits. H 30–50ft (10–15m), S 25ft (8m).

MYROXYLON

Three closely related species of evergreen trees make up this tropical S American genus; *M. balsamum* is native to Mexico, Panama, and Peru. They yield balsams with a cinnamon–vanilla aroma, which have long been used in medicine, perfumery, and food flavoring. *M. balsamum* is widely cultivated for these purposes. It is often planted as a windbreak or shade tree and tolerates both moist and dry, alkaline conditions. *Myroxylon* is from the Greek *myron*, "myrrh," and *xylon*, "wood."

Myroxylon balsamum (Tolu balsam, *bálsamo*)
Spreading evergreen tree with fragrant bark and leathery, shiny leaves. Downy clusters of white flowers are followed by leathery winged fruits, 4½in (11cm) long, containing 2 seeds. H 40–50ft (12–15m), S 15–30ft (5–10m).

MYRRHIS

A single species of aromatic perennial makes up this genus, which is native to Europe but widely naturalized elsewhere. *M. odorata* is found wild in cool, damp areas in grassland and hedgerows, and is an excellent plant for rich, moist soil. It has soft, anise-scented foliage and relatively large, shiny black seeds. Its fernlike appearance complements other shade-tolerant herbs, such as *Chelidonium majus* (see p.106), and *Rheum palmatum* (see p.189).

Myrrhis odorata (sweet cicely, sweet chervil, garden myrrh)
Large, downy perennial with hollow stems and fernlike leaves up to 12in (50cm) long. Tiny white flowers appear in umbels from late spring, followed by ridged fruits about 1in (2.5cm) long. H 3–6ft (1–2m), S 2–4ft (60cm–1.2m).

3–7

MYROBALAN, see *Terminalia chebula*, p.210
MYRRH, see *Commiphora myrrha*, p.265
MYRTLE, see *Myrtus communis*, p.163
MYRTLE FLAG, see *Acorus calamus*, p.73
NAAWA, see *Aspidosperma quebracho-blanco*, p.245
NAKED LADIES, see *Colchicum autumnale*, p.110

MYRTUS

Two species of aromatic evergreen shrubs belong to this genus, which occurs in Mediterranean regions and northern Africa. *M. communis*, found in Mediterranean regions and southwestern Europe, makes a dense, wind-resistant hedge in mild areas. The dwarf *M. c.* subsp. *tarentina* is an ideal specimen plant when grown under cover. In ancient Greece, myrtle was sacred to Aphrodite, goddess of love and beauty. It is still carried today in wedding bouquets in the Middle East.

Myrtus communis (myrtle)
Erect shrub with lustrous, ovate-lanceolate leaves, which have a juniper-like aroma when crushed. Fragrant, white flowers, 1¼in (3cm) across with golden stamens, appear in spring and summer, followed by blue-black berries. H and S 10ft (3m).

9–10

***Myrtus communis* 'Variegata'**
An attractive foliage plant with leaves variegated gray-green and creamy white. It is less hardy than the species. H 10–15ft (3–5m), S 10ft (3m).

10–11

***Myrtus communis* 'Flore Pleno'**
This cultivar is similar to the species in habit and foliage, but has longer lasting, fully double white flowers. H 10–15ft (3–5m), S 10ft (3m).

9–10

Myrtus communis* subsp. *tarentina
A compact, free-flowering variant with narrow leaves, smaller, pink-tinged flowers in late summer and autumn, and white fruits. H 3–6ft (1–2m), S 3ft (1m).

9–10

NARDOSTACHYS

A single species of Asian perennial makes up this genus, which is closely related to *Valeriana* (see p.217). It is found on rock ledges and open, scrubby slopes in the Himalayas, and from Uttar Pradesh to southwestern China. This attractive plant is rarely seen in cultivation today but was recommended for the rock garden in Victorian times. The name *Nardostachys* comes from the Greek *nardos*, "spikenard," and *stachys*, "ear of corn," or "spike."

Nardostachys grandiflora (nard, spikenard)
Small perennial with elongated, very fragrant roots and aromatic stems. Leaves are mostly basal and elliptic-lanceolate. Small purple to pink flowers appear in late summer. H 10–12in (25–30cm), S 8–12in (20–30cm).

7–9

NASTURTIUM

A genus of six species of perennials distributed through Europe to central Asia. Commercial cultivation of watercress began in the 19th century and it is now grown in most parts of Europe. In some countries, such as New Zealand, it has become a serious weed. The name *Nasturtium* comes from the Latin *nasus tortus*, "twisted nose," and refers to the pungent taste of these plants. The plant commonly known as nasturtium is *Tropaeolum majus* (see p.215).

Nasturtium officinale (watercress)
Aquatic perennial with floating, freely rooting stems and dark green, pungent-tasting leaves. Tiny white flowers are produced throughout summer, followed by upward-pointing, narrow pods, about ½in (1cm) long. H 4–24in (10–60cm), S indefinite.

6–9

NELUMBO

This genus of two species of aquatic perennials occurs in eastern N America and warm parts of Asia to Australia. *N. nucifera*, native to Asia, is grown worldwide in tropical pools for its large, circular leaves and exquisite, chalice-shaped flowers. To Hindus, it is sacred to Brahma and revered as the jewel in the lotus (*om mani padma hum*). In Buddhist mythology, Buddha first appeared floating on a lotus and is traditionally depicted on a lotus throne.

Nelumbo nucifera (sacred lotus, *padma*)
Aquatic perennial with thick rhizomes and round, glaucous, peltate leaves up to 32in (80cm) in diameter. Large, fragrant, pink to white flowers are followed by pepperpot receptacles containing hard nuts. H 8ft (2.5m), S 4ft (1.2m) in the wild; less in cultivation.

5–10

***Nelumbo nucifera* 'Alba Grandiflora'**
This cultivar has the same characteristically round leaves as the species, but bears larger, pure white flowers. H 3–5ft (1–1.5m), S 24–36in (60–90cm).

5–10

***Nelumbo nucifera* 'Rosea Plena'**
A favorite cultivar for ornamental pools, with double pink flowers. H 3–5ft (1–1.5m), S 24–36in (60–90cm).

5–10

NASTURTIUM, see *Tropaeolum majus*, p.215
NATIVE HOPS, *Dodonaea viscosa*, see p.119
NEEM, see *Azadirachta indica*, p.91
NEPETA, see *Glechoma hederacea* 'Variegata', p.134
NETTLE, see *Urtica dioica*, p.217
NEW JERSEY TEA, see *Ceanothus americanus*, p.103
NIGHTSHADE, see *Atropa*, p.91; *Solanum*, p.204
NIGHT-BLOOMING CEREUS, see *Selenicereus grandiflorus*, p.202
NIMBA, see *Azadirachta indica*, p.91
NINDE, NINDI, see *Aeollanthus gamwelliae*, p.229
NINGPO FIGWORT, see *Scrophularia*

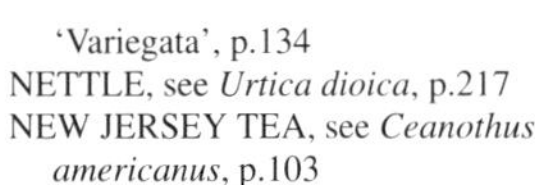

NEPETA

There are about 250 species of perennials in this genus occurring in Eurasia, northern Africa, and on tropical African mountains. The true catmint, *N. cataria*, is a medicinal herb with little merit as a garden plant. It owes its name to its stimulant effect on cats, which eat and roll in the plant with obvious pleasure. The hybrid *N.* x *faassenii*, commonly known as "catmint," is a popular ornamental but has less effect on cats and no medicinal properties.

Nepeta cataria (catnip, catmint)
Pungent, hairy perennial with erect, branched stems and gray-green, ovate, toothed leaves. White, purple-spotted, tubular flowers are borne in whorls from summer to midautumn.
H 1–3ft (30cm–1m), S 9–24in (23–60cm).

4–9

NIGELLA

Fourteen species of annuals belong to this Eurasian genus; *N. sativa* is native to the Mediterranean region. Several are grown as ornamentals and for dried floral arrangements. The most commonly grown species is *N. damascena* (love-in-a-mist), which differs in appearance from *N. sativa* and has different properties. In the Old Testament *N. sativa* was referred to as "fitches," from the Hebrew *ketzah*, "vetch." *Nigella* is the diminutive of the Latin *niger*, "black," and refers to the black seeds.

Nigella sativa (black cumin, nutmeg flower, Roman coriander)
Erect, branched annual with pinnately divided leaves up to 2in (5cm) long. Small, white, blue-tinged flowers about 1½in (3.5cm) across appear in summer, followed by inflated fruits with hornlike styles. H 12in (30cm), S 9in (23cm).

A

***Nymphaea odorata* 'Sulphurea Grandiflora'**
This cultivar has maroon-blotched leaves and semidouble, intensely fragrant yellow flowers up to 6in (15cm) in diameter. S to 3ft (1m).

3–11

NYMPHAEA

A cosmopolitan genus of 50 species of aquatic perennials with floating leaves; *N. lotus* occurs in warm parts of Asia and Africa. *N. odorata* is native to N America. Several species and many hybrids are grown as ornamentals, including both tropical and hardy plants, in a great variety of colors and sizes. These include the European *N. alba* and American *N. tuberosa*, which resemble *N. odorata* in appearance. The generic name *Nymphaea* is from the Greek *nymphaia*, "water nymph."

Nymphaea odorata (white pond lily, sweet-scented water lily)
Aquatic perennial with stout rhizomes and round, floating leaves, which are cleft at the base and often have purple-green undersides. Fragrant white to pink flowers with tapering petals, are borne in summer. S to 3ft (1m).

3–11

Nymphaea lotus (Egyptian lotus, white lotus)
Aquatic perennial with a tuberous rootstock and floating leaves. Large, fragrant flowers appear above the surface, opening night and morning only. Globose fruits containing numerous ribbed seeds ripen under water. S 3–5ft (1–1.5m).

3–11

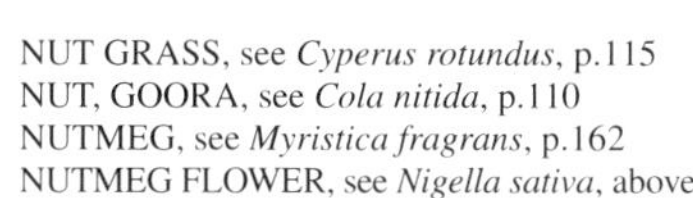

ningpoensis, p.201
NISPERO, see *Eriobotrya japonica*, p.123
NORTHERN PRICKLY ASH, see *Zanthoxylum americanum*, p.222
NUT GRASS, see *Cyperus rotundus*, p.115
NUT, GOORA, see *Cola nitida*, p.110
NUTMEG, see *Myristica fragrans*, p.162
NUTMEG FLOWER, see *Nigella sativa*, above
NUX-VOMICA, see *Strychnos nux-vomica*, p.206
OAK, see *Quercus*, p.187
OAK MOSS, see *Evernia prunastri*, p.126
OAT, see *Avena sativa*, p.91

OCIMUM

About 150 species of aromatic annuals, perennials, shrubs, and subshrubs belong to this genus, which occurs in most warm and tropical regions, especially Africa. The most widely grown basil is *O. basilicum*. It is a highly variable species and many of the variants offered in the horticultural trade are not recognized by botanists. Some variants are difficult to obtain outside the country of origin. Of those that are available, *O. b.* 'Dark Opal' and *O. b.* 'Purple Ruffles' are both worth growing as ornamentals. As with other basils, *O. basilicum* needs ample warmth and light, and is rarely successful outdoors in cool temperate areas. The name *Ocimum* is from the Greek *okimon*, used by Theophrastus for basil.

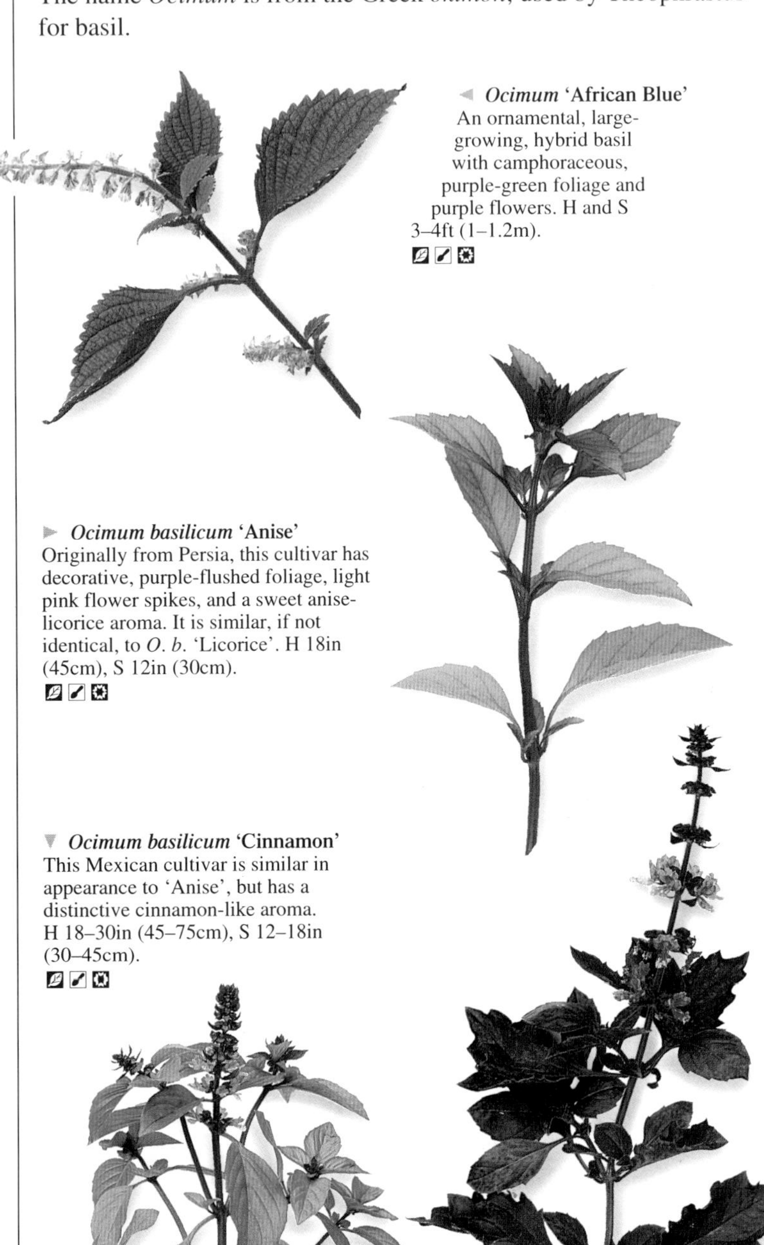

◄ ***Ocimum* 'African Blue'**
An ornamental, large-growing, hybrid basil with camphoraceous, purple-green foliage and purple flowers. H and S 3–4ft (1–1.2m).

► ***Ocimum basilicum* 'Anise'**
Originally from Persia, this cultivar has decorative, purple-flushed foliage, light pink flower spikes, and a sweet anise-licorice aroma. It is similar, if not identical, to *O. b.* 'Licorice'. H 18in (45cm), S 12in (30cm).

▼ ***Ocimum basilicum* 'Cinnamon'**
This Mexican cultivar is similar in appearance to 'Anise', but has a distinctive cinnamon-like aroma. H 18–30in (45–75cm), S 12–18in (30–45cm).

▲ ***Ocimum basilicum* 'Mini Purpurascens Wellsweep'**
This compact cultivar makes a mound of purple-flushed foliage that is ideal for containers. It may be a cultivar of *O. b.* var. *minimum*. H 6–8in (15–21cm), S 10–12in (24–30cm).

▲ ***Ocimum basilicum* 'Dark Opal'**
An attractive, highly aromatic cultivar, bred at the University of Connecticut in the 1950s, with purple-black leaves, 2–3in (5–7cm) long, and cerise-pink flowers. It differs from *O. b.* var. *purpurascens*, which has purplish leaves. H 24in (60cm), S 12in (30cm).

▲ ***Ocimum basilicum* 'Genovese'**
An Italian strain, widely regarded as the best for *pesto* and garlic-flavored dishes. It has dark green leaves, 2in (5cm) long, a tall, uniform habit, and is slow to bolt. H 18–24in (45–60cm), S 12-15in (30–38cm).

▲ ***Ocimum basilicum*** (basil, sweet basil)
Erect, much-branched, highly aromatic annual with ovate, bright green leaves up to 2in (5cm) long. Whorls of small, white, tubular flowers are borne in terminal racemes from summer to mid-autumn. H 8–24in (20–60cm), S 6–18in (15–45cm).

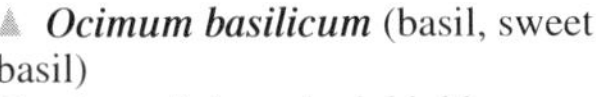

▲ ***Ocimum basilicum* 'Purple Ruffles'**
An outstanding cultivar with large, shiny, purple-black leaves that are interestingly fringed and crinkled. It makes a bushy, ornamental pot plant, with ample foliage for culinary use. An All America Selections (A.A.S.) winner. H and S 18–24in (45–60cm).

▲ ***Ocimum basilicum*** var. ***citriodorum*** (lemon basil, Indonesian *kemangie*)
A basil from northwestern India with a bushy habit and narrowly ovate, citrus-scented leaves. The white flowers are followed by lemon-scented seeds. It complements herb vinegars and fish dishes. H 18–24in (45–60cm), S 10–14in (25–35cm).

◄ ***Ocimum basilicum*** var. ***crispum*** (curly basil)
A robust basil with deeply curled foliage. The sweet flavor make this variety ideal for culinary use. Often referred to as 'Neapolitana' in the horticultural trade. H 8–24in (20–60cm), S 6–18in (15–45cm).

► ***Ocimum basilicum*** var. ***minimum*** (bush basil, Greek basil)
This dwarf variety has very small, pungent leaves, less than ½in (1cm) long. Tiny, white flowers occur in whorls or in terminal spikes. It makes a neat plant for pot culture or edging. H and S 6–12in (15–30cm).

► ***Ocimum gratissimum*** (East Indian basil, tree basil, fever plant)
Large, shrubby, pungently clove-scented annual or perennial with ovate-oblong, toothed leaves up to 6in (15cm) long. Pale greenish flowers are borne in 5–6in (12–15cm) spikes. H 6ft (2m), S 4ft (1.2cm).

▲ ***Ocimum sanctum*** (holy basil, sacred basil, *tulsi*)
Much-branched, softly hairy, shrubby perennial with elliptic-oblong to ovate leaves up to 1¼in (3cm) long, which have a spicy, pungent aroma. Violet or white flowers are borne in slender racemes in summer. H 18–24in (45cm–60cm), S 29–36in (3cm–1m).

OENOTHERA

Eighty species of annuals, biennials, and perennials belong to this N American genus, many of which are widely naturalized elsewhere. They are related to willow herbs (*Epilobium* species), but not to the primroses (*Primula* species, see p.183). *O. biennis* is a tall plant with scented flowers which grows well on very poor soil. *Oenothera* may derive from the Greek *oinos*, "wine", and *thera*, "hunt", from a name given by Theophrastus to a plant whose roots were eaten to arouse desire for wine.

Oenothera biennis (common evening primrose)
Erect biennial with a rosette of oblanceolate basal leaves, to 8in (20cm) long. In summer, night-scented, yellow flowers are followed by downy pods containing tiny seeds. H 1–5ft (30cm–1.5m), S 9–12in (22–30cm).

5–8

OLEA

This genus of 20 species of evergreen trees and shrubs occurs throughout the tropics and warm temperate regions of Africa and Eurasia. *O. europaea* needs specific growing conditions and will only thrive successfully outdoors in the Mediterranean area and similar climates. The tradition of the olive branch as a symbol of peace began with the biblical account of the dove returning to Noah's Ark with an olive branch after the flood waters had abated. *Olea* (Greek *elaio*), is the Latin for "olive" or "oil."

Olea europaea (olive)
Rugged, evergreen tree with gray, fissured bark, gray twigs, and dark gray-green, leathery, oblanceolate leaves. Numerous, off-white, fragrant flowers are borne in summer, followed by black fruits. H 28–40ft (9–12m), S 22–28ft (7–9m).

9–10

OPHIOPOGON

About 40 species of evergreen, tuft-forming perennials make up this genus, which occurs in southern and eastern Asia as far as Japan. *O. japonicus* is found in open, sunny areas in Japan. Several species are grown for their grass-like foliage, violet to white flowers, and mostly blue or black fruits. *O. japonicus* is especially attractive as ground cover and edging. It is widely used in landscaping in Australia and Hawaii.

Ophiopogon japonicus (lily turf, Mondo grass)
Evergreen perennial, with large, underground stolons, tuberous roots, and glossy, linear leaves, up to 16in (40cm) long. Spikes of lilac to white flowers appear from spring, followed by blue berries. H 12in (30cm), S indefinite.

6–10

OLD MAN, see *ARTEMISIA*, pp.88–9
OLIBANUM, see *Boswellia sacra*, p.95
OLIVE, see *Olea europea*, above
ONION, see *ALLIUM*, pp.80–81
ORACHE, see *Atriplex hortensis*, p.90
ORANGE, see *Citrus*, p.108
ORDEAL BEAN, see *Physostigma venenosum*, p.327

ORIGANUM

There are 36 species of perennials and subshrubs in this genus, which is Eurasian in distribution. About 20 are grown as ornamentals for their attractive, aromatic foliage and purple-pink to white flowers, which in certain species are surrounded by conspicuous bracts. They vary in habit and cultural requirements. Some are bushy perennials suitable for the border; others vary from arching to prostrate subshrubs, which are best grown on an elevation or in containers. All dislike winter wet and poor air circulation; *O. dictamnus* is especially sensitive and is usually grown in the alpine house. The name *Origanum* comes from *origanon* ("bitter herb"), the original Greek name used by Hippocrates for these plants. *Origanum vulgare* is found wild from Europe to central Asia, and is naturalized in eastern US. It hybridizes readily in cultivation, notably with *O. majorana* to give *O.* x *applii,* which is intermediate in appearance between the two species, and is often wrongly labeled *O. heracleoticum.* Hybrids between other cultivated marjorams abound, causing confusion over identification and naming.

▲ ***Origanum dictamnus*** (dittany of Crete, hop marjoram)
Prostrate subshrub with arching stems of woolly, gray-white leaves. Tiny pink flowers within large purple bracts are produced in pendant heads in summer. H 5–6in (12–15cm), S 16in (40cm).
8–9

▲ ***Origanum majorana*** (sweet marjoram, knotted marjoram)
Perennial shrub with wiry, red-brown stems and downy, gray-green leaves up to 1¼in (3cm) long. Very small white to pink flowers are produced in clustered spikes from late summer to midautumn. H 24in (60cm), S 18in (45cm).
9–10

▲ ***Origanum vulgare* 'Aureum Crispum'**
An ornamental cultivar with rounded, wrinkled, yellow-green leaves up to ½in (1cm) long that are at their best in spring. Tends to scorch in full sun and is less vigorous, and more tender, than *O. v.* 'Aureum'. H and S 12in (30cm).
7–9

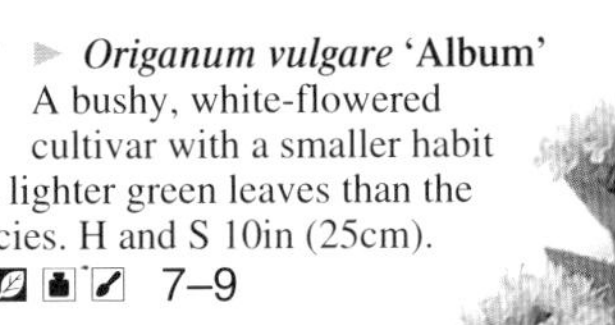

► ***Origanum vulgare* 'Album'**
A bushy, white-flowered cultivar with a smaller habit and lighter green leaves than the species. H and S 10in (25cm).
7–9

▲ ***Origanum vulgare* 'Aureum'** (golden marjoram)
This popular cultivar has small, bright, yellow-green leaves and lavender flowers. It makes colorful mounds in the spring, fading as flowering begins. The leaves scorch in full sun. H and S 30in (75cm).
6–9

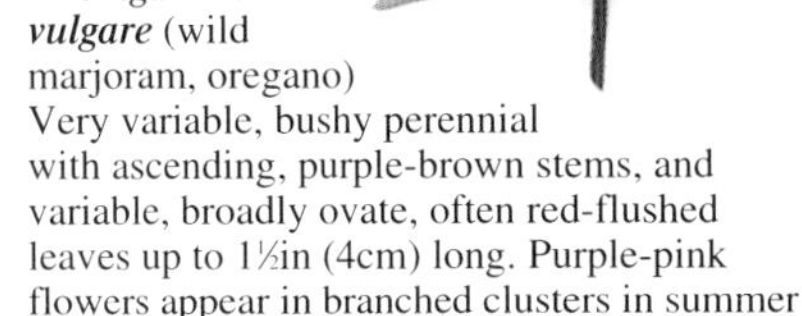

► ***Origanum vulgare*** (wild marjoram, oregano)
Very variable, bushy perennial with ascending, purple-brown stems, and variable, broadly ovate, often red-flushed leaves up to 1½in (4cm) long. Purple-pink flowers appear in branched clusters in summer and early autumn. H and S 18in (45cm).
5–9

► ***Origanum onites*** (pot marjoram, Greek oregano)
Perennial with erect, hairy stems and ovate, toothed, downy leaves up to 1in (2.5cm) long. Clusters of white, sometimes purple-tinged, flowers are borne in summer and early autumn. H and S 24in (60cm).
8–10

◀ ***Origanum vulgare*** **'Acorn Bank'**
This golden marjoram was named in 1995 after Acorn Bank House, Cumbria, England. It has pointed leaves, 1in (2.5cm) long, with inward-curling margins. The flowers are white with pink stamens. H and S 20in (50cm).
6–9

▲ ***Origanum vulgare*** **'Gold Tip'**
A fine foliage plant in spring, when each green leaf is symmetrically tipped with yellow. H and S 30in (75cm).
8–9

◀ ***Origanum vulgare*** **'Polyphant'**
A white-variegated, white-flowered cultivar that appeared as a sport of *O. v.* 'Aureum Crispum' at the Polyphant Herb Nursery, Cornwall, England in the 1980s. It is an attractive subject for containers and edging, but tends to scorch in full sun. H and S 12in (30cm).
8–9

▲ ***Origanum vulgare*** **'Compactum'**
(compact marjoram)
This dwarf, dense cultivar is ideal for containers, edging, and the rock garden. It forms a cushion of small rounded dark green leaves and bears numerous, pink-violet flowers. H 6in (15cm), S 12in (30cm).
7–9

▲ ***Origanum vulgare*** **'White Anniversary'**
An unusual cultivar with bright green, white-margined leaves, and inconspicuous flowers. It is smaller and less vigorous than the species and is a good subject for containers. The light, fresh coloration gives interesting uses in summer bedding and as groundcover or edging in a white border. H 6–10in (15–25cm), S 6–8in (15–20cm).
8–9

ORYZA

There are about 20 species of annual and perennial grasses in this tropical Asian genus. Rice is now grown in parts of Europe and the US, as well as in its native Asia. Wild rice comes from another species, *Zizania aquatica*, a native grass of eastern Canada and northeastern US. Pots of rice plants, easily raised from untreated, long-grained brown rice, make an ornamental feature for tropical pools. *Oryza* may be from the Greek *orusso*, meaning "to dig a trench," referring to the method of rice cultivation.

Oryza sativa (rice)
Annual, rhizomatous, wetland grass with stout, upright, arching stems and narrow leaves up to 5ft (1.5m) long. Panicles of spikelets, each containing a single flower, are followed by hard, pale brown seeds. H 20in–5ft (50cm–1.7m), S 8in–3ft (20cm–1m).
A

Oryza sativa **subsp.** ***japonica*** **'Arborio'**
This short-grained cultivar has 5–10 stems per plant, and leaf blades up to 20in (50cm) long. The red-brown grains are ¼in (7mm) long, borne in panicles 7in (17cm) long. H 3½ft (1.1m), S 24–30in (60–75cm).
A

OREGANO, see *ORIGANUM*, above; *Plectranthus amboinicus*, p.179
OREGON GRAPE, see *Mahonia aquifolium*, p.155
ORIENTAL BUSH CHERRY, see *PRUNUS*, pp.184–5
ORIENTAL SWEET GUM, see *Liquidambar orientalis*, p.152

PAEONIA

There are 33 species of perennials and small deciduous shrubs in this genus found in Eurasia and western N America. *P. lactiflora* and *P. suffruticosa* are native to eastern Asia; *P. officinalis* to Europe. Peonies are among the loveliest plants for borders. They have a long history of cultivation: *P. lactiflora* has been grown in the East since 900BC, and *P. suffruticosa* was the favorite flower of Chinese emperors for over 1,000 years. *Paeonia* is named after Paeon, physician to the Greek gods.

Paeonia lactiflora (Chinese peony)
Perennial with fleshy roots, red-marked stems, and dark green, divided leaves. Fragrant, single white flowers, 3–4in (7–10cm) across, appear in late spring and early summer. H and S 24–36in (60–90cm).

2–8

***Paeonia lactiflora* 'Duchesse de Nemours'**
Vigorous cultivar dating back to 1856, with medium-sized, fragrant, double flowers with large white outer petals and cream inner ones, produced in late spring and early summer. H and S 24–36in (60–90cm).

2–8

Paeonia officinalis (common peony)
Perennial with thick, knotted, dark brown roots and deeply divided midgreen leaves. Single, crimson, occasionally pink to white, 8-petaled flowers up to 5in (13cm) across are produced in late spring and early summer. H and S 24in (60cm).

2–8

Paeonia suffruticosa (tree peony, moutan peony)
Shrubby perennial with branching stems and light green, divided leaves. Single or semidouble, white to pink flowers up to 6in (15cm) across, appear in spring and early summer. H and S 4ft (1.2m).

5–8

PANAX

The number of species in this genus of perennials is disputed and may be three or six, depending on whether *P. pseudo-ginseng* is regarded as a single species with variants or four separate species. They are distributed in southern and eastern Asia, and N America. *P. ginseng* is native to montane woods in northeastern China. *P. pseudo-ginseng* is rapidly approaching extinction in the wild, and *P. zingiberensis*, which is collected for use as a substitute for *P. notoginseng*, is listed as endangered.

Panax ginseng (ginseng)
Perennial with a carrot-shaped, aromatic rootstock and upright stems bearing a whorl of 2–5 divided leaves. Umbels of small, green-yellow, 5-petaled flowers appear in spring and summer, followed by red berries. H 28–36in (70–90cm), S 30in (75cm).

4–8

Panax quinquefolius (American ginseng)
Perennial with an aromatic rootstock and leaves divided into 3–7 toothed leaflets up to 6in (16cm) long. Small green-white flowers appear in spring, followed by red berries. H 12–20in (30–50cm), S 18–24in (45–60cm).

4–8

PANDANUS

This large genus includes about 600 species of evergreen trees, shrubs, and scramblers, which occur in tropical Africa, Eurasia, and Australia. *P. odoratissimus* is found from western India to the central Moluccas. Various species are grown for their architectural appearance, either as landscape plants or as ornamentals under cover. They are known as "screw pines," since the strap-shaped leaves are arranged spirally; otherwise they resemble pineapple plants (*Ananas* species).

Pandanus odoratissimus (screw pine, *ketaki*)
Small tree with a stout trunk, aerial prop roots, and sword-shaped leaves up to 6ft (2m) long. Fragrant yellow flowers appear in summer, male and female separately, followed by red, woody fruits. H 20–30ft (6–10m), S 10ft (3m).

PAPAYA, see *Carica papaya*, p.101
PAPOOSE ROOT, see *Caulophyllum thalictroides*, p.103
PARAGUAY TEA, see *Ilex paraguensis*, p.142
PAREIRA, PAREIRA BRAVA, see *Chondrodendron tomentosum*, p.260
PARSLEY, see *Petroselinum crispum*, p.174
PARSLEY PIERT, see *Aphanes arvensis*, p.85
PARSLEY VINE, see *Vitis vinifera* 'Ciotat', p.221
PARSLEY-LEAVED ELDER, see *Sambucus nigra* var. *laciniata*, p.197
PARTRIDGE BERRY, see *Mitchella repens*, p.160
PASQUE FLOWER, see *Pulsatilla vulgaris*,

PAPAVER

Fifty species of annuals and perennials belong to this genus, which ranges through Eurasia, southern Africa, and Australia. *P. rhoeas* is a weed of disturbed ground in Europe and temperate Asia. It is the Flanders poppy, also renowned as the parent of the Shirley poppies, raised in Shirley, England, in the 19th century. All poppies contain bitter latex and have showy, short-lived, four-petaled flowers, followed by pepperpot capsules. They make colorful subjects for the border.

Papaver rhoeas (corn poppy, field poppy)
Annual with upright stems and long-stalked, usually red flowers, 2–4in (5–10cm) across, which have a dark basal spot and purple filaments, followed by dark brown seeds. H 8–36in (20–90cm), S 4–18in (10–45cm).

A

***Papaver rhoeas* 'Shirley Single Mixed'**
A recent selection of this Victorian strain, this cultivar produces the finest shades of pink, rose, salmon, crimson, and white. H 24in (60cm), S 12in (30cm).

A

Papaver somniferum (opium poppy)
Annual with glaucous, wavy leaves up to 10in (25cm) long. Lilac, pink, or white flowers, 3–7in (8–18cm) across, appear in summer, followed by capsules containing numerous gray seeds. H 1–5ft (30cm–1.5m), S 9–36in (23–90cm).

A

***Papaver somniferum* 'Danebrog'**
A 19th-century cultivar with brilliant red, often fringed petals, which have large white basal blotches. H 30in (75cm), S 12in (30cm).

A

***Papaver somniferum* 'Peony-flowered Mixed'**
This popular cultivar has double flowers, 4in (10cm) across, in shades of lilac, pink, purple, and white, followed by large seed capsules. H 26–36in (65–90cm), S12–18in (30–45cm).

A

PARIETARIA

There are about 20 species of annuals and perennials in this genus, which is almost cosmopolitan, especially in temperate regions. *P. judaica* is found from western and southern Europe to northern Africa and makes a picturesque sight on old roofs, walls, and hedge banks. It begins to grow early in the year and has fresh, green foliage when most other deciduous plants are still bare. The generic name *Parietaria* is from the Latin *parietarius*, "belonging to walls."

Parietaria judaica (pellitory-of-the-wall)
Softly hairy perennial with red-green, spreading stems and ovate to lanceolate leaves up to 3in (7cm) long. Insignificant green flowers are borne in forked clusters in summer. H and S 16in (40cm).

5–8

PASSIFLORA

There are about 500 species in this large genus, which occurs in tropical America, Asia, and Australia. It consists mainly of tendril climbers and climbing shrubs, with some perennials, small trees, and shrubs. Many of the climbing species are grown as ornamentals for their unique flowers and often edible fruits. They may be grown outdoors where the climate permits. The American *P. incarnata* is occasionally grown in herb gardens. It is one of the hardiest passion flowers.

Passiflora incarnata (maypops, passion flower)
Perennial climber with deeply lobed leaves about 6in (15cm) long. Fragrant lavender to white flowers, up to 2½in (6cm) across, appear in summer, followed by ovoid, yellow fruits, about 2in (5cm) long. H 25ft (8m).

7–10

PAULLINIA

This genus of almost 200 species of evergreen, woody lianas and climbing shrubs occurs mainly in tropical America. *P. cupana*, native to rainforest in Brazil, Uruguay, and Venezuela, is important to tribes in central Amazonian Brazil and was first noted by a Jesuit missionary in 1669. By the 18th century its use had spread widely in Brazil as an aphrodisiac and as protection against malaria and dysentery. Commercial plantations were established in the 1970s, and it is now a major cash crop.

Paullinia cupana (guaranà, Brazilian cocoa, zoom)
Liana with pinnately divided leaves that have toothed margins. Inconspicuous yellow flowers appear in spikes up to 4in (10cm) long. Red capsules split open when ripe to reveal 1–3 shiny, purple-brown seeds. H 30ft (10m).

T

p.186
PASSIONFLOWER, see *Passiflora incarnata*, above
PATCHOULI, see *Pogostemon cablin*, p.180
PAU D'ARCO, see *Tabebuia impetiginosa*, p.207
PAU ROSA, see *Aniba roseaodora*, p.239
PAWPAW, see *Carica papaya*, p.101
PEACH, see *PRUNUS*, pp.184–5
PEAT MOSS, see *Sphagnum*, p.205
PEDUNCULATE OAK, see *Quercus robur*, p.187

PELARGONIUM

This genus contains about 250 species of annuals, perennials, and subshrubs, which occur mainly in S Africa, with a few in tropical Africa, the Middle East, and Australia. Pelargoniums are commonly known as geraniums, confusing them with members of the related genus, *Geranium* (see p.133). Scented geraniums have been cultivated in Europe since the 17th century, and numerous hybrids and cultivars exist. They have become popular in recent years for their intensely aromatic leaves and subtle coloring. They are quite different in appearance and uses from the more popular zonal, regal, and ivy-leaved geraniums, commonly grown for summer display. The true species of *P. capitatum* has been superseded by the hybrid *P.* 'Attar of Roses', which has a stronger scent and more upright habit. The name *Pelargonium* comes from the Greek *pelargos*, "stork," because the shape of the fruit resembles a stork's beak.

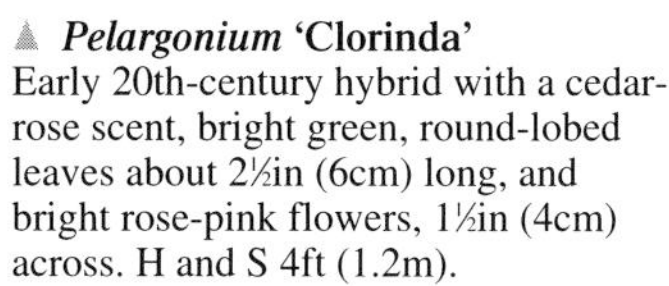

▲ ***Pelargonium citronellum***
An upright, bushy species with strongly lemon-scented leaves about 3½in (8cm) wide. Clusters of 5–8 purple-pink flowers with dark purple markings appear in summer. H 4–6ft (1.2–2m), S 3ft (1m).

▲ ***Pelargonium* 'Clorinda'**
Early 20th-century hybrid with a cedar-rose scent, bright green, round-lobed leaves about 2½in (6cm) long, and bright rose-pink flowers, 1½in (4cm) across. H and S 4ft (1.2m).

▲ ***Pelargonium odoratissimum***
(apple geranium)
Low-growing perennial with trailing flower stems and rounded, wavy-edged leaves which have a pronounced apple aroma. Small, white, red-veined flowers appear in spring and summer. H 12in (30cm), S 2ft (60cm).

▲ ***Pelargonium crispum***
(lemon geranium)
Stiffly upright subshrub with numerous rough and crinkled, kidney-shaped leaves, ½in (1cm) long, which are strongly lemon-scented. Pink flowers, ¾in (2cm) across, are borne in spring and summer. H 24–28in (60–70cm), S 12–18in (30–45cm).

◄ ***Pelargonium crispum* 'Major'**
This differs from the species in having larger leaves, up to 1in (2.5cm) long. The miniature version, *P. c.* 'Minor', has a stiff, compact habit. H 24–28in (60–70cm), S 12–18in (30–45cm).

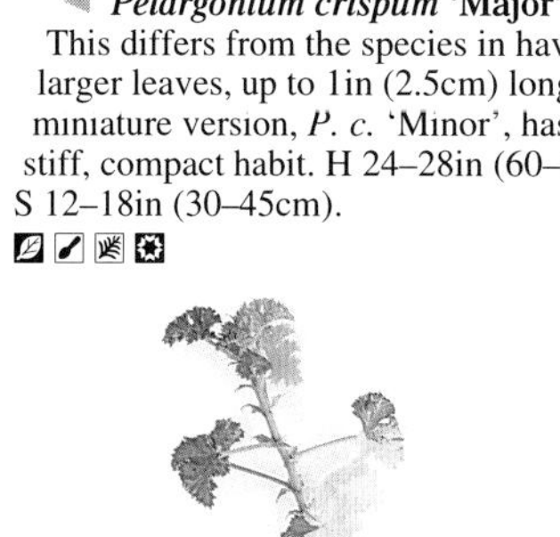

► ***Pelargonium crispum* 'Peach Cream'**
Unusual fruit-scented cultivar with irregular creamy white variegation. H 24–28in (60–70cm), S 12–18in (30–45cm).

◄ ***Pelargonium crispum* 'Variegatum'**
A favorite cultivar with crinkled, cream-edged leaves and the same lemon scent as the species. Can be trained as a standard, reaching 3ft (1m). H 24–28in (60–70cm), S 12–18in (30–45cm).

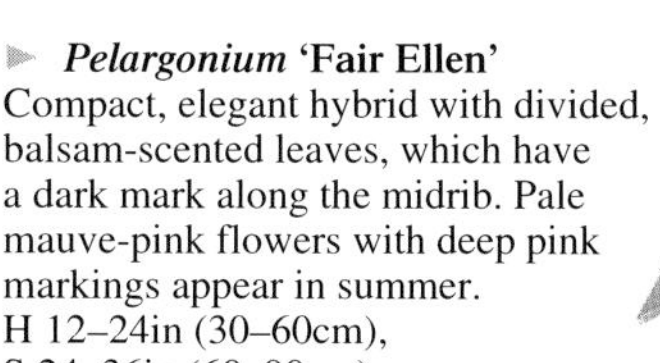

► ***Pelargonium* 'Fair Ellen'**
Compact, elegant hybrid with divided, balsam-scented leaves, which have a dark mark along the midrib. Pale mauve-pink flowers with deep pink markings appear in summer. H 12–24in (30–60cm), S 24–36in (60–90cm).

▲ *Pelargonium* 'Fragrans Variegatum'
The attractive silky leaves have irregular cream margins, which age to pale green; they have the same nutmeg-pine aroma as 'Fragrans'. H and S 12–16in (30–40cm).

▲ *Pelargonium* 'Fragrans'
(nutmeg geranium)
Erect subshrub with gray-green, silky, rounded leaves, which have a spicy, pinelike aroma. White flowers, about ½in (1cm) across marked with 2 red lines, are borne in spring and summer. H and S 18in (45cm).

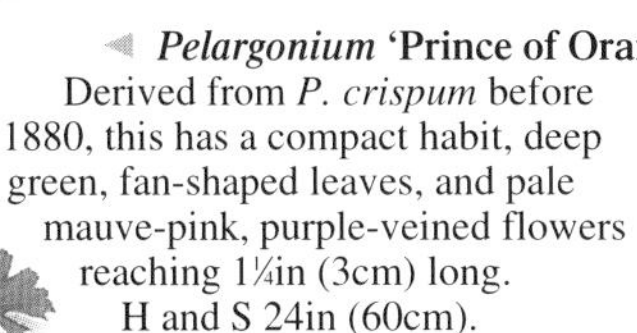

◄ *Pelargonium* 'Prince of Orange'
Derived from *P. crispum* before 1880, this has a compact habit, deep green, fan-shaped leaves, and pale mauve-pink, purple-veined flowers reaching 1¼in (3cm) long. H and S 24in (60cm).

► *Pelargonium radens* (rasp-leaved geranium)
Tall, bushy subshrub, introduced to the UK in 1774. It has a pungent lemon aroma and rough, finely divided leaves. Pale purple-pink flowers appear in summer. H and S 3–5ft (1–1.5m).

◄ *Pelargonium* 'Radula'
Similar to *P.* 'Graveolens' but with more deeply cut leaves, 4in (10cm) across. Scent is a camphoraceous rose-lemon. Small pink-purple flowers are borne in summer. H 3–5ft (1–1.5m), S 2–5ft (60cm–1.5m).

▲ *Pelargonium* 'Graveolens'
(rose geranium)
Upright subshrub with gray-green, rose-scented, triangular, toothed leaves up to 2½in (6cm) long. Pale pink flowers with two purple spots are borne in spring and summer. Dates back to the 1790s. H 3–5ft (1–1.5m), S 2–5ft (60cm–1.5m).

◄ *Pelargonium* 'Galway Star'
Outstandingly attractive, with small cream-edged, toothed leaves, deeply cut and with a strong lemon scent. Flowers are pale pink, with cerise and purple markings. H 18–24in (45–60cm), S 12–18in (30–45cm).

► *Pelargonium* 'Radula Rosea'
This cultivar makes a colorful pot plant with deep rose pink flowers. H 3–5ft (1–1.5m), S 2–5ft (60cm–1.5m).

◄ *Pelargonium* 'Rober's Lemon Rose'
Tall, vigorous variant of *P.* 'Graveolens' with soft, gray-green, irregularly lobed leaves about 2in (5cm) long. It has a lemon-rose scent and small pink flowers. H 5ft (1.5m), S 4ft (1.2m).

▲ *Pelargonium capitatum*
(wild rose geranium)
Low, spreading, evergreen, perennial with velvety, crinkled, rose-scented leaves up to 3in (8cm) long. Mauve-pink flowers, ¾in (2cm) across, are borne in clusters in summer. H 1–3ft (30–90cm), S 1½–5ft (45cm–1.5m).

▲ *Pelargonium* 'Lady Plymouth'
First recorded about 1800, this hybrid's triangular leaves have irregular cream margins and a minty rose-lemon scent. 'Grey Lady Plymouth' has mainly gray-green foliage. H 3–5ft (1–1.5m), S 2–5ft (60cm–1.5m).

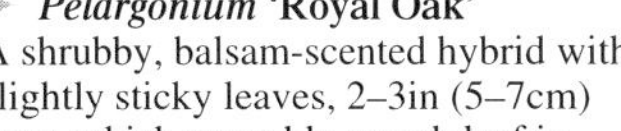

► *Pelargonium* 'Royal Oak'
A shrubby, balsam-scented hybrid with slightly sticky leaves, 2–3in (5–7cm) long, which resemble an oak leaf in shape. The relatively large pink-purple flowers have darker spots. H 2–5ft (60cm–1.5m), S 2–4ft (60cm–1.2m).

▲ *Pelargonium* 'Old Spice'
A cultivar derived from *P.* 'Fragrans', with a compact habit and crinkled leaves. H and S 1½–2ft (45–60cm).

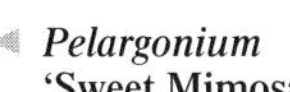

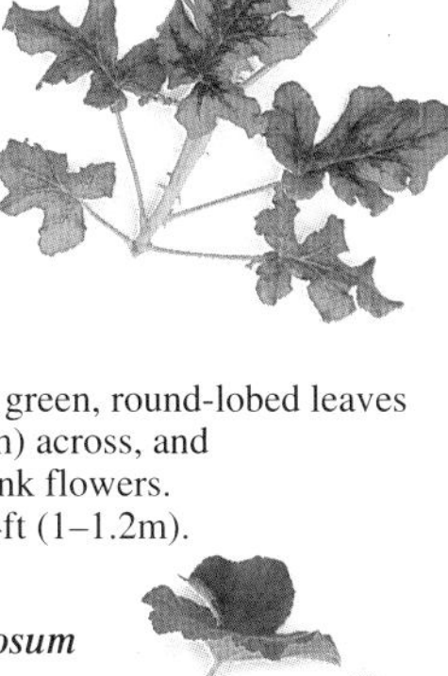

◄ *Pelargonium* 'Sweet Mimosa'
A sweetly scented hybrid with bright green, round-lobed leaves about 3½in (9cm) across, and bright shell pink flowers. H and S 3–4ft (1–1.2m).

► *Pelargonium tomentosum*
(peppermint geranium)
Large, semiprostrate, shrubby perennial with soft, velvety leaves, 4–5in (10–12cm) across, which are strongly peppermint-scented. Small white flowers appear in spring and summer. H 12–20in (30–50cm), S 3–4ft (1–1.2m).

PEGANUM

A genus of five or six species of branched perennials distributed in dry parts of the tropics and subtropics of both hemispheres, especially from Mediterranean regions to central and eastern Asia. The aromatic *P. harmala*, found in southern Europe, northern Africa, and Asia, is a hardy desert plant that adapts well to cultivation. Revered in many parts of Asia as a hallucinogen, research suggests it formed the intoxicating drink *soma*, or *huoma*, of ancient Persia and India.

Peganum harmala (Syrian rue, harmal)
Perennial with shrubby leaves divided into narrow lobes. Green-white, veined flowers up to 1in (2.5cm) across appear in spring and summer, followed by dry capsules containing numerous dark brown seeds. H 20–36in (50–90cm), S 18–24in (45–60cm).

7–9

PERILLA

Six species of aromatic annuals make up this genus, which occurs from India to Japan. *P. frutescens* is found from the Himalayas to Japan and is naturalized in parts of N America. It is widely grown as a culinary herb in eastern Asia and is increasingly popular as an ornamental for summer bedding. It is similar in appearance to coleus (*Solenostemon* species). Plants with curly leaves were once described as a separate species, *P. crispa*, but are now regarded as a cultivated variety.

Perilla frutescens (*shiso*)
Bushy annual with ovate leaves that are distinctly veined and strongly scented. Insignificant white flowers appear in spikes in summer, followed by pale brown nutlets. H 2–4ft (60cm–1.2m), S 12–24in (30–60cm).

A

***Perilla frutescens* 'Atropurpurea'**
(beefsteak plant)
This variant has deeply cut, crinkled, dark bronze-purple leaves and red or pink flowers. Considerable variation exists in seed-raised plants, and cultivar names may vary accordingly. H 2–4ft (60cm–1.2m), S 12–24in (30–60cm).

A

PETIVERIA

A single species of perennial belongs to this genus, which occurs in tropical and warm parts of America, and is naturalized in parts of tropical Asia and Africa. It is related to pokeweeds (*Phytolacca*, see p.176). *P. alliacea* is not in general cultivation but may be seen in many botanic gardens. It is an important medicinal and ritual plant in southern Florida, C America, and the Caribbean, especially in the Santeria religion, and has common names in many languages.

Petiveria alliacea (Guinea hen weed, conga root, strong man's weed)
Perennial with a thick taproot, slender stems, and pointed, garlic-smelling leaves up to 6in (16cm) long. Tiny white to green-white, starlike flowers appear all year, followed by spiny fruits. H 3–5ft (1–1.5m), S 3ft (1m).

PETROSELINUM

Three species of biennials belong to this European genus; *P. crispum* is found wild mainly in southeastern Europe and western Asia. Parsley is the most widely cultivated herb in Europe. It became popular in Roman times; a curly variant was first mentioned in AD42 and rapidly gained favor for its appearance. Curly parsleys are neat, attractive plants that may be grown as edging or in containers. *P. c.* var. *tuberosum* has been grown for its edible roots since the 16th century but remains a small-scale crop.

Petroselinum crispum (parsley)
Aromatic biennial with a white taproot and triangular pinnate leaves. Leaf margins are variably curled. Tiny yellow-green flowers are produced in flat-topped umbels in summer, followed by tiny ribbed, ovoid fruits. H 12–32in (30–80cm), S 12in (30cm).

6–9

***Petroselinum crispum* 'Italian'**
(French parsley, Italian parsley, plain-leaved parsley)
This cultivar has flat, dark green foliage, not curly, with a strong flavor. Plants are hardier, more weather-resistant, and larger than curly variants. H and S 15–24in (38–60cm).

6–9

PELLITORY, see *Anacyclus pyrethrum*, p.83
PELLITORY OF SPAIN, see *Anacyclus pyrethrum*, p.83
PELLITORY-OF-THE-WALL, see *Parietaria judaica*, p.171
PENNYROYAL, see *MENTHA*, pp.158–9
PEONY, see *Paeonia*, p.170
PEPPER, see *CAPSICUM*, p.100; *Piper nigrum*, p.178
PEPPER TREE, see *Drimys*, p.120
PEPPERMINT, see *MENTHA*, pp.158–9
PEPPERMINT GERANIUM, see *PELARGONIUM*, pp.172–3
PERFORATE ST. JOHN'S WORT, see *Hypericum perforatum*, p.141
PERIWINKLE, see *Vinca*, p.220

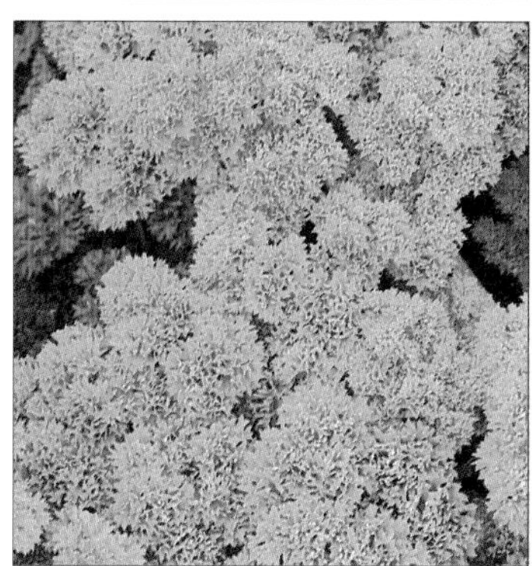

Petroselinum crispum **'Moss Curled'**
A tall, vigorous cultivar with densely curled foliage. It is one of many curly-leaved parsleys, equally good for garnishing and flavoring. H and S 12in (30cm).

6–9

Petroselinum crispum var. ***tuberosum*** (Hamburg parsley, turnip-rooted parsley)
A distinctive variety with large, swollen roots and noncurly foliage with a parsley–celery flavor, inferior to that of flat- and curly-leaved variants. H 12–24in (30–60cm), S 12in (30cm).

6–9

PEUMUS

This genus consists of a single species of evergreen shrub or small tree, which is found only in Chile. It belongs to the Monimiaceae, a family with an unusually high number of single-species genera, most of which yield aromatic oils. *P. boldus* is economically important in Chile, yielding hardwood, tannins, and dye from the bark, as well as edible fruits and medicinal compounds. It is hardy only in mild areas and is seldom seen in cultivation. The foliage has a lemon–camphor aroma.

Peumus boldus (boldo)
Shrubby tree with smooth brown bark and ovate, leathery, aromatic leaves. Pale green, scented flowers appear in clusters in late summer, male and female flowers on separate plants; females bear pale yellow fruits. H 22ft (7m), S 15ft (5m).

T

PHELLODENDRON

Ten species of deciduous trees belong to this genus, which is eastern Asian in distribution; *P. amurense* is found in northern China and Manchuria. They resemble *Ailanthus* species (see p.76) in appearance, with a graceful, spreading habit. *P. amurense* is grown as an ornamental for its attractive habit, corky, pale gray bark, and aromatic leaves that turn yellow in autumn. *Phellodendron* is from the Greek *phellos*, "cork," and *dendron*, "tree," an allusion to the bark of these trees.

Phellodendron amurense (Amur cork tree)
Aromatic deciduous tree with glossy, dark green leaves up to 14in (35cm) long. Tiny, pale green flowers appear in early summer, followed by black fruits that have a strong turpentine aroma. H 40–50ft (12–15m), S 50–60ft (15–18m).

3–9

PHRAGMITES

Fewer than six species of perennial reed grasses make up this cosmopolitan genus, which occurs in both temperate and tropical regions. *P. australis* is extremely fast-growing and adaptable, forming large stands in wetlands throughout the world. The flower heads are excellent for dried flower arrangements. The name *Phragmites* comes from the Greek *phragma*, "fence" or "screen." It is an abbreviation of the description of these plants as *kalamos phragmata*, "reed of hedges."

Phragmites australis (common reed, *carrizo*)
Tall rhizomatous reed with robust stems and tapering leaves up to 24in (60cm) long. Purple-brown flower heads up 18in (45cm) long appear in late summer and autumn, persisting into winter. H 11ft (3.5m), S indefinite.

4–10

Phragmites australis **'Variegatus'**
This tall, yellow-striped reed is smaller than the species but spreads vigorously. It may be grown in a large container in water or in moist soil. H 5ft (1.5m), S 3ft (1m).

4–10

PERSIAN LILAC, see *Melia azederach*, p.157
PERSIMMON, see *Diospyros*, p.119
PERUVIAN BALSAM, see *Myroxylon pereirae*, p.315
PERUVIAN BARK, see *Cinchona pubescens*, p.108

PHYLLOSTACHYS

This genus of 60 species of medium to large bamboos occurs in India, China, and Burma; *P. nigra* is found in damp areas in eastern and central China. It includes some of the most ornamental bamboos for gardens and large containers, with graceful foliage and rather zigzag canes, which are often beautifully colored and patterned. They are less invasive than most bamboos and may be planted as focal points in lawns or large borders.

Phyllostachys nigra (black bamboo) Evergreen, rhizomatous, clump-forming bamboo with arching, slender stems turning from green-brown to black in the 2nd or 3rd year, and narrow, lanceolate leaves up to 5in (13cm) long. H 10–30ft (3–10m), S indefinite.

6–10

***Phyllostachys nigra* 'Boryana'**
This Japanese cultivar has young, green canes that turn yellow with purple streaks when mature, and luxuriant leaves up to 3½in (9cm) long. H 8–25ft (2.5–8m), S indefinite.

6–10

Phyllostachys nigra* var. *henonis
This is the most common variety in the wild. It has green stems, which age yellow-green, and very fine, glossy foliage. Widely used in Chinese medicine. H 30ft (10m), S 6–10ft (2–3m).

6–10

PHYTOLACCA

A genus of 35 species of perennials, evergreen shrubs, and trees distributed in both warm and temperate regions; *P. acinosa* is found from Kashmir to southwestern China. *P. americana*, found in N and C America, is one of several species cultivated for their imposing habit and ornamental but poisonous berries. *Phytolacca* comes from the Greek *phyton*, "plant," and the Hindi *lakh*, a dye extracted from the lac insect, the color of which resembles that found in the berries of the plant.

Phytolacca acinosa (Indian pokeberry) Robust perennial with succulent stems and lanceolate, pointed leaves up to 10in (25cm) long. Small, green-white flowers appear in summer, followed by stout spikes, 4–8in (10–20cm) long, of dark purple berries. H and S 3–5ft (90cm–1.5m).

T

Phytolacca americana (pokeweed, pokeroot, red-ink plant)
Fetid perennial with succulent stems and pointed leaves up to 12in (30cm) long. Clusters of small, pink-white flowers appear in summer, followed by fleshy purple berries. H 4–10ft (1.2–3m), S 4–8ft (1.2–2.5m).

3–9

PHYSALIS

A cosmopolitan genus of around 80 species of occasionally rhizomatous, upright or sprawling annuals and perennials. *P. alkekengi* is found wild from SE Asia to Japan. All produce numerous seeds in a globose berry enclosed in an inflated calyx. *P. alkekengi* is popular as an ornamental for the papery, orange-red calyces surrounding the ripe fruits, and may be grown as an annual. It should not to be confused with *Solanum capicastrum*, which is also called "winter cherry."

Physalis alkekengi (Chinese lantern, winter cherry, bladder cherry)
Rhizomatous perennial with broadly ovate, pointed leaves up to 3½in (9cm) long. 5-lobed, white flowers appear in summer, followed by edible, orange to red berries surrounded by a papery calyx. H 24in (60cm), S indefinite.

3–9

PIMPINELLA

This genus of about 150 species of annuals, biennials, and perennials ranges through Eurasia and northern Africa. *P. anisum* needs a hot summer to thrive and for seed to ripen. Neither *P. major* nor *P. saxifraga* has much garden merit, but *P. m.* 'Rosea' is an attractive pink-flowered cultivar. *Pimpinella* may be from the Latin *bipinnula*, referring to the twice-pinnately divided leaves, or from "pimpernel" (Latin *piper*, "pepper"), perhaps referring to a spicy flavor.

Pimpinella anisum (anise, aniseed)
Aromatic, downy annual with kidney-shaped to ovate, toothed or divided leaves. Tiny off-white flowers are produced in umbels during summer, followed by ribbed seeds about ¼in (5mm) long. H 20in (50cm), S 10–18in (24–45cm).

A

PICK-POCKET, see *Capsella bursa-pastoris*, p.99
PIGWEED, see *Chenopodium*, p.106
PILEWORT, see *Ranunculus ficaria*, p.188
PILL-BEARING SPURGE, see *Euphorbia hirta*, p.126
PIMENTO, see *Pimenta dioica*, p.328
PIMPERNEL, see *Anagallis*, p.83
PINE, see *Pinus*, above
PINELLIA, see *Pinellia ternata*, above
PINK, see *Dianthus chinensis*, p.117

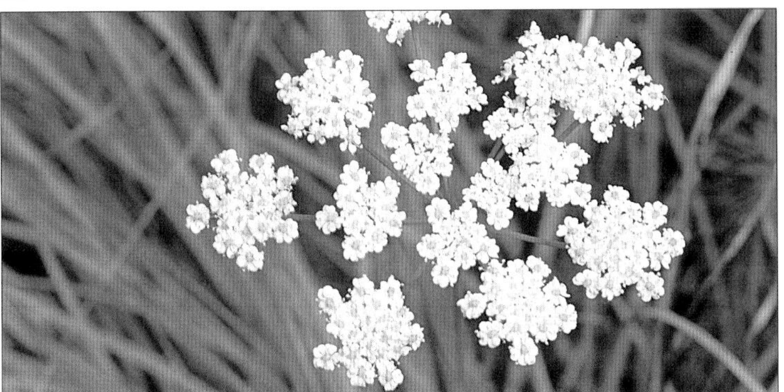

Pimpinella saxifraga (burnet saxifrage, small pimpernel)
Perennial with fetid taproot, slightly ridged stems, pinnate lower leaves, and bipinnate stem leaves. Tiny white flowers, occasionally tinged pink or purple, appear in umbels in summer. H to 36in (90cm), S 12–30in (30–75cm).

6–8

PINELLIA

Six species of small tuberous perennials belong to this genus, which occurs in eastern Asia. *P. ternata*, found in China, Japan, and Korea, has an unusual flower head with a green spathe and an erect, purple-green spadix, and it makes an eyecatching plant for a shady corner. It thrives beneath trees and shrubs and may be invasive, spreading by bulbils. *Pinellia* is named after Giovanni Pinelli (1535–1601), owner of a botanic garden in Naples, Italy.

Pinellia ternata (pinellia)
Slender perennial with a tuber up to ¾in (2cm) across, bulbil-bearing stalks, and trifoliate adult leaves. A long-stalked inflorescence appears in summer, followed by a cluster of green berries. H 24in (60cm), S 12in (30cm).

6–9

Pinus sylvestris (Scots pine)
Upright tree with a tall, bare trunk and rounded crown in older specimens, red-brown to purple-gray bark, paired leaves 1¼–4in (3–10cm) long, and gray-brown cones about 2in (5cm) long. H 50–80ft (15–25m), S 25–30ft (8–10m).

2–8

PINUS

This genus includes about 95 species of evergreen coniferous trees and shrubs, which occur throughout northern temperate regions, C and S America, Sumatra, and Java; *P. mugo* is native to central European Alps. Pines of all types are grown as ornamentals for their long, needlelike leaves. Dwarf variants are available, suitable for small spaces. Most pines dislike shade and polluted air, but some will tolerate very poor soils and coastal sites, and make excellent windbreaks.

Pinus mugo* var. *pumilio (dwarf mountain pine)
Spreading, often prostrate, shrubby conifer with thick, ascending branches, resinous buds, paired leaves, and almost globose brown cones up to 2½in (6cm) long. H 6–10ft (2–3m), S 3–6ft (1–2m).

2–8

***Pinus sylvestris* 'Aurea'** (golden Scots pine)
A slow-growing, small cultivar that turns yellow in winter. It makes a striking specimen in plantings for winter interest, especially with heathers and early flowering bulbs. H 30ft (10m), S 12ft (4m).

2–8

PIPER

This pantropical genus contains over 1,000 species of evergreen pungent-smelling climbers, shrubs, and small trees. *P. betle* is found in India, Sri Lanka, and Malaysia; *P. cubeba* in SE Asia; *P. longum* and *P. nigrum* in southern and eastern India. *P. nigrum* is attractive as a pot plant. One of the oldest known spices, pepper was the main commodity traded along caravan routes of the east. It was the inspiration for early European exploration of sea routes, which created the wealth of cities such as Venice.

Piper betle (betel)
Shrubby vine with semiwoody stems and glossy, pointed leaves up to 6in (15cm) long. Yellow-green male and female flowers are borne on separate plants: males in 6in (15cm) long spikes; females slightly shorter, followed by fleshy fruits. H 15ft (5m), S 30ft (10m).

Piper cubeba (cubeb, tailed pepper)
Climbing shrub with flexuous stems and tapering, ovate-elliptic, leathery leaves, 3–6in (7–15cm) long. Insignificant flowers are produced in spikes up to 4in (10cm) long; females bear round, ¼in (6mm), green fruits that ripen orange-brown. H 20ft (6m).

Piper longum (Indian long pepper, Jaborandi pepper, *pippali*)
Small climbing subshrub. Male flowers are borne in a lax spike about 2in (5cm) long; females in a dense spike, elongating up to 1½in (3.5cm) as the fused mass of small red-brown fruits develops. H 10ft (3m), S 15–20ft (5–6m).

Piper nigrum (pepper)
Woody-stemmed climber with ovate leaves 5–7in (12–18cm) long. Tiny white flowers are borne on pendulous spikes, with males and females usually on separate plants, followed by globose red berries ¼in (6mm) across.
H 12ft (4m).

PISTACIA

A genus of about nine species of trees and shrubs found in Mediterranean areas, Asia, C America, and southern US. Both *P. lentiscus* and *P. terebinthus* are native to Mediterranean regions. *P. lentiscus* has been valued since Classical times for its resin, known as "mastic," used to fill teeth and sweeten the breath. Turpentine, from *P. terebinthus*, and mastic were among the 17 ingredients of *kyphi*, an Egyptian incense. *Pistacia* is from the Greek *pistake*, pistachio tree (*P. vera*).

Pistacia lentiscus (mastic tree, lentisc)
Large evergreen shrub or small tree with leathery, pungently scented, divided leaves. Clusters of red-green flowers appear in spring, with males and females on separate plants; females bear globose, fleshy red fruits, ripening to black. H 15ft (5m), S 10ft (3m).

Pistacia terebinthus (terebinth tree, Cyprus turpentine)
Rounded deciduous tree or shrub with aromatic, dark green foliage that is red when new. Minute flowers appear in dense panicles in early summer. Female plants bear purple-brown fruits. H 20–28ft (6–9m), S 10–20ft (3–6m).

PLANTAGO

This large, cosmopolitan genus includes about 250 species of annuals, biennials, and perennials. *P. asiatica* is native to China; *P. psyllium* to the Mediterranean. *P. major* (greater plantain), common in Europe and temperate Asia, is a pernicious weed of lawns and paths but has several variants that are grown in borders as ornamentals. The common name "white man's foot," describes how the plant's seeds were spread worldwide during colonial times in the trouser cuffs of Europeans.

Plantago asiatica (Asian plantain)
Weedy perennial with a basal rosette of long-stalked, veined leaves up to 6in (15cm) long. Minute green flowers are borne in spikes up to 20in (50cm) long, followed by capsules containing 4–9 dark brown seeds. H 8–24in (20–60cm), S 6–12in (15–30cm).

3–9

PIPPALI, see *Piper longum*, above
PIPSISSEWA, see *Chimaphila umbellata*, p.107
PISTACHIO, see *Pistacia*, above
PLAIN-LEAVED PARSLEY, see *Petroselinum crispum* 'Italian', p.174
PLANTAIN, see *Plantago*, above

***Plantago asiatica* 'Variegata'**
This cultivar has irregular white variegation on the leaves and has considerably more ornamental value than the species. H 8–24in (20–60cm), S 6–12in (15–30cm).

3–9

Plantago major (greater plantain, rat-tail plantain)
Small perennial with a basal rosette of long-stalked, ovate to elliptic leaves up to 6in (15cm) long. Inconspicuous yellow-green flowers, up to 6in (15cm) long, are produced in cylindrical spikes in summer. H and S 16in (40cm).

3–9

***Plantago major* 'Rubrifolia'**
This popular cultivar has bold, beet red leaves, which contrast well with finely cut, gray-leaved herbs, such as artemisias. H and S 12–15in (30–38cm).

3–9

Plantago psyllium (Spanish psyllium, fleaseed, fleawort)
Annual with narrow, gray-green, glandular leaves, mostly arranged in whorls of 3–6. Globose flower spikes appear in the axils in summer, followed by tiny, glossy seeds. H 24in (60cm), S 12in (30cm).

A

PLATYCODON

This genus contains a single species of perennial that occurs in eastern Asia. It is closely related to *Campanula*. *P. grandiflorus* is an easily grown border plant and has single, and double-flowered cultivars in shades of pink, blue, and white. Dwarf variants are available, suited to rock gardens and containers. It is cultivated specifically as a medicinal plant in China. *Platycodon* is from the Greek *platys*, "broad," and *kodon*, "bell," referring to the wide, bell-shaped flowers.

Platycodon grandiflorus (balloon flower, Chinese bellflower)
Erect, clump-forming perennial with thick roots and blue-green, ovate, toothed leaves. Large inflated buds open into bell-shaped, usually blue, flowers in summer. H 16–36in (40–90cm), S 12–18in (30–45cm).

3–8

Platycodon grandiflorus* var. *apoyama
A Japanese variant with slightly larger, deeper blue flowers than the species, produced on very dwarf plants. It is ideal for alpine troughs and rock gardens. H 4–5in (10–13cm), S 8–12in (20–30cm).

3–8

PLECTRANTHUS

This genus of about 300 species of evergreen perennials and subshrubs occurs in warm and tropical parts of Africa, Asia, and Australia. *P. amboinicus*, known only in cultivation, originated in Vietnam and India; *P. barbatus* is found in India, western Asia, and eastern Africa. Several species are easily grown as indoor pot plants in cool temperate regions. The attractive *P. amboinicus* deserves to be more widely grown. *P. barbatus* was popular as an ornamental in the 19th century.

Plectranthus amboinicus (Indian borage, oregano, Spanish thyme)
Lemon-scented evergreen perennial with thick, succulent stems and crinkly, light green, fleshy leaves. In summer, small lilac flowers are borne in spikes up to 16in (40cm) long. H 12–36in (30cm–1m), S 9–24in (23–60cm).

Plectranthus barbatus
Aromatic, semisucculent perennial with erect stems and downy, ovate leaves, which have scalloped margins and are dotted with red glands on the undersurfaces. Whorls of lavender-blue flowers are produced in racemes in the rainy season. H and S 24in (60cm).

POLEMONIUM

A genus of 25 species of rhizomatous and clump-forming perennials and spreading annuals, often with unpleasant-smelling foliage. They occur in temperate regions of the northern hemisphere, mainly in N America, but also in southern S America and Asia. Most have blue or white saucer-shaped flowers. *P. caeruleum* is easily grown in borders and wild flower meadows. The less vigorous *P. reptans* is also popular as a border perennial, with cultivars in shades of blue and pink.

Polemonium caeruleum (Jacob's ladder, Greek valerian, charity)
Upright, clump-forming perennial with arching, pinnately divided leaves to 5in (12cm) long. Terminal clusters of blue (rarely white) flowers open from late spring and summer. H 12–36in (30–90cm), S 12–18in (30–45cm).

3–9

PODOPHYLLUM

A genus of about 10 species of perennials distributed throughout N America and the Himalayas. *P. peltatum*, found in eastern N America, is a distinctive plant suited to woodland conditions, with umbrella-shaped leaves, anemonelike flowers, and plumlike fruits. The lemon-flavored fruits are edible but all other parts are extremely poisonous. *Podophyllum* comes from the Greek *pous*, "foot," and *phyllon*, "leaf," describing the leaf shape.

Podophyllum peltatum (May apple, American mandrake, wild lemon)
Perennial with a red-brown rhizome up to 6ft (2m) long, and upright stems bearing drooping, deeply cleft leaves. In spring, white flowers are followed by yellow fruits, 2in (5cm) long. H 12–18in (30–45cm), S 12in (30cm).

3–9

***Polemonium caeruleum* 'Album'**
Almost as widely grown as the species, this white-flowered cultivar makes an excellent, early-flowering perennial for the white border and moist, shady corners of the garden. H 12–36in (30–90cm), S 12–18in (30–45cm).

3–9

POGOSTEMON

A genus of about 70 species of perennials and subshrubs occurring in India and Malaysia. *P. cablin* and various other species are widely cultivated in India and the Far East for patchouli, a heavy, distinctive, mint–sandalwood fragrance, once used to distinguish fabrics of Indian origin. Fashionable in Europe during the 1860s, patchouli regained popularity in the 1960s. *Pogostemon* is from the Greek *pogon*, "beard," and *stemon*, "stamen," and refers to the bearded filaments.

Pogostemon cablin (patchouli)
Aromatic, hairy perennial with ovate to triangular leaves up to 5in (12cm) long. White, violet-marked flowers with violet filaments are produced in spikes up to 5½in (14cm) long. H and S 3ft (1m).

Polemonium reptans (abscess root, Greek valerian)
Spreading to upright perennial with a creeping rhizome and pinnate leaves consisting of 7–19 elliptic to oblong, pointed leaflets. Small blue flowers are borne from spring to early summer. H 6–12in (15–30cm), S 15in (38cm).

3–9

PLEURISY ROOT, see *Asclepias tuberosa*, p.89
PLUM, see *PRUNUS*, pp.184–5
POHL, see *Brunfelsia uniflora*, p.95
POISON NUT, see *Strychnos nux-vomica*, p.206
POISON PARSLEY, see *Conium maculatum*, p.111
POKEWEED, POKEROOT, see *Phytolacca americana*, p.176
POLECAT WEED, see *Symplocarpus foetidus*, p.206

POLYGONATUM

A genus of about 30 species of rhizomatous perennials found in Europe, Asia, and the northern US. *P. odoratum* is one of several rather similar species grown for their arching stems and pendent, tubular flowers. Solomon's seals are elegant cut flowers, especially with peonies. The generic name *Polygonatum* is from the Greek *polys*, "many," and *gonu*, "knee joint," referring to the jointed rhizomes. Care should be taken not to confuse *Polygonatum multiflorum* and *Polygonum multiflorum* (see below).

Polygonatum odoratum (angled Solomon's seal)
Rhizomatous perennial with angled, arching stems and stalkless, ovate, pointed leaves up to 4in (10cm) long. Fragrant, white, green-tipped flowers, about ¾in (2cm) long, appear in early summer. H 34in (85cm), S 18in (45cm).

3–9

***Polygonatum odoratum* 'Variegatum'**
This decorative cultivar has white-striped leaves. As in the species, the flowers appear in the axils on the underside of the leaves, followed by globose, blue-black berries, ¼in (6mm) in diameter. H 24in (60cm), S 12in (30cm).

3–9

***Polygonum bistorta* 'Superbum'**
This is the most widely grown variant. It is larger all around than the species, with showier flowers. H 24–30in (60–75cm), S 24in (60cm).

POLYGONUM

This cosmopolitan genus of annuals, perennials, and deciduous shrubby climbers has about 150 species, distributed mainly in temperate regions. Many are weedy and often invasive in the garden. The true knotweed, *P. bistorta*, found through Europe and Asia to Japan, is rarely grown, but its variants are popular as groundcover, especially in damp situations. *P. multiflorum* is similar to the rampant *P. baldshuanicum* (Russian vine) in appearance, but it is less vigorous and less hardy.

Polygonum bistorta (bistort, snakeweed, English serpentary)
Erect perennial with a stout, contorted rhizome and broadly ovate basal leaves up to 6in (15cm) long. Numerous tiny pale pink flowers appear in dense spikes in summer, followed by hard nutlets. H 10–20in (25–50cm), S 18in (45cm).

3–9

POLYPODIUM

A genus of about 75 species of deciduous, evergreen and semievergreen, terrestrial, epiphytic, and lithophytic ferns with fleshy, creeping rhizomes, occurring mainly in northern temperate regions. *P. vulgare*, found in N America, Europe, and eastern Asia, has numerous cultivars grown as ornamentals for their elegant fronds. Polypodies make good groundcover for damp, shady areas beneath trees. The name is from the Greek *polys*, "many," and *pous*, "foot," and refers to the much-branched rhizomes.

Polypodium vulgare (polypody)
Evergreen, creeping, often epiphytic fern with rhizomes about ½in (1cm) thick, which are densely clad in red-brown scales when young. Fronds are pinnately lobed, almost to the midrib, into 20–40 lanceolate segments. H 4–16in (10–40cm), S indefinite.

5–8

***Polypodium vulgare* 'Cornubiense'**
This cultivar has finely cut, light green fronds, which may be tripinnate or quadripinnate. Pinnately cut fronds, resembling those of the species, should be removed. Like the species, spores are released in summer. H 4–16in (10–40cm), S indefinite.

5–8

POPULUS

There are 35 species of fast-growing deciduous trees in this genus, which occurs throughout northern temperate regions. Poplars grow in a wide range of situations, tolerating wet soils, coastal conditions, and urban pollution. They make excellent screens, avenues, and windbreaks. The new leaves of some are scented in spring, and many have ornamental variants. *Populus* may be derived from *arbor populi*, "the people's tree," since poplars have long been planted along town streets.

Populus alba (white poplar, abele)
Robust, suckering tree with broadly ovate leaves up to 3½in (9cm) long, which have white, downy undersides. Male and female flowers are borne on separate plants, females being followed by capsules containing cottony seeds. H 80ft (25m), S 15–25ft (5–8m).

3–8

***Populus alba* 'Richardii'**
This cultivar is smaller-growing and less vigorous than the species, with golden yellow, white-backed leaves. H 50ft (15m), S 40ft (12m).

3–8

Populus* x *candicans (balm of Gilead, Ontario poplar)
Conical tree with shiny buds and heart-shaped leaves up to 6in (15cm) long, balsam-scented when young. Male trees are not known; females produce catkins up to 6in (16cm) long when in fruit. H 80ft (25m), S 30ft (10m).

3–8

***Populus* x *candicans* 'Aurora'**
A distinctive cultivar with conspicuous new leaves irregularly variegated creamy-white, often pink-flushed, which age to green. H 50ft (15m), S 20ft (6m).

3–8

PORTULACA

A genus of 40 species of fleshy, trailing annuals and biennials found widely in warm temperate regions. *P. oleracea* is grown as a vegetable in many parts of the world. It was known to the ancient Egyptians and has also been grown for thousands of years in India and China. France is the main European producer and consumer of the plant. Cultivated purslane is sometimes treated as a distinct variety, *P. o.* var. *sativa.* Portulaca is the original Latin name used by Pliny.

Portulaca oleracea (purslane)
Annual with thick, soft, trailing stems and fleshy, spoon-shaped leaves up to 1¼in (3cm) long. Small yellow flowers with 4–6 petals, are produced in summer. H 8–18in (20–45cm), S 18–24in (45–60cm).

A

***Portulaca oleracea* var. *aurea* (golden purslane)**
This unusual variant has golden leaves, which make a colorful contrast with other salad vegetables. H 8–18in (20–45cm), S 9in (23cm).

A

POLYPODY, see *Polypodium vulgare*, p.181
POMEGRANATE, see *Punica granatum*, p.187
POOR MAN'S WEATHERGLASS, see *Anagallis arvensis*, p.83
POPLAR, see *Populus*, above
POPPY, see *Papaver*, p.171
PORTER'S LOVAGE, see *Ligusticum porteri*, p.303
POTENTWOOD, see *Dulacia inopiflora*, p.276
POT MARIGOLD, see *Calendula officinalis*, p.97
PRAIRIE HYSSOP, see *Pycnanthemum virginianum*, p.187
PRICKLY ASH, see *Zanthoxylum*, p.222

POTENTILLA

There are about 500 species in this large genus, which is distributed throughout the northern hemisphere; *P. erecta* is distributed widely in northern Europe, western Asia, and Siberia. Most species are perennials or shrubs, together with some annuals and biennials, and many are found on heaths and in woodland. Some make good garden plants, but the main medicinal species are rather weedy. *Potentilla* means "powerful," from the Latin *potens*, alluding to the curative powers of these plants.

Potentilla erecta (tormentil, bloodroot)
Perennial with a thick, woody rootstock, red inside, and thin, branched stems bearing 3-lobed basal leaves and 5-lobed stem leaves. Small, bright yellow, 4-petaled flowers are borne from early summer. H 20in (50cm), S 8–12in (20–30cm).

3–9

Primula vulgaris subsp. ***sibthorpii***
This pink-flowered variant is native to southeastern Europe. It was introduced to Britain in the 1630s as Tradescant's 'Turkie Purple'. H 6in (15cm), S 10in (24cm).

5–9

PRIMULA

This genus includes about 400 species of perennials occurring mostly in temperate and mountainous areas of the northern hemisphere. *P. veris*, found in Europe and western Asia, and *P. vulgaris*, found in Europe, northern Asia, and the Caucasus, thrive in borders and naturalize well in grass. They should be planted well apart to avoid hybridization, which produces yellow polyanthus. Many primulas are grown as ornamentals in a wide range of situations, including rock gardens and watersides.

Primula veris (cowslip, paigle)
Small clump-forming perennial with a short, stout rhizome, long, thin roots, and ovate-oblong leaves, 2–8in (5–20cm) long. Small, deep yellow, fragrant, orange-marked flowers are borne in long-stalked clusters in spring. H and S 6–8in (15–20cm).

5–9

Primula vulgaris (primrose)
Small clump-forming perennial with a short, thick rhizome and oblanceolate leaves, 2–10in (5–25cm) long. Solitary, pale yellow flowers, 1¼–1½in (3–4cm) across, with darker centers and notched petals, appear in late winter and spring. H 6in (15cm), S 10in (24cm).

5–9

***Primula vulgaris* 'Alba Plena'**
A choice cultivar with double white flowers, which makes a good specimen for pots. It is also effective grown with the unusual mauve, double-flowered *P. v.* 'Lilacina Plena'. H 6in (15cm), S 10in (24cm).

5–9

PROSTANTHERA

A genus of about 70 species of evergreen, sticky shrubs found throughout Australia. *P. rotundifolia* is native to southern and southeastern Australia. Most have a strong mintlike aroma. Several are grown as ornamentals for their neat, fragrant foliage and profuse flowering, both outdoors in warm climates and under glass in colder regions. *Prostanthera* is from the Greek *prosthema*, "addition," and *anthos*, "growth," since the anthers have spurlike appendages.

Prostanthera rotundifolia (round-leaved mint bush)
Large, bushy shrub with rounded to obovate leaves about ½in (1cm) long. Numerous lilac to mauve, occasionally pink, broadly bell-shaped flowers, ½in (1cm) across, are produced in spring. H 6–12ft (2–4m), S 4–8ft (1.2–2.5m).

PRUNELLA

A genus of seven species of perennials occurring in northern temperate regions and northwestern Africa. *P. vulgaris*, which has white- and lilac-flowered variants, is less often grown as a garden plant than other, more ornamental species. Often sold for naturalizing in wild-flower meadows, it is also planted as groundcover and in rock gardens. *Prunella* is an alternative spelling of *Brunella*, from the German *Bräune*, "quinsy," for which *P. vulgaris* was a standard treatment.

Prunella vulgaris (selfheal, heal-all)
Creeping, aromatic perennial with 4-angled stems and oblong-ovate, toothed leaves, 1½–2in (4–4cm) long. Deep purple, 2-lipped flowers are produced in compact spikes from summer to autumn. H 20in (50cm), S indefinite.

4–9

PRICKLY LETTUCE, see *Lactuca serriola*, p.146
PRICKLY MOSES, see *Acacia farnesiana*, p.71
PRICKLY WATERLILY, see *Euryale ferox*, p.126
PRIMROSE, see *Primula vulgaris*, above
PRINCE'S FEATHER, see *Amaranthus hypochondriacus*, p.82
PRINCE'S PINE, see *Chimaphila umbellata*, p.107
PRIVET, see *Ligustrum*, p.151

PRUNUS

There are about 430 species of deciduous, occasionally evergreen trees and shrubs in this genus, which occurs mostly throughout northern temperate regions and S America. It includes many economically important fruit and nut trees and numerous ornamentals, which are grown mainly for their blossoms. Both *P. armeniaca* and *P. persica* are probably Chinese in origin; the former reached Italy in Roman times and the latter, which has been cultivated in China for over 2,500 years, was recorded in Greece as early as the fourth century BC. Prunes are dried plums from cultivars of *P. domestica* subsp. *domestica*, which have large, oval, black-skinned fruits. *P. dulcis* is the world's most widely grown nut tree. *P. laurocerasus*, a shade-tolerant species, is extensively grown for hedging, screening, and game cover. Its many cultivars include low, spreading variants for groundcover. *P. laurocerasus* is popular for hedging. *P. mume* is the classic winter-flowering "plum blossom," used in Japanese bonsai.

◄ ***Prunus domestica* 'Prune d'Agen'**
This cultivar bears large, dark-skinned, very sweet plums, grown for drying as prunes. H 30–40ft (10–12m), S 12–15ft (4–5m) on its own roots, but smaller when grafted onto others.
5–8

► ***Prunus dulcis*** (almond)
Shrub or bushy deciduous tree with oblanceolate, toothed leaves up to 4in (10cm) long. Pink or white, solitary or paired flowers about 2in (5cm) across appear before the new leaves, followed by pale green, velvety fruits about 1½in (4cm) long, containing 2 seeds.
H and S 25ft (8m).
6–8

◄ ***Prunus armeniaca*** (wild apricot)
Deciduous tree with ovate to rounded leaves up to 5in (12cm) long. Single white flowers, about 1½in (4cm) across, appear in spring, followed by globose, white to orange-red or yellow fruits, 2in (5cm) in diameter. H 30ft (10m), S 15–22ft (5–7m).
5–9

► ***Prunus armeniaca* 'Hemskerk'**
This cultivar was introduced by Lee of Hammersmith, London, in 1820. The yellow, red-flushed fruits have an excellent flavor and ripen early in the season. H 30ft (10m), S 20–30ft (6–10m), though usually pruned to H 10ft (3m), S 15ft (5m).
5–9

◄ ***Prunus domestica*** (plum)
Variable deciduous tree or shrub with ovate leaves and green-white flowers about ¾in (2cm) across, followed by oval, mostly blue-black fruits. Possibly originated as a cross between *P. spinosa* and *P. cerasifera*.
H 30–40ft (10–12m), S 25–30ft (8–10m).
5–8

▲ ***Prunus laurocerasus***
(cherry laurel, English laurel)
Evergreen bushy shrub with oblong, shiny, pointed leaves up to 10in (25cm) long, which are poisonous and almond-scented when crushed. Strongly scented, white flowers appear in spring, followed by purple-black fruits. H 20ft (6m), S 30ft (10m).
6–10

Prunus laurocerasus **'Castlewellan'**
A slow-growing evergreen shrub with variegated gray-green and white foliage. H and S 5–6ft (1.5–2m).
6–10

Prunus laurocerasus **'Schipkaensis'**
This variant was found in 1888 near the Schipka Pass in Bulgaria. It is very hardy and has a low, spreading habit, narrow leaves, and abundant, upright flower spikes. H 6ft (2m), S 10ft (3m).
6–10

Prunus mume **'Beni-chidori'**
This cultivar makes a small tree with very fragrant, single, deep pink flowers, which appear slightly later than those of the species. H 20–22ft (6–7m), S 15–20ft (5–6m).
7–10

Prunus persica (peach)
Small, bushy, deciduous tree or large shrub with lanceolate, tapering leaves. Pale pink to white, solitary or paired flowers appear in spring, followed by globose, fleshy, yellow or white fruits. H and S 25ft (8m).
5–9

Prunus serotina (black cherry, wild rum cherry)
Deciduous tree with shiny, narrowly ovate leaves which turn yellow in autumn. Fragrant white flowers are borne in early summer, followed by small black fruits. H 60–100ft (18–30m), S 30–80ft (10–25m).
3–9

PTELEA

There are about a dozen shrubs and small trees in this N American genus. Most have musky-smelling leaves. Found in moist, rich woods and thickets in eastern and central US, *P. trifoliata* was a sacred herb of the native Menominee people. It is grown for its foliage and attractive clusters of fruits. *P. trifoliata* 'Aurea' is an outstanding golden tree for small gardens. *Ptelea* is the ancient Greek name for the elm, given to this genus because its fruits appear similar to those of the true elm.

Ptelea trifoliata (hop tree, wafer ash)
Low, spreading deciduous tree or large shrub with trifoliate leaves up to 5in (12cm) long. Pale green-white, star-shaped, scented flowers are borne in branched clusters in early summer, followed by round, pale green winged fruits. H and S 22ft (7m).
4–10

Ptelea trifoliata **'Aurea'**
This cultivar has light yellow leaves, which contrast well with bronze-leaved shrubs, such as *Sambucus nigra* 'Guincho Purple'. H and S 22ft (7m).
4–10

PTEROCARPUS

Twenty species of leguminous trees and woody climbers belong to this genus, which occurs throughout the tropics. *P. marsupium* is native to forests in southern and central India and Sri Lanka. It was cultivated under cover in the 19th century, but is seldom seen today outside the tropics. The flowers are followed by conspicuous pods, which contain kidney-shaped seeds. *Pterocarpus* comes from the Greek *pteron*, "wing," and *karpos*, "fruit," referring to the winged pods.

Pterocarpus marsupium (kino, Malabar kino, bastard teak)
Large deciduous tree with gray bark, red gum, and leathery leaves. Pale yellow flowers appear in lax clusters in late spring, followed by pods up to 2in (5cm) across, encircled by a broad wing. H 60ft (18m), S 30ft (10cm).

PUERARIA

This genus of climbers includes about 20 species that are found in southeast Asia and Japan. *P. lobata*, native to thickets and sparse woodland, was introduced to the southern US in the 1870s and became an invasive weed. In warm areas it can grow 60ft (18m) in a single season; the flowers, although attractive, are largely hidden beneath the luxuriant foliage. *Pueraria* is named after Marc Puerari (1766–1845), born in Geneva, who was a professor of botany in Copenhagen.

Pueraria lobata (kudzu, Japanese arrowroot)
Vigorous, twining climber with hairy stems and divided leaves. Fragrant purple flowers are produced in racemes up to 12in (30cm) long, in summer, followed by flat, hairy fruits that split open when ripe. H 15–70ft (5–20m).

7–10

***Pulmonaria officinalis* 'Sissinghurst White'**
This vigorous cultivar has white flowers. It is very good as an early-flowering edging plant with spring bulbs. H and S 12in (30cm).

3–9

PULMONARIA

This genus of 14 species of hardy, low-growing, rhizomatous perennials occurs in woodland areas of Europe, Asia, and western N America. The common name "soldiers and sailors" refers to the two flower colors, which resembled the red and blue uniforms of the British army and navy. The name derives from the Latin *pulmo*, "lung," because the plants were used for treating bronchial diseases. *P. officinalis* should not be confused with *Lobaria pulmonaria*, also known as "lungwort."

Pulmonaria officinalis (lungwort, Jerusalem cowslip, soldiers and sailors)
Perennial with hairy stems and white-spotted, ovate leaves up to 3in (7.5cm) long, covered in bristly hairs. The funnel-shaped flowers appear in spring, pink at first, turning blue. H 4–12in (10–30cm), S up to 12in (30cm).

3–9

***Pulmonaria officinalis* 'Cambridge Blue'**
A cultivar that bears an abundance of eggshell-blue flowers opening from pink buds. It is especially effective near dark-leaved evergreens. H and S 12in (30cm).

3–9

PULSATILLA

This genus of 30 species of clump-forming perennials occurs in temperate Eurasia and northern Africa; *P. vulgaris* is becoming rare in the wild through loss of habitat and overcollection. The common name for *P. vulgaris* was given by John Gerard, the 16th-century herbalist, who wrote, "They floure for the most part about Easter, which has moved mee to name it *Pasque-Floure*, or Easter floure." The flowers yield a green dye once used to color eggs at Easter.

Pulsatilla vulgaris (pasque flower)
Small, hairy perennial with divided, feathery leaves up to 9in (22cm) long. Blue-violet, nodding, bell-shaped flowers about 1¼in (3cm) long appear in spring, followed by silky, feathery seedheads on elongated stalks. H and S 6–9in (15–23cm).

5–8

Pulsatilla vulgaris* var. *alba
This variety is like the species, except for its white flowers. It provides a good contrast to purple, lilac, and red variants. H and S 6–9in (15–23cm).

5–8

Pulsatilla vulgaris* var. *rubra
A richly colored variety with ruby red flowers, bettered only by the more vigorous *P. vulgaris* 'Eva Constance'. H and S 6–9in (15–23cm).

5–8

PUFFBALL, see *Lycoperdon perlatum*, p.154
PUKEWEED, see *Lobelia inflata*, p.153
PUMILIO PINE, see *Pinus mugo* var. *pumilio*, p.177
PUMPKIN, see *Cucurbita maxima*, p.114
PURPLE ASTER, see *Aster tataricus*, p.245
PURPLE CLOVER, see *Trifolium pratense*, p.214
PURPLE CONEFLOWER, see *Echinacea purpurea*, p.121
PURPLE LOOSESTRIFE, see *Lythrum salicaria*, p.154
PURSLANE, see *Portulaca oleracea*, p.182
PUSSY-TOES, see *Antennaria*, p.84
QUACKGRASS, see *Elymus repens*, p.122
QUASSIA, see *Picrasma excelsa*, p.327;

PUNICA

Two species of shrubs or small trees belong to this genus distributed from eastern Mediterranean regions to the Himalayas. *P. granatum*, which is evergreen in the subtropics and deciduous in temperate regions, bears funnel-shaped, waxy flowers in summer, followed by yellow-brown, red-flushed pomegranate fruits. There are many cultivars, including ones with double, white, and white-striped flowers. *Punica* is a contraction of the Latin *punicum malum*, "Carthaginian apple."

Punica granatum (pomegranate)
Dense, twiggy shrub or small tree with spine-tipped branches and light green, shiny, ovate-lanceolate leaves. Orange-red flowers are followed by leathery-skinned fruits that contain numerous seeds in a pink, juicy pulp. H and S 6–20ft (2–6m).

7–10

Punica granatum var. ***nana***
This dwarf variety has been popular since at least the 18th century. It is slightly hardier than the species and has narrower leaves, smaller flowers, and fruits about the size of a nutmeg. Excellent for containers.
H and S 3ft (1m).

7–10

PYCNANTHEMUM

Seventeen species of perennials found in N America belong to this genus. All have a mintlike aroma. *P. virginianum*, which can be used as a substitute for mint in cooking, is often seen in herb gardens and in the wild in dry fields, but is little known in Europe. Various native N American peoples have used *Pycnanthemum* species medicinally. The generic name *Pycnanthemum* comes from the Greek *pyknos*, "dense," and *anthos*, "flower," and refers to the crowded flower heads.

Pycnanthemum virginianum
(Virginia mountain mint, wild basil, prairie hyssop)
Branched perennial with whorls of pointed, linear-lanceolate leaves. White to lilac flowers are borne in dense, flat-topped heads in late summer. H 28–36in (70–90cm), S 8–24in (20–60cm).

5–10

QUERCUS

A genus consisting of about 600 species of evergreen and deciduous trees and a few shrubs distributed throughout the northern hemisphere and in some montane regions of the southern hemisphere. Various species of oak are of particular importance in the lumber and tanning industries, and they have a long history of use in shipbuilding. They are long-lived, and many are planted in parks and open spaces. The rigidly narrow *Q. robur* f. *fastigiata* is particularly useful for confined areas.

Quercus robur (English oak, common oak, pedunculate oak)
Large deciduous tree with a broad crown, rugged branches, and fissured bark. Male flowers are borne in catkins; females in spikes of 1–5in spring, followed by acorns 1½in (4cm) long.
H and S 80ft (25m).

4–8

Quercus robur **'Atropurpurea'**
This slow-growing cultivar has red-purple young leaves, which mature to gray-purple. H and S 30ft (10m).

4–8

Simaba cedron, p.353
QUEBRACHO, see *Aspidosperma quebracho-blanco*, p.245
QUEEN'S DELIGHT, see *Stillingia sylvatica*, p.356
QUEEN ANNE'S LACE, see *Ammi majus*, p.82; *Daucus carota*, p.116
QUEEN OF THE MEADOW, see *Eupatorium purpureum*, p.126; *Filipendula ulmaria*, p.128
QUEEN-OF-THE-NIGHT, see *Selenicereus grandiflorus*, p.202

***Quercus robur* 'Concordia'** (golden oak)
An unusual small, slow-growing, and rounded cultivar with golden young foliage that becomes yellow-green in summer. Originating from Ghent in 1843, it is recommended for smaller gardens. H and S 30ft (10m).

4–8

Quercus robur* f. *fastigiata (upright English oak)
An extremely narrow form that makes a tall, impressive specimen in a restricted space. H 80ft (25m), S 15–20ft (5–6m).

4–8

QUILLAJA

Four species of evergreen trees and shrubs belong to this genus, which occurs in temperate parts of S America. *Q. saponaria*, found in Chile and Peru, is grown for its attractive, glossy foliage, large flowers, and curious soapy bark. It succeeds outdoors if given a sheltered position, and it is cultivated commercially in California and India. *Quillaja* is from the Chilean term *quillai*, "to wash," and refers to the soaplike properties of the genus.

Quillaja saponaria (soapbark tree, quillai, Panama bark)
Large tree with thick, dark, ashy bark and leathery, ovate leaves. White to green-yellow, purple-centered flowers appear in spring, followed by star-shaped fruits containing 10–18 oblong seeds. H 50–60ft (15–18m), S 20–22ft (6–7m).

T

RANUNCULUS

Distributed throughout temperate, far northern, and tropical montane regions, this genus contains about 400 species of annuals, biennials, and perennials. Found in Europe, western Asia, and northern Africa, *R. ficaria* is too invasive for garden use, but it has variants with neat foliage and numerous, often double, glossy flowers. *Ranunculus* is the diminutive of the Latin *rana*, "frog," because many species are aquatic or grow in wet places.

Ranunculus ficaria (lesser celandine, pilewort)
Small, mat-forming, tuberous perennial with heart-shaped leaves up to 1½in (4cm) long, often forming bulbils at the leaf bases. Bright yellow, solitary flowers appear in spring. H 2–6in (5–15cm), S 12in (30cm).

4–9

Ranunculus ficaria* var. *albus
This variety is like the species, except for its pure white flowers, which combine well with variegated plants. H 2–6in (5–15cm), S 12in (30cm).

4–9

***Ranunculus ficaria* 'Brazen Hussy'**
An unusual cultivar, which has bronze foliage and yellow flowers with bronze undersides. It is attractive beneath golden-leaved shrubs. H 2–6in (5–15cm), S 12in (30cm).

4–9

Ranunculus ficaria* var. *flore pleno
A double-flowered celandine that flowers slightly later and lasts longer than the species. H 2–6in (5–15cm), S 12in (30cm).

4–9

QUICKSET, see *Crataegus laevigata*, p.112
QUINCE, see *Chaenomeles*, p.105
QUININE, see *Cinchona*, p.108
QUINSY BERRY, see *Ribes nigrum*, p.190
RADISH, see *Raphanus sativus*, p.189
RAINBOW PINK, see *Dianthus chinensis*, p.117
RAMPS, see *ALLIUM*, pp.80–81
RAMSONS, see *ALLIUM*, pp.80–81
RASPBERRY, see *Rubus idaeus*, p.194
RAT-TAIL PLANTAIN, see *Plantago major*, p.178
RATTLESNAKE ROOT, see *Polygala senega*, p.332
RED GUM, see *Eucalyptus camaldulensis*, p.125

RAPHANUS

Eight species of annuals and perennials belong to this genus, which ranges through western and central Europe to central Asia. *R. sativus* is not known in the wild and is probably a hybrid from the wild radish, *R. raphanistrum*. It was cultivated 4,500 years ago in Egypt and at least 2,000 years ago in China. Black radishes probably originated in Spain during the Middle Ages. Radishes reached Britain in 1548, and four varieties were recorded by John Gerard in 1597.

Raphanus sativus (radish)
Bristly annual or biennial with a swollen, white-fleshed taproot, sometimes white on the outside. The leaves are toothed with a large terminal lobe. White or lilac flowers appear in summer, followed by inflated fruits that contain 6–12 seeds. H 8–36in (20–90cm).

A

RHAMNUS

A genus of about 140 species of deciduous and evergreen, often thorny trees and shrubs that occur mainly in northern temperate regions; *R. catharticus* is found in temperate Europe, northwestern Africa, and Asia. *R. frangula*, found on damp, peaty ground throughout Europe, is an attractive shrub for autumn color and is sometimes grown as a hedge. *R. purshiana* is particularly noticeable in winter, forming groups of upright, silver-gray stems. It is now very rare in the wild.

Rhamnus catharticus (buckthorn)
Deciduous shrub or small tree with gray-brown bark and ovate to elliptic, finely toothed leaves. Small clusters of pale green, 4-petaled flowers are borne in late spring, followed by globose black berries about ¼in (7mm) across. H 12–20ft (4–6m), S 8–15ft (2.5–5m).

2–9

RAUVOLFIA

Over 100 species of evergreen and deciduous shrubs and small trees make up this genus occurring in most tropical and subtropical regions. *R. serpentina*, found in Burma, was introduced to cultivation in Europe in 1690 and was recommended for pots under cover during the 19th century. A few species are occasionally seen in botanic gardens today, but none is now obtainable as an ornamental. *Rauvolfia* is named after Leonhart Rauwolf, a 16th-century German physician.

Rauvolfia serpentina (rauwolfia, serpentwood, Indian snakeroot)
Low evergreen shrub with lanceolate, pointed leaves up to 2–5in (5–13cm) long. Tiny white to pale pink flowers appear in spring, followed by glossy, crimson, 2-lobed berries about the size of a pea. H and S 3ft (1m).

Rhamnus frangula (alder buckthorn)
Deciduous, thornless shrub or small tree with ovate leaves up to 3in (7cm) long, turning yellow and brown in autumn. Insignificant green flowers appear in late spring, followed by red berries, ½in (1cm) across, ripening to black. H 15ft (5m), S 10–15ft (3–5m).

2–9

REHMANNIA

A genus of 10 species of perennials occurring in eastern Asia. Reminiscent of foxgloves, these attractive plants thrive outdoors only in warmer areas. *R. glutinosa*, which is native to China, has now been replaced by *R. elata* as an ornamental. However, due to its long cultivation for medicinal purposes, many variants of *R. glutinosa* are available in China, differing in size, habit, and root flavor. *Rehmannia* was named after Joseph Rehmann (1799–1831), a German physician.

Rehmannia glutinosa (Chinese foxglove)
Downy, purple-green perennial with tuberous orange roots and a basal rosette of ovate, toothed leaves up to 4in (10cm) long. In spring, purple-brown to dull yellow flowers are followed by ovoid capsules containing numerous seeds. H 6–12in (15–30cm), S 8in (20cm).

8–10

RHEUM

Fifty species of stout perennials make up this genus, which is Eurasian in distribution. Rhubarbs of various kinds have been cultivated in China as medicinal herbs for over 2,000 years and were recorded as imports by the ancient Greeks. The Kiakhta Rhubarb Commission, or Rhubarb Office, on the border between Siberia and Mongolia, maintained Russian and Chinese trade monopolies and prevented international trade until its final abolition in 1782.

Rheum palmatum (Chinese rhubarb, *chinghai* rhubarb)
Robust perennial with a thick rhizome, nearly round leaf stalks, and palmately lobed leaves up to 36in (90cm) long. In summer, deep red flowers in a spirelike panicle are followed by 3-winged fruits. H 6ft (2m), S 24–30in (60–75cm).

5–8

RED PEPPER, see *CAPSICUM*, p.100
REDROOT, see *Ceanothus americanus*, p.103
RED ROSE OF LANCASTER, see *Rosa gallica* var. *officinalis*, p.191
RED SORREL, see *Hibiscus sabdariffa*, p.138
RED-INK PLANT, see *Phytolacca americana*, p.176
RED-ROOTED GROMWELL, see *Lithospermum erythrorhizon*, p.153
REED, COMMON, see *Phragmites australis*, p.175
RESURRECTION LILY, see *Kaempferia galanga*, p.146
RHATANY, see *Krameria triandra*, p.300

***Rheum palmatum* 'Atrosanguineum'**
This cultivar has red-purple young leaves, which turn green with purple undersides, and cherry red flowers followed by pink fruits. H 6ft (2m), S 24–30in (60–75cm).

5–8

RIBES

A genus of about 150 species of small to medium-sized, mainly deciduous shrubs widely distributed in northern temperate regions. *R. nigrum* is the most widely grown and economically important member of the genus in Europe. *R. nigrum* is less common in the US because it hosts pine blister rust (*Cronartium ribicola*), which can devastate forests. Cultivated plants differed little from wild species until recent commercial breeding.

Ribes nigrum (blackcurrant, quinsy berry)
Aromatic shrub with yellow-brown shoots and 5-lobed leaves. Insignificant green-white flowers are borne in pendent clusters of 4–10, followed by many-seeded black berries, ½in (1cm) in diameter. H and S6ft (2m).

3–9

RHUS

A genus of about 200 species of mostly hardy deciduous or evergreen trees, shrubs, and scrambling climbers widely distributed in temperate and subtropical regions. *R. glabra*, common in northeastern US and southern Canada, provides vivid autumn color and, in female plants, upright clusters of scarlet fruits. It is an excellent subject for mass planting. The common name "sumac" comes from the Arabic *summaq*, a preparation used for tanning and dyeing.

Rhus glabra (smooth sumac)
Deciduous shrub or small tree with smooth, wax-coated branches and large, pinnate leaves that turn red in autumn. Green flowers are borne in late summer; male and female on separate plants, females bearing downy scarlet fruits. H 10–15ft (3–5m), S 5–7ft (1.5–2.2m).

2–9

***Rhus glabra* 'Laciniata'**
This cultivar is not fully hardy, and the leaves have deeply incised leaflets, giving a fernlike appearance. Many cultivated plants bearing this name are thought to belong to the hardier hybrid *R.* x *pulvinata*, Autumn Lace Group. H 10–15ft (3–5m), S 5–7ft (1.5–2.2m).

2–9

RICINUS

This genus of a single species of evergreen shrub is found wild throughout the Middle East into northeastern Africa, and is naturalized in many parts of the tropics. It reaches treelike proportions in the tropics, but may be grown as an annual in temperate regions. The large, luxuriant leaves are effective as a focal point or background in subtropical bedding. The generic name is from the Latin *ricinus*, "tick," because the mottled seeds of the plant are similar in shape to these insects.

Ricinus communis (castor bean, palma-christi)
Upright shrub with dark red stems and long-stalked, toothed leaves up to 24in (60cm) long. In summer, green, petal-less, female flowers are followed by red capsules containing 3 gray-brown seeds. H 6–40ft (2–12m), S 3–30ft (1–10m).

T

***Ricinus communis* 'Carmencita'**
An early flowering cultivar with bronze leaves, bright red flower buds, and spiny red capsules. H 5–6ft (1.5–2m), S 3ft (1m).

T

***Ricinus communis* 'Impala'**
This cultivar is smaller than the species and has maroon to carmine young foliage, cream-yellow flower buds, and maroon capsules. H 3–4ft (1–1.2m), S 24–36in (60–90cm).

T

RHEUMATISM ROOT, see *Dioscorea villosa*, p.273
RHUBARB, see *Rheum palmatum*, p.189
RIBBED MELILOT, see *Melilotus officinalis*, p.157
RICE, see *Oryza sativa*, p.169
RICHWEED, see *Collinsonia canadensis*, p.110
ROCAMBOLE, see *ALLIUM*, pp.80–81
ROCK HYSSOP, see *Hyssopus officinalis* subsp. *aristatus*, p.141
ROCK ROSE, see *Cistus*, p.108
ROCK SWEET FLAG, see *Acorus gramineus*, p.73
ROCKET, see *Eruca vesicaria*, p.123
ROCOTO, see *CAPSICUM*, p.100

ROSA

A genus consisting of about 100 species of deciduous and semievergreen shrubs, widespread in northern temperate regions. The cultivation of roses dates back thousands of years. *R. gallica* var. *officinalis* is descended from the southern European *R. rubra*, and was named in the 13th century when it spread into Gaul. In the 14th century *R. damascena* was brought from Persia by knights returning from the Crusades. *R. rugosa* and *R. laevigata* are both of Asian origin.

Rosa canina (dog rose)
Variable deciduous shrub with arching stems, curved prickles, and blue-gray leaves up to 2in (5cm) long. Scented, pink or white, 5-petaled flowers are produced in clusters of 1–4 from early to midsummer, followed by ovoid, scarlet hips. H and S 10ft (3m).

5–8

Rosa rugosa (Japanese rose, Ramanas rose)
Suckering deciduous shrub with densely prickly stems and dark green, divided leaves. In summer, clove-scented, purple-pink or white flowers are followed by red, globose hips that have a conspicuous crown of sepals. H and S 3–6ft (1–2m).

2–8

Rosa eglanteria (sweet briar, eglantine)
Dense, arching to upright, deciduous shrub with hooked thorns. Divided, apple-scented leaves bear rust-colored, sticky hairs on undersides. Fragrant, bright pink flowers appear in summer, followed by scarlet round to ovoid hips. H and S 8ft (2.5m).

5–8

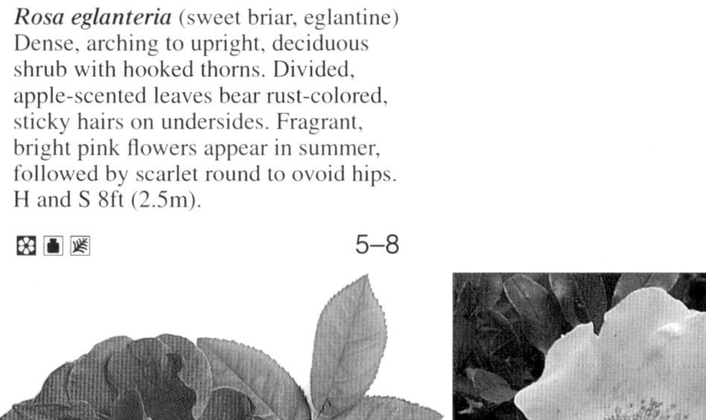

Rosa gallica* var. *officinalis
(apothecary's rose, red rose of Lancaster)
Bushy deciduous shrub with bristly stems and leathery divided leaves. In summer, fragrant flowers, 1½–3in (4–8cm) across, are followed by brick-red hips. H 32in (80cm), S 3ft (1m).

4–8

Rosa laevigata (Cherokee rose)
Vigorous, semievergreen, climbing shrub with glossy divided leaves. White, solitary, fragrant flowers 2–4in (5–10cm) across, with persistent, bristly sepals, appear in early summer, followed by pear-shaped, orange-red hips up to 1½in (4cm) long. H and S 30ft (10m).

7–9

***Rosa rugosa* 'Alba'**
This cultivar has a vigorous habit and luxuriant foliage, which is leathery, wrinkled, and glossy. Fragrant, single white flowers, 3½in (9cm) across, are produced from pink-flushed buds in summer, followed by large, tomato-like hips. H and S 3–6ft (1–2m).

2–8

ROMAN CHAMOMILE, see *Chamaemelum nobile*, p.105
ROMAN CORIANDER, see *Nigella sativa*, p.165
ROOIBOS, see *Aspalathus linearis*, p.89
ROSE, see *Rosa*, above
ROSE GERANIUM, see *PELARGONIUM*, pp.172–3
ROSE MALLOW, see *Hibiscus*, p.138
ROSÉE DU SOLEIL, see *Drosera rotundifolia*, p.120
ROSELLE, see *Hibiscus sabdariffa*, p.138

ROSMARINUS

A genus of one or more species of evergreen shrub native to dry, mainly coastal areas around the Mediterranean. Opinion differs on the number of species in the genus; some authorities regard *R. officinalis* as the only species, and others as variants. *R. officinalis* and its many variants are popular worldwide as garden and container plants. Low-growing variants make attractive specimens for pots, steep banks, or the tops of walls. *Rosmarinus* is from the Latin "dew of the sea," referring to the dewlike appearance of its pale blue flowers from a distance.

▲ ***Rosmarinus officinalis*** (rosemary)
Variable, aromatic, evergreen shrub with upright branches, and tough, blunt-ended, needlelike leaves, 1in (2.5cm) long. Pale to dark blue, rarely pink or white, tubular, two-lipped flowers appear in spring. H 6ft (2m), S 5–6ft (1.5–2m).
8–10

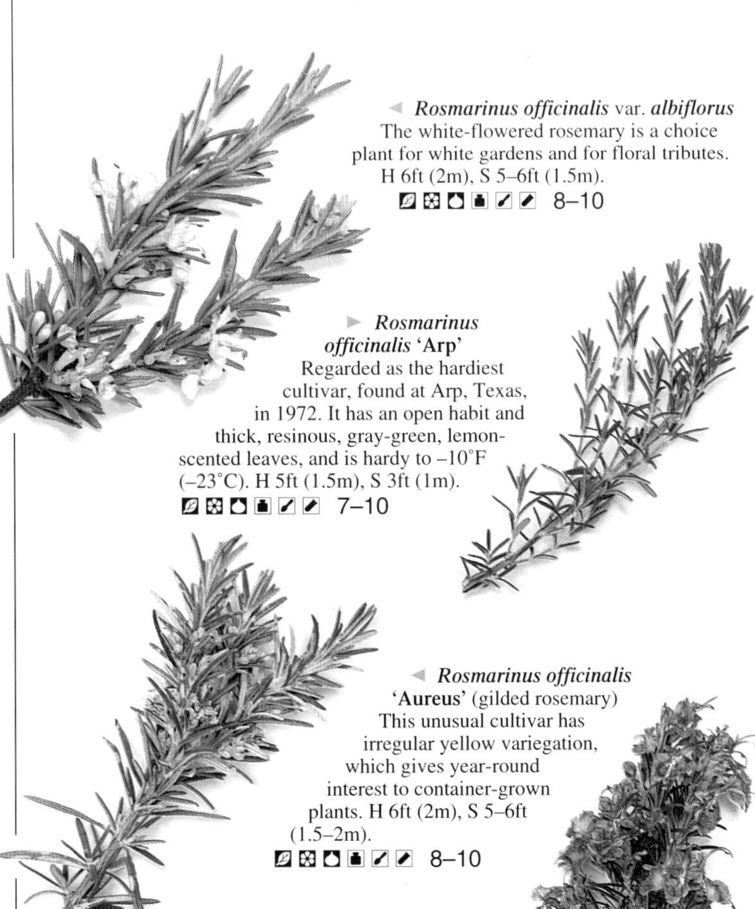

◄ ***Rosmarinus officinalis*** var. ***albiflorus***
The white-flowered rosemary is a choice plant for white gardens and for floral tributes. H 6ft (2m), S 5–6ft (1.5m).
8–10

► ***Rosmarinus officinalis* 'Arp'**
Regarded as the hardiest cultivar, found at Arp, Texas, in 1972. It has an open habit and thick, resinous, gray-green, lemon-scented leaves, and is hardy to –10°F (–23°C). H 5ft (1.5m), S 3ft (1m).
7–10

◄ ***Rosmarinus officinalis* 'Aureus'** (gilded rosemary)
This unusual cultivar has irregular yellow variegation, which gives year-round interest to container-grown plants. H 6ft (2m), S 5–6ft (1.5–2m).
8–10

► ***Rosmarinus officinalis* 'Benenden Blue'**
A small-growing cultivar with a dense, cascading habit, handsome, very narrow, dark green, glossy foliage, and medium blue flowers. Highly recommended for containers. H and S 3ft (1m).
8–10

► ***Rosmarinus officinalis* 'McConnell's Blue'**
A spreading, prostrate rosemary, with broad leaves and clear blue flowers. H 12–16in (30–40cm), S 3ft (1m).
8–10

▲ ***Rosmarinus officinalis* 'Miss Jessopp's Upright'**
A valuable, relatively hardy rosemary for the formal herb garden and confined spaces. It has a vigorous, upright habit and pale blue flowers.
H 6ft (2m), S 5–6ft (1.5–2m).
8–10

◄ ***Rosmarinus officinalis* 'Fota Blue'**
A rather tender, variable rosemary, semiprostrate in habit and free-flowering, with very dark blue flowers.
H 12–18in (30–45cm), S 24–36in (60–90cm).
8–10

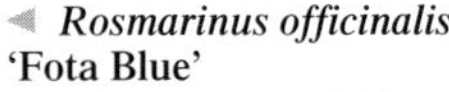

◄ ***Rosmarinus officinalis* 'Majorca Pink'**
This rather tender cultivar has a columnar, arching habit, small, dull green leaves, and mauve-pink flowers. H 4ft (1.2m), S 12–24in (30–60cm).
8–10

◄ ***Rosmarinus officinalis* 'Pinkie'**
This American cultivar is distinguished by its pink flowers and shorter gray-green leaves. H 4ft (1.2m), S 3ft (1m).
8–10

► ***Rosmarinus officinalis* 'Primley Blue'**
A relatively hardy cultivar with an upright habit and clear blue flowers. H 3ft (1m), S 24in (60cm).
8–10

◄ ***Rosmarinus officinalis* 'Roseus'**
This cultivar is like the species, except for its pink flowers and brighter green foliage. H 6ft (2m), S 5–6ft (1.5m).
8–10

▲ ***Rosmarinus officinalis,* Prostratus Group** (creeping rosemary)
This prostrate, rather tender rosemary is a good subject for containers, hanging baskets, banks, walls, rock gardens, and bonsai. H 6–12in (15–30cm), S 24–36in (60–90cm).
8–10

◄ ***Rosmarinus officinalis* 'Severn Sea'**
An especially fine cultivar for containers or over walls, with a spreading, arching habit, narrow leaves, and violet-blue flowers. H and S 3ft (1m).
8–10

◄ ***Rosmarinus officinalis* 'Sissinghurst Blue'**
An exceptionally free-flowering, relatively hardy rosemary with an upright habit. H 3–4ft (1–1.2m), S 3ft (1m).
8–10

► ***Rosmarinus officinalis* 'Sudbury Blue'**
One of the hardier cultivars, with dense, blue-green foliage, an upright habit, and midblue flowers. H 5–6ft (1.5–2m), S 4–5ft (1.2–1.5m).
8–10

► ***Rosmarinus officinalis* 'Tuscan Blue'**
This fast-growing cultivar has a tall, upright habit, red-brown stems, light green, slightly glossy leaves, and dark blue flowers. H and S 3–6ft (1–2m).
8–10

RUBIA

A genus of about 60 species of perennials and subshrubs occurring in Europe, Asia, and Africa; *R. cordifolia* is found in Asia, extending into Europe and Africa. *R. tinctorum*, found in southeastern Europe and western and central Asia, produces the red dye known as "Turkey red," traditionally used to color Turkish fezzes. It was originally exported from Turkey for cultivation in the main textile centers of northern Europe. *Rubia* is from the Latin *ruber*, "red," referring to the red dye yielded by the roots.

Rubia cordifolia (Indian madder, *munjeet, manjishta*)
Perennial climber with long, red roots, greenish white, prickly stems, and slender, heart-shaped leaves up to 3in (8cm) long. Tiny flowers appear from summer to autumn, followed by globose, black fruits with red juice. H 20ft (6m).
T

Rubia tinctorum (madder)
Rough perennial climber with a red, branched rhizome and whorls of rough, narrow, stalkless leaves. Tiny pale yellow-green flowers are borne in loose clusters in summer and autumn, followed by tiny, fleshy, red-brown to black berries. H 10–36in (25cm–1m).
6–10

ROSEMARY, see *ROSMARINUS*, pp.192–3
ROUGH HORSETAIL, see *Equisetum hyemale*, p.123
ROUND-LEAVED MINT BUSH, see *Prostanthera rotundifolia*, p.183
ROUND-LEAVED SUNDEW, see *Drosera rotundifolia*, p.120

RUBUS

A cosmopolitan genus of about 250 species of deciduous, semievergreen, and evergreen shrubs, scramblers, woody-stemmed climbers, and trailers found in the northern hemisphere. *R. coreanus* is native to Korea, Japan, and China; *R. fruticosus* is widespread in Europe, and *R. idaeus* in Europe, Asia, and N America. Raspberries were cultivated in England by the mid-16th century. Blackberries remained a wild-collected food until the 19th century.

Rubus coreanus (Chinese raspberry)
Deciduous, suckering shrub with dark, wax-coated, arching stems bearing stout prickles and divided leaves. Small pink to white flowers appear in summer, followed by red to black fruits.
H 12ft (4m), S indefinite.

6–9

Rubus fruticosus (blackberry, bramble)
Very variable semievergreen shrub with prickly, biennial stems and trifoliate or palmate leaves about 6in (15cm) long. Clusters of white to pink flowers are borne from midsummer, followed by juicy black fruits, ½–¾in (1–2cm) long. H and S 12ft (4m).

3–8

Rubus idaeus (raspberry)
Suckering deciduous shrub with prickly or almost smooth stems and pinnately divided leaves. Small white flowers are produced in drooping clusters in summer, followed by aromatic, juicy, usually red fruits. H 3–5½ft (1–1.7m), S 3–6ft (1–2m).

3–8

***Rubus idaeus* 'Aureus'**
This cultivar is grown for its foliage. It is smaller-growing than the species and has bright golden leaves, making good groundcover in semishade. H 3–4ft (1–1.2m), S 24–36in (60–90cm).

3–8

RUMEX

Some 200 species of annuals, biennials, and perennials make up this genus, which ranges throughout northern temperate regions. *R. crispus* is found in Europe and Africa. *R. scutatus*, found in Europe, western Asia, and northern Africa, is one of the few species with any merit as an ornamental, though it may be difficult to eradicate when well established. According to Pliny, Julius Caesar's soldiers were cured of scurvy by the use of *herba britannica* (since identified as *R. aquatica*).

Rumex crispus (curled dock, yellow dock)
Variable, erect perennial with a stout rootstock and lanceolate leaves up to 12in (30cm) long. Inconspicuous green flowers appear in summer, followed by tiny, woody fruits. H 1–5ft (30cm–1.5m), S 18–36in (45–90cm).

4–8

Rumex acetosa (sorrel)
Perennial with pale green stems and thick, long-stalked leaves up to 6in (15cm) long. Inconspicuous red-brown flowers, borne in slender, loose spikes from early summer, are followed by tiny, hard fruits. H 20–48in (50cm–1.2m), S 10–18in (25–45cm).

4–8

Rumex scutatus (French sorrel, buckler-leaf sorrel)
Low-growing, mat-forming perennial with a slightly woody base and long-stalked, spear-shaped leaves. In summer, inconspicuous red-green flowers appear, turning pale brown as fruits ripen.
H 6–20in (15–50cm), S 4ft (1.2m).

4–8

***Rumex scutatus* 'Silver Shield'**
This cultivar has silver-green leaves. It makes good, if rampant, groundcover beside paths and at the front of borders. H 6–20in (15–50cm), S 4ft (1.2m).

4–8

RUCOLA, see *Eruca vesicaria*, p.123
RUE, see *Ruta graveolens*, p.195
RUM CHERRY, see *PRUNUS*, p.184–5
RUNNING BOX, see *Mitchella repens*, p.160
RUSSIAN COMFREY, see *Symphytum* x *uplandicum*, p.206
RYNTEM ROOT, see *Gentiana scabra*, p.132
SACRED LOTUS, see *Nelumbo nucifera*, p.164
SAFFLOWER, see *Carthamus tinctorius*, p.101
SAFFRON CROCUS, see *Crocus sativus*, p.113
SAFFRON THISTLE, see *Carthamus tinctorius*, p.101

RUSCUS

Six species of evergreen clump-forming subshrubs belong to this genus, which occurs in the Azores, northern Africa, and through western Europe to the Caspian Sea. They are unusual in having flattened, leaflike branches, the true leaves being reduced to scales. An attractive plant with disproportionately large fruits, *R. aculeatus* makes excellent groundcover beneath trees. "Butcher's broom" gains its name from being traditionally tied in bundles to clean floors in butchers' shops.

Ruscus aculeatus (butcher's broom, box holly, Jew's myrtle)
Small, erect subshrub with stiff, ovate, leaflike branches up to 1in (2.5cm) long, tipped with spines. Inconspicuous green flowers appear in late winter and spring, followed by globose red fruits.
H 2½–4ft (75cm–1.2m), S 3ft (1m).

7–9

RUTA

A genus of eight species of strong-smelling evergreen or semievergreen subshrubs found from eastern Europe to southwestern Asia. *R. graveolens*, found in dry Mediterranean regions, is a useful shrub for narrow, sunny borders, and can have attractive foliage all year. *Ruta* may derive from the Greek *rhutos*, "shielded," in view of its long history as an antidote. "Herb of grace," the common name, comes from the tradition of sprinkling holy water during Mass with a brush made of rue.

Ruta graveolens (rue, herb of grace, herbygrass)
Small evergreen or semievergreen subshrub with deeply divided leaves. Mustard yellow flowers up to ½in (1cm) across with 4 fringed petals are borne in summer, followed by 4-lobed capsules.
H 24in (60cm), S 18in (45cm).

4–8

***Ruta graveolens* 'Jackman's Blue'**
This cultivar has blue-gray leaves.
H 24in (60cm), S 18in (45cm).

4–8

***Ruta graveolens* 'Variegata'**
A variegated cultivar with irregular, creamy white markings and the occasional entirely white leaf. It is unusual among variegated cultivars in coming true from seed. H 24in (60cm), S 18in (45cm).

4–8

SALIX

In this genus there are about 300 species of deciduous trees and shrubs, which occur in temperate and cold regions of the northern hemisphere; *S. alba* is common beside watercourses in Europe and central Asia. *S. alba* 'Britzensis' and *S. a.* var. *vitellina* are widely planted as a winter feature for their colorful bare stems. The golden weeping willow is a hybrid between the latter and *S. babylonica*. In parts of England, sprays of willow are woven into crosses at Easter.

Salix alba (white willow)
Large tree with deeply fissured, gray-brown bark, ascending branches, and lanceolate, tapering leaves up to 4in (10cm) long. Flowers appear in catkins with the new leaves in spring. H 80ft (25m), S 30ft (10m).

2–9

Salix alba* var. *vitellina (golden willow)
An attractive cultivar with yellow-green young stems, usually coppiced to maintain its ornamental value. H 80ft (25m), S 30ft (10m).

2–9

***Salix alba* var. *vitellina* 'Britzensis'** (scarlet willow)
This cultivar has bright orange-red young stems. It is usually coppiced annually to provide colorful new shoots. H 80ft (25m), S 30ft (10m).

2–9

SAGE, see *SALVIA*, pp.196–7
ST. JOHN'S WORT, see *Hypericum*, p.141
SALT BUSH, see *Salvadora persica*, p.345

Salvia

A genus of some 900 species of mostly aromatic annuals, biennials, perennials, and mainly evergreen shrubs and subshrubs, which, with the exception of only a few, are mostly tender or half hardy. They occur worldwide, especially in warmer temperate regions, favoring dry, sunny hillsides, and open ground. The flowers secrete abundant nectar, making them important bee plants. Salvias have interesting aromas, textures, and colors. The floral spikes of *S. viridis* and *S. sclarea* are excellent as fresh or dried cut flowers. About 80 species and many variants are available as ornamentals, some of which have medicinal and culinary uses. *Salvia* is from the Latin *salvere*, meaning "to be well," in reference to the health-giving properties of the plants.

▲ ***Salvia elegans*** **'Scarlet Pineapple'** (pineapple sage)
Evergreen, perennial, downy subshrub with bright green, ovate, pointed leaves up to 3½in (9cm) long, which have a pineapple-like scent. Spikes of slender red to pink flowers appear in winter. H and S 3ft (1m).
9–10

► ***Salvia clevelandii*** (blue sage, Jim sage)
Evergreen Californian shrub with downy stems and lanceolate, aromatic, wrinkled leaves to 1in (2.5cm) long. Spikes of blue to violet or white flowers appear in summer. H 18–24in (45–60cm), S 12–18in (30-45cm).
9–10

▲ ***Salvia dorisiana*** (fruit-scented sage)
Shrubby evergreen perennial with hairy stems and velvety, ovate leaves, sweet-scented and up to 7in (18cm) long. Magenta to rose-pink flowers are borne in spikes up to 6in (15cm) long in winter. H and S 3–5ft (1–1.5m).
10–11

▲ ***Salvia fruticosa*** (Greek sage)
Evergreen shrub with lavender-scented, ovate to oblong, gray-green leaves which have white, downy undersides. Mauve to pink, occasionally white, flowers appear in panicles up to 8in (20cm) long in spring and summer. H and S 3ft (1m).
8–9

▲ ***Salvia coccinea*** (Texas sage)
Annual with much-branched, downy stems and ovate to deltoid leaves up to 2in (5cm) long, with wavy to indented margins. Whorls of red, occasionally white, flowers almost ¾in (2cm) long open in branched spikes in summer. H 3ft (1m), S 18in (45cm).
8–10

◄ ***Salvia lavandulifolia*** (narrow-leaved sage, Spanish sage)
Spreading, evergreen perennial with hairy stems and narrowly oblong, gray- to white-woolly wrinkled leaves, up to 1in (2.5cm) long, that have a balsam-lavender aroma. Spikes of blue-violet flowers appear in summer. H 12–20in (30–50cm), S 24in (60cm).
7–9

▲ ***Salvia officinalis*** (common sage)
Shrubby evergreen perennial with much-branched stems and wrinkled, velvety, gray-green leaves about 2in (5cm) long. Spikes of violet to purple, pink, or white flowers, ½in (1cm) long, appear in summer.
H 24–32in (60–80cm), S 3ft (1m).
5–8

▲ ***Salvia officinalis*** **'Albiflora'**
This cultivar has white flowers and is a most elegant plant for white and silver gardens. H 24–32in (60–80cm), S 3ft (1m).
5–8

◄ ***Salvia officinalis* 'Berggarten'**
This distinctive German cultivar has a dense, compact habit, broad, almost rounded leaves in a light gray-green, and purple-blue flowers. H 18in (45cm), S 3ft (1m).
5–8

▲ ***Salvia officinalis* 'Icterina'**
A popular cultivar with yellow-variegated leaves that provide interest among plain green herbs. H 24–32in (60–80cm), S 3ft (1m).
7–9

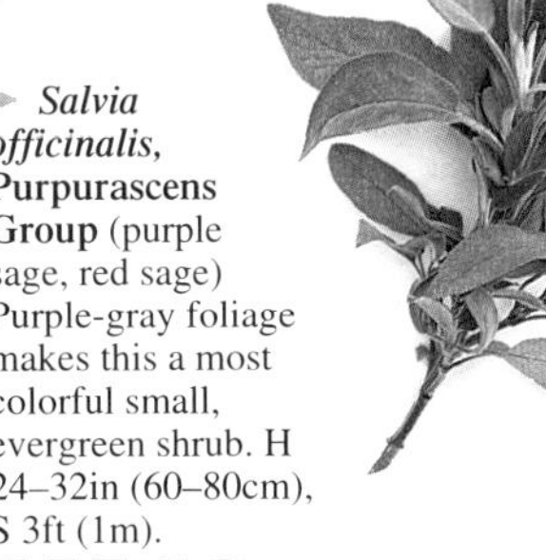

► ***Salvia officinalis* 'Kew Gold'**
This choice cultivar has yellow leaves and a compact, dwarf habit. It associates well with *Tagetes patula* and dwarf cultivars of *Tanacetum parthenium*. H 12in (30cm), S 18in (45cm).
7–9

▲ ***Salvia pomifera*** (apple-bearing sage)
Evergreen shrub, often bearing fleshy galls produced by gall wasps in the wild, and wrinkled, velvety light green leaves. Whorls of violet-blue flowers are borne in branched spikes in spring and summer. H and S 3ft (1m).
8–9

► ***Salvia officinalis,* Purpurascens Group** (purple sage, red sage)
Purple-gray foliage makes this a most colorful small, evergreen shrub. H 24–32in (60–80cm), S 3ft (1m).
7–9

◄ ***Salvia sclarea*** (clary sage, cleareye, muscatel sage)
Biennial with wrinkled, strong-smelling leaves. Bicolored cream and lilac flowers, with white to mauve bracts, in spring and summer. H 3ft (1m), S 24in (60cm).
4–9

▲ ***Salvia sclarea* var. *turkestanica***
A more colorful variety than the species, with pink stems, pink to white bracts, and pale blue and white flowers. H 3ft (1m), S 2ft (60cm).
4–9

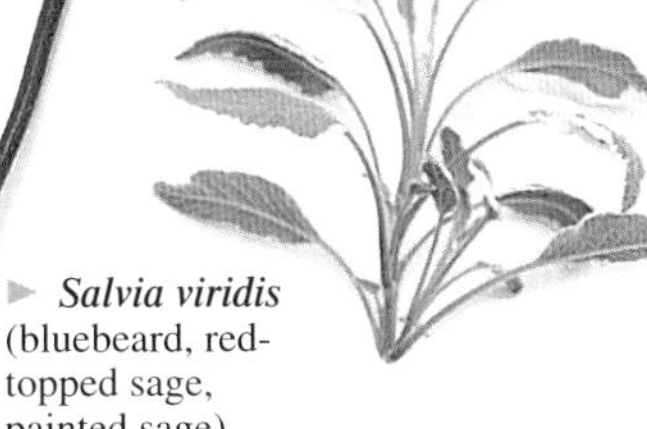

► ***Salvia viridis*** (bluebeard, red-topped sage, painted sage)
Annual or biennial with erect stems and downy leaves. Inconspicuous flowers with pink or purple bracts, appear in summer. H18in (45cm), S 8in (20cm).
A

◄ ***Salvia viridis* 'Claryssa'**
This cultivar has a more compact habit than the species and colorful bracts in blue-purple, pink, and green-veined white. H 18in (45cm), S 8in (20cm).
A

SAMBUCUS

This genus of about 20 species of small deciduous trees, shrubs, and perennials occurs in most temperate and subtropical regions; *S. nigra* is widely found in Europe, western Asia, and northern Africa. The species is seldom grown in gardens, having been superseded by a number of attractive cultivars, tolerant of a wide range of conditions, that have colorful foliage. *Sambucus* is from the Greek *sambuke*, "a musical pipe," for which the new shoots of elder bushes were traditionally used.

Sambucus nigra (common elder)
Large deciduous shrub with corky, gray-brown bark and pinnate leaves. The foliage has an unpleasant smell when crushed. Tiny, scented, cream flowers are borne in early summer, followed by black berries. H 15–30ft (4.5–10m), S 11–15ft (3.5–4.5m).
5–9

***Sambucus nigra* 'Aurea'** (golden elder)
A resilient, golden-leaved shrub that withstands exposed areas and full sun. The young foliage is bright yellow-green, becoming lime green with age. H and S 20ft (6m).
5–9

***Sambucus nigra* 'Guincho Purple'** (bronze elder)
This cultivar has dark purple-bronze foliage and pink-stamened flowers. H and S 20ft (6m).
5–9

Sambucus nigra* f. *laciniata (fern-leaved elder, parsley-leaved elder)
The deeply dissected leaves of this cultivar contrast well with bold, large-leaved herbs. H and S 20ft (6m).
5–9

***Sambucus nigra* 'Marginata'**
The leaflets of this cultivar have irregular, creamy white margins. H and S 20ft (6m).
5–9

SAMPHIRE, see *Crithmum maritimum*, p.113
SAN QI GINSENG, see *Panax pseudo-ginseng*, p.321
SAND LEEK, see *ALLIUM*, pp.80–81
SANDALWOOD, see *Santalum album*, p.198

SANGUINARIA

A single species of perennial makes up this genus belonging to the poppy family (Papaveraceae). Found in eastern N American woodlands, *S. canadensis* is a choice plant for woodland borders, raised beds, and shady areas of the rock garden. It is at its best in spring, when exquisite white or pink flowers open as the scalloped new leaves emerge. The name *Sanguinaria* comes from the Latin *sanguis*, "blood," and refers to the red sap in the rhizomes.

Sanguinaria canadensis (bloodroot, red puccoon)
Rhizomatous perennial with kidney-shaped gray-green leaves. In spring, solitary white to pink flowers are followed by an oblong capsule containing many seeds. H 6–24in (15–60cm), S 12–18in (30–45cm).

3–8

***Sanguinaria canadensis* 'Plena'**
This cultivar has longer-lasting, double white flowers. H 6–24in (15–60cm), S 12–18in (30–45cm).

3–8

SANGUISORBA

There are about 20 species of rhizomatous perennials in this genus, which occurs throughout northern temperate regions. *S. officinalis*, found in damp grassland through Europe to China and Japan, is grown as a border plant for its elegant foliage and small, bottlebrush flowers. It is naturalized in parts of N America. The name *Sanguisorba* comes from the Latin *sanguis*, "blood," and *sorbere*, "to soak up," and refers to the use of these plants to control bleeding.

Sanguisorba officinalis (great burnet)
Erect perennial with a stout, woody rootstock and a basal rosette of pinnately divided, toothed leaves. Tiny maroon flowers are produced in dense, oblong heads in summer. H 1–3½ft (30cm–1.1m), S 9–24in (23–60cm).

4–8

SANTALUM

Nine species of evergreen trees and shrubs belong to this genus, which occurs in SE Asia, Australia, and the Pacific Islands; *S. album* is probably native to coastal Malaysia and Indonesia. Sandalwoods are semiparasitic, deriving some food from photosynthesis but relying on a host plant, via sucker roots, for water and minerals. Various species have long been prized for their fragrant wood. *S. album* takes at least 20–40 years to develop sufficient heartwood for oil extraction.

Santalum album (Indian sandalwood, white sandalwood)
Small, graceful tree with fragrant wood and ovate to lanceolate leaves up to 3in (8cm) long. Panicles of dull yellow to maroon flowers are followed by fleshy, dark red to black fruits, ½in (1cm) long. H 15–30ft (5–10m), S 10ft (3m).

SANTOLINA

A genus of about 15 species of small, aromatic, evergreen shrubs that are Mediterranean in origin. *S. chamaecyparissus*, found in western and central Spain, was grown in Classical times and became popular for knot garden hedges in northern regions in the 16th century. Its neat, silver-gray foliage contrasts well with darker hedging plants, such as dwarf boxwood (*Buxus sempervirens* 'Suffruticosa', see p. 96). *Santolina* comes from the Latin *sanctum linum*, "holy flax," a name given to *S. virens*.

Santolina chamaecyparissus (lavender cotton, cotton lavender)
Strongly aromatic shrub with white-woolly, linear leaves divided into closely packed, blunt segments. Solitary, globular heads of deep yellow tubular flowers are produced in summer. H 8–20in (20–50cm), S 24in (60cm).

6–8

***Santolina chamaecyparissus* 'Lemon Queen'**
In spite of its name, this dwarf cultivar has cream flowers and gray-green leaves that have a slightly sweeter aroma than the species. H 10–16in (25–40cm), S 12–20in (30–50cm).

6–8

Santolina chamaecyparissus* var. *nana
The smallest of the santolinas, which is ideal for containers or a miniature hedge. H and S 6in (15cm).

6–8

SARGASSO, see *Sargassum fusiforme*, p.349
SASSAFRAS, see *Sassafras albidum*, p.199

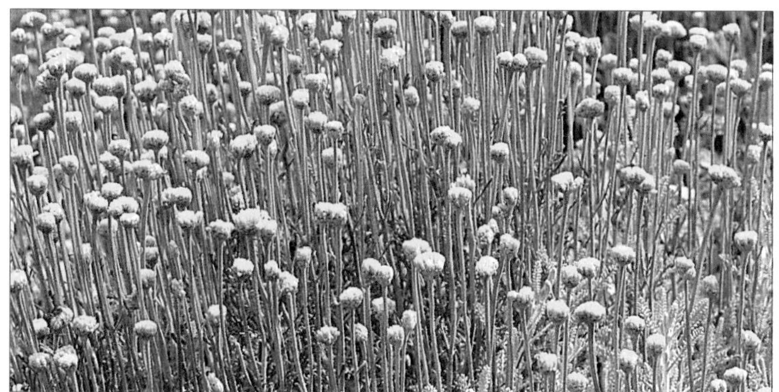

Santolina chamaecyparissus **'Pretty Carol'**
This cultivar has a very neat, compact habit, silver foliage, and bright yellow flowers. H 10–20in (25–50cm), S 24in (60cm).

6–8

Saponaria officinalis **'Rubra Plena'**
This cultivar has double, deep pink flowers. A cultivar known as *S. o.* 'Rosea Plena', with paler pink flowers, is also available. H 12–36in (30–90cm), S 24in (60cm).

2–8

SAPONARIA

A genus of about 30 species of annuals and perennials ranging throughout temperate Eurasia. *S. officinalis*, which is naturalized in N America, is a long-lived, late-flowering perennial for the border. It was used as a soap by the Assyrians (eighth century BC), and often occurs in the wild on the sites of old woollen mills, where it was once grown for cleaning cloth. The name *Saponaria* comes from the Latin *sapo*, "soap," and refers to the high saponin content of these plants, which lathers like soap.

Saponaria officinalis (soapwort, bouncing Bet)
Rhizomatous perennial with broadly ovate to elliptic, pointed leaves up to 4in (10cm) long. Scented pale pink flowers are borne in clusters from midsummer to midautumn. H 12–36in (30–90cm), S 24in (60cm).

2–8

Saponaria officinalis **'Dazzler'**
The leaves of this cultivar are cream-splashed, giving it interest as a foliage plant. The flowers are the same as in the species. H 24in (60cm), S 12in (30cm).

2–8

SASSAFRAS

A genus of three species of aromatic deciduous trees occurring in eastern N America and eastern Asia. *S. albidum*, found in thickets and disturbed woods, is grown for its scented, distinctively shaped foliage, which colors well in autumn. It was said that the scent of sassafras trees played a part in the discovery of the New World by Columbus, who detected their fragrance from afar and was thus guided to land. Sassafras was probably the first medicinal herb to reach Europe, c.1560.

Sassafras albidum (sassafras)
Suckering tree with deeply fissured bark, flexuous branches, and variously shaped leaves, up to 6in (15cm) long. Small yellow-green flowers appear in clusters in spring, followed by deep blue, ovoid fruits. H 70ft (20m), S 40ft (12m).

4–8

SATUREJA

This genus of 30 species of annuals, semievergreen perennials, and subshrubs occurs in temperate and warm areas of Eurasia and N America; *S. hortensis*, *S. montana*, and *S. thymbra* are Mediterranean in origin; *S. spicigera* is native to southwestern Asia. Savories are grown mainly for medicinal and culinary uses. *S. montana* may be planted as an informal dwarf hedge; it is hardier than *S. hortensis* and has a stronger, coarser aroma. *Satureja* may be from *satyrus*, "satyr," referring to its aphrodisiac effects.

Satureja hortensis (summer savory)
Annual with a single, widely branched stem and linear-oblanceolate, short-stalked leaves up to 14in (3cm) long. Whorls of lilac to white or purple flowers appear in summer. H 4–15in (10–38cm), S 7–30in (18–75cm).

A

Satureja montana (winter savory)
Shrubby evergreen perennial with woody rootstock and linear-lanceolate, stalkless, usually pointed leaves. Whorls of white to pale pink or purple flowers appear in summer. H 4–16in (10–40cm), S 3–8in (7–20cm).

5–8

Satureja spicigera (creeping savory)
Prostrate shrublet with 4-angled stems and linear-oblanceolate leaves. White flowers, about ¼in (6mm) long, are produced in late summer. H 2½in (6cm), S 12in (30cm).

7–8

Satureja thymbra (goat thyme, thyme-leaved savory)
Shrublet with wiry, erect stems and hairy, oblong leaves that have a thyme-pennyroyal aroma. Pink flowers appear in spring and summer, after which the calyces turn black. H 16in (40cm), S 12–16in (30–40cm).

8–9

SAUSSUREA

This genus of some 300 species of perennials is found in mountains of Europe, Asia, and N America. One or two species are occasionally seen, but most of these thistlelike plants have no ornamental value. *S. lappa*, native to the eastern Himalayas, is cultivated in China and parts of India for the herb trade, but India has banned the export of roots due to overcollection. *Saussurea* was named after the Swiss philosopher and botanist Horace Benedict de Saussure (1740–99).

Saussurea lappa (costus, *kuth*)
Perennial with a thick, tapering root, irregularly toothed upper leaves, and lyre-shaped lower leaves. Deep purple, very hard flower heads are produced in dense clusters of 2–3 in summer. H 10ft (3m), S 3ft (1m).

10

SCHISANDRA

A genus of some 25 species of deciduous and evergreen climbers occurring in eastern Asia and eastern N America. *S. chinensis*, found in northeastern China and Japan, was introduced to Western botanic gardens in the late 1850s. It is a large, handsome climber with scented flowers and brightly colored berries. Male and female flowers are borne on separate plants. *Schisandra* is from the Greek *schizo*, "to divide," and *andreios*, "male," and refers to the split anther cells.

Schisandra chinensis (schisandra)
Climbing deciduous shrub with elliptic to obovate, pointed leaves, 2½–6in (6–15cm) long. Solitary, cream to pink fragrant flowers are borne in late spring, followed on female plants by clusters of glossy scarlet fruits. H 25ft (8m).

5–8

SCOPOLIA

This genus of five species of perennials is found from the Mediterranean to the Himalayas, Japan, and Siberia. *S. carniolica*, found in central and southeastern Europe, is primarily a medicinal plant, but is occasionally grown as an ornamental. It is poisonous and should be sited with care. The distribution of the two species overlaps in central Europe, and the species have similar histories of medicinal uses. *Scopolia* was named after the botanist Giovanni Antonio Scopoli (1723–88).

Scopolia carniolica (scopolia, Japanese belladonna)
Clump-forming perennial with fleshy rhizomes and elliptic to ovate upper leaves up to 8in (20cm) long. Pendent, purple-brown, bell-shaped flowers, yellowish green inside, appear in spring and early summer. H and S 24in (60cm).

5–8

SAVORY, see *Satureja*, p.199
SAW PALMETTO, see *Serenoa repens*, p.203
SCABWORT, see *Inula helenium*, p.143
SCALLION, see *ALLIUM*, pp.80–81
SCARLET PIMPERNEL, see *Anagallis arvensis*, p.83
SCARLET WILLOW, see *Salix alba* 'Britzensis', p.195
SCENTED MAYWEED, see *Matricaria recutita*, p.156
SCHISANDRA, see *Schisandra chinensis*, above
SCOPOLIA, see *Scopolia carniolica*, above
SCOTCH BROOM, see *Cytisus scoparius*, p.116

SCROPHULARIA

This genus contains about 200 species of annuals, perennials, and subshrubs found in northern temperate parts; *S. ningpoensis* is native to China, *S. nodosa* to Europe. A few species are grown as border plants. In France, *S. nodosa* is known as *herbe du siège* since the tubers were eaten by Cardinal Richelieu's starving troops during the siege of La Rochelle (1627–8). It was an early remedy for scrofula, known as "King's Evil," from the belief that the disease could be cured by the king's touch.

Scrophularia ningpoensis (Ningpo figwort, black figwort)
Perennial with 4-angled stems and ovate leaves up to 6in (15cm) long. In spring, brown-red tubular flowers are borne in panicles on threadlike stalks, followed by ovoid capsules. H 2–4ft (60cm–1.2m), S 12–18in (30–45cm).
6–8

Scrophularia nodosa (common figwort)
Strong-smelling perennial with tuberous rhizomes and ovate, pointed, toothed leaves. In summer, green-brown flowers are borne in panicles, followed by ovoid capsules. H 16in–48in (40cm–1.2m), S 6–15in (15–38cm).
6–8

SCUTELLARIA

A cosmopolitan genus of about 300 species of annuals and perennials. *S. baicalensis*, found in eastern Asia, is an interesting border plant. *S. lateriflora*, found in N America, is common in herb gardens and nurseries, although many plants labeled as such are in fact *S. altissima*, a larger plant with showier flowers. Care should be taken to identify plants purchased for medicinal use. *Scutellaria* is from the Latin *scutella*, "a small dish," referring to the pouchlike appearance of the fruit's calyx.

Scutellaria baicalensis (Baikal skullcap)
Spreading perennial with stems often flushed purple and stalkless, slender, ovate leaves. Dense, one-sided racemes of hairy, tubular, blue-purple flowers are produced in summer. H to 16in (40cm), S 12–16in (30–40cm).
4–8

Scutellaria lateriflora (Virginia skullcap, mad dog skullcap)
Perennial with slender rhizomes and thin, ovate-lanceolate, toothed leaves. Blue, occasionally pink or white flowers are produced in one-sided, mostly axillary racemes in summer. H 6–30in (15–75cm), S to 18in (45cm).
3–8

SCOTS LOVAGE, see *Ligusticum scoticum*, p.151
SCOTS PINE, see *Pinus sylvestris*, p.177
SCREW PINE, see *Pandanus odoratissimus*, p.170
SCURF PEA, see *Psoralea corylifolia*, p.336
SEA FENNEL, see *Crithmum maritimum*, p.113
SEA HOLLY, see *Eryngium maritimum*, p.124
SEA LOVAGE, see *Ligusticum scoticum*, p.151
SEA ONION, see *Drimia maritima*, p.119
SEDGE ROOT, see *Cyperus rotundus*, p.115

SELENICEREUS

This genus contains about 20 species of epiphytic or lithophytic cacti occurring in tropical America and the Caribbean. *S. grandiflorus*, found in C American and W Indian forests, is one of several species grown for their exquisite blooms, which open in the evening and close at dawn. It was introduced into Britain from the W Indies in 1700 and became a favorite for greenhouses. *Selenicereus* is from the Greek *selene*, "moon," and *Cereus*, the name of another genus of cacti.

Selenicereus grandiflorus (queen-of-the-night, night-blooming cereus)
Climbing perennial cactus with tufts of white spines. Fragrant white flowers, up to 12in (30cm) across, with yellow-brown outer tepals and numerous stamens, are followed by globose red fruits. H 10–15ft (3–5m).

10–11

SEMPERVIVUM

This genus of about 40 evergreen species of small, fleshy, rosette-forming perennials occurs in Europe, northern Africa, and western Asia. Commonly known as "houseleeks," from the Anglo-Saxon *leac*, "a plant," they were grown in containers during Roman times. A large number of colorful cultivars and hybrids are available today. *Sempervivum* comes from the Latin *semper*, "always," and *vivus*, "alive," referring to the drought-tolerant nature of these plants.

Sempervivum tectorum (hens and chicks, houseleek)
Succulent perennial with rosettes up to 4in (10cm) across and thick, fleshy, spine-tipped, leaves. Clusters of pink star-shaped flowers are borne in summer. Individual rosettes die after flowering. H (when flowering) and S 12in (30cm).

5–10

***Sempervivum tectorum* 'Royal Ruby'**
This is one of several cultivars with a pronounced, deep red flush, in this case toward the center of the rosette. H (when flowering) and S 12in (30cm).

5–10

SENECIO

This large cosmopolitan genus contains some 3,000 species of annuals, biennials, perennials, evergreen shrubs, trees, and climbers. Many contain toxic alkaloids and some are widespread weeds, common in pasture, which cause serious poisoning and ill-health in livestock. *S. aureus*, native to eastern N America, is grown for the pharmaceutical industry in Belorussia, central Russia, and Ukraine. The name *Senecio* is from the Latin *senex*, "old man," referring to the white-haired seeds.

Senecio aureus (liferoot, squaw weed, golden ragwort)
Perennial with heart-shaped, toothed basal leaves and narrow, pinnately cut stem leaves. Yellow daisylike flowers are borne in branched, terminal clusters in spring and early summer. H 6–30in (15–75cm), S 6–24in (15–60cm).

5–9

SENNA

This genus of about 250 species of perennials, shrubs, and trees occurs mainly in the tropics and subtropics. *S. alexandrina* is native to Arabia, Djibouti, and Somalia; *S. marilandica* to midwestern US. A few species are grown as ornamentals in warm regions or under cover in temperate regions. *S. marilandica* is one of the hardiest, but prefers a sheltered situation outdoors in colder areas. The use of senna as a laxative was introduced to Europe by Arab physicians in the ninth and tenth centuries.

Senna alexandrina (Alexandrian senna, Tinnevelly senna)
Shrubby perennial with thin, hairy, divided leaves. In spring and summer, small, tawny flowers are borne in axillary racemes, followed by straight pods up to 3in (7cm) long. H 3ft (1m), S 20–24in (50–60cm).

Senna marilandica (wild senna)
Perennial with leafy, erect to sprawling stems and leaves up to 11in (28cm) long, dull yellow-green in color. Yellow flowers appear in racemes in summer, followed by stiff, hairy pods up to 4½in (11cm) long. H 2–6ft (60cm–2m), S 6in–4ft (15cm–1.2m).

3–9

SELFHEAL, see *Prunella vulgaris*, p.183
SENECA SNAKEROOT, see *Polygala senega*, p.332
SERPENTARY, see *Aristolochia serpentaria*, p.241
SERPENTWOOD, see *Rauvolfia serpentina*, p.189
SESAME, see *Sesamum indicum*, above
SEVEN BARKS, see *Hydrangea arborescens*, p.140
SEVILLE ORANGE, see *Citrus aurantium*, p.108
SHEEP'S PARSLEY, see *Petroselinum crispum* 'Italian', p.174
SHEPHERD'S PURSE, see *Capsella bursa-pastoris*, p.99

SERENOA

A single species of evergreen palm, *S. repens*, belongs to this genus. It occurs mainly in coastal areas of southeastern N America and forms dense thickets along the Atlantic coasts of Georgia and Florida. Its sweet, olive-shaped fruits are produced in abundance in early winter, and it is grown as an ornamental for its fan-shaped leaves. *Serenoa* is named after Sereno Watson (1826–92), an eminent Harvard botanist who described many new plant species during pioneering expeditions into N America.

Serenoa repens (saw palmetto)
Clump-forming rhizomatous palm with lanceolate, blue-green to yellow-green leaves, 18–36in (45cm–1m) wide. Tiny, fragrant, cream flowers are borne in summer, followed by ovoid, blue-black fruits about 1in (2.5cm) long. H 6–12ft (2–4m), S indefinite.

9–10

SIMMONDSIA

A genus of a single species of evergreen shrub native to southwestern US and northern Mexico. It is cultivated on a large scale in Arizona and the Middle East for the pharmaceutical industries, and elsewhere for erosion control and desert reclamation. It is slow-growing, and male and female bushes can be distinguished only after three years. *Simmondsia* is named after T. W. Simmonds (d. 1805), a botanist; jojoba (pronounced "hohoba") is the Mexican-Spanish word for the plant.

Simmondsia chinensis (jojoba, goat nut)
Variable shrub with thick, leathery, oblong-ovate leaves up to 1½in (4cm) long. Small, petal-less flowers appear in spring: males yellow, in clusters; females pale green, solitary, followed by ovoid capsules. H 6ft (2m), S 3–6ft (1–2m).

9–10

SESAMUM

This genus of 15 species of annuals and perennials is distributed in tropical Asia and southern Africa. *S. indicum* is a widespread crop in warmer parts of the world and is seen occasionally in collections of economic plants. The main producers are India, China, Myanmar (Burma), the Sudan, and Nigeria. Plants are easily raised from untoasted seed bought for culinary purposes. Those that produce black seeds were previously described as *S. orientale* but are now classed as a cultivar of *S. indicum*.

Sesamum indicum (sesame, benne, gingili)
Strong-smelling annual or short-lived perennial clad in sticky hairs, with large, divided, lower leaves. In summer, off-white, bell-shaped flowers are followed by capsules containing creamy white seeds. H 3ft (1m), S 18–36in (45–90cm).

A

SINAPIS

A genus of 10 species of annuals native to Europe and Mediterranean regions. *S. alba* is widely cultivated for mustard production and as a forage and green manure crop. Mustard was popular among the Romans, and its use spread through their influence to Gaul, then a region of western Europe. The name *Sinapis* comes from the Greek *sinapi*, "mustard." Mustard seeds were traditionally sown in baskets of "mustard and cress," but have now been replaced by the hardier *Brassica rapus*.

Sinapis alba (white mustard)
Annual with rough, hairy leaves up to 6in (15cm) long, which are deeply and irregularly cut, with a large terminal lobe. Yellow vanilla-scented flowers are produced in summer, followed by beaked pods containing about 3 seeds. H 2–4ft (60cm–1.2m), S 12in (30cm).

A

SILYBUM

A genus of two species of robust annuals or biennials found throughout Europe, Mediterranean regions, and the mountains of eastern Africa. *S. marianum* is grown as a foliage plant for its large, variegated leaves, and also for medicinal purposes. According to legend, the variegation was caused by the Virgin Mary's milk as it ran down the leaves, hence the plant's specific name, *marianum*. *Silybum* is from the Greek *silybon*, a term used by Dioscorides for thistlelike plants.

Silybum marianum (blessed thistle, milk thistle)
Stout annual or biennial with large, oblong, lobed or pinnately cut leaves, with spiny margins and variegated veins. Purple flowers are followed in summer by black seeds, each bearing a tuft of white hairs. H 4ft (1.2m), S 24in (60cm).

7–8

SISYMBRIUM

A genus of 80 species of annuals and perennials widespread in Europe, N America, the Andes, and southern Africa; *S. officinale* is also found in northern Africa and western Asia. Dioscorides, who knew *S. officinale* as *erysimon*, prescribed it with honey as an antidote to poisons and infections. It then became known as *herba erysimi*, hence its former species name, *Erysimum officinale*. One of its common names is "singer's plant" because it was used to remedy loss of voice.

Sisymbrium officinale (hedge mustard)
Stiffly upright, bristly annual, sometimes overwintering, with a basal rosette of pinnate leaves. Tiny pale yellow flowers appear throughout summer, followed by pods containing orange-brown seeds. H 12–36in (30–90cm), S 6–24in (15–60cm).

A

SIBERIAN GINSENG, see *Eleutherococcus senticosus*, p.122
SIBERIAN MILKWORT, see *Polygala tenuifolia*, p.332
SICKLE-LEAVED HARE'S EAR, see *Bupleurum falcatum*, p.96
SILK TREE, see *Albizia julibrissin*, p.78
SILKWEED, see *Asclepias tuberosa*, p.89
SILVER BIRCH, see *Betula pendula*, p.93
SILVER FIR, see *Abies alba*, p.70
SKULLCAP, see *Scutellaria*, p.201
SKUNK CABBAGE, see *Symplocarpus*, p.206
SLIPPERY ELM, see *Ulmus rubra*, p.217
SMALL-LEAVED LINDEN, see *Tilia cordata*, p.214
SMALLAGE, see *Apium graveolens*, p.85

SMILAX

This genus contains about 200 species of deciduous and evergreen climbing or scrambling vines ranging throughout tropical regions and temperate parts of Asia and Australia; *S. china* is native to uplands in Japan, China, and Korea. Several species were brought back by the Spanish from Mexico in the 16th century as a cure for syphilis. *S. ornata*, now regarded as synonymous with *S. regelii*, was introduced in 1865 and grown as an ornamental for its handsomely marked leaves.

Smilax china (China root)
Climbing deciduous shrub with a large, fleshy root, sparsely prickly stems, and leathery, broadly ovate leaves. Yellow-green flowers appear in early summer; females followed by globose red berries. Male and female flowers are borne on separate plants. H 15ft (5m), S indefinite.

7–10

SMYRNIUM

A genus of seven species of biennials and perennials occurring in western Europe and Mediterranean regions. *S. olusatrum*, a coastal species, is a celery-like plant that was known to Theophrastus in 322BC, and its cultivation as a pot herb was described by Pliny in the first century AD. Its specific name, *olus*, "pot herb," and *atrum*, "black" (referring to the black seeds), is derived from this use. *Smyrnium* is from the Greek *smyrna*, "myrrh," and refers to the aroma of these plants.

Smyrnium olusatrum (alexanders, black lovage)
Stout perennial with solid, furrowed stems and large, shiny, compound leaves. Umbels of tiny yellow-green flowers appear in spring and summer, followed by aromatic black seeds. H 1¾–5ft (50cm–1.5m), S 12–36in (30–90cm).

7–10

***Solanum dulcamara* 'Variegatum'**
This variant has creamy white-variegated foliage. It is less vigorous and slightly more tender than the species. It is especially attractive in autumn when the berries change in color from green to red. H 12ft (4m).

7–8

SOLANUM

This cosmopolitan genus consists of some 1,500 species of perennials, shrubs, trees, and climbers. It is one of the largest in the world. *S. dulcamara* is found in damp areas throughout Eurasia, and naturalized in N America. Most solanums contain toxic alkaloids. Dried fruits of *S. dulcamara* were found threaded on a collarette in Tutankhamun's third coffin. *S. dulcamara* 'Variegatum' is an attractive climber, tolerant of a wide range of conditions, which has a long period of interest.

Solanum dulcamara (deadly nightshade, bittersweet)
Shrubby, often climbing or trailing perennial with green stems and ovate, pointed leaves. Violet to blue or white flowers are borne in clusters in summer, followed by ovoid, bright red berries. H 12ft (4m), S indefinite.

6–8

SOLIDAGO

There are about 10 species of perennials in this genus, which is scattered throughout the northern hemisphere, but mainly in N America where they have had a long history in native medicine. *S. virgaurea* is native to dry areas in Europe. Virtually all the species, and various hybrids and variants, are grown in borders for their late show of color, which extends from midsummer to autumn. *Solidago* is from the Latin *solidare*, "to join," or "to make whole," and refers to the healing powers of these plants.

Solidago virgaurea (goldenrod)
Variable perennial with a knotted rhizome, upright stems, and oblanceolate, finely toothed, pointed leaves. Yellow flowers are borne in late summer, followed by brown fruits with a tuft of short, white hairs. H 32in (80cm), S 18–24in (45–60cm).

3–9

SNAKE GOURD, see *Trichosanthes kirilowii*, p.214
SNAKE-NEEDLE GRASS, see *Oldenlandia diffusa*, p.319
SNAKEROOT, see *Aristolochia*, p.87; *Liatris spicata*, p.151
SOAPBARK TREE, see *Quillaja saponaria*, p.188
SOAPWORT, see *Saponaria officinalis*, p.199
SOLOMON'S SEAL, see *Polygonatum*, p.181
SORREL, see *Rumex*, p.194
SPEARMINT, see *MENTHA*, pp.158–9
SPEEDWELL, see *Veronica*, p.218
SPHAGNUM MOSS, see *Sphagnum cymbilifolium*, above
SPICE BUSH, see *Lindera benzoin*, p.152

SOPHORA

A cosmopolitan genus of about 50 species of deciduous and evergreen trees, shrubs, and subshrubs. They have handsome, pinnate leaves and pea flowers. *S. japonica*, native to China and Korea, is widely grown as a landscape tree, especially in Japan. The red seeds of the N American *S. secundiflora* (mescal bean, coral bean) were important in initiation rites of tribes in the southwestern US and Mexico. *Sophora* is from the Arabic *sophero*, a name given to various trees with pea flowers.

Sophora japonica (Japanese pagoda tree)
Deciduous tree with large, divided, dark green, shiny leaves, which have downy or glaucous undersides. Creamy white, fragrant flowers appear in long panicles in late summer, followed by pods 2–3in (5–8cm) long. H 80ft (25m), S 70ft (20m).

5–8

***Sophora japonica* 'Pendula'**
This cultivar makes a small, weeping tree suitable as a lawn centerpiece.
H and S 10ft (3m).

5–8

STACHYS

This genus of about 300 species of annuals and perennials occurs in all parts of the world, except for Australia and New Zealand. *S. officinalis*, found throughout Europe, and its white- and pink-flowered cultivars are grown as border plants or naturalized in wildflower meadows. *S. palustris* is attractive for bog gardens and the margins of ponds. *Stachys* is a Greek word, meaning "ear of corn," or "spike," and refers to the arrangement of flowers on the stem.

Stachys officinalis (betony, bishopswort)
Mat-forming perennial with 4-sided, hairy stems and oblong, deeply veined, regularly toothed leaves. Spikes of bright magenta, pink, or white flowers are produced in summer. H 6–24in (15–60cm), S 12–18in (30–45cm).

4–8

***Stachys officinalis* 'Rosea Superba'**
A robust cultivar with large, clear pink flowers, which makes an outstanding summer-flowering border plant.
H 6–24in (15–60cm), S 12–18in (30–45cm).

4–8

Stachys palustris (marsh woundwort)
Rhizomatous perennial with tuberous roots and lanceolate, hairy leaves. Pale lilac flowers with darker markings are borne in whorled spikes in summer.
H 3ft (1m), S 12–18in (30–45cm).

4–8

SPHAGNUM

This genus consists of about 100 species of bog mosses found from tropical to Arctic and sub-Antarctic regions. *S. cymbilifolium* is found in wet bogs in northwestern Europe. The absorbent sponge-like tissues are important in regulating water loss from various habitats. Decomposed sphagnum is a major component of peat, known for its preservative properties, which has been exploited as a soil conditioner and basis for soil mixes by the horticultural industry.

Sphagnum cymbilifolium (sphagnum moss, bog moss)
Dense, clump-forming moss with pale yellow-green foliage, often tinged bright green or salmon pink. Dark brown fruit capsules are produced in summer. H and S 12in (30cm).

STELLARIA

There are some 120 species of annuals and perennials in this cosmopolitan genus, many of which have fragile stems. *S. media* is an abundant wild source of food and medicine, and its hardiness makes it available nearly all year. Historically, *S. media* was also valued in many countries as a food for birds and domestic fowl, hence its many common names associated with this use. The name *Stellaria* comes from the Latin *stella*, "star," referring to the star-shaped flowers.

Stellaria media (chickweed)
Spreading annual weed, often over-wintering, with a slender taproot, diffusely branched, brittle stems, and ovate leaves. White star-shaped flowers with deeply notched petals appear during much of the year.
H and S 2–16in (5–40cm).

A

SPINDLE TREE, see *Euonymus europaeus*, p.125
SPURGE, see *Euphorbia*, p.126
SQUASH, see *Cucurbita*, p.114
SQUAW VINE, see *Mitchella repens*, p.160
SQUILL, see *Drimia maritima*, p.119
SQUIRTING CUCUMBER, see *Ecballium elaterium*, p.121
STAG'S HORN CLUBMOSS, see *Lycopodium clavatum*, p.154
STAR ANISE, see *Illicium verum*, p.296
STINGING NETTLE, see *Urtica dioica*, p.217
STINKING ROGER, see *Tagetes minuta*, p.207

STROPHANTHUS

This genus of 38 species of evergreen or deciduous shrubs and small trees occurs in tropical Africa and Eurasia, many with a climbing habit; *S. gratus* is native to deciduous forest in tropical western Africa. Several species were cultivated in warm greenhouses in the 19th century for their interesting flowers with long, ribbonlike petals. A few are occasionally seen in botanic gardens. *Strophanthus* is from the Greek *strophos*, "twisted cord," and *anthos*, "flower," referring to the twisted petals.

Strophanthus gratus (smooth strophanthus, climbing oleander, *sawai*)
Robust evergreen climber with purple-stalked, leathery, oblong-elliptic leaves. Purple buds expand into night-scented, bell-shaped flowers. Forked fruits, up to 16in (40cm) long, containing brown seeds, develop over 12 months. H 28ft (9m).

STRYCHNOS

Approximately 200 species of mainly evergreen trees, shrubs, and climbers belong to this genus, which is pantropical in distribution; *S. nux-vomica* is found in wooded areas in India and Myanmar (Burma). They are important for their alkaloid content and have little or no ornamental value. Various species are used in curare by native American tribes. This was first observed by Alexander von Humboldt and Aimé Bonpland during their explorations in C and S America (1799–1804).

Strychnos nux-vomica (strychnine, nux-vomica, poison nut)
Evergreen tree with leathery, ovate leaves. Numerous white, green-tinged flowers are produced in terminal clusters in spring, followed by globose, juicy fruits containing 4 disc-shaped seeds. H 70ft (20m), S 50ft (15m).

SYMPHYTUM

A genus of 35 species of hairy perennials ranging through Europe from the Mediterranean to the Caucasus. *S. officinale* and *S.* x *uplandicum* may be grown in damp places and as perennial fodder crops. *S. officinale* was known to the Romans as *conferva* ("join together"), from which the common name "comfrey" is derived. *Symphytum* is derived from the Greek *symphyo*, "make grow together," and *phyton*, "plant." Both names refer to the use of these plants in healing fractures.

Symphytum officinale (comfrey, knitbone)
Stout, bristle-haired perennial with thick, mucilaginous roots and large, tapering, ovate-lanceolate leaves. Purple to white funnel-shaped flowers are borne in summer. H 2–4ft (60cm–1.2m), S 12–24in (30–60cm).

4–9

Symphytum* x *uplandicum (Russian comfrey)
Hybrid between *S. officinale* and *S. asperum*, similar in appearance to the former. It is extremely vigorous, with a thick rhizome and pink flowers that tend to turn blue as they age.
H 6ft (2m), S 3ft (1m).

4–9

***Symphytum* x *uplandicum* 'Variegatum'**
This cultivar has irregular ivory variegation and is less vigorous than *S.* x *uplandicum*. It tends to scorch in full sun. H 3ft (1m), S 24in (60cm).

4–9

SYMPLOCARPUS

This genus of a single species of deciduous perennial occurs in northeastern N America and northeastern Asia. *S. foetidus* is an unusual and interesting plant for the banks of streams and ponds. Its strange inflorescences appear at ground level early in the year, and produce their own internal heat to melt the surrounding snow and attract pollinators. *Symplocarpus* is from the Greek *symploke*, "union," and *karpos*, "fruit," and refers to the coalescence of the ovaries into a single fruit.

Symplocarpus foetidus (skunk cabbage, polecat weed)
Large perennial with a stout, vertical rhizome and ovate–heart-shaped leaves up to 20in (50cm) long. Inflorescences consist of a fleshy, incurved maroon spathe and a rotund, black-maroon spadix. H and S 30in (75cm).

3–7

SYZYGIUM

There are about 450 species of evergreen trees and shrubs in this genus, which occurs throughout Africa, Asia, and Australia. *S. aromaticum* is native to the Moluccas (Spice Islands). The dried flower buds of the plant are sold as cloves and were first used in China (where it was customary to hold a clove in the mouth as a breath-sweetener while addressing the Emperor). The name *Syzygium* comes from the Greek *syzygos*, "joined," and refers to the paired foliage of a Jamaican species.

Syzygium aromaticum (clove)
Small evergreen tree with ascending branches and shiny, leathery, aromatic, ovate-lanceolate leaves, which are salmon pink when young. Fragrant pink flowers are produced in summer, followed by aromatic, purple berries.
H 70ft (20m), S 20–30ft (6–10m).

STRYCHNINE, see *Strychnos nux-vomica*, above
SUCCORY, see *Cichorium intybus*, p.107
SUMAC, see *Rhus*, p.190
SUMMER SAVORY, see *Satureja hortensis*, p.199
SUN ROSE, see *Cistus*, p.108
SUNDEW, see *Drosera*, p.120
SUNFLOWER, see *Helianthus annuus*, p.137
SWALLOW WORT, see *Chelidonium majus*, p.106
SWEET ANNIE, see *ARTEMISIA*, pp.88–9
SWEET BAY, see *Laurus nobilis*, p.147; *Magnolia virginiana*, p.155

TABEBUIA

About 100 species of deciduous and evergreen, mainly spring-flowering trees and shrubs make up this genus, which occurs in C and S America and the W Indies; *T. impetiginosa* is found from northern Mexico to Argentina. Certain species yield extremely durable hardwoods, known to last hundreds of years in tropical climates. Several are grown as ornamentals in the tropics, producing a spectacular display of blossoms before the new leaves appear. They seldom flower in pots.

Tabebuia impetiginosa (*lapacho, pau d'arco, ipê roxa*)
Large tree with smooth, gray bark and dark brown wood. Leaves are divided into leaflets up to 8in (20cm) long. In spring, magenta flowers are followed by cylindrical capsules up to 22in (55cm) long. H 100ft (30m), S 50ft (15m).

TAGETES

A genus of about 50 species of annuals and perennials distributed mainly in tropical and warm parts of the Americas. The Mexican *T. patula* (French marigold), and *T. erecta* (African marigold), feature in religious rituals in both Mexico and India; the association of *T. patula* with All Saints' Day and All Souls' Day in Mexico dates back to pre-Columbian ceremonies. *Tagetes* is named after Tages, an Etruscan deity, who sprang from the earth and revealed the art of water divination.

Tagetes lucida (sweet mace, Mexican marigold, *anisillo*)
Perennial usually grown as an annual, with a thick, woody base and glossy, aromatic, narrowly lanceolate, sharply toothed leaves. Yellow flowers are borne in flat-topped clusters in late summer. H 12–32in (30–80cm), S 18in (45cm).

A

***Tagetes patula* 'Honeycomb'**
This cultivar bears numerous fully double blooms, 2in (5cm) across, with crinkled, deep orange petals edged with yellow. H 10in (25cm), S 8in (20cm).

A

Tagetes minuta (muster-John-Henry, khaki weed, stinking Roger)
Tall annual with leafy, branched stems and strongly aromatic leaves divided into segments up to 6in (15cm) long. Pale yellow flowers are produced in dense clusters in autumn. H 12–36in (30–90cm), S 4–30in (10–75cm).

A

Tagetes patula (French marigold)
Bushy annual with aromatic, deeply divided, sharply toothed leaves up to 3in (8cm) long. Yellow to orange or brown-red flowers, 1–2in (2.5–5cm) across, are borne from early summer to the first frosts. H and S 12in (30cm).

A

TAMARINDUS

This genus contains a single species of evergreen tree, which may have originated in Africa but is now widespread throughout the tropics. *T. indica* has been cultivated in India for centuries and was taken by the Spanish to the W Indies and Mexico in the 17th century. It is now widely grown in the tropics as an ornamental for shade. The name *Tamarindus* comes from the Arabic *tamar-Hindi*, "date of India," and refers to the datelike pulp inside the pods.

Tamarindus indica (tamarind, Indian date)
Graceful tree with spreading branches, rough, gray-black bark, and light green, pinnate leaves. In summer, pale yellow red-veined flowers are followed by brown pods containing kidney-shaped seeds in sticky, brown pulp. H and S 80ft (25m).

SWEET CHESTNUT, see *Castanea sativa*, p.102
SWEET CICELY, see *Myrrhis odorata*, p.162
SWEET FERN, see *Comptonia peregrina*, p.111
SWEET FLAG, see *Acorus calamus*, p.73
SWEET GALE, see *Myrica gale*, p.162
SWEET GRASS, See *Hierochloë odorata*, p.139
SWEET GUM, see *Liquidambar styraciflua*, p.152
SWEET RUSH, SWEET SEDGE, see *Acorus calamus*, p.73
SWEET TEA VINE, see *Gynostemma pentaphyllum*, p.291
SWEET VIOLET, see *Viola odorata*, p.220
SYRIAN RUE, see *Peganum harmala*, p.174

TANACETUM

There are about 70 species of annuals and perennials in this genus, which ranges throughout northern temperate regions. It includes members of the daisy family, formerly classified in *Balsamita*, *Chrysanthemum*, *Matricaria*, and *Pyrethrum*. Many are aromatic, containing pungent volatile oils and insecticidal compounds that may cause unpleasant reactions if handled, or consumed in excess. Some of the perennials become woody and shrublike with age. Many tanacetums tend to spread enthusiastically and need vigilant control in the garden. The name *Tanacetum* is from the Greek *athanasia*, "immortality," and refers to the long-lived flowers of certain species.

► ***Tanacetum balsamita***
(alecost, costmary)
Rhizomatous perennial with oblong, silver-green, mint-scented leaves up to 12in (20cm) long. Clusters of daisy-like flowers are borne on long stalks in late summer. H 32in (80cm), S 24in (60cm).
4–8

◄ ***Tanacetum parthenium* 'Aureum'**
An outstanding cultivar with bright golden foliage that comes true from seed. It makes a striking contrast to bronze-leaved herbs. H and S 8–18in (20–45cm).
4–9

▲ ***Tanacetum balsamita*** var. ***tomentosum*** (camphor plant)
This variety differs from the species in having camphor-scented foliage. H and S 3ft (1m).
4–8

▲ ***Tanacetum parthenium*** (feverfew)
Strong-smelling perennial with yellow-green, pinnately lobed leaves up to 3in (8cm) long. Clusters of daisylike flowers, about ½in (1cm) across, appear in summer. H 24in (60cm), S 18in (45cm).
4–9

▲ ***Tanacetum cinerariifolium***
(pyrethrum, Dalmatian pellitory)
Perennial with slender, hairy stems and oblong to ovate, divided leaves. Solitary flowers with white ray petals and yellow disc florets appear from early summer to early autumn. H 12–30in (30–75cm), S 12in (30cm).
4–9

▲ ***Tanacetum parthenium***
'Golden Ball'
The flowers of this cultivar differ from the species in being rounded and golden yellow. H and S 9in (23cm).
4–9

▲ ***Tanacetum parthenium***
'Golden Moss'
A dwarf cultivar with mosslike, golden foliage. It is mainly grown for edging and carpet bedding. The flowers may be removed as they appear, to retain the foliage effect. H and S 6in (15cm).
4–9

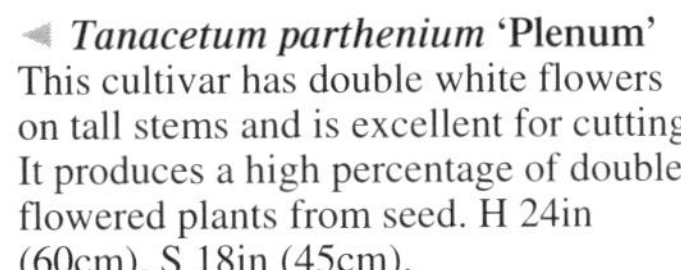

◀ *Tanacetum parthenium* 'Plenum'
This cultivar has double white flowers on tall stems and is excellent for cutting. It produces a high percentage of double-flowered plants from seed. H 24in (60cm), S 18in (45cm).
4–9

▲ *Tanacetum parthenium* 'Snowball'
A double white-flowered cultivar, similar to *T. p.* 'Rowallane', but smaller in habit. It has ivory pompom flowers. H 12in (30cm), S 8in (20cm).
4–9

▲ *Tanacetum parthenium*
'Tom Thumb White Stars'
An excellent cultivar for containers and edging, with a profusion of double white pompom flowers. It is effective with yellow-green herbs, such as *Salvia officinalis* 'Icterina' (see p.196). H and S 9in (23cm).
4–9

▲ *Tanacetum parthenium*
'White Bonnet'
A favorite cultivar among flower arrangers, with double white, green-flecked flowers. H 24in (60cm), S 18in (45cm).
4–9

▲ *Tanacetum vulgare* (tansy)
Strongly aromatic rhizomatous perennial with dark green, pinnately divided leaves up to 5in (12cm) long. Clusters of yellow buttonlike flowers are borne in late summer and autumn. H 2–4ft (60cm–1.2m), S indefinite.
4–9

▲ *Tanacetum vulgare* var. *crispum*
(fern-leaved tansy)
This variety has exquisitely cut leaves, which are particularly attractive in spring. It is a much better garden plant than the species, being more compact and less pungently scented. H 24in (60cm), S indefinite.
4–9

▲ *Tanacetum vulgare* 'Isla Gold'
This recent introduction is the most ornamental tansy to date, with golden foliage that withstands full sun. It arose as a sport at West Acre Gardens, Norfolk, England. H 2–4ft (60cm–1.2m), S indefinite.
4–9

▲ *Tanacetum vulgare* 'Silver Lace'
An unusual cultivar with irregular pale markings on the leaves. It should be planted where easily seen since the variegation is subtle and fades as flowering begins. H 2–4ft (60cm–1.2m), S indefinite.
4–9

TARAXACUM

A genus of about 60 species of perennials found in northern temperate regions and temperate parts of S America. *T. officinale* is grown as a vegetable, particularly in France, where improved forms were selected during the 19th century. Like chicory, it is bitter but may be blanched or soaked in water for an hour or so before use. The name *Taraxacum* comes from the medieval Latin, which in turn was derived from the Arabic *tarakhshaqún*, "wild chicory," or "bitter herb."

Taraxacum officinale (dandelion)
Variable perennial with a thick taproot, white latex, and a basal rosette of toothed to lobed leaves. Solitary bright yellow flowers appear from spring to autumn, followed by ribbed fruits bearing a tuft of fine white hairs. H 12in (30cm), S 18in (45cm).

3–10

TETRADIUM

This genus of about 10 species of evergreen and deciduous trees and shrubs occurs in the Himalayas and southern and eastern Asia. It is closely related to *Euodia* and *Ravensara*, and resembles *Phellodendron* in appearance. *T. ruticarpum* is found in well-drained forests and thickets in China and Taiwan. Several species are grown for their attractive leaves and large clusters of fruits. *Tetradium* is from the Greek *tetradeion*, "quaternion," since the floral parts are in fours.

Tetradium ruticarpum
Deciduous shrub or small tree with leaves to 16in (40cm) long, divided into 7–15 ovate leaflets. Small off-white flowers are produced in clusters in summer, followed by conspicuous warty rust-red fruits containing glossy black seeds. H 28ft (9m), S 15ft (5m).

TAXUS

This genus includes 10 species of evergreen coniferous trees and shrubs, occurring throughout northern temperate zones. Male and female flowers are usually borne on separate plants. *T. brevifolia* is found along the Pacific coast of N America and inland from southeastern British Columbia to northern Idaho. The English yew (*T. baccata*) is long-lived, with reliable records dating some British trees to at least 1,500 years ago. All parts of both species are very poisonous.

Taxus brevifolia (Pacific yew)
Small tree with slender, drooping branches, scaly, red-purple bark, and linear, leathery leaves. Small cream flowers appear in spring; female flowers are followed by poisonous, green-brown seeds, which are surrounded by a fleshy red aril. H 50ft (15m), S 30ft (10m).

5–8

TEUCRIUM

This cosmopolitan genus of about 240 species of perennials and small evergreen and semideciduous shrubs is centered on the Mediterranean region. *T. chamaedrys*, found throughout Europe and southwestern Asia, is a useful small evergreen for steep banks, walls, and edging; it is commonly confused with *T. divaricatum* (hedge germander) and *T.* x *lucidrys*. Both are often planted as a dwarf hedge in knot gardens, for which purpose the smaller, more spreading *T. chamaedrys* is unsuitable.

Teucrium chamaedrys (wall germander)
Shrubby perennial with a creeping rootstock, upright to spreading stems, and shiny, ovate leaves, resembling tiny oak leaves, that are aromatic when crushed. Small, purple-pink, 2-lipped, tubular flowers appear in summer and autumn. H and S 4–10in (10–24cm).

5–9

TERMINALIA

A genus of about 200 species of evergreen and deciduous, tropical trees and shrubs, which occurs in most tropical regions; *T. chebula* is found in Sri Lanka, India, Myanmar (Burma), and Nepal, and is widely grown in the tropics as a shade tree and an ornamental. They include lumber trees and sources of gums, dyes, and tannin. Trees characteristically have their foliage arranged in tiers at the tips of branches, hence the generic name, *Terminalia*, from the Latin *terminus*, "end."

Terminalia chebula (myrobalan, black chebulic, *haritaki*)
Evergreen tree with leathery, ovate, pointed leaves, which have woolly undersides. Tiny, odoriferous, cream flowers appear in summer, followed by ovoid-oblong, yellow-brown fruits. H 50–80ft (15–25m), S 70ft (20m).

THEOBROMA

A genus of 20 species of evergreen tropical American trees; *T. cacao* occurs in lowland tropical forests of C and S America. They are unusual in bearing flowers directly from the trunk or branches, a habit known as "cauliflory." Although cocoa fruits were first brought to Spain from S America by Christopher Columbus (1451–1506), the taste for cocoa did not develop until the 17th century. Africa began cocoa cultivation in the 19th century and now produces over half of all cocoa beans.

Theobroma cacao (cacao, cocoa, chocolate tree)
Small evergreen tree with thin, glossy leaves up to 16in (40cm) long, which are pink when young. Small pale yellow flowers are followed by pods containing numerous seeds in a mucilaginous pulp. H 25ft (8m), S 15–20ft (5–6m).

TAR WEED, see *Eriodictyon californicum*, p.279
TARRAGON, see *ARTEMISIA*, pp.88–9
TARWEED, see *Grindelia camporum*, p.290
TASMANIAN BLUE GUM, see *Eucalyptus globulus*, p.125
TATARIAN ASTER, see *Aster tataricus*, p.245
TAVOY CARDAMOM, see *Amomum xanthioides*, p.237
TEA, see *Camellia sinensis*, p.99
TEABERRY, see *Gaultheria procumbens*, p.132
TEINTURIER GRAPE, see *Vitis vinifera* 'Purpurea', p.221
TEREBINTH TREE, see *Pistacia terebinthus*, p.178

THUJA

This genus of five species of evergreen coniferous trees occurs in northeastern Asia and N America. *T. occidentalis* was important to many native N Americans, since it provided materials for bows, canoes, baskets, cordage, and roofing. Both *T. occidentalis* and *T. orientalis* have numerous cultivars varying in size, habit, and color, making them some of the most versatile conifers for garden use. *Thuja* is the original Greek name used by Theophrastus for a kind of juniper.

Thuja occidentalis (American arborvitae, eastern white cedar)
Narrow conifer with orange-brown bark and tiny scalelike leaves that turn bronze in winter and have an apple scent when crushed. Yellow-green cones, ½in (1cm) long, turn brown and pendulous when ripe. H 60ft (20m), S 22ft (7m).

2–9

***Thuja occidentalis* 'Rheingold'**
Probably the most popular and distinctive of all *T. occidentalis* cultivars on account of its gold foliage, which bronzes in winter. H 10–12ft (3–4m), S 6–12ft (2–4m).

2–9

Thuja orientalis (Chinese arborvitae)
Pyramidal shrub or small tree with red-brown, fibrous bark and vertical sprays of very small, scalelike leaves, which usually turn bronze or brown in winter. Upright, gray-bloomed cones, ¾in (2cm) long, are flask-shaped.
H 40ft (12m), S 15ft (5m).

5–9

***Thuja occidentalis* 'Holmstrup'**
This cultivar makes a dense, conical tree with rich green foliage. H 10–12ft (3–4m), S 3ft (1m).

2–9

***Thuja orientalis* 'Aurea Nana'**
A neat, dwarf cultivar with yellow-green foliage that bronzes in winter.
H and S 24in (60cm).

5–9

TETTERWORT, see *Chelidonium majus*, p.106
TEXAS SAGE, see *SALVIA*, pp.196–7
THORN, see *Crataegus*, p.112
THORN APPLE, see *Datura stramonium*, p.116
THOROUGHWORT, see *Eupatorium fortunei*, p.126; *Eupatorium perfoliatum*, p.126
THOROW-WAX, see *Bupleurum*, p.96

THYMUS

Some 350 species of small, evergreen, aromatic, mostly woody-based perennials, and subshrubs belong to this Eurasian genus. They have typical labiate flowers, with 5 sepals fused into a 2-lipped tube, a bearded throat, and a broad, 3-toothed upper lip. The taxonomy of thymes is complex, with numerous synonyms and invalid names. Many thymes are good garden plants, with a neat habit, fragrant foliage, and colorful flowers. They are ideal for rock gardens, walls, and containers. Although tiny, the numerous flowers produce copious nectar, and make many species important as bee plants. *Thymus* is the original Greek name used by Theophrastus for both thyme and savory.

▲ ***Thymus herba-barona***
(caraway thyme)
Wiry, carpeting subshrub with minute, dark green leaves, which may smell of caraway, nutmeg, or lemon. Loose clusters of pink to mauve flowers appear midsummer. H 2–4in (5–10cm), S 24in (60cm).
6–8

▲ ***Thymus caespititius* 'Aureus'**
A slow-growing cultivar with narrow, pale golden-green leaves and pink flowers. H 6in (15cm), S 18in (45cm).
8–9

◄ ***Thymus capitatus***
(conehead thyme)
Compact shrublet with gray stems and linear leaves. Pink flowers appear in summer. H and S 10in (25cm).
9

▲ ***Thymus cilicicus*** (Cilician thyme)
Compact, bushy shrublet with deep green, linear leaves. It bears dense clusters of mauve to lilac flowers in midsummer. H 4–6in (10–15cm), S 18in (45cm).
6–8

◄ ***Thymus* x *citriodorus***
(lemon thyme)
Variable hybrid between *T. pulegioides* and *T. vulgaris*, with lemon-scented, ovate to lanceolate leaves. Pale lilac flowers appear in summer. H 10–12in (25–30cm), S 24in (60cm).
5–9

▲ ***Thymus* x *citriodorus* 'Archer's Gold'**
A compact cultivar with bright yellow, lemon-scented foliage and pale purple flowers; named after Bill Archer who discovered it in Somerset, England. H 6–9in (15–23cm), S 18 in (45cm).
5–9

► ***Thymus* x *citriodorus* 'Bertram Anderson'**
This low-growing cultivar has red-tinged new growths and golden foliage. H 6–9in (15–23cm), S 12–24in (30–60cm).
5–9

◄ ***Thymus* x *citriodorus* 'Aureus'**
(golden lemon thyme)
Small, upright to spreading shrublet with gold-splashed leaves that are most colorful in winter and early spring. Tends to revert. H 4–6in (10–15cm), S 24in (60cm).
5–9

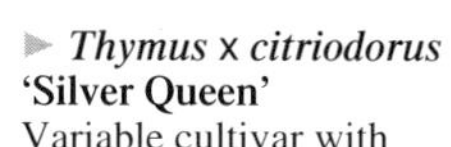

► ***Thymus* x *citriodorus* 'Silver Queen'**
Variable cultivar with silver-green to cream-marbled leaves. It differs from *T. vulgaris* 'Silver Posie' in being less hardy and more liable to revert, and in having more variable variegation, pink-tinged tips in winter, and a lemon scent. H 9in (23cm), S 12–16in (30–40cm).
5–9

▲ *Thymus praecox* (creeping thyme, wild thyme)
Variable mat-forming creeper with tiny, lanceolate-obovate, hair-fringed leaves. Mauve to purple, rarely off-white, flowers with purple leaflike bracts are borne in terminal clusters in summer. H 2in (5cm), S 18in (45cm).
5–8

▲ *Thymus pseudolanuginosus* (woolly thyme)
Prostrate shrublet with 4-sided, hairy stems and tiny, elliptic, gray-green, woolly leaves. Pale pink flowers appear sparsely in the leaf axils in midsummer. H 1–3in (2.5–7cm), S 3ft (1m).
6–8

▲ *Thymus serpyllum* 'Pink Chintz'
A vigorous cultivar with gray-green hairy leaves and pale, salmon-pink flowers. Discovered as a seedling on the rock garden at the Royal Horticultural Society's garden, Wisley, England, in 1939. H ½–3in (1–7cm), S 24in (60cm).
4–8

▲ *Thymus serpyllum* 'Rainbow Falls'
This colorful cultivar has small, gold-variegated, red-flushed leaves and mauve flowers. It has long stems and a rather lax habit. H ½–3in (1–7cm), S 3ft (1m).
4–8

► *Thymus pulegioides* (broad-leaved thyme, large thyme)
Sprawling, highly aromatic dwarf shrub with ovate-elliptic, flat leaves. Pink to purple flowers with leaflike bracts appear in summer. H 8–10in (20–25cm), S 16–18in (40–45cm).
4–8

► *Thymus serpyllum* 'Russetings'
The dark, bronze-tinted foliage of this cultivar is quite distinctive. Indispensable in plantings of mixed thymes. H ½–3in (1–7cm), S 3ft (1m).
4–8

► *Thymus serpyllum* 'Vey'
A very compact cultivar with upright heads of dark-budded, salmon-pink flowers. It was introduced in the 1980s and is a good choice for containers. H ½–3in (1–7cm), S 18in (45cm).
4–8

▲ *Thymus serpyllum* var. *coccineus* (red-flowered thyme)
One of the most vividly colored thymes, with bright crimson-magenta flowers and dark green leaves that turn bronze in autumn. H ½–3in (1–7cm), S 3ft (1m).
4–8

◄ *Thymus serpyllum* 'Annie Hall'
A popular cultivar dating back to 1924, with light green leaves and pale pink flowers. H ½–3in (1–7cm), S 3ft (1m).
4–8

▲ *Thymus vulgaris* (common thyme)
Variable shrub with gray-green leaves, and white to pale purple flowers in summer. H 12–18in (30–45cm), S 24in (60cm).
4–8

▲ *Thymus serpyllum* (wild thyme, creeping thyme, mother of thyme)
Variable, prostrate perennial with slender, creeping stems and tiny, ovate to oblong, hairy leaves. Clusters of pink to purple flowers appear in summer. H ½–3in (1–7cm), S 3ft (1m).
4–8

▲ *Thymus serpyllum* 'Elfin'
A diminutive, shy-flowering thyme with minute, glossy, rounded leaves and a hummock-forming habit. A few clusters of magenta-pink flowers may be produced in summer. H 2in (5cm), S 4-8in (10–20cm).
4–8

▲ *Thymus vulgaris* 'Erectus' (upright thyme)
This white-flowered cultivar resembles a diminutive conifer in habit, with strongly upright growth and narrow, gray-green, camphor-scented leaves. H 6–9in (15–23cm), S 4–6in (10–15cm).
5–8

▲ *Thymus vulgaris* 'Silver Posie'
The best of the silver thymes, with white-variegated leaves and pale, mauve-pink flowers. It remains in good condition through the winter. Ideal for edging and planting en masse for color effect. H 10in (25cm), S 18in (45cm).
7–8

TILIA

A genus of about 45 species of deciduous trees found throughout northern temperate regions; *T. cordata* is found in woods in central and eastern Europe. Most species are in cultivation and will hybridize readily. Linden honey and linden tea are important local products. *T. cordata* does not tend to sucker or become infested with aphids, and is thus a better subject for gardens than *T.* x *europaea* (common linden) or *T. platyphyllos* (broad leaved linden).

Tilia cordata (small-leaved linden)
Medium to large, spreading tree with dark green, shiny, heart-shaped leaves. Yellow-white flowers appear in mid-summer, followed by round, green fruits, 1/4in (6mm) across. H 70–130ft (20–40m), S 30–100ft (10–30m).

4–8

***Trifolium pratense* 'Susan Smith'**
This cultivar is prized by collectors of variegated plants. The leaves are patterned with a fine network of yellow veins. It may be grown as a semi-prostrate plant in the open ground or as a trailer in containers. H 8–20in (20–50cm), S 20in (50cm).

4–8

TRICHOSANTHES

A genus of 15 species of annual and perennial, half-hardy to tropical climbers, which ranges across Indo-Malaysia to the Pacific islands. *T. kirilowii*, found in Mongolia, China, and Vietnam, is probably the hardiest species in the genus and is cultivated as a medicinal herb in southern China, male plants being preferred for root production. It is rarely seen in the West. *Trichosanthes* is from the Greek *thrix*, "hair," and *anthos*, "flower," and refers to the fringed flowers.

Trichosanthes kirilowii (snake gourd, Chinese cucumber)
Perennial, tuberous, tendril climber with deeply lobed leaves. In summer, fringed white female flowers are followed by orange-red fruits containing pale brown seeds. Male and female flowers appear on separate plants. H 20–28ft (6–9m).

TRIGONELLA

This genus of 80 species of annuals extends from the Mediterranean to southern Africa and Australia. *T. foenum-graecum* is grown as a fodder crop in southern and central Europe, and as a spice in most Mediterranean countries, the Middle East, Russia, the Balkans, western Asia, and China. It is widely naturalized. *Trigonella* is from *trigonus*, "triangular," referring to the flower shape. *Foenum-graecum* means "Greek hay," because the plant was once grown as a fodder crop in Greece.

Trigonella foenum-graecum (fenugreek)
Erect, aromatic annual with trifoliate leaves. In spring and summer, solitary or paired yellow-white flowers tinged violet at the base are followed by beaked pods with yellow-brown seeds. H 24in (60cm), S 12–18in (30–45cm).

A

TRIFOLIUM

This large genus of about 230 species of annuals, biennials, and perennials is found through temperate and subtropical regions, and is naturalized in N America and Australia. *T. pratense* is found throughout Europe and has been important since the Middle Ages as a forage crop. The agricultural cultivar *T. p.* 'Broad Red' has been widely grown since the 17th century. *Trifolium* is from the Latin *tri*, "three," and *folium*, "leaf," and refers to the 3-lobed leaves.

Trifolium pratense (red clover, purple clover)
Erect to sprawling, short-lived perennial with long-stalked leaves divided into 3 obovate leaflets. Purple-pink, sometimes cream tubular flowers are borne in globose heads from late spring. H 8–24in (20–60cm), S 24in (60cm).

3–8

TRILLIUM

There are about 30 species of rhizomatous perennials in this genus, which occurs in N America and northeastern Asia. *T. erectum* is grown as an ornamental in the wild garden and shady border for its attractive, angular foliage and for its flowers, which contrast with more delicate spring-flowering woodland herbs, such as *Sanguinaria canadensis* (see p.198) and *Primula vulgaris* (see p.183). The name *Trillium* comes from the Latin *trilix*, "triple," because all parts of these plants are tripartite.

Trillium erectum (bethroot, wake robin, birthroot)
Variable perennial with a short, thick rootstock, erect stem, and 3 broadly ovate leaves up to 8in (20cm) long. The fetid flower has 3 pale green sepals and 3 maroon to white petals in late spring. H 12–20in (30–50cm), S 12in (30cm).

3–8

TINNEVELLY SENNA, see *Senna alexandrina*, p.202
TOADFLAX, see *Linaria*, p.152
TOLU BALSAM, see *Myroxylon balsamum*, p.162
TONKA BEAN, TONQUIN BEAN, see *Dipteryx odorata*, p.274
TOOTHACHE TREE, see *Zanthoxylum americanum*, p.222
TOOTHBRUSH TREE, see *Salvadora persica*, p.345
TORCHWOOD, see *Bursera*, p.251
TORMENTIL, see *Potentilla erecta*, p.183
TRAGACANTH, see *Astragalus gummifer*, p.245

Trillium erectum* f. *albiflorum
The white-flowered variety shows up well in shady positions, especially from a distance. H 12–20in (30–50cm), S 12in (30cm).

3–8

***Tropaeolum majus* 'Alaska'**
The leaves of this cultivar are irregularly marbled with creamy white. Flower color ranges from yellow to red, orange-red, and mahogany. It has a bushy habit and makes an excellent subject for hanging baskets and the front of borders. H and S 12in (30cm).

A

TROPAEOLUM

A genus of about 90 species of mostly climbing annuals and herbaceous perennials native to S America. Nasturtiums are among the most easily grown hardy annuals. Climbing or vining cultivars may cover large areas of a fence or bank within a few weeks of germination, and the more compact kinds are ideal for summer bedding and containers. *Tropaeolum* is from the Greek *tropaion*, "trophy," since the leaves are shaped like round shields, above which are the helmetlike flowers.

Tropaeolum majus (garden nasturtium, Indian cress)
Fast-growing trailing annual with almost circular, peltate leaves. Yellow to orange, long-spurred, slightly scented flowers, sometimes red-blotched, appear from early summer, followed by globose fruits. H 10ft (3m), S 5–6ft (1.5–2m).

A

***Tropaeolum majus* 'Empress of India'**
This cultivar dates back to the 19th century. It has dark, violet-green leaves and scented, vivid crimson flowers. H 9in (23cm), S 12in (30cm).

A

TRAILING ARBUTUS, see *Epigaea repens*, p.123
TREE OF HEAVEN, see *Ailanthus altissima*, p.76
TREE ONION, see *ALLIUM*, pp.80–81
TREE PEONY, see *Paeonia suffruticosa*, p.170
TREE WORMWOOD, see *ARTEMISIA*, pp.88–9
TRICOLOR SAGE, see *SALVIA*, pp.196–7
TRIFID BUR MARIGOLD, see *Bidens tripartita*, p.94

***Tropaeolum majus* 'Hermine Grashoff'**
One of the earliest double-flowered cultivars, listed in 19th-century gardening manuals, with orange-scarlet flowers. Being sterile, it must be propagated vegetatively. H 8in (20m) 18–24in (45–60cm).

A

***Tropaeolum majus* 'Peach Melba'**
A compact, floriferous cultivar with creamy yellow, single flowers blotched with scarlet in the throat. It is excellent for containers and for using in salads. H 9–12in (23–30cm), S 12in (30cm).

A

TUSSILAGO

A genus of 15 species of rhizomatous perennials ranging throughout northern temperate regions. *T. farfara* is found in Europe, western Asia, and northern Africa. Although too invasive for general garden use, it can be grown in the wild garden or where its spread can be contained. A variegated cultivar was known in the 19th century but is now lost to cultivation. *Tussilago* is from the Latin *tussis*, "cough," and refers to the antitussive effects of *T. farfara*.

Tussilago farfara (coltsfoot)
Robust, creeping perennial with large, heart-shaped to rounded, toothed leaves, which have a cobweblike covering. In early spring, dandelionlike flowers appear on woolly, scaly stalks before the leaves. H 12in (30cm), S indefinite.

3–7

TYPHA

A cosmopolitan aquatic genus of about 12 species of stout, rhizomatous, reedlike perennials. *T. latifolia* and its variegated cultivar are grown as ornamentals in ponds and lakes for their imposing foliage and decorative brown seedheads, which are dried for floral arrangements. Although sometimes called "bulrush," *T. latifolia* is quite different from the plant referred to by this name in the Bible, which is *Cyperus papyrus*. *Typha* is the original Greek name used by Theophrastus for this plant.

Typha latifolia (cattail, great reedmace)
Giant perennial with a long, branched rhizome and linear leaves up to 6ft (2m) long. Minute beige flowers appear on a long-stalked, cylindrical spike. Dark brown seedheads release seeds in spring. H 8ft (2.5m), S indefinite.

2–9

***Typha latifolia* 'Variegata'**
This variegated cultivar is smaller-growing than the species and better for garden pools. H 4ft (1.2m), S 2ft (60cm).

2–9

TRUE UNICORN ROOT, see *Aletris farinosa*, p.232
TRUMPET TREE, see *Tabebuia impetiginosa*, p.207
TUCKAHOE, see *Wolfiporia cocos*, p.372
TULSI, see *OCIMUM*, pp.166–7
TURMERIC, see *Curcuma longa*, p.114
TURNIP-ROOTED PARSLEY, see *Petroselinum crispum* var. *tuberosum*, p.174
TURTLEHEAD, see *Chelone glabra*, p.106
TWITCH, see *Elymus repens*, p.122
TWO-TOOTHED AMARANTHUS, see *Achyranthes bidentata*, p.72
UVA-URSI, see *Arctostaphylos uva-ursi*, p.86
VALERIAN, see *Valeriana officinalis*, above

ULMUS

Some 45 species of deciduous trees and shrubs belong to this genus, distributed in northern temperate regions from Mexico to central Asia. *U. rubra*, found from southern Canada to C America, is one of the most distinctive elms with its woolly buds and large, velvety leaves, which are red-flushed when young. It is planted as a street tree in the US, but it is rarely cultivated elsewhere. Stocks of the trees have been severely depleted by overexploitation and Dutch elm disease.

Ulmus rubra (slippery elm, red elm)
Medium to large tree with a broad crown and obovate, hairy, deeply veined leaves, reaching 8in (20cm) long. In early summer, inconspicuous flowers are followed by red-brown winged fruits consisting of a single seed.
H 70ft (20m), S 60ft (18m).

3–10

VACCINIUM

This large genus includes some 450 species of evergreen and deciduous, often stoloniferous shrubs, which range throughout the northern hemisphere and southern Africa. *V. myrtillus* is seldom cultivated, but bilberries are commonly harvested from the wild in parts of Europe. Highbush blueberries, derived from *V. corymbosum*, and rabbit-eye blueberries, from *V. ashei*, are preferred commercially and are grown on a large scale in the US, Australia, and New Zealand.

Vaccinium myrtillus (bilberry, huckleberry, whortleberry)
Deciduous shrub with creeping rhizomes, erect green stems, and ovate, bright green leaves. Small, bell-shaped, pink-green flowers appear in spring, followed by sweet fruits, blue-black when ripe. H and S 24in (60cm).

2–7

UMBELLULARIA

Two species make up this genus of evergreen trees, which occurs in western N America. *U. californica* is a baylike, shrubby tree, which needs a sheltered position in cold areas to prevent frost damage to new growth. It is generally found in canyon bottoms and flood plains below 5,000ft (1,500m). The leaves are so pungently aromatic that inhaling their scent may cause a headache. *Umbellularia* comes from the Latin *umbella*, "umbel," and refers to the shape of the inflorescence.

Umbellularia californica (California laurel, headache tree, California sassafras)
Large evergreen shrub with glossy leaves that have a strong, acrid aroma. Tiny pale green flowers appear in spring, followed by pearlike, purple-brown fruits. H 80ft (25m), S 50in (15m)

9–10

VALERIANA

A genus of 150–200 species of perennials, which occur worldwide except for Australia. *V. officinalis*, found widely in Europe and east to Japan, is a fine, tall plant for the back of borders and woodland gardens. The scent of the roots, especially when dried, attracts cats; some cats find the smell of valerian-based herb teas quite irresistible and will search out discarded tea bags. *V. officinalis* should not be confused with *Centranthus ruber* (red valerian), a garden plant with no medicinal uses.

Valeriana officinalis (common valerian, garden heliotrope)
Variable perennial with a short rhizome and pinnate, irregularly divided leaves. Dense clusters of small, scented, pink or white flowers appear in summer, followed by tiny seeds with a tuft of white hairs. H 5ft (1.5m), S 4ft (1.2m).

5–9

URTICA

A genus of about 50 species of annuals and perennials, widespread in temperate regions. *U. dioica*, found throughout Eurasia, is an all-too-familiar weed of human habitation, thriving in the nitrogen-rich soil of cultivated land. As Culpeper wrote, stinging nettles "need no description; they may be found by feeling, in the darkest night" (*The English Physitian Enlarged, or the Herball,* 1653). *Urtica* is the original Latin name used by Horace and Pliny for the plant.

Urtica dioica (stinging nettle, nettle)
Coarse perennial with creeping yellow roots and ovate, deeply toothed leaves covered with bristly, stinging hairs. In summer, minute green flowers, with male and female on separate plants, are borne in pendulous clusters up to 4in (10cm) long. H 5ft (1.5m), S indefinite.

3–10

VANILLA

There are about 100 species of climbing evergreen perennials in this genus of orchids, which occurs through the tropics and subtropics. *V. planifolia*, native to thickets in S America, the W Indies, and Florida, is the only member of the vast Orchidaceae family that is cultivated for a commercial product rather than as an ornamental. Orchid growers often train a vanilla vine on a greenhouse wall, and *V. planifolia* 'Variegata' is particularly attractive for this purpose.

Vanilla planifolia (vanilla)
Stout climbing orchid with green zigzag stems and fleshy, oblong leaves. Pale yellow-green flowers, 2in (5cm) across with a yellow-haired lip, appear in spring, followed by pendent capsules up to 7in (18cm) long, containing minute seeds. H 20ft (6m).

Vanilla planifolia 'Variegata'
An unusual, robust, variegated orchid with irregularly yellow-striped leaves. It is well worth planting in an orchid house because it differs in both habit and coloration from most ornamental orchids, and it provides year-round interest. H 20ft (6m).

VERONICA

This genus includes some 250 species of hardy, mostly blue flowered annuals, perennials, and both evergreen and semievergreen subshrubs, which occur in Europe, N America, and temperate parts of Asia. Those in cultivation range from elegant border plants and aquatics to shrubs and mat-forming plants suitable for the rock garden. Many speedwells have variants with pink, white, or purple flowers, as is common with most blue-flowered species.

Veronica officinalis (common speedwell, heath speedwell, fluellen)
Creeping, mat-forming, hairy perennial with ovate-elliptic, toothed leaves up to 2½in (5cm) long, and racemes of lilac, finely veined flowers from late spring through summer. H 4–20in (10–50cm), S indefinite.

3–9

VERBASCUM

A large genus of about 300 species of annuals, biennials, perennials, and subshrubs, which is distributed throughout Europe, northern Africa, and Asia. *V. thapsus*, found throughout Europe and east to western China, is a stately plant with woolly foliage and spires of yellow flowers. It tolerates a wide range of conditions, including dry, stony soils, and is suited to the border, steep banks, or the edges of a gravel drive. *Verbascum* is the Latin name used by Pliny for the plant.

Verbascum thapsus (great mullein, Aaron's rod)
Tall biennial with soft, gray-green, woolly leaves, obovate and up to 18in (45cm) long, forming a basal rosette in the first year. Yellow, 5-petaled flowers are borne in summer in a dense terminal spike. H 6ft (2m), S 3ft (1m).

5–9

VERONICASTRUM

A single species of perennial belongs to this genus, which occurs in eastern N America. *V. virginicum* is a tall, graceful plant for the back of the border and wild garden, introduced to European gardens in 1714. It varies in flower color, and named varieties are available to give reliably pink- or white-flowered plants. It played a role in certain native N American rituals, but the first settler to make use of this herb was Dr. Culver, hence the common names "Culver's root" and "Culver's physic."

Veronicastrum virginicum (Culver's root, blackroot)
Upright perennial with horizontal black rhizomes and whorls of pointed, finely toothed, oblanceolate leaves. Small, tubular, white or pink flowers are borne in terminal clusters of dense spikes in summer. H 6ft (2m), S 3ft (1m).

3–9

Veronicastrum virginicum var. ***roseum***
This variety has pale pink flowers and is especially handsome against bronze-leaved herbs. H 6ft (2m), S 3ft (1m).

3–9

VERBENA

This genus of about 250 species of annuals, perennials, and subshrubs is distributed mainly in tropical and temperate parts of the Americas, with two European species. *V. officinalis*, found in Europe, western Asia, and northern Africa, cannot compare in ornamental value with its S American relatives but is often grown for medicinal use. Verbena was revered in Celtic and Germanic cultures, used by the Druids, and held sacred by the Romans. It is reputed to heal holes in the aura.

Verbena officinalis (vervain)
Perennial with a woody base, 4-angled, branched stems, and ovate, often pinnately cut leaves up to 2½in (6cm) long. Tiny pale lilac flowers are borne on slender, terminal spikes in summer. H 32in (80cm), S 24in (60cm).

4–8

VANILLA, see *Vanilla planifolia*, p.217
VANILLA GRASS, see *Hierochloë odorata*, p.139
VARIEGATED GROUND IVY, see *Glechoma hederacea* 'Variegata', p.134
VASAK, see *Justicia adhatoda*, p.299
VEGETABLE MERCURY, see *Brunfelsia uniflora*, p.95
VERVAIN, see *Verbena officinalis*, above
VETIVER, see *Vetiveria zizanioides*, above

VETIVERIA

Ten species of perennial grasses make up this genus distributed throughout tropical Asia. *V. zizanioides* is an extremely useful, large, coarse grass. It is grown mainly in Haiti, Réunion, and Java for essential oil, and in many parts of the world to control erosion, since the aromatic roots grow straight down for 10ft (3m). In India the grass is traditionally woven into screens, which are hung in doorways and windows and sprayed with water to keep rooms cool and free from insects.

Vetiveria zizanioides (vetiver, *khus khus*)
Robust, giant grass with fibrous, spongy roots and rigid, linear leaves up to 3–6ft (1–2m) long. Brown to purple, tiny flowers are produced in long-stalked spikes up to 5ft (1.5m) tall in summer. H 6–9ft (2–3m), S indefinite.

9–10

***Viburnum opulus* 'Roseum'** (snowball bush)
A favorite garden shrub, on account of its conspicuous, creamy white, ball-shaped flower heads composed entirely of sterile flowers. This cultivar is of interest only in bloom because it does not bear fruit. H and S 12ft (4m).

3–9

VIBURNUM

A genus of about 150 species of evergreen and deciduous shrubs and small trees distributed widely in most temperate and warm areas, especially Asia and N America. *V. opulus*, found through Europe to northwestern Asia, is an excellent garden shrub with delightful flowers and early ripening, brightly colored fruits. *V. prunifolium* has the largest fruits of any viburnum and brilliant autumn color. It may be grown as a small garden tree if restricted to a single trunk.

Viburnum opulus (crampbark, guelder rose)
Deciduous shrub with 3- or 5-lobed, toothed leaves. Flat-topped clusters of tiny flowers, surrounded by conspicuous white, sterile flowers, appear in summer, followed by pendent clusters of glossy, scarlet, oval fruits. H and S 12ft (4m).

3–9

***Viburnum opulus* 'Aureum'**
This cultivar has a compact habit and bright golden leaves, which tend to scorch in full sun. H and S 12ft (4m).

3–9

***Viburnum opulus* 'Xanthocarpum'**
The fruits of this cultivar differ from the equally popular *V. o.* 'Fructuluteo' in being a translucent golden yellow with no hint of pink. H and S 12ft (4m).

3–9

VINCA

A genus of six species of low, evergreen subshrubs and herbaceous perennials, which ranges throughout Europe, northern Africa, and western Asia. *V. major* and its many cultivars are excellent for containers and groundcover, providing glossy, often variegated leaves and large, colorful flowers. They thrive in shade but flower more freely in sun. *Vinca* is from *pervinca*, the Latin for "periwinkle," derived from *vincire*, "to bind," because the long, trailing shoots were used to make wreaths.

Vinca major (greater periwinkle)
Arching to prostrate or trailing evergreen subshrub with stems rooting at the tips and broadly ovate, glossy leaves. Blue, propeller-shaped flowers, 1½in (4cm) across, appear in the axils of short, erect, flowering stems in spring. H 18in (45cm), S indefinite.

7–9

Vinca major 'Reticulata'
A choice cultivar, best grown on a bank or over a wall so that its unusual, gold-veined variegation can be appreciated. The flowers are the same color as those of the species. H 18in (45cm), S indefinite.

7–9

Vinca major 'Variegata'
This is probably the most widely grown cultivar, with flowers similar to those of the species and irregularly cream-variegated foliage, which gives a pleasantly light effect in shady positions. H 18in (45cm), S indefinite.

7–9

***Vinca major* 'Maculata'**
An unusual variegated cultivar with gold-splashed leaf centers and large, light blue flowers. H 18in (45cm), **S indefinite.**

7–9

VIOLA

A large genus of some 500 species of mostly annuals and perennials distributed throughout temperate regions. The European *V. odorata* was grown commercially in Greece as early as 400BC for sale in the market in Athens. It reached cult status during the reign of Queen Victoria (1837–1901), and was grown on a vast scale for cut flowers and perfumery. Most of the highly scented 19th-century cultivars became scarce or extinct during World Wars I and II.

Viola odorata (violet, sweet violet)
Perennial with long stolons and broadly ovate to heart-shaped leaves. Dark purple or white, occasionally yellow, sweetly scented flowers appear from late winter to late spring, followed by globose capsules. H 6in (15cm), S 12in (30cm).

6–9

***Viola odorata* 'Alba'**
This is the most widely grown cultivar. It has pure white flowers that are produced prolifically in good years. H 6in (15cm), S 12in (30cm).

6–9

Viola tricolor (heartsease, wild pansy)
Annual, biennial, or short-lived perennial with ovate to lanceolate, toothed to lobed leaves. Pansylike flowers in various combinations of purple, lilac, white, and yellow are produced in spring and summer. H and S 15in (38cm).

4–9

VIOLET, see *Viola odorata*, above
VIRGINIA BUGLEWEED, see *Lycopus virginicus*, p.154
VIRGINIA MOUNTAIN MINT, see *Pycnanthemum virginianum*, p.187
VIRGINIA SNAKEROOT, see *Aristolochia serpentaria*, p.241
VIRGINIA SKULLCAP, see *Scutellaria lateriflora*, p.201
WEST INDIAN WILD CINNAMON, see *Canella winterana*, p.99
WAFER ASH, see *Ptelea trifoliata*, p.185
WAHOO, see *Euonymus atropurpureus*, p.125
WAKE ROBIN, see *Trillium erectum*, p.214
WALL GERMANDER, see *Teucrium chamaedrys*, p.210

VISCUM

Occurring throughout temperate regions, this genus includes about 70 species of parasitic evergreen shrubs. *V. album* is found in Europe east to the Caucasus. It is not difficult to grow mistletoe if a suitable host plant is available, such as an apple tree, in the garden. Orchards are often used for commercial crops, thereby yielding a return in winter, when the trees are dormant, as well as in summer. *Viscum* is the original Latin name, meaning both "mistletoe," and "birdlime."

Viscum album (mistletoe)
Evergreen shrub, parasitic on apple, linden, poplar, maple, hawthorn, and mountain ash trees. It has regularly branched stems and leathery, obovate, yellow-green leaves. Tiny, yellow flowers are followed by poisonous, sticky white fruits. H and S 3ft (1m).
7–10

VITIS

A genus of some 65 species of sprawling deciduous vines and shrubs occurring throughout the northern hemisphere and most common in N America. *V. vinifera* probably originated in northwest Asia. It has hundreds of cultivars adapted to various climatic and pruning regimes, grown specifically for use as dessert or table grapes, raisins, juice, and red or white wines. Some are suited to greenhouse culture and make an attractive feature in conservatories.

Vitis vinifera (grape)
Deciduous tendril climber with fibrous bark, a twisted trunk, and palmately lobed leaves. Small pale green flowers are borne in summer, followed by clusters of ovoid to rounded, green to purple-black fruits. H 120ft (35m), pruned to 3–9ft (1–3m) in cultivation.
6–10

VITEX

A genus of about 250 species of mainly evergreen trees and shrubs, predominantly tropical and subtropical, with a few species in Europe. *V. agnus-castus*, found in southern Europe, and *V. negundo*, found in India, Taiwan, and China, are fine ornamental shrubs for warm temperate regions or sheltered positions in colder parts. They have elegant, compound leaves and spikes of mauve flowers. *V. negundo* is a very variable species, with seven or more recognized variants.

Vitex agnus-castus (chaste tree, agnus castus)
Deciduous aromatic shrub or small tree with palmate leaves divided into elliptic, pointed leaflets. In summer, small, tubular, lilac, scented flowers are borne in spikes, followed by tiny, fleshy, red-black fruits. H and S 15ft (5m).
7–10

itis vinifera **'Ciotat'** (parsley grape)
This ornamental cultivar has attractive leaves with fringed lobes and small blue-black fruits. H 20ft (6m).

6–10

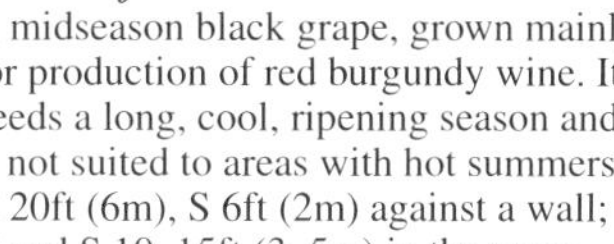

Vitis vinifera **'Pinot Noir'**
A midseason black grape, grown mainly for production of red burgundy wine. It needs a long, cool, ripening season and is not suited to areas with hot summers. H 20ft (6m), S 6ft (2m) against a wall; H and S 10–15ft (3–5m) in the open; H 2ft (60cm), S 4ft (1.2m) as cordons.
6–10

Vitex negundo (Chinese chaste tree)
Deciduous shrub with 4-angled stems and palmate leaves divided into 3–5 lanceolate, sometimes toothed leaflets. Small, tubular, lavender flowers are borne in loose panicles in late summer, followed by small, fleshy fruits. H and S 15ft (5m).
6–10

Vitex negundo var. ***heterophylla***
This variety has leaflets with deeply toothed margins, which in some plants almost divide them into segments. It differs from *V. n.* var. *cannabinifolia*, which has a more southern distribution, and leaves resembling those of *Cannabis sativa* (see p.99). H and S 15ft (5m).
6–10

Vitis vinifera **'Purpurea'** (Teinturier grape)
Probably the most striking cultivar for foliage, with beet red young leaves darkening to bronze, and tiny green to purple fruits. It makes an effective background to a border of gray-leaved herbs. H 20ft (6m).
6–10

WALNUT, see *Juglans regia*, p.145

WASABIA

Only two species of perennials occur in this genus, which is endemic to Japan and is generally found beside mountain streams. *W. japonica* is the Asian equivalent of horseradish (*Armoracia rusticana*, see p.87), and belongs to the same family. It is widely grown in Japan as a flavoring and accompaniment to raw fish (*sashimi*), but is usually available in the West only as powder. The name *Wasabia* is derived from the Japanese word for these plants.

Wasabia japonica (wasabi)
Perennial with stout, creeping rhizomes, upright stems, and long-stalked, kidney-shaped basal leaves. Racemes of small white flowers appear in summer, followed by twisted pods containing a few large seeds. H 8–16in (20–40cm), S 12in (30cm).

6–9

WITHANIA

Ten species of mostly evergreen shrubs belong to this genus, which is distributed mainly in Asia and Africa, with two species in Europe. Like most other members of the nightshade family (Solanaceae), they are rich in alkaloids, and all parts should be regarded as poisonous. *W. somnifera* occurs as an undershrub in stony places up to 5,600ft (1,700m) in Africa and Mediterranean regions, east to India. It is occasionally seen in herb gardens, but is by no means common in cultivation in the West.

Withania somnifera (winter cherry, *ashwagandha*)
Upright evergreen shrub with ovate leaves. Inconspicuous green to yellow flowers are borne all year, followed by tiny red berries containing yellow seeds enclosed in a papery, inflated calyx. H 2–6ft (60cm–2m), S 1–3ft (30cm–1m).

XANTHIUM

Cosmopolitan in distribution, this genus consists of two species of large, branched annuals. *X. strumarium* is found from Europe to eastern Asia and is an invasive weed in many parts of the world, including Australia. It resembles burdock (*Arctium lappa*, see p.86) in appearance, with similar spiny burs that cling to clothing and passing animals. The specific name *strumarium* derives from the Latin *struma* "swollen gland," referring to the swelling fruits.

Xanthium strumarium (cocklebur)
Stout annual with ovate-triangular, shallowly 3-lobed, coarsely toothed leaves. Pale green male and female flowers are borne separately in clusters in the leaf axils, followed by oblong, spiny fruits. H 8–36in (20cm–1m), S 4–24in (10–60cm).

A

ZANTHOXYLUM

This genus of about 250 species of deciduous and evergreen trees and shrubs occurs worldwide in warm temperate and subtropical regions. *Z. americanum* is native to eastern N America; *Z. piperitum* to China and Japan. A number of species are cultivated in various parts of the world for lumber, and also for medicinal and culinary purposes. *Zanthoxylum* is from the Greek *xanthos*, "yellow," and *xylon*, "wood," referring to the yellow wood of certain species.

Zanthoxylum americanum (toothache tree, northern prickly ash)
Deciduous shrub or small tree with spiny branches and pinnately divided leaves. Small yellow-green flowers appear before the new leaves in spring, followed by clusters of tiny black fruits. H 12–25ft (4–8m), S 20ft (6m).

4–8

Zanthoxylum piperitum (Japanese pepper, Sichuan pepper, *fagara*)
Deciduous shrubby tree with pungent bark and lemon-scented, pinnately divided leaves. From spring, small, pale green flowers are followed by purple-red fruits, each containing a black seed. H 10–22ft (3–7m), S 5–15ft (1.5–5m).

6–10

WATER LILY, see *Nymphaea*, p.165
WATER PLANTAIN, see *Alisma plantago-aquatica*, p.79
WATERCRESS, see *Nasturtium officinale*, p.164
WATTLE, see *Acacia*, p.71
WAX GOURD, see *Benincasa hispida*, p.93
WEEPING PAPERBARK, see *Melaleuca*, p.157
WILD BASIL, see *Pycnanthemum virginianum*, p.187
WILD GINGER, see *Asarum canadense*, p.89
WILD INDIGO, see *Baptisia tinctoria*, p.92
WILLOW, see *Salix*, p.195
WINTER CHERRY, see *Physalis alkekengi*, p.176; *Withania somnifera*, above

ZEA

A genus of four species of usually annual grasses native to C America. *Z. mays* has been cultivated for over 5,500 years in the Americas, from Chile to Canada. It tolerates wide climatic variations and is a major crop in most parts of the world. Corn makes an exotic feature plant; varieties with variegated leaves and multicolored cobs have been grown in containers and borders since at least the 19th century. Today's corn plants are unable to shed seed without human intervention.

Zea mays (corn, sweet corn, ornamental corn)
Large annual with lanceolate leaves, 1–5ft (30cm–1.5m). Male and female flowers are borne on the same plant in early summer. Fruit consists of a cob with dense rows of angular seeds. H 6–10ft (2–3m), S 18–36in (45cm–1m).

A

***Zea mays* 'Gracillima Variegata'**
A bold, erect annual with yellow-seeded cobs and creamy-white striped foliage. It is an attractive feature for containers. H 36in (90cm), S 12–18in (30–45cm).

A

***Zea mays* 'Gigantea Quadricolor'**
This robust cultivar makes an excellent centerpiece for summer bedding with leaves striped white, pale yellow, and pink. H 5–6ft (1.5–2m), S 24in (60cm).

A

ZINGIBER

A genus of about 100 species of perennials native to tropical Asia. All have reedlike stems and aromatic rhizomes. Gingers of various kinds are grown commercially in all warm regions, notably in Jamaica, which produces some of the finest. Fresh rhizomes, bought for flavoring, may be grown in containers as exotic foliage plants, yielding a further supply of rhizomes when the stems die down in winter. *Zingiber* is from the Greek *zingiberis*, "ginger."

Zingiber officinale (ginger)
Deciduous perennial with thick, branching rhizomes, stout, upright stems, and pointed, lanceolate leaves. Yellow-green flowers with a deep purple, yellow-marked lip are produced in summer, followed by 3-valved, fleshy capsules. H 5ft (1.5m), S indefinite.

9–11

ZIZIPHUS

A cosmopolitan genus of about 85 species of deciduous and evergreen trees, shrubs, and subshrubs found in tropical and subtropical regions; *Z. jujuba* is native to temperate Asia. In the 19th century, various species were recommended for greenhouses but are rarely seen outside botanic gardens today. *Ziziphus* is from the Persian *zizfum*, or *zizafun*, the name for *Z. lotus* (African lotus, jujube lotus), mentioned in many ancient texts, including the Greek myth about the lotus eaters.

Ziziphus jujuba (Chinese date, French jujube, Indian plum)
Deciduous tree or large shrub with spiny twigs and ovate-elliptic, leathery leaves. Small yellow flowers are borne in spring and summer, followed by dark red-black fleshy fruits containing one or two seeds. H 28ft (9m), S 22ft (7m).

6–10

WINTERGREEN, see *Gaultheria procumbens*, p.132
WINTER'S BARK, see *Drimys winteri*, p.120
WITCH HAZEL, see *Hamamelis*, p.136
WOAD, see *Isatis tinctoria*, p.144
WOLFSBANE, see *Aconitum napellus*, p.72
WOODRUFF, see *Galium odoratum*, p.131
WORMWOOD, see *ARTEMISIA*, pp.88–9
WRACK, see *Fucus vesiculosus*, p.130
YAM, see *Dioscorea*, p.119
YARROW, see *Achillea millefolium*, p.71
YERBA SANTA, see *Eriodictyon californicum*, p.279
YEW, see *Taxus*, p.210
YLANG-YLANG, see *Cananga odorata*, p.99

THE HERB DICTIONARY

Detailed information on the uses of every species listed, with historical background on each genus and concise instructions for growing and harvesting

ABELMOSCHUS
(Malvaceae)

A. moschatus is grown throughout the tropics. Virtually all parts are useful, notably the seeds, which are widely used as a spice in the East.

A. moschatus, syn. *Hibiscus abelmoschus* (ambrette, musk seed, musk mallow) p.70

PARTS USED Leaves, bark, roots, flowers, pods, seeds, oil.
PROPERTIES An aromatic, stimulant herb that relaxes spasms, especially in the digestive tract. It is also insecticidal and regarded as an aphrodisiac.
USES OF THE HERB
CULINARY Leaves and new shoots are eaten as vegetables. Unripe pods, known as "musk okra," are eaten as a vegetable.
AROMATIC Oil is used in food flavoring, perfumery, and cosmetics as a musk substitute; it is free of the fecal note sometimes present in animal musk. Its use has now been largely discontinued since it can cause photosensitization.
MEDICINAL Internally as a digestive and breath-freshener (seeds). Externally for cramps, poor circulation, and aching joints, and in aromatherapy for anxiety and depression (oil).
ECONOMIC Bark is processed into fiber. Root mucilage provides sizing for paper. Flowers are used to flavor tobacco. Seeds are added to coffee.
VARIANT
A. m. **'Mischief'**, p.70.

GROWTH AND HARVEST
GROWTH Ornamental. Rich, well-drained soil in sun. Propagate by seed sown in spring at 75–81°F (24–27°C), or by semiripe cuttings in summer. Pinch out the growing tip of young plants for bushy growth. In spring, cut back plants grown as perennials to 6in (15cm). Plants under cover may suffer from whitefly.
HARVEST Foliage and pods are picked when young and tender, and flowers as they open, and used fresh. Bark and roots are harvested as required and processed to extract fiber and mucilage. Fruits are cut as they begin to ripen and dried until the seeds are shed. Seeds are stored separately to avoid persistent musk odor, and are distilled for oil. They are also steeped in vegetable oil for external use.

ABIES Fir
(Pinaceae)

Many firs are economically important for lumber and resin. *A. alba* was the original Christmas tree, later superseded by the Norway spruce (*Picea abies*). Its medicinal uses have also declined: it was the source of Strassburg turpentine, listed in the *London Pharmacopoeia* until 1788, but has now been replaced by various species of pine (*Pinus*, see p.329).

A. alba, syn. *A. pectinata* (silver fir) p.70

PARTS USED Leaves, resin.
PROPERTIES An aromatic, antiseptic herb that acts as a diuretic and expectorant, and irritates the tissues, causing greater blood flow.
USES OF THE HERB
MEDICINAL Internally and externally as a common ingredient in remedies for coughs and colds. Externally also in bath extracts, rubbing oils, and liniments for rheumatism and neuralgia.
ECONOMIC Oil of turpentine is an important solvent in the paint industry. The residue, known as "rosin oil," is used in the manufacture of varnishes, lacquers, and carbon black (for pigments and ink).

A. balsamea (balsam fir, balm of Gilead) p.70

PARTS USED Leaves, bark, oleo-resin, oil.
PROPERTIES An aromatic, astringent, antiseptic herb with a strong balsam scent. It stimulates the circulation and acts as a diuretic.
USES OF THE HERB
MEDICINAL
Internally in commercial mixtures to treat coughs and diarrhea (but in excess is purgative). Externally in bath extracts for rheumatic pain, and as a mouthwash.
Oleo-resin and oil, known as "Canada balsam," are used in traditional N American medicine for chest infections, venereal disease, wounds, and burns. Oil is used in ointments and creams, especially in the treatment of hemorrhoids.
ECONOMIC Oleo-resin is used as a lens cement and sealing agent for mounting microscope slides. Oil is used in dentistry in sealing preparations, and as a fixative and fragrance in soaps, cosmetics, and perfumes, and as a flavoring in food products.
VARIANT
A. b. **'Hudsonia'**, p.70.

GROWTH AND HARVEST
GROWTH Ornamental. Deep, moist, well-drained, slightly acid soil in sun or shade. Young trees and *A. b.* 'Hudsonia' are more tolerant of alkaline conditions. Propagate by seed sown in spring. Maintain a single leading shoot by cutting out competing shoots flush with the main stem in spring. Firs may be attacked by sap-sucking adelgids, and are prone to dieback and rust caused by fungal infections. Firs are sensitive to atmospheric pollution. Although hardy, they may also be damaged by late spring frosts. Planting in light shade, rather than full sun, minimizes damage.
HARVEST Leaves and young shoots are collected in spring. Bark is removed throughout the year. Resin is tapped from 60–80-year-old trees in spring for distillation of oil. Oleo-resin is collected in summer from blisters on the trunk, and used fresh, dried, or distilled for oil.

ABRUS
(Leguminosae)

The seeds of *A. precatorius* are traditionally used in India to weigh gemstones (a single seed equals 1.75g, or 1 carat): the Kohinoor diamond was first weighed by this means. In parts of S America and the Caribbean, necklaces of the seeds were traditionally made for infants to wear as a protection against illness. They are also popular worldwide as beads, both for ornament and in rosaries.

A. precatorius (jequirity, crab's eyes, Indian licorice) p.70

PARTS USED Leaves, seeds.
PROPERTIES A licorice-tasting herb that is soothing (leaves), emetic, irritant, and abortifacient (seeds).
USES OF THE HERB
MEDICINAL Internally for sore throats and dry coughs (leaves). Externally for sciatica, hair loss, skin disease, leprosy, nervous debility, and paralysis (seeds). The seeds are extremely poisonous: eating even one is sufficient to cause stomach cramps, vomiting, birth deformities, sterility, coma, or death. The roots contain glycyrrhizin and have been used as a substitute for licorice; they also contain toxic, emetic compounds that make this use inadvisable.
For use by qualified practitioners only.
WARNING This herb is subject to legal restrictions in some countries.

GROWTH AND HARVEST
GROWTH Ornamental. Rich, well-drained, sandy loam in sun or partial shade, minimum 61°F (16°C). A temperature of 21°C (70°F) is needed in summer for successful flowering. Tolerates saline conditions. Propagate by seed or softwood cuttings in late winter, at a minimum of 75°F (24°C). Soak the hard seeds in water for 24 hours before sowing to speed germination. Cut back straggly growth to two or three buds in early spring.
HARVEST Leaves are picked during the growing season and dried for infusions. Ripe seeds are collected in the autumn and ground for pastes.
WARNING Seeds are extremely toxic if eaten.

ACACIA Wattle
(Leguminosae/Mimosaceae)

Various wattles are cultivated for lumber and as ornamentals. Many contain valuable compounds that are used in medicine, flavoring, perfumery, dyes, tanning, adhesives, and insecticides. When boiled, the foliage and wood of *A. catechu* produces a dark brown, sticky substance known as "catechu," "cutch," or "cachou," which crystallizes on cooling. An important article since at least the 16th century, it was first exported from India to China, Arabia, and Persia, reaching Europe in the 17th century. *A. farnesiana* is widely grown for the perfume industry, mostly in the south of France. A substance known as cassie absolute is extracted from the flowers, and its violet fragrance is considered superior to that of violets. *A. senegal* is the main source of gum arabic, although some 25 other species are used; the finest quality resin is known as "Kordofan gum." Sudan produces 85 percent of the world's crop, which is wild-collected. Several desert species (e.g. *A. ancistrocarpa* and *A. trachycarpa*), have been used by Australian Aborigines to treat headaches. Infusions or decoctions from bark and roots of some Western Australian and other species (e.g. *A. bivenosa* subsp. *wayi*, *A. holosericea*, *A. monticola*, *A. tetragonophylla*) were used for coughs, colds, and laryngitis.

A. catechu (black catechu) p.71

Parts used Leaves, young shoots, bark.
Properties A bittersweet, antiseptic, astringent herb that checks bleeding and discharges.
Uses of the herb
Medicinal Internally for dysentery, chronic diarrhea, and excess mucus. Externally for nose bleeds, hemorrhoids, skin eruptions, bed sores, mouth ulcers, sore throats, and dental infections. Combines well with *Acorus calamus* (see p.228), *Mentha* x *piperita* (see p.311), *Agrimonia eupatoria* (see p.231), *Quercus robur* (see p.338), and *Filipendula ulmaria* (see p.283) for lower bowel conditions, and with *Commiphora* spp. (see p.265) and *Hamamelis virginiana* (see p.291) as a gargle for oral and dental infections. In India, catechu is an ingredient of *paan*, a digestive made with betel nuts or leaves. WARNING *A. catechu* in the form of catechu is subject to legal restrictions in some countries.
Economic Important locally for lumber and fuel wood. The bark is used in tanning and as a source of khaki dye.

A. farnesiana (prickly Moses, cassie) p.71

Parts used Bark, flowers, pods, seeds.
Properties An aromatic, stimulant herb that relieves tension and contains insecticidal compounds (in the flowers).
Uses of the herb
Culinary Ripe seeds are pressed for cooking oil.
Aromatic Flowers are used in perfumes and added to potpourris.
Medicinal Internally for diarrhea and skin complaints (bark). Externally in baths for dry skin (flowers).
Economic Flowers are used in food flavoring (distilled oil) and in insecticides. Bark and pods yield a black dye.

A. senegal (gum arabic)

Tropical, thicket-forming large shrub or small tree, height 10–28ft (3–9m), spread 10–15ft (3–5m); it has a flattened crown, gray branches, and gray-green, bipinnate leaves with three curved spines at the base. Pale yellow, fragrant flowers are produced in axillary spikes 2–4in (5–10cm) long. Found in hot, dry regions of northern Africa and the Middle East.

Parts used Resin.
Properties A soothing herb that forms a protective coating over inflamed tissues, reducing irritation and encouraging healing.
Uses of the herb
Medicinal Internally in lozenges for sore throats, coughs, and mucus, and in commercial mixtures for diarrhea and dysentery. Externally for burns, sores, and leprosy.
Economic Important in the food industry as a stabilizer, flavor fixative, and emulsifier, and as an additive to retard sugar crystallization. Products such as chewing gum and candy are likely to include gum arabic.

Growth and Harvest

Growth Crop (*A. catechu*, *A. farnesiana*). Wild-collected (*A. senegal*). Well-drained neutral to acid soil in full sun; minimum 45°F (7°C) for *A. catechu* and *A. farnesiana*, 59–64°F (15–18°C) for *A. senegal*. Propagate by seed sown in spring at 70°F (21°C). Seeds have hard coats that should be nicked and soaked in water for 24 hours before sowing. Also by semiripe cuttings of lateral shoots in late summer at 61–64°F (16–18°C). To keep pot plants bushy, pinch out sideshoots. To control size, cut back hard after flowering. Prone to spider mite and root mealybug when grown under cover. Caterpillars may damage the leaves and new shoots, or borers attack stems and trunk. Wattles dislike disturbance, forming long taproots that are sensitive to damage. Carry out repotting and transplanting when necessary; trees may take a year to recover. *Acacia* species are subject to statutory control as weeds in parts of Australia.
Harvest Bark and leaves (*A. catechu*) are cut as required for infusions and powders. Flowers (*A. farnesiana*) are picked as they open, and are dried for infusions and baths, or distilled for oil. Seeds and pods are collected when ripe and pressed for oil. Resin (*A. senegal*) is scraped from the trunk and branches in the winter, after the rainy season, as it oozes from the bark. Unhealthy trees are the best source, and incisions are sometimes made to increase the quantity. Resin is processed into powder or dissolved in water.

ACANTHOPANAX

A. senticosus. See *Eleutherococcus senticosus*.

ACHILLEA Yarrow

(Compositae/Asteraceae)

Yarrow is closely associated with divination, giving rise to sayings and verses in many parts of the world. In China, yarrow stalks are used in consulting the *I Ching* (Book of Changes). Over 40 different constituents have been isolated from yarrow. These include an essential oil, which contains anti-inflammatory azulene. The azulene content varies between plants, even in the same habitat.

A. millefolium (yarrow, milfoil, soldier's woundwort) p.71

Parts used Whole plant.
Properties An aromatic, bitter, astringent herb that reduces inflammation, increases perspiration, relieves indigestion, and has diuretic effects. It is also effective in lowering blood pressure, relaxing spasms, and arresting hemorrhage.
Uses of the herb
Medicinal Internally for feverish illnesses (especially colds, influenza, and measles), mucus, diarrhea, dyspepsia, rheumatism, arthritis, menstrual and menopausal complaints, hypertension, and to protect against thrombosis after stroke or heart attack. Externally for wounds, nosebleeds, ulcers, inflamed eyes, and hemorrhoids. Combines well with *Sambucus nigra* (see p.347) and *Mentha* x *piperita* (see p.311) for fevers, with *Tilia* spp. (see p.363) for hypertension, and with *Chamaemelum nobile* (see p.259) for digestive disorders. Used similarly in Ayurvedic medicine and also as a tonic (often combined with *Salvia officinalis*, see p.346) for the nervous system. Prolonged use of yarrow may cause allergic rashes and make the skin more sensitive to sunlight.
Variants
***A. m.* 'Cerise Queen'**, p.71.
***A. m.* 'Lilac Beauty'**, syn. *A. m.* 'Lavender Beauty', p.71.

Growth and Harvest

Growth Crop (*A. millefolium*). Ornamental (*A. m.* 'Cerise Queen', *A. m.* 'Lilac Beauty'). Well-drained soil in full sun. Propagate by division in spring, or by seed sown in spring. Prone to mildew in hot, dry conditions. Flowers attract many beneficial insects, including ladybugs, and parasitic wasps that prey on garden pests, notably aphids. It is invasive unless confined in a container. Variants do not come true from seed.
Harvest Plants are cut when in flower in summer and dried for use in infusions, liquid extracts, lotions, and tinctures.

ACHYRANTHES

(Amaranthaceae)

This important Chinese herb was first described in medical texts c.AD200. The Chinese name for *A. bidentata* – *huai niu xi* – means "ox knees from the Huai River," and refers to the enlarged nodes on the stem. The seeds of *A. bidentata* are a good substitute for cereal grains in breadmaking and have been used for this purpose in India during famine. The leaves of *A. aspera* are eaten as a vegetable in Java and burned as a source of vegetable salt.

A. bidentata (two-toothed amaranthus) p.72

Parts used Roots, leaves, stems.
Properties A bitter, acrid herb that stimulates the circulatory and digestive systems, liver, and kidneys, lowering blood pressure and relieving pain. Acts predominantly on the lower half of the body. Research suggests that it dilates the cervix and is therefore inadvisable for use during pregnancy.
Uses of the herb
Medicinal Internally for blood in the urine, lower back and joint pains, hypertension, menstrual and postpartum pain, nosebleeds, and bleeding gums.

GROWTH AND HARVEST

GROWTH Crop. Rich, sandy, slightly acid soil, in partial shade. Propagate by seed sown in late spring.
HARVEST Leaves and stems are picked in summer and crushed for juice or used in tinctures. Roots are lifted in autumn or winter from one- or two-year-old plants and sun-dried for decoctions, liquid extracts, powders, and pills. The drying process often involves a stage of stir-frying with rice wine. Fresh root is used in southern China.

ACINOS
(Labiatae/Lamiaceae)

Although basil thyme is described in many herb books as an aromatic herb that can be used as a substitute for thyme, it is without aroma or only faintly aromatic. It is considered obsolete by most medical herbalists today and is of little use in the kitchen.

A. arvensis, syn. *A. thymoides*, *Calamintha acinos*, *Clinopodium acinos*, *Satureja acinos* (basil thyme) p.72

PARTS USED Whole plant, oil.
PROPERTIES A stimulant, diuretic herb that benefits the digestive system and irritates the tissues, causing a temporary improvement in local blood supply.
USES OF THE HERB
MEDICINAL Internally, according to old herbals, for shortness of breath, melancholy, and improving the digestion. Externally, oil was once distilled to treat bruises, toothache, sciatica, and neuralgia.

GROWTH AND HARVEST

GROWTH Ornamental. Light, dry soil in sun. Prefers sandy and alkaline conditions. Propagate by seed sown in summer in sandy soil mix. Once established, self-seeds in suitable conditions.
HARVEST Plants are cut in summer when in flower and used fresh in infusions, or as a salad herb.

ACONITUM Monkshood
(Ranunculaceae)

Aconitum species all contain the alkaloid aconitine, which is one of the most toxic plant compounds known. *A. ferox* is regarded as the most deadly, followed by *A. napellus*. Nevertheless, a number of different species are used medicinally in various parts of the world, having beneficial therapeutic effects when used correctly. *A. carmichaelii* was first mentioned in Chinese medical literature c.AD200. It has two names in Chinese medicine: *wu tou* refers to the fresh root and *fu zi* to the root cooked with salt and sugar. The cooking process makes it safer for internal use. Recent research has found it to be effective in congestive heart failure.

A. carmichaelii, syn. *A. fischeri* (azure monkshood, Sichuan aconite) p.72

PARTS USED Roots.
PROPERTIES A sedative, painkilling herb that stimulates the heart and kidneys, and has diuretic and antirheumatic effects.
USES OF THE HERB
MEDICINAL Internally as a restorative following shock and trauma, for *yang* energy weakness, and in chronic osteoarthritis. Dosage is critical, excess causing numbness of lips, tongue, and extremities, vomiting, breathing difficulties, lowering of pulse rate and blood pressure, coma, and death. Not given to pregnant women or patients with severe debilitation. Externally for rheumatism and arthritis, headache, and as a local anesthetic. For use by qualified practitioners only. WARNING This herb is subject to legal restrictions in some countries.
VARIANT
A. c. **'Arendsii'**, p.72.

A. napellus (monkshood, aconite, wolfsbane) p.72

PARTS USED Roots.
PROPERTIES A sedative, painkilling herb that acts on the heart and central nervous system, and also lowers fever.
USES OF THE HERB
MEDICINAL Internally for facial neuralgia and to relieve the pain of arthritis and gout. Externally for sciatica and arthritis. Used in homeopathy for shock (especially after surgery or childbirth), chicken pox, measles, mumps, croup, toothache and teething, and complaints caused, or made worse, by getting chilled. For use by qualified practitioners only. WARNING This herb is subject to legal restrictions in some countries.
VARIANT
A. n. **'Carneum'**, p.73.

GROWTH AND HARVEST

GROWTH Ornamental. Deep, moisture-retentive soil in shade. Plants will also thrive in a sunny position if the soil is sufficiently damp throughout the growing season. Propagate by division when dormant, or by seed sown under cover in spring. Remove dead flower heads to encourage a second crop of flowers.
HARVEST Plants are lifted in autumn and young, thick roots are removed before replanting. Roots are processed professionally for use in decoctions, liniments, and tinctures.
WARNING All parts of *Aconitum* species are extremely toxic if eaten, and may cause systemic poisoning if handled.

ACORUS Sweet flag
(Acoraceae)

Used both for medicinal purposes and as a strewing herb, *A. calamus* was grown in large quantities in Norfolk, England, and gathered at an annual "gladdon harvest." Calamus candy, made by crystallizing tender slices of the rhizome of *A. calamus*, was popular in the 18th century as a medicinal lozenge to cure coughs and indigestion, and to ward off infection. The Penobscot Indians of Maine chewed a piece of the root to prevent illness when traveling. There are several distinct populations of *A. calamus* in the wild, differing in genetic conformation and in important details of chemistry. All contain 1–4 percent of volatile oil (oil of calamus) in the rhizome. The constituents may include asarone, a tranquilizing and antibiotic compound that is potentially toxic and carcinogenic. Oil from populations in N America and Siberia is asarone-free.

A. calamus (sweet flag, calamus, myrtle flag) p.73

PARTS USED Rhizomes, oil.
PROPERTIES An aromatic, bitter, stimulant herb that relaxes spasms and relieves indigestion.
USES OF THE HERB
MEDICINAL Internally for digestive complaints, bronchitis, and sinusitis. Externally for skin eruptions, rheumatic pains, and neuralgia. An important herb in Ayurvedic medicine, regarded as a restorative for the brain and nervous system, especially after a stroke; also given for bronchial complaints and bleeding disorders. Combined with *Elettaria cardamomum* (see p.277) to help digestion of dairy products. Used as snuff for nasal congestion, polyps, shock, and coma. Excess causes vomiting. WARNING This herb, especially in the form of oil of calamus, is subject to legal restrictions in some countries.
VARIANT
A. c. **'Variegatus'**, p.73.

A. gramineus (rock sweet flag, grass-leaved sweet flag) p.73

PARTS USED Rhizomes (*shi chang pu*).
PROPERTIES An aromatic, antibacterial, tonic herb that stimulates the digestive system, clears the bronchial passages, relieves indigestion, and has mild sedative effects.
USES OF THE HERB
MEDICINAL An important herb in Chinese medicine for poor appetite, gastritis, excess mucus, and depression. Considered to be a warming herb and therefore not given to patients with a tendency to perspire excessively.
VARIANTS
A. g. **'Ogon'**, syn. *A. c.* 'Oborozuki', p.73.
A. g. **'Pusillus'**, p.73.

GROWTH AND HARVEST

GROWTH Ornamental. Wet soil or shallow water (up to 10in/25cm of water) in a sunny position. *A. g.* 'Pusillus' can be grown as a submerged aquatic. The smaller variants – some are barely 1in (2.5cm) high – are good in containers. Propagate by division of rhizomes in autumn or early spring.
HARVEST Plants are lifted at any time, except during the flowering period. The required amount of rhizome is cut and the remainder replanted. The rhizome may be dried for decoctions, or distilled for oil (*A. calamus*), or used fresh for tinctures, liquid extracts, pastes, and powders.

ADENOPHORA
Gland bellflower, ladybell
(Campanulaceae)

Gland bellflowers are well known in the East, where they are grown as ornamentals, vegetables (for their rhizomes), and medicinal herbs. The fragrant *A. liliifolia* is cultivated as a root crop in Japan, and both *A. stricta* and *A. trachilioidis* are used in traditional Chinese medicine for lung complaints.

A. stricta (fickle ladybell) p.74

PARTS USED Roots (*nan sha shen*).
PROPERTIES A stimulant herb that acts mainly on the respiratory system and heart.
USES OF THE HERB
MEDICINAL Internally for dry coughs, chronic bronchitis, and tuberculosis.

GROWTH AND HARVEST
GROWTH Ornamental. Rich, well-drained, moist soil in sun. Propagate by seed sown in autumn or by basal cuttings in early spring. *Adenophora* may become invasive. It resents disturbance.
HARVEST Roots are lifted in autumn and dried for use in decoctions.

ADHATODA
A. vasica. See *Justicia adhatoda*.

ADIANTUM Maidenhair fern
(Adiantiaceae)

Medicinal uses of the maidenhair fern have been recorded since Classical times. Dioscorides mentioned "adianton" for asthma; Culpeper valued it as "a good remedy for coughs, asthmas, pleurisy, etc., and on account of its being a gentle diuretic also in jaundice and other impurities of the kidneys"; and Gerard claimed it was a hair restorative. It was once popular as *sirop de capillaire*, a cough mixture made from the rhizomes and fronds, flavored with orange blossoms. The hardier *A. pedatum* from America and Japan is used in similar ways. *A. aethiopicum*, which occurs in Australia, has been used by Aborigines to soothe bronchial complaints. *Capillus-veneris* means "Venus' hair" and may refer to the Roman goddess of love, who rose from the waves with miraculously dry hair.

A. capillus-veneris (maidenhair fern) p.74

PARTS USED Whole plant.
PROPERTIES A bittersweet, soothing herb that relieves coughing and acts as a diuretic and expectorant.
USES OF THE HERB
MEDICINAL Internally for bronchitis, dry coughs, excess mucus, and pharyngitis. Externally in hair lotions to treat dandruff and bald spots caused by ringworm. Used in Ayurvedic medicine as a cooling, moistening remedy for coughs.

GROWTH AND HARVEST
GROWTH Ornamental. Moist, well-drained soil, enriched with leaf mold and bonemeal, in a sheltered, humid, shady position, minimum 45°F (7°C). Propagate by division of rhizomes in early spring, or by spores, collected on clean paper and sown in early spring. Spores take about six weeks to germinate. A plant that temporarily dries out will lose most or all of its fronds, although it usually sprouts again from the base.
HARVEST Plants are cut throughout summer and used fresh in infusions, powders, and, in Ayurvedic medicine, as milk decoctions.

ADONIS
(Ranunculaceae)

A. vernalis contains glycosides that have both tonic and sedative effects on the heart. It is an ingredient of several commercial German preparations for heart complaints and low blood pressure; it is also found in Bechterew's Mixture, a Russian formulation for heart conditions of nervous origin.

A. vernalis (false hellebore, yellow pheasant's eye) p.74

PARTS USED Whole plant.
PROPERTIES A tonic, diuretic herb that stimulates the heart.
USES OF THE HERB
MEDICINAL Internally for cardiac insufficiency, irregular or rapid heart beat, mitral stenosis, and edema due to heart failure. Included in many commercial formulas for heart complaints. Similar in effects to *Digitalis lanata* (see p.273), but not cumulative. For use by qualified practitioners only.
WARNING This herb is subject to legal restrictions in some countries.

GROWTH AND HARVEST
GROWTH Ornamental. Light, well-drained soil, enriched with leaf mold, in sun or partial shade. The crown should be planted 1in (2.5cm) below the surface. Propagate by division in early autumn, or by seed sown under cover in summer, as soon as it is ripe. Germination may be slow and erratic. New growth may be damaged by slugs and snails. Plants die down in summer and should be labeled to prevent accidental damage.
HARVEST Plants are cut when in full flower, and dried for use in liquid extracts and tinctures. The dried herb does not keep well, so stocks are renewed each year.

AEGOPODIUM
(Umbelliferae/Apiaceae)

Goutweed was apparently introduced to the British Isles during medieval times, when it was cultivated in monastery gardens for medicinal purposes. It is often referred to as "bishopweed," "bishopwort," or "herb Gerard" in old herbals, on account of its ecclesiastical connection and its dedication to St. Gerard, who was invoked to cure gout.

A. podagraria (goutweed, ground elder) p.74

PARTS USED Leaves, roots.
PROPERTIES A mild sedative herb that has diuretic and anti-inflammatory effects.
USES OF THE HERB
CULINARY Leaves have a distinctive flavor and, when young, are used in salads and soups, and as a vegetable.
MEDICINAL Internally for gout and sciatica. Externally for hemorrhoids, gout, stings, and burns. In homeopathy for arthritis and rheumatism.
VARIANT
A. p. **'Variegatum'**, p.74.

GROWTH AND HARVEST
GROWTH Wild-collected (*A. podagraria*). Ornamental (*A. p.* 'Variegata'). Well-drained to moist soil in sun or shade. Propagate by division of rhizomes in spring or autumn. The species is too invasive for most areas of the garden, but it may be grown in containers for medicinal and culinary use. *A. p.* 'Variegatum' is slightly less invasive and looks good in containers.
HARVEST Roots and leaves are harvested in summer and used fresh, or dried for use in infusions, homeopathic remedies, liquid extracts, medicated oils, and poultices.

AEOLLANTHUS
(Labiatae)

This genus includes 35 species of annuals, perennials, and small shrubs native to tropical and warm parts of Africa, most of which have thick, aromatic leaves and an explosive pollination mechanism. Several species have rose-scented flowers and lemon-scented leaves. These are known generally as *nindi* and include *A. gamwelliae*, *A. heliotropioides*, *A. lamborayi*, *A. myrianthus*, and *A. pubescens*. Oil of *nindi* is used in soaps and perfumes; it is produced mainly in eastern Africa and in Assam.

A. gamwelliae, syn. *A. graveolens* (*nindi*, *ninde*)

Tender subshrub, height to 5ft (1.5m), spread 3ft (1m), with branched, downy stems and ovate–lanceolate, gland-dotted leaves up to 3½in (9cm) long, which have wavy margins and downy undersurfaces. Strongly scented mauve flowers, ¾in (2cm) long with woolly calyces, are produced in many-branched inflorescences. Grows on rocky outcrops at 4,600ft (1,400m) in eastern Africa.

PARTS USED Whole plant, leaves, flowers, oil.
PROPERTIES An aromatic herb rich in essential oils, including geraniol (as in *Pelargonium* 'Graveolens', see p.323).
USES OF THE HERB
CULINARY Leaves are added to soups and salads.
ECONOMIC Oil from leaves and flowers is used in soaps and perfumes, often as a substitute for *palmarosa* oil (from *Cymbopogon martinii*, see p.270).

GROWTH AND HARVEST

GROWTH Crop. Well-drained to dry, sandy soil in sun, minimum 59–64°F (15–18°C). Propagate by seed sown in sandy soil mix in spring.
HARVEST Whole plant, or leaves and flowers separately, are distilled for oil.

AESCULUS Horse chestnut, buckeye
(Hippocastanaceae)

The common name "horse chestnut" has apparently no connection with the horseshoe-shaped leaf scars visible on the twigs but may refer to the use of its fruits as fodder, and to treat coughs in horses and cattle. It also has medicinal and cosmetic applications. For edible chestnuts, see *Castanea* species, p.256.

A. hippocastanum (common horse chestnut) p.75

PARTS USED Bark, seeds.
PROPERTIES A bitter, astringent herb that lowers fever and reduces capillary permeability and local edema. It is diuretic and anti-inflammatory. The main constituent is aescin, a complex mixture of saponins, which has a potent anti-inflammatory effect.

USES OF THE HERB
MEDICINAL Internally for disorders of the venous system, including hardening of the arteries, stroke, heart attack, circulatory insufficiency, varicose veins, phlebitis, chilblains, hemorrhoids, and swelling following severe trauma; injected for swollen joints and fractures.
ECONOMIC Used in cosmetics and hair preparations. Fruits are ground for fodder.
VARIANT
***A. h.* 'Baumannii'**, syn. *A. h.* 'Flore Pleno', p.75.

GROWTH AND HARVEST

GROWTH Ornamental. Fertile, well-drained soil in sun or partial shade. Propagate by seed sown in autumn, except for *A. h.* 'Baumannii', which is sterile and can be propagated only by grafting onto stocks of the species. Germination and growth are rapid.
HARVEST Bark and ripe seeds are collected in autumn for use in liquid extracts and decoctions. Seeds are chopped, then roasted before use. Since the active ingredient, aescin, is poorly absorbed in its natural state, horse chestnut is processed commercially for better absorption.
WARNING Harmful if eaten unprocessed.

AFROMOMUM
(Zingiberaceae)

Fifty species of rhizomatous perennials make up this genus, which occurs in tropical Africa. *Afromomum* is a spice related to ginger and cardamom. Known in ancient Rome, it was also used during medieval times to flavor hippocras (a spiced wine) and as a pepper substitute – a use banned in Britain by George III (1760–1820) as being injurious to health. Several species are used, including *A. angustifolium* (Madagascar cardamom), which produces pleasant-tasting fruits and aromatic seeds. The most important is *A. melegueta*, popular in medieval times, traded by the Portuguese, and cultivated today as a perennial and for the spice trade.

A. melegueta (grains of paradise, melegueta pepper, Guinea grains)

Tender perennial, height 3–8ft (1–2.5m), with reedlike stems and narrow, elliptic leaves. Solitary, mauve, orchidlike flowers with a yellow patch in the throat are borne on short stems. Pear-shaped, scarlet fruits, 2½–4in (6–10cm) long, contain 60–100 brown seeds in a pulp. Found wild in tropical west Africa.

PARTS USED Roots, seeds.
PROPERTIES A pungent stimulant that benefits the digestion and relieves spasms.
USES OF THE HERB
CULINARY Seeds are used as a condiment and flavoring.
MEDICINAL Internally, in west Africa, for a range of conditions, including excessive lactation, painful menstruation, postpartum hemorrhage, infertility (root decoction), and aphrodisiac (seeds); in Nigeria, combined with *Rauvolfia serpentina* (see p.339) for mental disorders, and with *Momordica charantia* (see p.312) for cholera (seeds).

GROWTH AND HARVEST

GROWTH Crop. Well-drained soil in partial shade, minimum 59–64°F (15–18°C). Propagate by division of rhizomes as new growth begins.
HARVEST Fruits are collected as they ripen and seeds separated from pulp and dried. Roots are lifted throughout the year.

AGASTACHE Giant hyssop
(Labiatae/Lamiaceae)

A. foeniculum was widely planted by bee-keepers in N America in the 1870s to produce a fine honey with a slight aniseed flavor. Native Americans made it into a tea and used it as a sweetener. *A. rugosa* was first noted as a medicinal herb in China c.AD500.

A. foeniculum, syn. *A. anethiodora* (anise hyssop, blue giant hyssop, fennel giant hyssop) p.75

PARTS USED Leaves, flowers.
PROPERTIES An aromatic, pleasant-tasting herb that increases perspiration and relieves bronchial congestion.
USES OF THE HERB
CULINARY The aniseed-flavored leaves may be added to salads.
MEDICINAL Internally for coughs in the traditional medicine of several native N American tribes.
VARIANT
***A. f.* 'Alabaster'**, p.75.

A. rugosa, syn. *Lophanthus rugosus*, *Cedronella japonica* (Korean mint, wrinkled giant hyssop) p.75

PARTS USED Leaves, stems (aerial parts are known as *huo xiang*).
PROPERTIES An aromatic, antibacterial herb that stimulates the digestive system, relaxes spasms, and helps to lower fever by increasing perspiration.
USES OF THE HERB
CULINARY Fresh or dried leaves provide a mintlike flavoring for meat and salad dishes, and make a pleasant tea.
MEDICINAL Internally, in traditional Chinese medicine, to improve appetite and relieve dyspepsia, nausea, and vomiting; also for the common cold when characterized by chills. Unsuitable for feverish colds. Interchangeable with *Pogostemon cablin* (see p.332).

GROWTH AND HARVEST

GROWTH Ornamental. Well-drained soil in sun. *A. foeniculum* tolerates poorer soils and drier conditions than *A. rugosa*. Propagate by seed sown under cover in spring, or by division in spring, or by softwood cuttings in summer.
HARVEST Leaves (*A. rugosa*, *A. foeniculum*) are collected in spring and summer, and flowers in summer, for use fresh or dried as a flavoring, or for teas. Leaves and stems (*A. rugosa*) are cut before flowering and dried for medicinal use.

AGATHOSMA
(Rutaceae)

"Buchu," an African word for dusting powder, is used as a common name for several different *Agathosma* species, gathered for this and other medicinal and industrial purposes. *A. betulina* (syn. *Barosma betulina*), although slightly smaller, is similar in appearance to *A. crenulata* and is used in identical ways. Research has shown that buchus contain a substance that blocks ultraviolet light, and may have applications in skin preparations.

A. crenulata, syn. *A. serratifolia*, *Diosma crenulata* (oval buchu) p.75

PARTS USED Leaves.
PROPERTIES A strongly aromatic herb that stimulates and cleanses the urinary system and increases perspiration. The active ingredient is diosphenol, or "barosma camphor," which is a potent antiseptic and diuretic.
USES OF THE HERB
CULINARY Used with *Artemisia afra* to flavor brandy and wine in various parts of Africa.
MEDICINAL Internally for urinary tract infections (especially prostatitis and cystitis), digestive problems, gout, rheumatism, coughs, and colds, often combined with *Althaea officinalis* (see p.236). Externally in traditional African medicine as a powder to deter insects and in a vinegar-based lotion for bruises and sprains.
ECONOMIC Leaves are used to enhance the blackcurrant aroma of the liqueur *cassis*.

GROWTH AND HARVEST
GROWTH Ornamental. Well-drained acid soil in full sun, minimum 41°F (5°C). Propagate by semiripe cuttings in late summer, in sand. Cut back hard in spring to control size, and pinch out to encourage bushy habit.
HARVEST Leaves are gathered when the plant is flowering and fruiting, and dried for use in infusions, liquid extracts, tablets, and tinctures.

AGAVE
(Agavaceae)

Agaves are used for a variety of purposes in the dry tropics. *A. americana* is commonly planted in rows as an effective stockproof barrier and is used in arid land reclamation. Both *A. americana* and the related *A. sisalana* (sisal) are important fiber plants and sources of hecogenin, used in the manufacture of steroid drugs. The uses of agaves were developed by the German East Africa Company, which carried out research after plants were first introduced from C America to Tanganyika (now part of Tanzania) in 1893.

A. americana (century plant) p.76

PARTS USED Whole plant, leaves, roots, sap.
PROPERTIES A healing, anti-inflammatory, diuretic herb with hormonal and insecticidal constituents. It acts mainly on the digestive system, and lowers fever by increasing perspiration.
USES OF THE HERB
CULINARY The sweet, tender plant core is cooked as a vegetable. Sap is fermented in Mexico to make the alcoholic drinks *pulque* and *vino mescal*.
MEDICINAL Internally for indigestion, flatulence, constipation, jaundice, and dysentery. Externally for burns and minor injuries. Fresh sap may cause skin irritation or dermatitis. Leaf-waste concentrate provides steroid drug precursors.
ECONOMIC Roots are used in soap manufacture, and the coarse fibers woven into ropes, twine, and mats.
VARIANT
***A. a.* 'Variegata'**, p.76.

GROWTH AND HARVEST
GROWTH Ornamental. Well-drained soil in full sun, minimum 41°F (5°C). Propagate by seed sown in spring at 70°F (21°C), by offsets, removed from the parent plant in spring or summer and left for some days to dry off before potting. Prone to attack by mealybugs or root mealybugs. Rot may occur in cool winter temperatures if the plant is overwatered. *A. a.* 'Variegata' does not come true from seed.
HARVEST Parts are harvested and processed as required. Leaves and roots may be used fresh or dried; they last well when dried.
WARNING Skin allergen.

AGLAIA
(Meliaceae)

Little is known about this large genus of tropical trees and shrubs. *A. edulis* produces large, succulent fruits, which are eaten in Fiji and neighboring islands. *A. argentea* is used in Indonesia for feverish illnesses and in preparations to treat leprosy; *A. odorata* is also used medicinally, but remains primarily a perfume plant.

A. odorata (mock lime) p.76

PARTS USED Leaves, flowers.
PROPERTIES An aromatic, tonic herb that lowers fevers. Dried flowers retain perfume almost indefinitely.
USES OF THE HERB
AROMATIC Used to scent tea (China), joss sticks, and potpourris.
MEDICINAL Internally for feverish and convulsive illnesses, and menopausal problems.

GROWTH AND HARVEST
GROWTH Ornamental. Rich, well-drained soil with ample moisture, warmth, and humidity, in sun or partial shade, minimum 59–64°F (15–18°C). Propagate by semiripe cuttings in summer.
HARVEST Leaves are picked during the growing season and used fresh or dried in decoctions (sometimes with root). Flowers are gathered as they open and are dried for infusions and scented articles. Dried parts are renewed annually for medicinal use.

AGRIMONIA Agrimony
(Rosaceae)

Agrimony was once an important wound herb, known in Anglo-Saxon times as "garclive." It is an ingredient of *eau d'arquebusade*, a French herbal lotion now used for various complaints, but originally applied to wounds caused by an arquebus, a 15th-century long-barrelled gun. The related *A. pilosa* (shaggy speedwell) is used to promote clotting, due to its high vitamin K content, and is used largely to control bleeding. It is often combined with *Bletilla striata* (see p.249) and *Sanguisorba officinalis* (see p.348) in tablets for internal hemorrhage. This combination has also proved beneficial in relieving symptoms of silicosis, a serious lung disease.

A. eupatoria (agrimony, sticklewort, cocklebur) p.76

PARTS USED Whole plant.
PROPERTIES A bitter, mildly astringent, tonic, diuretic herb; it controls bleeding, improves liver and gall bladder function, and has anti-inflammatory effects.
USES OF THE HERB
MEDICINAL Internally for colitis, dyspepsia, food allergies, diarrhea, gallstones, cirrhosis, grumbling appendix, urinary incontinence, cystitis, and rheumatism. Not given to patients with stress-related constipation. Externally for sore throat, conjunctivitis, hemorrhoids, minor injuries, and chronic skin conditions.

GROWTH AND HARVEST
GROWTH Crop. Well-drained soil in sun; it tolerates dry and alkaline conditions. Propagate by seed sown in spring.
HARVEST Plants are cut when flowering, avoiding flower spikes that have started to develop spiny burs, and dried for use in infusions, liquid extracts, pills, and tinctures.

AGROPYRON
A. repens. See *Elymus repens*.

AILANTHUS
(Simaroubaceae)

A. altissima contains quassinoids, similar to those found in the related *Quassia amara*. Recent research has shown these to have anti-malarial and antineoplastic effects.

A. altissima, syn. *A. glandulosa* (tree of heaven, ailanto, Chinese sumac) p.76

PARTS USED Bark (*chun pi*).
PROPERTIES A nauseatingly bitter, astringent herb that lowers fever, relaxes spasms, and slows the heart rate. Readily causes vomiting.
USES OF THE HERB
MEDICINAL Internally for malaria, asthma, palpitations, diarrhea, dysentery, hemorrhoids, excessive menstruation, and tapeworms.

GROWTH AND HARVEST
GROWTH Ornamental. Any well-drained soil in sun or partial shade. By seed sown in autumn (may be slow to germinate), or by suckers or root cuttings in winter. In spring, cut back plants grown as shrubs hard to encourage production of very large leaves. Tolerates urban pollution. Weedy. *A. altissima* is subject to statutory control as a weed in parts of Australia.
HARVEST Bark is removed in spring and dried for decoctions and tinctures.

AJUGA Bugle
(Labiatae/Lamiaceae)

A. reptans was an ingredient of the "Traumatick Decoction" in the *London Dispensatory* of 1694, and was taken after injury. It was a favorite herb of Nicholas Culpeper, who wrote in *The English Physitian Enlarged* (1653), "If the virtues of it make you fall in love with it (as they will if you be wise) keep a syrup of it to take inwardly, an ointment and plaister of it to use outwardly, always by you." He regarded it as both a wound herb and a cure for hangovers. Other bugles are used medicinally: the Australian *A. australis* is primarily a wound herb, though also used to treat boils and sores; in Africa, *A. remota* is used to treat high blood pressure, and contains compounds with potential in both cancer therapy and biological pest control. The Mediterranean *A. iva* has anti-malarial properties.

A. chamaepitys (ground pine) p.77

Parts used Leaves.
Properties A stimulant, diuretic herb that acts mainly on the urinary system and uterus.
Uses of the herb
Medicinal Internally for gout, rheumatism, and menstrual problems.

A. reptans (bugle) p.77

Parts used Whole plant.
Properties A mild, painkilling and astringent herb with a slight laxative effect.
Uses of the herb
Medicinal Externally for bruises, wounds, and tumors.
Variants
A. r. **'Atropurpurea'**, syn. *A. r.* 'Purpurea', p.77.
A. r. **'Burgundy Glow'**, p.77.
A. r. **'Variegata'**, p.77.

Growth and Harvest
Growth Ornamental (*A. reptans* and cultivars). Crop (*A. chamaepitys*). *A. chamaepitys* thrives in poor dry soil in full sun. *A. reptans* needs moist soil in sun or partial shade. Propagate by seed in autumn or spring (*A. chamaepitys* and *A. reptans*), or by division at any time in moist, shady conditions (*A. reptans*). Germination may be erratic. Cultivars of *A. reptans* do not come true from seed.
Harvest Leaves (*A. chamaepitys*) are gathered in summer and dried for infusions and liquid extracts. Plants (*A. reptans*) are cut in summer and usually used fresh in ointments and medicated oils.

AKEBIA
(Lardizabalaceae)

The closely related species of *A. trifoliata* and *A. quinata* differ mainly in having three and five leaflets respectively, and *A. quinata* has darker purple fruits. The fruit pulp is edible and has a pleasant, sweet taste.

A. trifoliata (akebia) p.78

Parts used Stems (*mu tong*).
Properties A pungent, bitter herb that controls bacterial and fungal infections and stimulates the circulatory and urinary systems and female organs. It is a potent diuretic due to the high content of potassium salts.
Uses of the herb
Medicinal Internally for urinary tract infections, rheumatoid arthritis, absence of menstruation, and insufficient lactation. A traditional Chinese method of promoting lactation is a stew of *mu tong* and pork knuckles.

Growth and Harvest
Growth Ornamental. Well-drained soil in sun. Propagate by seed sown in spring or autumn, or by semiripe cuttings in summer, or by layering in winter. Akebias dislike disturbance.
Harvest Stems are cut in autumn and dried for use in decoctions and powders.

ALBIZIA
(Leguminosae/Mimosaceae)

A. julibrissin was first mentioned in Chinese medicine in *Omissions from the Materia Medica* (Tang Dynasty, c.AD700). Bark of the related *A. odoratissima*, which bears scented white flowers, is used externally in India and Sri Lanka for leprosy and ulcers.

A. julibrissin (silk tree) p.78

Parts used Bark, flowers (*he huan*).
Properties A bitter, astringent, sedative herb that is also diuretic and analgesic, with stimulant effects on the circulation, uterus, and appetite (bark); the flowers are tranquilizing and relieve indigestion.
Uses of the herb
Medicinal Internally for insomnia and irritability (bark, flowers), boils and carbuncles (bark), and breathlessness and poor memory (flowers). Externally for injuries, swellings, and lung abscesses (bark).

Growth and Harvest
Growth Ornamental. Well-drained, moisture-retentive soil in full sun. Tolerates poor, alkaline, and saline soils, drought, and windy positions. Propagate by seed sown in autumn, presoaked for 12 hours, or by semiripe cuttings in summer, or by root cuttings in spring. Size and shape may be controlled by cutting back the previous year's growth to 5–6 buds in spring. Plants may be attacked by scale insects, webworm, and nematodes. In the US the main trunk may be killed by vascular wilt disease, leaving the roots to sucker. Young specimens make attractive foliage plants and may be treated as annuals for the purpose. Mature specimens are hardier and more floriferous in relatively poor soils, and in areas with long hot summers.
Harvest Bark is removed in spring or late summer, and flowers as they open; both are dried for decoctions.

ALCEA Hollyhock
(Malvaceae)

The hollyhock is closely related to marsh mallow (*Althaea officinalis*, see p.236) and was once classified in the same genus. Both have similar properties, but *Alcea rosea* has largely been replaced by its more effective relative.

A. rosea, syn. *Althaea rosea* (hollyhock) p.78

Parts used Flowers.
Properties A soothing herb that relieves irritation and soreness, and has diuretic effects.
Uses of the herb
Medicinal Internally for gastritis, coughs, and cystitis. Externally as a gargle for sore throats. Often combined with *Inula helenium* (see p.296), *Tussilago farfara* (see p.365), or *Thymus* spp. (see p.362) in cough syrups.
Variants
A. r. **'Chater's Double'**, p.78.
A. r. **'Nigra'**, p.78.

Growth and Harvest
Growth Ornamental. Well-drained soil in sun. Propagate by seed sown *in situ* in spring or late summer. Rust may shrivel the foliage and kill the plant. May be damaged by Japanese beetles and caterpillars.
Harvest Flowers are picked when open and dried for infusions and syrups.

ALCHEMILLA
(Rosaceae)

"Lady's mantle," the common name for *A. xanthochlora*, refers to the plant's reputation as a herb for female disorders. It has historically been of greater importance than *A. alpina* as a medicinal herb; it appears, however, that the latter is more effective. *A. mollis* is widely planted in herb gardens but has no medicinal uses. *Alchemilla* means "little magical one," because the way in which the leaves hold water was thought to be magical.

A. alpina (alpine lady's mantle) p.79

Parts used Leaves.
Properties An astringent, anti-inflammatory herb that controls bleeding and discharges.
Uses of the herb
Medicinal Internally for menstrual, menopausal, and postpartum problems, and for diarrhea. Externally as a mouthwash after tooth extraction, douche for vaginal discharge, or skin lotion for sores and minor injuries. Also used in veterinary medicine to treat diarrhea.

A. xanthochlora, syn. *A. vulgaris* (lady's mantle, lion's foot) p.79

Parts used Whole plant.
Properties A bitter, astringent herb that controls bleeding and discharges.
Uses of the herb
Medicinal Internally for excessive or irregular menstruation, menopausal problems, and diarrhea. Externally for vaginal discharge and vulval itching.

Growth and Harvest
Growth Ornamental. Moist, well-drained soil in sun or semishade. *A. xanthochlora* dislikes lime. Propagate by seed sown in early spring, or by division in autumn or spring. Most alchemillas hybridize and self-seed readily.
Harvest Whole plants (*A. xanthochlora*) are cut as the flowers begin to open. Leaves (*A. alpina*) are cut after flowering, when the foliage is quite dry. All parts are dried for infusions and liquid extracts.

ALETRIS
(Liliaceae/Melanthiaceae)

Native to eastern N America and eastern Asia, this genus consists of ten species of rhizomatous, fibrous-rooted perennials. *A. farinosa* is an interesting plant for the peat bed but is seldom seen in cultivation. Its uses passed to settlers from native N American tribes, notably the Catawba, who made it into a tea to treat dysentery. It was listed as a tonic in the *U.S. Pharmacopoeia* (1831–1926).

A. farinosa (true unicorn root, star grass, colic root)

Small perennial, hardy to 23°F (–5°C), height 12–36in (30–90cm), spread 6in (15cm), with lanceolate, ribbed leaves up to 8in (20cm) long, pale yellow-green in color and arranged in a basal rosette. Tubular white flowers with a mealy surface are borne in spikes during summer. Found from southeastern US to Mexico, on acid or sandy soils.

PARTS USED Rhizomes.
PROPERTIES A bittersweet, soapy-tasting, tonic herb that relieves spasms, especially in the digestive and female pelvic organs.
USES OF THE HERB
MEDICINAL Internally for flatulent colic, nervous dyspepsia, anorexia, womb prolapse, and menstrual problems. Rhizomes are always used dried; if used fresh they can cause diarrhea, colic, and dizziness.

GROWTH AND HARVEST
GROWTH Wild-collected. Well-drained peaty or sandy soil in sun. Propagated by seed sown in spring.
HARVEST Rhizomes are lifted in late summer after flowering and dried for use in elixirs, liquid extracts, and powders.

ALISMA
(Alismataceae)

A. plantago-aquatica has a long history of use in Chinese medicine, and is mentioned in texts dating back to about AD200. The plant used in China is probably the smaller, white-flowered *A. p.* var. *orientale*.

A. plantago-aquatica (water plantain) p.79

PARTS USED Roots (*ze xie*).
PROPERTIES A sweet, cooling herb that lowers blood pressure, cholesterol, and blood sugar levels.
USES OF THE HERB
MEDICINAL Internally for kidney and cardiovascular disease, fluid retention, and acute diarrhea. Used in traditional Chinese medicine for kidney weakness, which manifests as deafness, tinnitus, and dizziness. Believed to stimulate the female genitalia.

GROWTH AND HARVEST
GROWTH Ornamental. Shallow water up to 10in (25cm) deep in an open, sunny position. Propagate by seed sown in late summer, or by division in spring.
HARVEST Roots are harvested before flowering and dried for decoctions.

ALKANNA Alkanet
(Boraginaceae)

Various alkanets are used as colorants, yielding reds, pinks, and flesh tones to products containing fat, oil, wax, or alcohol. Although primarily dye plants, alkanets contain compounds that also have medicinal applications. In common with many members of the family Boraginaceae, some contain a liver-damaging pyrrolizidine alkaloid, which makes internal use inadvisable.

A. tinctoria (dyer's bugloss, Spanish bugloss) p.79

PARTS USED Roots.
PROPERTIES An astringent, antibacterial herb that encourages healing and relieves itching.
USES OF THE HERB
MEDICINAL Externally for varicose and indolent ulcers, bed sores, and itching rashes. WARNING This herb is subject to legal restrictions in some countries.
ECONOMIC Used as a red colorant for wood, foodstuffs, pharmaceutical products, and cosmetics.

GROWTH AND HARVEST
GROWTH Crop. Well-drained to dry soil in sun or partial shade. *A. tinctoria* thrives in alkaline and sandy soils. Propagate by seed sown in spring, or by division in autumn. True alkanet is not grown in the US.
HARVEST Roots are lifted in autumn and dried for powders, or macerated fresh in oil or fat.

ALLIARIA
(Cruciferae)

A. petiolata was described by John Evelyn in *Acetaria, a Discourse on Sallets* (1699), under the names "Jack-by-the-hedge," "alliaria," and "sauce alone," as having many valuable medicinal properties, and "eaten as other sallets, especially by Country people, growing wild under their banks and Hedges." Its pungent flavoring is the result of volatile oils and a glycoside (sinigrin) that is similar to those found in other members of the cabbage family (Cruciferae), such as *Brassica juncea* (see p.250), *B. nigra* (see p.250), and *Sinapis alba* (see p.353).

A. petiolata, syn. *A. officinalis, Sisymbrium alliaria* (garlic mustard, hedge garlic, Jack-by-the-hedge) p.79

PARTS USED Leaves, stems.
PROPERTIES A pungent, stimulant herb that clears infection, encourages healing, and is expectorant and anti-inflammatory.
USES OF THE HERB
CULINARY Young leaves add a mild garlic flavor to salads and sauces.
MEDICINAL Internally for bronchitis, asthma, and eczema. Externally for minor injuries and slow-healing skin problems, neuralgia, rheumatism, and gout.

GROWTH AND HARVEST
GROWTH Wild-collected. Moist soil in sun or shade. Propagate by seed sown in spring where the plants are to flower. *A. petiolata* self-seeds readily.
HARVEST Leaves and stems are cut before flowering for use fresh as a juice, and fresh or dried as an infusion or poultice.

ALLIUM Onion
(Liliaceae)

Onions are a distinctive group, sometimes classified as a separate family, Alliaceae. Garlic (*A. sativum*) is one of the most ancient of man's herbs; it was used by the Babylonians (c.3000BC), found in the tomb of Tutankhamun (c.1370–52BC), and consumed in large quantities in ancient Greek and Roman times. The pervasive odor of garlic has always caused ambivalence, as in the Muslim legend that when Satan left the Garden of Eden after the Fall, garlic sprang up from his left footstep and onion from his right. There are many superstitions about garlic: it wards off vampires, causes moles to "leap out of the ground presently" (William Coles, *The Art of Simpling*, 1656), and, if chewed, prevents competitors from getting ahead in races. *A. sativum* was first mentioned in traditional Chinese medicine c.AD500. In Ayurvedic medicine it is known as *rashona*, "lacking one taste," referring to the absence of sourness, while possessing all five other tastes (pungent root, bitter leaf, astringent stem, saline top of stem, and sweet seed). The characteristic smell of alliums is caused by sulfur compounds; these have beneficial effects on the circulatory, digestive, and respiratory systems. Garlic is the most pungent of all alliums, and highest in therapeutic value. *A. cepa* is often subdivided into three main groups: the Cepa group (common onion), which has single large bulbs; the Proliferum group (tree, or Catawissa onion), which produces an inflorescence consisting largely of bulbils; and the Aggregatum group (shallot, ever-ready onion, and potato, or multiplier onion), once classified as a separate species, *A. ascalonicum*, which forms clusters of small bulbs. *A. fistulosum* is much used in Chinese cuisine, and is the most common onion grown in SE Asia. The medicinal uses were first described in Shen Nong's *Canon of Herbs*, c.AD25–200. *A. tuberosum* is less used in Chinese medicine; it was mentioned c.AD500 in *Ben Jing Ji Zhu* by Tao Hong Jin. *A. chinense* (*rakkyo*) is similar to *A. schoenoprasum*, but with brighter green, 3- to 5-angled stems; it is used mainly for pickles. Best known of the several varieties of *A. ampeloprasum* is

A. a. var. *kurrat* (*kurrat*). This Middle Eastern variety is smaller, with narrower leaves and a more developed bulb, and is used like chives. "Pearl onions" are produced for pickling from another variety, grown in central Europe and Italy.

A. ampeloprasum var. *ampeloprasum* (elephant garlic, round-headed garlic) p.80

PARTS USED Bulbs.
PROPERTIES Similar to garlic and onion.
USES OF THE HERB
CULINARY Flavor intermediate between onion and garlic, but milder.

A. cepa (onion) p.80

PARTS USED Bulb, fresh juice.
PROPERTIES A pungent herb that protects against infection, relaxes spasms, and reduces blood pressure, clotting, and blood sugar levels. It is expectorant and diuretic.
USES OF THE HERB
CULINARY Cooked or raw, onions are indispensable as vegetables or to give flavor to most meat and vegetable dishes, and relishes. They are also eaten raw or as pickles with bread and cheese. *A. c.* 'Sweet Sandwich' is ideal for eating raw, while *A. c.* 'Noordhollandse Bloedrode' is attractive in salads. The miniature onions produced by *A. c.* var. *proliferum* are used fresh or cooked in the same way as scallions.
MEDICINAL Internally for bronchial and gastric infections (liquid extract of bulbs). Externally for acne and boils.
VARIANTS
***A. c.* 'Ailsa Craig'**, p.80.
***A. c.* 'Noordhollandse Bloedrode'**, p.80.
***A. c.* 'Sweet Sandwich'**, p.80.
A. c.* var. *proliferum, p.80.

A. fistulosum (Welsh onion, scallion, spring onion) p.80

PARTS USED Whole plant, bulb (*cong bai*), roots (*cong xu*).
PROPERTIES A pungent, tonic, antibiotic herb that stimulates the digestion, lowers fever by increasing perspiration, and reduces blood cholesterol levels. It is also diuretic, anti-inflammatory, and expectorant.
USES OF THE HERB
CULINARY Much used in Chinese and Western cuisines, both raw and cooked.
MEDICINAL Internally in traditional Chinese medicine as a decoction of the fresh plant, for the early stages of the common cold, and for excess mucus following respiratory tract infections. Regarded as especially useful for complaints and injuries caused by extreme cold (such as frostbite), and low *yang* energy.
VARIANT
***A. f.* 'White Lisbon'**, p.80.

A. sativum, syn. *A. controversum* (garlic) p.80

PARTS USED Bulbs (*da suan*).
PROPERTIES A pungent, warming herb that wards off or clears bacterial infection; lowers fever by increasing perspiration; reduces blood pressure, cholesterol, and blood sugar levels; and is expectorant. Regarded as rejuvenative, detoxicant, and aphrodisiac in Ayurvedic medicine.
USES OF THE HERB
CULINARY Garlic enhances the flavor of most meats, seafood, and many vegetables. It is an essential ingredient of regional dishes in many parts of the world, notably in southern Europe, the Middle East, the Far East, the W Indies, Mexico, and S America. Raw garlic predominates in sauces such as *aïoli* (Spain and southern France), and *skordalia* (Greece), and is added as a condiment to butter, oil, vinegar, and salt.
MEDICINAL Internally to prevent infection and to treat colds, influenza, bronchitis, whooping cough, gastroenteritis, and dysentery. Externally for skin problems, especially acne, and fungal infections. In addition to these traditional uses, garlic has recently been found to reduce glucose metabolism in diabetes, slow the development of arteriosclerosis, and lower the risk of further heart attacks in myocardial infarct patients. It is taken raw (crushed or as juice), as a syrup or tincture, or in capsules.

A. schoenoprasum, syn. *A. sibiricum* (chives) p.80

PARTS USED Leaves, bulbs, flowers.
PROPERTIES Similar effects to other alliums, but is milder and rarely used medicinally.
USES OF THE HERB
CULINARY Chives are especially good with potatoes and eggs. Leaves and bulbs are used to garnish and flavor soups and salads, and in soft cheeses, omelettes, and sauces such as *remoulade* and *ravigote*. Flowers also have a mild onion flavor, and are sprinkled into salads.
VARIANT
***A. s.* 'Forescate'**, p.80.

A. scorodoprasum (rocambole, sand leek) p.81

PARTS USED Leaves, bulbs.
PROPERTIES A pungent herb, similar to garlic.
USES OF THE HERB
CULINARY Used to flavor salads, soups, and stir-fries.

A. tricoccum (ramps, wild leek)

Perennial, hardy to 5°F (–15°C), height 6–18in (15–45cm), spread 4–12in (10–30cm), with slender, onionlike bulbs and long-stalked umbels of white flowers. Leaves are elliptic, 8–10in (20–24cm) long, appearing in spring and fading before flowers are borne. Native to eastern N America, where annual ramps festivals are held.

PARTS USED Leaves, bulbs.
PROPERTIES A pungent herb with properties similar to *A. sativum*.
USES OF THE HERB
CULINARY Bulbs were traditionally baked in the fire or dried for use as a food to reduce acidity. Used today mainly as a flavoring.
MEDICINAL As a spring tonic in native N American medicine, and to treat colds, sore throat, and worms in children. Externally for earache.

A. tuberosum (Chinese chives, garlic chives, *cuchay*) p.81

PARTS USED Leaves, roots, flower buds, seeds (*jiu zi*).
PROPERTIES An antiemetic herb that improves kidney function. It has a mild onion–garlic flavor.
USES OF THE HERB
CULINARY Chopped leaves and flower buds are added to salads, soft cheeses, and stir-fries. Lengthy cooking destroys the flavor. Blanched leaves are used with rice and pork in Chinese cuisine.
MEDICINAL Internally for urinary incontinence, kidney and bladder weakness, and stomach chills with vomiting (seeds). Externally with *Gardenia augusta* (see p.286) as a poultice for knee injuries.

A. ursinum (ramsons) p.81

PARTS USED Whole flowering plant, leaves.
PROPERTIES A strong-smelling, pungent herb, similar in flavor and effects to garlic.
USES OF THE HERB
CULINARY Leaves are used according to taste in salads, sandwiches, and savory dishes.
MEDICINAL Internally for high blood pressure and hardening of the arteries (fresh herb, leaves).

GROWTH AND HARVEST

GROWTH Ornamental (*A. cepa* var. *proliferum*, *A. schoenoprasum* and cultivars). Crop (*A. ampeloprasum* var. *ampeloprasum*, *A. cepa* and cultivars, *A. fistulosum* and cultivars, *A. sativum*). Wild-collected (*A. scorodoprasum*, *A. tricoccum*, *A. ursinum*). Rich, well-drained soil in full sun. *A. schoenoprasum* tolerates damper conditions, heavier soil, and a less open position than most other alliums. *A. scorodoprasum* thrives in poor, dry soils. *A. tricoccum* and *A. ursinum* prefer moist soil in shade. Propagate by seed sown in spring, or by bulbils planted in autumn or spring (*A. ampeloprasum* var. *ampeloprasum*). By seed sown in autumn or spring, or by "sets" (small bulbs) planted in spring (*A. cepa*). Sowing and planting of cultivars of *A. cepa* vary widely in different climates. By seed sown in succession in spring for summer use, and in summer for autumn and spring use (*A. fistulosum*). By bulbs or individual cloves planted in autumn or winter (*A. sativum*). By seed sown in spring, or by division in autumn or spring (*A. schoenoprasum*, *A. tuberosum*). By bulbils or cloves, planted in autumn or early spring (*A. scorodoprasum*). By seed sown in spring, or by bulbs planted when dormant (*A. tricoccum*, *A. ursinum*). Cut *A. schoenoprasum* down to the ground after flowering to produce fresh leaves. Onion ►

► fly is common in some countries on light soils; downy mildew is prevalent in wet weather; rots may affect both growing and stored bulbs. Onions, garlic, and chives are often recommended in companion planting to deter pests, weeds, and diseases, though both are supposed to affect legumes adversely.
HARVEST *A. ampeloprasum* var. *ampeloprasum*, *A. cepa*, and *A. sativum* are harvested in late summer and early autumn. *A. cepa* and *A. sativum* are left to dry in the sun before being stored at 37–41°F (3–5°C). *A. fistulosum* is pulled when the stems are pencil-thick, and used fresh. *A. schoenoprasum* is cut as required during the growing season. It is best used fresh. *A. tricoccum*, *A. tuberosum*, and *A. ursinum* are gathered as required and used fresh. *A. tuberosum* is blanched in China using clay pots or straw "tents" to give tender leaves that are eaten raw in finger length pieces.

ALNUS Alder
(Betulaceae)

A number of different alders are used, for lumber, dyes, and medicinal purposes. These include *A. serrulata* (hazel alder) of eastern N America, *A. rubra*, a western N American species, and *A. rugosa* (speckled alder). All were major sources of astringent remedies to native people.

A. glutinosa, syn. *A. rotundifolia* (common alder, European alder, black alder) p.81

PARTS USED Bark, leaves.
PROPERTIES An astringent, tonic herb that encourages healing of damaged tissues.
USES OF THE HERB
MEDICINAL Internally and externally for rheumatism (bark). Externally for throat, mouth, dental infections, and scabies (bark); as a poultice for inflammatory conditions such as rheumatism (leaves).
ECONOMIC Various parts, notably the bark, are used as coloring agents, producing red and (with copper) black dyes.
VARIANT
A. g. **'Imperialis'**, p.81.

GROWTH AND HARVEST
GROWTH Ornamental. Rich, moist to wet soil in sun or partial shade. Propagate by seed sown in autumn or spring, or by suckers detached in autumn, or by hardwood cuttings in early winter. Trees may be coppiced to minimize damage from harvesting of bark.
A. g. 'Imperialis' does not come true from seed.
HARVEST Bark of young twigs and two- to three-year-old branches is peeled off lengthwise when fresh, and dried for decoctions and powders. Leaves are picked in summer and used fresh.

ALOE
(Liliaceae/Aloeaceae)

A. vera has been identified in wall paintings in ancient Egypt, where it was used to treat excess mucus. It was also an embalming ingredient; the body of Jesus was wrapped in linen impregnated with myrrh and aloes "as the manner of the Jews is to bury" (John 19: 39–40). Records in ancient Greece date back to the fourth century BC. The use of *A. vera* in Chinese medicine is rather later, being first mentioned in the 11th century. It appears in Anglo-Saxon medical texts, having been introduced to Europe in the 10th century. Various aloes have similar constituents to *A. vera* and are used in the same ways. These include *A. ferox* (Cape aloe) and *A. perryi* (Socotrine or Zanzibar aloe). "Aloes" or "bitter aloes" is the name given to a purgative drug made from the leaves of several species.
WARNING This herb, in the form of aloes, is subject to legal restrictions in some countries.

A. vera, syn. *A. barbadensis* (Barbados aloe, Curaçao aloe) p.81

PARTS USED Leaves (occasionally), sap (*lu hui*).
PROPERTIES An intensely bitter, purgative herb that controls fungal infection, is anti-inflammatory, and promotes healing. It also destroys intestinal parasites and stimulates the uterus.
USES OF THE HERB
MEDICINAL Internally for chronic constipation (especially following iron medication), poor appetite, digestive problems, and in colonic irrigation. Not given to pregnant women or to patients with hemorrhoids or irritable bowel syndrome. Leaves are a strong purgative and require great care over dosage. Externally for burns, scalds, sunburn, wounds, eczema, and to prevent nail biting. To prevent griping in laxative formulations, it is usually combined with *Foeniculum vulgare* (see p.283) or *Tamarindus indica* (see p.359).
ECONOMIC Used in cosmetic and pharmaceutical preparations.

GROWTH AND HARVEST
GROWTH Ornamental. Very well-drained soil in sun, minimum 41°F (5°C). Propagate by offsets at any time. Mealybug may attack pot plants. *A. vera* rarely sets seed.
HARVEST Leaves are cut as required from two- or three-year old plants. Sap is drained from cut leaves and used fresh, or evaporated to a brown crystalline solid for the preparation of creams, decoctions, lotions, pills, and tinctures.

ALOYSIA
(Verbenaceae)

Dried leaves of *A. triphylla* (lemon verbena) retain their fragrance well and are a useful ingredient for potpourris. Lemon verbena oil was once popular in perfumery, especially in the citrus cologne *eau de verveine*, but was expensive. Its use further declined following evidence that it may sensitize the skin to sunlight and it has largely been replaced by *Cymbopogon* species (see p.270).

A. triphylla, syn. *Lippia citriodora* (lemon verbena) p.82

PARTS USED Leaves, oil.
PROPERTIES An astringent, aromatic herb, rich in volatile oils, that acts as a mild sedative, relieving spasms, especially of the digestive system, and reducing fever. The essential oil is both insecticidal and bactericidal.
USES OF THE HERB
CULINARY Fresh leaves are used in herb teas, and to flavor stuffings and salads.
AROMATIC Dried leaves are used in potpourris.
MEDICINAL Internally for feverish colds and indigestion. In aromatherapy for nervous and digestive problems and for acne, boils, and cysts.

GROWTH AND HARVEST
GROWTH Ornamental. Light, well-drained soil in sun. Propagate by heel cuttings in spring at 64°F (18°C), or by softwood cuttings in summer. Cut back main stems to 12in (30cm) and sideshoots to within two or three buds of the old wood in spring, or remove dead wood in early summer. Plants grown outdoors may not show signs of new growth until early summer.
HARVEST Leaves are picked in summer and used mainly fresh for oil extraction or flavoring, or dried for infusions and potpourris.

ALPINIA
(Zingiberaceae)

A. officinarum is of great importance as a medicinal herb; it has been used in both Ayurvedic and Chinese medicine since very early times (c.AD500 in China), and in Europe since the Middle Ages. In addition to *A. officinarum* and *A. galanga*, several other species are used for flavorings and medicines. *Yi zhi*, from the southern Chinese *A. oxyphylla* (black cardamom), is a warming digestive and kidney tonic, used in traditional Chinese medicine for diarrhea, incontinence, and stomach chills.

A. galanga (galangal, greater galingal, Siamese ginger) p.82

PARTS USED Rhizomes, oil.
PROPERTIES An aromatic, bitter, pungent herb that stimulates the digestive system.
USES OF THE HERB
CULINARY Raw rhizome is a popular ingredient in many Indonesian and Malaysian dishes for its gingerlike flavor. Oil and extracts are used as flavoring, especially in liqueurs, soft drinks, and bitters.

A. officinarum (galangal, lesser galingal)

Tender perennial, height 2½–4ft (75cm–1.2m), spread indefinite, with a red-brown, scaly rhizome up to 1in (2cm) thick; the thick, lanceolate leaves are up to 16in (40cm) long, with panicles of white, red-streaked, orchidlike flowers. Native to grassland and thickets in China and Vietnam.

PARTS USED Rhizomes (*gao liang*), oil.
PROPERTIES A bitter, aromatic, stimulant herb that acts mainly on the digestive system. It also relieves pain, lowers fevers, and controls bacterial and fungal infections.
USES OF THE HERB
CULINARY Raw rhizome, oil, and extracts are used for flavoring as for *A. galanga*.
MEDICINAL Internally for digestive upsets, chronic gastritis and gastric ulceration, and epigastric and rheumatic pain. Externally for skin infections, skin cancer, and gum disease.

GROWTH AND HARVEST
GROWTH Crop. Well-drained, humus-rich soil in partial shade with high humidity, minimum 59–64°F (15–18°C). Propagate by division of rhizome as new growth begins. Spider mite may attack plants under cover.
HARVEST Rhizomes four to six years old are lifted at the end of the growing season and used fresh, or dried for use in decoctions, liquid extracts, and tinctures, or distilled for oil.

ALSTONIA
(Apocynaceae)

Alstonia bark is the trade name given to the bark of *A. scholaris* and the Australian *A. constricta* (fever bark, Australian quinine). Both contain indole alkaloids, though their exact constituents differ. The related African *A. boonei* contains alkaloids that act as an antidote to *Strophanthus* poisoning. *A. scholaris* is so named because the soft wood was once used for making writing slates before paper was widely available.

A. scholaris (devil tree, dita bark, milky pine) p.82

PARTS USED Bark.
PROPERTIES A bitter, astringent, alterative herb that lowers fever, relaxes spasms, stimulates lactation, and expels intestinal worms. It also stimulates the uterus, making it unsafe for pregnant women.
USES OF THE HERB
MEDICINAL Internally for malaria, chronic diarrhea, dysentery, and intestinal parasites.
ECONOMIC Light, soft wood is used for making masks and coffins.

GROWTH AND HARVEST
GROWTH Wild-collected. Moist to wet soil in sun or partial shade, minimum 59–64°F (15–18°C). Propagate by hardwood cuttings in moist sand in early spring, at 70°F (21°C).
HARVEST Bark is stripped and dried for liquid extracts, tinctures, decoctions, and powder.

ALTHAEA
(Malvaceae)

The healing properties of *A. officinalis* were first recorded in the ninth century BC, and were widely used in Greek medicine. They are concentrated in the roots. Powdered roots were once used to make soft lozenges (*pâté de guimauve*) for throat infections and coughs – forerunners of the popular candy "marshmallow," which no longer contains extracts of the herb. *Malva sylvestris* (see p.308) and *M. neglecta* have similar properties, but are considered less effective.

A. officinalis (marsh mallow) p.82

PARTS USED Leaves, roots.
PROPERTIES A sweet, mucilaginous herb that soothes and softens tissues, has expectorant effects, and controls bacterial infection.
USES OF THE HERB
MEDICINAL Internally for inflammation and ulceration of the digestive tract, hiatus hernia, bronchitis, excess mucus, asthma, whooping cough, and cystitis (roots); and for urinary tract infections, excess mucus, bronchitis, irritating coughs, and cystitis (leaves). Externally for boils, abscesses, eye and skin inflammations, insect bites, splinters, minor injuries, gingivitis, mastitis, and gangrene. Often combined with *Symphytum officinale* (see p.357) for digestive complaints; with *Glycyrrhiza glabra* (see p.289), *Marrubium vulgare* (see p.308), or *Lobelia inflata* (see p.305) for bronchial complaints; and with *Ulmus rubra* for external use. Peeled root is given to children to chew as a traditional aid to teething.

A. rosea. See *Alcea rosea.*

GROWTH AND HARVEST
GROWTH Ornamental. Moist to wet soil in sun. Propagate by seed sown when ripe in late summer, or by division in autumn. Germination is erratic.
HARVEST Leaves are gathered in summer and dried for infusions, ointments, and liquid extracts. Roots are lifted in autumn, preferably from two-year-old plants, and dried for liquid extracts, ointments, and syrups.

AMARANTHUS
(Amaranthaceae)

Many species of *Amaranthus* are used as vegetables and pot herbs, and some tropical American species are important locally as grain crops. *A. hypochondriacus* is best known as an herb, but it also has nutritious leaves and seeds with high protein levels (15 percent). Species with similar medicinal uses include: *A. retroflexus* (green amaranth), which originated in tropical America and is now naturalized in the US; *A. polygamus*, an Indian species with reputedly aphrodisiac seeds; and the Chinese *A. spinosus* (wild amaranth), which is used both as an astringent and a febrifuge.

A. hypochondriacus, syn. *A. hybridus* subsp. *hypochondriacus* (prince's feather) p.82

PARTS USED Whole plant, leaves, seeds.
PROPERTIES An astringent, soothing, cooling herb that controls bleeding.
USES OF THE HERB
CULINARY Leaves are eaten as a vegetable. Seeds are harvested as a grain crop.
MEDICINAL Internally for diarrhea and excessive menstruation. Externally for ulcerated mouth and throat, vaginal discharge, wounds, and nosebleeds.
ECONOMIC The red pigment is used as coloring in foods and medicines.

GROWTH AND HARVEST
GROWTH Ornamental. Rich, well-drained soil in sun. Ample water and humidity intensifies foliage color. Propagate by seed sown in spring at 59°F (15°C). Plants grown under cover may be attacked by aphids.
HARVEST Whole plants are cut when coming into flower and dried for infusions and liquid extracts. Leaves are picked as required and eaten fresh. Seeds are harvested when ripe.

AMMI
(Umbelliferae/Apiaceae)

These medicinal herbs have long been used in the Middle East; *A. visnaga* was mentioned in the Ebers papyri c.1550BC. The seeds contain a fatty oil, which includes khellin. Research into khellin in the 1950s led to the formulation of many commercial drugs for the management of asthma attacks. *A. majus* is widely grown in India for the treatment of vitiligo (blotchy skin): the active ingredient is psoralene, which stimulates pigment production in skin exposed to ultraviolet light. It also has a long history of use as a contraceptive in various cultures. A decoction of ground seeds taken after intercourse appears able to prevent implantation of the fertilized ovum in the uterus. It is known as *cure-dents du Prophète* in Morocco, where it is used as a gargle for toothache.

A. copticum. See *Trachyspermum ammi.*

A. majus (bullwort, bishopsweed, Queen Anne's lace) p.82

PARTS USED Seeds.
PROPERTIES A tonic, diuretic herb that affects skin pigmentation.
USES OF THE HERB
MEDICINAL Externally, in commercial preparations, for vitiligo and psoriasis. Excess causes nausea, diarrhea, and headaches.
WARNING This herb is subject to legal restrictions in some countries.

A. visnaga, syn. *Daucus visnaga* (khella) p.83

PARTS USED Seeds.
PROPERTIES An aromatic herb that dilates the

bronchial, urinary, and blood vessels without affecting blood pressure.
USES OF THE HERB
MEDICINAL Internally for asthma, angina, coronary arteriosclerosis, and kidney stones. WARNING This herb is subject to legal restrictions in some countries.

GROWTH AND HARVEST
GROWTH Ornamental (*A. majus*). Crop (*A. visnaga*). Well-drained soil in sun. Propagate by seed sown in spring or autumn.
HARVEST Seeds are gathered when ripe and dried for powders, tinctures, and liquid extracts. Fractions of the fatty oil are extracted for drug formulation.

AMOMUM
(Zingiberaceae)

Several species in this genus are known as cardamom and are used for culinary and medicinal purposes, mainly for gastro-intestinal complaints. They have aromatic seeds but are not as pleasant in flavor as the true cardamom (*Elettaria cardamomum*, see p.277). *A. xanthioides* was first mentioned in Chinese medicine during the Ming dynasty (1368–1654). It contains a camphoraceous volatile oil that includes borneol, used for infusions and decoctions.

A. xanthioides (Tavoy cardamom, bastard cardamom, grains of Paradise)

Tender rhizomatous perennial with reedlike stems up to 10ft (3m) tall, and two rows of lanceolate leaves about 14in (35cm) long. Orchidlike flowers are produced in dense spikes on short, leafy stalks near the base of the plant.

PARTS USED Seeds (*sha ren*).
PROPERTIES An aromatic, warming herb that stimulates the appetite, relieves indigestion, and controls nausea and vomiting.
USES OF THE HERB
CULINARY Used as a substitute for true cardamom in flavoring food and liqueurs.
MEDICINAL Internally for digestive disturbances, notably in irritable bowel syndrome and pregnancy.

GROWTH AND HARVEST
GROWTH Crop. Rich soil, with moisture and humidity in partial shade, minimum 64°F (18°C). Propagate by division as new growth begins. Spider mite may attack plants under cover.
HARVEST Seeds of ripe fruits are used in decoctions and for food flavoring.

ANACARDIUM
(Anacardiaceae)

The fruits of *A. occidentale*, or cashew apples, yield a pleasantly acidic pulp and juice. Shells contain a caustic oil that is extracted before the nuts are removed. Several species have resinous bark, containing a gum resembling gum arabic, used for making varnish.

A. occidentale (cashew, *marañon*, *acajou*) p.83

PARTS USED Leaves, bark, fruits, seeds, oil.
PROPERTIES Reduces fever (leaves) and blood sugar levels (bark), and is diuretic (fruits); the nuts (seeds) are a source of nutrients, and the shell oil is toxic to many disease-causing organisms, such as *Staphylococcus* bacteria.
USES OF THE HERB
CULINARY Juice from the fruits is made into drinks and jam. Nuts are eaten roasted and used in a variety of both sweet and savory dishes, and also ground when raw to make cashew milk, a substitute for dairy milk in special diets.
MEDICINAL Internally for diarrhea (bark and leaf extracts, fruit juice), hypoglycemia (bark extract), and influenza (fruit juice), and, in west Africa, for malaria (leaf and bark infusions). Externally for leprosy, ringworm, warts, and corns (fresh extract from shells), and, in west Africa, for toothache and sore gums (leaf and bark infusions). Bark extract is regarded by native Amazonians as having contraceptive properties. WARNING Oil is a skin irritant; oil vapor is irritant if inhaled.
ECONOMIC Shell oil is used in brake linings, synthetic rubbers, and to treat paper and wood against insect attack. Planted in erosion control.

GROWTH AND HARVEST
GROWTH Crop. Well-drained, sandy soil in sun, with ample moisture during the growing season, minimum 64°F (18°C). Propagate by hardwood cuttings at the end of the growing season.
HARVEST Leaves are picked at any time and dried. Bark is removed as required and used fresh or dried. Fruits are harvested when ripe and processed into fresh pulp and juice. Oil is extracted from the shells, and the seeds (nuts) are removed and used fresh or roasted.

ANACYCLUS Mount Atlas daisy
(Compositae/Asteraceae)

A. pyrethrum has been extensively used from medieval times to the present by Arabian, Asian, and European physicians. Culpeper recommended that "the herb or root dried and chewed in the mouth, purges the brain of phlegmatic humours; thereby not only easing pains in the head and teeth, but also hinders the distilling of the brain upon the lungs and eyes, thereby preventing coughs, phthisicks and consumption, the apoplexy and falling sickness" (*The English Physitian Enlarged*, 1653). *A. pyrethrum* should not be confused with the insecticidal pyrethrum, which is from *Tanacetum cinerariifolium* (see p.359).

A. pyrethrum (pellitory, pellitory of Spain) p.83

PARTS USED Roots.
PROPERTIES A pungent, acrid herb that stimulates the salivary glands and irritates the tissues, thereby increasing blood flow to the area.
USES OF THE HERB
MEDICINAL Externally for toothache, facial neuralgia, and excess mucus.

GROWTH AND HARVEST
GROWTH Ornamental. Well-drained soil in sun. Propagate by seed sown in spring or autumn, or by softwood cuttings in spring.
HARVEST Roots are lifted in autumn and dried for decoctions, lozenges, and tinctures, and as a powder.

ANAGALLIS Pimpernel
(Primulaceae)

Once highly regarded as a medicinal herb, with uses dating back to Pliny (AD23–79) and Dioscorides, *A. arvensis* is no longer recommended. It contains irritant saponins, which recent research shows have antiviral effects, and cucurbitacins (as found in *Bryonia*, see p.251), which are highly toxic.

A. arvensis (scarlet pimpernel, poor man's weatherglass) p.83

PARTS USED Whole plant.
PROPERTIES An acrid, mucilaginous herb that lowers fever and has diuretic and expectorant effects.
USES OF THE HERB
MEDICINAL Traditionally prescribed internally for depression, tuberculosis, liver complaints, epilepsy, dropsy, and rheumatism. No longer considered safe by most medical herbalists, but of interest to medical researchers. Externally, as pimpernel water, for improving the complexion, especially for freckles.
VARIANT
A. a. var. *caerulea*, p.83.

GROWTH AND HARVEST
GROWTH Wild-collected (*A. arvensis*). Ornamental (*A. arvensis* var. *caerulea*). Well-drained to dry or sandy soil in sun. Propagate by seed sown in spring at 61–64°F (16–18°C). Aphids may attack plants under cover.
HARVEST Whole plants are gathered in summer and used fresh, often as expressed juice, or dried for infusions, liquid extracts, tinctures, and powder.
WARNING Harmful if eaten.

ANEMARRHENA
(Liliaceae/Asphodelaceae)

This genus has only one species, found in Japan and northern China. *A. asphodeloides* is a night-flowering member of the lily family, resembling an asphodel in appearance, as its name suggests. This attractive plant has potential as an ornamental but is little known in the West. Though not widespread or common, it has largely been collected in the wild for medicinal use. *Anemarrhena* was first recorded in traditional Chinese medicine c.AD200. It contains steroidal saponins, including asphonin, which has proven antipyretic effects. Studies are currently being carried out in China with the aim of establishing it as a cultivated crop.

A. asphodeloides

Rhizomatous perennial, hardy to 23°F (-5°C), 1½–3ft (45cm–1m) in height, of indefinite spread, with linear leaves 8in (20cm) long and 2in (5cm) wide. Small, yellow-white 6-petaled flowers, which are fragrant and open in the evening, are borne in spikes 3ft (1m) tall from late summer to autumn. They are followed by globose capsules containing one or two triangular black seeds.

Parts used Rhizomes (*zhi mu*).
Properties A bitter, mucilaginous, tonic herb that has expectorant and diuretic effects, lowers fever, reduces blood sugar levels, and clears bacterial and fungal infections.
Uses of the herb
Medicinal Internally for high fever in infectious diseases, tuberculosis, chronic bronchitis, and urinary problems. Not given to patients with diarrhea. Excess may cause a sudden drop in blood pressure. Externally as a mouthwash for mouth ulcers. Therapeutic action is slightly altered by cooking with wine or salt.

Growth and Harvest
Growth Wild-collected. Moist soil in partial shade. Propagate by division in spring, or by seeds sown when ripe.
Harvest Rhizomes are lifted in autumn and dried for use in decoctions.

Anemone

A. hepatica. See *Hepatica nobilis*.
A. pulsatilla. See *Pulsatilla vulgaris*.

Anethum Dill

(Umbelliferae/Apiaceae)

Dill has been an important medicinal herb in the Middle East since Biblical times; the Talmud (ancient Jewish law) records that it was subject to a tithe. Numerous uses were described by Pliny (AD23–79) and various European writers from the 10th century onward. According to Culpeper (*The English Physitian Enlarged*, 1653), "It stays the hiccough, being boiled in wine…and is used in medicines that serve to expel wind, and the pains proceeding therefrom." Dill also has a long history of both culinary and medicinal use in India.

A. graveolens, syn. *Peucedanum graveolens* (dill) p.83

Parts used Leaves, seeds, oil.
Properties A pungent, cooling, aromatic herb that calms and tones the digestive system, controls infection, and has diuretic effects.
Uses of the herb
Culinary Both seeds and leaves are widely used in cooking, especially in Scandinavian cuisine, with eggs, fish, seafood, and potatoes. Sprigs of dill are added to pickles and vinegar; chopped dill is a main ingredient of gravadlax (preserved salmon). Seeds of *A. g.* subsp. *sowa* are used in curry powder and leaves are added to rice and soups.
Medicinal Internally for digestive disorders, including indigestion, colic, flatulence (especially as an ingredient of gripe water for babies), and hiatus hernia.
Economic Oil is used in commercial medicines, soaps, detergents, and food flavoring.
Variants
***A. g.* 'Bouquet'**
Regarded as the best American cultivar for seed production, this plant has compact, prolific seedheads. Height 24–36in (60–90cm), spread 6–12in (15–30cm).
***A. g.* 'Fernleaf'**
An American dwarf cultivar, height 18in (45cm), spread 18–24in (45–60cm), with luxuriant, dark blue-green foliage. It is slow to bolt and excellent for containers.
***A. g.* 'Mammoth'**, p.84.
A. g.* subsp. *sowa (Indian dill)
Slightly taller than the species, height 4ft (1.2m), spread 18in (45cm), Indian dill has a white stem and very finely divided leaves. Containing less carvone, it also differs slightly in flavor.

Growth and Harvest
Growth Ornamental (*A. graveolens* subsp. *sowa*: crop). Well-drained, neutral to slightly acid soil in sun. Propagate by seed sown in spring or summer, thinned to 8in (20cm) apart. For a regular supply of leaves, make successional sowings every 3–4 weeks from early spring to midsummer. Dill bolts if overcrowded or in poor dry soil. It should not be grown near fennel because the two may hybridize, producing plants intermediate in flavor and appearance. Dill reputedly has an adverse effect on carrots, but is beneficial to cabbage if planted nearby. The flowers attract many beneficial insects that prey on aphids.
Harvest Leaves are cut in spring and summer for use fresh or dried in cooking. Seeds are gathered in summer and dried for infusions and dill water, ground in powders, or distilled for oil.

Angelica

(Umbelliferae/Apiaceae)

All angelicas contain furocoumarins, which increase skin photosensitivity and may cause dermatitis. *A. archangelica* became popular in Europe during the 15th century and was rated as the most important of all medicinal herbs by Parkinson (*Paradisi in Sole*, 1629). *A. polymorpha* var. *sinensis* (commonly referred to as *A. sinensis*) is probably the most important Chinese tonic after ginseng, dating back to about AD200. It is a component of many Chinese patent medicines in Hong Kong, San Francisco, and Singapore, as well as in China. A number of other angelicas are used in similar ways throughout the world, including *A. atropurpurea*, American angelica; the European wild angelica, *A. sylvestris*; the Chinese *A. gigas*, *A. keiskei*, *A. anomala*, and *A. pubescens*; and the Indian *A. glauca*. The tonic properties are thought to be highest in *A. glauca* and *A. polymorpha* var. *sinensis*. Known as *choraka* in Ayurvedic medicine, angelicas of various kinds are used mainly as a tonic for women, and are often combined with *Asparagus racemosus* (see p.245).

A. archangelica (angelica) p.84

Parts used Leaves, stems, roots, seeds.
Properties A bittersweet, aromatic, anti-inflammatory herb that relaxes spasms, increases perspiration, lowers fever, and has expectorant effects. It acts mainly on the bronchial, digestive, urinary, and female reproductive systems.
Uses of the herb
Culinary Foliage is eaten as a vegetable in Greenland and Scandinavia. Young stalks are candied for decorating cakes and desserts, or may be added to stewed rhubarb and orange marmalade. Roots and seeds are used to flavor liqueurs.
Medicinal Internally for digestive problems, including gastric ulcers, anorexia, and migraine sickness (for which it may be combined with *Chamaemelum nobile*, see p.259), bronchitis, excess mucus, and influenza (often combined with *Achillea millefolium*, see p.227, or *Tussilago farfara*, see p.365), chronic fatigue, and menstrual and obstetric problems. Not given to pregnant women, nor to patients suffering from diabetes. Externally for rheumatic pain, neuralgia, and pleurisy.

A. polymorpha var. ***sinensis***, syn. *A. sinensis* (Chinese angelica) p.84

Parts used Roots (*dang gui*).
Properties A bittersweet, aromatic herb that acts primarily as a tonic, especially for the female reproductive system and liver. It is also a mild laxative, sedative, and painkiller with some anti-bacterial activity.
Uses of the herb
Medicinal Internally for menstrual, postpartum, and menopausal complaints, and anemia. Not given to pregnant women. Also used as an injection into acupuncture points, for painful injury, neuralgia, angina, and arthritis. Chicken soup with angelica root is a popular Chinese folk remedy after childbirth.

Growth and Harvest
Growth Ornamental (*A. archangelica*). Crop (*A. polymorpha* var. *sinensis*). Rich, moist soil in sun or partial shade. Propagate by seed sown *in situ* in autumn or spring. Seed is viable for one year only, but most plants tend to self-seed freely. Removing the flower heads before seed develops will prolong the life of short-lived species. The flowers attract many beneficial insects, such as wasps, that prey on garden pests.
Harvest Roots are lifted in autumn, leaves gathered before flowering, and seeds harvested as they ripen; all are dried for decoctions. Stems of *A. archangelica* are cut in early summer.
Warning Skin allergen.

ANIBA
(Lauraceae)

Forty species of evergreen trees and shrubs make up this genus, which is found in tropical American and W Indian rainforests, with one species in India. Several are used for essential oils, hardwood lumber, and medicinal compounds. Native peoples use some species medicinally. Commercially, the most important is *A. roseaodora*, which has been exploited since 1875, when a Frenchman first distilled its exquisite fragrant oil, known as *bois de rose* or rosewood oil. First harvested from the wild in French Guiana, where supplies are now exhausted, stocks are currently taken from rainforests in Brazil. One or two plantations have been established, but little natural regeneration takes place. The need for urgent research into the life cycle and cultivation requirements of this rainforest tree was recognized by the Food and Agriculture Organization of the United Nations (FAO) in 1986.

A. roseaodora (*pau rosa, cara-cara*)

Tender, aromatic evergreen tree up to 80ft (25m) in height, 50ft (15m) spread. It has a slender habit, with leathery, obovate-elliptic leaves about 5½in (14cm) long, which have downy, yellow-brown undersides. Insignificant flowers are borne in downy, dull red panicles, up to 7in (18cm) long, at various times of the year. Found in understory rainforest in Amazonia and the Guianas.

PARTS USED Wood, oil.
PROPERTIES Rich in linalol, a volatile oil with a lily fragrance.
USES OF THE HERB
AROMATIC Oil gives fragrance to pharmaceutical products, detergents, and perfumes.
ECONOMIC This species yields a valuable hardwood. Oil is used to flavor candy, frozen desserts, chewing gum, and baked goods.

GROWTH AND HARVEST
GROWTH Wild-collected. Tender. Moist, well-drained soil in shade, with high humidity, minimum 59–64°F (15–18°C). Propagates by seed sown when ripe; needs light to germinate. Seeds are difficult to harvest.
HARVEST Trees are cut when 10–15 years old and chipped for steam-distillation of oil.

ANTENNARIA Pussy-toes
(Compositae/Asteraceae)

Although *A. dioica* is the only species in the genus with widespread use as a medicinal herb, several species in the closely related genus *Gnaphalium* (see p.289) feature in traditional medicine. *A. dioica* was formerly classified as *G. dioica*.

A. dioica (pussy-toes, catsfoot, cat's ear) p.84

PARTS USED Whole plant, flowers.
PROPERTIES An astringent, aromatic herb that has diuretic effects and stimulates the liver and gall bladder.
USES OF THE HERB
MEDICINAL Internally for liver and gall bladder complaints, hepatitis, and diarrhea. Externally as a gargle for tonsillitis and a douche for vaginitis.
VARIANT
A. d. **'Rosea'**, p.85.

GROWTH AND HARVEST
GROWTH Ornamental. Well-drained soil in sun. Propagate by seed under cover or by division in spring.
HARVEST Whole plants or flower heads are cut before the flowers are fully open, and dried for use in infusions.

ANTHEMIS

A. nobilis. See *Chamaemelum nobile*.
A. n. **'Flore Pleno'**. See *Chamaemelum nobile* 'Flore Pleno'.
A. n. **'Treneague'**. See *Chamaemelum nobile* 'Treneague'.

ANTHOXANTHUM
(Graminaeae/Poaceae)

Several species in this genus produce the scent of new-mown hay because of the coumarin glycosides they contain. These break down to dicoumarol if cut grass becomes damp or is fermented. Dicoumarol is a toxic compound used in rat poison, but it is medicinally important as an anticoagulant.

A. odoratum (sweet vernal grass) p.85

PARTS USED Flowers.
PROPERTIES An aromatic herb that stimulates the circulation and relieves pain and spasms.
USES OF THE HERB
AROMATIC Dried flowers are added to floral arrangements and potpourris.
MEDICINAL Internally and as a nasal lotion for hay fever. Externally for painful joints, chilblains, nervous exhaustion, and insomnia.

GROWTH AND HARVEST
GROWTH Wild-collected. Well-drained soil in sun. Propagates by seed sown in spring, or by division in autumn or spring.
HARVEST Flowers are cut as they open and dried for ornament or tinctures.

ANTHRISCUS
(Umbelliferae/Apiaceae)

A. cerefolium is an indispensable culinary herb that has been used since Roman times. Its medicinal uses are primarily as a "spring tonic" herb, but it is not widely used today. According to the herbalist Juliette de Baïracli Levy, it is good for "poor memory and mental depression" (*Herbal Handbook for Everyone*, London, 1972).

A. cerefolium (chervil) p.85

PARTS USED Leaves.
PROPERTIES A bitter, aromatic, anise-flavored herb that acts as a cleansing tonic, especially for liver and kidney functions, and as an expectorant.
USES OF THE HERB
CULINARY Leaves are added to dishes based on potatoes, eggs, or fish, especially in French cuisine. It is an essential ingredient of *ravigote* sauces and *fines herbes*. The delicate anise flavor does not withstand drying or prolonged cooking; chervil is therefore usually added just before serving. It is also used raw in salads and as a garnish, in sprigs or finely chopped.
MEDICINAL Internally for fluid retention, rheumatism, eczema, and jaundice. Externally for conjunctivitis, inflamed eyelids, and hemorrhoids.

GROWTH AND HARVEST
GROWTH Ornamental. Rich, light, moisture-retentive soil in partial shade. Propagate by seed sown at intervals of three to four weeks from early spring to early autumn, and thinned to 8in (20cm) apart. For a winter crop in cold areas, chervil may be protected with cloches or grown under cover, minimum 45–50°F (7–10°C). It bolts in high temperatures and dry, sunny positions. Seeds are viable for about a year. Chervil is reputed to give radishes a hotter flavor if planted beside them; it is also said to protect lettuces from ants and aphids, and to repel slugs.
HARVEST Leaves are cut before flowering and usually used fresh. If storage is necessary, it is better to freeze than to dry them for this purpose.

APHANES
(Rosaceae)

Once used as a salad herb and pickled for winter use, *A. arvensis* is rarely eaten today, although it remains important as a medicinal herb.

A. arvensis (parsley piert, breakstone parsley) p.85

PARTS USED Leaves.
PROPERTIES An astringent herb that has diuretic effects and soothes irritated or inflamed tissues.
USES OF THE HERB
MEDICINAL Internally for kidney and bladder stones, and chronic kidney and liver disorders. Often combined with *Agathosma* spp. (see p.230) or *Cytisus scoparius* (see p.271) for kidney and bladder complaints, and with *Althaea officinalis* (see p.236) to increase demulcent effect for kidney stones.

GROWTH AND HARVEST
GROWTH Crop. Well-drained soil in sun or partial shade. *A. arvensis* tolerates stony or gravelly soils, and both acidic and alkaline conditions. Propagate by seed sown in dry weather.
HARVEST Leaves are gathered in early summer and used fresh, or dried for infusions, liquid extracts, and tinctures. They also freeze well.

APIUM
(Umbelliferae/Apiaceae)

A. graveolens has been used as a food and flavoring since earliest times; it was present in the tomb of Tutankhamun (c.1370–52BC). The cultivated celery (*A. g.* var. *dulce*), with its pale, succulent stems and mild flavor, was developed during the 17th century in Italy and became popular in the rest of Europe and N America in the 19th century.

A. graveolens (wild celery, smallage) p.85

PARTS USED Whole plant, roots, seeds, oil.
PROPERTIES An aromatic, bitter, tonic herb that reduces blood pressure, relieves indigestion, stimulates the uterus, and has diuretic and anti-inflammatory effects. Sedative and aphrodisiac effects have also been reported.
USES OF THE HERB
CULINARY Wild celery is rarely used for culinary purposes on account of its bitterness – and toxicity in large amounts – although the seeds may be used in small quantities to flavor soups and stews, or mixed with salt as a condiment.
MEDICINAL Internally for osteoarthritis, rheumatoid arthritis, gout, and inflammation of the urinary tract. Externally for fungal infections and tumors (oil). Combined with *Menyanthes trifoliata* (see p.312) and *Guaiacum officinale* (see p.290) for rheumatic complaints, and with *Taraxacum officinale* (see p.360) to increase its potency. Internally in Ayurvedic medicine, for asthma, bronchitis, hiccups, and flatulence, and as a stimulating nerve tonic. Not given to pregnant women.

GROWTH AND HARVEST
GROWTH Crop. Rich, damp soil in a sheltered position in sun or partial shade. Tolerates saline soils. Propagate by seed sown in spring at 55–61°F (13–16°C). *A. graveolens* is less prone to pests and diseases than the cultivated variety, but may be damaged by slugs, celery-fly maggots, celery leafspot, and mosaic virus. *A. graveolens* fruits better in a warm climate and may be damaged by hard frost. Seeds sold for cultivation may be treated with fungicides and should not be used for medicinal purposes.
HARVEST Whole plants are harvested when fruiting and processed to extract the juice. Roots are dug in autumn and used fresh, or dried for use in tinctures. Seeds are collected as they ripen in autumn and dried for infusions, liquid extracts, and powders, or distilled for oil.

APOCYNUM
(Apocynaceae)

Both *A. cannabinum* and *A. androsaemifolium* are used medicinally, their similar properties being well known to native N Americans long before they were listed in the *Dispensatory of the United States* "as a substitute for digitalis in the treatment of chronic heart disease."

A. cannabinum (dogbane, Canadian hemp, black Indian hemp) p.85

PARTS USED Rhizomes, roots.
PROPERTIES An unpleasantly bitter, stimulant, irritant herb that acts on the heart, respiratory and urinary systems, and the uterus. It has diuretic and expectorant effects, increases perspiration, and causes vomiting.
USES OF THE HERB
MEDICINAL Internally for heart failure, intermittent fevers, and tumors. Used by the Cherokee for kidney failure. Externally for venereal warts and alopecia. For internal use by qualified practitioners only. WARNING This herb is subject to legal restrictions in some countries.

GROWTH AND HARVEST
GROWTH Ornamental. Well-drained, moist soil in sun. Propagate by seed sown in autumn, or by division in autumn or spring. Seeds require stratification in warm areas and need exposure to cold for successful germination.
HARVEST Rootstock is lifted in autumn after the plant has seeded and dried for decoctions, liquid extracts, powders, and tinctures.
WARNING Toxic if eaten.

AQUILARIA
(Thymelaeaceae)

A. malaccensis is valued throughout Asia for its decorative, fine-grained wood and scent of sandalwood. It has a long history of use in traditional Chinese, Ayurvedic, and Unani medicine. Similar species include the Chinese *A. sinensis*, which is cultivated as a substitute for *A. malaccensis*, and *A. crassna* from Cambodia.

A. malaccensis, syn. *A. agallocha* (eaglewood, aloewood) p.86

PARTS USED Bark, wood, resin.
PROPERTIES An astringent, stimulant, tonic herb that relieves spasms, especially of the digestive and respiratory systems, and lowers fevers.
USES OF THE HERB
CULINARY Used in Malaysia to flavor curries.
MEDICINAL Internally for digestive and bronchial complaints, fevers, and rheumatism (bark, wood).
ECONOMIC Used for perfumery and incense (resin). Wood is carved as settings for precious stones.

GROWTH AND HARVEST
GROWTH Crop. Well-drained, humus-rich soil in partial shade, with ample humidity, minimum 59–64°F (15–18°C). Propagate by seed sown when ripe at 66–77°F (19–25°C). Seeds are short-lived and take 15–30 days to germinate. Saplings are planted out when 24–32in (60–80cm) tall, in a shady site.
HARVEST Heartwood and bark are taken from trees at least 50 years old, then dried for decoctions or distilled for resin.

ARALIA
(Araliaceae)

Several N American aralias were adopted as medicinal herbs by settlers, who learned their uses from native tribes. The Ojibwa made poultices of *A. racemosa* and *Asarum canadense* (see p.244) for fractured limbs. The former was also used as a tea to ease childbirth and for menstrual irregularities. Various tribes took *A. nudicaulis* for coughs. *A. spinosa* (Hercules club) and *A. hispida* were also used as a tonic and to increase perspiration. In traditional Chinese medicine, *A. chinensis* (Chinese angelica tree) is used as a warming, painkilling herb for rheumatoid arthritis.

A. nudicaulis (wild sarsaparilla) p.86

PARTS USED Roots.
PROPERTIES A tonic, diuretic, cleansing herb that lowers fever.
USES OF THE HERB
CULINARY Makes a pleasant-tasting tea.
MEDICINAL Internally for coughs and in blood-purifying tonics. Externally for boils, arthritis, and swellings. Important in homeopathy for cystitis.

A. racemosa (American spikenard, life-of-man) p.86

PARTS USED Rhizomes, roots.
PROPERTIES A sweet, pungent, tonic herb that acts as an alterative. It also lowers fever and has diuretic and expectorant effects.
USES OF THE HERB
MEDICINAL Internally for bronchial complaints, rheumatic disorders, gout, skin disease, and blood poisoning. Externally for sores and inflammations. Regarded as a rejuvenative in Ayurvedic medicine.

GROWTH AND HARVEST
GROWTH Wild-collected (*A. nudicaulis*). Ornamental (*A. racemosa*). Rich, moist soil in partial shade. By seed sown in spring, or by division in spring.
HARVEST Rootstock is lifted in autumn and dried for use in liquid extracts, decoctions, infusions, powders, and poultices.

ARCTIUM
(Compositae/Asteraceae)

A. lappa has a number of variants. The various kinds are used similarly in traditional European medicine. In addition, burdock is cultivated as a root crop in Japan. The best-known cultivar is *A. l.* 'Gobo' (*gobo* is the Japanese word for "burdock"), traditionally slivered, soaked in water to remove bitterness, then stir-fried with carrots, sesame oil, and soy sauce.

A. lappa (burdock, lappa, beggar's buttons) p.86

PARTS USED Stems, roots, seeds (*niu bang zi*).
PROPERTIES An alterative herb with bitter foliage and sweet, mucilaginous roots, that reduces inflammation and controls bacterial infection. Seed extracts have been shown recently to lower blood sugar levels.
USES OF THE HERB
CULINARY Stalks of young leaves are scraped and then cooked like celery. Roots are eaten raw in salads, cooked like carrots, or added to stir-fries.
MEDICINAL Internally for skin diseases and inflammatory conditions due to chronic toxicity (notably eczema, psoriasis, rheumatism, gout, boils, and sores). Often combined with *Rumex crispus* (see p.344) or *Trifolium pratense* (see p.364). In traditional Chinese medicine the seeds are used for similar purposes and to treat colds, pneumonia, and throat infections.

GROWTH AND HARVEST
GROWTH Wild-collected. Moist, neutral to alkaline soil in sun or light shade. By seed sown in spring. *A. lappa* self-seeds freely.
HARVEST Young leaf stalks are cut in spring for use as a vegetable. Roots are lifted in autumn and used fresh as a vegetable or dried for use in decoctions, liquid extracts, tablets, and tinctures. Seeds are collected when ripe for use in decoctions.

ARCTOSTAPHYLOS Bearberry
(Ericaceae)

A. uva-ursi contains hydroquinones, notably arbutin, which is strongly antibacterial. It is effective mainly against *Klebsiella* and *Escherichia coli*, which are associated with urinary infections.

A. uva-ursi (bearberry, mountain box, uva-ursi) p.86

PARTS USED Leaves.
PROPERTIES An astringent, antibacterial herb that is an effective urinary antiseptic, possibly with some diuretic action.
USES OF THE HERB
MEDICINAL Internally for urinary infections (especially cystitis) and vaginitis. Often combined with *Althaea officinalis* (see p.236), *Elymus repens* (see p.277), *Zea mays* (see p.372), and *Agathosma* spp. (see p.230). Recently found useful in treating cystitis in paraplegics – a recurrent condition, frequently resistant to conventional antibiotics. Contains irritant substances and is not given to pregnant women, children, or to patients with kidney disease.

GROWTH AND HARVEST
GROWTH Ornamental. Moist, peaty or sandy soil in sun or partial shade. *A. uva-ursi* needs acid conditions (pH5); acid soil mix must be used for container-grown plants. Propagate ► by seed sown fresh into a mixture of peat and sand in the autumn, or by layering of long branches in early spring, or by semiripe cuttings with a heel in summer.
HARVEST Leaves are picked individually at any time during spring and summer, then dried for use in infusions, liquid extracts, medicinal tea bags, and tablets.

ARECA Areca palm
(Palmae/Arecaceae)

The chewing of betel "nuts" is a common practice in SE Asia. The hard seed is sliced, mixed with a piece of lime and spices, wrapped in a leaf of betel pepper (*Piper betle*, see p.329), and chewed. Elaborately decorated cutters and repositories are used to prepare and store the betel quids. Betel seeds contain tannins and alkaloids that stimulate saliva flow, accelerate heart and perspiration rates, and suppress hunger, while offering positive protection against intestinal worms. They also possess a pigment that turns the saliva red and blackens the teeth.

A. catechu (betel palm, areca palm) p.86

PARTS USED Fruit rind (*da fu pi*), seeds (*bing lang*).
PROPERTIES An astringent, stimulant herb that relieves hunger, abdominal discomfort, and weariness. It kills intestinal parasites and other pathogens, and has diuretic and laxative effects.
USES OF THE HERB
MEDICINAL Mainly in veterinary medicine to expel tapeworms. Internally, in traditional Chinese medicine, to destroy intestinal parasites, and for dysentery and malaria (seeds); as a laxative in constipation with flatulence and bloating, and a diuretic in edema (rind). Excess causes profuse salivation, vomiting, and stupor. WARNING This herb is subject to legal restrictions in some countries.

GROWTH AND HARVEST
GROWTH Crop. Moist, well-drained soil in sun, with high humidity, minimum 61°F (16°C). Propagate by seed sown in spring at 75–81°F (24–27°C).
HARVEST Fruits are collected when ripe and dried for use in decoctions and liquid extracts, or as a powder.

ARISAEMA
(Araceae)

In common with other members of the aroid family (Araceae), arisaemas contain crystals of calcium oxalate, which cause irritation to the mouth and throat if the plants are eaten raw, and to the eyes on accidental contact. In traditional Chinese medicine three different preparations are made from the corms: *tian nan xing* (sun-dried); *shi nan xing* (cooked with raw ginger); and *dan nan xing* (processed with ox bile). In China the term *nan xing* refers to the corms of several species, including those of *A. amurense* and *A. heterophyllum*, which have similar properties to *A. consanguineum*. The herb entered Chinese medicine at a late date, being first mentioned in 1765, during the Qing dynasty. Although poisonous when fresh, *A. triphyllum* was eaten by native N Americans, who destroyed the toxins by either roasting the tubers or pounding them with water before drying them to make flour. *A. triphyllum* varies greatly in size and appearance, and some botanists regard the main variants as separate species, such as *A. atrorubens* and *A. stewardsonii*, or as subspecies.

A. consanguineum (dragon /plant) p.87

PARTS USED Corms (*nan xing*).
PROPERTIES An acrid, irritant herb that acts as an expectorant and relaxes convulsions. Recent reports indicate some anticancer effects.
USES OF THE HERB
MEDICINAL Internally for coughs with profuse phlegm, tumors, cervical cancer, epilepsy, tetanus, and complaints involving convulsions and spasmodic twitching.

A. triphyllum (Jack-in-the-pulpit, Indian turnip) p.87

PARTS USED Corms.
PROPERTIES An acrid, antiseptic herb that has expectorant effects and increases perspiration.
USES OF THE HERB
MEDICINAL Internally, a traditional native N American remedy for asthma, whooping cough, and bronchitis. Externally for rheumatism, boils, and snake bite. Native people used dried, aged roots, since these are less acrid but maintain their active constituents. The Pawnee and Hopi used dried, powdered roots, taken in water, as a contraceptive, inducing permanent sterility by increasing the dose and water temperature.

GROWTH AND HARVEST
GROWTH Ornamental. Moist, well-drained, humus-rich soil in dappled shade. Propagate by offset corms removed when dormant, or by seeds sown in autumn. Corms rot if too wet or cold. New foliage may be damaged by spring frosts.
HARVEST Corms are lifted in autumn or winter when plants are dormant, and dried for decoctions.
WARNING All parts are harmful if eaten. Skin, eye, and mucous membrane irritant.

ARISTOLOCHIA Birthwort, snakeroot
(Aristolochiaceae)

The common names "birthwort" and "snakeroot" refer to the use of several species of *Aristolochia* in traditional medicine for postpartum infections and snakebite respectively. These uses may have originated in the medieval Doctrine of Signatures, which stated that the color or shape of a herb indicated its purpose. The flowers of

Aristolochia were seen to resemble a curved fetus or a snake. *A. clematitis* has a long history of use in childbirth, being recorded in ancient Egyptian times. It closely resembles *Asarum canadense* (see p.244) in its properties and uses. *A. debilis* was first mentioned in ancient Chinese medical texts in about AD600. *A. serpentaria* was valued by native N Americans as a remedy for snakebite. It was introduced into European medicine in the 17th century as a remedy for the bites of snakes and rabid dogs. Following modern research into its medicinal properties, it enjoyed a vogue during the 1970s and 1980s, resulting in overcollection from the wild and consequent rarity. *A. reticulata* (Red River or Texas snakeroot) is a similar but larger species. Various other species of *Aristolochia* are used medicinally, including *A. indica*, an Ayurvedic herb, used to induce abortion; *A. bracteata*, used in both India and tropical Africa; the N American *A. longa*; and *A. rotunda*, a southern European species.

A. clematitis (birthwort, heartwort) p.87

PARTS USED Roots.
PROPERTIES An aromatic, tonic herb that stimulates the uterus, reduces inflammation, controls bacterial infection, and promotes healing.
USES OF THE HERB
MEDICINAL Internally for gynecological and obstetric disorders. A toxic herb, prescribed in small doses for short-term use only and not given during pregnancy. For use by qualified practitioners only. Externally for skin infections and diseases, and wounds (especially snake and insect bites). WARNING This herb is subject to legal restrictions in some countries.

A. debilis (frail birthwort)

Scrambling perennial, hardy to 23°F (–5°C), height and spread to 3ft (1m), with branching, dark purple stems. Narrowly ovate-triangular leaves are 1½–3in (4–7cm) long and 2in (5cm) wide. Solitary, slender, yellow-green flowers appear in the axils during summer, followed by globose capsules. Found in lowland meadows in China and Japan.

PARTS USED Roots (*qing mu xiang*), fruits (*ma dou ling*).
PROPERTIES An herb with painkilling and anti-inflammatory effects (roots). It also lowers blood pressure, controls coughing, relaxes bronchial spasms, and acts as an expectorant (fruits).
USES OF THE HERB
MEDICINAL Internally for arthritis, purulent wounds, hypertension, snake and insect bites, and gastric disorders involving bloating (roots); for asthma, wet coughs, bronchitis, hypertension, and hemorrhoids (fruits). For use by qualified practitioners only. WARNING This herb is subject to legal restrictions in some countries.

A. serpentaria (Virginia snake root, serpentary)

Perennial, hardy to 23°F (–5°C), height and spread 4–18in (10–45cm), with upright, zigzag stems and thin, heart-shaped leaves, 1½–6in (4–15cm) long. Solitary or clustered brown-purple, S-shaped flowers, about ½in (1cm) long, appear at the base of the plant in early summer, followed by hard capsules, ½in (1cm) across. It is found in dry woods in eastern and southern US.

PARTS USED Roots.
PROPERTIES A bitter, aromatic, tonic herb that induces perspiration, is anti-inflammatory, and acts as a diuretic.
USES OF THE HERB
MEDICINAL Internally for rheumatism, gout, arthritis due to fevers, pneumonia, typhoid, and malaria. Externally for pleurisy, herpes, and slow-healing wounds. Included in a number of commercial tonics for the circulation, skin, and kidneys. For use by qualified practitioners only. WARNING This herb is subject to legal restrictions in some countries.

GROWTH AND HARVEST

GROWTH Ornamental (*A clematitis*). Crop (*A. debilis*). Wild-collected (*A. serpentaria*). Well-drained soil in sun or partial shade, or under cover in cold areas. Propagate by seed sown in spring at 55–61°F (13–16°C), or by semiripe cuttings in summer, or by division in early spring or autumn, or by layering in autumn. Thin out previous year's growths or cut back to two or three nodes in late winter. Aphids, whitefly, and spider mite may damage foliage of plants under cover.
HARVEST Roots are harvested in autumn, and fruits collected when ripe, and dried for liquid extracts, decoctions, powders, and tinctures.
WARNING Toxic if eaten.

ARMORACIA
(Cruciferae/Brassicaceae)

John Gerard (*The Herball, or Generall Historie of Plantes*, 1597) commented that "the Horse Radish stamped with a little vinegar put thereto, is commonly used among the Germans for sauce to eate fish with and such like meates as we do mustarde." By the mid-17th century both Britain and France had acquired the taste for horseradish sauce, which today is popular worldwide.

A. rusticana, syn. *A. lapathifolia, Cochlearia armoracia* (horseradish) p.87

PARTS USED Leaves, roots.
PROPERTIES A very pungent, stimulant herb that controls bacterial infection and lowers fever by increasing perspiration; it is diuretic, and irritates the tissues, causing improved circulation locally.
USES OF THE HERB
CULINARY Young, fresh leaves have a mild, pleasant flavor and are excellent in salads and sandwiches, especially with smoked mackerel. Fresh root is grated alone, or with apple, as a condiment for fish, or with vinegar and cream to accompany roast beef, cold chicken, or hard-boiled eggs. Horseradish sauces may be gently warmed, but cooking destroys the volatile oils responsible for the pungency.

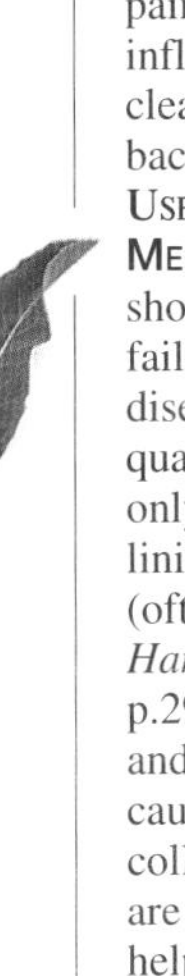

MEDICINAL Internally for general debility, arthritis, gout, sciatica, respiratory and urinary infections, and fevers characterized by coldness. Excess causes vomiting and may provoke allergic responses. Not given to patients with stomach ulcers or thyroid problems. Externally as a poultice for infected wounds, pleurisy, arthritis, and pericarditis.
VARIANT
***A. r.* 'Variegata'**, p.87.

GROWTH AND HARVEST

GROWTH Crop (*A. rusticana*). Ornamental (*A. rusticana* 'Variegata'). Well-drained, rich soil in sun or partial shade. Propagate by division in autumn or early spring, or by seed sown *in situ* in spring and thinned to 12in (30cm) apart. Old plants are prone to mosaic virus and leafspot. Horseradish is difficult to eradicate when well established because bits of root left in the ground grow into new plants. It is said to protect potatoes from Colorado beetles.
HARVEST Leaves are picked in spring and used fresh. Roots are lifted in autumn and used fresh for culinary purposes and in poultices and syrups, or macerated in vinegar and honey for medicinal use. They store well in damp sand.

ARNICA
(Compositae/Asteraceae)

A. montana has long been a popular remedy in Germany and Austria, especially for bruises, sprains, and heart complaints; Goethe (1749–1832) apparently took arnica tea in old age for angina. Recent research has proved both its therapeutic effects and its toxicity. It remains widely used in Germany for heart conditions, but is restricted to external use in the UK and ruled unsafe in the US. The exploitation and wild collection of *A. montana* may be subject to management measures.

A. montana (arnica, leopard's bane, mountain tobacco) p.87

PARTS USED Flowers.
PROPERTIES An aromatic, bitter, astringent herb that stimulates the immune system and heart, relieves pain and inflammation, and clears fungal and bacterial infections.
USES OF THE HERB
MEDICINAL Internally for the short-term treatment of heart failure and coronary artery disease. For use by qualified practitioners only. Externally in liniments and creams (often combined with *Hamamelis virginiana*, see p.291) for dislocations, sprains, bruises, chilblains and varicose ulcers, and as a throat gargle. May cause contact dermatitis when used externally, and collapse when taken internally. These side effects are not present in homeopathic preparations to help healing after accidents. WARNING This herb is subject to legal restrictions in some countries.

GROWTH AND HARVEST

GROWTH Crop. Well-drained, humus-rich, acid soil in a sunny position. Propagate by seed sown in autumn (stratification is required in mild areas), or by division in spring.

HARVEST Flowers are picked when fully open and dried for use in creams, infusions, liniments, and tinctures.

ARTEMISIA Sage brush, wormwood

(Compositae/Asteraceae)

Many wormwoods are used medicinally and include some of the most bitter herbs known. *A. abrotanum* (southernwood) has been cultivated since antiquity to repel insects and contagion. It was popular in nosegays (posies carried to ward off infection and unpleasant smells); until the 19th century, a bunch of southernwood and rue was placed in court to protect against the spread of jail fever from the prisoner. Another traditional use was as a cure for baldness: "The ashes [of southernwood] mingled with old salad oil helps those that have their hair fallen and are bald, causing the hair to grow again, either on the head or the beard" (Culpeper, *The English Physitian Enlarged*, 1653). *A. absinthium* (wormwood) has been a household remedy since biblical times, its bitterness becoming a metaphor for the consequences of sin: "For the lips of a strange woman drop as an honeycomb, And her mouth is smoother than oil: But her end is bitter as wormwood" (Proverbs 5:3–4).

Essential oil of wormwood was an ingredient in absinthe, an alcoholic aperitif first made by Henri Pernod in 1797. Consumption of absinthe became a serious problem in the 19th century, both in Europe and the US. The use of wormwood oil as a flavoring was banned in various countries, beginning in 1908 with Switzerland, after the discovery that the thujone content is addictive, excess causing hallucinations and damage to the central nervous system. Today's successors to absinthe – anisette and vermouth – do not contain thujone, although illicit absinthe liqueurs are still found in southern France, Italy, and Spain. *Absinthium*, the species name, means "without sweetness," and refers to the intensely bitter taste. Its common name "wormwood" comes from the German *Wermut*, "preserver of the mind," since the herb was thought to enhance mental functions. *A. dracunculus* var. *sativa* (French tarragon) used to be known as a dragon herb, a cure for poisonous stings and bites, hence the species name. *A. d.* subsp. *dracunculoides* (Russian tarragon) is similar in appearance but hardier, with a pungent, less pleasant flavor.

A. vulgaris (mugwort) was important in Druidic and Anglo-Saxon times, being one of the nine herbs used to repel evil and poisons. It was known as the "Mother of Herbs" and was associated with witchcraft (in old goddess religions) and fertility rites. On the Isle of Man mugwort is worn on the national day, July 5 (midsummer day in the Old Calendar), and is known as "Bollan bane." The herb is mentioned frequently in first-century AD Greek and Roman writings, and appears in Chinese medical literature dating back to c.AD500. It was reputedly planted beside roads by the Romans for soldiers to put in their sandals on long marches. Both the plant and its reputation for soothing sore feet persisted: "if a footman take mugwort and put it into his shoes in the morning he may goe forty miles before noon and not be weary" (William Coles, *The Art of Simpling*, 1656). Other wormwoods with medicinal uses include *A. afra*, used in southern Africa for digestive and menstrual problems, and feverish illnesses; *A. anomala*, used externally in China for burns and inflamed skin; *A. cina* (Levant wormseed) is used in homeopathy for worms in children, having a high content of santonin, a substance used to expel roundworms; *A. pallens* (*davana*), a fragrant Indian species, used in perfumery, food flavoring, and ritual; and *A. tilesii*, with properties similar to codeine, used by native N Americans.

WARNING Artemisias, and extracts from them such as cineole and santoxin, are subject to legal restrictions in some countries.

A. abrotanum (southernwood, lad's love, old man) p.88

PARTS USED Leaves.

PROPERTIES A strongly aromatic, bitter herb that improves digestion and liver function, encourages menstrual flow and stimulates the uterus, lowers fever, relaxes spasms, and destroys intestinal worms. It is reputed to stimulate hair growth.

USES OF THE HERB

MEDICINAL Internally for delayed or painful menstruation (often combined with *Chamaelirium luteum*, see p.258), poor appetite and digestion, threadworms in children, and hair loss. Not given to pregnant women. Externally for frostbite, extracting splinters, sciatic pains, swellings, and hair loss.

ECONOMIC Leaves are used in sachets and powders to repel moths and fleas.

A. absinthium (wormwood) p.88

PARTS USED Whole plant, leaves.

PROPERTIES An aromatic, diuretic, bitter herb that has anti-inflammatory effects and acts as a tonic for the liver, digestive system, and nerves. It stimulates the uterus and expels intestinal worms.

USES OF THE HERB

MEDICINAL Internally for digestion, poor appetite, gall bladder complaints, and roundworms. Taken in small doses for short-term treatment only. Not given to children or pregnant women. Externally for bruises and bites.

VARIANT

A. a. **'Lambrook Silver'**, p.88.

A. annua (sweet wormwood, sweet Annie) p.88

PARTS USED Whole plant (*qing hao*).

PROPERTIES An aromatic, antibacterial herb that destroys malarial parasites, lowers fevers, and checks bleeding.

USES OF THE HERB

AROMATIC Dried branches are used in wreaths.

MEDICINAL Internally for feverish illnesses, notably malaria and heat stroke. Externally for nose bleeds, bleeding rashes, and sores. Research in Thailand and the US shows that *A. annua*, in the preparation Artesunate, is an effective antimalarial against drug-resistant strains of the disease.

A. arborescens (tree artemisia, tree wormwood) p.88

PARTS USED Leaves.

PROPERTIES An aromatic herb.

USES OF THE HERB

AROMATIC Leaves are used fresh or dried in posies.

A. capillaris (fragrant wormwood) p.88

PARTS USED Leaves, young shoots (*yin chen hao*).

PROPERTIES A bitter, aromatic, diuretic herb that acts as a tonic for the liver and gall bladder, and lowers fever.

USES OF THE HERB

MEDICINAL Internally for jaundice, hepatitis, gall bladder complaints, and feverish illnesses.

A. caucasica, syn. *A. assoana*, *A. lanata*, *A. pedemontana* p.88

PARTS USED Leaves.

PROPERTIES An aromatic herb.

USES OF THE HERB

AROMATIC Leaves used fresh or dried in herbal posies.

A. dracunculus var. *sativa* (tarragon, French tarragon, *estragon*) p.88

PARTS USED Leaves, oil.

PROPERTIES A bitter, warming, aromatic herb that stimulates the digestive system and uterus, acts as a diuretic, lowers fevers, and destroys intestinal worms.

USES OF THE HERB

CULINARY Leaves are used in cooking, especially to flavor chicken and egg dishes, sauces, salad dressings, and mustard.

MEDICINAL Internally for poor digestion, indigestion, and worms in children. Not given to pregnant women. Externally for rheumatism and toothache. In aromatherapy for digestive and menstrual problems.

ECONOMIC Oil is used in commercial flavorings, perfumery, and detergents.

VARIANT

A. d. subsp. ***dracunculoides***, p.89.

A. lactiflora (white mugwort) p.89

PARTS USED Leaves, flowering stems.

PROPERTIES A bitter, aromatic, tonic herb.

USES OF THE HERB

AROMATIC Leaves and flowering stems are used in herbal posies.

MEDICINAL A traditional Chinese remedy for menstrual and liver disorders.

VARIANT
A. l., **Guizhou Group**, p.89.

A. ludoviciana (western mugwort, white sage, cudweed) p.89

PARTS USED Leaves, flowering stems.
PROPERTIES An aromatic herb.
USES OF THE HERB
AROMATIC Leaves and stems are used in herbal posies.
VARIANT
A. l. **'Silver Queen'**, p.89.

A. pontica (Roman wormwood, small absinthe) p.89

PARTS USED Leaves.
PROPERTIES Similar to *A. absinthium*, but milder.
USES OF THE HERB
ECONOMIC Mainly as a flavoring for wine (especially in Germany) and vermouth.

A. 'Powis Castle' p.88

PARTS USED Leaves
PROPERTIES An aromatic herb.
USES OF THE HERB
AROMATIC Leaves are used fresh or dried in herbal posies.

A. vulgaris (mugwort, felon herb, Chinese *moxa*) p.89

PARTS USED Leaves (*ai ye*).
PROPERTIES A bitter, aromatic, tonic herb that acts as a digestive stimulant, diuretic, and nerve tonic, and increases perspiration. It stimulates the uterus and expels intestinal parasites.
USES OF THE HERB
CULINARY One of the few palatable wormwoods, used in traditional recipes (especially in the UK, Germany, and Spain) in dishes of eels or carp, and in stuffings for geese, duck, pork, and game.
MEDICINAL Internally for depression with loss of appetite, dyspepsia, threadworm and roundworm infestations, and menstrual complaints (in the West mainly to encourage menstruation; in the East to control uterine bleeding and threatened miscarriage). In traditional Chinese medicine the compressed, dried leaf, known as *moxa*, is burned briefly on the skin to warm the acupuncture points in cases of internal cold. Used mainly in Ayurvedic medicine for the female reproductive system, nervous complaints, and as a wash for fungal infections. Not given internally to pregnant or lactating women.
VARIANT
A. v. **'Variegata'**, p.89.

GROWTH AND HARVEST

GROWTH Ornamental (*A. absinthium*, *A. abrotanum*, *A. a.* 'Lambrook Silver', *A. annua*, *A.* 'Powis Castle', *A. arborescens*, *A. capillaris*, *A. caucasica*, *A. lactiflora*, *A. l.* Guizhou Group, *A. ludoviciana*, *A. l.* 'Silver Queen', *A pontica*, *A. vulgaris* 'Variegata'). Crop (*A. dracunculus*, *A. vulgaris*). Wild-collected (*A. dracunculus* subsp. *dracunculoides*). Well-drained, neutral to slightly alkaline soil in sun. *A. absinthium*, *A. a.* 'Lambrook Silver', and *A. ludoviciana* tolerate drought. *A. lactiflora* prefers moist, ► neutral to acid soil, and tolerates light shade. Hardiness varies with species: protect *A. dracunculus* in cold winters. Propagate by seed in spring (annuals and *A. d.* subsp. *dracunculoides*), or by semiripe cuttings in summer (shrubby species), or by division in autumn or spring (perennials), or by root cuttings (*A. dracunculus*). In spring cut back shrubby species near to ground level, or remove dead stems and trim to shape. Rust may attack foliage.
HARVEST Whole plants (*A. absinthium*, *A. annua*) are cut when flowering; leaves are picked before flowering. All parts are dried for decoctions, infusions, powders, tablets, and tinctures, or oil extraction. *A. vulgaris* is pressed into moxibustion sticks. Young shoots are cut in spring, and used fresh or dried in decoctions.

ASARUM Wild ginger
(Aristolochiaceae)

Several *Asarum* species are used medicinally. In addition to *A. canadense*, they include the western N American *A. caudatum*, asarabacca (*A. europaeum*) from northern and eastern Europe, and the Chinese wild ginger (*A. sieboldii*). All have similar properties and are used in similar ways: as a stimulating, warming remedy for cold conditions. *A. canadense* was used by native North Americans for its mild ginger flavor.

A. canadense (wild ginger) p.89

PARTS USED Rhizomes.
PROPERTIES A bitter, pungent, aromatic, antibiotic herb that stimulates the digestive and respiratory systems and uterus, and increases perspiration. It acts as a diuretic, expectorant, and decongestant.
USES OF THE HERB
MEDICINAL Internally for coughs, asthma, chills, and rheumatic disorders. Women of the N American Pomo tribe take wild ginger as a contraceptive, and in Western medicine it is used to regulate menstruation and as a stimulant in difficult labor (but not in earlier stages of pregnancy). The Ojibwa tribe combined it with *Aralia racemosa* (see p. 240) in poultices for fractures.

GROWTH AND HARVEST

GROWTH Ornamental. Well-drained, moist soil enriched with leaf mold, in a shady, sheltered site. Propagate by division in spring.
HARVEST Sections of rhizome are removed in autumn and dried for powders, decoctions, liquid extracts, and tinctures.

ASCLEPIAS Milkweed, silkweed
(Asclepiadaceae)

A. tuberosa is widely regarded as one of the finest plant expectorants. The common name "pleurisy root" refers to its primary role in treating pleurisy. It was used by native Americans for over 1,000 years before entering European pharmacopoeias in the 18th century.

A. tuberosa (pleurisy root, butterfly weed) p.89

PARTS USED Roots.
PROPERTIES A bitter, nutty-flavored tonic herb that increases perspiration, relieves spasms, and acts as an expectorant.
USES OF THE HERB
MEDICINAL Internally for pleurisy, bronchitis, pneumonia, asthma, dry cough, gastritis, eruptive fevers, rheumatic fever, feverish stages of colds and influenza, and uterine disorders. Excess causes diarrhea and vomiting. Not given to pregnant women. Externally for bruises, wounds, ulcers, and rheumatism.

GROWTH AND HARVEST

GROWTH Ornamental. Dry, sandy, neutral to acid soil in sun. Propagate by seed in spring at 59°F (15°C), or by root cuttings in autumn or spring. May be attacked by cucumber mosaic virus. *A. tuberosa* is sensitive to disturbance and difficult to establish.
HARVEST Roots are lifted in autumn and used fresh in a syrup or dried for compresses, powders, decoctions, ointments, and tinctures.

ASPALATHUS
(Leguminosae)

Rooibos tea, made from the dried, fermented leaves of *A. linearis*, tastes similar to oriental tea (*Camellia sinensis*, see p.252), but is less astringent due to the lower tannin content. It is caffeine-free but has a higher fluoride content than oriental tea, which may help protect against tooth decay. Japanese research in the 1980s showed that rooibos contains a substance similar to the enzyme superoxide dismutase (SOD), an antioxidant compound thought to retard aging.

A. linearis, syn. *A. contaminatus*, *Psoralea linearis* (rooibos) p.89

PARTS USED Leaves, stems.
PROPERTIES An aromatic, pleasant-tasting, mildly astringent herb that benefits the digestion and relaxes spasms. It relieves some allergic symptoms and skin conditions.
USES OF THE HERB
CULINARY Mainly infused as a refreshing drink and as a base for soups, sauces, fruit drinks, and in baking. Extract is used locally in liqueur (*buchenbosch*) and schnapps.
MEDICINAL Internally for allergies, especially eczema, hay fever, and asthma in infants. Externally for skin infections and irritations.

GROWTH AND HARVEST

GROWTH Crop. Acid sand in full sun. Propagate by seed in spring. Pinch out to encourage bushy growth. Cut back plants hard to control growths from old wood.
HARVEST Plants are cut 14in (35cm) above ground, fermented, and sun dried for use in infusions, liquid extracts, and lotions.

ASPARAGUS
(Liliaceae/Asparagaceae)

Various *Asparagus* species are used medicinally in similar ways. Most contain asparagin, a diuretic that gives the urine a characteristic odor in those who lack the gene to break it down. *A. cochinchinensis* was first mentioned in Chinese medical texts c.AD200. *A. officinalis* has been cultivated for over 2,000 years as a vegetable, and as a medicinal herb with noticeable diuretic and laxative effects. In common with many popular medicinal plants, it was given the name *officinalis* to recognize its status as an "officinal" – a plant with a long commercial history as a medicinal herb. The common name of *A. racemosus*, *shatavari*, means "she who possesses a hundred husbands," and refers to the herb's rejuvenative effect on the female reproductive organs.

A. cochinchinensis, syn. *A. lucidus*, *Melanthium cochinchinensis* (Chinese asparagus)

Much-branched perennial, hardy to 5°F (–15°C), up to 5ft (1.5m) in height and 3ft (1m) spread, with linear cladodes ½in (1–2cm) long, arranged singly or in pairs up the stem. Clusters of pale yellow-green flowers appear in summer, followed by pale green-white berries, ¼in (7mm) across. Found in Japan, China, and Korea, near the sea.

PARTS USED Tubers (*tian men dong*).
PROPERTIES An antibacterial, cleansing herb that controls coughs, clears bronchial congestion, soothes inflammation, acts as a diuretic, and increases salivation.
USES OF THE HERB
MEDICINAL Internally for fevers, debility, sore throats, coughs, rhinitis, diphtheria, tuberculosis, and bronchitis.

A. officinalis (asparagus) p.90

PARTS USED Young shoots, rhizomes.
PROPERTIES A restorative, cleansing herb that acts on the bowels, liver, and kidneys. It contains asparagusic acid, which is nematocidal.
USES OF THE HERB
CULINARY Young shoots are steamed and served hot or cold as a vegetable, and puréed or finely chopped in soups.
MEDICINAL Internally for cystitis, pyelitis, kidney disease, rheumatism, gout, and edema from heart failure. Asparagusic acid is used to treat schistomiasis.

A. racemosus (*shatavari*) p.90

PARTS USED Rhizomes.
PROPERTIES A soothing, tonic herb that acts mainly on the circulatory, digestive, respiratory, and female reproductive organs.
USES OF THE HERB
MEDICINAL Internally for infertility, loss of libido, threatened miscarriage, menopausal problems, hyperacidity, stomach ulcers, dysentery, and bronchial infections. Externally for stiffness in joints and neck. The most important herb in Ayurvedic medicine for women, as *ashwagandha* (*Withania somnifera*, see p.371) is for men. Used internally by Australian Aborigines for digestive upsets, and externally for sores.

GROWTH AND HARVEST
GROWTH Crop. Rich, light, well-drained soil, in a sunny position. Propagate by seed in spring, thinned to 12in (30cm) apart, then to 3ft (1m) apart. *A. officinalis* is often purchased as a dormant one-year-old male "crown," and renewed after 10 years. *A. racemosus* may be grown as an annual in cold areas; protect under cover in winter. Asparagus beetle may attack young shoots and foliage.
HARVEST Young shoots (*A. officinalis*) are cut when about 9in (23cm) high from established plants in late spring, and eaten fresh or juiced for medicinal purposes. Rhizomes and tubers are lifted when dormant and boiled before drying for decoctions and powders; those of *A. racemosus* are used fresh for dysentery, dried for decoctions, powders, and medicated oils.
WARNING Berries are harmful if eaten.

ASPIDIUM
A. filix-mas. See *Dryopteris filix-mas.*

ASPIDOSPERMA
(Apocynaceae)

Eighty or so species of evergreen trees are included in this S American genus. They have fine wood and a milky sap containing alkaloids. Those contained in *A. quebracho-blanco* include the aphrodisiac quebrachine or yohimbine, also present in the unrelated *Pausinystalia yohimbe* (see p.323). The medicinal bark of *A. quebracho-blanco* first reached Europe in 1878, having long been used medicinally by native S Americans as a febrifuge. *Quebracho*, the Spanish for "axe breaks," refers to the hardness of the wood. *Blanco*, "white," distinguishes it from the red quebracho (*Schinopsis quebracho-colorado*), which is used as a mild digestive stimulant.

A. quebracho-blanco (quebracho, white quebracho, *naawa*)

Tender evergreen tree, height to 100ft (30m), spread 20–40ft (5–12m), with thick, corky bark, pendulous young twigs, and leathery, elliptic to lanceolate, spine-tipped leaves. Fragrant yellow, funnel-shaped flowers are produced in short, branched clusters, followed by woody capsules that split open to release numerous winged seeds. Found in dry forests, mainly in Argentina.

PARTS USED Bark.
PROPERTIES A bitter, tonic herb that stimulates the circulatory, respiratory, and genitourinary systems, lowers fever, and relaxes spasms.
USES OF THE HERB
MEDICINAL Internally for asthma, bronchitis, emphysema, and feverish illnesses. Excess causes nausea and vomiting. WARNING This herb is subject to legal restrictions in some countries.

GROWTH AND HARVEST
GROWTH Wild-collected. Well-drained to sandy soil in sun, minimum 59–64°F (15–18°C). Propagates by seed sown when ripe.
HARVEST Bark is removed as required and dried for alkaloid extraction or use in liquid extracts.

ASTER
(Compositae/Asteraceae)

About 250 species of rhizomatous and fibrous-rooted perennials, and a few annuals and biennials, are included in this genus, widely distributed in N America, Africa, and Eurasia. *A. amellus* is used in Chinese medicine for coughs and pulmonary ailments. *A. tataricus* was first mentioned in Chinese medical literature c.AD200. The British common name "Michaelmas daisy" was given to a N American species when the Gregorian calendar was introduced, which brought the feast day of Michaelmas forward by 11 days (to September 29), the time of flowering.

A. tataricus (Tatarian aster)

Tall perennial, hardy to 5°F (–15°C), height 5–6ft (1.5–2m), spread 3–4ft (1–1.2m), with a thickened stem base and long-stalked, elliptic, hairy leaves up to 16in (40cm) long, with toothed margins. Flat-topped corymbs of purple to blue daisylike flowers, about 1in (2.5cm) across, open in summer and autumn. Found in meadows and beside rivers in eastern Asia.

PARTS USED Roots (*zi wan*).
PROPERTIES A stimulant, expectorant herb for the bronchial system that helps clear infection.
USES OF THE HERB
MEDICINAL Internally for chronic bronchitis and tuberculosis. Often taken raw with honey to increase the expectorant effect.

GROWTH AND HARVEST
GROWTH Crop. Moist soil in sun or partial shade. Propagate by softwood cuttings in spring, or by division in spring or autumn. May suffer from mildew in dry conditions.
HARVEST Roots are lifted in autumn and used raw, or dried for decoctions.

ASTRAGALUS Milk vetch
(Leguminosae)

Milk vetches are used both medicinally and as food and fodder crops in many parts of the world. Gum tragacanth is collected from at least 20 species, mainly *A. gummifer*, which was known and used in ancient Greece. *A. complanatus* has been used in China as a liver and kidney tonic since the first century AD. The roots of *A. membranaceus* have provided traditional Chinese medicine with a tonic on a par with ginseng.

A. gummifer (tragacanth, gum tragacanth)

Low evergreen or semievergreen, umbrella-shaped shrub, hardy to 23°F (–5°C), height and spread to 12in (30cm), with spiny-stalked, pinnate leaves, and axillary clusters of downy, white pea flowers. Found in upland forests and grassland in the Middle East, and especially in Kurdistan.

PARTS USED Gum.
PROPERTIES A mucilaginous herb that has recently been shown to stimulate the immune system and suppress tumors.
USES OF THE HERB
ECONOMIC Mainly used as a stabilizing and thickening agent in the food and pharmaceutical industries, and in products such as toothpaste, processed cheese, and candy.

A. membranaceus (milk vetch) p.90

PARTS USED Roots (*huang qi*).
PROPERTIES A sweet, tonic herb that stimulates the immune system, spleen, lungs, liver, circulatory and urinary systems, and lowers blood pressure and blood sugar levels.
USES OF THE HERB
MEDICINAL An important ingredient in many traditional Chinese formulas; combined with *Angelica polymorpha* var. *sinensis* (see p.238) for poor circulation and low energy, and with *Atractylodes macrocephala* (see below) and *Ledebouriella seseloides* for allergies and frequent colds. Also for diabetes, kidney problems, prolapsed organs, and slow-healing skin eruptions.

GROWTH AND HARVEST
GROWTH Crop. Well-drained soil in sun. *A. membranaceus* prefers sandy, slightly alkaline soil. Propagate by seed in spring or autumn.
HARVEST Gum is collected from second-year plants of *A. gummifer* by incising the stem base; it is dried for use as a powder. Roots of *A. membranaceus* are lifted in autumn and dried for decoctions, powders, and tinctures.

ATRACTYLODES
(Compositae)

All seven species are used in traditional Chinese medicine, the most important being *A. macrocephala*, first recorded in AD659 in the *Tang Materia Medica*. In addition to its tonic properties, this herb is reputed to calm a restless fetus. *A. chinensis* is also widely used, mainly as a digestive tonic, and for glaucoma and night blindness.

A. macrocephala (Chinese thistle daisy) p.90

PARTS USED Rhizomes (*bai zhu*).
PROPERTIES A bittersweet, tonic herb that acts mainly on the digestive system. It is diuretic, lowers blood sugar levels, and controls bacterial infections.
USES OF THE HERB
MEDICINAL Internally for weak and disturbed digestion; often combined with *Wolfiporia cocos* (see p.372), *Codonopsis tangshen* (see p.264), and *Glycyrrhiza uralensis* (see p.289) in patent tonics, and with *Scutellaria baicalensis* (see p.351) as a blood tonic in pregnancy.

GROWTH AND HARVEST
GROWTH Crop. Any well-drained soil in sun or partial shade. Propagate by seed sown in spring.
HARVEST Rhizomes are lifted in autumn and baked for use in tonics.

ATRIPLEX Orache
(Chenopodiaceae)

Oraches are closely related to goosefoots (*Chenopodium* species, see p.259). Most contain large amounts of saponins, which are toxic in excess. Various species are used: the Australian *A. nummularia* tolerates drought and saline soils and was used by early settlers as a soap substitute, vegetable, and cure for scurvy and blood diseases. *A. halimus*, the ornamental northern African tree purslane, is burned to produce an antacid powder. A number of these plants are pot herbs, added to a dish to enhance its flavor or nutritional value but rarely eaten as a vegetable on their own. An exception is the European *A. patula*, eaten for its spinachlike leaves, which have a high vitamin C content.

A. hortensis (orache) p.90

PARTS USED Leaves.
PROPERTIES A mildly irritant herb that stimulates the metabolism.
USES OF THE HERB
CULINARY It may be eaten raw or cooked, on its own, or mixed with other vegetables, such as spinach.
MEDICINAL Internally to dispel sluggishness.
VARIANT
A. h. **'Rubra'**, p.90.

GROWTH AND HARVEST
GROWTH Wild-collected (*A. hortensis*). Ornamental (*A. h.* 'Rubra'). Well-drained soil in sun; grows well in coastal locations. Propagate by seed sown in autumn. *A. hortensis* and *A. h.* 'Rubra' self-seed freely.
HARVEST Leaves are picked as required and used fresh.

ATROPA Nightshade
(Solanaceae)

A. belladonna is of major importance in modern medicine, and is widely cultivated for the pharmaceutical industry, mainly in eastern Europe. Like other *Atropa* species, it contains various alkaloids that have valuable medicinal applications and a macabre history of use by poisoners. The genus gives its name to one of these alkaloids, atropine, which dilates the pupil of the eye. Before the advent of modern anesthetics, *A. belladonna* was applied to the skin as "sorcerer's pomade" to make the patient unconscious before surgery.

A. belladonna (deadly nightshade, dwale) p.91

PARTS USED Whole plant, roots.
PROPERTIES A narcotic herb that relieves spasms and reduces secretions of mouth, bronchi, and stomach.

USES OF THE HERB
MEDICINAL Internally for asthma, kidney stones and gallstones, Parkinson's disease, myocardial infarction, hypotension, hyperacidity, gastric ulcers, travel sickness, and as a premedication before surgery. Excess causes dry mouth, loss of voice, enlarged pupils, aversion to light, confusion, respiratory failure, and death. Externally, in liniments and plasters for rheumatic and muscular pain, and in eye drops for opthalmic diagnosis and surgery. For use by qualified practitioners only. Important in homeopathy for sunstroke, painful menstruation, and infections or inflammations characterized by sudden onset, redness, and violent pain. WARNING This herb and its alkaloids are subject to legal restrictions in some countries.

GROWTH AND HARVEST
GROWTH Crop. Well-drained, moisture-retentive, alkaline soil in sun or partial shade. Propagate by seed sown in spring, or by division in spring. The alkaloid content of the plant is higher in a sunny position and in warm, dry summers.
HARVEST Whole plants are cut when flowering and dried for processing into dry and liquid extracts, tinctures, liniments, plasters, and glycerin preparations. Roots of two- to three-year-old plants are lifted in autumn and processed similarly.
WARNING Toxic if eaten. Skin irritant and possible allergen.

AVENA Oat
(Gramineae/Poaceae)

A. sativa is on the boundary between a food and a herb. It is grown as fodder and also for oats, eaten as rolled oat, cereal, or in bread and cookies. It is known to medical herbalists as a "tropho-restorative." In addition to protein, starch, and minerals, oats contain an alkaloid, glycosides, and fixed oils, which are an important source of vitamin E.

A. sativa (oat, groats) p.91

PARTS USED Seeds.
PROPERTIES A mealy, nutritive herb that acts as a tonic to the heart, nerves, and thymus gland, and is externally emollient. Regular consumption of oat germ reduces blood cholesterol levels.
USES OF THE HERB
CULINARY Cooked oats are a popular breakfast dish; rolled oats are an important ingredient of muesli and toasted cereal snacks.
MEDICINAL Internally for depression, nervous exhaustion, shingles, herpes, menopausal symptoms, and debility following illness. Externally in preparations for eczema and dry skin. Often combined with *Cypripedium parviflorum* var. *pubescens* (see p.271) or *Scutellaria lateriflora* (see p.351) for depression.

> **GROWTH AND HARVEST**
> **GROWTH** Crop. Well-drained, fertile soil in sun. Propagate by seed sown in spring.
> **HARVEST** Plants are cut in summer before fully ripe and threshed to separate the grains, which are then dehusked and rolled for use as cereals, and in liquid extracts and tinctures. Dried stalks are sometimes included in tonics.

AZADIRACHTA
(Meliaceae)

A. indica has similar properties to its close relative, *Melia azederach* (see p.310). It is one of the most important detoxicants in Ayurvedic medicine and is a potent febrifuge, long used to treat intermittent fevers and recently shown to contain effective anti-malarial compounds. The seeds yield margosa oil, a nondrying oil with insecticidal and antiseptic properties. The wood is so highly prized for its insecticidal properties that in parts of Africa it is grown in hedges to provide easily harvested material for protection against insect-borne diseases.

A. indica, syn. *Melia azadirachta*, *M. indica* (neem, *nimba*, *margosa*) p.91

PARTS USED Leaves, bark, seeds, oil, resin.
PROPERTIES A bitter, tonic herb that acts as an alterative, clearing toxins, reducing inflammation, lowering fever, promoting healing, and improving all functions. It destroys a wide range of parasitic organisms and is also insecticidal and spermicidal.
USES OF THE HERB
MEDICINAL Internally for malaria, tuberculosis, rheumatism, arthritis, jaundice, intestinal worms, and skin diseases. Not given to the weak, old, or very young. Externally for ringworm, eczema, lice, fungal infections, and painful joints and muscles.
ECONOMIC Leaves are used in libraries and herbaria to protect against insect damage. Oil is used in hair dressings and insecticides (especially to protect crops against locust attack). Resin is added to soap, toothpaste, and skin lotions.

> **GROWTH AND HARVEST**
> **GROWTH** Crop. Well-drained soil in sun, minimum 59–64°F (15–18°C). Tolerates poor soils and prolonged drought. Propagate by seed sown as soon as ripe.
> **HARVEST** Leaves, bark, and resin are collected as required and used fresh or dried in decoctions, infusions, medicated oils, powders, and pastes. Seeds are harvested when ripe for oil extraction.

B

BALLOTA
(Labiatae/Lamiaceae)

B. nigra is an example of an herb which is widely grown in herb gardens, but seldom used today by medical herbalists, who prefer the similar, more pleasant-tasting *Marrubium vulgare* (white horehound, see p.308). The oil extracted from *B. nigra* is used to adulterate that of *Marrubium vulgare*.

B. nigra (black horehound) p.91

PARTS USED Whole plant.
PROPERTIES An unpleasant-tasting, expectorant herb that stimulates the uterus and calms spasms, especially in the digestive and bronchial systems. It is effective in controlling nausea and vomiting.
USES OF THE HERB
MEDICINAL Internally for nervous dyspepsia, motion sickness, morning sickness in pregnancy, menstrual disorders, and bronchial complaints.
VARIANT
B. n. **'Archer's Variety'**, syn. *B. n.* 'Variegata', p.91.

> **GROWTH AND HARVEST**
> **GROWTH** Wild-collected (*B. nigra*). Ornamental (*B. n.* 'Archer's Variety'). Well-drained soil in sun or partial shade. Propagate by seed in spring, or by division when dormant. *B. n.* 'Archer's Variety' does not come true from seed. *B. nigra* self-seeds readily.
> **HARVEST** Whole plants are cut as flowering begins and dried for infusions, liquid extracts, and tinctures. Fresh herb may be used to make a syrup. Renew stocks of dried herb annually.

BALSAMITA
B. major. See *Tanacetum balsamita*.

BAPTISIA False indigo
(Leguminosae/Papilionaceae)

B. tinctoria was well known to various native N American tribes before entering the *U.S. Pharmacopoeia* (1831–42). The Mohicans and Meskwaki made a decoction of the roots as an antiseptic wash for wounds. Other species, such as *B. leucantha*, *B. leucophaea*, and *B. australis*, were also used medicinally.

B. tinctoria (wild indigo, indigoweed, rattleweed) p.92

PARTS USED Roots.
PROPERTIES An acrid, bitter, antiseptic herb that stimulates the immune system and is particularly effective against bacterial infections. It also lowers fever and has laxative and emetic effects.
USES OF THE HERB
MEDICINAL Internally for tonsillitis, pharyngitis, and upper respiratory tract infections; excess causes nausea and vomiting. Externally for boils, ulcers, gum disease, sore nipples, and vaginitis. Regarded in Ayurvedic medicine as a cooling alterative, which can have a deleterious effect if taken for too long or in excess. Combines well with *Echinacea purpurea* (see p.276), *Capsicum frutescens* (see p.254), and *Commiphora myrrha* (see p. 265) for throat infections; with *Phytolacca americana* (see p.327), *Viola odorata* (see p.370), and *Arctium lappa* (see p.240) for boils and swollen lymph glands; and with *Cephaelis ipecacuanha* (see p.258) for aphthous ulcer. Used in homeopathy for influenza and sore throat associated with nervous exhaustion.

> **GROWTH AND HARVEST**
> **GROWTH** Crop. Deep, rich soil in sun. Propagate by seed sown in spring; by division when dormant. Large roots resent disturbance.
> **HARVEST** Roots are lifted in autumn and dried for use in decoctions, liquid extracts, and tinctures. They can be kept for up to two years.

BAROSMA
B. crenulata. See *Agathosma crenulata.*

BELAMCANDA
(Iridaceae)

Widely used in traditional Chinese medicine, *B. chinensis* was first mentioned in the *Shen Nong Canon of Herbs* (AD25–220). It is valued in southern China as a treatment for "rice-field dermatitis," a fungal skin infection common among paddyfield workers.

B. chinensis, syn. *Ixia chinensis*, *Pardanthus chinensis* (blackberry lily, leopard lily) p.92

PARTS USED Rhizomes (*she gan*).
PROPERTIES A bitter, cooling herb that acts mainly on the lungs and liver, lowering fever and reducing inflammation. It is effective against a number of bacterial, fungal, and viral organisms.
USES OF THE HERB
MEDICINAL Internally for throat infections and for coughs characterized by profuse phlegm. Not given to pregnant women.

> **GROWTH AND HARVEST**
> **GROWTH** Ornamental. Well-drained, sandy, humus-rich soil in sun. Needs protection in cold areas or during severe winters. Propagate by seed sown in spring; it takes about 15 days to germinate.
> **HARVEST** Rhizomes are lifted in summer and autumn, and dried for use in decoctions.

BELLIS English daisy
(Compositae/Asteraceae)

B. perennis is a traditional wound herb at present under investigation for possible use in HIV therapy. The flowers contain compounds similar to those in *Castanospermum australe* (see p.256). The English daisy has a long history of medicinal use. Gerard wrote that "The daisies do mitigate all kinde of paines, but especially in the joints, and gout, if they be stamped with new butter unsalted, and applied upon the pained place…" (*The Herball, or Generall Historie of Plantes*, 1597).

B. perennis (English daisy) p.92

PARTS USED Leaves, flowers.
PROPERTIES An astringent, healing, expectorant herb that relaxes spasms.
USES OF THE HERB
CULINARY Young leaves, flower buds, and petals have a pleasant sour flavor and may be added to salads.
MEDICINAL Internally for coughs and excess mucus. Externally for ruptures, varicose veins, minor wounds, and sore or watery eyes. A homeopathic remedy for deep bruising.
VARIANTS
B. p. **'Alba Plena'**, p.92.
B. p. **'Pomponette'**, p.92.
B. p. **'Prolifera'**, p.92.

GROWTH AND HARVEST
GROWTH Crop (variants: ornamental). Well-drained soil in sun or partial shade. Propagate by seed sown under cover in spring (or in early summer or autumn to flower the following year), or by division in spring. Deadhead regularly to prolong flowering. Extremely double-flowered cultivars are usually sterile and cannot be raised from seed.
HARVEST Leaves are picked in spring and summer and used fresh in decoctions, ointments, and poultices. Flowers are picked in spring and summer and used fresh in infusions and ointments.

BENINCASA
(Cucurbitaceae)

Wax gourds are widely cultivated for their edible fruits, which store well, and are a source of wax (*petha*) for candles. Chinese medicinal uses were first recorded in the *Tang Materia Medica* (AD659). The fruits are eaten in China in reducing diets. Recent research has shown that they contain anticancer terpenes.

B. hispida, syn. *B. cerifera* (wax gourd, white gourd, ash pumpkin) p.93

PARTS USED Fruit rind (*dong gua pi*), seeds (*dong gua zi* or *dong gua ren*).
PROPERTIES A cooling, pleasant-tasting herb that has diuretic effects (fruit rind), is anti-inflammatory and expectorant, and lowers fever (seeds).
USES OF THE HERB
CULINARY The unripe flesh of the fruit is eaten as a vegetable, especially in curries, and may be pickled; ripe fruits are candied. Seeds are eaten roasted.
MEDICINAL Internally, in Chinese medicine, for urinary dysfunction and summer fevers (rind); cough characterized by thick phlegm, internal abscesses, and vaginal discharge (seeds). Internally, in Ayurvedic medicine, for epilepsy, lung disease, asthma, coughs and hiccups, urine retention, internal hemorrhage (fruit); diabetes (rind), tapeworm (seeds); as an antidote to poisoning from mercury, alcohol, snakebite, and toxic plants (fresh juice).
ECONOMIC Wax is scraped from the rind to make candles.

GROWTH AND HARVEST
GROWTH Crop. Well-drained, humus-rich soil in sun, with ample water, minimum 61°F (16°C). Propagate by seed sown in spring at 64°F (18°C).
HARVEST Fruits picked as required. Seeds and rind from ripe fruits are dried for decoctions.

BERBERIS Barberry
(Berberidaceae)

The medicinal uses of *Berberis* are an example of the Doctrine of Signatures, in which the color or structure of a plant was thought to be a divine indication of its healing properties. Many plants with mainly yellow coloration were thus used as liver remedies. Various species of *Berberis* are used medicinally in different parts of the world, including the Himalayan *B. aristata* and *B. asiatica*. In Ayurvedic medicine, these species are known generally as *daruharidra*, "wood turmeric," because they have similar properties to *Curcuma longa* (see p.270). They contain an important antibacterial alkaloid, known as berberine, which is used extensively in Japan and SE Asia to control tropical diarrhea and certain eye diseases. The drug is obtained from the roots and rhizomes of various species of *Berberis* and the closely related *Mahonia* (see p.308). India produces up to 7 tons of the drug per year, extracted from 600–700 tons of roots.

B. vulgaris (common barberry) p.93

PARTS USED Leaves, stem and root bark, roots, fruits.
PROPERTIES A very bitter, sedative herb that is highly effective against many disease-causing organisms. It stimulates the liver, spleen, and uterus; lowers fever and blood pressure; controls bleeding; and reduces inflammation. Anticancer effects have been demonstrated.
USES OF THE HERB
CULINARY Ripe fruits are sour, with a high vitamin C content. They were once made into jelly for mutton dishes, and pickled or candied for decoration.
MEDICINAL Internally for dysentery, leishmaniasis, malaria, hepatitis, liver tumor, gallstones, hypertension, and cancer chemotherapy. Often combined with *Chionanthus virginicus* (see p.260) and/or *Veronicastrum virginicum* (see p.368) for gall bladder complaints. Highly regarded as a liver tonic and detoxicant in Ayurvedic medicine, and combined with *Curcuma longa* (see p.270) for liver complaints and diabetes. Not given to pregnant women.

GROWTH AND HARVEST
GROWTH Crop. Neutral to calcareous soil in sun or partial shade. Propagate by seed in autumn, or by softwood or semiripe cuttings in summer. Cut back old stems and straggly growths in late winter. May be attacked by *Armillaria* root rot. As a host of wheat rust, many *Berberis* may not be grown in some states and certain countries.
HARVEST Fruits are gathered in autumn and used fresh; stems and roots are collected in autumn and stripped of bark when fresh. Bark and roots are dried for use in decoctions and liquid extracts, and as powder.
WARNING All parts, except ripe berries, are harmful if eaten.

BETONICA
B. officinale. See *Stachys officinalis*.

BETULA Birch
(Betulaceae)

Birches are highly regarded as medicinal plants in Russia and Siberia, especially for treating arthritis. Large quantities of birch tar oil are produced in these regions, where silver birch is one of the most common trees. Many different birches are used medicinally, including the Eurasian *B. pubescens* (downy or white birch), which is used in identical ways to *B. pendula* (silver birch); the N American *B. alleghaniensis* (yellow birch) and *B. nigra* (river birch), used mainly for skin complaints and wounds; and *B. lenta* (cherry birch, black birch), the source of sweet birch oil, which contains large amounts of methyl salicylate and is used in perfumery and in dental products. The wood is used for a wide range of purposes, e.g., charcoal, paper, cotton reels, toys, and fish smoking. The bark is used in the tanning industry, imparting a delicate fragrance to leather (notably *peau d'Espagne*). The slender, flexible twigs are ideal for brooms – and for making "the birch," a rod or whip of birch twigs that was used to flog offenders.

B. pendula, syn. *B. alba*, *B. verrucosa* (silver birch) p.93

PARTS USED Leaves, bark, oil (occasionally buds, sap).
PROPERTIES A bitter, astringent, tonic herb that has diuretic and mild laxative effects, reduces inflammation, relieves pain, and increases perspiration.

USES OF THE HERB
MEDICINAL Internally for rheumatism, arthritis, gout, arteriosclerosis, water retention, cystitis, kidney stones, skin eruptions, and fevers. Some practitioners find that alternating *B. pendula* and *Urtica dioica* (see p.366) every three days is especially effective in conditions caused by chronic toxicity. Externally, mainly in the form of birch tar oil, for psoriasis and eczema.
ECONOMIC Sap is fermented to make beer, wine, spirits, or vinegar.

Betula pendula 'Laciniata'

VARIANTS
***B. p.* 'Laciniata'**, syn. *B. p.* 'Dalecarlica', p.93.
***B. p.* 'Tristis'**, p.93.
***B. p.* 'Youngii'**, p.93.

GROWTH AND HARVEST
GROWTH Ornamental. Well-drained soil in sun or shade. *B. pendula* prefers sandy soils below pH6.5 and dislikes shallow alkaline conditions, although it is extremely hardy and tolerates drier conditions than *B. pubescens*. Propagate by ripe seed sown in a mixture of peat and sand, in spring or summer. Seed does not store well and germination is erratic. Leaves may be damaged by aphids, caterpillars, sawfly larvae, and miners, and are also affected by rust. Birches are attacked by trunk borers and various fungi, including bracket fungi (notably birch polypore), witches' broom, and *Armillaria* root rot.
HARVEST Leaf buds and young leaves are gathered in spring for use in infusions, poultices, and tinctures. Bark is stripped from cut timber as required for distillation of oil. Sap is tapped from mature trees for a week during early spring, at a rate of up to 18 gallons (82 liters) per tree.

BIDENS Bur marigold
(Compositae/Asteraceae)

B. tripartita was once known as *Hepatorium* and was used for "obstruction of the liver" and many other complaints, as well as being burned to repel insects. *B. bipinnata* (Spanish needles) was used in traditional N American medicine for menstrual problems and for infections of the throat and lungs.

B. tripartita (trifid bur marigold, water agrimony) p.94

PARTS USED Whole plant.
PROPERTIES A bitter, astringent, diuretic herb that controls bleeding.
USES OF THE HERB
MEDICINAL Internally for blood in the urine, uterine bleeding, ulcerative colitis, and peptic ulcer. Externally, in Russia, for alopecia. Often combined with *Symphytum officinale* (see p.357), *Agrimonia eupatoria* (see p.231), *Acorus calamus* (see p.228), or *Zingiber officinale* (see p.373).

GROWTH AND HARVEST
GROWTH Crop. Damp to wet soil in sun. Propagate by seed sown in spring.
HARVEST Plants are cut as flowering begins, and dried for use in infusions, liquid extracts, and tinctures.

BIOTA
B. orientalis. See *Thuja orientalis*.

BIXA Annatto
(Bixaceae)

B. orellana has an ancient history of use by native Amazonians as a red or orange body dye, which may have insect-repellant properties. Today, it is of great importance as a food coloring, since it is virtually tasteless. The dye is reputedly an antidote to prussic acid poisoning, caused by eating manioc (*Manihot esculenta*) from which the toxin has not been completely removed. Its medicinal properties are poorly understood. In Brazil it is widely known as *urucú*.

B. orellana (annatto, *achiote*, lipstick tree) p.94

PARTS USED Leaves, fruits, seeds.
PROPERTIES A bitter, astringent, purgative herb that reputedly destroys intestinal worms, lowers fever, improves digestion, and has expectorant effects.
USES OF THE HERB
CULINARY Seeds are eaten cooked in butter and are used to flavor rice, soups, meat, and chocolate.
MEDICINAL Internally for mouth cancer (seed pulp, Mexico); worms in children, colic, and fevers (leaves, W Indies); fevers, especially in children and after childbirth (infusions of leaves, Indo-China). Externally on burns to prevent blistering and scarring (ground seeds, Philippines).
ECONOMIC Fruit pulp yields colorant, used mainly in foods (especially in margarine, cheese, soups, and smoked fish), and also to dye maggots for fish bait.

GROWTH AND HARVEST
GROWTH Crop. Tender. Well-drained, moist soil with high humidity, minimum 61°F (16°C). Propagate by fresh seed sown in sand in autumn, at 64–68°F (18–20°C), or by cuttings of ripened wood at 86°F (30°C). Seed-raised plants are slow to reach flowering size. Plants from cuttings of mature plants will flower when small. Clip hard if grown as a hedge. Trim specimen plants as required.
HARVEST Leaves are picked as required and dried for use in infusions. Seeds are collected as the fruits split open, and are soaked in hot water; the resulting sediment is pressed into cakes for use in medicines and dyes.

BLETIA
B. hyacinthina. See *Bletilla striata*.

BLETILLA
(Orchidaceae)

B. striata is an important wound herb in traditional Chinese medicine and was first described c.AD500.

B. striata, syn. *Bletia hyacinthina* (bletilla) p.94

PARTS USED Pseudobulbs.
PROPERTIES A bitter, sweet, and sour herb that checks bleeding, controls bacterial infection, reduces swelling, and promotes healing.
USES OF THE HERB
MEDICINAL Internally for hemorrhage of the lungs or stomach (e.g., in tuberculosis, gastric ulcer), uterine bleeding, and nosebleeds. Externally, often mixed with sesame oil, for burns, bleeding injuries, abscesses, and sores.

GROWTH AND HARVEST
GROWTH Ornamental. Well-drained, humus-rich soil with added peat, or peat substitute, and leaf mold, in shade. Propagate by offsets of pseudobulbs in early spring, or division if overcrowded. Slugs may damage young leaves. Aphids and spider mite can attack under cover.
HARVEST Pseudobulbs are lifted when dormant, and sliced and dried for use in decoctions and powder.

BOMBAX
B. pentandra. See *Ceiba pentandra*.

BORAGO Borage
(Boraginaceae)

Borage has a reputation for lifting the spirits, summarized by John Gerard in *The Herball, or Generall Historie of Plantes* (1597): "Those of our time do use the floures in sallads to exhilerate and make the minde glad. There be also many things made of them, used for the comfort of the heart, to drive away sorrow, & increase the joy of the minde. The leaves and floures of Borrage put into wine make men and women glad and merry, driving away all sadnesse, dulnesse, and melancholy, as Dioscorides and Pliny affirme. Syrrup made of the floures of Borrage comforteth the heart, purgeth melancholy, and quieteth the phrenticke or lunaticke person."

B. officinalis (borage) p.94

PARTS USED Leaves, flowers, seeds, oil.
PROPERTIES A cooling, saline, diuretic herb that soothes damaged or irritated tissues, increases perspiration, and has mild sedative and antidepressant effects. Seeds are a rich source of gamma-linolenic acid. Oil regulates hormonal systems and lowers blood pressure. Plant (but not oil) contains small amounts of pyrrolizidine alkaloids (as found in *Symphytum officinale*, see p.357) that may cause liver damage and liver cancer.

USES OF THE HERB
CULINARY Leaves give a cucumber flavor to drinks and are added whole to Pimms and wine-based drinks; they are also chopped in salads and cream cheese, and in parts of Italy are cooked as a vegetable. Fresh flowers are added to salads or used as a garnish, but turn pink on contact with acids such as lemon juice or vinegar; they are also made into a syrup or candied as cake decorations.

MEDICINAL Internally for fevers, bronchial infections (including pleurisy and tuberculosis), mouth and throat infections, dry skin conditions, cirrhosis, and chronic nephritis; as an alternative to evening primrose oil for skin complaints and premenstrual syndrome (oil). Externally in eyewashes, gargles, mouthwashes, and poultices.
WARNING All parts of the herb, except the seed oil, are subject to legal restrictions in some countries.
VARIANT
B. o. 'Alba', p.94.

GROWTH AND HARVEST

GROWTH Ornamental. Well-drained moist soil in full sun. Tolerates poor dry soil but makes a much larger plant in better conditions. Propagate by seed sown *in situ* in spring, and thinned to 18in (45cm) apart. May develop mildew in dry conditions or toward the end of the growing season.
HARVEST Leaves are gathered in spring and summer as the plant starts to flower, and are used fresh, or dried for use in infusions and liquid extracts. Flowers are picked as they open and separated from the calyx before using fresh, making into a syrup, or candying. Borage develops a thick taproot and does not transplant well. It is recommended in companion planting to deter Japanese beetles and tomato hornworms; also reputed to benefit strawberries. The flowers attract bees. Properties deteriorate rapidly; leaves and flowers must be processed promptly and stocks of dried herb renewed annually. Seeds are harvested when ripe for oil extraction.
WARNING Skin irritant and possible allergen.

BOSWELLIA Frankincense
(Burseraceae)

Frankincense has been used for cosmetic and medicinal purposes since earliest times, especially as an ingredient in theriacs and panaceas. It was associated with longevity and memory in Classical times, and burned as incense to drive away evil spirits. One of the most valuable articles of trade in early Middle Eastern cultures, frankincense had numerous domestic, medicinal, and ritual uses. Reliefs (c.1512–1482BC) on Queen Hatshepsut's temple at Luxor in Egypt show frankincense trees in pots, grown to make rejuvenating face masks.

B. sacra, syn. *B. carteri* (frankincense, olibanum, mastic tree) p.95

PARTS USED Gum resin (*ru xiang*).
PROPERTIES A bitter, pungent, warming herb that stimulates the circulation, calms the nerves, and has antiseptic, expectorant, and decongestant effects.
USES OF THE HERB
AROMATIC Used in incense and perfumery.
MEDICINAL Internally for bronchial and urinary infections. Not given to pregnant women (although traditionally used as a fumigant during and after childbirth in Oman). Externally as an inhalant for mucus and a douche for vaginal infections. In Chinese medicine, internally for menstrual pain and externally for injuries, skin eruptions, and as a wash for gum, mouth, and throat complaints. Regarded as a rejuvenative in Ayurvedic medicine. Important in aromatherapy for relieving anxiety.
ECONOMIC Used in antiwrinkle creams.

GROWTH AND HARVEST

GROWTH Wild-collected. Well-drained to dry soil in full sun, minimum 50–59°F (10–15°C). Propagate by semiripe cuttings in summer. Light pruning may be carried out in early spring.
HARVEST Gum resin is collected all year, although quality is dependent on location and season, that from the driest areas in the hottest months being the finest; it is used fresh or dried for distillation, decoctions, or powders.

BRASSICA Mustard
(Cruciferae/Brassicaceae)

Mustards have provided pungent flavorings, green vegetables, and medicinal compounds from very early times. Use as a condiment in the West dates back to at least 400BC and medicinal uses were first mentioned in China in AD659. Pungency of mustard develops when cold water is added to the ground seed; an enzyme (myrosin) acts on a glycoside (sinigrin) to produce the sulfur compound, allyl isothiocyanate. The reaction takes 10–15 minutes. Mixing with hot water or vinegar, or adding salt, inhibits the enzyme, producing a mild, bitter mustard. The three main kinds of commercially prepared mustard are: American, using white mustard (*Sinapis alba*, see p.353); English, using a mix of white and black (*S. alba* and *B. nigra*) or brown (*B. juncea*) mustards; and French, which is based on black (*B. nigra*) or, more usually today, on brown mustard (*B. juncea*).

B. alba. See *Sinapis alba*.

B. hirta. See *Sinapis alba*.

B. juncea, syn. *Sinapis juncea* (brown mustard, Indian mustard, Chinese mustard) p.95

PARTS USED Leaves, seeds.
PROPERTIES A warming, stimulant herb with antibiotic effects.
USES OF THE HERB
CULINARY Young leaves are cooked as a vegetable. Seeds are ground and blended with other mustards or used alone as Russian, brown, or Sarrepta mustard, which has an especially strong flavor; used whole in curries and pickles, they are often heated in fat to destroy pungency and give a nutty flavor.

B. nigra, syn. *Sinapis nigra* (black mustard) p.95

PARTS USED Leaves and flowers, seeds, oil.
PROPERTIES A pungent, warming herb that stimulates the circulatory and digestive systems, and irritates the skin and mucous membranes. It is a potent emetic in large doses.
USES OF THE HERB
CULINARY Young leaves and flowers add pungency to salads. Seeds are ground to make mustard and used whole in curries and pickles.
MEDICINAL Externally in poultices, mustard plasters, and baths for rheumatism, muscular pain, chilblains, and respiratory tract infections. A mustard footbath is a traditional remedy for colds and headaches. Skin contact with mustard causes reddening, thus increasing blood flow and removal of toxins. Prolonged contact may result in blistering, especially in those with sensitive skin.

GROWTH AND HARVEST

GROWTH Crop. Rich, well-drained soil in full sun. Propagate by seed sown in spring.
HARVEST Leaves and flowers are picked when young and used fresh. Pods are harvested as they begin to change color, and dried to complete the ripening process; this prevents the seeds from being shed in the field. Seeds store indefinitely if kept dry. Volatile oil is distilled from seeds for medicinal use.

BRUCEA
(Simaroubaceae)

B. javanica was first recorded in Chinese medicine c.AD720. It is used in folk medicine to kill maggots and also internally for hemorrhoids.

B. javanica (kusam seeds) p.95

PARTS USED Seeds (*ya dan zi*).
PROPERTIES A bitter herb that lowers fever and is effective against a wide range of pathogens.
USES OF THE HERB
MEDICINAL Internally for malaria, amebic dysentery, and vaginal thrush. Externally for warts and corns. Seeds are usually given whole, with dose and duration of treatment varying according to the complaint.

GROWTH AND HARVEST

GROWTH Crop. Well-drained soil in sun or partial shade, minimum 59–64°F (15–18°C). Propagate by seed sown in spring, or by ripewood cuttings in sand.
HARVEST Seeds are collected when ripe and the hard outer coating is removed.

BRUNFELSIA
(Solanaceae)

Brunfelsias contain various alkaloids and a furocoumarin that is reputed to be anti-inflammatory. Several are used by native

S Americans, both medicinally and as hallucinogens; they include *B. chiricaspi* and *B. grandiflora*, which both characteristically produce a chilling, tingling sensation.

B. uniflora, syn. *B. hopeana* (*manaca, pohl*, vegetable mercury) p.95

PARTS USED Roots.
PROPERTIES A sweet, slightly aromatic herb that has alterative, diuretic, and antirheumatic effects.
USES OF THE HERB
MEDICINAL Internally for syphilis, rheumatism, and arthritis.

GROWTH AND HARVEST
GROWTH Wild-collected. Rich, well-drained soil in partial shade and high humidity; minimum 55°F (13°C). Propagate by semiripe cuttings in summer at 70°F (21°C). Pinch out shoot tips in the growing season to encourage branching. Whitefly and mealybug may damage plants under cover.
HARVEST Roots are collected and dried for use in decoctions and liquid extracts.

BRYONIA
(Cucurbitaceae)

B. dioica is closely related to *B. alba*, differing mainly in having black, rather than red, berries. They are used in similar ways, although homeopathic remedies contain only *B. alba*. The tuber of *B. dioica* used to be known as "English mandrake" and was traditionally hung in herb shops, often trimmed to a manlike shape to resemble the true mandrake, *Mandragora officinarum* (see p.308). It can reach a great size: "The Queen's chief surgeon … shewed me a root hereof that waied half an hundredweight, and of the bignes of a child of a yeare old" (Culpeper, *The English Physitian Enlarged*, 1653).

B. dioica, syn. *B. cretica* subsp. *dioica* (white bryony, red bryony, English mandrake) p.95

PARTS USED Roots.
PROPERTIES A bitter, purgative herb that irritates the tissues, increasing blood supply to the area. It is known to have antitumor and antirheumatic effects. Highly toxic in large doses.
USES OF THE HERB
MEDICINAL Formerly used internally in small doses for bronchial complaints, asthma, intestinal ulcers, hypertension, and arthritis. Externally, as a rubefacient, in muscular and joint pains, and pleurisy.

GROWTH AND HARVEST
GROWTH Crop. Hardy. Well-drained neutral to alkaline soil in sun. Propagate by seed sown in autumn; by division of tuber when dormant.
HARVEST Root is lifted in autumn, then sliced and dried for use in liquid extracts.
WARNING Fresh root is a severe skin irritant.

BUPLEURUM Thorow-wax
(Umbelliferae/Apiaceae)

B. falcatum was first mentioned in Chinese medical texts c.AD200.

B. falcatum, syn. *B. scorzoneraefolium*, *B. chinense* (sickle-leaved hare's ear) p.96

PARTS USED Roots (*chai hu*).
PROPERTIES A bitter herb that acts as a tonic for the liver and circulatory system, lowers fevers, and has antiviral effects.
USES OF THE HERB
MEDICINAL Internally for malaria, blackwater fever, uterine and rectal prolapse, herpes simplex, hemorrhoids, sluggish liver associated with emotional instability, menstrual disorders, and abdominal bloating. Often used raw with wine for feverish illnesses, with vinegar as a circulatory stimulant, and mixed with tortoise blood for malaria.

GROWTH AND HARVEST
GROWTH Ornamental. Well-drained soil in full sun. Propagate by seed sown in spring; by division when dormant.
HARVEST Roots are lifted in autumn and used fresh, or dried for decoctions.

BURSERA Torchwood
(Burseraceae)

This tropical American genus contains about 50 species of deciduous trees and shrubs. The essential oils in various species were used as incense by the Mayas. Several species are sources of linalol, a fragrant liquid found in many essential oils and important in perfumes with woody or floral notes. Commonly used are *B. glabrifolia* (76 percent linalol) and *B. delpechiana*, as well as *B. penicillata* (Indian lavender), *B. simarda*, *B. simarouba*, and *B. spinosa*. *B. glabrifolia* was increasingly exploited after World War II, when production of linalol from *Aniba roseaodora* (see p.239) gave way to rubber plantations for the US military. Recent research has also shown interesting medicinal properties: antimicrobial in *B. delpechiana* and antitumor in *B. klugii* and *B. morelensis*.

B. glabrifolia, syn. *B. aloexylon* (linaloe, Mexican linaloe)

Tender, deciduous tree, height 15–20ft (5–6m), spread 10ft (3m), with pinnate leaves arranged at the tips of branches. Clusters of white flowers, ½in (1cm) long, are produced at the start of the wet season, followed by ovoid, pea-sized, red berries.

PARTS USED Wood, fruits, oil.
PROPERTIES A bitter, aromatic, antiseptic herb that reduces inflammation and controls convulsions.
USES OF THE HERB
MEDICINAL Internally for nervous tension. Externally for acne, wounds, and dermatitis.
ECONOMIC Oil is used in perfumery, and in the food industry for its slightly bitter limelike flavor.

GROWTH AND HARVEST
GROWTH Wild-collected. Well-drained to stony soil in sun or partial shade, with high humidity; minimum 54°F (12°C). Propagate by mallet cuttings in late summer at 59°F (15°C). In the tropics, by ripewood cuttings in the open ground.
HARVEST Wood is cut from trees at least 20 years old, and chipped and distilled for oil between December and June. Ripe fruits are collected in late summer for oil distillation.

BUXUS Boxwood
(Buxaceae)

B. sempervirens is reputedly comparable in effectiveness to quinine (*Cinchona* species, see p.261) for treating malaria. However, it is rarely used as a herb today on account of its toxicity. The wood is extremely hard and heavy and gave its name to boxes; it was used for printing blocks and mathematical, nautical, and musical instruments.

B. sempervirens (boxwood) p.96

PARTS USED Leaves, bark, wood.
PROPERTIES A strong-smelling, narcotic herb that lowers fever and may have antirheumatic effects. Destroys intestinal parasites.
USES OF THE HERB
MEDICINAL Internally for recurrent fevers (such as malaria). Dosage is critical: excess causes vomiting, convulsions, and death. Also used in homeopathy for rheumatism.
ECONOMIC Often included in preparations to stimulate hair growth. Wood is used in engraving.
VARIANTS
B. s. **'Elegantissima'**, p.96.
B. s. **'Kingsville Dwarf'**, p.96.
B. s. **'Latifolia Maculata'**, syn. *B. s.* 'Japonica Aurea', p.96.

GROWTH AND HARVEST
GROWTH Ornamental. Well-drained neutral to alkaline soil in sun or shade. *B. sempervirens* is hardy to 10°F (–23°C) but prefers higher winter temperatures. Plant 8in (20cm) apart for hedges. Propagate by softwood or semiripe cuttings in a mixture of peat or peat substitute and sand. Cut back hard to encourage new growth in late spring. Trim hedges and topiary specimens to shape in summer. Leaves may be affected by leafspot or rust. Young leaves may be attacked by boxwood psyllids, mites, and leaf miners. Older plants may suffer from "boxwood decline," a condition that is especially severe in poorly drained soil.
HARVEST Leaves are gathered in early spring, before flowering, and dried for infusions. Bark is stripped from wood and dried for decoctions.
WARNING All parts are toxic if eaten. Possible skin irritant or allergen.

CALAMINTHA Calamint
(Labiatae)

Calamints were "officinal" herbs of the pharmacopoeia in medieval times, but are regarded as more ornamental than useful by medical herbalists today. *Calamintha grandiflora* (ornamental savory) produces leaves with a minty aroma and is useful as a seasoning or tea. *C. g.* 'Variegata' maintains its speckled variegation in partial shade but will tolerate full sun. The active constituent is pulegone, as found in *Mentha pulegium* (see p.311), which is known to cause abortion.

C. acinos. See *Acinos arvensis.*

C. nepeta, syn. *C. nepetoides, Satureja nepeta* (lesser calamint) p.97

PARTS USED Whole plant.
PROPERTIES An aromatic herb that acts as a nerve tonic, stimulates the uterus, and relieves indigestion.
USES OF THE HERB
MEDICINAL Internally for indigestion, nervous tension, depression, insomnia, and painful menstruation. Not given to pregnant women.
VARIANT
C. nepeta subsp. ***nepeta,*** p.97.

C. sylvatica, syn. *C. ascendens, C. officinalis* (common calamint) p.97

PARTS USED Whole plant, leaves.
PROPERTIES Similar to *C. nepeta*, but not as strong.
USES OF THE HERB
CULINARY Used to flavor roasts, especially "gamey" meat.
MEDICINAL As for *C. nepeta.*

GROWTH AND HARVEST
GROWTH Ornamental (*C. nepeta* and subsp.). Wild-collected (*C. sylvatica*). Well-drained to dry, neutral to alkaline soil in sun. Propagate by seed sown under cover in spring or autumn, or by softwood cuttings in early summer, or by division in spring.
HARVEST Flowering plants and leaves are cut in summer and used fresh, or dried for infusions.

CALENDULA Pot marigold
(Compositae)

C. officinalis was used in early Indian and Arabic cultures, and in ancient Greece and Rome, as a medicinal herb and as a colorant for fabrics, foods, and cosmetics. The common name "marigold" is used for various species, notably for *Tagetes* species (see p.358), which are used in very different ways.

C. officinalis (pot marigold) p.97

PARTS USED Flower petals.
PROPERTIES A bittersweet, salty herb that stimulates the liver, gall bladder, and uterus, soothes the digestive system, supports the heart, and clears infections. It benefits the skin especially, reducing inflammation, controlling bleeding, and healing damaged or irritated tissues.
USES OF THE HERB
CULINARY Petals are used as a substitute for saffron in rice and soup, and infused to give color to cheese, butter, milk desserts, and cakes; also added fresh to salads.
MEDICINAL Internally for gastric and duodenal ulcers (with *Geranium maculatum*, see p.288), colitis, diverticulitis, hepatitis, swollen glands, menstrual problems, and pelvic inflammatory disease. Not given during pregnancy. Externally for eczema, conjunctivitis, thrush infections, herpes, gingivitis, athlete's foot, varicose veins (with *Hamamelis virginiana*, see p.291), cysts, minor injuries (with *Ulmus rubra* and *Chondrus crispus*, see p.260), and skin problems. As a general antiseptic, *C. officinalis* is often combined with *Hydrastis canadensis* (see p.294) and *Commiphora myrrha* (p.265). Used internally and externally in homeopathy for injuries where the skin is broken.
VARIANT
***C. o.* 'Prolifera'**, p.97.

GROWTH AND HARVEST
GROWTH Ornamental. Well-drained to poor soil in full sun. Propagate by seed sown *in situ* in spring or autumn. *C. officinalis* self-seeds readily. Remove dead flower heads to prolong flowering and prevent excessive self-seeding. Dies out in hot summers. Caterpillars, powdery mildew, rust, or cucumber mosaic virus may attack foliage.
HARVEST Flowers are cut in dry conditions and stripped of petals, for use fresh or dried in infusions, liquid extracts, tinctures, and for culinary purposes; they are also macerated in oil for external use.

CALLUNA Heather
(Ericaceae)

Heather is widely used as a medicinal plant in northern and upland Europe, due to its easy availability. Heather honey is an important product in these areas, also having reputed therapeutic properties. The honey has a pungent flavor, clear, dark amber color, and a thixotropic texture, which makes it difficult to extract, but is excellent for cut honeycomb.

C. vulgaris (heather, ling) p.98

PARTS USED Whole plant.
PROPERTIES An astringent, diuretic, mildly sedative herb that induces perspiration and has antiseptic effects, especially on the urinary system.
USES OF THE HERB
MEDICINAL Internally for coughs and colds, diarrhea, kidney and urinary tract infections, arthritis, rheumatism, and nervous exhaustion. Used in homeopathy for arthritis, rheumatism, and insomnia.

VARIANTS
***C. v.* 'Alba Plena'**, p.98.
***C. v.* 'Darkness'**, p.98.
***C. v.* 'Multicolor'**, p.98.
***C. v.* 'Silver Queen'**, p.98.

GROWTH AND HARVEST
GROWTH Ornamental (*C. vulgaris*: wild-collected). Well-drained, lime-free soil in an open, sunny position. Best in areas with cool summers. Propagate by cuttings of young sideshoots in summer, or by layering in spring. Trim after flowering. Heather dieback or *Armillaria* root rot may affect plants.
HARVEST Flowering shoots are cut in summer and dried for use in infusions.

CAMELLIA
(Theaceae)

Several different products are obtained from *C. sinensis*: green tea, made from leaves that are steamed and then dried; black tea, from fermented, dried leaves; and tea absolute, an essential oil distilled from black tea. Tea has been drunk in China for over 3,000 years. Both black and green teas contain antioxidants known as polyphenols, which help protect against heart disease, strokes, and cancer. *C. sinensis* contains 10–24 percent tannins, which are a possible cause of esophageal cancer. Drinking tea with milk eliminates this risk because the tannins are neutralized.

C. sinensis, syn. *Thea sinensis* (tea) p.99

PARTS USED Leaves (shoot tips only), oil.
PROPERTIES An aromatic, slightly bitter, astringent herb that stimulates the nervous system and has diuretic and bactericidal effects.
USES OF THE HERB
CULINARY Occasionally used to flavor food, notably as a soaking liquid for dried fruits and ham.
MEDICINAL Internally for diarrhea, dysentery, hepatitis, and gastroenteritis. Excess causes constipation, indigestion, dizziness, palpitations, irritability, and insomnia. Externally for sore eyes, minor injuries, and insect bites.
ECONOMIC Essential oil is used in perfumes, hair oil, and commercial food flavoring.

GROWTH AND HARVEST
GROWTH Crop. Rich, moist soil in sun or partial shade. Propagate by seed sown as soon as ripe, or in spring, at 59–64°F (15–18°C), or by semiripe cuttings in summer at minimum 64°F (18°C). Dried seeds need chipping. Bushes are normally pruned to 3ft (1m).
HARVEST Leaves are picked during the year from bushes over three years old, and dried for use in infusions.

CANANGA Ylang-ylang

(Annonaceae)

Ylang-ylang (*C. odorata*) is cultivated for the perfumery industry in Réunion, Indonesia, Madagascar, the Philippines, and the Comoro Islands. One tree produces approximately 265lb (120kg) of flowers, yielding 12oz (350g) of essential oil. Ylang-ylang perfume is also produced from the flowers of the closely related *Artabotrys hexapetalus*.

C. odorata, syn. *Canangium odoratum* (ylang-ylang, ilang-ilang) p.99

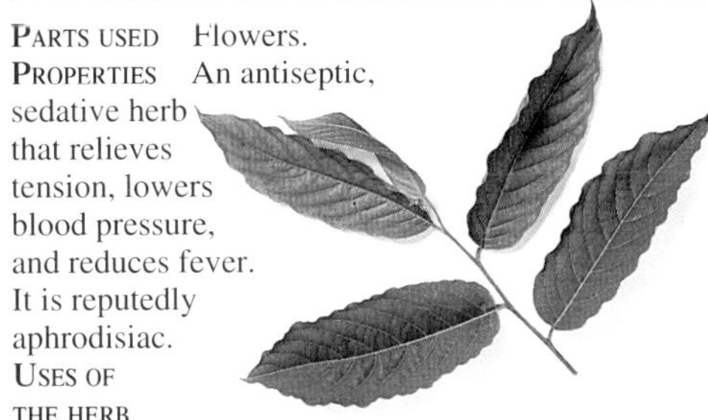

PARTS USED Flowers.
PROPERTIES An antiseptic, sedative herb that relieves tension, lowers blood pressure, and reduces fever. It is reputedly aphrodisiac.
USES OF THE HERB
MEDICINAL Internally for malaria and fevers. Externally for skin irritations, conjunctivitis, boils, and gout, and in baths for impotence and frigidity. Ylang-ylang is important in aromatherapy for treating tachycardia, rapid breathing, hypertension, gastrointestinal infections, and psychosexual complaints.
ECONOMIC The distilled oil (cananga oil) is used in perfumery and cosmetics, and with coconut oil in Macassar hair oil; also in the food industry, especially in peach and apricot flavorings.

GROWTH AND HARVEST
GROWTH Crop. Well-drained, moist soil in sun, with high humidity, minimum 59–64°F (15–18°C). Remove the terminal bud when the tree is 6ft (2m) tall, after about three years. Propagate by seed sown when ripe.
HARVEST Flowers are picked at night and dried for infusions, or distilled for oil.

CANANGIUM

C. odoratum. See *Cananga odorata*.

CANELLA

(Canellaceae)

Canella is a familiar spice in the W Indies. It was introduced to Europe in the early 17th century, as a species of *Cinnamomum* (see p.261). The fruits are fed to pigeons in Jamaica, giving their flesh a spicy flavor. Dried flowers emit a musklike scent when placed in warm water. *C. winterana* is one of the 21 plants of the *Omiero*, the sacred elixir of Afro-Caribbean Santeria initiation.

C. winterana, syn. *C. alba* (canella, white cinnamon, W Indian wild cinnamon) p.99

PARTS USED Leaves, bark, oil.
PROPERTIES A bitter, aromatic herb that improves digestion and has antimicrobial effects.
USES OF THE HERB
AROMATIC Oil is used occasionally in perfumes with an oriental bouquet.
MEDICINAL Internally for poor digestion. Externally for rheumatic pains (Cuba). Combined with aloes (*Aloe vera*, see p.235) for constipation and menstrual problems (W Indies). An aromatic adjunct in prescriptions for treating digestive complaints.
ECONOMIC Bark and leaves are used in seasoning mixtures and added to tobacco (W Indies); bark is used as fish poison (Puerto Rico).

GROWTH AND HARVEST
GROWTH Crop. Well-drained, sandy soil in sun. Propagate by ripewood cuttings with a heel, in spring.
HARVEST Leaves are picked locally as required and used fresh or dried. Bark is dried in long quills for oil distillation or for use in condiments, decoctions, and tinctures, and as a powder with aloes.

CANNABIS Hemp

(Cannabidaceae)

Cannabis has been grown in Asia and the Middle East for over 4,000 years, both as a fiber plant and as a drug. Therapeutic uses were described in Indian medical texts before 1000BC and in the Chinese herbal *Rh-ya* in the fifth century BC. Today its possession and use are illegal, or subject to strict controls, in most Western countries and in Australia and New Zealand, but legal and socially acceptable in many parts of Asia and the Middle East, where the dried plant or resin is commonly smoked or eaten. The various common names for cannabis refer to specific preparations: *hasheesh* – resin from the female plant, usually smoked in water pipes; *bhang* – dried plant mixed into water, fruits, or candy; *charas* – resin smoked or eaten with spices; and *ganja* – dried tops of the female plant. European herbals of the 16th century include the plant, which John Gerard called "Indian dreamer." Cannabis was listed in the pharmacopoeias of many countries, including the US, until its restriction in the 1930s. While modern research confirms its value for a wide range of conditions, its illegal status has suppressed therapeutic use in the West. It is still widely used in traditional Chinese medicine.

C. sativa (hemp, marijuana, *hasheesh*) p.99

In this variable species, two subspecies are recognized: the hardier *C. s.* subsp. *sativa* (hemp), which is cultivated for fiber, and *C. s.* subsp. *indica* (marijuana), which is richer in essential oils and other chemical compounds.
PARTS USED Whole plant (*C. s.* subsp. *sativa*); flowering tops, seeds (*C. s.* subsp. *indica*).
PROPERTIES *C. s.* subsp. *indica* has analgesic, anti-emetic, anti-inflammatory and sedative properties; it is also a laxative and hypotensive.
USES OF THE HERB
MEDICINAL Internally *C. s.* subsp. *indica* is used for nausea and vomiting associated with cancer chemotherapy, to reduce ocular pressure in glaucoma, and to help AIDS patients gain weight. Externally for corns, sores, and varicose ulcers. Seeds (*huo ma ren*) are used in traditional Chinese medicine to treat constipation caused by debility or fluid deficiency. WARNING This herb is subject to legal restrictions in most countries.
ECONOMIC *C. s.* subsp. *sativa* is a source of fibers for rope making.

GROWTH AND HARVEST
Cultivation, harvesting, and processing of *Cannabis* plants are subject to legal restrictions in many countries. Approved varieties for fiber (hemp) production, with no or low narcotic content, are permitted by license in producer countries. Subject to statutory control as a weed in some countries, notably in parts of Australia.

CAPPARIS Caper bush

(Capparaceae)

C. spinosa is the only species of commercial importance, although several other species are used (notably *C. brevispina*, *C. decidua*, and *C. zeylanica*). Pickled capers have been used as a condiment in southern Europe for over 2,000 years. Caper buds are both wild-collected and cultivated; plants grown in cultivation tend to be spineless (*C. spinosa* var. *inermis*). The unripe seeds of nasturtiums (*Tropaeolum majus*, see p.365) make satisfactory substitutes; when pickled they develop a similar taste, caused by capric acid.

C. spinosa (caper) p.99

PARTS USED Root bark, flower buds.
PROPERTIES An astringent, diuretic, expectorant herb that is regarded as a stimulating tonic.
USES OF THE HERB
CULINARY Pickled or dry-salted caper buds are used in caper sauce for lamb, *tartare*, *ravigote*, *gribiche*, and *remoulade* sauces, fish dishes, and hors d'oeuvres. Often combined with olives and with anchovies.
MEDICINAL Internally for gastrointestinal infections, diarrhea, gout, and rheumatism (root bark); for coughs (flower buds). Externally for eye infections (flower buds).

GROWTH AND HARVEST
GROWTH Ornamental. Well-drained, sandy soil in sun. Plants may be grown in or on top of walls. Propagate by ripewood cuttings in summer at 66–75°F (19–24°C).
HARVEST Flower buds are picked in early morning and wilted before pickling in salted white vinegar or dry salting. Fruits and leaves are also pickled in the countries of origin. Bark is stripped from roots lifted in autumn, and then dried.

CAPSELLA
(Cruciferae)

Shepherd's purse has been used as a food for thousands of years. Seeds were found in the stomach of Tollund man (c.500BC–AD400), and during excavation of the Catal Huyuk site, which dates back to 5950BC.

C. bursa-pastoris, syn. *Thlaspi bursa-pastoris* (shepherd's purse, witches' pouches, pick-pocket) p.99

PARTS USED Whole plant (*ji cai*), leaves.
PROPERTIES An astringent, diuretic herb that also acts as a urinary antiseptic and blood coagulant.
USES OF THE HERB
CULINARY The leaves are rich in vitamins A, B, and C, and may be added to salads.
MEDICINAL Internally and externally to stop bleeding, especially heavy menstruation, blood in urine, hemorrhoids, nosebleed, and wounds. Also internally for cystitis, and externally for varicose veins. In Chinese medicine, to cool the blood, with uses similar to the above; also for hypertension and postpartum bleeding.

GROWTH AND HARVEST
GROWTH Crop. Well-drained soil in sun or partial shade. Tolerates poor conditions. Propagate by seed in spring. Self-seeds freely.
HARVEST Whole plants are cut from late spring to autumn and used fresh, or dried in bunches, for infusions, decoctions, or liquid extracts. Leaves are picked fresh for culinary use.

CAPSICUM Pepper
(Solanaceae)

Most cultivated capsicums belong to *C. annuum* var. *annuum*, and may be divided into five main groups: Cerasiforme (cherry); Conioides (cone); Fasciculatum (red cone); Grossum (pimento, sweet or bell pepper); and Longum (cayenne, chili). They are rich in vitamin C. Pungency is due to a bitter, acrid alkaloid (capsaicin). Its presence depends on a single gene, and cultivars without it have sweet fruits. Capsaicin is the main therapeutic and flavoring compound in cayenne or chili powder; *C. annuum* var. *annuum* has both pungent and sweet cultivars, used respectively for cayenne and paprika. WARNING Capsicum oleoresin is subject to legal restrictions in some countries.

C. annuum var. *annuum* (sweet pepper, bell pepper, chili pepper)

Tender, variable annual or short-lived perennial, height 5ft (1.5m), spread to 6ft (2m), with branched stems and simple, ovate-lanceolate leaves. Bell-shaped, white to green flowers appear in spring and summer, followed by hollow fruits up to 6in (15cm) long which ripen to varying colors.

PARTS USED Fruits.
PROPERTIES Pungent-fruited cultivars have tonic and antiseptic effects, stimulate the circulatory and digestive systems, and increase perspiration. They also irritate the tissues, increasing blood supply to the area and reducing sensitivity to pain.
USES OF THE HERB
CULINARY Both pungent-fruited and sweet-fruited cultivars are used ripe or unripe, fresh or dried, as vegetables (raw or cooked), and in pickles and chutneys, in many parts of the world, especially S and C America, Mexico, India, and SE Asia. Ripe fruits are dried to make cayenne, chili powder, or paprika. Pungent-fruited peppers may cause painful inflammation in excess, or after accidental contact with eyes or broken skin.
MEDICINAL Internally for the cold stage of fevers, debility in convalescence or old age, varicose veins, asthma, and digestive problems. Externally for sprains, unbroken chilblains, neuralgia, lumbago, and pleurisy, and combined with *Commiphora myrrha* (see p.265), as a gargle for laryngitis. Pungent-fruited peppers are important as a gastrointestinal detoxicant and food preservative in the tropics. They contain a valuable antioxidant.
VARIANTS
C. a. var. ***annuum* 'Anaheim'**, p.100.
C. a. var. ***annuum* 'Chili Serrano'**, p.100.
C. a. var. ***annuum* 'Hungarian Wax'**, p.100.
C. a. var. ***annuum* 'Jalapeño'**, p.100.
C. a. var. ***annuum* 'Purple Tiger'**, p.100
C. a. var. ***annuum* 'Super Cayenne'**, p.100.
C. a. var. ***glabriusculum***, syn. *C. a.* var. *minimum* (bird pepper)
Tender, small-fruited variety, height 6ft (2m), spread 3–4ft (1–1.2m), with ovate to lanceolate leaves up to 1¼in (3cm) long, white flowers, and very pungent, red, pea-sized fruits, known as *chiltepins*; the ancestor of most cultivated chili peppers.

C. baccatum, syn. *C. microcarpum* p.100

PARTS USED Fruits.
PROPERTIES As for pungent-fruited cultivars of *C. annuum* var. *annuum*.
USES OF THE HERB
CULINARY As for pungent-fruited cultivars of *C. annuum* var. *annuum*.
MEDICINAL As for pungent-fruited cultivars of *C. annuum* var. *annuum*.
VARIANT
C. b. var. ***pendulum***, syn. *C. pendulum* (Andean *aji*)
Shrubby perennial, hardy to 32°F (0°C), height 1½–6ft (45cm–2m), spread 4ft (1.2m), with ovate-elliptic leaves, and solitary or paired white flowers, ½in (1cm) across, which have golden markings and yellow anthers. Fruits are red, medium to very hot, and up to 5in (13cm) long. Common in the southern Andes and Ecuador.

C. chinense, syn. *C. sinense*

Tender shrub, height and spread 5ft (1.5m), with clusters of two or more white or green-tinged flowers. Fruits are pendulous, red-brown to cream. Native to W Indies, southern C America and northern S America, not to China; ancestor of some of the hottest peppers.
PARTS USED Fruits.

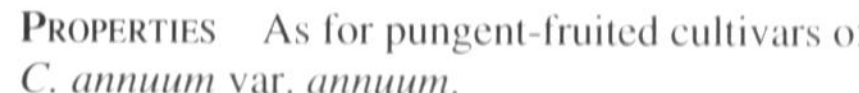

PROPERTIES As for pungent-fruited cultivars of *C. annuum* var. *annuum*.
USES OF THE HERB
CULINARY As for pungent-fruited cultivars of *C. annuum* var. *annuum*.
MEDICINAL As for pungent-fruited cultivars of *C. annuum* var. *annuum*.
VARIANT
C. c. **'Habañero'**, p.100.

C. frutescens, syn. *C. minimum* (Tabasco pepper, hot pepper, spur pepper) p.100

PARTS USED Fruits.
PROPERTIES As for pungent-fruited cultivars of *C. annuum* var. *annuum*.
USES OF THE HERB
CULINARY As for pungent-fruited cultivars of *C. annuum* var. *annuum*.
MEDICINAL As for pungent-fruited cultivars of *C. annuum* var. *annuum*.
VARIANT
C. f. **'Tabasco'**, p.100.

C. pubescens (*rocoto, chili manzano*, tree pepper)

Sprawling, shrubby perennial, hardy to 23°F (–5°C), height 10ft (3m), spread 6ft (2m), with striped stems, purple nodes, and wrinkled, hairy, ovate leaves. Solitary, violet, white-eyed flowers are followed by pendent to erect yellow, red, or brown fruits. The most cold-tolerant species, and able to fruit for 15 years in cool, moist climates. Known in Brazil as *malagueta*.

PARTS USED Fruits.
PROPERTIES As for pungent-fruited cultivars of *C. annuum* var. *annuum*.
USES OF THE HERB As for pungent-fruited cultivars of *C. annuum* var. *annuum*.

GROWTH AND HARVEST
GROWTH Crop. Rich, well-drained soil in sun, minimum 64–70°F (18–21°C). *C. baccatum* var. *pendulum* and *C. pubescens* withstand cooler conditions. Propagate by seed in early spring. *C. pubescens* may be espaliered or pruned. Several insects may damage growing points and leaves; plants under cover may be affected by spider mite, whitefly, and aphids.
HARVEST Unripe fruits are picked as required and used raw, pickled, or cooked. Ripe fruits are picked in summer and used fresh, pickled, or dried for condiments, decoctions, ointments, powders, tinctures, tablets, and oleoresin.

CARBENIA
C. benedicta. See *Cnicus benedictus*.

CARDAMINE Bitter cress
(Cruciferae/Brassicaceae)

Like many genera of the cabbage family (Cruciferae), cardamine contains mustard oil glycosides. This gives the flavor a characteristic tang and endows the oil with medicinal properties similar to the true mustards, *Sinapis alba* (see p.353), *Brassica nigra* (see p.250), and *B. juncea* (see p.250).

C. pratensis (cuckoo flower, lady's smock, meadow cress) p.101

PARTS USED Leaves.
PROPERTIES A tonic, cleansing herb with a high level of vitamin C. It arrests spasms and encourages productive coughing.
USES OF THE HERB
CULINARY Young leaves are added to salads.
MEDICINAL Internally for chronic skin complaints, asthma, and hysteria.
VARIANT
C. p. **'Flore Pleno'**, p.101.

GROWTH AND HARVEST
GROWTH Ornamental. Moist soil in sun or partial shade. Propagate by seed sown in spring, or by leaf-tip cuttings in midsummer, or by division in spring or autumn. *C. p.* 'Flore Pleno' is propagated vegetatively.
HARVEST Leaves are picked in spring and summer and used fresh in infusions, or frozen.

CARDUUS

C. benedictus. See *Cnicus benedictus*.
C. marianus. See *Silybum marianum*.

CARICA
(Caricaceae)

The unripe fruits, leaves, sap, and seeds of *C. papaya* contain papain, an enzyme that breaks down protein. Fruits of the American pawpaw or custard apple (*Asimina triloba*) have different properties, with edible flesh, and unpleasant-smelling seeds that have an emetic effect.

C. papaya (papaya, pawpaw) p.101

PARTS USED Leaves, fruits, seeds, sap.
PROPERTIES An enzyme-rich herb that improves digestion of protein, reduces scarring, and expels intestinal worms.
USES OF THE HERB
CULINARY Ripe fruits are eaten raw in desserts and salads. Seeds have a pungent, mustard-and-cress flavor and are used as a seasoning in countries of origin. Fresh leaves and unripe fruits are used to tenderize meat.
MEDICINAL Internally for digestive disorders, and externally for deep or slow-healing wounds (papain). Internally in countries of origin to expel threadworms and roundworms (leaves, seeds).
ECONOMIC Papain is used in the manufacture of chewing gum, in clarifying beer, termite control, and shrinkproofing wool and silk.

GROWTH AND HARVEST
GROWTH Crop. Rich, moist soil in sun and high humidity, minimum 55–59°F (13–15°C). Propagate by seed in spring at 75–86°F (24–30°C). Spider mite, aphids, and whitefly may damage plants under glass.
HARVEST Leaves are picked as required. Seeds are taken from ripe fruits and used fresh. Papain is extracted mainly from unripe fruits and from sap, which is collected from incisions in bark, and dried to a powder for medicinal and industrial uses.

CARLINA Carline thistle
(Compositae/Asteraceae)

The carline thistle was an important herb in medieval times, classed as alexipharmic (antidote to poison). It is little used today since there are more effective thistles, such as *Cnicus benedictus* (see p.264) and *Silybum marianum* (see p.353). In some areas the receptacles are eaten as a substitute for artichoke hearts. The flowers dry well.

C. acaulis (stemless carline thistle) p.101

PARTS USED Roots.
PROPERTIES A tonic, cleansing herb that benefits the liver and gall bladder, genitourinary system, and skin.
USES OF THE HERB
MEDICINAL Internally for fluid retention, liver, gall bladder, and prostate problems, bronchitis, and skin complaints, such as acne and eczema.

GROWTH AND HARVEST
GROWTH Ornamental. Well-drained, neutral to alkaline soil in full sun. Propagate by seed sown under cover when ripe.
HARVEST Roots are dug in autumn and dried for decoctions, liquid extracts, and tinctures.

CARTHAMUS
(Compositae/Asteraceae)

C. tinctorius has been in great demand since ancient times as a coloring agent for foods, fabrics, feathers, and rouge; the robes of Buddhist monks and nuns are traditionally dyed with saffron thistle flowers. Found in Egyptian tombs dating back to 3500BC, it was first described in traditional Chinese medicine in AD1061. Today it is grown mostly for the oil content of the seeds.

C. tinctorius (safflower, saffron thistle, false saffron) p.101

PARTS USED Flowers (*hong hua*), seeds, oil.
PROPERTIES A bitter, aromatic herb that stimulates the circulation, heart, and uterus, reducing fevers and inflammation, relieving pain, and lowering blood cholesterol levels.
USES OF THE HERB
CULINARY Oil is used in cooking and as part of cholesterol-reducing diets.
MEDICINAL Internally for coronary artery disease, menstrual and menopausal problems, jaundice, and measles. Not given to pregnant women. Externally for bruising, sprains, skin inflammations, wounds, and painful or paralyzed joints (flowers).

GROWTH AND HARVEST
GROWTH Crop. Well-drained soil in full sun. Propagate by seed sown in spring.
HARVEST Flower heads are harvested in summer and used fresh or dried for infusions. Alternatively, florets are carefully picked from fully opened flowers, leaving ovaries to develop into seeds for oil extraction. Flowers keep for one year only.

CARUM
(Umbelliferae/Apiaceae)

Various herbs were once included in *Carum*, including *Petroselinum crispum* (see p.325), formerly known as *C. petroselinum*, and *Trachyspermum ammi* formerly known as *Carum copticum* (see p.363). The typical smell of caraway (*C. carvi*) is produced by carvone, which forms 40–63 percent of the volatile oil in the seeds.

C. carvi (caraway) p.101

PARTS USED Leaves, roots, seeds, oil.
PROPERTIES A pungently aromatic, stimulant herb that reduces gastro-intestinal and uterine spasms, and encourages productive coughing.
USES OF THE HERB
CULINARY Leaves have a mild parsley–dill flavor, pleasant in soups and salads. Roots may be cooked as a vegetable. Seeds are especially popular in the cuisines of northern and eastern Europe, flavoring cakes and bread (notably rye bread), goulash, cabbage, cheese, cooked apples, liqueur (kümmel), and spirits (schnapps); also sugar-coated as digestive comfits or "sugar plums."
MEDICINAL Internally for indigestion, flatulence, colic (especially in children), hiatus hernia, stomach ulcer, diarrhea, menstrual cramps, and bronchitis. Externally as a gargle for laryngitis. Added to laxatives to reduce griping and to various products for digestive problems. Seeds may be chewed for prompt relief of indigestion.
ECONOMIC Oil is used for flavoring and perfumery.

C. copticum. See *Trachyspermum ammi*.

GROWTH AND HARVEST
GROWTH Crop. Well-drained soil in full sun. Propagate by seed sown in spring or early autumn. Seeds may not ripen from spring sowings in cold climates. Does not transplant well; self-seeds in suitable conditions. Flowers attract parasitic wasps, which prey on aphids.
HARVEST Leaves and roots are gathered to be used fresh as vegetables. Seeds are gathered as they ripen and are dried for use in infusions, pills, and tinctures. Oil is distilled commercially for flavoring and pharmaceutical products.

CASSIA

C. angustifolia. See *Senna alexandrina*.
C. marilandica. See *Senna marilandica*.

CASTANEA Chestnut
(Fagaceae)

Culpeper wrote in *The English Physitian Enlarged* (1653) that chestnuts "provoke lust exceedingly" and are "an admirable remedy for the cough and spitting of blood." Cultivars vary in flavor, keeping qualities, and ease of peeling; *C. sativa* 'Marron de Lyon' and *C. s.* 'Paragon' produce fruits with a single kernel, preferred for commercial production.

C. sativa (sweet chestnut, Spanish chestnut) p.102

PARTS USED Leaves, seeds.
PROPERTIES An astringent herb that controls coughing and has antirheumatic effects.
USES OF THE HERB
CULINARY Chestnuts are used in sauces, soups, stuffings, and desserts, and eaten roasted or boiled as a snack or vegetable. They are also puréed (*purée de marrons*) and crystallized (*marrons glacés*).
MEDICINAL Internally for paroxysmal coughs, whooping cough, excess mucus, diarrhea, and rheumatism (leaves). Externally as a gargle for pharyngitis (leaves).
VARIANT
C. s. **'Albomarginata'**, p.102.

GROWTH AND HARVEST
GROWTH Ornamental. Well-drained soil in sun. Propagate by seed sown in autumn. Cultivars do not come true from seed, but are grafted onto stocks of *C. sativa*.
HARVEST Leaves are gathered in summer and dried for infusions and liquid extracts. Seeds are collected in autumn and cooked before use.

CASTANOSPERMUM
(Leguminosae)

The seeds of *C. australe* have a high saponin content. Australian Aborigines soaked them for 8–10 days to reduce toxicity, then roasted and ground them when dry to make a coarse meal. *C. australe* is included as a herb following the discovery in 1981 of castanospermine, a new type of alkaloid, which mimics sugars and is currently being tested against human immunodeficiency virus (HIV). Disappearing in the wild.

C. australe (Moreton Bay chestnut, black bean) p.102

PARTS USED Seeds.
PROPERTIES An irritant, purgative herb.
USES OF THE HERB
MEDICINAL Possible use in HIV therapy.

GROWTH AND HARVEST
GROWTH Ornamental. Rich, moist, well-drained soil in sun, minimum 50–59°F (10–15°C). Propagate by seed sown in spring.
HARVEST Seeds are collected when ripe and processed for pharmaceutical research.
WARNING Toxic if eaten.

CATHARANTHUS
(Apocynaceae)

The use of alkaloids from *C. roseus* was developed in the 1950s, after the plant was screened by a US pharmaceutical company for possible therapeutic properties. It was found to reduce numbers of white blood cells, leading to applications that revolutionized cancer therapy. Isolated alkaloids are highly toxic and quite different in effect from the whole plant.

C. roseus, syn. *Vinca rosea* (Madagascar periwinkle, rosy periwinkle, Cayenne jasmine) p.102

PARTS USED Leaves.
PROPERTIES An astringent herb that reduces blood sugar levels, increases perspiration, and stimulates the uterus.
USES OF THE HERB
MEDICINAL Internally for diabetes (W Indies); diabetes, hypertension, chronic constipation, and indigestion (Mauritius, Vietnam, Surinam); asthma (Bahamas); menstrual regulation (Africa, Philippines). Isolated alkaloids treat acute leukemia (especially in children), Hodgkin's disease, and other cancers, with side effects such as nausea, alopecia, and bone marrow depression.
VARIANT
C. roseus, Pacifica Series, p.102.

GROWTH AND HARVEST
GROWTH Ornamental. Moist, well-drained soil in sun, minimum 65°F (18°C) for seedlings, and 55°F (13°C) for flowering plants. Propagate by seed sown in spring, or by cuttings of nonflowering shoots in spring. Cut back in spring to maintain compact shape. Low temperatures and wet conditions may cause fungal diseases.
HARVEST Leaves are picked before or during flowering and dried for infusions, liquid extracts, and tinctures; and for extraction of alkaloids.
WARNING Toxic if eaten.

CAULOPHYLLUM
(Berberidaceae)

C. thalictroides is one of the most important herbs for women and was used by various native American tribes to facilitate childbirth, giving rise to several common names. Its popularity led to inclusion in the *U.S. Pharmacopoeia* (1882–1905).

C. thalictroides (blue cohosh, squaw root, papoose root) p.103

PARTS USED Rhizomes, roots.
PROPERTIES An acrid, bitter, warming herb that stimulates the uterus, reduces inflammation, expels intestinal worms, and has diuretic effects.
USES OF THE HERB
MEDICINAL Internally for pelvic inflammatory disease, endometriosis, slow, erratic menstruation and parturition, and retained placenta. Taken in the last four weeks of pregnancy and during labor, to facilitate contractions and cervical dilation. Also for rheumatism, arthritis, and gout. Not given to patients with hypertension and heart disease. For use by qualified practitioners only.

GROWTH AND HARVEST
GROWTH Wild-collected. Rich, moist soil in shade. Propagate by seed sown when ripe, or by division of rhizome in autumn.
HARVEST Rhizomes and roots are lifted in autumn and dried for decoctions, liquid extracts, powders, and tinctures.

CEANOTHUS Redroot
(Rhamnaceae)

The Cherokee people of N America used *C. americanus* externally to treat skin cancer and venereal sores. Little is known about the constituents of *Ceanothus*, although *C. integerrimus* (deer bush) and *C. sanguineus* have been shown to contain alkaloids.

C. americanus (New Jersey tea, redroot) p.103

PARTS USED Roots.
PROPERTIES A bitter, astringent, cleansing herb that is expectorant, relaxes spasms, and stimulates the lymphatic system.
USES OF THE HERB
MEDICINAL Internally for colds, bronchitis, whooping cough, tonsillitis, diphtheria, sinusitis, enlarged spleen, abnormal uterine bleeding, nosebleeds, hemorrhoids, and depression.

GROWTH AND HARVEST
GROWTH Crop. Well-drained soil in sun. Dislikes alkaline conditions but tolerates poor, dry soils. Propagate by seed sown in autumn, or by semiripe cuttings in summer. Cut back to within 3–4in (8–10cm) of the previous season's growth in spring. Scale insects may attack stems. Dislikes disturbance.
HARVEST Roots are dug up and partially harvested in late autumn or early spring, when the red color is at its deepest, and dried for use in decoctions and liquid extracts.

CEDRONELLA
(Labiatae)

C. canariensis is known as "balm of Gilead" because of its camphoraceous odor. It bears no resemblance to the balm of Gilead obtained from various *Populus* species (see p.334), nor to the original balm of Gilead (*Balsamodendron opobalsamum*), no longer used commercially.

C. canariensis, syn. *C. triphylla* (balm of Gilead, Canary balm) p.103

PARTS USED Leaves.
PROPERTIES An aromatic herb with no known therapeutic uses.

USES OF THE HERB
CULINARY Leaves are infused for tea.
AROMATIC Leaves are dried for potpourris with a musky, woody scent.

C. japonica. See *Agastache foeniculum.*

GROWTH AND HARVEST
GROWTH Ornamental. Well-drained soil in sun. Propagate by seed under cover in spring, or by division in spring, or by stem cuttings in early autumn. Cut back in spring.
HARVEST Leaves are picked before flowering and dried for infusions and scented articles.

CEDRUS Cedar
(Pinaceae)

Cedrus species are rich in volatile oils that have medicinal properties. Cedar oil was used for embalming in ancient Egypt and is burned as temple incense by the Tibetans. Turkish carpet shops are often constructed or lined with cedar wood to deter moths. Closely related to larches (*Larix* species, p.301), cedars are among the most ornamental of conifers.

C. libani **subsp.** ***atlantica*** (Atlas cedar) p.103

PARTS USED Wood, oil.
PROPERTIES A good antiseptic and fungicide that stimulates the circulatory and respiratory systems, and calms the nerves. The odor repels insects.
USES OF THE HERB
AROMATIC Oil is used in perfumery, notably in jasmine-scented soap.
MEDICINAL Externally for skin diseases, ulcers, and dandruff, and as an inhalation for bronchitis, tuberculosis, and nervous tension.
ECONOMIC Wood is used in joinery, and for making insect-repellent articles for storing textiles.
VARIANT
C. l. subsp. ***atlantica*****, Glauca Group,** p.103.

GROWTH AND HARVEST
GROWTH Ornamental. Well-drained soil in sun. *C. l.* subsp. *atlantica* tolerates chalky soils. Propagate by seed sown in spring. *C. l.* subsp. *atlantica*, Glauca Group is usually grafted commercially, but comes fairly true from seed. To maintain a single leader, remove competing branches in autumn. *Armillaria* root rot may attack trees.
HARVEST Branches are chipped for oil distillation or dried for use in decoctions.

CEIBA
(Bombacaceae)

The most interesting product of this tree is kapok fiber, a downy material that surrounds the seeds. Kapok is eight times lighter than cotton, and absorbs sound. A single tree bears 300–400 pods a year, yielding up to 44lb (20kg), from its fifth year until it is about 60 years old. *C. pentandra* is used medicinally wherever it occurs, but little is known of its chemistry. The dark red-brown gum resembles tragacanth (*Astragalus gummifer*, see p.245).

C. pentandra, syn. *Bombax pentandra* (kapok, silk-cotton tree) p.104

PARTS USED Leaves, bark, seeds, gum.
PROPERTIES An astringent, diuretic herb that lowers fever, relaxes spasms, and controls bleeding.
USES OF THE HERB
CULINARY Although the seeds are toxic, they yield edible oil.
MEDICINAL Internally for abnormal uterine bleeding, dysentery, diarrhea in children (gum), bronchial congestion (bark, leaves). Externally in baths, for fevers and headaches (bark, leaves), and as a poultice for erysipelas, sprains (leaves), and wounds (bark).
ECONOMIC Kapok is used in acoustic insulation and flotation cushions. Seeds are used for making cattle feed.

GROWTH AND HARVEST
GROWTH Crop. Rich, deep, moisture-retentive, but well-drained, soil in sun, minimum 59°F (15°C). May be damaged by wind. Propagate by seed sown when ripe, or by semiripe cuttings in summer. In the tropics, *Ceiba* is propagated by cutting branches, or "post cuttings," 4–6ft (1.2–2m) long, which are spaced 10ft (3m) apart in the open ground. They may also be inserted closer together and used as poles for the cultivation of *Piper* spp. (see p.329). Prune pot-grown plants to shape in spring.
HARVEST Leaves are picked during the growing season and used fresh or dried in infusions and poultices. Wood is cut in the dry season ("when spirits are absent") and bark removed for use in decoctions. Gum is collected from incisions into young trees, made as the sap is rising at the end of the dry season. Fruits are collected when ripe and are dried before removal of seeds, separation of fiber, and processing for kapok.

CENTAUREA Knapweed
(Compositae/Asteraceae)

The cornflower (*C. cyanus*) is the best-known herb in the genus, although greater knapweed (*C. scabiosa*), black knapweed (*C. nigra*), and perennial cornflower (*C. montana*) all have similar properties. Cornflowers were common grainfield weeds until the 1920s, but have been greatly reduced through modern farming practices.

C. cyanus (cornflower, bluebottle) p.104

PARTS USED Flowers.
PROPERTIES An astringent herb that reduces inflammation.
USES OF THE HERB
CULINARY Florets may be used fresh in salads.
AROMATIC Florets may be dried for potpourris.
MEDICINAL Externally for corneal ulcers, conjunctivitis, minor wounds, and mouth ulcers.
ECONOMIC Extracts of cornflower are added to hair shampoos and rinses.
VARIANT
C. c., Florence Series, p.104.

GROWTH AND HARVEST
GROWTH Ornamental. Well-drained soil in sun. Propagate by seed sown in autumn or spring. Flowers may be affected by petal blight; leaves may be damaged by rust.
HARVEST Flowers are cut as they open and dried whole or as florets, according to use.

CENTAURIUM Centaury
(Gentianaceae)

C. erythraea contains bitter glycosides that stimulate the liver and gall bladder, increasing bile flow and improving the appetite and digestion. Bitter compounds are also present in *C. chilensis* (canchalagua), a similar plant that grows on the west coast of N America. Bitters are at their most effective taken 30 minutes before eating.

C. erythraea, syn. *Erythraea centaurium* (centaury, feverwort) p.104

PARTS USED Whole plant.
PROPERTIES A very bitter, dry herb that acts as a tonic for the digestive system and lowers fever.
USES OF THE HERB
MEDICINAL Internally for dyspepsia, liver and gall bladder complaints, hepatitis, jaundice, anorexia, postviral syndrome, poor appetite in convalescence, and feverish illnesses. Combined with *Chamaemelum nobile* (see p.259), *Filipendula ulmaria* (see p.283), and *Althaea officinalis* (see p.236) for dyspepsia, and with *Berberis vulgaris* (see p.248) and *Rumex crispus* (see p.344) for jaundice. Not given to pregnant women.

GROWTH AND HARVEST
GROWTH Crop. Sandy, neutral to alkaline soil in sun. Propagate by seed in spring.
HARVEST Flowering plants are cut in summer and dried for infusions and liquid extracts.

CENTELLA
(Umbelliferae/Apiaceae)

C. asiatica is one of the most important herbs in Ayurvedic medicine. Known as *brahmi*, "bringing knowledge of *Brahman* [Supreme

Reality]," it has long been used medicinally and to aid meditation in India. Traditionally used in both India and Africa for leprosy, it entered the French pharmacopoeia via Madagascar. Recent research has shown that *C. asiatica* reduces scarring, improves circulatory problems in lower limbs, and speeds healing.

C. asiatica, syn. *Hydrocotyle asiatica* (gotu kola, Indian pennywort, tiger grass) p.104

PARTS USED Whole plant, leaves.
PROPERTIES A rejuvenating, diuretic herb that clears toxins, reduces inflammation and fever, improves healing and immunity, and has a balancing effect on the nervous system.
USES OF THE HERB
CULINARY Leaves are eaten in salads and curries in SE Asia.
MEDICINAL Internally for wounds, chronic skin conditions (including leprosy), venereal diseases, malaria, varicose veins and ulcers, nervous disorders, and senility. Excess causes headaches and transient unconsciousness. Externally for wounds, hemorrhoids, and rheumatic joints. WARNING This herb is subject to legal restrictions in some countries.
ECONOMIC Extracts are added to cosmetic masks and creams to increase collagen and firm the skin.

GROWTH AND HARVEST
GROWTH Crop. Moist to wet soil in sun or partial shade. Propagate by seed or layers in spring.
HARVEST Whole plants or leaves are gathered at any time and used fresh or dried in infusions, milk decoctions, powder, medicated ghee, or medicated oil.
WARNING Skin irritant.

CEPHAELIS Ipecacuanha
(Rubiaceae)

Ipecacuanha was known to native Brazilians for centuries before its introduction to Portugal by a monk in colonial times. A Parisian doctor confirmed its effectiveness against dysentery and in 1688 sold his patent medicine to the court of Louis XIV for 1,000 *louis d'or*. *C. ipecacuanha* contains a potent emetic that as a side effect stimulates mucus secretion in the lungs. Now grown in the Far East, it is an ingredient of most commercial cough remedies.

C. ipecacuanha (ipecacuanha, ipecac) p.104

PARTS USED Roots.
PROPERTIES A violent irritant that stimulates the gastric and bronchial systems, lowers fevers, and prevents cyst formation in amebic dysentery.
USES OF THE HERB
MEDICINAL Internally for coughs, bronchitis, whooping cough, and amebic dysentery. Also used in a syrup to induce vomiting in children who have swallowed poisons, being preferable to the use of a stomach pump for the very young. Excess causes severe vomiting and diarrhea. Used in homeopathy for nausea. For use by qualified practitioners only.

GROWTH AND HARVEST
GROWTH Crop. Well-drained, humus-rich soil in shade, with ample moisture and humidity, minimum 59–64°F (15–18°C). Propagate by greenwood cuttings in late spring, in sandy soil mix at 70–75°F (21–24°C), or by root cuttings during harvesting. Difficult to cultivate outside its natural habitat.
HARVEST Roots are dug when the plants are in flower and dried for use by the pharmaceutical industry. Cultivated plants are replanted after partial removal of roots.

CETRARIA
(Parmeliaceae)

Recent research has shown that lichen acids are effective against organisms such as *Salmonella* species, *Trichomonas vaginalis*, and *Mycobacterium tuberculosis*.

C. islandica (Iceland moss) p.105

PARTS USED Whole plant.
PROPERTIES A bittersweet, cooling, antibiotic herb that is expectorant, soothes irritated tissues, and controls vomiting.
USES OF THE HERB
MEDICINAL Internally for gastroenteritis, food poisoning, tuberculosis, and bronchitis. Externally for vaginal discharge, boils, and impetigo. Extracts are added to antiseptics and to lozenges for dry coughs and sore throats.

GROWTH AND HARVEST
GROWTH Wild-collected. Propagates on bark of trees, and rocks on acid substrate. Must have clean air. There has apparently been no research into the possibility of growing lichens from spores.
HARVEST Whole plants are collected all year and dried for use in decoctions, liquid extracts, powder, and tinctures.

CHAENOMELES Flowering quince, japonica
(Rosaceae)

Medicinal use of *C. speciosa* was first mentioned in China c.AD470; it was introduced to Kew in 1796 by Sir Joseph Banks. Its popularity as a subject for bonsai has spread to the West from China and Japan.

C. speciosa, syn. *C. lagenaria* (flowering quince, Japanese quince, japonica) p.105

PARTS USED Fruits (*mu gua*).
PROPERTIES An anti-inflammatory and anti-spasmodic herb that acts mainly as a circulatory and digestive stimulant.
USES OF THE HERB
CULINARY Fruits may be used as a substitute for quince (*Cydonia oblonga*) in jams and fruit compote.
MEDICINAL Internally for rheumatism, arthritis, cramps (especially in the calf muscles), painful, weak, or swollen lower limbs, stomach cramps due to indigestion, diarrhea, and vomiting.
VARIANTS
C. s. **'Moerloosii'**, p.105.
C. s. **'Nivalis'**, p.105.

GROWTH AND HARVEST
GROWTH Ornamental. Well-drained soil in sun, either in the open or trained against a wall. Propagate by seed sown in autumn and placed in a cold frame, or by softwood cuttings of lateral shoots with a heel in summer, or by layering long shoots in early autumn. Plants grown in the open need little pruning other than thinning out or shaping branches after flowering. Prune wall trained specimens after flowering, reducing the previous year's growth to two or three buds and cutting back any outward-growing shoots. Plants may be affected by fireblight, and may suffer from chlorosis on alkaline soils. Cultivars do not come true from seed.
HARVEST Fruits are gathered when ripe in the autumn and dried for use in decoctions, or consumed fresh.

CHAMAELIRIUM
(Liliaceae/Melanthiaceae)

There is only one species in this genus, which is closely related to *Helonias*. The name *Chamaelirium* comes from the Greek *chamai*, "slow growing," and *leirion*, "lily" (*luteum* means "yellow"). *C. luteum* is called "false unicorn root" to distinguish it from true unicorn root, *Aletris farinosa* (see p.232). First used by native N Americans to prevent miscarriage, it won favor with settlers in the 18th and 19th centuries for depression and "derangements of women." It was listed in the U.S. *National Formulary* (1916–47) and is still regarded by present-day herbalists as invaluable for gynecological problems.

C. luteum, syn. *Helonias dioica* (false unicorn root, fairy wand, devil's bit)

Tuberous, summer-flowering perennial hardy to 5°F (–15°C), height 12–36in (30–90cm), spread 6–15in (15–38cm), with a basal rosette of obovate to spoon-shaped leaves up to 8in (20cm) long. Flowering stem is erect, bearing smaller, linear-lanceolate leaves and a dense, cylindrical raceme of tiny white, star-shaped flowers, yellowing with age. Male and female flowers occur on different plants; female plants are leafier. Found in damp woods and bogs in eastern N America.

PARTS USED Rhizomes, roots.
PROPERTIES An astringent, bitter, diuretic herb that acts mainly as an ovarian and uterine tonic. It also expels intestinal worms.
USES OF THE HERB
MEDICINAL Internally for menstrual and menopausal complaints, infertility, pelvic inflammatory disease, endometriosis, fibroids, threatened miscarriage, and morning sickness. Excess causes vomiting. Often combined with *Trillium erectum* (see p.364). Also as a tonic for digestive and genitourinary complaints, and to expel intestinal parasites. For use by qualified practitioners only.

GROWTH AND HARVEST
GROWTH Wild-collected. Moist, well-drained, humus-rich soil in partial shade. Propagate by seed sown in autumn, or by division in spring.
HARVEST Rhizomes with roots are lifted in autumn and dried for use in infusions, liquid extracts, and tinctures.

CHAMAEMELUM Chamomile
(Compositae/Asteraceae)

"Chamomile" is the name given to several different daisylike plants, but only two species are important as herbs: *C. nobile* (Roman chamomile) and *Matricaria recutita* (wild or German chamomile, also known as "scented mayweed," see p.309). Both are used for similar purposes. Chamomile tea is one of the most popular tisanes, immortalized in Beatrix Potter's *Tale of Peter Rabbit.*

C. nobile, syn. *Anthemis nobilis* (chamomile, Roman chamomile) p.105

PARTS USED Flowers, oil.
PROPERTIES A bitter, aromatic herb with sedative properties that acts mainly on the digestive system.
USES OF THE HERB
CULINARY Important as an herb tea.
MEDICINAL Internally for digestive problems (including colic, diverticulitis, morning sickness, and stress-induced dyspepsia), painful menstruation, and insomnia, and for feverish illnesses, hyperactivity, and temper tantrums in children (flowers). Oil is a uterine stimulant, and not used in pregnancy. It is used in inhalations for asthma and bronchial congestion, and in aromatherapy. Externally for irritated or sore skin. Used in homeopathy for complaints caused by anger or too much caffeine. WARNING This herb, in the form of essential oil, is subject to legal restrictions in some countries.
ECONOMIC Oil is used in beauty preparations to lighten and condition the hair.
VARIANTS
C. n. **'Flore Pleno'**, p.105.
C. n. **'Treneague'**, p.105.

GROWTH AND HARVEST
GROWTH Ornamental. Light, well-drained soil in full sun. Propagate by seed sown in spring or autumn, or by division in spring. Variants are sterile and can only be divided. Chamomile for lawns is planted 4in (10cm) apart, and weeded regularly until established. Plants may deteriorate in very cold or wet winters, but usually recover. Handling chamomile may cause dermatitis. *C. nobile* has been called "the plant's physician": ailing garden plants are supposedly cured by planting chamomile beside them, and cut flowers revive and last longer with the addition of chamomile tea to the water. An infusion of it is also said to prevent damping off in seedlings. ►

► HARVEST Flowers are gathered in summer and distilled for oil, or dried for use in infusions, liquid extracts, and dermatological creams. Dried flowers keep for one year only.

CHAMOMILLA
C. recutita. See *Matricaria recutita.*

CHELIDONIUM Celandine
(Papaveraceae)

C. majus contains a bright orange sap, which exudes when the plant is cut or bruised. The juice is dabbed on the skin direct from the plant, as a treatment for warts and corns. According to the Doctrine of Signatures, the sap resembled bile in color, and the herb was thus a remedy for liver disorders.

C. majus (greater celandine, swallow wort, tetterwort) p.106

PARTS USED Whole plant, sap.
PROPERTIES A cleansing, anti-inflammatory herb that improves bile flow, stimulates the uterus and circulatory system, and acts as an antispasmodic, diuretic, and laxative.
USES OF THE HERB
MEDICINAL Internally for inflammation of the gall bladder and biliary duct, jaundice, hepatitis, gout, arthritis, and rheumatism; remittent fevers, spasmodic cough, and bronchitis; skin eruptions, ulcers, and cancer (especially of skin and stomach). Excess causes sleepiness, skin irritation, irritant coughing, and difficulty in breathing. Not given to pregnant women. Externally for eye inflammations and cataract, bruises and sprains, warts, ringworm, psoriasis, and malignant tumors. Also used in Chinese medicine (as *bai qu cai*) and homeopathy for similar complaints. WARNING This herb is subject to legal restrictions in some countries.
VARIANTS
C. m. **'Laciniatum Flore Pleno'**, p.106.
C. m. **'Flore Pleno'**, p.106.

GROWTH AND HARVEST
GROWTH Ornamental. Most soils in sun or shade. Propagate by seed sown in spring, or by root division in spring. *C. majus* and its variants self-seed readily, often becoming weedy. The orange sap produces yellow stains when handled.
HARVEST Flowering plants are cut in summer and used fresh in infusions or tinctures, or as juice. Sap is used fresh; the properties are largely lost on drying.

CHELONE Turtlehead
(Scrophulariaceae)

C. glabra yields a digestive tonic that is increasingly favored by herbalists because the aerial parts of the plant are used rather than the roots, with the effect that less ecological damage is done when the herb is collected from the wild.

C. glabra (turtlehead, balmony) p.106

PARTS USED Whole plant.
PROPERTIES A very bitter herb with a tealike flavor that acts mainly as a tonic for the liver and digestive system. It also has antidepressant and laxative effects.
USES OF THE HERB
MEDICINAL Internally for gallstones with jaundice, chronic liver disease, colic, constipation, anorexia, and poor digestion (especially in the elderly and during convalescence). Combines well with *Juglans cinerea* for constipation, and with *Gentiana lutea* (see p.287) and *Hydrastis canadensis* (see p.294) for jaundice.

GROWTH AND HARVEST
GROWTH Ornamental. Moist soil in partial shade. Propagate by soft tip cuttings in summer, or by seed sown under cover in spring, or by division in early autumn.
HARVEST Plants are cut when in flower and dried for use in infusions, liquid extracts, powder, or tinctures.

CHENOPODIUM Goosefoot, pigweed
(Chenopodiaceae)

Oil of chenopodium contains a broad-spectrum vermifuge that is widely used in veterinary medicine. It is produced from both *C. ambrosioides* and *C. ambrosioides* var. *anthelminticum*, the latter having a higher content of the active constituent.

C. ambrosioides (wormseed, Mexican tea, *epazote*) p.106

PARTS USED Whole plant, leaves, oil.
PROPERTIES An acrid, astringent, strongly aromatic herb that destroys intestinal parasites, increases perspiration, and relaxes spasms. It also has expectorant, anti-fungal and insecticidal effects.
USES OF THE HERB
CULINARY Leaves flavor corn, bean, and fish dishes (Mexico, Guatemala).
MEDICINAL Internally for roundworms, hookworms, small tapeworms, amebic dysentery, asthma, and excess mucus. Not given to pregnant women. Excess causes dizziness, vomiting, convulsions, and death. Externally for athlete's foot and insect bites. WARNING This herb is subject to legal restrictions in some countries.
ECONOMIC Used as a fumigant against mosquitoes and in fertilizer to inhibit insect larvae.

GROWTH AND HARVEST
GROWTH Crop. Rich, well-drained soil in sun. Propagate by seed in spring. Pinch out tips to encourage bushiness. Self-seeds in warm climates. ►

► **HARVEST** Plants are cut in autumn for oil, or dried for liquid extracts and powder. Leaves are picked as required and used fresh.
WARNING Skin allergen.

CHIMAPHILA Pipsissewa
(Ericaceae)

C. umbellata was an important herb among native N Americans, who used it for various problems, including rheumatism. It became popular with settlers, especially the Pennsylvania Dutch, as a tonic and diuretic for kidney complaints and rheumatism. It was listed in the *U.S. Pharmacopoeia* (1820–1916). It contains quinone glycosides, such as are found in *Arctostaphylos uva-ursi* (see p.241), but it is less astringent and more diuretic, making it better for long-term use.

C. umbellata (pipsissewa, prince's pine, ground holly) p.107

PARTS USED Whole plant, leaves.
PROPERTIES A bitter, astringent, cooling herb that has tonic effects on the kidneys and spleen. It is considered an alterative.
USES OF THE HERB
CULINARY A traditional ingredient of root beer.
MEDICINAL Internally for urinary infections, prostatitis, urethritis, kidney stones, arthritis, and rheumatism.

GROWTH AND HARVEST
GROWTH Wild-collected. Well-drained, acid, sandy soil in shade. Propagate by seed sown in autumn, or by division in spring.
HARVEST Whole plants are picked when in flower, leaves during the growing season; both are dried for infusions and liquid extracts.

CHIONANTHUS Fringe tree
(Oleaceae)

C. virginicus is one of the most reliable remedies for disorders of the liver and gall bladder. The bark was used in traditional native American medicine, mainly for malaria but also as a poultice for wounds.

C. virginicus (fringe tree) p.107

PARTS USED Root bark.
PROPERTIES A bitter, tonic, alterative herb that stimulates the liver and gall bladder, and has both diuretic and laxative effects.
USES OF THE HERB
MEDICINAL Internally for jaundice, cirrhosis, chronic hepatitis, pancreatitis, gallstones, enlarged spleen, poor liver function, bilious headache, and migraine.

GROWTH AND HARVEST
GROWTH Ornamental. Rich, well-drained, moist soil in sun. Propagate by seed sown ► in autumn, which requires stratification, or by softwood cuttings in spring, or by budding in summer. Slow-growing in regions with cool summers.
HARVEST Bark is peeled from roots, which are removed as required, and dried for use in infusions, liquid extracts, and tinctures.

CHONDRODENDRON
(Menispermaceae)

A genus of 10 species of lianas native to C and S America. Several species are key ingredients of curare, an arrow poison used by native S Americans. The name comes from the Greek *chondros*, "cartilage," and *dendron*, "tree," and refers to the flexible, branchlike stems. *C. tomentosum* contains various alkaloids, notably *d*-tubocurarine, a skeletal muscle relaxant which acts instantaneously when injected but is unstable if taken orally. Supplies are dependent on wild stocks because the species is not cultivated and attempts to synthesize it have so far been unsuccessful. The stems and roots are used by native S Americans to treat various ailments including dropsy, madness, and bruising. The closely related *Cissampelos pareira* is also an ingredient of curare and source of a potent muscle relaxant, known as "cissampeline."

C. tomentosum (*pareira, pareira brava*)

Tender canopy liana reaching 100ft (30m) in height, with a hairy trunk, up to 4in (10cm) across at the base, and ovate to rounded leaves up to 8in (20cm) long, which have woolly stalks and undersides. Panicles of tiny, green-white, male and female flowers are borne on separate plants. Found in tropical rainforest in Panama, Brazil, Bolivia, and Peru.

PARTS USED Stems, roots.
PROPERTIES A bittersweet, diuretic, laxative herb that lowers fever and stimulates the uterus when taken orally.
USES OF THE HERB
MEDICINAL Mainly intravenously as a source of *d*-tubocurarine, used to relax muscles during surgery. WARNING This herb, especially in the form of curare, is subject to legal restrictions in some countries.

GROWTH AND HARVEST
GROWTH Wild-collected. Rich, moist soil in shade, with high humidity, minimum 59–64°F (15–18°C). There is no information on propagation requirements.
HARVEST Roots and stems are collected from the wild as available and processed by the pharmaceutical industry into liquid extracts.

CHONDRUS
(Gigartinaceae)

A genus of around 15 species of marine algae. Several species are collected from the wild for their uses in various industries. *C. crispus* is an important edible seaweed on both sides of the Atlantic. Plants are harvested by boat, using a rake, which causes minimal damage to the holdfasts, and by hand from rocks. Gel-forming polysaccharides, known as carragheenans, are found in *C. crispus*. Various grades are produced, those of high molecular weight being used in the food industry, on the grounds that they pass through the gut and are therefore nontoxic. However, carragheenans are suspected of being carcinogenic and a possible cause of ulcerative colitis.

C. crispus (Irish moss, carragheen)

Red-purple to green, cartilaginous alga, height and spread 3–6in (7–15cm), with a disc-shaped holdfast. The basal growth is narrow, expanding into branched fronds, often crimped along the margin, with narrow and broader forms occurring. Found in the lower littoral zone of the Atlantic, English Channel, and North Sea.

PARTS USED Whole plant.
PROPERTIES A mucilaginous, sweet, salty herb that has a softening, soothing effect on tissues, and is a mild laxative and expectorant.
USES OF THE HERB
MEDICINAL Internally for dry coughs, sore throat, cystitis, bronchitis, gastritis, and dyspepsia with nausea and heartburn; often combined with *Cinnamomum cassia* (see p.261), and *Glycyrrhiza glabra* (see p.289) for bronchitis, and with *Althaea officinalis* (see p.236) and *Ballota nigra* (see p.247) for dyspepsia. Externally, in lotions or creams, for chapped skin and dermatitis.
ECONOMIC Important in the food industry as a stabilizer in dairy products, desserts, salad dressings, sauces, and in pharmaceutical products, such as cod liver oil and toothpaste. Also used in air freshener gels and for various processes in the textile, leather, brewing, and paint industries.

GROWTH AND HARVEST
GROWTH Wild-collected. Grows on rocks and stones in pools and shallow salt water. Plants are left intact after harvesting to allow regeneration.
HARVEST Plants are cut in autumn and dried for extraction of polysaccharides.

CHRYSANTHEMUM
C. parthenium. See *Tanacetum parthenium.*
C. x morifolium. See *Dendranthema* x *grandiflorum.*

CICHORIUM Chicory
(Compositae/Asteraceae)

Chicory was grown as a vegetable in Roman times and remains an important crop throughout continental Europe. The leaves and roots have quite different uses. There are three main kinds of leaf chicory: bitter, loose-leaved cultivars, grown as a green winter vegetable, especially in southern Italy; narrow-leaved, Witloof or Belgian kinds, with a compact, elongate head (chicon), which is blanched for use in salads or cooked dishes; and broad-leaved, red chicory or radicchio types, which form cabbagelike heads, eaten cooked or raw. Roots are roasted as a coffee substitute (especially in France) and medicinal preparations. In England, a law forbidding its use was passed in 1832 but repealed in 1840, provided that the ingredient appeared on the label. Young chicory roots give a slightly bitter, caramel flavor when roasted; roots over two years old are much more bitter.

C. intybus (chicory, succory) p.107

PARTS USED Leaves, roots.
PROPERTIES A bitter, diuretic, laxative herb that reduces inflammation and has a tonic effect on the liver and gall bladder.
USES OF THE HERB
CULINARY Loose-leaved chicories are boiled to remove bitterness and served with white or cheese sauce; heads of Witloof and radicchio chicories are eaten in salads or cooked as a vegetable. Roasted root is added to coffee.
MEDICINAL Internally for liver complaints, rheumatism, gout, and hemorrhoids. Regarded as a cooling, alterative herb in Ayurvedic medicine.
VARIANT
C. i. **'Red Devil'**, p.107.

GROWTH AND HARVEST
GROWTH Ornamental (*C. intybus*). Crop (*C. i.* 'Red Devil'). Rich, well-drained, neutral to alkaline soil in sun. Propagate by seed in spring, thinned to 10in (25cm) apart. May self-seed, becoming a weed in dry, alkaline soil.
HARVEST Roots are lifted in early spring in the second year, and sliced before roasting at 350°F (180°C) as a coffee additive, or drying for decoctions and liquid extracts. Chicons are produced by lifting roots in autumn of first year, cutting off leaves, and packing in boxes kept in complete darkness at 50°F (10°C) for four weeks.

CIMICIFUGA Bugbane
(Ranunculaceae)

A number of different species are used for similar purposes. These include *C. americana* (American bugbane) and *C. dahurica*, an Asian species, used interchangeably with *C. foetida* (as *sheng ma*) in traditional Chinese medicine. The drug *sheng ma* was first noted in a Chinese medical text c.AD25–200. *C. racemosa* has long been used by native N Americans for female problems, for which reason it is also known as "squawroot."

C. foetida (fetid bugbane) p.107

PARTS USED Rhizomes (*sheng ma*).
PROPERTIES An anti-infective herb that lowers fevers and relieves pain.
USES OF THE HERB
MEDICINAL Internally for coughs, colds, headaches, gum disease, and feverish infections, e.g. measles.

C. racemosa (black cohosh, cohosh bugbane, black snakeroot) p.107

PARTS USED Rhizomes.
PROPERTIES A bitter, tonic herb that soothes aches and pains, controls coughing, lowers fevers, and stimulates the uterus.

USES OF THE HERB
MEDICINAL Internally for bronchial infections, menstrual and menopausal problems, labor and postpartum pains; arthritic and rheumatic diseases (often combined with *Menyanthes trifoliata*, see p.312, and *Petroselinum crispum*, see p.325), sciatica and tinnitus (with *Zanthoxylum americanum*, see p.372). Excess causes nausea and vomiting. Not given during pregnancy and lactation. Used in homeopathy for discomfort in late pregnancy, labor pains, and for headaches and depression. WARNING This herb is subject to legal restrictions in some countries.

GROWTH AND HARVEST
GROWTH Crop. (*C. foetida*). Ornamental (*C. racemosa*). Moist, humus-rich soil in partial shade. Propagate by seed sown under cover when ripe in autumn, or by division at any time.
HARVEST Rhizomes are lifted in autumn and used fresh in tinctures, or dried for use in decoctions, liquid extracts, and tinctures.

CINCHONA Quinine
(Rubiaceae)

C. pubescens is one of several cinchonas, including *C. calisaya*, *C. ledgeriana* (both known as yellow cinchona), and *C. officinalis*, from which the alkaloid quinine, a potent anti-malarial, is extracted. The story of cinchona's discovery by the eponymous Countess of Chinchon, wife of the Viceroy of Peru, after a bout of malaria, has been disproved by historians. It is certain, however, that Jesuits in the Lima area were familiar with its uses c.1630 (hence the name "Jesuit's bark"); it was first mentioned in medical literature by Herman van der Heyden (*Discours et advis sur les flus de ventre douloureux*, 1643). By the early 19th century, populations of wild cinchona were severely depleted, leading to competition between the Dutch and English to establish plantations. The Dutch succeeded, cultivating *C. ledgeriana* in Java, which became the world center for quinine production. Largely replaced by synthetic drugs in recent decades, *Cinchona* and other plants, such as *Artemisia annua* (see p.243), are again important, as various strains of malaria become resistant to synthetics. Another alkaloid, quinidine, has become important recently as a cardiac depressant. Quinine is famous as the first substance that Samuel Hahnemann (1755–1843), founder of homeopathy, tested on himself, leading to the formulation of the Law of Similars (*similia similibus curentur*, "like cures like").

C. pubescens (red cinchona, Peruvian bark, Jesuit's bark) p.108

PARTS USED Stem and root bark.
PROPERTIES A bitter, astringent herb that lowers fever, relaxes spasms, and is antimalarial (quinine), and slows the heart (quinidine).
USES OF THE HERB
CULINARY Quinine is used as a bitter in tonic water and carbonated drinks.
MEDICINAL Internally for malaria, neuralgia, muscle cramps, cardiac fibrillation; an ingredient of most commercial cold and influenza remedies. Excess causes cinchonism: headache, rash, abdominal pain, deafness, and blindness. Not given to pregnant women unless suffering from malaria. A gargle for sore throat. Used in homeopathy (as *China officinalis*) for nervous exhaustion, anemia, and convalescence. WARNING This herb, especially in the form of quinine, is subject to legal restrictions in some countries.

GROWTH AND HARVEST
GROWTH Crop. Well-drained, moist soil, with high humidity, in sun or partial shade, minimum 59–64°F (15–18°C). Propagate by nodal greenwood cuttings in late spring, or by semiripe cuttings in summer at 59–64°F (15–18°C). Commercial plantations are usually coppiced when about 6 years old. In late winter, cut back specimen plants hard to encourage strong new growth.
HARVEST Bark is collected from May until September, and dried for liquid extracts, tablets, tinctures, or powder. It may be shaved off *in situ* or peeled from coppiced branches.

CINNAMOMUM Camphor tree
(Lauraceae)

Cinnamomum species provide two different commodities: camphor, and cinnamon or cassia. Camphor (often called camphorated oil) is an aromatic terpene ketone, familiar as mothballs, which is used medicinally, and in the manufacture of celluloid. It is best known in the compound camphorated oil, in which camphor is blended with peanut oil. Similar compounds are extracted from *Blumea balsamifera* (Ngai camphor), and *Dryobalanops aromatica* (Borneo camphor, see p.275). Cinnamon and cassia are usually produced as barkquills, from which powdered cinnamon and essential oil are produced. They are of major importance in food flavoring, and are ingredients in numerous medicinal formulas for their warming, stimulant properties. *C. cassia* is one of the oldest spices known, first recorded in China in 2700BC and in Egypt in 1600BC. Oil from *C. camphora* contains safrole (as in *Sassafras albidum*, see p.349), which can be extracted for flavoring, but is now banned in many countries because it is potentially carcinogenic. *C. zeylanicum* is a major world spice that played a significant role in colonial expansion. Commercially less important species include: *C. burmanii* (Indonesian cassia), a good cinnamon substitute, also used in incense; *C. iners* (wild cinnamon), used in SE Asia for curries;

C. loureirii (Saigon cinnamon), a sweet variety used for baking and made into a cordial; *C. massoia* (massoia bark) from New Guinea, which has a clovelike aroma, used for flavoring and perfumery; *C. oliveri* (Oliver bark or black sassafras), an Australian species with a pungent, clove–sassafras flavor; and *C. tamala* (Indian cassia), with aromatic leaves (*tejpat*), used in Indian cuisine, and coarsely flavored bark, used to adulterate cinnamon.

C. camphora, syn. *Laurus camphora* (camphor) p.108

PARTS USED Wood and leaves (*zhang nao*), from which a crystalline camphor extract is prepared.
PROPERTIES A bitter, strongly aromatic herb that stimulates the circulatory and nervous systems, reduces inflammation, and relieves pain and spasms. It also benefits the digestion and destroys parasites.
USES OF THE HERB
MEDICINAL Externally in liniments, for joint and muscle pain, balms for chilblains, chapped lips, cold sores, and as an inhalant for bronchial and nasal congestion; in traditional Chinese medicine, for skin diseases, wounds, and as a stimulant in unconsciousness; in aromatherapy, for digestive complaints and depression. Internally, in Ayurvedic medicine, for bronchitis, asthma, sinusitis, eye complaints, epilepsy, painful menstruation, gout, rheumatism, and insomnia. Excess causes vomiting, palpitations, convulsions, and death; it may be absorbed through the skin, causing systemic poisoning. WARNING This herb, especially in the form of camphorated oil, is subject to legal restrictions in some countries.

C. cassia, syn. *C. aromaticum* (cassia bark, Chinese cinnamon) p.108

PARTS USED Inner bark (*rou gui*), leafy twigs (*gou zhi*), fruits, oil.
PROPERTIES The inner bark is a pungent, sweet, hot herb that stimulates the circulatory system, improves digestion, relieves spasms and vomiting, and controls infections. The twigs increase perspiration and lower fever.

USES OF THE HERB
CULINARY Used in western Asia in curries, the US for baked foods, and China for meat dishes (especially with anise, star anise, cloves, and fennel seeds, as one of the Chinese "five spices").
MEDICINAL Internally, in Western medicine, mainly in preparations for diarrhea, flatulent dyspepsia and colic, and colds; in Chinese medicine, for diarrhea, poor appetite, low vitality, kidney weakness (*yang* deficiency manifesting in edema and scanty urination), rheumatism, and coldness (*rou gui*); and for colds, influenza, fevers, arthritic and rheumatic complaints, angina, palpitations, and digestive complaints related to cold and chills (*gou zhi*).
ECONOMIC Fruits (known as "cassia buds") resemble cloves in appearance and are widely used for flavoring in the food industry. Cassia oil contains 80–90 percent cinnamaldehyde, used mainly in medicines, foods, and cosmetics.

C. zeylanicum, syn. *C. verum* (cinnamon, Ceylon cinnamon) p.108

PARTS USED Inner bark, leaves, oil.
PROPERTIES A pungent, sweet, warming herb that stimulates peripheral circulation, relieves spasms, lowers fever and blood pressure, controls bleeding and infections, and improves digestion.
USES OF THE HERB
MEDICINAL Internally for diarrhea, nausea and vomiting, gastroenteritis, colds, influenza, hypertension, arthritis, rheumatism, and candidiasis; used especially for cold people. Not given to pregnant women.
ECONOMIC Bark and bark oil, which contain cinnamaldehyde, are widely used in flavoring baked foods, meat products, candy, pickles, cola-type soft drinks, ice cream, and liqueurs; in oral hygiene products and cosmetics. The leaf oil is more delicate, containing 70–80 percent eugenol, which is used in carnation-type perfumes.

GROWTH AND HARVEST

GROWTH Crop (*C. camphora*: ornamental). Moist, well-drained soil in sun or partial shade, minimum 59°F (15°C) for *C. cassia* and *C. zeylanicum*, 50°F (10°C) for *C. camphora*. Propagate by seed sown under cover when ripe, or by semiripe cuttings in summer. Trees tolerate coppicing.
HARVEST Leaves of *C. camphora* are picked as required; wood is cut from trees over 50 years old and boiled to extract camphor, which is steam-distilled for oil or use in infusions, liniments, powder, and other medicated preparations. Bark of *C. cassia* is dried in quills without fermentation for use in infusions, powder, and tinctures; branches and leaves are distilled for oil. Unripe fruits of *C. cassia* are picked in summer and dried as cassia buds. Shoots of coppiced plants of *C. zeylanicum* are cut every 2nd year during the rainy season and stripped of leaves for distillation. The bark is left 24 hours to ferment; outer bark is then scraped away to expose inner bark, which is peeled and dried for use, whole or powdered, in infusions and tinctures, or distilled for oil.

CISTUS Rock rose, sun rose
(Cistaceae)

Ladanum, or labdanum, is an oleoresin from several species of *Cistus*, including *C. albiflorus*, *C. creticus*, *C. ladanifer*, and *C. maculatus*. It is the best plant substitute for ambergris from sperm whales and is important in perfume manufacture. It is traditionally collected by whipping the bushes, so that the exudate adheres to the leather thongs, or, in Crete, by combing it from the hides of sheep and goats with a leather rake, or *ladanisterion*. Ladanum is now produced commercially in France and Spain.

C. ladanifer (gum cistus) p.108

PARTS USED Leaves, oleoresin, oil.
PROPERTIES An aromatic, stimulant, expectorant herb that controls bleeding and has antibiotic effects.
USES OF THE HERB
MEDICINAL Internally for excess mucus and diarrhea.
ECONOMIC Used in Turkey as a fumigant. Important as a fixative in lavender, fern, and *chypre* perfumes, and as a commercial food flavoring for baked foods, soft drinks, ice cream, and candy.

GROWTH AND HARVEST

GROWTH Ornamental. Well-drained, light to poor soil in sun. Propagate by seed sown in autumn or spring, or by softwood cuttings in summer. Trim young plants in spring or after flowering to remove dead, damaged, or straggly growths. The genus dislikes disturbance.
HARVEST Leaves are collected in late spring and early summer for use in infusions and production of oleoresin and oil. Oil is steam-distilled commercially from the oleoresin.

CITRUS
(Rutaceae)

The medicinal uses of citruses are complex. Various parts of the tree are used, and also various parts of the fruit at different stages of ripeness. Commonly, the leaves, fruits, juice, and bark are used (as in the Indonesian *C. hystrix*), while in China several quite different drugs are prepared from the fruits – one of the most valuable being peel of *C. reticulata*, which becomes more potent with age. Citruses were unknown in Europe until the 12th century, though *C. aurantium* and *C. bergamia* were first mentioned in Chinese medicine in the first century AD. The related *Poncirus trifoliata* (hardy orange, Japanese bitter orange) is used in identical ways to *C. aurantium*. Citruses are high in vitamin C, flavonoids, acids, and volatile oils. They also contain coumarins, such as bergapten, which sensitize the skin to sunlight. Bergapten is sometimes added to tanning preparations and may cause dermatitis or allergic responses. Their most recent uses are as antioxidants and chemical exfoliants in specialized cosmetics.

C. aurantiifolia (lime) p.108

PARTS USED Leaves, fruits, peel, oil.
PROPERTIES An aromatic, cooling, astringent herb.
USES OF THE HERB
CULINARY Fruits are used in marmalade and drinks. Peel is used in similar ways to lemon peel.
AROMATIC Oil is used as a source of citral in perfumery.
MEDICINAL Internally for minor complaints such as bilious headache (infusions of leaves); juice is added to many medicinal preparations in SE Asia and Guyana, notably for diarrhea.

C. aurantium (bitter orange, Seville orange) p.109

PARTS USED Leaves, stems, flowers, ripe fruits with pips and peel removed (*zhi ke*), whole unripe fruits (*zhi shi*), peel, oil.
PROPERTIES A bitter, aromatic, expectorant herb that has diuretic effects, lowers blood pressure, and improves digestion. It also reduces inflammation and controls bacterial and fungal infections.
USES OF THE HERB
CULINARY Fruits are used to make marmalade. Orange-blossom water is used in desserts.
MEDICINAL Internally for flatulent indigestion and diarrhea, stubborn coughs, colic in babies, and shock. Externally in aromatherapy for tension, depression, and skin problems.
ECONOMIC Neroli oil and petitgrain are used in perfumery.

C. bergamia, syn. *C. aurantium* var. *bergamia* (bergamot orange)

Similar in appearance to *C. aurantium*, but with broader leaves and more aromatic rind. Height 30ft (10m), spread 22ft (7m).
PARTS USED Flowers, ripe fruit peel.
PROPERTIES A bitter, aromatic herb that relieves tension, relaxes spasms, and improves digestion. Neroli oil is stimulant and reputedly aphrodisiac; bergamot oil is more sedative and healing.
USES OF THE HERB
CULINARY Orange-blossom water is used in desserts (especially blancmange) and pastries.
MEDICINAL Internally for colic in babies (orange-blossom water). Externally in douches and baths for vaginal infections (bergamot oil), and in aromatherapy for stress-related complaints and skin conditions (bergamot and neroli oils).
ECONOMIC Bergamot oil is used to flavor Earl Grey tea. Neroli oil is used in perfumery.

C. limon (lemon)

Tender tree, height 6–22ft (2–7m), spread 3–10ft (1–3m), with light green leaves up to 4in (10cm) long. Red-budded flowers with white petals appear in spring and summer. Ovoid, yellow fruits, up to 6in (15cm) across, have very sour pulp.
PARTS USED Fruits, juice, peel, oil.
PROPERTIES A bitter, aromatic, cooling herb that has diuretic and anti-inflammatory effects, and improves peripheral circulation.
USES OF THE HERB
CULINARY Juice is used to set jam. It is also used in lemonade and other soft drinks, salad dressings, preserves, and marinades. Fruits are used in marmalade and pickles. Peel is used in cooking.
AROMATIC Peel is dried for potpourris.
MEDICINAL Internally for varicose veins, hemorrhoids, kidney stones, feverish minor illnesses, and bronchial congestion. Externally for eczema, poisonous stings, and sore throats.
ECONOMIC Oil is used as a flavoring in candy and also to scent soaps, detergents, and perfumery.
VARIANT
C. l. **'Variegata'**, p.109.

C. reticulata (mandarin orange, tangerine, clementine) p.109

PARTS USED Fruits, dried ripe peel (*chen pi*), unripe peel (*qing pi*), seeds (*ju he*).
PROPERTIES A bitter, spicy, warming herb that stimulates the digestion, lungs, and spleen (*chen pi*); acts mainly on the liver, gall bladder, and breasts (*qing pi*); an energy stimulant, affecting the liver and kidneys, and relieving pain (*ju he*).
USES OF THE HERB
CULINARY Fruits are eaten fresh or canned.
MEDICINAL Internally for indigestion, flatulence, vomiting, and wet coughs (*chen pi*); liver and gall bladder disorders, bronchial congestion, mastitis, breast cancer, and pain in liver, chest, or breasts (*qing pi*); lumbago, orchitis, mastitis (*ju he*).
VARIANT
C. r. **'Clementine'**
Tender N American cultivar, height 6–25ft (2–8m), spread 4–20ft (1.2–6m); it has an upright bushy habit and sweet, orange-red fruit.

GROWTH AND HARVEST
GROWTH Crop (*C. limon* and cultivars and *C. reticulata* 'Clementine' also ornamental). Rich, well-drained soil in sun, with ample moisture during the growing season, minimum 41°F (5°C) for *C. limon*, 45°F (7°C) for *C. reticulata*, *C. aurantium*, *C. bergamia*, 55°F (13°C) for *C. aurantiifolia*. Propagate by seed sown when ripe at 61°F (16°C), or by semiripe cuttings in summer. Scale insects, mealybugs, and spider mites may affect plants under cover. Citruses do not transplant well. Cultivars do not come true from seed.
HARVEST Leaves (*C. aurantiifolia*) are picked as required for infusions. Oil is distilled from foliage, unripe fruits (*C. aurantium*) and ripe fruits (*C. bergamia*). Fruits of *C. aurantium* are picked ripe for culinary use. Fruits (*C. aurantium*, *C. reticulata*) are picked unripe or ripe in Chinese medicine, and used whole or in parts for processing. Fruits of *C. limon* and *C. aurantiifolia* are picked ripe and used fresh; peel is used fresh or dried, and is distilled for oil.

CLAVICEPS
(Clavicipitaceae)

C. purpurea has been used to strengthen contractions in childbirth since the 16th century. It is rarely used in its crude state today, but is split into component alkaloids, such as ergometrine (a uterine stimulant) and ergotamine (a vasoconstrictor). Corn ergot (*Ustilago zeae*), a fungus found on corn, also contains alkaloids that stimulate the uterus. The chemistry of ergot is similar to that of lysergic acid diethylamide (LSD), and supplies of the fungus are carefully monitored to prevent its use in the manufacture of the illicit drug.

C. purpurea (ergot) p.109

PARTS USED Sclerotia (resting stage of fungus).
PROPERTIES An unpleasant-smelling herb that stimulates the uterus, constricts blood vessels, and acts on the central nervous system, blocking release of adrenaline.
USES OF THE HERB
MEDICINAL Internally in childbirth (expulsion of placenta only), postpartum hemorrhage (ergometrine), and migraine (ergotamine). For use by qualified practitioners only. WARNING This herb, especially in the form of ergometrine and ergotamine, is subject to legal restrictions in some countries.

GROWTH AND HARVEST
GROWTH Crop. Saprophytic on grasses. Propagates by spores raised in the laboratory and sprayed on a cereal crop (usually rye).
HARVEST Sclerotia are harvested mechanically and processed commercially into liquid extracts and alkaloids.

CLEMATIS
(Ranunculaceae)

Some 230 species of tender and hardy, deciduous or evergreen climbers and woody perennials are included in this genus, which is found in most temperate regions. Many species are grown as ornamentals for their showy flowers and often attractive foliage. Clematis are acrid plants, containing glycosides, which have a burning taste and blistering effect. A few are used medicinally, including the European *C. recta* and *C. vitalba*, found in homeopathic preparations for rheumatism and skin eruptions. The latter is known as *herbe aux gueux* ("beggar's weed") in France, having once been used by beggars to irritate the skin in order to simulate sores. *C. chinensis* was first described in Chinese medicinal formulas 1,000 years ago. An Australian species, *C. glycinoides*, is a traditional Aboriginal remedy for colds and headaches, the acrid smell of the foliage causing profuse watering of the eyes and nose when inhaled.

C. chinensis (Chinese clematis)

Deciduous climber or scrambler, hardy to 5°F (–15°C), reaching 25ft (8m) in height and spread. It has a ribbed stem and pinnately divided leaves, which have five ovate to heart-shaped leaflets up to 3in (8cm) long. Panicles of white flowers, ¾in (2cm) across, are produced in autumn. It is found in open woods, hedges, and thickets in central and western China.

PARTS USED Roots (*wei ling xian*).
PROPERTIES A pungent, warming herb that has painkilling, sedative, and diuretic effects, lowering fever and relieving spasms.
USES OF THE HERB
MEDICINAL Internally for rheumatism and arthritis, usually taken in wine. A decoction in rice vinegar is a traditional remedy for dissolving fish bones lodged in the throat.

GROWTH AND HARVEST
GROWTH Ornamental. Well-drained neutral to alkaline soil in sun. Propagate by seed sown in autumn, or by semiripe cuttings in early summer. In spring cut back shoots and dead stems after flowering. Plants may suffer from powdery mildew and clematis wilt.
HARVEST Roots are lifted in autumn and dried for use in decoctions.
WARNING Harmful if eaten. Mild skin irritant.

CLINOPODIUM

C. acinos. See *Acinos arvensis*.

CNICUS Blessed thistle

(Compositae)

Blessed thistle, originally cultivated in monastery gardens, was once regarded as a cure-all, and in the 16th century was widely recommended for the plague.

C. benedictus, syn. *Carbenia benedicta*, *Carduus benedictus* (blessed thistle, holy thistle) p.109

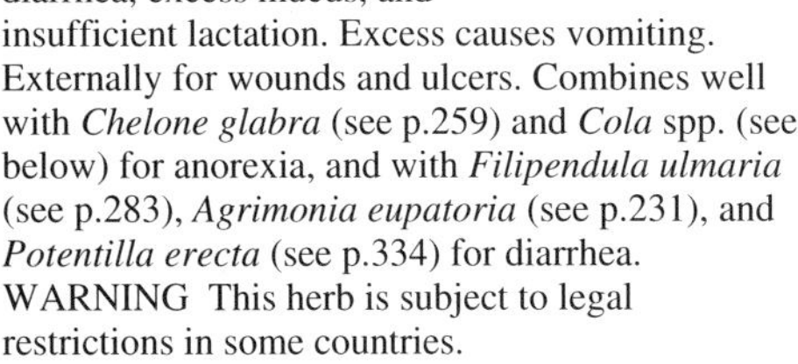

PARTS USED Whole plant.
PROPERTIES A very bitter, antiseptic, antibiotic herb that acts mainly as a digestive tonic. It is also expectorant, checks bleeding, encourages healing, lowers fever, and stimulates lactation.
USES OF THE HERB
MEDICINAL Internally for anorexia, poor appetite associated with depression, dyspepsia, flatulent colic, diarrhea, excess mucus, and insufficient lactation. Excess causes vomiting. Externally for wounds and ulcers. Combines well with *Chelone glabra* (see p.259) and *Cola* spp. (see below) for anorexia, and with *Filipendula ulmaria* (see p.283), *Agrimonia eupatoria* (see p.231), and *Potentilla erecta* (see p.334) for diarrhea.
WARNING This herb is subject to legal restrictions in some countries.

GROWTH AND HARVEST
GROWTH Crop. Well-drained soil in sun. Propagate by seed sown in spring.
HARVEST Whole plants are cut when flowering and dried for infusions, liquid extracts, and tablets.

COCHLEARIA

C. armoracia. See *Armoracia rusticana*.

CODONOPSIS Bonnet bellflower

(Campanulaceae)

C. tangshen is highly regarded in traditional Chinese medicine as a substitute for *Panax ginseng* (see p.321). Several other species are used interchangeably, including *C. pilosula* (eastern *dang shen)* and *C. tubulosa* (white *dang shen*). A famous Chinese energy tonic is the "soup of the four gentlemen," first described c.AD1200, which contains *C. tangshen*, *Wolfiporia cocos* (see p.372), *Glycyrrhiza uralensis* (see p.289), and *Atractylodes macrocephala* (see p.246).

C. tangshen (*dang shen*) p. 109

PARTS USED Roots (*tiao dang shen*).
PROPERTIES A sweet, warm, soothing herb, taken as an energy tonic. It acts mainly on the spleen, lungs, and stomach, raising secretion of body fluids and blood sugar levels, lowering blood pressure, and stimulating the immune system.
USES OF THE HERB
CULINARY May be roasted with millet.
MEDICINAL Internally for low energy, poor appetite and digestion, anemia, shallow breathing, and debility after illness. Often cooked with rice until glutinous as a tonic food.

GROWTH AND HARVEST
GROWTH Ornamental. Light, well-drained soil in semishade. Propagate by seed sown under cover in spring or autumn, or by cuttings of basal shoots in spring.
HARVEST Roots are lifted in autumn from plants at least three years old and used fresh, or threaded onto strings and rubbed vigorously at intervals until completely dry.

COFFEA Coffee

(Rubiaceae)

C. arabica is the most widely grown species, notably in the American tropics. It is popular worldwide as a stimulant beverage and food flavoring. The lower-quality *C. canephora* (robusta coffee) is grown mainly in Africa, but is longer-lived and higher-yielding. *C. liberica* is grown for local consumption in Malaysia and Guyana. Coffee contains up to 0.32 percent caffeine when fresh. It also contains chlorogenic acid, a stimulant and diuretic, which remains after decaffeination and is a known allergen. Caffeine is used in many commercial painkillers to potentiate aspirin and paracetamol, and in homeopathic remedies for hyperactivity and tension headaches.

C. arabica (coffee, Arabian coffee) p.110

PARTS USED Seeds.
PROPERTIES A bitter, aromatic, stimulant herb that has diuretic effects and controls vomiting.
USES OF THE HERB
MEDICINAL Internally for nausea and vomiting, and collapse after narcotic poisoning. Externally for burns and scalds (powdered seeds).
ECONOMIC Coffee extract is used in many commercial food and drink products. Combined with chocolate to give mocha flavor.

GROWTH AND HARVEST
GROWTH Ornamental. Well-drained, moisture-retentive soil in semishade, minimum 50°F (10°C). Propagate by seed sown as soon as ripe, at 86°F (30°C), or by tip cuttings at 86°F (30°C). Trim container-grown plants in spring to maintain shape. Plants under cover may be damaged by scale insect and mealybug.
HARVEST Fruits are picked when ripe and the seeds are dried, fermented, or roasted for infusions and essence. Homeopathic tinctures are made from unroasted beans.

COIX

(Gramineae/Poaceae)

C. lacryma-jobi was first described in Chinese medicine c.AD200, and is still used in Chinese patent remedies. The pearl gray fruits are worn to prevent tooth decay.

C. lacryma-jobi (Job's tears) p.110

PARTS USED Fruits (*yi yi ren*).
PROPERTIES A sweet, cooling herb that reduces inflammation, relieves pain and spasms, lowers fever, and controls bacterial and fungal infections. It acts mainly as a spleen tonic and has sedative effects. Large doses lower blood sugar levels.
USES OF THE HERB
CULINARY May be eaten as a grain.
MEDICINAL Internally for arthritis (especially rheumatoid arthritis), urinary problems, lung abscesses, and diarrhea associated with spleen weakness; liquor from fermented seeds is given for rheumatic pain. Not given to pregnant women.

GROWTH AND HARVEST
GROWTH Ornamental. Moist soil in sun. Propagate by seed sown in spring at 55–61°F (13–16°C). May be affected by powdery mildew.
HARVEST Fruits are collected when ripe in autumn, and the husks are removed before using fresh, roasted, or fermented.

COLA

(Sterculiaceae)

Originally a stimulant chewed to alleviate fatigue, hunger, and thirst, "cola" is now a household name for cola-flavored soft drinks. Cola nuts contain up to 1.25–2.4 percent caffeine (3.5 percent in *C. nitida*), some theobromine, and "cola red," a pigment that dyes the mouth and teeth. They are obtained from various species, including *C. acuminata* (Abata cola), *C. anomala* (Bamenda cola), *C. nitida* (*gbanja* cola), and *C. verticillata* (Owé cola). Trees fruit at 12–15 years old, producing 22–35lb (10–16kg) annually until 70–100 years old, and are often planted as shade trees for *Theobroma cacao* (cocoa).

C. nitida, syn. *C. vera* (cola, kola, *goora* nut) p.110

PARTS USED Seeds.
PROPERTIES An astringent, bittersweet, antidepressant herb that has a stimulant effect, especially on the heart.
USES OF THE HERB
MEDICINAL Internally in tonics for exhaustion, low energy, and poor appetite; also for diarrhea. Not given to patients with hypertension. Chewed fresh as an energy and digestive stimulant in countries of origin.
ECONOMIC Extracts added to soft drinks.

GROWTH AND HARVEST
GROWTH Crop. Rich, well-drained soil in sun, minimum 55–59°F (13–15°C). Propagate by seed sown when ripe at 68–75°F (20–24°C), or by hardwood cuttings in sand at 70–75°F (21–24°C).
HARVEST Seeds are taken from ripe fruits and used fresh or dried for liquid extracts, powder, tablets, and tinctures.

COLCHICUM
(Liliaceae/Colchicaceae)

The ancient Greeks took *Colchicum* in tiny amounts for gout, asthma, dropsy, and kidney complaints. Therapeutic doses were evaluated by Anton von Stoerck in 1763, and it has been the standard treatment for gout since then. It contains an important alkaloid, colchicine, which affects cell division and is used today in genetic engineering.

C. autumnale (meadow saffron, naked ladies, autumn crocus) p.110

PARTS USED Corms, seeds.
PROPERTIES A bitter, acrid herb that relieves pain and reduces inflammation.
USES OF THE HERB
MEDICINAL Used to treat acute gout, Behÿet's syndrome, familial Mediterranean fever, and scleroderma. Excess causes gastric pain, diarrhea, and renal damage. May cause fetal abnormalities; not given to pregnant women or patients with kidney disease. Prolonged use may cause hair loss, blood disorders, muscular pain and weakness, and tingling in hands and feet. Used in homeopathy for joint pains, diarrhea, and nausea brought on by damp weather. WARNING This herb and its alkaloids are subject to legal restrictions in some countries.
VARIANTS
C. a. var. ***album***, p.110.
C. a. **'Pleniflorum'**, p.110.

GROWTH AND HARVEST
GROWTH Ornamental. Moist, well-drained soil in sun or semishade. Propagate by seed in autumn, or by offsets in summer. Seeds may take 18 months to germinate. Slugs may damage corms.
HARVEST Corms are lifted in summer and seeds collected in early summer; both are dried for use in liquid and dry extracts, and tinctures.
WARNING All parts are highly toxic if eaten. Handling of corms may cause skin allergy.

COLEUS
C. amboinicus. See *Plectranthus amboinicus*.
C. barbatus. See *Plectranthus barbatus*.
C. forskohlii. See *Plectranthus barbatus*.

COLLINSONIA
(Labiatae/Lamiaceae)

C. canadensis is an unusual herb in that the root is well tolerated, but even small amounts of the fresh leaves may cause vomiting. It is always used with other herbs, forming part of many herbal remedies for kidney complaints. The exact nature of its constituents is unknown.

C. canadensis (horse balm, stone root, richweed) p.110

PARTS USED Rhizomes, roots.
PROPERTIES A bitter, astringent, unpleasant-tasting herb, which has diuretic and anti-inflammatory effects, and acts as a tonic for the capillaries and digestive system.
USES OF THE HERB
MEDICINAL Internally for kidney and urinary stones, cystitis, diarrhea, gastroenteritis, and hemorrhoids. Combines well with *Aphanes arvensis* (see p.239), *Eupatorium purpureum* (see p.281), and *Hydrangea arborescens* (see p.294).

GROWTH AND HARVEST
GROWTH Wild-collected. Moist soil in partial shade. Propagate by seed in spring or autumn.
HARVEST Rhizomes and roots are lifted in autumn and dried for decoctions, liquid extracts, and tinctures.

COMMIPHORA
(Burseraceae)

About 180 species of small, deciduous, mostly thorny shrubs and trees belong to this genus occurring in eastern and western Africa, Arabia, India, S America, and the W Indies. They exude an oleogum resin known as myrrh, an ingredient of incense, perfumes, medicines, and ritual oils; the composition varies slightly from one species to another. It has been a standard medicament in the Middle East since biblical times for infected wounds and bronchial and digestive complaints, and is especially associated with women's health and purification rituals. Being a symbol of suffering, myrrh was one of the three gifts presented by the Magi to the infant Jesus and was used to embalm Christ's body after the crucifixion. Chinese medical texts first described it c.AD600, and it has a long history of use in Ayurvedic medicine as a rejuvenative. Myrrh is obtained from several species, including *C. gileadensis* (balm of Gilead, opalbalsamum), *C. foliacea*, *C. habessinica*, and *C. mukul* (guggulu). The term "bdellium" can refer to these trees collectively, or to the resin. *C. mukul* has recently been found to contain unique saponins, known as guggulipid, that have anti-inflammatory effects in arthritis, and lower blood cholesterol.

C. myrrha, syn. *C. molmol* (myrrh, *bola*)

Tender, deciduous, spiny shrub, height and spread to 16ft (5m), with trifoliate leaves, which have obovate leaflets, the terminal leaflet about ½in (1cm) long. Yellow-red, 4-petaled flowers with a persistent calyx appear after the rains, often before the new leaves, followed by pointed, ellipsoid fruits up to ¼in (7mm) long. Native to desert scrubland in northern Somalia, Arabia, and Yemen.

PARTS USED Oleo-gum resin (*mo yao*).
PROPERTIES A pungent, astringent, aromatic herb that is strongly stimulant, antiseptic, and expectorant. It relieves spasms, inflammation, and digestive discomfort, and encourages healing.
USES OF THE HERB
MEDICINAL Internally for dyspepsia, bronchial and ear infections, glandular fever, tonsillitis, pharyngitis, gingivitis, and menstrual and circulatory problems. Externally for mouth ulcers, wounds, and boils. Added to oral hygiene preparations. Combined with *Hamamelis virginiana* (see p.291) for bruises; with *Cephaelis ipecacuanha* (see p.258) for mouth ulcers and diseased gums; and with *Echinacea* spp. (see p.276) and *Baptisia tinctoria* (see p.247) for various throat infections.

GROWTH AND HARVEST
GROWTH Wild-collected. Well-drained soil in sun, minimum 50–60° F (10–15° C). Propagate by seed sown in spring, or by hardwood cuttings at the end of the growing season.
HARVEST Resin is collected from cut branches and dried to a solid, which is distilled for oil, ground for tablets, or dissolved in tinctures.

COMPTONIA
(Myricaceae)

C. peregrina was used by native N Americans as a poultice for toothache and in a wash for poison-ivy rash. The leaves were used by the Iroquois to line berry baskets to preserve the fruit.

C. peregrina (sweet fern) p.111

PARTS USED Leaves.
PROPERTIES An aromatic, astringent herb that controls bleeding and discharges.
USES OF THE HERB
MEDICINAL Internally for diarrhea, dysentery, vaginal discharge, and vomiting of blood. Externally for minor hemorrhage, rashes, stings.

GROWTH AND HARVEST
GROWTH Ornamental. Well-drained to dry, acid soil in sun or partial shade. Propagate by seed sown when ripe, overwintered in a cold frame, or by removal of rooted suckers in spring, or by layering in spring. Difficult to transplant successfully.
HARVEST Leaves are cut in early summer and dried for use in infusions.

CONIUM Hemlock
(Umbelliferae/Apiaceae)

Hemlock is one of the most poisonous plants in northern temperate regions. The plant contains alkaloids, chiefly coniine, which paralyze the respiratory nerves, so that the victim dies of suffocation before the heart stops beating. The medicinal uses of hemlock date back to the first century AD, when Dioscorides used it externally to treat herpes and erysipelas. Death by hemlock poisoning was the method of execution adopted in ancient Athens, its most famous victim being the philosopher Socrates in 399BC. Under

Jewish law hemlock was also administered to criminals who were crucified or stoned to death, in order to deaden the pain. Coniine was the first alkaloid to be synthesized, in 1886.

C. maculatum (hemlock, poison parsley) p.111

PARTS USED Leaves, fruits (young foliage and unripe seeds have the highest alkaloid content).
PROPERTIES A narcotic herb that sedates and relieves pain.
USES OF THE HERB
MEDICINAL Formerly used internally for epilepsy, mania, chorea, cramps, and asthma. Excess causes dilation of pupils, difficulty in breathing, paralysis (especially of hind legs in animals), stupor, and death. Externally, usually in ointments or oils, for mastitis, malignant tumors (especially breast cancer), anal fissure, and hemorrhoids. In homeopathy for dizziness, anxiety and depression, and premenstrual tension. For use by qualified practitioners only. WARNING This herb is subject to legal restrictions in some countries.

GROWTH AND HARVEST
GROWTH Wild-collected. Damp, rich soil in sun or partial shade. Propagate by seed sown in spring. Subject to statutory control as a weed in some countries, notably in parts of Australia.
HARVEST Leaves are gathered in early summer, and the fruits slightly later, for industrial processing into ointments and oils.
WARNING All parts are extremely toxic if eaten. Skin irritant.

CONVALLARIA
Lily of the valley
(Liliaceae/Convallariaceae)

Forced lilies of the valley were popular for winter decoration during Victorian times, and were exported (as "Berlin crowns") from Germany in great quantities. The use of *C. majalis* as a medicinal herb dates back to at least the second century AD, when it was described in a herbal written by Apuleius. Research has revealed a range of constituents and effects that have increased its importance. *C. majalis* is similar in action to *Digitalis* species (see p.273) but is less cumulative and therefore safer for elderly patients.

C. majalis (lily of the valley, May lily) p.111

PARTS USED Whole plant, leaves, flowers, oil.
PROPERTIES A bitter, diuretic herb that acts as a tonic for the heart and cardiovascular system.
USES OF THE HERB
MEDICINAL Internally for congestive heart failure, arteriosclerosis with angina, and arterial hypotension. Often combined with *Crataegus* spp. (see p.268). For use by qualified practitioners only. WARNING This herb is subject to legal restrictions in some countries.
ECONOMIC The volatile oil, rich in farnesol, is used in perfumery and snuff.

VARIANTS
C. m. **'Albostriata'**, p.111.
C. m. **'Hardwick Hall'**, p.111.

GROWTH AND HARVEST
GROWTH Ornamental. Rich, moist soil in partial shade. Propagate by seed sown in spring, or by division after flowering or in autumn. May become weedy and persistent if allowed to invade other plantings. Leaves have a tendency to develop *Botrytis* in wet conditions. Cultivars do not come true from seed.
HARVEST Leaves, or leaves and flowers, are picked in spring and used fresh or dried in liquid extracts and tinctures. The glycoside content diminishes in the dried leaf. Flowers are collected in spring for extraction of volatile oil.
WARNING All parts, especially fruits and seeds, are toxic if eaten.

CONYZA
(Compositae)

C. canadensis was a native N American herb before entering the *U.S. Pharmacopoeia* (1836–1916). It was used by various tribes, including the Houma, Ojibwa, Meskwaki, Catawba, and Cree, to deter insects (hence the name "Canadian fleabane") and to cure diarrhea, hemorrhage, and menstrual irregularities.

C. canadensis, syn. *Erigeron canadensis* (horseweed, Canadian fleabane) p.112

PARTS USED Whole plant, oil.
PROPERTIES A slightly aromatic, bitter, tonic herb that acts as a diuretic and checks bleeding.
USES OF THE HERB
MEDICINAL Internally for diarrhea, hemorrhage, excessive menstruation, hemorrhoids, kidney disorders, and bronchial complaints. Externally for eczema and ringworm.

GROWTH AND HARVEST
GROWTH Crop. Light, sandy soil in sun. Tolerates most conditions, varying in size accordingly. Propagate by seed sown in spring.
HARVEST Plants are cut when in flower and are best used fresh for oil extraction and liquid extracts. They may also be frozen or made into syrup. Dried herb deteriorates within a year.

COPAIFERA
(Leguminosae)

This genus consists of 35-40 species of evergreen trees native to tropical America and Africa. Copaiba balsam, one of the most plentiful natural perfumery ingredients, is an oleoresin. It is collected from several species, including *C. guyanensis*, *C. martii*, *C. multijuga*, *C. officinalis*, and *C. reticulata*, as well as *C. lansdorffii*. The balsam varies considerably in color, viscosity, and odor, according to the source; balsam from *C. reticulata* has an unpleasant smell and taste, while that from *C. multijuga* has a delightful coumarin-like odor. The balsam contains 30–90 percent volatile oil, and unusual condensed tannins; it is tapped by drilling holes in the trunk, each tree yielding up to 12 gallons (55 liters). The name *Copaifera* comes from *copai*, the native American Tupi word for the tree and its resin.

C. lansdorffii, syn. *C. nitida*, *C. sellowii* (copaiba, copaiva)

Tender evergreen tree, height to 60ft (18m), spread variable, with aromatic bark and pinnate leaves up to 5in (13cm) long, which have 3–5 pairs of ovate leaflets. Very small yellow flowers are followed by dehiscent, yellow-brown to dark red fruits with black seeds. Found mainly in Brazilian rainforest.

PARTS USED Oleoresin.
PROPERTIES An aromatic, antiseptic, stimulant herb with a bitter, burning taste. It improves digestion, has diuretic and expectorant effects, and controls bacterial infections.
USES OF THE HERB
MEDICINAL Internally for cystitis, bronchitis, vaginal discharge, and gonorrhea. Externally for chilblains, sores, and psoriasis. Often combined with *Agathosma* spp. (see p.230), *Piper cubeba* (see p.329), and *Santalum album* (see p.348). Excess is purgative and may cause skin rashes and kidney damage.
ECONOMIC An important fixative in perfumes (especially those with violet, woody, and spicy notes) and a main source of copal, a resin used in varnishes and lacquers. It is also usable direct from the tree as a substitute for diesel oil.

GROWTH AND HARVEST
GROWTH Crop. Well-drained, sandy soil in shade and high humidity, minimum 55–59°F (13–15°C). Propagate by firm softwood cuttings in spring.
HARVEST Resin is tapped from trees at intervals (the hole is sealed afterward) and used in infusions or distilled for oil.

COPTIS Goldthread
(Ranunculaceae)

Ten species of low, moisture-loving perennials belong to this genus distributed throughout northern temperate regions. A few are grown in rock gardens or in peat beds for their anemone-like flowers. Goldthreads contain alkaloids, notably berberine (as found in *Berberis vulgaris*, see p.248, and *Hydrastis canadensis*, see p.294). *C. chinensis* was first mentioned in Chinese medical texts c.AD200. It has similar uses to *C. japonica* and *C. teeta*, with which it is sometimes adulterated. Other useful species include the N American *C. groenlandica* (goldthread, canker root, mouth root) and *C. trifolia* (Indian goldthread). The latter was a standard remedy among many N American tribes for mouth ulcers and was listed as a treatment for mouth and eye inflammations in the *U.S. Pharmacopoeia* (1820–82), and the U.S. *National Formulary* (1916–36). The common name "goldthread" describes the fine yellow roots that grow near the surface.

C. chinensis (mishmi bitter, Chinese goldthread)

Perennial, hardy to 5°F (–15°C), height 10in (25cm), spread 6in (15cm), with long-stalked, tripartite toothed leaves. Three to four small yellow-white flowers, consisting of 5–8 sepals up to ½in (1cm) long, have nectar-secreting petals half the size of the sepals. Native to bogs and damp coniferous woods in China.

PARTS USED Roots (*huang lian*).
PROPERTIES A pungent, very bitter, cooling herb that controls bacterial and viral infections, relaxes spasms, lowers fever, and stimulates the circulation. It is locally analgesic and anesthetic.
USES OF THE HERB
MEDICINAL Internally for "hot" conditions, such as dysentery, enteritis, high fever, inflamed mouth and tongue, conjunctivitis, middle ear infection, and palpitations. Externally for inflamed mucous membranes in mouth and eyes. An ingredient of the Chinese drug *san huang zhe she ye* ("injection of three yellow herbs"), given intramuscularly for upper respiratory tract infections.
ECONOMIC Bright yellow pigments in roots have been used in dyeing.

GROWTH AND HARVEST
GROWTH Crop. Moist, acid soil in shade. Propagate by seed sown in spring, or by division in autumn or spring.
HARVEST Roots are lifted in autumn and used fresh or dried in decoctions.

CORDYCEPS
(Ascomycetes)

A genus of 100 species of parasitic fungi found worldwide. *C. sinensis* is parasitic on caterpillars of a rare Himalayan moth. It has been harvested by the Yung in western China for thousands of years, a process aided by annual burning of the alpine meadows. The fungus is now produced more cheaply on wheat in California, but may still be bought in China as small bundles tied with red thread, identical to those collected by 19th-century explorers. *C. sinensis* was first described in Chinese medical texts c.AD200. A later account, c.AD1600, compared this bizarre, medicinal caterpillar-fungus to ginseng as a tonic. Traditionally, *dong chong xia cao* consists of both the parasitized larva and stroma (spore-producing body) of the fungus, which protrudes from the head of the caterpillar. According to the *Chinese Materia Medica* "large, fat larvae with yellow insides and short stromata are marks of good quality." It is, however, the fungus and not the caterpillar that possesses the medicinal properties – which explains why modern production techniques, cultivating the fungus on wheat, are equally effective. In China, *dong chong xia cao* is usually cooked with chicken to make a tonic broth, in early spring and early winter, to help the body adjust to seasonal changes. It is also a popular aphrodisiac for men, cooked with gin and soy sauce inside the head of a duck.

C. sinensis (Chinese caterpillar fungus)

Fungus which is parasitic on the larvae of *Hepialus armoricanus*. The larva measures 1¼in–2½in (3–6cm) long and up to ¼in (7mm) in diameter. Spores invade the host through the nostrils and consume the entire body contents to form a sclerotium which overwinters beneath the snow. The spring thaw triggers production of stromata (spore-producing bodies), which emerge from the carcass and infect the surrounding soil. The stromata are club-shaped, hollow in the center, and brown to black-brown with white interior tissue. They are 1½–3in (4–8cm) long and ⅛in (3mm) in diameter. Found only in the foothills of the eastern Himalayas in grassland above 11,000ft (3,353m).

PARTS USED Whole fungus (*dong chong xia cao*).
PROPERTIES A sweet energy tonic for lungs and kidneys, and a tranquilizer and muscle relaxant, controlling coughs and having antibacterial and anticancer effects.
USES OF THE HERB
MEDICINAL Internally for coughs, tuberculosis, conditions associated with kidney weakness (impotence, back pains, night sweats), menopausal problems, convalescence, and naso-pharyngeal cancer.

GROWTH AND HARVEST
GROWTH Crop. Parasitic on moth larvae in the wild. May be cultivated on wheat. Propagates by spores on suitable host.
HARVEST Fungus is collected in the wild in early spring as the snow melts, or from a cultivated grain base, and dried for capsules, compressed slices, powder, or tinctures.

CORIANDRUM Coriander
(Umbelliferae/Apiaceae)

Coriander was introduced to Chinese cooking and medicine c.AD600, and has been known as *hu*, "foreign," since then. In *Chinese Materia Medica* (G.A. Stuart, 1911), it was recommended for certain types of nonpathogenic food poisoning caused by decaying matter. The fresh foliage and ripe seeds have quite different aromas and uses.

C. sativum (coriander, cilantro) p.112

PARTS USED Leaves, seeds, oil.
PROPERTIES Both leaves and seeds are rich in volatile oils that act mainly on the digestive system, stimulating the appetite, and relieving irritation. They are also expectorant. Oil is fungicidal and bactericidal.

USES OF THE HERB
CULINARY Leaves are widely used to flavor food, especially in the Middle East, and SE Asia. Seeds and roots are also an ingredient of curries and of pickling spices, dishes *à la grecque*, and bakery products.
AROMATIC Oil is prized in perfumery.
MEDICINAL Internally for minor digestive problems. Externally for hemorrhoids and painful joints (seeds). Seeds reduce griping in laxative preparations based on *Rheum officinale* and *Senna alexandrina* (see p. 255).

GROWTH AND HARVEST
GROWTH Ornamental. Well-drained soil in a sunny position. *C. sativum* prefers a cool, damp spring, followed by a hot, dry summer. Plants grown for leaves do best in partial shade. Propagate by seed sown in spring, or in summer for an autumn harvest. Tends to bolt if too dry at the seedling stage, and during warm summers. Recommended in companion planting to improve germination in anise, and to repel aphids and carrot fly. May reduce seed yield in fennel if planted nearby.
HARVEST Leaves are gathered when young and used fresh. Seeds are harvested when ripe and used whole or ground for culinary purposes. Medicinal preparations usually call for powdered seeds, liquid extracts, or distilled oil.

CORIDOTHYMUS
C. capitatus. See *Thymus capitatus*.

CORNUS Dogwood
(Cornaceae)

C. officinalis was first described in Chinese medicine c.AD200. Other species with therapeutic properties are *C. florida* (flowering dogwood), used as a tonic for nervous exhaustion and tension headaches, and *C. sericea* (American red osier), a traditional remedy for indigestion, diarrhea, and vomiting.

C. officinalis (Japanese cornel, Japanese cornelian cherry) p.112

PARTS USED Fruits (*shan zhu yu*).
PROPERTIES A sour, astringent, diuretic herb that acts mainly as an energy tonic for the liver and kidneys. It also checks bleeding, lowers blood pressure, and controls bacterial and fungal infections.
USES OF THE HERB
MEDICINAL Internally for conditions associated with weak kidney and liver energy (such as urinary dysfunction and impotence), nocturnal sweats, and excessive menstruation.

GROWTH AND HARVEST
GROWTH Ornamental. Well-drained soil in sun or semishade. Propagate by seed in spring or autumn, or by softwood cuttings in summer.
HARVEST Fruits are collected when ripe and dried for use in decoctions.
WARNING Skin allergen.

CORYDALIS
(Papaveraceae)

C. solida is very similar to *C. cava,* the main differences being that the former has hollow, rather than solid, tubers, and a more westerly distribution. It is likely that both species are wild-collected for medicinal purposes. *C. solida* has been used as a painkiller in traditional Chinese medicine since at least the eighth century, when it was mentioned in the *Omissions from the Materia Medica* by Chen Cang-Zi. Its capsule fruit splits open when ripe to release the numerous black seeds.

C. solida (bulbous corydalis) p.112

PARTS USED Tubers (*yan hu suo*).
PROPERTIES A painkilling herb that stimulates the circulation, controls spasms and nausea, and has sedative and antibacterial properties. Research also suggests action on the thyroid and adrenal cortex.
USES OF THE HERB
MEDICINAL Internally as a sedative for insomnia, and as a stimulant and painkiller, especially in painful menstruation, traumatic injury, and lumbago. Not given to pregnant women.
VARIANT
C. s. **'George Baker'**, p.112.

GROWTH AND HARVEST
GROWTH Ornamental. Well-drained, humus-rich, moist soil in partial shade. The position of plants should be clearly marked because they die down completely in summer. Propagate by seed sown in early spring or autumn, or by division of tubers in their dormant period. All parts of *Corydalis* are very brittle and must be handled carefully.
HARVEST Tubers are collected during dormancy and dried for use in decoctions.

COUMAROUNA

C. odorata. See *Dipteryx odorata.*

CRATAEGUS Hawthorn

(Rosaceae)

Many species of *Crataegus* are variable, which in the past has led to the naming of over 1,000 different species, some of which were probably hybrids. Recent research has reduced this number considerably, but the numerous forms and hybrids still present a problem of identification. The common names of *C. laevigata* refer to different aspects of the plant: "may" from its time of flowering; "quickset" from its use as a "quick" or "living" hedge; also "bread-and-cheese" from the tasty young leaves, which were traditionally added to sandwiches in country areas. Many practices are associated with the hawthorn, notably the custom of going "a-Maying," and choosing a May queen, which predates Christian times. In pagan times the king and queen of the May were killed at the end of the growing season – hence the ambiguity today of hawthorn being both a symbol of hope and an omen of death. It has been used in Europe since the Middle Ages as a heart remedy, and has recently been adopted for this purpose, and as a digestive aid, by practitioners of traditional Chinese medicine. *C. laevigata* and *C. monogyna*, and their hybrids, are used interchangeably for medicinal purposes. *C. pinnatifida* was first mentioned as a herb in the *Supplement to the Extension of the Materia Medica* by Zhu Zhen Heng (c.1347). Fruits of another Chinese species, *C. cuneata*, have a sour but pleasant taste, and are used mainly to control diarrhea.

C. laevigata, syn. *C. oxyacantha* (hawthorn, may, quickset) p.112

PARTS USED Fruits.
PROPERTIES A sweet and sour, warming herb that improves peripheral circulation and regulates heart rate, blood pressure, and coronary blood flow.
USES OF THE HERB
MEDICINAL Internally for circulatory disorders and heart disease of all kinds, often combined with *Selenicereus grandiflorus* (see p.351), *Tilia* spp. (see p.363), *Viscum album* (see p.370), or *Scutellaria lateriflora* (see p.351). Unlike most medicinal plants that act on the heart, hawthorn is relatively nontoxic, although its use for such serious conditions should be confined to qualified practitioners.
VARIANTS
C. l. **'Paul's Scarlet'**, p.113.
C. l. **'Plena'**, p.113.
C. l. **'Rosea'**, p.113.

C. pinnatifida (Chinese haw) p.113

PARTS USED Fruits (*shan zha*).
PROPERTIES A digestive, circulatory, and uterine stimulant that also has hypotensive and antibacterial properties.
USES OF THE HERB
MEDICINAL Internally for "food stagnation" (a term used in Chinese medicine to cover irritable bowel syndrome or gall bladder weakness), hypertension associated with coronary artery disease, failure to menstruate, and postpartum pain. Fruits are used raw for circulatory disorders and baked for digestive problems.

GROWTH AND HARVEST
GROWTH Ornamental (*C. pinnatifida*: crop). Most soils, including alkaline, in sun or partial shade. *C. laevigata* flowers and fruits better in an open, sunny position. Propagate by seed gathered when ripe and stratified for 18 months before sowing in early spring. Cultivars do not come true from seed, and are propagated by grafting or budding onto stocks of *C. monogyna* in spring. Trim to shape at any time from late summer to early spring, or in winter for shrubs in which autumn color is a feature. Leaves may be attacked by caterpillars or affected by leafspot, powdery mildew, or rust. *Armillaria* root rot is a cause of rapid death. *C. laevigata* and *C. monogyna*, and their hybrids, are subject to certain plant controls in parts of Australia.
HARVEST Fruits are collected when ripe and used raw or cooked, or dried whole for use in decoctions, liquid extracts, and tinctures. Alternatively, the juice is extracted and freeze-dried.

CRITHMUM Samphire

(Umbelliferae/Apiaceae)

C. maritimum has been gathered from coastal rocks and cliffs for pickling and salads since time immemorial. John Evelyn in *Acetaria* (1699) remarked on "its excellent Vertues and effects against the Spleen, Cleansing the Passages, sharpning Appetite, etc. so far preferrable to most of our hotter Herbs." This succulent coastal plant contains high levels of vitamin C. It has a powerful, salty flavor, described by Tom Stobart in *Herbs, Spices and Flavourings* (1970) as like "a mixture of celery and kerosene." *C. maritimum* (rock samphire) is sometimes confused with *Salicornia* species (marsh samphire), as both are commonly referred to as "samphire."

C. maritimum (samphire, rock samphire, sea fennel) p.113

PARTS USED Whole plant, leaves.
PROPERTIES A strongly aromatic, salty herb that has diuretic effects, cleanses toxins, and improves digestion. It has a reputation for encouraging weight loss.
USES OF THE HERB
CULINARY Leaves are eaten in salads, cooked in butter, or pickled.
MEDICINAL Internally for obesity, kidney complaints, and sluggishness.

GROWTH AND HARVEST
GROWTH Wild-collected. Well-drained to dry soil in sun. Needs a warm, sheltered position inland and protection in cold winters. Propagate by seed sown when ripe, or by division in spring. Seeds lose viability rapidly.
HARVEST Whole plants are gathered in late spring and used fresh for infusions. Leaves are picked fresh for use as a vegetable.

CROCUS

(Iridaceae)

Saffron, from the Arabic *za'fân*, "yellow," is the world's most costly spice, requiring some 150,000 flowers and 400 hours' work to produce 2.2lb (1kg) of dried saffron. The Chinese value saffron as a medicinal herb; it reached China in the Yuen dynasty (1280–1368) from Persia and India. It has been prized as a flavoring and colorant for over 4,000 years, but especially since the early Crusades in the 11th century, when it became widely grown in Europe and the Middle East. Centers of saffron cultivation included Valencia, Spain; Nuremberg, Germany; and Saffron Walden, England. Today it is grown mainly in Kashmir and Spain. Over the centuries the high price of saffron gave rise to a thriving trade in adulterants, such as dyed fibers from beef and pomegranates. The penalties were severe: a trader in 15th-century Nuremberg was buried alive with his adulterated product. Genuine saffron consists of bright orange, threadlike fibers. The red coloring matter dissolves readily in warm water, diluting to yellow. Powdered saffron is cheaper but commonly contains adulterants. As well as its role as a spice and medicinal herb, saffron was once important as a dye for hair, nails, and fine textiles. *C. nudiflorus*, from the Pyrenees, was once grown as a saffron substitute. It was introduced into England by the Knights of St. John of Jerusalem, and is still found growing on properties belonging to the Order. *C. sativus* must not be confused with the poisonous meadow saffron (*Colchicum autumnale*, see p.265).

C. sativus (saffron crocus) p.113

PARTS USED Flower stigmas (*fan hong hua*).
PROPERTIES A pungent, bittersweet herb that improves the digestion, increases perspiration, stimulates the circulation and menstruation, and reduces high blood pressure.
USES OF THE HERB
CULINARY Used as a flavoring and colorant for cakes, eastern sweetmeats, and sauces; in rice dishes, such as *paella* (Spain) and *risotto Milanese* (Italy); and in fish stews, such as *zarzuela* (Spain) and *bouillabaisse* (France).
MEDICINAL Internally, in Chinese traditional medicine, for "stagnant liver energy," as in depression and menstrual disorders.
ECONOMIC A flavoring and colorant in liqueurs.

GROWTH AND HARVEST
GROWTH Crop. Well-drained soil in a warm situation, in full sun. Propagate by offsets removed from the parent corm in late spring. *C. sativus* thrives, but fails to flower, in areas with cool, wet summers.
HARVEST Flowers are picked when open and the stigmas removed for drying. Saffron does not store well and should be used within a year of harvesting.

CROTON
(Euphorbiaceae)

Many species contain resins used in making varnishes, and have medicinal properties used in the country of origin. Apart from *C. tiglium*, the only species with wide usage is the W Indian *C. eleuteria* (cascarilla), which has aromatic bark used in remedies for digestive upsets and to flavor tobacco.

C. tiglium (croton) p.114

PARTS USED
Seeds (*ba dou*), oil.
PROPERTIES
A pungent, unpleasant-smelling herb that is exceedingly irritant and purgative. Croton oil is the strongest of all purgatives.
USES OF THE HERB
MEDICINAL Internally in minute amounts for constipation, dysentery, biliary colic, intestinal obstructions, food poisoning, malaria, and mastitis. Externally for warts, dermatitis, abscesses, and boils (seeds, often after oil extraction to reduce toxicity). Croton oil is carcinogenic; excess causes shock (1ml can be fatal), and skin contact with it should be avoided. Side effects include blistering of skin and mucous membranes, edema, hypotension, and abdominal pain. WARNING This herb is subject to legal restrictions in some countries.

GROWTH AND HARVEST
GROWTH Crop. Damp soil in partial shade, minimum 59–64°F (15–18°C). Propagate by seed sown in spring. Cut back in early spring to control growth.
HARVEST Seeds are collected when ripe and used whole or crushed for oil extraction or use in pills.

CRYPTOTAENIA
(Umbelliferae/Apiaceae)

The celery-flavored foliage of *C. canadensis* is a common ingredient in traditional Japanese cuisine.

C. canadensis (honewort, Japanese wild chervil, *mitsuba*) p.114

PARTS USED Leaves.
PROPERTIES An aromatic herb with a celery-like flavor.
USES OF THE HERB
CULINARY Young leaves are cooked as a green vegetable, often served cold with soy sauce. Leaf stalks are added to soups, salads, and savory dishes.

GROWTH AND HARVEST
GROWTH Crop. Rich, moist soil in shade. Propagate by seed sown successively, from early spring to midsummer, or by division in spring or autumn.
HARVEST Young leaves are picked as required and used fresh.

CUCUMIS
(Cucurbitaceae)

Culpeper wrote of the cucumber in *The English Physitian Enlarged* (1653) that "there is not a better remedy for ulcers in the bladder" and "the face being washed with their juice, cleanses the skin." The bitter cucumber, *C. colocynthis*, is an important homeopathic remedy for colic.

C. sativus (cucumber) p.114

PARTS USED Fruits, seeds.
PROPERTIES A cooling, diuretic, alterative herb that clears and softens the skin. Seeds expel intestinal parasites.
USES OF THE HERB
CULINARY Fruits are eaten fresh, cooked, or pickled, and added to summer drinks and to yogurt to make *raita*.
MEDICINAL Internally for blemished skin, heat rashes, and overheating in hot weather (fruit); tapeworm (ground seeds). Externally for sunburn, scalds, sore eyes, and conjunctivitis.
ECONOMIC Used in cleansing and toning lotions for the face (fruits).

GROWTH AND HARVEST
GROWTH Crop. Rich, well-drained soil in sun or partial shade, minimum 50°F (10°C). Propagate by seed sown in spring at 64°F (18°C). Pinch out growing tips when plants have three leaves and again when lateral shoots have four or five leaves. Prone to various diseases, including mosaic virus, *Botrytis*, anthracnose, *Verticillium* wilt, powdery mildew, root rot, and *Sclerotinia*. Cucumbers may be grown on poles or trellis, or on the ground, according to variety.
HARVEST Fruits are picked unripe and used fresh as slices, pulp, or juice. Seeds are collected from ripe fruits and dried.

CUCURBITA Squash, pumpkin
(Cucurbitaceae)

Pumpkins, marrows, and winter and summer squashes belong to several different species, with interchangeable common names and the same medicinal properties. Pumpkin seeds are rich in oil, vitamins, and minerals, especially zinc, which is useful in treating enlarged prostate. As a remedy for intestinal parasites they are less potent than *Dryopteris filix-mas* (see p.276), but safer for pregnant women, debilitated patients, and children. Use of pumpkin seeds in Chinese medicine was adopted in the 17th century.

C. maxima (pumpkin, winter squash) p.114

PARTS USED Seeds (*nan gua zi*).
PROPERTIES A sweet, warming, nutty-flavored herb that acts as a diuretic, soothes irritated tissues, and expels intestinal worms.
USES OF THE HERB
CULINARY Dehusked seeds are eaten raw or roasted as a snack, or added to bread.
MEDICINAL Internally, often combined with *Serenoa repens* (see p.352) and *Echinacea purpurea* (see p.276), for prostatitis and with *Senna alexandrina* (see p.352), for tapeworms and roundworms; also for travel sickness and early stages of schistosomiasis.

GROWTH AND HARVEST
GROWTH Crop. Rich, well-drained soil in sun. Propagate by seed sown in spring at 61–64°F (16–18°C). Pinch out tips to encourage growth of lateral shoots. May be affected by mosaic virus, *Botrytis*, and powdery mildew. Growing on poles or supports protects fruits from slugs.
HARVEST Seeds are collected from ripe fruits in autumn and dried whole (not dehusked for medicinal use) before grinding.

CUMINUM Cumin
(Umbelliferae/Apiaceae)

Cumin was once a familiar spice in Europe, particularly in ancient Rome. Today, it is used mainly in Asia and the Middle East, as it has been since biblical times. Its pungent, aromatic, rather bitter flavor is essential to curries and many spicy dishes. Several kinds of cumin are recognized in India, the most common being *safed* (white) and *kala* (black). Caraway (*Carum carvi*, see p.255) is sometimes confused with it in Indian recipes.

C. cyminum (cumin, *comino, jeera*) p.114

PARTS USED Seeds.
PROPERTIES An aromatic, astringent herb that benefits the digestive system and acts as a stimulant to the sexual organs. The oil is anti-bacterial and larvicidal.
USES OF THE HERB
CULINARY Seeds are an ingredient in spice mixtures such as *garam masala* (India) and in *couscous* (Middle East); they may also be roasted, and give a characteristic flavor to Eastern dishes based on lamb and to side dishes of cucumber and yogurt.
MEDICINAL Internally for minor digestive problems and migraine of digestive origin. Widely used in Ayurvedic medicine to promote the assimilation of other herbs and to improve liver function; also used in veterinary medicine.

GROWTH AND HARVEST
GROWTH Crop. Well-drained soil in full sun. Propagate by seed sown in spring. Seeds may not ripen in cold climates.
HARVEST Seeds are collected when ripe and stored whole. They are used whole or ground for culinary use, or distilled for oil as a commercial flavoring and for veterinary use.

CURCUMA
(Zingiberaceae)

C. longa (turmeric) is one of the most common food flavorings and colorings in Asian cuisine. Many medicinal uses are recorded for the plant, especially in China, India, and Indonesia. Recent research has also shown significant anti-inflammatory and liver-protective effects. *C. longa* and *C. aromatica*, both native to India, were described in Chinese medicine in the seventh century. The term *yu jin* is applied to *C. aromatica* on its own and to a mixture of tubers from *C. aromatica*, *C. longa*, and *C. zedoaria*. Next in importance after *C. aromatica* and *C. longa* are *C. amada* (mango ginger), an Indian species that is candied or pickled, and *C. zedoaria* (zedoary), which has similar applications to *Zingiber officinale* (see p.373) and is used in China to treat cervical cancer.

C. aromatica (wild turmeric) p.114

PARTS USED Rhizomes (*yu jin*).
PROPERTIES A pungent, bitter, cooling herb that improves digestion and stimulates the gall bladder and circulatory system, both checking bleeding and dissolving clots.
USES OF THE HERB
MEDICINAL Internally for jaundice, nosebleeds, internal hemorrhage, painful menstruation, shock, chest pains associated with low liver energy, and angina.

C. longa, syn. *C. domestica* (turmeric, *haridra*) p.115

PARTS USED Rhizomes (*jiang huang*).
PROPERTIES A pungent, bitter, astringent herb with a characteristic smell and deep yellow color. It stimulates the digestive, circulatory, and respiratory systems, and uterus, normalizes energy flow, and has anti-inflammatory and antibiotic effects.
USES OF THE HERB
CULINARY An essential ingredient of curries and curry powder.
MEDICINAL Internally for digestive and skin complaints, poor circulation, uterine tumors, jaundice, liver disease, and menstrual problems. Often combined with *Berberis vulgaris* (see p.248) or *Mahonia aquifolium* (see p.308) for liver complaints and diabetes. Externally for injuries, sores, and ringworm.
ECONOMIC Used for piccalilli and as a natural food coloring; it cannot be substituted for saffron or annatto, on account of its strong flavor. A source of orange and yellow dyes for silk and wool, notably as a coloring for the robes of Buddhist monks.

GROWTH AND HARVEST
GROWTH Crop. Well-drained soil in sun, with ample humidity, minimum 59–64°F (15–18°C). Propagate by seed sown in autumn, or by division when dormant.
HARVEST Rhizomes are lifted during the dormant period and steamed or boiled before drying and grinding for use in decoctions, pills, poultices, and powders.

CUSCUTA Dodder
(Convolvulaceae)

About 100 twining, parasitic annuals belong to this genus, which occurs throughout temperate and warm regions. These unusual plants have no roots and no green parts, their leaves being reduced to scales. They obtain nutrients from the host plant, which they penetrate with suckers. Several are used medicinally, including *C. epithymum* (common dodder), which was once popular among European herbalists for "melancholy diseases" and disorders of the spleen, kidneys, and liver. Descriptions of *C. japonica* appeared in Chinese medical literature of the first century AD, based on texts going back to 1500BC.

C. japonica, syn. *C. systyla* (Japanese dodder)

Twining annual, hardy to 5°F (–15°C), 3ft (1m) in height, with thin, much-branched yellow stems, which are striped or spotted red. Numerous pale yellow, bell-shaped flowers are produced in short spikes in late summer. Found at low altitudes in eastern Asia.

PARTS USED Seeds (*tu si zi*).
PROPERTIES A sweet, pungent herb that acts mainly as a kidney and liver stimulant.
USES OF THE HERB
MEDICINAL Internally for diarrhea, impotence, urinary frequency, vaginal discharge, and poor eyesight associated with liver and kidney energy weakness.

GROWTH AND HARVEST
GROWTH Wild-collected. Grows only on suitable host plants. Propagates by seed sown in autumn, lodged among stems of host plant. Some species are subject to certain plant controls in parts of Australia.
HARVEST Seeds are collected when ripe in autumn and dried for use in decoctions.

CYMBOPOGON
(Gramineae/Poaceae)

These aromatic grasses contain large amounts of citral and geraniol, which are lemon- and rose-scented respectively. The following species are important: *C. martinii* (*palmarosa, rosha*) from India, source of Turkish geranium oil, used to adulterate rose oil and widely used in rose perfumes, soaps, and insect repellants; *C. martinii* var. *sofia* (ginger grass), which has a cruder scent; *C. flexuosus* (East Indian lemon grass), which yields lemon grass oil, used for food flavoring; and *C. nardus* (citronella), grown in Sri Lanka and Java for citronella oil, which is similar in fragrance and properties to *Melissa officinalis* (see p.310).

C. citratus (lemon grass) p.115

PARTS USED Leaves, stems, oil.
PROPERTIES A bitter, aromatic, cooling herb that increases perspiration and relieves spasms. Also effective against fungal and bacterial infections.
USES OF THE HERB
CULINARY Base of leaves is used fresh, or as *sereh* powder, in SE Asian cooking, especially with fish and meat. Leaves are infused for tea.
AROMATIC Oil is used in perfumes.
MEDICINAL Internally for digestive problems in children and minor feverish illnesses. Externally for ringworm, lice, athlete's foot, and scabies.
ECONOMIC Oil is used in soaps, hair oils, herbal baths, and cosmetics, and for flavoring.

GROWTH AND HARVEST
GROWTH Crop. Well-drained soil in sun, minimum 45°F (7°C). Propagate by division in spring.
HARVEST Stems are cut at ground level and used fresh for oil extraction, dried for powder, and either fresh or dried for infusions. The leaf blades may be removed and the lower 3–4in (7–10cm) used as a fresh herb.

CYNARA
(Compositae/Asteraceae)

Globe artichokes (*C. cardunculus*, Scolymus Group) and the closely-related cardoons (*C. cardunculus*) were both grown as vegetables by the Greeks and Romans. In recent years the globe artichoke has become important as a medicinal herb, following the discovery of cynarin. This compound, which is found in the leaves, improves liver and gall bladder function, and lowers blood cholesterol levels.

C. cardunculus, **Scolymus Group** (globe artichoke) p.115

PARTS USED Leaves, roots, flower heads.
PROPERTIES A bitter, slightly salty herb that detoxifies and regenerates liver tissues, stimulates the gall bladder, and reduces blood lipids, serum cholesterol, and blood sugar.
USES OF THE HERB
CULINARY Unopened flower heads are boiled and eaten hot with hollandaise sauce or melted butter, or cold with vinaigrette. Hearts are baked or fried.
MEDICINAL Internally for chronic liver and gall bladder diseases, jaundice, hepatitis, arteriosclerosis, and diabetes.

GROWTH AND HARVEST
GROWTH Ornamental. Deep, rich, well-drained soil in sun. Propagate by seed sown in spring, or by suckers (sideshoots) in spring or autumn. Flower heads may be affected by petal blight.
HARVEST Leaves are cut just before flowering, for use fresh or dried in liquid extracts, syrup, and tablets. Flower heads are cut before the bracts open for use as a vegetable.

CYNOGLOSSUM Houndstongue
(Boraginaceae)

C. officinale contains pyrrolizidine alkaloids similar to those in *Symphytum officinale* (see p.357). Internal use of *S. officinale* is now banned in some countries, hence the safety of *C. officinale* must also be questioned. *C. officinale* also contains allantoin, a highly effective healing substance, and the leaves were traditionally used as a compress for insect bites and other minor injuries such as bruises and burns.

C. officinale (houndstongue, rats-and-mice) p.115

PARTS USED Whole plant, leaves, roots.
PROPERTIES A painkilling herb that soothes inflamed tissues and speeds healing.
USES OF THE HERB
MEDICINAL Formerly used internally for coughs and diarrhea. Now mostly externally for minor injuries, bites, and leg ulcers, and as a suppository for hemorrhoids. Not prescribed for children or lactating women. WARNING This herb is subject to legal restrictions in some countries.

GROWTH AND HARVEST
GROWTH Wild-collected. Well-drained soil in sun or partial shade. Propagate by seed sown in spring or autumn.
HARVEST Flowering plants and leaves are collected in early summer and dried for use in infusions. Roots are lifted in autumn and dried for use in decoctions.
WARNING Skin irritant and allergen.

CYPERUS Sedge
(Cyperaceae)

The volatile oils and astringent substances found in a number of sedges are used in perfumery and as remedies for digestive problems. *C. longus* (sweet galingale) was once made into an aromatic tonic, but its uses are now limited to perfumery. The black tubers of *C. articulatus* (adrue) have a lavender aroma and are useful in treating nausea and dyspepsia. *C. rotundus* is important in traditional Chinese medicine today and is also used in Ayurvedic medicine.

C. rotundus (nut grass, sedge root, coco grass) p.115

PARTS USED Rhizomes, roots and tubers (*xiang fu*).
PROPERTIES A pungent, bittersweet herb that relieves spasms and pain, acting mainly on the digestive system and uterus.
USES OF THE HERB
MEDICINAL Internally for digestive problems related to blocked liver energy, and menstrual complaints. Often combined with *Angelica polymorpha* var. *sinensis* (see p.238) for irregular menstruation, and with *Atractylodes macrocephala* (see p.246) for nausea and vomiting.

GROWTH AND HARVEST
GROWTH Wild-collected. Damp soil in sun, minimum 55°F (13°C). Propagates by seed sown in spring, or by division in autumn. Subject to statutory control as a weed in some countries, notably in parts of Australia.
HARVEST Rootstocks are lifted in summer or winter and dried for use in decoctions.

CYPRIPEDIUM Lady's slipper orchid
(Orchidaceae)

C. parviflorum (yellow lady's slipper) has two variants in N America: *C. p.* var. *pubescens* (larger yellow lady's slipper) and *C. p.* var. *parviflorum* (smaller yellow lady's slipper). Both have similar uses and are rare in the wild. Claims that they are cultivated for medicinal use are mostly spurious, and stocks are largely wild-collected. The plants were used by native N Americans as tranquilizers, and were listed in the *U.S. Pharmocopoeia* from 1863 to 1916. Medical herbalists now recommend the use of suitable substitutes, such as *Scutellaria lateriflora* (see p.351) and *Lavandula angustifolia* (see p.301).

C. parviflorum var. ***pubescens,*** syn. *C. pubescens* (larger yellow lady's slipper, nerve root, American valerian) p.115

PARTS USED Rhizomes.
PROPERTIES A pungent, bittersweet herb with an unpleasant odor similar to that of *Valeriana officinalis* (see p.367). It relieves spasms and has sedative and tonic effects on the nervous system.
USES OF THE HERB
MEDICINAL Internally for anxiety, nervous tension, insomnia, depression, and tension headaches. Often combined with *Scutellaria lateriflora* (see p.351) and *Avena sativa* (see p.246) for anxiety.

GROWTH AND HARVEST
GROWTH Wild-collected. Humus-rich soil in an open, shady situation. Propagates by division in spring, or professionally by seed sown under sterile laboratory conditions.
HARVEST Rhizomes are lifted in autumn and dried for infusions, liquid extracts, powder, and tinctures.
WARNING Handling *C. parviflorum* var. *pubescens* may cause an allergic reaction.

CYTISUS Broom
(Leguminosae/Papilionaceae)

C. scoparius contains alkaloids, notably sparteine, which affect the heart and nerves in similar ways to curare (see *Chondrodendron* species, p.260, and *Strychnos* species, p.357). Its medicinal uses are listed in all the early European herbals under *Planta genista*, from which the British royal house of Plantagenet took its name.

C. scoparius, syn. *Sarothamnus scoparius* (broom, Scotch broom) p.116

PARTS USED Whole plant.
PROPERTIES A bitter, narcotic herb that depresses respiration, regulates heart action, and has diuretic and purgative effects.
USES OF THE HERB
MEDICINAL Internally, mainly for heart complaints, especially with *Convallaria majalis* (see p.266) in heart failure. Excess causes respiratory collapse. Not given to pregnant women or patients with high blood pressure. For use by qualified practitioners only. WARNING This herb is subject to legal restrictions in some countries.
VARIANT
C. s. var. ***prostratus***, p.116.

GROWTH AND HARVEST
GROWTH Ornamental. Well-drained soil in sun. Propagate by seed sown under cover in spring or autumn, or by semiripe cuttings in summer. Germination is erratic. Cut back shoots by two-thirds after flowering. Cytisus does not transplant well. Subject to statutory control as a weed in some countries, notably in parts of Australia.
HARVEST Tops of shoots are cut as flowering begins and dried for use in decoctions, infusions, liquid extracts, and tinctures; stocks are renewed annually.
WARNING Toxic if eaten.

DAPHNE
(Thymelaeaceae)

Daphnes of various kinds have therapeutic properties. *D. mezereum* (mezereon) was once prescribed for rheumatism and indolent ulcers, but is no longer considered safe. It contains similar toxic compounds to *D. laureola* (spurge laurel) and *D. gnidium*. These are currently being investigated for antileukemic effects. *D. genkwa* was first described in Chinese medical literature c.AD25–200, based on texts going back to 1500BC.

D. genkwa p.116

PARTS USED Flower buds (*yuan hua*).
PROPERTIES A bitter, acrid herb that controls coughs and has germicidal, diuretic, expectorant, and laxative effects.
USES OF THE HERB
MEDICINAL Internally for bronchitis, constipation, edema, and skin diseases (especially scabies); used in Chinese hospitals as an abortifacient. Externally for frostbite.

GROWTH AND HARVEST
GROWTH Ornamental. Well-drained, neutral to alkaline soil in sun or partial shade. Propagate by seed sown under cover when ripe or by semiripe cuttings in summer. Remove weak and badly placed shoots in spring.
HARVEST Flower buds are picked in spring and dried for use in decoctions.
WARNING Toxic if eaten.

DATURA Thorn apple
(Solanaceae)

Daturas are extremely poisonous, containing tropane alkaloids similar to those in *Atropa belladonna* (see p.246) and *Hyoscyamus niger* (see p.295). Alkaloids are extracted from several species, including *D. metel* and *D. meteloides*. All daturas have a long history of medicinal and ritual use in their countries of origin.

D. stramonium (jimson weed, thorn apple, devil's apple) p.116

PARTS USED Leaves, flowering tops, seeds.
PROPERTIES A bitter, narcotic herb that relaxes spasms, relieves pain, and encourages healing.
USES OF THE HERB
MEDICINAL Internally for asthma and Parkinson's disease. Excess causes giddiness, dry mouth, hallucinations, and coma. Externally for fistulas, abscesses, and severe neuralgia. WARNING This herb and its alkaloids are subject to legal restrictions in some countries.

GROWTH AND HARVEST
GROWTH Crop. Rich, light soil in sun. Propagate by seed sown in spring at 61°F (16°C). Subject to statutory control as a weed, notably in some parts of Australia.
HARVEST Leaves and flowering tops are collected in summer, and seeds in autumn, for commercial extraction of alkaloids or use in antiasthmatic smoking mixtures, liquid extracts, powders, and tinctures.
WARNING Toxic if eaten.

DAUCUS Carrot
(Umbelliferae/Apaceae)

D. carota has been an important vegetable crop in Europe, northern Africa, and many parts of Asia since at least Classical times. The familiar orange-fleshed carrot is eaten mainly in Europe, but Asian varieties range from orange to yellow, white, dark red, and purple, while fodder varieties are mostly larger and yellow to white. They are versatile vegetables, easily digested and nutritious; they contain large amounts of sugar and carotene (a source of vitamin A). Including carrots regularly in the diet improves vision, especially at night.

D. carota (wild carrot) p.116

PARTS USED Whole plant, seeds, oil.
PROPERTIES An aromatic herb that acts as a diuretic, soothes the digestive tract, and stimulates the uterus.
USES OF THE HERB
AROMATIC Oil has an orrislike scent and is used in perfumery.
MEDICINAL Internally for urinary stones, cystitis, gout (whole plant); edema, flatulent indigestion, menstrual problems (seeds).
ECONOMIC Oil is used in antiwrinkle creams.

D. c. subsp. *sativus* (carrot) p.117

PARTS USED Roots.
PROPERTIES A rich source of beta carotene, which improves eyesight and skin health, and has anticancer effects.
USES OF THE HERB
CULINARY Fresh carrots are used raw in salads (especially coleslaw), crushed for juice (especially in anticancer diets), or cooked as a vegetable.
ECONOMIC Processed as a source of carotene for food supplements.

D. visnaga. See *Ammi visnaga*.

GROWTH AND HARVEST
GROWTH Crop. Well-drained, fertile, alkaline soil in sun or partial shade. Propagate by seed sown in either spring, summer, or autumn. Carrot fly may damage the roots. Virus disease may cause chlorosis and twisting of the leaf stalks.
HARVEST Whole plants (*D. carota*) are cut in summer and dried for use in infusions and liquid extracts. Seeds are collected when ripe and dried for use in infusions or distilled for oil. Roots of *D. c.* subsp. *sativus* are harvested when young or mature.

DELPHINIUM
(Ranunculaceae)

D. staphisagria and the closely related *Consolida ajacis*, or larkspur, contain diterpene alkaloids, which are extremely poisonous and are rarely used by herbalists today. *D. staphisagria* was used as a parasiticide in Greek and Roman times.

D. staphisagria (stavesacre) p.117

PARTS USED Seeds.
PROPERTIES An acrid, bitter herb with potent insecticidal and parasiticidal effects.
USES OF THE HERB

GROWTH AND HARVEST
GROWTH Wild-collected. Well-drained, neutral to alkaline soil in sun. Propagate by seed sown in spring.
HARVEST Seeds are collected when ripe for use in lotions and ointments.
WARNING Harmful if eaten.

DENDRANTHEMA
Chrysanthemum
(Compositae/Asteraceae)

Florists' chrysanthemums were introduced to the West from China in the 18th century and rapidly became popular as ornamentals. In the East they have been valued for medicinal purposes since at least the first century AD. The edible chrysanthemum leaves featured in oriental cooking (commonly known as chop suey greens) are from *Chrysanthemum coronarium* (garland chrysanthemum, *shungiku*), an attractive, easily grown annual with spicy foliage and yellow flowers.

D. x *grandiflorum*, syn. *Chrysanthemum* x *morifolium* (florists' chrysanthemum, mulberry-leaved chrysanthemum) p.117

PARTS USED Flowers (*ju hua*).
PROPERTIES A bitter, aromatic herb that lowers fevers, soothes inflammation, dilates the coronary artery (increasing blood flow to the heart), and inhibits the growth of pathogens.
USES OF THE HERB
MEDICINAL Internally for hypertension, coronary artery disease, angina, feverish colds, and liver-related disorders.

GROWTH AND HARVEST
GROWTH Ornamental. Rich, well-drained soil in a sunny, sheltered position. Many cultivars require protection during the autumn and winter in cold areas. Propagate by cuttings in spring or early summer, or by seed in late winter at 70–75°F (21–24°C), or by basal softwood, or by cuttings in spring. Pinch out plants when 6–8in (15–20cm) tall to encourage sideshoots. *Botrytis*, mildew, blight, virus diseases, leafminer larvae, earwigs, aphids, slugs, snails, and nematodes may attack plants outdoors. Plants under cover are prone to whitefly, spider mite, and thrips.
HARVEST Flowers are gathered in late ►

► autumn and dried for use in infusions and tinctures. Steamed in China before drying to reduce bitterness.
WARNING Skin allergen.

DENDROBIUM
(Orchidaceae)

D. nobile has a very long history in Chinese medicine, dating back to at least 2000BC. It features in Taoist longevity formulas and is reputedly aphrodisiac. Known by its Korean name, *suk gok*, in the patent remedies market.

D. nobile p.117

PARTS USED Stems (*shi hu*).
PROPERTIES A mildly analgesic herb that lowers fever and acts as a tonic for the lungs and stomach. It also increases salivation.
USES OF THE HERB
MEDICINAL Internally for fever with vomiting and abdominal pain, dry cough, and complaints with symptoms such as dry mouth and severe thirst. Combined with *Glycyrrhiza uralensis* (see p.289) in tonic formulas.

GROWTH AND HARVEST
GROWTH Ornamental. Light position on tree branch or in orchid potting mix, with ample water and humidity during the growing season and a cool, dry, winter rest at minimum 41°F (5°C). Propagate by division in spring, or by seed or micropropagation in sterile laboratory conditions. Flower buds and new growths may be damaged by aphids.
HARVEST Stems are cut before flowering and dried for use in decoctions and tinctures.

DIANTHUS Pink
(Caryophyllaceae)

D. chinensis was first mentioned in Chinese medical texts during the Han dynasty (AD23–206). The first seeds of it were sent from China to Paris in 1705 under the name *Caryophyllus sinensis*. It remains widely used in China, though in Europe the medicinal applications of *D. caryophyllus* are now obsolete. Both *D. chinensis* and the closely related *D. superbus* (fringed pink) provide the Chinese drug *qu mai*, but the former species is more widely used.

D. caryophyllus (clove pink, carnation, gillyflower) p.117

PARTS USED Flowers, oil.
PROPERTIES An aromatic, stimulant herb that lowers fevers.
USES OF THE HERB
CULINARY Fresh flowers may be added to salads.
AROMATIC Flower heads are dried for potpourris.
MEDICINAL Internally, once used in tonic cordials to treat fevers, but now obsolete in medicine.
ECONOMIC Flowers are used mainly

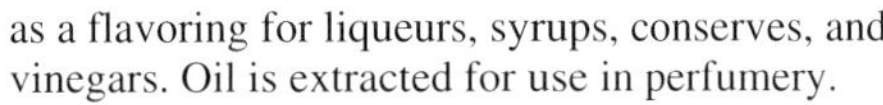

as a flavoring for liqueurs, syrups, conserves, and vinegars. Oil is extracted for use in perfumery.

D. chinensis (rainbow pink, Chinese pink) p.118

PARTS USED Whole plant (*qu mai*).
PROPERTIES A bitter, tonic herb that stimulates the digestive and urinary systems and bowels. It also lowers blood pressure, relieves fevers, and controls bacterial infections.
USES OF THE HERB
MEDICINAL Internally for acute urinary tract infections (especially cystitis), urinary stones, constipation, and failure to menstruate. Externally in Chinese medicine for skin inflammations and swellings.
VARIANT
D. c. **'Strawberry Parfait'**, p.118.

GROWTH AND HARVEST
GROWTH Ornamental. Well-drained, neutral to alkaline soil in full sun. Propagate by seed sown under cover in spring. Also (*D. caryophyllus*) by softwood cuttings in late spring, or by layering in late summer. May be affected by a number of diseases, especially when grown under cover, including *Botrytis*, *Fusarium* and *Verticillium* wilts, powdery mildew, and leaf and stem rots.
HARVEST Flowers of *D. caryophyllus* are picked after 3 hours' exposure to morning sunshine and used fresh for oil extraction, and culinary use, or dried for potpourris. Plants of *D. chinensis* are cut just before the flower buds open and dried for use in decoctions, pills, powders, and poultices.

DICTAMNUS Gas plant
(Rutaceae)

D. albus was first described in Chinese medical texts c.AD600, and it remains an important herb for dispelling pathogenic heat.

D. albus, syn. *D. dasycarpus*, *D. fraxinella* (gas plant, dittany, burning bush) p.118

PARTS USED Root bark (*bai xian pi*).
PROPERTIES A bitter, strong-smelling herb that lowers fever and controls bacterial and fungal infections.
USES OF THE HERB
MEDICINAL Internally and externally for skin diseases (especially scabies and eczema), German measles, arthritic pain, and jaundice. May be combined with *Sophora flavescens* (see p.355) as an external wash.
VARIANT
D. a. var. ***purpureus***, p.118.

GROWTH AND HARVEST
GROWTH Ornamental. Well-drained neutral to alkaline soil in sun. Propagate by seed sown under cover when ripe in late summer. Does not transplant well.
HARVEST Bark is peeled from roots lifted in autumn and dried for use in decoctions.
WARNING Skin irritant in sunlight.

DIGITALIS Foxglove
(Scrophulariaceae)

Foxgloves contain cardioactive glycosides, which vary from species to species and according to weather and site. *D. lanata* is a major source of digitoxin, digoxin, and gitoxin, while the glycosides in *D. purpurea* include digitoxin, gitoxin, and gitaloxin. (*D. grandiflora* and *D. lutea* have similar properties, but are seldom used.) Digoxin is the most rapidly excreted, and least cumulative. In pharmaceutical terms, "digitalis" refers to the powdered leaf of *D. purpurea*; it is used in the form of tablets or capsules for certain conditions. Leaves of *D. purpurea* are easily confused with those of comfrey (*Symphytum officinale*, see p.357), and have caused poisoning when accidentally included in herbal preparations. Digitalin is a standardized mixture of glycosides from *D. purpurea*, formerly used in solution for injection. Isolated glycosides are now used in preference to the whole herb, so that the dose can be more accurately monitored.

D. lanata (woolly foxglove) p.118

PARTS USED Leaves.
PROPERTIES A very bitter, diuretic herb that strengthens heart contractions.
USES OF THE HERB
MEDICINAL Internally for heart failure and irregular heart beat. Excess causes nausea, vomiting, slow pulse, visual disturbance, anorexia, and fainting.
WARNING This herb and *D. purpurea*, especially in the form of glycosides, are subject to legal restrictions in some countries.

GROWTH AND HARVEST
GROWTH Ornamental. Well-drained, neutral to acid soil in partial shade. Propagate by seed sown under cover in autumn. May develop crown rot and root rot in damp conditions.
HARVEST Leaves are picked before flowering and dried for commercial extraction of alkaloids.
WARNING All *Digitalis* species are toxic if eaten.

DIOSCOREA Yam
(Dioscoreaceae)

Many species contain steroidal saponins, used in the preparation of steroids by the pharmaceutical industry. Until the hormone was synthesized in 1970, *D. macrostachya* (Mexican yam) was the sole source of diosgenin for contraceptive pills. *D. opposita* contains allantoin, a cell proliferant also in *Symphytum officinale* (see p.357). Various yams are used in traditional medicine. *D. opposita*, *D. hypoglauca*, and *D. nipponica* are used in Chinese medicine for rheumatic, digestive, or urinary complaints. The N American *D. quaternata* has similar uses to *D. villosa*. Known as *aluka*, yams are also used in Ayurvedic medicine for sexual and hormonal problems, and hysteria.

D. opposita, syn. *D. batatas* (Chinese yam, cinnamon yam) p.119

PARTS USED Tubers (*shan yao*).
PROPERTIES A sweet, soothing herb that stimulates the stomach and spleen and has a tonic effect on the lungs and kidneys.
USES OF THE HERB
MEDICINAL Internally for poor appetite, chronic diarrhea, asthma, dry coughs, frequent or uncontrollable urination, diabetes, and emotional instability associated with *qi* deficiency. Externally for boils and abscesses.

D. villosa (colic root, wild yam, rheumatism root)

Perennial climber, hardy to 5°F (–15°C), height 15ft (5m), with slender rhizomes and pointed, heart-shaped ovate leaves up to 4in (10cm) long. Drooping axillary spikes of minute green-yellow flowers appear in the summer, with male and female borne separately. Found in moist woods, and along roads in N America.

PARTS USED Roots, rhizomes.
PROPERTIES An acrid, anti-inflammatory herb that relaxes spasms, stimulates bile flow, and dilates blood vessels.
USES OF THE HERB
MEDICINAL Internally for arthritis, colitis, irritable bowel syndrome, diverticulitis, gastritis (especially in alcoholics), gall bladder complaints, Crohn's disease, morning sickness, painful menstruation, ovarian and labor pains, bronchitis, excess mucus, asthma, whooping cough, and cramps. Used in homeopathy for colic (especially in babies).

GROWTH AND HARVEST
GROWTH Crop. Rich, well-drained soil in sun or partial shade. Propagate by seed sown in spring, or by division or sections of tubers in autumn or early spring. Tubers may rot in cool, damp conditions when dormant.
HARVEST Tubers, roots, and rhizomes are lifted in autumn. *D. opposita* is used raw or baked with flour or clay, according to the diagnosis. *D. villosa* is dried for use in liquid extracts, or used fresh for homeopathic preparations.

DIOSMA

D. crenulata. See *Agathosma crenulata.*

DIOSPYROS Persimmon

(Ebenaceae)

D. kaki was first recorded in Chinese medicine c.AD720. It is a renowned cure for hiccups, taken with clove (*Syzygium aromaticum*, see p.358) and fresh ginger (*Zingiber officinale*, see p.373). *D. kaki* is now grown as a commercial crop in southern Europe. The N American *D. virginiana* was used as an astringent by native peoples and was listed in the *U.S. Pharmacopoeia* (1820–82).

D. kaki (Chinese persimmon, Japanese persimmon, kaki) p.119

PARTS USED Calyces (*shi di*), fruits (including juice and powder, or "saccharum").
PROPERTIES An astringent, expectorant herb that checks bleeding and lowers blood pressure.
USES OF THE HERB
CULINARY Ripe fruits are eaten fresh or cooked in desserts, and used in making jam.
MEDICINAL Internally for hiccups, internal bleeding (calyx), bronchial complaints (dried ripe fruits), dry coughs (saccharum), high blood pressure (juice of unripe fruit), constipation, hemorrhoids (raw ripe fruit), and diarrhea (cooked ripe fruit).

GROWTH AND HARVEST
GROWTH Crop. Fertile, well-drained soil in sun. Propagate by seed sown in autumn, or by softwood cuttings in summer, or by rooted suckers, or by grafting. Remove crowded or badly placed growths and cut back leaders by one-third during dormancy. Plants grown outdoors may be damaged by thrips, mealybugs, scale insects, fruit flies, and fungal leafspots. Spider mites and whitefly may attack plants under cover. For successful fruiting, *D. kaki* requires one male tree to pollinate 8–10 female trees.
HARVEST Calyces are usually collected during flowering, and dried for decoctions. Fruits are gathered when unripe for juice, or ripe for using fresh, dried, or powdered as saccharum.

DIPTERYX

(Leguminosae)

Ten species of evergreen trees make up this tropical American genus. The seeds of *D. odorata* and other species, such as *D. oppositifolia*, contain coumarin (1–3 percent) and coumarin glycosides, which release the scent of sweet hay in the course of drying. *D. odorata* was grown in Victorian times to scent snuff, but the value of the species in perfumery has decreased since the discovery of synthetic coumarin in 1868. Medicinal uses are also largely discontinued following recent findings that coumarin may damage the heart and liver and cause cancer. The seeds are available dried for use in potpourris, but unfortunately cannot be germinated; like most rainforest seeds, they are viable for only a short time and have no dormant period. Most are collected from the wild in Venezuela or from cultivated trees in Trinidad, which are grown both in plantations and as a windbreak for cocoa trees. The name comes from the Greek *dis*, "double," and *pteron*, "wing," and refers to the winglike upper lobes of the calyx.

D. odorata, syn. *Coumarouna odorata* (tonka bean, tonquin bean)

Tender, compact rainforest tree, height 80–130ft (25–40m), spread 50–70ft (15–20m), with a trunk up to 3ft (1m) in diameter, and smooth, pale gray bark. The leathery, glossy, pinnate leaves have 3–6 elliptic leaflets up to 6in (15cm) long. Showy panicles of rose-violet, very fragrant pea flowers are followed by fleshy, pale yellow-brown, oval fruits up to 4in (10cm) long, each containing a single mahogany-colored seed 1¼–2in (3–5cm) long. Often found beside rivers, mainly in Venezuela and also in Colombia and the Guianas.

PARTS USED Seeds.
PROPERTIES An aromatic herb that improves the lasting qualities of perfumes.
USES OF THE HERB
MEDICINAL Formerly used to treat whooping cough.
ECONOMIC Now used as a flavoring for candy, cocoa, liqueurs, and medicinal preparations, such as cod liver oil (banned in some countries, including the US); a perfume fixative in potpourris and scented goods; aromatic ingredient in tobaccos and snuff.

GROWTH AND HARVEST
GROWTH Wild-collected. Well-drained, gravelly or sandy, acid soil, with ample rainfall and humidity, minimum 59–64°F (15–18°C). Propagate by fresh seed sown *in situ*, which takes about 6 weeks to germinate. Seedlings do not transplant well. Remove leading shoots of saplings when 6ft (2m) tall.
HARVEST Fallen ripe fruits are collected and dried to remove seeds, which are then cured by soaking in rum for 2–3 days. This process causes the coumarin to crystallize on the surface, known as "frosting."

DODONAEA

(Sapindaceae)

D. viscosa is used medicinally in many different countries, including Peru, Burma, India, Taiwan, S Africa, and by Aborigines in Australia. The leaves contain up to 18 percent tannin, comparable with amounts in *Potentilla erecta* (see p.334). In cases of toothache, the leaves are apparently effective if chewed, without swallowing the juice.

D. viscosa (sticky hop bush, native hops) p.119

PARTS USED Leaves.
PROPERTIES A strongly astringent herb that lowers fever and relieves pain.
USES OF THE HERB
MEDICINAL Internally for fevers. Externally for pain relief of toothache, sore throat, wounds, and stings.
VARIANT
D. v. **'Purpurea'**, p.119.

GROWTH AND HARVEST
GROWTH Ornamental. Well-drained soil in sun, minimum 37–41°F (3–5°C). Propagate by seed sown in spring, or by semiripe cuttings in late summer. Cut back in spring, and again in late summer if necessary, to maintain shape.
HARVEST Leaves are picked in summer and used fresh for gargles and poultices or dried for infusions.

DOREMA
(Umbelliferae)

Sixteen species of short-lived, large-leaved perennials and subshrubs belong to this genus occurring in central and southwestern Asia. All are monocarpic. *D. ammoniacum* is listed in Victorian gardening manuals as "of easy culture" and "increased readily by seed." This imposing umbellifer would make an interesting feature in the herb garden, but it seems to have disappeared from cultivation. *D. ammoniacum* was named after the temple of Ammon, because the gum resin was first extracted from plants in this area of Libya, its use being mentioned by Hippocrates in the first century AD. The gum resin exudes naturally from holes in the stems caused by beetles.

D. ammoniacum (ammoniac, gum ammoniac)

Giant perennial, hardy to 23°F (–5°C), height 6–10ft (2–3m), spread 3–5ft (1–1.5m), with branched, hairy stems, woody at the base and 1¼–2½in (3–6cm) in diameter. It has large, divided leaves and umbels of small white flowers in spring and summer, followed by elliptic seeds about ¼in (7mm) long. Found in dry, rocky areas from Iran to Afghanistan and Pakistan.

PARTS USED Gum resin.
PROPERTIES A strong-smelling, acrid, stimulant herb that has expectorant effects, relaxes spasms, and increases perspiration.
USES OF THE HERB
MEDICINAL Internally for chronic bronchitis, asthma, and excess mucus. Externally for swollen joints and indolent tumors.
ECONOMIC Formerly used in perfumery and in porcelain cement.

GROWTH AND HARVEST
GROWTH Crop. Well-drained to dry soil in sun. Propagate by seed sown in autumn or spring.
HARVEST Gum resin is collected from incisions in stems and leaf stalks during the flowering and fruiting periods. It is solidified into "tears" or blocks before grinding into powder.

DRIMIA
(Liliaceae/Hyacinthaceae)

D. maritima is cultivated for the drug industry in various Mediterranean countries, including Egypt and Turkey. Bulbs are harvested after six years, with a yield of about 10,000 bulbs per acre (25,000 per hectare). *D. maritima* contains scillarin, which affects the heart. It is known in the trade as "white squill" or "red squill," depending on the color of the bulb, which varies across the area of distribution. Although similar in constituents, only red bulbs contain the rat poison scilliroside, which has the interesting property of poisoning only rodents (other animals vomit). *D. indica* (Indian squill) is another source of scillarin. Squill is often given as "squill vinegar," a preparation described by Dioscorides.

D. maritima, syn. *Urginea maritima* (squill, sea onion) p.119

PARTS USED Bulbs.
PROPERTIES A bitter, acrid, very poisonous herb that has diuretic and expectorant effects, stimulates the heart, and acts as a tonic for the scalp.
USES OF THE HERB
MEDICINAL Internally for bronchitis, bronchitic asthma, whooping cough, and edema. Large doses are emetic. For use by qualified practitioners only. Externally for dandruff and seborrhea.
ECONOMIC Extracts are added to cough mixtures and hair tonics. Once used in rat poison.

GROWTH AND HARVEST
GROWTH Ornamental. Free-draining, sandy or stony soil in sun, minimum 19°F (–7°C), with bulb partly above surface. Propagate by seed sown in autumn, or by offsets in late summer, when bulbs are dormant.
HARVEST Bulbs are lifted in late autumn, sliced transversely, and dried for use in infusions, liquid extracts, squill vinegar, and tinctures.

DRIMYS Pepper tree
(Winteraceae)

D. winteri was first described as a medicinal herb by Captain John Winter, on Sir Francis Drake's voyage around the world (1577–80); he introduced it to Europe from S America in 1578. It was apparently "very powerful against the scurvy," caused by lack of vitamin C and a common complaint on long voyages. The bark is no longer used for this, but is recognized as having similar effects on the digestive system to both *Canella winterana* (see p.253) and *Cinnamomum zeylanicum* (see p.261), though less commonly available. Commercial supplies of Winter's bark may also include bark from *D.granadensis* and *Cinnamodendron corticosum* (false Winter's bark). The closely related *Tasmannia lanceolata* (pepper tree, mountain pepper) is the only other species in common cultivation. It is an Australasian shrub with aromatic, edible berries. It is widely grown as a hedge in mild temperate regions.

D. winteri (Winter's bark) p.120

PARTS USED Bark.
PROPERTIES A pungent, bitter, tonic herb that relieves indigestion. It resembles *Acorus calamus* (see p.228) in aroma.
USES OF THE HERB
MEDICINAL Internally for indigestion and colic.

GROWTH AND HARVEST
GROWTH Ornamental. Moist, fertile, well-drained soil in sun or partial shade. In cold areas plants need the protection of a wall or any other sheltered position. Propagate by seed sown in autumn, or by semiripe cuttings in summer.
HARVEST Bark is removed from branches in autumn and winter, and dried for powders and infusions.

DROSERA Sundew
(Droseraceae)

D. rotundifolia has a long history of use in medicine. William Turner wrote in 1568 that "Our Englishmen nowadays set very much faith by it, and hold it good for consumptions and swooning, and faintness of the harte" (*A New Herball*, 1551–68). A sundew liqueur, known as *Rosa Solis*, was popular in Britain, France, and Germany during the 17th century for its reputedly fortifying and aphrodisiac effects.

D. rotundifolia (round-leaved sundew, *rosée du soleil*, dewplant) p.120

PARTS USED Whole plant.
PROPERTIES An acrid, warming, soothing herb that has diuretic and expectorant effects, relaxes spasms, and controls coughing. It contains pigments that are active against a wide range of pathogens.
USES OF THE HERB
MEDICINAL Internally for asthma, whooping cough, bronchitis, influenza, gastritis, and gastric ulcer. Combined with *Grindelia camporum* (see p.290), *Euphorbia hirta* (see p.281), and *Polygala senega* (see p.332) for asthma. In homeopathy for whooping cough, dry coughs, sore throat, and laryngitis. Imparts a dark color to the urine.

GROWTH AND HARVEST
GROWTH Ornamental. Wet peat in sun. Propagate by seed sown in spring, by division in spring, or by leaf cuttings with base in summer.
HARVEST Plants are collected as flowering begins and dried for use in infusions, liquid extracts, and tinctures.

DRYOBALANOPS
(Dipterocarpaceae)

Camphor is an aromatic, crystalline substance that forms in cavities in the trunks of trees such as *D. aromatica* and *Cinnamomum camphora* (see p.261). Young trees produce a clear yellow liquid, known as "oil of camphor," which sometimes crystallizes in older specimens.

D. aromatica (Borneo camphor, borneol) p.120

PARTS USED Crystallized exudate, oil.
PROPERTIES A bitter, pungent, stimulant herb that relieves pain, lowers fever, relaxes spasms, and reduces inflammation. It also has antibacterial effects.
USES OF THE HERB
MEDICINAL Internally for fainting, convulsions associated with high fever, cholera, and pneumonia. Externally for rheumatism, ringworm, abscesses, boils, cold sores, mouth ulcers, sore throat, chest infections, and conjunctivitis. Used in aromatherapy internally and externally as an antiseptic, sedative, and tonic for the heart and adrenal cortex, mainly in skin problems, rheumatism, infectious diseases, depression, and convalescence.
ECONOMIC Source of *d*-borneol, a volatile oil used in perfumes with a camphoraceous note. Wood is valued for resistance to termites.

GROWTH AND HARVEST

GROWTH Crop. Well-drained, moist soil in sun or partial shade, with high humidity, minimum 59–64°F (15–18°C). Propagate by seed when ripe.
HARVEST Camphor crystals are collected from fissures in trunk; oil of camphor by tapping young trees or by distillation of wood. Both crystals and oil are used in capsules, infusions, lotions, pills, powders, and rubbing oils.

DRYOPTERIS Buckler fern
(Dryopteridaceae)

A number of species contain phloroglucinol derivatives ("filicin"), which paralyze intestinal parasites. In addition to *D. filix-mas*, *D. cristata* (crested field fern or buckler fern), *D. oreades* (dwarf male fern), and *D. crassirhizoma* are used. Drugs derived from these ferns are used in conjunction with an effective purgative. *D. crassirhizoma* has been recorded in Chinese medicine since at least the later Han dynasty (AD25–220). Known as *guan zhong*, it also reduces inflammation, controls bleeding, and lowers fever.

D. filix-mas, syn. *Aspidium filix-mas* (male fern) p.120

PARTS USED Rhizomes.
PROPERTIES A bitter, unpleasant-tasting herb that expels intestinal worms and has antibacterial and antiviral effects. It also controls bleeding, relieves pain, reduces inflammation, and lowers fever.
USES OF THE HERB
MEDICINAL Internally for all intestinal parasites, liver flukes, internal hemorrhage, uterine bleeding, mumps, and feverish illnesses (including colds, influenza, measles, pneumonia, and meningitis). Doses for intestinal worms are critical; poisoning is prevented by combining with a saline purgative, such as magnesium sulfate – not castor oil, which increases absorption. Excess causes nausea and vomiting, delirium, breathing difficulties, and heart failure. Externally for abscesses, boils, carbuncles, and sores. For use by qualified practitioners only. WARNING This herb is subject to legal restrictions in some countries.
VARIANTS
D. f.-m. **'Crispa Cristata'**, p.120.
D. f.-m. **'Linearis'**, p.121.

GROWTH AND HARVEST

GROWTH Ornamental. Humus-rich soil in shade. Propagates by spores in early spring, or by division in autumn or spring. Variants do not come true from spores. Foliage may be affected by rust.
HARVEST Rhizomes are lifted in autumn, leaving bases of fronds but removing roots, and are dried for use in liquid extracts and powders. Stocks are renewed annually.

DUBOISIA
(Solanaceae)

D. myoporoides and the related *D. leichardtii* provide the main source of tropane alkaloids for the pharmaceutical industry. These include atropine, hyoscine, hyoscyamine, and scopolamine, which occur in other members of the nightshade family, such as *Atropa belladonna* (see p.246), *Hyoscyamus niger* (see p.295), and *Scopolia carniolica* (see p.350). In Australia, hybrids between *D. myoporoides* and *D. leichardtii* have been developed that yield over three percent total alkaloids.

D. myoporoides (corkwood, cork tree, eyeplant) p.121

PARTS USED Leaves.
PROPERTIES A bitter, hypnotic herb that dilates the pupils, stimulates respiration, and acts as a sedative.
USES OF THE HERB
MEDICINAL In homeopathy for eye complaints. For use by qualified practitioners only. WARNING This herb and *D. leichardtii* are subject to legal restrictions in some countries.
ECONOMIC A source of pharmaceutical alkaloids.

GROWTH AND HARVEST

GROWTH Crop. Sandy soil in sun with high humidity, minimum 59–64°F (15–18°C). Propagate by seed sown when ripe. Trim plants regularly to control size.
HARVEST Leaves are collected during the flowering season and dried for processing.
WARNING All parts are toxic if eaten.

DULACIA
(Olacaceae)

Thirteen species of tropical trees and shrubs belong to this S American genus. Little is known about *D. inopiflora*, though it has a long history of use in the Amazonian region. The active constituents are reported to include an alkaloid and sterols.

D. inopiflora, syn. *Liriosma ovata* (*muira-puama, marapuama*, potentwood)

Tender tree, height 30–50ft (10–15m), spread 10–15ft (3–5m), with gray, fissured trunk and oblong, rather leathery, dark brown leaves. Tiny white flowers are followed by orange-yellow fruits. Found in Amazonian rainforests.

PARTS USED Roots, bark, wood, balsam.
PROPERTIES A spicy, warming, astringent herb that has aphrodisiac and stimulant effects, probably acting mainly on the kidney energy.
USES OF THE HERB
MEDICINAL Internally for impotence and diarrhea.

GROWTH AND HARVEST

GROWTH Wild-collected. Moist soil in shade, minimum 60–65°F (15–18°C). This species does not appear to be in cultivation.
HARVEST Roots, bark, wood, and balsam are collected for liquid extracts.

ECBALLIUM
(Cucurbitaceae)

E. elaterium has been used medicinally since Classical times. Theophrastus mentioned the root as a cure for mange in sheep, and the fruit extract was recommended as an emetic. It contains cucurbitacins.

E. elaterium, syn. *Momordica elateria* (squirting cucumber) p.121

PARTS USED Fruits.
PROPERTIES A purgative herb that causes evacuation of water from the bowels.
USES OF THE HERB
MEDICINAL Internally for edema associated with kidney complaints, rheumatism, paralysis, and shingles. Excess causes irritation to the stomach and bowels, and may be fatal. Externally for sinusitis and painful joints. For use by qualified practitioners only. WARNING This herb is subject to legal restrictions in some countries.

GROWTH AND HARVEST

GROWTH Crop. Well-drained to poor soil in sun. Propagate by seed sown in spring at 61°F (16°C). Subject to statutory control as a weed in some countries, notably in parts of Australia.
HARVEST Fruits are picked underripe and left in containers until contents are expelled. Juice is then dried in flakes to be used as the drug elaterium.
WARNING Toxic if eaten. Repeated handling of seeds and other parts may cause poisoning. Ripe fruits eject contents forcibly and may cause injuries, especially to the eyes.

ECHINACEA Coneflower
(Compositae/Asteraceae)

E. purpurea is one of several species, including *E. angustifolia* and *E. pallida*, used by native N Americans, mainly to treat wounds. In particular, the Plains tribes regarded *E. angustifolia* as a cure-all, and it was listed in the U.S. *National Formulary* (1916–50). These three species have similar constituents and are used interchangeably. *E. purpurea* is the most widely used, being much more easily cultivated. It is now considered the most effective detoxicant in Western medicine for the circulatory, lymphatic, and respiratory systems, and has been adopted by Ayurvedic practitioners. Research into this species followed the import of seed by the German herbal company Madaus in 1939.

E. purpurea (purple coneflower, purple echinacea) p.121

PARTS USED Roots, rhizomes.
PROPERTIES A bitter, slightly aromatic, alterative herb that stimulates the immune system, promotes

healing, and has antiviral and antibacterial effects.
USES OF THE HERB
MEDICINAL Internally for skin diseases, fungal infections, septicemia, gangrene, boils, abscesses, slow-healing wounds, upper respiratory tract infections, and venereal diseases; excess causes throat irritation. Externally for herpes, acne, psoriasis, and infected injuries. Often combined with *Hypericum perforatum* (see p.295) for herpes, with *Arctium lappa* (see p.240) for boils, and with *Baptisia tinctoria* (see p.247) or *Commiphora myrrha* (see p.265) for throat infections.
VARIANTS
***E. p.* 'Robert Bloom'**, p.121.
***E. p.* 'White Swan'**, p.122.

GROWTH AND HARVEST
GROWTH Ornamental. Rich, well-drained soil in sun. Propagate by seed sown in spring, or by root cuttings in late winter, or by division when dormant.
HARVEST Roots and rhizomes are lifted in autumn and dried for use in decoctions, infusions, liquid extracts, powders, tablets, and tinctures.

ECLIPTA
(Compositae)

E. prostrata is regarded as the best remedy for the hair in Ayurvedic medicine and is also widely used as a rejuvenative and liver tonic. Traditional Chinese medicine describes it as a good general tonic for liver and kidney *yin*, for which purpose it is often combined with *Centella asiatica* (see p.257). The plant yields thiophene derivatives that are used in preparations to destroy bodily nematodes.

E. prostrata, syn. *E. alba* (false daisy, *bhringaraja*) p.122

PARTS USED Whole plant (*han lian cao*).
PROPERTIES A bitter, sweet and sour, cooling herb that has a tonic effect on the circulatory, nervous, and digestive systems, and checks bleeding.
USES OF THE HERB
MEDICINAL Internally for kidney and liver weakness (manifesting as tinnitus, premature graying of hair, poor teeth and eyesight, nervous disorders), cirrhosis, hepatitis, complaints involving bleeding (especially postpartum and abnormal uterine bleeding), anemia, and diphtheria. Used in Chinese folk medicine for eczema, athlete's foot, dermatitis, and child malnutrition; in Ayurvedic medicine, both internally and externally as an oil, for hair loss. Externally, combined with *Senna obtusifolia* in an oil for ringworm (India, Burma).
ECONOMIC Source of a black dye used as a hair dye and in tattooing.

GROWTH AND HARVEST
GROWTH Crop. Damp to wet soil in shade, minimum 50–59°F (10–15°C). Propagate by seed sown in spring.
HARVEST Whole plants are cut when flowering and dried for use in decoctions, infusions, medicated oil, powders, and tinctures.

ELETTARIA
(Zingiberaceae)

There are several varieties of cardamom and many other *Elettaria* species that produce similar fruits, all varying in flavor and appearance. True cardamom seeds have a eucalyptus-like aroma, which deteriorates rapidly when ground, while substitutes often have a strong, camphoraceous odor. *E. cardamomum* was first mentioned as a medicinal plant in China c.AD720. True cardamom plants are difficult to find in the US. Plants sold as *E. cardamomum* are often in fact a species of *Afromomum*; they rarely flower or set seed but they do have fragrant leaves.

E. cardamomum (cardamom) p.122

PARTS USED Seeds, oil.
PROPERTIES A pungent, warm, aromatic herb that has stimulating, tonic effects, especially on the lungs and kidneys. It relaxes spasms, is expectorant, and improves digestion. Reputedly detoxifies caffeine and counteracts mucus-forming foods, such as dairy products.
USES OF THE HERB
CULINARY Seeds are used to flavor bakery products (especially in northern Europe), coffee (Middle East), curries, pickles, milk-based desserts, fruit compotes, and mulled wine.
AROMATIC Essential oil is important in perfumery.
MEDICINAL Internally for indigestion, nausea and vomiting, enuresis, and pulmonary disease with copious phlegm. Used in Ayurvedic medicine for bronchial and digestive complaints. WARNING This herb, as a tincture, is subject to legal restrictions in some countries.

GROWTH AND HARVEST
GROWTH Crop. Rich, moist, well-drained soil in partial shade, minimum 64°F (18°C). Propagate by seed sown in autumn, or by division in spring or summer. Plants grown under cover may suffer from spider mite.
HARVEST Fruits are collected during the dry season and dried whole; seeds are removed for oil extraction or used in liquid extracts, powders, and tinctures.

ELEUTHEROCOCCUS
(Araliaceae)

The active constituents of *E. senticosus* are similar in effect to those of *Panax* species (see p.321), but stronger. Several related species, together with *E. senticosus*, are known in Chinese medicine as *wu jia pi*. They have been used for rheumatic complaints, low vitality, and weak liver and kidney energy for 2,000 years, and are regarded as less heating than *Panax ginseng* (see p.321).

E. senticosus, syn. *Acanthopanax senticosus* (Siberian ginseng, *eleuthero*) p.122

PARTS USED Roots, root bark.
PROPERTIES A pungent, bitter-sweet, warming herb that stimulates the immune and circulatory systems, regulates blood pressure, lowers blood sugar, and reduces inflammation. It is adaptogenic, having a tonic effect on all organs.
USES OF THE HERB
MEDICINAL Internally for convalescence, menopausal complaints, geriatric debility, physical and mental stress, and insomnia caused by prolonged anxiety. Used in the background treatment of cancer and exposure to toxic chemicals and radiation, and to improve resistance to infection. Not given to children, or taken for longer than three weeks at a time. Contraindicated with caffeine.

GROWTH AND HARVEST
GROWTH Crop. Well-drained, rich, moist soil in sun or partial shade. Propagate by seed sown in spring or autumn (needs stratification), or by root cuttings in late summer, or by hardwood cuttings, 6–12in (15–30cm) long, in autumn.
HARVEST Roots are lifted in autumn and dried whole or decorticated. Both roots and root bark are used in decoctions, powders, teas, and tinctures.

ELYMUS
(Gramineae/Poaceae)

Couch grass (*E. repens*) is a most useful medicinal herb, included in many preparations for the treatment of prostatitis. It is a gentle, well-tolerated remedy with no side effects.

E. repens, syn. *Agropyron repens* (couch grass, quack grass, twitch) p.122

PARTS USED Rhizomes.
PROPERTIES A soothing herb that improves excretion from kidneys and bowels, lowers blood cholesterol levels, and clears infection.
USES OF THE HERB
MEDICINAL Internally for kidney and bladder complaints (especially enlarged prostate and cystitis), gout, and rheumatism. Combines well with *Agathosma* spp. (see p.230) for cystitis and *Hydrangea arborescens* (see p.294) for prostatitis.

GROWTH AND HARVEST
GROWTH Crop. Most soils in sun or shade. Light, sandy soils give highest yields of rhizomes. Propagate by division in autumn or spring. *E. repens* is extremely invasive and difficult to eradicate. It should be grown in containers and not allowed to seed.
HARVEST Rhizomes are dug in spring and used fresh in homeopathic preparations or dried for use in decoctions, liquid extracts, and tinctures.

EOPEPON

E. vitifolius. See *Trichosanthes kirilowii.*

EPHEDRA Joint fir

(Ephedraceae)

Ephedra species contain alkaloids, notably ephedrine, that are included in many patent medicines for excess mucus and asthma. Species used include *E. equisetina*, *E. intermedia*, the Indian *E. gerardiana*, and *E. sinica*, which usually has a higher alkaloid content. The Chinese name *ma huang* is now used for any of these species. Recent research has shown antiviral effects, notably against influenza. The American *E. trifurca* (Mormon or Brigham tea) is diuretic rather than antiasthmatic. A similar stimulant to ephedrine, norpseudoephedrine or cathine, which is used in geriatric medicine, is found in *Catha edulis* (khat, kat) in southwest Arabia and Ethiopia.

E. distachya (joint fir, *ma huang*, shrubby horsetail) p.122

PARTS USED Stems.
PROPERTIES A pungent, bitter, warm herb that dilates the bronchial vessels, stimulates the heart and central nervous system, is diuretic, and increases perspiration.
USES OF THE HERB
MEDICINAL Internally for asthma, hay fever, and allergic complaints; Chinese *ma huang* is used for kidney weakness, and combined with *Prunus dulcis* (see p.335) for asthma, *Cinnamomum cassia* (see p.261) for colds, and *Mentha arvensis* (see p.311) for allergies. Used in Ayurvedic medicine for arthritis and edema. Often combined with *Thymus vulgaris* (see p.362), *Primula veris* (see p.334), *Marrubium vulgare* (see p.308), or *Hyssopus officinalis* (see p.295) for asthma and serious bronchial complaints, and with *Urtica dioica* (see p.366) or *Chamaemelum nobile* (see p.259) for allergic reactions. For use by qualified practitioners only. Not given to patients taking monoamine oxidase (MAO) inhibitors or suffering from high blood pressure, glaucoma, or hyperthyroidism. WARNING *Ephedra* species are subject to legal restrictions in some countries.

GROWTH AND HARVEST
GROWTH Crop. Well-drained to dry soil in sun. Propagate by seed sown in autumn, or by division in autumn or spring.
HARVEST Stems are collected at any time and dried for use in powders, decoctions, tinctures, or liquid extracts.

EPIGAEA

(Ericaceae)

Native N Americans made a leaf tea from *E. repens* to treat kidney disorders and purify the blood. The Shakers used it for "gravel" (kidney stones), hence its name "gravel plant." It is used by herbalists today in much the same way as *Agathosma* (see p.230) and *Arctostaphylos uva-ursi* species (see p.241).

E. repens (trailing arbutus, Mayflower) p.123

PARTS USED Whole plant.
PROPERTIES An astringent, diuretic herb.
USES OF THE HERB
MEDICINAL Internally for cystitis, kidney stones, and kidney and urinary tract infections.

GROWTH AND HARVEST
GROWTH Ornamental. Moist, acid, humus-rich soil in cool shade. Propagate by seed sown in autumn, or by softwood cuttings in summer, or by division of clumps in autumn.
HARVEST Plants are cut in summer and dried for use in infusions, liquid extracts, and tinctures.

EPIMEDIUM

(Berberidaceae)

E. sagittatum was first described as a medicinal herb in the *Shen Nong Canon of Herbs* (written AD25–220).

E. sagittatum (horny goat weed, barrenwort) p.123

PARTS USED Whole plant (*yin yang huo*).
PROPERTIES A pungent, sweet herb that acts mainly as an aphrodisiac and as a tonic to liver and kidneys. It dilates blood vessels, lowers blood pressure, controls coughing, and is expectorant.
USES OF THE HERB
MEDICINAL Internally for asthma, bronchitis, cold or numb extremities, arthritis, lumbago, impotence, involuntary and premature ejaculation, high blood pressure, and absent-mindedness. Excess causes vomiting, dizziness, thirst, and nosebleed.
ECONOMIC An ingredient of Chinese "spring wine."

GROWTH AND HARVEST
GROWTH Ornamental. Moist, well-drained, rich soil in partial shade. Propagate by seed sown in late summer, or by division in spring or autumn. Cut back before new growth appears in spring. Young shoots are damaged by frost.
HARVEST Whole plants are cut in the growing season and dried for decoctions.

EQUISETUM Horsetail

(Equisetaceae)

Horsetails have an unusual chemistry, containing alkaloids (including nicotine) and various minerals. They are rich in silica, giving abrasive properties that were used from the Middle Ages until the 18th century for scouring pots and pans, especially pewter. The Dutch rush (*E. hyemale*) was once exported from the Netherlands, where it grows abundantly, for this purpose. Certain horsetails concentrate gold in their tissues (although not sufficient to warrant extraction) and are useful indicators for gold prospectors.

E. arvense (field horsetail, bottlebrush, shave grass) p.123

PARTS USED Stems.
PROPERTIES An astringent, healing herb that acts mainly on the genitourinary system and controls both internal and external bleeding.
USES OF THE HERB
MEDICINAL Internally for prostatitis, incontinence, cystitis, and urethritis. Often used with *Hydrangea arborescens* (see p.294) for prostate problems. Internally and externally for hemorrhage. An irritant, best combined with demulcent herbs, and restricted to short-term use.

E. hyemale (Dutch rush, rough horsetail) p.123

PARTS USED Stems (*mu zei*).
PROPERTIES A bittersweet, astringent herb that has diuretic and anti-inflammatory effects.
USES OF THE HERB
MEDICINAL Internally in traditional Chinese medicine for cataracts, conjunctivitis, and sore or watering eyes related to feverish colds. Often combined with *Dendranthema* x *grandiflorum* (see p.272) to treat eye problems associated with the liver meridian. Also used internally in Ayurvedic medicine for kidney, gall bladder, and urinary problems, venereal diseases, and fractures.

GROWTH AND HARVEST
GROWTH Crop (*E. arvense*). Ornamental (*E. hyemale*). Moist soil in sun or partial shade. Propagate by division in early spring. Horsetails are invasive and difficult to eradicate. *Equisetum* species are subject to statutory control as a weed in parts of Australia.
HARVEST Stems are cut at any time during the growing season and dried for use in decoctions, infusions, liquid extracts, and powders.

ERIGERON

E. canadensis. See *Conyza canadensis.*

ERIOBOTRYA

(Rosaceae)

E. japonica is the most popular cough remedy in the Far East and is used in many patent remedies, such as loquat leaf jelly.

E. japonica (loquat, Japanese medlar, *nispero*) p.123

PARTS USED Leaves (*pi pa ye*), fruits.
PROPERTIES A bitter, expectorant herb that controls coughing and vomiting; it is effective against bacterial and viral infections (leaves).
USES OF THE HERB
CULINARY Fruit is eaten raw or made into jam or jellies.
MEDICINAL Internally for bronchitis, coughs with feverish colds, nausea, vomiting, hiccups, and persistent burping.

GROWTH AND HARVEST
GROWTH Ornamental. Good, well-drained soil in sun. Propagate by seed sown in autumn or ►

► spring, or by softwood cuttings in summer. Trim shoots in spring.
HARVEST Leaves are picked as required and, after hairs have been removed (to prevent irritation of the throat), used fresh or dried in decoctions, or made into jelly. Fruits are harvested in late spring when ripe.

ERIODICTYON
(Hydrophyllaceae)

Eight species of woolly or sticky evergreen shrubs make up this genus, which occurs in southwestern N America and Mexico. The name comes from the Greek *erion*, "wool," and *dictyon*, "net," referring to the white hairs and network of veins on the leaf undersides. *E. californicum* is most important in the traditional medicine of Mendocino County, California. Rich in flavonoids and resin, it was revered as a holy herb (*yerba santa*) and was found in every household medicine chest. Spanish missionaries learned its uses from the native N Americans and it was listed in the *U.S. Pharmacopoeia* (1894–1905) and (1916–47), after which it entered the U.S. *National Formulary* as an expectorant.

E. californicum (*yerba santa*, wild balsam, gum leaves, tar weed, mountain balm)

Tender shrub, height 8ft (2.5m), spread 6ft (2m), with lanceolate leaves that have resinous upper surfaces, white, woolly undersides, and wavy or toothed margins. Clusters of 5-lobed, funnel-shaped lilac to white flowers, about ½in (1cm) long, appear in summer, followed by 4-valved capsules.

PARTS USED Leaves.
PROPERTIES An aromatic, pleasant-tasting, tonic herb that reduces spasms, expels phlegm, and lowers fever.
USES OF THE HERB
MEDICINAL Internally for asthma, bronchitis, laryngitis, sinusitis, and hay fever. An ingredient in patent cough mixtures; added to bitter medicines to improve the taste. Smoked by native N Americans for asthma and chewed for mouth hygiene.

GROWTH AND HARVEST
GROWTH Wild-collected. Sandy soil in dry, sunny conditions, minimum 41–45°F (5–7°C). Propagate by seed sown in spring or autumn. If required, trim to shape in spring or summer, cutting into new or one-year-old wood only.
HARVEST Leaves are picked in summer and dried for use in infusions and liquid extracts.

ERUCA Rocket
(Cruciferae/Brassicaceae)

Rocket was once used medicinally but is now known only as a salad herb. Dioscorides wrote in *De Materia Medica libri quinque* (first century AD) that "This being eaten raw in any great quantitie doth provoke Venery, and the seed of it also doth work ye like effect, being ureticall and digestive, and good for ye belly. They doe also use the seed of it in making Sawces."

E. vesicaria subsp. *sativa* (rocket, arugula, rucola) p.123

PARTS USED Leaves.
PROPERTIES A bitter, pungent, tonic herb with a peppery flavor.
USES OF THE HERB
CULINARY Mainly as a salad herb, notably in *mesclun*, a traditional mixed salad of tiny leaves from the Nice area of France. May also be added to stir-fries and pasta sauces. Flowers, seeds, and oil are also edible.

GROWTH AND HARVEST
GROWTH Crop. Most soils in sun. Leaves from plants grown in cool, moist, rich soil are more tender and less pungent than those from plants in hot, dry ground. Propagate by seed sown in succession from late winter to early summer. Leaves may be damaged by flea beetles.
HARVEST Leaves are picked before the flowering stem appears, when they are less pungent than those picked later.

ERYNGIUM
(Umbelliferae/Apiaceae)

Several species are used medicinally in various parts of the world: the N American *E. aquaticum* (button snakeroot) and *E. yuccifolium* (rattlesnake master), used mainly for disorders of the kidneys and sexual organs; *E. planum*, from eastern Europe, used in Transylvania for whooping cough; and the European *E. campestre* (field eryngo), which can be substituted for *E. maritimum*, taken for urinary tract infections, skin complaints, and whooping cough. The roots of *E. maritimum* were collected on a large scale in England during the 17th and 18th centuries for candying as restorative, quasi-aphrodisiac lozenges, known as "eryngoes." Old records of Colchester in eastern England show that it was famous for "oysters and eringo root."

E. foetidum, syn. *E. antihystericum* (culantro, fitweed, perennial coriander) p.124

PARTS USED Leaves, roots.
PROPERTIES A pungent, aromatic herb that lowers fever, relaxes spasms, and benefits the digestion.
USES OF THE HERB
CULINARY Important in Latin American cuisine and increasingly used in SE Asia in soups, curries, and rice and fish dishes. Flavor similar to that of *Coriandrum sativum* (see p.267), but stronger.
MEDICINAL In Carib medicine as a cure-all, and, specifically for epilepsy, high blood pressure, and fevers, fits, and chills in children.

E. maritimum (sea holly, eryngo) p.124

PARTS USED Roots.
PROPERTIES A sweet, mucilaginous herb that is diuretic, anti-inflammatory, and expectorant.
USES OF THE HERB
CULINARY Sometimes made into a conserve and used to flavor jellies and toffee.
MEDICINAL Internally for urinary infections, especially cystitis, urethritis, excessive urine production (as in diabetes), prostate complaints, and renal colic.

GROWTH AND HARVEST
GROWTH Crop (*E. foetidum*). Ornamental (*E. maritimum*). Damp, heavy soil in sun or shade (*E. foetidum*), minimum 59–64°F (15–18°C); well-drained, sandy or stony soil in sun (*E. maritimum*). Propagate by seed sown in spring, or by root cuttings in late winter. *E. maritimum* is best sown in autumn or stratified for 4 weeks before sowing in spring.
HARVEST Leaves (*E. foetidum*) are picked before flowering; roots of 2nd-year plants are lifted in autumn and used fresh for flavoring, and fresh or dried in infusions and decoctions. Roots of *E. maritimum* are lifted in autumn and used fresh for conserves, or dried for use in powders, decoctions, and flavorings.

ERYSIMUM

E. officinale. See *Sisymbrium officinale*.

ERYTHRAEA

E. centaurium. See *Centaurium erythraea*.

ERYTHROXYLUM
(Erythroxylaceae)

E. coca and several other species, such as *E. cataractacum* and *E. novogranatense*, contain tropane alkaloids. The most important is cocaine, first extracted in 1860, but this has now been largely replaced by synthetic derivatives. *E. coca* has an ancient history of use as a medicinal, psychoactive, and ritual plant, featuring in the origin myths of several S American tribes. The use of powdered dried leaves, mixed with the ashes of other plants as a stimulant, was first recorded c.AD500.

E. coca (coca) p.124

PARTS USED Leaves.
PROPERTIES A bitter, locally anesthetic herb that stimulates the central nervous system.
USES OF THE HERB
MEDICINAL Externally in preparations for eczema, nettle rash, hemorrhoids, facial neuralgia, and as a local anesthetic in surgery (cocaine). Combined with morphine (see *Papaver somniferum*, p.322) as a "Brompton cocktail" to

relieve pain in the terminally ill; for use by qualified practitioners only. Fresh or dried powdered leaves are held in the mouth (not chewed or swallowed) in countries of origin to relieve fatigue and hunger. Excess or persistent use of cocaine (but not coca) causes tremors, convulsions, loss of memory, delusions, hyperactivity, and emaciation. WARNING This herb, especially in the form of cocaine and coca leaf, is subject to legal restrictions in most countries.

GROWTH AND HARVEST
Cultivation, harvesting, and processing of coca plants are subject to legal restrictions in many countries. Subject to statutory control as a weed in some countries, notably in parts of Australia.

ESCHSCHOLZIA
California poppy
(Papaveraceae)

The watery sap of *E. californica* is mildly narcotic and was used by native N Americans to relieve toothache. It is similar in effect to *Papaver somniferum* (see p.322), but much milder, and does not depress the central nervous system.

E. californica (California poppy) p.124

PARTS USED Whole plant.
PROPERTIES A bitter, sedative herb that acts as a diuretic, relieves pain, relaxes spasms, and promotes perspiration.
USES OF THE HERB
MEDICINAL Internally for nervous tension, anxiety, insomnia, and incontinence (especially in children).
VARIANT
***E. californica*, Ballerina Series**, p.124.

GROWTH AND HARVEST
GROWTH Ornamental. Well-drained to poor soil in full sun. Propagate by seed sown *in situ* in late summer, or spring to early summer.
HARVEST Whole plants are cut when flowering and dried for use in infusions and tinctures.

EUCALYPTUS Gum tree
(Myrtaceae)

Gum trees are rich in volatile oils, with over 40 different kinds recorded. The most common are: cineole (eucalyptol) with the typical eucalyptus scent; citronellal (lemon-scented); piperitone (peppermint-scented); and pinene, with a turpentine-like odor. Eucalypts also exude an oleoresin, known as kino, containing tannins. Australian Aboriginal uses of eucalypts are little known, but bark, kino, and leaves were used in remedies. Bark decoctions were used to bathe sores and treat dysentery, and bark charcoal was considered antiseptic; water solutions of kino (of, for example, *E. gummifera*) were used against dysentery and bladder inflammation. People in the north preferred *Melaleuca* species (see p.309), since northern eucalypts have relatively low oil contents. In addition to those described below, the species *E. polybractea*, *E. radiata* var. *australiana*, and *E. smithii* are distilled for eucalyptus oil; others, such as *E. gummifera*, *E. haemastoma*, and *E. racemosa*, are sources of kino; the rutin contained in *E. macrorhyncha* is used to strengthen capillaries; and *E. macarthurii* is rich in geranyl acetate, used in perfumery. The leaves of several species, including *E. mannifera* and *E. viminalis*, exude a sweet substance when damaged by insects. This "manna" has a mild laxative effect, as found in the exudate from *Fraxinus ornus* (see p.284). Commercial production of eucalyptus oils began in 1860 in Victoria, Australia, pioneered by Joseph Bosisto, an emigrant from England. In common with all volatile oils, eucalyptus oils are toxic, requiring caution in handling, storage, and use. WARNING This herb, in the form of eucalyptus oil, is subject to legal restrictions in some countries.

E. camaldulensis (river red gum, Murray red gum, red gum) p.125

PARTS USED Leaves, oil, resin (kino).
PROPERTIES An aromatic, astringent, tonic herb that sticks to the teeth and turns the saliva red.
USES OF THE HERB
MEDICINAL Internally for diarrhea; externally for sore throats, colds, fevers, sores, and wounds.

E. citriodora (lemon-scented gum) p.125

PARTS USED Leaves, oil, resin (kino).
PROPERTIES An aromatic, astringent herb that is effective against some bacterial and fungal infections.
USES OF THE HERB
AROMATIC Dried leaves are included in potpourris and linen sachets.
MEDICINAL Externally for athlete's foot, dandruff, herpes, candidiasis, infections caused by *Staphylococcus aureus* (such as boils, impetigo, and septicemia), and as an inhalation for fevers, asthma, and laryngitis.
ECONOMIC Richest known source of citronellal, used in perfumery, detergents, and insect repellants.

E. dives (broad-leaved peppermint, Australian peppermint) p.125

PARTS USED Leaves, oil; the predominant oil varies according to chemotype; several are known, with volatile oil consisting mainly of piperitone, cineole (eucalyptol), or thymol.
PROPERTIES An aromatic, antiseptic herb that has anti-inflammatory and antiseptic effects. Plants containing mainly piperitone are the most used.
USES OF THE HERB
MEDICINAL Externally for bronchitis, mouth and throat infections, influenza, colds, neuralgia, sciatica, arthritis, and sprains. Used in the manufacture of menthol and thymol for oral hygiene preparations.

E. globulus (blue gum, Tasmanian blue gum) p.125

PARTS USED Leaves, oil.
PROPERTIES An aromatic, stimulant, decongestant herb that is expectorant, relaxes spasms, and lowers fever. It is effective against many bacterial organisms, especially *Staphylococcus*.
USES OF THE HERB
MEDICINAL Externally, in inhalations and vapor rubs for excess mucus, bronchitis, sinusitis, colds, and influenza; in liniments for bruises, sprains, and muscular pains; and in ointments for wounds and abscesses. Excess causes headaches, convulsions, and delirium, and may prove fatal.
ECONOMIC Used as a flavoring in pharmaceutical products and in spot removers for oil and grease. An important lumber species, used for the keels of ships in the 19th century. Widely planted to dry out swampy ground, notably in Italy and California.

GROWTH AND HARVEST
GROWTH Crop. Ornamental (*E. citriodora*, *E. globulus*). Hardiness varies with species and provenance: *E. camaldulensis* and *E. dives*, minimum 19°F (–7°C); *E. citriodora*, minimum 41–45°F (5–7°C). *E. globulus*, minimum 5°F (–15°C), is hardier, often cut down to the ground by frost, but usually surviving. Fertile, well-drained neutral to acid soil in sun, average 61°F (16°C). Propagate by seed sown under cover in spring or autumn. Cut back in spring only to restrict size or retain juvenile foliage.
HARVEST Leaves are cut as required and dried for use in decoctions and infusions, or distilled for oil. Kino is collected from bark incisions and dried for use in lozenges, powders, and tinctures.
WARNING Skin irritant.

EUGENIA
***E. caryophyllata*.** See *Syzygium aromaticum*.

EUONYMUS Spindle
(Celastraceae)

Several species were used by native N Americans, the most important being *E. atropurpureus*, used for various ailments from uterine discomfort to sore eyes. It was adopted by settlers in the 19th century as a diuretic, and became popular as a heart medicine following reports of digitalis-like effects. *E. atropurpureus* has also found its way into Ayurvedic medicine as a diuretic, purgative, and antipyretic.

E. atropurpureus (wahoo, burning bush, Indian arrowwood) p.125

PARTS USED Bark of stems and roots.
PROPERTIES An acrid, bitter herb that stimulates the gall bladder and circulatory system, has diuretic and laxative effects, and acts as a mild cardiac tonic.

USES OF THE HERB
MEDICINAL Internally for constipation and skin eruptions associated with liver and gall bladder dysfunction. Often combined with *Berberis vulgaris* (see p.248), *Chionanthus virginicus* (see p.260), *Pulsatilla vulgaris* (see p.338), and *Taraxacum officinale* (see p.360) for liver and gall bladder disorders.

E. europaeus (spindle tree) p.125

PARTS USED Bark, root bark.
PROPERTIES A bitter, astringent herb that is diuretic and emetic, and stimulates bile flow.
USES OF THE HERB
MEDICINAL Internally for liver and gall bladder complaints. Externally for chilblains, abscesses, acne, and wounds.
VARIANT
E. e. **'Red Cascade'**, p.125.

> **GROWTH AND HARVEST**
> **GROWTH** Wild-collected. Ornamental (*E. europaeus, E. e.* 'Red Cascade'). Well-drained soil in sun or partial shade. Propagate by seed sown when ripe, or by semiripe cuttings in late summer. Seed needs stratifying and is viable for 2 years. Thin out shoots in late winter to maintain shape. *E. europaeus* may be affected by aphids, scale insects, and spider mite.
> **HARVEST** Bark is collected in autumn and dried for use in decoctions, tablets, and tinctures.
> **WARNING** All parts, especially fruits and seeds, are harmful if eaten.

EUPATORIUM
(Compositae/Asteraceae)

In the 19th century *E. perfoliatum* was the standard household remedy in N America for coughs and colds. *E. cannabinum* has recently been found to contain a compound with possible antitumor activity. As well as *E. fortunei*, the Chinese also use *E. lindleyanum* for bronchitis and dysentery, and *E. chinense* for colds, diphtheria, and rheumatoid arthritis.

E. cannabinum (hemp agrimony) p.126

PARTS USED Whole plant.
PROPERTIES A bittersweet, slightly aromatic herb that is diuretic and has a tonic effect, stimulating the immune system and arresting the growth of tumors. It contains pyrrolizidine alkaloids that may cause damage or cancer to the liver.
USES OF THE HERB
MEDICINAL Internally for arthritis, rheumatism, feverish colds, and influenza. Excess is purgative and emetic. Combined with other herbs as a tonic for low energy with biliousness or constipation. Externally for ulcers, sores, and as an insect repellant for animals. Used in homeopathic tinctures for influenza.

E. fortunei, syn. *E. japonicum* var. *fortunei*, *E. stoechadasum* (thoroughwort)

Perennial, hardy to 5°F (–15°C), height 3–5ft (1–1.5m), spread 1–3ft (30cm–1m), with divided oppositely arranged leaves, and with toothed margins. Corymbs of white flowers are borne in late summer. Native to Korea, China, and Japan.

PARTS USED Whole plant (*pei lan*).
PROPERTIES A tonic herb that acts mainly on the stomach and spleen; considered cooling and drying in traditional Chinese medicine.
USES OF THE HERB
MEDICINAL Internally for indigestion, nausea and vomiting, diarrhea, heat stroke, and feverish summer colds. Excess is irritant to the stomach.

E. perfoliatum (boneset, thoroughwort, feverwort) p.126

PARTS USED Whole plant.
PROPERTIES A bitter, astringent herb that lowers fevers, relieves bronchial congestion and constipation, and stimulates the immune system.
USES OF THE HERB
MEDICINAL Internally for influenza, colds, acute bronchitis, excess mucus, and skin diseases. Combined with *Achillea millefolium* (see p.227), *Sambucus nigra* (see p.347), *Asclepias tuberosa* (see p.244), *Zingiber officinale* (see p.373), and/or *Capsicum annuum* (see p.254) for influenza.

E. purpureum (Joe Pye weed, gravel root, queen of the meadow) p.126

PARTS USED Rhizomes, roots.
PROPERTIES A slightly bitter, restorative, cleansing herb that acts especially on the genitourinary organs and uterus.
USES OF THE HERB
MEDICINAL Internally for kidney and urinary disorders, including stones, cystitis, and urethritis; for prostate problems (combined with *Lamium album*, see p.300); and for painful menstruation or a history of miscarriage and difficult labor.

> **GROWTH AND HARVEST**
> **GROWTH** Ornamental. Crop (*E. fortunei*, *E. perfoliatum*). Moist soil in sun or partial shade. Propagate by division when dormant, or by seed sown in spring. Cut stems almost down to ground level in autumn after flowering. Some *Eupatorium* species are subject to statutory controls as weeds in parts of Australia.
> **HARVEST** Plants are cut when in bud, and dried for use in infusions, liquid extracts, and tinctures. Rhizomes and roots are lifted in autumn, and dried for use in decoctions and tinctures.

EUPHORBIA Spurge
(Euphorbiaceae)

Most spurges contain carcinogenic, highly irritant, diterpene esters and are strong purgatives. The Chinese species *E. kansui* (*gan sui*) is used in this way, as is *E. pekinensis*, which also has diuretic and antibacterial effects. The northern African *E. resinifera* (euphorbium) is another drastic purgative, now considered too dangerous for medicinal use. *E. lathyrus* is too toxic for medicinal use, since it contains a violently purgative oil similar to croton oil (see *Croton tiglium*, p.269). *E. hirta* is ester-free and regarded worldwide as a safe, effective herb. In Chinese medicine the genus is considered incompatible with licorice (*Glycyrrhiza uralensis*, see p.289).

E. hirta, syn. *E. pilulifera* (asthma weed, pill-bearing spurge) p.126

PARTS USED Whole plant, juice.
PROPERTIES An acrid, bitter, antiseptic herb that expels phlegm and relieves spasms.
USES OF THE HERB
MEDICINAL Internally for asthma, bronchitis, emphysema, nervous cough, excess mucus, hay fever, and amebic dysentery. Externally for burns and warts (juice). Combined with *Grindelia camporum* (see p.290) for bronchitis and asthma.

> **GROWTH AND HARVEST**
> **GROWTH** Crop. Dry, sandy soil in sun, minimum 50–59°F (10–15°C). Propagate by seed sown in spring. Some species are subject to statutory control as weeds in certain countries, notably in parts of Australia.
> **HARVEST** Plants are cut when flowering and used fresh for juice, or dried for use in infusions, liquid extracts, and tinctures.
> **WARNING** All euphorbias are toxic if eaten. The sap (latex) is a serious skin and eye irritant.

EUPHRASIA
(Scrophulariaceae)

E. officinalis was first recorded as a medicinal herb for "all evils of the eye" in the 14th century. It gained credence through the Doctrine of Signatures: "the purple and yellow spots and stripes which are upon the flowers of the eyebright doth very much resemble the diseases of the eye, as bloodshot, etc., by which signature it hath been found out that this herb is effectual for the curing of the same."

E. officinalis (eyebright) p.126

PARTS USED Whole plant.
PROPERTIES A bitter, astringent herb that reduces inflammation.
USES OF THE HERB
MEDICINAL Internally for excess mucus, sinusitis, allergic rhinitis, hayfever, and upper respiratory tract infections. Externally for conjunctivitis, eye injuries, herpes, and weeping eczema.

> **GROWTH AND HARVEST**
> **GROWTH** Crop. Grows in natural grassland near host plants. Propagate by seed scattered around host plants. Tolerates a wide range of soils and conditions.
> **HARVEST** Plants are cut when flowering and dried for use in infusions, liquid extracts, tinctures, and homeopathic preparations.

EURYALE
(Nymphaeaceae)

E. ferox was first mentioned in traditional Chinese medicine c.AD1600. It is also used in Ayurvedic medicine, where it is known as *makhanna*. It has been cultivated in China for 3,000 years for its edible, floury seeds.

E. ferox (prickly waterlily, Chinese foxnut) p. 126

PARTS USED Seeds (*qian shi*).
PROPERTIES A sweet and sour, astringent herb that acts as a spleen and kidney tonic.
USES OF THE HERB
CULINARY Seeds are eaten roasted in China.
MEDICINAL Internally for chronic diarrhea, vaginal discharge, kidney weakness associated with frequent urination, impotence, premature and involuntary ejaculation, and nocturnal emissions.

GROWTH AND HARVEST
GROWTH Ornamental. Rich mud in still water, at least 24in (60cm) deep, minimum 41°F (5°C), in full sun. Propagate by seed sown in spring. Seeds are rarely produced when cultivated under cover.
HARVEST Seeds are collected in autumn and dried for use in decoctions.

EUTREMA
E. wasabi. See *Wasabia japonica*.

EVERNIA
(Lecanorales)

Approximately 9,000 tons of *E. prunastri* are collected annually, mainly from cork oak and fruit trees. France, the Balkan countries, and Morocco are the main producers. The volatile oils found in the plant are extracted in benzene and evaporated to a viscous solid. *E. prunastri* is often mixed with the related *Pseudoevernia purpuracea*, which is more aromatic but inferior when used as a perfume fixative.

E. prunastri (oak moss) p.126

PARTS USED Whole plant, oil.
PROPERTIES An aromatic, antibiotic herb containing lichen acids that inhibit the tuberculosis bacillus.
USES OF THE HERB
ECONOMIC Mainly as a fixative in perfumes with a mossy note, such as *chypre*, *ambre*, and *fougère*.

GROWTH AND HARVEST
GROWTH Wild-collected. Grows mainly on trunks of deciduous trees, occasionally on spruces (*Picea* species). Also on fences, walls, rocks, and soil. The ecology and reproductive biology of lichens are complex and there are no known propagation experiments. Plants are damaged by sulfur levels above 0.021 p.p.m.
HARVEST Plants are collected in dry winter weather for oil extraction.

FAGOPYRUM
(Polygonaceae)

F. esculentum was introduced into Europe from Asia by the Crusaders, hence the common names such as "Saracen corn," *sarrasin*, *grano saraceno*, *trigo sarraceno*. It is cultivated in parts of Europe and central Asia as a grain crop, a food plant, and as cover for game birds. It contains large amounts of rutin, a flavonoid glycoside also found in *Ruta graveolens* (see p.345) and *Citrus* species (see p.262), which has beneficial effects on the blood vessels.

F. esculentum (buckwheat) p.127

PARTS USED Leaves, flowers, seeds.
PROPERTIES A bitter but pleasant-tasting herb that controls bleeding, dilates blood vessels, reduces capillary permeability, and lowers blood pressure.
USES OF THE HERB
CULINARY Grain is roasted before boiling to make *kasha* (Poland, Russia) and *polenta* (northern Italy), and is ground into flour for buckwheat pancakes.
MEDICINAL Internally for varicose veins, chilblains, spontaneous bruising, frostbite, radiation damage, retinal hemorrhage, and hypertension. Combined with vitamin C and/or *Equisetum arvense* (see p.278) to strengthen capillaries. May cause light-sensitive dermatitis.

GROWTH AND HARVEST
GROWTH Crop. Well-drained, sandy soil in sun. Propagate by seed sown in spring.
HARVEST Leaves and flowers are collected as flowering begins and dried for infusions and tablets. Seeds are harvested when ripe and dried for use whole or ground. Buckwheat products are stored in the dark because their properties deteriorate rapidly on exposure to light.

FAGUS Beech
(Fagaceae)

Beech nuts, known as beech mast when fallen, were once an important food for pigs, forming part of the rights of pannage (the right to pasture pigs in a forest). They have been eaten in times of famine and roasted as a coffee substitute, but contain several toxins that make it inadvisable to consume them in any quantity. Beech wood is the main source of the creosote used for medicinal purposes, which is distilled from wood tar. It should not be confused with creosote prepared from coal tar, which is used to preserve wood. The active ingredient in beech creosote is guaiacol, which is also extracted from *Guaiacum officinale* (see p.290).

F. sylvatica (European beech) p.127

PARTS USED Creosote (from wood), oil (from seeds).
PROPERTIES An antiseptic, stimulating, expectorant herb with a burning taste and penetrating odor.
USES OF THE HERB
CULINARY Oil is used in salads and cooking.
MEDICINAL Internally for chronic bronchitis and upper respiratory tract infections; externally for skin diseases (creosote).
VARIANTS
***F. s.* 'Dawyck'**, p.127.
***F. s.* Heterophylla Group**, p.127.
***F. s.* Purpurea Group**, p.127.

GROWTH AND HARVEST
GROWTH Ornamental. Well-drained, moist to dry, acid to alkaline soil in sun or partial shade. For hedging space 18–24in (45–60cm) apart. Propagate by seed sown in autumn (species only), or by budding in late summer. Specimen trees require no pruning. Hedges should have the top quarter removed after planting, and again in the first summer, then trim to shape in following summers. Trees may be attacked by bracket fungi, canker, root rot, scale, aphids, or weevils. Foliage may be damaged by late frosts and scorching.
HARVEST Wood is cut and distilled for tar and creosote, from which guaiacol is then extracted. Seeds are collected when ripe, peeled, and pressed for oil, leaving a poisonous residue.

FERULA Giant fennel
(Umbelliferae/Apiaceae)

F. assa-foetida and *F. gummosa* are important for their gum resins, which have been used since earliest times. *F. assa-foetida is* probably the most foul-smelling of all herbs, with a sulfurous odor. However, in judicious quantities, it gives a surprisingly pleasant flavor to many foods. It is also a very effective medicinal herb, much used in the Ayurvedic tradition. Airtight storage is necessary to avoid contamination of surroundings. A similar gum resin is also collected from related species, such as *F. rubicaulis*. The pleasant-smelling musk root (*F. sumbul*) is used like *F. gummosa* in incense and to treat hysteria.

F. assa-foetida (asafoetida, devil's dung) p.127

PARTS USED Gum resin (*e wei*).
PROPERTIES A pungent herb that acts mainly on the digestive system, cleansing and strengthening the gastrointestinal tract. It also relieves pain and spasms, encourages productive coughing, and has hypotensive and anticoagulant effects.
USES OF THE HERB
CULINARY Minute amounts give flavor to legumes, vegetables, sauces, and pickles, especially in Indian cuisine.
MEDICINAL Internally for indigestion, flatulence, colic, constipation, intestinal worms, dysentery, whooping cough, bronchitis, and convulsive illnesses. Externally for painful joints.

F. gummosa, syn. *F. galbaniflua* (galbanum)

Perennial, hardy to 5°F (–15°C), height and spread 3ft (1m), with solid stems and divided, gray-green, hairy leaves, up to 1ft (30cm) long, which smell like celery. Lax panicles bearing flat umbels of tiny yellow flowers appear in spring, followed by thin, flat seeds. Found in central Iran, Turkey, and the south of Russia.

PARTS USED Gum resin.
PROPERTIES A bitter, stimulant, antiseptic herb that is expectorant and anti-inflammatory, relieves indigestion, and reduces spasms.
USES OF THE HERB
CULINARY Gives a celery flavor to condiments.
AROMATIC An ingredient of incense.
MEDICINAL Internally for bronchitis, asthma, and minor digestive complaints. Externally for ulcers, boils, wounds, abscesses, and skin disorders.

GROWTH AND HARVEST
GROWTH Crop. Rich, well-drained soil in sun. Propagate by seed sown when ripe in late summer.
HARVEST *F. assa-foetida* is cut down as it begins to flower, and the gum resin is scraped from the top of the root. Slices are removed and scraped until the root is finally exhausted. Stems and roots of *F. gummosa* are incised to collect gum resin during the growing season. Resins are formed into lumps, which are then processed into paste, or are used in pills, powders, or tinctures.

FICUS Fig
(Moraceae)

F. carica has been cultivated since earliest times. It was a major crop in ancient Greece, and 29 cultivars were later described by Pliny (AD23–79). The fruits are important as food and medicine, containing laxative substances, flavonoids, sugars, vitamins A and C, acids, and enzymes.

F. carica (fig) p.127

PARTS USED Fruits, leaves, sap.
PROPERTIES A sweet, laxative herb that soothes irritated tissues.
USES OF THE HERB
CULINARY Fruits are eaten raw or stewed, made into jam, and used to flavor coffee.
MEDICINAL Internally for constipation, sore throat, cough, bronchial infections, and inflammation of the trachea. Externally for hemorrhoids, sore eyes (leaves), corns, and warts (sap).
VARIANTS
F. c. **'Brown Turkey'**, p.128.
F. c. **'White Ischia'**
A dwarf cultivar, height and spread 15ft (5m), with an abundance of small, green-white, thin-skinned fruits, ideal for pot culture. Hardy to 23°F (–5°C), depending on site.

GROWTH AND HARVEST
GROWTH Ornamental. Rich, well-drained, neutral to alkaline soil in sun. Propagate by semiripe or hardwood cuttings in late summer, or by layering in summer, or by rooted suckers. Shorten and thin out shoots in early spring to maintain an open, compact bush. Harder pruning is required in cool climates to encourage well-ripened shoots. Shoots may be damaged by *Botrytis*. Fruits are often attacked by birds and wasps. Plants under cover may be affected by scale insect, mealybug, and spider mite. Fruits may not ripen in cool regions. Protect plants from frost in hard winters, or bring under cover.
HARVEST Fruits are picked when ripe and used fresh or dried. For medicinal use, they are soaked or made into an elixir.
WARNING Skin irritant in sunlight. Skin allergen. Sap is a serious eye irritant.

FILIPENDULA Meadowsweet
(Rosaceae)

Meadowsweet was one of the three most sacred herbs of the Druids, the others being water mint (*Mentha aquatica*, see p.311) and vervain (*Verbena officinalis*, see p.368). In medieval times it was important as a strewing herb. It was from *F. ulmaria* that salicylic acid was first isolated in 1838. This substance was later synthesized as "aspirin," a name derived from the plant's older name, *Spiraea ulmaria*.

F. ulmaria (meadowsweet, queen of the meadow) p.128

PARTS USED Whole plant, flowers.
PROPERTIES An astringent, aromatic, antacid herb that heals, soothes, and relieves pain, especially in the joints and digestive tract. It is effective against organisms causing diphtheria, dysentery, and pneumonia.
USES OF THE HERB
AROMATIC Oil of meadowsweet, distilled from flower buds, has a wintergreen-like scent and is used in potpourri.
MEDICINAL Internally for hyperacidity, heartburn, gastritis, and peptic ulcers, for which meadowsweet is among the most effective of plant remedies. Also for diarrhea in children, dysentery, rheumatic and joint pains, influenza, and cystitis. Combined with *Althaea officinalis* (see p.236) and *Melissa officinalis* (see p.310) for gastric complaints. Not given to patients hypersensitive to aspirin.
ECONOMIC The whole plant yields a greenish yellow dye, and the roots produce a black dye.
VARIANTS
F. u. **'Aurea'**, p.128.
F. u. **'Flore Pleno'**, p.128.
F. u. **'Variegata'**, p.128.

GROWTH AND HARVEST
GROWTH Ornamental. Rich, moisture-retentive to wet soil in sun or partial shade. Propagate by seed sown in early spring, or by division in autumn or spring. Dislikes acid soil; prone to powdery mildew in dry conditions.
HARVEST Plants are cut as flowering begins and dried for use in tablets, infusions, liquid ► extracts, and tinctures. Flowers may be gathered separately to make infusions.

FOENICULUM Fennel
(Umbelliferae/Apiaceae)

The flavor of fennel oil depends on the proportions of its two main constituents: fenchone, a bitter-tasting element, and anethole, which has a sweet anise aroma. These vary according to strain and region; sweet, or Roman, fennel predominates in the Mediterranean, and the bitter, or wild, fennel is most common in central Europe and Russia. The seeds were eaten in medieval times as a flavoring, and during Lent to allay hunger.

F. vulgare (fennel) p.128

PARTS USED Leaves, stems, roots, seeds, oil.

PROPERTIES A sweet, aromatic, diuretic herb that relieves digestive problems, increases milk flow, relaxes spasms, and reduces inflammation.
USES OF THE HERB
CULINARY Fennel leaves and seeds are popular in fish dishes. Leaf bases, especially of the variety *azoricum*, have a delicate anise flavor and are eaten raw in salads (as *cartucci* in Italy) or cooked as a vegetable. Fennel also gives the characteristic flavor to *finocchiona*, an Italian salami, and the French liqueur, *fenouillette*. Bruised or crushed seeds are infused as a pleasant tea.
AROMATIC Oil is used in perfumes.
MEDICINAL Internally for indigestion, wind, colic, and insufficient lactation (seeds), and urinary disorders (root). Externally as a mouthwash or gargle for gum disease and sore throat. Combines with *Chamaemelum nobile* (see p.259), *Filipendula ulmaria* (see this page), *Mentha* **x** *piperita* (see p.311), and *Geranium maculatum* (see p.288) for digestive problems. Oil is combined with oils of *Thymus vulgaris* (see p.362) and *Eucalyptus globulus* (see p.280), and diluted with vegetable oil as a rub for bronchial congestion; also added to laxative preparations to prevent griping and to "gripe water" for babies. Oil is not given to pregnant women.
ECONOMIC Oil is used in food flavorings, toothpastes, soaps, and air fresheners.
VARIANTS
F. v. var. ***azoricum***, p.128.
F. v. **'Purpureum'**, p.128.

GROWTH AND HARVEST
GROWTH Ornamental (*F. vulgare* var. *azoricum*: crop). Well-drained soil in full sun. ►

► *F. vulgare* is not reliably hardy in areas with cold, damp winters. *F. v.* var. *azoricum* needs rich, light soil, a warm position, and ample moisture to produce compact "bulbs" that are hilled up as they develop. Propagate by seed sown in autumn or spring, or by division in spring. *F. v.* var. *azoricum* is grown as a half-hardy annual. *F. v.* 'Purpureum' comes true from seed. Fennel self-seeds freely in most soils. The flowers attract beneficial insects, such as hoverflies, parasitic wasps, and tachinid flies, which prey on garden pests. It should not be planted near beans, kohlrabi, or tomatoes, since it is said to affect their growth adversely, and also that of coriander (*Coriandrum sativum*, see p.267). Fennel and dill (*Anethum graveolens*, see p.238) should not be grown close together since hybridization produces seedlings with an indeterminate flavor. Subject to statutory control as a weed in some countries, notably in parts of Australia.
HARVEST Leaves are picked for use at any time during the growing season; leaf bases are most tender in spring. Stems for use in cooking are cut as required. Roots are lifted in autumn and dried for use in decoctions. Unripe seeds are collected in summer for using fresh. Ripe seeds are harvested before they fall by cutting the seedheads and upturning into a paper bag for drying; they are used whole, ground, or distilled for oil.

FORSYTHIA
(Oleaceae)

F. suspensa has an extremely long history as a medicinal herb, being mentioned in some of the very earliest Chinese medical texts, which date back to at least 2000BC.

F. suspensa (weeping forsythia) p.129

PARTS USED Fruits (*lian qiao*).
PROPERTIES A bitter, astringent herb that stimulates the nervous system, heart, and gall bladder, and is diuretic. It also lowers fevers and clears bacterial infections. The vitamin P content strengthens capillaries.
USES OF THE HERB
MEDICINAL Internally for acute infectious diseases (such as mumps and erysipelas), tonsillitis, urinary tract infection, abscesses, allergic rashes, and retinal hemorrhage. Often combined with *Lonicera japonica* (see p.306).
VARIANT
F. s.* f. *atrocaulis, p.129.

GROWTH AND HARVEST
GROWTH Ornamental. Most soils in sun or partial shade. Propagate by softwood cuttings in summer, or by hardwood cuttings in autumn or winter. Remove old wood after flowering and trim vigorous shoots to shape. Cut back wall-trained plants of *F. suspensa* and its cultivars to within one or two buds of the old wood after flowering.
HARVEST Fruits are collected when ripe and dried for use in decoctions.

FRAGARIA Strawberry
(Rosaceae)

Strawberries of various kinds have always been a popular source of household remedies. Both roots and leaves contain tannins. Culpeper regarded strawberries as a cooling remedy for "wheals and other breakings forth of hot and sharp humours in the face and hands…and to take away any redness in the face, or spots, or other deformities in the skin, and to make it clear and smooth" (*The English Physitian Enlarged*, 1653).

F. vesca (wild strawberry) p.129

PARTS USED Leaves, roots, fruits.
PROPERTIES A cooling, astringent, tonic herb, with mild diuretic and laxative effects, that improves digestive function and benefits the skin.
USES OF THE HERB
CULINARY Leaves are included in blended herb teas. Fruits are eaten fresh, added to summer drinks, and made into desserts, juice, jam, syrup, and wine.
MEDICINAL Internally for diarrhea, digestive upsets, and gout (leaves, roots). Externally for sunburn, skin blemishes, and discolored teeth (fruit juice).
VARIANTS
***F. v.* 'Fructu Albo'**, p.129.
***F. v.* 'Multiplex'**, syn. *F. v.* 'Flore Pleno', p.129.

GROWTH AND HARVEST
GROWTH Ornamental. Humus-rich soil in sun or partial shade. Propagate by seed sown in autumn at 64–75°F (18–24°C). Plants deteriorate after a few years and need replacing.
HARVEST Leaves are gathered in early summer and dried for use in infusions. Roots are lifted in autumn and dried for use in decoctions. Fruits are picked in summer and used fresh.

FRANGULA
F. alnus. See *Rhamnus frangula*.

FRAXINUS Ash
(Oleaceae)

F. excelsior (common ash) is a laxative, anti-inflammatory herb, once taken for rheumatism and arthritis; *F. bungeana* (northern ash) is similarly anti-inflammatory, and also diuretic and analgesic, controlling bacterial infections and coughs. The common name of *F. ornus*, manna ash, refers to the sugary sap that oozes from the bark when the tree is tapped, and granulates as "manna." In Italy manna has been collected from *F. ornus*, mainly grown in plantations in Sicily, since the 15th century. The word "manna" has been used since biblical times to describe the sweet exudates of various plants, but in 1927 an Italian law reserved the name for the product of the manna ash and defined its constituents.

F. ornus (manna ash) p.129

PARTS USED Sap.
PROPERTIES A sweet, mildly laxative herb that soothes irritated tissues.
USES OF THE HERB
MEDICINAL Internally, dissolved in water, as a gentle laxative for children and pregnant women. Also added to other laxatives.
ECONOMIC Used as a sweetener in sugar-free preparations and as an anticaking agent.

GROWTH AND HARVEST
GROWTH Ornamental. Well-drained, neutral to alkaline soil, in an open position. Propagate by seed sown in autumn.
HARVEST Manna is obtained from trees aged 8 years or more, with trunks at least 3in (7.5cm) across. A series of slanting incisions is made on alternate sides of the trunk during warm, dry weather in summer and the exudate scraped off the surface when solidified.
WARNING Contact may cause skin or systemic allergic reactions.

FRITILLARIA Fritillary
(Liliaceae)

Several species are used medicinally. Those gathered from the wild or cultivated for medicinal use in China are known as *bei mu* and include *F. pallidiflora* and *F. cirrhosa*.

F. verticillata p.130

PARTS USED Bulbs (*zhe bei mu*).
PROPERTIES A sweet, pungent herb that controls coughs, is expectorant, relaxes bronchial spasms, and lowers fever and blood pressure.
USES OF THE HERB
MEDICINAL Internally for coughs, bronchitis, pneumonia, feverish illnesses, abscesses, and tumors of the breast or lungs. Excess causes breathing difficulties and heart failure. For use by qualified practitioners only.

GROWTH AND HARVEST
GROWTH Ornamental. Well-drained soil in sun or partial shade.The scaly bulbs are best planted on their sides or surrounded by sand, to prevent water from collecting in the crowns. Propagate by bulbils or offsets of mature bulbs when dormant, or by seed sown under cover when ripe, which germinates the following spring.
HARVEST Bulbs are lifted in winter, before new growth, and dried for decoctions and powder.

FUCUS Wrack
(Fucaceae)

Bladderwrack is an important seaweed manure, soil conditioner, and a high potash fertilizer, especially for potatoes. It also has a reputation for being a food supplement that improves the condition of skin and hair. *F. serratus* (toothed wrack) is used similarly, and both are used to make kelp tablets. The discovery of iodine in the 19th century was made by distilling *Fucus*.

F. vesiculosus (bladderwrack, black-tang) p.130

PARTS USED Whole plant.
PROPERTIES A mucilaginous, salty, tonic herb that stimulates the thyroid, helps control weight, and has antibiotic effects.
USES OF THE HERB
MEDICINAL Internally for goiter and obesity associated with thyroid deficiency. Externally for rheumatic complaints.
ECONOMIC Used for fertilizers, livestock feed, and mineral supplements. Source of alginates for the food, textile, cosmetic, and pharmaceutical industries.

GROWTH AND HARVEST
GROWTH Wild-collected. Found in the wild on unpolluted shores; not cultivated.
HARVEST Plants are collected in summer, when the nutrient content is highest; washed-up plants are not suitable for medicinal use, having lost important nutrients. They are dried in thin layers, being turned regularly; when brittle, the blackish brown strips are chopped and ground. As a fertilizer, it is spread, fresh or dried, directly onto the soil and dug in, rather than being composted in heaps. Small amounts are also added to compost piles as an activator.

FUMARIA Fumitory
(Papaveraceae)

There are many old prescriptions containing *F. officinalis*, once used for a wide range of complaints. A syrup made from the juice of the herb, mixed with the syrup of damask roses, peach blossoms, or senna, was "a most singular thing against hypochondriack melancholy in any person whatsoever" (quoted without reference by Mrs. Grieve in A *Modern Herbal*, 1931).

F. officinalis (fumitory, earth smoke) p.130

PARTS USED Flowering plant.
PROPERTIES A bitter, tonic herb, with mild diuretic and laxative effects, that improves liver and gall bladder function and reduces inflammation.
USES OF THE HERB
MEDICINAL Internally for biliary colic and migraine with digestive disturbances. Externally for conjunctivitis. Both internally and externally for skin complaints, including eczema and dermatitis. Excess causes drowsiness.

GROWTH AND HARVEST
GROWTH Crop. Light, well-drained soil in sun. Propagate by seed sown in spring where the plants are to flower. Self-seeds readily.
HARVEST Plants are collected as flowering begins and dried for use in infusions, liquid extracts, pills, and tinctures.

GALEGA
(Leguminosae/Papilionaceae)

G. officinalis was once important in the treatment of plague, fevers, and infectious diseases, hence the German name of *Pestilenzkraut*. Its ancient reputation as a galactagogue was validated by research in France, which in 1873 showed that, in cows given goat's rue, milk yields were increased by 35–50 percent.

G. officinalis (goat's rue, French lilac) p.130

PARTS USED Whole plant.
PROPERTIES A bitter, mildly diuretic herb that increases milk flow, lowers blood sugar levels, and improves digestion.
USES OF THE HERB
MEDICINAL Internally for insufficient lactation, late-onset diabetes, pancreatitis, and digestive problems, especially chronic constipation caused by lack of digestive enzymes.
ECONOMIC Fed directly to livestock to increase milk yield.
VARIANT
G. o. **'Alba'**, p.130.

GROWTH AND HARVEST
GROWTH Ornamental. Moist, well-drained soil in sun or partial shade. Propagate by seed sown in spring, or by division in autumn or spring.
HARVEST Plants are cut as flowering begins and dried for use in infusions, liquid extracts, powders, and tinctures.

GALIPEA
(Rutaceae)

There are eight to ten species of evergreen trees and shrubs in this genus, which occurs in tropical C and S America. *G. officinalis* has a long history of use as a bitter tonic by native S Americans before its introduction to Europe in 1759. Aromatic bitters were first made in Angostura (now Ciudad Bolivar), Venezuela, and the recipe (originally a medicine for fevers) patented by Dr. J. G. B. Siegert in 1824. When added to the water, the active constituents of *G. officinalis* have the effect of stunning fish. Fishing by means of ichthyotoxic plants does not affect edibility or cause pollution, since the compounds break down rapidly. The skill has been developed by many tribes in S America, using various species of *Galipea*.

G. officinalis, syn. *G. cusparia* (Angostura, cusparia bark)

Tender rainforest shrub or small tree, height 50ft (15m), spread 30ft (10m), with smooth, gray bark. The shiny, trifoliate leaves, in which the terminal leaflet is up to 12in (30cm) long, smell of tobacco. White, tubular, 5-lobed flowers with an unpleasant scent are produced in panicles about 3in (8cm) long, followed by 5-celled capsules containing round black seeds. Native to tropical S America.

PARTS USED Bark.
PROPERTIES A bitter, musty-smelling, tonic herb that stimulates the liver and gall bladder, lowers fever, and relaxes spasms.
USES OF THE HERB
CULINARY Used to flavor alcoholic and soft drinks.
MEDICINAL Internally for dysentery, bilious diarrhea, poor appetite, and feverish illnesses; laxative and emetic in large doses.

GROWTH AND HARVEST
GROWTH Wild-collected. Humus-rich soil in partial shade, minimum 59–64°F (15–18°C). This species does not appear to be cultivated, and no information has been found as to its requirements.
HARVEST Bark is removed as required and dried for use in concentrated infusions, liquid extracts, and powders.

GALIUM
(Rubiaceae)

A number of species contain asperuloside, which produces coumarin, giving the sweet smell of new-mown hay as the foliage dries. Asperuloside can be converted to prostaglandins (hormonelike compounds that stimulate the uterus and affect the blood vessels), making *Galium* species of great interest to the pharmaceutical industry. Roots of some species contain a red dye, similar to that produced by the closely related *Rubia tinctorum* (see p.343).

G. aparine (goosegrass, cleavers, sticky Willie) p.131

PARTS USED Whole plant, seeds.
PROPERTIES A bitter, cooling, salty herb that acts as a tonic for the lymphatic system and has mild laxative, diuretic, and astringent effects. Also alterative, it lowers blood pressure and promotes healing.
USES OF THE HERB
CULINARY In China as a weight-reducing vegetable; seeds roasted as coffee substitute.
MEDICINAL Internally for glandular fever, tonsillitis, myalgic encephalomyelitis (ME), hepatitis, benign breast tumors and cysts, cystitis, eczema, and psoriasis. Externally for swollen lymph glands, breast lumps, ulcers, skin inflammations, minor injuries, and psoriasis. Combined with *Althaea officinalis* (see p.236) for cystitis; with *Echinacea purpurea* (see p.276) or *Hydrastis canadensis* (see p.294) for throat infections; with *Trifolium pratense* (see p.364), *Urtica dioica* (see p.366) and *Scrophularia nodosa* (see p.350) for psoriasis.

G. odoratum, syn. *Asperula odorata* (sweet woodruff) p.131

PARTS USED Whole plant.
PROPERTIES An astringent, slightly bitter herb, aromatic when dried, with tonic, diuretic, and sedative effects. It improves liver function, relaxes spasms, and reduces blood clotting.
USES OF THE HERB
CULINARY The herb is soaked in white wine to make *Maitrank*, a tonic drink made in Alsace.
AROMATIC Dried herb may be added to potpourris.
MEDICINAL Internally for thrombophlebitis, varicose veins, biliary obstruction, hepatitis, jaundice, and insomnia in children. Used in homeopathy for inflammation of the uterus.

G. verum (lady's bedstraw, yellow bedstraw, cheese rennet) p.131

PARTS USED Whole plant.
PROPERTIES An astringent, acidic, slightly bitter herb that is alterative and diuretic, and relaxes spasms.
USES OF THE HERB
MEDICINAL Internally, especially useful for kidney and bladder complaints.
ECONOMIC Foliage was once important as a stuffing for mattresses. It yields a yellow dye used to color food, such as cheese and butter; the roots provide a red dye.

GROWTH AND HARVEST

GROWTH Crop (*G. aparine*). Ornamental (*G. odoratum*, *G. verum*). Moist, well-drained, neutral to alkaline soil in shade (*G. aparine*, *G. odoratum*); dry, well-drained, neutral to alkaline soil in sun (*G. verum*). Propagate by seed sown when ripe in summer, or by division in early spring or autumn.
HARVEST Plants are cut when flowering and dried. *G. aparine* is used fresh, either juiced or in oil for external use. Seeds are collected when ripe. Roots are lifted in autumn.

GANODERMA
(Ganodermataceae)

G. lucidum is one of the most important Taoist longevity herbs. It was much valued by early Chinese emperors, including the Yellow Emperor (c.2500BC). Recent scientific research has shown that it contains substances that may be of value in treating cancer, virus infections, and allergies, and new drugs are being developed from the spores.

G. lucidum (lacquered bracket fungus, *reishi*) p.131

PARTS USED Whole plant (*ling zhi*).
PROPERTIES A tonic, sedative herb that is expectorant, lowers blood sugar and cholesterol levels, controls coughing, relieves pain, and stimulates the immune system. It improves heart and liver function, and has antiallergenic, antiviral, and antibacterial effects.
USES OF THE HERB
MEDICINAL Internally for bronchitis, asthma, liver disorders, rheumatoid arthritis, heart disease, palpitations, high blood pressure, high cholesterol levels, nervous disorders, insomnia, and debility.

GROWTH AND HARVEST

GROWTH Crop. On living or dead wood of deciduous trees, often *Quercus* spp. (see p.187), often near the base. Propagates by spores.
HARVEST Fungi are collected when mature and sun-dried for use in syrups, powders, tablets, and tinctures.

GARDENIA
(Rubiaceae)

G. augusta was first described in traditional Chinese medicine during the Han dynasty (AD25–220). It is an ingredient in several patent remedies for feverish colds or coughs.

G. augusta, syn. *G. florida*, *G. jasminoides* (gardenia, Cape jasmine) p.131

PARTS USED Fruits (*zhi zi*), flowers.
PROPERTIES A bitter, cold, alterative herb that lowers fever and blood pressure, checks bleeding, stimulates bile flow, and promotes healing.
USES OF THE HERB
CULINARY Used in China to flavor tea.
AROMATIC Flowers yield an important essential oil, widely used in perfumery.
MEDICINAL Internally for feverish illness, hepatitis, jaundice, and hemorrhage. Externally for wounds, sprains, skin inflammations, and toothache.
VARIANT
G. a. **'Fortuniana'**, p.132.

GROWTH AND HARVEST

GROWTH Ornamental. Well-drained, fibrous, acid soil in sun or partial shade, minimum 55°F (13°C). Plants should be kept evenly moist. Avoid sudden changes in temperature and cold drafts. Propagate by greenwood cuttings in spring, or by semiripe cuttings in summer. Young plants flower more freely. Cut back after flowering to maintain a bushy habit. Grows well in containers. Plants under cover may be damaged by spider mites, aphids, whitefly, and mealybugs.
HARVEST Fruits are collected when ripe and dried for use in decoctions.

GASTRODIA
(Orchidaceae)

A genus of 20 saprophytic species of orchids found from eastern Asia to New Zealand. They are very difficult to cultivate because of their lack of green parts and complete dependence on a fungus for food. *G. elata* was first described in traditional Chinese medicine c.AD470. Due to its increasing rarity in the wild, techniques for cultivating this saprophytic orchid have now been devised in China.

G. elata

Perennial, leafless saprophyte, hardy to 5°F (–15°C), height 2–3ft (60cm–1m), spread 12in (30cm). The angular, horizontal, tuberlike rhizome, 4–6in (10–15cm) long and 2–2½in (5–6cm) wide, has a brown stem clad in scalelike sheaths. Small, pale green-brown flowers appear in summer. Native to China, Japan, Korea, Tibet, and Siberia.

PARTS USED Rhizomes (*tian ma*).
PROPERTIES A sweet, acrid, sedative herb that lowers blood pressure, relieves pain, stimulates bile flow, and relaxes spasms.
USES OF THE HERB
MEDICINAL Internally for convulsive illnesses (such as epilepsy and tetanus), rheumatoid arthritis, vertigo, and numbness associated with liver disharmony.

GROWTH AND HARVEST

GROWTH Crop. Damp, humus-rich soil in shade, in association with fungal partner. Propagate by seed when ripe in the natural habitat near existing colonies or onto a bed of *Quercus* wood, inoculated with the fungus *Armillaria mellea*, or by division of rhizomes during dormancy.
HARVEST Rhizomes are lifted in autumn and dried for use in decoctions.

GAULTHERIA
(Ericaceae)

G. procumbens was used for aches and pains in native N American medicine, and to help breathing while hunting or carrying heavy loads. Wintergreen leaves were listed in the *U.S. Pharmacopoeia* (1820–94); oil of wintergreen is still listed. It was a major source of methyl salicylate (an anti-inflammatory, similar in effect to aspirin), which was produced mainly in Monroe County, Pennsylvania. Most methyl salicylate is now synthesized.

G. procumbens (wintergreen, checkerberry, teaberry) p.132

PARTS USED Leaves, oil, fruits.
PROPERTIES An astringent, aromatic, warming herb that is anti-inflammatory, diuretic, and expectorant. It is a good antiseptic and counterirritant.
USES OF THE HERB
CULINARY Leaves are used for tea. Fresh fruits have a pleasant taste.
AROMATIC Used in perfumery with woody notes.
MEDICINAL Mainly externally for rheumatism, arthritis, sciatica, myalgia, sprains, neuralgia, and excess mucus. Oil of wintergreen is toxic in excess, causing liver and kidney damage. Not given to patients hypersensitive to salicylates (aspirin).
ECONOMIC Oil was important in flavoring root beer and toothpaste.

GROWTH AND HARVEST

GROWTH Ornamental. Acid soil in partial shade. Propagate by seed sown on soil surface in autumn, or by semiripe cuttings in summer, or by division in autumn. ►

► HARVEST Leaves are gathered from spring to early autumn and dried for use in infusions and liquid extracts. Oil is extracted from fresh leaves for use in rubbing oils, inhalers, liniments, and ointments.

GELIDIUM
(Rhodophyceae)

A genus of about 20 species of red seaweeds, found mainly in waters off Japan, Spain, Portugal, western Scotland and Ireland, northern, southern, and western Africa, Madagascar, California, and Chile. They are collected with rakes from boats and by divers from deep water, and are now cultivated by the Japanese on poles in coastal waters. The earliest observations of the properties of *G. amansii* (agar-agar) were made by a Japanese innkeeper, Minoya Tarozaemon, in 1660. Its use as agar, a culture medium for bacteria, was developed in the 1880s by Robert Koch, who thus discovered the organisms that cause tuberculosis. Some 30 species of algae, belonging to about 10 different genera, are used worldwide for agar production; the main ones are *G. amansii* (Japan), *G. cartilagineum* (US), *Gracilaria verrucosa*, syn. *Gr. confervoides* (Australia), and *Pterocladia pinnata* (New Zealand). The 20th century has seen demand for *Gelidium* increasing in many varied areas, including medicine, dentistry, forensic science, and the food industry. The constituents of the plant are nontoxic and are not absorbed. It is prepared as strips of solidified mucilaginous extract, which gels at 90°F (32°C), liquefies at 105°F (42°C), and melts at 185°F (85°C). The high melting point makes agar-agar useful in foods which might otherwise melt in warm temperatures.

G. amansii (agar-agar, Japanese isinglass)

Perennial, tuft-forming seaweed, length and spread 4–12in (10–30cm), with pinnately branched, rigid, cartilaginous fronds divided into threadlike segments. Found in intertidal and subtidal zones around China, Japan, Korea, and the Pacific coasts of Russia.

PARTS USED Whole plant.
PROPERTIES A nutritive, almost tasteless, gelatinous herb that acts as a bulk laxative.
USES OF THE HERB
MEDICINAL Internally for constipation.
ECONOMIC Used in foods for invalids, and as a gelling and stabilizing agent in canned meats, ice cream, sauces, desserts, and dairy products.

GROWTH AND HARVEST
GROWTH Crop. In shallow coastal water on poles. Propagates by spores, which spread naturally.
HARVEST Plants are collected during the growing season and sun-dried before processing into dried agar strips and powder.

GELSEMIUM
(Loganiaceae)

The uses of *G. sempervirens* were discovered by a Mississippi farmer, who drank an infusion made from the roots of the plant, mistaking it for another. He developed serious symptoms of poisoning, but recovered to find himself cured of the bilious fever from which he had been suffering. *G. sempervirens* was listed in most pharmacopoeias in the mid-19th century.

G. sempervirens (Carolina jessamine, false jasmine) p.132

PARTS USED Roots and rhizomes.
PROPERTIES A bitter, slightly aromatic, sedative herb that lowers fever, increases perspiration, relieves pain, and relaxes spasms.
USES OF THE HERB
MEDICINAL Internally for neuralgia, migraine, sciatica, toothache, severe pain (especially in terminal illness or accidents), and meningitis. May be combined with *Lavandula angustifolia* (see p.301), or *Rosmarinus officinalis* (see p.343) and *Piscidia piscipula*, for migraine. Excess causes respiratory depression, giddiness, double vision, and death. Not given to patients with heart disease, hypotension, or myasthenia gravis. Also in homeopathy for feverish illnesses (including influenza and measles) and acute anxiety. For use by qualified practitioners only. WARNING This herb and its alkaloids are subject to legal restrictions in some countries.

GROWTH AND HARVEST
GROWTH Ornamental. Rich, well-drained soil in sun. Propagate by seed in spring (species only), or by semiripe cuttings in summer. Thin out oldest stems in spring after flowering.
HARVEST Roots and rhizomes are lifted in autumn and dried for decoctions and tinctures.
WARNING Toxic if eaten. Skin allergen. Contact may cause systemic poisoning.

GENISTA Broom
(Leguminosae/Papilionaceae)

All parts of *G. tinctoria* contain glycosides, notably luteolin glycosides, which produce a yellow dye that has been used since Roman times for dyeing fabrics. Other constituents include alkaloids, some of which are similar to those found in the closely related *Cytisus scoparius* (see p.271). Comparatively little research has been done on *Genista*, but it should be treated with caution, given that the alkaloids in *Cytisus* are known to affect the heart and respiration. In the 14th century both *G. tinctoria* and *Cytisus scoparius* were used to make *Unguentum geneste*, an ointment for gouty limbs.

G. tinctoria (dyer's greenweed) p.132

PARTS USED Flowering plant.
PROPERTIES A bitter, diuretic, purgative emetic herb that acts as a weak cardiac stimulant and vasoconstrictor.
USES OF THE HERB
MEDICINAL Formerly used internally for gout, rheumatism, and dropsy; externally for fractures, sciatica, abscesses, and tumors.
ECONOMIC Used in domestic dyeing of natural fabrics.

GROWTH AND HARVEST
GROWTH Ornamental. Light, well-drained soil in sun. Tolerates dry, poor, or sandy soils. Propagate by seed sown under cover in spring or autumn, or by semiripe cuttings in summer. Established plants do not transplant well. No regular pruning is required, but shoots can be thinned and/or pinched out after flowering to improve shape. Some *Genista* species are subject to certain plant controls in parts of Australia.
HARVEST Leafy branches are cut before the plant sets seed, and dried for infusions. Dried herb should not be stored for more than a year.

GENTIANA Gentian
(Gentianaceae)

Gentians contain some of the most bitter compounds known, against which the bitterness of other substances is scientifically measured. Bitter-tasting herbs benefit the digestive system, stimulating gastric secretions and protecting against indigestion. *G. lutea* is the classic bitter digestive, so much so that the taste can still be detected when diluted to 1 in 12,000 parts. Many different species are used similarly in different parts of the world, the choice being largely dependent on local availability. The exploitation and wild-collection of *Gentiana* species may be subject to management measures.

G. lutea (great yellow gentian) p.132

PARTS USED Roots and rhizomes.
PROPERTIES An intensely bitter (though sweet at first), tonic herb that stimulates the liver, gall bladder, and digestive system. It reduces inflammation and lowers fever.
USES OF THE HERB
MEDICINAL Internally for liver complaints, indigestion, gastric infections, and anorexia. Not given to patients with gastric and duodenal ulcers.
ECONOMIC Used in commercial tonics, bitter aperitifs, and Enzian schnapps.

G. macrophylla, syn. *G. burserii* var. *villarsi* (large-leaved gentian) p.133

PARTS USED Roots (*qin jiao*).
PROPERTIES A bitter, pungent, sedative herb that has a tonic effect on the liver, gall bladder, and stomach, and increases blood sugar levels. It lowers fever, relieves pain, and reduces inflammation.
USES OF THE HERB
MEDICINAL Internally for rheumatism, arthritis, low-grade fevers associated with chronic disease,

allergic inflammations, hepatitis, jaundice, and constipation related to liver complaints.

G. scabra (Japanese gentian, *ryntem* root) p.133

PARTS USED Roots (*long dan cao*).
PROPERTIES A bitter, cooling, anti-inflammatory herb that stimulates the appetite and digestion, increases blood sugar levels, and potentiates the sedative and analgesic properties of other herbs.
USES OF THE HERB
MEDICINAL Internally for liver disorders, eye complaints related to liver disharmony (such as conjunctivitis), acute urinary infections, hypertension with dizziness or tinnitus, and tantrums in children. Included in many Chinese patent remedies for "liver heat."

GROWTH AND HARVEST
GROWTH Ornamental (*G. lutea*). Crop (*G. macrophylla, G. scabra*). Well-drained, humus-rich, neutral to acid soil in sun or partial shade. *G. lutea* prefers alkaline soil. Propagate by seed sown in autumn, or by cuttings of basal shoots, or by division, or by offshoots in spring. Root rot may affect plants in wet conditions.
HARVEST Roots and rhizomes are lifted in autumn and dried for use in decoctions, tablets, and tinctures.

GERANIUM Cranesbill
(Geraniaceae)

Geraniums are high in tannins, providing astringent remedies important in traditional medicine for the emergency treatment of injuries and diarrhea. *G. maculatum* has a history of use among native N Americans and *G. dissectum* (cut-leaved cranesbill), a European species, appears to have similar properties. The Chinese *G. wilfordii* is used for rheumatic pain and gastrointestinal infections with diarrhea.

G. maculatum (American cranesbill, alumroot, spotted cranesbill, wild geranium) p.133

PARTS USED Whole plant, roots.
PROPERTIES A highly astringent, tonic herb that is antiseptic, checks bleeding, controls discharges, and promotes healing.
USES OF THE HERB
MEDICINAL Internally for diarrhea (especially in children and the elderly), dysentery, cholera, gastroenteritis, colitis, peptic ulcer, hemorrhage, and excessive menstruation. Externally for purulent wounds, hemorrhoids, thrush, vaginal discharge, and inflammations of the mouth, gums, and throat. Combined with *Bidens tripartita* (see p.249) for hemorrhage in the digestive tract; with *Trillium erectum* (see p.364) as a douche for vaginal discharge; with *Geum urbanum* (see this page), *Agrimonia eupatoria* (see p.231), and *Symphytum officinale* (see p.357) for peptic ulcer; and with *Agrimonia eupatoria* (see p.231), *Althaea officinalis* (see p.236), *Filipendula ulmaria* (see p.283), or *Chamaemelum nobile* (see p.259) for digestive upsets.
VARIANT
G. m. f. ***albiflorum***, p.133.

G. robertianum (herb Robert) p.133

PARTS USED Whole plant.
PROPERTIES A bitter, astringent, mildly diuretic herb that checks bleeding and mucous discharge, and promotes healing.
USES OF THE HERB
MEDICINAL Internally for diarrhea, gastrointestinal infections, peptic ulcer, and hemorrhage. Externally for skin eruptions, wounds, inflamed gums and throat, and herpes.
VARIANT
G. r. **'Celtic White'**, p.133.

GROWTH AND HARVEST
GROWTH Ornamental. Moist to wet soil in sun or partial shade (*G. maculatum*); well-drained to dry soil in sun or shade (*G. robertianum*). Propagate by division when dormant (*G. maculatum*), or by seed sown in early autumn or spring. Rust may attack foliage.
HARVEST Plants are cut as flowering begins, and roots (*G. maculatum*) are harvested in autumn; both are dried for use in decoctions, infusions, liquid extracts, powder, tablets, and tinctures. *G. robertianum* is often used fresh.

GEUM Avens
(Rosaceae)

G. urbanum has been used medicinally since Roman times. The root contains eugenol, as found in *Syzygium aromaticum* (see p.358); *G. rivale* (water avens) has similar but weaker properties.

G. urbanum (avens, wood avens, herb Bennet) p.134

PARTS USED Whole plant, roots.
PROPERTIES An astringent, antiseptic herb that reduces inflammation, checks bleeding and discharges, lowers fever, and has a tonic effect on the digestive system.
USES OF THE HERB
MEDICINAL Internally for diarrhea, gastrointestinal infections, bowel disease, uterine hemorrhage, and intermittent fever. Externally for hemorrhoids, vaginal discharge, and inflammations of the mouth, gums, and throat.

GROWTH AND HARVEST
GROWTH Crop. Rich, moist soil in shade. Propagate by seed sown in autumn or spring. Self-seeds freely.
HARVEST Plants are cut as flowering begins and dried for infusions and liquid extracts. Roots are lifted in spring and used fresh or dried for decoctions and liquid extracts.

GILLENIA
(Rosaceae)

G. trifoliata was known to many N American tribes and was adopted by the early colonists. It was listed in the *U.S. Pharmacopoeia* (1820–82). The same common names are generally shared between *G. trifoliata* and *G. stipulata*, although some authorities call the latter "American ipecac."

G. trifoliata, syn. *Porteranthus trifoliatus* (Indian physic, Bowman's root, American ipecac) p.134

PARTS USED Root bark.
PROPERTIES An emetic herb, similar in effects to *Cephaelis ipecacuanha* (see p.258). It also has purgative and expectorant effects. Small doses act as a stimulant.
USES OF THE HERB
MEDICINAL Internally in small doses for feverish illnesses, chronic diarrhea, constipation, and bronchial and asthmatic complaints.

GROWTH AND HARVEST
GROWTH Ornamental. Light, rich, moist soil in partial shade. Propagate by seed sown in autumn, or by division in autumn or spring.
HARVEST Roots are lifted in early autumn and stripped of bark, which is dried for use in decoctions and powder.

GINKGO Maidenhair tree
(Ginkgoaceae)

Ginkgo is often referred to as a living fossil, because trees alive today are almost identical to those that have been found in fossil records. It is classified in the same group as conifers and cycads, but is distinct from both. Seeds were sent back from China and Japan to Europe about 1727, and ginkgos were soon in cultivation. Seeds have long been used in traditional Chinese medicine, but in recent years Western research has concentrated on the leaves. One of the plant's main constituents are ginkgolides, which are not known in any other plant; these are PAF (platelet activating factor) blockers, which inhibit allergic responses. Ginkgo flavonoids appear to be effective in improving the circulation.

G. biloba (ginkgo, maidenhair tree) p.134

PARTS USED Leaves, seeds (*bai guo*).
PROPERTIES A bittersweet, astringent herb that dilates bronchial tubes and blood vessels, controls allergic responses, and stimulates the circulation; has antifungal and antibacterial effects.
USES OF THE HERB
CULINARY "Nuts" (seeds) are eaten after roasting.
MEDICINAL Internally for asthma, allergic inflammatory responses, cerebral insufficiency in the elderly, circulatory complaints such as Raynaud's disease and varicose veins, and irregular heartbeat (leaves); also for asthma, coughs with thick phlegm, and urinary incontinence (seeds). Combined with *Tilia* spp. (see p.363), and *Vinca major* (see p.369) or *Crataegus laevigata* (see p.268) for circulatory disorders, and with *Melilotus officinalis* (see p.310) for venous complaints (leaves); with *Ephedra* spp. (see p.278), *Tussilago*

farfara (see p.365), and leaves of *Morus alba* (see p.313) for asthma and coughs (seeds). Excess may cause dermatitis, headaches, diarrhea, and vomiting.
VARIANT
G. b. **'Pendula'**, p.134.

GROWTH AND HARVEST
GROWTH Ornamental. Rich, well-drained soil in sun. Propagate by seed sown when ripe in autumn (species only), or by softwood cuttings in spring, or by side-veneer grafting in winter. Ginkgos die back if pruned.
HARVEST Leaves are picked as they change color in autumn, and are dried for use in distilled extracts, infusions, powders, and tinctures. Kernels from ripe fruits are cooked for use in decoctions.

GLECHOMA
(Labiatae/Lamiaceae)

G. hederacea was important in brewing until about the 16th century, giving rise to its common name "alehoof" ("hoof" meant a herb); it was superseded by the hop (*Humulus lupulus*, see p.294). It was also made into a cough medicine known as "gill tea," from the French *guiller*, "to ferment" (beer).

G. hederacea, syn. *Nepeta glechoma*, *N. hederacea* (ground ivy, alehoof) p.134

PARTS USED Whole plant.
PROPERTIES A bitter, aromatic, astringent herb; it has a tonic effect on the bronchial, digestive, and urinary systems. It is diuretic and expectorant.
USES OF THE HERB
MEDICINAL Internally for excess mucus, sinusitis, ear infections, bronchitis, gastritis, and cystitis. Externally for inflammations of throat and mouth, and hemorrhoids.
VARIANT
G. h. **'Variegata'**, p.135.

GROWTH AND HARVEST
GROWTH Crop (*G. hederacea*). Ornamental (*G. hederacea* 'Variegata'). Moist, well-drained soil in sun or shade. Propagate by seed sown in spring (species only), or by division in autumn or spring. May be invasive.
HARVEST Flowering plants are dried for infusions and liquid extracts.

GLORIOSA Glory lily
(Liliaceae/Colchicaceae)

G. superba contains alkaloids, including colchicine. The species is grown in India as a commercial source of this compound, which is used in medicine and genetic engineering.

G. superba (glory lily, Malabar glory lily, Mozambique lily) p.135

PARTS USED Tubers.
PROPERTIES A bitter, stimulant herb, with anti-bacterial effects.

USES OF THE HERB
MEDICINAL Internally, use of fresh tuber causes abortion; it has been used to speed labor, soaked in milk to reduce toxicity. Mainly externally for lice, scabies, and leprosy. Excess causes numbness, nausea, spasms, and unconsciousness. For use by qualified practitioners only.
ECONOMIC Used in countries of origin for making arrow poison and to poison vermin.

GROWTH AND HARVEST
GROWTH Ornamental. Rich, well-drained soil in sun, minimum 46–50°F (8–10°C), with high humidity. Propagate by seed sown in spring at 70–75°F (21–24°C), or by offsets in early spring, started into growth at 61–66°F (16–19°C). Overwatering causes discolored foliage and premature leaf fall.
HARVEST Tubers are lifted in autumn and dried for use in pastes and powder.
WARNING All parts, especially tubers, are extremely toxic if eaten. Repeated handling of tubers causes skin irritation.

GLYCYRRHIZA Licorice
(Leguminosae/Papilionaceae)

Several different species and variants of licorice are used medicinally, including *G. glabra* var. *typica* (Spanish or Italian licorice), *G. g.* var. *violacea* (Persian or Turkish), and *G. g.* var. *glandulifera* (Russian). The main ingredient of *G. glabra* is glycyrrhizin, a substance 50 times sweeter than sucrose, with cortisone-like effects. *G. lepidota* (American or wild licorice) was used by native N Americans and by early settlers for problems with childbirth and menstruation. *G. uralensis* is a key herb in traditional Chinese medicine, its use being associated with longevity.

G. glabra (licorice) p.135

PARTS USED Roots, stolons.
PROPERTIES A very sweet, moist, soothing herb that is anti-inflammatory and expectorant, controls coughing, and has hormonal effects. It detoxifies and protects the liver.
USES OF THE HERB
MEDICINAL Internally for Addison's disease, asthma, bronchitis, coughs, peptic ulcer, arthritis, allergic complaints, and following steroid therapy. Not given to pregnant women or patients with high blood pressure, kidney disease, or taking digoxin-based medication. Excess causes water retention and raised blood pressure. Externally for eczema, herpes, and shingles. For use by qualified practitioners only.
ECONOMIC Roots are boiled to extract the familiar black substance used in licorice candy, and is sold dried to eat. A basis for most commercial laxatives. Extracts flavor tobacco, beer, soft drinks, and pharmaceutical products, and are used as a foaming agent in beers and fire extinguishers.

G. uralensis, syn. *G. viscida* (Chinese licorice, Manchurian licorice) p.135

PARTS USED Roots (*gan cao*).
PROPERTIES A sweet, tonic herb that stimulates adrenocorticol hormones, relaxes spasms, reduces pain and inflammation, is expectorant, and controls coughing. It also neutralizes toxins and balances blood sugar levels.
USES OF THE HERB
MEDICINAL Internally for Addison's disease, asthma, coughs, and peptic ulcer, externally for acne (combined with flowers of *Lonicera japonica*, see p.306), boils, and sore throat. Added to almost all formulas to harmonize and direct the effects of the various ingredients. Combined with *Panax ginseng* (see p.321) as an energy tonic. Precipitates many compounds, therefore considered incompatible with *Daphne genkwa* (see p.272), *Euphorbia kansui* (see p.281), *E. pekinensis*, and *Sargassum fusiforme* (see p.349); reduces effectiveness of *Coptis chinensis* (see p.266), *Corydalis solida* (see p.267), and *Tetradium ruticarpum* (see p.361); increases toxicity of salicylates, ephedrine, adrenaline, oral hypoglycemics, and cortisone. Contraindicated in pregnancy, hypertension, kidney disease, and for patients taking digoxin-based medication. Excess causes water retention, and raised blood pressure. Hormonal effects may cause impotence. For use by qualified practitioners only.

GROWTH AND HARVEST
GROWTH Crop. Deep, rich, sandy soil in sun. Slightly alkaline, moisture-retentive conditions give the best results. Propagate by seed sown in autumn or spring, or by division in autumn or spring, or by stolon cuttings in autumn or spring. Slow to grow from seed. Remove flower heads to encourage stronger roots and stolons, unless seed is required. Difficult to eradicate when well established.
HARVEST Roots and stolons are lifted in early autumn, 3–4 years after planting, and dried for decoctions, liquid extracts, lozenges, and powder.

GNAPHALIUM
(Compositae/Asteraceae)

According to Culpeper, "the juice of the herb taken with wine and milk, is, as Pliny saith, a sovereign remedy against the mumps and quinsey" (*The English Physitian Enlarged*, 1653). The American *G. obtusifolium* (sweet everlasting) was similarly used by the Creek people, who boiled the leaves in water, added lard, and wrapped cloths soaked in the liquid around the swollen neck. Others include *G. polycephalum*, an Indian remedy for mouth ulcers and *G. multiceps*, a Chinese cough cure.

G. uliginosum, syn. *Filaginella uliginosa* (marsh cudweed, low cudweed, cottonweed) p.135

PARTS USED Whole plant.
PROPERTIES An astringent, slightly aromatic herb

that is diuretic, anti-inflammatory, and increases perspiration. May have antidepressant and aphrodisiac effects.
USES OF THE HERB
MEDICINAL Internally and externally for laryngitis, upper respiratory mucus, and tonsillitis. Combined with *Sambucus nigra* (see p.347), *Xanthium strumarium* (see p.372), or *Solidago virgaurea* (see p.354) for excess mucus, and with *Echinacea purpurea* (see p.276) or *Galium aparine* (see p.285) for throat infections.

GROWTH AND HARVEST
GROWTH Crop. Moist to wet, acid soil in sun or partial shade. Propagate by seed sown in spring.
HARVEST Plants are cut when in flower and dried for use in infusions, liquid extracts, and tinctures.

GOSSYPIUM
(Malvaceae)

G. herbaceum was introduced from India to Egypt and China c.500BC and to the US in 1774. Cotton is also produced from *G. arboreum*, a species found in Asia and Africa, and from the American *G. barbadensis* (Sea Island cotton) and *G. hirsutum* (Upland cotton). Various parts of the cotton plant are also used in the traditional medicine of producer countries. The flower petals are used to produce brown and yellow dyes. Scientific research into its potential as a male contraceptive began in the 1970s, following the use in China of cottonseed oil for cooking, which caused infertility in men. The active constituent appears to be gossypol, a fraction of the oil that also stimulates the uterus.

G. herbaceum (cotton, Levant cotton) p.136

PARTS USED Leaves, root bark, seeds, flowers.
PROPERTIES An astringent, slightly acidic, aromatic herb that causes uterine contractions, depresses sperm production, lowers fever, reduces inflammation, and soothes irritated tissues. It also has antibacterial and antiviral effects.
USES OF THE HERB
MEDICINAL Internally for painful menstruation (root bark); dysentery, intermittent fever, and fibroids (seeds); gastroenteritis (leaves). Externally for thrush, scalds, bruises, and sores (leaves); herpes, scabies, wounds, and orchitis (seeds). For use by qualified practitioners only.
ECONOMIC Seed oil is used for cooking (with gossypol removed) and in making margarine, soaps, and animal feeds. Seed fibers account for 56 percent of all natural fibers used in fabrics, cordage, cotton balls, paper, and rayon. Other uses include X-ray and photographic films, and explosives. Petals yield brown and yellow dyes.

GROWTH AND HARVEST
GROWTH Crop. Rich, well-drained soil in sun, minimum 55–64°F (13–18°C). Propagate by seed sown in spring at 75–85°F (24–30°C). Pinch out tips in spring to encourage bushiness. Commercial crops are prone to numerous pests and diseases.
HARVEST Leaves are picked during the growing season for use in poultices or lotions. ►

► Roots are lifted in autumn, then peeled and dried for decoctions, liquid extracts, and tinctures. Seeds are separated from fibers in autumn for oil extraction and decoctions.

GRATIOLA
(Scrophulariaceae)

G. officinalis was once a well-known "officinal" plant. It is now obsolete as a herb on account of its toxicity; it contains cucurbitacins, which are poisonous to living cells, and glycosides similar in effect to those in *Digitalis* spp. (see p.273). Plants are, however, widely grown in herb gardens and sold as medicinal herbs by specialist nurseries. Hedge hyssop has quite different properties from true hyssop (*Hyssopus officinalis*) and cannot be used as a substitute.

G. officinalis (hedge hyssop) p.136

PARTS USED Whole plant.
PROPERTIES A bitter, acrid, diuretic herb that stimulates the heart and uterus, and has purgative and emetic effects.
USES OF THE HERB
MEDICINAL Internally, formerly used for liver complaints, jaundice, dropsy, enlarged spleen, and intestinal worms. Excess causes abortion, kidney damage, and bowel hemorrhage.

GROWTH AND HARVEST
GROWTH Ornamental. Damp, alkaline soil in sun. Propagate by seed sown under cover in spring, or by division in spring.
HARVEST Plants are cut when flowering and dried for use in infusions.
WARNING Toxic if eaten.

GRINDELIA Gumplant
(Compositae/Asteraceae)

Some 60 species of annuals, biennials, evergreen perennials, and subshrubs are included in this genus, distributed in western N and S America. A few are grown for their daisylike yellow flowers. Several species, including *G. squarrosa* and *G. lanceolata*, were used by native N Americans for bronchial complaints and poison-ivy rash. The latter use was observed by Dr. Canfield of Monterey, California, in 1863, and *Grindelia* became an official drug, listed in the *U.S. Pharmacopoeia* (1882–1926) and in the U.S. *National Formulary* (1926–60). It is unusual among perennials in containing up to 21 percent resin.

G. camporum, syn. *G. robusta* var. *rigida* (gumplant, gumweed, tarweed)

Annual or short-lived perennial, hardy to 23°F (–5°C), height 20in–4ft (50cm–1.2m), spread 30in (75cm), with narrowly oblong, toothed, resinous leaves up to 3in (8cm) long, and resinous yellow daisies, about 2in (5cm) across, in late summer. All parts have a balsamic odor. Found in dry situations in California.

PARTS USED Whole plant.
PROPERTIES A bitter, pungent, aromatic herb that is anti-inflammatory and expectorant, relaxes spasms, and has sedative effects.
USES OF THE HERB
MEDICINAL Internally for bronchitis, whooping cough, asthma, and cystitis. Externally for poison-ivy rash, dermatitis, eczema, and skin eruptions. Combined with *Lobelia inflata* (see p.305), *Glycyrrhiza glabra* (see p.289), *Euphorbia hirta* (see p.281), *Inula helenium* (see p.296), or *Primula veris* (see p.334) for bronchial complaints. Excess may irritate the kidneys.

GROWTH AND HARVEST
GROWTH Crop. Well-drained soil in sun. Propagate by seed sown in early spring at 61–66°F (16–19°C), or by semiripe cuttings in late summer.
HARVEST Plants are cut in full bloom and dried for use in infusions, liquid extracts, and tinctures, or used fresh in poultices.

GUAIACUM
(Zygophyllaceae)

The Spanish began exporting *G. officinale* to Europe in 1503, monopolizing the trade in its fine, bicolored wood and medicinal by-products. It was used by native people in northeastern S America to treat syphilis, which had been introduced by the colonists; Europeans also adopted this use for the next 200 years. The medicinal properties of *G. officinale* were described by Sir Hans Sloane (1660–1753), who practiced medicine in Jamaica. The wood contains about 20 percent resin, which can be used as a chemical reagent to detect bloodstains. *G. sanctum* is also exploited as a source of lignum vitae, as are the related *Bulnesia sarmienti* (Paraguay lignum vitae) and *B. arborea* (Maracaibo lignum vitae). Essential oil is also extracted from *B. sarmienti* and *B. arborea* for use as a fixative and fragrance in soaps, cosmetics, and perfumery. Another resinous species in this family is the southwestern American *Larrea divaricata* (creosote bush, chaparral), which contains nordihydroguaiaretic acid (NDGA), a potent antioxidant and alterative.

G. officinale (lignum vitae, guaiacum, guaiac) p.136

PARTS USED Wood, resin.
PROPERTIES A bitter, aromatic herb that stimulates the peripheral circulation, increases perspiration rate, is diuretic, anti-inflammatory, and expectorant, and clears toxins from the tissues. A mild laxative.
USES OF THE HERB
MEDICINAL Internally for upper respiratory tract infections. Internally and externally for rheumatic and arthritic complaints, and gout. Formerly used to treat syphilis. WARNING This herb is subject to legal restrictions in some countries.
ECONOMIC The wood is heavier than water and is used in the propeller shafts of ships, as well as for bowling balls and carving.

GROWTH AND HARVEST

GROWTH Crop. Rich, sandy, fibrous soil, minimum 59°F (15°C). Propagate by seed, sown with orange-yellow pericarp intact, in spring or summer, at 79°F (26°C); by softwood cuttings in spring. Seedlings and saplings do not transplant well from small pots and should be given relatively large containers at each stage.
HARVEST Wood (preferably heartwood) is cut as required and processed into chips and shavings, which are heated to extract resin for use in decoctions, liquid extracts, and tinctures.

GYNOSTEMMA
(Cucurbitaceae)

This genus occurs in southern and eastern Asia, and consists of two climbers, which attach themselves by means of tendrils. *G. pentaphyllum* was first described in traditional Chinese medicine during the Ming dynasty (1368–1644) as a folk remedy for hepatitis, bronchitis, and peptic ulcers. A better understanding of its properties was gained in the 1980s, as part of a Japanese research program into herbs with possible anticancer effects. It was rated among the ten most important tonic herbs at the 1991 International Conference on Traditional Medicine, in Beijing, China.

G. pentaphyllum (sweet tea vine, gospel herb)

Japanese annual or short-lived perennial climber, reaching 25ft (8m), hardy to 23°F (–5°C). Leaves are palmate, with 3–7 toothed leaflets, the terminal leaflet being up to 3in (8cm) long. Small, yellow-green, star-shaped flowers are produced in panicles up to 6in (15cm) long in summer, followed by smooth, very dark green fruits, up to 3in (8cm) across, marked with white lines.

PARTS USED Whole plant.
PROPERTIES A tonic herb that improves the circulation, stimulates liver function, strengthens the immune and nervous systems, and reduces blood sugar and cholesterol levels. It also has sedative effects, relaxing spasms and lowering blood pressure.
USES OF THE HERB
MEDICINAL Internally for nervous tension and exhaustion, peptic ulcer, asthma, bronchitis, diabetes, cardiovascular disease, and cancer.
ECONOMIC Used in antiaging tonics and cosmetics.

GROWTH AND HARVEST

GROWTH Crop. Moist, well-drained soil in partial shade. Propagate by seed sown in spring, soaked for 24 hours before sowing.
HARVEST Plants are cut in summer and dried for use in capsules, decoctions, extracts, tablets, and teabags.

HAMAMELIS Witch hazel
(Hamamelidaceae)

Various native N American tribes knew the medicinal properties of *H. virginiana*, including the Mohawk, who made a wash for bruised eyes by steeping the bark in water. It was adopted by settlers and listed in the *U.S. Pharmacopoeia* (1862–1916) and in the U.S. *National Formulary* (1916–55). Distilled witch hazel can be bought in any pharmacy for first aid or for making cosmetics, but is less effective than the tincture for treating more serious conditions.

H. virginiana (common witch hazel) p.136

PARTS USED Leaves, branches, bark.
PROPERTIES An astringent, slightly aromatic herb that checks bleeding and mucous discharge, and reduces inflammation.
USES OF THE HERB
MEDICINAL Internally for diarrhea, colitis, dysentery, hemorrhoids, vaginal discharge, excessive menstruation, hemorrhage in stomach or lungs, and prolapsed organs. Externally for varicose veins, sprains, bruises, burns, hemorrhoids, sore nipples, muscular aches, eye and skin inflammations, and sore throat. Combined with *Agrimonia eupatoria* (see p.231) and *Quercus robur* (see p.338) for diarrhea; *Ranunculus ficaria* (see p.339) or *Plantago major* (see p.331) for hemorrhoids; and *Aesculus hippocastanum* (see p.230) and *Calendula officinalis* (see p.252) for varicose veins.
ECONOMIC An important ingredient of commercial eye drops, skin creams, ointments, and skin tonics.

GROWTH AND HARVEST

GROWTH Ornamental. Moist, humus-rich, neutral to acid soil in sun or partial shade. Propagate by seed sown in autumn, or by layering in early autumn, or by softwood cuttings in summer. Germination is slow and erratic. Cut back untidy growths after flowering.
HARVEST Leaves are picked in summer for dry and liquid extracts, and ointments. Branches are cut in spring and decorticated for use in tinctures. Twigs are cut in spring for use in distilled extracts.

HARPAGOPHYTUM
(Pedaliaceae)

Nine species of perennials make up this genus found in southern Africa. In the Transvaal *H. procumbens* is a common wild plant, hazardous to animals that pick up the thorny fruits in their coats. It has large, colorful flowers, but is rarely cultivated; the fruits are apparently used as mouse traps in Madagascar. It was introduced to Western medicine by G. H. Mehnert, a South African farmer who observed local people using decoctions of the dried tubers to treat various ailments, notably digestive and rheumatic complaints. It contains bitter compounds, on a par with *Gentiana lutea* (see p.287), and harpagide, an iridoid glycoside, as found in the distantly related *Scrophularia nodosa* (see p.350).

H. procumbens (devil's claw, grapple plant)

Tender trailing perennial, reaching 3–5ft (1–1.5m), with tubers up to 8in (20cm) long and 2½in (6cm) thick, and many stems bearing round to ovate, toothed to pinnately lobed leaves about 3in (7cm) long, with white, hairy undersides. Solitary, red to purple, trumpet-shaped flowers, up to 2½in (6cm) long, appear in spring, followed by dehiscent capsules, up to 3in (7cm) long, armed with 1in (2.5cm) long, barbed thorns.

PARTS USED Tubers.
PROPERTIES A bitter, astringent, sedative, pain-killing herb that reduces inflammation and stimulates the digestive and lymphatic systems.
USES OF THE HERB
MEDICINAL Internally for arthritis, rheumatoid arthritis, spondylosis, neuralgia, and digestive problems involving the gall bladder and pancreas. Externally for arthritic and rheumatic joints. Not given to patients with gastric or duodenal ulcers.

GROWTH AND HARVEST

GROWTH Wild-collected. Sandy soil in sun, minimum 41–50°F (5–10°C). Propagate by seed sown in spring.
HARVEST Tubers are lifted when dormant and dried for use in decoctions, ointments, powders, and tinctures.

HEDEOMA
(Labiatae/Lamiaceae)

H. pulegioides had a long history of use by native N Americans for headaches, feverish colds, menstrual cramps, and abortion, before becoming a household remedy among settlers for the same purposes, and a popular digestive herb tea. It was listed in the *U.S. Pharmacopoeia* (1831–1916). *H. pulegioides* has a similar chemistry to *Mentha pulegium* (see p.311). *H. floribunda* (*mapá*, oregano) is used for flavoring and, in northern Mexico, as a tea for indigestion. The closely related *Poliomintha longiflora* (Mexican oregano) is also used for flavoring.

H. pulegioides (American pennyroyal, squaw mint, mosquito plant) p.136

PARTS USED Whole plant, oil.
PROPERTIES A pungently aromatic herb that stimulates the uterus, induces perspiration, improves digestion, and is expectorant.

USES OF THE HERB
MEDICINAL Internally for colds, whooping cough, indigestion, flatulence, nausea, painful menstruation, and childbirth (plant). Essential oil is extremely toxic and may cause death if taken internally. For use by qualified practitioners only.
ECONOMIC Oil is used in insect repellants and cleaning products.

GROWTH AND HARVEST
GROWTH Crop. Rich, sandy soil in sun or partial shade. Propagate by seed in spring.
HARVEST Plants are cut when flowering and dried for use in infusions and liquid extracts, or distilled for oil.

HEDERA Ivy
(Araliaceae)

Ivy contains emetine, an amebicidal alkaloid also found in *Cephaelis ipecacuanha* (see p.258), and triterpene saponins, which are effective against liver flukes, mollusks, intestinal parasites, and fungal infections. There are over 300 cultivars of *H. helix*. It was widely used by the ancient Greeks.

H. helix (English ivy) p.136

PARTS USED Leaves.
PROPERTIES A bitter, aromatic, antibacterial herb with a nauseating taste. It lowers fever, relaxes spasms, is expectorant, and constricts veins.
USES OF THE HERB
MEDICINAL Internally for gout, rheumatic pain, whooping cough, and bronchitis. Excess destroys red blood cells and causes irritability, diarrhea, and vomiting. Externally for skin eruptions, swollen tissues, painful joints, neuralgia, toothache, burns, warts, impetigo, scabies, and cellulitis. For use by qualified practitioners only.
VARIANTS
H. h. **'Erecta'**, p.137.
H. h. **'Glacier'**, p.137.
H. h. **'Goldheart'**, syn. *H. h.* 'Oro di Bogliasco', p.137.

GROWTH AND HARVEST
GROWTH Crop (*H. helix*). Ornamental (*H. h.* 'Erecta', *H. h.* 'Glacier', *H. h.* 'Goldheart'). Any soil or situation, except waterlogged. Tolerates heavy shade. Variegated cultivars are less hardy and need more light. Propagate by rooted layers, or by softwood cuttings in late summer. Trim to shape in spring and summer to control new growths. Scale insects, spider mites, and leafspot may attack leaves.
HARVEST Leaves are picked as required and used fresh for decoctions, liquid extracts, ointments, poultices, and tinctures, or macerated in vinegar.
WARNING All parts, especially young leaves and berries, are harmful if eaten. Severe skin irritant and allergen.

HELIANTHUS Sunflower
(Compositae/Asteraceae)

H. annuus is a plant on the borderline between food and herb. It was, however, widely used for medicinal purposes in Russia, following its introduction as a crop in the 18th century. A treatment for malaria, involving the maceration of sunflower stems and heads in vodka to stimulate perspiration, was used successfully by a healer in Siberia and passed into the repertoire of folk remedies.

H. annuus (sunflower) p.137

PARTS USED Whole plant, seeds, oil.
PROPERTIES A nutritious herb that lowers blood cholesterol levels and soothes irritated tissues.
USES OF THE HERB
CULINARY Seeds are eaten fresh or roasted, added to bread, or ground into flour for bakery products. Oil is used for cooking and salads.
MEDICINAL Internally for bronchial infections (seeds), tuberculosis, and malaria (whole plant). Externally as a base for massage oils and liniments used for rheumatic complaints and muscular aches.
ECONOMIC Oil is used for manufacture of margarine. Residue is important in animal feeds.
VARIANTS
H. a. **'Italian White'**, p.137.
H. a. **'Teddy Bear'**, p.137.

GROWTH AND HARVEST
GROWTH Ornamental. Well-drained soil in sun. Propagate by seed in spring. Flower heads may be affected by *Botrytis* in cool, damp conditions. Stems may collapse through *Sclerotinia* disease. Flowers attract beneficial insects, such as lacewings and parasitic wasps, that prey on garden pests, notably aphids.
HARVEST Whole plants are cut as flowering begins and used fresh for liquid extracts and tinctures. Seeds are collected in autumn and used fresh, pressed for oil, or roasted.

HELICHRYSUM
Everlasting flower
(Compositae/Asteraceae)

A few species have minor uses. *H. orientale* (immortelle) yields essential oil, used in perfume blending, and *H. serpyllifolium* (Hottentot tea) was popular as a tea in southern Africa, until doubts were cast on its safety. The flowers and leaves of many helichrysums dry well for floral arrangements and potpourris.

H. italicum, syn. *H. angustifolium* (curry plant) p.137

PARTS USED Leaves.
PROPERTIES An aromatic herb.
USES OF THE HERB
CULINARY Sprigs are added to rice, vegetables, deviled eggs and savory dishes to give a mild curry flavor.

GROWTH AND HARVEST
GROWTH Ornamental. Light, well-drained soil in sun. Propagate by heel or semiripe cuttings in summer. Cut back to old wood in spring.
HARVEST Sprigs are picked as required and used fresh.

HELONIAS
H. dioica. See *Chamaelirium luteum*.

HEPATICA
(Ranunculaceae)

H. nobilis has a long history of use in traditional European medicine. Culpeper wrote that "it fortifies the liver exceedingly, and makes it impregnable" (*The English Physitian Enlarged*, 1653). Early settlers in N America valued it for hepatitis and found that native tribes used the closely related *H. acutiloba* (sharplobe hepatica) in similar ways.

H. nobilis, syn. *H. triloba*, *Anemone hepatica* (American liverwort, liverleaf, kidneywort) p.138

PARTS USED Whole plant.
PROPERTIES An astringent, diuretic, antibiotic herb that acts as a mild tonic for the liver, and digestive and bronchial systems. It also promotes healing.
USES OF THE HERB
MEDICINAL Internally for bronchial and digestive complaints, and liver and gall bladder disorders. Externally for minor injuries and ringworm. It is little used today.
VARIANT
H. n. **'Rubra Plena'**, p.138.

GROWTH AND HARVEST
GROWTH Ornamental. Deep, moist, humus-rich, alkaline soil in shade. Propagate by seed sown when ripe (species only), or by division in late summer. Dislikes disturbance.
HARVEST Plants are cut from late spring to midsummer and dried for use in infusions, liquid extracts, and tinctures.

HERACLEUM
(Umbelliferae/Apiaceae)

Gerard's *Herball* (1597) recommended *H. sphondylium* for headaches, poor memory, melancholy, and agitation. It contains volatile oil and bergapten, a furanocoumarin that can cause photosensitivity. The fruits of the N American cow parsnip, *H. lanatum*, were used by Eclectic physicians in the 19th century to treat epilepsy, while various native N American tribes used the roots externally for healing and pain relief. *H. maximum* (also known as "cow parsley"), was similarly used for rheumatic pain and palpitations, and internally for indigestion and asthma. The difficulty in identifying white-flowered umbellifers, many of which are poisonous, makes it potentially dangerous to use these plants for food or medicine.

H. sphondylium (hogweed, cow parsnip, keck) p.138

PARTS USED Whole plant, leaves, leaf stalks, fruits.
PROPERTIES An aromatic, sedative, mildly expectorant herb that has a tonic effect on the digestion, lowers blood pressure, and is reputedly aphrodisiac.
USES OF THE HERB
CULINARY Leaf stalks are tied in bundles and sun-dried until yellow, exuding a sugar substance eaten as a delicacy in Russia and Siberia. Young shoots are eaten raw or cooked like asparagus.
MEDICINAL Internally for laryngitis, bronchitis, and debility, though little used today.

GROWTH AND HARVEST
GROWTH Crop. Moist or wet soil in sun or partial shade. Propagate by seed in spring. *H. sphondylium* should not be confused with *H. mantegazzianum* (giant hogweed).
HARVEST Plants are cut just before flowering for use fresh or dried in infusions. Leaves are cut before flowering, and fruits (when ripe) for use in infusions, liquid extracts, and tinctures.
WARNING Skin irritant in sunlight.

HEUCHERA
(Saxifragaceae)

H. americana was an important healing herb among native N Americans. It was adopted by settlers and was listed briefly in the *U.S. Pharmacopoeia* (1880–82).

H. americana (alumroot, American sanicle) p.138

PARTS USED Roots.
PROPERTIES A bitter, astringent herb that controls bleeding and discharge, and promotes healing.
USES OF THE HERB
MEDICINAL Internally for diarrhea, dysentery, and gastric ulcers. Excess irritates the stomach and causes kidney and liver failure. Externally for sores, wounds, sore throat, and vaginal discharge.

GROWTH AND HARVEST
GROWTH Ornamental. Moist, well-drained soil in partial shade. Propagate by seed in autumn or spring, or by division in autumn or spring. Shoots may be distorted by leafy gall.
HARVEST Roots are lifted in autumn and dried for decoctions and powders.

HIBISCUS Rose mallow
(Malvaceae)

H. sabdariffa was introduced to Jamaica in the 18th century and is now grown in many parts of Asia, Africa, C America, and in California and Florida. It reached Europe in the late 19th century as "Sudanese tea," but was initially unpopular due to its blood red color. Today it is used to color and flavor most fruit-based herb teas. *H. sabdariffa* var. *altissima* is widely grown for fiber; it has a taller, narrower habit. The related *Malvaviscus arboreus* (sleeping hibiscus, *tulipan del monte*) is used in C America and the Caribbean to stimulate hair growth and promote sweating.

H. abelmoschus. See *Abelmoschus moschatus*.

H. rosa-sinensis (Chinese hibiscus) p.138

PARTS USED Flowers, juice from petals.
PROPERTIES A sweet, astringent, cooling herb that checks bleeding, soothes irritated tissues, and relaxes spasms.
USES OF THE HERB
MEDICINAL Internally for excessive and painful menstruation, cystitis, venereal diseases, feverish illnesses, coughs, and to promote hair growth.
ECONOMIC Juice from petals is used in China as shoe polish and mascara.
VARIANT
H. r.-s. **'Cooperi'**, p.138.

H. sabdariffa (roselle, Jamaica sorrel, *karkadé*) p.139

PARTS USED Leaves, stems, flower calyces, seeds.
PROPERTIES An aromatic, astringent, cooling herb that has diuretic effects, helps lower fever, and provides vitamin C.
USES OF THE HERB
CULINARY Leaves, eaten raw or cooked, have a rhubarblike flavor. Calyces are added to jams, curries, and chutneys, and made into a cranberry-like sauce. Seeds are eaten roasted or made into an oily sauce.
MEDICINAL Internally as a tonic tea for digestive and kidney functions.
ECONOMIC Stems are a source of fiber (rosella hemp). Calyces are used to give color and flavor to herb teas.

GROWTH AND HARVEST
GROWTH Ornamental (*H. rosa-sinensis*, *H. r.-s.* 'Cooperi'). Crop (*H. sabdariffa*). Well-drained soil in sun, minimum 45–50°F (7–10°C). Propagate by seed in spring (species only), or by greenwood cuttings in late spring, or semiripe cuttings in summer. Cut back hard in spring. Whitefly, aphids, and spider mite may attack plants under cover.
HARVEST Stems are cut for fiber. Leaves are picked when young and used fresh; flowers are cut and dried for infusions and powders. Calyces are collected when mature and used fresh or dried. Seeds for roasting are collected when ripe.

HIERACIUM Hawkweed
(Compositae/Asteraceae)

H. pilosella was recommended by Culpeper in *The English Physitian Enlarged* (1653) as a "cooling, somewhat drying and binding" herb for a wide range of ailments.

H. pilosella, syn. *Pilosella officinarum* (mouse-ear hawkweed) p.139

PARTS USED Whole plant.
PROPERTIES A bitter, antibiotic herb that is diuretic and expectorant, promotes healing, relaxes spasms, reduces inflammation, and increases salivation.
USES OF THE HERB
MEDICINAL Internally for asthma, bronchitis, excess mucus, whooping cough, bronchial infections with hemorrhage, influenza, cystitis, inflammation of the kidney, kidney stones, diarrhea, and brucellosis. Externally for wounds, fractures, hernia, and nosebleed. Combined with *Marrubium vulgare* (see p.308), *Verbascum thapsus* (see p.368), and *Tussilago farfara* (see p.365) for whooping cough; with *Drosera rotundifolia* (see p.275), *Grindelia camporum* (see p.290), *Euphorbia hirta* (see p.281), or *Polygala senega* (see p.332) for asthma.

GROWTH AND HARVEST
GROWTH Crop. Well-drained to dry, poor soil in sun or partial shade. Propagate by seed sown in autumn or spring, or by division in autumn or spring.
HARVEST Plants are cut in summer and used fresh or dried in infusions, liquid extracts, syrups, and tinctures. Preparations are made fresh each year.

HIEROCHLOË Sweet grass
(Gramineae/Poaceae)

H. odorata contains glycosides, which on drying produce coumarin, a sweet-smelling, crystalline compound important in perfumery. It was synthesized from tar in 1868, but is still in demand from natural sources.

H. odorata, syn. *H. borealis* (sweet grass, holy grass, vanilla grass) p.139

PARTS USED Leaves, oil.
PROPERTIES An aromatic herb with a strong vanilla scent that acts as an excitant in perfumes and as a fixative for other scents.
USES OF THE HERB
AROMATIC Essential oil is used in perfumery.
ECONOMIC Leaves are added to vodka as a flavoring. They are also in demand for sachet and basket weaving, because they hold their fragrance for years. Oil is used to flavor candy, soft drinks, and tobacco.

GROWTH AND HARVEST
GROWTH Crop. Well-drained, moisture-retentive soil in sun. Propagate by division of rhizomes in spring and summer.
HARVEST Leaves are cut in summer, dried, and stored whole, or distilled for oil.

HORDEUM Barley
(Gramineae/Poaceae)

Barley was domesticated in the Middle East c.10,000 years ago. Grains were found in ancient Egyptian and Swiss Lake remains (c.2000BC). There are many cultigens, belonging to the two principal types (both included in *H. vulgare*): two-rowed barley (*H. distichum*) and six-rowed barley (*H. polystichum*). Medicinal uses of barley were first mentioned in the Ebers papyri (c.1550BC), in recipes for laxatives, expelling intestinal parasites, and poultices for burns and fractures. Barley was first mentioned in traditional Chinese medicine in the 16th century. Both decorticated ("pearl" barley) and germinated, or sprouted ("malted" barley) seeds are used. Barley has a low gluten content and is unsuitable for leavened bread or baking.

H. vulgare (barley) p.139

PARTS USED Seeds (*mai ya*).
PROPERTIES A sweet, warming herb that soothes irritated tissues, stimulates appetite, improves digestion, and suppresses lactation.
USES OF THE HERB
CULINARY Pearl barley is cooked in soups and stews, and infused with lemon or orange as barley water.
MEDICINAL Internally for indigestion, especially in babies, or after eating cereals, and for *Candida albicans* infection. Also for excessive lactation, hepatitis, abdominal bloating (germinated seed); coughs, weak digestion (malt extract), and poor appetite and digestion during convalescence (barley water). Not given to nursing mothers.
ECONOMIC Seeds are germinated and kiln-dried to produce "wort" for brewing beer, distilling whisky, and making malt extracts.

> **GROWTH AND HARVEST**
> GROWTH Crop. Well-drained soil in sun. Propagate by seed sown in spring.
> HARVEST Seeds are collected in autumn and decorticated or germinated for malt extracts.

HOUTTUYNIA
(Saururaceae)

H. cordata has two distinct chemotypes: the Japanese, with an orange scent, and the Chinese, which has a smell resembling that of coriander leaves.

H. cordata (*doku-dami, giáp cá*) p.139

PARTS USED Whole plant, leaves (*yu xing cao*).
PROPERTIES A pungent, cooling herb that is aromatic and diuretic, clears fevers and toxins, and reduces swelling.
USES OF THE HERB
CULINARY Leaves are used in Vietnamese cuisine as a garnish for fish stew and boiled duck eggs; also eaten raw in parts of China.
MEDICINAL Internally, in traditional Chinese medicine, for upper respiratory tract infections and for inflammation of the urinary tract. Externally for snakebites and skin disorders.
VARIANTS
***H. c.* 'Chameleon'**, p.139.
***H. c.* 'Flore Pleno'**, p.139.

> **GROWTH AND HARVEST**
> GROWTH Ornamental. Moist to wet soil, or shallow water in partial shade. Propagate by division in spring or autumn.
> HARVEST Whole plants and leaves are cut in the growing season and used fresh for decoctions.

HUMULUS Hop
(Cannabaceae)

Hops were used medicinally by several native N American tribes for insomnia and pain, and were well established in European medicine by the 17th century. Culpeper recommended them for skin infections, jaundice, headaches, and "heat of the liver and stomach" (*The English Physitian Enlarged*, 1653). Extracts of hop were listed in the *U.S. Pharmacopoeia* (1831–1916).

H. lupulus (hop) p.140

PARTS USED Leaves, shoots, female flowers (hops, strobili), oil.
PROPERTIES A bitter, tonic herb that is aromatic and diuretic, relieves pain, and relaxes spasms. It is a potent sedative and has hormonal and antibacterial effects.
USES OF THE HERB
CULINARY Young shoots are eaten raw or cooked like asparagus.
AROMATIC Dried hops are added to sleep pillows. Used in perfumes of the *chypre* and *fougère* types.
MEDICINAL Internally for insomnia, nervous tension, anxiety, irritability, nervous intestinal complaints (including irritable bowel syndrome), priapism, and premature ejaculation. Externally for skin infections, eczema, herpes, and leg ulcers. Combined with *Valeriana officinalis* (see p.367) as a sedative, and with *Chamaemelum nobile* (see p.259) or *Mentha* x *piperita* (see p.311) for nervous digestive problems. Not given to patients with a history of depression.
ECONOMIC Hops are the main flavoring in beers. Distilled oil and extracts are also used in food flavorings and soft drinks.
VARIANT

> **GROWTH AND HARVEST**
> GROWTH Crop (*H. lupulus*). Ornamental (*H. l.* 'Aureus'). Moist, well-drained soil in sun or partial shade. Propagate by tip cuttings in spring from female plants, or by division in spring. Remove previous season's growths during dormancy. Thin new shoots as required.
> HARVEST Flowers are picked in autumn and used fresh or dried for infusions, liquid extracts, tinctures, and oil distillation. Young shoots are cut in spring for culinary use.
> WARNING Skin irritant and allergen.

HYDNOCARPUS
(Flacourtiaceae)

H. kurzii was first mentioned in Chinese medical literature in 1347, and its use spread worldwide as a treatment for serious skin diseases, especially leprosy. The oil has a unique chemistry, containing acids which are unknown in any other oils.

H. kurzii, syn. *Taraktogenos kurzii* (chaulmoogra) p.140

PARTS USED Seeds (*da feng zi*), oil.
PROPERTIES An acrid, sedative herb, with an unpleasant smell, that lowers fever and expels intestinal worms. It is a potent antibiotic and alterative. In excess, it is a cardiovascular depressant.
USES OF THE HERB
MEDICINAL Internally for leprosy, scabies, eczema, psoriasis, scrofula, ringworm, and intestinal worms. May cause vomiting, dizziness, and breathing difficulties. Externally as a dressing for skin diseases; combined with walnut oil and pork lard for ringworm; with calomel and sesame oil for leprosy; and with sulfur and camphor for scabies. For use by qualified practitioners only.

> **GROWTH AND HARVEST**
> GROWTH Crop. Rich, moist, well-drained soil in moderate humidity, minimum 54–57°F (12–14°C). Propagate by seeds sown when ripe at 64–70°F (18–21°C), or by grafting in late spring or early summer.
> HARVEST Seeds are separated from berries when ripe and used whole for decoctions, powdered for pills and pastes, or crushed for oil. Oil is given as an emulsion or by injection.

HYDRANGEA
(Hydrangeaceae)

H. arborescens is an old native N American remedy for urinary stones, adopted by settlers and later established in herbal medicine. *H. a.* subsp. *radiata*, which has white undersides to the leaves, is occasionally grown for foliage effect. Its cultivars have some of the largest flower heads of the species, consisting almost entirely of sterile flowers.

H. arborescens (wild hydrangea, seven barks) p.140

PARTS USED Roots.
PROPERTIES A sweet, pungent herb that is antiseptic and diuretic, soothes irritated tissues, and reduces formation of urinary stones.
USES OF THE HERB
MEDICINAL Internally for kidney and bladder stones, cystitis, urethritis, prostatitis, rheumatoid arthritis, gout, and edema. Works well with *Aphanes arvensis* (see p.239), *Eupatorium purpureum* (see p.281), and *Arctostaphylos uva-ursi* (see p.241). Excess may cause dizziness and bronchial congestion.
VARIANT
***H. a.* 'Annabelle'**, p.140.

> **GROWTH AND HARVEST**
> GROWTH Crop (*H. arborescens*). Ornamental (*H. arborescens* 'Annabelle'). Moist, well-drained, humus-rich soil in sun or partial shade, avoiding early morning sun in frosty areas. Propagate by softwood cuttings in summer. Cut back previous year's flowering shoots in early spring. Remove dead flower heads.
> HARVEST Roots are lifted in autumn and dried for decoctions, liquid extracts, and tinctures.

HYDRASTIS
(Ranunculaceae)

H. canadensis was used for a variety of purposes by native N Americans. The Cherokees pounded the roots with bear fat as an insect-repellent unguent, and made decoctions to treat sore eyes and digestive problems. It became a popular home remedy among settlers and was listed in the *U.S. Pharmacopoeia* (1831–42 and 1863–1936). Goldenseal contains isoquinoline alkaloids, including berberine (as found in *Berberis vulgaris*, see p.248), which suggests that berberis is equally effective in treating complaints for which *Hydrastis* is used. After centuries of exploitation, populations in the wild are now severely depleted, and rhizomes have become increasingly expensive. The Trades Records Analysis of Flora and Fauna in Commerce (TRAFFIC) stated in 1992 that "all goldenseal in trade originates from wild sources" and is "susceptible to becoming endangered in some states."

H. canadensis (goldenseal, yellowroot, orangeroot) p.141

PARTS USED Rhizomes.
PROPERTIES A bitter, fetid, alterative herb that checks bleeding, reduces inflammation, stimulates bile flow and uterine contractions, and acts as a mild laxative. It also improves digestion, is decongestant, and is effective against bacterial and amebic infections.
USES OF THE HERB
MEDICINAL Internally for digestive disorders, peptic ulcers, excess mucus, sinusitis, excessive and painful menstruation, postpartum hemorrhage, and pelvic inflammatory disease. Not given to pregnant women or patients with high blood pressure. Destroys beneficial intestinal organisms as well as pathogens, so it is prescribed for limited periods only (maximum three months). Externally for eczema, ear inflammations, conjunctivitis, vaginal infections, and gum disease. Combined with *Filipendula ulmaria* (see p.283) and *Chamaemelum nobile* (see p.259) for digestive problems; with *Trillium erectum* (see p.364) for uterine bleeding; and *Hamamelis virginiana* (see p.291) and *Euphrasia officinalis* (see p.281) for eye infections.

GROWTH AND HARVEST
GROWTH Crop. Rich, moist, well-drained soil in shade, pH6.0–7.0. Propagate by seed in autumn, or by division when dormant. Germination from seed is slow.
HARVEST Rhizomes are lifted in autumn after foliage has died down, and dried for use in decoctions, liquid extracts, tablets, and tinctures.

HYDROCOTYLE

H. asiatica. See *Centella asiatica.*

HYOSCYAMUS Henbane
(Solanaceae)

H. niger was recommended by Dioscorides in the first century AD as a soporific and painkiller. It contains tropane alkaloids (mainly hyoscyamine and hyoscine), as found in the related *Atropa belladonna* (see p.246). Other species grown for alkaloid extraction include *H. muticus* (Egyptian henbane) and *H. albus* (Russian henbane). Henbane is notorious as a herb of sorcery, used to cause hallucinations and delirium. It has also been used as a poison: Hamlet's father was dispatched by having henbane juice poured into his ear.

H. niger (henbane, hogbean) p.141

PARTS USED Whole plant, leaves.
PROPERTIES A narcotic, sedative herb, with an unpleasant taste, that relaxes spasms, relieves pain, and dilates the pupils.
USES OF THE HERB
MEDICINAL Internally for asthma, whooping cough, motion sickness, Menière's syndrome, tremor in senility or paralysis, and as preoperative medication. Excess causes impaired vision, convulsions, coma, and death from heart or respiratory failure. Externally for neuralgia and dental and rheumatic pain. Added to laxatives to prevent griping, and to antiasthma and herbal cigarettes. For use by qualified practitioners only. WARNING This herb is subject to legal restrictions in some countries.

GROWTH AND HARVEST
GROWTH Crop. Light, well-drained soil in sun. Propagate by seed in spring or autumn. Potato beetle may cause damage.
HARVEST Flowering tops and leaves are collected in summer for use in dry and liquid extracts, medicated oil, and tinctures.
WARNING All parts are extremely toxic if eaten. Possible skin irritant or allergen.

HYPERICUM St. John's wort
(Guttiferae)

The ancient alleged magical properties of *H. perforatum* were partly due to the fluorescent red pigment, hypericin, which oozes like blood from the crushed flowers. Hypericin is an antidepressant and has been used in drug trials for acquired immune deficiency syndrome (AIDS).

H. perforatum (perforate St. John's wort, common St. John's wort) p.141

PARTS USED Whole plant.
PROPERTIES A bittersweet, cooling herb that is astringent, calms the nerves, reduces inflammation, and promotes healing. Locally antiseptic and analgesic.
USES OF THE HERB
MEDICINAL Internally for enuresis (especially in children), anxiety, nervous tension, menopausal disturbances, premenstrual syndrome, shingles, sciatica, and fibrositis. Not given to patients with chronic depression. Externally for burns, bruises, injuries (especially deep or painful wounds involving nerve damage), sores, sciatica, neuralgia, cramps, sprains, and tennis elbow. Works well with *Hamamelis virginiana* (see p.291) or *Calendula officinalis* (see p.252) for bruises. Used in homeopathy for pain and inflammation caused by nerve damage.
ECONOMIC Plant yields a red dye, and extracts are used in cosmetics.

GROWTH AND HARVEST
GROWTH Crop. Well-drained to dry soil in sun or partial shade. Propagate by seed in autumn or spring, or by division in autumn or spring. Subject to statutory control as a weed in some countries, notably in Australia.
HARVEST Plants are cut as flowering begins and used fresh or dried in creams, infusions, liquid extracts, medicated oils, and tinctures.
WARNING Harmful if eaten. Skin allergen in sunlight.

HYSSOPUS Hyssop
(Labiatae/Lamiaceae)

Hyssop is an ancient herb, mentioned several times in the Old Testament for purification (although these references may possibly be to *Origanum maru* var. *aegypticum* or to *O. syriacum*, rather than *H. officinalis*). It contains a camphoraceous volatile oil and compounds similar to those found in *Marrubium vulgare* (see p.308); hence its effectiveness for bronchial complaints.

H. officinalis (hyssop) p.141

PARTS USED Whole plant, leaves, flowers, oil.
PROPERTIES A bitter, aromatic, astringent herb that is expectorant, reduces inflammation, and lowers fever. It has a tonic effect on the digestive, urinary, nervous, and bronchial systems.
USES OF THE HERB
CULINARY Leaves have a bitter, sage–mint flavor, and are used sparingly with legumes and meat dishes.
MEDICINAL Internally for bronchitis, upper respiratory tract infections and congestion, feverish illnesses and coughs in children, flatulence, and colic (flowering plant); coughs (flowering plant or flowers). Externally for cuts and bruises (flowering plant); bronchial infections (medicated oil); nervous exhaustion (bath oil). Combined with *Verbascum thapsus* (see p.368) or *Glycyrrhiza glabra* (see p.289) for persistent coughs, and with *Thymus vulgaris* (see p.362) and *Eucalyptus globulus* (see p.280) for bronchial congestion. Excessive use of essential oil may cause epileptic fits and death. WARNING This herb, in the form of essential oil, is subject to legal restrictions in some countries.
ECONOMIC Used to flavor liqueurs, such as Chartreuse.
VARIANTS
H. o. f. ***albus***, p.141.
H. o. subsp. ***aristatus***, p.142.

GROWTH AND HARVEST
GROWTH Ornamental. Well-drained to dry, neutral to alkaline soil in sun. Propagate by seed in autumn or spring, or by softwood cuttings in summer. Variants may not come true from seed. Trim hedges and cut specimen plants back hard in spring.
HARVEST Leaves and flowering tops are picked as the buds open, and dried for infusions, syrup, liquid extracts, and tinctures, or distilled for oil.

I

ILEX Holly
(Aquifoliaceae)

Several different hollies are used medicinally. Some contain bitter compounds and stimulants, such as caffeine and theobromine, as found in tea, coffee, and cocoa. The N American *I. opaca* (American holly) has been given for bronchial complaints, fevers, constipation, intestinal worms, gout, and rheumatism; *I. vomitoria* was important as the emetic "black drink" in native N American rituals. Holly is also an important evergreen in the originally pagan custom of Christmas indoor decoration, symbolizing the continuation of life during winter dormancy.

I. aquifolium (English holly) p.142

PARTS USED Leaves.
PROPERTIES A bitter, astringent, tonic herb that is diuretic and lowers fever.
USES OF THE HERB
MEDICINAL Internally for malaria, bronchial complaints, influenza, and rheumatism.
VARIANTS
***I. a.* 'Ferox Argentea'**, p.142.
***I. a.* 'Madame Briot'**, p.143.

I. paraguensis, syn. *I. paraguariensis* (*maté*, *yerba maté*, Paraguay tea) p.143

PARTS USED Leaves.
PROPERTIES A pleasant-tasting, stimulant herb that is mildly analgesic and diuretic, relaxes spasms, and clears toxins. Reputed to reduce appetite.
USES OF THE HERB
MEDICINAL Internally for nervous tension headaches, migraine, neuralgia, mild depression, and rheumatic pain.
ECONOMIC A commercially important beverage in S America.

I. verticillata, syn. *Prinos verticillatus* (black alder, winterberry) p.143

PARTS USED Bark.
PROPERTIES A bitter, astringent, antiseptic herb that has tonic and laxative effects.
USES OF THE HERB
MEDICINAL Internally for fevers, hepatitis, and jaundice. Externally for skin inflammations, herpes, and gangrenous ulcers. Combined with *Ulmus rubra* (see p.366) for skin problems.

GROWTH AND HARVEST

GROWTH Ornamental (*I. paraguensis*: crop). Moist, well-drained soil in sun or shade. Deciduous or variegated hollies need sun or partial shade. *I. paraguensis* needs minimum 45°F (7°C). *I. verticillata* tolerates wet conditions. Propagate by seed sown in spring (species only), or by semiripe cuttings in late summer and autumn, or by layering in autumn. Cut back or trim in spring. Prune *I. paraguensis* into a low bush for ease of harvesting in the same way as tea (*Camellia sinensis*, see p.252). Leaves may be damaged by holly leaf miner or leafspot. Hollies dislike root disturbance.
HARVEST Leaves are picked in early summer (*I. aquifolium*) and dried for infusions and liquid extracts. Leafy shoots (*I. paraguensis*) may be picked at intervals throughout the year, in the same way as tea, and dried for infusions. Bark is peeled from twigs of *I. verticillata* in spring and dried for use in decoctions and liquid extracts.
WARNING Berries are harmful if eaten.

ILLICIUM Anise tree
(Illiciaceae)

A genus of about 40 species of evergreen shrubs and small trees, with aromatic bark, widely distributed in SE Asia and SE N America. The leathery leaves are aniseed-scented, and the flowers are produced directly from the bark. *I. verum* should not be confused with *I. anisatum*, which contains poisonous sikimitoxin and whose smaller, odorless fruits are sometimes used to adulterate star anise.

I. verum (star anise, *badian*)

Evergreen tree, hardy to 23°F (–5°C), height 60ft (18m), spread 22–40ft (7–12m), with pointed, elliptic leaves up to 6in (15cm) long. Solitary, yellow-white, magnolia-like flowers about ½in (1cm) across, often tinged red to pink inside, appear in summer, followed by 8-pointed, woody fruits, with a single seed in each segment. Found in woodland in China and Vietnam.

PARTS USED Fruits (*ba jiao hui xiang*), oil.
PROPERTIES A warm, stimulant herb that benefits the digestion, relieves pain, and has antifungal and antibacterial effects.
USES OF THE HERB
CULINARY Used to flavor curries, tea, and pickles; also an ingredient of "five spice powder" in Chinese and Vietnamese cuisine.
MEDICINAL Internally for abdominal pain, digestive disturbances, and complaints associated with cold conditions (such as lumbago). Often included in remedies for digestive disturbances and cough mixtures, and as aniseed flavoring for medicines. Chewed after meals as a digestive and breath sweetener in the East.
ECONOMIC Used to flavor coffee and candy. Essential oil is used to flavor liqueurs (such as anisette), soft drinks, and bakery products.

GROWTH AND HARVEST

GROWTH Crop. Moist, well-drained, neutral to acid soil in partial shade. Propagate by semi-ripe cuttings in summer.
HARVEST Fruits are collected unripe for chewing, and ripe for oil distillation or use in decoctions and powders.

IMPATIENS Jewelweed
(Balsaminaceae)

Jewelweeds have long been used by native N Americans to relieve the pain and irritation of rashes and eczema, particularly by the Potawatomi, who applied the juice to poison-ivy rash. *I. pallida* is very similar in appearance to the more common *I. capensis*.

I. pallida (pale touch-me-not, jewelweed) p.143

PARTS USED Whole plant, juice.
PROPERTIES An acrid herb that has diuretic, purgative, and emetic effects if taken internally.
USES OF THE HERB
MEDICINAL Externally for rashes caused by *Rhus* spp. (see p.341), corns, warts, ringworm (juice), and hemorrhoids (ointment).

GROWTH AND HARVEST

GROWTH Wild-collected. Moist soil in sun or shade. Propagate by seed in spring.
HARVEST Plants are cut when flowering and used fresh for ointments and juice extraction.

INULA
(Compositae/Asteraceae)

Several species are used medicinally and as dye plants. The shrubby *I. cappa* is a popular remedy in southern China for bronchial and rheumatic complaints, migraine, and skin infections. *Inula* is known as *pushkaramula* in Ayurvedic medicine and is highly regarded as a lung tonic and analgesic. *I. helenium* contains up to 44 percent inulin, a slightly sweet polysaccharide, which is of little food value but is often recommended to diabetics as a sweetener.

I. britannica var. *chinensis*, *syn. I. japonica* (Japanese elecampane,yellow starwort)

Robust perennial, hardy to 5°F (–15°C), height 8–24in (20–60cm), spread 20in (50cm). It has stalkless, lanceolate to oblong leaves, up to 4in (10cm) long, and yellow, daisylike flowers in summer. Native to wetlands and river banks in China, Japan, Manchuria, and Korea.

PARTS USED Flowers (*xuan fu hua*).
PROPERTIES A bitter, pungent, antibacterial herb that stimulates the digestive system, is expectorant, and controls vomiting.
USES OF THE HERB
MEDICINAL Internally for bronchial complaints with profuse phlegm, nausea and vomiting, hiccups, and flatulence. Combined with honey as an expectorant, and with *Zingiber officinale* (see p.373) and *Glycyrrhiza glabra* (see p.289) for digestive problems.

I. helenium (elecampane, scabwort) p.143

PARTS USED Roots, flowers, oil.
PROPERTIES A bitter, pungent, aromatic herb that is expectorant and diuretic; it relaxes spasms, reduces inflammation, and increases perspiration. Effective against bacterial and fungal infections, and acts as an alterative, cleansing toxins and stimulating the immune and digestive systems.

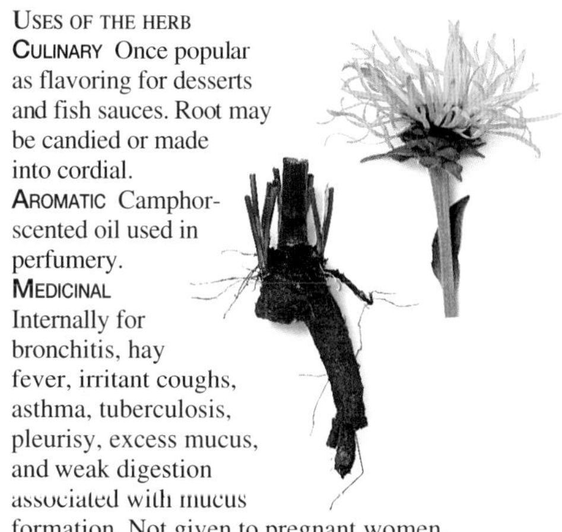

USES OF THE HERB
CULINARY Once popular as flavoring for desserts and fish sauces. Root may be candied or made into cordial.
AROMATIC Camphor-scented oil used in perfumery.
MEDICINAL Internally for bronchitis, hay fever, irritant coughs, asthma, tuberculosis, pleurisy, excess mucus, and weak digestion associated with mucus formation. Not given to pregnant women. Combines well with *Marrubium vulgare* (see p.308), *Tussilago farfara* (see p.365), *Asclepias tuberosa* (see p.244), and *Achillea millefolium* (see p.227). Sometimes recommended externally as a wash for skin inflammations and varicose ulcers, but may cause allergic reactions.
ECONOMIC Once favored as flavoring for candy and liqueurs.

GROWTH AND HARVEST
GROWTH Crop (*I. britannica* var. *chinensis*). Ornamental (*I. helenium*). Moist, well-drained soil in sun. Propagate by division or seed sown in spring or autumn.
HARVEST Roots are lifted in autumn and distilled for oil, used fresh to make extracts and syrup, or dried for decoctions, liquid extracts, powders, and tinctures. Flower heads are picked when fully open and dried whole for use in decoctions (prepared using a muslin bag to contain irritant fibers), infusions, and powders.

IPOMOEA Morning glory
(Convolvulaceae)

This large genus consists of 450–500 species of annuals, perennials, small trees, and shrubs, many of which are climbers. Several different species, including *I. turpeth* (turpeth) and the closely related *Convolvulus arvensis*, contain resins with a strong purgative effect. *I. arvensis* has also been used for fevers and to control bleeding. *I. digitata* (*vidari-kanda*) is used in Ayurvedic medicine as a diuretic, aphrodisiac, and rejuvenative tonic.

I. purga, syn. *I. jalapa*, *Convolvulus jalapa* (jalap)

Evergreen climber, hardy to 32°F (0°C), height to 10ft (3m), with a turniplike tuber, purple-red, twining stems, and pointed, ovate to heart-shaped leaves. Purple-pink, funnel-shaped flowers, 5in (12cm) across, appear in autumn. Native to woodland on the eastern slopes of the Mexican Andes.

PARTS USED Tuber, resin.
PROPERTIES A resinous, acrid herb, with an unpleasant taste, that acts as a purgative.
USES OF THE HERB
MEDICINAL Internally for constipation, colic, and intestinal parasites. Added to laxative and carminative preparations to prevent griping. WARNING This herb, in the form of jalap resin, is subject to legal restrictions in some countries.

GROWTH AND HARVEST
GROWTH Crop. Well-drained, humus-rich soil in sun. Propagate by seed sown in spring, or by semiripe cuttings in summer. Cut back or thin out in spring. Whitefly, aphids, and spider mites may damage plants under cover.
HARVEST Roots are lifted in autumn and dried for use in powders, resin extraction, and tinctures.
WARNING Seeds of many *Ipomoea* species are harmful if eaten.

IRIS
(Iridaceae)

The use of dried iris root, known as "orris," was recorded in ancient Egypt, Greece, and Rome, and remains important in perfumery. Orris contains volatile oil, consisting partly of irone, which gives a violet scent that intensifies as the dried rhizome ages. Several different species are grown as sources of orris, including *I. pallida* (Dalmatian iris). *I. versicolor* was one of the most widely used medicinal plants among native N Americans; its importance to the Creek people was such that they grew it near their villages. Blue flag was listed in the *U.S. Pharmacopoeia* (1820–95) as an emetic and purgative, but it has a far wider range of medicinal applications today. Some authorities maintain that *I. germanica* var. *florentina*, which is common near Florence, is a separate species (*I. florentina*), while others regard it as a hybrid.

I. germanica var. *florentina* (orris) p.143

PARTS USED Rhizomes.
PROPERTIES A soothing, aromatic herb that has diuretic and expectorant effects. It is both purgative and antidiarrheal.
USES OF THE HERB
MEDICINAL Internally for coughs, excess mucus, and diarrhea. Externally for deep wounds.
ECONOMIC Added to dental preparations, breath fresheners, and dusting powders. Used as a fixative in perfumery and potpourris.

I. versicolor (blue flag, wild iris) p.143

PARTS USED Rhizomes.
PROPERTIES An acrid, slightly aromatic, alterative herb that stimulates the liver and gall bladder, reduces inflammation, increases rates of perspiration and salivation, and acts as a diuretic and laxative.
USES OF THE HERB
MEDICINAL Internally for psoriasis, acne, herpes, migraine due to liver dysfunction, arthritis, fibroids, swollen glands, septicemia, and pelvic inflammatory disease. Fresh rhizome causes nausea and diarrhea. Not given to pregnant women. Externally for skin diseases, rheumatism, and infected wounds. Combines well with *Rumex crispus* (see p.344), *Trifolium pratense* (see p.364), *Phytolacca americana* (see p.327), or *Stillingia sylvatica* (see p.356) for skin disease.
VARIANT
***I. v.* 'Kermesina'**, p.144.

GROWTH AND HARVEST
GROWTH Ornamental. Well-drained, neutral to alkaline soil in sun (*I. germanica* var. *florentina*); rich, moist to wet, acid soil or shallow water in sun (*I. versicolor*). Propagate by division in summer, or by seed sown in autumn. Cultivars do not come true from seed.
HARVEST Rhizomes are lifted in late summer and early autumn, and dried for use in decoctions, liquid extracts, and powders.
WARNING All parts of *Iris* species are harmful if eaten, especially rhizomes. Skin irritant and allergen.

ISATIS
(Cruciferae/Brassicaceae)

Both Julius Caesar and Pliny described how the Britons painted their bodies with woad, the blue dye produced from *I. tinctoria.* The process of fermentation gave off such a foul smell that it was banned by Queen Elizabeth I within 5 miles (8km) of any of her palaces. It remained a popular dye for fabrics until the 1630s, when it was superseded by indigo (from *Indigofera* species). According to Mrs. Grieve (*A Modern Herbal*, 1931), *I. tinctoria* "is so astringent that it is not fit to be given internally as a medicine, and has only been used medicinally as a plaster, applied to the region of the spleen, and as an ointment for ulcers, inflammation, and to stanch bleeding." It was first mentioned in traditional Chinese medicine in the 1590s and is often prescribed in large doses with apparently no ill effects. In practice, high doses are recommended to maintain high levels of active ingredients. Recent research suggests pronounced antiviral effects. The Chinese drug *qing dai* (from the leaf pigment of *I. tinctoria*) is also prepared from *Polygonum tinctorium* and *Indigofera suffruticosa*.

I. tinctoria (woad) p.144

PARTS USED Leaves (*da qing ye*), roots (*ban lang gen*).
PROPERTIES A bitter, chilling herb that lowers fever and reduces inflammation. It controls a wide range of pathogenic organisms, including viruses, and reputedly has anticancer effects.
USES OF THE HERB
MEDICINAL Internally for meningitis, encephalitis, mumps, influenza, erysipelas, heat rash, sore throat, abscesses and swellings (leaves, roots); convulsions and high fevers in children, coughing of blood, and as a detoxifier in infections such as mumps, erysipelas, and thrush (pigment).

GROWTH AND HARVEST
GROWTH Ornamental. Rich, well-drained, neutral to alkaline soil in sun. Propagate by seed sown *in situ* in spring or under cover in autumn. Self-seeds readily, but does not thrive in the same soil for more than 2 years.
HARVEST Leaves are picked in summer and used fresh or dried in decoctions, or macerated for extraction of blue pigment, which is then dried as a powder. Roots are lifted in autumn and dried for use in decoctions.

J

JASMINUM Jasmine
(Oleaceae)

J. officinale was introduced to Europe in the mid-16th century and is widely grown for the perfumery industry. *J. grandiflorum* and the yellow-flowered *J. odoratissimum* are also used. Traditionally, the essential oil was produced by *enfleurage*, a method in which the volatile scents were taken up by odorless oils. *J. sambac*, especially in its double forms, is sacred to Vishnu and is used in Hindu ceremonies. *J. sambac* 'Grand Duke of Tuscany' is a rare double-flowered cultivar, first established in Europe in the garden of the Grand Duke, having been imported to Pisa from Goa c.1691. *J. sambac* is the main species used for flavoring tea. Good-quality jasmine tea does not necessarily contain jasmine flowers; it can be made by storing loose tea alongside the flowers for several weeks. Medicinal jasmines include *J. angustifolium*, mixed with *Acorus calamus* (see p.228) in Ayurvedic medicine as a cure for ringworm, and *J. lanceolarium* stems, used in southern China for rheumatic pains, injuries, boils, and abscesses.

J. grandiflorum (royal jasmine, Spanish jasmine, *jati*) p.144

PARTS USED Roots, flowers, oil.
PROPERTIES A bitter, astringent, cooling herb that calms the nerves, checks bleeding, and stimulates the uterus. Regarded as an aphrodisiac for women and an alterative, reputedly effective against various cancers and bacterial and viral infections.
USES OF THE HERB
MEDICINAL Internally, mainly in Ayurvedic medicine, for infectious illnesses with high fever, complaints involving bleeding, sunstroke, conjunctivitis, dermatitis, urethritis, cancer (especially Hodgkin's disease and cancers of the bone, lymph nodes, and breast), emotional upsets, and headaches. Often combined with *Santalum album* (see p.348).
ECONOMIC Oil is used in the perfumery industry.

J. officinale (common jasmine, poets' jessamine) p.144

PARTS USED Flowers, oil.
PROPERTIES An aromatic, tonic, euphoric herb that relieves spasms, increases milk flow, and stimulates the uterus. It also has aphrodisiac and antiseptic effects.
USES OF THE HERB
MEDICINAL Mainly in aromatherapy for depression, nervous tension, impotence, frigidity, menstrual disorders, respiratory disorders of nervous origin, and weak digestion.
ECONOMIC Essential oil is used in perfumes with a floral note, and in food flavorings (notably Maraschino cherries).
VARIANTS
***J. o.* 'Aureum'**, syn. *J. o.* 'Aureovariegatum', p.144.
J. o.* f. *affine, syn. *J. o.* 'Grandiflorum', p.144.

J. sambac (Arabian jasmine) p.145

PARTS USED Flowers.
PROPERTIES Similar to both *J. grandiflorum* and *J. officinale*.
USES OF THE HERB
ECONOMIC Mainly as a flavoring for green (Hyson) tea in China. An important garland flower in India.
VARIANTS
***J. s.* 'Grand Duke of Tuscany'**, syn. *J. s.* 'Trifoliatum', p.145.

GROWTH AND HARVEST

GROWTH Ornamental. Rich, well-drained soil in sun. *J. grandiflorum* and *J. officinale* need minimum 45°F (7°C), *J. sambac* minimum 50°F (10°C). Propagate by seed sown in spring, or by semiripe cuttings in summer. *J. s.* 'Grand Duke of Tuscany' does not root from cuttings and may be layered during the growing season. Thin out shoots or cut back after flowering. Climbing and trailing forms are excellent for hanging baskets. Plants under cover may be affected by spider mite, aphids, whitefly, and mealybugs.
HARVEST Roots are lifted in autumn and dried for use in decoctions (*J. grandiflorum*). Flowers are picked soon after opening each morning and used fresh for oil extraction, as flavorings, or dried for infusions, medicated oil, pastes, and powders.

JATEORHIZA
(Menispermaceae)

This genus of two species of herbaceous climbers occurs in tropical east Africa. It was introduced to Europe in the 17th century by the Portuguese as an antidote to poisons but was not widely used until the end of the 18th century. It contains substances similar to those found in *Berberis vulgaris* (see p.248).

J. palmata, syn. *J. calumba*, *Menispermum palmatum* (*calumba*, *colombo*)

Tender, perennial, rhizomatous vine, reaching 45ft (15m), with fleshy roots and hairy, palmately lobed leaves up to 16in (40cm) long. Small green-white flowers are borne in axillary clusters: males in panicles up to 16in (40cm) long; females in racemes up to 4in (10cm) long, followed by globose fruits, 1in (2.5cm) long and almost as wide. Found in lowland rainforest and riverine forest.

PARTS USED Roots.
PROPERTIES A very bitter, mucilaginous herb that acts mainly as a tonic for the digestive system. It also lowers blood pressure and has antifungal effects.
USES OF THE HERB
MEDICINAL Internally for morning sickness, atonic dyspepsia with low stomach acid, diarrhea, and dysentery. Combines well with *Zingiber officinale* (see p.373) and *Senna alexandrina* (see p.352).

GROWTH AND HARVEST

GROWTH Crop. Moist, humus-rich soil in shade, with high humidity, minimum 59–64°F (15–18°C). Propagate by seed sown in spring, by division in spring, or by cuttings of semiripe shoots in summer. Cut back stems in early spring or train on supports.
HARVEST Roots are lifted in dry weather and dried for use in concentrated infusions, liquid extracts, powders, and tinctures.

JUGLANS Walnut
(Juglandaceae)

The N American *J. cinerea* (butternut, white walnut) was a native remedy for digestive disorders and became one of the most widely used laxatives in the last century. It was listed in the *U.S. Pharmacopoeia* (1820–1905) and is now used by herbalists for constipation associated with dyspepsia, liver dysfunction, and skin eruptions. Although strongly purgative, it is quite safe for pregnant women. Walnut leaves and husks were the main source of brown hair dyes until the early 20th century, a use first described by Pliny (AD23–79). Lumber and veneers come from a number of different species, including *J. nigra* (black walnut), prized for its rich brown, attractively grained, durable wood.

J. regia (English walnut) p.145

PARTS USED Leaves, bark, fruits (unripe rind), kernels (*hu tao ren*), oil.

PROPERTIES A bitter, astringent herb that is expectorant and laxative, soothes irritated tissues, and dissolves kidney stones. It controls many disease-causing organisms and has anticancer properties.
USES OF THE HERB
CULINARY Nuts are included in Middle Eastern chicken dishes, Provençal *raito* (salt cod), and Italian *pesto* sauce for pasta. Oil is also much used in a variety of dishes. Unripe fruits are pickled, preserved in syrup, and made into the French liqueur *brou de noix*.
MEDICINAL Internally for constipation, chronic coughs, asthma, and urinary stones (leaves); diarrhea and anemia (rind); and menstrual problems and dry skin conditions (oil). Externally for eczema, herpes, eruptive skin complaints, eye inflammations, and hair loss. Regarded in traditional Chinese medicine as a tonic for weak kidney energy.

ECONOMIC Leaves and husks yield brown dye used in hair tints and conditioners for dark hair. Wood is used in furniture, veneers, and gunstocks. Oil is used in cosmetics and artists' paints.
VARIANT
J. r. **'Laciniata'**, p.145.

GROWTH AND HARVEST
GROWTH Ornamental. Deep, rich, well-drained soil in sun. Propagate by seed sown under cover in autumn (species only), by whip-and-tongue grafting, or by chip-budding onto *J. nigra*. Self-fertile cultivars produce more reliable crops. Certain plants are sensitive to an exudate from the leaves and roots of black walnuts and will not grow under or near them. Remove badly placed and dead branches in winter. Leaves may be marked by bacterial leaf blotch and blight. Young shoots and flowers may be damaged by frost in cold sites.
HARVEST Leaves are picked during the growing season and dried for use in infusions and liquid extracts. Fruits are collected unripe, or when ripe in autumn, and separated into husks, shells, and kernels. Green rinds are used fresh for infusions, husks are infused for dye, and kernels pressed for oil.

JUNIPERUS Juniper
(Cupressaceae)

Various junipers are used medicinally. Native N Americans treated a wide range of illnesses, from kidney complaints to dandruff and syphilis, with extracts of *J. scopulorum* (Rocky Mountain juniper). *J. virginiana* (red cedar) was used for ailments such as coughs and colds, headaches, dysentery, and mumps. Red cedar oil is pleasantly aromatic but is extremely toxic. *J. sabina* (savin) is also considered too poisonous for internal use because it contains podophyllotoxin (as found in *Podophyllum peltatum*, see p.332), which destroys cells and has resulted in fatalities.

J. communis (common juniper) p.145

PARTS USED Fruits ("berries"), oil.
PROPERTIES A bitter, aromatic herb that is antiseptic and diuretic, improves digestion, stimulates the uterus, and reduces inflammation.
USES OF THE HERB
CULINARY Juniper berries are added to pickles, sauerkraut, game, pâtés, ham, and pork.
AROMATIC Oil is used in spicy fragrances.
MEDICINAL Internally for cystitis, urethritis, kidney inflammation, rheumatism, gout, arthritis, and poor digestion with flatulence and colic. Externally for rheumatic pain and neuralgia. Combines well with *Aphanes arvensis* (see p.239) for cystitis. Juniper is an irritant, best combined with demulcent herbs, such as *Althaea officinalis* (see p.236) or *Zea mays* (see p.372). Not given to pregnant women or to patients with kidney disease.
ECONOMIC Oil gives flavor to gin (the word gin, a shortened form of the Dutch *genever*, derives from the Latin *juniperus*).

GROWTH AND HARVEST
GROWTH Ornamental. Most soils in sun or partial shade. Tolerates acid and alkaline conditions, dry and wet soils, and exposed positions. Propagate by seed sown under cover in autumn or spring, or by cuttings of lateral shoots with a heel in autumn. Plants may be damaged by juniper scale, blight, mites, and bagworms.
HARVEST Fruits are collected by shaking branches over a groundsheet; they are used fresh for oil distillation or dried for infusions, liquid extracts, tablets, and tinctures.
WARNING Junipers may cause skin irritation and allergic responses.

JUSTICIA
(Acanthaceae)

In India, *J. adhatoda* has long been an important medicinal herb for treating a wide range of bronchial diseases. It was introduced to Europe in 1699. Recent research has shown that it contains various alkaloids, including vasicine (also known as peganine), which stimulates contraction of uterine muscles, thus inducing or accelerating labor. It is now important as a source of this clinically useful drug. Another substance found in *J. adhatoda* is adhatodic acid. According to Mrs. Grieve (*A Modern Herbal*, 1931), adhatodic acid "exerts a strong poisoning influence upon the lower forms of animals and vegetable life, though nonpoisonous to the higher animals."

J. adhatoda, syn. *Adhatoda vasica* (Malabar nut, *vasak*) p.145

PARTS USED Leaves.
PROPERTIES A bitter, expectorant herb with a strong tealike odor. It relaxes spasms, lowers fever, and stimulates the uterus.
USES OF THE HERB
MEDICINAL Internally for asthma, chronic bronchitis, tuberculosis, and intermittent fever. Leaves are smoked to relieve asthma.

GROWTH AND HARVEST
GROWTH Crop. Well-drained soil in sun or partial shade, minimum 50–59°F (10–15°C). Propagate by softwood cuttings in spring or early summer. Cut back ornamental specimens hard in early spring to control size. Plants under cover may be attacked by whitefly.
HARVEST Leaves are collected during the growing season and dried for use in herbal smoking mixtures, liquid extracts, and tinctures.

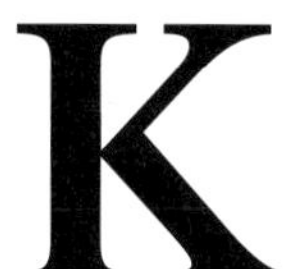

KAEMPFERIA
(Zingiberaceae)

K. galanga is used for flavoring in tropical Africa and Asia, as an hallucinogen in New Guinea, and is added to arrow poison in Malaysia. In the Middle Ages it was familiar in European cooking as galingale, perhaps because it resembled *Cyperus longus* (sweet galingale, see p.271). The related *K. rotunda* and *K. pandurata* are also used for flavoring and as spicy vegetables in their countries of origin.

K. galanga (resurrection lily) p.146

PARTS USED Rhizomes.
PROPERTIES A bitter, stimulant herb with a camphoraceous aroma. It is antibacterial, improves digestion, and has diuretic effects.
USES OF THE HERB
CULINARY Used to flavor rice and as a substitute for turmeric. Rhizomes and young shoots are pickled, eaten raw, or cooked as vegetables.
AROMATIC Powdered rhizome is used in linen sachets.
MEDICINAL Internally for bronchial complaints, dyspepsia, and headaches. Externally for wounds, dandruff, rheumatic joints, and as a gargle for sore throat. Combined with *Alpinia galanga* (see p.235), *Curcuma longa* (see p.270), and *Zingiber* spp. (see p.373) as *awas empas*, an Indonesian remedy for headaches, stiff joints, and urinary tract complaints.
ECONOMIC Powdered rhizome is added to body powders and cosmetics.

GROWTH AND HARVEST
GROWTH Crop. Rich, moist soil in shade, with high humidity, minimum 64°F (18°C). Propagate by division in late spring. Kaempferias must be kept dry when dormant.
HARVEST Rhizomes are lifted during dormancy and used fresh as a vegetable, or dried for use in decoctions, poultices, and powders.

KALMIA
(Ericaceae)

The toxicity of *K. latifolia* is legendary. Some native Americans used it as a suicide plant. Game birds and livestock may be poisonous to eat if they have ingested the leaves. According to Pehr Kalm (1715–79), after whom the genus is named, sheep are especially susceptible (hence one of Kalmia's common names, lambkill), while deer are unharmed (*Travels in North America*, i, 1753). Though the flesh of affected animals is apparently not contaminated, the intestines will cause poisoning if fed to dogs, so that they "become quite stupid, and, as it were, intoxicated, and often fall so sick that they seem to be at the point of death" (Kalm). Symptoms of poisoning in humans include vertigo, headache, loss of sight, salivation, thirst, nausea, vomiting, palpitations, slow pulse, and difficulty in breathing. *K. latifolia* contains arbutin (as in *Arctostaphylos uva-ursi*, see p.241), a urinary antiseptic, but this is of minor importance compared with the plant's narcotic effects.

K. latifolia (mountain laurel, calico bush, ivybush) p.146

PARTS USED Leaves.
PROPERTIES An astringent, slightly bitter herb that acts as a cardiac sedative.
USES OF THE HERB
MEDICINAL Internally for syphilis, inflammatory fevers, diarrhea, bowel hemorrhage, neuralgia, paralytic conditions, tinnitus, and angina. Externally for herpes, scalp conditions, and skin irritations. For use by qualified practitioners only. It is seldom used today.
VARIANTS
***K. l.* 'Clementine Churchill'**, p.146.
***K. l.* 'Ostbo Red'**
Dense shrub, hardy to –15°F (–26°C), height and spread 10ft (3m), with red buds and deep pink flowers. This cultivar was the first red-budded kalmia in cultivation. It originated in the US during the 1940s. Many cultivars are available.

GROWTH AND HARVEST
GROWTH Ornamental. Acid soil in sun or partial shade. Propagate by seed in autumn (species only), or by softwood cuttings in summer. Prefers cooler regions.
HARVEST Leaves are picked when plants are flowering and used fresh for infusions, tinctures, and ointments, or dried for powder.
WARNING All parts, including the nectar, are harmful if eaten.

KRAMERIA
(Krameriaceae)

This genus is the only one in the family Krameriaceae; it contains 15–25 species of semiparasitic trees, shrubs, and perennials occurring in dry areas of southwestern N America and southern S America. Rhatany root is collected mainly from *K. triandra*, but *K. cistoidea* and *K. argentea* are also exploited. Supplies are exported from Peru, where they are collected from the wild. *K. triandra* was introduced to cultivation during the 19th century, but is no longer seen, presumably because it proved too difficult. Aqueous extracts of rhatany are red, like those from other tannin-rich herbs, such as *Agrimonia eupatoria* (see p.231) and *Potentilla erecta* (see p.334). The extracts of rhatany contain 10–20 percent condensed tannins and also a red pigment, phlobaphene (rhatany red). Rhatany extracts were once widely used to improve the color, astringency, and richness of red wine, and their source was a closely guarded secret among Portuguese and Spanish merchants during colonial times.

K. triandra (rhatany, *ratanhia*, *mapato*)

Tender, low-growing shrub, height 20–36in (50–90cm), spread 2–4ft (60cm–1.2m), with a wide-spreading, red-black rootstock, orange-red within, and procumbent stems. The stalkless, ovate, hairy leaves are about ½in (1cm) long, and 1in (2.5cm) across; shining scarlet flowers with pointed petals are followed by rounded, spiny fruits, ¼in (6mm) across. Found on western slopes of the Andes in Peru, at 3,000–9,000ft (915–2,785m).

PARTS USED Roots.
PROPERTIES A strongly astringent herb that checks bleeding, controls discharges and diarrhea, and encourages healing.
USES OF THE HERB
MEDICINAL Internally for diarrhea, hemorrhage, and excessive menstruation. Externally for vaginal discharge, hemorrhoids, chilblains, wounds, gingivitis, and pharyngitis.
ECONOMIC Added to port wine to increase astringency, and to oral hygiene preparations.

GROWTH AND HARVEST
GROWTH Wild-collected. Well-drained, sandy or stony soil in sun, minimum 41–50°F (5–10°C). This species does not appear to be in cultivation at present.
HARVEST Roots are lifted from wild plants as available and dried for use in tinctures and dry extracts.

L

LACTUCA Lettuce
(Compositae/Asteraceae)

Lactuca species contain mildly narcotic compounds in the latex, which is known as "lactucarium" when dried. The active constituents increase during flowering and are relatively low in young plants. In addition to *L. serriola*, the main sources of lactucarium now are *L. virosa* (wild or great lettuce) and *L. canadensis* (American wild lettuce). Centuries of breeding have reduced the amounts in the garden lettuce (*L. sativa*). Lactucarium entered medical practice as a sedative in the 18th century. It was used to adulterate opium (see p.322, *Papaver somniferum*) and became known as "lettuce opium" because of its similar, but non-addictive, effects.

L. serriola (prickly lettuce, wild lettuce, compass plant) p.146

PARTS USED Whole plant, leaves, latex.
PROPERTIES A very bitter, sedative herb, with an unpleasant smell, that relieves pain, is expectorant, and soothes irritated tissues.
USES OF THE HERB
MEDICINAL Internally for insomnia, anxiety, neuroses, hyperactivity in children, dry coughs, bronchitis, whooping cough, and rheumatic pain. Combined with *Humulus lupulus* (see p.294), *Passiflora incarnata* (see p.323), *Valeriana officinalis* (see p.367), *Scutellaria lateriflora* (see p.351), and *Cypripedium parviflorum* (see p.271) for insomnia. May cause drowsiness. Excess causes restlessness.

GROWTH AND HARVEST
GROWTH Crop. Well-drained to dry, alkaline soil in sun. Propagate by seed in autumn.
HARVEST Latex is extracted from leaves and stems of flowering plants in summer and dried for use as lactucarium, and in extracts, infusions, tablets, and tinctures.

LAMIUM Deadnettle
(Labiatae/Lamiaceae)

L. album has been used for gynecological and obstetric problems since at least medieval times; no modern research has yet been done.

L. album (white deadnettle, archangel) p.146

PARTS USED Whole plant, flowers.
PROPERTIES A slightly bitter, astringent, decongestant herb that checks bleeding and reduces inflammation.
USES OF THE HERB
CULINARY Flowers make a pleasant herb tea.
MEDICINAL Internally for menstrual problems, bleeding after childbirth, vaginal discharge, and prostatitis. Externally as a douche for vaginal

discharge. Combines well with *Achillea millefolium* (see p.227) for vaginal discharge, with *Vinca major* (see p.369) or *Geranium maculatum* (see p.288) for excessive menstruation, and with *Hydrangea arborescens* (see p.294), *Elymus repens* (see p.277), or *Zea mays* (see p.372) for prostate problems.
VARIANT
***L. a.* 'Friday'**, p.146.

> **GROWTH AND HARVEST**
> GROWTH Crop (*L. album*). Ornamental (*L. a.* 'Friday'). Moist, well-drained soil in sun or partial shade. Propagate by seed sown in autumn or spring (species only), or by division in autumn or early spring, or by cuttings of nonflowering shoots in summer.
> HARVEST Whole plants are cut when in flower, or flowers are removed individually; both are dried for use in infusions and tinctures.

LARIX Larch
(Pinaceae)

The American larch, or tamarack (*L. laricina*), is less used medicinally than the European larch (*L. decidua*). The bark was once used to treat rheumatism, jaundice, and skin complaints, and as a poultice for wounds. Resin exuding from the bark was collected by native N Americans as a chewing gum, which also relieved indigestion.

L. decidua, syn. *L. europaea* (common larch, European larch) p.147

PARTS USED Bark, resin.
PROPERTIES A bitter, astringent herb with a turpentine-like smell. It relieves bronchial congestion, is diuretic, and promotes healing.
USES OF THE HERB
MEDICINAL Internally for bronchitis and urinary tract inflammation (bark); for tapeworm, diarrhea, failure to menstruate, and as an antidote to phosphorus poisoning (resin). Not given to patients with kidney complaints. Externally for infected wounds (bark), and for wounds and skin problems (resin).
VARIANT
***L. d.* 'Pendula'**, p.147.

> **GROWTH AND HARVEST**
> GROWTH Ornamental. Moist, well-drained soil in an open, sunny position. Propagate by seed sown in spring, or by tip cuttings in summer. Remove lower branches of specimen trees to give a clean trunk. To maintain a single leading shoot, remove secondary leaders. Larches may suffer from rust and *Armillaria* root rot.
> HARVEST Bark is stripped in late spring and dried for use in decoctions, powders, and tinctures. Tree is tapped for resin in autumn.

LAURUS Bay laurel
(Lauraceae)

The large, brittle, dried leaves of the bay tree (*L. nobilis*) are an important ingredient of both sweet and savory dishes in European cuisines. Little use is made of *L. nobilis* medicinally, although it was long regarded as a potent antiseptic. Bay rum, an aromatic liquid used in hair dressings, cosmetics, and medicines, does not contain bay leaves but is made by distilling the leaves of *Pimenta acris* in rum.

L. camphora. See *Cinnamomum camphora.*

L. nobilis (bay, bay laurel, sweet bay) p.147

PARTS USED Leaves, oil.
PROPERTIES A bitter, aromatic, stimulant herb that improves digestion and is locally antiseptic.
USES OF THE HERB
CULINARY Leaves are an important ingredient of bouquet garni and are commonly added to sauces, soups, stews, and desserts.
MEDICINAL Internally for indigestion, poor appetite, colic, and flatulence. Externally for dandruff, rheumatism, sprains, bruises, atonic ulcers, and scabies.
ECONOMIC Leaves are used in packing dried figs and licorice in order to deter weevils. Essential oil gives flavor to commercial condiments, meat products, and liqueurs.
VARIANTS
***L. n.* 'Angustifolia'**, p.147.
***L. n.* 'Aurea'**, p.147.

> **GROWTH AND HARVEST**
> GROWTH Ornamental. Well-drained soil in sun or partial shade, with shelter from frost and cold in areas with hard winters. Excellent for containers. Propagate by semiripe cuttings or removal of suckers in summer, or by layering in autumn. Trim to shape in summer, removing suckers from standards and topiaries as they appear. Prone to scale insect.
> HARVEST Leaves are collected in summer and dried whole, or as branches, for infusions, powders, and oil distillation. Although fragrance increases upon drying, dried leaves lose flavor after about a year.

LAVANDULA Lavender
(Labiatae/Lamiaceae)

The two most important lavenders with medicinal uses are *L. angustifolia* and *L. latifolia*. Both are rich in essential oils but differ in constituents; *L. angustifolia* yields an exquisitely scented oil, used in aromatherapy and high-quality perfumes; *L. latifolia* yields the pungent, camphoraceous, spike lavender oil, which is mainly used in cleaning products, as an insect repellant, and as a dressing for burns. *L. latifolia* is rarely seen as a garden plant but is grown in Spain for its oil. Hybrid lavenders, such as *L.* x *intermedia* (from crosses between *L. angustifolia* and *L. latifolia*) are often preferred by the perfume industry, but are not recommended for medicinal use. *L. stoechas* was widely used as an antiseptic and toiletry herb in ancient times by the Greeks, Romans, and Arabs.

L. x *allardii* (giant lavender) p.148

PARTS USED Flowers, oil.
PROPERTIES An aromatic herb with a strong camphoraceous aroma.
USES OF THE HERB
AROMATIC Flowers are dried for potpourris and other scented articles.
ECONOMIC Oil is distilled from the flowers for the perfume industry in S Africa.

L. angustifolia, syn. *L. officinalis*, *L. spica* in part, *L. vera* in part (common lavender, English lavender) p.148

PARTS USED Flowers, oil.
PROPERTIES An aromatic, tonic herb with a sweet scent. It relaxes spasms, benefits the digestion, stimulates the peripheral circulation and uterus, and lowers fevers. It has antidepressant effects and is antiseptic.
USES OF THE HERB
CULINARY Fresh flowers are crystalized or added to jams, ice creams, and vinegars.
AROMATIC Dried flowers are used in potpourris.
MEDICINAL Internally for indigestion, depression, anxiety, exhaustion, irritability, tension headaches, migraine, and bronchial complaints (including tuberculosis). Externally for burns, sunburn, rheumatism, muscular pain, neuralgia, skin complaints, cold sores, insect and snakebites, head lice, halitosis, vaginal discharge, and anal fissure. Combines well with *Rosmarinus officinalis* (see p.343) for depression and tension headaches, with *Verbena officinalis* (see p.368) for migraine and nervous tension, and with *Filipendula ulmaria* (see p.283) and *Cimicifuga racemosa* (see p.261) for rheumatism. Added to baths for patients suffering from debility, nervous tension, and insomnia.
ECONOMIC Oil is used in perfumery and toiletries.
VARIANTS
***L. a.* 'Folgate'**, p.148.
***L. a.* 'Hidcote'**, p.148.
***L. a.* 'Hidcote Pink'**, p.148.
***L. a.* 'Imperial Gem'**, p.148.
***L. a.* 'Miss Katherine'**, p.148.
***L. a.* 'Munstead'**, p.148.
***L. a.* 'Nana Alba'**, syn. *L. a.* 'Alba Nana', p.148.
***L. a.* 'Rosea'**, p.148.
***L. a.* 'Royal Purple'**, p.148.

L. dentata (French lavender, fringed lavender) p.149

PARTS USED Flowers.
PROPERTIES An aromatic herb with a rosemary-like scent.
USES OF THE HERB
AROMATIC Mainly grown as an aromatic ornamental, but flower heads may be dried for potpourris.

VARIANT
L. d. var. ***candicans***, syn. *L. d.* 'Silver Form', p.149.

L. x *intermedia* (lavandin) p.149

PARTS USED Flowers.
PROPERTIES An aromatic herb with a slightly camphoraceous lavender scent.
USES OF THE HERB
CULINARY Fresh flowers are crystallized, or added to jams and vinegars.
AROMATIC Dried flowers are added to herb pillows and potpourris.
ECONOMIC Essential oil is used in perfumery, toiletries, and cleaning products.
VARIANTS
L. x *i.* **Dutch Group**, p.149.
L. x *i.* **'Grappenhall'**, p.149.
L. x *i.* **'Grosso'**, p.149.
L. x *i.* **'Provence'**, p.149.
L. x *i.* **'Seal'**, p.149.
L. x *i.* **'Twickel Purple'**, p.149.

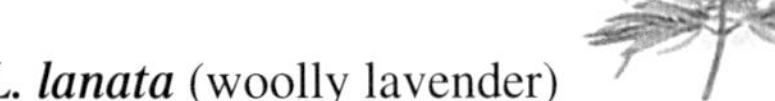

L. lanata (woolly lavender) p.148

PARTS USED Flowers.
PROPERTIES An aromatic herb with a balsam–lavender scent.
USES OF THE HERB
AROMATIC Grown mainly as an aromatic ornamental, but flower heads may be dried for potpourris.

L. multifida (branched lavender) p.149

PARTS USED Flowers.
PROPERTIES An aromatic herb.
USES OF THE HERB
AROMATIC As for *L. lanata*.

L. pinnata p.149

PARTS USED Flowers.
PROPERTIES An aromatic herb.
USES OF THE HERB
AROMATIC As for *L. lanata*.

L. 'Sawyers' p.149

PARTS USED Flowers.
PROPERTIES An aromatic herb with a balsam scent.
USES OF THE HERB
AROMATIC Flowers may be dried for potpourris and other scented articles.

L. stoechas (French lavender, Spanish lavender) p.149

PARTS USED Flowers.
PROPERTIES An antiseptic, aromatic herb with a balsamlike scent. It benefits the digestion, relaxes spasms, promotes healing, repels insects, has mild sedative effects on the nervous system, and stimulates the peripheral circulation.
USES OF THE HERB
AROMATIC Dried flowers are added to potpourris and linen sachets.
MEDICINAL Used in southern Europe to alleviate nausea, and externally as an insect repellant, antiseptic, and relaxant.
VARIANTS
L. s. f. ***leucantha***, p.149.
L. s. subsp. ***pedunculata***, p.149.

L. viridis (green lavender) p.149

PARTS USED Flowers.
PROPERTIES An aromatic, lemon-scented herb.
USES OF THE HERB
AROMATIC Grown mainly as an unusual aromatic plant for the garden and containers, but flower heads may be dried for potpourris.

GROWTH AND HARVEST

GROWTH Ornamental (*L.* x *intermedia*: crop). Well-drained, neutral to alkaline soil in an open, sunny position. *L. dentata* and *L. lanata* may withstand 23°F (5°C) in very sheltered, well-drained conditions; *L. lanata* is very susceptible to damage from overwatering. *L. multifida* and *L. pinnata* need frost-free conditions. Many of the barely hardy and tender lavenders are excellent subjects for container culture under cover. Propagate by seed in autumn (species, subspecies, and varieties only), or by semiripe cuttings in summer, or by layering. Trim hedges and cut specimen plants back in spring to encourage bushiness. Deadhead and trim lightly after flowering. Plants may be damaged by frost and affected by gray mold, scab, leaf spot, and root rot. Lavenders become woody with age and are best replaced every 3–4 years. *L. stoechas* is subject to statutory control as a weed in parts of Australia.
HARVEST Flowers of *L. angustifolia* and *L.* x *intermedia* are picked as they begin to open and used fresh, distilled for oil, or (*L. angustifolia* only) dried for use in infusions, spirits, and tinctures. Flower heads and flowers of other lavenders are gathered as they open, and are dried.

LAWSONIA Henna
(Lythraceae)

In spite of its medicinal applications, henna is mainly used as a dye plant. *L. inermis* has been important as an orange-red colorant for hair, skin, and nails in the Middle East since ancient times; introduced to Europe at the end of the 19th century, it became an important constituent of hair tints and conditioners.

L. inermis, syn. *L. alba* (henna, mignonette tree, Egyptian privet) p.150

PARTS USED Leaves, flowers, oil.
PROPERTIES An astringent herb, with a tealike aroma, that controls bleeding and is antibacterial. It is regarded as an alterative and nerve tonic in Ayurvedic medicine.
USES OF THE HERB
AROMATIC Lilac-scented oil is used in perfumery.
MEDICINAL Internally for amebic dysentery. Externally for skin diseases (including leprosy), wounds, ulcers, and herpes.
ECONOMIC Used for dyeing hair, feet, and hands.

GROWTH AND HARVEST

GROWTH Crop. Well-drained, sandy soil in sun, minimum 50°F (10°C). Propagate by seed in spring, or by softwood cuttings in spring, or by hardwood cuttings in winter. Remove dead wood and trim to shape in late spring.
HARVEST Young leafy shoots, 8–10in (20–25cm) long, are picked during the growing season and dried for use in powders. Flowers are gathered in early morning and distilled for oil.

LEDUM
(Ericaceae)

Ledum contains substances similar to those found in the related *Arctostaphylos uva-ursi* (see p.241). It is reputedly narcotic, causing "a peculiar delirium" when taken in excess. It is also said to deter insect pests and vermin, and was once placed among clothes and in grain bins. *L. palustre* (marsh tea, wild rosemary) has similar narcotic properties.

L. groenlandicum, syn. *L. latifolium* (Labrador tea) p.150

PARTS USED Leaves, shoots.
PROPERTIES A bitter, astringent herb with a camphoraceous aroma. It has expectorant, diuretic, and insecticidal effects.
USES OF THE HERB
MEDICINAL Internally for bronchial congestion and diarrhea. Externally for dandruff, scabies, and skin irritations.
ECONOMIC Tincture used against mosquitoes, bed bugs, lice, fleas, and beetle larvae.

GROWTH AND HARVEST

GROWTH Ornamental. Moist to wet, acid soil in sun or partial shade. Does not grow in warm regions. Propagate by seed sown in autumn, or by semiripe cuttings in summer.
HARVEST Leaves and shoots are collected in late summer and dried for infusions and tinctures.

LEONURUS Motherwort
(Labiatae/Lamiaceae)

L. cardiaca was prescribed in ancient Greece for anxiety in pregnant women; hence the name "motherwort." Research has proved that it is effective in calming the heart and reduces the risk of thrombosis. All species are thought to have similar properties. *L. sibiricus* was first mentioned in the *Illustrated Classic of the Materia Medica* by Su Song (AD106). It is unusual among Chinese herbs in being often prescribed as a "simple" (that is, not mixed with other herbs).

L. cardiaca (motherwort) p.150

PARTS USED Whole plant.
PROPERTIES A very bitter, diuretic herb that acts as a circulatory and uterine stimulant, lowers blood pressure, and relaxes spasms. It is a sedative and nerve tonic, and has antibacterial and antifungal effects.
USES OF THE HERB
MEDICINAL Internally for heart complaints (notably palpitations) and problems associated with menstruation, childbirth, and menopause, especially of nervous origin. Not given to pregnant women.

L. sibiricus, syn. *L. heterophyllus* (Chinese motherwort) p.150

PARTS USED Whole plant (*yi mu cao*), seeds (*chong wei zu*).
PROPERTIES A bitter, diuretic herb that stimulates the circulation and uterus, lowers blood pressure,

regulates menstruation, and clears toxins. It is also effective against bacterial and fungal infections. Seeds are slightly sweet and have similar actions but are less effective as a diuretic and detoxicant.
USES OF THE HERB
MEDICINAL Internally for eye problems related to the liver meridian (seeds); painful and excessive menstruation, postpartum bleeding (whole plant, seeds); edema, kidney complaints, kidney stones, eczema, and abscesses (whole plant). Not given to pregnant women.

GROWTH AND HARVEST
GROWTH Crop. Well-drained, moist soil in sun or partial shade. Propagate by seed in spring, or by division in spring or autumn (*L. cardiaca*).
HARVEST Plants are cut when flowering, but before the seeds are set, and dried for infusions, liquid extracts, and tinctures (*L. cardiaca*), or in decoctions, pills, powder, and poultices (*L. sibiricus*). Seeds (*L. sibiricus*) are collected when ripe in autumn by drying the whole plant, and threshing and sifting it to remove seeds.

LEPTANDRA
L. virginica. See *Veronicastrum virginicum*.

LEVISTICUM Lovage
(Umbelliferae/Apiaceae)

L. officinale has an interesting flavor, resembling celery and yeast extract. Medicinally, it resembles the Chinese *Angelica polymorpha* var. *sinensis* (see p.238), for which it has at times been substituted.

L. officinale, syn. *Ligusticum levisticum* (lovage, love parsley) p.150

PARTS USED Leaves, stems, roots, seeds, oil.
PROPERTIES A bittersweet, sedative, pungently aromatic herb that benefits the digestion, relaxes spasms, increases perspiration, and acts as a diuretic and expectorant. It is effective against many disease-causing organisms.
USES OF THE HERB
CULINARY Young shoots are blanched and eaten as a vegetable. Stalks are candied like angelica or used fresh as straws for Bloody Marys. Seeds are added to bread and cheese crackers. Leaves are added to soups, stews, salads, and savory dishes.
AROMATIC Oil is used in perfumery.
MEDICINAL Internally for indigestion, flatulence, colic, poor appetite, kidney stones, cystitis, painful menstruation, and slow labor. Externally for sore throat and aphthous ulcers.

GROWTH AND HARVEST
GROWTH Ornamental. Deep, rich, moist soil in sun or partial shade. Propagate by seed sown in autumn, or by division in spring. Leaves may be damaged by leaf miners.
HARVEST Leaves are picked before flowering and distilled for oil or dried for infusions. ► Stems are cut in spring, when tender and succulent. Roots are lifted in the third year and used fresh, or dried for decoctions, liquid extracts, tinctures, and oil distillation. Seeds are collected when ripe and dried for use in decoctions.

LIATRIS Blazing star
(Compositae/Asteraceae)

Various blazing stars are used locally in N America: *L. squarrosa* and *L. scariosa* are interchangeable with *L. spicata* as diuretics and provide poultices for snakebites; root decoctions of *L. punctata* are applied as a wash for itching skin complaints; and *L. chapmannii* contains liatrin, which has anticancer properties. Blazing stars are known to contain coumarins, which were banned as flavorings in the US in the early 1950s because they are a possible cause of liver damage and reduced blood clotting. The related *Trilisa odoratissima* (vanilla leaf, deer's tongue) is especially rich in coumarins, which crystallize on the tongue-shaped leaves.

L. spicata (blazing star, gay feather, button snakeroot) p.151

PARTS USED Leaves, roots.
PROPERTIES A bitter, aromatic herb that is tonic and astringent, and has antibacterial and diuretic effects.
USES OF THE HERB
AROMATIC Leaves and roots are added to potpourris.
MEDICINAL Internally for kidney disease and gonorrhea. Externally for sore throat.
ECONOMIC Leaves and roots are added to insect-repellent herbal mixtures.
VARIANT
L. s. **'Alba'**, p.151.

GROWTH AND HARVEST
GROWTH Ornamental. Moist to wet soil in an open, sunny position. Propagate by seed in spring or early autumn (species), or by division in spring. Shoots may be damaged by slugs.
HARVEST Leaves are collected during summer, and roots in autumn, and are used fresh in syrups or dried for use in decoctions.

LIGUSTICUM Alpine lovage
(Umbelliferae/Apiaceae)

Several different species of *Ligusticum* are used medicinally. They contain volatile and fixed oils, and a very bitter alkaloid that has been shown to increase blood flow to coronary arteries and the brain. The Chinese drug *chuan-xiong* is a mixture of several herbs, the main ones being *L. sinense* and *Carthamus tinctorius* (see p.255). *L. canbyi* (Canby's lovage) is used by the Flathead people of N America for colds, and *L. porteri* was an important herb among Rocky Mountain tribes. The latter has been adopted by Chinese, Ayurvedic, and western herbalists as superior to *L. sinense*.

L. levisticum. See *Levisticum officinale*.

L. porteri (*osha*, Porter's lovage, Colorado cough root)

Tall perennial, hardy to 5°F (–15°C), height 18–36in (45–90cm), spread 24in (60cm), with thin, dark green compound leaves divided into segments, and flattened umbels of small white flowers. Found in upland meadows and ravines at 8,000–12,000ft (2,400–3,600m) in the southern Rocky Mountains.

PARTS USED Roots, seeds, oil.
PROPERTIES A bitter, camphoraceous, warming herb that stimulates the circulation, kidneys, and uterus; it improves digestion, relieves spasms, is expectorant, and increases perspiration.
USES OF THE HERB
MEDICINAL Internally for eruptive fevers, bronchial infections, digestive complaints, toothache, painful menstruation, and retained placenta.

L. scoticum (Scots lovage, sea lovage) p.151

PARTS USED Leaves, stems, seeds.
PROPERTIES An aromatic, diuretic herb that improves digestion and stimulates the circulation and uterus.
USES OF THE HERB
CULINARY Young leaves and stalks have a pungent, celery-like flavor and are eaten raw, cooked, or added to soups and stews.
MEDICINAL Once used to treat digestive problems, uterine disorders, and rheumatism.
ECONOMIC Seeds are ground as a condiment and used to improve the taste of medicines.

L. sinense (Chinese lovage, Szechuan lovage)

Perennial, hardy to 5°F (–15°C), height 3ft (1m), spread 18–24in (45–60cm), with a ribbed stem and compound, toothed leaves 6–8in (15–20cm) long and 4–6in (10–15cm) wide, which are deltoid-ovate in outline. Umbels of tiny white flowers are borne in summer, followed by oblong, ribbed fruits about ⅙in (2mm) long. Native to the southern Yellow River basin and Nei Mongol, China.

PARTS USED Roots.
PROPERTIES An aromatic, sedative herb that is antibacterial, stimulates the circulation, lowers blood pressure, relieves pain, and causes uterine contractions.
USES OF THE HERB
MEDICINAL Internally for menstrual problems, postpartum bleeding, coronary heart disease, poor circulation, headaches (especially those caused by concussion), and aches and pains caused by cold.

GROWTH AND HARVEST
GROWTH Crop. Well-drained to dry soil in sun. *L. sinense* tolerates damp conditions. Propagate by seed sown in spring, or by division in autumn.
HARVEST Leaves and stems (*L. scoticum*) are cut in spring for use as a vegetable and at any time as a flavoring. Roots are lifted in autumn and used fresh or dried for oil extraction (*L. porteri*), decoctions, and tinctures. Seeds are collected when ripe and ground (*L. scoticum*) or distilled for oil (*L. porteri*). Roots are lifted in autumn and dried for decoctions (*L. sinense*).

LIGUSTRUM Privet
(Oleaceae)

L. lucidum was first mentioned in traditional Chinese medicine in a text that was probably written before AD1000. In recent years it has been increasingly used to prevent bone marrow loss in cancer chemotherapy patients, and it has potential in the treatment of acquired immune deficiency syndrome (AIDS). Chinese research has also shown good results in the treatment of respiratory tract infections, hypertension, Parkinson's disease, and hepatitis.

L. lucidum (glossy privet, Chinese privet) p.151

PARTS USED Fruits (*nu zhen zi*).
PROPERTIES A bitter, slightly sweet herb that acts as a tonic for the kidneys and liver. It has diuretic, antitumor, antibacterial, and possibly antiviral effects.
USES OF THE HERB
MEDICINAL Internally for complaints associated with weak kidney and liver energy, such as menopausal problems (especially premature menopause), blurred vision, cataracts, tinnitus, graying of hair, rheumatic pains, palpitations, backache, and insomnia.
VARIANT
L. l. **'Excelsum Superbum'**, p.151.

GROWTH AND HARVEST
GROWTH Ornamental. Well-drained soil in sun or shade. Variegated cultivars are best in sun. Propagate by semiripe cuttings in summer, or by ripe seed in winter (species only). Leafspot may damage leaves.
HARVEST Fruits are collected when ripe and dried, then usually mixed with honey and steamed before further drying for use in decoctions, powders, and pills.
WARNING Harmful if eaten.

LILIUM Lily
(Liliaceae)

Various lilies have edible bulbs and are important as vegetables in parts of China and Japan (where they are cultivated for the purpose), and among native N Americans. *L. candidum* has a long history of medicinal use, being recorded by Pliny as a cure for foot complaints and skin problems. It is seldom used today on account of its scarcity. Several Chinese species, including *L. concolor*, are used in traditional medicine for bronchial complaints.

L. candidum (madonna lily) p.151

PARTS USED Bulbs, flowers.
PROPERTIES An astringent, mucilaginous herb that soothes and heals damaged or irritated tissues.
USES OF THE HERB
MEDICINAL Externally for burns, abscesses, chapped or inflamed skin, chilblains, ulcers, and alopecia.

GROWTH AND HARVEST
GROWTH Ornamental. Well-drained alkaline soil in sun, with the bulb just below the surface. Propagate by seed sown in autumn or spring, or by scales in summer, or by offsets in late summer. Prone to *Botrytis* infection. *L. candidum* resents disturbance.
HARVEST Bulbs are lifted in late summer, and flowers picked as they open; they are used fresh for juice, ointments, and tinctures, or may be frozen for later use.

LINARIA Toadflax
(Scrophulariaceae)

L. vulgaris has a long history of medicinal use and was once highly regarded as a diuretic for edema. It is seldom used now but undoubtedly merits investigation.

L. vulgaris (butter-and-eggs) p.152

PARTS USED Whole plant.
PROPERTIES A bitter, acrid, astringent herb that cleanses toxins from the tissues, and is diuretic and laxative. It acts mainly on the liver.
USES OF THE HERB
MEDICINAL Internally for skin diseases, enteritis, hepatitis, gall bladder complaints, and edema. Not given to pregnant women. Externally for hemorrhoids, skin eruptions, sores, and malignant ulcers. For use by qualified practitioners only; dosage is apparently critical.

GROWTH AND HARVEST
GROWTH Ornamental. Well-drained, neutral to alkaline soil in sun or partial shade. Propagate by seed in autumn or spring, or by division in autumn or spring. Self-seeds freely.
HARVEST Plants are cut when flowering and dried for use in infusions.

LINDERA
(Lauraceae)

L. benzoin was important to early settlers in N America as a source of medicines, food flavoring, and beverages. The powdered fruits were a good substitute for allspice (*Pimenta dioica*, see p.328) in the US during the Revolutionary period in the 18th century, and the leaves make a refreshing tea. *L. glauca* is one of several oriental species used in the manufacture of incense and joss sticks, and *L. strychnifolia* is a warming remedy in Chinese medicine for menstrual pain, stomach chills, and urinary incontinence.

L. benzoin (spice bush, Benjamin, feverbush) p.152

PARTS USED Leaves, twigs, bark, fruits.
PROPERTIES An aromatic, warming, tonic herb that improves the circulation, increases perspiration rate, and expels intestinal worms.
USES OF THE HERB
CULINARY For food flavoring and beverages.
MEDICINAL Internally formerly used as a household remedy for colds, dysentery, and intestinal parasites.

GROWTH AND HARVEST
GROWTH Ornamental. Moist, acid soil (pH4.5–6.0) in partial shade. Propagate by seed sown in autumn, or by softwood cuttings in summer.
HARVEST Leaves are collected during the growing season, twigs in spring, bark as required, and berries in autumn; all are used fresh, or dried for decoctions and infusions.

LINUM Flax
(Linaceae)

Although it is classified as a species, *L. usitatissimum* is probably an ancient cultigen derived from *L. bienne*. Two distinct kinds of *L. usitatissimum* have evolved: the taller flax, with fewer branches and flowers, which yields fiber; and the shorter, more floriferous and fruitful linseed, which is now grown for oil and as a fodder crop. Seeds contain 30–40 percent of a fixed oil, known as linseed oil, which consists mainly of linoleic and linolenic acids. In common with many members of the Linaceae, Rosaceae, and Caprifoliaceae families, they also contain cyanogenic glycosides, or prussic acid. In small amounts, these compounds stimulate respiration and improve digestion but, in excess, cause respiratory failure and death. There is no indication that recommended doses of *L. usitatissimum* pose any threat. The related *L. catharticum* (mountain or purging flax) is described as a laxative and an antirheumatic, but is now seldom used.

L. usitatissimum (flax, linseed, flaxseed) p.152

PARTS USED Whole plant, stems, seeds, oil.
PROPERTIES A sweet, mucilaginous herb that is laxative and expectorant, soothes irritated tissues, controls coughing, and relieves pain.
USES OF THE HERB
MEDICINAL Internally as a bulk laxative for chronic constipation and diverticulitis (crushed seeds mixed with breakfast cereals and ample liquid), gastritis, pharyngitis (macerated seeds), chronic bronchial complaints, coughs, and sore throat; as a diet supplement for eczema,

menstrual problems, hardening of the arteries, and rheumatoid arthritis (oil). Externally for bronchitis, pleurisy, sore throat, burns, scalds, boils, abscesses, and ulcers. Crushed seeds are combined, as a poultice, with *Sinapis alba* (see p.353) for chest complaints, and with honey and lemon as a cough remedy.
ECONOMIC Fibers yield flax, used to make linen. Seeds are pressed for oil, used in foods and animal fodder, and in the paint and flooring industries. Seed residue is made into linseed cake for animal feed.

GROWTH AND HARVEST
GROWTH Crop. Well-drained to dry sandy soil in sun. Propagate by seed in spring where plants are to flower. Dislikes being transplanted.
HARVEST Plants are cut when mature for fiber extraction. Seeds are collected when ripe, then stored whole, or pressed for oil.

LIPPIA
(Labiatae/Verbenaceae)

The aromatic foliage of various lippias is used medicinally, or for food flavoring and teas. *L. dulcis* (*yerba dulce*, cimarron) is an expectorant with a pleasant, camphoraceous odor, and is used as a sweetener.
L. graveolens and *L. palmeri* have oregano-scented leaves, exported from Mexico as dried oregano. *L. alba* is similar in aroma to *Cymbopogon citratus* (see p.270), and the West Indian *L. micromera* (false thyme) can be used as a thyme substitute.
L. adoensis, an African species, and the Brazilian *L. pseudo-thea* are infused for tea.

L. citriodora. See *Aloysia triphylla.*

L. graveolens (Mexican oregano) p.152

PARTS USED Leaves.
PROPERTIES An aromatic herb with an oregano scent.
USES OF THE HERB
CULINARY Source of commercial dried oregano, used for flavoring seafood, cheese, and dishes based on tomatoes, eggplant, and zucchini (especially in Italian cuisine).

GROWTH AND HARVEST
GROWTH Crop. Light, sandy soil in sun, minimum 41–50°F (5–10°C). Propagate by seed in spring, or by softwood cuttings in spring and early summer. Cut back and remove dead wood in late winter. Spider mites, whitefly, and aphids may attack plants under cover.
HARVEST Leaves are picked in spring and summer and dried for culinary use.

LIQUIDAMBAR Sweet gum
(Hamamelidaceae)

L. styraciflua was widely used by native N Americans to heal wounds, and by settlers for skin complaints. It was first listed as an antiseptic in the *U.S. Pharmacopoeia* in 1926. *L. orientalis* appeared in Chinese medicine c.AD500. *L. formosana* (Chinese sweet gum), an analgesic, antirheumatic, and wound herb, is also used, as is *L. taiwaniana*, whose fruits are used to stimulate the circulation and treat menstrual irregularities, joint pains, and allergies. The gum obtained from these species is a syrupy balsam, with an aroma like cinnamon or hyacinth.

L. orientalis (oriental sweet gum, storax) p.152

PARTS USED Balsam (*su he xiang*).
PROPERTIES An aromatic, stimulant herb that is antiseptic, and anti-inflammatory, has expectorant effects, and also promotes healing.
USES OF THE HERB
MEDICINAL Internally for strokes, infantile convulsions, coma, heart disease, and pruritus. Externally, mixed with olive oil for scabies. (Leaves, fruits, and roots are also used in similar ways in folk medicine.)

L. styraciflua (sweet gum, American storax) p.152

PARTS USED Balsam.
PROPERTIES An aromatic, stimulant herb that has antiseptic, expectorant, and anti-inflammatory effects.
USES OF THE HERB
AROMATIC Used in perfumery, especially in jasmine types.
MEDICINAL Internally for sore throats, coughs, colds, asthma, bronchitis, cystitis, and vaginal discharge. Externally for sores, hemorrhoids, ringworm, scabies, and frostbite. An ingredient of friar's balsam, a preparation based on benzoin (*Styrax benzoin*, see p.357), which relieves colds and skin problems.
ECONOMIC Used in commercial flavoring of foods and tobacco.
VARIANTS
L. s. **'Aurea'**, syn. *L. s.* 'Variegata', p.153.
L. s. **'Worplesdon'**, p.153.

GROWTH AND HARVEST
GROWTH Ornamental. Deep, rich, moist, neutral to slightly acid soil in sun or partial shade. Propagate by seed sown in autumn, or by softwood cuttings in summer. Remove badly placed branches in autumn.
HARVEST Balsam is collected as a natural exudate, or from cuts in the bark, and made into syrups and tinctures. It is also extracted from the bark after beating the trees to increase flow.

LIRIOSMA
L. ovata. See *Dulacia inopiflora.*

LITHOSPERMUM Gromwell
(Boraginaceae)

Little is known of the chemistry of this genus, but the effectiveness of several species as contraceptives and as depuratives for skin conditions warrants further investigation.
L. erythrorhizon has an ancient history of use in Chinese medicine. *L. ruderale* (gromwell, puccoon) was one of several species used by native N Americans: by the Algonquin as dyes and body paints, and by the Shoshoni as a contraceptive, which caused permanent sterility after six months of use.

L. erythrorhizon, syn. *L. officinale* subsp. *erythrorhizon* (red-rooted gromwell) p.153

PARTS USED Whole plant, roots (*zi cao*).
PROPERTIES A sweet, soothing, healing herb that lowers fever and clears toxins. It stimulates the liver, heart, and circulation, and has contraceptive and anticancer effects.
USES OF THE HERB
MEDICINAL Internally for irritant skin conditions, measles, chicken pox, boils, carbuncles, hepatitis, and skin cancer. Externally for eczema, diaper rash, burns, abscesses, poison oak or ivy rash, vaginal discharge, and herpes.
ECONOMIC Added to skin-care creams.

GROWTH AND HARVEST
GROWTH Crop. Well-drained, neutral to alkaline soil in sun or partial shade. Propagate by seed sown in autumn, or by division in autumn.
HARVEST Whole plants are cut when flowering and roots are lifted in autumn; all parts are dried for use in decoctions.

LOBELIA
(Campanulaceae)

A number of lobelias contain piperidine alkaloids, notably lobeline, that stimulate respiration and cause vomiting. These include the ornamental *L. cardinalis*; *L. tupa* (devil's tobacco), used to treat toothache, and smoked as a narcotic by Chilean tribes; and *L. siphilitica* (great lobelia), used with *Podophyllum peltatum* (see p.332) as a remedy for venereal diseases. *L. inflata* was used by native N Americans for bronchial complaints and was popularized by Samuel Thomson (1769–1843), a pioneer herbalist and founder of Physiomedicalism. He was prosecuted, but found not guilty, of its misuse in 1809.

L. chinensis, syn. *L. radicans* (Chinese lobelia) p.153

PARTS USED Whole plant (*ban bian lian*).
PROPERTIES An acrid, antifungal herb that is diuretic, reduces inflammation, lowers fever, contracts tissues, and clears toxins. It acts mainly on the liver and kidneys.

USES OF THE HERB
MEDICINAL Internally for dysentery, gastroenteritis, cirrhosis, edema, jaundice, schistomiasis, stomach cancer, eczema, and snakebite with depressed respiration. Excess causes nausea, vomiting, drowsiness, and respiratory failure. For use by qualified practitioners only.

L. inflata (Indian tobacco, asthma weed, pukeweed) p.153

PARTS USED Whole plant.
PROPERTIES An acrid, emetic herb that stimulates respiration, increases perspiration rate, reduces inflammation, and is expectorant.
USES OF THE HERB
MEDICINAL Internally for asthma, bronchitis, whooping cough, and pleurisy. Excess causes nausea, vomiting, drowsiness, and respiratory failure. Not given to pregnant women or patients with heart complaints. Externally for pleurisy, rheumatism, tennis elbow, whiplash injuries, boils, and ulcers. For use by qualified practitioners only.
WARNING This herb and its alkaloids are subject to legal restrictions in some countries.
ECONOMIC An important ingredient of antismoking tobaccos (imitating effects of nicotine) and cough mixtures.

GROWTH AND HARVEST
GROWTH Crop. Rich, moist soil in sun or partial shade. *L. inflata* prefers slightly acid soil. Many are short-lived. Propagate by seed sown in autumn or spring.
HARVEST Whole plants are cut when flowering (*L. inflata* when lower fruits are ripe); used fresh, or dried in decoctions (*L. chinensis*), infusions, liquid extracts, and tinctures.
WARNING Harmful if eaten. Skin irritant and allergen.

LONICERA Honeysuckle
(Caprifoliaceae)

L. caprifolium (perfoliate honeysuckle, Dutch honeysuckle) and *L. periclymenum* (honeysuckle, woodbine) are often listed as medicinal herbs, but are seldom used today. The former has laxative and expectorant effects; the latter is an expectorant, antiseptic, and diuretic that causes vomiting but, in small doses, is a useful addition to cough mixtures. *L. japonica* has played an important role in Chinese medicine since the time of the *Tang Materia Medica* (AD659).

L. japonica (Japanese honeysuckle) p.153

PARTS USED Stems (*jin yin teng*), flower buds (*jin yin hua*).
PROPERTIES A slightly sweet, cooling herb that is antibacterial, diuretic, lowers fever, reduces inflammation and blood pressure, relaxes spasms, and increases perspiration. Regarded as an alterative.
USES OF THE HERB
MEDICINAL Internally for acute rheumatoid arthritis, mumps, hepatitis (stems); upper respiratory tract infections, including pneumonia, and dysentery (flowers, stems); high fevers, conjunctivitis, throat inflammations, childhood infections (including measles and chicken pox), boils, nettle rash, infected wounds, gastroenteritis, food poisoning, urinary tract infections, mastitis, and breast cancer (flowers). Externally for skin inflammations, infectious rashes, and sores (flowers).
VARIANT
L. j. **'Aureoreticulata'**, p.153.

GROWTH AND HARVEST
GROWTH Crop (*L. japonica*). Ornamental (*L. j.* 'Aureoreticulata'). Well-drained soil in sun or partial shade. Propagate by seed sown in autumn or spring (species only), or by semiripe cuttings in summer or hardwood cuttings in late autumn, or by division in spring or autumn. Cut back or remove surplus stems after flowering. Aphids may attack leaves and flowers. *L. japonica* is an invasive weed in Australia and parts of the US.
HARVEST Stems are cut in autumn and winter, and dried for decoctions, pills, poultices, powders, tinctures, and dry extracts. Flowers are collected in the early morning, before they open, and are dried for decoctions.

LUFFA Loofah, loofa
(Cucurbitaceae)

The loofah is a surprisingly useful plant. Fibers of fully ripe loofah fruits have been used in traditional Chinese medicine since the 10th century AD. Before World War II, 60 percent of the harvest in the US was used to filter out oil from water in ships' boilers. Today loofah gourds are used medicinally and also as vegetables, dried sponges, and material for shock-absorbent helmets. Japan is now the main producer. Pieces of loofah are boiled in water to make a strong decoction for internal use, or gently heated in a sealed container until reduced to charcoal for external application. Loofahs are popular in exfoliant treatments.

L. cylindrica, syn. *L. aegyptica* (loofah, sponge gourd, dishcloth gourd) p.154

PARTS USED Fruits, fibers (*si gua luo*), seeds, oil.
PROPERTIES An astringent, painkilling herb that controls bleeding, promotes healing, improves circulation, and increases milk flow. It acts mainly on the lungs, liver, and stomach.
USES OF THE HERB
CULINARY Young fruits are cooked like squash or pickled. Seeds are pressed for cooking oil.
MEDICINAL Internally for rheumatism, chest pains, backache, orchitis, hemorrhoids, internal hemorrhage, and insufficient lactation. Externally for shingles and boils. Dried fruit fibers are used as abrasive sponges in skin care to remove dead skin and stimulate the peripheral circulation.

GROWTH AND HARVEST
GROWTH Crop. Rich, sandy soil in sun, minimum 50°F (10°C). Propagate by seed sown in spring. Pinch out side branches when the first fruit is set to encourage development. Shorten growths as necessary to train against a wall or trellis. Spider mites, whitefly, and aphids may attack plants under cover.
HARVEST Fruits are cut when 6in (15cm) long for culinary use or left on vine to dry, before skinning and retting to clean flesh from fibers. Seeds are pressed for oil.

LYCIUM Boxthorn
(Solanaceae)

According to European folklore, boxthorn caused discord between husband and wife if planted near their home: hence its common name "matrimony vine." The root bark and fruits of *L. barbarum* are both used in Chinese medicine. The former was first mentioned c.AD500 and the latter described in texts, dating back to 206BC–AD23, which were based on much earlier records. In common with most members of the Solanaceae (nightshade family), *L. barbarum* contains poisonous alkaloids.

L. barbarum, syn. *L. chinense* (Duke of Argyll's tea-tree, Chinese boxthorn, matrimony vine) p.154

PARTS USED Root bark (*di gu pi*), fruits (*gou qi zi*).
PROPERTIES Fruits produce a sweet, tonic decoction that lowers blood pressure and blood cholesterol levels, acting mainly on the liver and kidneys. The bitter, cooling, antibacterial root bark controls coughs and lowers fever, blood pressure, and blood cholesterol levels.
USES OF THE HERB
MEDICINAL Internally for high blood pressure, diabetes, poor eyesight, vertigo, lumbago, impotence, and menopausal complaints (fruits); chronic fevers, internal hemorrhage, nosebleed, tuberculosis, coughs, asthma, verrucas, and childhood eczema (root bark). Externally for genital itching.

GROWTH AND HARVEST
GROWTH Ornamental. Sandy, alkaline, moist but well-drained soil in sun. Propagate by seed sown in autumn, by softwood cuttings in summer, or by hardwood cuttings in winter. Remove dead wood in winter and cut back to control growth in spring. Prune plants grown for commercial use two or three times a year to encourage a compact, well-branched shrub for heavier fruiting and easier harvesting.
HARVEST Bark is stripped from roots in winter and dried for decoctions, pills, and powders. Fruits are collected in autumn and dried for decoctions.

LYCOPERDON Puffball
(Lycoperdaceae)

Puffballs have long been used as food in many parts of the world, and feature in both native N American and Chinese traditional medicine.

L. perlatum, syn. *L. gemmatum* (puffball) p.154

PARTS USED Whole plant, spores (*ma bo*).
PROPERTIES An astringent herb that controls bleeding.
USES OF THE HERB
CULINARY The firm white flesh of young puffballs is eaten as a delicacy, often fried in batter.
MEDICINAL Externally for bleeding wounds and hemorrhoids. In traditional Chinese medicine spores are given internally, combined with honey or syrup, for inflammations of the respiratory tract, and used externally, as a powder, to stop bleeding.

GROWTH AND HARVEST
GROWTH Wild-collected. Well-drained, moist, sandy soil. Propagates by spores.
HARVEST Whole fungi are collected in summer and used fresh for food, or in autumn and dried for use as pills and powders. Spores are collected in autumn and dried for powder.

LYCOPODIUM Clubmoss
(Lycopodiaceae)

In ancient times the whole clubmoss plant was used as a diuretic and digestive. The use of the spores alone dates from the 17th century. According to Mrs. Grieve (*A Modern Herbal*, 1931), "they have a strong repulsive power, that if the hand is powdered with them, it can be dipped in water without becoming wet." This property is put to use in coating pills, to seal in any unpleasant taste and to prevent their sticking together. *L. complanatum* (American ground pine) has similar properties to *L. clavatum* and is often combined with *Taraxacum officinale* (see p.360) and *Agrimonia eupatoria* (see p.231) for liver complaints. The Chinese *L. cernuum* is decocted in water or sweet wine for internal use and crushed for topical treatment of aches, pains, and spasms in the arms or legs. The exploitation and wild collection of *Lycopodium* species may be subject to management measures.

L. clavatum (stag's horn clubmoss, ground pine) p.154

PARTS USED Whole plant (*shen jin cao*), spores.
PROPERTIES A sedative, antibacterial herb that is diuretic, lowers fever, benefits the digestion, and stimulates the uterus.
USES OF THE HERB
MEDICINAL Internally for urinary and kidney disorders, cystitis, gastritis, and in Chinese medicine for rheumatoid arthritis and traumatic injury. Externally for skin diseases and irritation. Spores are the basis for a homeopathic preparation for dry coughs, rheumatic pains, mumps, and complaints that characteristically cause pain or discomfort on the right side of the body.

GROWTH AND HARVEST
GROWTH Crop. Damp, acid soil in sun or shade. Propagate by spores.
HARVEST Plants are cut all year and used fresh, or dried for use in decoctions and infusions. Spores are shaken out into a sieve from plants cut in summer.

LYCOPUS Bugleweed
(Labiatae/Lamiaceae)

L. virginicus was listed in the *U.S. Pharmacopoeia* in the late 19th century as an effective antihemorrhagic. *L. europaeus* (gipsywort) and *L. americanus* (water horehound) are regarded as very similar in effects to *L. virginicus* and are often substituted. *L. lucidus* has been used for over 2,000 years in Chinese medicine for menstrual pain, painful injuries, and incontinence.

L. virginicus (Virginia bugleweed) p.154

PARTS USED Whole plant.
PROPERTIES A bitter, faintly aromatic herb that controls bleeding, suppresses coughs, and lowers blood sugar levels. It slows and strengthens heart contractions and inhibits thyroid-stimulating hormones.
USES OF THE HERB
MEDICINAL Internally for hyperthyroidism, nervous tachycardia, coughs (especially in patients with heart disease), tuberculosis, and excessive menstruation. Not given to pregnant women or patients with hypothyroidism. For use by qualified practitioners only.

GROWTH AND HARVEST
GROWTH Crop. Moist to wet soil in sun or partial shade. Propagate by seed in autumn or spring, or by division in autumn or spring.
HARVEST Plants are cut as flowering begins and dried for use in infusions, liquid extracts, and tinctures.

LYTHRUM Loosestrife
(Lythraceae)

L. salicaria has a long history of use in European folk medicine. It was widely used in cholera epidemics in England during the 19th century, with reputedly "electrical" effects. Its astringency is such that it was once used for tanning leather, but it apparently leaves mucous surfaces moist.

L. salicaria (purple loosestrife) p.154

PARTS USED Whole plant.
PROPERTIES A highly astringent, antibacterial herb that is diuretic, soothes irritated tissues, and controls bleeding.
USES OF THE HERB
MEDICINAL Internally for diarrhea, dysentery, cholera, typhoid, hepatitis, hemorrhage, excessive menstruation, and vaginal discharge. Externally for wounds, sores, impetigo, eczema, eye infections, and vaginal discharge. Combined with *Gnaphalium uliginosum* (see p.289) as a gargle for sore throat.

GROWTH AND HARVEST
GROWTH Ornamental. Moist to wet, neutral to alkaline soil, or shallow water in sun or partial shade. Propagate by seed sown in autumn or spring (species only), or by division in autumn or spring, or by basal cuttings in spring. Self-seeds readily in damp conditions. Importation of plants and seeds is prohibited in parts of the US and Canada, because of their extensive invasion of wetlands.
HARVEST Plants are cut when in flower and used fresh, or dried for use in decoctions and infusions.

M

MAGNOLIA
(Magnoliaceae)

Magnolias of various kinds are used medicinally in N America, originally by native tribes. The active constituents of magnolia bark dissolve readily in alcohol, which gave rise to the use by N American settlers of bitter, alcoholic extracts to prevent malaria. The nonastringent bark of *M. acuminata* (cucumber tree) and *M. tripetala* (umbrella tree), as well as of *M. virginiana*, were listed in the *U.S. Pharmacopoeia* (1820–94), mainly for intermittent fevers and rheumatism. *M. liliiflora* and *M. officinalis* have been important in Chinese traditional medicine for over 2,000 years. *M. officinalis* contains magnocurarine, which is similar to curare (a muscle relaxant obtained from various species of *Chondrodendron*, see p.260, and *Strychnos*, see p.357).

M. liliiflora, syn. *M. quinquepeta* (lily-flowered magnolia) p.155

PARTS USED Flowers, flower buds (*xin yi*).
PROPERTIES A pungent, warming, sedative herb whose main action is to constrict blood vessels in the nasal passages. It also lowers blood pressure, relieves pain, and has antifungal effects.
USES OF THE HERB
MEDICINAL Internally for sinusitis, allergic rhinitis, and colds with excess mucus or runny nose. Excess causes dizziness. Incompatible with *Astragalus membranaceus* (see p.245).
VARIANT
***M. l.* 'Nigra'**, p.155.

M. officinalis (magnolia) p.155

PARTS USED Bark, flowers (*hou po hua*).
PROPERTIES A bitter, warming, relaxant herb that improves digestion, lowers blood pressure, and has antibacterial and antifungal effects. The flowers act mainly as an aromatic, digestive tonic.
USES OF THE HERB
MEDICINAL Internally for abdominal distention, stomach pains, diarrhea and vomiting associated with indigestion, asthma, coughs with profuse phlegm (bark); pressure and fullness in the abdomen and chest, and shortness of breath associated with disturbed stomach energy (flowers). Bark is often combined with *Zingiber officinale* (see p.373) and *Paeonia* spp. (see p.321).

M. virginiana, syn. *M. glauca* (sweet bay, beaver tree) p.155

PARTS USED Bark.
PROPERTIES A bitter, aromatic, tonic herb that increases perspiration and reduces inflammation.
USES OF THE HERB
MEDICINAL Internally for bronchial diseases, upper respiratory tract infections, malaria, rheumatism, and gout.

GROWTH AND HARVEST

GROWTH Ornamental (*M. officinalis*: crop). Moist, neutral to acid, humus-rich soil in sun or partial shade, with shelter from cold winds and late frosts. *M. virginiana* tolerates wet soils. Propagate by seed sown in autumn (species only), or by semiripe cuttings in summer, or by grafting in winter. Plants may be killed by root rot. Buds and open flowers turn brown when damaged by frost.
HARVEST Bark is collected in autumn and dried for use in decoctions, liquid extracts, powders, and tinctures. Its aromatic properties do not keep well, so stocks are renewed annually. Flower buds and flowers are picked in spring (*M. liliiflora*) or when open in summer (*M. officinalis*), and are used fresh or dried in decoctions, or dried for powders.

MAHONIA
(Berberidaceae)

M. aquifolium closely resembles *Berberis vulgaris* (see p.248) in its chemistry and is used in similar ways. One of the main differences is the lower content of the antiseptic, anti-inflammatory berberine, which makes it less effective for infectious diseases but better as a liver tonic. It has been called *yerba de la sangre* ("herb of the blood"), indicating its importance as a blood purifier. The smaller *M. repens* (creeping Oregon grape) is also used.

M. aquifolium (Oregon grape, mountain grape) p.155

PARTS USED Roots, root bark, fruits.
PROPERTIES A bitter, astringent, decongestant herb that stimulates bile flow and releases toxins.
USES OF THE HERB
CULINARY Jelly is made from the grapelike juice of the fruits.
MEDICINAL Internally for skin diseases (especially dry eczema), gall bladder complaints, chronic hepatitis B, gastritis, and diarrhea.
ECONOMIC The whole plant yields a greenish yellow dye.
VARIANT
***M. a.* 'Apollo'**, p.155.

GROWTH AND HARVEST

GROWTH Ornamental. Well-drained, humus-rich soil in sun or partial shade. *M. aquifolium* colors better in winter when planted in full sun. Propagate by seed sown in autumn (species only), or by leaf-bud or semiripe cuttings in summer. Cut back groundcover plants and old, straggly specimens hard in spring. Leafspot, powdery mildew, and rust may attack foliage.
HARVEST Roots and root bark are collected in late autumn or early spring, and dried for use in decoctions and liquid extracts. Fruits are collected when ripe and used fresh.

MAJORANA
M. hortensis. See *Origanum majorana.*
M. onites. See *Origanum onites.*

MALVA Mallow
(Malvaceae)

M. sylvestris been grown as a medicinal plant and pot herb since Roman times. In the 16th century it was known as a "cure-all," or omnimorbia. Several species have very similar constituents, and *M. sylvestris* is used interchangeably with the less potent *M. moschata* (musk mallow) and the stronger *M. neglecta* (dwarf mallow). All are regarded as inferior to the closely related *Althaea officinalis* (marsh mallow, see p.236). Rather different in effects is the Chinese *M. verticillata* (farmer's tobacco), a soothing diuretic, used for urinary tract infections. It also promotes lactation.

M. sylvestris (common mallow, blue mallow, high mallow) p.156

PARTS USED Leaves, flowers, fruits.
PROPERTIES A mucilaginous, slightly astringent herb that is expectorant, soothes irritated tissues, and reduces inflammation.
USES OF THE HERB
CULINARY Young leaves and shoots are eaten raw in salads or cooked in vegetable dishes. Flowers are used to make tea. Unripe seed capsules, known as "cheeses" because of their shape, make an unusual addition to salads.
MEDICINAL Internally for bronchitis, coughs, throat infections, excess mucus, asthma, emphysema, and gastritis. Large doses are laxative. Externally for weeping eczema, boils, abscesses, and insect bites.
VARIANTS
***M. s.* 'Cottenham Blue'**, p.156.
***M. s.* 'Zebrina'**
This cultivar, height 18–36in (45–90cm), spread 24–36in (60–90cm), is hardy to 5°F (–15°C). It has pink to white, veined flowers with purple centers.
***M. s.* subsp. *mauritiana* 'Bibor Felho'**, p.156.

GROWTH AND HARVEST

GROWTH Ornamental. Well-drained to poor soil, in sun or partial shade. Propagate by seed sown in spring or autumn, or by division during dormancy, or by cuttings of basal shoots in spring or summer. Mallows are prone to rust.
HARVEST Leaves and flowers are gathered in summer and used fresh for compresses or dried for infusions and liquid extracts. Fruits (seed capsules) are picked when green and used fresh.

MANDRAGORA Mandrake
(Solanaceae)

The mandrake is a strange plant, both in appearance and associations. The forked root resembles the human form and was once esteemed as an aphrodisiac and cure for sterility. Its narcotic, hallucinogenic properties were exploited in witchcraft and magic rituals during ancient and medieval times. It was held to be fatal for anyone to dig up a mandrake since its shrieks would scare them to death: hence the tradition of tying a dog to the root for the final pull. Like the closely related *Atropa belladonna* (deadly nightshade, see p.246) and *Hyoscyamus niger* (henbane, see p.295), *M. officinarum* is poisonous, containing a potent sedative and painkiller. In sufficient quantities, these induce a state of oblivion, properties which were used in early surgery. *M. officinarum* became an official homeopathic preparation in 1877, and is rarely used for any other purpose today. *M. officinarum* should not be confused with *Podophyllum peltatum* (American mandrake or May apple, see p.332), a major medicinal herb, often loosely referred to as mandrake.

M. officinarum (mandrake, devil's apples) p.156

PARTS USED Roots.
PROPERTIES A sedative, painkilling herb that has purgative and emetic effects.
USES OF THE HERB
MEDICINAL Internally, used formerly as a painkiller, aphrodisiac, and treatment for nervous disorders. Externally for ulcers. For use by qualified practitioners only. WARNING This herb is subject to legal restrictions in some countries.

GROWTH AND HARVEST

GROWTH Ornamental. Deep, well-drained, humus-rich soil in a sunny or partly shaded, sheltered position. Propagate by seed sown in autumn or spring, or by root cuttings in winter. Resents root disturbance.
HARVEST Roots are collected during dormancy and grated fresh for extraction of juice, or dried for use in decoctions.
WARNING Toxic if eaten.

MARRUBIUM Horehound
(Labiatae/Lamiaceae)

M. vulgare contains a potent expectorant and was first used as a cough remedy in ancient Egyptian times. The most popular way of taking horehound today is in the form of candy, which is sucked to relieve chesty coughs and bronchitis. It has also been used as a cure for cankerworm in trees, and can be made into horehound ale.

M. vulgare (horehound, hoarhound, white horehound) p.156

PARTS USED Whole plant.
PROPERTIES A bitter, aromatic herb that is antiseptic and expectorant, reduces inflammation, and relieves spasms. It also increases perspiration rate, stimulates bile flow, and has a sedative effect on the heart.
USES OF THE HERB
MEDICINAL Internally for bronchitis, asthma, excess mucus, chesty coughs and colds, whooping cough, liver

and gall bladder disorders, typhoid fever, and palpitations. Externally for minor injuries and skin eruptions. Combines well with *Zingiber officinale* (see p.373) for whooping cough, and with *Cephaelis ipecacuanha* (see p.258), *Lobelia inflata* (see p.305), and *Tussilago farfara* (see p.365) for bronchial congestion.

GROWTH AND HARVEST
GROWTH Crop. Well-drained, neutral to alkaline soil in sun. Propagate by seed sown in spring, or by division in spring, or by softwood cuttings in summer. Cut back plants after flowering for a second crop of new leaves. Subject to statutory control as a weed in some countries, notably in parts of Australia.
HARVEST Plants are cut when flowering and used fresh or dried, in cough mixtures, candy, infusions, liquid extracts, powders, and syrups.

MARSDENIA
(Asclepiadaceae)

There are about 100 species of tender evergreen or deciduous woody climbers and shrubs in this genus, which occurs in tropical and warm parts of Africa, Eurasia, and the Americas. All contain a poisonous white latex, which in some species is processed as rubber. Research has been carried out into several marsdenias since the 1970s. They are reported to contain unusual glycosides, which have potential in cancer treatment. *M. tinctoria* (Java indigo), which is grown as a dye plant, also has antifertility properties. Several species are known to be extremely toxic, with strychninelike effects, and have been used to poison wild dogs.

M. cundurango, syn. *Gonolobus condurango* (condurango, eagle vine)

Tender, twining, evergreen climber, reaching 30ft (9m) in height, with an aromatic stem up to 24in (60cm) in diameter, and oblong to rounded leaves. Waxy, off-white, bell- to funnel-shaped flowers are produced in summer, followed by fleshy fruits containing seeds that each have a tuft of hairs. Found in wooded valleys in C America.

PARTS USED Bark.
PROPERTIES A bitter, slightly aromatic, acrid herb that improves appetite and digestion. It is regarded as an alterative and gastric sedative.
USES OF THE HERB
MEDICINAL Internally for anorexia and nervous dyspepsia. Combined with *Gentiana lutea* (see p.287), *Acorus calamus* (see p.228), *Chelone glabra* (see p.259), *Humulus lupulus* (see p.294), and *Chamaemelum nobile* (see p.259) for anorexia.

GROWTH AND HARVEST
GROWTH Wild-collected. Sandy, humus-rich soil in partial shade, minimum 60–65°F (15– 18C°). Propagate by seed when ripe, or by semiripe cuttings with a heel in summer, or by layering during the growing season. Cut back leading shoots after flowering to restrict growth and encourage production of laterals. ►

► **HARVEST** Bark is beaten from the stems after drying and stored as liquid extracts, powders, or quills.

MATRICARIA
(Compositae/Asteraceae)

German chamomile is similar in chemistry to Roman chamomile (*Chamaemelum nobile*, see p.259) but has a less pronounced aroma. Some herbalists combine the flowers, using two parts German to one part Roman, while others prefer Roman chamomile, especially in its double variant, *C. n.* 'Flore Pleno' (see p.259). German chamomile has a slightly higher proportion of volatile oil, containing an anti-inflammatory and analgesic that is particularly effective in healing burns and preventing ulceration and infection. It is less bitter as an ingredient of herb teas than is Roman chamomile.

M. parthenium. See *Tanacetum parthenium*.

M. recutita, syn. *M. chamomilla*, *Chamomilla recutita* (German chamomile, scented mayweed) p.156

PARTS USED Flowers.
PROPERTIES A bitter, aromatic, sedative herb that relaxes spasms, reduces inflammation, relieves pain, and promotes healing. It benefits the digestion and stimulates the immune system.
USES OF THE HERB
MEDICINAL Internally for nervous digestive upsets, insomnia, travel sickness, and children's complaints, such as teething, colic, and infantile convulsions. Externally for wounds, sunburn, burns, hemorrhoids, mastitis, and leg ulcers.
ECONOMIC Added to cosmetics as an anti-allergenic agent and to hair preparations as a conditioner and lightener.

GROWTH AND HARVEST
GROWTH Crop. Well-drained, moist to dry, neutral to slightly acid soil in sun. Propagate by seed sown in autumn or spring.
HARVEST Flowers are collected when first fully opened and used fresh, frozen, or dried in infusions, liquid extracts, and powders. For long-term storage, flowers are better used fresh or frozen, because they lose volatile oil rapidly when dried.

MEDICAGO Medick
(Leguminosae/Papilionaceae)

M. sativa (alfalfa) is of major importance as a fodder crop. It is a long-lived, deep-rooted plant that can be cut up to five times each season for hay or silage, transforming the agricultural potential of areas with poor pasture. Excellent honey is obtained from alfalfa fields. Less tolerant of competition than clovers (*Trifolium* species, see p.364), *M. sativa* is usually grown on its own. It is rich in nutrients, including protein, minerals (notably calcium), pro-vitamin A, and vitamins of the B group, C, D, E, and K. While beneficial in moderation, consumption of alfalfa is known to trigger attacks in patients with systemic lupus erythematosus (SLE). It also contains porphyrins, which affect liver function and may cause photosensitization, and other substances that, if given in excess, cause breakdown of the red blood cells.

M. sativa (lucerne, alfalfa) p.157

PARTS USED Whole plant, leaves, seeds.
PROPERTIES A sweet, astringent, cooling herb that cleanses toxins from the tissues, controls bleeding, stimulates appetite, lowers cholesterol levels, and is diuretic. It acts mainly on the circulatory and urinary systems, and influences hormones.
USES OF THE HERB
CULINARY Leaves are eaten raw or cooked as a vegetable; seeds are sprouted for use in salads, giving a sweet, pealike flavor.
MEDICINAL Internally for debility in convalescence or anemia, hemorrhage, menopausal complaints, premenstrual tension, fibroids, and other conditions indicating hormonal imbalance. Not given to patients with autoimmune diseases, such as rheumatoid arthritis.
ECONOMIC A commercial source of chlorophyll, carotene, and vitamin K.

GROWTH AND HARVEST
GROWTH Crop. Light, well-drained to dry, neutral to alkaline soil in sun. Propagate by seed sown in autumn or spring.
HARVEST Plants are cut before flowering and dried for infusions. Young leaves are used fresh. Seeds are germinated for 3–6 days for eating raw.

MELALEUCA
(Myrtaceae)

Melaleucas are rich in germicidal volatile oils, notably cineole (as found in *Eucalyptus*, see p.280), which can vary according to the tree's genetic constitution and growing conditions. The cineole content and yield are lower than in *Eucalyptus*. Several different species are used medicinally, especially by Aborigines in northern regions of Australia. Cajuput oil was first exported from Malaysia in the 17th century – hence its name, which is derived from the Malaysian *kayu-puti*, "white wood." It is now obtained mainly from *M. leucadendron* and the closely related *M. cajuputi*, widely grown in Malaysia. *M. quinquenervia* and *M. viridiflora* yield a similar oil (niaouli) that is used in perfumery and has strong antiseptic properties, especially against thrush. Tea tree oil, from *M. alternifolia*, was used by Australian forces in World War II for dressing wounds.

M. alternifolia (medicinal tea tree)

Shrub or small tree, hardy to 32°F (0°C), height 15–22ft (5–7m), spread 10–15ft (3–5m), with papery bark in several layers, and pointed leaves up to 1½in (3.5cm) long. In spring small, white, 5-petaled flowers are borne in dense spikes up to 2½in (5cm) long, followed by tiny woody capsules. Found in New South Wales and Queensland.

PARTS USED Oil.
PROPERTIES An aromatic, antiseptic herb that is expectorant, increases perspiration, and stimulates the immune system. It is effective against bacterial and fungal infections. Oil is nonirritant.
USES OF THE HERB
MEDICINAL Externally for thrush, vaginal infection, acne, athlete's foot, verrucas, warts, insect bites, cold sores, nits (eggs of head lice). May be applied directly to verrucas, warts, and nits, but dilute with a carrier oil (such as almond) for other uses.
ECONOMIC Used in deodorants, soaps, mouthwashes, and toilet waters.

M. leucadendron (weeping paperbark, weeping tea tree, cajuput) p.157

PARTS USED Oil.
PROPERTIES A stimulant, antiseptic herb with a strong, camphoraceous aroma. It is expectorant, relieves spasms, increases perspiration, and expels intestinal parasites.
USES OF THE HERB
MEDICINAL Internally for bronchitis, tuberculosis, colds, sinusitis, gastric infections, and roundworms. Not given to pregnant women. Externally for rheumatism, gout, neuralgia, acne, nasal congestion, sinusitis, toothache, chilblains, and skin diseases. An antiseptic and painkiller in aromatherapy.
WARNING This herb, in the form of cajuput oil, is subject to legal restrictions in some countries.
ECONOMIC Used to flavor candy, also in perfumery, detergents, soaps, and insect repellants.

GROWTH AND HARVEST

GROWTH Ornamental (*M. alternifolia*). Crop (*M. leucadendron*). Moisture-retentive to wet, neutral to acid soil in sun, minimum 59–64°F (15–18°C). *M. leucadendron* tolerates light and saline soils. Propagate by seed in spring, or by semiripe cuttings in summer. Pinch out young, pot grown plants to induce bushiness.
HARVEST Oil is distilled from leaves and twigs, used directly, or in spirits and ointments.

MELANTHIUM

M. cochinchinensis. See *Asparagus cochinchinensis*.

MELIA
(Meliaceae)

M. azederach was first described in Chinese medicine in AD1082. It is closely related to *Azadirachta indica* (see p.247), which has similar properties and uses in Ayurvedic medicine, but it is a hardier plant.

M. azadirachta. See *Azadirachta indica*.

M. azederach (chinaberry, bead tree, Persian lilac) p.157

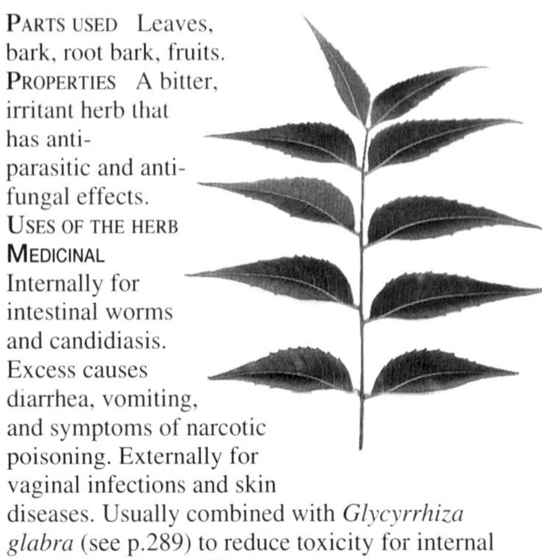

PARTS USED Leaves, bark, root bark, fruits.
PROPERTIES A bitter, irritant herb that has anti-parasitic and anti-fungal effects.
USES OF THE HERB
MEDICINAL
Internally for intestinal worms and candidiasis. Excess causes diarrhea, vomiting, and symptoms of narcotic poisoning. Externally for vaginal infections and skin diseases. Usually combined with *Glycyrrhiza glabra* (see p.289) to reduce toxicity for internal use. For use by qualified practitioners only.

M. indica. See *Azadirachta indica*.

GROWTH AND HARVEST

GROWTH Ornamental. Well-drained to dry soil in sun. Tolerates very dry, coastal sites in warm areas. Propagate by seed sown as soon as ripe in autumn.
HARVEST Leaves are collected during the growing season, bark and root bark at any time, and fruits in autumn; all parts are used fresh or dried in decoctions, ointments, and pills.

MELILOTUS Melilot
(Leguminosae/Papilionaceae)

M. officinalis contains coumarins, which release the pleasant smell of new-mown hay when drying. Poorly dried or fermented melilot produces dicoumarol, a potent anti-coagulant that is extremely poisonous in excess; it is used in rat poison. Melilot is effective in drawing out toxins and reducing inflammation; melilot plasters were used from ancient Greek times until the 19th century for this purpose. Several species have a limited use in food flavoring; the blue-flowered *M. caerulea* is specially grown in Switzerland to flavor *sapsago* (Schabziger) cheese.

M. officinalis, syn. *M. arvensis* (yellow sweet clover, yellow melilot, ribbed melilot) p.157

PARTS USED Whole plant.
PROPERTIES An aromatic, sedative herb that is diuretic, relieves spasms and pain, clears congestion, reduces inflammation, and has anti-thrombotic effects.
USES OF THE HERB
CULINARY Dried herb is used to flavor marinades, stews (especially of rabbit), and Gruyère cheese.
MEDICINAL Internally for tension headaches, neuralgia, palpitations, insomnia, varicose veins, painful congestive menstruation, and to prevent thrombosis. Not given to patients with a history of poor blood clotting, or taking warfarin medication. Externally for eye inflammations, rheumatic pain, swollen joints, severe bruising, boils, and erysipelas.
ECONOMIC Dried herb is added as flavoring to snuff and tobacco, and used as a moth repellant.

GROWTH AND HARVEST

GROWTH Crop. Well-drained to dry, neutral to alkaline soil in sun. *M. officinalis* is drought-tolerant. Propagate by seed sown in autumn or spring.
HARVEST Plants are cut when flowering and dried for compresses, infusions, and tinctures.

MELISSA
(Labiatae/Lamiaceae)

M. officinalis contains a lemon-scented volatile oil that has antiviral activity. Commercial sources of oil are often adulterated with oils of *Citrus limon* (see p.262) or *Cymbopogon citratus* (see p.270). Lemon balm is most popular as an ingredient of herb teas, having a pleasant flavor and calming effect. Paracelsus (1493–1541) called it "the elixir of life" and John Evelyn (1620–1706) described it as "sovereign for the brain, strengthening the memory, and powerfully chasing away melancholy."

M. officinalis (lemon balm, balm, melissa) p.157

PARTS USED Whole plant, leaves, oil.
PROPERTIES An aromatic, cooling, sedative herb that lowers fever, improves digestion, relaxes spasms and peripheral blood vessels, and inhibits thyroid activity. It has antiviral, antibacterial, and insect-repellent effects.
USES OF THE HERB
CULINARY Fresh leaves give a lemon flavor to salads, soups, sauces, herb vinegars, game, and fish (especially in Spain), and are an ingredient in *eau de mélisse des Carmes* (melissa cordial), liqueurs such as Benedictine and Chartreuse, and wine cups.
AROMATIC Dried leaves are added to potpourris and herb pillows.
MEDICINAL Internally for nervous disorders, indigestion associated with nervous tension, excitability with digestive upsets in children, hyperthyroidism, depression, anxiety, palpitations, and tension headaches. Externally for herpes, sores, gout, insect bites, and as an insect repellant. Combines well with *Chamaemelum nobile* (see p.259), *Filipendula ulmaria* (see p.283), and *Humulus lupulus* (see p.294) for nervous indigestion. Oil is used in aromatherapy to relax and rejuvenate, especially in cases of depression and nervous tension.
VARIANTS
***M. o.* 'All Gold'**, p.157.
***M. o.* 'Aurea'**, syn. *M. o.* 'Variegata', p.157.

GROWTH AND HARVEST

GROWTH Ornamental. Moist soil in sun or partial shade. Propagate by seed sown in ►

► autumn or spring (species only), or by division or stem cuttings in autumn or spring. Cut back plants after flowering to produce a fresh crop of leaves.
HARVEST Plants are cut as flowering begins and used fresh or dried in infusions, liquid extracts, ointments, and tinctures. Fresh foliage is distilled for oil.

MENISPERMUM

M. palmatum. See *Jateorhiza palmata.*

MENTHA Mint

(Labiatae/Lamiaceae)

The mints are a complex group, involving hybridization in both the wild and cultivation, which makes individual plants often difficult to identify. They are rich in volatile oils of variable composition. It is menthol that gives mints their typical smell and taste, which are simultaneously cool and warming. Menthol is an antiseptic, decongestant, analgesic compound that predominates in *M.* x *piperita*. It is mildly anesthetic, giving the cooling, numbing sensation experienced when smelling or tasting peppermint. Menthol-rich mints are used only with sweet foods, such as chocolate, ice cream, and candy, becausethe anesthetic effect overwhelms more subtle flavors. Spearmint and peppermint are among the world's most popular flavors, and crops for leaf and oil production are grown on a large scale in Europe, US, the Middle East, and Asia. Less pleasant in aroma is pulegone, a toxic compound, notorious for causing abortion, which is present in the oils of both *M. pulegium* and *Hedeoma pulegioides* (see p.291). *M. longifolia* also contains the diuretic diosphenol, which predominates in *Agathosma* species (see p.230). Other mints, such as *M. spicata*, have high concentrations of carvone, a compound that characterizes the aroma of *Carum carvi* (caraway, see p.255). The Australian *M. diemenica* (slender mint) has been used as a substitute for *M. pulegium*. It is taken to relieve colic and cramps, though should not to be taken in excess, or during pregnancy, due to the pulegone content. It is also a good insect repellant.

M. aquatica, syn. *M. hirsuta* (watermint) p.158

PARTS USED Whole plant, leaves.
PROPERTIES A strongly aromatic, astringent herb that stimulates bile flow, improves digestion, and relieves spasms.
USES OF THE HERB
MEDICINAL Internally for diarrhea, gastroenteritis, colds, and painful menstruation. Excess causes vomiting.

M. arvensis, syn. *M. austriaca* (corn mint, field mint) p.158

PARTS USED Whole plant (*bo he*), leaves, oil.
PROPERTIES A pungently aromatic, stimulant, antibacterial herb that benefits the digestion, relaxes spasms, reduces inflammation, and increases perspiration rate. It also relieves pain and itching, and suppresses lactation. According to Chinese medicine, it acts mainly on the lung and liver energies.
USES OF THE HERB
CULINARY Traditionally used to prevent milk from curdling; also to make tea (*M. a.* var. *villosa*).
MEDICINAL Internally for colds, sore throat, headaches, measles, and indigestion; for nausea (*M. a.* var. *villosa*) by native N Americans. Externally for skin irritations. Combined with *Schizonepeta tenuifolia* and *Dendranthema* x *grandiflorum* (see p.272) in a powder for sore throat, blown down the throat through a tube. May reduce milk flow if taken when breastfeeding.
ECONOMIC Oil (especially of *M. a.* var. *piperascens*) is used as a substitute for, or adulterant of, peppermint oil.
VARIANTS
M. a.* var. *piperascens (Japanese mint)
Japanese variety, hardy to 5°F (–15°C), height 4–24in (10–60cm), spread indefinite; ovate, gland-dotted leaves have a strong peppermint scent.
M. a.* var. *villosa, syn. *M. canadensis* (American mint)
N American variety, hardy to 5°F (–15°C), height 8–20in (20–50cm), spread indefinite; it differs from *M. arvensis* in its hairier, lanceolate leaves, pink or white flowers, and pleasant aroma.

M. x *gracilis*, syn. *M. cardiaca*, *M.* x *gentilis* (gingermint, redmint) p.158

PARTS USED Whole plant, leaves, oil.
PROPERTIES A stimulant herb with a spicy, fruity aroma. It benefits the digestion and relieves spasms.
USES OF THE HERB
CULINARY May be used fresh as a flavoring, especially with melon, tomatoes, and fruit salads.
ECONOMIC A source of spearmint oil in the US.
VARIANT
***M.* x *g.* 'Variegata'**, syn. *M.* x *g.* **'Aurea'**, p.158.

M. longifolia, syn. *M. sylvestris*, *M. incana* (horsemint) p.158

PARTS USED Whole plant, leaves, oil.
PROPERTIES A peppermint-scented herb.
USES OF THE HERB
CULINARY Mainly in Asian cuisine as a seasoning in Indian chutneys. Leaves are candied.
ECONOMIC A source of oil, used as a substitute for peppermint oil in candy.

M. x *piperita*, syn. *M. nigricans* (peppermint) p.158

PARTS USED Whole plant, leaves, oil.
PROPERTIES A strongly aromatic, bitter, decongestant herb that relieves spasms, increases perspiration, improves digestion, and has antiseptic, mildly anesthetic effects. It acts mainly on the digestive system, especially on the lower bowel.
USES OF THE HERB
CULINARY Leaves are used in teas, in iced drinks, and in salads.
AROMATIC Leaves are added to potpourris.
MEDICINAL Internally for nausea, morning sickness, indigestion, gastric ulcer, gastroenteritis, irritable bowel syndrome, colic, influenza (especially in the feverish stage), and colds. Externally for upper respiratory tract infections, sinusitis, excess mucus, asthma, itching skin conditions, burns, ringworm, neuralgia, rheumatism, and as an insect repellant. Excessive use of essential oil causes irritation to mucous membranes. May cause allergic reaction. Not given to infants in any form. *M.* x *piperita* 'Citrata' has uses (for infertility, nervous exhaustion, and rapid heartbeat) more akin to *Lavandula angustifolia* (see p.301) than to peppermint.
ECONOMIC Oil (*M.* x *piperita*, *M.* x *piperita* 'Citrata') is used in oral hygiene preparations, cold or influenza remedies, antacids, and toiletries; as flavoring in medicines, perfumery, cigarettes, candy, ice cream, and liqueurs (*crème de menthe*). *M.* x *piperita* 'Citrata' is a source of lavender oil for perfumery.
VARIANT
***M.* x *p.* 'Citrata'**, p.158.

M. pulegium (pennyroyal) p.159

PARTS USED Whole plant, leaves, oil.
PROPERTIES A pungently aromatic, bitter, astringent herb that improves digestion, increases perspiration, and stimulates the uterus.
USES OF THE HERB
CULINARY Leaves are added to black pudding (northern England) and sausages (Spain).
AROMATIC Leaves added to potpourris.
MEDICINAL Internally for indigestion, colic, feverish colds, and menstrual complaints. Not given to pregnant women. Externally for skin irritations.
ECONOMIC Traditionally used to repel mice and insects. Oil is used in soaps and detergents.
VARIANT
***M. p.* 'Cunningham Mint'**, syn. *M. p.* 'Dwarf Pennyroyal', p.159.

M. requienii (Corsican mint) p.159

PARTS USED Whole plant.
PROPERTIES An aromatic herb with a strong peppermint scent.
USES OF THE HERB
AROMATIC An aromatic garden ornamental.
ECONOMIC Used to flavor liqueurs.

M. satureioides (Australian pennyroyal, Brisbane pennyroyal)

Upright, creeping perennial, hardy to 5°F (–15°C), height 12in (30cm), spread indefinite, with smooth, oblong, untoothed leaves and clusters of white flowers in spring. It has a pungent, peppermint–pennyroyal aroma. Native to eastern Australia.

PARTS USED Whole plant, leaves.
PROPERTIES A pungently aromatic, tonic, decongestant herb that improves the digestion, stimulates the uterus, and relieves spasms and pain.
USES OF THE HERB
MEDICINAL Internally for colds, excess mucus, indigestion, colic, and menstrual complaints. Used as a substitute for both *M.* x *piperita* and *M. pulegium*. Not given to pregnant women.

M. x smithiana, syn. *M. rubra* (red raripila mint) p.159

PARTS USED Leaves.
PROPERTIES An aromatic herb with a spearmintlike flavor.
USES OF THE HERB
CULINARY As for *M. spicata*.

M. spicata, syn. *M. crispa*, *M. viridis* (spearmint) p.159

PARTS USED Whole plant, leaves, oil.
PROPERTIES An aromatic, stimulant herb that improves digestion and relieves spasms. Oil is less pungent than peppermint oil and is nonirritant.
USES OF THE HERB
CULINARY Leaves are an important ingredient of mint sauce and jelly to accompany lamb, *tzatziki* (eastern Europe), and *tabbouleh* (Middle East); also used for garnishing and flavoring, and for herb teas and iced drinks.
MEDICINAL Internally for indigestion, colic, flatulence, hiccups, and feverish childhood illnesses. Combined with *Ballota nigra* (see p.247) for upper respiratory tract infections in children.
ECONOMIC Oil is used in commercial food flavoring (notably in chewing gum) and oral hygiene preparations.
VARIANTS
***M. s.* 'Crispa'**, p.159.
***M. s.* 'Moroccan'** (Moroccan spearmint) A favorite cultivar, hardy to 5°F (–15°C), height 12–36in (30cm–1m), spread indefinite, with close-set leaves and a fine flavor.

M. suaveolens, syn. *M. insularis*, *M. macrostachya* (applemint, woolly mint) p.159

PARTS USED Leaves.
PROPERTIES An aromatic herb with a fruity, spearmint flavor.
USES OF THE HERB
CULINARY As for *M. spicata* (considered superior in flavor, but hairy leaves are less suitable for garnishing). Leaves may be candied.
VARIANT
***M. s.* 'Variegata'**, p.159.

M. x villosa var. **alopecuroides**, syn. *M. nemorosa* var. *alopecuroides* (Bowles' mint) p.159

PARTS USED Leaves.
PROPERTIES An aromatic herb with a spearmint flavor.
USES OF THE HERB
CULINARY As for *M. spicata*.

GROWTH AND HARVEST
GROWTH Ornamental (*M. arvensis*, *M. a.* var. *piperascens*, *M. a.* var. *villosa*: crop, *M. satureioides*: wild-collected). Rich, moist soil in sun or partial shade. *M. aquatica* thrives in wet soil; *M. arvensis* tolerates dry conditions; *M. pulegium* prefers damp, sandy, acid soil; *M. requienii* needs moist, shady conditions. Propagate by seed sown in spring (*M. pulegium*, *M. requienii*, *M. satureioides* only), or by division in spring or autumn, or by cuttings during the growing season, placed in moist soil mix or water (not *M. requienii*). Foliage may be damaged by ► mildew and rust, though *M.* x *villosa* var. *alopecuroides* is resistant to rust. Most mints are invasive and are best grown in a confined space. *M. requienii* usually self-seeds, even when the parent plant is killed by frost. *M. pulegium* is subject to statutory control as a weed in some countries, notably in parts of Australia.
HARVEST Whole plants are cut as flowering begins, and leaves are cut during the growing season and used fresh or dried for use in concentrated waters, infusions, liquid extracts, powders, spirits, or oil distillation. *M. arvensis* is mainly decocted or powdered in Chinese remedies.

MENYANTHES Bog bean
(Menyanthaceae)

Menyanthes is closely related to *Gentiana* species (see p.287) and contains similarly bitter glycosides. It is used as a substitute for *Gentiana lutea* (see p.287) but may irritate the digestive system in patients with gastric inflammation or infection.

M. trifoliata (bog bean, buckbean, marsh trefoil) p.160

PARTS USED Leaves.
PROPERTIES A very bitter herb that is diuretic and laxative, stimulates the digestion, and improves lymphatic drainage.
USES OF THE HERB
MEDICINAL Internally for indigestion, anorexia, arthritis, rheumatism, muscular weakness in myalgic encephalomyelitis (ME), and chronic infections with debility and exhaustion. May be combined with *Cimicifuga racemosa* (see p.261) or *Apium graveolens* (see p.240) to relieve joint and muscular pain. Excess causes vomiting. Not given to patients with diarrhea, dysentery, or colitis.

GROWTH AND HARVEST
GROWTH Ornamental. Shallow, acid water or wet soil in sun. Propagate by seed in spring, or by stem cuttings or division of rhizomes in spring.
HARVEST Leaves are picked in summer and dried for use in infusions, liquid extracts, and tinctures.

MITCHELLA
(Rubiaceae)

M. repens was first used by N American tribes, such as the Cherokee and Penobscot, to ease labor; hence the common name "squaw vine." Its uses were adopted by colonists and it was listed as an astringent, tonic, and diuretic in the U.S. *National Formulary* (1926–47).

M. repens (partridge berry, squaw vine, running box) p.160

PARTS USED Whole plant.
PROPERTIES A bitter, astringent herb that is diuretic, relaxes the uterus, strengthens uterine contractions, and calms the nerves.
USES OF THE HERB
MEDICINAL Internally for menstrual disorders, preparation for childbirth, labor pains, nervous exhaustion, and irritability. Not given during the first six months of pregnancy but may be given alone, or combined with *Rubus fruticosus* (see p.343), as a uterine tonic during the last two months.

GROWTH AND HARVEST
GROWTH Ornamental. Moist, humus-rich, neutral to acid soil in shade. Propagate by seed in autumn, or by division in spring. May be invasive.
HARVEST Plants are cut in summer and dried for infusions, liquid extracts, and tinctures.

MOMORDICA
(Cucurbitaceae)

Bitter substances, known as cucurbitacins, are common in the family. In edible species they have been either largely bred out (as in cucumbers) or must be removed by careful soaking of the fruits before use. *M. charantia* is an important food plant in parts of the tropics and is used medicinally in most countries of origin. Other species with medicinal applications include the oriental *M. cochinchinensis*, whose poisonous seeds are used externally for skin eruptions and infections, hemorrhoids, mastitis, and enlarged lymph nodes, and *M. grosvenori*, an expectorant and lymphatic cleanser.

M. charantia (balsam pear, bitter gourd) p.160

PARTS USED Leaves, fruits.
PROPERTIES A laxative, diuretic herb that soothes irritated tissues, lowers fever, kills parasites, and cleanses toxins from the system. It is probably a uterine stimulant.
USES OF THE HERB
CULINARY Young fruits are added to curries or eaten raw, boiled, or fried, after soaking in salt water to remove bitterness.
MEDICINAL Internally for colitis and dysentery (fresh juice), intestinal worms, jaundice, and fevers (leaves). Externally for hemorrhoids, chapped skin, and burns (fruit).

M. elateria. See *Ecballium elaterium.*

GROWTH AND HARVEST
GROWTH Crop. Rich, well-drained soil in sun, minimum 59–64°F (15–18°C). Propagate by seed sown in spring. Plants flower in 30–35 days, producing fruits 15–20 days later. Pinch shoots after fruits have set. Plants under cover may be damaged by whitefly, spider mites, and aphids. Plants grown outdoors may be protected by individual paper covers against insect damage.
HARVEST Leaves are collected during the growing season and used fresh or dried in infusions. Fruits are picked when young, and used fresh as pulp or juice.

MONARDA Horsemint
(Labiatae/Lamiaceae)

Several native N American tribes made great use of horsemints. These should not be confused with the European horsemint, *Mentha longifolia* (see p.311). *M. fistulosa* was used extensively for bronchial complaints and as a seasoning for meat. *M. punctata* was listed in the *U.S. Pharmacopoeia* (1820–82) as a digestive and antirheumatic. The volatile oil is rich in thymol (as found in *Thymus vulgaris*, see p.362), a potent antiseptic and expectorant. *M. didyma* is famous as the source of "Oswego tea," named after an area of New York near Lake Ontario, where it grew abundantly. Other species include: *M. citriodora* (lemon bergamot) from the southwestern US, whose lemon-scented leaves are used in teas and to flavor wild game; *M. menthaefolia* of western N America, which has antiseptic, anesthetic, and diaphoretic effects; and the oregano-flavored *M. austromontana* from northern Mexico.

M. didyma (Oswego tea, bee balm, bergamot) p.160

PARTS USED Whole plant, leaves, flowers.
PROPERTIES An aromatic, stimulant, expectorant herb that lowers fever and benefits the digestion.
USES OF THE HERB
CULINARY Leaves are infused as tea, and give an Earl Grey flavor to tea and iced drinks. Flowers are added to salads.
AROMATIC Leaves and flowers scent and color potpourris.
MEDICINAL Internally for minor digestive complaints.

M. fistulosa (wild bergamot, horsemint) p.160

PARTS USED Whole plant, leaves.
PROPERTIES An aromatic, stimulant herb that improves the digestion and increases perspiration.
USES OF THE HERB
CULINARY Leaves are used to flavor meat and beans; young shoots and leaves are infused for tea.
MEDICINAL Internally for colds, sore throat, excess mucus, headaches, fevers, and gastric disorders. Externally for skin eruptions.

M. punctata (horsemint) p.160

PARTS USED Whole plant, leaves.
PROPERTIES A bitter, pungent, diuretic herb with a mint–thyme aroma. It increases perspiration, benefits the digestion, and is rubefacient when applied topically.
USES OF THE HERB
MEDICINAL Internally for indigestion, colic, nausea and vomiting, diarrhea, feverish chills, colds, and backache. Externally for neuralgia and rheumatism.

GROWTH AND HARVEST
GROWTH Ornamental. Rich, moist soil in sun (*M. didyma*); light, dry, alkaline soil in sun (*M. fistulosa* and *M. punctata*). Propagate by seed sown in spring, or by division in spring, or by softwood cuttings in spring. *M. didyma* is prone to mildew in dry conditions.
HARVEST Plants are cut when flowering, and leaves before flowering, and used fresh, or dried for infusions.

MORINDA
(Rubiaceae)

M. officinalis was first mentioned in Chinese medical literature during the Han Dynasty (206BC–AD23) as a tonic, warming herb that acts mainly on the kidney energy. The roots (*ba ji*) are combined with *Glycyrrhiza uralensis* to reduce toxicity. *M. tinctoria* (dyer's mulberry) is best known as a source of red dye, but both leaves and roots have astringent properties. *M. citrifolia* is the most widely used species.

M. citrifolia (Indian mulberry, awl tree) p.161

PARTS USED Roots (*ba ji*), leaves, fruits.
PROPERTIES An astringent, purgative herb that reduces inflammation.
USES OF THE HERB
CULINARY Fruits are eaten in curries.
MEDICINAL Internally for dysentery, hemorrhage (fruits), constipation (roots), and tuberculosis (leaves). Externally for gout (leaf juice), chronic ulcers, snakebite (leaves), and gum disease (fruits).

GROWTH AND HARVEST
GROWTH Crop. Well-drained, sandy soil in sun, minimum 59–64°F (15–18°C). Tolerates saline conditions. Propagate by seed sown when ripe at 64–70°F (18–21°C), or by semi-ripe cuttings in summer at 64°F (18°C).
HARVEST Roots are lifted as required and used in decoctions. Leaves are collected during the growing season for juice extraction, decoctions, or pastes. Fruits may be picked ripe or unripe, and are often charred and mixed with salt for medicinal use.

MORINGA
(Moringaceae)

M. oleifera is by far the most commonly used species. Nearly all parts of the tree are edible, and the seeds yield *ben* oil, a useful ingredient in foods and pharmaceutical products, since it does not go rancid. *M. pterygosperma* is important in India; the young leaves and unripe pods are eaten as vegetables, and the flowers added to curries, while various parts of the tree have medicinal uses. *M. peregrina*, a graceful African tree, has edible, potato-like roots and yields an oil that is used to treat infantile convulsions.

M. oleifera (horseradish tree, *ben*) p.161

PARTS USED Leaves, bark, roots, flowers, fruits, seeds, oil, gum.
PROPERTIES A nutritious, diuretic, laxative herb that is expectorant, increases milk flow, controls bacterial infections, and is rubefacient when applied topically. It contains a potent antibiotic. *Ben* oil has no taste, smell, or color, and is exceptionally resistant to oxidation. Gum has similar properties to tragacanth (see *Astragalus gummifer*, p.245).
USES OF THE HERB
CULINARY Leaves, flowers, and young pods are eaten as vegetables (leaves are often added to shellfish dishes to counteract any toxins). Roots make an acceptable substitute for horseradish. Seeds are roasted like nuts.
MEDICINAL Internally for insufficient lactation (young leaves), tuberculosis, septicemia (bark, gum); asthma, gout, rheumatism, enlarged spleen and liver, bladder and kidney stones, and inflammatory conditions (juice of root). Externally for boils, ulcers, glandular swellings, infected wounds, skin diseases, dental infections, snakebites, and gout (bark, root, gum).
ECONOMIC Oil is used in salad dressings, lubricants, artists' paints, soaps, and ointments. Wood is used in the manufacture of rayon and cellophane; bark is used in tanning. Older leaves are fed to livestock.

GROWTH AND HARVEST
GROWTH Crop. Well-drained, sandy soil in sun, minimum 59–64°F (15–18°C). Propagate by seed when ripe, or by semiripe cuttings in summer. Cut plants back hard when harvesting, or to control growth.
HARVEST Leaves, flowers, and immature fruits are collected as available and used fresh. Seeds are removed from pods when ripe and roasted for eating, or pressed for oil, which stores well. Bark, roots, and root bark are harvested as required for juice extraction, or used fresh or dried for decoctions. Gum is collected from bark for use in infusions and decoctions.

MORUS Mulberry
(Moraceae)

M. alba and *M. nigra* have similar constituents and are considered to be interchangeable for medicinal purposes. Being Chinese in origin, however, *M. alba* has been used exclusively in traditional Chinese medicine since AD659. The leaves, root bark, branches, and fruits are listed in the *Chinese Pharmacopoeia* (1985), but other parts, including sap and wood ash, are also widely used. All parts are prepared in a great variety of ways. Recent research has shown improvements in elephantiasis when treated with leaf extract injections, and in tetanus following oral doses of sap mixed with sugar. *M. alba* is also the preferred food of silkworms and is widely cultivated for this purpose. In China the start of silk production using mulberry leaves is generally attributed to the Empress Si-Ling, who lived c.2960BC.

M. alba (white mulberry) p.161

PARTS USED Leaves (*sang ye*), branches (*sang zhi*), root bark (*sang bai pi*), fruits (*sang shen*).
PROPERTIES A pleasant-tasting, bitter or sweet herb (depending on the part). It increases perspiration rate and has antibacterial, cooling effects (leaves), is anti-rheumatic (branches), controls coughing, is expectorant and diuretic (root bark), and has a tonic effect on kidney energy (fruits). Both root bark and branches reduce blood pressure.
USES OF THE HERB
CULINARY Fruits are eaten fresh and made into jellies, jams, syrup, and wine.
MEDICINAL Internally for colds, influenza, eye infections, and nosebleeds (leaves); rheumatic pains and hypertension (branches); coughs, asthma, bronchitis, edema, hypertension, and diabetes (root bark); urinary incontinence, tinnitus, premature graying of hair, thirst, and constipation in the elderly (fruits).
ECONOMIC Leaves are fed to silkworms. Wood is used in the manufacture of sports equipment, such as tennis rackets and bats, especially in India.
VARIANT
M. a. 'Pendula', p.161.

GROWTH AND HARVEST
GROWTH Ornamental. Rich, deep, well-drained soil in sun. Propagate by seed sown in autumn (species only), or by softwood cuttings in summer, or hardwood cuttings in autumn. Mulberries have brittle roots and need careful handling when planting. Prune only when fully dormant in winter because mulberries bleed when cut. Ideally prune only badly placed branches and dead wood. Canker and dieback may damage young shoots.
HARVEST For medicinal use, leaves are collected after frost in autumn, branches in late spring or early summer, roots in winter, and fruits when nearly ripe. Leaves and root bark are traditionally processed with honey. Fresh leaves and fruits are sometimes juiced but otherwise all parts are dried for use in decoctions or poultices. Fruits may be steamed or blanched before drying to improve storage qualities; for culinary use they are harvested when ripe.

MUCUNA Velvet bean
(Leguminosae/Papilionoideae)

About 100 species of woody lianas, climbers, and shrubs belong to this leguminous genus found in the tropics and subtropics. Some species are bat-pollinated, and most contain alkaloids. A few are grown as ornamentals, notably the scarlet-flowered *M. bennettii*, which is among the world's most spectacular climbers. *M. pruriens* (often given incorrectly as *M. prurita*) is a species with several variants; the main one is *M. p.* var. *utilis* (syn. *M. deeringiana*, *M. utilis*), which lacks irritant hairs and is widely grown in the tropics as a fodder crop. *M. pruriens* is unusual among herbs in that the parts used are the bristly hairs on the pods. The use of this species as an anthelmintic was first recorded by Patrick Browne in his *Civil and Natural History of Jamaica*, 1756. Ancient Sanskrit texts indicate that it was used as an aphrodisiac. Seeds of *M. pruriens*, or possibly a variety, yield L-dopa, which revolutionized the treatment of Parkinson's disease in the 1960s. They also contain hallucinogenic, toxic compounds. Though poisonous, the seeds are a common famine food, edible if boiled in several changes of water.

M. pruriens, syn. *Dolichos pruriens*, *Stizolobium pruriens* (cowhage, cowitch, *kaunch*)

Tender, evergreen, twining climber, height to 12ft (3m), with downy leaves up to 18in (45cm) long, divided into 3 ovate, pointed leaflets. Clusters of purple or white pealike flowers, about 2in (5cm) long, appear in summer, followed by flattened pods up to 3½in (9cm) long and ¾in (2cm) wide, with a pointed, often hooked, apex. The pods contain 3–6 seeds, about ½in (1cm) long, and are covered in orange or dark brown, irritant bristles. Found in tropical Asia, Africa, and America.

PARTS USED Roots, hairs from pods, seeds.
PROPERTIES An irritant, rubefacient herb that destroys intestinal parasites (hairs), and acts as a diuretic (roots) and aphrodisiac (seeds).
USES OF THE HERB
CULINARY Seeds are boiled in milk, decorticated, fried, and made into a confection with honey.
MEDICINAL Internally for nervous and kidney complaints, and paralysis (roots), roundworms (hairs); externally for elephantiasis and dropsy (roots). Internal use of the hairs is highly irritant; excess may prove fatal.

GROWTH AND HARVEST
GROWTH Crop. Well-drained, moist, humus-rich soil in sun or partial shade, minimum 64°F (18°C). Propagate by seed sown in spring, or by layering in late summer. Remove crowded branches in winter and cut back flowered shoots to within 2–3in (5–8cm) of the base. Spider mite and whitefly may attack plants under cover.
HARVEST Roots are lifted as required and dried for decoctions and powders. Pods are collected when ripe and scraped to remove hairs, which are powdered and mixed with honey or added to ointment. Seeds are removed from ripe pods, cooked, and ground to a paste.
WARNING Pods, hairs, and powder are extremely irritant to skin, eyes, and mucous membranes.

MURRAYA
(Rutaceae)

The fresh leaves of *M. koenigii* are an indispensable ingredient of curries in southern India and Sri Lanka. It is grown throughout these regions for this purpose. Curry leaf remains unknown in the West largely because the leaves lose their flavor on drying, but can be preserved in oil. *Murraya* is closely related to *Citrus* (see p.262); lemon trees (*C. limon*) can be grafted onto the rootstock of *M. koenigii*.

M. koenigii (curry leaf) p.161

PARTS USED Leaves, bark, root, seeds, oil.
PROPERTIES A warming, strongly aromatic herb that improves appetite and digestion.
USES OF THE HERB
CULINARY Locally in curries (leaves).
MEDICINAL Internally for digestive problems (leaves, roots, bark), constipation, colic, diarrhea (leaves).

GROWTH AND HARVEST
GROWTH Crop. Moist, humus-rich, well-drained soil in sun or partial shade, minimum 59–64°F (15–18°C). Propagate by seed in spring, or by semiripe cuttings in summer. Remove excessive growth in late winter.
HARVEST Leaves are picked all year and used fresh for juice, infusions, and poultices. Bark and roots are collected as required, and used fresh or dried in decoctions. Oil is extracted from ripe seeds.

MYRICA Wax myrtle
(Myricaceae)

The fruits of various species are boiled to produce wax for making candles that are aromatic and smokeless. *M. gale* and *M. cerifera* contain tannins, resins, gums, and bactericidal substances. *M. gale* was once an important herb for tea and flavoring in some communities and it is the badge of the Scottish Campbell clan. *M. cerifera* is a key herb in the Thomsonian system of medicine, being the main astringent used for "any stomach or bowel derangement, particularly after fevers." *M. californica* is similarly used for gastrointestinal disorders and infections.

M. cerifera (bayberry, wax myrtle, candleberry) p.162

PARTS USED Bark, root bark, wax.
PROPERTIES A bitter, astringent, aromatic herb that stimulates the circulation, increases perspiration, and controls bacterial infections.
USES OF THE HERB
CULINARY Fruits may be used with strongly flavored meat dishes, such as game, in the same way as juniper berries.
MEDICINAL Internally for fevers, colds, influenza, excess mucus, diarrhea, colitis, excessive menstruation, and vaginal discharge. Externally for sore throat, ulcers, sores, itching skin conditions, dandruff, and hair loss. Combined with *Sambucus nigra* (see p.347) and *Mentha x piperita* (see p.311) for feverish illnesses; with *Capsicum annuum* var. *annuum* (see p.254), *Zingiber officinale* (see p.373), and *Syzygium aromaticum* (see p.358) as a circulatory stimulant, and with *Lavandula* (see p.301) in hair preparations.

ECONOMIC Wax from fruits is used in making candles and soap.

M. gale (sweet gale, bog myrtle) p.162

PARTS USED Whole plant, leaves, fruits.
PROPERTIES A bitter, astringent, antiseptic herb with a resinous, baylike aroma.
USES OF THE HERB
CULINARY Whole plant was used as a substitute for hops to flavor ale. Leaves are infused for tea and added to soups and stews.
ECONOMIC Fruits are a source of candle wax.

GROWTH AND HARVEST
GROWTH Crop (*M. cerifera*). Ornamental (*M. gale*). Well-drained to wet, acid, sandy soil in sun or partial shade. Propagate by seed in autumn or spring, or by layering in spring, or by suckers (*M. gale*), or by semiripe cuttings in summer.
HARVEST Whole plants or leaves are collected during the growing season, and bark and root bark in late autumn or early spring. All are dried for decoctions, infusions, liquid extracts, and powders. Fruits are gathered when ripe for wax extraction.

MYRISTICA Nutmeg
(Myristicaceae)

Fruits of *M. fragrans* are rich in volatile oils, which differ in concentration (and hence flavor) in the seed (nutmeg) and aril (mace). These include safrole (as found in *Sassafras albidum*, see p.349), and myristicin, a hallucinogenic compound. Nutmeg and mace probably reached Europe via Arab traders in the first century AD, and were mainly used for medicinal purposes. Although now used almost exclusively as a spice, *M. fragrans* was promoted as a tonic after the Portuguese took the Moluccas and obtained a monopoly on its production in 1512. The first recorded case of nutmeg poisoning came in 1576, when a "pregnant English lady" consumed 10–12 fruits and became "deliriously inebriated." *M. fragrans* has been listed as a Chinese medicinal herb since c.600AD.

M. fragrans (nutmeg, *jatiphala*) p.162

PARTS USED Seeds (*rou dou kou*), oil.
PROPERTIES A bitter, astringent, spicy herb that acts as a warming, digestive tonic. It controls vomiting and relaxes spasms. Topical application is anti-inflammatory.
USES OF THE HERB
CULINARY Ground or grated nutmeg gives flavor to bakery products, puddings, drinks, meat dishes, vegetables (notably spinach and mushrooms), cheese dishes, sauces (such as onion, bread, and *béchamel*), and pasta stuffings. Powdered or whole mace gives a similar but less pungent flavor and is better suited to soufflés, fish, clear soups, and sauces where nutmeg would spoil the appearance.
MEDICINAL Internally for diarrhea, dysentery, vomiting, abdominal distention, indigestion, and colic. Excess causes severe headache, nausea, dizziness, and delirium. Externally for toothache, and rheumatic and abdominal pains (including labor pains). Used in Ayurvedic medicine for poor digestion, insomnia, urinary incontinence, and premature ejaculation.
ECONOMIC Fatty oil, known as "nutmeg butter," is used in the pharmaceutical industry, mainly in perfume, soap, and candle manufacturing.

GROWTH AND HARVEST
GROWTH Crop. Well-drained, humus-rich, sandy soil, minimum 59–64°F (15–18°C). Propagate by seed sown when ripe, or by hardwood cuttings at the end of the growing season. Dried nutmegs are prone to insect attack; they are usually limed and stored in sealed containers.
HARVEST Seeds are removed from ripe fruits and separated from arils; both are dried for oil distillation or used in decoctions and powders.

MYROXYLON *Bálsamo*
(Leguminosae/Papilionoideae)

Bálsamo trees were cultivated by the Incas. The first European to record their medicinal uses was Nicolas Monardes in 1565, who noted that balsam was collected by either cutting the bark or by boiling the branches in water. Following the Spanish conquest, balsam was exported to Europe for medicines and perfumery. It was also approved for use in anointing oils: papal bulls of 1562 and 1571 declared it sacrilege to destroy balsam trees. Tolu balsam (*M. balsamum*) is named after Santiago de Tolu, Colombia; the resin differs only slightly in chemistry from the oily, fluid balsam of Peru (*M. pereirae*), originally shipped from Callao, Peru. Both contain benzoic acid, which is a common cause of allergic reaction. Tolu balsam is collected from V-shaped incisions in the tree bark and solidifies to a yellow-red or brown, crystalline consistency. A different method is employed for balsam of Peru: the bark is beaten, left a few days, then burned off; balsam exudes from the wounded areas and is soaked up by rags, which are boiled in water to separate the balsam into an oily layer.

M. balsamum, syn. *M. toluiferum* (Tolu balsam, *bálsamo*) p.162

PARTS USED Seeds, oleoresin, oil.
PROPERTIES A sweet, acid-tasting, aromatic herb that acts as an antiseptic and stimulating expectorant.
USES OF THE HERB
AROMATIC Oil is used in perfumery.
MEDICINAL Mainly as a pleasant-tasting ingredient in friar's balsam and cough mixtures; also as a base for lozenges (oleoresin).
ECONOMIC Extract is used in food flavoring (mainly for chewing gum, ice cream, candy, soft drinks, and bakery products).

M. pereirae, syn. *M. peruiferum*, *M. balsamum* var. *pereirae* (Peruvian balsam, balsam of Peru)

Tender, spreading evergreen tree, height 40–50ft (12–15m), spread 30ft (10m). It is very similar to *M. balsamum*, but leaves have 7–11 leaflets, less downy flower clusters, and single-seeded pods. Native to the Pacific coast of C America.

PARTS USED Seeds, oleoresin.
PROPERTIES A bitter, acrid herb with a vanilla-like aroma. It is antiseptic and a stimulating expectorant.
USES OF THE HERB
MEDICINAL Internally for excess mucus, diarrhea, coughs, asthma, and bronchitis. Externally for minor injuries, rheumatic pains, ulcers, eczema, diaper rash, and sore nipples.
ECONOMIC Used as incense in C America and in commercial food flavoring. An important constituent of oriental-type perfumes, soaps, and hand creams.

GROWTH AND HARVEST
GROWTH Crop.Well-drained soil with added sand and leaf mold, in sun, with ample water when in growth; minimum 59–64°F (15–18°C). *M. pereirae* tolerates alkaline and poor soils. Propagate by seed sown when ripe, or by semi-ripe cuttings in late summer. Balsam trees are resilient, tolerating heavy tapping and often reaching 100 years old.
HARVEST Oleoresin is collected at any time of the year, but mostly during the dry season, by wounding the bark; it is used raw or processed into extracts, oils, syrups, and tinctures. Oil is distilled from oleoresin. Seed are collected when ripe and used whole.

MYRRHIS Sweet cicely
(Umbelliferae/Apiaceae)

M. odorata contains a volatile oil, which includes anethole, as found in *Foeniculum vulgare* (see p.283), *Pimpinella anisum* (see p.328), and *Illicium verum* (see p.296). This same constituent is present in the American sweet cicely (*Osmorhiza claytoni*) and in aniseroot (*O. longistylis*), both of which have aromatic roots.

M. odorata (sweet cicely, sweet chervil, garden myrrh) p.162

PARTS USED Leaves, roots, seeds.
PROPERTIES A sweet, aromatic, expectorant herb that benefits the digestion.
USES OF THE HERB
CULINARY Leaves are added to soups, stews, and wine cups, and are used as a low-calorie sweetener and flavoring for stewed fruit, yogurt, and whipped cream. Roots are cooked as a vegetable and eaten cold in salads. Seeds are eaten raw in salads.
MEDICINAL Internally for coughs, minor digestive complaints, and anemia.

GROWTH AND HARVEST
GROWTH Ornamental. Moist, humus-rich soil in sun or shade. Propagate by seed in spring. It may be slow to germinate, but may self-seed ►

► prolifically in good conditions. Does not like summer heat.
HARVEST Leaves are picked during the growing season and used fresh or frozen. Roots are lifted in autumn and used fresh, or dried for use in decoctions. Seeds are collected when green and used fresh.

MYRTUS Myrtle
(Myrtaceae)

The active compounds in *M. communis* are rapidly absorbed and give a violet-like scent to the urine within 15 minutes.

M. communis (myrtle) p.163

PARTS USED Whole plant, leaves, fruits, oil.
PROPERTIES An aromatic, astringent herb that is antiseptic and an effective decongestant.
USES OF THE HERB
CULINARY Leaves give flavor to dishes of pork, lamb, and small birds. Fruits (known as *mursins*) are used as a spice in the Middle East.
AROMATIC Oil is used in perfumery.
MEDICINAL Internally for urinary infections (as a substitute for *Agathosma crenulata*, see p.230), vaginal discharge, bronchial congestion, sinusitis, and dry coughs. Externally for acne (oil), gum infections, and hemorrhoids.
ECONOMIC Oil is used in soaps and skin-care products.
VARIANTS
***M. c.* 'Flore Pleno'**, p.163.
***M. c.* 'Variegata'**, syn. *M. c.* 'Tricolor', p.163.
M. c.* subsp. *tarentina, syn. *M. c.* 'Jenny Reitenbach', *M. c.* 'Microphylla', *M. c.* 'Nana', p.163.

GROWTH AND HARVEST
GROWTH Ornamental. Well-drained, neutral to alkaline soil in sun. Given sharply drained soil and protection from cold, *M. communis* may survive down to 14°F (–10°C) outdoors. Even with optimum conditions, *M. c.* 'Variegata' rarely survives below 23°F (–5°C). Excellent, traditional subject for container-grown topiary. Propagate by seed sown in spring (species only), or by semiripe cuttings in late summer. Trim plants in spring and remove damaged or dead shoots. Plants under cover may be damaged by whitefly and spider mites.
HARVEST Plants are cut with or without flowers and distilled for oil. Leaves are picked as required and used fresh, or dried for use in infusions. Fruits are collected when ripe and dried for use whole or ground.

NARDOSTACHYS Spikenard
(Valerianaceae)

N. grandiflora, the spikenard of the Bible, is mentioned in the Song of Solomon and was the substance used to anoint the feet of Jesus at the Last Supper. The perfume extracted from the roots was a valuable commodity in the Roman Empire, worth 300 denarii per pound weight (0.66kg). (A denarius was a laborer's average daily wage.) It was used by the Moghul empress Nur Jehan to make rejuvenating cosmetics. It contains borneol acetate (similar to the main constituent of *Dryobalanops aromatica*, see p.275) and patchouli alcohol, as found in *Pogostemon cablin* (see p.332). It is regarded as similar but superior to *Valeriana officinalis* (see p.367) in Ayurvedic medicine, harmonizing the constitution and strengthening the mind.

N. grandiflora, syn. *N. jatamansi* (nard, spikenard) p.164

PARTS USED Roots, oil.
PROPERTIES A bitter, astringent, aromatic herb that improves digestion, calms the nerves, relaxes spasms, and lowers blood pressure.
USES OF THE HERB
AROMATIC Oil is used in perfumery.
MEDICINAL Internally for nervous indigestion, insomnia, depression, and tension headaches. Externally for rashes and as a deodorant.

GROWTH AND HARVEST
GROWTH Wild-collected. Well-drained, gritty, moisture-retentive soil in partial shade or shade from midday sun. Needs a cool root run. Dislikes rich soil. Propagate by seed sown when ripe. Requires light for germination.
HARVEST Roots are dried for oil distillation or use in decoctions.

NASTURTIUM Watercress
(Cruciferae/Brassicareae)

N. officinale contains a volatile mustard oil and compounds similar to those in *Raphanus sativus* (see p.339), with a characteristic burning taste. It is also rich in vitamins and minerals, including iron, iodine, and calcium. Many watercress beds are stocked with hybrids of *N. officinale* that grow through the winter, allowing up to 10 crops a year.

N. officinale, syn. *Rorippa nasturtium-aquaticum* (watercress) p.164

PARTS USED Leaves.
PROPERTIES A bitter, pungent, stimulant herb that clears toxins, benefits the digestion, and has diuretic and expectorant effects.

USES OF THE HERB
CULINARY Traditionally taken as a spring tonic. Leaves are added to salads and to garnish butter; made into soup and a sauce for fish.
MEDICINAL Internally for edema, excess mucus, bronchitis, wet coughs, skin eruptions, rheumatism, anemia, debility associated with chronic disease, and gall bladder complaints.

GROWTH AND HARVEST
GROWTH Crop. Shallow, flowing, slightly alkaline water, in sun, at about 50°F (10°C). May be grown in pots, using rich soil mix and standing the pots in a dish of water, changing the water daily. Propagate by root cuttings in water during the growing season. Pinch out to encourage bushiness and delay flowering.
HARVEST Leaves are cut as required and used whole or liquified. Gathering from the wild is not recommended because of the frequent occurrence in watercourses of pollutants and pathogenic organisms, notably liver fluke.

NELUMBO Lotus
(Nelumbonaceae)

N. nucifera was revered in ancient Indian, Chinese, Tibetan, and Egyptian cultures, and the flowers are sacred to Buddhists. Specific parts of it are used in traditional Chinese medicine.

N. nucifera, syn. *Nelumbium speciosum* (sacred lotus, *padma*) p.164

PARTS USED Leaves (*he ye*), stems (leaf stalk, *lian geng*), flower stalk with receptacle attached (*lian fang*), rhizomes (*ou jie*), flower stamens (*lian xu*), seed plumule and radicle (*lian zi xin*), seeds (*lian zi*).
PROPERTIES An astringent, cooling herb that controls bleeding, lowers blood pressure and fever, sedates the heart energy, and acts as a tonic for the spleen and kidney energies.
USES OF THE HERB
CULINARY Seeds and roots are eaten as a vegetable.
MEDICINAL Internally for hemorrhage, nosebleed, excessive menstruation (rhizome); hypertension, insomnia, restlessness (plumule and radicle); diarrhea, poor digestion, insomnia, palpitations (seeds); urinary frequency, premature ejaculation (stamens); bleeding gastric ulcer, excessive menstruation, postpartum hemorrhage (flower stalk). In Ayurvedic medicine, mainly as cooling remedies for bleeding disorders.
VARIANTS
***N. n.* 'Alba Grandiflora'**, p.164.
***N. n.* 'Rosea Plena'**, p.164.

GROWTH AND HARVEST
GROWTH Ornamental. Sunny position in water at least 24in (60cm) deep or in large tubs of rich, wet soil mix under cover, minimum 34–45°F (1–7°C). Propagate by seed or by division in spring. May be invasive in good conditions outdoors. ►

► HARVEST Leaves and leaf stalks are collected in summer and autumn; rhizomes in autumn and winter; stamens from early to midsummer; seeds and flower stalks with receptacles from mid- to late summer. All parts are dried for use in decoctions and powders. (Plumule and radicle are separated from seeds before drying.)

NELUMBIUM

N. speciosum. See *Nelumbo nucifera.*

NEPETA

(Labiatae/Lamiaceae)

N. cataria contains citronellal (as found in *Melissa officinalis*, see p.310), thymol (as found in *Thymus vulgaris*, see p.362), and pulegone (as found in *Mentha pulegium*, see p.311). The constituent responsible for the stimulant effect on cats is thought to be actinidine, an iridoid glycoside, similar to that found in *Valeriana officinalis* (see p.367). The closely related *Schizonepeta tenuifolia* (Japanese catnip) is used in Chinese medicine for hemorrhages, especially postnatal bleeding and excessive menstruation, colds, measles, and nettle rash.

N. cataria (catnip, catmint) p.165

PARTS USED Whole plant, leaves.
PROPERTIES A bitter, astringent, cooling herb with a camphoraceous, pennyroyal–thyme aroma. It lowers fever, relaxes spasms, increases perspiration, and has a sedative effect.
USES OF THE HERB
CULINARY Leaves are infused for a mintlike tea (lemon-scented in the case of *N. c.* 'Citriodora'), and may be added to sauces and stews.
MEDICINAL Internally for feverish illnesses (especially colds and influenza), insomnia, excitability, palpitations, nervous indigestion, diarrhea, stomach upsets, and colic. May be combined with *Achillea millefolium* (see p.227) and *Sambucus nigra* (see p.347) for feverish stages of colds and influenza, and with *Glechoma hederacea* (see p.289) for congestive stages.
ECONOMIC Dried catnip is used to stuff cat toys.
VARIANT
N. c. 'Citriodora'
A fully hardy, lemon-scented cultivar, often preferred for tea. H 1–3ft (30cm–1m), S 9–24in (23–60cm).

N. glechoma. See *Glechoma hederacea.*

N. hederacea. See *Glechoma hederacea.*

GROWTH AND HARVEST

GROWTH Ornamental. Moist, well-drained soil in sun. Propagate by seed sown in autumn or spring, or by division in spring; by stem-tip or softwood cuttings in spring or summer. Seedlings reach flowering size in the first year. Cut back hard for a second harvest. Powdery mildew may damage leaves. *N. cataria* is said to repel cabbage pests, aphids (including peach aphids), flea beetles, cucumber beetles, squash bugs, and ants, if planted among garden plants and vegetables.
HARVEST Plants are cut when in bud and dried for use in infusions. Pick leaves when young for culinary purposes and use fresh or dried.

NIGELLA

(Ranunculaceae)

N. sativa is a popular spice in India, Turkey, Greece, and the Middle East (especially in Egypt and Tunisia). The seeds have a spicy, fruity taste and were important as a seasoning before the introduction of pepper (*Piper nigrum*, see p.329) to Europe from SE Asia in the fifth century AD. It has a long history of use in Islamic medicine: it is also important in Unani medicine and is exported to Malaysia for medicinal purposes. *N. sativa* should not be confused with *N. damascena* (love-in-a-mist), the familiar garden annual. The two species look similar but have no uses in common. Essential oil is distilled from *N. damascena* for lipsticks and perfumery.

N. sativa (black cumin, nutmeg flower, Roman coriander) p.165

PARTS USED Seeds, oil.
PROPERTIES A pungently aromatic, laxative herb that stimulates the uterus, increases lactation, benefits the digestion, and reduces inflammation.
USES OF THE HERB
CULINARY Seeds flavor bread, pastries, curries, meat, chutneys, sauces, and cooked vegetables. Oil is used as a substitute for spikenard (*Nardostachys grandiflora*, see p.316).
MEDICINAL Internally for painful menstruation, postpartum contractions, insufficient lactation, and bronchial complaints. Externally for abscesses, hemorrhoids, and orchitis.

GROWTH AND HARVEST

GROWTH Crop. Well-drained soil in sun. Propagate by seed sown in autumn or spring, where plants are to flower.
HARVEST Seeds are collected when ripe and dried for oil extraction; used whole or ground, or in infusions.

NYMPHAEA Water lily

(Nymphaeaceae)

N. odorata has a long history of medicinal use among native N Americans, but *N. alba* and *N. tuberosa* are used interchangeably as well. In the 19th century the powdered rhizome was widely sold by apothecaries for making poultices. *N. lotus* (white lotus) was one of the most important plants in ancient Egyptian art, ritual, food, and medicine. The flowers were a common ingredient of unguents, oils, poultices, and enemas; the leaves appear in remedies for liver disease; the roots were eaten either raw or cooked; the seeds were added to bread. White lotus flowers are still used by Egyptian herbalists for their cooling, calming effects. *N. caerulea* (blue lotus) was similarly venerated and used medicinally. It is found in parts of north, central, and southern Africa, where it is still used internally for kidney and bladder complaints, and externally as a soothing, antiseptic remedy for sunburn, heat rashes, and skin inflammations.

N. lotus (Egyptian lotus, white lotus) p.165

PARTS USED Rootstock, flowers, fruits, seeds.
PROPERTIES A soothing, astringent herb that has diuretic and tranquilizing effects, and is reputedly detoxicant and aphrodisiac.
USES OF THE HERB
CULINARY Rootstock is boiled as a starchy vegetable and ground into flour in parts of India, Sri Lanka, and China. Fruits and seeds are pickled, added to curries or mixed with flour and baked. Seeds, crushed in water, are an old remedy for diabetes, and may be fried as a nutritious food.
MEDICINAL Internally in Ayurvedic medicine for dyspepsia, enteritis, diarrhea, hemorrhoids, urinary problems, fevers, and insomnia (rootstock); palpitations (flowers); blood in urine from snake-bite (juice of fruits mixed with *Setaria italica*, or foxtail millet, and salt).

N. odorata (white pond lily, sweet-scented water lily) p.165

PARTS USED Rhizomes.
PROPERTIES An astringent, soothing herb that is antiseptic, relieves pain, and has alterative effects.
USES OF THE HERB
MEDICINAL Internally for tuberculosis, chronic bronchial complaints, diarrhea, dysentery, gastro-intestinal inflammation, gonorrhea, vaginal discharge, cystitis, prostatitis, uterine infections, and uterine cancer. Externally for boils, conjunctivitis, sore throat, and vaginitis. Combined with *Prunus serotina* (see p.335) for bronchial complaints, and with *Ulmus rubra* (see p.366) and *Linum usitatissimum* (see p.304) for boils.
VARIANT
***N. o.* 'Sulphurea Grandiflora'**, p.165.

GROWTH AND HARVEST

GROWTH Ornamental. Rich soil in still water up to 18in (45cm) deep (*N. odorata*); rich soil in still water at least 12in (30cm) deep, minimum 70°F (21°C) in winter (*N. lotus*). Both species need full sun. Dormant tubers of *N. lotus* may be taken from the pond and stored in moist sand. Propagate by seed in spring, or by offsets or division in spring or early summer. Aphids may attack plants. Water lily beetles and caterpillars may eat leaves. Deep water and overly rich soil inhibit flowering.
HARVEST Flowers are cut when open and used fresh for infusions. Rootstocks are lifted when dormant and used fresh or dried for decoctions (*N. lotus*). Fruits and seeds are harvested when ripe and used fresh. Rhizomes are lifted in autumn, after the leaves have died down, and dried for decoctions, liquid extracts, and powders (*N. odorata*).

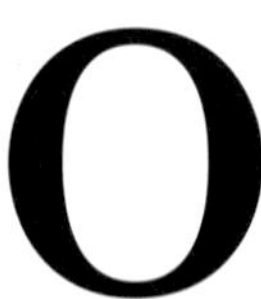

OCIMUM Basil
(Labiatae/Lamiaceae)

Basils are rich in volatile oils, which often vary considerably within the same species and according to growing conditions. Some 20 or more constituents have been isolated, the main ones being methyl chavicol (anise), methyl cinnamate (cinnamon), eugenol (clove), citral (lemon), geraniol (rose), linalol (lilac/orange blossom), thymol (thyme), and camphor. Those variants in which certain constituents predominate are known as "chemotypes." *O. americanum* (syn. *O. canum, O. micranthum,* hoary basil, or mosquito plant), which is very similar to *O. basilicum*, has three distinct chemotypes: floral–lemony, camphoraceous, and spicy. The composition of oils in a particular plant affects its aroma, flavor, and uses, and may make identification difficult. Mediterranean types of *O. basilicum* contain mainly linalol and methyl chavicol, with little or no camphor, which give the typical sweet basil flavor; eastern European types are characterized by methyl cinnamate; SE Asian types contain a high proportion of eugenol; and, in Réunion or African types, camphor and methyl chavicol predominate.

Hybridization in cultivation further complicates the picture. The most widely grown basils for commercial drying and oil extraction go under many different names, not necessarily recognized by botanists as distinct cultivars. These include 'Lettuce Leaf' (*O. b.* var. *crispum*), 'Italian', and 'Albahaca', all with a typically sweet basil aroma. Most basils also have seeds that are high in mucilage and have different uses from the foliage. *O. kilimandscharicum* (camphor basil) is used in Africa to lower fevers, as a commercial source of camphor, and as a mosquito repellant. *O. sanctum* is regarded in India as the most sacred plant after the lotus (*Nelumbo nucifera*, p.316) and is grown by most Hindu homes, and around temples, for its protective influence.

O. basilicum (basil, sweet basil) p.166

PARTS USED Whole plant, leaves, seeds, oil.
PROPERTIES A restorative, warming, aromatic herb that relaxes spasms, lowers fever, improves digestion, and is effective against bacterial infections and intestinal parasites.
USES OF THE HERB
CULINARY Leaves are used with tomatoes and tomato-flavored dishes, pasta sauces (notably *pesto*), vegetables (especially beans, peppers, and eggplant), soups (*soupe au pistou*), and stuffing for duck.
AROMATIC Oil is used in perfumery and aromatherapy.
MEDICINAL Internally for feverish illnesses (especially colds and influenza), poor digestion, nausea, abdominal cramps, gastroenteritis, migraine, insomnia, low spirits, and exhaustion. Externally for acne, loss of smell, insect stings, snakebites, and skin infections.
ECONOMIC Seeds (*O. b.* var. *citriodorum*) are made into a tonic drink. Oil is used in dental preparations and insect repellants.
VARIANTS
O. b. **'African Blue'**, p.166.
O. b. **'Anise'**, syn. *O. b.* 'Licorice', p.166.
O. b. **'Cinnamon'**, p.166.
O. b. **'Dark Opal'**, syn. *O. b.* 'Purpureum', p.166.
O. b. **'Genovese'**, p.166.
O. b. **'Mini Purpurascens Wellsweep'**, p.166.
O. b. **'Purple Ruffles'**, p.167.
O. b. var. ***citriodorum***, syn. *O. citriodorum,* p.167.
O. b. var. ***crispum***, syn. *O. b.* 'Lettuce Leaf', p.167.
O. b. var. ***minimum***, p.167.

O. gratissimum, syn. *O. viride, O. suave* (East Indian basil, tree basil, fever plant) p.167

PARTS USED Leaves, oil.
PROPERTIES An aromatic, stimulant, antiseptic herb that repels insects, expels intestinal parasites, and lowers fever.
USES OF THE HERB
CULINARY Leaves are infused for tea.
AROMATIC Oil is used in perfumery.
MEDICINAL Internally for fevers, headache, impotence, diarrhea, dysentery, postpartum problems, and worms in children. Externally for rheumatism and lumbago.
ECONOMIC Plants are grown to repel mosquitoes. Oil is used in insect repellants. Clove- and thyme-scented types are used for flavoring.

O. sanctum, syn. *O. tenuiflorum* (holy basil, sacred basil, *tulsi*) p.167

PARTS USED Whole plant, leaves, stems, seeds, oil.
PROPERTIES A pungently aromatic, warming, antiseptic herb that lowers fever, relaxes spasms, clears bacterial infections, strengthens the immune and nervous systems, and benefits the digestion.
USES OF THE HERB
CULINARY Leaves are added to salads and cold foods, but not used in cooking.
MEDICINAL Internally for feverish illnesses (especially in children), colds, influenza, sinusitis, headaches, rheumatism, arthritis, abdominal distention and cramps, low libido, and negativity. Externally for skin infections.
ECONOMIC Stems are cut into beads for rosaries. Seeds are made into tonics. Oil is used as an insect repellant and antibiotic.

GROWTH AND HARVEST

GROWTH Ornamental (*O. gratissimum*: crop). Rich, light, well-drained to dry soil in sun, minimum 50–59°F (10–15°C), pH5–8. ► Propagate by seed sown in spring, minimum 55°F (13°C), or by softwood cuttings in spring (perennials and shrubs only). Pinch out growing tips to encourage bushiness and delay flowering. Slugs, aphids, whitefly, spider mites, and *Botrytis* may attack plants. Basil is often used in companion planting because it is said to repel aphids, asparagus beetles, mites, and tomato hornworms, and to slow the growth of milkweed bugs.
HARVEST Whole plants (*O. basilicum, O. gratissimum, O. sanctum*) are cut as flowering begins and distilled for oil. Leaves are picked during the growing season and used fresh or juiced, or dried for infusions. (*O. sanctum* is also prepared as medicated ghee.) Seeds (*O. basilicum, O. sanctum*) are collected when ripe and dried for decoctions.

OENOTHERA
Evening primrose
(Onagraceae)

According to Mrs. Grieve (*A Modern Herbal*, 1931), a drug was made from the leaves and stem peelings of *O. biennis* to treat asthma, gastrointestinal disorders, whooping cough, and "certain female complaints, such as pelvic fullness." The medicinal uses of evening primrose oil are a recent discovery, following scientific research in the 1980s that demonstrated its effectiveness for a wide range of intractable complaints. The oil contains gamma-linoleic acid (GLA), an unsaturated fatty acid, which assists the production of hormonelike substances. This process is commonly blocked, causing disorders that affect uterine muscles, blood vessels, nervous system, and metabolism. GLA is also found in the seeds of *Borago officinalis* (see p.249) and *Ribes nigrum* (see p.341).

O. biennis (common evening primrose) p.167

PARTS USED Oil.
PROPERTIES An alterative herb that regulates hormonal systems.
USES OF THE HERB
MEDICINAL Internally for premenstrual and menopausal syndromes, eczema, acne, brittle nails, hyperactivity in children, rheumatoid arthritis, coronary artery disease, alcohol-related liver damage, and multiple sclerosis. Externally for dry skin.
ECONOMIC Oil is added to skin preparations and cosmetics. Often combined with vitamin E to prevent oxidation.

GROWTH AND HARVEST

GROWTH Ornamental. Dry soil, including coastal sands, in sun. Propagate by seed in ►

► autumn or spring. Plants may succumb to root rot in wet conditions. Powdery mildew may attack leaves. Self-seeds freely in optimum conditions.
HARVEST Seeds are collected when ripe and pressed for oil.

OLDENLANDIA
(Rubiaceae)

This is a large genus, consisting of about 300 species of annuals, perennials, and shrubs that occur throughout the tropics and subtropics. There are no particularly ornamental species, and few have practical uses, though *O. umbellata* (Indian madder) yields a dye used for turbans. *O. diffusa* is an herb with a long history in Chinese folk medicine, and has come to prominence in recent years following pharmacological research. It is a traditional Chinese remedy for snakebites, especially of pit vipers (*Trimeresurus* species). *O. hedyotidea* is used in some parts of China for similar purposes. Leaves and roots have expectorant properties, and the root is a specific for snakebite.

O. diffusa (snake-needle grass)

Densely branched, prostrate annual, hardy to 23°F (–5°C), height 8–12in (20–30cm), spread 12in (30cm), with linear leaves about 1¼in (3cm) long. Tiny purple-white flowers are produced in axillary pairs all year, mainly in late summer. A weed of moist ground and fields in China.

PARTS USED Whole plant (*bai hua zhe she cao*).
PROPERTIES A pleasant-tasting, cooling, alterative herb that lowers fever, reduces inflammation, relieves pain, and is diuretic and antibacterial. It acts mainly on the liver and stimulates the immune system.
USES OF THE HERB
MEDICINAL Internally for fever, coughs, asthma, jaundice, urinary tract infections, and cancers of the digestive tract. Externally for snakebites, boils, abscesses, and severe bruising.

GROWTH AND HARVEST
GROWTH Crop. Damp soil in partial shade. Propagate by seed sown in spring.
HARVEST Plants are cut in summer and dried for use in decoctions and syrups.

OLEA Olive
(Oleaceae)

The olive has been cultivated since prehistoric times, providing the oil and fruits that characterize the cuisines of most Mediterranean countries. Both oil and olives vary greatly in flavor, depending on variety, time of harvesting, and processing techniques. The finest oil (extra virgin) often comes from unpalatable varieties and is pressed without using heat or chemical solvents. It has the lowest percentage (about one percent) of acidity and therefore the best flavor. The culinary uses of the olive are well known; less familiar are the medicinal applications, which involve leaves as well as the oil. Olive oil is monounsaturated, and regular consumption is thought to reduce the risk of circulatory disease. It reduces gastric secretions, which is of benefit to patients suffering from hyperacidity.

O. europaea (olive) p.167

PARTS USED Leaves, fruits, oil.
PROPERTIES An antiseptic, astringent herb that lowers fever and blood pressure, and has a calming effect. It is also a laxative and emollient.
USES OF THE HERB
CULINARY Olives are an important ingredient of *hors d'oeuvres*, salads, spreads (such as *tapenade*), pasta sauces, tomato and eggplant dishes, pizzas, and breads. Olive oil gives flavor and texture to cooked dishes, salads, sauces, and mayonnaise, and accompanies bread in Mediterranean regions. Fruits are soaked in water before preserving in brine or oil and may be picked unripe (green), semiripe (purple-mauve), or ripe (black).
MEDICINAL Internally for minor feverish illnesses, nervous tension, and hypertension (leaves); constipation and peptic ulcers (oil). Externally for abrasions (leaves), dry skin and hair, dandruff (oil).
ECONOMIC Oil is added to liniments, ointments, skin and hair preparations, and soap.

GROWTH AND HARVEST
GROWTH Ornamental. Well-drained soil in sun. Propagate by seed sown in autumn, or by semiripe cuttings in summer. Remove leading shoot when the plant reaches 5ft (1.5m). Remove old branches to encourage new growths, since fruits are mostly produced on one-year-old wood. Trees may be damaged by scale insects, root-knot nematodes, and *Verticillium* wilt. Plants under cover may suffer from whitefly, thrips, and spider mites. Subject to statutory controls as a weed in parts of Australia.
HARVEST Leaves are collected as required and dried for infusions, liquid extracts, and tinctures. Fruits are harvested in autumn and winter; the oil pressed from them is stored in cool, dark conditions.

OPHELIA
O. chirata. See *Swertia chirata*.

OPHIOPOGON
Japanese hyacinth
(Liliaceae/Convallariaceae)

O. japonicus contains substances that "replenish vital essence and promote secretion of body fluids." It has been used in traditional Chinese medicine as a *yin* tonic since the first century AD.

O. japonicus (lily turf, Mondo grass) p.167

PARTS USED Tubers (*mai men dong*).
PROPERTIES A sweet, soothing, sedative herb that controls coughs and lubricates the digestive and bronchial tracts.
USES OF THE HERB
MEDICINAL Internally for dry coughs, fevers, thirst, dry constipation, insomnia, anxiety, and palpitations. Often mixed with cinnabar (mercuric sulfide) to increase sedation.

GROWTH AND HARVEST
GROWTH Ornamental. Rich, well-drained soil in sun or partial shade. Propagate by seed sown in autumn, or by division in spring.
HARVEST Tubers are lifted in spring and dried for use in decoctions.

ORIGANUM
(Labiatae/Lamiaceae)

Marjorams are mainly used as culinary herbs but are rich in flavonoids and volatile oils, notably carvacrol and thymol, which have medicinal applications. Theophrastus (370–285BC) wrote, in his *Enquiry into Plants*, that *O. dictamnus* "is marvelous in virtue and is useful for many purposes, but especially for women in childbirth." However, there is no evidence that it is used for any specific purposes in present-day herbalism. *O. vulgare* is extremely variable in appearance and in chemical composition. It differs from *O. majorana* in containing a higher proportion of thymol, which gives it a more thymelike aroma. Although several species of *Origanum* are known as "oregano," commercial dried oregano is produced from several different, unrelated plants. Sources include *Lippia graveolens* (Mexican oregano, see p.305) and *L. palmeri*, *O. vulgare* subsp. *hirtum* (winter marjoram) from Greece and Turkey, and the Middle Eastern *O. syriacum*, as well as from *O. vulgare* itself. Much commercial oregano oil comes from *Thymus capitatus* (conehead thyme, see p.362). *O. dictamnus* is rare in the wild.

O. dictamnus (dittany of Crete, hop marjoram) p.168

PARTS USED Leaves, flowers.
PROPERTIES An aromatic herb.
USES OF THE HERB
CULINARY Leaves are added to salads. Flowers are infused for tea.
MEDICINAL Medicinal uses appear to be obsolete.
ECONOMIC Used to flavor vermouth.

O. majorana, syn. *Majorana hortensis* (sweet marjoram, knotted marjoram) p.168

PARTS USED Whole plant, leaves, seeds, oil.
PROPERTIES Similar to *O. vulgare*, but more relaxing.
USES OF THE HERB
CULINARY *O. majorana* has a more delicate flavor than *O. vulgare*, and is best used fresh toward the end of cooking. Leaves and flowering sprigs are

popular in Italian and Greek cooking, with meat dishes, soups, tomato sauces, and pasta, and to flavor oil and vinegar.
MEDICINAL Internally for bronchial complaints, tension headaches, insomnia, anxiety, minor digestive upsets, and painful menstruation. Not given to pregnant women. Externally for bronchial congestion, muscular pain, arthritis, sprains, and stiff joints.
ECONOMIC Seeds are added to condiments and meat products. Oil is used in commercial food flavoring, liqueurs, perfumery, soaps, and hair products.

O. x *majoricum* (Italian oregano, hardy marjoram)

This sterile hybrid, height 24in (60cm), spread 18in (45cm), is probably a cross between *O. majorana* and the yellow-bracted *O. vulgare* subsp. *virens*. It resembles *O. majorana* in appearance and aroma, but it is hardier, to 23°F (–5°C).

PARTS USED Leaves.
PROPERTIES Very similar to *O. majorana*.
USES OF THE HERB
CULINARY Whole plant and leaves may be substituted for *O. majorana* in cooking.

O. onites, syn. *Majorana onites* (pot marjoram, Greek oregano) p.168

PARTS USED Leaves, flowers.
PROPERTIES A slightly bitter, aromatic herb with a thymelike aroma.
USES OF THE HERB
CULINARY As a culinary substitute for *O. majorana* or *O. vulgare*, but inferior in flavor.
AROMATIC Leaves and flowering sprigs are added to potpourris and scented articles.
VARIANT
***O. o.* 'Aureum'**
This cultivar, hardy to 23°F (–5°C), height and spread 24in (60cm), has golden foliage that has less tendency to scorch in the sun than *O. vulgare* 'Aureum'.

O. vulgare (wild marjoram, oregano) p.168

PARTS USED Whole plant, leaves, oil.
PROPERTIES A pungently aromatic, antiseptic, warming herb that relaxes spasms, increases perspiration, benefits the digestion, stimulates the uterus, and acts as a mild expectorant.

USES OF THE HERB
CULINARY An important herb in Italian, Greek, and Mexican cooking, often used dried rather than fresh, in strongly flavored dishes in which ingredients such as chili, garlic, tomatoes, onions, and wine predominate. Leaves and flowering tops are infused for tea.
AROMATIC Leaves and flowering tops are added to potpourris.
MEDICINAL Internally for colds, influenza, minor feverish illnesses, indigestion, flatulence, stomach upsets, and painful menstruation. Externally for bronchitis, asthma, arthritis, and muscular pain. Not given to pregnant women. Oil used in aromatherapy for similar conditions and, externally, to kill lice; it may cause skin irritation.
ECONOMIC Oil is used in commercial food flavoring, toiletries, and men's colognes.

VARIANTS
***O. v.* 'Album'**, p.168.
***O. v.* 'Acorn Bank'**, p.169.
***O. v.* 'Aureum'**, p.168.
***O. v.* 'Aureum Crispum'**, p.168.
***O. v.* 'Compactum'**, syn. *O. v.* 'Humile', p.169.
***O. v.* 'Gold Tip'**, p.169.
***O. v.* 'Nanum'**
Dwarf cultivar, hardy to 5°F (–15°C), height 8in (20cm), spread 12in (30cm), with purple flowers.
***O. v.* 'Polyphant'**, p.169.
***O. v.* 'White Anniversary'**, p.169.

GROWTH AND HARVEST

GROWTH Ornamental. Well-drained to dry, neutral to alkaline soil in sun. *O. dictamnus* needs sharp drainage and protection from excessive winter moisture. *O.* x *majoricum* and *O. onites* are normally frost hardy but may prove hardier in a warm, sharply drained situation. Propagate by seed sown in autumn or spring (species only), or by cuttings of non-flowering shoots in early summer, or by division in autumn or spring.
HARVEST Plants are cut as flowering begins, and leaves during the growing season, to be used fresh, distilled for oil, or dried for infusions.

ORYZA Rice
(Gramineae)

Rice has been cultivated in India and China for at least 4,000 years and is the staple food of over half the world's population. It was introduced to SE Asia from India in the first century AD and to Spain by the Arabs in the eighth or ninth century. *O. sativa* was first mentioned in traditional Chinese medicine in the seventh century, as a sprouted grain used in diet therapy. It is often prescribed with germinated barley (*Hordeum vulgare*, p.293), notably in *yi tang*, a digestive tonic and cough remedy. Rice water is used in the East for stomach upsets in the same way as barley water is used in the West. Rice syrup has similar properties to (barley) malt extract, strengthening the bronchial and digestive systems, especially in children. Rice paper, however, is made from the pith of *Tetrapanax papyrifera* (Araliaceae). *O. sativa* has numerous cultivars, mostly belonging to *O. s.* subsp. *indica*, which produce long grains suitable for "dry" dishes, such as *pilau,* while the hardier, short-grained *O. s.* subsp. *japonica* is more suitable for "wet" dishes, such as *risotto, paella,* and rice pudding.

O. sativa (rice) p.169

PARTS USED Rhizomes (*nuo dao gen xu*), seeds (*jing mi*), germinated seeds (*gu ya*).
PROPERTIES A nutritive, soothing, tonic herb that is diuretic, reduces lactation, improves the digestion, and controls sweating.
USES OF THE HERB
CULINARY Rice is eaten boiled or steamed, and may be fried before or after boiling; it is an essential accompaniment of curries and Far Eastern dishes and a key ingredient of *pilau* (Turkey, Middle East, India), *paella* (Spain), and *risotto* (Italy). It is also used in milk desserts, such as rice pudding. Grains are "popped" as breakfast cereals, used as bakery ingredients, and fermented to make *saki* (Japanese rice wine).
MEDICINAL Internally for urinary dysfunction (seeds); excessive lactation (seeds, germinated seeds); poor appetite, indigestion, and abdominal discomfort and bloating (germinated seeds); night sweats, especially in tuberculosis and chronic pneumonia (rhizomes). In Chinese medicine, grains are often often cooked with herbs to make a medicinal gruel.
VARIANT
O. s. subsp. ***japonica* 'Arborio'**, p.169.

GROWTH AND HARVEST

GROWTH Crop. Inundated soil in sun, minimum 59–64°F (15–18°C) for *O. s.* subsp. *indica*, and 50–54°F (10–12°C) for *O. s.* subsp. *japonica*. Optimum average growing temperatures for the former are 77–86°F (25–30°C), and 64°F (18°C) for the latter. *O. s.* subsp. *japonica* stops growing below 41°F (5°C) but may survive frost damage. Propagate by seed sown in nursery bed and transplanted in clumps of 2–6 seedlings. Seed viability of *O. s.* subsp. *japonica* is poor after a cold summer.
HARVEST Rhizomes are lifted in autumn and dried for use in decoctions. Seeds are collected when ripe and germinated as required, or dried for use in decoctions and powders.

P

PAEONIA Peony
(Paeoniaceae)

P. officinalis was a popular medicinal herb in Europe until the 16th century, but is seldom used today. Culpeper distinguished two variants: the male peony, with purple red flowers, little-divided leaves, and both black and crimson seeds; and the female peony, with leafier, more divided foliage, smaller, scented, darker purple flowers, and black seeds. They were used for male and female complaints respectively. The uses of *P. lactiflora* date back to at least AD500. *P. suffruticosa* was first mentioned in Chinese medicine in *Pouch of Pearls*, a 12th-century work by Zhang Yuan-Su. Regardless of flower or root color, the roots of cultivated and wild plants are considered to be different drugs by Chinese herbalists. Cultivated ("white peony") *P. lactiflora* is a *yin* tonic for the liver and circulation, known as *bai shao yao*; wild-collected plants are termed "red peony" (*chi shao yao*) and considered mainly as a remedy for cooling the blood. The roots of both *P. lactiflora* and *P. veitchii* are harvested from the wild as the drug *chi shao*. *Chi shao* is one of the Chinese herbs used successfully to treat eczema at the Great Ormond Street Children's Hospital, London.

P. lactiflora, syn. *P. albiflora* (Chinese peony) p.170

PARTS USED Roots (*bai shao yao*, white peony; *chi shao yao*, red peony).
PROPERTIES A bitter, cooling, astringent herb that reduces inflammation, relaxes spasms, and lowers fever and blood pressure. It has a sour taste and analgesic, tranquilizing, and antibacterial effects.
USES OF THE HERB
MEDICINAL Internally for menstrual complaints, injuries, and skin conditions associated with heat excess, such as eczema (*chi shao*), hypertension, pre-menstrual syndrome, and liver disorders (*bai shao*). Not given during pregnancy. For use by qualified practitioners only.
VARIANT
P. l. **'Duchesse de Nemours'**, p.170.

P. officinalis (common peony) p.170

PARTS USED Roots.
PROPERTIES A diuretic, sedative, cleansing herb that relaxes spasms, stimulates the uterus, and constricts blood vessels.
USES OF THE HERB
MEDICINAL Formerly used internally for epilepsy, convulsions, whooping cough, kidney and gall bladder stones, hemorrhoids, intestinal spasms, menstrual and postpartum problems, and varicose veins. For use by qualified practitioners only.

P. suffruticosa, syn. *P. moutan* (tree peony, moutan peony) p.170

PARTS USED Root bark (*mu dan pi*).
PROPERTIES A pungent, bitter, analgesic herb that cools the blood, lowers blood pressure, and has anti-allergenic, antibacterial, and tranquilizing effects.
USES OF THE HERB
MEDICINAL Internally for fevers, boils, menstrual disorders, nosebleed, ulcers, irritability, and gastrointestinal infections. Used raw for blood heat, stir-baked for stagnant circulation, and carbonized to control bleeding. For use by qualified practitioners only.

GROWTH AND HARVEST

GROWTH Ornamental. Rich, well-drained soil in sun or partial shade, avoiding positions where frost damage is likely. Propagate by seed sown in autumn (species only), or by division in autumn or early spring, or by root cuttings in winter (*P. lactiflora* and *P. officinalis*), or by layering or semiripe cuttings in spring, or grafting in winter (*P. suffruticosa*). Seed may take 3 years to germinate. Remove dead wood from *P. suffruticosa* in early spring. Species prone to peony wilt. Foliage may be damaged by leafspot and virus diseases. Buds and stem bases may be affected by *Botrytis*.
HARVEST Roots (*P. lactiflora*) are lifted from cultivated plants 4–5 years old, in late summer to midautumn, and boiled and dried for use in decoctions, pills, and powders; wild plants are lifted in spring or (preferably) autumn and sun-dried. Roots (*P. officinalis*) are lifted from 2-year-old plants and dried for use in decoctions. Root bark (*P. suffruticosa*) is stripped from roots in autumn and used raw or dried in decoctions.

PANAX Ginseng
(Araliaceae)

P. ginseng is an ancient Taoist tonic herb, which has been used as a *qi* (vital essence) tonic in Chinese medicine for about 5,000 years. It was introduced to Europe several times from the ninth century onward but assumed no importance in Western medicine until studies by Soviet scientists in the early 1950s established it as an "adaptogen." To increase availability of the drug, they also searched for similar properties in related native species and discovered *Eleutherococcus senticosus* (Siberian ginseng, see p.277). *P. pseudo-ginseng* was first mentioned in Chinese medical texts in the 16th century. It is primarily a healing herb and was used extensively by the Vietcong during the Vietnam War to improve recovery from gunshot wounds. In medical literature, confusion exists between *P. pseudo-ginseng* and *P. notoginseng*, and whether or not they do differ notably in constituents is not clear. *P. quinquefolius* was discovered in the 18th century by Jesuit colleagues of Père Jartoux, who deduced that similar plants might exist in N America. It was first collected for export to China by backwoodsmen ("seng diggers"), and was first described in Chinese medicine c.1765. Regarded as more *yin* than *P. ginseng*, *P. quinquefolius* is given to children and young people, for whom *P. ginseng* would not be appropriate. The main medicinal species are now rare in the wild and are cultivated commercially in Korea, China, Russia, and the US (mainly in Wisconsin). Brazilian ginseng or *suma* is the root of *Pfaffia paniculata*, a member of the Amaranthaceae which grows in ravines of the upper Amazon rainforest. Known as *para tudo*, "for everything," it has long been used by native people as an aphrodisiac and cure-all. It contains up to 11 percent saponins, including pfaffic acid and derivatives that have been patented as antitumor drugs. The ground root is taken as a tonic, especially during convalescence and menopause.

P. ginseng (ginseng) p.170

PARTS USED Roots (*ren shen*), processed to produce red or white ginseng as required.
PROPERTIES A sweet, tonic herb that both relaxes and stimulates the nervous system, encourages secretion of hormones, improves stamina, lowers blood sugar and cholesterol levels, and increases resistance to disease.
USES OF THE HERB
MEDICINAL Internally for debility associated with old age or illness, lack of appetite, insomnia, stress, shock, and chronic illness. An ingredient in many important Chinese formulas; also taken as a "simple" (i.e. not mixed with other herbs), often as a *yang* tonic before winter or a period of great stress. Not usually prescribed for pregnant women or patients under 40 years old, or with depression, anxiety, or acute inflammatory disease. Use is normally restricted to three weeks. Excess may cause headaches, restlessness, raised blood pressure, and other side effects, especially if taken with caffeine, alcohol, turnips, and bitter or spicy foods.

P. pseudo-ginseng (*san qi* ginseng, *tienchi* ginseng)

Perennial, hardy to 5°F (–15°C), height 3ft (1m), spread 30in (75cm), with carrotlike roots, sometimes extending into creeping rhizomes. Leaves are divided into 5–7 lanceolate leaflets up to 7in (18cm) long. Small flowers appear in spring and summer, followed by globose red berries. Found mainly in Bhutan and northeastern India.

PARTS USED Roots (occasionally flowers).
PROPERTIES A sweet, slightly bitter, warming herb that controls bleeding, reduces inflammation, improves circulation, relieves pain, and has anti-bacterial effects.
USES OF THE HERB
MEDICINAL Internally for coronary heart disease and angina (roots), dizziness, and vertigo (flowers).

Internally and externally for nosebleed, and hemorrhage from lungs, digestive tract, uterus, or injuries (roots). Not given during pregnancy.

P. quinquefolius (American ginseng) p.170

PARTS USED Roots (*xi yang shen*).
PROPERTIES A bittersweet, tonic herb with similar properties to *P. ginseng*.
USES OF THE HERB
MEDICINAL Similar to *P. ginseng*, but mainly prescribed for younger patients with *yin* deficiency.

GROWTH AND HARVEST
GROWTH Crop. Moist, well-drained, rich soil in shade, with ample warmth and humidity during the growing season. Propagate by seed sown in spring. Germination is slow and erratic.
HARVEST Roots are lifted from 6–7-year-old plants in autumn and used fresh or dried in decoctions, liquid extracts, pills, and powders. Processing of *P. ginseng* varies according to product and quality. Red ginseng is steamed, heat-dried, then sun-dried; white ginseng is peeled and dried for chewing. Flowers are picked in spring and summer for decoctions.

PANDANUS Screw pine
(Pandanaceae)

P. odoratissimus is widely grown in the tropics, the thornless *P. o.* var. *laevis* being used for fibers for cordage and thatch. It is used to bind fragile soils, and in eastern India it is grown to produce kewda attar, a popular perfume. *P. amaryllifolius* is grown in Sri Lanka and parts of India for its aromatic leaves, which give a garliclike flavor to food.

P. odoratissimus, syn. *P. tectorius* (screw pine, *ketaki*) p.170

PARTS USED Aerial roots, leaf bud ("cabbage"), flowers, fruits, seeds, oil.
PROPERTIES A diuretic herb (roots and leaf bud) with a hyacinth–ylang-ylang scent (flowers).

USES OF THE HERB
CULINARY The fruits are eaten by Pacific Islanders; the seeds are a staple food in parts of New Guinea.
AROMATIC Oil from flowers is used in perfumery.
MEDICINAL Internally in folk medicine as a diuretic, depurative, and tonic (roots). Externally as a poultice for boils (leaf bud).
ECONOMIC Male flower bracts are distilled as an addition to sandalwood oil. Oil from flowers is used in skin preparations.

GROWTH AND HARVEST
GROWTH Crop. Well-drained soil in sun or partial shade, minimum 55–61°F (13–16°C). Propagate by seed or suckers in spring, or by cuttings of lateral shoots in summer. Plants take 3–4 years to flower.
HARVEST Flowers and bracts are collected during the flowering season and distilled for oil; other parts taken as required.

PAPAVER Poppy
(Papaveraceae)

Medicinal uses of opium, extracted from *P. somniferum*, were first described on clay tablets by the Sumerians, who dominated southwestern Asia in the fourth millenium BC. *P. somniferum* is now cultivated on a large scale as the source of major analgesics and the illicit drug heroin (diamorphine). It contains about 25 alkaloids, the most important being morphine and codeine. Morphine is an extremely potent painkiller, but is addictive and therefore normally reserved for patients with severely painful, terminal illnesses. Alkaloids are separated for specific uses or given as a total extract, known as "papaveretum," which is widely used as a preoperative analgesic and relaxant. Two main kinds of opium poppy are grown commercially for opium or for seeds for culinary use, respectively: *P. s.* subsp. *somniferum* and *P. s.* subsp. *hortense*. *P. rhoeas* contains different, less potent alkaloids and a red pigment. The seeds of both *P. rhoeas* and *P. somniferum* are alkaloid-free and safe for all culinary purposes. They are used in Ayurvedic medicine, mainly for digestive problems and to counteract the indigestibility of legumes.

P. rhoeas (corn poppy, field poppy) p.171

PARTS USED Flowers, seeds.
PROPERTIES A sweet, astringent, sedative herb that relieves pain, relaxes spasms, is expectorant, and improves digestion.
USES OF THE HERB
CULINARY Seeds are used, whole or ground, in similar ways to those of *P. somniferum*.
AROMATIC Petals of red-flowered plants give color to potpourris.
MEDICINAL Internally for coughs, insomnia, poor digestion, nervous digestive disorders, and minor painful conditions (petals).
ECONOMIC Petals of red-flowered plants are used to color medicines and wine.
VARIANT
***P. r.* 'Shirley Single Mixed'**, p.171.

P. somniferum (opium poppy) p.171

PARTS USED Fruits, seeds, latex, oil.
PROPERTIES A bitter, narcotic, sedative herb that relieves pain, relaxes spasms, controls coughing and diarrhea, and increases perspiration.
USES OF THE HERB
CULINARY Seeds, sometimes known as "maw seed," are used whole or ground in breads, biscuits, pastries, spiced meat dishes, and as a garnish for cooked food. Cold-pressed, almond-flavored oil (*huile d'oeillette*) is used for salad dressings.
MEDICINAL Internally, in commercial formulas for painful conditions, coughs, and diarrhea. In homeopathy for shock, torpor, apathy, alcohol poisoning, and breathing difficulties.
WARNING This herb, especially in the form of opium and its alkaloids, is subject to legal restrictions in most countries.
ECONOMIC Further pressings of cold-pressed oil are used in paints, soaps, and ointments.
VARIANTS
***P. s.* 'Danebrog'**, p.171.
***P. s.* 'Peony-flowered Mixed'**, p.171.

GROWTH AND HARVEST
GROWTH Ornamental. Well-drained soil in sun. Propagate by seed sown in autumn or spring. *P. rhoeas*, *P. somniferum*, and their cultivars self-seed freely, but cultivars tend to revert. Poppies resent disturbance and rarely transplant successfully. Leaves may be damaged by downy mildew. *P. somniferum* is subject to statutory control as a weed in some countries, notably in parts of Australia.
HARVEST Petals are collected as flowers open and dried for use whole, or in infusions and syrups (*P. rhoeas*). Seeds are harvested from ripe capsules and dried for use whole, ground, or in infusions. Oil is pressed from ripe seeds (mostly from *P. somniferum*). Latex (raw opium) and various alkaloids are extracted from green capsules after petals fall (*P. somniferum*).
WARNING All parts of *Papaver* species, except the seeds, are toxic if eaten. Cultivation of *P. somniferum* is subject to legal restrictions in some countries.

PARDANTHUS
P. chinensis. See *Belamcanda chinensis.*

PARIETARIA Pellitory
(Urticaceae)

P. judaica was once known as *P. officinalis*, indicating that it was formerly widely used medicinally. It is still a respected, nonirritating treatment for chronic urinary complaints.

P. judaica, syn. *P. diffusa* (pellitory-of-the-wall) p.171

PARTS USED Whole plant.
PROPERTIES An acrid, soothing, cooling herb that has diuretic and anti-inflammatory effects.
USES OF THE HERB
MEDICINAL Internally for cystitis, pyelitis, urinary stones, and edema associated with kidney complaints. Combines well with *Apium graveolens* (see p.240), *Petroselinum crispum* (see p.325), *Aphanes arvensis* (see p.239), *Arctostaphylos uva-ursi* (see p.241), *Agathosma crenulata* (see p.230), and *Juniperus communis* (see p.299) to control infection; and with *Elymus repens* (see p.277) and *Zea mays* (see p.372) to relieve pain and inflammation. Not given to patients with hay fever or other allergic conditions.

GROWTH AND HARVEST
GROWTH Crop. Well-drained to dry, alkaline soil in sun or partial shade. Propagate by seed in autumn or spring. Subject to statutory control as a weed in parts of Australia.
HARVEST Plants are cut when flowering and used fresh, or dried for liquid extracts and tinctures. Decoctions may be frozen, or the plant liquidized.

PASSIFLORA Passionflower
(Passifloraceae)

Spanish missionaries in S America regarded these flowers as symbols of Christ's passion – the three stigmas representing the nails, the five anthers the wounds, and the ten sepals the apostles (Peter and Judas Iscariot being absent). *P. incarnata* was used in native N American medicine, notably by the Houma tribe, who added it to drinking water as a tonic. It was described by a visiting European doctor in 1783 as a remedy for epilepsy and became a popular treatment for insomnia in the 19th century, with an entry in the U.S. *National Formulary* (1916–36). The herb contains alkaloids and flavonoids, which are effective, nonaddictive sedatives that do not cause drowsiness. One flavonoid, apigenin, is an antispasmodic and anti-inflammatory, and occurs in various unrelated plants, notably *Apium graveolens* (see p.240).

P. incarnata (maypops, passionflower) p.171

PARTS USED Whole plant, fruits.
PROPERTIES A bitter, sedative, cooling herb that relieves pain, relaxes spasms, and lowers blood pressure.
USES OF THE HERB
CULINARY Fruits are pulped for jam and desserts.
MEDICINAL Internally for nervous tension, insomnia, irritability, tension headache, asthma, irritable bowel syndrome, premenstrual tension, nervous tachycardia, hypertension, and shingles. Combines well with *Valeriana officinalis* (see p.367), *Chamaemelum nobile* (see p.259), and *Humulus lupulus* (see p.294) for insomnia. Not recommended during pregnancy.

GROWTH AND HARVEST
GROWTH Crop. Well-drained, sandy, slightly acid soil in sun. Propagate by seed sown in spring, at 18–21°C (64–70°F), or by semiripe cuttings in summer. Germination is slow and erratic. Cut back in early spring. Cucumber mosaic virus may attack leaves. The fruits ripen only in warm, sunny climates.
HARVEST Plants are cut when fruiting and dried for use in infusions, liquid extracts, tablets, and tinctures. Fruits for culinary use are picked when ripe in autumn and used fresh or cooked.

PAULLINIA
(Sapindaceae)

Seeds of *P. cupana* are used by the Guaranis of Brazilian Amazonia to make a stimulant drink, much as tea and coffee are. They contain up to seven percent of a caffeinelike compound, known as "guaranine." Unlike caffeine, it is not addictive and takes longer to be metabolized, giving it a gentler, more sustained stimulant effect. It has recently been promoted as a safe, natural stimulant by the health-food industry in the form of capsules and candy, and as a component of tonic drinks based on spring water, fruit juices, and herbal extracts. Stems of the closely related *P. yoco* (yoco) are used by native people in Colombia, Ecuador, and northern Peru to make a similar drink.

P. cupana, syn. *P. sorbilis* (guaranà, Brazilian cocoa, zoom) p.171

PARTS USED Seeds.
PROPERTIES An astringent, bitter herb with a strong stimulant effect.
USES OF THE HERB
CULINARY Seeds are roasted, ground, and pressed into paste (*pasta guaranà*), which is dried into sticks and then grated into water as a tealike drink.
MEDICINAL Internally to relieve fatigue, aid concentration, and lift the spirits. May cause sleeplessness, although reputedly less so than caffeine-based products. Not recommended for those with cardiovascular disease or hypertension.
ECONOMIC Added to diet foods, supplements for athletes, tonic drinks, and chewing gum. Seeds also fermented locally to make an alcoholic drink. Used as a source of caffeine and flavoring for soft drinks, liqueurs, and candy. Sweetened paste is known as "Brazilian chocolate."

GROWTH AND HARVEST
GROWTH Crop. Moist, humus-rich soil in partial shade, minimum 65°F (18°C). Propagate by ripewood cuttings at the end of the growing season.
HARVEST Seeds are collected when ripe, then roasted, ground, and stored as paste or powder.

PAUSINYSTALIA
(Rubiaceae)

This western African genus consists of 13 species of large trees characterized by panicles of tubular flowers with conspicuous appendages. Medicinal use of yohimbe bark appears to have reached Europe in the 1890s. *P. yohimbe* and the related *P. macroceras* and *P. tillesii* contain indole alkaloids, the principal one being yohimbine, which blocks the release of adrenalin and acts as a sexual stimulant. In Africa *P. lane-poolei* (*pamprana, igbepo*) is also used medicinally; dressings of ground bark are applied to yaws (a skin infection) and itching skin.

P. yohimbe, syn. *Corynanthe yohimbe* (*yohimbe, endone*)

Tender evergreen tree, height 90ft (27m), spread 40ft (12m), with red to yellow-ochre wood and glossy, oblanceolate, dark green leaves up to 14in (35cm) long. White or pink tubular flowers appear in clusters arranged in panicles up to 7in (18cm) long in winter in the wild, followed by capsules containing small, winged seeds.

PARTS USED Bark.
PROPERTIES A bitter, warming, antidiuretic herb with reputedly aphrodisiac effects. It has a stimulant effect on the heart, increases heart rate and blood pressure, and is locally anesthetic.
USES OF THE HERB
MEDICINAL Internally for impotence and frigidity. Interacts with certain antihypertension drugs. Not given to patients with hypertension, or renal or hepatic disease. Excess may cause depression.
WARNING This herb is subject to restrictions in some countries.

GROWTH AND HARVEST
GROWTH Wild-collected. Moist soil with high humidity, minimum 59–64°F (15–18°C). *P. yohimbe* does not appear to be in cultivation, and no information has been found on its requirements.
HARVEST Bark is dried in strips for pills, liquid extracts, and extraction of yohimbine.

PEGANUM
(Zygophyllaceae)

P. harmala is much used in Arab medicine and is mentioned in early Muslim medical literature. It contains hallucinogenic alkaloids and has a history of use in folk medicine.

P. harmala (Syrian rue, harmal) p.174

PARTS USED Fruits, seeds, oil.
PROPERTIES A bitter, spicy, diuretic herb that stimulates the uterus and digestive system, and is reputedly aphrodisiac.
USES OF THE HERB
CULINARY Seeds are used as a spice and purifying agent.
MEDICINAL Locally, internally for stomach complaints, urinary and sexual disorders, epilepsy, menstrual problems, nervous and mental illnesses. Excess causes hallucinations and vomiting. Externally for hemorrhoids and baldness.
ECONOMIC Fruits yield a red dye and oil.

GROWTH AND HARVEST
GROWTH Crop. Well-drained to dry, poor soil in sun. Propagate by seed sown in late spring, or by division in late spring. Subject to statutory control as a weed in parts of Australia.
HARVEST Fruits and seeds are collected when ripe. Fruits are pressed for dye and oil. Seeds are dried for use in infusions and ointments.

PELARGONIUM Geranium
(Geraniaceae)

Scented geraniums contain very complex volatile oils. Over 2,000 components have been found, including those with discernible similarities to orange, lemon, peppermint, rose, nutmeg, and eucalyptus. Most popular are the rose-scented species and cultivars such as *P.* 'Rober's Lemon Rose'. They yield geranium oil, which is a fragrance in its own right and is often used as an adulterant of attar of roses. *P. capitatum* and cultivars related to *P. graveolens* and 'Radula' are grown for the production of geranium oil in parts of France, Italy, India, Egypt, Algeria, and the former Soviet Union. The finest, known as "Bourbon oil," comes from the island of Réunion. Many species are used medicinally in southern Africa, mainly for digestive, bronchial, and skin problems. *P. betulinum* (camphor geranium, birch-leaf geranium) is a good decongestant and digestive; leaves of *P. antidysentericum* (dysentery geranium) are infused and taken with lemon juice for gastrointestinal complaints. The leaves of *P. acetosum* (sorrel leaf) have an acidic taste and may be eaten raw in salads or added to soups and stews; several species, such as *P. rapaceum* and *P. triste*, have tuberous roots that are cooked like potatoes. Most species are easily propagated and hybridized, and the feasibility of producing aromas for the food and perfumery industries from plant cells grown *in vitro* has recently been examined.

P. capitatum (wild rose geranium) p.173

PARTS USED Whole plant, leaves, oil.
PROPERTIES An aromatic, soothing, emollient herb with a roselike aroma.
USES OF THE HERB
AROMATIC Oil is used in perfumery. Leaves are dried for potpourris.
MEDICINAL Internally as a traditional Cape remedy for minor digestive ailments and kidney and bladder disorders. Externally for rashes and calloused and cracked skin. Oil is a major component of geranium oil, used in aromatherapy and skin care.

P. citronellum p.172

PARTS USED Leaves.
PROPERTIES An aromatic herb with a lemon scent.
USES OF THE HERB
CULINARY Leaves may be infused to make tea and used fresh to flavor desserts, punch, and vinegar.
AROMATIC Leaves are dried for potpourris and herb pillows.

P. 'Clorinda' p.172

PARTS USED Leaves.
PROPERTIES An aromatic herb with a cedar–rose perfume.
USES OF THE HERB
AROMATIC Mainly grown as an aromatic ornamental. Leaves may be dried for potpourris.

P. crispum (lemon geranium) p.172

PARTS USED Leaves.
PROPERTIES An aromatic herb with a lemon aroma.
USES OF THE HERB
CULINARY Leaves may be infused to make tea and used fresh to give a lemon flavor to sauces, sorbets, ice cream, cakes, fruit punch, and vinegar.
AROMATIC Leaves are dried for potpourris and herb pillows.

P. c. 'Major' p.172

PARTS USED Leaves.
PROPERTIES An aromatic herb with a lemon aroma.
USES OF THE HERB
Leaves may be used as for *P. crispum.*

P. c. 'Peach Cream' p.172

PARTS USED Leaves.
PROPERTIES An aromatic herb with a fruity scent.
USES OF THE HERB
Leaves may be used as for *P. crispum.*

P. c. 'Variegatum' p.172

PARTS USED Leaves.
PROPERTIES An aromatic herb with a lemon aroma.
USES OF THE HERB
Leaves may be used as for *P. crispum.*

P. 'Fair Ellen' p.172

PARTS USED Leaves.
PROPERTIES An aromatic herb with a balsamlike scent.
USES OF THE HERB
AROMATIC Mainly grown as an aromatic ornamental. Leaves may be dried for potpourris.

P. 'Fragrans' (nutmeg geranium) p.173

PARTS USED Leaves.
PROPERTIES An aromatic herb with a spicy scent.
USES OF THE HERB
AROMATIC Mainly grown as an aromatic ornamental. Dried leaves are added to potpourris.
MEDICINAL Externally as a rub for aching feet or legs (fresh leaves).
ECONOMIC Leaves give flavor to *pâté* and a spicy flavor to coffee.

P. 'Fragrans Variegatum' p.173

PARTS USED Leaves.
PROPERTIES An aromatic herb with a spicy scent.
USES OF THE HERB
Leaves may be used as for *P.* 'Fragrans'.

P. 'Galway Star' p.173

PARTS USED Leaves.
PROPERTIES An aromatic herb with a lemon scent.
USES OF THE HERB
Leaves may be used as for *P. crispum.*

P. graveolens (rose geranium) p.173

PARTS USED Whole plant, leaves, oil.
PROPERTIES An aromatic, rose-scented herb that has relaxant, antidepressant, and antiseptic effects, reduces inflammation, and controls bleeding.
USES OF THE HERB
CULINARY Fresh leaves are infused for tea and used in similar ways to those of *P. crispum.*
AROMATIC Oil is used in perfumery and aromatherapy. Dried leaves added to potpourris.
MEDICINAL Internally for premenstrual and menopausal problems, nausea, tonsillitis, and poor circulation. Externally for acne, hemorrhoids, eczema, bruises, ringworm, and lice.
ECONOMIC Oil is the main constituent of geranium oil, used in skin care and food flavoring,

P. 'Lady Plymouth' p.173

PARTS USED Leaves.
PROPERTIES An aromatic herb with a minty rose-lemon scent.
USES OF THE HERB
Fresh and dried leaves may be used in similar ways to *P. graveolens.*

P. 'Mabel Grey'

Tender, erect hybrid, height 3–5ft (1–1.5m), spread 3ft (1m), with a strong lemon scent similar to *P. citronellum.* It has small mauve flowers and rough-textured leaves up to 3in (7cm) long.
PARTS USED Whole plant, leaves, oil.
PROPERTIES An aromatic herb with a strong lemon scent.
USES OF THE HERB
CULINARY Leaves may be used as for *P. crispum.*
AROMATIC Leaves may be used as for *P. crispum.*
ECONOMIC Oil is a flavoring in the food industry.

P. odoratissimum (apple geranium) p.172

PARTS USED Whole plant, leaves, oil.
PROPERTIES An aromatic herb with a fruity scent. It has astringent, tonic, and antiseptic effects, controls bleeding, promotes healing, and repels insects.
USES OF THE HERB
CULINARY Leaves may be used as for *P. crispum.*
AROMATIC Leaves may be used as for *P. crispum.*
MEDICINAL Internally for debility, gastroenteritis, and hemorrhage. Externally for skin complaints, injuries, neuralgia, and throat infections. Oil used in aromatherapy for burns, sores and shingles.

P. 'Old Spice' p.173

PARTS USED Leaves.
PROPERTIES An aromatic herb with a spicy scent.
USES OF THE HERB
Leaves may be used as for *P.* 'Fragrans'.

P. 'Prince of Orange' p.173

PARTS USED Leaves.
PROPERTIES An aromatic herb with a citrus scent.
USES OF THE HERB
Leaves may be used as for *P. crispum.*

P. quercifolium (oak-leaved geranium)

Tender, erect subshrub, height 1½–5ft (45cm–1.5m), spread 12–36in (45–90cm),with rough-textured, balsam-scented leaves, 2–4in (5–10cm) long, which are triangular in outline and deeply divided. Purple-pink flowers with darker markings appear in spring and summer.
PARTS USED Leaves.
PROPERTIES An aromatic, stimulant herb with a resinous scent.
USES OF THE HERB
AROMATIC Dried leaves are added to potpourris.
MEDICINAL Internally as a Cape remedy for rheumatism, hypertension, and heart disease.
ECONOMIC Dried leaves are added to insect-repellent sachets.

P. radens (rasp-leaved geranium) p.173

PARTS USED Leaves.
PROPERTIES An aromatic herb with a lemony scent.
USES OF THE HERB
MEDICINAL Externally as a rub for aching feet or legs (fresh leaves).
ECONOMIC Dried leaves are added to insect-repellent sachets and act as a fixative for other perfumes in potpourris.

P. 'Radula' p.173

PARTS USED Whole plant, leaves, oil.
PROPERTIES Aromatic herb with a camphoraceous, rose-lemon scent.
USES OF THE HERB
CULINARY Fresh leaves may be used in cooking.
AROMATIC Oil is used in perfumery. Dried leaves may be added to potpourris and herb pillows.
ECONOMIC Oil, in geranium oil, is used in aromatherapy and skin care; also in food flavoring and moth-repellent sachets.

P. 'Radula Rosea' p.173

PARTS USED Leaves.
PROPERTIES Aromatic herb with a camphoraceous rose-lemon scent.
USES OF THE HERB
CULINARY Fresh leaves may be used in cooking.
AROMATIC Leaves are dried for potpourris.

P. 'Rober's Lemon Rose' p.173

PARTS USED Whole plant, leaves, oil.
PROPERTIES Aromatic herb with a lemon-rose scent.
USES OF THE HERB
CULINARY Fresh leaves may be used in the same ways as *P. graveolens*.
ECONOMIC Oil is a flavoring in the food industry.

P. 'Royal Oak' p.173

PARTS USED Leaves.
PROPERTIES An aromatic herb with a balsam scent.
USES OF THE HERB
AROMATIC Mainly grown as an aromatic ornamental.

P. 'Sweet Mimosa' p.173

PARTS USED Leaves.
PROPERTIES An aromatic herb with a fruity scent.
USES OF THE HERB
CULINARY Fresh leaves may be used in cooking.
AROMATIC Mainly grown as an aromatic plant; dried leaves may be added to potpourris.

P. tomentosum (peppermint geranium) p.173

PARTS USED Leaves.
PROPERTIES Aromatic herb with peppermint scent.
USES OF THE HERB
CULINARY Fresh leaves are infused for tea, fruit punches, and jellies.
AROMATIC Dried leaves are added to potpourris.
MEDICINAL As a poultice for bruises and sprains.

GROWTH AND HARVEST

GROWTH Ornamental. Well-drained, neutral to alkaline soil in sun, min. 45–50°F (7–10°C). *P. crispum*, *P. odoratissimum*, and *P. tomentosum* tolerate partial shade. Propagate by softwood cuttings from spring to autumn. Plants may be cut back in early spring. If grown outdoors in cool climates, they may also be cut back before bringing in for the winter. They do well on a sunny windowsill in winter. Aphids, spider mites, and whitefly may attack plants under cover.
HARVEST Plants are cut in late summer and distilled for oil. Leaves are picked as required.

PERILLA
(Labiatae/Lamiaceae)

The volatile oil in the leaves of *P. frutescens* contains perillaldehyde, which is 2,000 times sweeter than sugar and eight times sweeter than saccharin. The seed oil is high in linolenic acid. Perilla has been used medicinally in China since c.AD500. The green and purple leaves of *P. frutescens* are both used in cooking, but seeds of purple-leaved variants are preferred for all uses.

P. frutescens (*shiso*, beefsteak plant) p.174

PARTS USED Leaves (*zi su ye*), stems (*zi su geng*, *su gen*), seeds (*zi su zi*, *su zi*), oil.
PROPERTIES A pungent, aromatic, warming herb that relaxes spasms, increases perspiration, and is effective against bacterial infection. It is also laxative, expectorant, and controls coughing.
USES OF THE HERB
CULINARY Fresh or pickled leaves and seeds give flavor to Japanese raw fish, bean curd, tempura, and pickles. Purple leaves color preserved fruits, such as *Prunus mume*.
MEDICINAL Internally for colds and chills, nausea, abdominal pain, food poisoning, and allergic reactions, especially from seafood; bronchitis, asthma, and constipation (seeds). Stems are a traditional Chinese remedy for morning sickness.
ECONOMIC Oil from foliage is used in sauces, tobacco, candy, and dental products. Oil from seeds (*yegoma*) is used in waterproofing and in the paper, printing, and paint industries.
VARIANT
***P. f.* 'Crispa'**, p.174.

GROWTH AND HARVEST

GROWTH Crop (*P. frutescens*). Ornamental (*P. f.* 'Crispa'). Well-drained soil in sun or partial shade, doing best in moist, rich conditions. Propagate by seed sown in spring. Pinch out growing tips to encourage bushiness.
HARVEST Leaves are cut in summer and used fresh or pickled, or dried for decoctions. Stems are cut in summer, or after the plant has gone to seed (some prefer young stems). Ripe seeds are collected in autumn and dried for decoctions.
NOTE Quality is variable; selections of green *Perilla* are considered superior to the wild, weedy forms found throughout much of the US.

PERSICARIA
P. bistorta. See *Polygonum bistorta*.

PETIVERIA
(Phytolaccaceae)

The strong, garliclike smell of *P. alliacea* is caused by the presence of a compound containing sulfur. This pungent odor may account for its popularity as a medicinal herb.

P. alliacea (Guinea hen weed, conga root, strong man's weed) p.174

PARTS USED Whole plant, leaves, roots.
PROPERTIES A pungent, diuretic, antiseptic herb that reputedly calms the nerves, controls diarrhea, lowers fever, stimulates the uterus, and relaxes spasms.
USES OF THE HERB
MEDICINAL Internally for nervous spasms, paralysis, hysteria, asthma, whooping cough, pneumonia, bronchitis, hoarseness, fevers, headaches, influenza, cystitis, venereal disease, menstrual complaints, and abortion. Externally for earache, fever, and headache.

GROWTH AND HARVEST

GROWTH Wild-collected. Rich, moist soil in partial shade, minimum 45°F (7°C). Propagate by semiripe cuttings in summer.
HARVEST Whole plants, leaves, and roots are collected for use in decoctions. Fresh leaves are bound around the head for headaches or juiced for direct application for earache.

PETROSELINUM
(Umbelliferae/Apiaceae)

P. crispum and its variants are rich in vitamins A and C and contain apigenin, a flavonoid that reduces allergic responses and is an effective antioxidant. Although quite safe in the amounts given in recipes, *P. crispum* is toxic in excess, especially as essential oil.

P. crispum (parsley) p.174

PARTS USED Leaves, roots, seeds, oil.
PROPERTIES A bitter, aromatic, diuretic herb that relaxes spasms, reduces inflammation, and clears toxins. It stimulates the digestion and uterus.
USES OF THE HERB
CULINARY Leaves are used as garnish and to flavor sauces, butter, dressings, stuffings, and savory dishes. Plain or flat-leaved parsleys have a stronger flavor than curly-leaved cultivars. Eaten as a vegetable in some areas. The flavor of *P. c.* var. *tuberosum* is inferior.
MEDICINAL Internally for menstrual complaints, edema, cystitis, prostatitis, kidney stones, indigestion, colic, anorexia, anemia, arthritis, and rheumatism (roots, seeds); after delivery, for promoting lactation and contracting the uterus (roots, seeds). Excess causes nerve inflammation, abortion, liver and kidney damage, and gastrointestinal hemorrhage. Not given to pregnant women or patients with kidney disease.
ECONOMIC Oil is used in commercial food flavoring and perfumes for men.
VARIANTS
***P. c.* 'Italian'**, p.174.
***P. c.* 'Moss Curled'**, p.175.
P. c.* var. *tuberosum, p.175.

GROWTH AND HARVEST

GROWTH Crop (*P. crispum*, *P. c.* var. *tuberosum*). Ornamental (*P. c.* 'Italian', *P. c.* 'Moss Curled'). Rich, well-drained, neutral to alkaline soil in sun or partial shade. Propagate by seed sown from early spring to early summer and in autumn, or by seed sown in spring (*P. c.* var. *tuberosum*). Parsley seed takes 3–6 weeks to germinate, but may be sooner if seeds are soaked in hot water. Leaves may be damaged by leafspot or viral disease.
HARVEST Leaves are picked throughout the growing season and used fresh, frozen, as juice, or dried. Roots are lifted in late autumn of first year, or spring of second year, and dried for decoctions and liquid extracts. Seeds are collected when ripe and dried for infusions and liquid extracts. Oil is distilled from leaves and seeds.

PEUCEDANUM
P. graveolens. See *Anethum graveolens*.

PEUMUS
(Umbelliferae/Apiaceae)

P. boldus was first investigated by a French physician in 1869. It contains a volatile oil that destroys internal parasites, and alkaloids that stimulate the liver. Alkaloids extracted from the bark are more effective than leaf-based preparations.

P. boldus (boldo) p.175

PARTS USED Leaves, bark.
PROPERTIES A bitter, aromatic herb that improves liver and gall bladder function, and expels worms. It is diuretic and a mild urinary antiseptic.
USES OF THE HERB
MEDICINAL Internally for liver disease, gallstones, urinary tract infections, intestinal parasites, and rheumatism. Formerly given as a substitute for quinine. Often added to diet foods. Combines well with *Berberis vulgaris* (see p.248) and *Chionanthus virginicus* (see p.260) for liver and gall bladder complaints. WARNING This herb is subject to legal restrictions in some countries.

GROWTH AND HARVEST
GROWTH Crop. Well-drained, sandy, acid soil in sun. Propagate by seed sown in spring, or by semiripe cuttings in summer.
HARVEST Leaves are picked during the growing season and dried for infusions, liquid extracts, and tinctures. Alkaloids are extracted commercially from the bark.

PHELLODENDRON
(Rutaceae)

P. amurense was first described in Chinese medical texts in 1578. *P. chinense* is also used. All species are rich in alkaloids, such as berberine (as found in *Berberis vulgaris*, see p.248).

P. amurense (Amur cork tree) p.175

PARTS USED Bark (*huang bai*).
PROPERTIES A bitter, diuretic, cooling herb that stimulates the liver and gall bladder, lowers fever, reduces blood pressure and blood sugar levels, and is strongly anti-bacterial. It acts mainly on the kidneys and is traditionally regarded as a detoxicant for hot, damp conditions.
USES OF THE HERB
MEDICINAL Internally for diarrhea, dysentery, jaundice, acute urinary tract infections, enteritis, boils, abscesses, night sweats, and skin diseases. An ingredient of the Chinese drug *san huang zhe she ye* ("injection of three yellow herbs"), the others being *Scutellaria baicalensis*, see p.351, and *Coptis chinensis*, see p.266. The drug is given intramuscularly for upper respiratory tract infections.

GROWTH AND HARVEST
GROWTH Ornamental. Rich, well-drained, neutral to alkaline soil in sun. Young growth may be damaged by late frosts in cold areas. Propagate by seed sown in autumn, or by softwood cuttings in summer, or by root cuttings in late winter.
HARVEST Bark is stripped in winter and dried for use in decoctions.

PHRAGMITES
(Gramineae/Poaceae)

The common reed, *P. australis*, provides flood control, raw materials (including stems for thatching and matting, and fibers for the textile and paper industries), fuel, alcohol, and fertilizer. Roots, shoots, and seeds are edible, and stems contain a sweet gum that was used as a source of sugar by native N Americans. It was first recorded as a Chinese medicinal herb in the *Collection of Commentaries of the Classic Materia Medica*, by Tao Hong-Ying, c.AD500.

P. australis, syn. *P. communis* (common reed, carrizo) p.175

PARTS USED Rhizomes (*lu gen*).
PROPERTIES A sweet, cooling, sedative herb that is diuretic, controls coughing and vomiting, relieves pain, and lowers fever.
USES OF THE HERB
MEDICINAL Internally for fevers, vomiting, coughs with thick, dark phlegm, lung abscesses, urinary tract infections, and food poisoning (especially from seafood). Externally, combined with gypsum for halitosis and toothache.
VARIANT
P. a. **'Variegatus'**, p.175.

GROWTH AND HARVEST
GROWTH Ornamental. Wet soil or shallow water in sun. Propagate by division in spring. *P. australis* is a large, invasive plant, unsuited to garden ponds or areas where it might escape into the wild.
HARVEST Rhizomes are lifted in autumn and juiced, or dried for use in decoctions.

PHYLLOSTACHYS
(Gramineae/Poaceae–Bambusoideae)

Bamboos are of great economic importance in Asia. They probably have a wider range of uses than any other kind of plant, from paper and musical instruments to scaffolding, fishing rods, and drainpipes. The stems are particularly strong, due to their high silica content. Young shoots of many species, notably *P. pubescens*, are edible, and large quantities are canned for export. Various species are used medicinally in China, apparently interchangeably, as *zhu*. The first mention in medical texts of bamboo sap (*zhu li*) and stem shavings (*zhu ru*) was made c.AD500. A siliceous substance, known as *tabasher*, or *tabashir* (*tian zhu huang*), is used in similar ways to the dried sap. It occurs in fragile, angular concretions, up to the size of a hen's egg, inside the lower internodes.

P. nigra (black bamboo) p.176

PARTS USED Leaves, stem shavings, roots, sap.
PROPERTIES A sweet, cooling, diuretic herb that lowers fever, is expectorant, controls vomiting, checks bleeding, and is effective against bacterial infections.
USES OF THE HERB
MEDICINAL Internally for lung infections with cough and phlegm (stem, sap); vomiting, nosebleed (leaves, stem); fevers, especially infantile convulsions (leaves, roots); rabies (roots).
VARIANTS
P. n. **'Boryana'**, p.176.
P. n. var. ***henonis***, syn. *P. henonis*, p.176.

GROWTH AND HARVEST
GROWTH Ornamental. Moist soil in a sheltered, sunny position. Periodic applications of manure will help provide nutrients to keep bamboo growing well. Propagate by division in spring during wet weather, or by cuttings of young rhizomes in late winter. Divisions from open ground do not transplant well and should be nurtured in pots under cover until late spring. Small divisions are more successful than large clumps. Remove dead stems at any time. Clumps may be thinned in spring to leave the strongest stems, creating an open, grovelike effect. Many bamboos are very invasive.
HARVEST Leaves are collected during the growing season, young stems are cut for shavings in summer, and roots are lifted in winter; all are dried for use in decoctions. Sap is pressed from young stems and evaporated.

PHYSALIS
(Solanaceae)

According to Dioscorides, the fruits of *P. alkekengi* are a cure for epilepsy. In European folk medicine the fruits were taken to relieve scarlet fever, and the foliage was used in tonics for anemia and malaria. Fruits, though edible, are inferior to those of *P. peruviana* (Cape gooseberry), which is grown on a commercial scale.

P. alkekengi, syn. *P. franchetti* (Chinese lantern, winter cherry, bladder cherry) p.176

PARTS USED Fruits, fruit juice, leaves.
PROPERTIES A bittersweet herb that is diuretic and aperient, lowers fever, and reduces inflammation.
USES OF THE HERB
CULINARY Fruits may be eaten raw, stewed (with calyx removed), dipped in chocolate, or used as a garnish (with calyx peeled back).
MEDICINAL Internally for intermittent fevers, urinary disorders, arthritis, rheumatism, and gout (fruits, juice). Leaves formerly used externally for skin inflammations. Used in homeopathy for arthritic, rheumatic, and urinary disorders, and jaundice.

GROWTH AND HARVEST
GROWTH Ornamental. Well-drained soil in sun. Propagate by seed sown in spring, or by division in spring.
HARVEST Fruits are harvested when ripe and used fresh, as juice, or dried. For medicinal use, the calyx is removed. Leaves are picked in summer and used fresh as a poultice.
WARNING Foliage and unripe fruits are harmful if eaten.

PHYSOSTIGMA
(Leguminosae)

Four species of perennial climbers belong to this western African genus. Before its adoption by Western medicine, *P. venenosum* was notorious as the plant used in the "ordeal by poison" in the Calabar Province of Nigeria. In this ritual, an accused person drinks a solution of poisonous beans, dying if guilty and apparently surviving if innocent. The success of the method may be based on the probability that innocent people will tend to gulp the entire drink, causing vomiting and expulsion of toxins, while the guilty are perhaps more likely to sip cautiously and thereby ingest more poison. *P. venenosum* contains alkaloids, of which the most important is physostigmine (eserine), which influences the parasympathetic nervous system. It is mainly used in eyedrops to reduce pressure on the eyeball, and as an antidote to atropine (see *Atropa belladonna*, see p.246). Another alkaloid, calabarine, has opposite effects. Extracts of whole seeds differ in effects from isolated alkaloids.

P. venenosum (Calabar bean, *esere* bean, ordeal bean)

Tender evergreen climber, height to 50ft (15m), with trifoliate leaves, 6in (16cm) long and 4in (10cm) wide. Pink-purple pea flowers are produced in drooping clusters in spring, followed by oblong pods up to 6in (16cm) long, containing 2–3 brown-black seeds, 1¼in (3cm) long.

PARTS USED Seeds (with outer coat removed).
PROPERTIES A narcotic herb that depresses the central nervous system, mimics the parasympathetic nervous system, contracts the pupil of the eye, raises blood pressure, and stimulates peristalsis.
USES OF THE HERB
MEDICINAL As physostigmine, internally for neuromuscular diseases (notably myasthenia gravis), and postoperative constipation; externally as eyedrops (especially for glaucoma). Formerly used in the treatment of tetanus, epilepsy, and rheumatism. Excess causes muscular weakness, respiratory failure, and cardiac arrest. For use by qualified practitioners only.

GROWTH AND HARVEST
GROWTH Crop. Rich, well-drained soil in sun, minimum 59–64°F (15–18°C). Propagate by seed sown when ripe.
HARVEST Seeds are collected when ripe, mainly in the rainy season, and dried for use in decoctions and for extraction of alkaloids.

PHYTOLACCA
(Phytolaccaceae)

Phytolaccas have an unusual chemistry that is currently being researched for anti-AIDS drugs. They contain potent anti-inflammatory agents, antiviral proteins, and substances (referred to collectively as "pokeweed mitogens") that affect cell division. These compounds are toxic to many disease-causing organisms, including the water snails that cause schistosomiasis. *P. acinosa* was first recorded in Chinese medicine during the Han dynasty (206BC–AD23). Occasionally the roots are mistakenly sold in markets as ginseng, causing outbreaks of poisoning. *P. americana* was used by native N Americans as an emetic and antirheumatic, and was listed in the *U.S. Pharmacopoeia* (1820–1916) as an analgesic and anti-inflammatory . Although most parts are poisonous, very young shoots and young leaves are eaten, after boiling in several changes of water, in various countries.

P. acinosa (Indian pokeberry) p.176

PARTS USED Roots (*shang lu*).
PROPERTIES A bitter, pungent, cooling herb that has diuretic and expectorant effects, and controls coughing. It is effective against various bacterial and fungal infections.
USES OF THE HERB
MEDICINAL Internally for urinary disorders, nephritis, edema, and abdominal distension. Externally for boils, carbuncles, and sores.

P. americana, syn. *P. decandra* (pokeweed, pokeroot, red-ink plant) p.176

PARTS USED Roots, fruits (berries).
PROPERTIES A bitter, pungent, alterative herb that reduces inflammation, stimulates the immune and lymphatic systems, and clears toxins. It is effective against many organisms.
USES OF THE HERB
MEDICINAL Internally for autoimmune diseases (especially rheumatoid arthritis), tonsillitis, mumps, swollen glands (including glandular fever), chronic excess mucus, bronchitis, mastitis, skin diseases, and inflammations. Excess causes diarrhea and vomiting. Not given during pregnancy. Externally for skin complaints (including fungal infections), joint inflammation, hemorrhoids, mastitis, breast abscesses, and varicose ulcers. Combines well with *Guaiacum officinale* (see p.290) and *Zanthoxylum* spp. (see p.372) for rheumatic conditions; with *Galium aparine* (see p.285) and *Iris versicolor* (see p.297) for swollen glands. For use by qualified practitioners only. Used in homeopathic preparations for breast complaints, swollen tonsils, mumps, teething, halitosis, and shooting pains.
ECONOMIC When fermented with a vinegar mordant, the berries make a beet red dye.

GROWTH AND HARVEST
GROWTH Ornamental. Rich, moist, well-drained soil in sun or partial shade. Often weedy. Propagate by seed sown in autumn or spring, or by division in autumn or spring.
HARVEST Roots and fruits (*P. americana*) are collected in autumn and dried for decoctions, liquid extracts, powder, poultices, and tinctures.
WARNING All parts, notably leaves and berries, are toxic if eaten. Sap is irritant to skin and eyes.

PICRAENIA
P. excelsa. See *Picrasma excelsa.*

PICRASMA
(Simaroubaceae)

This genus has eight species of deciduous trees, which occur in tropical America, India, and Malaysia. *P. excelsa* (Jamaica quassia) has slightly different constituents from *P. ailanthoides* (Japanese quassia) or the related *Quassia amara* (Surinam quassia), but they are used interchangeably. *Q. amara* was introduced to Europe in 1756, and entered the *London Pharmacopoeia* in 1788. It was superseded by *P. excelsa* (*Q. excelsa*) in 1809. The term "quassia" refers to a bitter compound extracted from the bark and wood of either *P. excelsa* or *Q. amara.*

P. excelsa, syn. *Picraenia excelsa* (Jamaica quassia, bitter ash)

Tender ashlike tree, height 80ft (25m), spread 50ft (15m), with pinnate, coarsely toothed leaves up to 12in (30cm) long. Small green-white flowers are produced in panicles in late autumn, followed by black, shiny, globose berries, which ripen in winter. Found in hill forests in the West Indies.

PARTS USED Wood.
PROPERTIES An intensely bitter, nonastringent, odorless herb that lowers fever, stimulates appetite, and improves digestion. It is an effective insecticide and parasiticide, and is reputedly antileukemic.
USES OF THE HERB
MEDICINAL Internally for convalescent debility, poor appetite, malaria, and nematodes. Excess causes gastric irritation and vomiting. Externally as a lotion for parasites, such as lice, and an enema for threadworms.
ECONOMIC Quassia extract is used to give a bitter flavor to soft drinks, beer, and other alcoholic beverages, and in insecticides against flies, spider mites, aphids, and woolly aphids.

GROWTH AND HARVEST
GROWTH Crop. Moist, sandy, humus-rich soil in sun or partial shade, with moderate to high humidity, minimum 59–64°F (15–18°C). Propagate by seed sown when ripe, or by semi-ripe cuttings in late summer at 59–64°F (15–18°C). Trim plants to shape in late winter before new growth begins.
HARVEST Wood is chipped and dried for use in concentrated infusions, powders, and tinctures.

PILOCARPUS Jaborandi
(Rutaceae)

About 20 species of shrubs and small trees belong to this genus, which occurs in tropical America and the W Indies. Jaborandi is the source of an important alkaloid, pilocarpine, which is obtained from several species, including *P. jaborandi* (Pernambuco jaborandi), *P. microphyllus*, *P. pinnatifolius* (Paraguay jaborandi), and *P. trachylophus* (Ceara jaborandi). The medicinal uses of jaborandi were introduced to Europe about

1873 by Symphronio Coutinho (1832–87), a Brazilian physician. Pilocarpine stimulates the parasympathetic nervous system, and is now used mainly in ophthalmology to constrict the pupil of the eye. Supplies of foliage are still collected mainly from the wild, though plantations have been established in Brazil.

P. microphyllus (jaborandi, Maranham jaborandi)

Tender, evergreen shrub, height 4–5ft (1.2–1.5m), spread 3ft (1m), with smooth, gray bark and dull yellow-green, pinnate leaves. Small red-purple flowers are produced in lax racemes, followed by 2-valved fruits consisting of 1–5 nearly separate, one-seeded carpels. Found in Brazilian rainforests.

PARTS USED Leaves, leafy twigs.
PROPERTIES A bitter, slightly aromatic herb that stimulates the heart, causes copious perspiration and salivation, contracts the pupils, and reputedly increases hair growth.
USES OF THE HERB
MEDICINAL Internally for psoriasis, itching of the skin, syphilis, chronic excess mucus, and dropsy (leaf extracts). Internally and externally for glaucoma and as an antidote to atropine (pilocarpine); externally for hair loss (leaf extracts). Excess causes profuse perspiration and salivation, rapid pulse, contracted pupils, diarrhea, and vomiting, and may be fatal. WARNING This herb, especially in the form of pilocarpine and leaf extracts, is subject to legal restrictions in some countries. Use of jaborandi in cosmetics is prohibited in many countries.

GROWTH AND HARVEST
GROWTH Crop. Rich, well-drained soil in partial shade and high humidity, minimum 59–64°F (15–18°C). Propagate by seed when ripe, or by ripewood cuttings with leaves intact during the growing season.
HARVEST Leaves and leafy twigs are picked as required and dried for extraction of alkaloids and for use in liquid extracts and tinctures.

PILOSELLA

P. officinarum. See *Hieracium pilosella.*

PIMENTA

(Myrtaceae)

About four species of aromatic, evergreen trees belong to this tropical American genus. The fruits of *P. dioica* were first imported to Europe by the Spanish in the 16th century, and given the name "allspice" by John Ray (1627–1705), an English botanist, who likened their flavor to a combination of cloves, cinnamon, and nutmeg. Allspice is an important crop in Jamaica; trees are grown in plantations, known as "pimento walks," which fill the air with scent during the flowering season. *P. dioica* contains a volatile oil that consists mainly of eugenol (as found in *Syzygium aromaticum*, p.358). The related W Indian *P. acris* (syn. *P. racemosa*, bayberry tree, wild clove) was once important as the source of bay rum, an aromatic liquid used in hair dressings, which was distilled from the leaves and is now synthesized.

P. dioica (allspice, pimento, Jamaica pepper)

Tender, aromatic tree, height 30–50ft (10–15m), spread 15ft (5m), with thin, oblong-elliptic, leathery leaves, 2½in–8in (6–20cm) long. Many small white flowers are borne in panicles up to 5in (12cm) long in spring and summer, followed by dark brown, globose berries, about ¼in (6mm) in diameter. Found on wooded hillsides in C and S America.

PARTS USED Leaves, fruits (berries), oil.
PROPERTIES A pungent, warming, aromatic herb with a clovelike aroma. It improves the digestion, has a tonic effect on the nervous system, and is locally antiseptic and anesthetic. Oil of pimento is carminative and antioxidant.
USES OF THE HERB
CULINARY Dried, unripe berries are used whole in pickling spices, marinades, and mulled wine, and ground for flavoring cakes, biscuits, puddings, and chutneys. Leaves are infused for tea.
AROMATIC Oil and berries are used in perfumery, notably oriental fragrances and aftershave lotions.
MEDICINAL Internally for indigestion, flatulence, diarrhea, and nervous exhaustion. Externally for chest infections, and muscular aches and pains.
ECONOMIC Powdered berries are added to medicines to disguise the flavor, and to liniments and plasters. Oil and berries are used in commercial food flavoring in the countries of origin.

GROWTH AND HARVEST
GROWTH Crop. Rich, well-drained, sandy soil in sun, minimum 59–64°F (15–18°C). Propagate by semiripe cuttings in summer. Remove weak branches in spring.
HARVEST Leaves are picked as required and used fresh for infusions. Fruits are collected when fully grown, but unripe, and distilled for oil or dried for liquid extracts and powders.

PIMPINELLA

(Umbelliferae/Apiaceae)

P. anisum was first cultivated as a spice by the ancient Egyptians and later by the Greeks, Romans, and Arabs. Although widely grown commercially, it has declined in recent years through competition with cheaper anise flavorings, such as *Illicium verum* (see p.296) and synthetic anethole. *P. saxifraga*, which has a large proportion of coumarins in the roots, is used interchangeably with the larger-rooted *P. s.* var. *nigra* (black caraway) and the closely related *P. major* (greater burnet saxifrage, greater pimpernel).

P. anisum (anise, aniseed) p.176

PARTS USED Leaves, seeds, oil.
PROPERTIES A sweet, warming, stimulant herb that improves digestion, benefits the liver and circulation, and has expectorant and estrogenic effects.
USES OF THE HERB

CULINARY Fresh leaves are added to salads, vegetables, and various cooked dishes in countries of origin. Seeds are used to flavor candy (especially aniseed balls), dried figs, cakes, bread, and curries. Seeds and oil form the basis of anise-flavored drinks, such as Pernod, *ouzo*, *raki*, and *arak*, which turn milky when diluted with water.
MEDICINAL Internally for dry coughs, whooping cough, bronchitis, tracheitis, bronchial asthma, indigestion, flatulence, and insufficient lactation. Externally for lice, scabies, and as a chest rub for bronchial complaints. Combines well with *Mentha* x *piperita* (see p.311) for colic, *Prunus serotina* (see p.335) for tracheitis, *Lactuca* spp. (see p.300) for dry coughs; and with *Marrubium vulgare* (see p.308), *Tussilago farfara* (see p.365), *Lobelia inflata* (see p.305), and *Symplocarpus foetidus* (see p.358) for bronchial complaints. Oil is often mixed with oil of *Sassafras albidum* (see p.349) for skin parasites, and with that of *Eucalyptus globulus* (see p.280) as a chest rub. Traditionally regarded as an aphrodisiac.
ECONOMIC Oil is used commercially in perfumery, in tobacco manufacture, and in pharmaceutical products.

P. saxifraga (burnet saxifrage, small pimpernel) p.177

PARTS USED Whole plant, leaves, roots, oil.
PROPERTIES A bitter, pungent, diuretic herb that is expectorant, improves digestion, relieves spasms, and increases lactation. It is antiseptic and promotes healing.
USES OF THE HERB
CULINARY Young leaves are cucumber-flavored and are added to salads.
MEDICINAL Internally for infections of the throat and upper respiratory tract, excess mucus, measles, heartburn, cystitis, urinary stones, gout, and insufficient lactation. Externally for sore throat, inflamed gums, and wounds.
ECONOMIC Oil gives a bitter flavor to liqueurs and pharmaceutical products.

GROWTH AND HARVEST
GROWTH Crop. (*P. anisum*). Rich, well-drained, sandy soil, pH6.0–7.5, in sun. Crop (*P. saxifraga*). Dry, alkaline soil in sun or light shade. Propagate by seed sown in spring. All white-flowered umbellifers must be accurately identified before use because many look alike and a number are extremely poisonous.
P. anisum is recommended in companion planting to repel aphids and cabbage worms. The flowers attract parasitic wasps, which prey on a number of garden pests.
HARVEST Plants and leaves are cut in summer and used fresh; roots are lifted in autumn and dried for use in decoctions or distilled for oil (*P. saxifraga*). Seeds are collected as they ripen and distilled for oil, or dried for use whole, ground, or distilled in water, infusions, and liqueurs (*P. anisum*).

PINELLIA

(Araceae)

P. ternata was first recorded in Chinese medicine in the *Shen Nong Canon of Herbs*, which was completed during the later Han dynasty (AD25–220). Like most members of the aroid family, it is extremely acrid when fresh, containing toxins that are neutralized by drying or by soaking in tea or vinegar. Among the constituents are alkaloids that are thought to resemble coniine (as found in *Conium maculatum,* see p.265), and ephedrine (as found in *Ephedra* species, see p.278). Its reputation for controlling nausea and vomiting has been scientifically validated; it is part of a successful Chinese prescription for removing gallstones without surgery, a process causing severe nausea.

P. ternata (pinellia) p.177

PARTS USED Tubers (*ban xia*).
PROPERTIES A pungent, slightly bitter, warming herb that controls coughing and has expectorant and antimucus effects. It is a potent antiemetic.
USES OF THE HERB
MEDICINAL Internally for coughs with thin, watery phlegm, gastritis, nausea, and vomiting. Often combined with *Zingiber officinale* (see p.373) to control vomiting; with *Citrus reticulata* (*chen pi*, see p.262), *Scutellaria baicalensis* (see p.351), or *Coptis chinensis* (see p.266) for coughs; and with *Glycyrrhiza uralensis* (see p.289), calcium carbonate, and alum as an expectorant. In Chinese prescriptions, it is combined with *Zingiber officinale* (see p.373) or *Glycyrrhiza uralensis* (see p.289) to reduce its toxicity.

GROWTH AND HARVEST
GROWTH Ornamental. Humus-rich soil in partial shade. Propagate by offsets in early spring, or by bulbils in late summer. *P. ternata* is highly invasive in optimum conditions, spreading by bulbils.
HARVEST Tubers are lifted in summer and dried for use in decoctions.
WARNING Harmful if eaten. Irritant to skin, eyes, and mucous membranes.

PINUS Pine
(Pinaceae)

Pines of all kinds have been used medicinally in various countries from earliest times. All are rich in resins and camphoraceous volatile oils, including pinene, that are strongly antiseptic and stimulant. Pine oil is extracted from many different species and is widely used in massage oils for muscular stiffness, sciatica, and rheumatism, and in vapor rubs for bronchial congestion. In traditional Chinese medicine the main species used are *P. massoniana* (Masson pine, horsetail pine) and *P. tabuliformis* (Chinese red pine). Knotty pine wood (*song jie*) usually refers to the latter and was first mentioned in Chinese medical literature c.AD500 as an antiarthritic and analgesic. Various parts of *P. massoniana* are used: the needles for influenza and rheumatoid arthritis; resin for eczema and burns; and pollen, given internally for peptic ulcers, dizziness, and facial edema, and externally for boils and sores. Fossilized pine resin (amber, *hu po*) from *P. succinifera* (now extinct) is obtained from buried trees and used to treat urinary tract infections, urinary stones, heart disease, and infantile convulsions. A viscous oleoresin, known as turpentine, is tapped from various species, including *P. palustris* and *P. pinaster* (maritime pine). It is distilled to produce oil of turpentine or spirits of turpentine. Turpentine substitute, or white spirit, is a thinner for paints and varnishes based on petroleum. Rosin, or colophony, is a brittle, translucent substance produced in the distillation of turpentine. Resin is tapped from *P. halepensis* (Aleppo pine) in Greece to flavor *retsina*. A number of pines produce large, edible seeds, known as "pine nuts," which are added to salads, cooked vegetables, and rice, and ground for sauces, such as *pesto*.

P. mugo var. *pumilio* (dwarf mountain pine) p.177

PARTS USED Oil.
PROPERTIES An aromatic, stimulant, antiseptic herb that is expectorant, relieves bronchial and nasal congestion, and improves blood flow locally.
USES OF HERB
AROMATIC Oil is used in woody perfumes.
MEDICINAL Internally and externally for upper respiratory tract infections, chronic bronchitis, excess mucus, and asthma. Externally for rheumatism and muscular stiffness. WARNING This herb, in the form of pine oil, is subject to legal restrictions in some countries.

P. palustris (longleaf pine, southern pitch pine)

Conifer, hardy to 23°F (–5°C), height 100ft (30m), spread 15ft (5m), with an irregular crown, orange-brown, scaly bark, and white, fire-resistant buds up to 2½in (6cm) thick. Leaves, up to 18in (45cm) long, are arranged in threes. Red-brown cones are 10in (25cm) long. Found in dry, sandy areas in southeastern US.

PARTS USED Oil (turpentine), resin (colophony, rosin).
PROPERTIES An aromatic, antiseptic herb that improves blood flow locally.
USES OF THE HERB
AROMATIC Oil is used in perfumery
MEDICINAL Externally for boils, ulcers, bronchitis, and ringworm (resin), rheumatism and muscular stiffness (oil, resin).
ECONOMIC Oil is used a solvent. Resin is used in varnishes, printing inks, sealing waxes, and for treating bows of stringed instruments.

P. sylvestris (Scots pine) p.177

PARTS USED Leaves, young shoots and buds, tar, oil.
PROPERTIES A bitter, aromatic, warming herb that acts as a diuretic and expectorant, improves blood flow locally, and has a tonic effect on the nerves. It is strongly antiseptic.
USES OF THE HERB
MEDICINAL Internally for urinary and respiratory tract infections, and gall bladder complaints. Externally for arthritis, rheumatism, sciatica, poor circulation, bronchitis, excess mucus, sinusitis, asthma, pneumonia, neuralgia, acne, fatigue, and nervous exhaustion. Oil is used in aromatherapy for similar complaints. Not given to patients with allergic skin conditions.
ECONOMIC Oil and tar are added to disinfectants, bath preparations, detergents, and preparations to stimulate hair growth.
VARIANT
P. s. **'Aurea'**, p.177.

GROWTH AND HARVEST
GROWTH Ornamental. Well-drained, neutral to acid soil in sun. *P. sylvestris* thrives in both acid and alkaline soils. *P. palustris* tolerates drought and poor soil but needs warmth and humidity. Propagate by seed in autumn or spring (species and varieties only), or by layering (*P. m.* var. *pumilio*), or by grafting. Remove dead branches in winter. Restrict the leading shoots. Foliage may be damaged by adelgids, caterpillars, sawfly larvae, canker, dieback, *Botrytis*, and rust. Trees may be killed by *Armillaria* root rot.
HARVEST Leaves and young shoots are collected during the growing season and usually used fresh for decoctions and syrups (*P. sylvestris*). Resin is tapped by cutting vertical grooves in the bark and collecting the exudate; oil is distilled or solvent extracted from wood and bark (*P. palustris*). Oil is distilled from leaves (*P. mugo* var. *pumilio*). Tar is distilled from roots (*P. sylvestris*).

PIPER Pepper
(Piperaceae)

Pepper has always been one of the most valuable of spices: Attila the Hun demanded a huge quantity of it as a ransom during the siege of Rome (AD408), and its use as currency gave rise to the term "peppercorn rent." It accounts now for a quarter of the spice trade. India is the main producer. Most peppers are grown for their fruits, which are rich in volatile oil and pungent piperidine alkaloids. *P. guineense* (West African, or Ashanti pepper) produces mild-flavored peppercorns, and leaves that are used as a substitute for *P. betle* in betel quids.
P. methysticum is unusual in being a root crop; the roots may weigh 12–16lb (5.5–7.3kg).
P. auritum (*makulan*) and *P. angustifolia* (*matico*) are tropical American species grown for their leaves. Those of the former resemble spinach, and they are used as a flavoring in Guatemalan and Mexican cooking; the latter is an astringent, styptic herb with a tealike aroma, used in preparations for hemorrhoids, hemorrhage, and vaginal discharge.
Numerous species other than *P. nigrum* are grown for their fruits, but only *P. longum* and *P. retrofractum* (Javanese long pepper) are sufficiently similar in flavor to use as substitutes. Pink peppercorns come from a S American tree, *Schinus terebinthifolius*. They are often mixed with green, black, and white peppercorns for decorative effect, but

they have a resinous flavor and cannot be used as a substitute. Red and chili peppers are the fruits of *Capsicum* species (see p.254).

P. betle (betel) p.178

PARTS USED Leaves, oil.
PROPERTIES An aromatic, antibacterial, stimulant herb with a clovelike flavor. It increases salivation and may protect against intestinal parasites.
USES OF THE HERB
AROMATIC Main use of leaves is to wrap around betel nuts (seeds of *Areca catechu*, see p.241) to make a betel quid for chewing.
MEDICINAL Minor medicinal uses in countries of origin include external application for excess mucus, diphtheria, and breast abscesses (oil), and in Indonesia as a pessary after childbirth.

P. cubeba (cubeb, tailed pepper) p.178

PARTS USED Fruits, oil.
PROPERTIES A bitter, antiseptic, stimulant herb with a pungent, turpentine–allspice aroma. It has expectorant and diuretic effects, and improves digestion.
USES OF THE HERB
CULINARY Indonesian cookery uses the dried, unripe fruits.
AROMATIC Oil is used in perfumery and toiletries.
MEDICINAL Internally for coughs, bronchitis, sinusitis, throat and genitourinary infections, poor digestion, and amebic dysentery.
ECONOMIC Oil is used in commercial flavoring of pickles, sauces, bitters, and tobacco.

P. longum (Indian long pepper, Jaborandi pepper, *pippali*) p.178

PARTS USED Fruits (*bi ba*).
PROPERTIES An aromatic, hot, stimulant herb that improves digestion and has decongestant, antibiotic, and analgesic effects.
USES OF THE HERB
CULINARY Fruit clusters are used whole in curries and pickles.
MEDICINAL Internally, in traditional Chinese medicine, for stomach chills, vomiting, acid regurgitation, headache, and rhinitis; in Ayurvedic medicine, for epilepsy, colds, asthma, bronchitis, arthritis, rheumatism, lumbago, indigestion, sciatica, and flatulence. Externally, in traditional Chinese medicine, for toothache. Combined with *P. nigrum* and *Zingiber officinale* (see p.373) in *trikatu*, an Ayurvedic remedy for cold conditions.

P. methysticum (kava kava)

Tender, erect shrub, height 9–21ft (3–7m), spread 6–15ft (2–5m), with stout rhizomes, fleshy stems, and ovate, tapering leaves up to 10in (25cm) across. Small flowers are produced in spikes 3in (7.5cm) long. Native to Polynesian uplands.

PARTS USED Roots, rhizomes.
PROPERTIES A bitter, very pungent, warming herb with a lilac aroma. It acts as a diuretic, relieves pain, relaxes spasms, and has a stimulant effect on the circulatory and nervous systems.
USES OF THE HERB
CULINARY Chewed, fermented roots are the base of a ritual Melanesian drink, which has a calming effect, but promotes mental awareness.
MEDICINAL Internally for genitourinary infections, gall bladder complaints, arthritis, and rheumatism; externally for joint pains. Not given to pregnant women. Excess causes stupor.

P. nigrum (pepper) p.178

PARTS USED Fruits (*hu jiao*).
PROPERTIES A pungent, aromatic, warming herb that lowers fever and improves digestion. It is regarded as a stimulating expectorant in Western and Ayurvedic medicine, and as tranquilizing and antiemetic in Chinese practice.
USES OF THE HERB
CULINARY Black and white peppercorns are, respectively, the dried unripe and ripe berries; they give flavor and piquancy to most savory dishes, meat products, sauces, dressings, pickles, and coatings for fish, meat, and cheese. Ground white pepper is less aromatic. Mignonette pepper (also called "shot pepper," or *poivre gris*) is a blend of ground white and black peppercorns. Green (fresh, unripe) peppercorns are used in cream sauces, and to flavor duck; pickled for *pâtés*, butters, and sauces; and dried for stock, soup, and casseroles.
MEDICINAL Internally, in Western medicine, for indigestion and flatulence; in traditional Chinese medicine, for stomach chills, food poisoning (from fish, meat, crab, or fungi), cholera, dysentery, diarrhea, and vomiting caused by cold. Externally, in Ayurvedic medicine, mixed with *ghee* for nasal congestion, sinusitis, epilepsy, and inflammations such as nettle rash and erysipelas.

GROWTH AND HARVEST

GROWTH Crop. Rich, well-drained soil in light shade and high humidity (*P. longum*, *P. nigrum*). Deep, rich soil, including heavy clay, with ample moisture and shade (*P. betle*, *P. cubeba*). Well-drained, stony soil, with ample water, in shade (*P. methysticum*). All need minimum 59–64°F (15–18°C). Plants are usually grown on frames. Propagate by semiripe cuttings in summer. Remove weak or congested stems in late winter or early spring before new growth begins. For optimum fruiting (*P. nigrum*), cut back young plants to 12in (30cm) several times a year to stimulate growth of shoots, retaining the 10 strongest, and tying in at each node. Mature vines are pruned regularly to 12ft (4m).
HARVEST Leaves are picked as required, blanched in the dark, often pressed together, and dried for extracts or to use whole (*P. betle*). Roots are lifted as required, and used fresh, or dried for use in decoctions, liquid extracts, powders, and tablets (*P. methysticum*). Fruits are picked unripe and distilled for oleoresin and oil, or dried for use in liquid extracts, powders, and tinctures (*P. cubeba*). Fruit clusters are picked unripe and dried for use whole, ground, or in decoctions (*P. longum*). Fruits of *P. nigrum* are picked unripe and used fresh, pickled (green peppercorns), and dried (green and black peppercorns); or ripe, and retted for eight days before drying (white peppercorns); black peppercorns are ground or decocted for medicinal use.

PISCIDIA
(Leguminosae)

This genus includes eight or so species of trees occurring in C America, the W Indies, and Florida. *P. piscipula* was introduced to Europe from the W Indies in 1690. It was grown under cover during the 19th century but is seldom seen today. The name comes from the Latin *piscis*, "fish," and *caedere*, "to kill," and refers to the use of these plants by native N Americans to stupefy fish, so that they float to the surface and are easily caught. *Piscidia* is closely related, and similar in appearance, to *Lonchocarpus*, a much larger genus that is known for its fish poisons. Both genera contain rotenoids, which stun the fish but leave the flesh untainted and edible. One of these compounds is rotenone, a powerful insecticide, which is extracted from the East Indian legume *Derris elliptica* for commercial purposes. Although known as Jamaica dogwood, *Piscidia* is not related to dogwoods (*Cornus*, see p.267) and differs in appearance.

P. piscipula, syn. *P. erythrina* (Jamaica dogwood, fish poison tree)

Tender deciduous tree, height 50ft (15m), with pinnately divided leaves up to 10in (24cm) long. Blue-purple to white, red-striped flowers appear in panicles in spring before the new leaves, followed by winged pods, 3in (7cm) long. Found in dry woods in southern Florida and the W Indies.

PARTS USED Bark.
PROPERTIES A bitter, acrid, sedative herb with an opium-like aroma. It relaxes spasms, controls coughing, and relieves pain.
USES OF THE HERB
MEDICINAL Internally for whooping cough, asthma, neuralgia, migraine, nervous exhaustion, toothache, insomnia, painful menstruation, threatened miscarriage, and postpartum pain. Combined with *Viburnum prunifolium* (see p.369) for gynecological problems, and with *Passiflora incarnata* (see p.323), *Humulus lupulus* (see p.294), or *Valeriana officinalis* (see p.367) for severe symptoms of nervous tension, such as palpitations and panic attacks. Not given to pregnant women or patients with cardiac insufficiency. For use by qualified practitioners only.

GROWTH AND HARVEST

GROWTH Crop. Deep, well-drained soil in sun with high humidity, minimum 61–64°F (16–18°C). Propagate by seed sown in spring, or by semiripe cuttings in summer. Cut back hard after flowering to control size.
HARVEST Bark is collected as required and dried for use in liquid extracts and powders.

PISTACIA Pistachio
(Anacardiaceae)

P. lentiscus contains pinene, a strongly antiseptic volatile oil, more usually found in *Pinus* species (see p.329). *P. terebinthus* was described by Theophrastus in the first century BC as the source of turpentine, a viscous oleoresin, which is also obtained from various conifers, such as *Pinus palustris* (see p.329). Essence of turpentine, used in aromatherapy, is made by distilling this turpentine. Fioravanti's balm is a compound spirit of turpentine, made by distilling alcohol with turpentine and various other antirheumatic substances.

P. lentiscus (mastic tree, lentisc) p.178

PARTS USED Resin, oil.
PROPERTIES An aromatic, stimulant, antiseptic herb with a pinelike aroma. It has diuretic and expectorant effects, and controls bleeding.
USES OF THE HERB
MEDICINAL Externally for boils, ulcers, bronchitis, ringworm, and muscular stiffness.
ECONOMIC Resin and oil are used as fixatives in perfumery and also in the Greek confectionery *masticha* and in the liqueur *mastiche*. Resin is used in varnishes, lacquers, and for sealing edges of microscope mounts.

P. terebinthus (terebinth tree, Cyprus turpentine) p.178

PARTS USED Resin, essence.
PROPERTIES A bitter, aromatic, antiseptic herb that is expectorant, relaxes spasms, controls bleeding, promotes healing, and is effective against various parasitic organisms.
USES OF THE HERB
MEDICINAL Internally for streptococcal, urinary, and renal infections, chronic bronchial infections, hemorrhage, gallstones, tapeworm, and rheumatism. Externally for arthritis, gout, sciatica, scabies, and lice.

GROWTH AND HARVEST

GROWTH Crop. Well-drained to dry, sandy or stony, alkaline soil in sun, minimum 50°F (10°C). Propagate by seed sown in spring, or by semiripe cuttings in summer. Trim plants in spring to restrict size.
HARVEST Resin is obtained from incisions in bark from midsummer to midautumn, and dried for powder (*P. lentiscus*) or distilled for oil and essence (*P. lentiscus*, *P. terebinthus*).

PLANTAGO Plantain
(Plantaginaceae)

A number of different plantains are used medicinally, some for their leaves and others for their seeds. The main constituents in the foliage are tannins and iridoid glycosides, notably aucubin, which stimulates uric acid secretion from the kidneys. Plantain seeds contain up to 30 percent mucilage, which swells in the gut, acting as a bulk laxative and soothing irritated membranes. The husks, rather than whole seeds, are used in certain preparations. *P. asiatica*, the Chinese plantain, is very similar in appearance and chemistry to *P. major*. It was first recorded in Chinese medicine during the Han dynasty (206BC–AD23). *P. ovata* (blond psyllium, ispaghula) has pink- or gray-brown seeds, used interchangeably with those of *P. psyllium*. Other species, such as *P. indica* (black psyllium) and *P. arenaria* (golden psyllium), are also used.

P. asiatica, syn. *P. major* var. *asiatica* (Asian plantain) p.178

PARTS USED Whole plant (*che qian cao*), seeds (*che qian zi*).
PROPERTIES A cooling herb that is diuretic and expectorant, reduces inflammation, stops bleeding, and controls coughing.
USES OF THE HERB
MEDICINAL Internally for complaints associated with "overheating," such as acute infections of the lungs and urinary tract, hepatitis, and boils (whole plant); diarrhea, urinary complaints, coughs with profuse phlegm, conjunctivitis, and vertigo (seeds).
VARIANT
***P. a.* 'Variegata'**, p.179.

P. major (greater plantain, rat-tail plantain) p.179

PARTS USED Leaves.
PROPERTIES An astringent herb that is diuretic and expectorant, promotes healing, and is effective against bacterial infections.
USES OF THE HERB
MEDICINAL Internally for diarrhea, hemorrhage, hemorrhoids, cystitis, bronchitis, excesss mucus, sinusitis, asthma, hay fever, ear infections, dry coughs, and gastric ulcers. Externally for wounds, insect bites, ulcers, eye inflammations, shingles, hemorrhoids, and varicose ulcers. Often used to moderate the irritant effect of herbs containing volatile oils.
VARIANT
***P. m.* 'Rubrifolia'**, p.179.

P. psyllium (Spanish psyllium, fleaseed, fleawort) p.179

PARTS USED Seeds.
PROPERTIES A sweet, astringent, cooling herb that moistens membranes, soothes irritation, and absorbs digestive toxins.
USES OF THE HERB
MEDICINAL Internally for constipation and diarrhea. Externally for skin irritation and inflamed eyelids. Used in Ayurvedic medicine with buttermilk for diarrhea and with warm milk for constipation.
ECONOMIC Added to face masks and used as a fabric dressing.

GROWTH AND HARVEST

GROWTH Crop (*P. asiatica*, *P. major*, *P. psyllium*). Ornamental (*P.a.* 'Variegata', *P. m.* 'Rubrifolia'). Well-drained soil in sun (*P. asiatica*, *P. psyllium*); moist soil in sun or partial shade (*P. major*). The latter thrives in sandy, gravelly soil. Propagate by seed sown in spring (annuals and perennials), or by division in spring (perennials only). *P. major* and variants self-seed freely and may spread from borders. *P. m.* 'Rubrifolia' comes true from seed. *P. major* is prone to powdery mildew in dry conditions.
HARVEST Plants are cut during the growing season and used fresh, as juice, or dried for decoctions (*P. asiatica*). Leaves are cut before flowering and dried for infusions, liquid extracts, and tinctures (*P. major*). Ripe seeds are dried for decoctions and powders.

PLATYCLADUS
P. orientalis. See *Thuja orientalis*.

PLATYCODON
(Campanulaceae)

P. grandiflorus has a long history of use in traditional Chinese medicine, mentioned in the *Shen Nong Canon of Herbs* during the Han dynasty (206BC–AD23). It is widely used in patent remedies and sold as platycodi cough tablets.

P. grandiflorus (balloon flower, Chinese bellflower) p.179

PARTS USED Roots (*jie geng*).
PROPERTIES A bitter, pungent, warming herb that dilates the bronchial vessels; it is expectorant and effective against a number of disease-causing organisms.
USES OF THE HERB
CULINARY Roots are eaten in soup as a tonic vegetable (Korea), pickled, and preserved in sugar.
MEDICINAL Internally for coughs with profuse phlegm, colds, bronchitis, pleurisy, pulmonary abscess, and throat infections. Combined with *Glycyrrhiza uralensis* (see p.289) for throat infections.
VARIANT
P. g.* var. *apoyama, p.179.

GROWTH AND HARVEST

GROWTH Ornamental. Rich, well-drained, sandy soil in sun. Propagate by seed in autumn or spring, or by basal cuttings of nonflowering shoots in summer. Seedlings are very fragile and best planted when dormant.
HARVEST Roots are lifted in spring or autumn from plants 2–3 years old, peeled, and used fresh, or dried for decoctions and powders.

PLECTRANTHUS
(Labiatae/Lamiaceae)

P. amboinicus is SE Asian in origin but is widely used in Cuba, Mexico, and the W Indies as a food flavoring. *P. barbatus* has recently been the subject of scientific research because of its effects on the heart and circulation.

P. amboinicus, syn. *Coleus amboinicus* (Indian borage, oregano, Spanish thyme) p.179

PARTS USED Leaves.
PROPERTIES A strongly aromatic herb with the combined flavors of thyme, oregano, and savory. Little is known of its effects, other than that it reduces inflammation.
USES OF THE HERB
CULINARY Leaves are infused as tea, and added to beans, salads, and strong-smelling meat and fish, or cooked as tempura.
AROMATIC Fresh leaves scent hair and laundry.
MEDICINAL Internally for bronchitis, asthma, and postpartum pain. Externally for headache, sores, burns, and scorpion stings.

P. barbatus, syn. *Coleus barbatus*, *C. forskohlii* p.180

PARTS USED Whole plant.
PROPERTIES An aromatic herb that affects heart contractions and blood clotting.
USES OF THE HERB
AROMATIC Leaves have a strong, camphoraceous aroma, and are used as a body rub to cleanse and deodorize the skin.
MEDICINAL Under investigation for treating congestive heart disease, glaucoma, and chronic bronchial disease.

GROWTH AND HARVEST
GROWTH Ornamental (*P. amboinicus*). Crop (*P. barbatus*). Light, rich, well-drained soil in sun or partial shade, minimum 50–59°F (10–15°C). Provide ample moisture during the growing season but keep on the dry side in winter. Propagate by stem cuttings or division in spring or summer. Pinch out tips during the growing season to encourage bushy growth. Cut back straggly plants in spring.
HARVEST Plants are cut during the growing season and processed commercially (*P. barbatus*). Leaves of *P. amboinicus* are picked as required and used fresh.

PODOPHYLLUM
(Berberidaceae)

Podophyllums contain lignans, the most important of these being podophyllotoxin, and a resin known as podophyllin. These substances yield potent antitumor drugs, such as etoposide. They are highly toxic to cells, causing fetal death if ingested by pregnant women. The Himalayan *P. emodi* is especially rich in podophyllotoxin. *P. peltatum* was used in various ways by native N Americans: in minute doses as a purgative, emetic, vermifuge, and liver tonic, and externally for removing warts. The Menominee made a decoction of the plant as an insecticide for potato crops. It was also used in suicide.

P. peltatum (Mayapple, American mandrake, wild lemon) p.180

PARTS USED Rhizomes, resin.
PROPERTIES An acrid, caustic herb, with an unpleasant smell, that has anticancer and antiviral effects. It is a drastic purgative.
USES OF THE HERB
MEDICINAL Internally for certain cancers. Externally for venereal warts and verrucae. Not given to pregnant women. WARNING This herb is subject to legal restrictions in most countries.

GROWTH AND HARVEST
GROWTH Ornamental. Humus-rich, moist soil, pH4.0–7.0, in sheltered semishade. Young leaves may be damaged by frost in cold areas. Propagate by seed sown in autumn or spring, or by division in spring.
HARVEST Rhizomes are lifted in autumn and dried for use in tinctures and for commercial extraction of resin.
WARNING Extremely toxic if eaten. Handling may cause systemic poisoning.

POGOSTEMON
(Labiatae/Lamiaceae)

In the East, patchouli oil is thought to prevent the spread of infection and is widely used for this purpose. It is produced from various different and, in some cases, unrelated species. *P. heyneanus* yields an inferior oil, known as "Java patchouli," or "dilem." Other sources include *P. comosus*, *Microtaena cymosa*, and *Plectranthus patchouli*.

P. cablin, syn. *P. patchouli* (patchouli) p.180

PARTS USED Leaves, oil.
PROPERTIES An astringent, antiseptic, warming herb with a long-lasting, pervasive aroma. It acts as a diuretic, lowers fever, improves digestion, controls vomiting, has both a tonic and sedative effect on the nervous system, and is reputedly aphrodisiac.
USES OF THE HERB
AROMATIC Leaves are added to potpourris. Oil is of major importance in perfumery.
MEDICINAL Internally for colds, headache, nausea, vomiting, abdominal pain, and diarrhea. Externally for halitosis, snakebite, fungal skin infections, weeping eczema, acne, chapped skin, and impetigo. Used in aromatherapy for nervous exhaustion, depression, stress-related complaints, low libido, and frigidity.
ECONOMIC Oil is used in toiletries, cosmetics, breath fresheners, and incense; also used in insecticides and disinfectants.

GROWTH AND HARVEST
GROWTH Crop. Rich, moist soil with high humidity, minimum 61–64°F (16–18°C). Propagate by seed, when available, sown in spring (plants rarely set seed), or by greenwood cuttings (most usual method) with a heel in late spring, or by division in spring or autumn. Pinch out or cut back plants in spring to encourage bushy growth.
HARVEST Leaves are cut two or three times a year and dried, mainly for oil distillation.

POLEMONIUM Jacob's ladder
(Polemoniaceae)

Both *P. caeruleum* and *P. reptans* are often called "Greek valerian," though they are not related to true valerian (*Valeriana officinalis*, see p.367) and have quite different medicinal properties. The plants do, however, attract cats, who roll in them with evident pleasure. In ancient Greek times *P. caeruleum* was prescribed in wine for dysentery, toothache, and poisonous bites. It passed into various European pharmacopoeias as *herba valerianae graeca*, and was used mainly for rabies and syphilis. Being ornamental and easily grown, *P. caeruleum* and *P. reptans* are widely seen in herb gardens, though they are seldom used for medicinal purposes today. *P. caeruleum* is a variable species with a wide range of named variants. In *A Modern Herbal* (1931), Mrs. Grieve refers to a "handsome form, frequent in gardens" with variegated leaves and white flowers, which seems to have disappeared from cultivation.

P. caeruleum (Jacob's ladder, Greek valerian, charity) p.180

PARTS USED Whole plant.
PROPERTIES A slightly bitter, odorless, astringent herb that increases perspiration.
USES OF THE HERB
MEDICINAL Formerly used internally for a range of conditions, from headaches to fevers and epilepsy.
VARIANT
***P. c.* 'Album'**, p.180.

P. reptans (abscess root, Greek valerian) p.180

PARTS USED Rhizome.
PROPERTIES A slightly bitter, acrid, astringent herb that increases perspiration and has expectorant and alterative effects.
USES OF THE HERB
MEDICINAL Internally for coughs, colds, bronchitis, laryngitis, tuberculosis, and feverish and inflammatory conditions, including skin diseases and poisonous bites. Rarely used today.
VARIANT
***P. r.* 'Pink Beauty'**
This cultivar, height 6–12in (15-30cm), spread 15in (38cm), is hardy to 5°F (–15°C). It has pink flowers.

GROWTH AND HARVEST
GROWTH Ornamental. Moist soil in sun or partial shade. *P. caeruleum* tolerates alkaline conditions; *P. reptans* prefers humus-rich soil. Propagate by seed in spring, or by division in spring. Cultivars may not come true from seed. Cut back flower stems to base after flowering, unless seed is required. *P. caeruleum* may self-seed excessively in optimum conditions.
HARVEST Plants (*P. caeruleum*) are cut in summer for infusions. Rhizomes (*P. reptans*) are lifted in winter and dried for decoctions and tinctures.

POLYGALA Milkwort
(Polygalaceae)

This large genus includes about 500 species of annuals, perennials, shrubs, and trees, which are found almost worldwide. A few are grown as ornamentals for their pea flowers, but the medicinal species have little merit as garden plants. The N American Seneca people used *P. senega* against rattlesnake bite; its present uses were discovered in about 1735 by John Tennent, a Scottish physician, who observed that the symptoms of the bite were similar to those of pleurisy and the later stages of pneumonia. Experiments in using it for respiratory diseases were so successful that by 1740 the plant was being cultivated and used in Europe. *P. tenuifolia* was first recorded in traditional Chinese medicine during the earlier Han dynasty (206BC–AD23). Both *P. senega* and *P. tenuifolia* contain similar compounds but are used rather differently in European and Chinese herbal medicine. The European *P. vulgaris* (common milkwort) has similar properties but is less potent. The bitter-tasting *P. amarella* (dwarf milkwort) is also used.

Contrary to traditional belief, use of these plants does not increase lactation.

P. senega (Seneca snakeroot, rattlesnake root)

Perennial, hardy to 23°F (–5°C), height and spread 18in (45cm), with a thick root and linear-lanceolate leaves up to 2in (5cm) long. Small white flowers are produced in terminal racemes in summer. Found in rocky, dry woods in most mountainous areas of N America.

PARTS USED Roots.
PROPERTIES A bitter, acrid, warming herb that has expectorant effects and increases salivation and perspiration.
USES OF THE HERB
MEDICINAL Internally for bronchitis, excess mucus, asthma, and croup. Excess causes diarrhea and vomiting. Externally for pharyngitis and snakebite.

P. tenuifolia (Siberian milkwort)

Perennial, hardy to 5°F (–15°C), height and spread 10in (25cm), with thin stems and linear leaves, up to 1¼in (3cm) long. Pale violet to blue flowers appear in lateral branches, followed by capsules ¼in (5mm) in diameter. Found in dry meadows and stony slopes in Siberia, Mongolia, and China.

PARTS USED Roots (*yuan zhi*).
PROPERTIES A pungent, bitter, warming herb that lowers blood pressure and has expectorant, anti-bacterial, and tranquilizing effects. It acts mainly as a tonic for heart and kidney energies.
USES OF THE HERB
MEDICINAL Internally for coughs with profuse phlegm, bronchitis, insomnia, palpitations, poor memory, anxiety, depression, and nervous tension. Externally for boils and carbuncles. Combined with *Glycyrrhiza uralensis* (see p.289) for coughs in heavy smokers.

GROWTH AND HARVEST
GROWTH Crop. Well-drained, moisture-retentive soil in sun or part shade. Propagate by seed sown in spring, or by softwood cuttings in spring, or by semiripe cuttings in late summer.
HARVEST Roots are lifted in autumn and dried for use in decoctions, concentrated infusions, liquid extracts, powders, and tinctures.

POLYGONATUM Solomon's seal
(Liliaceae/Convallariaceae)

Several sources list *P. multiflorum*, rather than *P. odoratum,* as the species used medicinally. Both are quite rare in the wild. Most plants in cultivation are hybrids between *P. multiflorum* and *P. odoratum*, and there is probably little difference in their constituents.

P. odoratum, syn. *P. officinale* (angular Solomon's seal) p.181

PARTS USED Rhizomes (*yu zhu*).
PROPERTIES A bittersweet, astringent, tonic herb that acts as an expectorant, soothes irritated or damaged tissues, reduces inflammation, and clears toxins.
USES OF THE HERB
MEDICINAL Internally, in Chinese medicine, for

heart disease, tuberculosis, dry cough, dry throat in diabetes, and to encourage secretion of body fluids. In Western herbalism, internally for coughs and gastric irritation; externally for bruises, broken nose, hemorrhoids, rupture, and dislocations. Internally, in Ayurvedic medicine, as a rejuvenative and aphrodisiac; one of eight root herbs (mostly belonging to the lily family) known as *ashtavarga*, used for infertility, insufficient lactation, chronic wasting diseases, and bleeding disorders related to kidney weakness. Given with warm milk and *ghee* as a tonic.
VARIANT
P. o. **'Variegatum'**, p.181.

GROWTH AND HARVEST
GROWTH Ornamental. Well-drained, moist, humus-rich soil in part shade, or in sun with a cool root run. Propagate by seed sown in autumn, or by division in early spring. Leaves may be damaged by caterpillars.
HARVEST Rhizomes are lifted in autumn and used fresh in tinctures and ointments, or dried for use in decoctions and powders.
WARNING All parts, especially the berries, are harmful if eaten.

POLYGONUM Knotweed
(Polygonaceae)

P. bistorta was once known as "serpentaria" because of its contorted, snakelike rhizomes. *P. hydropiper* (smartweed, water pepper) is also used medicinally, mainly for failure to menstruate. *P. multiflorum* has a tonic effect on the kidneys and liver. It is a major Chinese tonic herb with a long history of use, being first described in medical literature in AD713. Its Chinese name means "black-haired mister," alluding to its fame as a hair restorative. Similar in appearance to *P. hydropiper* is the tender, moisture-loving *P. odoratum* (Vietnamese coriander, *rau ram*), used as a medicinal and culinary herb in SE Asia. It has a lemon–coriander aroma and is added to meat dishes (especially fowl), duck eggs, and the sauerkraut-like *du'a cân*.

P. bistorta, syn. *Persicaria bistorta* (bistort, snakeweed, English serpentary) p.181

PARTS USED Rhizomes.
PROPERTIES An astringent, soothing, cooling herb that reduces inflammation, controls diarrhea and bleeding, and promotes healing.
USES OF THE HERB
MEDICINAL Internally for diarrhea (especially in babies), cholera, dysentery, excess mucus, cystitis, mucous colitis, and excessive menstruation. Externally for pharyngitis, stomatitis, vaginal discharge, anal fissure, purulent wounds, hemorrhoids, mouth ulcers, and gum disease. Combines well with *Geranium maculatum* (see p.288), *Agrimonia eupatoria* (see p.231), or *Quercus robur* (see p.338) for diarrhea.

VARIANT
P. b. **'Superbum'**, p.181.

P. multiflorum (flowery knotweed, Chinese cornbind)

Deciduous climber, hardy to 5°F (–15°C), height 22–30ft (7–10m), with a tuberous rhizome, red stems when young, and light green, ovate leaves up to 3in (7cm) long. Small white or pink-tinted flowers are produced in slender panicles, 8–10in (20–24cm) long, in autumn, followed by 3-winged fruits. Native to southwestern China.

PARTS USED Roots (*he shou wu*, *fo ti*), stems (*shou wou teng*).
PROPERTIES A bittersweet, astringent, slightly warming herb that has a tonic, rejuvenative effect on the liver and the reproductive, urinary, and circulatory systems. It lowers blood sugar and cholesterol levels, clears toxins, and is effective against many bacterial infections.
USES OF THE HERB
MEDICINAL Internally for menstrual and menopausal complaints, weak kidney and liver energy, constipation in the elderly, swollen lymph glands, and high cholesterol (roots), insomnia and neurasthenia (stems). Externally for bleeding wounds and sores (roots), and ringworm (roots and stems). Roots are combined, in Chinese medicine, with *Panax ginseng* (see p.321) and *Angelica polymorpha* var. *sinensis* (see p.238) as a tonic. Excess may cause skin rash and numbness of the extremities.

GROWTH AND HARVEST
GROWTH Ornamental (*P. bistorta*, *P. b.* 'Superbum'). Crop (*P. multiflorum*). Rich, moist soil in sun or partial shade. *P. multiflorum* needs additional peat, sand, and leaf mold, and protection from severe weather. Propagate by seed in autumn or spring, or by division in autumn or spring, or by semiripe cuttings in summer (*P. multiflorum*), which root easily in soil or water. Cut back to 12in (30cm) above ground level in spring (*P. multiflorum*). Aphids may attack young growths of *P. multiflorum.*
HARVEST Rhizomes (*P. bistorta*) are lifted in autumn and dried for decoctions, infusions, liquid extracts, powders, and tinctures; roots of *P. multiflorum* similarly for decoctions, extracts, pills, powders, poultices, and tinctures. Crops of *P. multiflorum* are harvested for roots when 3–4 years old. Stems are cut in late summer and autumn, and sun-dried for decoctions and poultices.

POLYPODIUM Polypody
(Polypodiaceae)

P. vulgare was prescribed by Dioscorides as a laxative and used as a poultice for sprains and fractures. The rhizome is rich in mucilage that contains osladin, a sweet-tasting saponin. This sweetness is particularly noticeable in *P. glycyrrhiza* (licorice fern), which was used by native N Americans to treat measles and coughs.

P. vulgare (polypody) p.181

PARTS USED Rhizomes.
PROPERTIES A very sweet, slightly acrid, warming

herb that acts as an expectorant and diuretic, increases bile flow, promotes healing, improves digestion and liver function, and kills intestinal worms. It also has antirheumatic, alterative, and mild purgative effects.
USES OF THE HERB
MEDICINAL Internally for dry cough, excess bronchial mucus, chest infections, arthritis, indigestion, poor appetite, skin diseases, and intestinal parasites (especially tapeworm). Externally for wounds. May cause a harmless rash.
VARIANT
P. v. **'Cornubiense'**, p.182.

GROWTH AND HARVEST
GROWTH Ornamental. Moist, well-drained, humus-rich soil in semishade. Propagates by spores in late summer (species only), or by division in spring. Leaves may be damaged by rust.
HARVEST Rhizomes are lifted in autumn and used, usually fresh, in decoctions, liquid extracts, syrups, and tinctures.

POPULUS Poplar
(Salicaceae)

Poplars are closely related to willows (*Salix* species, see p.345) and similarly contain salicin, which reduces inflammation and relieves pain. Salicylates are the origin of aspirin, which was synthesized in the 19th century. The chemistries of many poplars are so alike that various different species are used interchangeably. Poplar bark comes mainly from *P. alba*, but *P. nigra* (black poplar), *P. tremuloides* (American aspen), and other species are also used. *P. alba* was listed in the *U.S. Pharmacopoeia* (1895–1936) as a remedy for fevers and menstrual pain. Poplar buds are collected mainly from *P.* x *candicans*, but again, other sources include *P. balsamifera* (balsam poplar) and *P. nigra*. Poplar buds were listed in the *U.S. Pharmacopoeia* (1916–65) as an expectorant and stimulant. *P.* x *candicans* is often confused with other plants known as "balm of Gilead," such as *Abies balsamea* (see p.226) and *Cedronella canariensis* (see p.256).

P. alba (white poplar, abele) p.182

PARTS USED Bark.
PROPERTIES An astringent, diuretic, cooling herb that reduces inflammation, relieves pain, and acts as a bitter tonic and alterative.
USES OF THE HERB
MEDICINAL Internally for rheumatoid arthritis, gout, fevers, lower back pain, urinary complaints, digestive and liver disorders, debility, and anorexia.
Externally for chilblains, hemorrhoids, infected wounds, and sprains. Combined with *Cimicifuga racemosa* (see p.261) and *Menyanthes trifoliata* (see p.312) for rheumatoid arthritis, and with *Mahonia aquifolium* (see p.308) and *Chelone glabra* (see p.259) for anorexia.
VARIANT
P. a. **'Richardii'**, p.182.

P. x *candicans*, syn. *P.* x *gileadensis* (balm of Gilead, Ontario poplar) p.182

PARTS USED Leaf buds.
PROPERTIES An antiseptic, expectorant herb that lowers fever and stimulates the circulation. Applied topically, it relieves pain and improves blood flow to the area.
USES OF THE HERB
AROMATIC Dried buds are added to potpourris.
MEDICINAL Internally for bronchitis and upper respiratory tract infections. Not given to patients sensitive to aspirin. Externally for colds, sinusitis, arthritis, rheumatism, muscular pain, and dry skin conditions. Widely used in cough mixtures, often with *Pinus strobus* and *Prunus serotina* (see p.335).
VARIANT
P. x *c.* **'Aurora'**, p.182.

GROWTH AND HARVEST
GROWTH Ornamental. Deep, moist, well-drained soil in sun. *P. alba* tolerates drier conditions than most poplars. Propagate by hardwood cuttings in winter. Prune *P.* x *candicans* 'Aurora' hard in late winter to encourage vigorous shoots and colorful new leaves. Prone to bacterial canker and fungal diseases. Aphids, poplar beetle larvae, and caterpillars may attack leaves. Poplars have extensive root systems and should not be planted close to buildings or drainage systems.
HARVEST Buds are collected in spring before opening (*P.* x *candicans*), and dried for infusions, liquid extracts, and tinctures. Bark is stripped from side branches or coppiced trees and dried for decoctions, liquid extracts, and powders.

PORIA
P. cocos. See *Wolfiporia cocos.*

PORTERANTHUS
P. trifoliatus. See *Gillenia trifoliata.*

PORTULACA Purslane
(Portulacaceae)

Recent research has shown that *P. oleracea* is a rich source of omega-3 fatty acids, which are thought to be important in preventing heart attacks and strengthening the immune system. *P. oleracea* was first described in Chinese medical literature c.AD500. *P. grandiflora* (moss rose) is also used, mainly in the form of fresh juice for hepatitis or as a lotion for snake and insect bites, burns, scalds, and eczema.

P. oleracea (purslane) p.182

PARTS USED Whole plant (*ma chi xian*), leaves.
PROPERTIES A sour, diuretic, cooling herb that lowers fever and clears toxins. It is effective against many bacterial infections.
USES OF THE HERB
CULINARY Leaves are cooked as a vegetable, pickled in vinegar, and added to sauces and salads, especially the Middle Eastern *fattoush*.
MEDICINAL Internally for dysentery, acute enteritis, appendicitis, mastitis, hemorrhoids, and postpartum bleeding. Not given to pregnant women or to patients with digestive problems. Externally for boils, snakebite, bee stings, and eczema.
VARIANT
P. o. var. ***aurea***, p.182.

GROWTH AND HARVEST
GROWTH Ornamental. Rich, moist, well-drained soil in sun. Propagate by seed sown in spring. Plants may be damaged by aphids and slugs.
HARVEST Plants are cut in summer, usually before flowering, and used fresh, or dried for use in decoctions. Leaves and young shoots are picked before flowering and used fresh. The cultivated forms have a superior flavor to the more common, weedy forms.

POTENTILLA Cinquefoil
(Rosaceae)

Several species are used medicinally for their high content of tannins, which in *P. erecta* approaches 20 percent. These include *P. anserina* (silverweed) and *P. reptans* (creeping cinquefoil, fiveleaf grass).

P. erecta, syn. *P. tormentilla* (tormentil, bloodroot) p.183

PARTS USED Roots.
PROPERTIES A bitter, astringent, cooling herb that controls bleeding, reduces inflammation, and promotes healing.
USES OF THE HERB
MEDICINAL Internally for diarrhea, enteritis, Crohn's disease, mucous colitis, ulcerative colitis, gastritis, diverticulitis, peptic ulcer, and inflammation of the colon. Externally for hemorrhoids, vaginal discharge, sore throat, mouth ulcers, cuts, sores, ulcers, burns, sunburn, frostbite, and shingles. Care is needed in topical application of strong tannins, which can cause scarring.

GROWTH AND HARVEST
GROWTH Crop. Moist or dry acid soil in sun or light shade. Propagate by seed in autumn or spring, or by division in autumn or spring.
HARVEST Roots are lifted in autumn or spring and dried for use in infusions, liquid extracts, powders, and tinctures.

POTERIUM
P. officinalis. See *Sanguisorba officinalis.*

PRIMULA
(Primulaceae)

P. veris and *P. vulgaris* have a long history of use as medicinal herbs. The latter was recommended by Pliny for paralysis, gout, and rheumatism, and by Culpeper for healing wounds. *P. veris* was once known as *herba paralysis*, *radix arthritica*, and "palsywort," on account of its widespread use, dating back to at least medieval times, for conditions involving spasms, cramps, paralysis, and rheumatic pain. Culpeper also prescribed the flowers, mixed with nutmeg, for "all infirmities of the head," and referred to the use of the leaves "by our city dames" in cosmetics to enhance beauty and to treat "spots and wrinkles of the skin, sun-burning and freckles." Until cowslips became quite rare in this century, through habitat loss and modern farming practices, the flowers were collected each spring to make wine, which was taken largely as a sedative and nervine. Both species have similar constituents that may be used interchangeably; these include saponins, which have an expectorant effect, and salicylates (as in aspirin). *P. veris* is the more widely used today.

P. veris (cowslip, paigle) p.183

Parts used Roots, flowers.
Properties A sedative, expectorant herb that relaxes spasms and reduces inflammation.
Uses of the herb
Culinary Flowers are added fresh to salads; also candied and used for making country wines and tea.
Medicinal Internally for bronchitis, dry cough, whooping cough, arthritis, insomnia, headache, and restlessness (especially in children). Not given during pregnancy, or to patients sensitive to aspirin or taking anticoagulant drugs (such as warfarin). Externally for facial neuralgia, arthritic pain, skin blemishes, sunburn, and migraine.

P. vulgaris (primrose) p.183

Parts used Whole plant, leaves, roots, flowers.
Properties An expectorant, anti-inflammatory herb that relieves pain, relaxes spasms, and promotes healing.
Uses of the herb
Culinary Flowers and young leaves are added to salads. Flowers are used to make desserts, such as primrose pottage, based on ground rice flavored with saffron, honey, and almonds.
Medicinal Internally for bronchitis, respiratory tract infections, insomnia, anxiety, rheumatic disorders, and gout. Not given during pregnancy, or to patients sensitive to aspirin or taking anti-coagulant drugs (such as warfarin). Externally for minor wounds, and nerve and joint pain. May be used as a substitute for *P. veris*, although generally considered less effective.
Variants
P. v. **'Alba Plena'**, p.183.
P. v. subsp. ***sibthorpii***, p.183.

Growth and Harvest
Growth Ornamental. Dry, neutral to alkaline soil in sun or partial shade (*P. veris*). Moist, well-drained soil in sun or shade (*P. vulgaris*). Propagate by seed sown in late summer (except for cultivars), or by division in late spring or early autumn. Regular division is necessary to ensure vigor. Plants may be affected by rust, *Botrytis*, leafspot, and other fungal and viral diseases. Aphids, caterpillars, cutworms, and vine weevils may damage leaves.
Harvest Flowers (including calyx) are picked in spring and used fresh, or dried for use in infusions, ointments, and tinctures. Whole plant (*P. vulgaris*) is cut when flowering and dried for use in infusions. Roots are lifted in spring (*P. veris*), or autumn of second year (*P. vulgaris*), and dried for decoctions and tinctures.
Warning Skin irritant and allergen.

PROSTANTHERA Mint bush
(Labiatae/Lamiaceae)

Mint bushes are rich in volatile oils, including menthol and cineole (as found in *Mentha* species, see p.311), which have bactericidal and fungicidal properties. Several species, including *P. cineolifera*, were used by Australian Aborigines in infusions to relieve headaches and colds.

P. rotundifolia (round-leaved mint bush) p.183

Parts used Leaves.
Properties An aromatic, decongestant herb that has antibacterial and antifungal effects.
Uses of the herb
Aromatic Leaves are added to potpourris.
Medicinal Externally for colds and headaches.

Growth and Harvest
Growth Ornamental. Well-drained soil in sun or partial shade, minimum 23°F (-5°C). Propagate by seed in spring, or by semiripe cuttings from late summer to autumn. Prune lightly immediately after flowering. Prostantheras dislike hard pruning.
Harvest Leaves are picked as required for infusions, and dried for potpourris.

PRUNELLA Selfheal
(Labiatae/Lamiaceae)

P. vulgaris has a long history of use in traditional medicine. It was first mentioned in Chinese medical literature during the Han dynasty (206BC–AD23), mainly for complaints associated with disturbed liver energy. European herbalists have always regarded it primarily as a wound herb.

P. vulgaris (selfheal, heal-all) p.183

Parts used Whole plant, flowers (*xia ku cao*).
Properties An astringent, slightly bitter, saline herb that lowers fever and blood pressure, stimulates the liver and gall bladder, and promotes healing. It has diuretic, antibacterial, and alterative effects.

Uses of the herb
Medicinal Internally, in Western medicine, for hemorrhage and excessive menstruation (whole plant); in Chinese medicine, often combined with *Dendranthema* x *grandiflorum* (see p.272), for headaches, high blood pressure, mumps, mastitis, conjunctivitis, and hyperactivity in children related to liver energy problems (flowers). Externally, in Western medicine, for minor injuries, sores, burns, bruises, sore throat, mouth inflammations, and hemorrhoids (whole plant).

Growth and Harvest
Growth Ornamental. Moist, well-drained soil in sun or light shade. Propagate by seed sown in autumn or spring, or by division in spring. *P. vulgaris* is rather invasive but easily controlled.
Harvest Plants are cut in summer when flowering and dried for use in infusions, ointments, and tinctures. Flower spikes are cut in late autumn and dried for use in decoctions.

PRUNUS Plum, cherry, peach
(Rosaceae)

Many species are used medicinally, yielding a range of therapeutic products, from emollient oils to cough cures and laxatives. The Chinese species have a particularly long history of use: *P. armeniaca* and *P. mume* were first mentioned in medical literature c.AD500, and references to *P. japonica* date back to the Han dynasty (206BC–AD23). Most of the medicinal properties result from the presence of amygdalin and prunasin, which break down in water to form hydrocyanic acid (cyanide). In small amounts, this exceedingly poisonous compound stimulates respiration, improves digestion, and gives a sense of well-being. Also present is benzaldehyde, which gives the typical almond scent. This is now synthesized as a substitute for bitter almond oil in food flavoring. *P. africana* (African cherry, red stinkwood) has become more important since the 1960s, when it was found to contain a liposoluble complex that has proved effective in treating prostate gland enlargement. The bark has long been used by traditional healers, but recent large-scale demand has led to severe shortages, notably in Cameroon, where restrictions on bark removal were imposed in 1991. Plantations are now being established to relieve pressure on wild populations. Although little used today, the fruit stalks of *P. avium* (wild cherry, gean) and various other species were infused to make a diuretic, astringent tonic for cystitis, edema, and diarrhea. *P. serotina* was first listed in the *U.S. Pharmacopoeia* in 1820 as a sedative and antitussive. It was used by the Cherokee people to relieve labor pains. *P. spinosa* (blackthorn) is a useful plant for hedging in cold, exposed, or coastal areas, and yields small, blue-black, very astringent fruits (sloes), which are the flavoring in sloe gin.

P. armeniaca (wild apricot) p.184

PARTS USED Fruits, kernels (*xing ren*), oil.
PROPERTIES A bittersweet, warming, lubricant herb that is expectorant and controls coughing. Extracted laetrile has been used in cancer therapy.

USES OF THE HERB
CULINARY Fruits are eaten fresh, dried, or preserved, and used to make jams and juice.
MEDICINAL Internally for dry coughs, bronchitis, asthma, emphysema, and dry constipation. Excess causes central nervous system depression and respiratory failure. Toxicity of amygdalin is reduced by stir-baking or steaming, and may be neutralized by a decoction of the outer bark.
ECONOMIC Oil is used in cosmetics. Fruits are used to make brandy and liqueurs.
VARIANT
***P. a.* 'Hemskerk'**, p.184.

P. domestica (plum) p.184

PARTS USED Dried fruits (prunes).
PROPERTIES A cooling, lubricant, laxative herb.
USES OF THE HERB
CULINARY Prunes are eaten dried, soaked, and cooked, preserved in brandy or vinegar, and in sauces or stews (especially the Arab *tadjub ahmar*), stuffings, desserts, and cakes.
MEDICINAL Internally for constipation. Often added to laxative preparations.
ECONOMIC Prunes are sold pitted and unpitted, and may have mineral oil and preservatives (such as sulfur dioxide) added to enhance their keeping qualities and appearance.
VARIANT
***P. d.* 'Prune d'Agen'**, p.184.

P. dulcis, syn. *P. amygdalus* (almond) p.184

PARTS USED Seeds, oil.
PROPERTIES A soothing, laxative herb that relaxes spasms.
USES OF THE HERB
MEDICINAL Internally for kidney stones, gallstones, and constipation. Externally for dry skin conditions.
ECONOMIC Sweet almond oil is used in the manufacture of emulsions for medicines, massage oils, skincare preparations, and cosmetics. Bitter almond oil is used in commercial food flavoring, especially in cakes, biscuits, candy, ice cream, maraschino cherries, and marzipan.
VARIANT
***P. d.* 'Macrocarpa'**
Deciduous shrub or tree, hardy to 5°F (–15°C), height and spread 25ft (8m). It has pale pink to white flowers, and large fruits.

P. japonica (oriental bush cherry, Chinese plum)

Deciduous shrub, hardy to 5°F (–15°C), height and spread 5ft (1.5m), with wiry branches and ovate, pointed leaves up to 3in (7cm) long. Small white or pale pink flowers are produced in spring, followed by dark red fruits, about ½in (1cm) across. Found in woods from central China to Korea and Japan.

PARTS USED Seeds (*yu li ren*).
PROPERTIES A bittersweet, pungent, laxative herb that is diuretic and lowers blood pressure.
USES OF THE HERB
MEDICINAL Internally for dry constipation and edema, and in folk medicine for insomnia following trauma. Often combined with *Cannabis sativa* (see p.253) for chronic constipation.

P. laurocerasus (cherry laurel, laurel) p.184

PARTS USED Leaves (distilled extract [cherry laurel water] and oil).
PROPERTIES A very poisonous, sedative herb that relaxes spasms, improves digestion, and controls coughing.
USES OF THE HERB
MEDICINAL Internally for nausea and vomiting. Externally for eye infections (cherry laurel water).
ECONOMIC Water and detoxified oil are used in commercial food flavoring.
VARIANTS
***P. l.* 'Castlewellan'**, syn. *P. l.* 'Marbled White', p.185.
***P. l.* 'Schipkaensis'**, p.185.

P. mume (Japanese apricot)

Deciduous tree, hardy to 5°F (–15°C), height 28ft (9m), spread 15–20ft (5–6m), with green twigs when young and broadly ovate to rounded, toothed leaves up to 4in (10cm) long. Pale pink, solitary or paired, almond-scented flowers, 1½in (3cm) across, appear along the bare branches in late winter, followed by globose, slightly downy, yellow fruits, 1¼in (3cm) in diameter. Native to southern Japan.

PARTS USED Unripe fruits (*wu mei*).
PROPERTIES An astringent, sour herb that expels intestinal parasites and stimulates bile flow.
USES OF THE HERB
CULINARY Fruits are pickled and also used to make plum wine and liqueurs.
MEDICINAL Internally for chronic coughs, chronic diarrhea, and roundworms. Externally for fungal skin infections, corns, and warts.
VARIANT
***P. m.* 'Beni-chidori'**, syn. *P. m.* 'Beni-shidori', p.185.

P. persica (peach) p.185

PARTS USED Leaves, bark, fruits, flowers, seeds (*tao ren*), oil.
PROPERTIES A bittersweet, soothing, laxative herb that controls coughing, stimulates the uterus and circulatory system, lowers fever, and is diuretic, sedative, and expectorant.
USES OF THE HERB
CULINARY Fruits are eaten fresh, cooked, and preserved.
MEDICINAL Internally, in Western medicine, for gastritis, coughs, whooping cough, and bronchitis (bark, leaves); in Chinese medicine, for malaria, boils, hemorrhoids, and eczema (leaves); constipation and edema (flowers); constipation in the elderly, coughs, asthma, and menstrual disorders (seeds). Not given to pregnant women.
ECONOMIC Oil is used in skin creams. Fruits are used to flavor candy and ice cream.

P. serotina (black cherry, wild rum cherry) p.185

PARTS USED Bark.
PROPERTIES A bitter, astringent, warming herb that controls coughing, increases perspiration rate, improves digestion, and has sedative, anti-bacterial, and antiviral effects.
USES OF THE HERB
MEDICINAL Internally for chronic and dry coughs, whooping cough, bronchitis, nervous dyspepsia, poor digestion, gastritis, diarrhea, and convalescent debility.

GROWTH AND HARVEST

GROWTH Crop (*P. armeniaca* 'Hemskerk', *P. dulcis* 'Macrocarpa', *P. laurocerasus*, *P. l.* 'Castlewellan', *P. l.* 'Schipkaensis', *P. mume*, *P. m.* 'Beni-chidori', *P. m.* 'Pendula', *P. serotina:* ornamental). Well-drained, neutral to alkaline soil in sun. *P. laurocerasus* tolerates shade. Propagate by seed in autumn (deciduous species), or by softwood cuttings in summer (deciduous species and variants), or by semiripe cuttings in summer (*P. laurocerasus*). Prune fruiting specimens in summer to restrict growth and encourage formation of fruit buds. Trim *P. laurocerasus* in spring. Leaves and young shoots are often attacked by aphids and caterpillars. Diseases and disorders include peach leaf curl, bacterial canker, chlorosis, witches' broom, and root rot. *P. laurocerasus* may be affected by borers, leafspot, and powdery mildew. Most *Prunus* spp. are shallow-rooted and will sucker if roots are damaged. Early-flowering species are prone to frost damage in cold springs.
HARVEST Leaves (*P. persica, P. laurocerasus*) are picked in summer and dried for infusions, or (*P. laurocerasus* only) distilled for aqueous extract and oil. Bark (*P. persica*, *P. serotina*) is stripped in autumn and dried for infusions, liquid extracts, powders, syrups, and tinctures. Flowers (*P. persica*) are gathered in spring, and unripe fruits (*P. armeniaca*, *P. domestica*, *P. mume*, *P. persica*) in summer, and dried for decoctions. Fruits of prune cultivars of *P. domestica* may be dried on or off trees. Seeds from ripe fruits are dried for decoctions (*P. japonica*) or crushed for oil (*P. armeniaca*, *P. dulcis*, *P. persica*).
WARNING All parts of *P. laurocerasus*, notably the leaves and seeds, are harmful if eaten.

PSORALEA Scurf pea
(Leguminosae/Papilionaceae)

About 130 species of perennials and subshrubs belong to this genus, which ranges through N and S America, S Africa, and Asia. A number of the Cape species were grown as ornamentals during the 19th century. *Psoralea* seeds are used medicinally in both Ayurvedic and Chinese medicine; they were first described in Chinese medical literature c.AD470. Some species, including the N American *P. esculenta*, have edible tubers.

P. corylifolia (Malay tea, scurf pea, *babchi*)

Tender, erect annual, height 3ft (90cm), spread 4–8in (10–20cm), with simple, broadly ovate, toothed leaves up to 3in (7.5cm) long. Yellow cloverlike flowers appear in long-stalked clusters from spring to summer, followed by short, black pods containing compressed, oval, yellow-black seeds, about ⅙in (4mm) long. Found on arable land in Asia (mainly in India and Iran).

PARTS USED Seeds (*bu gu zhi*).
PROPERTIES A bitter, astringent, warming herb that stimulates kidney (*yang*) energy, and has diuretic and antibacterial effects.
USES OF THE HERB
MEDICINAL Internally, in Chinese medicine, for disorders related to kidney weakness, such as early morning diarrhea, urinary complaints, impotence, asthma, and alopecia. May be mixed with salt to increase action on kidneys. Injection of psoralea extract has been used with considerable success in Chinese research to treat alopecia. Internally and externally, in Ayurvedic medicine, for skin diseases and hair loss.

P. linearis. See *Aspalathus linearis*.

GROWTH AND HARVEST
GROWTH Crop. Well-drained soil in sun, minimum 50–59°F (10–15°C). Propagate by seed sown in spring, soaked in hot water to speed germination.
HARVEST Seeds are collected when ripe and dried for use in decoctions.

PTELEA
(Rutaceae)

P. trifoliata was sacred to the Menominee people of N America, who added its root bark to other medicines to increase their effectiveness. The herb was first described in *Medical Flora* by Constantine Rafinesque (2 vols, 1828–30), and was rapidly adopted by practitioners.

P. trifoliata (hop tree, wafer ash) p.185

PARTS USED Root bark.
PROPERTIES A bitter, pungent, tonic herb that lowers fever and improves digestion; it expels intestinal parasites and has antibacterial effects.
USES OF THE HERB
MEDICINAL Internally for fevers (especially intermittent), heartburn, roundworms, poor digestion, and pinworms. Externally for wounds.
VARIANT
P. t. **'Aurea'**, p.185.

GROWTH AND HARVEST
GROWTH Ornamental. Moist, well-drained soil in sun. Propagate by seed in autumn (species only), or by softwood cuttings in summer.
HARVEST Roots are lifted in autumn and peeled for bark, which is dried for use in infusions and powders.

PTEROCARPUS
(Leguminosae)

P. marsupium yields a very astringent sap, known as "kino." It hardens into brittle, shiny, red-black pieces, which turn the saliva red when chewed. Kino resembles *Acacia catechu* (see p.226) in its chemistry. It contains compounds similar to those extracted from other *Pterocarpus* species, and from the unrelated *Coccoloba uvifera* (West Indian kino, Jamaica kino) and *Butea frondosa* (Bengal kino). *P. santalus* is valued for its purple-red wood, which has antidiabetic properties, and is also used as a coloring agent in medicines.

P. marsupium (kino, Malabar kino, bastard teak) p.185

PARTS USED Sap.
PROPERTIES A very astringent herb that controls diarrhea and discharges, promotes healing, and has antidiabetic effects.
USES OF THE HERB
MEDICINAL Internally for diarrhea, dysentery, and diabetes. Externally for sore throat and vaginal discharge.

GROWTH AND HARVEST
GROWTH Crop. Well-drained soil in sun, minimum 59–64°F (15–18°C). Propagate by seed sown when ripe.
HARVEST Sap is tapped from incisions in the trunk and dried for use in powders and tinctures.

PUERARIA
(Leguminosae/Papilionaceae)

The first mention of *P. lobata* in Chinese medicine was in the *Shen Nong Canon of Herbs*, begun during the Han dynasty (206BC–AD23). The plant has long been used in Chinese medicine to treat alcohol abuse and has recently been publicized as a potentially safe and effective treatment; it contains chemicals (daidzin and daidzein) in both roots and flowers that suppress the appetite for alcohol. (Existing drugs interfere with the way alcohol is metabolized and can cause a build-up of toxins.) It is also planted in the East to prevent soil erosion and as a fodder crop.

P. lobata, syn. *P. thunbergiana* (kudzu, Japanese arrowroot) p.186

PARTS USED Roots (*ge gen*), flowers (*ge hua*).
PROPERTIES A sweet, cooling, tonic herb that increases perspiration, relieves pain, relaxes spasms, lowers blood pressure, and soothes the digestive system.
USES OF THE HERB
CULINARY Ground root used in macrobiotic cooking to thicken sauces.
MEDICINAL Internally for colds, influenza, feverish illnesses, thirst in diabetes, and muscular tension in neck and shoulders; also for acute conditions, such as stiff neck and sudden deafness (roots), gastritis, nausea and vomiting, alcohol poisoning, and abdominal bloating (flowers). Externally for snakebite (roots). Ground root is widely used in remedies for colds, influenza, and minor digestive problems.

GROWTH AND HARVEST
GROWTH Crop. Well-drained soil in sun. Propagate by seed in spring, or by division in spring, or by layering during the growing season. Seeds germinate more quickly if soaked before sowing. Prune regularly to control growth. *P. lobata* is an invasive weed in warm areas.
HARVEST Roots are lifted from autumn to spring and used fresh as juice, or dried for use in decoctions and powders. Flowers are picked before fully open and dried for use in decoctions.

PULMONARIA Lungwort
(Boraginaceae)

Lungworts are an interesting and much-quoted example of the Doctrine of Signatures, which dominated European medical thinking in the 16th and 17th centuries. This held that herbs were given by God to heal human ills and that the use of a plant was indicated by its appearance: thus the mottled ovate leaves of lungwort suggested diseased lungs. This theory is fully described in *The Art of Simpling* (William Coles, 1656). In fact, many herbs are used to this day for the purposes described – if not for the fanciful reasons given. The genus *Pulmonaria* is closely related to *Symphytum* (see p.357), and is suspected of similar toxicity.

P. officinalis (lungwort, Jerusalem cowslip, soldiers and sailors) p.186

PARTS USED Flowering plant.
PROPERTIES A soothing, astringent, expectorant herb.
USES OF THE HERB
CULINARY Young leaves are added to salads and soups.
MEDICINAL Internally for coughs, bronchitis, excess mucus, hemorrhoids, and diarrhea. Externally for wounds and as an eyewash.
WARNING This herb is subject to legal restrictions in some countries.
ECONOMIC Extract is an ingredient of vermouth.
VARIANTS
P. o. **'Cambridge Blue'**, p.186.
P. o. **'Sissinghurst White'**, p.186.

GROWTH AND HARVEST
GROWTH Ornamental. Moist soil, including clay, in shade. Propagate by seed sown in spring, or by division in autumn or spring. Germination may be slow. Sawfly larvae may attack foliage.
HARVEST Plants are cut in early summer and dried for infusions and extracts.
WARNING Skin irritant and allergen.

PULSATILLA Pasque flower
(Ranunculaceae)

A number of different species are used medicinally in various parts of the world. *P. chinensis* (Chinese anemone) is an anti-inflammatory, astringent, antibacterial herb used since the Han dynasty (206BC–AD23). *P. patens* (pulsatilla) was known to the Thompson people of British Columbia as "bleeding nose plant." It was listed in the *U.S. Pharmacopoeia* (1882–1905) as a diuretic, expectorant, and uterine stimulant. *P. pratensis* (small pasque flower) is used in homeopathy for a range of conditions.

P. vulgaris, syn. *Anemone pulsatilla* (pasque flower) p.186

PARTS USED Flowering plant.
PROPERTIES A bitter, cooling, alterative herb that relaxes spasms, relieves pain, and calms the nerves.
USES OF THE HERB
MEDICINAL Internally for premenstrual syndrome, inflammations of the reproductive organs, tension headache, neuralgia, insomnia, hyperactivity, bacterial skin infections, septicemia, spasmodic coughs in asthma, whooping cough, and bronchitis. Not given to patients with colds. Excess causes diarrhea and vomiting, and convulsions. For use by qualified practitioners only.
VARIANTS
P. v. var. ***alba***, p.186.
P. v. var. ***rubra***, p.186.

GROWTH AND HARVEST
GROWTH Ornamental. Well-drained, neutral to alkaline soil in sun. Propagate by seed sown in summer, or by division after flowering, or by root cuttings in winter. *P. vulgaris* does not transplant well.
HARVEST Plants are cut when flowering for use fresh in elixirs, liquid extracts, and tinctures; these must be used within a year.
WARNING Harmful if eaten. Repeated handling may cause skin irritation.

PUNICA
(Punicaceae/Lythraceae)

P. granatum was mentioned as a cure for tapeworms in the Ebers papyri (c.1500BC), and as a Chinese medicinal herb around 470AD. It contains unusual alkaloids, known as pelletierines, which paralyze tapeworms so that they are easily expelled in conjunction with a laxative. In Classical times the pomegranate became a symbol of fertility, and was eaten by childless women.

P. granatum (pomegranate) p.187

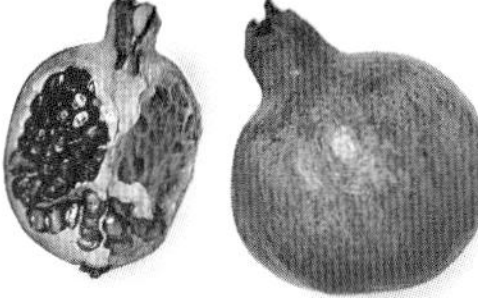

PARTS USED Root bark, fruit rind (*shi liu pi*) and juice, seeds.
PROPERTIES A bitter-sweet, astringent, warming herb that destroys intestinal parasites. It is also antiviral and controls diarrhea.
USES OF THE HERB
CULINARY Fruits are eaten fresh and the seeds used to garnish desserts. Juice is made into a cordial known as grenadine, an important ingredient of cocktails (especially daiquiris), and a flavoring for fruit salad, sorbet, and ice cream. Seeds are boiled to make pomegranate syrup, a flavoring in Middle Eastern dishes such as *faisinjan* (Iran).
MEDICINAL Internally for chronic diarrhea, amebic dysentery, and intestinal worms. Externally for vaginal discharge, mouth sores, and throat infections. WARNING This herb, especially in the form of bark extracts, is subject to legal restrictions in some countries.
VARIANT
P. g. var. ***nana***, p.187.

GROWTH AND HARVEST
GROWTH Ornamental. Well-drained soil in sun. Propagate by seed in spring at 72°F (22°C), or by semiripe cuttings in summer or hardwood cuttings in autumn, or by root suckers in autumn. Remove suckers as they appear, unless required for propagation. *P. granatum* and varieties tolerate short periods just below freezing. For successful fruiting, a warm climate and long, hot summers are required.
HARVEST Roots are lifted in autumn; the bark is peeled and dried for use in decoctions and liquid extracts. Fruits are picked when ripe in autumn, and the rind removed and dried for use in decoctions and powders; seeds and pulp are separated from the bitter pith and eaten fresh or pressed for juice.

PYCNANTHEMUM Mountain mint
(Labiatae/Lamiaceae)

P. virginianum is a traditional N American seasoning for soups and meat and is one of several species, including *P. incanum*, *P. muticum*, and *P. pilosum*, that can be used as a mint substitute in cooking. The Fox and Chippewa tribes are known to have used *P. virginianum* medicinally; *P. flexuosum* and *P. incanum* (hoary mountain mint) were used by the Cherokee, Choctaw, and Koasati as a general tonic and to treat stomach upsets, fevers, colds, and sinus headaches.

P. virginianum (Virginia mountain mint, wild basil, prairie hyssop) p.187

PARTS USED Whole plant, leaves, flowers, buds.
PROPERTIES An aromatic, tonic, stimulant herb that increases perspiration, relaxes spasms, and improves digestion.
USES OF THE HERB
CULINARY Leaves, flowering tops, and flower buds give a mintlike flavor to savory dishes.
MEDICINAL Internally for indigestion, colic, chills, and fevers.

GROWTH AND HARVEST
GROWTH Wild-collected. Rich soil in sun or partial shade. Propagates by seed sown in spring or autumn, or by division when dormant.
HARVEST Whole plants, leaves, and flowers are collected as flowering begins and used fresh for seasoning, or dried for use in infusions.

QUASSIA
Q. cedron. See *Simaba cedron*.

QUERCUS Oak
(Fagaceae)

In ancient times the oak was dedicated to Thor, the god of thunder. This gave rise to the belief that an oak tree could never be struck by lightning; acorn-shaped wooden pulls attached to Venetian blind cords are thought to protect a house. The bark, galls, and acorns of various oaks are a major source of tannic acid. They contain up to 20 percent tannin, reaching 36–58 percent in *Q. infectoria*, an eastern Mediterranean species widely exploited by the pharmaceutical industry. *Q. alba* (white oak) was important in native N American medicine as a remedy for diarrhea, wounds, and hemorrhoids. The Menominee and Potawatomi made syringes, using an animal bladder and hollow bone of a bird, for the injection of oak-bark infusion into the rectum. *Q. alba* was adopted by settlers as a substitute for the English oak, and was listed as an astringent, tonic, and antiseptic in the *U.S. Pharmacopoeia* (1820–1916). Boiled in milk and water with the root of *Verbena urticifolia* (white vervain), it makes a useful antidote to *Rhus radicans* (poison ivy).

Q. robur (English oak, common oak, pedunculate oak) p.187

PARTS USED Bark.
PROPERTIES A bitter, astringent, antiseptic herb that reduces inflammation and controls bleeding.
USES OF THE HERB
MEDICINAL Internally for diarrhea, dysentery, hemorrhage, and prolapsed uterus or anus. Externally for hemorrhoids, vaginal discharge, sore throat, bleeding gums, minor injuries, dermatitis, weeping eczema, ringworm, ulcers, and varicose veins.
ECONOMIC Bark and galls are used in tanning and also in dyeing, the color produced being dependent on the mordant.
VARIANTS
Q. r. **'Atropurpurea'**, p.187.
Q. r. **'Concordia'**, p.188.
Q. r. f. ***fastigiata***, p.188.

GROWTH AND HARVEST
GROWTH Ornamental. Deep, well-drained soil in sun or partial shade. Propagate by seed sown in autumn (species only), or by grafting in late winter. Remove lateral branches in late ►

▶ winter to maintain a clean trunk. Foliage may be damaged by mildew, gall mites, chafer beetles, and caterpillars. Gall wasps cause the formation of galls on various parts of the tree, the most serious being deformed acorns, known as "knopper galls."
HARVEST Bark is removed in spring from trees 10–25 years old and dried for use in decoctions and liquid extracts.

QUILLAJA Soapbark tree
(Rosaceae)

Nine percent of the bark of *Q. saponaria* is made up of complex saponins, known collectively as "quillajasaponin," together with calcium oxalate and tannins. It is now mainly used in pharmaceutical and cosmetic preparations, since research has shown that internal use may have unpleasant side effects.

Q. saponaria (soapbark tree, quillai, Panama bark) p.188

PARTS USED Inner bark.
PROPERTIES An acrid, astringent, cleansing herb that reduces inflammation and has expectorant effects.
USES OF THE HERB
MEDICINAL Internally for bronchial congestion. May cause irritation and inflammation of the digestive tract, and is no longer considered safe. Externally for skin ulcers and eruptions, and dandruff. Powdered bark causes violent sneezing.
ECONOMIC Extracts are added to dandruff shampoos and exfoliant cleansers. Used as a foaming agent in fire extinguishers.

GROWTH AND HARVEST
GROWTH Ornamental. Fertile, well-drained soil, sited in a sheltered position in cold areas. Propagate by ripe cuttings at the end of the growing season.
HARVEST Bark is dried for use in liquid extracts, powders, and tinctures.

R

RANUNCULUS Buttercup
(Ranunculaceae)

Most members of the buttercup family contain acrid compounds that are too irritant for internal use. *R. ficaria* is an exception and is often taken in tablet form for hemorrhoids (piles). The traditional use of this herb for treating piles gave rise to the common name, "pilewort." Its suitability for this purpose was in accordance with the Doctrine of Signatures (according to which a plant's appearance indicated its use), because the tuberous roots of pilewort were thought to resemble piles.

R. ficaria (lesser celandine, pilewort) p.188

PARTS USED Whole plant, including roots.
PROPERTIES An astringent, slightly bitter herb that is specifically antihemorrhoidal.
USES OF THE HERB
MEDICINAL Internally and externally for hemorrhoids. Externally for perineal damage after childbirth. Often combined with *Hamamelis virginiana* (see p.291) for external use, and with *Plantago major* (see p.331), *Calendula officinalis* (see p.252), or *Hamamelis virginiana* (see p.291) in suppositories.
VARIANTS
R. f. var. ***albus***, p.188.
R. f. **'Brazen Hussy'**, p.188.
R. f. var. ***flore pleno***, p.188.

GROWTH AND HARVEST
GROWTH Ornamental (except *R. ficaria*: crop). Moist, neutral to alkaline soil in sun or shade. Propagate by seed sown in summer (species only), or by division in spring or autumn. *R. ficaria* is particularly invasive when grown in moist shade, which encourages formation of bulbils at leaf bases.
HARVEST Plants are lifted after flowering, complete with roots, and used fresh for ointments and suppositories, or dried for use in infusions, liquid extracts, and tablets.
WARNING Harmful if eaten. Skin irritant.

RAPHANUS Radish
(Cruciferae)

Nicholas Culpeper recommended radishes for urinary problems but condemned them as food. "Garden radishes are in wantonness by the gentry eaten as a sallad, but they breed scurvy humours in the stomach, and corrupt the blood" (*The English Physitian Enlarged*, 1653). *R. sativus*, which contains the antibiotic raphinin, is less pungent than *R. raphanistrum* (wild radish), which is closer in chemistry to *Sinapis alba* (white mustard, see p.353). Radishes were first mentioned in Chinese medical literature during the 14th century. Those of oriental origin, sometimes classed as *R. s.* var. *macropodus*, have much larger roots, weighing up to 44lb (20kg). They include the white-rooted mooli, or *daikon*, which is harvested in autumn and stored for winter use. Black radishes, which are favored for homeopathic remedies, differ in having a pronounced effect on the liver.

R. sativus (radish) p.189

PARTS USED Leaves, roots, seeds (*lai fu zi*).
PROPERTIES A sweet, slightly pungent, tonic herb that improves digestion, acts as an expectorant, and is effective against many bacterial and fungal infections.
USES OF THE HERB
CULINARY Shredded or grated roots are served with fish, used to tenderize octopus, and added to soups, stews, and salads. Immature seed pods are pickled. Young leaves are eaten in salads. Roots are eaten raw, cooked, or pickled in Japan and Korea.
MEDICINAL Internally for indigestion, abdominal bloating, flatulence, acid regurgitation, "food stagnation" diarrhea, and bronchitis (seeds).

GROWTH AND HARVEST
GROWTH Crop. Rich, moist, well-drained soil in sun. Propagate by seed sown in spring for harvesting seeds, or by seed sown in succession from late winter to late summer for roots. Roots may be damaged by root rots and slugs. Radishes are said to repel cucumber beetles if planted around the base of cucumber plants, and also vine borers, which attack squashes and pumpkins.
HARVEST Leaves are picked when young and used fresh. Roots are lifted as required and used fresh. Seeds are collected when ripe and dried for use in decoctions and pills.

RAUVOLFIA
(Apocynaceae)

R. serpentina, known as *sarpagandha* in Sanskrit, was mentioned in Hindu texts c.600BC. A tea made from the whole plant has been used for centuries in India for treating madness, hysteria, and restlessness. Mahatma Gandhi is said to have drunk it regularly for its calming effect. It contains about 25 alkaloids, the most important of which is reserpine, a potent hypotensive. Other useful species include *R. vomitoria* (African serpentwood), which is even richer in alkaloids, notably ajmaline, which has largely superseded reserpine because it has fewer side effects. Roots of *R. vomitoria* have long been used in traditional African medicine for calming mentally disturbed patients. It is collected mainly from Zaïre, Rwanda, and Mozambique for processing in Europe.

R. serpentina (rauwolfia, serpentwood, Indian snakeroot) p.189

PARTS USED Roots.
PROPERTIES A tranquilizing, sedative herb that lowers blood pressure and slows heartbeat.
USES OF THE HERB
MEDICINAL Internally for high blood pressure,

abnormally rapid heartbeat, and nervous and mental disorders. Side effects include dry mouth, nasal congestion, depression, and slowed heartbeat.
WARNING This herb is subject to legal restrictions in some countries.

GROWTH AND HARVEST
GROWTH Crop. Well-drained soil in sun or partial shade, minimum 50–55°F (10–13°C), with an almost-dry winter resting period. Propagate by seed sown at 75°F (24°C) in spring, or by stem cuttings in spring and summer, or by root cuttings in winter. Seeds have a low germination rate.
HARVEST Roots ½in (1cm) in diameter are lifted in winter from plants at least 15 months old, and dried for use in decoctions and powders, or for commercial extraction of alkaloids. Bark and inner root may be separated before drying.

REHMANNIA Chinese foxglove
(Scrophulariaceae)

R. glutinosa is one of the most popular tonic herbs in Chinese medicine and among the 50 most important Chinese herbs. The fresh or dried roots (*sheng di huang*) were first mentioned in Chinese medical literature during the Han dynasty (206BC–AD23). Roots steamed in rice wine, known as *shu di huang*, were described in the *Illustrated Classic of the Materia Medica* by Su Song (AD1061). *R. glutinosa* was the first species of the genus to be cultivated in the West.

R. glutinosa (Chinese foxglove) p.189

PARTS USED Roots (*di huang*).
PROPERTIES A sweet, cooling (*sheng di huang*) to slightly warming (*shu di huang*) herb that controls bleeding, lowers fever, reduces blood sugar, and has diuretic and antibacterial effects (*sheng di huang*). It acts as a tonic for the heart, blood, and kidney energy, regulates menstruation, and strengthens women after childbirth (*shu di huang*).
USES OF THE HERB
MEDICINAL Internally for thirst associated with feverish illnesses, heat rash, hemorrhage of all kinds, excessive menstruation, and diabetes (*sheng di huang*); anemia, night sweats, menopausal problems, weakness following childbirth, and involuntary ejaculation (*shu di huang*). Not given to patients with digestive problems. Often combined with *Angelica polymorpha* var. *sinensis* (see p.238), the peel of *Citrus reticulata* (see p.262), and *Ziziphus jujuba* (see p.373).

GROWTH AND HARVEST
GROWTH Crop. Light, moist, well-drained, neutral to acid, sandy soil in sun. Propagate by seed sown in autumn or spring, or by root cuttings in winter, or by division in spring, or by stem cuttings of basal shoots in spring. Plants ► are prone to fungal infections, especially in damp conditions.
HARVEST Roots are lifted in autumn and early winter (cultivated crops), or early spring (wild plants), and used fresh, or dried for use in decoctions, extracts, pills, powders, and tinctures.

RHAMNUS
(Rhamnaceae)

The bark of several species contains anthraquinone glycosides, which act as a strong purgative and cause severe griping pains, nausea, and vomiting unless stored for at least a year after drying. Anthraquinones are pigments, so plants that contain them are almost always used for dyeing – a purpose that usually predates their importance in medicine. *R. infectoria* (Avignon berry) was once an important source of yellow dye; *R. davurica* and *R. utilis* were sources of the pigment known as "Chinese green indigo," used in dyeing silk. Fruits of *R. catharticus*, known as "Rhine berries," also yield an artist's pigment. It has been used since at least the ninth century and was included in the *British Pharmacopoeia* in 1650. Its effect is so drastic that it is no longer prescribed, although buckthorn syrup, made from the berries, is used in veterinary practice. *R. frangula* and *R. purshiana* have superseded *R. catharticus* in medicine, having a gentler effect. *R. purshiana* was first listed in the *U.S. Pharmacopoeia* in 1890. It is mild enough for use in treating children and the elderly. Indiscriminate stripping of bark, leading to the destruction of some 100,000 trees a year, was reported as early as 1909, and shortages led to the exploitation of the much smaller *R. alnifolia* (alderleaf buckthorn), once the similarity of their chemistry was realized. *R. frangula* was formerly grown to make charcoal for small-arms gunpowder.

R. catharticus (buckthorn) p.189

PARTS USED Bark, fruits.
PROPERTIES A bitter, cooling, purgative herb that cleanses toxins from tissues and has diuretic effects.
USES OF THE HERB
MEDICINAL Internally for constipation. Small amounts are occasionally used in alterative formulas to treat skin diseases, intestinal parasites, and gallstones.
ECONOMIC Bark and fruits yield a yellow dye, once used to color paper and maps. Fruits are mixed with gum arabic and limewater to make a green pigment used in watercolor painting.

R. frangula, syn. *Frangula alnus* (alder buckthorn) p.189

PARTS USED Inner bark.
PROPERTIES A bitter, astringent, antiseptic herb that stimulates the liver and gall bladder, and acts as a purgative.
USES OF THE HERB
MEDICINAL Internally for chronic, atonic constipation, abdominal bloating, hepatitis, cirrhosis, jaundice, and liver and gall bladder complaints. Externally for gum disease and scalp infestations.

R. purshiana (cascara sagrada)

Lax evergreen shrub or tree, hardy to 5°F (–15°C), height 10–40ft (3–12m), spread 10–30ft (3–10m), with obovate, irregularly toothed, deeply veined leaves up to 6in (15cm) long. Umbels of small flowers appear in late spring, followed by poisonous black berries, ½in (1cm) in diameter. Native to forests on the Pacific coast of N America.

PARTS USED Bark.
PROPERTIES A bitter, astringent, cooling herb that has a tonic effect on the liver and digestive system, and acts as a laxative.
USES OF THE HERB
MEDICINAL Internally for chronic constipation, colitis, digestive complaints, hemorrhoids, liver problems, and jaundice. Fruits taken in excess cause diarrhea and vomiting. Not given to pregnant or lactating women, or patients with intestinal obstruction. Externally to deter nail biting.

GROWTH AND HARVEST
GROWTH Ornamental (*R. purshiana*: wild-collected). Well-drained soil in sun or partial shade. *R. catharticus* prefers alkaline soil, *R. frangula* neutral to acid soil. Propagate by seed sown in autumn, or by semiripe cuttings in summer, or by layering in late winter or early spring. Shorten or thin out branches and remove dead wood in late winter or early spring.
HARVEST Bark is stripped from young plants in spring and early summer, and dried for one to two years before use in decoctions, liquid extracts, powders, and tablets. Bark from two-year-old plants is preferred in the case of *R. frangula*. Fruits (*R. catharticus*) are collected when ripe and made into syrup.
WARNING All parts, especially the berries, are harmful if eaten. Sap and berries are skin irritants.

RHEUM Rhubarb
(Polygonaceae)

The two main medicinal species of rhubarb are *R. palmatum*, introduced into Europe in 1762, and *R. officinale*, introduced in 1867. The cultivation of *R. palmatum* was given high priority in the 18th century. A map of the Royal Botanic Garden Edinburgh (originally a physic garden), dated 1777, indicates a very large area devoted to its cultivation. *R. palmatum* is one of the most widely used Chinese herbs. It was first mentioned in the *Shen Nong Canon of Herbs*, which dates back to the Han dynasty (206BC–AD23). Rhubarbs contain anthraquinone glycosides (as found in *Rhamnus* species, see p.340), which act as strong laxatives. Several species are used medicinally, including *R. officinale*, *R. australe* (Himalayan rhubarb, Indian rhubarb), and the hybrid *R. palmatum* x *R. coreanum* (Japanese rhubarb). Many other names exist, such as "Turkey rhubarb," and "Dutch rhubarb," which usually refer to the commercial source of the drug, rather than the country of origin. These rhubarbs vary slightly in chemistry but are used interchangeably. Only the roots are used; the leaves are poisonous. The familiar edible rhubarb was derived from *R. rhabarbarum* (syn. *R. rhaponticum*), developed through hybridization during the 19th century. The roots of edible rhubarbs are not used for medicinal purposes.

R. palmatum (Chinese rhubarb, *chinghai* rhubarb) p.189

PARTS USED Rhizomes (*da huang*).
PROPERTIES A bitter, astringent, cooling herb that improves digestion, stimulates the uterus, promotes healing, and has a laxative effect.
USES OF THE HERB
MEDICINAL Internally for chronic constipation, diarrhea, liver and gall bladder complaints, hemorrhoids, menstrual problems, heat-related symptoms (such as nosebleed), and skin eruptions due to the accumulation of toxins. Not given to pregnant or lactating women, or patients with intestinal obstruction. Externally for burns. Used in homeopathy for irritability and teething in children.
ECONOMIC Extract with bitterness removed is used in commercial food flavoring.
VARIANTS
***R. p.* 'Atrosanguineum'**, syn.
R. p. 'Atropurpureum', p.190.
R. p.* var. *tanguticum
Unusual variety from China, hardy to 5°F (–15°C), height 6ft (2m), spread 24–30in (60–75cm), with vivid, red-purple young leaves and spires of white flowers in early summer.

GROWTH AND HARVEST
GROWTH Ornamental. Well-drained, moist, humus-rich soil in sun. Propagate by seed sown in spring or autumn (species and varieties only), or by division in spring or autumn.
HARVEST Rhizomes are lifted in autumn from plants at least three years old and dried for use in decoctions, dry extracts, powders, tinctures, and tablets.
WARNING Leaves are harmful if eaten.

RHUS Sumac
(Anacardiaceae)

Various sumacs have a high tannin content and are valued for their astringent properties. These include the N American *R. aromatica*, used mainly for urinary incontinence, and *R. coriaria* (tanner's or Sicilian sumac), whose acidic fruits are made into a condiment and sour drink in the Middle East. *Rhus typhina* (staghorn sumac) was used extensively by native N Americans. The leaves were smoked with tobacco by the Potawatomi, and the Menominee harvested the fruits to make a "lemonade" for winter and boiled the roots to make a yellow dye. The hollowed stems served as maple sugar conduits for the Chippewa. Sumacs commonly bear galls caused by parasitic insects. Those of *R. chinensis* (Chinese sumac) contain up to 70 percent tannins, and were first described in traditional Chinese medicine c.AD720 for coughs, diarrhea, hemorrhage, injuries, mouth ulcers, and hemorrhoids. *R. radicans* (poison ivy) differs from most species in containing toxins that cause severe contact dermatitis.

R. glabra (smooth sumac) p.190

PARTS USED Root bark, fruits.
PROPERTIES An astringent, antiseptic, mucilaginous herb with tonic effects. The bark is regarded as an alterative; the fruits are cooling and diuretic.
USES OF THE HERB
MEDICINAL Internally for diarrhea and dysentery (root bark), feverish illnesses and urinary complaints (fruits). Externally for skin irritations, sores, ulcers, vaginal discharge, and hemorrhoids (root bark).
VARIANT
***R. g.* 'Laciniata'**, p.190.

GROWTH AND HARVEST
GROWTH Ornamental. Well-drained soil in sun. Propagate by seed sown in autumn (species only), or by semiripe cuttings in summer, or by root cuttings in winter. Remove suckers in autumn. Cut back to the ground in early spring to encourage vigorous new growth and large leaves. Plants may be damaged by dieback and *Verticillium* wilt. Sumacs are short-lived and brittle, especially as single-stemmed specimens. Growing them as coppiced shrubs prolongs life and minimizes damage from wind and snow.
HARVEST Roots are lifted as required, then bark is peeled and dried for use in decoctions and liquid extracts. Fruits are collected when ripe and dried for use in decoctions, liquid extracts, and powders.

RIBES Currant
(Grossulariaceae)

The distinctive flavor of blackcurrants was not as popular in the past as it is now. John Gerard, in his *Generall Historie of Plantes* (1597) described them as "of a stinking and somewhat loathing savour." The fruits were also thought to breed worms in the stomach. Blackcurrant leaves were once important as a substitute for Indian and China tea. In the UK, at various times during the 18th and 19th centuries, shortages and high prices led to the widespread practice of making substitute blends. Dried blackcurrant leaves were also added to Indian blends to make them go further. Most present-day cultivars were developed by growers and research institutes after World War II, when food shortages stimulated an interest in the nutritional value of the genus. The medicinal properties of *R. nigrum* were first described by Peter Forestus, who used the leaves to treat urinary retention and bladder stones. The leaves contain tannins and the fruits are high in vitamin C, 120mg per 100g (0.12 percent by weight) of fresh fruit. The common name, "quinsy berry," refers to its effectiveness in treating quinsy, a severe throat inflammation. The seeds are a source of gamma-linolenic acid (see *Oenothera biennis*, p.318), used in cosmetics.

R. nigrum (blackcurrant, quinsy berry) p.190

PARTS USED Leaves, fruits.
PROPERTIES A sweet-sour, astringent, tonic herb that reduces inflammation, strengthens capillaries, and controls bacterial infections.
USES OF THE HERB
MEDICINAL Internally for colds, capillary fragility, and mouth and throat infections. Externally for sore throat.
ECONOMIC Dried leaves are added to blended herb teas. Fruits and fruit extracts are used in desserts and in jams, jellies, drinks, and liqueurs (*cassis*).

GROWTH AND HARVEST
GROWTH Crop. Well-drained, preferably clay soil in sun or partial shade, with protection from cold winds and late frosts. Propagate by hardwood cuttings in winter. Remove weak growths and one third of older (gray or black) shoots in autumn. Bushes tend to lose vigor with age and are usually replaced every 10 years or so. Buds may be damaged by birds, aphids, and blackcurrant ("big bud") gall mites.
HARVEST Leaves are gathered during the growing season and used fresh, or dried for use in infusions. Fruits are picked when ripe; oil is extracted from ripe seeds.

RICINUS Castor bean
(Euphorbiaceae)

R. communis has been cultivated for over 6,000 years and was a source of oil for lamps and for cosmetics in ancient Egypt. All parts of the plant are poisonous, and the seeds contain ricin, an exceedingly toxic protein. As a result of a political assassination in London that was carried out using an umbrella tipped with the plant's toxins, the toxicity of the plant has been well publicized. Necklaces were also made from the attractive seeds, although as few as two may prove fatal if swallowed. When the seeds are pressed for oil, some ricin remains in the residue. Greek physicians of the first century AD regarded the oil as suitable only for external application. This view persisted until the 1780s, when castor oil was listed in many pharmacopoeias as a purgative, following a report of its use for this purpose in the W Indies.

R. communis (castor bean, palma-christi) p.190

PARTS USED Oil.
PROPERTIES A purgative, emollient herb with an unpleasant taste.
USES OF THE HERB
MEDICINAL Internally for constipation and acute diarrhea due to food poisoning. Excess causes severe colic, vomiting, and purgation. Externally as an enema in severe constipation, and for irritating skin and eye conditions. Used in Ayurvedic medicine for nervous disorders.
ECONOMIC Oil is added to soaps, cosmetics, and ophthalmic products, and is used in the making of candles, crayons, varnishes, lubricating oils, high-performance fuels, carbon paper, polyamide fiber, leather preservatives, fabric waterproofing, and dyes for cotton. It repels insects, notably cockroaches. The residue is used in fertilizers, and in fiber and board manufacture.
VARIANTS
***R. c.* 'Carmencita'**, p.190.
***R. c.* 'Impala'**, p.190.

GROWTH AND HARVEST
GROWTH Ornamental. Well-drained, humus-rich soil in sun. Propagate by seed sown in spring. Subject to statutory control as a weed in some countries, notably in parts of Australia.
HARVEST Ripe seeds are collected and pressed for oil.
WARNING All parts, especially seeds, are extremely toxic if eaten. Repeated handling of foliage or seeds may cause skin irritation or allergic reactions.

RORIPPA

R. nasturtium-aquaticum. See *Nasturtium officinale.*

ROSA Rose
(Rosaceae)

Roses have been important since earliest times in ritual, cosmetics, perfumes, and medicines. Various kinds were used medicinally by the ancient Greeks, Romans, and Persians; in AD77 Pliny recorded 32 different disorders that responded well to treatment by rose preparations. *R. gallica* var. *officinalis* and *R. damascena* were widely grown in medieval times for medicinal purposes. The oriental species *R. laevigata* was first mentioned in Chinese medical literature about AD470, and seems to have been introduced to the US by the East India Company in 1759; known as the Cherokee rose, it became the state flower of Georgia. *R. rugosa* is used to a lesser extent and is fairly recent, being first mentioned in *Food as Materia Medica* during the Ming dynasty (AD1368– 1644); it reached Europe, the US, and Australia during the 19th century from its homelands in Japan and northern China. Red rose petals were listed in the *British Pharmacopoeia* until the 1930s as an astringent and flavoring for medicines. Rose oil, or attar (otto) of roses, consists mainly of beta-damascenone, which gives the typical rose fragrance; its constituents include citronellol, an insecticidal, antirheumatic compound which is isolated commercially (but mainly from *Pelargonium* spp.) for use in rose-scented perfumes, cosmetics, and soap. The oil was originally made by macerating rose petals in oil or molten fat. Sixteenth-century Persian chemists produced a superior oil by distillation. It is a costly commodity, taking 0.98 ton (1 tonne) of petals to produce 11oz (300g) of oil and, for this reason, is now largely synthesized. Some 96 percent of women's perfumes and about 42 percent of men's fragrances contain rose oil, putting it on par with jasmine in popularity. Rose water was first produced by the Persian physician, Avicenna, in the first century AD. "Cold cream" was originally known as ointment of rose water, since both rose water and rose oil were ingredients. Several different roses are grown for rose oil and water, including *R. gallica*, *R. damascena*, *R. centifolia*, and variants of *R.* x *alba*. Any strongly scented rose can be used. Rose hips contain large amounts of vitamins, notably vitamin C.

R. canina (dog rose) p.191

PARTS USED Fruits (hips).
PROPERTIES An acidic, astringent, tonic herb, rich in vitamins.
USES OF THE HERB
MEDICINAL Internally for colds, influenza, minor infectious diseases, scurvy, diarrhea, and gastritis.
ECONOMIC Fruits are made into syrup as a nutritional supplement, especially for babies, and into commercial pills. Syrup is also added to cough mixtures and used to flavor medicines. Fruit extracts are added to vitamin C tablets. Traditionally, fruits are also used in making wine, vinegar, and preserves.

R. eglanteria, syn. *R. rubiginosa* (sweet briar, eglantine) p.191

PARTS USED Oil (seeds).
PROPERTIES A healing herb that promotes tissue regeneration.
USES OF THE HERB
MEDICINAL Externally for burns, scars, and wrinkles.

R. gallica var. *officinalis* (apothecary's rose, red rose of Lancaster) p.191

PARTS USED Flowers.
PROPERTIES An aromatic, astringent, tonic herb that controls bacterial infections, promotes healing, and improves morale.

USES OF THE HERB
CULINARY Petals are added to salads.
AROMATIC Dried petals and buds are used in potpourris.
MEDICINAL Internally for colds, bronchial infections, gastritis, diarrhea, depression, and lethargy; externally for sore throat, eye irritations, minor injuries, and skin problems. Internally in Ayurvedic medicine for inflammations, circulatory congestion, sore throat, mouth sores, and menstrual complaints. Combined with *Asparagus racemosus* (see p.245) as a tonic, and with *Hibiscus rosa-sinensis* (see p.293) or *Carthamus tinctorius* (see p.255) for menstrual irregularity. Used in aromatherapy to counter depression, anxiety, and negative feelings.
ECONOMIC Rose oil and rose water are used in bath preparations and skin care. Rose water gives flavor to candy (notably Turkish Delight), desserts, sorbets, mousses, and jellies. Petals are crystallized and made into syrup and preserves. Dried petals and rosebuds are important ingredients of the northern African spice mixture, *ras-el-hanout*.

R. laevigata (Cherokee rose) p.191

PARTS USED Fruits (*jing ying zi*).
PROPERTIES An acidic, astringent herb that regulates kidney energy, stimulates the digestion, and is effective against many bacterial and viral infections.
USES OF THE HERB
MEDICINAL Internally for urinary dysfunction, infertility, and chronic diarrhea.

R. rugosa (Japanese rose, Ramanas rose) p.191

PARTS USED Flowers (*mei gui hua*), fruits.
PROPERTIES An aromatic, tonic herb that stimulates the liver, improves circulation, and acts as an antidote in antimony poisoning (flowers).
USES OF THE HERB
MEDICINAL Internally for poor appetite and digestion, and menstrual complaints arising from constrained liver energy (flowers). Combined with *Leonurus cardiaca* (see p.302) or *L. sibiricus* (see p.150) for excessive menstruation. Fruits are used as a source of vitamin C and flavonoids, especially in the US.
VARIANT
***R. r.* 'Alba'**, p.191.

GROWTH AND HARVEST
GROWTH Ornamental. Well-drained but moist, fertile, neutral to slightly acid soil in sun. *R. eglanteria* enjoys dry, calcareous conditions, *R. laevigata* poor soils. *R. rugosa* tolerates dry, sandy, or coastal conditions. Propagate by seed sown in autumn (species only), or by budding in summer, or hardwood cuttings in autumn. Remove dead and damaged wood, and prune lightly in late winter, removing weak growths. Most species and old roses flower on the previous year's growth and should not be cut back hard. Rose hips, especially of *R. rugosa*, are eaten by birds. Leaves may be damaged by blackspot, rust, and mildew. Aphids often attack flowers. *R. canina* and *R. eglanteria* ►

► are subject to statutory control as weeds in some countries, notably in parts of Australia.
HARVEST Petals (*R. gallica* var. *officinalis*, *R. rugosa*) are collected when flowers first open and distilled for oil and rose water, used fresh for syrups, crushed into paste, or dried for use in decoctions. Fruits (*R. canina*, *R. laevigata*) are picked when ripe and used fresh or dried in decoctions, or made into syrups and confections. Seeds (*R. eglanteria*) from ripe fruits are processed commercially for oil extraction.
WARNING Seeds contain irritant hairs.

ROSMARINUS Rosemary
(Labiatae/Lamiaceae)

Rosemary is rich in volatile oils, flavonoids, and phenolic acids, which are strongly antiseptic and anti-inflammatory. Rosmarinic acid has potential in the treatment of toxic shock syndrome. The flavonoid diosmin is reputedly more effective than rutin (see *Ruta graveolens*, p.345) in reducing capillary fragility. A symbol of friendship, loyalty, and remembrance, rosemary is traditionally carried by mourners at funerals and by the bride at her wedding. Greek scholars wore garlands of rosemary when they were taking examinations to improve their memory and concentration. In the 14th century Queen Izabella of Hungary claimed that, at the age of 72 years, when crippled with gout and rheumatism, she had so regained her strength and beauty by using Hungary water (rosemary tops macerated in alcohol) that the King of Poland proposed to her.

R. officinalis (rosemary) p.192

PARTS USED Leaves, flowering tops, oil.
PROPERTIES An aromatic, restorative herb that relaxes spasms, relieves pain, and increases perspiration rate. It also stimulates the liver and gall bladder, improves digestion, and controls many pathogenic organisms.
USES OF THE HERB

CULINARY Fresh or dried leaves are used to flavor meat (especially lamb and kid), soups, and stews; they have a bitter, resinous taste and a tough texture, so should be used either finely chopped or in sprigs that can be removed before serving. Very small amounts (usually as powder) are added to biscuits and jams. Fresh sprigs steeped in vinegar, wine, or olive oil flavor sauces and dressings.
MEDICINAL Internally for depression, apathy, nervous exhaustion, headaches and migraines associated with nervous tension or feeling cold, poor circulation, and digestive problems associated with anxiety. Excess causes abortion in pregnant women and convulsions. Externally for rheumatism, arthritis, neuralgia, muscular injuries, wounds, dandruff, and scurf. May be combined with *Avena sativa* (see p.246), *Scutellaria lateriflora* (see p.351), or *Verbena officinalis* (see p.368) for depression.
ECONOMIC Extracts are used in hair, skin, and bath preparations.
VARIANTS
R. o. var. *albiflorus*, p.192.
***R. o.* 'Arp'**, p.192.
***R. o.* 'Aureus'**, syn. *R. o.* 'Variegatus', p.192.
***R. o.* 'Benenden Blue'**, syn. *R. o.* 'Collingwood Ingram', p.192.
***R. o.* 'Fota Blue'**, p.192.
***R. o.* 'Majorca Pink'**, syn. *R. o.* 'Roseus-Cozart', p.192.
***R. o.* 'McConnell's Blue'**, p.192.
***R. o.* 'Miss Jessopp's Upright'**, syn. *R. o.* 'Erectus', *R. o.* 'Fastigiatus', p.192.
***R. o.* 'Pinkie'**, p.193.
***R. o.* 'Primley Blue'**, p.193.
***R. o.* Prostratus Group**, syn. *R. lavandulaceus*, p.193.
***R. o.* 'Roseus'**, p.193.
***R. o.* 'Severn Sea'**, p.193.
***R. o.* 'Sissinghurst Blue'**, p.193.
***R. o.* 'Sudbury Blue'**, p.193.
***R. o.* 'Tuscan Blue'**, p.193.

GROWTH AND HARVEST
GROWTH Ornamental. Well-drained, neutral to alkaline soil in sun, with shelter in cold areas. Rosemary makes an excellent subject for container culture and may be trained into topiary and other fanciful shapes. To help prevent mildew infestation, provide good air circulation during winter. Propagate by seed sown in spring (species only), or by semiripe cuttings in summer. Remove dead stems and straggly shoots in spring. Prune after flowering to encourage bushy growth. Rosemaries dislike cold, wet winters and poorly drained soil.
HARVEST Leaves and flowering tops are collected in spring and early summer, and distilled for oil or dried for infusions, decoctions, extracts, spirits, and tinctures.

ROUPELLIA
R. grata. See *Strophanthus gratus.*

ROXBURGHIA
R. gloriosa. See *Stemona tuberosa.*

RUBIA Madder
(Rubiaceae)

Various species contain pigments, which include alizarin (madder red), purpurin (madder purple), rubiacin (madder orange), and xanthine (madder yellow). These compounds are similar to those in the related *Galium aparine* (see p.285) and *G. verum* (see p.285). *R. cordifolia* was first described in Chinese medicine in the *Shen Nong Canon of Herbs*, during the Han dynasty (206BC–AD23). It also has a long history of use in Ayurvedic medicine. *R. tinctorum* was mentioned by Pliny (AD23–79) as a cure for jaundice. Alizarin, its main pigment, once known as Turkey red, was synthesized in 1868; this greatly reduced its commercial cultivation.

R. cordifolia, syn. *R. manjith* (Indian madder, *munjeet*, *manjishta*) p.193

PARTS USED Rhizome, roots (*qian cao gen*).
PROPERTIES A bittersweet, cooling herb that is diuretic and expectorant, checks bleeding, controls coughing, reduces inflammation, and has anti-bacterial effects (Chinese medicine). It also stimulates the circulation, dissolves and inhibits formation of kidney stones, and has alterative effects (Ayurvedic medicine).
USES OF THE HERB
MEDICINAL Internally for abnormal uterine bleeding, internal and external hemorrhage, bronchitis, and rheumatism (Chinese medicine); menstrual and menopausal complaints, jaundice, hepatitis, kidney stones, bladder stones and gallstones, herpes, skin complaints, and dysentery (Ayurvedic medicine). Externally, combined with honey for skin inflammations and with *Glycyrrhiza glabra* (see p.289) for burns and injuries (Ayurvedic medicine).
ECONOMIC Roots are used as a source of dye.

R. tinctorum (madder) p.193

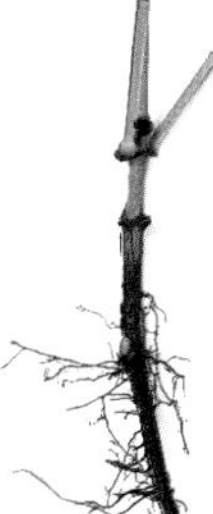

PARTS USED Roots.
PROPERTIES An antiseptic, diuretic, laxative herb that stimulates the liver and uterus, and relaxes spasms.
USES OF THE HERB
MEDICINAL Internally for kidney and bladder stones. Externally for wounds.
ECONOMIC Fermented roots are used as a source of natural dyes, which vary in color according to the mordant. Alizarin is used in making dyes and yields pigments for inks and paints.

GROWTH AND HARVEST
GROWTH Crop. Well-drained soil in sun or partial shade. *R. tinctorum* prefers light, dry soil. Propagate by seed when ripe, or by division at any time between spring and autumn.
HARVEST Rhizomes and roots are lifted in autumn from plants at least three years old, and peeled and dried for decoctions and powders. Chinese herbalists also lift roots in spring. Roots for dye production are lifted from three-year-old plants in spring and autumn. Internal use of madders stains the urine red.

RUBUS Bramble
(Rosaceae)

Fossil evidence shows that raspberries (*R. idaeus*) and blackberries (*R. fruticosus*) have formed part of the human diet from very early times. Mention is made of the raspberry by the Roman poet Propertius (c.50-16BC), and of the blackberry by the Greek dramatist

Aeschylus (c.525–456BC) and the Greek physician Hippocrates (c.460–357BC). The roots and foliage of most *Rubus* species contain tannins and flavonoids, while the fruits are rich in vitamin C, organic acids, sugars, and pectin. Recent research into the active constituents of *R. idaeus*, which relax the uterus in pregnancy, has isolated a substance known as "fragarine." *R. fruticosus* was used by the ancient Greeks to treat gout, and by the Romans for sore mouths and inflammation of the bowel. It is considered to be interchangeable with *R. villosus* (the American blackberry), which entered the *U.S. Pharmacopoeia* in 1820 as an astringent tonic. Various species were used by native N Americans to cure diarrhea and dysentery, including *R. hispidus* (swamp dewberry), *R. odoratus* (purple-flowered raspberry, thimbleberry), *R. parviflorus* (thimbleberry), and *R. procumbens* (creeping blackberry), as well as *R. villosus*. *R. idaeus* was brought to the US by colonists, but proved less successful than native species such as *R. occidentalis* (thimbleberry, black raspberry), with which it was crossed to give black-red or purple raspberries. The fruits of *R. idaeus* were used by several tribes to flavor medicines. This use was first listed in the *U.S. Pharmacopoeia* in 1882 and remains important. *R. coreanus* was first mentioned in Chinese medical literature c.AD500. It is one of several oriental species known as "ghost brambles" or "whitewashed brambles" on account of their stems, which are coated in a gray-white wax. It is used interchangeably with *R. chingii*. The red-fruited *R. parvifolius* (Japanese bramble) is also used, its leaves and roots for skin problems, and unripe dried fruits as a tonic and aphrodisiac.

R. coreanus (Chinese raspberry) p.194

PARTS USED Fruits (*fu pen zi*).
PROPERTIES An astringent herb that acts as a kidney and liver tonic.
USES OF THE HERB
MEDICINAL Internally for complaints associated with disturbed liver and kidney functions, such as urinary dysfunction, premature graying, blurred vision, infertility, impotence, and premature ejaculation.

R. fruticosus (blackberry, bramble) p.194

PARTS USED Leaves, roots, root bark, fruits.
PROPERTIES An astringent, tonic, mildly diuretic herb.
USES OF THE HERB
CULINARY Dried leaves are added to herbal tea blends. Fruits are eaten raw or cooked, and made into syrups, cordials, jams, jellies, and wine.
MEDICINAL Internally for diarrhea, dysentery, hemorrhoids, and cystitis. Externally for sore throat, mouth ulcers, and gum inflammations (leaves, roots, and root bark).

R. idaeus (raspberry) p.194

PARTS USED Leaves, fruits.
PROPERTIES An astringent herb that tones the uterine muscles during pregnancy.
USES OF THE HERB
CULINARY Fruits are eaten raw or cooked.
MEDICINAL Internally for diarrhea and as a preparation for childbirth. Given to pregnant women in the last three months and during labor, but not in early pregnancy. Externally for tonsillitis, mouth inflammation, sores, conjunctivitis, minor wounds, burns, and varicose ulcers. Combines well with *Agrimonia eupatoria* (see p.231) and *Geum urbanum* (see p.288) for diarrhea; with *Euphrasia officinalis* (see p.281) as an eye lotion; and with *Salvia officinalis* (see p.346) as a mouthwash and gargle.
ECONOMIC Fruit is made into syrups, cordials, jams, jellies, wine, and purées, and used to flavor vinegar. Fruit essence is added to shampoos and bath preparations. Fruit syrup is a flavoring agent for medicines.
VARIANT
R. i. **'Aureus'**, p.194.

GROWTH AND HARVEST

GROWTH Crop (except *R. i.* 'Aureus': ornamental). Moist, well-drained soil in sun or partial shade. Propagate by seed sown in spring (species only), or by softwood cuttings in summer, or by leaf-bud cuttings in late summer, or by hardwood cuttings in winter, or by tip layering in summer (*R. fruticosus*), or by root cuttings and suckers during dormancy (*R. idaeus*), or by division in early spring or autumn. *R. fruticosus* may be trained against a wall. Remove old stems after fruiting. In spring, lightly prune plants grown for fruit. Plants may be damaged by aphids, raspberry fruit worm, raspberry beetle, crown gall, cane blight, *Botrytis*, and virus disease. *R. fruticosus* is subject to statutory control as a weed in some countries, notably in parts of Australia.
HARVEST Leaves (*R. fruticosus*, *R. idaeus*) are picked before flowering and dried for use in infusions, liquid extracts, and tablets. Roots (*R. fruticosus*) are lifted in summer and dried for use in decoctions. Fruits are harvested when ripe and dried for use in decoctions (*R. coreanus*), or used fresh or frozen for juice, syrups, and culinary purposes.

RUMEX Dock, sorrel
(Polygonaceae)

R. crispus and *R. obtusifolius* (broad-leaved dock, lapathum), long used to treat skin complaints, are similar in constituents, containing the laxative anthraquinone. *R. crispus* gained ascendancy among 19th-century American Physiomedicalists and predominates in modern practice. The roots of *R. aquatica* (water dock) are powdered as a dentifrice and used internally in similar ways to *R. crispus*. *R. acetosella* (sheep's sorrel) is more diuretic and is used for urinary complaints. Most species also contain oxalates, similar to those found in spinach and rhubarb. Oxalates are poisonous in excess, especially for those with a tendency to rheumatism, arthritis, gout, kidney stones, and hyperacidity. They are also acidic, which may affect sensitive teeth. In the past, young leaves of several species of *Rumex* were picked as pot herbs. Culpeper regarded docks as "exceeding strengthening to the liver… and as wholesome a pot herb as any" (*The English Physitian Enlarged*, 1653). Most people today would find docks unpalatable, but sorrels remain popular.

R. acetosa (sorrel) p.194

PARTS USED Leaves.
PROPERTIES An acidic, astringent, cooling herb with diuretic effects.
USES OF THE HERB
CULINARY Fresh, young leaves are added to salads, sauces, soups, cream cheese, and egg dishes, or puréed to add color and acidity to mayonnaise and pancake batter.
MEDICINAL Seldom used.
ECONOMIC Juice is used to remove rust, mold, and ink stains from linen, wood, silver, and wicker.

R. crispus (curled dock, yellow dock) p.194

PARTS USED Roots.
PROPERTIES A bitter, astringent, cooling herb that stimulates the liver and gall bladder, cleanses toxins, and has a laxative effect.
USES OF THE HERB
MEDICINAL Internally for chronic skin diseases, jaundice, constipation (especially associated with skin eruptions), liver disorders, and anemia. Excess may cause nausea and dermatitis. Combined with *Taraxacum officinale* (see p.360) or *Smilax* spp. (see p.354) for skin conditions, and with molasses as a blood tonic. Used in homeopathy for laryngitis, dry cough, and sore throat.

R. scutatus (French sorrel, buckler-leaf sorrel) p.194

PARTS USED Leaves.
PROPERTIES A mildly acidic, astringent, cooling herb that has diuretic effects.
USES OF THE HERB
CULINARY The leaves are used in the same ways as *R. acetosa*, and are often preferred because of their lower acidity.
VARIANT
R.s. **'Silver Shield'**, p.194.

GROWTH AND HARVEST

GROWTH Ornamental (*R. crispus*: crop). Moist soil in sun or partial shade. They grow poorly ►

in hot weather. Propagate by seed sown in spring, or by division in autumn or spring. *R. crispus* is subject to statutory control as a weed in some countries, notably in parts of Australia.
HARVEST Leaves (*R. acetosa*, *R. scutatus*) are picked before flowering and used fresh. Roots (*R. crispus*) are lifted in autumn and dried for use in decoctions, liquid extracts, and tinctures. *R. acetosa* and *R. crispus* have deep roots and may be difficult to eradicate when well established. *R. scutatus* is invasive.

RUSCUS
(Liliaceae/Ruscaeae)

R. aculeatus is used for medicinal, decorative, and culinary purposes. It contains saponins that reduce vascular permeability. Dioscorides (first century AD) mentioned it as a remedy for kidney stones. Exploitation and wild collection of *Ruscus* species may be subject to management measures.

R. aculeatus (butcher's broom, box holly, Jew's myrtle) p.195

PARTS USED Whole plant, young shoots, roots.
PROPERTIES An aromatic, diuretic, mildly laxative herb that reduces inflammation, increases perspiration, and constricts the veins.
USES OF THE HERB
CULINARY Young shoots are eaten like asparagus.
MEDICINAL Internally, formerly for jaundice, gout, and kidney and bladder stones; now for venous insufficiency and hemorrhoids. Not given to patients with hypertension. Externally for hemorrhoids.
ECONOMIC Fruiting branches are used in Christmas decorations.

GROWTH AND HARVEST
GROWTH Ornamental. Well-drained to dry soil in sun or shade. Propagate by seed sown in autumn, or by division in spring or autumn. Seeds may take 18 months to germinate. Remove dead shoots in spring. To ensure good fruiting, plants should be set in groups of several females to each male.
HARVEST Plants are cut in late spring and roots lifted in autumn, then dried for use in decoctions, ointments, and suppositories. Young shoots are gathered in spring for culinary use.

RUTA Rue
(Rutaceae)

R. graveolens contains flavonoids (notably rutin) that reduce capillary fragility, which may explain why rue is a traditional remedy for failing eyesight. The potent chemistry of rue has always been regarded as protective: it was an ingredient of Mithridates' antidotes and of "four thieves' vinegar," which protected from contagion a band of thieves who plundered the bodies of plague victims; posies of rue and southernwood (*Artemisia abrotanum*, see p.243) were once placed in courtrooms to ward off jail fever. Rue is also mentioned a number of times in the Bible, though this is more likely to refer to *R. chalapensis* (fringed rue), since it has a more southerly distribution. Rue was much more widely used in the past, largely because there is little demand now for an antidote to poisons, witches, and plagues!

R. graveolens (rue, herb of grace, herbygrass) p.195

PARTS USED Leaves.
PROPERTIES A bitter, pungent, warming herb that stimulates the uterus, relaxes spasms, improves digestion, increases perspiration, and strengthens capillaries.
USES OF THE HERB
CULINARY Rue is sometimes recommended for use with food, but the flavor is strong and bitter.
MEDICINAL Internally for menstrual problems, colic, epilepsy, and rheumatic pain. Excess affects central nervous system and may prove fatal. Not given to pregnant women. Externally for sore eyes, earache, skin diseases, neuralgia, and rheumatism. Used in homeopathy for sprains, bruising over bones, tennis elbow, backache, weak eyesight, and eye strain.
ECONOMIC Leaves are used to flavor Italian grape liqueur (*grappa*), and were an ingredient of sack (mead).
VARIANTS
R. g. **'Jackman's Blue'**, p.195.
R. g. **'Variegata'**, p.195.

GROWTH AND HARVEST
GROWTH Ornamental. Well-drained, neutral to alkaline soil in sun. Propagate by seed (except *R. g.* 'Jackman's Blue') sown in spring, or by semiripe cuttings in summer. Cut back hard in spring. *R. g.* 'Variegata' is unusual among variegated cultivars in coming true from seed.
HARVEST Leaves are picked in spring and summer, and dried for use in infusions, liquid extracts, and powders.
WARNING Serious skin irritant in sunlight, causing severe blistering.

SALIX Willow, osier
(Salicaceae)

Willow bark has been used since the time of Dioscorides (first century AD) for pain relief and to lower fever. Willows yield salicylic acid, which was first synthesized in 1838 and provides the basis of aspirin. *S. cinerea* (gray willow), *S. fragilis* (crack willow), the American *S. nigra* (black willow), *S. pentandra* (bay willow), and *S. purpurea* (purple osier), are all used interchangeably with *S. alba*. Several other species were used by native N Americans, who drank strong willow-bark tea to induce sweating as a cure for fever, and the stems were used in basketmaking. The willow was also once regarded as a symbol of desolation and grief: garlands of the plant were worn by those deserted by their loves.

S. alba (white willow) p.195

PARTS USED Leaves, bark.
PROPERTIES A bitter, astringent, cooling herb that relieves pain, lowers fever, and reduces inflammation.
USES OF THE HERB
MEDICINAL Internally for minor feverish illnesses and colic (leaves), rheumatism, arthritis, gout, inflammatory stages of autoimmune diseases, diarrhea and dysentery, feverish illnesses, neuralgia, and headache (bark). Combined with *Cimicifuga racemosa* (see p.261), *Guaiacum officinale* (see p.290), and *Apium graveolens* (see p.240) for rheumatoid arthritis.
VARIANTS
S. a. var. ***vitellina***, p.195.
S. a. var. ***vitellina* 'Britzensis'**, syn.
S. a. 'Chermesina', p.195.

GROWTH AND HARVEST
GROWTH Ornamental. Moist to wet, heavy soil in sun. Propagate by semiripe cuttings in summer, or by hardwood cuttings in winter. Willows are susceptible to aphids, caterpillars, scale insects, sawfly, leaf beetles, willow heart rot, galls, and rust.
HARVEST Leaves are collected during the growing season and used fresh or dried for infusions. Bark is removed throughout the summer and dried for use in decoctions, liquid extracts, powders, tablets, and tinctures.

SALVADORA
(Salvadoraceae)

Four or five species of evergreen, salt-tolerant trees and shrubs make up this genus found in drier areas of Africa, the Middle East, India, and China. The seeds of *Salvadora* species are rich in volatile mustard oils, which are similar in effect to those found in true mustards (*Brassica juncea* and *B. nigra*, see p.250, and *Sinapis alba*, see p.353). Research suggests that *S. persica*, which was first found in Persia, is the plant described in the parable of the mustard seed (Matthew 13: 31–2): "which indeed is the least of all seeds: but when it is grown, it is the greatest among herbs, and becometh a tree." All parts of *S. persica* are used locally for medicinal and veterinary purposes. Toothbrushes are made from sections of root by removing the bark from one end and fraying the inner wood, which is then chewed and applied to teeth and gums.

S. persica (toothbrush tree, salt bush, mustard tree)

Tender shrub or small tree, height 6–20ft (2–6m), spread 15ft (5m), with gray, pendulous branches and bright green, elliptic leaves up to 2½in (6cm) long. Small, green-white, bell-shaped flowers are produced throughout the year, followed by globose, red to purple, aromatic fruits. Found in seasonally flooded areas of Africa, Arabia, and India.

PARTS USED Leaves, twigs, wood, root bark, roots, fruits, seeds.
PROPERTIES An astringent, stimulant herb that is diuretic and expectorant and cleanses toxins (leaves), destroys parasites (leaves, root bark), promotes healing (wood), improves appetite and bowel function, regulates the menstrual cycle (fruits), and stimulates the circulation (fruits, seeds).
USES OF THE HERB
MEDICINAL Internally for colds, skin complaints, urinary problems, syphilis, intestinal parasites, constipation, enlarged spleen, poor appetite, menstrual problems, rheumatism, and arthritis. Externally for abscesses and swellings (leaves), poisonous bites, bruises, and oral hygiene.
ECONOMIC Leaves are burned as a source of salt. Seeds yield a wax used on skin and for candles.

GROWTH AND HARVEST

GROWTH Wild-collected. Well-drained, seasonally moist to wet soil in sun, minimum 50–55°F (10–13°C). Propagate by semiripe cuttings in summer, rooted in sand, at 64°F (18°C).
HARVEST Leaves are picked as required for use fresh, or dried and powdered. Both leaves and wood are burned to a fine ash for external veterinary applications. Bark and wood are dried and powdered. Twigs and roots are cut as required for use fresh. Fruits are collected when ripe for use fresh, cooked, or dried. Seeds may be removed for use whole or crushed in oil.

SALVIA Sage
(Labiatae/Lamiaceae)

S. officinalis has been cultivated in northern Europe since medieval times, and was introduced to N America in the 17th century. Known as *Salvia salvatrix* ("sage the savior"), its reputation for promoting longevity began in Classical times. Sages are rich in volatile oils, which vary from species to species, producing a wide range of aromas. *S. officinalis* contains a camphoraceous oil, consisting of about 50 percent thujone. In excess, this compound is hallucinogenic, addictive, and toxic. *S. fruticosa* has less thujone, and *S. lavandulifolia* has none. *S. officinalis* also contains rosmarinic acid. It has the effect of stopping perspiration within about two hours of the correct dose being given, and the medicinal uses of both it and *S. sclarea* were known to Dioscorides. The ancient Egyptians used *S. officinalis* to increase fertility. In C America the flowers and minty leaves of *S. microphylla* (red bush) are infused to treat fevers, and the mucilaginous seeds of the Mexican *S. hispanica* are mixed with water, lemon juice, and sugar to make a drink known as *chia*. *S. miltiorhiza* (known as "red ginseng" because of its red roots), has been an important Chinese medicinal herb since 206BC. *S. officinalis* is a widely used culinary herb; the dried leaves are often mixed with those of *S. fruticosa*, *S. pomifera*, and *S. lavandulifolia* as commercial dried sage.

S. clevelandii (blue sage, Jim sage) p.196

PARTS USED Leaves.
PROPERTIES A highly aromatic herb.
USES OF THE HERB
AROMATIC Dried leaves may be added to potpourris. Used ceremonially by native Americans.

S. coccinea (Texas sage) p.196

PARTS USED Leaves.
PROPERTIES An aromatic herb.
USES OF THE HERB
AROMATIC Mainly grown as an aromatic ornamental.
VARIANT
***S. c.* 'Lady in Red'.**
Very free-flowering dwarf cultivar for bedding, with brilliant red flowers. Height 12–15in (30–38cm), spread 9–12in (23–30cm).

S. dorisiana (fruit-scented sage) p.196

PARTS USED Leaves.
PROPERTIES An aromatic herb with a fruity scent.
USES OF THE HERB
CULINARY Leaves are used in salads and dressings.
AROMATIC Leaves are dried for potpourris.

S. elegans 'Scarlet Pineapple', syn. *S. rutilans* (pineapple sage) p.196

PARTS USED Leaves and flowers.
PROPERTIES An aromatic herb with a pineapple scent.
USES OF THE HERB
CULINARY Sprigs are added to cold drinks and fruit salads. Fresh leaves may be placed under sponge cake mixtures to give a subtle scent, and fresh or dried leaves give a sagelike aroma to pork dishes. The delicious flowers are made into fritters.

S. fruticosa, syn. *S. triloba* (Greek sage) p.196

PARTS USED Leaves, oil.
PROPERTIES Similar to *S. lavandulifolia*.
USES OF THE HERB
CULINARY Leaves are infused for *chanomilia* (Cyprus) and mixed with those of *S. pomifera* for *faskomelo* tea (Greece).
MEDICINAL Internally for influenza, coughs, and rheumatic pains.
ECONOMIC Dried leaves make up 50–95 percent of commercial sage. Oil is used to adulterate spike lavender oil (from *Lavandula latifolia*).

S. lavandulifolia (narrow-leaved sage, Spanish sage) p.196

PARTS USED Leaves, oil.
PROPERTIES An antiseptic, astringent, tonic herb with a lavender–balsam aroma. It improves digestion, lowers fever, strengthens the immune and nervous systems, cleanses toxins, stimulates the uterus, and has expectorant and estrogenic effects.
USES OF THE HERB
AROMATIC Oil is used in perfumery.
MEDICINAL Internally for digestive and respiratory complaints, menstrual problems, infertility, nervous tension, and depression. Not given in pregnancy.
ECONOMIC Leaves are used as a substitute for *S. officinalis* in food flavoring and made into tea. Oil is used in food flavoring, soaps, and cosmetics.

S. miltiorhiza (red sage, Chinese sage)

Hairy, herbaceous perennial, hardy to 5°F (–15°C), height 12–32in (30–80cm), spread 9–12in (23–30cm), with red-purple roots and toothed leaves. Spikes of blue-purple flowers, about ¾in (2cm) long, appear from late spring to autumn.
PARTS USED Roots (*dan shen*).
PROPERTIES A bitter, sedative, cooling herb that controls bleeding, stimulates the circulatory and immune systems, lowers cholesterol levels, promotes healing, and inhibits many disease-causing organisms. It acts mainly on the heart energy.
USES OF THE HERB
MEDICINAL Internally for coronary heart disease, poor circulation, palpitations, irritability, insomnia, breast abscesses, mastitis, ulcers, boils, sores, bruises, menstrual problems, and postnatal pains. Often combined with *Angelica polymorpha* var. *sinensis* (see p.238) for suppressed menstruation.

S. officinalis (common sage) p.196

PARTS USED Leaves, oil, flowers.
PROPERTIES An astringent, antiseptic, anti-inflammatory herb with a camphoraceous aroma. It relaxes spasms, suppresses perspiration and lactation, improves liver function and digestion, and has antidepressant and estrogenic effects. Many herbalists regard *S. o.* Purpurascens Group as more potent than the species.
USES OF THE HERB
CULINARY Leaves are made into tea, and used to flavor *saltimbocca* and liver (Italy), Sage Derby cheese, sausages, eels, and stuffings for goose and pork (northern Europe). Flowers are edible.
MEDICINAL Internally for indigestion, wind, liver complaints, excessive lactation, night sweats, excessive salivation (as in Parkinson's disease), profuse perspiration (as in tuberculosis), anxiety, depression, female sterility, and menopausal problems. Toxic in excess or over long periods.

Not given in pregnancy or to epileptics. Externally for insect bites; throat, mouth, gum, and skin infections; and vaginal discharge. Combined with *Potentilla erecta* (see p.334) as a gargle and with *Chamaemelum nobile* (see p.259) and *Filipendula ulmaria* (see p.283) for digestive problems.
ECONOMIC Oil is used as a fixative for perfumes and added to toothpastes and bioactivating cosmetics.
VARIANTS
S. o. **'Albiflora'**, syn. *S. o.* 'Alba', p.196.
S. o. **'Berggarten'**, p.197.
S. o. **'Icterina'**, p.197.
S. o. **'Kew Gold'**, p.197.
S. o. **Purpurascens Group**, p.197.
S. o. **'Purpurascens Variegata'**
Similar to *S. o.* 'Purpurascens' but with irregularly pink-splashed purple leaves. Hardy to 5°F (–15°C), height 24–32in (60–80cm), spread 3ft (1m).
S. o. **'Tricolor'**
Less vigorous than the species, making it a good subject for containers. The gray-green leaves are irregularly variegated pink and ivory. Hardy to 5°F (–15°C), height and spread 18–24in (45–60cm).

S. pomifera, syn. *S. calycina* (apple-bearing sage) p.197

PARTS USED Leaves, galls.
PROPERTIES Similar to *S. officinalis* but stronger.
USES OF THE HERB
ECONOMIC Leaves are used instead of *S. officinalis* in food flavoring, and blended with *S. fruticosa* as *faskomelo* tea (Greece). Galls are made into a conserve and medicinal candy (Greece).

S. sclarea (clary sage, clear eye, muscatel sage) p.197

PARTS USED Leaves, flowers, seeds, oil.
PROPERTIES A bitter, astringent, warming herb with mucilaginous seeds and a vanilla–balsam aroma. It relaxes spasms, aids digestion, stimulates the uterus, calms nerves, controls vomiting, and is reputedly aphrodisiac.
USES OF THE HERB
CULINARY Fresh young leaves are made into fritters. Flowers may be added to salads and made into tea.
MEDICINAL Internally for vomiting, poor appetite, and menstrual complaints. Not given in pregnancy. Externally for foreign bodies in the eye or skin (seeds), minor injuries, and ulcers.
ECONOMIC Young leaves are infused with elder-flowers to give a muscatel bouquet to Rhine wines. "Muscatel oil" has an ambergris aroma and is used in soaps and cosmetics, and as a fixative in perfumery.
VARIANT
S. s. var. ***turkestanica***, p.197.

S. viridis, syn. *S. horminum* (bluebeard, red-topped sage, painted sage) p.197

PARTS USED Leaves, flowering spikes, seeds, oil.
PROPERTIES An aromatic, antiseptic herb.
USES OF THE HERB
CULINARY Seeds and leaves may be used to flavor food.
MEDICINAL Externally for sore gums and as snuff.
ECONOMIC Oil gives flavor to wine and beer.
VARIANT
S. v. **'Claryssa'**, p.197.

GROWTH AND HARVEST

GROWTH Ornamental, except *S. miltiorhiza* and *S. pomifera* (crop). Well-drained to dry, neutral to alkaline soil in sun. *S. miltiorhiza* needs moist, sandy soil. *S. dorisiana* and *S. elegans* 'Scarlet Pineapple' require minimum 41°F (5°C). Some hardy sages will survive 14°F (–10°C), but may succumb to lower temperatures, especially if conditions are damp. Propagate by seed sown in spring (species and annual cultivars only), or by softwood cuttings in spring and summer, or by division (*S. miltiorhiza*), or by layering in autumn or spring. *S. sclarea* self-seeds freely in sandy soil. If grown under cover, pinch out new growths regularly to encourage a compact habit. Plants under cover are prone to spider mite, aphids, and whitefly. Sages become woody and sparse with age and should be replaced every 4–7 years.
HARVEST Leaves are picked for immediate use, or before flowers open for oil distillation and drying; dried leaves are used in infusions, liquid extracts, and tinctures. Roots (*S. miltiorhiza*) are lifted in late autumn and winter, and dried for pills, decoctions, and tinctures. Ripe seeds (*S. sclarea*) are dried for use in macerations. Flower spikes (*S. viridis*) are cut in summer when the bracts are most colorful. Galls (*S. pomifera*) are picked in spring and candied.

SAMBUCUS Elder
(Caprifoliaceae)

Elder has been called "the medicine chest of the people," providing remedies for most common complaints. It is revered by gypsies and is associated with the Jewish kabbalah. Historically, all parts of *S. nigra* are used medicinally, but modern usage favors the flowers. They contain a plant acid that is apparently anti-inflammatory, flavonoids (including rutin, as found in *Ruta graveolens*, see p.345), and fixed oil. The leaves contain toxic cyanogenic glycosides (as found in *Prunus* species, see p.335).

S. nigra (common elder) p.197

PARTS USED Leaves, bark, flowers, fruits.
PROPERTIES A bitter, pungent, cooling herb that lowers fever, reduces inflammation, soothes irritation, and has diuretic, alterative, and antimucus effects (flowers, fruits); leaves are insecticidal, antiseptic, and healing.
USES OF THE HERB
CULINARY Flower heads are fried in batter (elderflower fritters). Flowers give a muscatel flavor to stewed fruit, jellies, and jam (especially gooseberry). Fruits are made into sauce and used to flavor and color stewed fruit and jellies (dried fruits are less bitter). Juice is boiled with sugar to make a cordial (elderberry rob), flavored with ginger and cloves.
MEDICINAL Internally for influenza, colds, excess mucus, sinusitis, and feverish illnesses (flowers, fruits), rheumatic complaints (fruits), and constipation and arthritic conditions (bark). Externally for minor burns and chilblains (leaves, bark); sore eyes, irritated or inflamed skin, mouth ulcers, and minor injuries (flowers). Combined with *Mentha* x *piperita* (see p.311), *Achillea millefolium* (see p.227), *Hyssopus officinalis* (see p.295), or *Tilia cordata* (see p.363) for upper respiratory tract infections (flowers, fruits); and with *Menyanthes trifoliata* (see p.312) or *Salix alba* (see p.345) for rheumatism (fruits).
ECONOMIC Flowers are used in skin lotions (elderflower water, or *Aqua Sambuci*), oils, and ointments. Flowers are also used to make white wine and "elderflower champagne." Fruits are made into wine and ketchup. Leaves are boiled and strained to make a natural insecticidal spray.
VARIANTS
S. n. **'Aurea'**, p.197.
S. n. **'Guincho Purple'**, syn. *S. n.* 'Purpurea', p.197.
S. n. f. ***laciniata***, p.197.
S. n. **'Marginata'**, syn. *S. n.* 'Albovariegata', *S. n.* 'Argenteomarginata', p.197.

GROWTH AND HARVEST

GROWTH Ornamental. Rich, moist, neutral to alkaline soil in sun or partial shade. Propagate by seed sown in autumn (species only), or by softwood cuttings in summer, or by hardwood cuttings in winter. Cut back almost to ground level during the winter to ensure large, colorful leaves in ornamental varieties. Do not prune hard if flowers and fruit are required. Elders are prone to aphids in poor conditions and may be affected by *Arabis* mosaic virus.
HARVEST Leaves are picked in summer and used fresh. Bark is stripped in late winter, before new leaves appear, or in autumn before leaves change color, and dried for decoctions. Fully open flower heads are collected and dried whole; the flowers are then stripped off for infusions, floral water, liquid extracts, ointment, and tinctures. Fruits are harvested when ripe, separated from the stalks, and used fresh or as juice, or dried for use in decoctions, syrups, and tinctures.
WARNING Leaves and raw berries are harmful if eaten.

SANGUINARIA Bloodroot
(Papaveraceae)

In common with most members of the poppy family, *S. canadensis* contains a number of opium-like alkaloids. This toxic herb was used by various native N American peoples to dye skin (often ceremonially) and implements red, and to induce therapeutic vomiting. Also used to treat sore throats, ringworm, and rheumatism, it appears in the *U.S. Pharmacopoeia* (1820–1926) as a stimulating expectorant. In recent years it has become important as a source of sanguinarine, a dental plaque inhibitor.

S. canadensis (bloodroot, red puccoon, red Indian paint) p.198

PARTS USED Rhizomes.
PROPERTIES A bitter, acrid, warming herb that has expectorant and diuretic effects, lowers fever,

relaxes spasms, and slows the heart rate. It is locally anesthetic and effective against many pathogenic organisms.

USES OF THE HERB

MEDICINAL Internally for bronchial, respiratory tract, and throat infections, and poor peripheral circulation. Excess depresses the central nervous system, causes nausea and vomiting, and may prove fatal. Not given to pregnant and lactating women. For use by qualified practitioners only. Externally for skin diseases, warts, nasal polyps, benign skin tumors, sore throat, and chilblains. Combined with *Lobelia inflata* (see p.305) for bronchial asthma; with *Salvia officinalis* (p.346) and *Capsicum annuum* (see p.254) as a gargle for pharyngitis; with *Myrica cerifera* (see p.314) in snuff for polyps, and with *Chelidonium majus* (see p.259) for warts. Used in homeopathy for migraine.

ECONOMIC Extracts are added to toothpaste and mouthwash as an antiplaque agent.The rhizome yields an orange-red dye.

VARIANT

S. c. **'Plena'**, syn. *S. c.* 'Flore Pleno', *S. c.* 'Multiplex', p.198.

> **GROWTH AND HARVEST**
>
> GROWTH Ornamental. Well-drained, humus-rich soil in sun or partial shade. Propagate by seed sown in autumn (species only), or by division after flowering.
>
> HARVEST Rhizomes are lifted in autumn and dried for liquid extracts, ointments, and tinctures.

SANGUISORBA
(Rosaceae)

S. officinalis is used for its unique tannins, known as sanguiins, and glycosides (sanguisorbins). Use of the roots was first recorded in Chinese medicine in the *Shen Nong Canon of Herbs* during the Han dynasty (206BC–AD23). Western medicine favors the leafy parts. Culpeper described its astringent qualities graphically: "to staunch bleeding inward or outward, lasks, scourings, the bloody flux, women's too abundant flux of courses, the whites, and the choleric belchings and castings of the stomach." *S. minor*, burnet, is a cooling herb valued for its cucumber flavor. The leaves are added to salads, vinegars, and tomato juice.

S. officinalis, syn. *Poterium officinalis* (great burnet) p.198

PARTS USED Leaves, roots (*di yu*).

PROPERTIES A bitter, astringent, cooling herb that controls bleeding, reduces inflammation, promotes healing, and destroys many pathogenic organisms.

USES OF THE HERB

MEDICINAL Internally for diarrhea, dysentery, ulcerative colitis, hemorrhoids, hemorrhage, and abnormal uterine bleeding. Externally for burns, scalds, sores, and skin diseases. An ingredient in Chinese formulas to treat cervical erosion and uterine and gastrointestinal hemorrhages, and in a dentifrice for periodontal disease. Roots are often stir-baked or charred to increase astringency.

> **GROWTH AND HARVEST**
>
> GROWTH Ornamental. Rich, moist soil in sun. Propagate by seed sown in autumn or spring, or by division in spring.
>
> HARVEST Leafy parts are cut before flowers open and dried for use in infusions, liquid extracts, and tinctures. Roots are lifted in autumn and dried for decoctions.

SANTALUM Sandalwood
(Santalaceae)

Sandalwood has been used as medicine, incense, and perfume in the East for 4,000 years, having special importance in Hindu devotional practices. Traditionally the wood is burned at Buddhist funerals and is ground to make Hindu caste marks. It reached Europe in the 1880s and was soon used in perfumery. *S. fernandezianum*, a native of the Juan Fernandez Islands in the south Pacific, was recorded as rare by 1740 and extinct by 1916. *S. album* is cultivated in a semiwild state alongside the natural host. It is rich in volatile oil, with at least 90 percent sesquiterpene alcohols, known as "santalols." The oil is present in all parts of the tree: six percent of the root, four percent of leaves, five percent of heartwood, two percent of bark. Dry, rocky areas give high yields and quality. It was reported in a 19th-century gardening manual that *S. album* was being grown successfully at Kew Gardens in London in "very sandy loam," but it is now seen mostly in the tropics. Sandalwood oil is often adulterated with castor oil and oil of cedar; oil from the related *S. spicatum* (Australian sandalwood) and *Osyris tenuifolia* may also be substituted, or the quite different *Amyris balsamifera* (a relative of *Phellodendron* and *Ptelea*). Various parts of *S. lanceolatum* (plumbush), a small tree or shrub common on rocky ground in Australia, are used in Aboriginal medicine for sores, boils, itching, gonorrhea, constipation, and rheumatism; the tree contains a bactericidal volatile oil.

S. album (Indian sandalwood, white sandalwood) p.198

PARTS USED Heartwood, roots, oil.

PROPERTIES An aromatic, bittersweet, astringent herb that cools the body, calms the mind, relieves spasms, and improves digestion. It has diuretic, analgesic, and antiseptic effects.

USES OF THE HERB

AROMATIC Oil is used in perfumery.

MEDICINAL Internally for genitourinary disorders, fever, sunstroke, digestive problems, and abdominal pain. Externally for skin complaints.

ECONOMIC Sapwood is used for carved objects. Ground wood provides a Hindu caste-mark pigment. Oil is used in soaps, body oils, food flavoring, and incense.

> **GROWTH AND HARVEST**
>
> GROWTH Crop. Well-drained, moist, fertile soil in partial shade, minimum 59°F (15°C). Propagate by seed when ripe, presoaked in a 1:9 solution of bleach, sown in vermiculite at 59–70°F (15–21°C). Seedlings are planted alongside host when roots reach 1½in (4cm) long.
>
> HARVEST Trees are usually felled when at least 50 years old. Wood is dried for use in decoctions, liquid extracts, powders, and tinctures. Oil is pressed or extracted from heartwood and roots.

SANTOLINA Lavender cotton
(Compositae)

Culpeper described *S. chamaecyparissus*, in *The English Physitian Enlarged* (1653), as a remedy for poisonous bites, intestinal worms, and skin irritations. Although seldom used today, research in the 1980s showed it to be an effective anti-inflammatory.

S. chamaecyparissus (lavender cotton, cotton lavender) p.198

PARTS USED Leaves, flowering stems.

PROPERTIES A bitter, stimulant herb with a strong, chamomile-like aroma. It reduces inflammation, improves digestion, stimulates the uterus and liver, and expels intestinal parasites.

USES OF THE HERB

AROMATIC Dried leaves are added to potpourris as a fixative.

MEDICINAL Internally for poor digestion, digestive and menstrual problems, worms in children, and jaundice. Externally for stings, bites, minor wounds, and skin inflammations.

ECONOMIC Dried leaves are blended with *Tussilago farfara* (see p.365) and *Chamaemelum nobile* (see p.259) in herbal tobacco.

VARIANTS

S. c. **'Lemon Queen'**, p.198.

S. c. var. ***nana***, p.198.

S. c. **'Pretty Carol'**, p.199.

> **GROWTH AND HARVEST**
>
> GROWTH Ornamental. Light, well-drained to dry soil in sun. Tolerates sandy and poor, alkaline soils. Propagate by semiripe cuttings in summer. Remove dead flower heads and trim in autumn. Cut back hard in spring.
>
> HARVEST Leaves are picked in the growing season, flowering stems in summer; both are dried for use in infusions and powders.

SAPONARIA Soapwort
(Caryophyllaceae)

Saponin-rich plants such as *S. officinalis* were widely used for cleaning purposes before commercial production of soap in the 1800s. *S. officinalis* is still used in the Middle East and by museums for cleaning furniture, tapestries, and pictures. In *The English Physitian Enlarged* (1653), Culpeper described *S. officinalis* as "an absolute cure in the French pox [syphilis]." The plant's use in treating these symptoms, and in other venereal diseases, was also recommended by Mrs. Grieve (*A Modern Herbal*, 1931), especially where the treatment with mercury (standard for nearly 400 years) had failed.

S. officinalis (soapwort, bouncing Bet) p.199

PARTS USED Leafy stems, rhizomes.
PROPERTIES A diuretic, laxative, expectorant herb that clears toxins and stimulates the liver.
USES OF THE HERB
MEDICINAL Internally for gout and skin diseases, bronchial congestion, and jaundice. Rarely used today, due to its irritant effect on the digestive system. Excess destroys red blood cells and causes paralysis of the vasomotor center. Externally for skin diseases.
ECONOMIC Dried herb is used as a soap substitute for delicate materials. Although sometimes recommended as a shampoo, it can cause severe eye irritation.
VARIANTS
***S. o.* 'Dazzler'**, syn. *S. o.* 'Variegata', p.199.
***S. o.* 'Rubra Plena'**, p.199.

> **GROWTH AND HARVEST**
> **GROWTH** Ornamental. Well-drained, moist, neutral to alkaline soil in sun or partial shade. Propagate by seed sown in spring or autumn (species only), or by division when dormant, or by softwood cuttings in summer. May be invasive. Poisonous to fish; roots or foliage should not contact pond water.
> **HARVEST** Leafy stems are collected in summer, rhizomes in late autumn; both are dried for decoctions.

SARGASSUM Gulfweed
(Laminariaceae)

A genus of 150 species of brown algae found in warm seas, mainly from Australia north to Japan in the Pacific, and to Cape Cod in the Atlantic. *Sargaçao* was a description given by Portuguese navigators to floating seaweed, hence the name Sargasso Sea. *S. fusiforme* was first mentioned in the *Shen Nong Canon of Herbs* during the later Han dynasty (AD25–220). It contains 0.2 percent iodine and is effective in treating iodine deficiencies. In the 1940s Japanese research discovered anticoagulant action similar to that of heparin. It also contains alginic acid which, when combined with calcium in plasters, stops bleeding in major trauma.

S. fusiforme (gulfweed)

Yellow-brown seaweed with a broad, cylindrical holdfast and thick, fleshy, leaflike branches with midribs, toothed to lobed margins, and axillary spindle-shaped air sacs. Plants are attached to rocks when young and later become free-floating. Found off the coasts of China, Japan, and Korea.

PARTS USED Whole plant (*hai zao*).
PROPERTIES A bitter, saline, cooling herb that is expectorant and diuretic, controls bleeding, lowers blood pressure and lipid levels, softens hard swellings, acts on the thyroid, and suppresses appetite.
USES OF THE HERB
MEDICINAL Internally for goiter, tuberculosis of lymph nodes, cysts, bronchitis, edema, and hydrocele. Externally for hemorrhage.

> **GROWTH AND HARVEST**
> **GROWTH** Wild-collected. Grows on partly submerged rocks between high tide and low tide zones. Propagates by holdfasts being left to regenerate.
> **HARVEST** Whole plants are collected in winter and spring, then dried for decoctions and powders.

SAROTHAMNUS
S. scoparius. See *Cytisus scoparius.*

SASSAFRAS
(Lauraceae)

Sassafras may have been the first American plant drug to reach Europe. Discovered in Florida by the Spanish, it was used medicinally in Spain c.1560. *S. albidum* contains volatile oil, which consists of 80–90 percent safrole, as well as alkaloids, lignins, tannin, and resin. Safrole is carcinogenic in animals, and many countries no longer use the oil as a food flavoring; safrole-free bark extracts may be used instead, although their flavor is inferior.

S. albidum (sassafras) p.199

PARTS USED Leaves, roots (bark, pith, oil).
PROPERTIES A sweet, warming herb with a fennel-like aroma. It increases perspiration, relieves pain, improves digestion, and has antirheumatic, antiseptic, diuretic, and alterative effects.
USES OF THE HERB
CULINARY Leaves are dried and ground for *filé* powder to thicken soup.
ECONOMIC Extracts used as a perfumery ingredient.
MEDICINAL Internally for gastrointestinal complaints, colic, menstrual pain, skin diseases, acne, syphilis, gonorrhea, arthritis, and rheumatism (root bark). Excess (1 tsp or more of oil) causes vomiting, dilated pupils, stupor, collapse, and kidney and liver damage. Externally for sore eyes (root pith), lice, and insect bites (oil), though oil may irritate skin. Combined with *Guaiacum officinale* (see p.290) and *Smilax glabra* (see p.354) in a tea to induce therapeutic sweating in feverish illnesses.
ECONOMIC Extracts are used as flavoring by food and drink industries (especially in root beer) and in oral hygiene products. Wood shavings or roots are used to make sassafras tea. WARNING This herb, especially in the form of oil and safrole, is subject to legal restrictions in some countries.

> **GROWTH AND HARVEST**
> **GROWTH** Ornamental. Deep, rich, neutral to acid soil in sun or shade, sheltered from late spring frosts. Propagate by seed sown in autumn, by suckers in autumn, or by root cuttings in winter.
> **HARVEST** Leaves are picked and dried in spring for powder. Roots are lifted in autumn and dried for decoctions, liquid extracts, powders, and tinctures. Root bark is distilled for oil. Root pith is dried for macerations.

SATUREJA Savory
(Labiatae/Lamiaceae)

Savories are rich in volatile oils, which vary in constituents from species to species. They are similar in aroma to thymes and marjorams. In spite of their medicinal properties, savories are mainly used as culinary herbs. *S. hortensis* has been valued as a flavoring for 2,000 years.

S. acinos. See *Acinos arvensis.*

S. hortensis (summer savory) p.199

PARTS USED Leaves, flowering tops.
PROPERTIES An antiseptic, astringent, warming herb with a peppery flavor and high carvacrol content. It improves digestion, increases perspiration, has expectorant effects, stimulates the uterus and nervous system, and is reputedly aphrodisiac.
USES OF THE HERB
CULINARY Leaves flavor legumes, sausages, stuffings, meat dishes, and are used in *herbes de Provence* (with *Rosmarinus officinalis*, see p.343, *Thymus vulgaris*, see p.362, and *Origanum* species, see p.319).
MEDICINAL Internally for indigestion, nausea, colic, diarrhea, bronchial congestion, sore throat, and menstrual disorders. Not given to pregnant women. Externally for sore throat and insect stings.
ECONOMIC Extracts are used commercially in liqueurs. Often used as a salt substitute.

S. montana (winter savory) p.200

PARTS USED Leaves, shoots.
PROPERTIES As for *S. hortensis*, but with a higher proportion of thymol.
USES OF THE HERB
CULINARY Culinary uses as for *S. hortensis*.
MEDICINAL Medicinal uses as for *S. hortensis*. As an ingredient in herbal cordials for gastric complaints. Not given to pregnant women.

S. nepeta. See *Calamintha nepeta.*

S. spicigera, syn. *S. repandra* (creeping savory) p.200

PARTS USED Leaves.
PROPERTIES Similar to *S. hortensis*, but more strongly flavored.

USES OF THE HERB
CULINARY As for *S. hortensis*.
MEDICINAL As for *S. hortensis*.

S. thymbra (thyme-leaved savory) p.200

PARTS USED Leaves.
PROPERTIES A pungent, aromatic herb that improves digestion and has bactericidal and expectorant effects.
USES OF THE HERB
CULINARY Leaves have a thymelike flavor and may be added to savory breads, meat, and legume dishes.
MEDICINAL Internally, in countries of origin, as an infusion to relieve minor digestive discomfort and bronchial congestion.
ECONOMIC Oil, rich in carvacrol, and thymol is distilled from the leaves for the pharmaceutical industry.

GROWTH AND HARVEST
GROWTH Ornamental (except *S. thymbra*: crop). Well-drained to dry, neutral to alkaline soil in sun. Propagate by seed sown in spring (all species), or by division in autumn or spring, or by softwood cuttings in summer (*S. montana*, *S. spicigera*, *S. thymbra*), or by layering in spring (*S. montana*). Pinch out new shoots in spring to encourage bushiness (*S. hortensis*, *S. montana*). Cut back in autumn or spring (*S. montana*). Winter crops of *S. hortensis* may be grown in pots under cover at 45–50°F (7–10°C) or from seed sown in early autumn. It reputedly deters Mexican bean beetles if planted along rows of legumes.
HARVEST Leaves are picked during the growing season; flowering tops (*S. hortensis*) are picked in summer. Both are used fresh, or dried for infusions and oil extraction.

SAUSSUREA
(Compositae/Asteraceae)

S. lappa has been used in both Chinese and Ayurvedic medicine for thousands of years. The species is currently listed on CITES Appendix I as having become endangered through overcollecting. The roots have a pervasive scent (*mu xiang* means "wood fragrance"). Crops of *mu xiang* come mainly from Guangdong Province in China. Essential oil for perfumery comes mainly from India.

S. lappa, syn. *S. costus* (costus, *kuth*) p.200

PARTS USED Roots (*mu xiang*), oil.
PROPERTIES A bitter, pungent, warming herb that relaxes spasms, lowers blood pressure, relieves pain, and has antibacterial effects. It regulates spleen and stomach energy.
USES OF THE HERB
AROMATIC Oil has a strong, lingering scent used in perfumery.
MEDICINAL Internally for abdominal distension and pain, chest pains due to liver problems and jaundice, gall bladder pain, constipation associated with energy stagnation, and asthma. Used in Ayurvedic medicine for digestive problems, coughs, asthma, cholera, and as an alterative in skin diseases and rheumatism.

GROWTH AND HARVEST
GROWTH Crop. Moist soil in sun or partial shade. Propagate by seed sown when ripe, or by division in spring.
HARVEST Roots are lifted in autumn and spring, and dried for use in decoctions, liquid extracts, and powders, or processed for oil extraction.

SCHISANDRA
(Schisandraceae)

Schisandra was first mentioned in Chinese medical texts during the later Han dynasty (AD25–220). Different schisandras are used in northern and southern China; these were first differentiated in 1596 by Li Shi Zhen in his *Compendium of Materia Medica*. *S. chinensis* is used by both men and women as a tonic for sexual energy and is popular with women because of its reputation for improving the complexion. The Chinese name means "five-flavor fruit," because it has sweet and sour flavors in the peel and pulp, and acrid, bitter, and salty flavors in the seeds. The red-flowered *S. sphenanthera* (southern schisandra), which grows farther south and west, is used in the same ways as *S. chinensis* but is seldom exported.

S. chinensis (schisandra) p.200

PARTS USED Fruits (*wu wei zi*).
PROPERTIES A sweet and sour, astringent, warming herb that regulates secretion of body fluids, controls coughing, and moistens dry and irritated tissues. It acts as a tonic for the nervous system and kidney and heart energies.
USES OF THE HERB
MEDICINAL Internally for dry coughs, asthma, night sweats, urinary disorders, involuntary ejaculation, chronic and early morning diarrhea (associated with kidney weakness), palpitations, insomnia, poor memory, hyperacidity, hepatitis, and diabetes. Externally for irritating and allergic skin conditions. Combined with *Ophiopogon japonicus* (see p.319) and *Panax ginseng* (see p.321) as an injectable drug for shock.

GROWTH AND HARVEST
GROWTH Ornamental. Rich, well-drained, moist soil in sun or partial shade. Both male and female plants must be grown for successful fruiting. Propagate by seed sown in autumn, or by seed sown in spring after soaking overnight, or by semiripe cuttings in summer, or by layering in spring or early autumn. Remove unwanted shoots in late winter from plants trained against a wall or fence. Leaves and young growths may be damaged by aphids.
HARVEST Fruits are collected after the first frosts and sun-dried for use in decoctions, powders, and tinctures.

SCLEROTIUM
S. cocos. See *Wolfiporia cocos.*

SCOPOLIA
(Solanaceae)

Scopolia resembles *Atropa* (see p.246) and *Hyoscyamus* (see p.295) in chemistry. Four species, *S. carniolica*, *S. physaloides*, *S. lurida*, and *S. tangutica*, are all major sources of tropane alkaloids. *S. carniolica* contains hyoscine and hyoscyamine. It became popular in the US during the 19th century as a substitute for belladonna (*Atropa belladonna*, see p.246). In 1900 an alkaloid from this plant was combined with morphine from *Papaver somniferum* (see p.322) to produce "twilight sleep"; this compound was used as a pre-anesthetic prior to the administration of chloroform or ether. The Chinese *S. tangutica* yields hyoscyamine, anisdamine, and anisodine.

S. carniolica, syn. *S. atropoides* (scopolia, Japanese belladonna) p.200

PARTS USED Rhizomes.
PROPERTIES A narcotic, warming herb that dilates the pupils, relaxes spasms, and relieves pain.
USES OF THE HERB
MEDICINAL Internally, in Chinese medicine, for chronic diarrhea, dysentery, stomachache, and manic-depressive states. Mainly as a source of hyoscine, and sometimes as a substitute for *Atropa belladonna* (see p.246), notably in the manufacture of belladonna plasters, and for *Hyoscyamus niger* (see p.295). For use by qualified practitioners only.
WARNING This herb and its alkaloids are subject to legal restrictions in some countries.

GROWTH AND HARVEST
GROWTH Ornamental. Well-drained, fertile soil in shade. Propagate by seed sown in autumn, or by division in spring.
HARVEST Rhizomes are lifted in autumn and processed for extraction of alkaloids.
WARNING Toxic if eaten.

SCROPHULARIA Figwort
(Scrophulariaceae)

The use of *S. ningpoensis* in medicine dates back to the later Han dynasty (AD25– 220). *S. nodosa* contains aucubin, a mild laxative that increases excretion of uric acid from the kidneys, and harpagide. In Europe it has long been used as a medicinal herb for treating skin diseases. Culpeper felt that "a better remedy cannot be found for the king's evil" (*The English Physitian Enlarged*, 1653). "King's evil" was a term once used for scrofula (tuberculosis of the lymphatic glands). *S. auriculata* (water figwort) is used externally for healing wounds and ulcers.

S. ningpoensis (Ningpo figwort, black figwort) p.201

PARTS USED Roots (*xuan shen*).
PROPERTIES A bitter, saline, cooling herb that lowers fever, blood pressure, and blood sugar, and has antibacterial effects. Small doses act as a heart tonic; large doses depress cardiac function.

USES OF THE HERB
MEDICINAL Internally for feverish illnesses with symptoms such as rashes, delirium, and insomnia (associated with excess heat), dry cough, throat infections, abscesses, and carbuncles.

S. nodosa (common figwort) p.201

PARTS USED Whole plant.
PROPERTIES A diuretic, alterative herb that is mildly laxative, relieves pain, and stimulates the liver, heart, and circulation.
USES OF THE HERB
MEDICINAL Internally for chronic skin diseases (such as eczema, psoriasis, pruritus), mastitis, swollen lymph nodes, and poor circulation. Not given to patients with heart conditions. Externally for skin diseases (including fungal infections), wounds, burns, ulcers, and skin inflammations. Combines well with *Rumex crispus* (see p.344) for skin diseases.

GROWTH AND HARVEST
GROWTH Crop. Moist to wet soil in sun or partial shade. Propagate by seed sown in autumn or spring, or by division in spring, or by semiripe cuttings in summer. Plants may be damaged by slugs, spider mites, and whitefly.
HARVEST Roots (*S. ningpoensis*) are lifted in autumn and dried for use in decoctions. Plants (*S. nodosa*) are cut when flowering and dried for use in infusions, liquid extracts, ointments, poultices, and tinctures.

SCUTELLARIA Skullcap
(Labiatae/Lamiaceae)

S. baicalensis was mentioned in the *Shen Nong Canon of Herbs*, which dates back to the later Han dynasty (AD25–220). It has been researched in China and found to contain flavonoids that greatly improve liver function and have anti-inflammatory and anti-allergenic effects. *S. barbata* (barbed skullcap) is used as a detoxicant, mainly for certain kinds of cancer, liver diseases, poisonous bites, and pharyngitis. *S. lateriflora* was used by the Cherokee to promote menstruation. It was investigated by Dr. Van Deveer in 1772 and found to be useful in treating rabies, hence its common name, "mad dog skullcap." The plant was first listed as a sedative and antispasmodic in the *U.S. Pharmacopoeia* in 1863 and is still regarded by herbalists as a very effective remedy. *S. galericulata* (European skullcap) appears to have similar constituents to *S. baicalensis*, and is used as a substitute for *S. lateriflora*.

S. baicalensis, syn. *S. macrantha* (Baikal skullcap) p.201

PARTS USED Roots (*huang qin*).
PROPERTIES A bitter, sedative, cooling herb that lowers fever, blood pressure, and cholesterol levels, relaxes spasms, stimulates the liver, improves digestion, controls bleeding, and has diuretic, antibacterial, and anti-toxic effects. It reputedly calms the fetus in pregnant women.
USES OF THE HERB
MEDICINAL Internally for enteritis, dysentery, diarrhea, jaundice, chronic hepatitis, urinary tract infections, hypertension, threatened miscarriage, nosebleed, and hemorrhage from lungs or bowel. It is an ingredient of the Chinese drug *san huang zhe she ye* ("injection of three yellow herbs"), the others being *Coptis chinensis* (see p.266) and *Phellodendron amurense* (see p.326).

S. lateriflora (Virginia skullcap, mad dog skullcap) p.201

PARTS USED Whole plant.
PROPERTIES A bitter, sedative, tonic herb that relaxes spasms, lowers fever, and stimulates the kidneys.
USES OF THE HERB
MEDICINAL Internally for nervous and convulsive complaints, insomnia, irritability, delirium tremens, neuralgia, and withdrawal from barbiturates and tranquilizers. Excess causes giddiness, stupor, confusion, and twitching. Not given in pregnancy.

GROWTH AND HARVEST
GROWTH Ornamental (*S. baicalensis*). Crop (*S. lateriflora*). Light, well-drained soil in sun or partial shade. *S. lateriflora* enjoys damp conditions. *S. baicalensis* needs sharp drainage and tolerates drought. Propagate by seed sown in autumn or spring, or by division in spring, or by semiripe cuttings in summer. Cut back to within 3–4in (7–10cm) of the base in early spring and pinch out in spring to encourage bushy growth.
HARVEST Roots (*S. baicalensis*) are lifted in autumn or spring from plants 3–4 years old and dried for use in decoctions. Plants (*S. lateriflora*) are cut when flowering for use in infusions, liquid extracts, and tinctures, or dried for tablets.

SELENICEREUS
(Cactaceae)

A rapturous description of *S. grandiflorus* in *The Illustrated Dictionary of Gardening* (ed. George Nicholson, 1885) concludes that "there is hardly any flower of greater beauty." It also contains cactine, an alkaloid which reputedly has an effect comparable to that of *Digitalis* (see p.273) on the heart. It is cultivated in Mexico for the preparation of a drug used in the treatment of rheumatism.

S. grandiflorus (queen-of-the-night, night-blooming cereus) p.202

PARTS USED Stems, flowers.
PROPERTIES A diuretic, sedative, tonic herb that stimulates the heart.
USES OF THE HERB
MEDICINAL Internally for palpitations, angina, edema, rheumatism, kidney congestion, and nervous headaches. Excess causes gastric irritation, confusion, and hallucinations.

GROWTH AND HARVEST
GROWTH Ornamental. Epiphytic soil mix, below pH6, in partial shade with high humidity, minimum 50°F (10°C). Propagate by seed sown in spring or summer, or by stem cuttings in spring or summer. Plants under cover may be damaged by mealybugs.
HARVEST Stems and flowers are cut in summer and dried for infusions, liquid extracts, and tinctures.

SEMPERVIVUM Hens and chicks
(Crassulaceae)

The Emperor Charlemagne decreed that his subjects should grow houseleeks on their roofs to ward off lightning; they are still traditionally planted for this purpose. *S. tectorum* contains tannins and mucilage, which soothe and heal damaged tissues; the leaves were traditionally halved and applied directly to the affected part.

S. tectorum (hens and chicks, houseleek) p.202

PARTS USED Leaves.
PROPERTIES An astringent, acidic, saline herb that is diuretic and has cooling, soothing, and healing effects.
USES OF THE HERB
MEDICINAL Internally for shingles, skin complaints, and hemorrhoids. Excess is emetic and purgative. Externally for stings, bites, warts, burns, sunburn, inflamed or itching skin conditions, and corns.
VARIANT
S. t. **'Royal Ruby'**, p.202.

GROWTH AND HARVEST
GROWTH Ornamental. Well-drained, gritty or stony soil in sun. May also be planted in crevices of roofing tiles, thatch, walls, and paving. Propagate by seed sown in spring (species only), or by division of overcrowded clumps, or by offsets, in spring. Leaves may be damaged by rust. Sempervivums require minimal attention, and will survive without water for long periods.
HARVEST Leaves are collected as required and used fresh in infusions, poultices, and tinctures.

SENECIO Groundsel
(Compositae/Asteraceae)

S. aureus is a classic herbal "female regulator" and was used by several native N American tribes to ease childbirth and to treat complaints of the female reproductive system. Although declared a "completely safe aid in gynecological disorders" (Hutchens, *Indian Herbology of North America*, 1973), it contains pyrrolizidine alkaloids (as found in *Symphytum officinale*, see p.357), which cause liver damage, and is no longer thought safe for internal use. *S. vulgaris* (groundsel) has similar uses but is also no longer regarded as safe. *S. jacobaea* (ragwort, tansy ragwort) is used externally, often combined with *Lobelia inflata* (see p. 305) and *Gaultheria procumbens* (see p. 286) in lotions to relieve arthritis, rheumatism, muscular pain, and sciatica.

S. aureus (liferoot, squaw weed, golden ragwort) p.202

PARTS USED Whole plant, rhizomes.
PROPERTIES A bitter, astringent herb that is diuretic, stimulates the uterus, and controls bleeding.
USES OF THE HERB
MEDICINAL Internally for failure to menstruate, menopausal symptoms, prolonged labor, and pulmonary hemorrhage. Externally for vaginal discharge. Not given to pregnant women. For use by qualified practitioners only. WARNING This herb is subject to legal restrictions in some countries.

GROWTH AND HARVEST
GROWTH Crop. Damp to wet soil in sun or partial shade. Propagate by division or by seed sown in autumn or spring.
HARVEST Plants are cut before flowering and dried for use in infusions and liquid extracts. Roots are lifted in autumn and dried for powder.

SENNA
(Leguminosae/Caesalpiniaceae)

Apart from their long history of use as a laxative, sennas are useful for a wide range of other complaints, ranging from ringworm (*S. alata*, *S. obtusifolia*, and *S. sophera*) to venereal disease (*S. sieberiana* and *S. surattensis*). *S. reticulata* yields the antibiotic Rhein-cassic acid, which is effective against various bacterial and fungal infections. The pods of *S. fistula* (pudding pipe tree) are up to 20in (50cm) long and contain a black pulp, which is used as a mild substitute for *S. alexandrina*. *S. obtusifolia* (sickle senna) was recorded in Chinese medicine during the later Han dynasty (AD25–220). It is used in patent medicines and to treat hypertension, high cholesterol levels, constipation, skin diseases, and eye disorders. The seeds of *S. laevigata*, *S. obtusifolia*, *S. occidentalis*, and *S. sericea* are used as coffee substitutes in various parts of the world.

S. alexandrina, syn. *Cassia angustifolia*, *C. senna* (Alexandrian senna, Tinnevelly senna) p.202

PARTS USED Leaves (*fan xie ye*), pods.
PROPERTIES A sweet, cooling, laxative herb with a tealike aroma and antibacterial effects.
USES OF THE HERB
MEDICINAL Internally for constipation; it is the main ingredient of most laxative preparations. Usually prescribed with carminatives (such as *Zingiber officinale*, see p.373, or *Coriandrum sativum*, see p.267) to reduce griping. Excess or frequent usage may cause nausea, vomiting, abdominal pain, inflammation of the gastrointestinal tract, and deterioration in bowel function (laxative dependency). Not given to pregnant women or patients with colitis or spastic constipation.

S. marilandica, syn. *Cassia marilandica* (wild senna) p.202

PARTS USED Leaves, pods.
PROPERTIES A laxative herb with a milder, slower effect than *S. alexandrina*.
USES OF THE HERB
MEDICINAL Internally for constipation.

GROWTH AND HARVEST
GROWTH Ornamental (*S. marilandica*). Crop (*S. alexandrina*). Well-drained soil in sun, minimum 41°F (5°C) for *S. alexandrina*; rich, moist, sandy soil in sun (*S. marilandica*). Propagate by seed sown in spring, or by semi-ripe cuttings in summer. In spring, prune plants grown under cover or in a confined space. Pot-grown plants may be damaged by root mealybugs.
HARVEST Leaves are picked before and during flowering, and pods are collected in autumn when ripe. Both are dried for use in infusions, powders, tablets, and tinctures.

SERENOA
(Palmae/Arecaceae)

The seeds of *S. repens* provided food for native peoples of southeastern N America, who also recognized the sedative, tonic properties of the edible fruits. Animals feeding on the fruits were renowned for their health, and similar effects of improved digestion and increased strength and weight were observed by settlers who regularly ate the fruits or products derived from them. Among such products are the best-selling herbal remedies for male impotence. In spite of claims that it has specific hormonal effects on the male reproductive system, little research has been done on its chemistry.

S. repens, syn. *S. serrulata* (saw palmetto) p.203

PARTS USED Fruits.
PROPERTIES A sedative, warming, tonic herb with a soapy taste and pungent, vanilla-like aroma. It affects the endocrine system, is a urinary antiseptic, diuretic, and expectorant, and is reputedly aphrodisiac.
USES OF THE HERB
MEDICINAL Internally for impotence, debility in elderly men, prostate conditions, cystitis, bronchial complaints associated with coldness, and wasting diseases. May be combined with *Equisetum arvense* (see p.278) and *Hydrangea arborescens* (see p.294) for prostate enlargement.

GROWTH AND HARVEST
GROWTH Ornamental. Well-drained, moist soil in sun, minimum 50–55°F (10–13°C). ► Propagate by suckers and by seed sown in spring. Divided clumps do not reestablish. Plants grown under cover may be attacked by spider mites.
HARVEST Fruits are collected when ripe and partly dried for elixirs, infusions, liquid extracts, and tinctures, or dried and powdered for use in tablets.

SESAMUM Sesame
(Pedaliaceae)

A crop of African origin, *S. indicum* has been cultivated in parts of Asia and Africa for thousands of years. It is mentioned as being important 5,000 years ago in Egypt, and in Babylonia (2200–538BC). A plant named *semsent*, mentioned in the Egyptian Ebers papyri (c.1500BC), is probably the earliest record of *S. indicum*. Sesame was grown in Italy during the time of Pliny (AD23–79), and Dioscorides described the custom of sprinkling the seeds on bread in Sicily. In Africa the seeds are often stewed whole; in India they are ground into meal; and in the Middle East, India, and China, they are made into candy. Roasted sesame oil is widely used in Japan. Seeds of *S. indicum* are rich in unsaturated oil, vitamins A, B, and E, and calcium salts. There are indications that the calcium is well absorbed, providing an excellent dietary source. *S. indicum* has been used in Chinese medicine since the 16th century, and it is an important rejuvenative tonic in Ayurvedic medicine.

S. indicum (sesame, benne, gingili) p.203

PARTS USED Leaves, seeds (*hei zhi ma*), oil.
PROPERTIES A sweet, warming, soothing herb that strengthens bones and teeth, lubricates dry tissues, relaxes spasms, and has a tonic effect on the liver and kidneys. It is a mild laxative.
USES OF THE HERB
CULINARY Sesame oil (also known as "benne oil" or "gingili") is a high-quality, distinctively flavored oil for cooking and salads. Seeds are sprinkled over vegetables. Ground seeds are mixed with honey as *halva* (Middle East, India), or made into a paste used as a spread (*tahini*), or in *hummus* (Middle Eastern chick-pea dip), sauces, and *pâtés*.
AROMATIC Sesame oil is used in perfumery.
MEDICINAL Internally for premature hair loss and graying, convalescence, chronic dry constipation, tooth decay, osteoporosis, stiff joints, dry cough, and symptoms such as tinnitus, poor vision, dizziness, headache associated with weak liver and kidney energy (seeds); infantile cholera, diarrhea, dysentery, excess mucus, and cystitis (leaves); dry constipation in the elderly (oil). Seeds and oil are high in calories (kilojoules), and may not be advisable in the treatment of obese patients. Externally for hemorrhoids (seeds), and burns, boils, and ulcers (oil mixed with lime water).
ECONOMIC Seeds are added whole to bakery products. The oil is used in the manufacture of margarine, lubricants, soaps, and pharmaceutical drugs. Residue is used in livestock feeds.

GROWTH AND HARVEST

GROWTH Crop. Well-drained, sandy soil in sun. Propagate by seed sown in spring or autumn. Plants are easily raised from untoasted seed bought for culinary purposes.
HARVEST Leaves are picked during the growing season for use in infusions. Seeds are collected when ripe and stored whole for decoctions, pressed for oil, or ground into paste.

SILYBUM Milk thistle
(Compositae/Asteraceae)

S. marianum was once cultivated as a vegetable: the roots resembled salsify when boiled; the flower heads made a substitute for artichokes; and the young leaves, similar in flavor to spinach, were cooked or eaten in salads. *S. marianum* contains unique substances collectively referred to as "silymarin." They protect the liver against toxins and are apparently so effective that animals given it are unaffected by *Amanita phalloides* (death cap), a fungus that often causes irreversible liver damage.

S. marianum, syn. *Carduus marianus* (blessed thistle, milk thistle) p.203

PARTS USED Whole plant, seeds.
PROPERTIES A bitter, diuretic, tonic herb that regenerates liver cells, stimulates bile flow, and relaxes spasms.
USES OF THE HERB
MEDICINAL Internally for liver and gall bladder diseases, jaundice, cirrhosis, hepatitis, and poisoning (especially by *Amanita phalloides*, alcohol, drugs, and chemicals).

GROWTH AND HARVEST

GROWTH Ornamental. Well-drained soil in sun. Propagate by seed sown in spring (if as annual), or summer/early autumn (as biennial). Remove flowering stems from plants to prolong attractive appearance of foliage. Slugs and snails may damage leaves. Subject to control as a weed in some countries, notably in parts of Australia.
HARVEST Plants are cut when flowering and seeds are collected when ripe. All parts are dried for use in infusions and tinctures, or for extraction of silymarin.

SIMABA
(Simaroubaceae)

A genus of 14 species of deciduous and evergreen trees and shrubs, occurring in S and C America. *S. cedron* was first imported for medicinal use in Europe in the 1890s. The seeds contain antimalarial quassinoids, found in *Picrasma excelsa* (see p.327), which belongs to the same family. *Quassia amara* (syn. *Simaruba amara*), also closely related, is used to treat malaria and amebic dysentery. In medicine, "quassia" refers to a bitter compound extracted from the wood of either *P. excelsa* or *Q. amara*, but not from *Simaba cedron*. Once used as a treatment for lice and roundworms, quassia is used today mainly as a bitter and in denaturing alcohol. Sale, supply, and use of quassia extracts are subject to restrictions in certain countries.

S. cedron, syn. *Quassia cedron* (cedron)

Tender tree, height 15–50ft (5–15m), spread 10–30ft (3–10m), with leaves reaching 3ft (1m) long, divided into narrow leaflets. Dark yellow, slightly fragrant, 5-petaled flowers are borne in summer, followed by ovoid fruits each containing one seed. Found in C America and northern Brazil.

PARTS USED Seeds.
PROPERTIES An exceedingly bitter, tonic herb with a coconut-like aroma. It lowers fevers, reduces inflammation, and relaxes spasms.
USES OF THE HERB
MEDICINAL Internally for malaria or fevers; internally and externally for snakebite.

GROWTH AND HARVEST

GROWTH Crop. Well-drained soil in sun, minimum 59–64°F (15–18°C). Propagate by seed when ripe, or by hardwood cuttings at the end of the growing season.
HARVEST Seeds are collected when ripe and powdered for use in infusions.

SIMMONDSIA Jojoba
(Simmondsiaceae)

S. chinensis yields jojoba oil, long used by native N Americans for cosmetic purposes and leather softening. It is unusual in being a liquid wax and has exceptional lubricant qualities. Scientific investigations in the 1970s showed it to be an excellent substitute for sperm whale oil. Tissue culture of female plants has greatly increased production.

S. chinensis, syn. *S. californica* (jojoba, goat nut) p.203

PARTS USED Oil (from seeds).
PROPERTIES A soothing, softening herb.
USES OF THE HERB
MEDICINAL Externally for dry skin and hair, psoriasis, acne, and sunburn.
ECONOMIC Added to shampoos, moisturizers, and sunscreens. Used as a lubricant, especially in engines, detergents, and wetting agents.

GROWTH AND HARVEST

GROWTH Crop. Well-drained to dry, sandy, or gravelly soil in sun. *S. chinensis* is drought-tolerant. Propagate by seed sown in spring, or by nodal cuttings in spring, or by heel cuttings in autumn.
HARVEST Seeds are collected when ripe and crushed to extract oil.

SINAPIS
(Cruciferae)

The flavor of mustard depends on the kind of seeds used and the method of preparation, which may be with water, unfermented wine, vinegar, or verjuice. The seeds of *S. alba* are larger than those of *Brassica nigra* (black mustard, see p.250) and are pale brown with a mild flavor. They are the main ingredient in American mustard and are blended with seeds of *B. nigra* to make English mustard; they are not used in French mustards. In *The English Physitian Enlarged* (1653), Culpeper highly recommends mustard for all manner of complaints, from weak stomachs and cold diseases to toothache, joint pains, skin problems, and a crick in the neck. John Evelyn described mustard as "exceeding hot and mordicant, not only in Seed but Leaf also … of incomparable effect to quicken and revive the Spirits; strengthening the Memory, expelling heaviness, preventing the Vertiginous Palsie [giddiness] and is a laudable Cephalic." (*Acetaria, a Discourse on Sallets*, 1699).

S. alba, syn. *Brassica alba*, *B. hirta* (white mustard) p.203

PARTS USED Seeds (*bai jie zi*), oil.
PROPERTIES A pungent, stimulant, warming herb that improves digestion and circulation, relieves pain, and is expectorant, diuretic, and antibiotic.
USES OF THE HERB
MEDICINAL Externally (usually in mustard plasters, baths, or poultices) for respiratory infections, arthritic joints, chilblains, and skin eruptions. In traditional Chinese medicine, for complaints characterized by cold and torpor: internally for bronchial congestion, coughs, and joint pains; externally for painful extremities, neuralgia, sprains, sores, boils, and bruises. Like other mustards, seeds of *S. alba* contain substances that are extremely irritant to skin and mucous membranes. For use by qualified practitioners only.
ECONOMIC Ground seeds provide the basis for mustards to accompany meats. Whole seeds are an important component of pickles. Seeds are sprouted with those of *Lepidium sativum* as "mustard and cress"; the mustard seeds grow more quickly than the cress, so are sown three days later.

S. juncea. See *Brassica juncea.*

S. nigra. See *Brassica nigra.*

GROWTH AND HARVEST

GROWTH Crop. Most soils in sun. Propagate by seed sown in spring.
HARVEST Seeds are harvested as they ripen, then dried, and stored whole, ground, or crushed for oil.

SISYMBRIUM
(Cruciferae/Brassicaceae)

Sisymbrium contains glucosinolates, as found in the true mustards (*Brassica nigra*, see p.250, *B. juncea*, see p.250, and *Sinapis alba*, see p.353), and a glycoside similar to digitalin.

S. alliaria. See *Alliaria petiolata.*

S. officinale, syn. *Erysimum officinale* (hedge mustard) p.203

PARTS USED Whole plant, leaves, flowering tops.
PROPERTIES A tonic herb with a mustardlike aroma. It has laxative, diuretic, and expectorant effects, and benefits the digestion.
USES OF THE HERB
CULINARY Young leaves give flavor to salads, soups, sauces, and omelettes.
MEDICINAL Internally for bronchitis, pharyngitis, coughs, laryngitis, and excess bronchial mucus. Excess may affect the heart.

GROWTH AND HARVEST
GROWTH Crop. Moist to dry, acid to alkaline soil in sun or light shade. Propagate by seed sown in autumn or spring.
HARVEST Plants and flowering tops are cut in summer for infusions and liquid extracts. Leaves are picked in spring and used fresh.

SMILAX Greenbrier
(Liliaceae)

Sarsaparilla is derived from a number of different species. By 1685 three main species were imported into Europe for medicinal use: *S. aristolochiaefolia* (Mexican sarsaparilla), *S. febrifuga* (Ecuadorian sarsaparilla), and *S. regelii* (Honduran sarsaparilla). It gained a reputation as a cure-all, and was listed in most national pharmacopoeias until the early 20th century. The roots contain steroidal saponins, antibiotic compounds that provide the basis for sarsaponin tablets, which are effective in many cases of psoriasis. They also have hormonal effects, and may improve fertility in women with ovarian dysfunction. Also used in Chinese medicine is *S. glabra*, first mentioned in the *Materia Medica of South Yunnan* during the Qing dynasty (1644–1911). It is used internally to clear toxins, and to treat rheumatoid arthritis, syphilis, urinary tract infections, jaundice, skin ulcers, boils, and mercury poisoning. The leaves of *S. glyciphylla*, an Australian species, have been used medicinally and as a substitute for S American sarsaparillas in soft drinks.

S. china (China root) p.204

PARTS USED Tuberous rhizomes.
PROPERTIES A cooling, slightly bitter, alterative herb that has antibiotic, anti-inflammatory, diuretic, and antirheumatic properties.
USES OF THE HERB
MEDICINAL Internally for rheumatoid arthritis, gout, syphilis, skin disorders (including psoriasis), enteritis, urinary tract infections, jaundice, skin ulcers, boils, abscesses, and various kinds of cancer.

S. regelii, syn. *S. ornata*, *S. officinalis* (Honduran sarsaparilla)

Tender, variable evergreen climber, height and spread 5ft (1.5m), with angled, spiny stems and ovate, glossy leaves. White to pale green, 6-petaled flowers appear in summer: male flowers solitary or in clusters; females solitary, on stalks, followed by black berries.

PARTS USED Roots, rhizomes.
PROPERTIES A sweet, acrid, alterative herb that reduces inflammation, controls itching, improves digestion and elimination, and is antiseptic.
USES OF THE HERB
MEDICINAL Internally for skin diseases, liver disorders, venereal diseases, herpes, and vaginal discharge. May be combined with other alteratives, such as *Rumex crispus* (see p.344), *Arctium lappa* (see p.240), *Taraxacum officinale* (see p.360), and *Trifolium pratense* (see p.364).
ECONOMIC Root extracts flavor soft drinks, ice cream, candy, and bakery products.

GROWTH AND HARVEST
GROWTH Crop. Well-drained soil in sun or partial shade. *S. regelii* needs minimum 54°F (12°C). Propagate by seed, suckers, or division in spring, or by semiripe cuttings in summer.
HARVEST Roots and rhizomes are lifted by severing larger roots near the crown, leaving smaller roots to increase. They are dried for use in decoctions, elixirs, liquid extracts, and powders.

SMYRNIUM
(Umbelliferae/Apiaceae)

S. olusatrum is primarily a pot herb and is now obsolete as a medicinal plant. It was used for asthma, menstrual problems, and wounds.

S. olusatrum (alexanders, black lovage) p.204

PARTS USED Leaves, young stems and shoots, roots, flowers, seeds.
PROPERTIES A bitter, diuretic herb, with a celery-like flavor, that benefits the digestion.
USES OF THE HERB
CULINARY Leaves, young stems and shoots, and roots are cooked as vegetables and added to soups and stews. Flower buds make a pleasant addition to salads. Seeds may be ground as a condiment.
MEDICINAL Medicinal uses are obsolete.

GROWTH AND HARVEST
GROWTH Ornamental. Moist, rich, sandy soil in sun. Propagate by seed sown in late summer or early spring.
HARVEST Leaves, young stems and shoots, flower buds are picked in spring and early summer. Roots are lifted in autumn. All parts are used fresh. Seeds are collected when ripe and stored whole or ground.

SOLANUM Nightshade
(Solanaceae)

S. dulcamara has a long history of use for skin diseases, warts, tumors, and felons (inflammations of finger-end joints, hence another of its common names, "felonwort"), and is regarded as a substitute for sarsaparilla (see *Smilax* species, this page). The N American *S. carolinense* (horsenettle), which also contains alkaloids, has a similar bitter, then sweet, taste. Its effects are antibacterial, antispasmodic, and sedative. With some *Solanum* species, certain parts are edible while other parts of the same plant are very poisonous. The best-known example is the potato (*S. tuberosum*), which has edible tubers (although these become poisonous when they turn green on exposure to light) and poisonous foliage and fruits.

S. dulcamara (bittersweet, deadly nightshade) p.204

PARTS USED Stems, root bark.
PROPERTIES An astringent, cooling herb with a bitter, then sweet, taste. It lowers fever and has diuretic, expectorant, sedative, alterative, and antirheumatic effects.
USES OF THE HERB
MEDICINAL Internally for skin diseases, bronchial congestion, rheumatism, jaundice, and ulcerative colitis. Excess paralyzes the central nervous system, slows heart and respiration, and lowers temperature, causing vertigo, delirium, convulsions, and death. Externally for skin eruptions, ulcers, rheumatism, and cellulite. For use by qualified practitioners only.
VARIANT
S. d. **'Variegatum'**, p.204.

GROWTH AND HARVEST
GROWTH Ornamental. Dry to wet, neutral to alkaline soil in sun or shade. Propagate by seed sown in spring (species only), or by semiripe cuttings in summer. Thin out or cut back in spring. Subject to statutory control as a weed in parts of Australia.
HARVEST Stems 2–3 years old are cut in spring, or after the leaves have fallen in autumn. Roots are lifted in autumn and peeled. Both are dried for infusions, liquid extracts, and ointments.
WARNING All parts, especially leaves and unripe berries, are toxic if eaten.

SOLIDAGO Goldenrod
(Compositae/Asteraceae)

The constituents of *S. virgaurea* include saponins (similar to those found in *Polygala* species, see p.332), which are antifungal; rutin (as found in *Ruta graveolens*, see p.345); and phenolic glycosides, which are anti-inflammatory. Many other species have been recorded in native N American medicine: the flowers of *S. canadensis* (Canada goldenrod) were chewed for sore throats, *S. odora* (sweet goldenrod) was listed as a stimulant and diaphoretic in the *U.S. Pharmacopoeia* (1820–82), and *S. rigida* (stiff goldenrod) was made into a lotion for bee stings.

S. virgaurea (goldenrod) p.204

PARTS USED Leaves, flowering tops.
PROPERTIES A bitter, astringent, relaxant herb that stimulates the liver and kidneys and reduces inflammation; it is expectorant, improves digestion, and promotes healing. It is also a good urinary antiseptic.
USES OF THE HERB
MEDICINAL Internally for urinary infections, chronic excess mucus, skin diseases, influenza, whooping cough, flatulent dyspepsia associated with nervous tension, and kidney stones. Externally for wounds, insect bites, ulcers, and sore throat. Combines well with *Gnaphalium uliginosum* (see p.289) for excess nasal mucus.

GROWTH AND HARVEST

GROWTH Crop. Well-drained, moisture-retentive soil in sun or partial shade. Propagate by seed sown in spring, or by division in autumn or spring. Leaves may be damaged by caterpillars and powdery mildew. The flowers of *Solidago* attract many different beneficial insects, such as lacewings and ladybugs, which are effective in controlling pests, especially aphids.
HARVEST Leaves and flowering tops are picked before flowers are fully opened and dried for use in infusions, liquid extracts, ointments, powders, and tinctures.

SOPHORA
(Leguminosae/Papilionaceae)

The members of this genus are rich in cytisine, which resembles nicotine and is similarly toxic. *S. flavescens* was first mentioned during the later Han dynasty (AD25–220), and uses of *S. japonica* can be dated back to c.AD600. *S. subprostrata* (pigeon pea) was first recorded in Chinese medicine c.AD973, as an anti-inflammatory and detoxicant for mouth and throat infections, and for snakebite. Recent research suggests use in the treatment of various cancers. The seeds of *S. secundiflora* (mescal bean, coral bean) were important to native people in Wisconsin for the external treatment of earache.

S. flavescens (yellow pagoda tree)

Deciduous shrub, hardy to 5°F (–15°C), height 5ft (1.5m), spread 6ft (2m), with upright stems and leaves up to 10in (25cm) long, divided into 15–40 narrowly oblong leaflets. Pale green-yellow, rarely purple flowers are produced in erect racemes in summer, followed by leathery pods about 3in (8cm) long. Found in grassland in Japan, China, Siberia, and Korea.

PARTS USED Roots (*ku shen*).
PROPERTIES A bitter, cooling, diuretic herb that controls itching and has antibacterial, antifungal, and antitumor effects.
USES OF THE HERB
MEDICINAL Internally for jaundice, dysentery, diarrhea, and urinary infections. Internally and externally for vaginitis, eczema, pruritus, ringworm, leprosy, syphilis, scabies, and itching allergic reactions.

S. japonica (Japanese pagoda tree) p.205

PARTS USED Flowers (including buds, *huai hua*), fruits (*huai jiao*).
PROPERTIES A bitter, cooling, antibacterial herb that controls bleeding. It also lowers blood pressure and cholesterol levels, strengthens capillaries, reduces inflammation, and relaxes spasms (flowers); soothes irritated and damaged tissues, increases blood sugar levels, expels intestinal parasites, and improves liver function (fruits).
USES OF THE HERB
MEDICINAL Internally for internal hemorrhage; hypertension and poor peripheral circulation; intestinal worms; and liver energy imbalance with symptoms such as tight chest, dizziness, headache, red eyes, and hypertension. Not prescribed during pregnancy.
ECONOMIC The fruits yield a yellow dye.
VARIANT
S. j. **'Pendula'**, p.205.

GROWTH AND HARVEST

GROWTH Ornamental (*S. japonica*). Crop (*S. flavescens*). Well-drained soil in sun, with shelter in cold areas. Propagate by seed sown in autumn (species only), or by semiripe cuttings in summer.
HARVEST Roots (*S. flavescens*) are lifted in autumn. Flowers and flower buds (*S. japonica*) are picked in late summer. Fruits are collected in autumn. All parts are dried for use in decoctions.

SPHAGNUM Peat moss
(Sphagnaceae)

Bog mosses have a long history of use by Eskimos, Lapps, Kashmiris, and Gaelic peoples for absorbent and antiseptic purposes, such as for menstruation, babies' diapers, and as stable litter. Sphagnum dressings have also been widely used in military field hospitals. *S. japonicum* is used internally in a Chinese formula to treat epidemic dysentery. Extracts of decomposed peat moss, such as peat tar and sphagnol, are cheap and effective astringent, antibiotic, and antipruritic treatments for skin diseases and irritations. Exploitation and wild-collection of *Sphagnum* species may be subject to management measures.

S. cymbilifolium (sphagnum moss, bog moss) p.205

PARTS USED Whole plant.
PROPERTIES An astringent, antiseptic, absorbent herb.
USES OF THE HERB
MEDICINAL Externally for wounds and to absorb discharges.
ECONOMIC Dried sphagnum is added to orchid potting mixes and used to line hanging baskets.

GROWTH AND HARVEST

GROWTH Wild-collected. Wet, acid soil in sun or partial shade. Propagates by division and by stem cuttings during the growing season.
HARVEST Plants are dried whole.

STACHYS
(Labiatae/Lamiaceae)

S. officinalis was endowed with magical powers in ancient Egypt and was an important medicinal and magical herb in Anglo-Saxon times. According to Culpeper, "Antonius Musa, physician to the Emperor Augustus Caesar, wrote a peculiar book of the virtues of this herb; and among other virtues saith of it, that it preserves the liver and bodies of men from the danger of epidemical diseases, and from witchcraft also" (*The English Physitian Enlarged,* 1653). *S. officinalis* and *S. palustris* contain tannins and alkaloids; in addition, *S. palustris* contains allantoin.

S. officinalis, syn. *S. betonica*, *Betonica officinale* (betony, wood betony) p.205

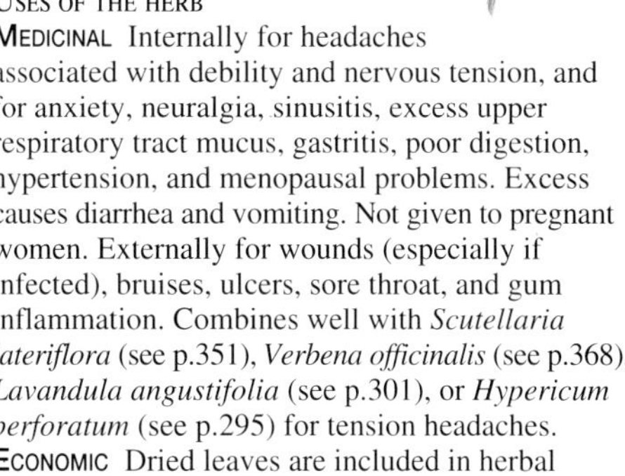

PARTS USED Whole plant.
PROPERTIES A bitter, astringent, sedative herb that improves digestion and cerebral circulation.
USES OF THE HERB
MEDICINAL Internally for headaches associated with debility and nervous tension, and for anxiety, neuralgia, sinusitis, excess upper respiratory tract mucus, gastritis, poor digestion, hypertension, and menopausal problems. Excess causes diarrhea and vomiting. Not given to pregnant women. Externally for wounds (especially if infected), bruises, ulcers, sore throat, and gum inflammation. Combines well with *Scutellaria lateriflora* (see p.351), *Verbena officinalis* (see p.368), *Lavandula angustifolia* (see p.301), or *Hypericum perforatum* (see p.295) for tension headaches.
ECONOMIC Dried leaves are included in herbal tobacco and snuff.
VARIANT
S. o. **'Rosea Superba'**, p.205.

S. palustris (marsh woundwort) p.205

PARTS USED Whole plant.
PROPERTIES An astringent, antiseptic herb with an unpleasant smell. It relaxes spasms, controls bleeding, and promotes healing.
USES OF THE HERB
MEDICINAL Internally for gout, cramps, vertigo, and hemorrhage. Externally for minor injuries.

GROWTH AND HARVEST

GROWTH Ornamental. Dry, neutral to acid soil in sun or partial shade; damp to wet soil, or water to 3in (8cm) deep, in sun or partial shade (*S. palustris*). Propagate by seed sown in autumn or spring, or by division when dormant. ►

► HARVEST Flowering plants are cut in summer and dried for use in infusions, liquid extracts, and tinctures.

STELLARIA
(Caryophyllaceae)

Chickweed has been used as a healing herb for centuries. Culpeper's recipe for ointment was "Boil a handful of Chickweed, and a handful of red rose leaves [petals] dried, in a quart of muscadine, until a fourth part be consumed; then put to them a pint of oil of trotters of sheep's feet; let them boil a good while, still stirring them well; which being strained, anoint the grieved place therewith, warm against the fire, rubbing it well with one hand" (*The English Physitian Enlarged*, 1653). It is an easy herb to use, being available in most gardens much of the year and readily infused in oil.

S. media (chickweed) p.205

PARTS USED Whole plant.
PROPERTIES A soothing, cooling, slightly saline herb that relieves itching, promotes healing, and has alterative, antirheumatic effects.
USES OF THE HERB
CULINARY Sprigs are added to salads and cooked as a vegetable.
MEDICINAL Internally for rheumatism. Externally for itching skin conditions, eczema, psoriasis, vaginitis, ulcers, boils, and abscesses. Often blended with *Althaea officinalis* (see p.236) or *Ulmus rubra* (see p.366) in antipruritic ointments.
ECONOMIC Sprigs are fed to domestic fowl and pet birds.

GROWTH AND HARVEST
GROWTH Crop. Moist soil in sun or shade. Propagate by seed sown at any time.
HARVEST Plants are cut and used fresh as juice or poultices, and fresh or dried in infusions, liquid extracts, medicated oils, ointments, and tinctures.

STEMONA
(Stemonaceae)

A genus of 25 species of perennial climbers, which occur throughout Indo-Malaysia to eastern Asia and tropical Australia. Most species contain alkaloids, and a number are effective insecticides. According to a 19th-century gardening manual, *S. tuberosa* was introduced in 1803 from the E Indies; it has large, attractive but fetid flowers and is seldom seen in cultivation today. *S. japonica* and *S. sessilifolia* are used interchangeably.

S. tuberosa, syn. *Roxburghia gloriosa* (stemona)

Tender, shrubby, evergreen climbing perennial, height 15–20ft (5–6m), with tuberous roots and pointed, ovate-cordate leaves up to 12in (30cm) long, which have wavy margins. Bell-shaped, purple-veined green flowers are produced in small clusters in summer, followed by 1in (2.5cm) long capsules, containing 5–8 seeds. Found in upland areas of India, China, and northern Malaysia.

PARTS USED Tubers (*bai bu*).
PROPERTIES A bittersweet, cooling herb that lubricates the lungs, controls coughing, destroys parasites, and is antibacterial and antifungal.
USES OF THE HERB
MEDICINAL Internally for bronchitis, tuberculosis, dry cough, whooping cough, amebic dysentery, and pinworms. Externally for lice and fleas. Baked with honey for coughs. Used fresh to make insecticidal washes.

GROWTH AND HARVEST
GROWTH Crop. Light, well-drained soil in sun or partial shade, minimum 59–64°F (15–18°C). Propagate by seed sown in autumn, or by semiripe cuttings in spring, or by division when dormant. Cut back in early spring to restrict growth.
HARVEST Tubers are lifted during dormancy, scalded in boiling water, and sun-dried for decoctions.

STILLINGIA
(Euphorbiaceae)

This genus includes about 30 species of perennials and evergreen or deciduous shrubs, which range throughout tropical and warm parts of the Americas to Madagascar and eastern Malaysia. No species appears to be in cultivation. In common with most members of the family Euphorbiaceae, they contain an irritant milky sap. In *S. sylvatica* the irritant properties are similar to those in *Daphne* species (see p.272) but are mostly lost in preparations of the dried root. The boiled, mashed roots of *S. sylvatica* were eaten by native N American women after childbirth and used by settlers as an external treatment for menstrual irregularity. The herb was popular in the southern US as a cure for constipation and by 1828 was used to relieve pain and ulceration after mercurial treatment for syphilis. The acrid, fresh root was chewed for bronchial complaints, and a tincture was made with *Drosera rotundifolia* (see p.275) and *Passiflora incarnata* (see p.323) to treat the early stages of tuberculosis.

S. sylvatica (queen's delight, yaw root)

Perennial, hardy to 32°F (0°C), height 2–4ft (60cm–1.2m), spread 24–36in (60–90cm), with stalkless, leathery, ovate leaves up to 3in (8cm) long. Small, green-yellow, male and female flowers without petals are borne separately in erect spikes, 2–4in (5–10cm) long in summer, followed by 3-seeded capsules. Found in dry woods in eastern N America.

PARTS USED Roots.
PROPERTIES A bitter, acrid, tonic herb with an unpleasant odor. It is alterative, diuretic, expectorant, and laxative.
USES OF THE HERB
MEDICINAL Internally for syphilis, and for liver, genitourinary, and bronchial complaints. Combined with other depurative or alterative herbs, such as *Trifolium pratense* (see p.364), in tonic and "blood-purifying" formulas. Excess causes diarrhea and vomiting. For use by qualified practitioners only.

GROWTH AND HARVEST
GROWTH Wild-collected. Dry, sandy, acid or alkaline soil in sun or partial shade. Propagate by seed sown in autumn or spring, or by division in spring, or by semiripe cuttings in spring at 59–64°F (15–18°C). Cuttings may be dipped in powdered charcoal to control the flow of latex.
HARVEST Roots are lifted in late summer and early autumn and dried for use in decoctions, elixirs, liquid extracts, tablets, and tinctures. They should be processed as soon as possible after harvesting because their properties deteriorate rapidly. Dried roots should be discarded after 2 years.

STROPHANTHUS
(Apocynaceae)

S. gratus contains cardiac glycosides, such as ouabain, and strophanthin, which was first isolated in 1885. These compounds are poorly absorbed when taken orally and are usually given by injection. Unlike digitalis (see *Digitalis purpurea*, p.273), they are not cumulative. Similar glycosides are found in *S. intermedius*, *S. kombe*, *S. hispidus*, and *S. strophanthus*. Locally, these plants are used in the preparation of arrow and fish poisons. The seeds are soaked in water to obtain a highly toxic liquid that is mixed with adhesive and applied to the tips of weapons. The effects of *S. kombe* were noted by David Livingstone, the explorer, in 1861.

S. gratus, syn. *Roupellia grata* (smooth strophanthus, climbing oleander, *sawai*) p.206

PARTS USED Seeds.
PROPERTIES An extremely poisonous, diuretic, tonic herb that stimulates the heart.
USES OF THE HERB
MEDICINAL Internally, usually by injection, for heart failure, angina, hypertension, pulmonary edema, and hypotension during anesthesia and surgery. Excess causes cardiac arrest. For use by qualified practitioners only. WARNING This herb is subject to legal restrictions in many countries.

GROWTH AND HARVEST
GROWTH Crop. Moist, well-drained, humus-rich soil in sun, with high humidity, minimum 61°F (16°C). Propagate by seed sown in spring, or by ripewood cuttings in early spring. Plants take 3 years to reach flowering size; maximum fruit production occurs after 6–10 years. Many flowers do not set seeds.
HARVEST Seeds are collected when ripe and processed commercially for the extraction of glycosides.
WARNING Seeds are extremely toxic if eaten.

STRYCHNOS
(Loganiaceae)

The genus is rich in alkaloids, including strychnine. A dozen or more species are used in the preparation of curare, a black, resinous arrow poison made by native American tribes, which causes instantaneous muscular paralysis. Extracts of *S. nux-vomica* and *S. ignatii* (St. Ignatius' bean) are used in minute amounts in tonic and restorative preparations.

S. nux-vomica (strychnine, nux-vomica, poison nut) p.206

PARTS USED Seeds.
PROPERTIES A very bitter, tonic herb that stimulates the nervous system and improves appetite.
USES OF THE HERB
MEDICINAL Internally, in minute amounts, for nervous exhaustion, debility, and poor appetite (especially in the elderly and children). It is also used as a central nervous system stimulant in chloroform or chloral poisoning, surgical shock, and cardiac arrest. Excess causes paralysis (notably *risus sardonicus*, a fixed grin), convulsions, respiratory failure, and death. WARNING This herb and strychnine are subject to legal restrictions in most countries.
ECONOMIC Strychnine is extracted commercially for use in vermin poisons.

GROWTH AND HARVEST
GROWTH Crop. Well-drained, humus-rich soil in sun or partial shade, minimum 59°F (15°C). Propagate by seed sown in spring, or by semiripe cuttings in summer.
HARVEST Seeds are collected when ripe, and dried for use in elixirs, liquid extracts, pills, and tinctures, and for the commercial extraction of alkaloids.

STYRAX
(Styracaceae)

This genus includes some 100 species of deciduous and evergreen shrubs and small trees, widely distributed in the Americas, Asia, and Europe. *S. benzoin* was first described by Ibn Batuta, an Arab who explored Sumatra between 1325 and 1349. He referred to it as *luban jawi*, "frankincense of Java," from which the name "gum Benjamin" derives. *S. benzoin* yields benzoin, a gum resin, best known as an ingredient of friar's balsam. The resin became popular in Europe toward the end of the 16th century and was subject to tax at Worms, under the name *asa dulcis*. It also entered Chinese medicine about this time, being first mentioned in Li Shi Zhen's herbal of 1596. *S. tonkinensis* (Siam benzoin) and *S. hypoglauca* are alternative sources of benzoin. The term "storax" refers to a vanilla-scented, solid resin obtained from the Eurasian species *S. officinalis*, and used in incense, perfumery, and medicine. The liquid, aromatic balsam from *Liquidambar* species (see p.305) is also called storax.

S. benzoin (benzoin, gum Benjamin)

Tender, evergreen tree, height 25ft (8m), spread 15–20ft (5–6m), with gray, resinous bark and ovate, minutely toothed leaves up to 5½in (14cm) long, which have downy, gray undersides. Clusters of 10–20 fragrant, cup-shaped white flowers, about 1¼in (3cm) across, appear in spring and summer. Found in rich woodland and swamps in Sumatra.

PARTS USED Gum resin (*an xi xiang*).
PROPERTIES An astringent, expectorant, and antiseptic herb with a cinnamon–camphor aroma. It is regarded as a circulatory stimulant in Chinese medicine and as a sedative in aromatherapy.
USES OF THE HERB
MEDICINAL In Western medicine, internally for coughs, colds, bronchitis, sore throat, wounds, ulcers, and mouth ulcers. In Chinese medicine, internally for chest and abdominal pains. In aromatherapy for influenza, chills, and itching skin conditions.
ECONOMIC Used as an antioxidant in cosmetics, a fixative in perfumes, and in friar's balsam, and as flavoring in the food industry.

GROWTH AND HARVEST
GROWTH Wild-collected. Moist to wet soil in sun or partial shade, minimum 59–64°F (15–18°C). Propagate by seed sown in autumn, or by semiripe cuttings in summer.
HARVEST Gum is collected from deep incisions made in the trunks of trees at least 7 years old. Hardened gum is stored in pieces ("tears"), compressed into a solid mass, or made into tinctures.

SWERTIA
(Gentianaceae)

Fifty species of mostly annuals and perennials belong to this genus, which occurs in montane regions of N America, Eurasia, and Africa. About half a dozen species, mainly of Indian annuals, were listed in 19th-century gardening manuals, but few are seen today outside botanic gardens. Chirata is the common name for several bitter, gentianlike plants sold in Indian bazaars. *S. chirata* has an interesting chemistry, similar in many respects to that of *Gentiana lutea* (see p.287). It also contains xanthones, reputedly effective against malaria and tuberculosis, and amarogentin, an iridoid glycoside that may protect the liver against carbon tetrachloride poisoning. Bitter compounds are also found in other species; *S. japonica* is cultivated in China as a source of bitterness agents. Green chiretta, a fever remedy, is obtained from *Andrographis paniculata*, an unrelated member of the Acanthaceae.

S. chirata, syn. *Ophelia chirata* (chiretta, brown chirata, Indian balmony)

Robust annual, hardy to 5°F (–15°C), height 5ft (1.5m), spread 2ft (60cm), with pointed, lanceolate-ovate leaves. Many lurid green-yellow, 4-lobed, purple-veined flowers are produced in large, leafy panicles in autumn, followed by tiny 2-valved capsules. Native to Himalayan pastures and slopes.

PARTS USED Whole plant.
PROPERTIES An extremely bitter, tonic herb that lowers fever and improves digestion.
USES OF THE HERB
MEDICINAL Internally for liver and gall bladder complaints, dyspepsia, constipation, malaria, and convalescent debility.

GROWTH AND HARVEST
GROWTH Crop. Moist, well-drained soil in sun or partial shade. Propagate by seed sown in autumn or spring.
HARVEST Plants are cut toward the end of flowering and dried for use in infusions, liquid extracts, and powder.

SYMPHYTUM Comfrey
(Boraginaceae)

S. officinale contains allantoin, which promotes cell proliferation and is now synthesized for use in healing creams, and pyrrolizidine alkaloids (in higher quantities in the roots than in the foliage). The alkaloids have been shown to cause liver damage and tumors in laboratory animals. As a result, *S. officinale* is now banned in the form of tablets and capsules (made from roots or leaves) in several countries. Comfrey teas, tinctures, and preparations for external use are considered safe. However, the advice remains against self-medication with comfrey products or its regular use as a food or food supplement. Culpeper wrote that it is "special good for ruptures and broken bones; yea it is said to be so powerful to consolidate and knit together, that if they be boiled with dissevered pieces of flesh in a pot, it wil join them together again" (*The English Physitian Enlarged*, 1653). He also recommended it for sore breasts and hemorrhoids, for which purposes it is still used by the pharmaceutical industry today, though in a synthesized form.

S. officinale (comfrey, knitbone) p.206

PARTS USED Leaves, roots.
PROPERTIES A sweet, mucilaginous, cooling herb that has expectorant, astringent, soothing, and healing effects. It reduces inflammation and controls bleeding.
USES OF THE HERB
CULINARY Fresh young leaves have been recommended as a raw or cooked vegetable, but recent suspicions of toxicity makes such uses inadvisable.

MEDICINAL Internally for chronic bronchial diseases, gastric and duodenal ulcers, colitis, and rheumatism (leaf tea only). Externally for psoriasis, eczema, sores, varicose veins and ulcers, arthritis, sprains, bunions, hemorrhoids, sore breasts during lactation, and injuries, including fractures.
WARNING This herb is subject to legal restrictions in some countries.

S.* x *uplandicum, syn. *S. peregrinum* (Russian comfrey) p.206

PARTS USED Leaves, roots.
PROPERTIES As for *S. officinale*.
USES OF THE HERB
CULINARY As for *S. officinale*.
MEDICAL As for *S. officinale*.
ECONOMIC Preferred species for livestock fodder.
VARIANT
S. x *u.* **'Variegatum'**, p.206.

GROWTH AND HARVEST
GROWTH Ornamental. Moist to wet soil in sun or partial shade. Propagate by seed sown in autumn or spring (species only), or by division in spring or autumn. Comfrey is invasive and deep-rooted, and difficult to eradicate when established. Plants may be affected by rust.
HARVEST Leaves are picked in early summer before flowering and dried for infusions, liquid extracts, and poultices. Roots are lifted during dormancy and dried for decoctions, liquid extracts, and ointments.
WARNING Skin irritant.

SYMPLOCARPUS
Skunk cabbage
(Araceae)

The roots of *S. foetidus* are known to contain volatile oil, resins, and a slightly narcotic alkaloid, 5-hydroxytryptamine, but the pharmacology is poorly understood. Uses among native N Americans include an inhalation of crushed leaves for headaches and a decoction of root hairs for external bleeding.

S. foetidus (skunk cabbage, polecat weed) p.206

PARTS USED Rhizomes, roots.
PROPERTIES A pungent, warming, antispasmodic, sedative herb with a fetid odor. It acts as an expectorant and diuretic, and increases perspiration.
USES OF THE HERB
MEDICINAL Internally for bronchitis, asthma, hay fever, excess mucus, whooping cough, and irritating coughs. Combines well with *Grindelia camporum* (see p.290) and *Euphorbia hirta* (see p.281) for bronchitis and asthma. Excess causes vomiting.

GROWTH AND HARVEST
GROWTH Ornamental. Deep, humus-rich, moist to wet, acid soil in sun or shade. *S. foetidus* is very hardy, tolerating –31°F (–35°C). Propagate by seed kept wet until sown in autumn or spring (germinating in spring), or by division of large plants during dormancy. *S. foetidus* does not transplant easily. ►

► **HARVEST** Rhizomes and roots are lifted during dormancy and dried for use in decoctions, infusions, liquid extracts, powders, and tinctures.

SYZYGIUM
(Myrtaceae)

Cloves are pink when fresh, turning brown as they dry and exuding oil when squeezed. First known in China, they reached Europe by AD300. Main producers today include Madagascar, Tanzania, Indonesia, and the Comoro Islands. *S. aromaticum* was first mentioned in Chinese medicine c.AD600. The volatile oil contains eugenol, which gives the characteristic aroma, and methyl salicylate. *S. cumini* has equally interesting, although rather different properties, regulating blood sugar levels in diabetes.

S. aromaticum, syn. *Eugenia caryophyllata* (cloves) p.206

PARTS USED Flower buds (*ding xiang*), oil.
PROPERTIES A spicy, warming, stimulant herb that relieves pain, controls nausea and vomiting, improves digestion, protects against intestinal parasites, and causes uterine contractions. It is strongly antiseptic. Regarded mainly as a kidney tonic in Chinese medicine.
USES OF THE HERB
CULINARY Whole or ground cloves, and oil, give flavor to preserves, pickles, ham, cooked apples, and cakes.

AROMATIC Whole cloves are used in potpourris and pomanders. Oil is used in perfumery.
MEDICINAL Internally for gastroenteritis and intestinal parasites. Externally for toothache and insect bites. In Chinese medicine, internally for nausea, vomiting, hiccups, stomach chills, and impotence.
ECONOMIC Whole or ground cloves, and oil, give flavor to Indian and Indonesian cigarettes. Oil is used in toothpaste.

GROWTH AND HARVEST
GROWTH Crop. Well-drained, fertile soil in sun, minimum 59–64°F (15–18°C). Propagate by seed sown in spring, or by semiripe cuttings in summer.
HARVEST Unopened flower buds are picked as they develop and sun-dried for use in infusions and powders, and for oil extraction.

T

TABEBUIA Trumpet tree
(Bignoniaceae)

The heartwood of *T. impetiginosa* contains lapachol, a naphthoquinone that was shown to have antibiotic properties in 1956 and anti-tumor effects in 1967. Under the common name *ipê*, a number of species have long been used medicinally by native S Americans. Some have a reputation for curing cancer; these include *T. incana* and *T. impetiginosa*, used by the Campas in Peru, *T. rosea* by the Mayas in Mexico (and to treat rabies in Guatemala), and *T. serratifolia* in Colombia. In addition, *T. insignis* var. *monophylla* and *T. neochrysantha* are used to treat stomach ulcers. *T. heptaphylla*, an important lumber species, is reputedly effective against syphilis.

T. impetiginosa, syn. *T. avellanedae* (*lapacho, pau d'arco, ipê-roxa*) p.207

PARTS USED Wood, inner bark.
PROPERTIES A bitter, pungent, cooling herb that lowers fever and reduces inflammation. It suppresses many pathogenic organisms and has anticancer effects.
USES OF THE HERB
MEDICINAL Internally for inflammatory diseases, chronic degenerative diseases, cancers, tumors, ulcers, cysts, fungal infections (especially candidiasis), and venereal, rheumatic, and skin diseases (notably eczema, herpes, and scabies). Combined with other alterative herbs, such as *Echinacea purpurea* (see p.276), *Trifolium pratense* (see p.364), and *Panax ginseng* (see p.321), in formulas to clear toxins, resolve congestion, and strengthen the immune system. Excess may cause nausea, vomiting, dizziness, and diarrhea.
ECONOMIC Lumber, known as *lapacho*, is valued for cabinetmaking.

GROWTH AND HARVEST
GROWTH Crop. Well-drained, fertile soil in sun, minimum 61–64°F (16–18°C). Propagate by seed or air layering in spring, or by semiripe cuttings in summer. Young plants may be trimmed in autumn.
HARVEST Wood and inner bark are dried for decoctions, powder, tablets, and extraction of active constituents.

TAGETES Marigold
(Compositae/Asteraceae)

Marigolds grown as bedding plants come from two main species: *T. patula* (French marigold) and *T. erecta* (African or Aztec marigold, *cempazuchil*). Native to Mexico, these have similar properties. Both are used for severe constipation and colic and, like *T. lucida* and *T. minuta*, are also grown as culinary herbs. *T. lucida* was used to flavor *chocólatl*, the foaming, cocoa-based drink of the Aztecs. *T. minuta* is grown mainly for medicinal purposes but also has unusual importance in horticulture because of its root extracts, known as "thiophenes"; these sulfur compounds inhibit the growth of nematodes (eelworms), which cause extensive damage to a wide range of plants. Thiophenes may also inhibit the growth of other plants – an effect that has been put to good use in the control of invasive weeds. *Tagetes* marigolds should not be confused with the pot marigolds (*Calendula officinalis,* see p.252), which have quite different properties.

T. lucida (sweet mace, Mexican marigold, *anisillo*) p.207

PARTS USED Whole plant, leaves.
PROPERTIES A stimulant, diuretic, anise-scented herb that reduces fever, lowers blood pressure, and improves digestion. It depresses the central nervous system; reputedly hallucinogenic and anesthetic.
USES OF THE HERB
CULINARY Dried leaves and flowering tops make a popular tea in Latin America. Leaves are a substitute for tarragon (*Artemisia dracunculus*, see p.243).
AROMATIC Dried plant is burned as incense and to repel insects.
MEDICINAL Internally for diarrhea, indigestion, nausea, colic, hiccups, malaria, and feverish illnesses. Externally for scorpion bites and to remove ticks.

T. minuta (muster-John-Henry, khaki weed, stinking Roger) p.207

PARTS USED Whole plant, oil.
PROPERTIES A strongly aromatic, diuretic, purgative herb that relaxes spasms, improves digestion, destroys intestinal parasites, and is effective against many pathogenic organisms. It is an effective insecticide.
USES OF THE HERB
CULINARY Dried leaves give an applelike aroma to soups, meat dishes, and vegetables.
AROMATIC Oil is used in perfumery.
MEDICINAL Internally for gastritis, indigestion, and intestinal worms. Externally for hemorrhoids and skin infections.
ECONOMIC Plants are grown to protect crops against nematodes and slugs, and to suppress perennial weeds, such as *Aegopodium podagraria* (ground elder, see p.229), *Calystegia sepium* (bindweed), and *Elymus repens* (couch grass, see p.277). Dried plants are hung indoors or added to bedding to deter insects (Africa). Oil is used in commercial food flavoring and tobacco.

T. patula (French marigold) p.207

PARTS USED Whole plant, leaves, flowers, oil.
PROPERTIES An aromatic, diuretic, calming herb that improves digestion. It is reputedly effective against a number of garden pests.
USES OF THE HERB
CULINARY Leaves may be used to flavor food.
AROMATIC Oil is blended with sandalwood oil in India to produce *attar genda* perfume.
MEDICINAL Internally for indigestion. Externally for sore eyes and rheumatism.
ECONOMIC Dried flowers occur as adulterants of saffron (*Crocus sativus*, see p.268). Flower extracts give color to dairy products, poultry feed, and textiles. Oil is used in food flavoring but is inferior to that of *T. minuta*.
VARIANT
***T. p.* 'Honeycomb'**, p.207.

GROWTH AND HARVEST
GROWTH Crop (*T. patula* 'Honeycomb': ornamental). Well-drained, fertile soil in sun. Propagate by seed in spring at 64°F (18°C). Deadhead plants to prolong flowering. *Botrytis* and spider mites may affect plants. *T. minuta* and, to a lesser extent, *T. patula*, are widely used in companion planting. *T. patula* is often used to repel soil nematodes, slugs, and whitefly from tomatoes, although cultivars vary in effectiveness. *T. minuta* has an irritant sap that may cause dermatitis.
HARVEST Plants are cut when flowering and distilled for oil, or dried for infusions. *T. lucida* and *T. minuta* are used in ointments for external use. Leaves (*T. lucida, T. patula*) and flowers (*T. patula*) are picked in summer for use either fresh or dried in infusions.

TAMARINDUS Tamarind
(Leguminosae)

Tamarind fruits are usually sold compressed into a block. They contain sugars, plant acids, and a complex volatile oil that includes elements characteristic of lemons (limonene), rose geranium (geraniol), sassafras (safrole), cinnamon (cinnamaldehyde), mint (menthol), and wintergreen (methyl salicylate). Since its introduction in the 17th century, *T. indica* has become important in the cuisines of the W Indies and Mexico.

T. indica (tamarind, Indian date) p.207

PARTS USED Fruits.
PROPERTIES A sweet and sour, astringent, stimulant herb with a pleasant aroma. It lowers fever, improves digestion, and has antiseptic and laxative effects.
USES OF THE HERB
CULINARY Fruits are eaten fresh and made into a refreshing drink. Fresh or dried fruits act as a souring agent, similar to lemon juice or vinegar, in curries, fish dishes, chutneys, sauces (notably Worcestershire sauce), satays, sweet and sour dishes, and sweets.
MEDICINAL Internally for fevers, jaundice, asthma, dysentery, and nausea in pregnancy. Externally for sore eyes, ulcers, and rheumatism. Combined with *Senna alexandrina* (see p.352) in laxative preparations.

GROWTH AND HARVEST
GROWTH Crop. Light, well-drained soil in sun, minimum 59–64°F (15–18°C). Propagate by seed in spring at 70°F (21°C), or by air layering in spring, or by grafting in spring.
HARVEST Fruits are picked when ripe and used fresh, or dried for use in concentrates and decoctions.

TANACETUM Tansy
(Compositae/Asteraceae)

These members of the daisy family are rich in volatile oils, bitters, and sesquiterpene lactones, which inhibit allergic, inflammatory responses and are insecticidal. They are extremely pungent, potent herbs and should be used with caution. *T. parthenium* has undergone a great deal of research since the 1970s, and has proved an effective and relatively safe remedy in many cases of migraine and rheumatism. Insecticides based on pyrethrins were first made from the flowers of *T. coccineum* (red pyrethrum, syn. *Chrysanthemum coccineum*, *Pyrethrum roseum*), and were known as Persian Insect Powder. The flowers of *T. cinerariifolium* were later found to be more effective. Dried flowers and powder retain their insecticidal properties almost indefinitely. Pyrethrins are nontoxic to mammals. *T. vulgare* was important as a strewing herb in the 16th century. It contains thujone, an insecticidal substance also found in *Artemisia absinthium* (see p.243), which is highly toxic in excess. Tansy featured in a number of Easter rituals in the British Isles, as a cleansing herb after the Lenten fast, and symbol of the bitter Passover herbs. Tansy cakes were also traditionally eaten at this season, originally awarded to the victor in handball games.

T. balsamita, syn. *Balsamita major* (alecost, costmary) p.208

PARTS USED Leaves.
PROPERTIES A bitter, astringent, laxative herb with a balsam–mint aroma. It improves digestion and liver function.
USES OF THE HERB
CULINARY Fresh leaves may be added with discretion to meat and vegetable dishes; dried leaves are infused as tea.
AROMATIC Dried leaves are added to potpourris.
MEDICINAL Now obsolete medicinally, but once used internally as a liver and gall bladder remedy, and externally for insect stings.
ECONOMIC Formerly used in brewing beer (hence the common name, alecost), as a strewing herb, and as "bible leaf" (a bookmark).
VARIANT
T. b. var. ***tomentosum***, p.208.

T. cinerariifolium, syn. *Chrysanthemum cinerariifolium, Pyrethrum cinerariifolium* (pyrethrum, Dalmatian pellitory) p.208

PARTS USED Flowers.
PROPERTIES An aromatic herb with strong insecticidal effects.
USES OF THE HERB
ECONOMIC Dried flowers are used in insecticides and fumigants, especially in sprays to control pests and insect-borne diseases in aircraft.

T. parthenium, syn. *Matricaria parthenium, Chrysanthemum parthenium* (feverfew) p.209

PARTS USED Whole plant, leaves.
PROPERTIES A bitter, tonic, cooling herb with a pungent odor and nauseating taste.

It relieves pain, relaxes spasms, dilates blood vessels, lowers fever, improves digestion, stimulates the uterus, and has laxative effects.

USES OF THE HERB

MEDICINAL Internally for migraine caused by excess heat, headache, rheumatism, arthritis, minor feverish illnesses, and digestive and menstrual complaints. Externally for insect bites and bruising. Not given to pregnant women. Fresh leaves may cause dermatitis and mouth ulcers if consumed.

VARIANTS

T. p. **'Aureum'**, p.208.
T. p. **'Golden Ball'**, p.208.
T. p. **'Golden Moss'**, p.208.
T. p. **'Plenum'**, syn. *T. p.* 'Flore Pleno', p.209.
T. p. **'Snowball'**, p.209.
T. p. **'Tom Thumb White Stars'**, p.209.
T. p. **'White Bonnet'**, p.209.

T. vulgare (tansy) p.209

PARTS USED Whole plant, oil.

PROPERTIES A bitter, acrid, warming herb with a pungent aroma. It expels intestinal parasites, benefits the digestion, and stimulates the uterus.

USES OF THE HERB

CULINARY Leaves are added to a kind of custard, known as a tansy, and to tansy cakes.

AROMATIC Flowers are added to potpourris.

MEDICINAL Mainly used as a enema for expelling worms in children, and topically in lotions for scabies. The herb is possibly unsafe for internal use, especially in pregnancy, although sometimes recommended for failure to menstruate and nausea. Tansy oil is highly toxic for both internal and external use, and very small amounts may prove fatal; excess causes abortion, venous congestion of abdominal organs, and convulsions. It is rarely used internally.

WARNING This herb, especially as tansy oil, is subject to legal restrictions in some countries.

ECONOMIC Tansy was once important in preserving meat, and colonists planted it by their front doors to repel ants.

VARIANTS

T. v. var. ***crispum***, p.209.
***T. v.* 'Isla Gold'**, p. 209.
***T. v.* 'Silver Lace'**, p.209.

GROWTH AND HARVEST

GROWTH Ornamental. Well-drained to dry, stony soil in sun. Propagate by seed sown in spring or autumn (species and some variants only), or by division in spring or autumn, or by basal cuttings in spring, or by semiripe cuttings in summer. Remove dead flower heads of *T. parthenium* to prevent excessive self-seeding. *T. vulgare* is invasive.

HARVEST Whole plants (*T. parthenium*, *T. vulgare*) are cut when flowering, and leaves are picked as required, and used fresh or dried for use in infusions, liquid extracts, powders, and tinctures. *T. vulgare* is distilled for oil. Leaves (*T. parthenium*) are sometimes eaten fresh, or dried for use in tablets to treat migraine, rheumatism, and arthritis. Flowers (*T. cinerariifolium*) are picked as they open and dried for powder.

TARAKTOGENOS

T. kurzii. See *Hydnocarpus kurzii.*

TARAXACUM Dandelion

(Compositae/Asteraceae)

The best-known member of the genus is *T. officinale*, which is a potent diuretic, hence the French name, *pissenlit*, "wet-the-bed." It contains high levels of potassium salts, particularly important in a strong diuretic, because large amounts are lost in the urine. It was first described in Chinese medicine c.AD659 and in European medicine in 1485, although there are possible mentions dating back to Pliny (AD23–79). Promoted by Arab physicians in the 11th century, it became an "officinal" drug by the 16th century.

T. officinale (dandelion) p.210

PARTS USED Whole plant (*pu gong ying*), leaves, roots, flowers.

PROPERTIES A bittersweet, cooling herb that has diuretic, laxative, and antirheumatic effects, stimulates liver function, improves digestion, and reduces swelling and inflammation.

USES OF THE HERB

CULINARY Fresh leaves, usually blanched, are eaten in salads or cooked like spinach (often mixed with sorrel). Flower petals are made into wine.

MEDICINAL Internally for gall bladder and urinary disorders, gallstones, jaundice, cirrhosis, dyspepsia with constipation, edema associated with high blood pressure and heart weakness, chronic joint and skin complaints, gout, eczema, and acne. In Chinese medicine, internally for breast and lung tumors, mastitis, and abscesses, and jaundice, hepatitis, and urinary tract infections; externally for snakebite. Combines well *with Veronicastrum virginicum* (see p.368), *Berberis vulgaris* (see p.248), and *Chelone glabra* (see p.259) for gall bladder complaints.

ECONOMIC Leaves and roots flavor herbal beers and soft drinks, such as dandelion and burdock. Roots are roasted and ground as a caffeine-free substitute for coffee.

GROWTH AND HARVEST

GROWTH Crop. Moist to dry, neutral to alkaline soil in sun. Propagate by seed sown in spring. Dandelion crops should be dead-headed to prevent seeding into neighboring land.

HARVEST Plants are cut in early summer and dried for use in decoctions (Chinese medicine only). Leaves are picked in spring and used fresh as a vegetable, juiced, or dried for use in infusions, liquid extracts, and tinctures. They may be blanched, like chicory, to reduce bitterness. Roots are lifted in autumn from 2-year-old plants and pressed for juice, roasted for coffee, or dried for decoctions, infusions, liquid extracts, and tinctures. Stocks of preserved leaves and roots are replaced annually. Flowers for winemaking are picked in spring and all the green parts are removed.

TAXUS Yew

(Taxaceae)

Yew trees were sacred to the Druids, who built their temples nearby – an association continued by the Christian practice of planting yew trees around churches. The wood of *T. baccata* (common yew) is very hard and durable, and was once used for longbows. *T. brevifolia* contains taxol, which, since clinical trials in the US, has been hailed as one of the most promising drugs of the 1990s for treating ovarian and other cancers. However, an enormous number of trees are needed to supply the bark for the drug; in order to provide sufficient taxol to treat a cancer patient, the bark of six trees is required. In the US this exploitation of *T. brevifolia* led to the Pacific Yew Act (1992), which provides for the management of the tree on federal lands, covering both its harvesting and conservation. *T. baccata* also contains taxol but in amounts not worth exploiting, although it is used in research. The bark and twigs of *T. canadensis* (Canadian yew) have been used by several native N American tribes in a tea to treat influenza. Eating the leaves of yews is a common cause of death among livestock, which succumb so quickly that the foliage of the plant is often found still in the mouth of the animal.

T. brevifolia (Pacific yew) p.210

PARTS USED Extracts of leaves, bark.

PROPERTIES A toxic herb that has anticancer effects.

USES OF THE HERB

MEDICINAL Internally mainly for cancers of the lungs, ovaries, and breasts. Side effects include nausea and a reduction in the numbers of white blood cells. For use by qualified practitioners only.

GROWTH AND HARVEST

GROWTH Wild-collected. Well-drained soil in sun or shade. Propagate by seed sown in autumn, or by cuttings of lateral shoots with a heel in early autumn.

HARVEST Leaves are picked in early autumn or spring, and bark is collected from autumn to spring, for commercial extraction of taxol.

WARNING All parts are extremely toxic if eaten.

TERMINALIA Myrobalan

(Combretaceae)

T. chebula is of central importance in Ayurvedic medicine and is sacred to Shiva. The *triphala* ("three fruits"), a rejuvenative, laxative tonic, is based on *T. chebula* (*haritaki*), *Phyllanthus emblica* (*amalaki*, emblic myrobalan, ambal), and *T. belerica* (*bibhitaki*, bastard myrobalan, beleric myrobalan). *T. chebula* was first mentioned in Chinese medicine in 1061. In Tibetan medicine it is known as "king of medicines" and, with *T. belerica* and *T. arjuna*, features in most formulas.

T. chebula (myrobalan, black chebulic, *haritaki*) p.210

PARTS USED Fruits (*he zi*).
PROPERTIES A sweet, astringent, warming herb with an unpleasant taste; it regulates colon function, improves digestion, is expectorant, controls bleeding and discharges, and destroys intestinal parasites. It also has a tonic, rejuvenative effect, especially on the digestive, respiratory, and nervous systems.
USES OF THE HERB
MEDICINAL Internally for constipation, digestive and nervous disorders, diarrhea, dysentery, intestinal worms, hemorrhoids, rectal prolapse, abnormal uterine bleeding and inflammation, vaginal discharge, involuntary ejaculation, coughs, and asthma. Not given to pregnant women or patients with severe exhaustion or dehydration. Externally for ulcers, wounds, mouth inflammation, and gum disease.

GROWTH AND HARVEST
GROWTH Crop. Well-drained soil in sun, minimum 61–64°F (16–18°C). Propagate by seed sown in spring, or by semiripe cuttings in summer.
HARVEST Fruits are collected when ripe and sun-dried for use in decoctions, pastes, and powders.

TETRADIUM
(Rutaceae)

T. ruticarpum was first recorded in Chinese medicine before AD200, during the later Han dynasty. In contrast to its unpleasant-tasting, poisonous fruits, those of the Madagascan tree, *Ravensara aromatica*, to which *Tetradium* is closely related, are clove-scented and used in food flavoring.

T. ruticarpum, syn. *T. officinalis* p.210

PARTS USED Fruits (*wu zhu yu*).
PROPERTIES A pungent, bitter, very warming herb that relieves pain, destroys intestinal parasites, stimulates the uterus, controls vomiting, and is antibacterial. It increases both body temperature and blood pressure.
USES OF THE HERB
MEDICINAL Internally for stomach chills and pains, vomiting and acid regurgitation, diarrhea (especially in early morning), painful menstruation, and threadworm infestations. Usually combined with *Glycyrrhiza glabra* (see p.289) to reduce toxicity and with *Zingiber officinale* (see p.373) for abdominal chills. Excess causes diarrhea, dyspepsia, and delirium.

GROWTH AND HARVEST
GROWTH Crop. Well-drained soil in sun, minimum 41–50°F (5–10°C). Propagate by seed sown in autumn, or by semiripe cuttings in summer, or by root cuttings in late winter. Remove dead or congested growths in early spring.
HARVEST Fruits are collected when ripe and dried for use in decoctions.
WARNING Fruits are poisonous.

TEUCRIUM Germander
(Labiatae/Lamiaceae)

T. chamaedrys has been used medicinally since ancient Greek times, when Dioscorides recommended it for coughs and asthma. The Holy Roman Emperor, Charles V (1500–1558), was apparently cured of gout by taking decoctions of the herb for 60 days. *T. scorodonia* (wood sage, sage-leaved germander) has very bitter, hop-scented leaves that have been used in brewing. In cultivation, *T. chamaedrys* is often confused with *T. divaricatum* and the hybrid *T.* x *lucidrys* (*T. chamaedrys* x *T. lucidum*). Both of these are taller, and more upright, with glossier, more leathery, darker green leaves, and are difficult to tell apart. *Teucrium canadense*, American germander, is often grown in herb gardens. *Teucrium marum*, source of herba mariveri, contains an essential oil, a bitter principle, and resin. Plants in herb gardens are often wrongly labeled, so it is important to establish correct identification when purchasing for medicinal use.

T. chamaedrys (wall germander) p.210

PARTS USED Whole plant, leaves.
PROPERTIES A bitter, astringent, antirheumatic herb that reduces inflammation, stimulates the digestion, and lowers fever. It has antiseptic, diuretic, and decongestant effects.
USES OF THE HERB
MEDICINAL Internally for loss of appetite, gall bladder and digestive disorders, summer diarrhea in children, gout, rheumatoid arthritis, excess nasal mucus, and bronchitis. Externally for gum disease, skin eruptions, and injuries (including snakebite). Combined with *Apium graveolens* (see p.240), *Filipendula ulmaria* (see p.283), and *Guaiacum officinale* (see p.290) for rheumatoid arthritis; and with *Lobelia inflata* (see p.305) and *Marrubium vulgare* (see p.308) for bronchitis. May cause liver damage and is subject to a voluntary ban by practitioners in certain countries, notably in France.
ECONOMIC Leaves are used to flavor liqueurs, vermouths, and tonic wines.

GROWTH AND HARVEST
GROWTH Ornamental. Light, well-drained to dry or stony soil in sun. *T. chamaedrys* is hardy to –20°F (–29°C). Propagate by seed sown in spring, or by division in autumn, or by softwood or semiripe cuttings in spring and summer. Cut off dead flower spikes to encourage bushy new growth.
HARVEST Plants are cut when flowering, and dried for use in infusions and liquid extracts.

THEA

T. sinensis. See *Camellia sinensis.*

THEOBROMA
(Sterculiaceae)

The fermented, dried, and roasted seeds of *T. cacao* produce cocoa butter and cocoa powder, which are used in a range of ways medicinally, and in the preparation of cocoa beverages and chocolate. Cocoa was the basis of the Aztec drink *chocólatl* and was held in such high esteem by the Incas, Mayas, and Aztecs that the seeds were used as currency. Although cocoa contains caffeine, the stimulant effect is weaker than that of coffee. Both cocoa powder and paste are bitter and are usually sweetened when used as a food or flavoring. Chocolate will vary greatly in flavor depending upon the type of bean, and the methods of processing and manufacture used: dark chocolate has the highest percentage of cocoa solids and lowest sugar content; milk chocolate contains dried or condensed milk; white chocolate is cocoa butter with milk and sugar added.

T. cacao (cacao, cocoa, chocolate tree) p.210

PARTS USED Fruits, seeds, fat, butter.
PROPERTIES A bitter, stimulant, diuretic herb that lowers blood pressure and dilates coronary arteries. Cocoa powder and butter are nutritive; the latter also softens and soothes damaged skin.
USES OF THE HERB
CULINARY As well as being a food, chocolate is used to flavor game, sauces, and milk drinks.
MEDICINAL Internally for angina and high blood pressure (cocoa powder). Externally for chapped skin and burns (cocoa butter). Not given internally to patients with irritable bowel syndrome. Chocolate may cause allergies or migraine.
ECONOMIC Chocolate is used to flavor liqueurs. Cocoa butter is used in cosmetics, skin creams, and as a suppository base. By-products from cocoa processing include fertilizer, fodder, fuel (husks), jelly, alcohol, and vinegar (pulp).

GROWTH AND HARVEST
GROWTH Crop. Fertile, moist, well-drained soil in shade, with high humidity and shelter from wind, minimum 61°F (16°C). Propagate by seed sown when ripe, or by air layering in spring or summer, or by semiripe cuttings in summer. All methods require a minimum temperature of 79°F (26°C). Cut back to required shape in early spring to control growth under cover.
HARVEST Fruits are cut all year, especially from early summer to early winter. Seeds are fermented, dried, roasted, and ground as paste (cocoa mass). Cocoa butter is extracted from cocoa mass, leaving powder.

THLASPI

T. bursa-pastoris. See *Capsella bursa-pastoris*.

THUJA Arborvitae

(Cupressaceae)

T. occidentalis has long been used by native N Americans to provide everyday materials, and medicines to treat menstrual problems, headache, and heart disease. Twigs were made into an antirheumatic tea by loggers and were listed in the *U.S. Pharmacopoeia* (1882–94) as a uterine stimulant and diuretic. *T. orientalis* was first described in Chinese medicine in the *Tang Materia Medica* (c.AD659). Both species are rich in volatile oil, which consists mainly of thujone (as found in *Artemisia absinthium*, see p.243). This compound is toxic in excess and requires discretion when used internally.

T. occidentalis (American arborvitae, Eastern white cedar) p.211

PARTS USED Foliage, bark.
PROPERTIES A bitter, astringent, cooling herb with a camphoraceous, fruity aroma. It stimulates the heart, uterus, and nerves; reduces inflammation; clears toxins; and is expectorant, antifungal, and antiviral.
USES OF THE HERB
MEDICINAL Internally in cancer therapy and for bronchial complaints (especially associated with congestive heart failure), urinary infections (including cystitis), psoriasis, eczema, failure to menstruate, and side effects of vaccinations. Not given to pregnant women or patients with dry, irritant coughs. Externally for vaginal infections, warts, muscular aches, and rheumatism. Combined with *Hamamelis virginiana* (see p.291) as a lotion for exudative eczema. For use by qualified practitioners only.
VARIANTS
T. o. **'Holmstrup'**, p.211.
T. o. **'Rheingold'**, p.211.

T. orientalis, syn. *Biota orientalis*, *Platycladus orientalis* (Chinese arborvitae) p.211

PARTS USED Foliage (*ce bai ye*), seeds (*bai zi ren*).
PROPERTIES A bitter, astringent, cooling herb that controls bleeding and coughing, stimulates the uterus, encourages hair growth, and is expectorant and antibacterial (foliage); a sweet, sedative, mildly laxative herb (seeds).
USES OF THE HERB
MEDICINAL Internally for coughs, hemorrhage, excessive menstruation, bronchitis, asthma, skin infections, mumps, bacterial dysentery, arthritic pain, and premature baldness (foliage); and for palpitations, insomnia, nervous disorders, and constipation in the elderly (seeds). Leaf preparations are not given to pregnant women.
VARIANT
T. o. **'Aurea Nana'**, p.211.

GROWTH AND HARVEST

GROWTH Ornamental. Deep, moist soil in a sheltered, sunny position. *T. occidentalis* is hardy to –50°F (–46°C). Propagate by seed sown in late winter (species only), or by semiripe cuttings in summer or early autumn. *Thuja* spp. may be permanently damaged by pruning. Trees may be infected by *Armillaria* root rot.
HARVEST Foliage and bark are removed as required and dried for use in decoctions, liquid extracts, and tinctures. Seeds (*T. orientalis*) are collected from ripe cones in autumn and dried for use in decoctions, powders, and tinctures.
WARNING Leaves are toxic if eaten. Skin allergen.

THYMUS Thyme

(Labiatae/Lamiaceae)

In common with many pleasant-smelling plants, thyme came to symbolize death, because the souls of the dead were thought to rest in the flowers; the smell of thyme has apparently been detected at several haunted sites. It is also associated with various rituals once carried out by young women to reveal their true love. Thymes vary in aroma, but the majority can be used to flavor food. Most widely used are *T. vulgaris*, *T.* x *citriodorus*, and their cultivars. The main medicinal thymes are *T. vulgaris* and *T. serpyllum*. All thymes are rich in volatile oil, which consists mainly of thymol, a powerful antiseptic. The oil varies considerably in composition between species and from plant to plant. Commercial thyme oil is largely derived from *T. zygis* (Spanish sauce thyme), a white-flowered species found in Spain and Portugal. Oil from *P. serpyllum* (sometimes known as serpolet oil) differs from *T. vulgaris* in being lower in carvacrol and higher in linalol and cymol, and thus having a sedative effect. Red and white thyme oil refer to the color of the oil, which turns red when oxidized by contact with metal, but remains clear otherwise.

T. caespititius, syn. *T. azoricus* (Azores thyme)

Hummock-forming shrublet, hardy to 5°F (–15°C), height 6in (15cm), spread 18in (45cm), with upright flowering stems and narrow, slightly sticky leaves about ¼in (6mm) long, which have a resinous aroma. Pink, lilac, or white flowers appear in small clusters, close to the mat, from late spring to summer. Found on dry, stony slopes and gullies in the Azores, northwestern Spain, and Portugal.

PARTS USED Leaves.
PROPERTIES An aromatic herb with a citrus–pine scent.
USES OF THE HERB
CULINARY As a substitute for *T.* x *citriodorus* in cooking, and as a flavoring in custards.
VARIANT
T. c. **'Aureus'**, p.212.

T. capitatus, syn. *Coridothymus capitatus* (conehead thyme) p.212

PARTS USED Whole plant, leaves, flowering tops, oil.
PROPERTIES Similar to *T. vulgaris*.
USES OF THE HERB
ECONOMIC Mainly as a source of essential oil, known as Spanish oregano oil, used in commercial food flavoring, soaps, and men's toiletries. Flowering plants are worked by bees to produce Greek Hymettus honey. Highly irritant to mucous membranes and should not be used in aromatherapy.

T. cilicicus (Cilician thyme) p.212

PARTS USED Leaves.
PROPERTIES An aromatic herb with a lemon scent.
USES OF THE HERB
CULINARY Leaves may be used for flavoring.

T.* x *citriodorus (lemon thyme) p.212

PARTS USED Whole plant, leaves, flowering tops, oil.
PROPERTIES An aromatic, decongestant, relaxant herb with a strong lemon scent.
USES OF THE HERB
CULINARY Leaves flavor savory dishes, especially fish, stuffings for poultry, and vegetables.
AROMATIC Dried leaves are added to potpourris and herb pillows.
MEDICINAL Oil is thought less irritant than other thyme oils, and is used in aromatherapy for asthma and other respiratory complaints, notably in children.
VARIANTS
T. x *c.* **'Archer's Gold'**, p.212.
T. x *c.* **'Aureus'**, p.212.
T. x *c.* **'Bertram Anderson'**, syn. *T.* x *c.* 'Anderson's Gold', *T.* x *c.* 'E. B. Anderson', p.212.
T. x *c.* **'Golden King'**
An upright, bushy cultivar, hardy to 5°F (–15°C), height 9in (23cm), spread 12in (30cm). The yellow-edged leaves tend to revert.
T. x *c.* **'Silver Queen'**, p.212.

T. herba-barona (caraway thyme) p.212

PARTS USED Leaves.
PROPERTIES An aromatic herb with a caraway, nutmeg, or lemon scent, depending on genotype.
USES OF THE HERB
CULINARY Used to flavor game and meat dishes in which wine and garlic predominate.

T. mastichina (mastic thyme, Spanish wood marjoram)

Erect shrub, hardy to 5°F (–15°C), height 8–12in (20–30cm), spread 24–30in (60–75cm), with clusters of ovate, wavy-edged, downy leaves up to ½in (1cm) long, which have a pungent, camphoraceous aroma. Small, off-white flowers are produced in almost spherical heads in summer. Found in Spain and Portugal on rocky ground and beside roads.

PARTS USED Whole plant, leaves, flowering tops, oil.
PROPERTIES A pungent, bittersweet, aromatic herb with a eucalyptus-like scent.

USES OF THE HERB
CULINARY Leaves may be added to strong-flavored meat dishes.
ECONOMIC Oil, known as "oil of wild marjoram," is used in the food industry to flavor meat sauces and soups.

Thymus praecox (creeping thyme, wild thyme) p.213

PARTS USED Leaves.
PROPERTIES An aromatic herb with typical thyme scent. Not recognized as a source of oil or extracts, but may have similar properties to *T. serpyllum*.
USES OF THE HERB
CULINARY Leaves may be used to flavor food.

T. pseudolanuginosus, syn. *T. serpyllum* subsp. *lanuginosus*, *T. lanuginosus* (woolly thyme) p.213

PARTS USED Leaves.
PROPERTIES An aromatic herb with a thyme scent.
USES OF THE HERB
AROMATIC Mainly as an aromatic ornamental, but leaves may be used for flavoring.

T. pulegioides (broad-leaved thyme, large thyme) p.213

PARTS USED Leaves.
PROPERTIES An aromatic herb with a thyme scent.
USES OF THE HERB
CULINARY May be used instead of *T. vulgaris* in cooking.

T. serpyllum (wild thyme, creeping thyme, mother of thyme) p.213

PARTS USED Whole plant, leaves, oil.
PROPERTIES An aromatic, sedative herb that is diuretic and expectorant, reduces spasms, and improves digestion. It is strongly antiseptic and promotes healing.
USES OF THE HERB
CULINARY Leaves may be used as for *T. vulgaris* in cooking.
MEDICINAL Internally for bronchitis, excess mucus, whooping cough, laryngitis, flatulent indigestion, painful menstruation, colic, and hangovers. Reputedly effective in treating alcoholism. Not given to pregnant women. Externally for minor injuries, mastitis, rheumatism, sciatica, and mouth, gum, and throat infections. Combined with *Prunus serotina* (see p.335) and *Marrubium vulgare* (see p.308) for whooping cough; and with astringent herbs, such as *Rubus idaeus* (see p.243) and *Commiphora myrrha* (see p.265), for throat infections. Source of serpolet oil, which has similar effects to thyme oil from *T. vulgaris* for stress-related conditions, but may cause allergic reactions.
VARIANTS
T. s. var. ***albus***
This cultivar has pure white flowers. Hardy to 5°F (–15°C), height ½–3in (1–7cm), spread 3ft (1m).
T. s. **'Annie Hall'**, p.213.
T. s. var. ***coccineus***, p.213.
T. s. **'Elfin'**, p.213.
T. s. **'Goldstream'**
This vigorous cultivar has variegated gold and light green leaves, and lilac flowers. Hardy to 5°F (–15°C), height ½–3in (1–7cm), spread 3ft (1m).
T. s. **'Minor'**,
A slow-growing, compact cultivar with tiny leaves and pink flowers. Hardy to 5°F (–15°C), height ½in (1cm), spread 24in (60cm).
T. s. **'Pink Chintz'**, p.213.
T. s. **'Rainbow Falls'**, p.213.
T. s. **'Russetings'**, p.213.
T. s. **'Vey'**, p.213.

T. vulgaris (common thyme) p.213

PARTS USED Whole plant, leaves, flowering tops, oil.
PROPERTIES An aromatic, thyme-scented, warming, astringent herb that is expectorant, improves digestion, relaxes spasms, and controls coughing. It is strongly antiseptic and antifungal.
USES OF THE HERB
CULINARY Thyme is an essential ingredient of *bouquet garni* and many classic French dishes. It is also used to flavor soups, marinades (especially for olives), stuffings, casseroles, and baked or sautéed vegetables (especially mushrooms and zucchini); it retains its flavor well in slowly cooked dishes.
AROMATIC Dried leaves are added to potpourris and moth-repellent sachets.
MEDICINAL Internally for dry coughs, whooping cough, bronchitis, excess bronchial mucus, asthma, laryngitis, indigestion, gastritis, and diarrhea and enuresis in children. Not given to pregnant women. Externally for tonsillitis, gum disease, rheumatism, arthritis, and fungal infections. Combined with *Lobelia inflata* (see p.305) and *Ephedra* species (see p.278) for asthma; and with *Marrubium vulgare* (see p.308), *Prunus serotina* (see p.335), and *Drimia maritima* (see p.275) for whooping cough. Oil is used in aromatherapy for aches and pains, exhaustion, depression, upper respiratory tract infections, and skin and scalp complaints. Not given to pregnant women. Oil may cause irritation to skin and mucous membranes, and allergic reactions.
ECONOMIC Thymol is an important ingredient of toothpastes, mouthwashes, and topical anti-rheumatic preparations.
VARIANTS
T. v. **'Erectus'**, p.213.
T. v. **'Silver Posie'**, syn. *T. v.* 'Variegatus', p.213.

GROWTH AND HARVEST

GROWTH Ornamental (*T. capitatus*: crop). Well-drained soil in sun. *T. cilicicus* thrives in stony situations. *T. herba-barona* is one of the best thymes to grow in crevices. *T.* x *citriodorus*, *T. praecox*, *T. serpyllum*, *T. vulgaris*, and *T. pseudolanuginosus* are hardy to 5°F (–15°C), others to at least 14°F (–10°C). Thymes dislike winter wet and benefit from a layer of gravel to protect the foliage from contact with wet soil. Propagate by seed in spring (species only), by softwood or semiripe cuttings in summer, or by division in spring or late summer. Established plants may be pruned quite hard in early spring, or lightly after flowering; remove dead flower heads to encourage bushiness. Remove green shoots of variegated cultivars to maintain variegation. *T. vulgaris* is used in companion planting to control flea beetles, cabbage white butterflies, and other cabbage pests.
HARVEST Whole plants and flowering tops are collected in summer, as flowering begins, and distilled for oil, or dried for elixirs, liquid extracts (*T. vulgaris*), and infusions. Sprigs are picked during the growing season and used fresh, or dried for infusions.

TILIA Linden
(Tiliaceae)

Linden (or lime) trees are tolerant of most conditions and withstand hard pruning, which makes them well-suited to street planting. The wood from various kinds is prized for its pale color, light weight, and suitability for carving, turning, and musical instruments. In folklore, linden flowers were thought to cure epilepsy if the sufferer sat under the tree. Linden flowers are collected from various species and hybrids, including *T. cordata*, *T. platyphyllos* (broad-leaved linden), *T. americana* (basswood), and *T.* x *europaea* (common linden). Lindens yield excellent honey.

T. cordata, syn. *T. parvifolia* (small-leaved linden) p.214

PARTS USED Flowers.
PROPERTIES An aromatic, mucilaginous herb that is diuretic and expectorant, calms the nerves, lowers blood pressure, increases perspiration rate, relaxes spasms, and improves digestion.
USES OF THE HERB
MEDICINAL Internally for hypertension, hardening of the arteries, cardiovascular and digestive complaints associated with anxiety, urinary infections, feverish colds, influenza, excess respiratory mucus, migraine, and headaches. Combines well with *Crataegus laevigata* (see p.268) for high blood pressure, with *Ginkgo biloba* (see p.288) for hardening of the arteries, with *Humulus lupulus* (see p.294) for nervous tension, and with *Sambucus nigra* (see p.347) for colds and influenza.

GROWTH AND HARVEST

GROWTH Ornamental. Moist, well-drained, neutral to alkaline soil in sun or partial shade. Propagate by seed sown in spring, or by suckers in spring, or by grafting in late summer. Remove suckers from base and trunk as they appear. Aphids, caterpillars, gall mites, and leafspot may attack leaves. Shoots may be affected by dieback and canker. Linden flowers develop narcotic properties as they age and should only be collected when first opened.
HARVEST Flowers are picked in summer and dried for infusions, liquid extracts, and tinctures.

TRACHYSPERMUM
(Umbelliferae)

Twenty species of aromatic annuals belong to this genus, distributed throughout northern Africa to central Asia, India (where it is grown on a large scale), and western China. The seeds of *T. ammi* are rich in volatile oil, particularly thymol, as found in *Thymus* species (see p.362).

T. ammi, syn. *T. copticum*, *Ammi copticum*, *Carum copticum* (ajowan, ajwain)

Tender annual, height 1–3ft (30–90cm), spread 12–18in (30–45cm) with stems branching from the base, and finely divided, pinnate leaves. Small white flowers, hairy outside, appear in long-stalked, dense umbels in summer, followed by tiny, pungently aromatic, ovoid fruits about ¾in (2cm) long. Found in damp ground in Asia.

PARTS USED Seeds, oil.
PROPERTIES A bitter, aromatic, warming herb with a thymelike aroma and tonic, diuretic and expectorant effects. It relaxes spasms, improves digestion, increases perspiration, and is strongly antiseptic.
USES OF THE HERB
CULINARY Seeds are used to flavor savory dishes, including curries, legumes, breads (*naan*, *pakora*, *paratha*), and pastry snacks, especially in India, Iran, and Afghanistan. Not suitable as a substitute for thyme in Western cooking.
MEDICINAL Internally for colds, coughs, influenza, asthma, diarrhea, cholera, colic, indigestion, flatulence, edema, arthritis, and rheumatism. Not given to patients with hyperacidity. Externally for vaginal discharge and rheumatism. Used mainly in Ayurvedic medicine as a stimulating decongestant for the respiratory and digestive systems.
ECONOMIC Seed extracts are added to cough medicines and epoxy derivatives.

GROWTH AND HARVEST
GROWTH Crop. Moist soil in sun. Propagate by seed sown in autumn or spring.
HARVEST Seeds are collected when ripe and distilled for oil, or dried for use in infusions and powders.

TRICHOSANTHES
(Cucurbitaceae)

T. kirilowii was first described in Chinese medicine in the *Shen Nong Canon of Herbs* during the later Han dynasty (AD25–220). It is best known in China for inducing abortion, but recent interest has been shown in it as a possible remedy for AIDS. The active constituent is trichosanthin, a protein that is undergoing trials as "Compound Q." Chinese medicine also uses *T. japonica* and *T. rosthornii*, as well as *T. kirilowii*. The dried fruits of *T. cucumeroides* are rich in saponins and are used as a soap substitute. *Cucurbita foetidissima* (buffalo gourd) is also used for washing; native N Americans crushed the plant in water for use as a washing agent.

T. kirilowii, syn. *Eopepon vitifolius* (snake gourd, Chinese cucumber) p.214

PARTS USED Tubers (*gua lou gen*, *tian hua fen*), fruit peel (*gua lou pi*), seeds (*gua lou zi*).
PROPERTIES A bittersweet, anti-inflammatory, cooling herb that lowers fever, promotes secretions (notably lactation), and stimulates the uterus (tubers). A sweet, expectorant, laxative herb that stimulates the circulation, dilates the bronchial vessels, moistens dry tissues, and is antibacterial and antifungal (fruits).
USES OF THE HERB
MEDICINAL Internally for diabetes, dry coughs, abscesses, childbirth (second stage of labor), and abortion (tubers); bronchial infections with thick phlegm, chest pain and tightness, dry constipation, and lung and breast tumors (fruits). Not given to pregnant women. Fruits are traditionally prepared as a winter soup to ward off colds and influenza.

GROWTH AND HARVEST
GROWTH Crop. Moist, well-drained soil in partial shade. Propagate by seed sown in spring, soaked for 24 hours before sowing, or by division in spring. Thin out overcrowded branches to allow air to circulate around developing fruits.
HARVEST Tubers and fruits are harvested in autumn and dried for use in decoctions, pills, and powders.

TRIFOLIUM Clover
(Leguminosae/Papilionaceae)

Agricultural cultivars, varying in persistence and flowering time, were developed by medieval times. *T. pratense* is the most important leguminous forage crop in northern Europe. It contains flavonoids that are estrogenic, at least in livestock that consume large amounts of the plant.

T. pratense (red clover, purple clover) p.214

PARTS USED Flowering tops.
PROPERTIES A sweet, cooling, alterative herb that relaxes spasms and has diuretic and expectorant effects.
USES OF THE HERB
MEDICINAL Internally for skin complaints (especially eczema and psoriasis), cancers of the breast, ovaries, and lymphatic system, chronic degenerative diseases, gout, whooping cough, and dry cough. Combined with *Larrea divaricata* (chaparral, creosote bush) in background treatment of cancer, and with *Rumex crispus* (see p.344) for skin disease.
VARIANT
***T. p.* 'Susan Smith'**, syn. *T. p.* 'Gold Net', p.214.

GROWTH AND HARVEST
GROWTH Crop (*T. p.* 'Susan Smith': ornamental). *T. pratense* is hardy to 9°F (–23°C). Moist, well-drained, neutral soil in sun. Propagate by seed in spring, or by division in spring. Powdery mildew may affect leaves.
HARVEST Flower heads with upper leaves are picked in summer as they open and dried for infusions, liquid extracts, ointments, and tinctures.

TRIGONELLA
(Leguminosae/Papilionaceae)

T. foenum-graecum was mentioned in the Ebers papyri (c.1500BC) as an herb to induce childbirth, and was cultivated in Assyria (seventh century BC), spreading eastward to India. It is grown for fodder in parts of Europe. Dried plants are sold as *hilba* in Egypt as a remedy for painful menstruation. It was first mentioned in Chinese medicine in the 11th century and has a long tradition as a tonic herb in both Chinese and Ayurvedic medicine. Western interest in the herb centers on one of its constituent alkaloids, trigonelline, which has potential in cancer therapy, and its saponins, which are extracted for use in oral contraceptives and other pharmaceutical products.

T. foenum-graecum (fenugreek) p.214

PARTS USED Leaves, seeds (*hu lu ba*).
PROPERTIES A bitter, pungent, warming herb that increases milk flow, stimulates the uterus, soothes irritated tissues, lowers fever, reduces blood sugar, improves digestion, promotes healing, and has laxative, expectorant, diuretic, antiparasitic, and antitumor effects.
USES OF THE HERB
CULINARY Dried leaves (*methi*) flavor root vegetables in Indian and Middle Eastern dishes; fresh leaves are cooked as a vegetable curry (India). Seeds are lightly roasted to reduce bitterness, and ground as an ingredient of curry powder, pickles, and Ethiopian spice mixes; they are also used as a flavoring for bread (Egypt, Ethiopia), stews, and fried foods. Seeds are sprouted as a salad vegetable, which is also eaten as a tonic for the liver, kidneys, and male sexual organs. *Helba*, a dish of northern Yemen, is made from boiled seeds, served as a purée with a garnish of fried onion and meat.
MEDICINAL Internally for late-onset diabetes, poor digestion (especially in convalescence), gastric inflammation, digestive disorders, tuberculosis, painful menstruation, labor pains, and insufficient lactation. Not given to pregnant women. Externally for skin inflammations and cellulitis. In Chinese medicine, mainly for kidney-related disorders, such as back pain, premature ejaculation, loss of libido, edema of the legs, and hernia. Regarded as a rejuvenative and aphrodisiac in Ayurvedic medicine, and used to treat digestive and bronchial complaints, debility, allergies, neurasthenia, gout, and arthritis.
ECONOMIC Seed extracts are used in synthetic maple syrup, and maple, vanilla, caramel, and butterscotch flavors for the food industry.

GROWTH AND HARVEST
GROWTH Crop. Well-drained, fertile soil in sun. Propagate by seed sown in spring.
HARVEST Leaves are picked in summer and used fresh or dried in infusions, or as a vegetable. Seeds are collected when ripe and dried for decoctions, pastes, and powders, or commercially processed for extracts.

TRILLIUM
(Liliaceae)

T. erectum was introduced to herbal medicine by Constantine Rafinesque in his *Medical Flora* (2 vols, 1828–30) and was listed in the U.S. *National Formulary* (1916–47). It and the related Asiatic *T. kamtschaticum* and

T. tschonoskii are known to contain steroidal saponins, which have hormonal effects; hence their use in gynecological and obstetric medicine. The white-flowered variety of *T. erectum* was preferred by native N Americans for treating sore nipples, inducing labor, and controlling postpartum hemorrhage, vaginal discharge, and heavy menstruation.

T. erectum (bethroot, wake robin, birthroot) p.214

PARTS USED Rhizomes.
PROPERTIES A sweet-sour, astringent, warming herb that is expectorant, controls bleeding, and benefits the female reproductive system.
USES OF THE HERB
MEDICINAL Internally for hemorrhage from uterus, urinary tract, and lungs, and for excessive menstruation. Externally for vaginal discharge, ulcers (especially varicose), skin complaints, and insect bites and stings. Combined with *Vinca major* (see p.369) or *Geranium maculatum* (see p.288) for excessive menstruation; with *Bidens tripartita* (see p.249) for blood in the urine; and with *Ulmus rubra* (see p.366) and *Lobelia inflata* (see p.305) for ulcers.
VARIANT
T. e. f. ***albiflorum***, p.215.

GROWTH AND HARVEST
GROWTH Ornamental. Moist, well-drained, neutral to slightly acid, humus-rich soil in partial shade. *T. erectum* is hardy to –31°F (–35°C). Propagate by seed sown in spring, or by division during dormancy. Seed takes up to 3 years to germinate. Slugs may damage leaves.
HARVEST Rhizomes are lifted after leaves have died back in late summer, and dried for use in decoctions, liquid extracts, and tinctures.

TROPAEOLUM
(Tropaeolaceae)

T. majus was introduced to Europe from Peru in the 16th century by the conquistadors, and was first known as *Nasturtium indicum*, "Indian cress," on account of its pungent, watercress-like flavor. The species is seldom seen now, having been superseded by a wide range of cultivars. *T. majus* has several interesting properties that make it a useful medicinal and culinary herb. It contains large amounts of sulfur, which reputedly retards baldness, and a glycoside that reacts with water to produce an antibiotic. The pickled, unripe seeds are the only acceptable substitute for capers; they develop capric acid, which gives the characteristic flavor.

T. majus (garden nasturtium, Indian cress) p.215

PARTS USED Whole plant, leaves, flowers, seeds.
PROPERTIES A bitter, antiseptic, tonic herb that has diuretic and expectorant effects, and controls fungal and bacterial infections.
USES OF THE HERB
CULINARY Leaves, flowers, flower buds, and nectar spurs are eaten in salads. Chopped fresh leaves give a peppery flavor to cream cheese or egg dishes. Flowers are used to make nasturtium vinegar. Unripe seeds are pickled as a substitute for capers.
MEDICINAL Internally for genitourinary and respiratory infections, scurvy, and poor skin and hair. Externally for baldness, minor injuries, and skin eruptions.
ECONOMIC Combined with *Urtica dioica* (see p.366), *Buxus sempervirens* (see p.351), and *Quercus robur* (see p.338) in hair lotion.
VARIANTS
T. m. **'Alaska'**, p.215.
T. m. **'Empress of India'**, p.215.
T. m. **'Hermine Grashoff'**, p.216.
T. m. **'Peach Melba'**, p.216.

GROWTH AND HARVEST
GROWTH Ornamental. Well-drained, moist, average to poor soil in sun. Propagate by seed sown in late spring or early summer. Self-seeds freely in some gardens and may be invasive. Rich soil promotes leaf growth at the expense of flowers. Often used in companion planting to deter cucumber beetles and whitefly. Growth slows during hot, dry weather. Prone to viral diseases. However, nasturtiums are reputed to deter woolly aphids if plants are grown at the base of apple trees.
HARVEST All parts are picked in summer and used fresh for infusions and tinctures. Plants are also cut for juice extraction.

TURNERA
(Turneraceae)

Sixty species of shrubs and short-lived perennials belong to this genus, which occurs mainly in C and S America, with one species in Africa. Despite its name, *T. diffusa* var. *aphrodisiaca* has not been proved to have an aphrodisiac action, though antidepressant effects have been reported. The closely related *T. ulmifolia* (sage rose, W Indian holly) has similar effects. It is common as an ornamental, having more attractive foliage and much larger, hibiscus-like flowers.

T. diffusa var. *aphrodisiaca* (damiana)

Aromatic, shrubby perennial, hardy to 23°F (–5°C), height 3ft (1m), spread 2ft (60cm), with light green, obovate toothed leaves up to 1in (2.5cm) long. Yellow-orange, 5-petaled flowers about ½in (1cm) long are borne in summer, followed by globose, aromatic, 3-valved fruits about ¾in (2cm) across, with numerous tiny, pear-shaped seeds. Found in dry, sandy, or rocky places in northern S America, C America, southern N America, and Namibia.

PARTS USED Whole plant.
PROPERTIES A bitter, pungent, warming herb with a figlike flavor. It improves digestion, lifts the spirits, calms the nerves, regulates hormone function, stimulates the genitourinary tract, and rejuvenates kidney energy.
USES OF THE HERB
MEDICINAL Internally for nervous exhaustion, anxiety, depression, debility in convalescence, impotence, premature ejaculation, prostate complaints, urinary infections, frigidity, vaginal discharge, painful menstruation, menopausal problems, poor appetite and digestion, and atonic constipation. Combines well with *Serenoa reopens* (see p.352) as a tonic for sexual neurosis: with *Avena sativa* (see p.246) for depression, and with *Scutellaria lateriflora* (see p.351) or *Stachys officinalis* (see p.355) for anxiety states.

GROWTH AND HARVEST
GROWTH Crop. Dry soil in sun. Propagate by seed sown in spring, or by division in spring or autumn, or by cuttings in summer. Cut back in early spring.
HARVEST Plants are cut when flowering and dried for use in compound mixtures, infusions, liquid extracts, and tablets.

TUSSILAGO Coltsfoot
(Compositae/Asteraceae)

T. farfara was smoked as a cough remedy in classical times. Pliny (AD23–79) recommended that the leaves and roots be burned over cypress charcoal, and the smoke swallowed rather than inhaled. It has similar applications in Chinese medicine, but only the flower buds and flowers are used. The herb contains pyrrolizidine alkaloids, which have not proved toxic at low dosages in tests, and there is no suggestion that *T. farfara* should be banned for internal use, as is the case with *Symphytum officinale* (see p.357).

T. farfara (coltsfoot) p.216

PARTS USED Leaves, flowers.
PROPERTIES A bittersweet, astringent, expectorant herb with a licorice-like flavor. It relaxes spasms, controls coughing, soothes irritated tissues, reduces inflammation, and stimulates the immune system.
USES OF THE HERB
CULINARY Leaves are eaten raw in salads, added to soups, and cooked as a vegetable. Flowers are used to make country wine.
MEDICINAL Internally for coughs, whooping cough, asthma, excess mucus, bronchitis, and laryngitis. Externally for ulcers, sores, eczema, insect bites, and skin inflammations. Combined with *Marrubium vulgare* (see p.308) and *Verbascum thapsus* (see p.368) for irritating coughs. WARNING This herb is subject to legal restrictions in some countries.
ECONOMIC Dried leaves are an ingredient of herbal tobaccos and are used in curing pipe tobaccos.

GROWTH AND HARVEST
GROWTH Crop. Moist, neutral to alkaline soil in sun or partial shade. *T. farfara* is hardy to –20°F (–29°C). Propagate by seed sown in spring, or by division in spring or autumn; it is an invasive weed.
HARVEST Leaves are cut when full grown and used fresh, or dried for smoking mixtures, liquid and solid extracts, and tinctures. Flowers are picked when they first open and are used fresh or dried in decoctions (in Chinese medicine), liquid extracts, syrups, and tinctures.

TYPHA Cattail
(Typhaceae)

T. angustifolia, *T. bungeana*, *T. davidiana*, *T. minima*, and *T. orientalis* are used interchangeably with *T. latifolia* as the Chinese drug *pu huang*. The pollen contains flavonoids, volatile oil, and hormonal substances.

T. latifolia (cattail, great reedmace) p.216

PARTS USED Pollen from male flowers (*pu huang*), leaves, fruit hairs.
PROPERTIES A sweet, acrid herb that is diuretic, controls bleeding, improves the circulation, promotes healing, and stimulates the uterus. Dried pollen is anticoagulant; roasted with charcoal, it becomes hemostatic.
USES OF THE HERB
MEDICINAL Internally for hemorrhage, painful menstruation, abnormal uterine bleeding, post-partum pains, abscesses, and cancer of the lymphatic system. Not given to pregnant women. Externally for tapeworms, diarrhea, and injuries. May be combined with honey for abscesses and with powdered cuttlefish bone for bleeding injuries.
ECONOMIC Leaves are used in basketry and for making woven chair seats. Fruit hairs are used to stuff mattresses and pillows.
VARIANT
T. l. **'Variegata'**, p.216.

GROWTH AND HARVEST
GROWTH Ornamental. Wet soil or shallow water in sun or shade. Propagate by seed sown in spring (species only), or by division in spring. Subject to statutory control as a weed in parts of Australia.
HARVEST Pollen is gently shaken from flower spikes when blooming, and dried for use in decoctions, pastes, powders, and suppositories.

ULMUS Elm
(Ulmaceae)

Native N Americans made a healing salve from the outer bark of *U. rubra*, and an infusion for sore throats and to ease childbirth. Contact with settlers led to the bark being used as a mechanical irritant to abort half-breed fetuses. Its use as an abortifacient became so widespread that it is now banned in many countries, though the powdered inner bark, which is useless for that purpose, is available commercially for other medicinal applications. *U. rubra* bark, when mixed with water, makes a pale, pink-brown gruel, which may be flavored with honey and spices; it is often taken in this form. The unrelated *Fremontodendron californicum*, which is widely grown as an ornamental, apparently has similar properties. *U. minor* var. *vulgaris* (English elm) may be used in lotions for skin complaints but is not of major importance as an herb, particularly since the demise of many elms from Dutch elm disease.

U. rubra, syn. *U. fulva* (slippery elm, red elm) p.217

PARTS USED Inner bark.
PROPERTIES A sweet, mucilaginous, laxative herb with a fenugreek-like odor. It soothes and lubricates tissues, draws out toxins, and promotes healing.
USES OF THE HERB
MEDICINAL Internally for gastric and duodenal ulcers, gastritis, colitis, and digestive problems in infants. Externally for sore throat, coughs, wounds, burns, boils, abscesses, and chilblains. Often added as a soothing element to cough mixtures. Combines well with *Althaea officinalis* (see p.236) for digestive disorders and with *Linum usitatissimum* (see p.304) in poultices for skin inflammations.
WARNING This herb, especially as whole bark, is subject to legal restrictions in some countries.

GROWTH AND HARVEST
GROWTH Crop. Moist, deep soil in sun. Hardy to –35°F (–37°C). Propagate by seed sown in autumn, or by suckers in autumn, or by layering in autumn, or by semiripe cuttings in summer, or by grafting. Plants may be damaged by aphids, caterpillars, gall mites, fungal infections, and Dutch elm disease.
HARVEST Inner bark is stripped from trunks and larger branches in spring, then dried and powdered for use in decoctions, liquid extracts, ointments, poultices, powders, and tablets. Fine powder is used internally; coarse powder is better suited to poultices.

UMBELLULARIA
(Lauraceae)

U. californica is pungently aromatic; inhaling the scent of the leaves may cause a headache. The herb is nevertheless a traditional remedy for headaches, and may be taken as an infusion, or the leaves bound to the forehead for this purpose. Native Californians also found the leaves useful as insect repellants.

U. californica (California laurel, headache tree, California sassafras) p.217

PARTS USED Leaves.
PROPERTIES A pungent, analgesic herb with a camphoraceous aroma.
USES OF THE HERB
CULINARY Leaves may be used very sparingly with meat dishes as a substitute for bay leaves.
MEDICINAL Internally for headache, neuralgia, intestinal cramps, and gastroenteritis. Externally for headache and fainting.

GROWTH AND HARVEST
GROWTH Ornamental. Well-drained, moist soil in sun. Propagate by seed sown in autumn, or by semiripe cuttings in summer, or by layering in spring or summer. May require winter protection when young.
HARVEST Leaves are picked as required and used fresh, or dried whole for use in infusions.

URGINEA
U. maritima. See *Drimia maritima*.

URTICA Nettle
(Urticaceae)

U. dioica is a fibrous plant, used in cloth manufacture from the Bronze Age to the early 20th century. It is rich in vitamins, notably A and C, and minerals, especially iron; it also contains indoles (mainly histamine and serotonin) and large amounts of chlorophyll. *U. urens* (annual nettle) and *U. pilulifera* (Roman nettle) have similar properties to *U. dioica*. The name comes from the Latin *urere*, "to burn," and refers to the stinging hairs, which in some species contain substances toxic enough to cause death.

U. dioica (stinging nettle, nettle) p.217

PARTS USED Whole plant, leaves.
PROPERTIES An astringent, diuretic, tonic herb that controls bleeding, clears toxins, and slightly reduces blood pressure and blood sugar levels.
USES OF THE HERB
CULINARY Young leaf tips are cooked as a spinachlike vegetable, puréed for soup,

and used to make nettle beer. Raw leaves are highly irritant, and recommendations for using them chopped in salads and soft cheeses should be disregarded. Older leaves contain crystals of calcium oxalate that give a gritty texture, even after cooking. Leaves are dried for tea, which is bland and nonaromatic; it may be added to Indian tea as a tonic.

MEDICINAL Internally for anemia, hemorrhage (especially of the uterus), excessive menstruation, hemorrhoids, arthritis, rheumatism, gout, and skin complaints (especially eczema). Externally for arthritic pain, gout, sciatica, neuralgia, hemorrhoids, scalp and hair problems, burns, insect bites, and nosebleed. Combines well with *Arctium lappa* (see p.240) for eczema.

ECONOMIC Plants are processed commercially for extraction of chlorophyll, which is used as a coloring agent in foods and medicines.

GROWTH AND HARVEST

GROWTH Crop. Moist, nitrogen-rich soil in sun or dappled shade. Propagate by seed sown in spring, or by division in spring. Cut stands of nettles to the ground in summer to provide a second crop of new leaves. Nettles are invasive but are easily controlled by pulling out dormant rhizomes. They provide food for the caterpillars of various butterflies, such as red admirals.

HARVEST Whole plants for medicinal use are cut as flowering begins in summer and dried for use in infusions, liquid extracts, ointments, powders, and tinctures. For culinary use, pick young leaf tips from plants less than 4in (10cm) high, before they develop oxalate crystals.

VACCINIUM
(Ericaceae)

The leaves of *V. myrtillus* contain glucoquinones, which reduce blood sugar, and the fruits are rich in anthocyanosides, shown experimentally to dilate blood vessels. Arbutin, which acts as a urinary antiseptic, has not been found in *V. myrtillus*, although it is present in most other *Vaccinium* species and in other members of the heather family (such as *Arctostaphylos uva-ursi*, see p.241). Leaves of *V. vitis-idaea* (cowberry), which contain up to seven percent arbutin, are used to treat urinary tract infections, cystitis, diabetes, and diarrhea.

V. myrtillus (bilberry, huckleberry, whortleberry) p.217

PARTS USED Leaves, fruits.

PROPERTIES A bittersweet, astringent, cooling herb that acts as a diuretic, lowers blood sugar levels, and has a tonic effect on the blood.

USES OF THE HERB

CULINARY Fruits are added to salads and made into jams, syrups, and desserts.

MEDICINAL Internally for diabetes (leaves), edema, anemia, diarrhea, dysentery, and urinary complaints. Externally for gum inflammations, hemorrhoids, skin complaints, and burns (fruits).

ECONOMIC Fruits are added to wine; extracts are used to flavor liqueurs.

GROWTH AND HARVEST

GROWTH Crop. Moist, acid soil in sun or partial shade. Propagate by seed sown in autumn, or by semiripe cuttings in summer. Trim in spring to encourage bushy growth.

HARVEST Leaves are picked in spring and dried for decoctions. Fruits are collected in late summer and dried for decoctions and liquid extracts.

VALERIANA Valerian
(Valerianaceae)

V. officinalis was used by Hippocrates in the fourth century BC, and it appears in Anglo-Saxon herbals. Its name, gained in the 10th century when the herb was recommended by Arab physicians, may derive from the Latin *valere*, "to be well." The active constituents are complex and are not fully understood. The roots contain iridoids, known as "valepotriates," that regulate the functioning of the nervous system. Some authorities claim that the valepotriates are not present in the root itself, or in preparations derived from it, but actually develop during processing. Valerian tincture was widely used in World War I to treat shell shock (loss of memory and other functions due to prolonged psychological strain). Similar constituents are found in *V. jatamansi* and *V. mexicana*.

V. officinalis (common valerian, garden heliotrope) p.217

PARTS USED Rhizomes, roots, oil.

PROPERTIES A bitter, sedative, warming herb with a musty aroma. It calms the nerves, relaxes spasms, improves digestion, relieves pain, and lowers blood pressure.

USES OF THE HERB

AROMATIC Oil is used in "mossy" perfumes.

MEDICINAL Internally for insomnia, hysteria, anxiety, cramps, migraine, indigestion of nervous origin, hypertension, and painful menstruation. Excess causes headaches, palpitations, and stupor; extended use may lead to addiction. Not given to patients with liver problems. Externally for eczema, ulcers, and minor injuries (especially splinters). Best on people with cold, nervous dispositions. Combined with *Viscum album* (see p.370) and *Scutellaria lateriflora* (see p.351) for hysteria; with *Humulus lupulus* (see p.294) and *Passiflora incarnata* (see p.323) for insomnia; with *Dioscorea villosa* (see p.273), *Pulsatilla vulgaris* (see p.338), and *Caulophyllum thalictroides* (see p.256) for painful menstruation.

ECONOMIC Extracts are used in flavoring ice cream, bakery products, condiments, soft drinks, liqueurs, beers, and tobacco, and are especially important in apple flavors; they are also used as a bait for trapping wild cats and rodents.

GROWTH AND HARVEST

GROWTH Ornamental. Moist soil in sun or shade. Propagate by seed sown in spring, or by division in spring or autumn. Remove flowers to encourage rhizome growth.

HARVEST Rhizomes and roots are lifted in the second year after the leaves have died off and used fresh, dried for use in decoctions, infusions, liquid extracts, tablets, and tinctures, or distilled for oil.

VANILLA
(Orchidaceae)

Vanilla is one of the world's most important flavorings; it was introduced to Europe in the 16th century by the Spanish, who found it used by the Aztecs as a flavoring for chocolate. Production is now concentrated in Madagascar, Réunion, Tahiti, Java, and the Seychelles. Vanilla flowers are short-lived and have specific pollinators. In cultivation they must be pollinated by hand to produce fruits (vanilla pods), which take five to seven months to ripen. The aromatic compounds are developed during fermentation of the unripe pods. *V. planifolia* fruits contain about 3.5 percent vanillin, which is present in many natural balsams and resins. There is a large market for synthetic vanilla, which occurs as a by-product of paper manufacturing and is extracted from both *Ferula assa-foetida* (see p.282) and the eugenol fraction in oil of cloves (*Syzygium aromaticum*, see p.358). The flavor does not compare in richness with that of natural vanilla, which contains some 35 other aromatic compounds. *V. tahitensis* (Tahiti vanilla) and *V. pompona* (W Indian vanilla) are alternative, though inferior, sources of natural vanilla.

V. planifolia (vanilla) p.217

PARTS USED Fruits.
PROPERTIES An aromatic herb that improves digestion.
USES OF THE HERB
AROMATIC Extracts used in perfumery.
ECONOMIC Whole pods are stored in sugar, which is used to sweeten and give a vanilla flavor to desserts and cakes. Extracts are used in flavoring of ice cream, syrups, candy, bakery products, breakfast cereals, soft drinks, liqueurs, and tobacco.
VARIANT
V. p. **'Variegata'**, p.218.

GROWTH AND HARVEST
GROWTH Crop (*V. p.* 'Variegata': ornamental). Epiphytic soil mix with ample moisture, shade, and humidity, at 81°F (27°C). Propagate by cuttings 5–6ft (1.5–2m) long at any time (but best toward the end of the dry season), kept loosely coiled in a dry, shady place for 2–3 weeks before insertion in loose soil mix. For optimum fruiting, plants are trained in loops, rather than allowed to climb upwards. This encourages both formation of new shoots and, where the loop touches the ground, of adventitious roots that help feed the plant. Plants may be damaged by scale insects, mildew, vanilla root rot, and snails.
HARVEST Fruits are picked when fully ripe before they split open, and scalded before undergoing various stages of fermentation and drying, which can take 6 months. Cured pods are stored whole, or processed commercially for solvent extractions (vanilla resinoid), and alcoholic tinctures (vanilla essence).

VERBASCUM Mullein
(Scrophulariaceae)

A number of verbascums have been used medicinally for respiratory complaints since Classical times, but none are well researched. *V. densiflorum* (large-flowered mullein) contains iridoid glycosides, similar to those found in *Plantago major* (see p.331), that stimulate the secretion of uric acid from the kidneys. These may also be a constituent of other verbascums. *V. densiflorum*, *V. nigrum* (dark mullein), and the rare *V. phlomoides* (orange mullein) are used in similar ways to *V. thapsus*.

V. thapsus (great mullein, Aaron's rod) p.218

PARTS USED Whole plant, leaves, flowers.
PROPERTIES A bitter, cooling, mucilaginous herb that soothes and lubricates tissues, promotes healing, and has expectorant, diuretic, analgesic, and antiseptic effects.
USES OF THE HERB
MEDICINAL Internally for coughs, whooping cough, bronchitis, laryngitis, tonsillitis, tracheitis, asthma, influenza, excess respiratory mucus, tuberculosis, urinary tract infections, nervous tension, and insomnia. Externally for earache (flowers in olive oil), sores, wounds, boils, rheumatic pain, hemorrhoids, and chilblains. Combines well with *Marrubium vulgare* (see p.308), *Lobelia inflata* (see p.305), and *Tussilago farfara* (see p.365) for bronchitis.
ECONOMIC Leaves are smoked alone, or with *Tussilago farfara* (see p.365) and *Eriodictyon californicum* (see p.279) as a substitute for tobacco.

GROWTH AND HARVEST
GROWTH Ornamental. Well-drained to dry soil in sun. Propagate by seed in autumn or spring, or by root cuttings in late winter. *V. thapsus* self-seeds freely in suitable conditions. Caterpillars may attack plants. Subject to statutory control as a weed in some countries, notably in parts of Australia.
HARVEST Whole plants are collected when flowering, and leaves and flowers in summer, and dried for use in infusions, liquid extracts, and tinctures. Flowers may also be used fresh or frozen for use in infusions, medicated oil, and syrup.

VERBENA Vervain
(Verbenaceae)

V. officinalis is used mainly for nervous complaints in Western medicine, and for conditions associated with disturbances of the liver, spleen, and bladder meridians in Chinese medicine. The N American *V. hastata* (blue vervain) has similar constituents but is considered more alterative, acting mainly on the liver and lungs. It is used for liver disorders, respiratory, and menstrual complaints.

V. officinalis (vervain) p.218

PARTS USED Whole plant (*ma bian cao*).
PROPERTIES A very bitter, aromatic, cooling herb that is diuretic, calms the nerves, increases perspiration and lactation, reduces inflammation, and relieves pain; it controls bleeding, improves liver and gall bladder function, and stimulates the uterus. Regarded as antimalarial in Chinese medicine.
USES OF THE HERB
MEDICINAL Internally for nervous exhaustion, depression, convalescent debility, asthma, migraine, jaundice, gall bladder problems, and insufficient lactation. Excess causes nausea and vomiting. Not recommended during pregnancy, although it may assist contractions during labor. Externally for minor injuries, eczema, sores, neuralgia, and gum disease. In Chinese medicine, for malaria, menstrual complaints, influenza, feverish illnesses, gum disease, abscesses, urinary disorders, and schistosomiasis. Combines well with *Scutellaria lateriflora* (see p.351), *Avena sativa* (see p.246), and *Cypripedium parviflorum* var. *pubescens* (see p.271) for depression.

GROWTH AND HARVEST
GROWTH Crop. Well-drained, moist soil in sun. Propagate by seed sown in spring or autumn, or by division in spring, or by stem cuttings in late summer. Pinch out tips to encourage branching.
HARVEST Plants are cut as flowering begins, and dried for use in decoctions (Chinese medicine), infusions, liquid extracts, ointments, and tinctures.

VERONICA Speedwell
(Scrophulariaceae)

"Common speedwell" and "speedwell" are names applied to several different species, and for medicinal purposes care should be taken to identify the correct plant. *V. officinalis* was a popular healing herb in Europe during the Middle Ages, under the name *herba Veronica majoris*. In 1690 it was the subject of a 300-page treatise (*Polchresta Herba Veronica* by Johannes Francus). By the 19th century it was used mostly as a tea substitute, and was known in France as *thé d'Europe*. It is regarded as obsolete by herbalists today. *Veronica* is thought to be named after St. Veronica. The common name "speedwell" (goodbye) refers to the rapid fall of the corollas if the flower spikes are picked.

V. officinalis (common speedwell, heath speedwell, fluellen) p.218

PARTS USED Whole plant.
PROPERTIES A bitter, astringent, alterative herb with a tealike odor when dried. It has weak diuretic and expectorant effects.
USES OF THE HERB
MEDICINAL Formerly, internally for upset stomach and bronchial, arthritic, rheumatic, and skin complaints; externally for minor injuries.
ECONOMIC Dried herb may be added to tea blends.

GROWTH AND HARVEST
GROWTH Crop. Dry, slightly acid soil in sun or partial shade. Propagate by seed in autumn, or by division in spring or autumn, or by semiripe cuttings in summer. Prone to downy and powdery mildews.
HARVEST Plants are cut when flowering and dried for infusions.

VERONICASTRUM Blackroot
(Scrophulariaceae)

V. virginicum is a powerful purgative and emetic that has a long history of use among native N Americans; they used it to induce vomiting, which was an important part of the healing process and played a role in certain rituals. *V. virginicum* contains a bitter compound (leptandrin), saponins, hormonal substances, tannins, volatile oil (including esters of cinnamic acids), and a glycoside resembling senegin (as found in *Polygala senega*, see p.332).

V. virginicum, syn. *Leptandra virginica* (Culver's root, blackroot) p.218

PARTS USED Rhizomes, roots.
PROPERTIES A bitter, laxative, tonic herb that increases perspiration, relaxes spasms, and stimulates the liver and gall bladder.
USES OF THE HERB
MEDICINAL Internally for chronic constipation and indigestion associated with liver disorders, and gall bladder inflammation. Combined with *Taraxacum officinale* (see p.360) and *Berberis vulgaris* (see p.248) for liver complaints; and with *Acorus calamus* (see p.228) and *Hydrastis canadensis* (see p.294) for constipation with flatulence and bloating.
VARIANT
V. v. var. ***roseum***, p.218.

GROWTH AND HARVEST
GROWTH Ornamental. Well-drained, moist to dry soil in sun or partial shade. Propagate by seed sown in autumn, or by division in spring or late autumn, or by semiripe cuttings of lateral shoots in late summer. Tall flowering stems may need staking. Plants may be affected by downy mildew.
HARVEST Rhizomes and roots are lifted in autumn and dried for use in decoctions, liquid extracts, powders, tablets, and tinctures.

VETIVERIA Vetiver
(Gramineae)

Vetiver roots are rich in volatile oil, known as "the oil of tranquility" in India and Sri Lanka. It has a heavy, earthy aroma, and is strongly repellent to flies, cockroaches, bedbugs, and clothes moths.

V. zizanioides (vetiver, *khus khus*, cuscus) p.219

PARTS USED Roots, oil.
PROPERTIES An aromatic, sedative, antiseptic herb that increases production of red blood corpuscles.
USES OF THE HERB
AROMATIC Oil is an ingredient in oriental "woody" perfumes.
MEDICINAL Internally for nervous and circulatory problems. Externally for lice.
ECONOMIC Dried roots are woven into scented mats, screens, and fans; also used as insect repellants. Oil is used in soaps and cosmetics, and as a fragrance fixative. Some applications in food flavoring, mainly in canned asparagus and Indian fruit drinks.

GROWTH AND HARVEST
GROWTH Crop. Wet to dry soil in sun, minimum 59–64°F (15–18°C). Propagate mainly by division, or "slips," and layering at the start of the growing season, or commercially by tissue culture. Trim plants grown as a hedge to encourage dense growth; burn over to destroy crop-pest larvae. Plants may be damaged by fungal diseases and termites.
HARVEST Roots are lifted as required and distilled for oil, or processed for solvent extraction.

VIBURNUM
(Caprifoliaceae)

Common to *V. opulus* and *V. prunifolium* is scopoletin, a coumarin that has a sedative effect on the uterus. *V. prunifolium* also contains salicin, an analgesic that occurs in *Salix alba* (see p.345). The two herbs are sometimes prescribed alternately or together, *V. opulus* being considered the weaker in action. In parts of the eastern US, fruits of *V. prunifolium* have been used for preserves since colonial times, and larger-fruited, palatable clones are grown for fruit production. These and the fruits of *V. opulus* are poisonous when raw but edible when cooked.

V. opulus (crampbark, guelder rose) p.219

PARTS USED Bark.
PROPERTIES A bitter, astringent, sedative herb that relaxes spasms and regulates uterine function.
USES OF THE HERB
MEDICINAL Internally for painful menstruation, postpartum and ovarian pain, threatened miscarriage, hypertension, nervous constipation, and muscular cramps. Externally for muscular cramps. Combines well with *Dioscorea villosa* (see p.273) and *Zanthoxylum americanum* (see p.372) for cramps; and with *V. prunifolium* and *Chamaelirium luteum* (see p.258) for uterine pain and threatened miscarriage.
VARIANTS
V. o. **'Aureum'**, p.219.
V. o. **'Roseum'**, syn. *V. o.* 'Sterile', p.219.
V. o. **'Xanthocarpum'**, p.219.

V. prunifolium (black haw, stagbush)

Deciduous shrub or bushy tree, hardy to –30°F (–35°C), height 15–28ft (5–9m), spread 3–20ft (1–6m), with red-tinged shoots and shiny, ovate leaves up to 3in (8cm) long, which turn red in autumn. White flowers, ⅛in (3mm) across, are produced in flat clusters up to 4in (10cm) across in late spring and early summer, followed by blue-black, oval fruits, almost ¾in (2cm) long. Native to eastern US.

PARTS USED Stem bark, root bark.
PROPERTIES A bitter, astringent, sedative herb that relaxes spasms, relieves pain, calms the nerves, lowers blood pressure, and regulates uterine function.
USES OF THE HERB
MEDICINAL Internally for painful menstruation, threatened miscarriage, convulsive disorders, hysteria, muscular cramps, asthma, and palpitations of nervous origin. Combined with *Chamaelirium luteum* (see p.258) and *Hydrastis canadensis* (see p.294) for threatened miscarriage.

GROWTH AND HARVEST
GROWTH Ornamental. Deep, moist soil in sun or partial shade. Propagate by seed sown in autumn (species only), or by semiripe cuttings in summer. Remove dead wood and older stems after flowering. Plants may be damaged by aphids, especially *V. o.* 'Roseum'. Leaves may be affected by leafspot.
HARVEST Bark is stripped before leaves change color in autumn, or before leaf buds open in spring, and dried for decoctions, liquid extracts, and tinctures (*V. opulus*, *V. prunifolium*), creams (*V. opulus*), and infusions, elixirs, and powders (*V. prunifolium*).

VINCA Periwinkle
(Apocynaceae)

V. major and *V. minor* (lesser periwinkle) are both sources of the alkaloid vincamine, used by the pharmaceutical industry as a cerebral stimulant and vasodilator. *V. major* also contains reserpine, as found in *Rauvolfia serpentina* (see p.339), which reduces high blood pressure. It does not contain the anti-cancer alkaloids found in the related *Catharanthus roseus* (see p.256). *V. minor* is also used by herbalists as a diuretic and remedy for stomach disorders.

V. major (greater periwinkle) p.220

PARTS USED Whole plant.
PROPERTIES An acrid, slightly bitter, astringent herb that controls bleeding.
USES OF THE HERB
MEDICINAL Internally for excessive menstruation, abnormal uterine bleeding, vaginal discharge, and hardening of the arteries (especially the cerebral arteries). Not given to patients with constipation. Externally for vaginal discharge, nosebleed, sore throat, and mouth ulcers. Combined with *Trillium erectum* (see p.364) for excessive menstruation and with*Ginkgo biloba* (see p.288) for hardening of the cerebral arteries.
VARIANTS
V. m. **'Maculata'**, p.220.
V. m. **'Reticulata'**, p.220.
V. m. **'Variegata'**, p.220.

V. rosea. See *Catharanthus roseus.*

GROWTH AND HARVEST
GROWTH Ornamental. Moist soil in sun or partial shade. Propagate by division from autumn to spring, or by semiripe cuttings in summer. *V. major* is invasive, sending out shoots up to 3ft (1m) long, which root at every node. Cut back plants in autumn or winter to control spread. Remove excess shoots in summer to restrict spread before rooting at nodes takes place.
HARVEST Plants are cut when flowering and processed commercially for alkaloid extraction, or dried for use in infusions, liquid extracts, powders, and tinctures.
WARNING Toxic if eaten.

VIOLA Violet
(Violaceae)

Violets were extolled by Muslims in the saying "the excellence of the violet is as the excellence of Islam above all other religions." The Romans drank violet-flavored wine and were criticized by Horace (65–8BC) for spending more time growing violets than olives. They were the favorite flower of Napoleon, who was nicknamed *Caporal Violette* and died wearing a locket of violets taken from Josephine's grave. The main aromatic element in *V. odorata*, known as ionone, was synthesized in 1893; since then the cultivation of violets for perfumery has declined. Violets are regarded as cleansing herbs and have been used in the background treatment of cancer. *V. yezoensis* has featured in recent trials for treating childhood eczema at the Great Ormond Street Children's Hospital in London. *V. striata* is also used medicinally and apparently has antitumor effects. Chinese herbals feature a number of other species, including *V. diffusa*, *V. inconspicua*, and *V. patrinii*. High doses of violets cause nausea and vomiting because of the irritant effect of the saponins on the digestive system.

V. odorata (violet, sweet violet) p.220

PARTS USED Leaves, flowers, oil.
PROPERTIES A bitter-sweet, mucilaginous, cooling herb that cleanses toxins and has expectorant, antiseptic, and anti-cancer effects.
USES OF THE HERB
CULINARY Flowers are used in salads, as a garnish for desserts.
AROMATIC Oil is used in perfumery.
MEDICINAL Internally for bronchitis, excess respiratory mucus, coughs, asthma, and cancer of the breast, lungs, or digestive tract. Externally for mouth and throat infections. In aromatherapy, for bronchial complaints, exhaustion, or skin problems.
ECONOMIC Flowers are used fresh to flavor and color candy and breath fresheners; also candied as cake decorations.
VARIANT
V. o. **'Alba'**, p.220.

V. tricolor (heartsease, wild pansy) p.220

PARTS USED Whole plant.
PROPERTIES A bittersweet, cooling herb that is laxative and diuretic, lowers fever, cleanses toxins, and reduces inflammation. It is also expectorant, relieves pain, and promotes healing.
USES OF THE HERB
MEDICINAL Internally for bronchitis, whooping cough, rheumatism, skin complaints (especially weeping eczema), urinary complaints, capillary fragility, and autoimmune disease involving several of these symptoms. Externally for skin complaints and varicose ulcers. Combines well with *Galium aparine* (see p.285), *Rumex crispus* (see p.344), *Trifolium pratense* (see p.364), and *Urtica dioica* (see p.366) for eczema; with *Agathosma crenulata* (see p.230), *Elymus repens* (see p.277), and *Eupatorium purpureum* (see p.281) for cystitis; and with *Tussilago farfara* (see p.365) or *Drimia maritima* (see p.275) for whooping cough.

V. yezoensis (Chinese violet)

Perennial, hardy to –15°F (5°C), height 8in (20cm), with slender rhizomes and ovate, toothed leaves up to 2½in (6cm) long. White, purple-striped flowers about 1¼in (3cm) long are produced in spring, followed by 3-lobed capsules. Found in Japan.

PARTS USED Whole plant (*zi hua di ding*).
PROPERTIES A bitter, pungent, cooling herb that clears toxins, reduces inflammation, and is anti-bacterial.
USES OF THE HERB
MEDICINAL Internally for boils, carbuncles, snake-bite, skin disorders (especially erysipelas), mumps, and "hot" disorders with inflammation of the eyes, throat, or ears.

GROWTH AND HARVEST

GROWTH Ornamental. Well-drained, moisture-retentive soil in sun or partial shade. Propagate by seed sown in spring or autumn, or by cuttings of nonflowering basal shoots in summer, or by division in autumn. *V. tricolor* self-seeds freely. Remove dead flowers promptly in order to prolong flowering. Plants may be damaged by slugs, snails, grasshoppers, and viral and fungal diseases (notably pansy sickness).
HARVEST Whole plants, leaves, and flowers are collected during the flowering season and dried for use in decoctions (*V. yezoensis*), infusions, and liquid extracts. Leaves of *V. odorata* are often used fresh, and flowers may also be picked in spring for extraction of essential oil. *V. tricolor* is often powdered when dried and used in skin creams.

VISCUM Mistletoe
(Viscaceae)

The tradition of "kissing under the mistletoe" originated in Scandinavian legend. Balder, the god of peace, was killed by an arrow made from mistletoe and was resurrected by the other deities. Mistletoe was then entrusted to the goddess of love, who established it as a symbol of love, with the custom that anyone passing beneath it should receive a kiss. Mistletoe was also an important Druidic herb, associated with welcoming the New Year. It was cut only from oak trees at a particular phase of the moon, using a golden sickle. The constituents of *V. album* appear to vary according to the host plant, which may explain why the Druids regarded mistletoe on oak as superior. These include compounds that affect protein synthesis, the immune and circulatory systems, and heart. *V. album* is sometimes used in Chinese medicine, but more commonly used are *V. coloratum*, which grows farther east and has yellow to orange-red fruits, and *Loranthus europaeus* (mulberry mistletoe), a parasite on plants of the beech family (Fagaceae). In certain countries, sale and use of *V. album* for therapeutic purposes are restricted.

V. album (mistletoe) p.221

PARTS USED Leaves, stems.
PROPERTIES A pungent, bittersweet, warming herb that lowers blood pressure, stimulates the immune system, slows heartbeat, relaxes spasms, and has sedative, diuretic, and anticancer effects.
USES OF THE HERB
MEDICINAL Internally for mild hypertension, hardening of the arteries, nervous tachycardia, nervous tension, St. Vitus's dance, and cancer (especially of lungs and ovaries). Externally for arthritis, rheumatism, chilblains, leg ulcers, and varicose veins. Combines well with *Crataegus laevigata* (see p.268) and *Melissa officinalis* (see p.310) for mild hypertension; and with *Ginkgo biloba* (see p.288) or *Vinca major* (see p.369) for hardening of the arteries. For use by qualified practitioners only.

GROWTH AND HARVEST

GROWTH Crop. Grows on young branches of host tree, such as oak or apple. Propagate by crushing fruit into crevices of bark, protected from birds, from autumn to spring.
HARVEST Leafy stems are cut in spring and dried for use in infusions, liquid extracts, tablets, and tinctures.
WARNING All parts, especially stems and leaves, are toxic if eaten.

VITEX
(Verbenaceae)

V. agnus-castus has long been associated with chastity, white-flowered plants in particular being a traditional symbol of virtue in southern Europe. Ground seeds were used in monasteries as a condiment to suppress libido, hence one of the plant's common names, "monk's pepper." Both *V. agnus-castus*, which affects the hormonal balance both in men and women, and *V. negundo* and its variants are rich in volatile oil and glycosides. The cut-leaved Chinese chaste tree, *V. n.* var. *cannabinifolia* (often treated as synonymous with *V. n.* var. *heterophylla* by Western botanists) is listed in the *Chinese Pharmacopoeia* (1985) as a different drug, *mu jing*, which has expectorant, antitussive, antiasthmatic, sedative, antispasmodic, and antibacterial effects. *V. canescens* and *V. quinata* are used as a substitute for *V. negundo* in Tibet. Chinese herbalists also use *V. trifolia* and *V. rotundifolia*, which are both known as *man jing zi*.

V. agnus-castus (chaste tree, agnus castus) p.221

PARTS USED Fruits.
PROPERTIES A pungent, bittersweet, slightly astringent, relaxant herb that regulates hormonal

functions, promotes lactation, and relieves spasms and pain.

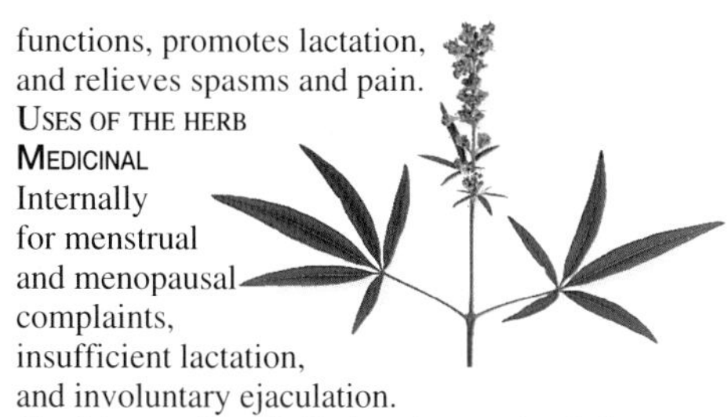

USES OF THE HERB

MEDICINAL Internally for menstrual and menopausal complaints, insufficient lactation, and involuntary ejaculation. Combines well with *Hydrastis canadensis* for menopausal problems. Excess causes nerve disorder known as formication (sensation of insects crawling under the skin).

V. negundo (Chinese chaste tree) p.221

PARTS USED Leaves, stems, roots, fruits (*huang jing zi*), oil.
PROPERTIES A sedative, cooling, detoxifying herb that lowers fever, relieves pain, improves digestion, and is expectorant and antibacterial.
USES OF THE HERB
MEDICINAL Internally for malaria, poisonous bites, arthritis, and breast cancer. Not given to patients with heart disease or hypertension. Externally for ringworm (leaves), rheumatic and arthritic pain, toothache, and sore throat (stems), colds and coughs (all parts), asthma and digestive disturbances (leaves, roots, fruits), bronchitis (roots, fruits, oil), hemorrhoids, migraine, and eye problems (fruits). In Ayurvedic medicine, internally for headache, excess mucus, and gonorrhea (leaves), fevers and bronchial congestion (roots); externally for ulcers (juice of leaves), and sores (medicated oil).
ECONOMIC Fresh leaves are burned with grass as a fumigant against mosquitoes.
VARIANT
V. n. var. ***heterophylla***, syn. *V. n.* var. *cannabinifolia*, p.221.

GROWTH AND HARVEST

GROWTH Ornamental. Rich, moist to poor dry soil in sun. Propagate by seed in spring or autumn, or by layering or by softwood cuttings in spring, or by semiripe cuttings in summer. Cut back the previous year's growths to 1–2in (2.5–5cm) in spring.
HARVEST Leaves are picked in early summer, and used fresh as juice, or in infusions and poultices, or dried for use in decoctions. Stems are cut in late summer or autumn and dried for use in decoctions and charcoal powder. Roots are lifted in late summer or autumn and dried for use in decoctions. Fruits (*V. agnus-castus*, *V. negundo*) are collected in autumn and used fresh or dried in decoctions or powder. Oil is extracted mainly from *V. n.* var. *heterophylla*.

VITIS Grape
(Vitaceae)

The grape is central to Jewish and Christian rituals and is an integral part of most European cultures and cuisines, especially those of Mediterranean regions. *V. vinifera* was cultivated in Egypt over 4,000 years ago. The Romans introduced it to Burgundy and to the Rhineland, where vineyards predominate to this day. In the 19th century the aphid *Phylloxera vastatrix* devastated European vineyards. American species fortunately proved resistant, enabling European varieties to be grafted onto American rootstocks, and vineyards to be replanted. Various parts of the plant have long-established medicinal uses, mainly to relieve conditions associated with chronic congestion and excess heat.

V. vinifera (grape) p.221

PARTS USED Leaves, stems, fruits.
PROPERTIES A sour, astringent, cooling herb that is diuretic, reduces inflammation, controls bleeding, improves circulation, and clears toxins.
USES OF THE HERB
CULINARY Blanched fresh leaves, or leaves preserved in brine, are used to contain fillings, such as minced meat, fish, and rice (*dolmades*). Fruits are eaten fresh or briefly cooked.
MEDICINAL Internally for varicose veins, excessive menstruation, menopausal syndrome, hemorrhage, urinary complaints, hypertension, high blood cholesterol, skin rashes, and torpor with overweight and cellulite. Internally and externally for inflammations of the mouth, gums, throat, or eyes. Fruits are the basis of a cure for poor liver function.
ECONOMIC Fruits are made into wine, vinegar, juice, and jelly. Dried fruits are known as "raisins" or "sultanas," according to the variety. Seeds yield a polyunsaturated oil, suitable for mayonnaise and cooking, especially frying. Cream of tartar, or potassium bitartrate, a crystalline salt, is extracted from the residue of pressed grapes known as "marc," and from the sediment of wine barrels. It is used in baking powders, laxatives, and soldering fluxes.
VARIANTS
***V. v.* 'Ciotat'**, syn. *V. v.* 'Apifolia', *V. v. 'Laciniosa'*, p.221.
***V. v.* 'Incana'** (dusty miller grape)
Unusual cultivar, hardy to 32°F (0°C), height 12–15ft (4–5m), with gray-green, unlobed or 3-lobed leaves that have a white, cobweblike covering on the upper surface, and black fruits.
***V. v.* 'Pinot Noir'**, syn. *V. v.* 'Spätburgunder', p.221.
***V. v.* 'Purpurea'**, p.221.

GROWTH AND HARVEST

GROWTH Ornamental (*V.v.* 'Ciotat', *V. v.* 'Incana', *V.v.* 'Purpurea'). Crop (*V. v.* 'Pinot Noir'). Wild-collected (*V. vinifera*). Hardiness varies according to cultivar. Deep, moist, humus-rich, neutral to alkaline soil in sun. Propagate by hardwood cuttings in late autumn, or by semiripe cuttings in summer, or by seed sown in autumn (species only), or by grafting, or by eye cuttings in late winter. Prune young plants to within 9–12in (23–30cm) of the ground in winter. In older vines, thin out old growths and shorten young growths in late summer. Plants may be damaged by scale insects, mealybugs, aphids, weevils, and caterpillars. Cultivars grown for fruit are prone to magnesium deficiency, gray mold, shanking, and various physiological disorders in unfavorable conditions.
HARVEST Leaves and stems are collected in early summer and used fresh, preserved, or dried for decoctions, liquid extracts, and tinctures. Stems yield drops of liquid that are used directly as an eyewash and diuretic. Ripe fruits are used fresh for medicinal purposes.

WX

WASABIA Wasabi
(Cruciferae/Brassicaceae)

W. japonica belongs to the same family as horseradish, radishes, and mustard, all of which contain pungent sulfur glycosides.

W. japonica, syn. *Eutrema wasabi* (wasabi) p.222

PARTS USED Roots.
PROPERTIES A pungent, warming herb that stimulates the digestion.
USES OF THE HERB
CULINARY Used in Japanese cuisine: grated fresh root is served with *sashimi* (raw fish); powdered root is made into a paste to flavor meat and fish dishes, or blended with other ingredients as a dip.
MEDICINAL Internally as an antidote to fish poisoning.

GROWTH AND HARVEST

GROWTH Crop. Moist to wet soil, ideally in clear, running spring water, in partial shade, at 50–59°F (10–15°C) in the growing season. Propagate by seed sown in spring and kept constantly moist, or by division in spring or autumn (most easily done when harvesting).
HARVEST Roots are lifted in spring or autumn, 15–24 months after planting, and used fresh, or dried and ground.

WITHANIA
(Solanaceae)

W. somnifera is little known in the West but holds an important place in Ayurvedic medicine, similar to that of *Panax ginseng* (see p.321) in Chinese medicine.

W. somnifera (winter cherry, *ashwagandha*) p.222

PARTS USED Roots.
PROPERTIES A bittersweet, astringent, warming herb with a horselike smell. It acts mainly on the reproductive and nervous systems, and has sedative, rejuvenative, and aphrodisiac effects.
USES OF THE HERB
MEDICINAL Internally for debility, convalescence, nervous exhaustion, insomnia, geriatric complaints, wasting diseases, failure to thrive in children, impotence, infertility, joint and nerve pains, and multiple sclerosis. Usually given as a milk decoction, often with raw sugar or honey.

GROWTH AND HARVEST

GROWTH Crop. Dry, stony soil in sun or partial shade. Propagate by seed sown in spring, or by greenwood cuttings with a heel in late spring. Cut back plants in early spring.
HARVEST Roots are dried for use in medicated *ghee*, medicated oil, pastes, and powders.
WARNING Toxic if eaten.

WOLFIPORIA
(Polyporaceae)

A genus of 250 species of fungi that live on tree roots and wood in Asia and temperate N America. *W. cocos* is unusual in being distributed in both regions, which has resulted in a long history of use in both Chinese and native N American medicine.

W. cocos, syn. *Poria cocos*, *Sclerotium cocos* (Indian bread, tuckahoe)

Subterranean fungus, hardy to 5°F (–15°C), height 2–6in (5–15cm), spread 4–12in (10–30cm), with large, globose to elliptic, tuberlike bodies, which have a hard, wrinkled, dark brown surface and a granular, pale pink interior. Found on roots of hardwoods and conifers, often up to 24in (60cm) below the surface.

PARTS USED Whole plant (*fu ling*).
PROPERTIES A sweet, sedative herb that is diuretic, regulates fluid metabolism, and calms the heart energy.
USES OF THE HERB
MEDICINAL Internally for urinary dysfunction, insomnia, palpitations, emotional disturbances, diarrhea, and abdominal bloating. Used in many classic Chinese formulas, such as *si jun zi tang* ("soup of four noble things"), which combines *W. cocos* with *Panax ginseng* (see p.321), *Glycyrrhiza uralensis* (see p.289), and *Atractylodes macrocephala* (see p.246).

GROWTH AND HARVEST
GROWTH Crop. Base of hardwood or coniferous trees. Information is not available on Chinese techniques for cultivating this fungus.
HARVEST Fungi are collected in winter and dried for decoctions and tinctures.

XANTHIUM Burweed
(Compositae)

The use of *X. strumarium* was first mentioned in Chinese medicine during the Tang dynasty (AD618–907), in the *Thousand Ducat Prescriptions*. It is a common ingredient of Chinese patent remedies and is used to adulterate *Datura stramonium*.

X. strumarium, syn. *X. sibiricum* (cocklebur) p.222

PARTS USED Fruits (*cang er zi*).
PROPERTIES A pleasant-tasting, warming herb that relieves pain, relaxes spasms, and has antibacterial, antifungal, and antirheumatic effects.
USES OF THE HERB
MEDICINAL Internally for allergic rhinitis, sinusitis, excess mucus, rheumatism, rheumatoid arthritis, lumbago, leprosy, and pruritus. Externally for pruritus.

GROWTH AND HARVEST
GROWTH Crop. Poor, dry soil in sun. Propagate by seed in autumn or spring. Subject to statutory control as a weed in some countries, notably in parts of Australia.
HARVEST Fruits are collected when ripe and dried for use in decoctions.

Z

ZANTHOXYLUM Prickly ash
(Rutaceae)

Most prickly ashes contain alkaloids, including chelerythrine, an effective antimicrobial, and fagarine, which also occurs in *Ruta graveolens* (see p.345). *Z. americanum* is a traditional native N American remedy for toothache and was introduced into mainstream medicine in 1894 by John Nash, who used it to treat typhus and cholera epidemics. In the central and southern US it is replaced by *Z. clavaherculis* (southern prickly ash). Fruits of *Z. acanthopodium* are sold as a pice in Sikkim. Various parts of *Z. armatum*, which grows from Kashmir to SE Asia, are used to clean teeth and relieve toothache, as well as for poisoning fish and flavoring food. *Z. capense* and *Z. zanthoxyloides* are used medicinally in S Africa. *Z. planispinum* (winged prickly ash, Chinese pepper) has similarly diverse uses. *Z. schinifolium* and *Z. simulans* are used interchangeably with *Z. piperitum* in Chinese medicine.

Z. americanum (toothache tree) p.222

PARTS USED Bark, fruits.
PROPERTIES A spicy, warming, stimulant herb that relieves pain, lowers fever, stimulates the circulation, improves digestion, controls diarrhea, and is antirheumatic.
USES OF THE HERB
MEDICINAL Internally for rheumatic and arthritic complaints, lumbago, toothache, fevers, peripheral circulatory problems, diarrhea, indigestion, abdominal chills, and chronic skin conditions. Externally for chronic joint pain and rheumatism. Combined with *Myrica cerifera* (see p.314) and *Zingiber officinale* (see p.373) for circulatory insufficiency; with *Cimicifuga racemosa* for tinnitus; and with *Guaiacum officinale* (see p.290), *Menyanthes trifoliata* (see p.312), and *Capsicum annuum* (see p.254) for rheumatic complaints.

Z. piperitum (Japanese pepper, Sichuan pepper, *fagara*) p.222

PARTS USED Leaves, bark, fruits, fruit pericarp (*hua jiao*).
PROPERTIES A spicy, warming, stimulant herb that acts mainly on the spleen and stomach. It lowers blood pressure, has diuretic, antibacterial, and antifungal effects, and is locally anesthetic.
USES OF THE HERB
CULINARY Leaves flavor soups and meat dishes, and are boiled with sugar and soy sauce as a condiment. Bark and unripe fruits are ground as a flavoring in Japan, China, and Hawaii. Ground dry-roasted fruits are one of the ingredients of Chinese five-spice powder.
MEDICINAL Internally for digestive complaints associated with cold.

GROWTH AND HARVEST
GROWTH Crop. Fertile soil in sun or shade. Propagate by seed sown in autumn, or by root cuttings in late winter. Remove dead wood and cut back in late winter or early spring. Rarely troubled by pests.
HARVEST Leaves (*Z. piperitum*) are picked during the growing season and used fresh. Bark is stripped in spring and dried for use in decoctions, liquid extracts, and tinctures. Fruits are collected in summer and dried for use in decoctions and liquid extracts.

ZEA Corn
(Gramineae)

The culinary uses of corn are well known. There are five principal kinds: dent corn (mostly white to yellow grains); flint corn (which shrinks on drying, and may have white, yellow, red, purple, or blue-black grains, often striped or mottled); popcorn (a primitive strain with hard grains, specifically grown for popcorn); sweet corn (with a higher sugar content and best as a vegetable); and waxy corn (containing starch with a waxy appearance). Dent and flint corns are widely grown for oil, cereals, flour, and animal fodder. Waxy corn yields a tapioca-like starch, used mainly in the Far East. Less familiar is its role as a medicinal herb. The female flowers of *Z. mays* contain allantoin (as found in *Symphytum officinale*, see p.357), and alkaloids that were extracted by native Peruvians and used in religious rites. Aztec herbals mention the plant, which was apparently used to clear heat from the heart. *Z. mays* reached China from N America after Li Shi Zhen's time (1518–93) and was first mentioned as a herb in the *Sichuan Journal of Chinese Herbal Medicine* in the 20th century.

Z. mays (corn, sweet corn, ornamental corn) p.223

PARTS USED Stigmas and styles of female flowers (cornsilk, *yu mi xu*), fruits, seeds, oil.
PROPERTIES A sweet, cooling, soothing herb that is diuretic, lowers blood sugar levels, stimulates bile flow, and prevents formation of urinary stones.
USES OF THE HERB
CULINARY Immature ears are eaten whole as a vegetable. Fresh, ripe seeds are cooked as a vegetable. Corn husks are not edible but are used in C and S American cooking to give a sweet, nutty flavor.
MEDICINAL Internally for cystitis, urethritis, prostatitis, urinary stones, and enuresis in children. Combines well with *Elymus repens* (see p.277) and *Arctostaphylos uva-ursi* (see p.241) for cystitis; with *Agrimonia eupatoria* (see p.231) and *Equisetum arvense* (see

p.278) for enuresis; and with *Aphanes arvensis* (see p.239) and *Eupatorium purpureum* (see p.281) for urinary stones. Used similarly in Chinese medicine for urinary problems, and for gallstones, jaundice, hepatitis, and cirrhosis.
ECONOMIC Dried, ripe seeds are processed as cereals and flour (cornflour, cornmeal, grits, polenta, cornflakes), and yield corn oil, an all-purpose culinary oil that tastes strongly of sweet corn when cold-pressed. Corn syrup is extracted from fresh corn and may be blended with molasses.
VARIANTS
***Z. m.* 'Black Aztec'**
Vigorous, pre-Columbian cultivar, hardy to 32°F (0°C), height 5ft (1.5m), spread 18in (45cm), with medium-sized ears, bearing white, unripe seeds that turn blue-black when ripe. They may be eaten fresh when young, or ground when mature for blue cornmeal.
***Z. m.* 'Gigantea Quadricolor'**,
syn. *Z. m. 'Quadricolor'*, p.223.
***Z. m.* 'Gracillima Variegata'**, p.223.
***Z. m.* 'Strawberry Corn'**
Ornamental cultivar, hardy to 32°F (0°C), height 3–4ft (1–1.2m), spread 18in (45cm), with strawberry-shaped ears, 2in (5cm) long, of mahogany red seeds, which are dried for floral decorations when ripe.

GROWTH AND HARVEST

GROWTH Ornamental. Hardiness varies according to cultivar. Rich, well-drained soil in sun. *Z. mays* is wind-pollinated and fruits better if grown in a block. Propagate by seed sown in spring. Birds, raccoons, and other animals may damage the ears.
HARVEST Cornsilk is collected in summer before the strands wither and is dried for use in decoctions, infusions, liquid extracts, and syrup. Ears are cut when immature or ripe for use as vegetables, and cut when ripe for processing as cereals, flour, oil, and syrup.

ZINGIBER Ginger
(Zingiberaceae)

Z. officinale has been cultivated for medicinal and culinary purposes since earliest times. It was listed as a taxable commodity by the Romans in AD200. It was first mentioned in Chinese medical literature during the later Han dynasty (AD25–220). In Ayurvedic medicine *Z. officinale* is known as *vishwabhesaj*, "universal medicine," and in both Ayurvedic and Chinese medicine occurs in about half of all prescriptions. Ginger is rich in volatile oil, gingerols, and shogaols. Shogaols, which are a breakdown product of gingerols, produced only on drying, are twice as pungent as gingerols. Thus dried ginger is hotter than fresh and is used for different purposes in Chinese medicine. *Z. officinale* is also of worldwide importance as a flavoring. Other species used for culinary purposes include: the SE Asian *Z. cassumar* (cassumar ginger); *Z. mioga* (Japanese ginger, *mioga* ginger), which has a bergamot-like flavor; and *Z. zerumbet* (wild ginger, bitter ginger), an Indo-Malaysian species. *Z. zerumbet* contains zerumbone, a cytotoxic compound used to treat cancer in China.

Z. officinale (ginger) p.223

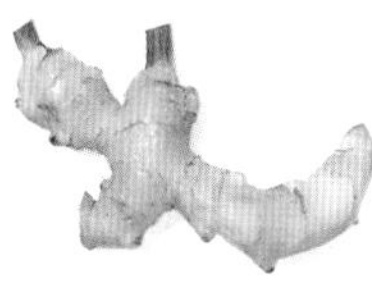

PARTS USED Rhizomes (*jiang*), oil.
PROPERTIES A sweet, pungent, aromatic, warming herb that is expectorant, increases perspiration, improves digestion and liver function, controls nausea, vomiting, and coughing, stimulates the circulation, relaxes spasms, and relieves pain.
USES OF THE HERB
CULINARY Fresh, young rhizomes (green ginger) are eaten raw, preserved in syrup, and candied; also used in curries, chutneys, pickles, meat and fish dishes, soups, and marinades. In India, the rhizomes are combined with cinnamon to make a warming, healthful tea. Pickled ginger (*gari*) is used in Japanese cooking, especially to flavor *sushi*. Dried, ground ginger gives flavor to cakes, biscuits, and sauces.
AROMATIC Oil is used in perfumery.
MEDICINAL Internally for motion sickness, morning sickness, indigestion, colic, abdominal chills, colds, coughs, influenza, and peripheral circulatory problems. Not for patients with inflammatory skin complaints, ulcers of the digestive tract, or high fever. Externally for spasmodic pain, rheumatism, lumbago, menstrual cramps, and sprains. Often combined with *Rheum palmatum* (see p.340) and *Gentiana lutea* (see p.287) for digestive complaints. In Chinese medicine, internally, for coughs, colds, diarrhea, vomiting, and abdominal pain associated with colds (fresh rhizome); uterine bleeding and blood in the urine (fresh, carbonized rhizome); abdominal fullness and edema (rhizome peel); coldness associated with shock, digestive disturbances arising from deficient spleen energy, and chronic bronchitis (dried rhizome).
ECONOMIC Oil is used in food flavoring. Dried, ground ginger flavors candy, soft drinks, and condiments.

GROWTH AND HARVEST

GROWTH Crop. Well-drained, humus-rich, neutral to alkaline soil, in sun or partial shade, with high humidity, minimum 30°F (–1°C). Propagate by division in late spring as growth begins. Ginger is treated as an annual or biennial crop; plants need a 10-month growing season for optimum rhizome production. Oldest growths may be removed when new shoots appear.
HARVEST Rhizomes are lifted during the growing season for uses where lack of fibrousness is important, or when dormant for drying. Young, fresh rhizomes bought for cooking will keep for 2–3 months in a cool, dry place, and they freeze well; they are soaked in brine and vinegar before processing in sugar syrup as "crystallized ginger." Mature rhizomes are peeled ("white ginger"), limed ("bleached"), or left unpeeled ("coated") before storing whole, or ground for use in infusions, decoctions, tinctures, and powders. Oil is distilled from unpeeled, dried, ground rhizomes.

ZIZIPHUS
(Rhamnaceae)

Z. jujuba has long been cultivated in China for its fruits, known in China as *da zao*, "big date," which are "to the Chinese what apples are to Americans" (Foster, *Herbal Emissaries*, 1992). Plants were introduced from China to western Asia some 3,000 years ago, and they have been used in Chinese medicine since at least the later Han dynasty (AD25–220). Jujubes were also grown by the ancient Greeks and Romans, who introduced the plant to Spain, where it became naturalized. By the 17th century there were 43 cultivars: now there are hundreds. The closely related *Z. vulgaris* (common jujube) has similar properties to *Z. jujuba*.

Z. jujuba (Chinese date, French jujube, Indian plum) p.223

PARTS USED Fruits (*da zao*), seeds (*suan zao ren*).
PROPERTIES A mucilaginous, nutritive, sedative herb, with a sweet and sour taste; it controls allergic responses, relieves coughing, soothes irritated or damaged tissues, protects the liver, prevents stress ulcer formation, and has a tonic effect on spleen and stomach energies. It also moderates the actions of other drugs.
USES OF THE HERB
CULINARY Fruits are left to become wrinkled and spongy, which increases their sweetness, and are eaten fresh or cooked.
MEDICINAL Internally for chronic fatigue, loss of appetite, diarrhea, anemia, irritability, and hysteria (fruits); palpitations, insomnia, nervous exhaustion, night sweats, and excessive perspiration (seeds). Often combined with *Panax ginseng* (see p.321) or *Angelica polymorpha* var. *sinensis* (see p.238), and added to tonic prescriptions as a buffer to improve synergy and minimize side effects. Long-term use reputedly improves the complexion. Fruits are also used to sweeten and flavor medicines.

GROWTH AND HARVEST

GROWTH Ornamental. Well-drained, moist to dry soil in sun. Propagate by seed, which needs stratification, sown in sandy soil mix in autumn, or by suckers in spring, or by hardwood cuttings in autumn and winter, or by root cuttings in late winter at 41–50°F (5–10°C). Cut back in winter to encourage the new growth on which fruits are borne. *Z. jujuba* tolerates a wide range of growing conditions but needs a hot, dry summer to fruit well. *Zizyphus* species are subject to certain plant controls as a weed in parts of Australia.
HARVEST Fruits are collected in early autumn when ripe, then parboiled, and sun-dried. Seeds are removed from the ripe fruits and dried. Both are used in decoctions.

CULTIVATING HERBS

THE GROWING OF HERBAL plants is a rich and varied pastime, combining the delights of the flower garden and productivity of the vegetable plot with the allure of the ancient myths linked to many of them. Herbal plants include trees, shrubs, climbers, annuals, perennials, lichens, mosses, seaweeds, and fungi. They come from all climatic zones and are used in all cultures. In this section you will find many suggestions for growing herbs in a variety of situations, as well as advice for their propagation, harvest, and storage.

A RICH HARVEST
A wide selection of herbs, ready for drying and use.

Even without a garden, plenty of herbs can be grown in pots that are small enough for a windowsill, or in containers to hang from walls. Perhaps you may wish to produce fresh parsley all year, or supply your own raw materials for homemade potpourri, cosmetics, or tisanes. Maybe you aspire to an entire herb garden, a peaceful retreat with soft colors, sweet fragrances, and the hum of bees. Whatever you want from your garden, the practical advice in the following pages will help you to achieve your aims.

The Herb Dictionary in this book (pp. 224–373) gives an outline of how each herb is grown. This section covers all stages for the home gardener, from planning a garden to storing the produce.

CHOOSING SUITABLE PLANTS

Not every herb described in the Herb Dictionary is suitable for growing at home, and some are not cultivated at all. These include some of the rainforest trees, such as angostura (*Galipea officinalis*), and lichens, such as oak moss (*Evernia prunastri*). In these cases, growing conditions can be deduced from their natural habitat, but information on their care and cultivation is scarce. Some herbs, notably some weeds, are cultivated by specialists for the herb trade, but are not practical for the ordinary garden. A successful herb garden will be planned with regard to its site, its purpose, and the plants that are suited to it.

BLENDING DIFFERENT STYLES
This formal diamond pattern sits well in this informal border.

HERBS IN SMALL GARDENS

It is fun to allocate a special part of the garden to herbs. A popular choice is to make a small bed of culinary herbs within easy reach of the kitchen. Another possibility is a collection of herbs for making teas, planted in a bed or pots around the garden table or sitting area. The "tea garden" could include fragrant lemon balm (*Melissa officinalis*), chamomile (*Matricaria recutita*), lemon verbena (*Aloysia triphylla*), or peppermint (*Mentha* x *piperita*). Growing them in containers makes it easy to rearrange them and saves space, especially with an invasive herb such as mint. Herbs can also be grown with other plants in the border; annuals such as sunflowers (*Helianthus* spp.) can provide focal points or they can be used to fill gaps, giving color as well as culinary ingredients – perhaps borage (*Borago officinalis*), corn poppies (*Papaver rhoeas*) or pot marigolds (*Calendula officinalis*), against the dark foliage of red perilla (*Perilla frutescens* var. *crispa*) or perhaps bronze basil (*Ocimum basilicum* 'Dark Opal').

PLANTING WITH ROOM TO SPREAD
Seedheads of Angelica archangelica, *right, are a focal point of this country garden. The trained fig (*Ficus carica*) acts as a windbreak to the greenhouse.*

SCENT AND COLOR

Citrus trees make excellent perfumed pot plants for the patio or conservatory. Blue lavender or yellow evening primroses (*Oenothera biennis*) near a window will scent the air of a summer evening. The bronze-purple *Salvia officinalis* Purpurascens Group or *Ajuga reptans* 'Atropurpurea' would combine well with silver-leaved artemisias (*Artemisia* spp.). Or plant a golden border with yellow-variegated cultivars of meadowsweet (*Filipendula* spp.), sage (*Salvia* spp.), thyme (*Thymus* spp.), or perhaps marjoram (*Origanum* spp.); or golden shrubs, such as *Ptelea trifoliata* 'Aurea', *Viburnum opulus* 'Aureum', and raspberry (*Rubus idaeus* 'Aureus').

CLIMBERS AND CREEPERS

Many interesting herbs are naturally climbers. The golden hops (*Humulus lupulus* 'Aureus') could climb over a garden shed or old tree stump, as could a passionflower

◄ STRIKING COLORS AND SHAPES *Warm, vibrant colors and strong foliage give impact to the herb garden. The dominant angelica is framed by feathery bronze fennel, bold alliums, and mounds of* Alchemilla mollis. *Purple sage and* Lavandula stoechas *subsp.* pedunculata *give rich, long-lasting color.*

MAKING THE MOST OF SPACE ► *The planting in this narrow bed combines parsley (*Petroselinum crispum, *front), tall stems of onions (*Allium cepa*), silvery sprigs of* Santolina, *and purple* Lavandula *flowers.*

(*Passiflora incarnata*), or akebia (*Akebia quinata*). Walls and fences give protection, enabling less hardy herbs to be grown out of doors in cooler areas. Some are low-growing creepers and can be grown in very small spaces. Plants that are suited to this include creeping thymes (*Thymus* spp.), basil thyme (*Acinos arvensis*), or creeping savory (*Satureja spicigera*), which all prefer full sun; and parsley piert (*Aphanes arvensis*), or Corsican mint (*Mentha requienii*), which prefer moist shade.

THE HERB KITCHEN GARDEN

Kitchen gardens mix business with pleasure, producing food for the family and herbs to delight the senses. These plots make sense in terms of husbandry, since a changing mixture of short-lived plants is less likely to suffer from pests and diseases than a large amount of one crop. Salad crops and tomatoes could have parsley (*Petroselinum crispum*) or basil (*Ocimum* spp.) planted nearby, ready to combine in cooking or salads.

GROWING WITHOUT A GARDEN

The would-be herb gardener without a garden is at no great disadvantage. Many herbs are quite small plants, easily grown in almost any type of container. The cottage garden traditionally had its own wheelbarrow and watering can brimming with plants, and in many parts of the world tin cans and oil drums are turned into miniature gardens. Herb pots can be hung on walls or fences, or placed on steps. Containerized plants can also be changed from year to year, and the growing season extended with pots under cover in winter. Elderly and disabled gardeners often find containers easier to manage than plants in open ground, provided that there is help with lifting and repotting.

GARDEN MICROCLIMATES

The majority of herbs in this book can be grown in the garden or under cover. Success is largely dependent on providing conditions closest to those in the natural habitat. Even small gardens provide microclimates; fences and hedges give shelter from winds, and walls and paving retain warmth, ideal for creeping thymes. Drainage for Mediterranean herbs, such as rosemary (*Rosmarinus officinalis*), can be improved by sloping beds and by adding sharp sand to the soil. Given the additional warmth and protection of a cold frame or greenhouse, a wider range of herbs can be grown: scented geraniums and balm of Gilead (*Cedronella canariensis*) make excellent container plants in summer, needing frost-free, fairly dry conditions during winter.

GROWING TEMPERATURES

Plants from different climatic zones (see pp. 8–9 for zone information) differ in their requirements for growing medium, water, humidity, light levels, and temperature. Most critical is the temperature range tolerated. The maximum tolerated by most plants, unless they have special adaptations, is 96°F (35°C), but minimum temperatures vary greatly from plant to plant. For this reason, the hardiness of a plant is the first thing to consider before trying to grow it. The United States Department of Agriculture has produced a map of 11 hardiness zones based on the average annual minimum temperatures recorded from 1974 to 1986; this hardiness map appears on the endpapers of this book. Many gardening books, nursery catalogs, and local public gardens and gardeners provide established hardiness zones for plants. Knowing your particular hardiness zone is very helpful when considering plants for your garden, but use that information only as a guide. Many plants may be able to withstand the normal winter conditions in an area, but cannot survive the high heat and humidity of summer. This is especially true in much of the US South and lower Midwest. Familiarity with hardiness zones and microclimates (see above) can be useful when attempting to grow plants not considered "hardy" in a given area. Some plants from Mediterranean climates, such as some *Lavandula* and *Salvia* species, tolerate slightly below-freezing temperatures occasionally, but succumb to more severe or prolonged cold. Growing those plants in "hot spots" or giving them extra winter protection may give them the edge to survive. Many other plants unable to stand any frost may be grown outdoors in the open ground as bedding plants, replaced every year, or they may be grown in containers that are brought under cover during cold weather. "Under cover" may mean a cold frame, slightly heated basement or garage, or a greenhouse, sun porch, or conservatory where the minimum temperatures they require can be maintained.

DESIGN FOR A SMALL SPACE *Culinary herbs grouped in pots, as here, can be moved to catch the sun. Using a barrow to display the herbs gives them extra height and adds visual interest to the grouping.*

Style and Site

Herbs may be grown in a variety of situations, depending on personal preference and resources. There is no need to have an herb garden as such; whatever herbs you use can be grown and enjoyed in containers or a patch of ground near the kitchen, or be mixed in with flowers and vegetables elsewhere in the garden. A special herb garden does have its advantages, though; it is an attractive feature for any property, combining visual impact, delightful aromas, and colors with practical uses.

Deciding on the Style

You will need to consider the style of the herb garden at an early stage, and decide on the general size and shape. Whether formal or informal, the design can complement the rest of the garden and the style of your home. An informal garden would be the obvious choice for a rambling old house on the side of a hill, whereas a formal design would be an excellent solution for a city apartment with a paved courtyard. Suggestions for styles to suit a wide variety of situations are given in the section *Designing an Herb Garden* on pp.20–41, and these can be adapted to individual taste. Costs and maintenance should be taken into account at the planning stage. Formal herb gardens are often labor-intensive and expensive to construct, and may be tedious to keep up if there are many yards of hedging to clip or paths to weed. An informal herb design usually needs less initial structural work and is easier to maintain. However, a successful informal garden still requires a well thought-out design.

Formal Designs

Formal gardens are usually based on geometric patterns and framed by low hedges or paths, which take on a mature look soon after planting. For maximum impact, each small bed is planted with one kind of herb, giving bold blocks of color and texture. In general, tall, invasive, or sprawling herbs spoil the pattern and proportion of a formal herb garden, and may damage dwarf hedges. Where used as focal points, large shrubs and trees are trained or clipped – a standard bay (*Laurus nobilis*), often in a handsome container, is the classic centerpiece. At its simplest, the design may take the form of a cartwheel with a different herb planted in each segment, or a group of species of one genus, as in the illustration on the opposite page. Formal designs are most impressive when viewed from above, and ideally are sited where they can be overlooked from an upper window or a slope.

Informal Designs

An informal herb garden is more appropriate to an irregularly shaped plot; it depends for its success largely on the plants themselves, and on plant groupings. There is far greater scope here for a mixture of elements – perhaps a water feature for aquatic herbs, or a paved area for creeping ones. Plants of varying heights and sprawling habits are more suited to an informal setting than a formal one. Herbs of complementary or contrasting colors and textures are best planted to achieve particular effects – for instance, a tapestry of various creeping thymes (*Thymus* spp.) underfoot; tall spires and soft colors of foxgloves (*Digitalis* spp.), or a group of golden evening primroses (*Oenothera biennis*) in a corner lit by low shafts of evening sunlight. The prostrate, pale blue rosemary

An Informal Country Garden
Lavandula angustifolia *'Hidcote Blue' is interspersed with a yellow-leaved ivy and gray-white eryngiums in this relaxed cottage garden.*

Chamomile

Although often recommended for planting as a lawn, the non-flowering *Chamaemelum nobile* 'Treneague' is a slow-growing and difficult plant to establish. A more practical solution is to have a small planting that can be easily maintained, perhaps to break up an area of paving, or as a broad link between stones in a path, where walking on it will release its fragrance. The plants need a rich, well-drained soil, and diligent weeding.

Formal Design of Contrasts
*This design contrasts the daisy-like clusters of the white garden feverfew (*Tanacetum parthenium 'Aureum', *front) with the single-flowered* T. cinerariifolium.*in the central bed.*

Height as a Focal Point
This combination of open ground planting and small containers at varying levels creates an interesting focal point and gives prominence to the mix of unusual leaf shapes.

CULINARY CARTWHEEL BED
*Here the spokes of the wheel serve to separate different species of low-growing thymes (*Thymus *spp.), a neat and attractive way of displaying a small group of plants.*

PLANTING AN HERB BED TO A THEME

A bed of herbs reflecting a special interest can make an interesting feature. It can be integrated in an existing border, perhaps outlined by a dwarf hedge of lavender (*Lavandula* spp.) or winter savory (*Satureja montana*). Tender herbs may be grown in pots out of doors in summer, and brought in under cover in winter.

COSMETIC HERBS – for simple skin and hair preparations: *Pot marigold (*Calendula officinalis*); chamomile (*Chamaemelum nobile *or* Matricaria recutita*); wild strawberry (*Fragaria vesca*); rosemary (*Rosmarinus officinalis*); elder (*Sambucus nigra*).*

HERBS TO SOOTHE THE NERVES – gentle herbal sedatives: *Chamomile (*Chamaemelum nobile *or* Matricaria recutita*); hops (*Humulus lupulus*); lemon balm (*Melissa officinalis*); skullcap (*Scutellaria lateriflora*); betony (Stachys officinalis); valerian (*Valeriana officinalis*); vervain (*Verbena officinalis*).*

PERFUMERY HERBS – aromatic herbs used to extract natural scents: *Bitter orange (*Citrus aurantium*); lemon (*Citrus limon*); lemon grass (*Cymbopogon citratus*); Arabian jasmine (*Jasminum sambac*); patchouli (*Pogostemon heyneanus*).*

(*Rosmarinus officinalis,* Prostratus Group) overhanging a garden wall or fence, or some giant angelica (*Angelica archangelica*) as an architectural feature in the border, would be two possibilities.

ASSESSING THE SITE

While planning an herb garden you must assess the site and decide on the size, shape, and exposure. You will need to determine the kind of soil and other environmental factors, such as climate, the direction in which the plot faces, its slope and drainage, and surrounding features. Make allowances for seasonal changes; deciduous trees look innocuous in winter, but for much of the year they cast heavy shade, and in autumn drop leaves onto small herbs, rotting their foliage. The ideal site is sunny, open but sheltered, with slightly acid to alkaline, well-drained, fertile soil. As far as possible, it should be free from perennial weeds and overhanging trees, and have good access from the house so that the herbs can be harvested in all kinds of weather. If your proposed site has serious disadvantages, then it is worth considering hiring professional help to landscape, clear, and drain the area, to improve the condition of the soil, to lay paths, and to do any other heavy work that requires skill and experience. If the site is overgrown or neglected, it may take an entire growing season to ensure that the site is completely free from weeds and prepared for planting.

PREPARING THE GROUND

If the ground is infested with perennial weeds, clear it as far in advance of planting as possible, and allow it to lie fallow for several weeks to allow any weeds that have been missed to resurface. Digging them out is hard work, but may be more successful eventually than applying chemical weedkiller, which may fail to destroy the deepest rhizomes. When the ground is "clean," fork in well-rotted organic matter, such as garden or mushroom compost, and rake the soil to a fine, level tilth. The aim is to provide a reasonably fertile, well-drained soil. Heavy feeding with manure or inorganic fertilizers is not needed for most Mediterranean herbs, since it produces soft growth with poor aroma and little resistance to pests, diseases, and cold. On heavy clay soils it may be necessary to improve drainage by the addition of coarse sand; this can be done immediately in and around the planting holes rather than throughout the whole garden. Most herbs thrive in slightly acid to alkaline soil, though many Mediterranean herbs tolerate alkaline conditions. If the pH is below 6.5, add a dressing of lime in the recommended quantity when preparing the soil for planting.

MAKING A PLAN

To draw up a plan, first measure the site and relevant surrounding features accurately. Be sure to include such factors as the spread of existing trees, and take account of any changes in ground level. Take note where shade is cast at different times of the day and at different seasons; this will determine the best sites for garden seats, as well as for herbs that have specific requirements for full sun or shade. Whether your design is formal or informal in style, the herbs should ideally be planted within arm's length for convenient harvesting. In large beds or borders, plan to provide stepping stones for access so that the soil is not compacted by being stepped on to reach the herbs. Stones or paving should be laid before planting, so that you have a surface to walk on while preparing and laying out the garden. When all the measurements have been made, transfer them to graph paper, working to scale, and including all the surrounding features. This will be your master plan; if you have several different designs to consider, draw each one on tracing paper, laid over the master plan. Decide which herbs will best suit your design (see *Choosing and Planting Herbs* on pp.378–9), and make notes on their cultivation requirements, habit, and color, and their eventual height and spread.

PREPARING AND MARKING OUT THE SITE

1 *Use a fork to dig up the roots of perennial weeds. Hold the main stem close to the ground, so that the whole root system is removed.*

2 *Having prepared the soil, the design can be marked out. Use string and stakes, measure to scale, and include any paths or paving.*

CHOOSING AND PLANTING HERBS

If you aim to create an herb garden, the ideal plan of attack would be to spend the autumn and winter planning the design and compiling orders for seeds and plants. Then, when spring is in the air, you will be ready to start work out of doors, preparing the site and transferring your plans from paper to ground.

PREPARING THE SITE

The amount of time this may take depends on the size and complexity of the proposed garden and the state of the ground (see *Style and Site*, pp.376-377). If the design is large and ambitious, and the existing garden a wilderness, it may be necessary to spend the entire first year preparing the site. In the meantime, your garden can begin with herbs in grown containers; you can raise herbs from seed, acquire surplus plants and cuttings from friends, and buy stock plants to grow on or use for propagating.

CHOOSING SUITABLE HERBS

Perhaps the most enjoyable stage in planning an herb garden is deciding which herbs to grow. Be sure, though, that they are suitable for the conditions and the design of your garden. Herbs should be grown in conditions that, as far as possible, resemble their natural habitat. Many popular culinary and aromatic herbs are Mediterranean in origin; these mainly prefer ample sunshine, mild winters, and free-draining soil. Some herbs prefer a damp, shaded position, however, or even wet soil. Sweet flag (*Acorus calamus*) and bogbean (*Menyanthes trifoliata*) are true aquatics, and can be grown in mud or shallow water. Most variegated and golden-leaved cultivars do best in a position that is lit by morning or evening sun, but shaded at midday, since full sun tends to scorch the colorful foliage. Find out about your chosen plant's natural habitat and try to match it with a niche in the garden. For example, primroses (*Primula vulgaris*) love shady banks and can be sited at the foot of a slope which stays damp all year; the houseleek (*Sempervivum tectorum*), an inhabitant in the wild of rock faces, may be placed growing out from a wall.

PLANTING A SEMPERVIVUM
The roots are inserted into a crevice of a wall or rockery, and held in position while clayey soil is added to firm the plant into place.

BUYING HERBS

Many culinary herbs can be bought at most garden centers. Those most commonly stocked include parsley (*Petroselinum* spp.), chives (*Allium schoenoprasum*), common sage (*Salvia officinalis*) or purple sage (*S. o.* Purpurascens Group), as well as peppermint (*Mentha* x *piperita*), spearmint (*Mentha spicata*), common thyme (*Thymus vulgaris*), rosemary (*Rosmarinus officinalis*), lemon balm (*Melissa officinalis*), curry plant (*Helichrysum italicum*), and bronze fennel (*Foeniculum vulgare* 'Purpureum'). Medicinal herbs such as valerian (*Valeriana officinalis*), rue (*Ruta graveolens*), and boxwood (*Buxus sempervirens*) are often sold alongside culinary herbs with little or no explanation of their uses. An interesting selection of thymes (*Thymus* spp.) can often be found, and the water-gardening section may have herbs such as sweet flag (*Acorus calamus*), watercress (*Nasturtium officinale*), watermint (*Mentha aquatica*), and *Houttuynia cordata*. Ornamental cultivars of herbal trees, shrubs, and perennials are usually well represented, too. Some herbs are not good buys for planting out from pots since they dislike root disturbance; borage (*Borago* spp.), chervil (*Anthriscus cerefolium*), dill (*Anethum graveolens*), and poppies (*Papaver* ssp.) are all better grown from seed, sown where the plants are to flower.

SPECIALIST HERB NURSERIES

Specialist herb nurseries offer a much wider choice and may be able to give better advice than garden centers. Most of them stock medicinal herbs, dye plants, larger-than-average sizes of culinary herbs, and preplanted containers.

POT-BOUND CONTAINER PLANT
Pot-bound root balls like this should be avoided; roots poking through the bottom of the pot indicate that the plant has outgrown its container.

Nursery plants are often of better quality too, due to the staff's greater interest and knowledge. If you are planning to start a thyme collection, or grow a lavender hedge, for instance, it is well worth visiting a herb nursery at flowering time to make your selection; there is a surprising range of colors and habits to choose from, and decisions are much more easily reached when the cultivars are in front of you and looking at their best.

POINTS TO LOOK FOR

When making your selection, check plants for pests and diseases, and choose the one that has the best shape and condition. Try to ignore

SPECIALIST HERB NURSERY
Well-established herb nurseries offer the widest range of culinary, medicinal, and aromatic plants for the herb garden, and expert advice on cultivation. Specialist nurseries are listed in gardening magazines, books on herbs, and by local herb societies.

▲ Planting out Herbs
Planting holes should be big enough to take some organic fertilizer or conditioner as well as the plants. Some extra plants will improve the coverage until they are all larger.

Checking the Design ►
Place all the pots of herbs in the positions they will occupy in the bed; this will enable you to check the spacing and the overall effect before you commit to planting.

flowers, which may mislead you into buying an inferior specimen; concentrate instead on the number of growths or new shoots, and look for richly colored, vigorous foliage. Ensure that it is not potbound, since it may take many months for a plant to send out new roots from a very compressed root ball; in the meantime it will be almost as dependent upon watering as if it were still containerized.

Principles of Planting

Container-grown herbs can be planted during much of the year, but will establish more quickly in spring when they are starting to grow vigorously and there is regular rainfall. If they have been kept under glass during the winter, or bought from under cover at a nursery, they will need hardening off in a cold frame or unheated greenhouse before planting out. Herbs for culinary and medicinal use should be planted away from possible contamination by pets, roadside pollution, and pesticides. A number of commonly grown herbs, such as foxgloves (*Digitalis* spp.), castor beans (*Ricinus communis*), monkshood (*Aconitum* spp.), as well as opium poppies (*Papaver somniferum*), boxwood (*Buxus sempervirens*), and meadow saffron (*Colchicum autumnale*) are highly poisonous and need careful siting in gardens used by children.

Planting Methods

Water well before planting since dry root balls are difficult to wet thoroughly when underground. Bare roots can be submerged in water for a thorough soaking. To avoid trampling and compacting the soil, which restricts root growth, stand on a board in order to reach the planting position. If you are following a planting plan, first set out the herbs in their positions, as shown above. Space them according to their expected height and spread so that they have room to reach their full potential – an angelica (*Angelica archangelica*) only 6in (15cm) high when planted will eventually exceed 6ft (2m) in height and 4ft (1.2m) in width. Seedlings of smaller herbs may be planted out more densely and thinned to leave one at each station. Planting out is best done on a calm, damp day to minimize stress to the plants; sunny, windy days increase moisture loss. Incorporate some organic soil conditioner or concentrated organic fertilizer, such as bone or fish meal. Sharp sand may also be added to heavy soils for herbs that need free drainage. Firm the soil gently around the plant and water thoroughly to settle the soil and provide ample moisture for new root growth. After planting, pinch out the tips of shrubby herbs to encourage a bushy habit.

An Easy Selection for New Gardeners

Herbs for Dry, Sunny Positions

Culinary
Artemisia dracunculus, Ocimum basilicum, Origanum vulgare, Rosmarinus officinalis, Salvia officinalis, Satureja montana, Thymus vulgaris.

Aromatic
Agastache foeniculum, Artemisia abrotanum, Helichrysum italicum, Lavandula spp., *Salvia clevelandii, Santolina chamaecyparissus.*

Medicinal
Calendula officinalis, Eschscholzia californica, Galega officinalis, Hyssopus officinalis, Nepeta cataria, Sempervivum tectorum, Verbascum thapsus.

Herbs for Moist Soil in Shade

Culinary
Allium schoenoprasum, Angelica archangelica, Levisticum officinale, Mentha spicata, Myrrhis odorata, Petroselinum crispum.

Aromatic
Artemisia lactiflora, Galium odoratum, Houttuynia cordata, Mentha requienii, Myrica gale.

Medicinal
Ajuga reptans, Digitalis spp., *Filipendula ulmaria, Melissa officinalis, Mentha* x *piperita, Sambucus nigra, Symphytum officinale, Vinca major.*

Herbs for a Bog or Pool

Acorus calamus / A. gramineus, Cardamine pratensis, Iris versicolor, Mentha aquatica, Menyanthes trifoliata, Myrica gale, Typha latifolia.

Planting Invasive Herbs in Open Ground

Some very useful garden herbs can be a nuisance on account of their invasive tendencies. These include mints (*Mentha spp.*), woodruff (*Galium odoratum*), and tansy (*Tanacetum vulgare*). In open ground the spread of these plants can be restricted by planting them in sunken containers, hidden below ground; any large pot or old bucket with drainage holes will do. The plant should be divided each spring and the pot filled with fresh soil or soil mix, or a mixture of the two, before replanting.

1 *Dig a hole large enough to take the container. Check for drainage holes and fill with a soil and soil mix mixture.*

2 *Plant the herb (this is mint,* Mentha x piperita*), adding enough soil to cover the pot. Water thoroughly to establish.*

HERBS IN CONTAINERS

Herbs grown in containers need more care than those in the open ground. Almost any container is suitable, provided that it has a drainage hole to prevent waterlogging, but is covered with crocks to prevent loss of soil mix. However, watertight containers can be used for herbs that enjoy wet conditions, such as galingale (*Cyperus longus*). Terracotta pots are well suited to Mediterranean herbs, and they age beautifully to complement the subtle colors of flowers and foliage. The disadvantages are that they dry out quickly in warm weather and must be brought under cover in winter unless they can resist frost. Very different effects are obtained by planting a formal clipped bay or boxwood tree in a rectangular Versailles tub or half-barrel. A large container or group of smaller ones can provide a focal point for an herb garden or add interest beside a garden seat or entrance. An entire herb garden may consist of containers, on walls, steps, and windowsills, as well as at ground level. Where space is at a premium, a number of different herbs can be grown in a very small area, using a half-barrel, cartwheel, or windowbox. A strawberry jar (a pot with planting pockets) is an attractive container for growing a selection of herbs. It is convenient for regularly used culinary herbs, but can also be planted with interesting collections, such as home remedies.

ADVANTAGES OF GROWING HERBS IN CONTAINERS

- Pots can be sited conveniently for easy harvesting of your herbs.
- Containers are easy to keep looking good all year, since unsightly plants can simply be replaced.
- Invasive herbs, given separate containers, are easily controlled.
- Tender herbs can be positioned in a "sun trap" and brought under cover in bad weather.
- Herbs with special soil requirements are not a problem since they can be grown using suitable soil mix.
- Succulent herbs that appeal to slugs, such as basil (*Ocimum* spp.) and purslane (*Portulaca oleracea*), are protected when grown in pots.

A MINIATURE WATER GARDEN
*An attractive feature of miniature water lilies (*Nymphaea *species).*

PLANTING AND SITING

The key to success with containers of herbs is to plant the appropriate kind and number of plants in each pot. If they are overplanted, the containers become top heavy, dry out quickly, and soon exhaust nutrients. When choosing herbs for a mixed planting in a single container, consider eventual size and habit carefully. Dwarf cultivars (such as *Origanum vulgare* 'Compactum') or naturally small-growing herbs, such as heartsease (*Viola tricolor*) and houseleeks (*Sempervivum tectorum*), are good choices. Prostrate or trailing herbs are useful for softening outlines. Large, deep-rooted herbs, such as angelica (*Angelica* spp.), lovage (*Levisticum officinale*), and fennel (*Foeniculum vulgare*), are unsuitable for shallow containers. Use a half-and-half mixture of commercial soilless mix and loamy soil, since soil is heavier than soilless mix and retains moisture better. Containers tend to dry out more quickly as the growing season advances, and may be given additional water by standing them in trays. In order to reduce evaporation, place containers in a sheltered position, so that they are protected from the wind. Large shrubs and trees trained as standards give height to the containerized garden. Spiky herbs, such as standard hollies and agaves planted as specimens, are very attractive and also wind-resistant, but they can be hazardous in confined spaces.

HIGH-LEVEL HERB GARDENS

Growing herbs on high – on balconies, roof gardens, window ledges, and in hanging baskets – is a challenge. The restricted space limits choice, and extra air movement accelerates drying out. In confined spaces, the habit of a plant can be put to practical use. Where a large tub can be accommodated, several evergreen herbs with different habits make the best use of available space and give a pleasing display all year. Try combining a climber such as jasmine (*Jasminum officinale*), trained on a fan-shaped trellis at the back, with dwarf lavender (*Lavandula* spp.) or hyssop (*Hyssopus* spp.) around the

HERBS ON DIFFERENT LEVELS
*A display of herbs in terracotta pots makes an attractive feature for small spaces. The gold-variegated and purple sages (*Salvia *species) add a touch of color.*

A STRAWBERRY JAR
This is a popular and practical container for growing herbs in a confined area. It allows for seasonal flexibility since most of the plants are replaced regularly.

Planting a Windowbox

A Golden Combination
*Marjoram (*Origanum vulgare *cv.), feverfew (*Tanacetum parthenium*), zinnias, and gazanias.*

Herbs for Windowboxes

Dianthus chinensis cvs.
Glechoma hederacea 'Variegata'
Hedera helix cvs.
Helichrysum italicum subsp. *microphyllum*
Lavandula angustifolia 'Nana Alba'
Origanum vulgare 'Compactum'
Rosmarinus officinalis 'Benenden Blue'
Rosmarinus officinalis, Prostratus Group
Salvia officinalis 'Tricolor'
Salvia viridis cvs.
Santolina chamaecyparissus var. *nana*
Tagetes patula cvs.
Tanacetum parthenium 'Golden Moss'
Thymus vulgaris cvs.
Vinca minor and cvs.
Viola tricolor

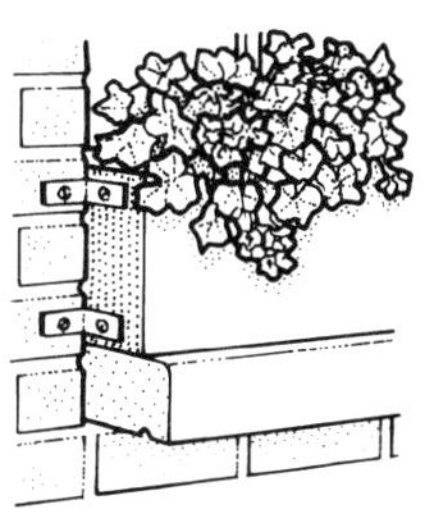

Attaching a Windowbox
Choose a durable windowbox at least 6in (15cm) deep, and attach it as shown, either to the wall or the window frame.

Suggested Plants for Containers

Specimen Shrubs and Trees

Aloysia triphylla
Buxus sempervirens and cvs.
Citrus species
Eucalyptus globulus
Ilex aquifolium 'Ferox Argentea'
Juniperus communis
Laurus nobilis and cvs.
Myrtus communis 'Variegata'
Olea europaea
Pelargonium spp. and hybrids
Phyllostachys nigra and cvs.
Pinus sylvestris 'Aurea'
Punica granatum var. *nana*

Centerpieces for Large Containers

Agave americana 'Variegata'
Helianthus annuus 'Teddy Bear'
Laurus nobilis and cvs.
Ricinus communis 'Carmencita'
Zea mays 'Gracillima Variegata'

Compact Herbs

Arctostaphylos uva-ursi
Buxus sempervirens 'Suffruticosa'
Buxus sempervirens 'Kingsville Dwarf'
Dianthus chinensis cvs.
Hedera helix 'Erecta'
Hyssopus officinalis subsp. *aristatus*
Lavandula angustifolia 'Nana Alba'
Myrtus communis subsp. *tarentina*
Ocimum basilicum 'Mini Purpurascens Wellsweep'
Ocimum basilicum var. *minimum*
Origanum vulgare 'Compactum'
Pinus mugo var. *pumilio*
Salvia officinalis 'Tricolor'
Santolina chamaecyparissus var. *nana*
Sempervivum tectorum
Tagetes patula cvs.
Thymus serpyllum 'Elfin'
Thymus vulgaris 'Erectus'

An Attractive Contrast
*A pot of pale alliums set against a bed of pink chives (*Allium schoenoprasum*) and silver thyme (*Thymus vulgaris *'Silver Posie').*

Trailing Herbs

Acinos arvensis
Cytisus scoparius subsp. *maritimus*
Fragaria vesca
Glechoma hederacea 'Variegata'
Hedera helix cvs.
Rosmarinus officinalis, Prostratus Group
Thymus herba-barona
Tropaeolum majus 'Empress of India'
Vinca minor and cvs.

Aquatic Herbs

Acorus gramineus and cvs.
Cyperus longus
Houttuynia cordata
Iris versicolor
Mentha aquatica
Menyanthes trifoliata
Nasturtium officinale

trellis base, and a prostrate rosemary (*Rosmarinus* spp.) or creeping savory (*Satureja spicigera*) to tumble down the front. If you intend to grow herbs on a window ledge, the choice of herbs depends on its position. Woody-stemmed herbs with resilient foliage, such as sage (*Salvia* spp.), thyme (*Thymus* spp.), rosemary (*Rosmarinus* spp.), and bay (*Laurus nobilis*), are more wind-resistant than soft-stemmed herbs like parsley (*Petroselinum* spp.), chives (*Allium schoenoprasum*), and chervil (*Myrrhis odorata*). All need a fairly sunny spot.

Care and Maintenance

Regular watering is essential. Check soil moisture daily, especially in hot or windy conditions. Water in the evening or early morning, giving the pot a thorough soaking, rather than an overhead sprinkle. During the growing season, feed every two weeks with a liquid fertilizer. In the winter, bring the containers under cover. Frost-proof pots may be left outdoors, but in severe weather you may need to wrap them to protect the herbs' roots from freezing. This may be done with old carpet or burlap, bound securely with string. Horticultural fleece can be used to clad both containers and plants, since it lets in sufficient light. In the spring, check the condition of each plant. If a plant is pot-bound (has outgrown the container) there will be roots protruding through the base of the pot, pale foliage, and weak new growth. A pot-bound plant can either be transferred into a larger pot, or split for replanting in the original pot. Cutting back the herbs after they have been repotted will stimulate new growth, remove many pests on the foliage, and compensate for any root damage. If repotting is impractical, the container can be top-dressed by renewing the top 1–2in (2.5–5cm) of soil mix, incorporating well-rooted organic matter or slow-release fertilizer. Bay trees thrive in relatively small containers and, provided they are not too top-heavy, are better top-dressed than repotted.

An Elegant Standard
*Growing a standard boxwood (*Buxus sempervirens*) in a container allows room around it for bushy or creeping herbs, such as thymes (*Thymus *spp.).*

GROWING UNDER COVER

There are herbs for all tastes that can be grown in various situations under cover or indoors. The additional warmth and shelter are ideal for tender subjects and extend the growing season for hardy and half-hardy plants. Whether in a greenhouse, in a conservatory, or on a windowsill, the herbs will be close at hand for harvesting and for the enjoyment of their fragrance.

LIGHT AND WARMTH

Although the covered environment offers protection against the elements, it may cut down the amount of available light. Most herbs thrive in bright light, and therefore need a sunny position with 12–14 hours of daylight per day and as much overhead light as possible. Variegated plants need more light than others, since they have a smaller green area for photosynthesis. Plants receiving directional light can be turned each time they are watered to counteract one-sided growth. A fan heater, designed for use in humid conditions, can control temperature and also function as a cooling fan for summer. Most tender plants come from tropical regions where humidity rises as the temperature increases. Humid conditions can be created by misting plants in the morning, or by standing containers on a layer of moisture-retentive material, such as gravel, sand, or capillary matting. Greenhouses may be "damped down" by splashing water on the floor and shelving. If the humidity is too low, tender plants may develop brown tips on leaves and become prone to spider mites; if it is too high, plants may develop fungal diseases, such as gray mold (*Botrytis*) or mildew.

HERBS INDOORS

One of the easiest ways to grow culinary herbs is in pots on a windowsill. The only limiting factors are size and the length of time that any herb can be kept in good condition in lower light levels. Pots of seedlings for cutting like salad cress can be bought from supermarkets, or they may be raised from seed. Rocket (*Eruca vesicaria* subsp. *sativa*), coriander (*Coriandrum sativum*), and dill (*Anethum graveolens*) are especially suitable for cropping as seedlings: rocket seeds sprout within three to four days; coriander takes about five or six days; and dill is usually up within about 10 days. Herbs such as parsley (*Petroselinum crispum*), thyme (*Thymus vulgaris*), sage (*Salvia officinalis*), rosemary (*Rosmarinus officinalis*), savory (*Satureja* spp.), and basil (*Ocimum basilicum*) can be grown as single plants in pots, or in a hanging basket or wall-mounted container. Baskets tend to dry out easily, but moisture retention can be improved by adding granules that absorb water. Nasturtiums (*Tropaeolum majus*) can trail to give color. Seed onions ("sets," *Allium cepa*) and cloves of garlic (*A. sativum*), left whole as a bulb or separated, can be planted several to a pot at any time from autumn to spring. Within about three weeks they will sprout succulent, flavorsome leaves that can be snipped when they reach 2in (5cm) long. Tall-growing herbs will soon outgrow a windowsill, but even giants such as lovage (*Levisticum officinale*) and fennel (*Foeniculum vulgare*) will provide useful amounts of flavoring at the seedling stage. Most of these culinary herbs are hardy, and therefore unlikely to thrive indefinitely in the warmth and relatively low light of even the sunniest windowsill, but they will provide color and flavor for a few months. Aim to replace single plants twice or three times a year, and seedlings every month or so.

CULINARY HANGING BASKET
The light weight of soilless mixes is useful for baskets, but they dry out easily and need plenty of watering.

GROWING WATERCRESS
Plant 3 or 4 shoots in a 6in (15cm) pot of rich soil mix, standing it in water that is changed daily.

HERBS FOR THE GREENHOUSE

The greenhouse is an ideal place to raise culinary herbs in variety and quantity. Light levels are good, and even unheated greenhouses provide a more sheltered environment than outdoors, enabling out-of-season crops to be grown. Clumps of chives (*Allium schoenoprasum*), French tarragon (*Artemisia dracunculus*), and mint (*Mentha* spp.) can be lifted, divided, and potted up for early spring crops, or for winter use, under glass where frost-free temperatures can be maintained. Discard forced plants in spring, or plant them out and do not harvest again for an entire growing season to allow them time to recover. Sown in late summer or early autumn, a number of herbs such as chervil (*Anthriscus cerefolium*), coriander, and parsley will continue to grow throughout the winter if protected from severe cold.

THE GREENHOUSE IN SUMMER

The best use of a greenhouse in the summer is to grow tender herbs that often give disappointing results in the open ground in cool summers. A wider range of plants can also be grown. Basil rarely thrives outdoors in cold areas, but it luxuriates in warmth and light under glass. Growing several different cultivars,

PHOTOSYNTHESIS
Leaves contain the green pigment chlorophyll. This absorbs the energy of sunlight in order to convert carbon dioxide in the air and water in the soil into carbohydrates, by the process of photosynthesis. Variegated-leaved plants, which have a smaller amount of green leaf area, need more light than plants with plain green leaves. Oxygen is essential to all life, and is a by-product of photosynthesis. The energy required to drive the plant's metabolism is produced through respiration when the leaves take in oxygen and break down carbohydrates to release energy, carbon dioxide, and water.

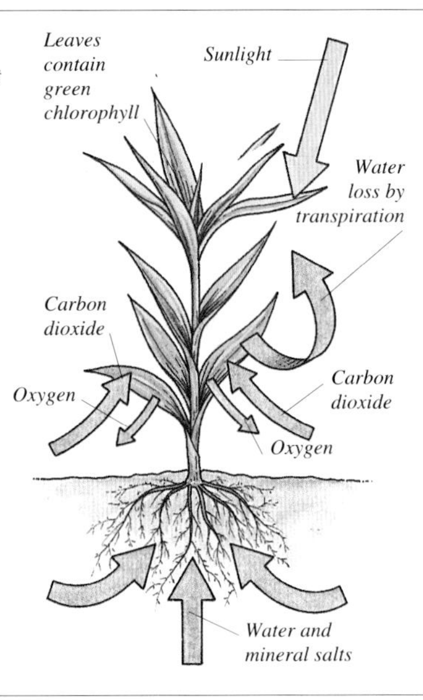

WINDOWSILL HERBS
*Pots of sweet marjoram (*Origanum *spp.), chives (*Allium *spp.), purple sage (*Salvia *spp.), and applemint (*Mentha suaveolens*) are easily kept near at hand for culinary use.*

GREENHOUSE SUN AND SHADE *This grapevine (*Vitis vinifera*) fruits well in warmth and has been trained along the roof of the greenhouse to benefit from the sunlight and to provide shade for foliage plants.*

for example, *Ocimum basilicum* 'Cinnamon', 'Dark Opal', or the curly-leaved *O. b.* var. *crispum*, will give visual interest and a choice of flavors. *Perilla frutescens* is another herb that benefits from extra warmth, and again has a handsome purple-leaved cultivar (*P. frutescens* 'Crispa') for added interest. Chili peppers (*Capsicum* spp.) enjoy temperatures above 70°F (21°C) and are much more likely to produce ripe fruits under glass than in the open ground. They have a long growing season, taking 15–18 weeks to reach flowering size, so seeds should be sown in warmth in early spring. If the greenhouse gets too hot and sunny, shade can be provided by climbing herbs, such as grapes (*Vitis vinifera*), cucumbers (*Cucumis sativus*), or a loofah (*Luffa cylindrica*). Young half-hardy plants must be acclimatized to lower temperatures and higher levels of ventilation before being planted outdoors. This is known as "hardening off," since the plant's tissues harden in response to tougher conditions. It is usually done by moving plants to a cooler, more airy position in the greenhouse or on the windowsill. When they have been hardened off, half-hardy plants can be set out either in containers or in the open ground, provided that all danger of frost has passed.

ORNAMENTAL HERBS INDOORS

A garden room or conservatory is a refuge in which to sit and enjoy the fragrance and beauty of herbs in all weathers and throughout the seasons. A few large, well-chosen plants with a long period of interest may give more pleasure and will need less maintenance than an assortment of smaller ones. Citrus trees make attractive specimens, with glossy, evergreen leaves, delightfully fragrant blossoms, and colorful fruits. The variegated lemon (*Citrus limon* 'Variegata') is one of the finest, suited to indoor cultivation, with its yellow-edged leaves and striped young fruits. Variegated myrtle (*Myrtus communis* 'Variegata') also offers greater interest than its plain green counterpart and, being less hardy, is a suitable candidate for cosseting under glass. It has small, neat, aromatic foliage, delicate white flowers in summer, and blue-black fruits.

Scented geraniums are very varied in leaf shape, texture, and aroma, and give much pleasure under glass. They tolerate hard pruning and dry conditions, and are easily propagated when they become too woody or untidy. Site them near doors, so their fragrance fills the air as you pass. The brilliant green, velvety peppermint pelargonium (*Pelargonium tomentosum*) is happy in partial shade. Tender sages (*Salvia* spp.) and lavenders (*Lavandula* spp.) are similarly generous with scent and color; the pineapple sage, *Salvia elegans* 'Scarlet Pineapple', will produce scarlet flowers in midwinter. For a more exotic touch, try growing pots of ginger (*Zingiber officinale*) or turmeric (*Curcuma longa*) from fresh rhizomes bought at the grocery store. They will make elegant foliage plants, with canes several feet tall, and they conveniently die down in the autumn, making space for plants brought in from the garden. You could then complete your tropical paradise with the heavy fragrance of Arabian jasmine (*Jasminum sambac*), which at room temperature will flower on and off all year.

PESTS AND DISEASES

Ventilation and hygiene are of paramount importance in controlling pests and diseases. To keep fungal diseases at bay, remove dead leaves and flowers regularly, and open windows on fine days, or use a fan. Spring clean the area at the change of each season. Keep glass clean inside and out to ensure maximum light. If containers of plants are brought in from the garden in the autumn, remove dead parts, check for pests and diseases, and treat appropriately. Ample warmth encourages the growth of pests as well as plants. Inspect indoor herbs regularly, especially under the leaves and around the growing tips, for aphids, whitefly, spider mites, and other pests.

BIOLOGICAL PEST CONTROL

Most people are averse to using chemical sprays on culinary herbs, especially when growing indoors, but biological pest control, which does not eliminate the pest altogether but reduces it to acceptable levels, may be used. The term means the use of predators, parasites, and diseases that affect a particular pest. These agents may sound alarming, but they are smaller than the pests, and work invisibly. There are now excellent biological predators for aphids, whitefly, spider mites, mealybugs, scale insects, thrips, and caterpillars. For best results, introduce the control before plants become heavily infested, since it may take a few weeks to have a noticeable impact. Make sure you order enough predators for the area, or they may not keep pace with the pests. Most predators and parasites need a minimum temperature of 70°F (21°C) and bright light in order to breed successfully. If pest populations get out of hand in early spring before conditions are suitable for controls, cut back affected plants, discard foliage, and repot or feed them well to encourage healthier growth. Do not use pesticides after controls have been introduced, other than those specified in the instructions, since even organic ones may harm predators.

SOME COMMON AILMENTS

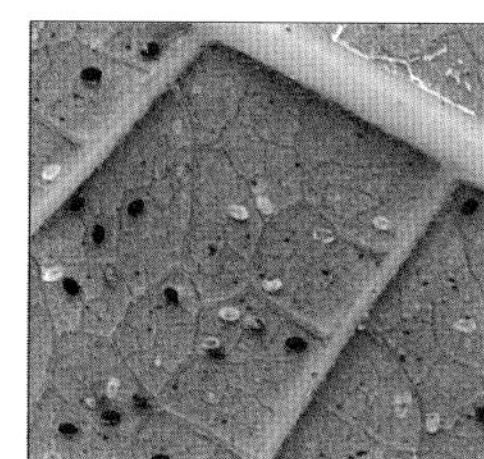

Whitefly nymphs

Adult whitefly

These common pests can be controlled by chemical sprays or by introducing predators that will attack them. Improved air circulation and the use of fungicide sprays should help to control fungal diseases.

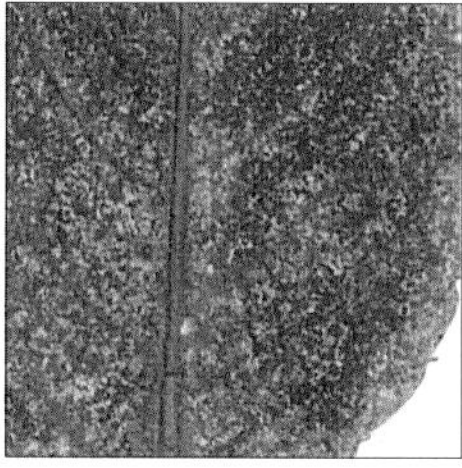

◄ *Spider mites*

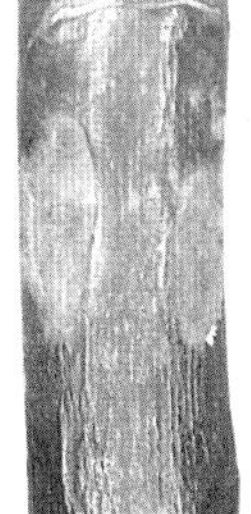

▲ *Gray mold* (Botrytis)

ROUTINE GARDEN CARE

However well the herb garden is designed and planted initially, it needs regular care to look good from year to year. General maintenance is obviously important, but plants need individual attention, too. Tasks such as deadheading and pruning will also give you the opportunity to enjoy the aromas, textures, and habits of the herbs at close quarters.

WATERING

Many Mediterranean herbs, such as rosemary (*Rosmarinus officinalis*) and thymes (*Thymus* spp.), are naturally drought-resistant when established and need watering only in periods of prolonged drought. Newly planted herbs need regular watering until strong new growth is apparent and the root system has extended beyond the original root ball. It is better to water thoroughly and less frequently rather than little and often, which encourages production of shallow surface roots. The best time to water is in the late afternoon or early evening; this minimizes evaporation and allows for drying before nightfall.

FEEDING AND MULCHING

Few of the popular culinary herbs are rich feeders, but heavy cropping – of chives (*Allium schoenoprasum*), for example – increases their nutritional requirements. An annual mulch of bulky organic fertilizer, such as compost or finely chipped bark, replenishes nutrients and inhibits weeds. This should be spread in spring after rain and when the ground has warmed up, since covering dry, frozen soil retards growth. On damp, heavy soils, feed and mulch only established herbs that thrive in rich, moist conditions, such as mint (*Mentha* spp.), bergamot (*Monarda didyma*), and angelica (*Angelica archangelica*. Spread a layer of grit around Mediterranean and gray-leaved herbs to reduce the risk of rotting. Inorganic fertilizers and heavy manuring are not recommended for herbs. These encourage sappy growth that lacks flavor and is more prone to frost damage, pests, and diseases.

WEEDING

Removing weeds from the herb garden ensures that growth is not suppressed by competition for light, nutrients, air circulation, and moisture. It also provides the opportunity to check the condition of your herbs. Take care when weeding near rue (*Ruta graveolens*), since contact with the leaves, especially in sunlight, can cause skin irritation.

VARIEGATION AND REVERSION

Most variegated herbs are propagated from green-leaved species that have produced a freak variegated shoot. These "sports," or mutations, may be caused by environmental factors or by a particular virus. Variegated plants are usually less vigorous than their plain green counterparts, which is an advantage in invasive species, such as goutweed (*Aegopodium podagraria*). From time to time, variegated plants develop shoots that revert to plain green. These branches are more vigorous and should be removed. If they are left, the entire plant will eventually revert to plain green. Some variegated herbs, such as pineapple mint (*Mentha suaveolens* 'Variegata'), also put out the occasional plain cream shoot. Again, it is best to remove these since they scorch easily. Reverted shoots of culinary herbs can be used for flavoring.

DEADHEADING

Some herbs flower for longer or grow more vigorously if their faded flower heads are removed promptly, saving the energy that would otherwise be put into seed production. This is particularly true of annuals, such as pot marigold (*Calendula officinalis*) and chamomile (*Chamaemelum nobile*). Vigilant deadheading is required for herbs that self-seed freely. Red plantain (*Plantago major* 'Rubrifolia') and garlic chives (*Allium tuberosum*) self-seed prolifically and can be troublesome weeds. Dandelions grown for their roots and leaves should have flower buds removed as they appear. Individual flower heads may be picked off or cut with pruners; flower heads of shrubby herbs, such as lavender (*Lavandula* spp.), are best removed *en masse* with about 1in (2.5cm) of growth, which serves also as a midseason pruning.

CONTROLLING GROWTH

A number of commonly grown herbs are invasive. These include mint (*Mentha* spp.), periwinkle (*Vinca* spp.), tansy (*Tanacetum vulgare*), and woodruff (*Galium odoratum*). If grown in the open ground rather than containers, it is advisable to remove excess growth as it appears, especially if nearby plants are threatened.

Some shrubs and trees produce suckers from stems or roots, which may spoil the appearance of the plant. In grafted specimens, suckers resemble the more vigorous stock in foliage, and will dominate if allowed to grow. *Prunus* spp. tend to develop suckers if their roots are disturbed by digging. When small, suckers can be rubbed out easily with a thumb, but when further developed they should be cut off close to the stem or root.

VARIEGATION
The pale areas of variegated plants, such as Teucrium x lucidrys *'Variegatum', tend to scorch if planted in full sun. Most variegated plants occasionally produce plain green shoots that encourage reversion and must be removed.*

PRUNING

Pruning is an important part of routine care, stimulating vigorous fresh growth and creating well-shaped, manageable plants. Herbs that are grown for their fresh young foliage may be cut back hard once or twice during the growing season to produce a supply of new leaves. Mints (*Mentha* spp.) and lemon balm (*Melissa officinalis*) should be cut back before flowering and

PREVENTION OF SELF-SEEDING
*Remove the seed heads of angelica (*Angelica archangelica*), above, before the seeds ripen, to prevent an invasion of seedlings that will smother small garden plants.*

PRUNING AND COPPICING

MAINTAINING HEALTHY GROWTH
*Prune Mediterranean herbs, such as this lavender cotton (*Santolina chamaecyparissus*), hard in spring to encourage new growth. Trim again after flowering.*

COPPICING SHRUBS
*To encourage colorful, uniform growth, cut back plants such as this willow (*Salix alba *'Britzensis') to near ground level at the first sign of growth in spring.*

CLEARING DEBRIS
*Remove the dead stems of hops (*Humulus lupulus*) each winter since they are difficult to disentangle from the new growth in spring. If left from year to year, they will build up and become unmanageable.*

then again in late summer. It is best to leave chives (*Allium schoenoprasum*) and marjoram (*Origanum*) until after flowering, since the flowers are both attractive and also make useful flavorings. Remove the first flowering stems of sorrel (*Rumex acetosa*) as they appear to prolong leaf production. Unlike other Mediterranean herbs, sage (*Salvia officinalis*) dislikes hard pruning and should be trimmed only lightly after flowering. When pruning rue (*Ruta graveolens*), take care not to cut too far into the main stem since this may kill the plant.

Most deciduous trees are pruned when dormant in late winter and early spring. Care is needed with those that "bleed" (exude sap) excessively if pruned toward the end of dormancy. Examples are horse chestnut (*Aesculus*), birch (*Betula*), walnut (*Juglans*), and *Prunus* spp., which are best pruned in midsummer. The majority of evergreen trees require little pruning other than the removal of dead wood. Most conifers dislike it and will not regenerate from hard pruning. Boxwood (*Buxus sempervirens*) needs clipping two or three times during the growing season when grown as a hedge or topiary. If the aroma of boxwood is disliked, cut it after rain, or water it well after pruning to disperse the distinctive smell.

Pruning a shrub enhances the shape of the plant and encourages better foliage, flowers, and fruits. Elder (*Sambucus nigra*) should be pruned hard in late winter since it comes into growth early in the season. Hard pruning is particularly necessary for elder cultivars, since they will produce larger, more colorful leaves in response to it. White willow (*Salix alba*) and its cultivars can be cut back nearly to ground level in early spring. Many trees, shrubs, and climbers, especially those grown for their fruits, such as grapes (*Vitis* spp.), blackcurrants (*Ribes nigrum*), and raspberries or blackberries (*Rubus* spp.), require specialized pruning. The Herb Dictionary (pp.224–373) contains general pruning details for plants, and more detailed information can be found in books that deal more fully with the subject.

TRAINING

Various shrubs and climbers described in this book can be trained against a wall, pillar, or pergola to give interest and height in the herb garden and extend the range of plants grown in a small space. Walls act as storage heaters, offering considerable protection to less hardy subjects in cold areas. It is important to establish a framework for training when planting, using durable materials, and to tie in new growths when they are still soft and pliable. A combination of pruning and training is needed throughout the growing season to discipline growth so that the plant does not become so heavy and wide-spreading that it damages its supports and swamps nearby plants.

AUTUMN CLEARANCE

Cutting down the dead foliage of herbaceous perennials may look neater, but leaving this natural layer until spring helps protect the dormant crowns from frost and wind. Remove any dead leaves that have fallen on thymes and other small evergreen herbs, since they may encourage fungal disease.

WINTER PROTECTION

The hardiness of many common culinary herbs varies according to the species or cultivar. In cold areas, protect "borderline" herbs with a layer of insulating material. Alternatively, lift them and bring under cover. In spring, they can be cut back and planted out again, or used as a source of cuttings to propagate new plants. This works especially well for scented geraniums.

TRANSPLANTING

Even with careful planning, it is sometimes necessary to move a plant to avoid overcrowding or to create a more pleasing association. For perennials, shrubs, and trees, this is best done in autumn or early spring. Large plants should be lifted carefully to minimize root damage. Annuals usually need thinning out so that they have sufficient room to develop. Transplant on a damp, rainy day, and water the plants well afterward, since annuals tend to "bolt" (flower prematurely) when severely stressed by disturbance and shortage of water. Chervil (*Anthriscus cerefolium*) and dill (*Anethum graveolens*) are particularly prone to bolting. California poppies (*Eschscholzia californica*), flax (*Linum usitatissimum*), and borage (*Borago officinalis*) are some species that do not transplant well in any conditions.

PROTECTING THE ROOT BALL
*This young beech (*Fagus sylvatica*) should have the roots wrapped in burlap to keep the soil around them while the tree is in transit or being transplanted.*

METHODS OF PROPAGATION

Herbs may be propagated by a wide variety of methods, depending on the kind of plant. For information on individual species and cultivars, see the *Growth and Harvest* information given in the Herb Dictionary, pages 224–373.

RAISING HERBS FROM SEED

Many herbs are easy to grow from seed; they may be sown in containers or, where larger quantities are required, in a prepared bed of fine soil in the open. Seeds of small, creeping herbs, such as wild thyme (*Thymus serpyllum*) may also be sown directly into cracks between paving stones where it would be difficult to insert plants. Spring is the best time to sow most seeds. **HARDY ANNUALS**, such as borage (*Borago officinalis*), pot marigolds (*Calendula officinalis*), cornflowers (*Centaurea cyanus*), and poppies (*Papaver* spp.) should be sown either in spring to flower the following summer, or in early autumn for flowering the following spring. **BIENNIALS**, such as evening primrose (*Oenothera biennis*), angelica (*Angelica archangelica*), and caraway (*Carum carvi*), should be sown in late summer or early autumn to flower the following summer. Thin out seedlings after germination and again after a few weeks so that only the strongest are left to grow on. Short-lived, hardy herbs that are used in large quantities, such as parsley (*Petroselinum crispum*) or coriander (*Coriandrum sativum*), should be sown at intervals of 3–4 weeks from early spring to early autumn for a regular supply of young leaves. Dill (*Anethum graveolens*) and chervil (*Anthriscus cerefolium*) must be sown *in situ* since they tend to "bolt" (flower prematurely) if the roots are disturbed. In cold areas, basil (*Ocimum basilicum*) should not be sown until late spring when there is ample warmth and light. Seeds need a minimum temperature of 55°F (13°C) and good ventilation to prevent fungal diseases such as gray mold (*Botrytis*).

PERENNIALS should be sown in warmth in spring, growing on the seedlings in pots until they are large enough to be hardened off and planted out. Seeds of some hardy herbaceous perennials, trees, and shrubs need stratifying (subjecting to a period of cold) in order to break their dormancy. Soak the seeds overnight, put them in a plastic bag containing a mixture of moist peat and sand, and place the bag in a refrigerator for 4–12 weeks at 34–41°F (1–5°C). As an alternative, they may be sown in containers of soil mix, covered with a layer of grit to prevent mud-splashing, and left outdoors during the winter. Seeds needing stratification include those of aconite (*Aconitum napellus*), beech (*Fagus* spp.), birch (*Betula* spp.), and primrose (*Primula vulgaris*); also *Adonis*, *Euonymus*, and some *Viburnum* species. Alternate periods of warmth and cold are required for successful germination of *Trillium* and *Paeonia* species. Hard-coated seeds, such as those of *Galega officinalis*, *Baptisia tinctoria,* and *Paeonia* species, germinate more quickly if the seed coat is scarified (nicked or abraded) before sowing so that the seed can absorb moisture.

WARM-GROWING OR TROPICAL herbs require their seeds to be sown soon after they ripen, since in general they have a short period of viability and do not store well.

PLANTING SEEDS IN PAVING
Sow seeds in moist soil in the cracks to add interest to your patio.

SAVING SEED

If you save seed from garden plants, bear in mind that certain herbs may cross-pollinate, giving rise to seedlings that differ from the mother plant. When various kinds of thyme (*Thymus* spp.), marjoram (*Origanum* spp.), mint (*Mentha* spp.), and lavender (*Lavandula* spp.) are grown near each other, the chances of hybridization are high. Closely related genera may also interbreed if they are grown together and flower at the same time; dill and fennel (*Foeniculum vulgare*) are known to cross, resulting in plants that are indeterminate in flavor. More successful from home-grown seed are coriander, pot marigold, sweet cicely (*Myrrhis odorata*), angelica, caraway, and borage. Seed should be collected as soon as it is ripe, cleaned, and stored in envelopes (not plastic bags) in a dry, dark place at 34–41°F (1–5°C). It is important to remember when propagating from collected seed that most cultivars do not come true from seed. Some annuals and biennials, such as poppies, pot marigolds, and foxgloves (*Digitalis* spp.), produce a percentage of plants resembling the mother plant, but this tends to decrease each year. Very few variegated cultivars come true from seed; an exception is variegated rue (*Ruta graveolens* 'Variegata').

PLANTS FROM PRODUCE

An interesting range of herbs can be propagated from produce bought in a grocery store. Many suppliers sell pots of growing herbs, for example parsley (*Petroselinum crispum*), basil (*Ocimum basilicum*), and coriander (*Coriandrum sativum*), which consist of numerous seedlings crowded together. These can be split into three or four smaller clumps, potted up separately, and grown on for planting out in either containers or the herb garden. (If the seedlings are growing in fiber, rather than soil mix, you will find it easier to cut the root ball using scissors; some

SOWING SEEDS IN CONTAINERS

1 Sprinkle the dried seeds over the surface of firmed seed soil mix. Space larger seed by hand. Cover them lightly with sieved soil mix.

2 Once the seedlings are large enough to handle, tap the container to loosen the soil mix. Lift the seedlings out, holding them by the leaves, not the stems.

PLANTING OUT IN OPEN GROUND
When seedlings are sufficiently advanced, they can be planted out at the recommended spacing and depth. Firm the soil gently around the roots and water in well.

Saving Seed

1 Dry out seedheads on blotting paper or newspaper to absorb any moisture. In time, they will begin to split open and show signs of releasing their seeds.

2 When the seedheads are dry, shake out the seeds onto clean paper and clear away any debris. Store the seeds in a labeled envelope in a cool, dry place.

seedlings inevitably get damaged, but the majority will soon put out new roots and leaves). Bunches of watercress (*Nasturtium officinale*) can be treated as cuttings destined for the garden pond, and will thrive for a short time in a jar of water on the windowsill. Fresh roots of ginger (*Zingiber officinale*) and also turmeric (*Curcuma longa*) rapidly produce handsome new shoots if they are planted in a pot of moist soil mix and kept above 70°F (21°C). Spring is the best time to start rhizomes into growth. Bulbs of garlic (*Allium sativum*), split into separate cloves, should be planted out 6in (15cm) apart in the herb garden in the autumn. This will produce many bulbs of garlic for harvesting the following summer. Alternatively, the cloves will sprout garlic-flavored leaves if potted up 1in (2.5cm) apart. Fresh chili peppers (*Capsicum annuum* var. *annuum*) contain viable seeds from which useful and ornamental plants can easily be grown, given sufficient warmth and light. In addition, they are often of commercial cultvars from other countries that are not otherwise available.

Grapevine Grown from Pits
*A grapevine (*Vitis vinifera*) is easily grown from pits and should fruit successfully, but it will not come true from seed. However, it is valuable for its decorative qualities as well.*

Growing from Pits

A number of trees and shrubs are easily raised from pits. A plant propagated in this way will not be exactly the same as the parent; pits from a 'Pinot Noir' grape will produce grapevines but the fruits may differ considerably from 'Pinot Noir'. Oranges, tangerines, lemons, and limes make very handsome trees with fragrant foliage, regardless of whether they flower or fruit successfully. The best time to plant citrus pits is in the spring, so that the seedlings have ample warmth and light for growth. They take 3–4 weeks to germinate when sown in seed soil mix at 60–70°F (16–21°C). Most citruses produce polyembryonic pits, resulting in two or three seedlings from each pit. They can be grown on together or separated. Pomegranate seeds (*Punica granatum*) need about 70°F (21°C) for germination. They can be obtained from ripe fruits in the autumn for spring sowing. Wash and dry a few seeds extracted from the pink pulp, or store a fruit whole through the winter – the skin shrinks and hardens but the seeds remain plump. Golden loquat fruits (*Eriobotrya japonica*) ripen in the spring, germinating readily from fresh pits sown in sandy soil mix and kept above 64°F (18°C). Young loquats make exceptionally fine pot plants. A papaya, or pawpaw (*Carica papaya*), is probably the most exotic tree you can grow easily from a pit. Papaya needs 72–82°F (22–28°C) for germination. Use biodegradable pots for seeds and young papayas so that they can be potted on without root disturbance.

Eriobotrya japonica
A loquat can be grown from seed as a bush or standard for containers, or trained on a sunny wall. Flowering in autumn, it fruits the next spring.

Damping off

Seedlings grown under cover are prone to "damping off," a condition caused by various fungi which are soil- or water-borne. The roots of the seedlings rot and the plants collapse. It is a virulent disease which is especially prevalent in overcrowded seedlings and peat-based soil mixes, and usually spreads rapidly to all plants in the same container. There is no cure, but watering with a copper-based

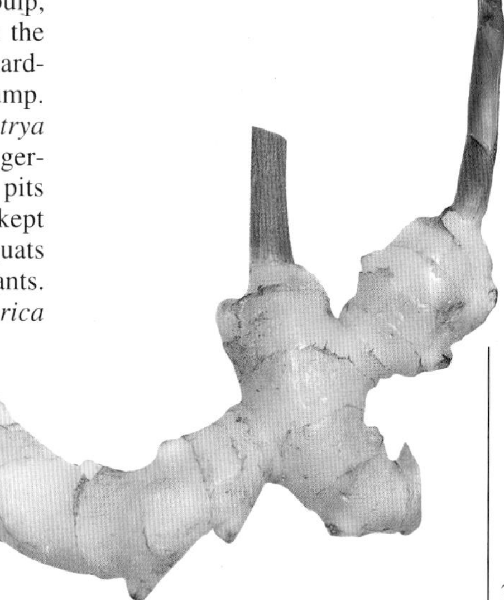

Propagating from a Ginger Root
*A good crop of ginger (*Zingiber officinale*) can be produced in warm conditions by planting rhizomes bought from a supermarket.*

VEGETATIVE PROPAGATION

Of the various methods of propagation that you can use, one of the most popular and reliable is by taking cuttings. This applies to herbs as much as to other plants and is often the quickest way to propagate perennial herbs.

TYPES OF CUTTINGS

Use a clean, sharp knife or pruners for taking cuttings and insert them as soon as possible in open, well-drained soil mix or a mixture of peat and sand. Warmth is needed for rooting: 64–77°F (18–25°C) for cool temperate species; 77–90°F (25–32°C) for warm-growing and tropical species. The cut surface may be dipped in a hormone preparation to encourage rooting. Humidity is important for leafy cuttings; this can be provided by a propagator or by enclosing the container in a plastic bag.

HARDWOOD (RIPEWOOD) CUTTINGS are taken from mature wood at the end of the growing season from both evergreen subjects, such as hollies, and deciduous trees and shrubs, such as poplars and roses. Cuttings of deciduous species will be leafless. Hardwood cuttings are slow to root, but are easily kept in good condition since they do not wilt.

SOFTWOOD CUTTINGS are taken from young, immature, nonflowering growth during the growing season. They may be tip cuttings in shrubby herbs, or basal cuttings in herbaceous plants, such as *Buxus*, *Hyssopus*, *Origanum*, *Pelargonium*, *Santolina*, *Tanacetum*, *Thymus*, and *Viola*. Remove lower leaves, which will rot if inserted into the soil mix. Softwood cuttings of most mints (*Mentha* species) root easily in water. Geranium cuttings should be left for a day so that the cut surfaces dry off; this helps prevent rot and improves rooting. Most softwood cuttings wilt easily; they need to be kept under cover and misted to retain turgidity.

SEMIRIPE CUTTINGS are taken from half-ripened wood during the growing season from plants such as *Artemisia*, *Buxus*, *Citrus*, *Helichrysum*, *Lavandula*, *Myrtus*, *Rosmarinus*, and *Thymus*.

STEM CUTTINGS can be taken from any section of the plant stem during the growing season, for example *Melissa, Pelargonium*, and *Salvia*.

BASAL CUTTINGS are taken from the base of a plant, on or just below ground level, as it begins new growth in spring. Used mainly for herbaceous perennials, such as *Adenophora*. "Irishman's cuttings" are cuttings that already have some roots and so "take" very easily.

ROOT CUTTINGS are small sections taken from a semimature or mature root from plants such as *Albizia*. Root cuttings of watercress (*Nasturtium officinale*) are easy to grow and root quickly in water during the growing season.

LEAF CUTTINGS consist of detached, healthy, mature leaves taken from the plant during the growing season, for example *Cardamine*.

HARDWOOD CUTTINGS
These willow (Salix alba) *cuttings are easy to keep healthy.*

SOFT TIP CUTTINGS are taken from the tip of a shoot. They may be either greenwood or softwood cuttings.

GREENWOOD CUTTINGS consist of the soft tips of new growth, taken later than softwood cuttings, when the main flush of spring growth has slowed down, for example *Pogostemon patchouli* or *Withania somnifera*. Nodal greenwood cuttings are taken just beneath a node or leaf joint.

LEAF-BUD CUTTINGS consist of short sections of stem, bearing a leaf-bud or pair of buds and a leaf, taken during the growing season.

HEEL CUTTINGS are taken with a sliver of wood at the base from such plants as *Helichrysum italicum*. They are obtained by gently pulling a semiripe sideshoot from the main stem.

EYE CUTTINGS are small, ripened, leafless stem sections, each with one bud, taken in late winter, for example *Vitis*.

LAYERING

In this method of propagation, a stem or shoot is induced to form roots while still attached to the parent plant. Choose a strong, flexible shoot that will easily bend to the ground. Make a small cut in the underside of the shoot, and insert it into the soil so that the growing tip protrudes above the surface. Secure the shoot tip to a stake, and anchor the buried section with a large stone. The following autumn, if the layer has rooted, it can be severed from the main plant and potted up or transplanted.

AIR LAYERING is used mainly for warm-growing trees and shrubs, for example *Ficus*, *Magnolia*, *Tabebuia*, and *Theobroma*. Choose a healthy shoot, 1–2 years old, and make a slit 6–15in (15–40cm) from the growing tip. Pack the slit and surrounding area with moist sphagnum moss and wrap in plastic, secured at each end with garden twine. Air layering is best done in the spring; rooting may take up to two years. When the roots can be seen through the plastic, cut the new plant from the parent and pot up separately.

TAKING LEAF CUTTINGS OF HALF-HARDY PERENNIALS

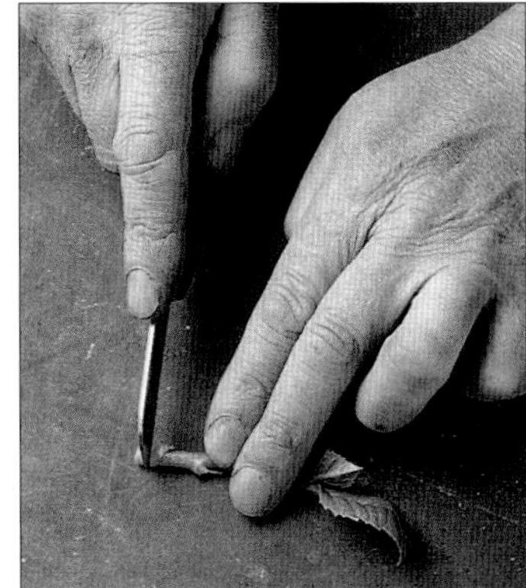

1 *Take a cutting with at least three leaves and a new shoot. Trim the stem just below the lowest leaf joint. Dip the stem into hormone rooting powder, tapping off any excess.*

2 *Put the cutting into a pot filled with well-drained soil mix. Make a hole and insert the cutting. Gently firm the soil mix down around the cutting, pressing it down with your fingers.*

3 *Bend a piece of wire to form an arch over the cutting and press it into the pot. Cover with a plastic bag. Alternatively, put the pot in the bag, blow into the bag to inflate it, and seal.*

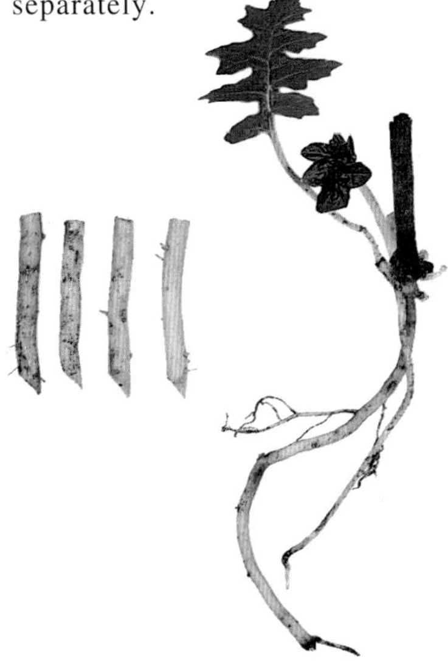

ROOT CUTTINGS
These are best taken in the dormant season. The warmer the environment for propagation, the shorter the cuttings can be, but keep to a minimum length of 1in (2.5cm).

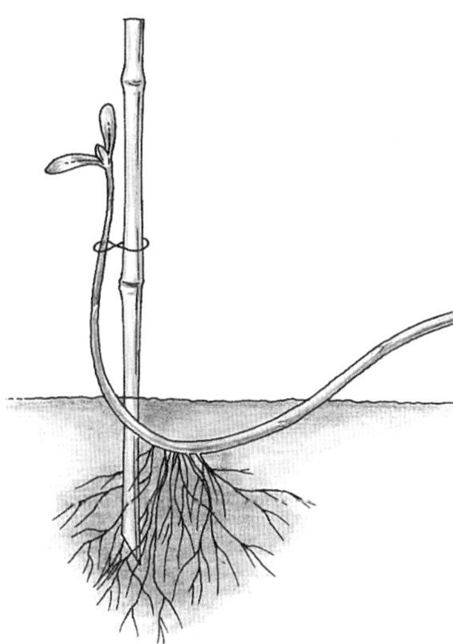

SIMPLE LAYERING
This form of propagation is best carried out on a young, vigorous plant between autumn and spring. If the plant has rooted well, it can be cut from the parent in the following autumn.

MOUND LAYERING is a useful method for shrubby herbs that are prone to becoming woody and sparse with age, such as thyme. In spring, mound free-draining soil over the base of the plant, leaving the tips of the shoots above the surface. This stimulates new shoots to develop roots. By late summer, the shoots should be sufficiently well rooted for you to cut them off and pot them up separately.

DIVISION

Clumps of herbaceous perennials need dividing every few years, or when they become too large. This can be done by lifting the plant and splitting it into smaller pieces by hand, or with a spade if the roots are too tough. It is important to divide primroses regularly to maintain vigor. The best time to divide herbs is when growth is minimal, from autumn to early spring, choosing fine, mild weather to avoid frost damage. To minimize disturbance, divide sensitive plants in early spring when new buds are visible. Water transplanted or divided plants well, even in damp weather, to settle the soil round the roots.

OFFSETS

Most herbs with storage organs increase naturally by producing offsets from the mature bulb or corm. They can be detached during dormancy and planted separately to grow on as new plants. The term "offsets" also refers to plantlets which are formed at the ends of stolons and runners. These usually form roots while still attached to the parent plant, or root rapidly when detached and potted up separately.

SUCKERS

Taking rooted suckers is a very easy method of propagation for herbs such as *Alnus glutinosa* and *Rosa rugosa*. It is not suitable for propagating grafted plants that are not growing on their own roots.

GRAFTING AND BUDDING

These are more specialized methods of propagation for woody plants in which a section of stem (a scion) is united with the rootstock or stock of a different plant. If the scion consists of a short piece of stem with a single bud, the method is referred to as "budding." The aim is to produce a new plant with certain characteristics, such as a greater resistance to root disease. Grafting is usually carried out from late winter to early spring; budding is done mostly in summer.

SPORES

Nonflowering plants, such as ferns, mosses, fungi, horsetails, and algae, reproduce by means of minute, dustlike spores. They need constant moisture for germination. Ferns such as *Adiantum capillus-veneris* are quick and easy to grow from spores. To propagate a fern in this way, select a frond that has ripe brown sporangia on the underside of the leaf blade, and position it over a piece of clean white paper to collect the spores. These can then be sown in a pot of moist, sterile soil mix and covered with plastic wrap. Germination takes 1–3 months. Spray the surface of the soil mix regularly. Pot on the ferns when they are large enough to handle.

MICROPROPAGATION

This technique requires sterile laboratory conditions and is used commercially to propagate large numbers of identical plants of the same cultivar in a short time. It is an important method of producing virus-free stock from infected plants, and of "bulking up" rare species for reintroduction to the wild or for the horticultural trade.

DIVISION OF RHIZOMATOUS PLANTS

1 Shake the clumps of rhizomes to remove any loose soil. Using your hands or a hand fork, split each clump into manageable pieces, checking for signs of disease.

2 Discard any old rhizomes, then detach the young rhizomes from the clump and neatly trim off their ends. Dust the cut areas with fungicide, shaking off excess powder.

MOUND LAYERING HERBS
To stimulate rooting from the lower stems, mound up 3–5in (7–12cm) of sandy soil over the crown of the plant, covering the lower stems, except for the tips of the shoots.

DIVISION OF PERENNIAL PLANTS

*1 Lift the plant to be divided, taking care to insert the fork far enough away from the plant so that the roots are not damaged. Shake off any surplus soil. The plant shown here is a sunflower (*Helianthus *spp.).*

2 Divide the plant into smaller pieces by hand, retaining only healthy, vigorous sections, each with several new shoots. Cut back old top-growth and replant the divided sections. Firm in and water thoroughly.

HARVESTING YOUR CROP

Gathering herbs is a delight and an adventure. It brings us into contact with the remarkable plants on which so much of the health and physical well-being of all the world's peoples depend. However, harvesting herbs is also a practical undertaking, and needs careful preparation and organization.

HARVESTING WILD HERBS

In many countries it is an offense to pick any parts of certain rare plants, or uproot *any* plant without the landowner's permission. You should thus harvest only those that you know are permitted, common, and plentiful, and which you can identify with certainty. Special care is needed with some groups of plants such as the carrot family (Umbelliferae), which even experts find hard to identify. However common they may be, respect wild plants and pick only a few of their leaves, flowers, or fruits to ensure that the plants survive and reproduce. Try to avoid collecting herbs that may be polluted by vehicle exhausts, agricultural sprays, or animals.

CUTTING

Do not cut garden plants at random, but take the opportunity to pinch out or prune the plant at the same time, removing unwanted shoots and encouraging bushiness. Harvesting time is also a good opportunity to cut out reverted shoots of variegated plants.

TIMING

The Herb Dictionary (see pages 224–373) will tell you the best time of the year to harvest the various parts of each herb. If you intend to process and store the herbs for future use, choose a dry, overcast morning, after any dew or rain has dried.

COMMERCIAL HARVESTING
Many herbs are grown on a commercial scale and can be harvested like other crops. Here a planting of lavender is being cut in southern Spain. The oil will be extracted from the cut flowers for use in perfume manufacture.

HARVEST FROM THE GARDEN
A mix of bay leaves, rosemary, lavender, basil, sage, and parsley. Sharp scissors or pruners are essential for a clean cut off the parent plant. The shallow trug ensures that cuttings are kept in their best condition for storing.

EQUIPMENT

You will need ordinary garden tools (including a sharp knife, scissors, or pruners) and it is advisable to wear gloves. Some herbs can trigger an allergic reaction, and a few (such as rue) may cause blistering if the sap contacts skin in the presence of sunlight.

QUANTITIES

Collect small quantities at a time, handle them as little as possible, and process them quickly to protect the active constituents from deterioration. Aromatic herbs are especially vulnerable – any scent they leave in the air or on your hands indicates that their volatile oils are being lost, and that the processed herbs will thus have less aroma and beneficial effect.

POINTS TO REMEMBER

Always try to harvest material from only clean, healthy plants in the peak of condition. The active constituents and properties will then be at their highest levels. Avoid damaged or diseased parts, and any that are immature, aging, or out of season – these factors also imply low levels of active constituents. Collect only one kind of herb at a time to avoid transfer of odors and mistakes in identification. Lay the parts you have cut carefully in a single layer in a shallow container, and use or process them quickly; even a small heap generates heat which will lead to wilting and deterioration of the herb.

WHICH PARTS, AND WHEN?

It is important to harvest the correct part of the plant for the purpose you intend: the leaves and seeds of coriander (*Coriandrum sativum*), for example, have quite different aromas and uses. In some cases, unusual plant elements are used – pistils of the saffron crocus (*Crocus sativus*), tangerine peel (*Citrus reticulata*), or spores of the puffball fungus (*Lycoperdon perlatum*). The most commonly used parts of plants are described below and on the opposite page, together with the best times to harvest them.

WHOLE PLANT

This is also known as the aerial parts, and means the parts growing above the soil, which are

SIMPLE DRYING
The flavor of some herbs, such as bay, is enhanced by drying. A drying rack can be simply made from an old slatted shelf or a mesh-covered wooden frame. Lay the herbs on it in a single layer and keep in a warm place.

usually cut off near ground level as the plant begins to flower.

LEAVES AND STEMS

Individual leaves or sprigs are generally harvested when young since foliage tends to toughen once flowering has begun. Large leaves may be picked individually. Cut stems or branches of small-leaved herbs and remove the leaves from them later.

FLOWERS

Occasionally picked when in bud, but for most purposes flowers are at their best when just opened. Large blooms can be picked individually, with or without stalks; small ones, such as elder (*Sambucus nigra*) are separated from the stalks after picking. In the case of some herbs, such as lavender (*Lavandula* species), the whole flower head is cut and may be used whole or in pieces. For certain uses, only specific parts may be required; the petals (as in pot marigold, *Calendula officinalis*), or the flower head or corolla (as in borage, *Borago officinalis*).

FRUITS AND BERRIES

Harvested mostly when ripe, but before they become squishy. They may be picked individually or in bunches, depending on habit of growth and intended use.

SEEDS

Harvested in pods or seedheads when ripe (that is, when no longer green), but before they become overripe and the plant sheds them. The ripening process will continue for a time after harvesting if the seedhead is kept intact.

ROOTS, RHIZOMES, TUBERS, AND BULBS

In most cases, these are harvested during autumn after the aerial parts have died down. It is often possible to avoid destroying the whole plant by carefully lifting and removing a portion of the underground parts. Bulbous plants will often produce small offsets that can be replanted.

BARK AND WOOD

The required age of the shrub or tree, and the time to harvest the bark or wood, may vary greatly. Wherever possible, remove only a few branches from each plant or grow them on a coppice basis. Cut the branch cleanly and remove bark later to avoid introducing infection. Do not bark-ring trees (that is, remove a band of the bark going around the trunk or branch) since this usually kills them. Remove lichen and mosses from the bark before it is processed.

SAP, GUM, AND RESIN

Sap from trees is usually collected in the spring as it rises. Gum and resin may be harvested by cutting grooves diagonally in the bark. Resin also often exudes naturally and can be scraped off the tree at any time.

PREPARING FOR PROCESSING

The purpose of storing herbs is to preserve the constituents – and thereby the flavor, aroma, and therapeutic properties – as fully as possible for later use. Exactly how this is done depends on the part used and the purpose for which it is intended. With few exceptions, herbs are best used freshly harvested. Certain constituents, such as the alkaloids in *Papaver somniferum*, remain potent for many years, but the majority are easily destroyed by the enzymatic processes at work within the cut plant, and by exposure to light, heat, and air. As a rule, stocks of preserved herbs should be replaced every year, since a certain amount of deterioration will inevitably take place, especially when they are stored at room temperature in the home.

CLEANING THE HARVEST

Check that all parts harvested are clean and free of dirt and insects. Avoid washing leaves, flowers, fruits, and seedheads, since this lengthens the time of air-drying and encourages deterioration. Underground parts, however, should be thoroughly washed to remove soil and grit, dried on paper towels, and then sliced into manageable pieces.

RIPE SEEDHEADS
*The seedheads of poppies (*Papaver *species) have a ribbed outer skin with a crownlike stigma. The chambers inside contain hundreds of seeds, which are used in cooking.*

DRYING FLOWER HEADS

1 Flower heads cut from their stalks are laid to dry on a tray lined with paper towels.

2 Only the dried petals of pot marigolds are used, so they are plucked from the center, which is then discarded.

3 Lavender flowers are dried on the stem. The whole flower head is used, and storing them upside down in a bag, as here, prevents any of the flowers or seeds from being lost. The stems could also be inverted over a tray.

DRYING AERIAL PARTS AND LEAVES

1 Small-leaved herbs like these are best dried on the stem. Tie in small bunches as soon as they are picked and cleaned; hang upside down to dry in a well-ventilated place.

2 When leaves are brittle, rub them off the stems onto dry paper. Crumble pieces together if all aerial parts are being used.

3 Transfer dried herbs from the paper to a storage container, which should be well sealed. Colored glass, used here, helps prevent light oxidization.

PROCESSING AND STORING

Most of the techniques used for preserving and storing herbs are traditional, and easily learned and carried out at home. Extraction of the constituents (through distillation, pressing, or by solvent extraction, for example) is much more complex, and requires equipment and expertise that is rarely available on a domestic scale. In many countries, too, it is an offense to be in possession of an unlicensed still.

AIR-DRYING

Hanging herbs up or spreading them out to dry is the most widely used method of preservation. In many countries, they are simply left on mats in the sun or strung under the house eaves. Speed is of the essence in air-drying (they should be dry in 24–48 hours), otherwise enzymes in the plant tissues continue to break down the chemical constituents, as do factors such as moisture, air, light, and heat. If the leaves turn black or show any mold, the drying process has been too slow and the herb will not be worth keeping.

The ideal place is dry and well ventilated, free from dust and fumes, and constantly at 68–90°F (20–32°C). To maximize the air circulation, hang whole plants, stems, and seedheads in small bundles, and thread sliced roots and fungi on strings. Solitary flower heads, such as chives (*Allium schoenoprasum*), and roses (*Rosa* species) can be dried on the stalk by slotting the stems through a wire mesh drying rack, or by laying them on it.

Fragile seedheads of herbs such as fennel, dill, and caraway should be cut with sufficient stalk to hang upside down, tied into small bundles; the heads should be hung either over clean paper or inside a paper bag to catch the seeds as they fall. Onions and garlic are traditionally harvested with the stalks attached, which are then braided into ropes and sun-dried. Large leaves, flowers, fruits, or petals can be arranged in a single layer on racks covered with wire mesh or muslin. On a small scale, a cake-cooling rack spread with paper towels can be used. Air movement can be boosted by a fan (or fan heater if more heat is also needed).

MICROWAVE-DRYING

Herbs can be washed before being dried if they need it. The cut parts should be spread out in a single layer on paper towels and dried in the microwave oven, according to the temperature guidelines provided by the manufacturer. On average, this should take only about 2–3 minutes, but progress should be checked every 30 seconds, rearranging the parts to ensure even drying. Cool first before storing as for air-dried herbs.

OVEN-DRYING

This is recommended only for cut underground plant parts that need lengthy drying and will tolerate higher temperatures than fragile leaves and flowers. Spread the slices out thinly on a baking sheet and dry them at 120–140°F (50–60°C). This may take 2–3 hours, depending on the size of the root material.

AIR-DRYING
*Here a bunch of long stems of lovage (*Levisticum officinale*) is hung up to dry. The leaves may be used fresh or dried; the seeds are dried, and the fresh stalks may be candied like angelica.*

FREEZE-DRYING

This method produces excellent retention of flavor in soft-leaved herbs, such as parsley, mint, basil, and chives. Pack individual leaves either whole or in sprigs into labeled plastic bags or boxes. There is no need to defrost before use since the leaves crumble easily when still frozen; chopped herbs can be thawed quickly in a sieve before use. Herbs can also be added when making ice cubes (see illustration opposite). Iced borage flowers, or sprigs of mint or lemon balm, may also be added directly to drinks to impart flavor and interest to them.

CONTAINERS

It is important to use scrupulously clean containers and lids (either sterilized in the oven or in pans of boiling water if being reused). Containers of preserved herbs should be stored in a cool, dry place, out of direct sunlight. Dark glass or ceramic jars and bottles are best for dried or liquid storage. Clear glass lets in light, leading to bleaching and oxidation of the product; if used, the container should be kept in a dark cupboard. Lids should be airtight to prevent the entry of moisture, molds, and bacteria, which cause rapid deterioration. Plastic containers may contaminate herbs and increase humidity. Food-grade plastic bags and plastic boxes or tubs, rather than glass, are, however, recommended for frozen herbs.

STORING DRIED HERBS

When quite dry, herbs should be packed into storage containers and labeled with name and date. In the case of aromatic herbs, keep the pieces as large as possible to avoid loss of volatile oils through exposure to air. At this stage, blends can be created for bouquets garnis, special recipes, potpourris, and teas. If large quantities of dried herbs are being processed, it may be advisable to wear a face mask to avoid inhaling dust. All dried herbs have a tendency to absorb moisture from the air, so when storing them use containers that are only just big enough so that as much air as possible is excluded. Check the contents regularly in case there has been any deterioration in quality. Certain herbs, such as the marsh

HERBS FOR DRYING
These bunches of thyme and bay are tied up ready for drying. Cuttings for processing and storing should always be in prime condition when they are taken from the plant.

DRYING FLOWER HEADS
These chive flowers are dried on wire mesh. The stalks are threaded through the mesh to suspend the flowers and preserve their shape.

PREPARING ROOTS FOR STORAGE

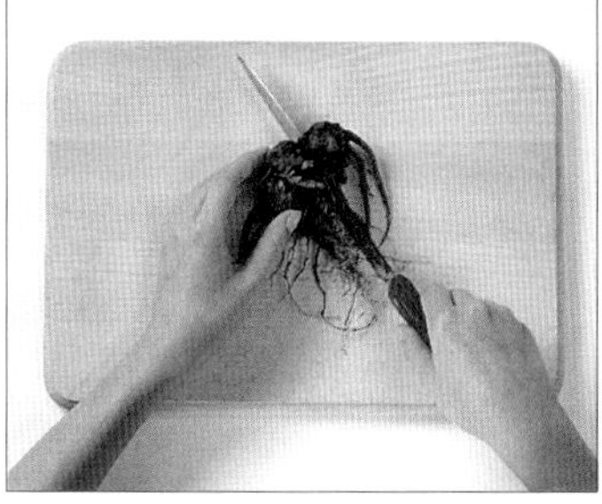

1 *Always try to remove only part of the root, so that the plant can regrow. Wash the parts well to remove all dirt.*

2 *Cut the root parts into slices or small pieces with a sharp knife. It is easier to cut the roots when they are still wet.*

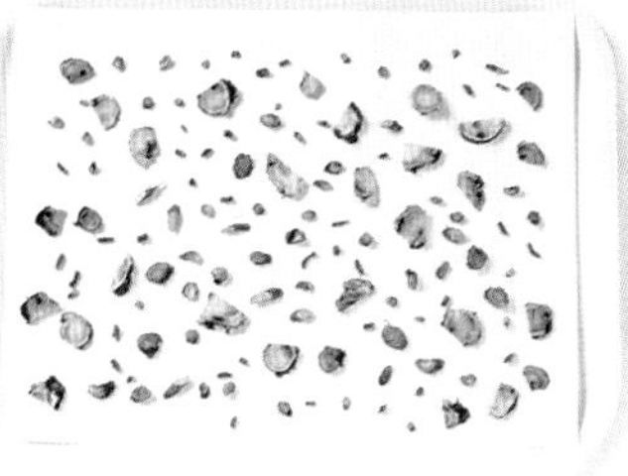

3 *Spread out the root pieces on a tray lined with paper. Dry them in an oven and then leave them out to cool.*

mallow (*Althaea officinalis*) and lady's mantle (*Alchemilla* species) are especially prone to the problem of moisture absorption and should be stored with care to avoid this.

HERB OILS AND VINEGARS

The flavors of many fresh herbs can be preserved in oils or vinegars. This is very simple to do, and will enhance salad dressings and marinades. Almost any herb can be used, either singly or in combination, in the preparation of a herb oil. Choose a good-quality oil, such as sunflower (or olive for a stronger flavor). Loosely fill a clear glass jar with the herb, pour over the oil, and seal. Leave the jar in a sunny place for at least two weeks, shaking daily. Strain the contents to remove the steeped herb, and refill into clean jars or bottles, adding a sprig of the fresh herb for identification. Basil (*Ocimum* species) leaves can be preserved by packing in jars of oil; the leaves can be used in sauces and cooked dishes, and the oil in salad dressings.

FREEZING HERBS
Freezing is a simple way to store herbs, and is convenient for small quantities. Contents can be identified easily in clear plastic bags with labels.

For herb vinegars, it is best to lightly crush the herb first. Warm either wine or cider vinegar, and proceed as for herb oil. Do not use containers with metal lids to hold vinegar; the acid will corrode the lids and taint the contents. Vinegar is used in processing certain Chinese herbs, such as *Corydalis solida*; it potentiates alkaloids and improves detoxifying and painkilling effects.

HERB JUICE

Some herbs, such as *Galium aparine*, are used in the form of juice, which is more easily prepared in batches, though a large amount of the herb is needed, since the amount of juice produced is not large. The fresh herb is liquefied or put through an electric juice extractor. It can then be sieved, and frozen in small plastic tubs. A herb paste can be made in the same way, ideal for using in herb butter.

PRESERVING IN SUGAR

In sufficient concentration, sugar or honey makes a useful preservative for certain herbs, such as *Glycyrrhiza uralensis*, and will also disguise unpleasant flavors. For syrup, the sugar content should never be less than 65 percent; unrefined sugar is often preferred. The fresh herb may be simmered in the sugar solution, or sugar (or honey) added to an infusion, decoction, or tincture of the herb, and then heated until dissolved. Honey is used in processing certain Chinese herbs for its soothing effects. Rosehips (*Rosa* spp.) should be minced and infused in boiling water, brought to a boil briefly, and left to stand for about 15 minutes; the infusion should then be finely strained to remove any irritant seed hairs before adding sugar. Angelica stems and ginger rhizomes are traditionally preserved by crystallizing. It is a long process, and recipes must be followed exactly.

HERBAL WINES

Alcohol is an excellent preservative, drawing out active constituents and prohibiting the growth of microorganisms. Recipes for herbal wines can be found in books on winemaking; favorites include elderflower and elderberry (*Sambucus nigra*), cowslip (*Primula veris*), and dandelion (*Taraxacum officinale*).

OTHER ALCOHOLIC DRINKS

Elderflower "champagne" and ginger beer are only slightly alcoholic, since they are fermented for only a very short time. Based on hops (*Humulus lupulus*), beers are essentially herbal, too. Homemade ale can be flavored with nettles (*Urtica dioica*) or ground ivy (*Glechoma hederacea*). A mint liqueur can easily be made by macerating leaves of spearmint (*Mentha spicata*) or peppermint (*M.* x *piperita*) in vodka or grappa for a week, and adding sugar after straining. It is important to follow herbal recipes with alcohol exactly in order to achieve the right concentration, upon which the benefits and flavor depend.

MAKING HERB ICE CUBES

1 *Several different herbs can be used for flavor or appearance in ice cubes and added to drinks. They include borage, pineapple mint, and parsley, as shown here.*

2 *Put chopped herbs, or herb flowers like this borage, in ice-cube trays, adding about one tablespoon of water to each tablespoon of herb.*

CONTAINERS
Airtight ceramic jars like these are good containers for storing herbs in dry or liquid form. They prevent the potential deterioration caused by exposure to light.

Glossary of Terms

Botanical

Acid [of soil]. With a pH value of less than 7; see also *alkaline* and *neutral*.

Adventitious [of roots]. Arising directly from a stem or leaf.

Aerial root. See *root*.

Aggregate species. A group of closely related species or microspecies that are often regarded as a single species.

Air layering. A method of propagation by which a portion of stem is induced to root by enclosing it in a suitable medium while still attached to the parent plant (see *Cultivating Herbs*, pp.374–393).

Alkaline [of soil]. With a pH value of more than 7.

Alpine. A plant that is native or suited to montane conditions, or that grows above the tree line in mountainous regions; loosely applied to rock garden plants that may be grown at relatively low altitudes.

Alternate [of leaves]. Borne singly at each node, on either side of a stem.

Annual. A plant that completes its life cycle, from germination through to flowering and then death, in one year.

Anther. The part of a stamen that produces pollen; it is usually borne on a filament.

Apex. The tip or growing point of an organ such as a leaf or shoot.

Aquatic. A plant that grows in water.

Architectural. A term used in horticulture to describe plants that have strong, often spectacular shapes.

Aril. A fleshy or hairy, often brightly colored outgrowth of certain seeds, such as those of nutmeg (*Myristica fragrans*).

Awn. A stiff, bristlelike projection commonly found on grass seeds and spikelets.

Axil. The upper angle between a leaf and stem, between a main stem and a lateral branch, or between a stem and a bract.

Axillary. Growing in an axil.

Basal. Growing at the base.

Beaked. Having a beak-shaped part or projection.

Bedding plant. A plant that is usually planted in quantity to provide a temporary display.

Biennial. A plant that flowers and dies in the second season after germination, producing only stems, roots, and leaves in the first season.

Bipinnate. A pinnate leaf in which the leaflets are further subdivided pinnately.

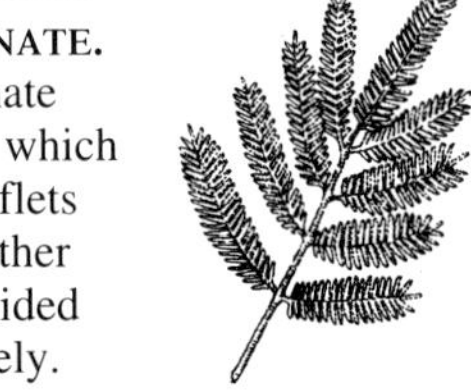

Bloom. 1. A flower or blossom. 2. A fine, waxy, whitish or bluish white coating on stems, leaves, or fruits.

Bole. The trunk of a tree from ground level to the first major branch.

Bolt. To produce flowers and seed prematurely.

Bract. A modified leaf at the base of a flower or flower cluster. Bracts may resemble normal leaves or be reduced and scalelike in appearance; they are often large and brightly colored.

Bud. A rudimentary or condensed shoot containing embryonic leaves and/or flowers.

Budding (bud grafting). A method of grafting in which a bud (the scion), together with a small piece of bark, is removed from the desired variety, and inserted into a slit made in the bark of the chosen rootstock (the stock).

Bulb. A storage organ consisting mainly of fleshy scales and swollen, modified leaf-bases on a much reduced stem. Bulbs usually, but not always, grow underground.

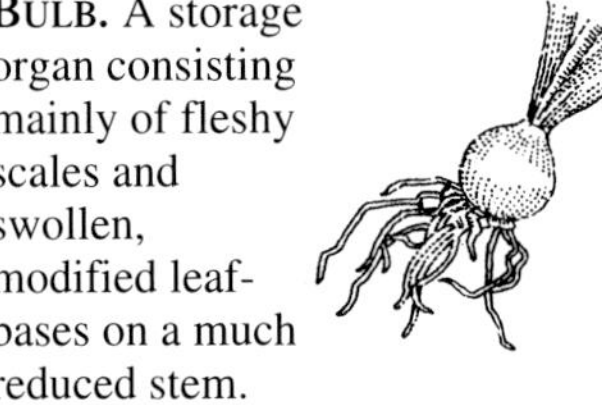

Bulbil. A small, bulblike organ, often borne in a leaf axil, occasionally in a flower head; it may be used for propagation.

Bulblet. A small bulb produced at the base of a mature one.

Bulbous. 1. Growing from or bearing bulbs. 2. Shaped like a bulb.

Bur. 1. A prickly or spiny fruit, or aggregate of fruits. 2. A woody outgrowth on the stems of certain trees.

Calcareous. Chalky.

Calyx (pl. calcyces). The outer part of a flower, usually small and green but sometimes showy and brightly colored, that is formed from the sepals and encloses the petals in bud.

Capsule. A dry fruit that splits open when ripe to release its seeds.

Catkin. A flower cluster, normally pendulous, in which the flowers lack petals, are often stalkless, and are surrounded by scalelike bracts. They are usually unisexual.

Chemotype. A population of plants within a species that differs consistently in certain chemical constituents.

Chicon. The blanched, compact shoots of chicory (*Cichoricum intybus*).

Chip-budding. A method of grafting (see *Cultivating Herbs*, pp.374–393).

Chlorophyll. The green pigment in plants that absorbs light, providing the energy for photosynthesis.

Cladode. A stem, often flattened, with the function and appearance of a leaf.

Climber. A plant that climbs using other plants or objects as a support: a leaf-stalk climber by coiling its leaf stalks around supports; a root climber by producing aerial, supporting roots; a self-clinging climber by means of suckering pads; a twining climber by coiling stems.

Cloud forest. A mountain forest that is constantly covered in mist, creating stunted trees and abundant epiphytes.

Compound. Made up of several or many parts, such as a leaf divided into two or more leaflets.

Cone. The reproductive or woody, seed-bearing structure of a conifer.

Coppice. To cut back to near ground level each year in order to produce vigorous shoots for ornamental or practical purposes.

Corm. A bulb-like, under-ground storage organ consisting mainly of a swollen stem base and often surrounded by a papery tunic.

Corolla. The often showy and colored part of a flower formed by the petals.

Corona (crown). A petal-like outgrowth borne on the corolla in some flowers.

Corymb. A racemose flower cluster in which the inner flower stalks are shorter than the outer, resulting in a rounded or flat-topped head.

Creeper. A plant that grows close to the ground, usually rooting as it spreads.

Crested. Shaped like a crest or ridge.

Crisped. Minutely wavy-edged.

Crop. A cultivated plant that is grown on a field scale.

Crown. 1. The part of the plant at or just below the soil surface from which new shoots are produced and to which they die back in autumn. 2. The upper, branched part of a tree above the trunk. 3. A corona.

Cultivar. A cultivated variety, usually produced by plant breeding, and not normally found in natural populations.

Cutting. A section of a plant which is removed and used for propagation (see *Cultivating Herbs*, pp.374–393).

Cyme. A flower cluster in which the first flower is the terminal bud of the main stem, and subsequent flowers develop as terminal buds of lateral stems.

Deadhead. To remove spent flower heads in order to promote further growth or flowering, prevent seeding or improve appearance.

Deciduous. Losing leaves annually at the end of the growing season; semideciduous plants lose only some leaves.

DEHISCENT. Splitting open along predetermined lines to release contents.

DELTOID–OVATE [of leaves]. Midway between triangular and egg-shaped.

DIEBACK. Death of the tips of shoots due, for example, to frost or disease.

DISC FLORET, disc flower. A small and often individually inconspicuous, usually tubular flower, one of many that make up the central portion of a composite flower head such as an English daisy (*Bellis perennis*).

DIVISION. Propagation by dividing a clump into several parts, often while dormant (see *Cultivating Herbs*, pp.374–393).

DORMANT. Alive but inactive.

ELLIPTIC [of leaves]. Broadening in the center and narrowing toward each end.

ENTIRE [of leaves]. With untoothed margins.

EPIPHYTE. A plant that in nature grows on the surface of another without being parasitic.

ERICACEOUS. 1. Plants of the family Ericaceae, which mostly require acid soils of pH6.5 or less. 2. Soil mix with a suitable pH for growing lime-hating plants.

ESCAPE. A non-native plant originally cultivated in an area but now found growing in the wild.

ESPALIER. A plant trained with the main stem vertical, and branches horizontally on either side in a single plane.

EVERGREEN. Retaining its leaves all year, although losing some older leaves regularly throughout the year. Semievergreen plants retain only some leaves or lose older leaves only when the new growth is produced.

F1 HYBRID. The first generation derived from crossing two distinct individuals of purebred lines. Offspring are vigorous, but seed from F1 hybrids does not come true to type.

FILAMENT. The stalk part of the stamen that bears the anther.

FLEXUOUS. Bending or curving readily.

FLORET. A single flower in a head of many flowers.

FLOWER. The basic reproductive unit of an angiosperm (flowering plant). The basic flower forms are: *single*, with one row of usually 4–6 petals; *semidouble*, with more petals, usually in two rows; *double*, with many petals in several rows and few or no stamens; *fully double*, usually rounded in shape, with densely packed petals and with the stamens obscured.

FLOWER HEAD. A mass of small flowers or florets that together appear as one flower.

FORCE. To induce artificially the early production of growth, flowers, or fruits.

FREE-FLOWERING. Flowering more easily or more generously than usual.

FROND. The compound leaf of a fern. Some ferns produce both barren and fertile fronds, the fertile fronds bearing spores.

FRUIT. The structure in plants that bears one or more seeds, such as a berry or nut.

GENUS. A group of related species, denoted by the first part of the scientific name, e.g. *Acacia*.

GLAND-DOTTED. Marked with small, round, secretory cells.

GLAUCOUS. Covered with a waxy or powdery bloom.

GLOBOSE. Spherical.

GRAFTING. A method of propagation by which an artificial union is made between different parts of individual plants (see *Cultivating Herbs*, pp.374–393).

HABIT. The characteristic growth or general appearance of a plant.

HALF-HARDY. Not tolerating frost, but withstanding temperatures down to 32°F (0°C).

HARDY. Normally withstands year-round climatic conditions in a given area without protection. Usually refers primarily to cold, but may also consider heat and humidity.

HEARTWOOD. The central core of wood in a tree trunk, consisting of nonfunctioning tissues that have become blocked with resins, tannins, gums, and oils.

HEEL. The small portion of old wood that is retained at the base of a cutting when it is removed from the stem.

HERBACEOUS. Dying down at the end of the growing season.

HIPS. The characteristic fruits of the genus *Rosa*. Also called rosehips.

HOLDFAST. A structure found at the base of many algae in flowing or tidal water, that serves to attach the plant to a support.

HOST. A plant or animal that supports and nourishes a parasite.

HUMUS. The soft, moist, dark brown to black content of soil, derived from decaying plant and animal matter.

HYBRID. The offspring of genetically different parents, usually produced accidentally or artificially in cultivation, but occasionally arising in the wild.

INFLORESCENCE. A cluster of flowers with a distinct arrangement, e.g. corymb, cyme, panicle, raceme, spike, umbel.

INTERTIDAL. The zone of the shore between high and low-water marks.

LANCEOLATE. Narrow and tapering at both ends.

LATERAL. A side growth that arises from a shoot or root.

LATEX. A fluid produced by many plants, containing substances such as starch, alkaloids, mineral salts, and sugars; often white in appearance.

LAX. Loose, or with loosely arranged parts.

LAYERING. Propagation method by which a stem pegged down into the soil will produce roots and shoots while still attached to the parent plant (see *Cultivating Herbs*, pp.374–393).

LEADER. The tip of the main stem of a plant.

LEAFLET. A subdivision of a compound leaf.

LEGUME. 1. A plant of the family Leguminosae, or of one of its three subfamilies, Caesalpiniaceae, Mimosaceae, and Papilionaceae. 2. A one-celled, dehiscent fruit, splitting into two when mature, produced by the family Leguminosae, as above.

LIANA. A woody climbing plant, found in tropical forests.

LICHEN. An organism formed by the symbiotic association of a fungus and an alga.

LIFT. To take out of the ground for transplanting or harvesting.

LIME. Compounds of calcium; the amount of lime in soil determines whether it is alkaline, neutral, or acid.

LINEAR [of leaves]. Very narrow with parallel sides.

LIP. A floral lobe consisting of two or more flat or sometimes pouched perianth segments. Prominent in flowers of the mint family (Menthaceae, or Labiatae) and the orchid family (Orchidaceae).

LITHOPHYTE. A plant that in nature grows on a rocky or stony substrate.

LOAM. Well-structured, fertile soil that is moisture-retentive but free-draining.

LOBE. A rounded projection, forming part of a larger structure.

MICROPROPAGATION. Propagation of plants by tissue culture.

MIDRIB. The main, central vein of a leaf, or the central stalk to which the leaflets of a pinnate leaf are attached.

MINERAL SALTS. Inorganic substances in plants, such as potassium, silicon, calcium, and selenium, that can supplement mineral shortages in the body.

MONOCARPIC. Flowering and fruiting only once before dying. Such plants may take several years to reach flowering size.

MONOTYPIC. A division that has only one subdivision, such as a family with just one genus, or a genus with a single species.

MONTANE. Inhabiting mountainous regions.

MOUND LAYERING. A method of propagation, suitable for small shrubs and subshrubs (see *Cultivating Herbs*, pp.374–393).

MULCH. A layer of organic matter applied to the soil over or around a plant to conserve moisture, protect the roots from frost, reduce the growth of weeds, and enrich the soil.

NATURALIZE. To establish and grow as if in the wild.

NECTAR. A sweet, sugary liquid secreted by the nectary glandular tissue, usually found in the flower, but sometimes on the leaves or stem.

NEEDLE. The linear, usually pointed, sometimes flattened leaf of a conifer, such as *Pinus*.

NEUTRAL [of soil]. With a pH value of 7, the point at which soil is neither acid nor alkaline.

NODE. The point on a stem from which a leaf or leaves arise.

NOTCH. A v-shaped indentation.

NUTLET. A one-seeded portion of a fruit that fragments when mature.

OBLANCEOLATE [of leaves]. Having a broad, rounded apex and a tapering base.

OBOVATE [of leaves]. Egg-shaped in outline, with the narrower end at the base.

OFFSET. A small plant that arises by natural vegetative reproduction, usually at the base of the mother plant.

OPPOSITE [of leaves]. Borne two to each node, one opposite the other.

ORNAMENTAL. A plant that has value or potential for decorative purposes.

OVARY. The swollen base of the female part of the flower. It is hollow, containing one or more ovules (embryonic seeds). After fertilization, the ovary wall forms the outer layer of the fruit.

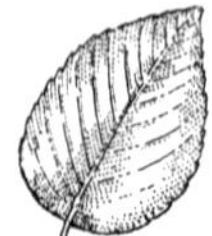

OVATE [of leaves]. Egg-shaped in outline, with the broader end at the base, becoming more pointed at the tip.

PALMATE [of leaves]. Having four or more leaflets arising from a single point, as in horse chestnut (*Aesculus hippocastanum*).

PANICLE. A compound, branched raceme in which the flowers develop on stalks (peduncles) arising from the main stem.

PANTROPICAL. Tropical regions in all parts of the world.

PARASITE. A plant that lives in or on another (the host), from which it obtains nourishment.

PEALIKE [of flowers]. Of the same structure as a pea flower.

PELTATE [of leaves]. Shield-shaped, with the stalk inserted toward or at the center of the blade and not at the margin.

PERENNIAL. Living for at least three seasons. In this book the term when used as a noun, and unless qualified, denotes a herbaceous perennial. A woody-based perennial dies down only partially, leaving a woody stem at the base.

PERFOLIATE [of leaves]. Having leaf bases that completely encircle the stem.

PETAL. One portion of the corolla.

pH. The scale by which the acidity of soil is measured. See also *acid*, *alkaline*, *neutral*.

PHOTOSYNTHESIS. The synthesis of carbohydrates in green plants from carbon dioxide and water, using light energy absorbed by chlorophyll.

PINCH OUT. To remove the growing tips of a plant to induce the production of sideshoots.

PINNATE [of leaves]. Describing a compound leaf in which the leaflets grow in two rows on each side of the midrib.

PISTIL. The female part of a flower, consisting of the ovary, stigma, and style.

PLUMULE. The embyonic shoot of a seed-bearing plant.

POLLINATION. The transfer of pollen from the anthers to the stigma of the same or different flowers, resulting in the fertilization of the embryonic seeds in the ovary.

PROSTRATE. With stems growing along the ground. Also called procumbent.

PSEUDOBULB. A swelling at the base of the stem in which epiphytic orchids store water and nutrients.

RACEME. An unbranched flower cluster with several or many stalked flowers borne singly along a main axis, the youngest at the apex.

RADICLE. The embryonic root, normally the first organ to emerge from a seed on germination.

RAY FLORET. One of the flowers, usually with strap-shaped petals, that together form the outer ring of flowers in a composite flower head, such as an English daisy (*Bellis perennis*).

RAY PETAL. The petal or fused petals, often showy, of a ray floret.

RECEPTACLE. The enlarged tip of the flower stalk that carries the parts of the flower.

RECURVED. Curved backward.

RESIN. A solid or semisolid compound, occuring with varying amounts of oil and/or gum, which is obtained directly as exudations from certain plants or trees.

RETTING. The process of soaking cut stems in order to promote bacterial action that helps separate fibrous tissues.

REVERT. To return to its original state, for example when a plain green leaf is produced on a variegated plant.

REVOLUTE. Rolled backward and downward at the margin.

RHIZOME. A branched, underground stem that gows horizontally and bears leafy shoots.

ROOT. The part of a plant, normally underground, that functions as anchorage, and through which water and nutrients are absorbed. An aerial root emerges from the stem at some distance above the soil level.

ROOTBALL. The roots and accompanying soil or soil mix visible when a plant is lifted.

ROOTSTOCK. A well-rooted plant onto which a scion is grafted: see *grafting*.

ROSETTE. A group of leaves radiating from approximately the same point, often at ground level at the base of a very short stem.

RUNNER. A horizontally spreading, usually slender stem that forms roots at each node; often confused with stolon.

SAPROPHYTIC. Lives and feeds on dead organic matter.

SCARIFY. To scar the coat of a seed by abrasion in order to speed water intake and hence germination.

SCLEROPHYLL. A woody plant with small, leathery, evergreen leaves, characteristic of hot, dry areas.

SCLEROTIUM. The compact, dormant phase of certain fungi, which gives rise to new growth or spore-producing structures.

SCREE. 1. An accumulation of rock fragments on a hillside. 2. A deep layer of stone chips mixed with a small amount of soil. It provides extremely fast drainage for plants that resent moisture at their base.

SEEDHEAD. Any usually dry fruit that contains ripe seeds.

SELF-SEED. To produce seedlings around the parent plant.

SELF-FERTILE. Producing viable seed when fertilized with its own pollen.

SEPAL. Part of a calyx, usually green. They can be insignificant but are sometimes showy.

SERIES. The name applied to a group of similar but not identical plants, usually annuals, linked by one or more common features.

SHEATH. A cylindrical structure that surrounds or encircles, partially or fully, another plant organ such as a stem.

SHOOT. The aerial part of a plant which bears leaves. A sideshoot arises from the side of a main shoot.

SHRUB. A plant with woody stems, usually well-branched from or near the base.

SHRUBLET. A miniature shrub.

SIMPLE [of leaves]. Not divided into leaflets.

SOILLESS MIX. A lightweight potting soil mix, based on peat or coir (coconut fiber). It often lacks nutrients.

SORI (sing. sorus). Clusters of spore-producing structures on the undersurface of fertile fern fronds.

SPADIX (pl. spadices). A spikelike flower cluster that is usually fleshy and bears numerous small flowers. Characteristic of the Aroid family (Araceae), such as *Arisaema*.

SPATHE. A large bract, frequently colored and showy, that surrounds a spadix (as in *Arisaema*).

SPHAGNUM. Mosses common to bogs; their moisture-retentive character makes them ideal components of some growing media.

SPECIES. Individuals that are alike and naturally breed with each other, denoted by the second part of the scientific name.

SPIKE. A racemose flower cluster with several or many unstalked flowers along a common axis.

SPIKELET. 1. The flowering unit of grasses consisting of one or several flowers with basal bracts. 2. A small spike, part of a branched flower cluster.

SPORE. The minute reproductive structure of flowerless plants, such as ferns and mosses.

SPORT. A mutation, caused by an accidental or induced change in the genetic makeup of a plant, which gives rise to a shoot with different characteristics from those of the parent plant.

SPUR. 1. A hollow projection from a petal, often producing nectar. 2. A short stem bearing a group of flower buds such as is found on fruit trees.

STAMEN. The anther and filament.

STANDARD. 1. A tree or shrub with a clear length of bare stem below the first branches. Certain shrubs, e.g. roses and bay, may be trained to form standards. 2. One of the three inner and often erect perianth segments of the iris flower. 3. The larger, usually upright back petal of a flower in the family Leguminosae, or in subfamilies Caesalpiniaceae, Mimosaceae, and Papilionaceae, e.g. *Abrus*.

STERILE. Infertile, not bearing spores, pollen, or seeds.

STIGMA. The part of the female portion of the flower, borne at the tip of the style, that receives pollen.

STOCK. See rootstock.

STOLON. A horizontally spreading or arching stem, usually above ground, which roots at its tip to produce a new plant.

STOP. To remove certain growing points of a plant to control growth or the size and number of flowers. See *pinch out*.

STOVE. An obsolete word for a warm greenhouse.

Strap-shaped [of leaves]. Long and narrow.

Stratify. To break the dormancy of some seeds by exposing them to a period of cold.

Strobilus or strobile (pl. strobili or strobiles). A cone or conelike structure.

Style. The stem-like part of the flower on which the stigma is borne.

Subalpine. Growing below the treeline in mountainous regions.

Subshrub. A small, bushy plant that is woody except for the herbaceous tips to the branches.

Succulent. A plant with fleshy, water-storing leaves or stems, adapted to growing where water is either in short supply or saline.

Sucker. A shoot that arises from below ground level, directly from the root or rootstock.

Taproot. The main, downward-growing root of a plant; also generally applied to any similar, downward-growing root.

Tender. Vulnerable to low temperatures. Tender plants are often categorized: cool-growing, withstanding a minimum temperature of 50°F (10°C); intermediate, 55°F (13°C); or warm-growing, 64°F (18°C).

Tendril. A threadlike structure, often used by climbing plants to provide support.

Tepal. A subdivision of the perianth in flowers that have no distinct calyx and corolla, as in *Crocus*.

Terminal. At the tip of a stem or branch.

Throat. The inner portion of a tubular or bell-shaped flower.

Tilth. The fine, crumbly nature of soil produced by cultivation.

Tip layering. A method of propagation for shrubs and climbers (see *Cultivating Herbs*, pp.374–393).

Tissue culture. The growth of small pieces of plant tissue under sterile conditions in artificial media.

Tooth. A small, marginal, often pointed part on a leaf, calyx, or corolla.

Topiary. The trimming or training of trees or shrubs into decorative shapes, often geometric or resembling animals or birds.

Transpiration. Loss of water by evaporation from a plant surface.

Trifoliate. With three leaves; loosely, with three leaflets.

Trifoliolate. With three leaflets.

Trilobed. With three lobes.

Trim. To prune lightly by clipping.

True [of seedings]. Retaining the distinctive characteristics of the parent when raised from seed.

Tuber. A thickened, usually underground, storage organ derived from a stem or root.

Umbel. A usually flat-topped or rounded flower cluster in which the individual flower stalks arise from a central point. In a compound umbel, each primary stalk ends in an umbel. Characteristic of the Umbelliferae, or carrot family.

Understory. A lower tier of shrubs and small trees.

Upright [of habit]. With vertical or semivertical main branches.

Valve. A section of dry, dehiscent fruit, especially of a capsule.

Variegated. Marked with patches or streaks of different-colored tissues.

Vegetative propagation. Any method of reproduction in plants, other than by seed.

Vermiculite. A lightweight, micalike mineral which is added to soil mixes to improve moisture retention and aeration.

Weeping. With slender branches that hang down.

Whip-and-tongue. A method of grafting (see *Cultivating Herbs*, pp.374–393).

Whorl. The arrangement of three or more organs arising from the same point, characteristic of the family Rubiaceae.

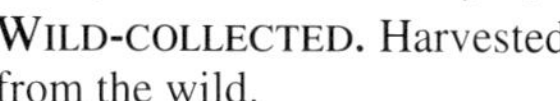

Wild-collected. Harvested from the wild.

Winged [of seeds or fruits]. Having a marginal flange or membrane.

Woody-stemmed. With a stem composed of woody fibers and therefore persistent, as opposed to soft-stemmed and herbaceous. A semiwoody stem contains some softer tissue.

x. The sign used to denote a hybrid plant derived from the crossing of two or more genetically distinct plants.

Medical

Abortifacient. Causes abortion.

Acrid. Unpleasantly pungent or caustic.

Adaptogenic. Improving resistance to stress.

Adrenal cortex. Part of the adrenal gland that produces corticosteroid hormones.

Adrenaline. A hormone secreted by the inner tissue of the endocrine glands, which prepares the body for "flight or fight" in response to stress.

Adrenocortical. Relating to the adrenal cortex.

Allergen. Any substance that produces an allergic reaction.

Alexipharmic. Acting as an antidote.

Alkaloid. A nitrogen-containing compound, produced by plants, that has a potent effect on body function.

Alterative. Increases vitality, mainly through improving the breakdown and excretion of waste products.

Amino acids. The basic structure units of proteins.

Amebic dysentery. Inflammation of the intestines caused by a parasitic ameba.

Anesthetic. Causes local or general loss of sensation.

Analgesic. Relieves pain.

Anethole. A volatile oil with an aniseed odor, extracted mainly from *Pimpinella anisum* and *Illicium verum*, which has carminative and mildly expectorant effects.

Anodyne. Soothes pain.

Antibacterial. Destroys or inhibits the growth of bacteria.

Anthelmintic. Another word for vermifuge.

Antibiotic. Destroys or inhibits the growth of microorganisms.

Anticoagulant. Prevents or slows clotting of the blood.

Anti-inflammatory. Reduces inflammation.

Antioxidant. Prevents or slows the deterioration of cells by oxidation.

Antipyretic. Relieves fever.

Antirheumatic. Mitigates the symptoms of rheumatism.

Antiseptic. Prevents or controls infection.

Antispasmodic. Reduces spasm or tension, especially of involuntary muscle.

Aperient. A mild laxative.

Aphrodisiac. Promotes sexual excitement.

Astringent. Precipitates proteins from the surfaces of cells, causing contraction of tissues; forms a protective coating, and reduces bleeding and discharges.

Bacillus. Any rod-shaped bacterium.

Bactericidal. Destroys bacteria.

Balsam. An aromatic oleoresin obtained from various woody plants, and used as a base for medicines, perfume, and ritual ointments.

Beta-carotene. The most important form of carotene, the orange-yellow plant pigment, which is converted in the body to vitamin A.

Bile. A thick, bitter fluid secreted by the liver and stored in the gall bladder; aids digestion of fats.

Bitter. Stimulates secretion of digestive juices, improving appetite.

Bittersweet. A flavor that combines bitter-tasting and sweet.

Blood coagulant. A substance that aids blood clotting.

Blood clotting. The process in which blood protein is changed by an enzyme from a liquid to a solid, in order to arrest bleeding.

Blood sugar. The concentration of glucose in the blood.

BORNEOL. A volatile oil with a camphoraceous aroma, extracted mainly from *Dryobalanops aromatica*, which is used in perfumery and which has expectorant and rubefacient effects.

BORNEOL ACETATE. A volatile, fragrant liquid made from borneol, used in perfumery.

BRONCHIAL. Relating to the air passages in the lungs.

CAMPHORACEOUS. Having a camphorlike aroma.

CAPILLARY PERMEABILITY. The exchange of oxygen, carbon dioxide, water, and salts between blood in the capillaries (fine blood vessels) and the tissues.

CARCINOGENIC. Causes cancer.

CARDIAC FIBRILLATION. Rapid and irregular beating of heart muscles.

CARDIOVASCULAR SYSTEM. The heart and blood vessels that circulate blood around the body, transporting oxygen and nutrients to the tissues, and removing waste products.

CARMINATIVE. Relieves flatulence, colic, and digestive discomfort.

CARVACROL. A volatile oil, found in various herbs (notably in *Thymus* species), which stimulates secretions from mucous membranes.

CARVONE. A volatile oil with a caraway aroma and carminative effects, found mainly in *Carum carvi*.

CAUSTIC. Capable of burning or corroding through chemical action.

CHOLESTEROL. A fatlike material, present in the blood and in most tissues, which is an important constituent of cell membranes, steroid hormones, and bile salts.

CINEOLE. A volatile oil with a camphoraceous aroma, extracted mainly from *Eucalyptus* species and *Melaleuca leucadendron*, which has rubefacient and antiseptic effects. Also known as eucalyptol.

CIRCULATORY STIMULANT. Dilates the blood vessels and increases blood flow.

CITRONELLAL. A volatile oil with a lemon aroma, extracted mainly from *Cymbopogon nardus*, which is used in flavorings, perfumery, and insect repellents.

CITRONELLOL. A volatile oil with a roselike aroma, extracted mainly from *Pelargonium* species, and used in perfumery and cosmetics.

CLEANSING HERB. A herb that improves excretion of waste products from the body.

COLONIC IRRIGATION. Washing out the contents of the large bowel by introducing copious amounts of water, often with soap or herb extracts, high into the colon.

COOLING. A remedy, often based on bitter or relaxant herbs, that reduces internal "heat" or physiological hyperactivity, mainly by clearing toxins.

COUMARIN. A vanilla-scented plant constituent, used in perfumes and flavorings, and in remedies to encourage blood clotting.

COUNTERIRRITANT. Causes superficial irritation of the skin, increasing blood flow to the area, speeding removal of toxins, and thereby relieving inflammation of deeper tissues.

CUCURBITACINS. Toxic compounds, found especially in pumpkin seeds and *Bryonia dioica*, which have anthelmintic and anti-tumor effects.

DECONGESTANT. Relieves congestion (especially nasal).

DEMULCENT. Soothes and softens damaged, irritated, or inflamed tissues (especially of the digestive tract).

DEPRESSANT. Reduces nervous or functional activity.

DEPURATIVE. Promotes the elimination of waste products from the body.

DETOXICANT. Removes poisons (especially waste products) from the body.

DIAPHORETIC. Causes sweating, thus eliminating toxins and lowering fever.

DIOSPHENOL. A volatile oil, common in *Agathosma* spp., which has diuretic effects.

DIURETIC. Increases volume of urine.

EDEMA. Excessive accumulation of fluid in the tissues.

EMETIC. Causes vomiting.

EMOLLIENT. Softens or soothes the skin.

ENZYME. A complex protein, produced by cells, that acts as a catalyst, speeding biological reactions without itself being used up in the reaction.

EPIGASTRIC. Relating to the epigastrium (upper central region of the abdomen, above the navel and below the breast).

ESSENTIAL OIL. A volatile oil or oils extracted from a plant, having the characteristic aroma or flavor of the plant.

ESTROGENIC. Similar in effects to the hormone estrogen, which plays an important role in the development and functioning of female sexual organs.

EUGENOL. A volatile oil with of female sexual organs.a clove aroma, which has carminative and local anesthetic effects; extracted mainly from *Syzygium aromaticum*.

EUPHORIC. Causing an increased sense of well-being.

EXCITANT. Causing stimulation.

EXPECTORANT. Encourages the expulsion of phlegm from the respiratory tract.

FEBRIFUGE. Reduces fever.

FIXATIVE. A substance added to a perfume to make it less volatile and longer-lasting.

FLAVONOIDS. Glycosides found widely in flowers, fruits and leaves, which improve the circulation and have diuretic, anti-spasmodic and anti-inflammatory effects.

FUMAROCOUMARIN. A type of coumarin, found widely in plants, that has antispasmodic effects, but may cause photosensitivity.

FUNGAL. Caused by a fungus.

FUNGICIDE. A substance that destroys fungi.

GALACTOGOGUE. Increases milk flow.

GAMMA-LINOLENIC ACID (GLA). An unsaturated fatty acid, essential for growth and repair of cells, and for production of hormone like substances. It is normally produced in the body, but in cases of deficit may be supplemented by the GLA component in oils of various plants.

GENITOURINARY. Relating to both the reproductive and excretory systems.

GERMICIDAL. Destroys germs.

GLYCOSIDE. A constituent of certain plants, such as digitoxin in *Digitalis* species, containing a sugar part or glycone, and a non-sugar part or aglycone.

GYNECOLOGICAL. Relating to the branch of medicine that concerns diseases affecting the female reproductive system.

HEMORRHAGE. Bleeding.

HEMOSTATIC. Stops bleeding.

HORMONE. A chemical substance produced in the endocrine glands and transported in the blood to a certain tissue on which it exerts a specific effect.

HYPERACIDITY. Excess acidity of the digestive tract (especially of the stomach), producing a burning sensation.

HYPERTENSION. High blood pressure.

HYPOGLYCEMIA. A deficiency of sugar in the blood, causing muscular weakness, mental confusion, and sweating.

HYPOTENSION. Low blood pressure.

HYSTERIA. A disorder characterized by emotional outbursts and instability.

IMMUNE SYSTEM. The body's defense mechanisms against infectious organisms and other foreign materials, such as allergens.

INDOLENT. Slow to heal (usually applied to painless ulcers of the skin or mucous membranes).

INSECTICIDAL. Destroys insects.

LACTATION. Secretion of milk by the mammary glands, which usually begins at the end of pregnancy.

LARVICIDAL. Destroys larvae (immature forms) of certain animals.

LAXATIVE. Encourages bowel movements.

LICHEN ACIDS. Bitter constituents of lichens, which have antibiotic effects.

LINALOL/LINALOOL. A fragrant liquid, found in many volatile oils, which has antiseptic effects, and is also used in perfumery.

LIPIDS. Fatlike substances, such as cholesterol, which are important structural materials in the body, and present in most tissues (especially the blood).

LUBRICANT. Reduces friction.

LYMPHATIC DRAINAGE. The return of lymph (fluid containg white blood cells) from the tissues of the body to the bloodstream via the lymphatic vessels.

MENTHOL. A volatile oil with a peppermint aroma, extracted mainly from *Mentha* species, which has antiseptic, carminative, and decongestant effects and a mild local anesthetic action.

MENSTRUATION. The "period" in the menstrual cycle, occurring at approximately monthly intervals, in which the lining of the womb breaks down and is discharged as blood and debris.

METABOLISM. The total chemical processes that occur in the body, resulting in growth, production of energy, elimination of wastes, etc.

MUCILAGE. A complex, sticky carbohydrate, secreted by certain plants, such as comfrey (*Symphytum officinale*).

NARCOTIC. A drug that causes stupor and insensibility, and relieves pain; in legal terms, usually applied to an addictive drug which is subject to illegal use.

NASOPHARYNGEAL. Relating to the part of the pharynx that lies above and behind the soft palate.

Nematocidal. Destroys nematodes (unsegmented worms, some of which are disease-causing parasites, such as hookworm).

Nerve tonic. A remedy that supports the proper functioning of the nervous system. Also called nervine.

Nutritive. A herb that also provides nourishment as a food.

Oat germ. The vitamin-rich embryo of the oat kernel.

Officinal. A plant with pharmacological properties, available in medicinal form; origin of specific name of many herbs, such as *Salvia officinalis*.

Ovarian. Relating to the ovary, the main female reproductive organ that produces ova and secretes estrogen hormones.

Paroxysmal. Convulsive.

Pathogen. A microorganism that causes disease.

Peripheral. Near the surface of the body.

Peristalsis. Waves of involuntary muscle contraction in the digestive tract, that push the contents along.

Phlegm. Thick mucus, secreted by the walls of the respiratory tract.

Photosensitivity. Sensitivity to light.

Photodermatitis. A condition in which the skin becomes sensitized to a certain substance that, when exposed to sunlight, causes dermatitis.

Pigmentation. Coloration responsible for normal skin color, produced in the body by pigments, such as melanin.

Pimento oil. Essential oil extracted from allspice (*Pimenta dioica*), which has carminative and antioxidant effects.

Piperitone. A constituent of the volatile oil of peppermint (*Mentha* x *piperita*).

Porphyrins. Pigments found widely in living things, which are constituents of blood and of chlorophyll, in animals and plants respectively.

Postpartum. Following childbirth.

Potassium salts. A form of potassium given to maintain potassium levels in the body, which have been depleted through excessive fluid loss (e.g. through diarrhea, burns, or use of diuretics).

Productive coughing. Resulting in expulsion of phlegm.

Protein. A compound which forms the main structural material of muscles, tissues, and organs, synthesized in the body from amino acids.

Pulegone. A volatile oil with a pennyroyal aroma, found mainly in *Mentha pulegium*, which has abortifacient and insect repellent effects.

Pungent. Having an acrid smell or strong, bitter flavor.

Purgative. A strong laxative.

Pyrrolizidine alkaloids. A group of alkaloids, found in herbs such as comfrey (*Symphytum officinale*), borage (*Borago officinalis*), and coltsfoot (*Tussilago farfara*), which in excess are associated with liver damage.

Rejuvenative. Restores vitality.

Relaxant. Relaxes tense, overactive tissues.

Restorative. Revives health or strength.

Rubefacient. Causes reddening of the skin, thus increasing blood flow and cleansing the tissues of toxins.

Safrole. A volatile oil, extracted mainly from *Sassafras albidum*, and widely used in flavorings and toiletries; restricted as a possible cause of cancer and liver damage.

Saline. Containing common salt.

Salivation. Secretion of saliva by the salivary glands in the mouth.

Saponins. A group of soaplike glycosides, found widely in plants, that have complex effects in herbal remedies; some resemble steroidal hormones.

Secretion. A substance released from a cell (especially a glandular cell), which is synthesized in the cell from constituents of the blood or tissue fluids.

Sedative. Reduces anxiety and tension.

Serum. 1. The fluid that separates from clotted blood or blood plasma when it is allowed to stand. 2. Antitoxin obtained from the blood serum of immunized animals.

Simple. A herb used as a remedy on its own.

Soporific. Inducing drowsiness or sleep.

Spermicidal. Destroys spermatozoa.

Staphylococci. Bacteria of the genus *Staphylococcus* that cause boils, infection in wounds, and septicemia.

Steroids. Compounds containing a characteristic chemical ring structure, notably the sex hormones, hormones of the adrenal cortex, and vitamin D.

Sterol. A waxy, steroid alcohol, such as cholesterol.

Stimulant. Increases physiological activity.

Synthesis. The process of producing a compound by chemical reaction from simpler materials.

Therapeutic. Beneficial to health.

Thixotropic. A gel that becomes less viscous when stirred.

Thrombotic. Forming a clot of coagulated blood in blood vessel or in the heart, that remains at the site of formation, impeding blood flow.

Thujone. A volatile oil, found mainly in *Salvia officinalis* and *Artemisia absinthium*, which has carminative and antiseptic effects.

Thymol. A constituent of the volatile oil of certain herbs, notably of thymes (*Thymus* species), which has antiseptic, fungicidal, and vermifugal effects.

Thyroid. Relating to the thyroid gland, near the base of the neck, which controls metabolism and growth.

Tone. To strengthen or restore, such as the muscles.

Tonic. Improves physiological functions and sense of well-being.

Topical. Applied to the body surface.

Toxic. Harmful or poisonous.

Toxicity. The degree of strength of a toxic substance.

Toxin. A poisonous substance.

Tranquilizing. Calming, without affecting clarity of consciousness.

Tropho-restorative. Nutritious and strengthening.

Uterus. Womb.

Vasoconstrictor. Causes narrowing of the walls of blood vessels.

Venereal. Relating to diseases transmitted by sexual intercourse.

Vermifuge. Destroys or expels intestinal worms.

Viral. Caused by a virus.

Virus. A disease-causing organism, capable of replication only within the cells of an animal or plant.

Volatile oils. Complex, aromatic plant constituents that may be extracted to produce essential oils, such as oil of geranium (from *Pelargonium* species), or as isolated constituents, such as linalol.

Warming. A remedy, often based on spicy, pungent herbs, that dispels internal "coldness" or hypoactivity, and increases vitality, mainly by stimulating the digestion and circulation.

Yin and yang. The two complementary principles of Chinese philosophy, whose interaction maintains the harmony of the universe, and influences all qualities and activity. *Yin* is the female energy: dark, negative, damp, cold, descending, and interior. *Yang* is the male aspect: bright, positive, dry, hot, ascending, and exterior.

INDEX

Page numbers in *italics* indicate illlustrations. Page numbers in **bold** indicate main plant entry in Dictionary section.

A

Aaron's rod see *Verbascum thapsus*
Abata cola 264
Abele see *Populus alba*
Abelmoschus
moschatus 70, **226**
'Mischief' *70*, **226**
Abies
alba 70, 226, **226**
balsamea 70, **226**, 334
'Hudsonia' *70*
pectinata see *A. alba*
Abrus precatorius 66, *70*, **226**
Abscess root see *Polemonium reptans*
Absinthe, small see *Artemisia pontica*
Acacia
ancistrocarpa 227
bivenosa subsp. *wayi* 227
catechu 71, 226, **227**, 337
farnesiana 71, 226, **227**
holosericea 227
monticola 227
senegal 60, 61, **227**
spp. 66
tetragonophylla 227
trachycarpa 227
Acajou see *Anacardium occidentale*
Account of Two Voyages to New England made during the years 1638-1663 13
Acetaria, a Discourse on Sallets 233, 268, 353
Achillea
millefolium 18, *71*, **227**, 238, 281, 297, 301, 317, 347, 361
'Cerise Queen' *71*, **227**
'Lavender Beauty' see *A. m.* 'Lilac Beauty'
'Lilac Beauty' *71*, **227**
Achiote see *Bixa orellana*
Achyranthes
aspera 227
bidentata 72, **227-8**
acids 11
Acinos
arvensis 32, *72*, **228**, 375, 381, 386
thymoides see *A. arvensis*
Aconite see *Aconitum napellus*
Sichuan see *Aconitum carmichaelii*
aconitine 228
Aconitum 386
carmichaelii 72, **228**
'Arendsii' *72*, **228**
ferox 228
fischeri see *A. carmichaelii*
napellus 15, 33, *33*, 57, *72*, **228**
'Carneum' *73*, **228**
spp. 43, 117, 379
Acorus
calamus 73, 227, **228**, 249, 275,298, 309, 369, 378, 379
'Oborozuki' see *A. gramineus* 'Ogon'
'Variegatus' 30, *73*, **228**
gramineus 73, **228**, 379, 381
'Ogon' *73*, 188, **228**
'Pusillus' *73*, **228**
'Variegatus' 30
actinidine 317
Adam in Eden 19
Adenophora 388
liliifolia 229
stricta 74, **229**
trachilioidis 229
Adhatoda vasica see *Justicia adhatoda*
adhatodic acid 299
adianton 229
Adiantum **229**
aethiopicum 229
capillus-veneris 74, **229**, 389
pedatum 229
Adonis 386
vernalis 74, **229**
Adrue see *Cyperus articulatus*
Aegopodium
podagraria 74, **229**, 359, 384
'Variegatum' 33, *74*, **229**
Aeollanthus
gamwelliae **229-30**
graveolens see *A. gamwelliae*
heliotropioides 229
lamborayi 229
myrianthus 229
pubescens 229
Aeschylus 344
aescin 230
Aesculus 385
hippocastanum 57, *75*, **230**, 291
'Baumannii' *75*, **230**
'Flore Pleno' see *A. h* 'Baumannii'
Africa, herbs in wild 58-9
African cherry see *Prunus africana*
African lotus see *Ziziphus lotus*
African marigold see *Tagetes erecta*
African serpentwood see *Rauvolfia vomitoria*
Afromomum
angustifolium 230
melegueta **230**
Agar-agar see *Gelidium amansii*
Agastache
anethiodora see *A. foeniculum*
foeniculum 26, 27, *75*, **230**, 379
'Alabaster' 35, *75*, **230**
rugosa 75, **230**
Agathosma
betulina 230
crenulata 75, **230-1**, 316, 322, 370
serratifolia see *A. crenulata*
spp. 59, 239, 241, 266, 277, 278
Agave
americana 32, 55, *76*, **231**
'Variegata' *76*, **231**, 381
sisalana 231
Aglaia
argentea 231
edulis 231
odorata 76, **231**
Agnus castus see *Vitex agnus-castus*
Agrimonia
cernuum 307
clavatum 154, **307**
eupatoria 76, 227, **231**, 249, 264,288, 291, 300, 307, 333, 344, 372-3
pilosa 231
Agrimony see *Agrimonia*
hemp see *Eupatorium cannabinum*
water see *Bidens tripartita*
Agropyron repens see *Elymus repens*
ai ye (*Artemisia vulgaris*) 244
Ailanthus
altissima 76, **231**
glandulosa see *A. altissima*
spp. 175
vilmoriniana 76
Ailanto see *Ailanthus altissima*
air layering 388
air-drying 392, *392*
ajmaline 339
Ajowan see *Trachyspermum ammi*
Ajuga
australis 231
chamaepitys 77, **232**
iva 231
remota 231
reptans 77, 231, **232**, 379
'Atropurpurea' 33, *77*, **232**, 374
'Burgundy Glow' *77*, **232**
'Purpurea' see *A. r.* 'Atropurpurea'
'Variegata' *77*, **232**
Ajwain see *Trachyspermum ammi*
Akebia
quinata 232
trifoliata 78, **232**
Albizia
julibrissin 78, **232**
'Rosea' 78
odoratissima 232
Alcea
rosea 78, **232**
'Chater's Double' *78*, **232**
'Nigra' *78*, **232**
Alchemilla
alpina 79, **232**
mollis 33, 232
spp. 57, 393
vulgaris see *A. xanthochlora*
xanthochlora 79, **232**
Alder see *Alnus*
black see *Alnus glutinosa*; *Ilex verticillata*
common see *Alnus glutinosa*
European see *Alnus glutinosa*
hazel see *Alnus serrulata*
speckled see *Alnus rugosa*
Alder buckthorn see *Rhamnus frangula*
Alderleaf buckthorn see *Rhamnus alnifolia*
Alecost see *Tanacetum balsamita*
Alehoof see *Glechoma hederacea*
Aleppo pine see *Pinus halepensis*
Aletris farinosa 53, **232-3**
Alexanders see *Smyrnium olusatrum*
Alexandrian senna see *Senna alexandrina*
Alfalfa see *Medicago sativa*
algae 10
alginic acid 349
Alisma
plantago-aquatica 79, **233**
var. *orientale* 233
alizarin 343
alkaloids 11
Alkanet see *Alkanna*
Alkanna tinctoria 79, **233**
allantoin 355, 357, 372
Alliaria
officinalis see *A. petiolata*
petiolata 79, **233**
Allium **233-5**
ampeloprasum
var. *ampeloprasum 80*, **234**, 235
var. *kurrat* 233-4
ascalonicum see *A. cepa* Aggregatum group
cepa 61, *80*, 233, **234**, 235, *375*,382
Aggregatum group 233
'Ailsa Craig' *80*, **234**
Cepa group 233
'Noordhollandse Bloedrode' *80*, **234**
var. *proliferum* 22, *80*, **234**
Proliferum group 233
'Sweet Sandwich' *80*, **234**
chinense 233
controversum see *A. sativum*
fistulosum 80, *80*, 233, **234**, 235
'White Lisbon' *80*, **234**
porrum 'Musselburgh' 38
sativum 11, 44-5, 61, *80*, 233, **234**, 235, 382, 387
schoenoprasum 22, *23*, 29, 36, 38, *40*, *80*, 233, **234**, 235, 378, 379, 382, *382*, 385, 392
'Forescate' 30, *80*, **234**
scorodoprasum 81, **234**
sibiricum see *A. schoenoprasum*
tricoccum 38, **234**, 235
tuberosum 34, 36, *81*, 233, **234**,235
ursinum 81, **234**, 235
Allspice see *Pimenta dioica*
allyl isothiocyanate 250
Almond see *Prunus dulcis*
Alnus
glutinosa 81, **235**, 389
'Imperialis' *81*, **235**
rotundifolia see *A. glutinosa*
rubra 235
rugosa 235
serrulata 235
Aloe 59
barbadensis see *Aloe vera*
ferox 235
perryi 60, 61, *61*, 235
vera 41, 49, 59, *81*, **235**, 253, 375
Aloewood see *Aquilaria malaccensis*
Aloysia triphylla 27, 41, *82*, **235**, 374, 375, 381
Alpine lady's mantle see *Alchemilla alpina*
Alpine lovage see *Ligusticum*
Alpinia
galanga 82, **235**, 299
officinarum 235, **236**
Alston, Charles 82
Alstonia
boonei 236
constricta 236
scholaris 82, **236**
Althaea
officinalis 11, 230, 232, 239, 241, 257, 260, 283, 285, 288, 299, 308, 356, 366, 393
rosea see *Alcea rosea*
aluka (*Dioscorea*) 273
Alumroot see *Geranium maculatum*; *Heuchera americana*
Amalaki see *Phyllanthus emblica*
Amaranth
green see *Amaranthus retroflexus*
two-toothed see *Achyranthes bidentata*
wild see *Amaranthus spinosus*
Amaranthus
hybridus subsp. *hypochondriacus* see *A. hypochondriacus*
hypochondriacus 82, **236**
polygamus 236
retroflexus 236
spinosus 236
amarogentin 56, 357
Ambal see *Phyllanthus emblica*
amber 329
ambergris 262
Ambrette see *Abelmoschus moschatus*
American angelica see *Angelica atropurpurea*
American arborvitae see *Thuja occidentalis*
American aspen see *Populus tremuloides*
American blackberry see *Rubus villosus*
American bugbane see *Cimicifuga americana*
American cranesbill see *Geranium maculatum*
American ginseng see *Panax quinquefolius*
American ground pine see *Lycopodium complanatum*
American holly see *Ilex opaca*
American ipecac see *Gillenia trifoliata*
American larch see *Larix laricina*
American licorice see *Glycyrrhiza lepidota*
American mandrake see *Podophyllum peltatum*
American mint see *Mentha arvensis* var. *villosa*
American pennyroyal see *Hedeoma pulegioides*
American Physitian 19
American red osier see *Cornus sericea*
American sanicle see *Heuchera americana*
American spikenard see *Aralia racemosa*
American storax see *Liquidambar styraciflua*
American valerian see *Cypripedium parviflorum* var. *pubescens*
American wild lettuce see *Lactuca canadensis*
Ammi
copticum see *Trachyspermum ammi*
majus 61, *82*, **236**, 237
visnaga 17, *83*, **236-7**
Ammoniac see *Dorema ammoniacum*
Amomum xanthioides **237**
Amur cork tree see *Phellodendron amurense*
amygdalin 335
Amyris balsamifera 348
an xi xiang (*Styrax benzoin*) 357
Anacardium occidentale 55, *83*, **237**
Anacyclus
pyrethrum 83, **237**
var. *depressus* 83
Anagallis
arvensis 83, **237**

var. *caerulea* *83*, **237**
Ananas spp. 170
Andrographis paniculata 63, 357
Anemarrhena asphodeloides **237-8**
Anemone
hepatica see *Hepatica nobilis*
pulsatilla see *Pulsatilla vulgaris*
Anemone, Chinese see *Pulsatilla chinensis*
anethole 283, 315, 328
Anethum
graveolens 29, 30, 36, 61, *83*, **238**, 284, 378, 382, 385, 386
'Bouquet' **238**
'Fernleaf' **238**
'Mammoth' *84*, **238**
subsp. *sowa* **238**
sowa see *A. graveolens* subsp. *sowa*
Angelica
anomala 238
archangelica 22, *84*, **238**, *374*, 377, 379, 384, *384*, 386
atropurpurea 238
glauca 238
keiskei 238
polymorpha var. *sinensis* 64, *84*, **238**, 246, 271, 333, 340, 346, 373
pubescens 238
sinensis see *A. polymorpha* var. *sinensis*
sylvestris 238
Angelica tree, Chinese see *Aralia chinensis*
angiosperms 10
Angostura see *Galipea officinalis*
Angular Solomon's seal see *Polygonatum odoratum*
Aniba roseaodora **239**, 251
anisdamine 350
Anise see *Pimpinella anisum*
star see *Illicium verum*
Anise hyssop see *Agastache foeniculum*
Anise tree see *Illicium*
Aniseed see *Pimpinella anisum*
Anisillo see *Tagetes lucida*
anisodine 350
Annatto see *Bixa*
Antennaria
dioica *84*, **239**
'Rosea' *85*, **239**
Anthemis nobilis see *Chamaemelum nobile*
anthocyanosides 367
Anthony, St. 12
Anthoxanthum
drogeanum 85
odoratum *85*, **239**
anthraquinones 11, 340, 341, 344
Anthriscus cerefolium 38, *85*, **239**, 378, 385, 386
Aphanes arvensis *85*, **239-40**, 265, 294, 299, 322, 373, 374
aphids 383
apigenin 323, 325
Apium graveolens *85*, **240**, 312, 322, 323, 345, 361
Apocynum
androsaemifolium 240
cannabinum *85*, **240**
Apothecary's rose see *Rosa gallica* var. *officinalis*
Apple
custard see *Asimina triloba*
devil's see *Datura stramonium*
May see *Podophyllum peltatum*
thorn see *Datura*
Apple geranium see *Pelargonium odoratissimum*
Apple-bearing sage see *Salvia pomifera*
Applemint see *Mentha suaveolens*
Apricot
Japanese see *Prunus mume*
wild see *Prunus armeniaca*
Apuleius 266
Aqua Sambuci 347
Aquilaria
agallocha see *A. malaccensis*
crassna 240
malaccensis 62, 67, *86*, **240**
sinensis 240
Aquilegia, Music Series 35, *35*
Arabian coffee see *Coffea arabica*
Arabian jasmine see *Jasminum sambac*
Aralia
chinensis 240
hispida 240
nudicaulis *86*, **240**
racemosa *86*, **240**, 244
spinosa 240
Arborvitae see *Thuja*
American see *Thuja occidentalis*
Chinese see *Thuja orientalis*
arbutin 241, 300, 367
Arbutus, trailing see *Epigaea repens*
Archangel see *Lamium album*
Arctium
lappa *86*, 222, **240-1**, 247, 277, 354, 367
'Gobo' 240
Arctostaphylos uva-ursi 56, 260, 278, 294, 300, 302, 322, 372, 381
Areca catechu *86*, **241**, 330
Arisaema
amurense 241
atrorubens 241
consanguineum *87*, **241**
heterophyllum 241
stewardsonii 241
Aristolochia **241-2**
bracteata 242
clematitis *87*, **242**
debilis **242**
indica 242
longa 242
reticulata 242
rotunda 242
serpentaria **242**
Aristotle 19
Armoracia
lapathifolia see *A. rusticana*
rusticana *87*, 222, **242**
'Variegata' *87*, **242**
Arnica montana 56, 57, *87*, **242-3**
Arnold Arboretum, Boston 65
Arrow-wood, Indian see *Euonymus atropurpureus*
Arrowroot, Japanese see *Pueraria lobata*
Arsenic, vegetable see *Colchicum autumnale*
Art of Simpling 19, 233, 243,337
Artabotrys hexapetalus 253
Artemisia 13, **243-4**, 388
abrotanum 26, 27, *88*, **243**, 345, 379
absinthium 57, *88*, **243**, 244, 359
'Lambrook Silver' 32, *88*, **243**, 244
afra 59, 230, 243
annua 65, *88*, **243**, 244, 261
anomala 243
arborescens *88*, **243**, 244
assoana see *A. caucasica*
capillaris *88*, **243**, 244
caucasica *88*, **243**
cina 243
dracunculus 29, *88*, **243**, 244, 359, 382
subsp. *dracunculoides* *89*, **243**,244
var. *sativa* *88*, **243**, 244
lactiflora *89*, **243**, 244, 379
Guizhou Group *89*, **244**
ludoviciana *89*, **244**
'Silver Queen' *32*, *89*, **244**
pallens 243
pedemontana see *A. caucasica*
pontica 22, *23*, *34*, 35, *89*, **244**
'Powis Castle' 35, *35*, *88*, **244**
schmidtiana 'Nana' 36
spp. 374
tilesii 243
vulgaris *89*, **244**
'Variegata' *89*, **244**
Artesunate 243
Artichoke, globe see *Cynara cardunculus*, Scolymus Group
Arugula see *Eruca vesicaria* subsp. *sativa*
asa dulcis (*Styrax benzoin*) 357
Asafoetida see *Ferula assa-foetida*
Asarabacca see *Asarum europaeum*
asarone 228
Asarum
canadense *89*, 240, 242, **244**
caudatum 244
europaeum 244
sieboldii 244
Asclepias tuberosa *89*, **244**, 281, 297
Ash see *Fraxinus*
bitter see *Picrasma excelsa*
common see *Fraxinus excelsior*
manna see *Fraxinus ornus*
northern see *Fraxinus bungeana*
northern prickly see *Zanthoxylum americanum*
prickly see *Zanthoxylum*
southern prickly see *Zanthoxylum clavaherculis*
wafer see *Ptelea trifoliata*
winged prickly see *Zanthoxylum planispinum*
Ash pumpkin see *Benincasa cerifera*
Ashanti pepper see *Piper guineense*
ashtavarga 333
Ashwagandha see *Withania somnifera*
Asia, southeast, herbs in wild 67
Asian plantain see *Plantago asiatica*
Asimina triloba see *Carica* 255
Aspalathus
contaminatus see *A. linearis*
linearis *58*, *89*, **244**
asparagine 326
Asparagus
cochinchinensis **245**
lucidus see *A. cochinchinensis*
officinalis 38, *39*, *90*, **245**
racemosus *90*, 238, **245**, 342
Asparagus, Chinese see *Asparagus cochinchinensis*
asparagusic acid 245
Aspen, American see *Populus tremuloides*
Asperula odorata see *Galium odoratum*
asperuloside 285
asphonin 237
Aspidium filix-mas see *Dryopteris filix-mas*
Aspidosperma quebracho-blanco **245**
aspirin 17, 283
Assyrians 18, 46
Aster tataricus **245**
Asthma weed see *Euphorbia hirta*; *Lobelia inflata*
Astragalus
complanatus 245
gummifer 61, **245-6**, 257, 313
membranaceus *90*, **246**, 307
Atlas cedar see *Cedrus libani* subsp. *atlantica*
Atlas of Commonly Used Chinese Traditional Drugs 19
Atractylodes
chinensis 246
macrocephala 64, *90*, **246**, 264, 271, 372
Atriplex
halimus 246
hortensis *90*, **246**
'Rubra' 38, *90*, **246**
nummularia 66, 246
patula 246
Atropa 350
belladonna 15, 43, 57, *91*, **246**, 272, 276, 295, 308, 327, 350
atropine 246, 276, 327
attar of roses 342
Attila the Hun 329
aucubin 331, 350
Augustus Caesar, Emperor 355
Australasia, herbs in wild 66
Australian Aborigines 66, 245, 309, 335
Australian pennyroyal see *Mentha satureioides*
Australian peppermint see *Eucalyptus dives*
Australian quinine see *Alstonia constricta*
Australian sandalwood see *Santalum spicatum*
autumn clearance 385
Autumn crocus see *Colchicum autumnale*
Avena sativa 61, *91*, **246-7**, 271, 343, 365, 368
Avens see *Geum*
wood see *Geum urbanum*
Avicenna 19, 342
Avignon berry see *Rhamnus infectoria*
awas empas (*Kaempferia galanga*: *Zingiber* spp.) 299
Awl tree see *Morinda citrifolia*
Ayurvedic medicine 18, 46, 62
Azadirachta indica *91*, **247**
Azores thyme see *Thymus caespititius*
Aztec marigold see *Tagetes erecta*
Aztecs 13, 361, 367, 372
azulene 227
Azure monkshood see *Aconitum carmichaelii*

B

ba dou (*Croton tiglium*) 269
ba ji (*Morinda citrifolia*; *M. officinalis*) 313
ba jiao hui xiang (*Illicium verum*) 296
Babchi see *Psoralea corylifolia*
Bacchus 136
Bachelor's buttons see *Centaurea cyanus*
Badian see *Illicium verum*
bai bu (*Stemona tuberosa*) 356
bai dou kou (*Elettaria cardamomum*) 277
bai guo (*Ginkgo biloba*) 288
bai hua zhe she cao (*Oldenlandia diffusa*) 319
bai jie zi (*Sinapis alba*) 353
bai qu cai (*Chelidonium majus*) 259
bai shao (*Paeonia lactiflora*) 321
bai shao yao (*Paeonia lactiflora*) 321
bai xian pi (*Dictamnus albus*) 273
bai zhu (*Atractylodes macrocephala*) 246
bai zi ren (*Thuja orientalis*) 362
Baikal skullcap see *Scutellaria baicalensis*
balconies, growing herbs on 380-1
Balder (Norse god) 15, 370
Balloon flower see *Platycodon grandiflorus*
Ballota
nigra *91*, **247**, 260, 312
'Archer's Variety' *91*, **247**
'Variegata' see *B. n.* 'Archer's Variety'
Balm see *Melissa officinalis*
bee see *Monarda didyma*
Canary see *Cedronella canariensis*
of Gilead see *Abies balsamea*; *Balsamodendron opobalsamum*; *Cedronella canariensis*; *Commiphora gileadensis*; *Populus* x *candicans*
horse see *Collinsonia canadensis*
lemon see *Melissa officinalis*
mountain see *Eriodictyon californicum*
Balmony see *Chelone glabra*
Indian see *Swertia chirata*
balsam
Canada 226
Balsam of Peru see *Myroxylon pereirae*
tolu see *Myroxylon balsamum*
wild see *Eriodictyon californicum*
Balsam fir see *Abies balsamea*
Balsam pear see *Momordica charantia*
Balsam poplar see *Populus balsamifera*
Balsamita major see *Tanacetum balsamita*
Bálsamo see *Myroxylon*
Balsamodendron opobalsamum 256
Bamboo, black see *Phyllostachys nigra*
Bamenda cola 264
ban bian lian (*Lobelia chinensis*) 305
ban lang gen (*Isatis tinctoria*) 297
ban xia (*Pinellia ternata*) 329
Banckes's Herbal 19
Banks, Sir Joseph 258
Baptisia
australis 247
leucantha 247

leucophaea 247
tinctoria 92, **247**, 265, 277, 386
Barbados aloe see *Aloe vera*
Barbed skullcap see *Scutellaria barbata*
Barberry see *Berberis*
common see *Berberis vulgaris*
bark 43, 391
Barley see *Hordeum*
six-rowed see *Hordeum polystichum*
two-rowed see *Hordeum distichum*
Barosma
betulina see *Agathosma betulina*
crenulata see *Agathosma crenulata*
barosma camphor 230
Barrenwort see *Epimedium sagittatum*
Bartolomaeus Anglicus 19
Basil see *Ocimum*
camphor see *Ocimum kilimandscharicum*
East Indian see *Ocimum gratissimum*
hoary see *Ocimum americanum*
holy see *Ocimum sanctum*
sacred see *Ocimum sanctum*
sweet see *Ocimum basilicum*
tree see *Ocimum gratissimum*
wild see *Pycnanthemum virginianum*
Basil thyme see *Acinos arvensis*
Basswood see *Tilia americana*
Bastard cardamom see *Amomium xanthioides*
Bastard myrobalan see *Terminalia belerica*
Bastard teak see *Pterocarpus marsupium*
Bay see *Laurus nobilis*
golden see *Laurus nobilis* 'Aurea'
sweet see *Laurus nobilis*; *Magnolia virginiana*
willow-leaf see *Laurus nobilis* 'Angustifolia'
Bay rum 301, 328
Bay willow see *Salix pentandra*
Bayberry see *Myrica cerifera*; *M. pensylvanica*
Bayberry tree see *Pimenta acris*
bdellium 265
Bead tree see *Melia azederach*
Bean
black see *Castanospermum australe*
bog see *Menyanthes*
Calabar see *Physostigma venenosum*
coral see *Sophora secundiflora*
esere see *Physostigma venenosum*
mescal see *Sophora secundiflora*
ordeal see *Physostigma venenosum*
St. Ignatius' see *Strychnos ignatii*
tonka see *Dipteryx odorata*
tonquin see *Dipteryx odorata*
velvet see *Mucuna*
Bearberry see *Arctostaphylos uva-ursi*
Beaver tree see *Magnolia virginiana*
Bechterew's Mixture 229
beds
cartwheel *377*
island 29, *29*
Mediterranean 32, *32*
raised 25, *25*
Bedstraw
lady's see *Galium verum*
yellow see *Galium verum*
Bee balm see *Monarda didyma*
Beech see *Fagus*
copper see *Fagus sylvatica*, Purpurea (Purple) Group
cut-leaved see *Fagus sylvatica*, Heterophylla Group
Dawyck see *Fagus sylvatica* 'Dawyck'
European see *Fagus sylvatica*
fern-leaved see *Fagus sylvatica*, Heterophylla Group
Beefsteak plant see *Perilla frutescens* 'Atropurpurea'
Beggar's buttons see *Arctium lappa*
Beggar's weed see *Clematis vitalba*
Begonia
semperflorens
'Cocktail' 36
'Excel Mixed' *36*
bei mu (*Fritillaria cirrhosa*; *F. pallidiflora*) 284
Belamcanda chinensis 92, **247**
Beleric myrobalan see *Terminalia belerica*
Bell pepper see *Capsicum annuum* var. *annuum*
Belladonna, Japanese see *Scopolia carniolica*
Bellflower
bonnet see *Codonopsis*
Chinese see *Platycodon grandiflorus*
gland see *Adenophora*
Bellis
perennis 92, **247-8**
'Alba Plena' *92*, **248**
'Pomponette' *92*, **248**
'Prolifera' *92*, **248**
Ben see *Moringa oleifera*
Ben Jing Ji Zhu 233
Benedict, St. 12
Bengal kino see *Butea frondosa*
Benincasa
cerifera see *B. hispida*
hispida *93*, **248**
Benjamin see *Lindera benzoin*
Benne see *Sesamum indicum*
benzaldehyde 335
benzoic acid 315
benzoin 305
Siam see *Styrax tonkinensis*
berberine 248, 266, 295, 308, 326
Berberis
aristata 63, 248
asiatica 63, 248
vulgaris *93*, **248**, 257, 266, 270, 281, 295, 298, 308, 326, 360, 369
Bergamot see *Monarda didyma*
lemon see *Monarda citriodora*
wild see *Monarda fistulosa*
Bergamot orange see *Citrus bergamia*
bergapten 262, 292
berries 391
beta carotene 272
Beta vulgaris, Cichla Group 38
beta-damascenone 342
Betel see *Piper betle*
Betel palm see *Areca catechu*
Bethroot see *Trillium erectum*
Betonica officinale see *Stachys officinalis*
Betony see *Stachys officinalis*
Betula 385, 386
alba see *Betula pendula*
alleghaniensis 248
lenta 248
nigra 248
pendula *93*, **248-9**
'Dalecarlica' see *B. p.* 'Laciniata'
'Laciniata' *93*, **249**
'Tristis' *93*, **249**
'Youngii' *93*, **249**
pubescens 248, 249
spp. 52
verrucosa see *Betula pendula*
Bhang see *Cannabis*
Bhringaraja see *Eclipta prostrata*
bi ba (*Piper longum*) 330
Bibhitaki see *Terminalia belerica*
Bible 216, 316, 345, 346
Bidens
atrosanguinea see *Cosmos atrosanguineus*
bipinnata 249
ferulifolia 94
tripartita *94*, **249**, 288, 365
Bilberry see *Vaccinium myrtillus*
Bindweed see *Calystegia sepium*
bing lang (*Areca catechu*) 241
biological pest control 383
Biota orientalis see *Thuja orientalis*
Birch see *Betula*
black see *Betula lenta*
cherry see *Betula lenta*
cutleaf see *Betula pendula* 'Laciniata'
downy see *Betula pubescens*
red see *Betula nigra*
silver see *Betula pendula*
white see *Betula pubescens*
Young's weeping see *Betula pendula* 'Youngii'
Bird pepper see *Capsicum annuum* var. *glabriusculum*
Birthroot see *Trillium erectum*
Birthwort see *Aristolochia*
frail see *Aristolochia debilis*
Bishopsweed see *Ammi majus*
Bishopweed see *Aegopodium podagraria*
Bishopwort see *Aegopodium podagraria*
Bistort see *Polygonum bistorta*
Bitter aloes 235
Bitter ash see *Picrasma excelsa*
Bitter cress see *Cardamine*
Bitter ginger see *Zingiber zerumbet*
Bitter gourd see *Momordica charantia*
Bitter orange see *Citrus aurantium*
Japanese see *Poncirus trifoliata*
bitters 11, 285
Bittersweet see *Solanum dulcamara*
Bixa orellana 55, *55*, *94*, **249**
Black alder see *Alnus glutinosa*; *Ilex verticillata*
Black bamboo see *Phyllostachys nigra*
Black bean see *Castanospermum australe*
Black birch see *Betula lenta*
Black caraway see *Pimpinella saxifraga* var. *nigra*
Black cardamom see *Alpinia oxyphylla*
Black catechu see *Acacia catechu*
Black chebulic see *Terminalia chebula*
Black cherry see *Prunus serotina*
Black cohosh see *Cimicifuga racemosa*
Black cumin see *Nigella sativa*
Black figwort see *Scophularia ningpoensis*
Black haw see *Viburnum prunifolium*
Black horehound see *Ballota nigra*
Black Indian hemp see *Apocynum cannabinum*
Black knapweed see *Centaurea nigra*
Black lovage see *Smyrnium olusatrum*
Black mustard see *Brassica nigra*
Black pepper see *Piper nigrum*
Black poplar see *Populus nigra*
Black psyllium see *Plantago indica*
Black raspberry see *Rubus occidentalis*
Black sassafras see *Cinnamomum oliveri*
Black snakeroot see *Cimicifuga racemosa*
Black willow see *Salix nigra*
Black-tang see *Fucus vesiculosus*
Blackberry see *Rubus fruticosus*
American see *Rubus villosus*
creeping see *Rubus procumbens*
Blackberry lily see *Belamcanda chinensis*
Blackcurrant see *Ribes nigrum*
Blackroot see *Veronicastrum*
Bladder cherry see *Physalis alkekengi*
Bladderwrack see *Fucus vesiculosus*
Blazing star see *Liatris*
Bleeding nose plant see *Pulsatilla patens*
Blessed thistle see *Cnicus benedictus*; *Silybum marianum*
Blet, Don Louis 94
Bletia hyacinthina see *Bletilla striata*
Bletilla striata *94*, 231, **249**
Blond psyllium see *Plantago ovata*
Bloodroot see *Potentilla erecta*; *Sanguinaria*
Blue cedar see *Cedrus libani* subsp. *atlantica*, Glauca Group
Blue cohosh see *Caulophyllum thalictroides*
Blue flag see *Iris versicolor*
Blue giant hyssop see *Agastache foeniculum*
Blue gum see *Eucalyptus globulus*
Blue mallow see *Malva sylvestris*
Blue pimpernel see *Anagallis arvensis* var. *caerulea*
Blue sage see *Salvia clevelandii*
Blue vervain see *Verbena hastata*
Bluebeard see *Salvia viridis*
Blueberry
highbush see *Vaccinium corymbosum*
rabbit-eye see *Vaccinium ashei*
Bluebottle see *Centaurea cyanus*
Blumea balsamifera 261
bo he (*Mentha arvensis*) 311
body-painting 49
Bog bean see *Menyanthes*
Bog moss see *Sphagnum cymbilifolium*
Bog myrtle see *Myrica gale*
bogs, herbs for 379
bois de rose 239
Bola see *Commiphora myrrha*
Boldo see *Peumus boldus*
Bollan bane see *Artemisia vulgaris*
bolting 385, 386
Bombax pentandra see *Ceiba pentandra*
Boneset see *Eupatorium perfoliatum*
Bonnet bellflower see *Codonopsis*
Bonpland, Aimé 206
Book of Changes (*I Ching*) 227
books, herbal 18-19
Borage see *Borago*
Indian see *Plectranthus amboinicus*
Borago
officinalis 22, *22*, 29, 30, *31*, 36, 57, *94*, **249-50**, 318, 374, 386, 391
'Alba' *94*, **250**
pygmaea 94
spp. 378
borders
formal 28, *28*
mixed 36, *36*, 374
white, with herbs 34-5, *34-5*
Borneo camphor see *Dryobalanops aromatica*
Borneol see *Dryobalanops aromatica*
borneol 237, 275
borneol acetate 316
Bosisto, Joseph 280
Boswellia
carteri see *B. sacra*
sacra 14, *43*, 60, 61, *61*, *95*, **250**
botanic gardens 13
Botanic Guide to Health 19
Botanologia. The English Herbal or History of Plants 19
Botrytis (gray mold) 382, *383*, 386
Bottlebrush see *Equisetum arvense*
Bouncing Bet see *Saponaria officinalis*
Bourbon oil 323
Bowles' mint see *Mentha* x *villosa* var. *alopecuroides*
Bowman's root see *Gillenia trifoliata*
Box holly see *Ruscus aculeatus*
Boxthorn see *Lycium*
Chinese see *Lycium barbarum*
Boxwood see *Buxus*
common see *Buxus sempervirens*
edging see *Buxus sempervirens* 'Suffruticosa'
mountain see *Arctostaphylos uva-ursi*
running see *Mitchella repens*
silver see *Buxus sempervirens* 'Elegantissima'
Bracket fungus, lacquered see *Ganoderma lucidum*
Brahmi see *Centella asiatica*

Bramble see *Rubus*
Japanese see *Rubus parviflorus*
Branched lavender see *Lavandula multifida*
Brassica
alba see *Sinapis alba*
hirta see *Sinapis alba*
juncea 61, *63*, *95*, 233, **250**, 254, 346
nigra 63, *95*, 233, **250**, 254, 346, 353
oleracea 'Red Drumhead' 38, *38*
rapus 203
Brazil medicine stall *46*
Brazilian cocoa see *Paullinia cupana*
Brazilian ginseng see *Pfaffia paniculata*
Bread-and-cheese see *Crataegus laevigata*
Breakstone parsley see *Aphanes arvensis*
Brekhman, I. I. 122
Brigham tea see *Ephedra trifurca*
Bringing Home the May 15
Brisbane pennyroyal see *Mentha satureioides*
British Pharmacopoeia 340, 342
Broad-leaved dock see *Rumex obtusifolius*
Broad-leaved linden see *Tilia platyphyllos*
Broad-leaved peppermint see *Eucalyptus dives*
Broad-leaved thyme see *Thymus pulegioides*
"Brompton cocktail" 279-80
Bronze elder see *Sambucus nigra* 'Guincho Purple'
Bronze fennel see *Foeniculum vulgare* 'Purpureum'
Broom see *Cytisus*; *Genista*
butcher's see *Ruscus aculeatus*
Scotch see *Cytisus scoparius*
Brown chiretta see *Swertia chirata*
Brown mustard see *Brassica juncea*
Browne, Patrick 314
Brucea
antidysenterica 95
javanica *95*, **250**
sumatrana 95
Brunella see *Prunella*
Brunfels, Otto 95
Brunfelsia 250-1
chiricaspi 251
grandiflora 251
hopeana see *B. uniflora*
uniflora *95*, **251**
Bryonia
alba 251
cretica subsp. *dioica* see *B. dioica*
dioica *95*, **251**
Bryony see *Bryonia dioica*
bryophytes 10
bu gu zhi (*Psoralea corylifolia*) 337
Buchu see *Agathosma*
Buckbean see *Menyanthes trifoliata*
Buckeye see *Aesculus*
Buckler fern see *Dryopteris*
Buckler-leaf sorrel see *Rumex scutatus*
Buckthorn see *Rhamnus catharticus*
alder see *Rhamnus frangula*
alderleaf see *Rhamnus alnifolia*
Buckwheat see *Fagopyrum esculentum*
Buddhism, sacred plants 14
budding 389
Buffalo gourd see *Cucurbita foetidissima*
Bugbane see *Cimicifuga*
American see *Cimicifuga americana*
cohosh see *Cimicifuga racemosa*
fetid see *Cimicifuga foetida*
Bugle see *Ajuga*
Bugleweed see *Lycopus*
Virginia see *Lycopus virginicus*
Bugloss see *Alkanna tinctoria*
bulb fennel see *Foeniculum vulgare* var. *azoricum*
bulbs 43, 391
Bullwort see *Ammi majus*
Bulnesia
arborea 290
sarmienti 290
Bupleurum
chinense see *B. falcatum*
falcatum *96*, **251**
scorzoneraefolium see *B. falcatum*
Bur marigold see *Bidens*
trifid see *Bidens tripartita*
Burdock see *Arctium lappa*
Burnet, great see *Sanguisorba officinalis*
Burnet saxifrage see *Pimpinella saxifraga*
greater see *Pimpinella major*
Burning bush see *Dictamnus albus*; *Euonymus atropurpureus*
Bursera
aloexylon see *B. glabrifolia*
delpechiana 251
glabrifolia **251**
klugii 251
morelensis 251
penicillata 251
simarda 251
simarouba 251
spinosa 251
Burweed see *Xanthium*
Bush cherry, oriental see *Prunus japonica*
bushfires *66*
Butcher's broom see *Ruscus aculeatus*
Butea frondosa 337
Butter-and eggs see *Linaria vulgaris*
Buttercup see *Ranunculus*
Butterfly weed see *Asclepias tuberosa*
Butternut see *Juglans cinerea*
Button snakeroot see *Eryngium aquaticum*; *Liatris spicata*
Buxus 13, 388
sempervirens *96*, **251**, 365, 378, 379, 381, *381*, 385
cvs 381
'Elegantissima' 28, *96*, **251**
'Japonica Aurea' see *B. s.* 'Latifolia Maculata'
'Kingsville Dwarf' *96*, **251**, 381
'Latifolia Maculata' *96*, **251**
'Suffruticosa' 24, *96*, 198, **251**, 381
buying herbs 378-9

C

Cabbage, skunk see *Symplocarpus foetidus*
Cacao see *Theobroma cacao*
cachou 226
cactine 351
caffeine 264, 296, 361
Cajuput see *Melaleuca leucadendron*
cajuput oil 309, 310
Calabar bean see *Physostigma venenosum*
calabarine 327
Calamint see *Calamintha*
common see *Calamintha officinalis*
lesser see *Calamintha nepeta*
Calamintha
acinos see *Acinos arvensis*
ascendens see *C. sylvatica*
grandiflora 97
'Variegata' 97
nepeta 22, *97*, **252**
subsp. *nepeta* *97*, **252**
nepetoides see *C. nepeta*
officinalis see *C. sylvatica*
sylvatica *97*, **252**
calamus, oil of 228
calcium 309, 316, 352
calcium oxalate 241, 339
Calendula
officinalis 22, 25, *26*, 27, 30, 38, 41, 47, 49, 57, *97*, **252**, 291, 295, 339, 359, 374, 377, 379, 384, 386, 391
'Prolifera' *97*, **252**
Calico bush see *Kalmia latifolia*
California laurel see *Umbellularia californica*
California poppy see *Eschscholzia californica*
California sassafras see *Umbellularia californica*
Callistemon 157
Calluna
vulgaris *98*, **252**
'Alba Plena' *98*, **252**
'Darkness' *98*, **252**
'Multicolor' *98*, **252**
'Silver Queen' *98*, **252**
Calumba see *Jateorhiza palmata*
Calumba wood see *Coscinium fenestratum*
Calystegia sepium 359
Camellia sinensis *99*, 244, **252**, 296
Camphire see *Lawsonia*
Camphor see *Cinnamomum camphora*
Borneo see *Dryobalanops aromatica*
Ngai see *Blumea balsamifera*
camphor 318
barosma 230
Camphor basil see *Ocimum kilimandscharicum*
Camphor plant see *Tanacetum balsamita* var. *tomentosum*
Camphor tree see *Cinnamomum*
camphorated oil 261, 262
Canada balsam 226
Canada goldenrod see *Solidago canadensis*
Canadian fleabane see *Conyza canadensis*
Canadian hemp see *Apocynum cannabinum*
Canadian yew see *Taxus canadensis*
Cananga odorata *48*, 67, *67*, *99*, **253**
Canangium odoratum see *Cananga odorata*
Canary balm see *Cedronella canariensis*
Canary Island laurel see *Laurus azorica*
Canby's lovage see *Ligusticum canbyi*
canchalagua 257
Candleberry see *Myrica cerifera*
Canella
alba see *C. winterana*
winterana 59, *99*, **253**, 275
Canfield, Dr. 290
cang er zi (*Xanthium strumarium*) 372
Canker root see *Coptis groenlandica*
Cannabis
sativa 15, 61, *99*, 221, **253**, 336
subsp. *indica* **253**
subsp. *sativa* **253**
Canon of Medicine 19
Cape aloe see *Aloe ferox*
Cape gooseberry see *Physalis peruviana*
Cape jasmine see *Gardenia augusta*
Cape Town, public gardens 13
Caper bush see *Capparis*
Caper spurge see *Euphorbia lathyrus*
Capparis
brevispina 253
decidua 253
spinosa *99*, **253**
var. *inermis* 253
zeylanica 253
capric acid 365
capsaicin 44, 254
Capsella bursa-pastoris 56, *99*, **254**
Capsicum
annuum 44, 281, 348, 372
var. *annuum* 50, **254**, 314, 387
'Anaheim' *100*, **254**
'Chili Serrano *100*, **254**
'Hungarian Wax' *100*, **254**
'Jalapeño' *100*, **254**
'Purple Tiger' *100*, **254**
'Super Cayenne' *100*, **254**
var. *glabriusculum* **254**
var. *minimum* see *C. a.* var. *glabriusculum*
baccatum *100*, **254**
var. *pendulum* **254**
chinense **254**
'Habañero' *100*, **254**
frutescens *100*, 247, **254**
'Tabasco' *100*, **254**
microcarpum see *C. baccatum*
minimum see *C. frutescens*
pendulum see *C. baccatum* var. *pendulum*
pubescens **254**
sinense see *C. chinense*
spp. *19*, 54, 55, 330, 383
Cara-cara see *Aniba roseaodora*
Caraway see *Carum carvi*
black see *Pimpinella saxifraga* var. *nigra*
Caraway thyme see *Thymus herba-barona*
Carbenia benedicta see *Cnicus benedictus*
carbon dioxide 382
Cardamine 254-5, 388
pratensis *101*, **255**, 379
'Flore Pleno' *101*, **255**
Cardamom see *Elettaria cardamomum*
bastard see *Amomum xanthioides*
black see *Alpinia oxyphylla*
Madagascar see *Afromomum angustifolium*
Tavoy see *Amomum xanthioides*
cardiac alkaloids 67
cardiac glycosides 11, 57, 356
Cardoon see *Cynara cardunculus*
Carduus
benedictus see *Cnicus benedictus*
marianus see *Silybum marianum*
Carica papaya 54, 55, *55*, *101*, **255**, 387
Carlina acaulis *101*, **255**
Carline thistle see *Carlina*
Carnation see *Dianthus caryophyllus*
Carolina jessamine see *Gelsemium sempervirens*
carotene 272, 309
Carragheen see *Chondrus crispus*
carragheenans 260
Carrizo see *Phragmites australis*
Carrot see *Daucus*
edible see *Daucus carota* subsp. *sativus*
wild see *Daucus carota*
Carthamus tinctorius 61, *101*, **255**, 303, 342
cartwheel bed *377*
Carum
carvi 61, *101*, 114, **255**, 270, 386
copticum see *Trachyspermum ammi*
petroselinum see *Petroselinum crispum*
carvacrol 319, 349, 350, 362
carvone 238, 255, 311
Caryophyllus sinensis see *Dianthus chinensis*
Cascade Range *52*
Cascara sagrada see *Rhamnus purshiana*
Cascarilla see *Croton eleuteria*
Cashew see *Anacardium occidentale*
Cassia
angustifolia see *Senna alexandrina*
marilandica see *Senna marilandica*
senna see *Senna alexandrina*
cassia 260, 261
Indian see *Cinnamomum tamala*
Indonesian see *Cinnamomum burmanii*
Cassia bark see *Cinnamomum cassia*
Cassie see *Acacia farnesiana*
cassie absolute 226
Cassumar ginger see *Zingiber cassumar*
Castanea
sativa *102*, **256**
'Albomarginata' *102*, **256**
'Marron de Lyon' 256
'Paragon' 256
castanospermine 256
Castanospermum australe *102*, 247, **256**
Castor bean see *Ricinus*
Cattail see *Typha latifolia*
Catal Huyuk 254

Catawissa onion see *Allium cepa* var. *proliferum*
catechu 226, 227
caterpillars 383
Catha edulis 61, 278
Catharanthus
  roseus 11, 17, 43, 58, 59, *102*, **256**, 369
    var. *alba* 102
    var. *ocellatus* 102
    Pacifica Series *102*, **256**
cathine 278
Catmint see *Nepeta cataria*; *N.* x *faassenii*
Catnip see *Nepeta cataria*
  Japanese see *Schizonepeta tenuiifolia*
Cat's ear see *Antennaria dioica*
Catsfoot see *Antennaria*
Caulophyllum thalictroides 103, **256**, 367
Cayenne jasmine see *Catharanthus roseus*
ce bai ye (*Thuja orientalis*) 362
Ceanothus
  americanus 53, *103*, **256**
  integerrimus 256
  sanguineus 256
Ceara jaborandi see *Pilocarpus trachylophus*
Cedar see *Cedrus*
  Atlas see *Cedrus libani* subsp. *atlantica*
  blue see *Cedrus libani* subsp. *atlantica*, Glauca Group
  Eastern white see *Thuja occidentalis*
  red see *Juniperus virginiana*
Cedron see *Simaba cedron*
Cedronella
  canariensis 103, **256-7**, 334, 375
  japonica see *Agastache foeniculum*
Cedrus
  libani 60, *61*
    subsp. *atlantica 103*, **257**
    Glauca Group *103*, **257**
  spp. 61
Ceiba pentandra 104, **257**
Celandine see *Chelidonium*
  greater see *Chelidonium majus*
  lesser see *Ranunculus ficaria*
Celery, wild see *Apium graveolens*
Cempazuchil see *Tagetes erecta*
Centaurea
  cyanus 30, *104*, **257**, 386
    Florence Series *104*, **257**
  montana 257
  nigra 257
  scabiosa 257
Centaurium
  chilensis 257
  erythraea 104, **257**
Centaury see *Centaurium*
Centella asiatica 63, *104*, **257-8**, 277
Central America, herbs in wild 54-5
Centranthus ruber 217
Century plant see *Agave americana*
Cephaelis ipecacuanha 54-5, *104*, 247, **258**, 265, 288, 292, 309
Cereus, night-blooming see *Selenicereus grandiflorus*
Cetraria islandica 105, **258**
Ceylon cinnamon see *Cinnamomum zeylanicum*
Chaenomeles 13
  speciosa 105, **258**, 388
chai hu (*Bupleurum falcatum*) 251
Chaldeans 18
Chamaelirium luteum 243, **258-9**, 369
Chamaemelum
  nobile 12, 47, 49, 57, *105*, 227, 238, 257, **259**, 278, 283, 288, 294, 295, 309, 310, 323, 347, 348, 376, 377, 384
    'Flore Pleno' 22, 41, *105*, **259**, 309
    'Treneague' 30, *30*, *105*, **259**, 376
Chamomile see *Chamaemelum*
  double see *Chamaemelum nobile* 'Flore Pleno'
  German see *Matricaria recutita*
  lawn see *Chamaemelum nobile* 'Treneague'
  Roman see *Chamaemelum nobile*
Chamomilla recutita see *Matricaria recutita*
Chaparral see *Larrea divaricata*
Charaka Samhita 17
Charas see *Cannabis*
Charity see *Polemonium caeruleum*
Charlemagne 128, 152, 351
Charles V, Holy Roman Emperor 361
Charles V, King of Spain 13
Chaste tree see *Vitex agnus-castus*
  Chinese see *Vitex negundo* var. *heterophylla*
Chauca, Dr. 100
Chaulmoogra see *Hydnocarpus kurzii*
che qian cao (*Plantago asiatica*) 331
che qian zi (*Plantago asiatica*) 331
Chebulic, black see *Terminalia chebula*
Checkerberry see *Gaultheria procumbens*
Cheese rennet see *Galium verum*
chelerythrine 372
Chelidonium
  majus 106, 162, **259**, 348
    'Flore Pleno' *106*, **259**
    'Laciniatum Flore Pleno' *106*, **259**
Chelone glabra 106, **259**, 264, 309, 334, 360
Chelsea Physic Garden 21
chemistry 10-11
Chen Cang-Zi 267
chen pi (*Citrus reticulata*) 263, 329
Chenopodium
  album 106
  ambrosioides 55, *106*, **259-60**
    var. *anthelminticum* 259
  bonus-henricus 106
Cherokee rose see *Rosa laevigata*
Cherry see *Prunus*
  African see *Prunus africana*
  black see *Prunus serotina*
  bladder see *Physalis alkekengi*
  Japanese cornelian see *Cornus officinalis*
  oriental bush see *Prunus japonica*
  wild see *Prunus avium*
  wild rum see *Prunus serotina*
  winter see *Physalis alkekengi*; *Solanum capsicastrum*; *Withania somnifera*
Cherry birch see *Betula lenta*
Cherry laurel see *Prunus laurocerasus*
Chervil see *Anthriscus cerefolium*
  Japanese wild see *Cryptotaenia canadensis*
  sweet see *Myrrhis odorata*
Chestnut see *Castanea*
  horse see *Aesculus*
  Moreton Bay see *Castanospermum australe*
  Spanish see *Castanea sativa*
  sweet see *Castanea sativa*
chi shao (*Paeonia lactiflora*) 321
chi shao yao (*Paeonia lactiflora*) 321
Chickweed see *Stellaria media*
Chicory see *Cichorium*
Childing daisy see *Bellis perennis* 'Prolifera'
Chili manzano see *Capsicum pubescens*
Chili pepper see *Capsicum annuum* var. *annuum*
Chimaphila umbellata 107, **260**
China 13, 14
  herbs in wild 64-5
  medicine 18, 46, 64-5
  medicine stall *42*
China officinalis (*Cinchona pubescens*) 261
Chinaberry see *Melia azederach*
Chinchon, Countess of 261
Chinese anemone see *Pulsatilla chinensis*
Chinese angelica see *Angelica keiskei*; *A. polymorpha* var. *sinensis*
Chinese angelica tree see *Aralia chinensis*
Chinese arborvitae see *Thuja orientalis*
Chinese asparagus see *Asparagus cochinchinensis*
Chinese bellflower see *Platycodon grandiflorus*
Chinese boxthorn see *Lycium barbarum*
Chinese caterpillar fungus see *Cordyceps sinensis*
Chinese chaste tree see *Vitex negundo* var. *heterophylla*
Chinese chives see *Allium tuberosum*
Chinese cinnamon see *Cinnamomum cassia*
Chinese clematis see *Clematis chinensis*
Chinese cornbind see *Polygonum multiflorum*
Chinese cucumber see *Trichosanthes kirilowii*
Chinese date see *Ziziphus jujuba*
Chinese foxglove see *Rehmanniia*
Chinese foxnut see *Euryale ferox*
Chinese goldthread see *Coptis chinensis*
Chinese hawthorn see *Crataegus pinnatifida*
Chinese hibiscus see *Hibiscus rosa-sinensis*
Chinese lantern see *Physalis alkekengi*
Chinese licorice see *Glycyrrhiza uralensis*
Chinese lobelia see *Lobelia chinensis*
Chinese lovage see *Ligusticum sinense*
Chinese Materia Medica 267
Chinese motherwort see *Leonurus sibiricus*
Chinese *moxa* see *Artemisia vulgaris*
Chinese mustard see *Brassica juncea*
Chinese peony see *Paeonia lactiflora*
Chinese pepper see *Zanthoxylum planispinum*
Chinese persimmon see *Diospyros kaki*
Chinese Pharmacopoeia 313, 370
Chinese pink see *Dianthus chinensis*
Chinese plum see *Prunus japonica*
Chinese privet see *Ligustrum lucidum*
Chinese raspberry see *Rubus coreanus*
Chinese red pine see *Pinus tabuliformis*
Chinese rhubarb see *Rheum palmatum*
Chinese sumac see *Ailanthus altissima*; *Rhus chinensis*
Chinese thistle daisy see *Atractylodes macrocephala*
Chinese violet see *Viola yezoensis*
Chinese wild ginger see *Asarum sieboldii*
Chinese yam see *Dioscorea opposita*
Chinghai rhubarb see *Rheum palmatum*
Chionanthus virginicus 53, *107*, 248, **260**, 281, 326
Chiretta see *Swertia chirata*
  brown see *Swertia chirata*
chiretta, green 357
Chives see *Allium schoenoprasum*
  Chinese see *Allium tuberosum*
  garlic see *Allium tuberosum*
chloral 357
chloroform 357
chlorogenic acid 264
chlorophyll 309, 366, 367, 382
Chocolate tree see *Theobroma cacao*
Chondrodendron
  spp. 271
  tomentosum 17, 55, **260**
Chondrus crispus 252, **260**
chong wei zu (*Leonurus sibiricus*) 302
choosing herbs 378-9
chop suey greens see *Chrysanthemum coronarium*
Choraka see *Angelica*
Chrysanthemum
  cinerariifolium see *Tanacetum cinerariifolium*
  coccineum see *Tanacetum coccineum*
  coronarium 272
  x *morifolium* see *Dendranthema* x *grandiflorum*
  parthenium see *Tanacetum parthenium*
Chrysanthemum
  florists' see *Dendranthema* x *grandiflorum*
  garland see *Chrysanthemum coronarium*
  mulberry-leaved see *Dendranthema* x *grandiflorum*
chuan-xiong (*Carthamus tinctorius*; *Ligusticum sinense*) 303
Chufa see *Cyperus esculentus* var. *sativus*
chun pi (*Ailanthus altissima*) 231
Cichorium 36, 260-1
  endivia 107
  intybus 107, **261**
    'Giulio' 36
    'Red Devil' *107*, **261**
Cilantro see *Coriandrum sativum*
Cilician thyme see *Thymus cilicicus*
Cimicifuga
  americana 261
  dahurica 261
  foetida 107, **261**
  racemosa 52, *107*, **261**, 301, 312, 334, 345, 372
Cimmaron see *Lippia dulcis*
Cinchona
  calisaya 261
  ledgeriana 17, 261
  officinalis 261
  pubescens 108, **261**
  spp. 17, *17*, 55, 251
cineole 243, 280, 309, 335
cinnamaldehyde 262, 359
cinnamic acids, esters of 369
Cinnamodendron corticosum 275
Cinnamomum
  aromaticum see *C. cassia*
  burmanii 261
  camphora 65, *108*, 261, **262**, 275
  cassia 64, *108*, 260, 261, **262**, 278
  iners 261
  loureirii 262
  massoia 262
  oliveri 262
  tamala 262
  verum see *C. zeylanicum*
  zeylanicum 62, 63, *108*, 261, **262**, 275
Cinnamon see *Cinnamomum zeylanicum*
  Ceylon see *Cinnamomum zeylanicum*
  Chinese see *Cinnamomum cassia*
  Saigon see *Cinnamomum loureirii*
  West Indian wild see *Canella winterana*
  white see *Canella winterana*
  wild see *Cinnamomum iners*
Cinnamon yam see *Dioscorea opposita*
Cinquefoil see *Potentilla*
  creeping see *Potentilla reptans*
cissampeline 260
Cissampelos pareira 260
Cistus
  albiflorus 262
  creticus 262
  ladanifer 108, **262**
  maculatus 262
Cistus, gum see *Cistus ladanifer*
CITES (Convention on International Trade in Endangered Species of Wild Fauna and Flora) 51, 52, 55, 60, 62, 350
citral 270, 318
Citronella see *Cymbopogon nardus*

citronellal 280, 317
citronellol 342
Citrus 388
aurantiifolia 108, **262**, 263
aurantium 108, *109*, 262, **263**, 377
var. *bergamia* see *C. bergamia*
bergamia 160, 262, **263**
hystrix 262
limon 27, 108, **263**, 310, 314, 377
'Variegata' *109*, **263**, 383
reticulata 42, *109*, 262, **263**, 329, 340, 390
'Clementine' **263**
spp. 49, 374, 381, 387
Civil and Natural History of Jamaica 314
Clary sage see *Salvia sclarea*
classification 10-11
Claviceps purpurea 16, *109*, **263**
cleaning herbs 391
Clear eye see *Salvia sclarea*
Cleavers see *Galium aparine*
Clematis
chinensis **263**
glycinoides 263
recta 263
vitalba 263
Clementine see *Citrus reticulata* 'Clementine'
climatic zones 8
climbers 39, 374-5
training 385
Climbing oleander see *Strophanthus gratus*
Clinopodium acinos see *Acinos arvensis*
Clove, wild see *Pimenta acris*
Clove pink see *Dianthus caryophyllus*
Clover see *Trifolium*
purple see *Trifolium pratense*
red see *Trifolium pratense*
yellow sweet see *Melilotus officinalis*
Cloves see *Syzygium aromaticum*
Clubmoss see *Locopodium*
stag's horn see *Lycopodium clavatum*
Cnicus benedictus 109, 255, **264**
Coca see *Erythoxylum coca*
cocaine 16, 54, 55, 279-80
Coccoloba uvifera 337
Cochlearia armoracia see *Armoracia rusticana*
Cocklebur see *Agrimonia eupatoria*; *Xanthium strumarium*
Coco grass see *Cyperus rotundus*
Cocoa see *Theobroma cacao*
Brazilian see *Paullinia cupana*
codeine 17, 322
Codiaeum 114
Codonopsis
pilosula 264
tangshen 109, 246, **264**
tubulosa 264
Coffea
arabica 110, **264**
'Nana' 110
canephora 264
liberica 264
Coffee see *Coffea*
Arabian see *Coffea arabica*
robusta see *Coffea canephora*
Coffin, Albert Isaiah19, 52
Cohosh
black see *Cimicifuga racemosa*
blue see *Caulophyllum thalictroides*
Cohosh bugbane see *Cimicifuga racemosa*
Coix lacryma-jobi 110, **264**
Cola
acuminata 264
anomala 264
nitida 110, **264-5**
spp. 264
vera see *C. nitida*
verticillata 264
cola red 264
colchicine 16, 59, 63, 265
Colchicum
autumnale 16, *110*, **265**, 269, 379
var. *album 110*, **265**
'Pleniflorum' *110*, **265**
spp. 43
Coles, William 19, 233, 243, 337
Coleus
amboinicus see *Plectranthus amboinicus*
barbatus see *Plectranthus barbatus*
forskohlii see *Plectranthus barbatus*
Colic root see *Aletris farinosa*; *Dioscorea villosa*
collecting herbs 51
Collection of Commentaries of the Classic Materia Medica 326
Collinson, Peter 110
Collinsonia canadensis 110, **265**
Colocasia esculenta 66
Colombo see *Jateorhiza palmata*
colophony 329
Colorado cough root see *Ligusticum porteri*
color
herbs for 374
planting for *375*
color wheel raised beds 25, *25*
Coltsfoot see *Tussilago*
Columbus, Christopher 45, 199, 210
Comfrey see *Symphytum*
Russian see *Symphytum* x *uplandicum*
Comino see *Cuminum cyminum*
Commiphora
foliacea 265
gileadensis 265
habessinica 265
molmol see *C. myrrha*
mukul 63, 265
myrrha 11, 14, 60, 61, 247, 252, 254, **265**, 277, 363
spp. 227
Compass plant see *Lactuca serriola*
Compendium Aromatorium 126
Compendium of Materia Medica 19, 350
compresses 47, *47*
Compton, Henry 111
Comptonia peregrina 111, **265**
Condurango see *Marsdenia cundurango*
Coneflower see *Echinacea*
Conehead thyme see *Thymus capitatus*
cong bai (*Allium fistulosum*) 234
cong xu (*Allium fistulosum*) 234
Conga root see *Petiveria alliacea*
coniine 265-6, 329
Conium 265-6
maculatum 111, **266**
conservation 50-1
Consolida ajacis 272
containers
advantages of 380
feeding plants in 381
growing herbs in *21*, 40-1, *40-1*, 374, 375, *375*, 380-1, *380-1*
planting 380
plants for 381
pot-bound plants *378*, 379, 381
siting 380
for storage 392, *393*
types 380
watering 381
Convallaria
majalis 33, *33*, 43, *111*, **266**, 271
'Albostriata' *111*, **266**
'Hardwick Hall' *111*, **266**
'Prolificans' 111
'Rosea' 111
Convolvulus
arvensis 297
jalapa see *Ipomoea purga*
Conyza canadensis 112, **266**
cooking tips 45
Copaiba see *Copaifera lansdorfii*
Copaifera
guyanensis 266
lansdorfii **266**
martii 266
multijuga 266
nitida see *C. lansdorfii*
officinalis 266
reticulata 266
sellowii see *C. lansdorfii*
Copaiva see *Copaifera lansdorfii*
copal 266
Copper beech see *Fagus sylvatica*, Purpurea (Purple) Group
Coptis
chinensis 63, 64, **266-7**, 289, 326, 329, 351
groenlandica 266
japonica 266
teeta 63, 266
trifolia 266
Copts 18
Coral bean see *Sophora secundiflora*
Cordyceps sinensis **267**
Coriander see *Coriandrum*
perennial see *Eryngium foetidum*
Roman see *Nigella sativa*
Vietnamese see *Polygonum odoratum*
Coriandrum sativum 26, 27, 29, 30, 36, 61, *112*, **267**, 279, 284, 352, 382, 386, 390
Coridothymus capitatus see *Thymus capitatus*
Cork tree see *Duboisia myoporoides*
Amur see *Phellodendron amurense*
Corkwood see *Duboisia* spp.
corms 43
Corn see *Zea mays*
Saracen see *Fagopyrum esculentum*
sweet see *Zea mays*
Corn ergot see *Ustilago zeae*
Corn mint see *Mentha arvensis*
Corn poppy see *Papaver rhoeas*
Cornbind, Chinese see *Polygonum multiflorum*
Cornel, Japanese see *Cornus officinalis*
Cornelian cherry, Japanese see *Cornus officinalis*
Cornflower see *Centaurea cyanus*
perennial see *Centaurea montana*
cornsilk 42, 372, 373
Cornus
florida 267
officinalis 112, **267**
sericea 267
Corsican mint see *Mentha requienii*
Cortés, Hernando 13
corticosteroids 17
cortisone 17
Corydalis
bulbosa 112
cava 267
solida 112, **267-8**, 289, 393
'George Baker' *112*, **268**
Corynanthe yohimbe see *Pausinystalia yohimbe*
Coscinium fenestratum 62, 63
cosmetic herbs 48-9, 377
Cosmos atrosanguineus 94
Costmary see *Tanacetum balsamita*
Costus see *Saussurea lappa*
Cotton see *Gossypium herbaceum*
Levant see *Gossypium herbaceum*
Sea Island see *Gossypium barbadensis*
upland see *Gossypium hirsutum*
Cottonweed see *Gnaphalium uliginosum*
Couch grass see *Elymus repens*
Cough root, Colorado see *Ligusticum porteri*
coumarins 11, 239, 262, 274, 285, 293, 303, 328
Coumarouna odorata see *Dipteryx odorata*
Countrie Housewife's Garden 25
Coutinho, Symphronio 328
Cow parsley see *Heracleum maximum*
Cow parsnip see *Heracleum sphondylium*
North American see *Heracleum lanatum*
Cowberry see *Vaccinium vitis-idaea*
Cowhage see *Mucuna pruriens*
Cowitch see *Mucuna pruriens*
Cowslip see *Primula veris*
Jerusalem see *Pulmonaria officinalis*
Crab's eyes see *Abrus precatorius*
Crack willow see *Salix fragilis*
Crambe cordifolia 34, 35
Crampbark see *Viburnum opulus*
Cranesbill see *Geranium*
American see *Geranium maculatum*
cut-leaved see *Geranium dissectum*
spotted see *Geranium maculatum*
Crataegus
cuneata 268
laevigata 112, **268**, 288, 363, 15, 370
'Paul's Scarlet' *114*, **268**
'Plena' *114*, **268**
'Rosea' *114*, **268**
x *media* 112
monogyna 15, 112, 268
oxyacantha see *C. laevigata*
pinnatifida 112, *113*, **268**
spp. 266
cream of tartar 371
creepers 374-5
Creeping blackberry see *Rubus procumbens*
Creeping cinquefoil see *Potentilla reptans*
Creeping Oregon grape see *Mahonia repens*
Creeping rosemary see *Rosmarinus officinalis*, Prostratus Group
Creeping savory see *Satureja spicigera*
Creeping thyme see *Thymus praecox*; *Thymus serpyllum*
creosote 282
Creosote bush see *Larrea divaricata*
Cress
bitter see *Cardamine*
Indian see *Tropaeolum majus*
meadow see *Cardamine pratensis*
Crested field fern see *Dryopteris cristata*
Crithmum maritimum 113, **268**
Crocus **268-9**
nudiflorus 269
sativus 42, *45*, 57, *113*, **269**, 359, 390
Crocus
autumn see *Colchicum autumnale*
saffron see *Crocus sativus*
cross-pollination 386
Croton
eleuteria 269
tiglium 67, *114*, **269**, 281
Crown imperial see *Fritillaria imperialis*
Cruÿdboeck 19, 119
Cryptotaenia canadensis 114, **269**
crystallization 393
Cubeb see *Piper cubeba*
Cuchay see *Allium tuberosum*
Cuckoo flower see *Cardamine pratensis*
Cucumber see *Cucumis sativus*
Chinese see *Trichosanthes kirilowii*
squirting see *Ecballium elaterium*
Cucumber tree see *Magnolia acuminata*
Cucumis
sativus 49, *114*, **269**, 383
'Telegraph Improved' 38
Cucurbita
foetidissima 364
maxima 114, **269**
moschata 114
pepo 114
'Cream of the Crop' 38
spp. 54
cucurbitacins 237, 276, 290, 312
Cudweed see *Artemisia ludoviciana*
low see *Gnaphalium uliginosum*
marsh see *Gnaphalium uliginosum*
Culantro see *Eryngium foetidum*
culinary uses 44-5
Culpeper, Nicholas 19, 104, 217, 229, 231, 237, 238, 243, 251, 252, 256, 269, 284, 289, 292, 293, 294, 321, 334, 339, 344, 348, 349, 350, 353, 355, 356, 357, 361
cultivation 374-89
Culver's root see *Veronicastrum virginicum*
Cumin see *Cuminum*

black see *Nigella sativa*
Cuminum **269-70**
  cyminum 61, *114*, **270**
Curaçao aloe see *Aloe vera*
curare 17, 54, 260, 307, 357
Curcuma
  amada 270
  aromatica *114*, **270**
  domestica see *C. longa*
  longa 114, *115*, 248, **270**, 299, 383, 387
  zedoaria 270
cure-dents du Prophète 236
Curled dock see *Rumex crispus*
Currant see *Ribes*
Curry leaf see *Murraya koenigii*
Curry plant see *Helichrysum italicum*
Cuscus see *Vetiveria zizanoides*
Cuscuta
  epithymum 270
  japonica **270**
  systyla see *C. japonica*
Cusparia bark see *Galipea officinalis*
Custard apple see *Asimina triloba*
Cut-leaf birch see *Betula pendula* 'Laciniata'
Cut-leaved beech see *Fagus sylvatica,* Heterophylla Group
Cut-leaved cranesbill see *Geranium dissectum*
Cut-leaved walnut see *Juglans regia* 'Laciniata'
cutch 226
cuttings 388, *388*
cyanide 335
cyanogenic glycosides 11, 304, 347
Cydonia
  oblonga 258
  speciosa
    'Moerloosii' *105*, **258**
    'Nivalis' *105*, **258**
Cymbopogon
  citratus *115*, **270**, 305, 310, 377
  flexuosus 115, 270
  martinii 270
    var. *sofia* 270
  nardus, 115 270
  spp. 235
cymol 362
Cynara
  cardunculus 270
    Scolymus Group *115*, **270-1**
  scolymus 30, 43
cynarin 271
Cynoglossum officinale *115*, **271**
Cyperus
  articulatus 271
  esculentus var. *sativus* 115
  involucratus 115
  longus 82, 271, 299, 380, 381
  papyrus 115, 216
  rotundus *115*, **271**
Cypripedium
  parviflorum 53, 271, 300
    var. *parviflorum* 271
    var. *pubescens* *115*, 246, **271**, 368
  pubescens see *C. parviflorum* var. *pubescens*
Cyprus turpentine see *Pistacia terebinthus*
cytisine 355
Cytisus
  scoparius *116*, 239, **271**, 287
    subsp. *maritimus* 381
    var. *prostratus* *116*, **271**

D

d-borneol 275
d-tubocurarine 260
da feng zi (*Hydnocarpus kurzii*) 294
da fu pi (*Areca catechu*) 241
da huang (*Rheum palmatum*) 341
da qing ye (*Isatis tinctoria*) 297
da suan (*Allium sativum*) 234
da zao (*Ziziphus jujuba*) 373
Dahlia 'Coltness Hybrids' 36
daidzein 337
daidzin 337
Daikon see *Raphanus sativus* var. *macropodus*
Daisy
  childing see *Bellis perennis* 'Prolifera'
  Chinese thistle see *Atractylodes macrocephala*
  English see *Bellis perennis*
  false see *Eclipta prostrata*
  hen-and-chicken see *Bellis perennis* 'Prolifera'
  Michaelmas see *Aster* p. 245
  Mount Atlas see *Anacyclus*
Dalmatian iris see *Iris pallida*
Dalmatian pellitory see *Tanacetum cinerariifolium*
Damiana see *Turnera diffusa* var. *aphrodisiaca*
dan nan xing (*Arisaema*) 241
dan shen (*Salvia miltiorhiza*) 346
Dandelion see *Taraxacum*
dang gui (*Angelica polymorpha* var. *sinensis*) 238
Dang shen see *Codonopsis tangshen*
dangerous plants 11
Daphne
  genkwa *116*, **272**, 289
  gnidium 272
  laureola 272
  mezereum 272
  spp. 43, 356
Dardymov, I. V. 122
Dark mullein see *Verbascum nigrum*
daruharidra (*Berberis*) 248
Date
  Chinese see *Ziziphus jujuba*
  Indian see *Tamarindus indica*
Date plum see *Diospyros lotus*
Datura
  metel 272
  meteloides 272
  spp. 55
Daucus
  carota *116*, **272**
    subsp. *sativus* *117*, **272**
  visnaga see *Ammi visnaga*
Davana see *Artemisia pallens*
Dawyck beech see *Fagus sylvatica* 'Dawyck'
De Materia Medica 19, 279
De Proprietatibus Rerum 19
De Simplicibus 19
deadheading 384
Deadly nightshade see *Atropa belladonna; Solanum dulcamara*
Deadnettle see *Lamium*
  white see *Lamium album*
decoctions 47
Deer bush see *Ceanothus integerrimus*
Deer's tongue see *Trilisa odoratissima*
Delphinium staphisagria *117*, **272**
Dendranthema
  x *grandiflorum* *117*, **272-3**, 278, 311, 335
  indicum 117
  'Suncharm' 36
Dendrobium nobile *117*, **273**
Denmark, folklore 15
Derris elliptica 330
designs 20-41, 376-7
  in containers 40-1, *40-1*
  formal 20-1, *20*, 22, *22*, 376, *376*
  formal border 28, *28*
  herbs with roses 37
  informal 20, 21, 376, *376*
  island bed 29, *29*
  knot gardens 24, *24*
  making plan 377
  Mediterranean bed 32, *32*
  mixed border 36
  potpourri garden 26-7, *26-7*
  potager 38-9, *38-9*
  small-scale 30-1, *30-1*
  theme planting 377
  white border with herbs 34-5, *34-5*
  woodland 33, *33*
Devil tree see *Alstonia scholaris*
Devil's apple see *Datura stramonium*
Devil's apples see *Mandragora officinarum*
Devil's bit see *Chamaelirium luteum*
Devil's claw see *Harpagophytum procumbens*
Devil's dung see *Ferula assa-foetida*
Devil's tobacco see *Lobelia tupa*
Dewberry, swamp see *Rubus hispidus*
Dewplant see *Drosera rotundifolia*
di gu pi (*Lycium barbarum*) 306
di huang (*Rehmannia glutinosa*) 340
di yu (*Sanguisorba officinalis*) 348
diamorphine 322
Dianthus
  caryophyllus *26*, 27, 37, *37*, *117*, **273**
  chinensis 117, *118*, **273**
    cvs 381
    'Strawberry Parfait' *118*, **273**
  'Mrs. Sinkins' 35
  superbus 273
dicoumarol 239, 310
Dictamnus
  albus *118*, **273**
    var. *purpureus* *118*, **273**
  dasycarpus see *D. albus*
  fraxinella see *D. albus*
digitalin 273
Digitalis 33, 351
  grandiflora 273
  lanata 11, 22, 33, *33*, *118*, 229, **273-4**
  lutea 273
  purpurea 273, 356
  spp. *37*, 43, 57, 266, 290, 376, 379, 386
digitoxin 273
digoxin 273
dilem 332
Dill see *Anethum*
  Indian see *Anethum graveolens* subsp. *sowa*
ding xiang (*Syzygium aromaticum*) 358
Dionysus 136
Dioscorea
  alata 119
  batatas see *D. opposita*
  deltoidea 63
  hypoglauca 273
  macrostachya 55, *55*, 273
  nipponica 65, 273
  opposita *119*, **273-4**
  quaternata 273
  spp. 17
  villosa *16*, 273, **274**, 367, 369
Dioscorides 19, *19*, 203, 229, 237, 249, 265, 275, 277, 279, 295, 326, 333, 345, 346, 352, 361
diosgenin 17, 55, 273
Diosma crenulata see *Agathosma crenulata*
diosmin 343
diosphenol 230, 311
Diospyros
  kaki *119*, **274**
  lotus 119
  virginiana 119, 274
Dipteryx
  odorata **274**
  oppositifolia 274
Discours et advis sur les flus de ventre douloureux 261
diseases 383
Dishcloth gourd see *Luffa cylindrica*
Dispensatory of the United States 240
diterpene alkaloids 272
diterpene esters 281
Ditta bark see *Alstonia scholaris*
Dittany see *Dictamnus*
Dittany of Crete see *Origanum dictamnus*
division 389, *389*
Dock see *Rumex*
  broad-leaved see *Rumex obtusifolius*
  curled see *Rumex crispus*
  water see *Rumex aquatica*
  yellow see *Rumex crispus*
Doctrine of Signatures 19, 46, 138, 241, 248, 259, 281, 337, 339
Dodder see *Cuscuta*
  common see *Cuscuta epithymum*
  Japanese see *Cuscuta japonica*
Dodoens, Rembert 19, 119
Dodonaea
  viscosa 66, *119*, **274**
    'Purpurea' *119*, **274**
Dog rose see *Rosa canina*
Dogbane see *Apocynum cannabinum*
Dogwood see *Cornus*
  Jamaica see *Piscidia piscipula*
Doku-dami see *Houttuynia cordata*
Dolichos pruriens see *Mucuna pruriens*
dong chong xia cao (*Cordyceps sinensis*) 267
dong gua pi (*Benincasa cerifera*) 248
dong gua ren (*Benincasa cerifera*) 248
dong gua zi (*Benincasa cerifera*) 248
Doré, Henri 64
Dorema ammoniacum **275**
Downy birch see *Betula pubescens*
Dragon plant see *Arisaema consanguineum*
Drake, Sir Francis 275
Drimia
  indica 275
  maritima 57, *119*, **275**, 363, 370
Drimys
  granadensis 275
  lanceolata see *Tasmannia lanceolata*
  winteri 54, *120*, **275**
    var. *andina* 120
Drosera rotundifolia *120*, **275**, 293, 356
Druids 11, 15, 18, 218, 360, 370
dry positions, herbs for 379
drying herbs *390-1*, 392, *392*
Dryobalanops aromatica *120*, 261, **275-6**, 316
Dryopteris
  crassirhizoma 276
  cristata 276
  filix-mas *120*, 269, **276**
    'Crispa Cristata' *120*, **276**
    'Linearis' *121*, **276**
  oreades 276
Du Bois, Charles 121
Duboisia
  leichardtii 276
  myoporoides *121*, **276**
  spp. 66
Duke of Argyll's tea-tree see *Lycium barbarum*
Dulacia inopiflora **276**
Dusty miller grape see *Vitis vinifera* 'Incana'
Dutch 13
Dutch honeysuckle see *Lonicera caprifolium*
Dutch rush see *Equisetum hyemale*
Dwale see *Atropa belladonna*
Dwarf male fern see *Dryopteris oreades*
Dwarf mallow see *Malva neglecta*
Dwarf milkwort see *Polygala amarella*
Dwarf mountain pine see *Pinus mugo* var. *pumilio*
Dyer's bugloss see *Alkanna tinctoria*
Dyer's greenwood see *Genista tinctoria*
Dyer's mulberry see *Morinda tinctoria*
Dysentery geranium see *Pelargonium antidysentericum*

E

e wei (*Ferula assa-foetida*) 282
Eagle vine see *Marsdenia cundurango*
Eaglewood see *Aquilaria malaccensis*
Earth smoke see *Fumaria officinalis*
East Indian basil see *Ocimum gratissimum*
East Indian lemon grass see *Cymbopogon flexuosus*
Eastern white cedar see *Thuja occidentalis*
eau d'arquebusade 231
Ebers Papyri 18, 236, 294, 338, 352, 364
Ecballium elaterium *121*, **276**
Echinacea
  angustifolia 52, 276
  pallida 52, 276
  purpurea 52, 53, *121*, 247,

269, **276-7**, 285, 290, 358
'Robert Bloom' *121*, **277**
'White Lustre' 122
'White Swan' *122*, **277**
spp. 265
Eclectic medicine 292, 372
Eclipta
alba see *E. prostrata*
prostrata 122, **277**
Ecuadorian sarsaparilla see *Smilax febrifuga*
Eglantine see *Rosa eglanteria*
Egypt 12, 14, 18, 46, 48, 49
Egyptian henbane see *Hyoscyamus muticus*
Egyptian lotus see *Nymphaea lotus*
Egyptian paper rush see *Cyperus papyrus*
Egyptian privet see *Lawsonia inermis*
elaterium 276
Elder see *Sambucus*
bronze see *Sambucus nigra* 'Guincho Purple'
common see *Sambucus nigra*
fern-leaved see *Sambucus nigra* f. *laciniata*
golden see *Sambucus nigra* 'Aurea'
ground see *Aegopodium podagraria*
Elecampane, Japanese see *Inula britannica* var. *chinensis*
elements, theories of 46
Elettaria, *cardamomum* 63, *122*, 228, 237, **277**
Eleuthero see *Eleutherococcus senticosus*
Eleutherococcus senticosus 64-5, *122*, **277**, 321
Elizabeth I 297
Elm see *Ulmus*
English see *Ulmus minor* var. *vulgaris*
red see *Ulmus rubra*
slippery see *Ulmus rubra*
Elymus repens 122, 241, **277**, 301, 322, 359, 370, 372
Emblic myrobalan see *Phyllanthus emblica*
emetine 292
Endive see *Cichorium endivia*
Endone see *Pausinystalia yohimbe*
English daisy see *Bellis perennis*
English elm see *Ulmus minor* var. *vulgaris*
English holly see *Ilex aquifolium*
English Husbandman 21
English ivy see *Hedera helix*
English laurel see *Prunus laurocerasus*
English lavender see *Lavandula angustifolia*
English mandrake see *Bryonia dioica*
English oak see *Quercus robur*
English Physitian 19
English Physitian Enlarged 19, 104, 216, 231, 237, 238, 243, 251, 252, 256, 269, 284, 289, 292, 293, 294, 339, 344, 349, 350, 353, 355, 356, 357, 361
English serpentary see *Polygonum bistorta*
English walnut see *Juglans regia*
Enquiry into Plants (*Historia Plantarum*) 19, 319
Eopepon vitifolius see *Trichosanthes kirilowii*
Epazote see *Chenopodium ambrosioides*
Ephedra
distachya 122, **278**
equisetina 65, 278
gerardiana 278
intermedia 278
sinica 64, 65, 278
spp. 288, 363
trifurca 278
ephedrine 64, 65, 278, 329
Epigaea repens 123, **278**
Epilobium spp. 167
Epimedium sagittatum 123, **278**
Equisetum
arvense 123, **278**, 282, 352, 372-3
hyemale 123, **278**
ergometrine 263
ergonovine 16
Ergot see *Claviceps purpurea*
corn see *Ustilago zeae*
ergotamine 16, 263
Erigeron canadensis see *Conyza canadensis*
Eriobotrya japonica 123, **278-9**, 387
Eriodictyon californicum **279**, 368
Eruca
vesicaria 382
subsp. *sativa 123*, **279**
Eryngium
antihystericum see *E. foetidum*
aquaticum 279
campestre 279
foetidum 124, **279**
giganteum 376
maritimum 32, *124*, **279**
planum 279
yuccifolium 279
Eryngo see *Eryngium maritimum*
field see *Eryngium campestre*
Erysimum officinale see *Sisymbrium officinale*
Erythraea centaurium see *Centaurium erythraea*
Erythroxylum
cataractacum 279
coca 16, *16*, 55, *124*, **279-80**
novogranatense 279
Eschscholzia
californica 32, 53, *53*, *124*, **280**, 379
Ballerina Series *124*, **280**
Esere bean see *Physostigma venenosum*
eserine 327
essential oils 44-5, 48
Estragon see *Artemisia dracunculus* var. *sativa*
Eternal flower see *Helichrysum stoechas*
etoposide 332
eucalyptol 280
Eucalyptus
camaldulensis 125, **280**
citriodora 125, **280**
dives 125, **280**
globulus 32, *125*, **280**, 283, 295, 328, 381
gummifera 280
haemastoma 280
macarthurii 280
macrorhyncha 280
mannifera 280
polybractea 280
racemosa 280
radiata var. *australiana* 280
smithii 280
spp. 66
viminalis 280
Eugenia caryophyllata see *Syzygium aromaticum*
eugenol 288, 318, 328, 358, 368
Euodia 210
Euonymus 386
atropurpureus 125, **280-1**
europaeus 125, **281**
'Red Cascade' *125*, **281**
Eupatorium
cannabinum 22, *126*, **281**
'Flore Pleno' 126
fortunei **281**
japonicum var. *fortunei* see *E. fortunei*
lindleyanum 281
perfoliatum 126, **281**
purpureum 126, 265, **281**, 294, 370, 373
stoechadasum see *E. fortunei*
Euphorbia
hirta 126, 275, **281**, 290, 293, 358
kansui 281, 289
lathyrus 126, 281
pekinensis 281, 289
pilulifera see *E. hirta*
pulcherrima 126
resinifera 281
tirucalli 59
Euphrasia
montana 126
officinalis 126, **281**, 295, 344
rostkoviana 126
Euphrosinum see *Borago*
Europe, herbs in wild 56-7
European alder see *Alnus glutinosa*
European beech see *Fagus sylvatica*
European galingal see *Cyperus longus*
European larch see *Larix decidua*
European liverwort see *Hepatica nobilis*
European skullcap see *Scutellaria galericulata*
Euryale ferox 126, **282**
Eutrema wasabi see *Wasabia japonica*
Evelyn, John 24, 233, 268, 310, 353
Evening primrose see *Oenothera*
common see *Oenothera biennis*
Ever-ready onion see *Allium cepa*, Aggregatum group
Everlasting flower see *Helichrysum*
Evernia prunastri 126, **282**, 374
Eyebright see *Euphrasia officinalis*
Eyeplant see *Duboisia myoporoides*

F

Fagara see *Zanthoxylum piperitum*
fagarine 372
Fagopyrum esculentum 11, *127*, **282**
Fagus 386
sylvatica 56, *127*, **282**
'Dawyck' *127*, **282**
Heterophylla Group *127*, **282**
Purpurea (Purple) Group *127*, **282**
Fairy wand see *Chamaelirium luteum*
False coriander see *Eryngium foetidum*
False daisy see *Eclipta prostrata*
False indigo see *Baptisia*
False jasmine see *Gelsemium sempervirens*
False saffron see *Carthamus tinctorius*
False thyme see *Lippia micromera*
False unicorn root see *Chamaelirium luteum*
False Winter's bark see *Cinnamodendron corticosum*
fan hong hua (*Crocus sativus*) 269
fan xie ye (*Senna alexandrina*) 352
Farmer's tobacco see *Malva verticillata*
farnesol 266
Farrer, Reginald 65
Fat hen see *Chenopodium album*
feeding 381, 384
Felon herb see *Artemisia vulgaris*
Felonwort see *Solanum dulcamara*
fenchone 283
Fennel see *Foeniculum*
bronze see *Foeniculum vulgare* 'Purpureum'
bulb see *Foeniculum vulgare* var. *azoricum*
Florence see *Foeniculum vulgare* var. *azoricum*
giant see *Ferula*
sea see *Crithmum maritimum*
sweet see *Foeniculum vulgare* var. *azoricum*
Fennel, giant hyssop see *Agastache foeniculum*
Fenugreek see *Trigonella foenum-graecum*
Fern-leaved beech see *Fagus sylvatica*, Heterophylla Group
Fern-leaved elder see *Sambucus nigra* f. *laciniata*
ferns, propagation by spores 389
Ferula
assa-foetida 61, *127*, **282**, 283, 368
galbaniflua see *F. gummosa*
gummosa 282, **283**
rubicaulis 282
sumbul 282
Fetid bugbane see *Cimicifuga foetida*
Fever bark see *Alstonia constricta*
Fever plant see *Ocimum gratissimum*
Feverbush see *Lindera benzoin*
Feverfew see *Tanacetum parthenium*
Feverwort see *Centaurium erythraea*; *Eupatorium perfoliatum*
Fickle ladybell see *Adenophora stricta*
Ficus 388
carica 60, 61, *127*, **283**, *374*
'Brown Turkey' *128*, **283**
'White Ischia' **283**
Fig see *Ficus carica*
Figwort see *Scrophularia*
black see *Scrophularia ningpoensis*
common see *Scrophularia nodosa*
Ningpo see *Scrophularia ningpoensis*
water see *Scrophularia auriculata*
Filaginella uliginosa see *Gnaphalium uliginosum*
filicin 276
Filipendula
spp. 374
ulmaria 11, *11*, 17, 57, *128*, 257, 264, **283**, 288, 295, 301, 310, 347, 361, 379
'Aurea' 30, *128*, **283**
'Flore Pleno' *128*, **283**
'Variegata' 30, *128*, **283**
Finocchio see *Foeniculum vulgare* var. *azoricum*
Fioravanti's balm 330-1
Fir
balsam see *Abies balsamea*
joint see *Ephedra*
silver see *Abies alba*
Fish poison tree see *Piscidia piscipula*
Fishmouth see *Chelone glabra*
Fitches see *Nigella sativa*
Fitweed see *Eryngium foetidum*
5-hydroxytryptamine 358
five-spice powder 45, 262, 296, 372
Fiveleaf grass see *Potentilla reptans*
Flag
blue see *Iris versicolor*
grass-leaved sweet see *Acorus gramineus*
myrtle see *Acorus calamus*
rock sweet see *Acorus gramineus*
sweet see *Acorus*
Flame lily see *Gloriosa superba*
Flanders poppy see *Papaver rhoeas*
flavones 11
flavorings 44
Flax see *Linum*
mountain see *Linum catharticum*
New Zealand see *Phormium tenax*
purging see *Linum catharticum*
Flaxseed see *Linum usitatissimum*
Fleabane, Canadian see *Conyza canadensis*
Fleaseed see *Plantago psyllium*
Fleawort see *Plantago psyllium*
Flora of Arabia 60
Flora Iranica 60
Flora Medica 19
Flora of Turkey 60
Florence fennel see *Foeniculum vulgare* var. *azoricum*
Florists' chrysanthemum see *Dendranthema* x *grandiflorum*
flowers 42, 391
drying *391*, 392, *392*
Flowery knotweed see *Polygonum multiflorum*
Fluellen see *Veronica officinalis*
fluid extracts 47
fluoride 244
fo ti (*Polygonum multiflorum*) 333
Foeniculum
vulgare 27, *27*, 29, 30, 38, 47, 57, *128*, 235, **283-4**, 379, 382
var. *carosella* 283
var. *azoricum 128*, **283-4**
'Purpureum' 22, *128*, **283-4**, 378
folk medicine 14-15
Food in England 341
Food as Materia Medica 342
Forestus, Peter 341

Forsythia 65
suspensa 65, 129, **284**
f. *atrocaulis 129*, **284**
Forsythia, weeping see *Forsythia suspensa*
Foster, 373
four thieves' vinegar 345
Foxglove see *Digitalis*
Chinese see *Rehmannia*
woolly see *Digitalis lanata*
Foxnut, Chinese see *Euryale ferox*
Foxtail millet see *Setaria italica*
Fragaria
x *ananassa* 129
chiloensis 129
vesca 38, *129*, **284**, 377, 381
'Alexandria' 129
'Baron Solemacher' 129
'Fructo Albo' *129*, **284**
'Multiplex' *129*, **284**
virginiana 129
fragarine 344
Fragrant wormwood see *Artemisia capillaris*
Frail birthwort see *Aristolochia debilis*
Francus, Johannes 368
Frangula alnus see *Rhamnus frangula*
Frankincense see *Boswellia*
Fraxinus
bungeana 284
excelsior 284
ornus 129, 280, **284**
freeze-drying 392
freezing herbs 392, *393*
Fremontodendron californicum 366
French jujube see *Ziziphus jujuba*
French lavender see *Lavandula dentata*; *L. stoechas*
French lilac see *Galega officinalis*
French marigold see *Tagetes patula*
French parsley see *Petroselinum crispum* 'Italian'
French sorrel see *Rumex scutatus*
French tarragon see *Artemisia dracunculus* var. *sativa*
Friar's balsam 357
Fringe tree see *Chionanthus*
Fringed lavender see *Lavandula dentata*
Fringed pink see *Dianthus superbus*
Fringed rue see *Ruta chalapensis*
Fritillaria
cirrhosa 284
imperialis 130
pallidiflora 284
verticillata 130, **284**
Fritillary see *Fritillaria*
frost hardiness 375
Fruit-scented sage see *Salvia dorisiana*
fruits 42, 391
fu ling (*Wolfiporia cocos*) 372
fu pen zi (*Rubus coreanus*) 344
fu zi (*Aconitum carmichaelii*) 228
Fuchs, Leonhard 18, 19
Fucus
serratus 284
spp. 49
vesiculosus 49, 130, **284-5**
Fumaria officinalis 130, **285**
Fumitory see *Fumaria*
fungal diseases 382, 383
fungi 10
furanocoumarins 292
furocoumarins 238

G

Galangal see *Alpinia galanga*
Gale, sweet see *Myrica gale*
Galega
cusparia see *G. officinalis*
officinalis 130, **285**, 379, 386
'Alba' 35, *130*, **285**
Galen 19, 46
Galingal
European see *Cyperus longus*
greater see *Alpinia galanga*
lesser see *Alpinia officinarum*
Galingale see *Kaempferia galanga*
sweet see *Cyperus longus*
Galipea
cusparia see *G. officinalis*
officinalis **285**, 374
Galium
aparine 47, 56, *131*, **285-6**, 290, 327, 343, 370
odoratum 33, 35, *131*, **286**, 379
verum 131, **286**, 343
gamma-linoleic acid (GLA) 318, 341
gan cao (*Glycyrrhiza uralensis*) 289
Gan sui see *Euphorbia kansui*
Gandhi, Mahatma 339
Ganja see *Cannabis*
Ganoderma lucidum 131, **286**
gao liang (*Alpinia officinarum*) 236
garclive see *Agrimonia*
Garden, Dr. Alexander 131
Gardenia
augusta 131, 234, **286**
'Fortuniana' *132*, **286**
vetchiana 132
florida see *G. augusta*
jasminoides see *G. augusta*
Garland chrysanthemum see *Chrysanthemum coronarium*
Garlic see *Allium sativum*
Elephant see *Allium ampeloprasum var. ampeloprasum*
hedge see *Alliaria petiolata*
round-headed see *Allium ampeloprasum* var. *ampeloprasum*
Garlic chives see *Allium tuberosum*
Garlic mustard see *Alliaria petiolata*
Gas plant see *Dictamnus albus*
Gastrodia elata 64, **286**
Gaultheria procumbens 132, **286-7**, 352
Gaulthier, Jean François 132
Gay feather see *Liatris spicata*
ge gen (*Pueraria lobata*) 337
ge hua (*Pueraria lobata*) 337
Gean see *Prunus avium*
Gelidium
amansii 64, **287**
cartilaginium 287
Gelsemium sempervirens 132, **287**
Generall Historie of Plantes 242, 248, 249, 283, 292, 341
Genista tinctoria 132, **287**
Gentian see *Gentiana*
great yellow see *Gentiana lutea*
Japanese see *Gentiana scabra*
large-leaved see *Gentiana macrophylla*
Gentiana
burserii var. *villarsi* see *G. macrophylla*
lutea 11, 56, *56*, 57, *132*, **287**, 288, 291, 309, 312, 357, 373
macrophylla 132, *133*, **287-8**
scabra 132, *133*, **288**
Gentius, King of Illyria 132
geraniol 229, 270, 318, 359
Geranium
dalmaticum 'Album' 35
dissectum 288
maculatum 133, 252, 283, **288**, 301, 333, 365
f. *albiflorum 133*, **288**
robertianum 33, *33*, *133*, **288**
'Celtic White' *133*, **288**
wilfordii 288
Geranium see *Pelargonium*
Geranium
apple see *Pelargonium odoratissimum*
dysentery see *Pelargonium antidysentericum*
lemon see *Pelargonium crispum*
nutmeg see *Pelargonium* 'Fragrans'
oak-leaved see *Pelargonium quercifolium*
peppermint see *Pelargonium tomentosum*
rasp-leaved see *Pelargonium radens*
wild see *Geranium maculatum*
geranium oil 323
geranyl acetate 280
Gerard, St. 229
Gerard, John 19, 186, 189, 229, 242, 248, 249, 253, 283, 292, 341
germanium 44
German chamomile see *Matricaria recutita*
Germander see *Teucrium*
sage-leaved see *Teucrium scorodonia*
wall see *Teucrium chamaedrys*
Germany, folklore 15
germination 386
Geum
rivale 288
urbanum 134, 288, **288**, 344
ghanja cola 264
Giáp cá see *Houttuynia cordata*
Gilded rosemary see *Rosmarinus officinalis* 'Aureus'
Gillenia
stipulata 288
trifoliata 34, 35, *134*, **288**
Gillyflower see *Dianthus caryophyllus*
Ginger see *Zingiber*
bitter see *Zingiber zerumbet*
cassumar see *Zingiber cassumar*
Japanese see *Zingiber mioga*
mango see *Curcuma amada*
mioga see *Zingiber mioga*
Siamese see *Alpinia galanga*
wild see *Asarum*; *Zingiber zerumbet*
Ginger grass see *Cymbopogon martinii* var. *sofia*
Gingermint see *Mentha* x *gracilis*
gingerols 373
Gingili see *Sesamum indicum*
Ginkgo
biloba 65, *65*, *134*, **288-9**, 363, 369, 370
'Pendula' *134*, **289**
ginkgolides 288
Ginseng see *Panax ginseng*; *Withania somnifera*
American see *Panax quinquefolius*
Brazilian see *Pfaffia paniculata*
red see *Salvia miltiorhiza*
san qi see *Panax pseudo-ginseng*
Siberian see *Eleutherococcus senticosus*
tienchi see *Panax pseudo-ginseng*
Gipsywort see *Lycopus europaeus*
gitaloxin 273
gitoxin 273
GLA see gamma-linoleic acid
Gladiolus communis subsp. *byzantinus* 36
Gland bellflower see *Adenophora*
Glechoma
hederacea 134, **289**, 317
'Variegata' 41, 134, *135*, **289**, 381
Globe artichoke see *Cynara cardunculus*, Scolymus Group
Gloriosa
spp. 43
superba 59, 63, *135*, **289**
'Rothschildiana' 63
Glory lily see *Gloriosa*
Malabar see *Gloriosa superba*
Glossy privet see *Ligustrum lucidum*
glucoquinones 367
glucosinolates 354
glycosides, types 11
Glycyrrhiza
glabra 135, 236, 260, **289**, 290, 295, 296, 310, 343, 361
var. *glandulifera* 289
var. *typica* 289
var. *violacea* 289
lepidota 289
uralensis 65, *135*, 246, 264, 273, 281, **289**, 313, 329, 331, 333, 372
viscida see *G. uralensis*
glycyrrhizin 226, 289
Gnaphalium
dioica see *Antennaria dioica*
multiceps 289
obtusifolium 289
polycephalum 289
uliginosum 135, **289-90**, 307, 355
Goat nut see *Simmondsia chinensis*
Goat's rue see *Galega officinalis*
Goat thyme see *Satureja thymbra*
Goethe, Johann Wolfgang von 242
Golden bay see *Laurus nobilis* 'Aurea'
Golden elder see *Sambucus nigra* 'Aurea'
Golden lemon thyme see *Thymus* x *citriodorus* 'Aureus'
Golden oak see *Quercus robur* 'Concordia'
Golden psyllium see *Plantago arenaria*
Golden purslane see *Portulaca oleracea* var. *aurea*
Golden ragwort see *Senecio aureus*
Goldenrod see *Solidago*
Canada see *Solidago canadensis*
stiff see *Solidago rigida*
sweet see *Solidago odora*
Golden Scots pine see *Pinus sylvestris* 'Aurea'
Golden willow see *Salix alba* var. *vitellina*
Goldenseal see *Hydrastis canadensis*
Goldthread see *Coptis*
Chinese see *Coptis chinensis*
Indian see *Coptis trifolia*
Gondwanaland 66
Gonolobus condurango see *Marsdenia cundurango*
Good King Henry see *Chenopodium bonus-henricus*
Goora nut see *Cola nitida*
Gooseberry, Cape see *Physalis peruviana*
Goosefoot see *Chenopodium*
Goosegrass see *Galium aparine*
Gospel herb see *Gynostemma pentaphyllum*
Gossypium
arboreum 290
barbadensis 290
herbaceum 136, **290**
hirsutum 290
gossypol 290
Gotu kola see *Centella asiatica*
gou qi zi (*Lycium barbarum*) 306
gou zhi (*Cinnamomum cassia*) 262
Gourd
bitter see *Momordica charantia*
buffalo see *Cucurbita foetidissima*
dishcloth see *Luffa cylindrica*
snake see *Trichosanthes kirilowii*
sponge see *Luffa cylindrica*
wax see *Benincasa cerifera*
white see *Benincasa cerifera*
Goutweed see *Aegopodium podagraria*
Graciliaria
confervoides see *G. verrucosa*
verrucosa 287
grafting 389
Grains of Paradise see *Afromomum melegueta*; *Amomium xanthioides*
Grape see *Vitis vinifera*
creeping Oregon see *Mahonia repens*
dusty miller see *Vitis vinifera* 'Incana'
mountain see *Mahonia aquifolium*
Oregon see *Mahonia aquifolium*
Parsley see *Vitis vinifera* 'Ciotat'
Teinturier see *Vitis vinifera* 'Purpurea'
Grass-leaved sweet flag see *Acorus gramineus*
Gratiola officinalis 136, **290**
Gravel plant see *Epigaea repens*
Gravel root see *Eupatorium purpureum*
Great Ormond Street Children's Hospital 321, 370
Greek oregano see *Origanum onites*
Greek sage see *Salvia fruticosa*
Greek valerian see *Polemonium caeruleum*; *P. reptans*
Greeks 14-15, 17, 18, 46
Green, Thomas 18
Green amaranth see *Amaranthus*

retroflexus
green chiretta 357
Green lavender see *Lavandula viridis*
Greenbrier see *Smilax*
greenhouses, growing herbs in 382-3
Greenwood, dyer's see *Genista tinctoria*
gray mold (*Botrytis*) 382, *383*, 386
Gray willow see *Salix cinerea*
Grieve, Mrs. M. 19, 99, 285,297, 299, 307, 318, 332, 349
Grindelia
camporum 275, 281, **290**, 293, 358
lanceolata 290
robusta var. *rigida* see *G. camporum*
squarrosa 290
Groats see *Avena sativa*
Gromwell see *Lithospermum*
red-rooted see *Lithospermum erythrorhizon*
groundcover 21
Ground elder see *Aegopodium podagraria*
Ground holly see *Chimaphila umbellata*
Ground ivy see *Glechoma hederacea*
variegated see *Glechoma hederacea* 'Variegata'
Ground pine see *Ajuga chamaepitys*; *Lycopodium clavatum*
American see *Lycopodium complanatum*
Groundsel see *Senecio*
Growth of Plants (*Causis Plantarum*) 19
gu ya (*Oryza sativa*) 320
gua lou gen (*Trichosanthes kirilowii*) 364
gua lou pi (*Trichosanthes kirilowii*) 364
gua lou zi (*Trichosanthes kirilowii*) 364
Guaiac see *Guaiacum officinale*
guaiacol 282
Guaiacum
officinale 54, 55, *136*, 240, 282, **290-1**, 327, 345, 349, 361, 372
sanctum 55, 290
Guan zhong see *Dryopteris crassirhizoma*
Guaranà see *Paullinia cupana*
guaranine 323
Guelder rose see *Viburnum opulus*
guggulipid 265
Guggulu see *Commiphora mukul*
Guibourt, 99
Guinea grains see *Afromomum melegueta*
Guinea hen weed see *Petiveria alliacea*
Gulfweed see *Sargassum*
Gum
blue see *Eucalyptus globulus*
lemon-scented see *Eucalyptus citriodora*
Murray red see *Eucalyptus camaldulensis*
oriental sweet see *Liquidambar orientalis*
red see *Eucalyptus camaldulensis*
river red see *Eucalyptus camaldulensis*
sweet see *Liquidambar*
Tasmanian blue see *Eucalyptus globulus*
Gum ammoniac see *Dorema ammoniacum*
Gum arabic see *Acacia senegal*
Gum Benjamin see *Styrax benzoin*
Gum cistus see *Cistus ladanifer*
Gum leaves see *Eriodictyon californicum*
Gum tragacanth see *Astragalus gummifer*
Gum tree see *Eucalyptus*
Gumplant see *Grindelia*
gums 11
collecting 391
Gumweed see *Grindelia camporum*
gymnosperms 10
Gynostemma pentaphyllum **291**

H

Hahnemann, Samuel 46, 261
hai zao (*Sargassum fusiforme*) 349
half-hardy plants 375
hallucinogenic alkaloids 323
Hamamelis virginiana 49, 53, *136*, 227, 242, 252, 265, **291**, 295, 339, 362
Hamburg parsley see *Petroselinum crispum* var. *tuberosum*
Hamersley ranges, Australia *66*
han lian cao (*Eclipta prostrata*) 277
han zi (*Nelumbo nucifera*) 316
hanging baskets 382, *382*
Haputale, Sri Lanka, plant nursery *62*
hardening off 379, 383
hardiness, levels of 8, 375
Haridra see *Curcuma longa*
Haritaki see *Terminalia chebula*
Harmal see *Peganum harmala*
harpagide 291, 350
Harpagophytum procumbens 58, 59, *59*, **291**
Hartley, Dorothy 341
harvesting 390-1, *390*
Hasheesh see *Cannabis sativa*
Hatfield House, knot gardens and parterres *13*
Hatshepsut, Queen 12, 250
Haw, black see *Viburnum prunifolium*
Hawkweed see *Hieracium*
mouse-ear see *Hieracium pilosella*
Hawthorn see *Crataegus*
hazardous herbs 11
Hazel
common witch see *Hamamelis virginiana*
witch see *Hamamelis*
Hazel alder see *Alnus serrulata*
he shou wu (*Polygonum multiflorum*) 333
he yi (*Nelumbo nucifera*) 316
he zi (*Terminalia chebula*) 361
Headache tree see *Umbellularia californica*
Heal-all see *Prunella vulgaris*
Healing Herbs 18
Heartsease see *Viola tricolor*
Heartwort see *Aristolochia clematitis*
Heath speedwell see *Veronica officinalis*
Heather see *Calluna*
hecogenin 231
Hedeoma
floribunda 291
pulegioides 136, **291-2**
Hedera
helix 136, **292**
cvs 381
'Erecta' *137*, **292**, 381
'Glacier' *137*, **292**
'Goldheart' *137*, **292**
'Oro di Bogliasco' see *H. h.* 'Goldheart'
Hedge garlic see *Alliaria petiolata*
Hedge hyssop see *Gratiola officinalis*
Hedge mustard see *Sisymbrium officinale*
Hedgehog holly, silver see *Ilex aquifolium* 'Ferox Argentea'
hedges, dwarf 24, *24*, 377
hei zhi ma (*Sesamum indicum*) 352
Helianthus
annuus 137, **292**
'Italian White' *137*, **292**
'Teddy Bear' *137*, **292**, 381
spp. 374
Helichrysum 388
angustifolium see *H. italicum*
italicum 22, *23*, 32, *137*, **292**, 378, 379, 388
subsp. *microphyllum* 381
orientale 292
serpyllifolium 292
stoechas 292
Heliotrope, garden see *Valeriana officinalis*
Hellebore, false see *Adonis vernalis*
Helonias dioica see *Chamaelirium luteum*
Hemlock see *Conium*
Hemp see *Cannabis sativa* subsp. *sativa*
black Indian see *Apocynum cannabinum*
Canadian see *Apocynum cannabinum*
rosella 293
Hemp agrimony see *Eupatorium cannabinum*
Hen-and-chickens daisy see *Bellis perennis* 'Prolifera'
Hen-and-chickens marigold see *Calendula officinalis* 'Prolifera'
Henbane see *Hyoscyamus*
Egyptian see *Hyoscyamus muticus*
Russian see *Hyoscyamus albus*
Henna see *Lawsonia*
Hens and chicks see *Sempervivum tectorum*
heparin 349
Hepatica
acutiloba 292
nobilis 138, **292**
'Rubra Plena' *138*, **292**
triloba see *H. nobilis*
Heracleum
lanatum 292
mantegazzianum 293
maximum 292
sphondylium 138, **292-3**
Herb Benedict see *Geum urbanum*
Herb Bennet see *Geum urbanum*
herb gardens
designing 20-41, 376-7
high level 380-1
history 12-13
Herb Gerard see *Aegopodium*
Herb of grace see *Ruta graveolens*
herb oils 393
Herb Robert see *Geranium robertianum*
herb vinegars 393
Herba paralysis see *Primula veris*
Herbal (Paracelsus) 19
Herbal Emissaries 373
Herbal Handbook for Everyone 239
herbal wines 393
herbalism 46-7
Herball, or Generall Historie of Plantes 19, 242, 248, 249, 283, 292, 341
herbals 18-19
herbarium *51*
Herbarius zu Teusch 18
Herbe aux gueux see *Clematis vitalba*
Herbe du siège see *Scrophularia nodosa*
herbs
buying 378-9
choosing 378-9
cultivating 374-89
definition 10
harvesting 390-1
invasive, planting *379*
parts used 42-3
poisonous 43, 379
processing and storing 392-3
using 42-9
in wild 50-67
Herbs, Spices and Flavorings 268
Herbygrass see *Ruta graveolens*
Hercules club see *Aralia spinosa*
heroin 322
Heucher, Johann Heinrich von 138
Heuchera americana 138, **293**
Hibiscus
abelmoschus see *Abelmoschus moschatus*
rosa-sinensis 138, **293**, 342
'Cooperi' *138*, **293**
sabdariffa 42, *139*, **293**
var. *altissima* 293
Hibiscus
Chinese see *Hibiscus rosa-sinensis*
sleeping see *Malvaviscus arboreus*
Hieracium pilosella 139, **293**
Hierochloë
borealis see *H. odorata*
odorata 139, **293**
High mallow see *Malva sylvestris*
Highbush blueberry see *Vaccinium corymbosum*
Himalayan rhubarb see *Rheum australe*
Himalayas 62, *62*
Hindu Kush Mountains *60*
Hindus 14, 18
Hippocrates 18, 46, 141, 275, 344, 367
histamine 366
Historia Stirpium, De 18
history 12-13
History of Mexico 13
ho pu (*Pinus succinifera*) 329
Hoarhound see *Marrubium vulgare*
Hoary basil see *Ocimum americanum*
Hoary mountain mint see *Pycnanthemum incanum*
Hogbean see *Hyoscyamus niger*
Hogweed see *Heracleum sphondylium*
giant see *Heracleum mantegazzianum*
Holly see *Ilex*
American see *Ilex opaca*
box see *Ruscus aculeatus*
English see *Ilex aquifolium*
ground see *Chimaphila umbellata*
sea see *Eryngium maritimum*
silver hedgehog see *Ilex aquifolium* 'Ferox Argentea'
West Indian see *Turnera ulmifolia*
Hollyhock see *Alcea rosea*
Holm oak see *Quercus ilex*
Holy basil see *Ocimum sanctum*
Holy grass see *Hierochloë*
Holy thistle see *Cnicus benedictus*
homeopathy 46
Honduran sarsaparilla see *Smilax regelii*
Honewort see *Cryptotaenia canadensis*
Honeysuckle see *Lonicera*
Dutch see *Lonicera caprifolium*
Japanese see *Lonicera japonica*
perfoliate see *Lonicera caprifolium*
hong hua (*Carthamus tinctorius*) 255
Hops see *Humulus*
native see *Dodonaea viscosa*
Hop bush, sticky see *Dodonaea viscosa*
Hop marjoram see *Origanum dictamnus*
Hop tree see *Ptelea trifoliata*
Horace 143, 217, 370
Hordeum 293-4
distychum 294
polystichum 294
vulgare 139, **294**, 320
Horehound see *Marrubium*
black see *Ballota nigra*
water see *Lycopus americanus*
white see *Marrubium vulgare*
Horny goat weed see *Epimedium sagittatum*
Horse balm see *Collinsonia canadensis*
Horse chestnut see *Aesculus*
Horsemint see *Mentha longifolia*; *Monarda*
Horsenettle see *Solanum carolinense*
Horseradish see *Armoracia rusticana*
Horseradish tree see *Moringa oleifera*
Horsetail see *Equisetum*
field see *Equisetum arvense*
rough see *Equisetum hyemale*
shrubby see *Ephedra distachya*
Horsetail pine see *Pinus massoniana*
Horseweed see *Conyza canadensis*
Hosta 'Royal Standard' 35
Hot pepper see *Capsicum frutescens*
Hottentot tea see *Helichrysum serpyllifolium*
hou po hua (*Magnolia officinalis*) 307
Houndstongue see *Cynoglossum*

officinale
Hours of the Duke of Burgundy 15
Houseleek see *Sempervivum*
Houttuyn, Maarten 139
Houttuynia
cordata 139, **294**, 378, 379, 381
'Chameleon' *139*, **294**
'Flore Pleno' *139*, **294**
'Variegata' 139
hu jiao (*Piper nigrum*) 330
hu lu ba (*Trigonella foenum-graecum*) 364
hu tao ren (*Juglans regia*) 298
hua jiao (*Zanthoxylum piperitum*) 372
hua niu xi see *Achyranthes bidentata*
huai hua (*Sophora japonica*) 355
huai jiao (*Sophora japonica*) 355
huang bai (*Phellodendron amurense*) 326
Huang Di 19
huang jing zi (*Vitex negundo*) 371
huang lian (*Coptis chinensis*) 267
huang qi (*Astragalus membranaceus*) 246
huang qin (*Scutellaria baicalensis*) 351
Huaxtepec 13
Huckleberry see *Vaccinium myrtillus*
Hughes, William 19
Humboldt, Alexander von 206
humidity 382
Humulus
lupulus 57, *140*, 289, **294**, 300, 309, 310, 323, 330, 363, 367, 377, 385, *385*, 393
'Aureus' *140 21*, 27, *27*, 30, *30*, **294**, 374
Hungary water 48, 343
huo ma ren (*Cannabis sativa* subsp. *indica*) 253
Hutchens, 351
Hyacinth, Japanese see *Ophiopogon*
hybridization 386
Hydnocarpus
anthelmintica 140
kurzii 67, *140*, **294**
wightiana 140
Hydrangea
arborescens 52, *52*, *140*, 265, 277, 278, **294**, 301, 352
'Annabelle' *140*, **294**
'Grandiflora' 140
subsp. *radiata* 294
Hydrangea, wild see *Hydrangea arborescens*
Hydrastis canadensis 52, 53, *141*, 252, 259, 266, 285, **294-5**, 369, 371
Hydrocotyle asiatica see *Centella asiatica*
hydrocyanic acid 335
hydroquinones 241
hygiene 383
hyoscine 276, 295, 350
hyoscyamine 276, 295, 350
Hyoscyamus 350
albus 295
muticus 295
niger 15, *141*, 272, 276, **295**, 308, 350
hypericin 295
Hypericum perforatum 47, *141*, 277, **295**, 355, 393
Hyssop see *Hyssopus*
anise see *Agastache foeniculum*
blue giant see *Agastache foeniculum*
fennel, giant see *Agastache foeniculum*
giant see *Agastache*
hedge see *Gratiola officinalis*
pink see *Hyssopus officinalis* f. *roseus*
prairie see *Pycnanthemum virginianum*
rock see *Hyssopus officinalis* subsp. *aristatus*
wrinkled giant see *Agastache rugosa*
Hyssopus
dwarf cvs 380
officinalis 22, 25, 41, *141*, 278, **295**, 347, 379, 384
f. *albus* 35, *141*, **295**
subsp. *aristatus* 28, 141, *142*, **295**, 381
f. *roseus* 37, *142*, **295**

I

I Ching 227
Ibn Batuta 357
Iceland moss see *Cetraria islandica*
Igbepo see *Pausinystalia lane-poolei*
Ilang-ilang see *Cananga odorata*
Ilex 388
aquifolium 142, **296**
'Ferox Argentea' *142*, **296**, 381
'Madame Briot' *143*, **296**
opaca 296
paraguariensis see *I. paraguensis*
paraguensis 55, 142, *143*, **296**
verticillata 142, *143*, **296**
vomitoria 296
Illicium
anisatum 296
verum 45, **296**, 328
Illustrated Classic of the Materia Medica 302, 340
Illustrated Dictionary of Gardening 95, 99, 351
illustration 18
Immortelle see *Helichrysum orientale*
Impatiens
capensis 296
pallida 143, **296**
Incas 13, 16, 361
incense 14
India 14, 46
Indian angelica see *Angelica glauca*
Indian arrow-wood see *Euonymus atropurpureus*
Indian balmony see *Swertia chirata*
Indian borage see *Plectranthus amboinicus*
Indian bread see *Wolfiporia cocos*
Indian cassia see *Cinnamomum tamala*
Indian cress see *Tropaeolum majus*
Indian date see *Tamarindus indica*
Indian dill see *Anethum graveolens* subsp. *sowa*
Indian goldthread see *Coptis trifolia*
Indian hemp, black see *Apocynum cannabinum*
Indian Herbology of North America 351
Indian lavender see *Bursera penicillata*
Indian licorice see *Abrus precatorius*
Indian long pepper see *Piper longum*
Indian madder see *Oldenlandia umbellata*; *Rubia cordifolia*
Indian mandrake see *Podophyllum hexandrum*
Indian mulberry see *Morinda citrifolia*
Indian mustard see *Brassica juncea*
Indian pennywort see *Centella asiatica*
Indian physic see *Gillenia trifoliata*
Indian plum see *Ziziphus jujuba*
Indian pokeberry see *Phytolacca acinosa*
Indian rhubarb see *Rheum australe*
Indian sandalwood see *Santalum album*
Indian snakeroot see *Rauvolfia serpentina*
Indian squill see *Drimia indica*
Indian subcontinent, herbs in wild 62-3
Indian tobacco see *Lobelia inflata*
Indian turnip see *Arisaema triphyllum*
Indigo
false see *Baptisia*
Java see *Marsdenia tinctoria*
wild see *Baptisia tinctoria*
Indigofera spp. 297
Indigoweed see *Baptisia tinctoria*
indole alkaloids 236, 323
indoles 366
Indonesia, herbs in wild 67
Indonesian cassia see *Cinnamomum burmanii*
indoor herbs 382, 383
infusions 47
Inula
britannica var. *chinensis* **296**, 297
cappa 296
helenium 143, 232, 290, **296-7**
japonica see *I. britannica* var. *chinensis*
inulin 296
invasive herbs
controlling growth 384
planting *379*
iodine 285, 316, 349
ionone 370
Ipecac see *Cephaelis ipecacuanha*
Ipê roxa see *Tabebuia impetiginosa*
Ipecacuanha (Ipecac) see *Cephaelis ipecacuanha*
American see *Gillenia trifoliata*
Ipomoea
digitata 297
jalapa see *I. purga*
purga **297**
turpeth 297
iridoid glycosides 291, 331, 357, 368
iridoids 367
Iris
florentina see *I. germanica* var. *florentina*
germanica var. *florentina* 26, 27, 32, 35, *143*, **297**
pallida 297
versicolor 143, 297, **297**, 327, 379, 381
'Kermesina' *144*, **297**
Iris
Dalmatian see *Iris pallida*
wild see *Iris versicolor*
Irish Herbal 252
Irish moss see *Chondrus crispus*
iron 316, 366
Isatis tinctoria 49, 132, *144*, **297**
Ishtar 14
Isinglass, Japanese see *Gelidium amansii*
Islam 14, 46, 60
gardens 12, *12*
island bed 29, *29*
isoquinoline alkaloids 295
Ispaghula see *Plantago ovata*
Italian licorice see *Glycyrrhiza glabra* var. *typica*
Italian parsley see *Petroselinum crispum* 'Italian'
IUCN (International Union for the Conservation of Nature) 51
Ivy see *Hedera*
ground see *Glechoma hederacea*
poison see *Rhus radicans*
variegated ground see *Glechoma hederacea* 'Variegata'
Ivybush see *Kalmia latifolia*
Ixia chinensis see *Belamcanda chinensis*
Izabella, Queen of Hungary 48, 343

J

Jaborandi see *Pilocarpus*
Ceara see *Pilocarpus trachylophus*
Paraguay see *Pilocarpus pinnatifolius*
Pernambuco see *Pilocarpus jaborandi*
Jaborandi pepper see *Piper longum*
Jack-by-the-hedge see *Alliaria petiolata*
Jack-in-the-pulpit see *Arisaema triphyllum*
Jacob's ladder see *Polemonium*
Jalap see *Ipomoea purga*
Jamaica dogwood see *Piscidia piscipula*
Jamaica kino see *Coccoloba uvifera*
Jamaica pepper see *Pimenta dioica*
Jamaica quassia see *Picrasma excelsa*
Jamaica sorrel see *Hibiscus sabdariffa*
jamu 67
Japan 13, 45
Japanese apricot see *Prunus mume*
Japanese arrowroot see *Pueraria lobata*
Japanese belladonna see *Scopolia carniolica*
Japanese bitter orange see *Poncirus trifoliata*
Japanese bramble see *Rubus parviflorus*
Japanese catnip see *Schizonepeta tenuifolia*
Japanese cornel see *Cornus officinalis*
Japanese cornelian cherry see *Cornus officinalis*
Japanese dodder see *Cuscuta japonica*
Japanese elecampane see *Inula britannica* var. *chinensis*
Japanese gentian see *Gentiana scabra*
Japanese ginger see *Zingiber mioga*
Japanese honeysuckle see *Lonicera japonica*
Japanese hyacinth see *Ophiopogon*
Japanese Isinglass see *Gelidium amansii*
Japanese medlar see *Eriobotrya japonica*
Japanese mint see *Mentha arvensis* var. *piperascens*
Japanese pagoda tree see *Sophora japonica*
Japanese pepper see *Zanthoxylum piperitum*
Japanese persimmon see *Diospyros kaki*
Japanese quassia see *Picrasma ailanthoides*
Japanese quince see *Chaenomeles japonica*
Japanese rhubarb see *Rheum palmatum* x *R. coreanum*
Japanese rose see *Rosa rugosa*
Japanese wild chervil see *Cryptotaenia canadensis*
Japonica see *Chaenomeles*
Jasmine see *Jasminum*
Arabian see *Jasminum sambac*
Cape see *Gardenia augusta*
Cayenne see *Catharanthus roseus*
common see *Jasminum officinale*
false see *Gelsemium sempervirens*
royal see *Jasminum grandiflorum*
Spanish see *Jasminum grandiflorum*
Tuscan see *Jasminum sambac* 'Grand Duke of Tuscany'
Jasminum
angustifolium 298
grandiflorum 144, **298**
lanceolarium 298
odoratissimum 298
officinale 27, *144*, **298**, 374, 380
f. *affine 144*, **298**
'Aureovariegatum' see *J. o.* 'Aureum'
'Aureum' *144*, **298**
'Grandiflorum' see *J. o.* f. *affine*
sambac 63, *145*, **298**, 377, 383
'Grand Duke of Tuscany' *145*, **298**
'Trifoliatum' see *J. s.* 'Grand Duke of Tuscany'
Jateorhiza
calumba see *J. palmata*
palmata **298**
Jati see *Jasminum grandiflorum*
Jatiphala see *Myristica fragrans*
Java indigo see *Marsdenia tinctoria*
Java patchouli 332
Javanese long pepper see *Piper retrifractum*

Jeera see *Cuminum cyminum*
Jequirity see *Abrus precatorius*
Jerome, St. 12
Jerusalem cowslip see *Pulmonaria officinalis*
Jessamine see *Jasminum officinale*
Jesuit's bark see *Cinchona pubescens*
Jewelweed see *Impatiens*
Jew's myrtle see *Ruscus aculeatus*
ji cai (*Capsella bursa-pastoris*) 254
jiang huang (*Curcuma longa*) 270
jiang (*Zingiber officinale*) 373
jie geng (*Platycodon grandiflorus*) 331
Jim sage see *Salvia clevelandii*
Jimson weed see *Datura stramonium*
jin yin hua (*Lonicera japonica*) 306
jin yin teng (*Lonicera japonica*) 306
jing mi (*Oryza sativa*) 320
jing ying zi (*Rosa laevigata*) 341
Job's tears see *Coix lacryma-jobi*
Joe Pye weed see *Eupatorium purpureum*
Johnson, Thomas 19
Joint fir see *Ephedra*
Jojoba see *Simmondsia*
Josselyn, John 13, 19
Joyfull Newes Out of the Newe Founde Worlde 19
ju he (*Citrus reticulata*) 263
ju hua (*Dendranthema* x *grandiflorum*) 272
Juglans 385
cinerea 298
lutea 259
nigra 299
regia 145, **298-9**
'Laciniata' *145*, **299**
juices 47, 393
Jujube
common see *Ziziphus vulgaris*
French see *Ziziphus jujuba*
Jujube lotus see *Ziziphus lotus*
Julius Caesar 194, 297
Juniper see *Juniperus*
common see *Juniperus communis*
Rocky Mountain see *Juniperus scopulorum*
Juniperus
communis 56, 57, *145*, **299**, 322, 381
sabina 299
scopulorum 299
virginiana 52, 299
Justice, James 145
Justicia
adhatoda 145, **299**
brandegeana 145

K

kabbalah 15
Kaempfer, Engelbert 146
Kaempferia
galanga 146, **299**
pandurata 299
rotunda 299
Kaki see *Diospyros kaki*
Kalm, Pehr 299-300
Kalmia
latifolia 146, **299-300**
'Clementine Churchill' *146* **300**
'Ostbo Red' **300**
Kamel, George Joseph 99
kapok 257
Karkadé see *Hibiscus sabdariffa*
Kat see *Catha edulis*
Kaunch see *Mucuna pruriens*
Kava kava see *Piper methysticum*
Keck see *Heracleum sphondylium*
Ketaki see *Pandanus odoratissimus*
Khaki weed see *Tagetes minuta*
Khat see *Catha edulis*
Khella see *Ammi visnaga*
khellin 17, 236
Khus khus see *Vetiveria zizanoides*
Kidneywort see *Hepatica nobilis*
kino 66, 280, 337
Kino see *Pterocarpus marsupium*
Bengal see *Butea frondosa*
Jamaica see *Coccoloba uvifera*
Malabar see *Pterocarpus marsupium*
West Indian see *Coccoloba uvifera*
kitchen garden, herbs in 375
Knapweed see *Centaurea*
black see *Centaurea nigra*
greater see *Centaurea scabiosa*
Knitbone see *Symphytum officinale*
knot gardens *13*, 24, *24*
Knotted marjoram see *Origanum majorana*
knotty pine 329
Knotweed see *Polygonum*
flowery see *Polygonum multiflorum*
Koch, Robert 287
Köhler, 59
kola see *Cola nitida*
Kordofan gum 227
Korean mint see *Agastache rugosa*
Krameria
argentea 300
cistoidea 300
triandra 49, **300**
Kreuterbuch 18
ku shen (*Sophora flavescens*) 355
Kudda-mulla see *Jasminum sambac* 'Grand Duke of Tuscany'
Kudzu see *Pueraria lobata*
Kurrat see *Allium ampeloprasum* var. *kurrat*
Kusam seeds see *Brucea javanica*
Kuth see *Saussurea lappa*
kyphi 178

L

L-dopa 314
labdanum 262
Labrador tea see *Ledum groenlandicum*
Lacquered bracket fungus see *Ganoderma lucidum*
Lactuca
canadensis 300
sativa 300
'Cocarde' 38, *39*
serriola 146, **300**
spp. 328
virosa 300
lactucarium 300
ladanum 262
Lad's love see *Artemisia abrotanum*
Ladybell see *Adenophora*
fickle see *Adenophora stricta*
Lady's bedstraw see *Galium verum*
Lady's mantle see *Alchemilla vulgaris*
alpine see *Alchemilla alpina*
Lady's slipper orchid see *Cypripedium*
yellow see *Cypripedium parviflorum*
Lady's smock see *Cardamine pratensis*
lai fu zi (*Raphanus sativus*) 339
Lambkill see *Kalmia latifolia*
Lamb's quarters see *Chenopodium album*
Lamium
album 146, 281, **300-1**
'Friday' *146*, **301**
landscape gardening 13
Lapacho see *Tabebuia impetiginosa*
Lapathum see *Rumex obtusifolius*
Lappa see *Arctium lappa*
Larch see *Larix*
American see *Larix laricina*
common see *Larix decidua*
European see *Larix decidua*
Larix
decidua 147, **301**
'Pendula' *147*, **301**
europaea see *L. decidua*
laricina 301
Larkspur see *Consolida ajacis*
Larrea divaricata 290, 364
Laurel
California see *Umbellularia californica*
Canary Island see *Laurus azorica*
cherry see *Prunus laurocerasus*
English see *Prunus laurocerasus*
mountain see *Kalmia latifolia*
spurge see *Daphne laureola*
Laurus
azorica 147
camphora see *Cinnamomum camphora*
nobilis 15, 22, 28, 30, *40*, 57, *147*, **301**, 376, 381, *381*
'Angustifolia' *147*, **301**
'Aurea' 25, *147*, **301**
cvs 381
Lavandin see *Lavandula* x *intermedia*
Lavandula 314, *375*, 388, *390*
allardii 148, **301**, 302
angustifolia 32, 38, *148*, 271, 287, **301**, 302, 311, 355
'Alba Nana' see *L. a.* 'Nana Alba'
'Folgate' 37, *37*, *148*, **301**
'Hidcote' *21*, 22, *23*, 26, 27, *27*, 28, 30, *39*, *148*, **301**
'Hidcote Pink' *148*, **301**
'Imperial Gem' 25, *148*, **301**
'Miss Katherine' *148*, **301**
'Munstead' *148*, **301**
'Nana Alba' 28, 35, *148*, **301**, 381
'Rosea' 22, *23*, 37, *148*, **301**
'Royal Purple' *148*, **301**
dentata 149, **301-2**
var. *candicans 149*, **302**
'Silver Form' see *L. d.* var. *candicans*
dwarf cvs 380
'Hidcote Blue' *376*
x *intermedia 149*, 301, **302**
Dutch Group *149*, **302**
'Grappenhall' *149*, **302**
'Grosso' *149*, **302**
'Provence' *149*, **302**
'Seal' *149*, **302**
'Twickel Purple' *149*, **302**
lanata 32, *148*, **302**
latifolia 301, 346
multifida 149, **302**
officinalis see *L. angustifolia*
pinnata 149, **302**
'Sawyers' *149*, **302**
spica (in part) see *L. angustifolia*
spp. 57, 374, 375, 377, 379, 383, 384, 391
stoechas 57, *149*, 301, **302**
f. *leucantha 149*, **302**
subsp. *pedunculata* 32, *149*, **302**
vera (in part) see *L. angustifolia*
viridis 149, **302**
Lavatera trimestris 'Mont Blanc' *34*, 35, *35*
Lavender see *Lavandula*
branched see *Lavandula multifida*
common see *Lavandula angustifolia*
English see *Lavandula angustifolia*
French see *Lavandula dentata*; *L. stoechas*
fringed see *Lavandula dentata*
giant see *Lavandula allardii*
green see *Lavandula viridis*
Indian see *Bursera penicillata*
Spanish see *Lavandula stoechas*
woolly see *Lavandula lanata*
Lavender cotton see *Santolina chamaecyparissus*
lavender water 48
law 11, 51
Law of Similars 261
Lawson, William 25
Lawsonia
alba see *L. inermis*
inermis 49, 61, *61*, *150*, **302**
layering 388-9, *389*
leaves 42, 391
drying *391*
Ledebouriella seseloides 246
Ledum
groenlandicum 53, *150*, **302**
latifolium see *L. groenlandicum*
palustre 302
Leech Book of Bald 18, 19
Leek
sand see *Allium scorodoprasum*
wild see *Allium tricoccum*
legal restrictions 11, 51
legends 14-15
Lemon see *Citrus limon*
wild see *Podophyllum peltatum*
Lemon balm see *Melissa officinalis*
Lemon bergamot see *Monarda citriodora*
Lemon grass see *Cymbopogon citratus*
East Indian see *Cymbopogon flexuosus*
Lemon geranium see *Pelargonium crispum*
Lemon thyme see *Thymus* x *citriodorus*
golden see *Thymus* x *citriodorus* 'Aureus'
Lemon verbena see *Aloysia triphylla*
Lemon-scented gum see *Eucalyptus citriodora*
Lentisc see *Pistacia lentiscus*
Leonurus
cardiaca 150, **302**, 303, 342
heterophyllus see *L. sibiricus*
sibiricus 150, **302-3**, 342
Leopard lily see *Belamcanda chinensis*
Leopard's bane see *Arnica montana*
Lepidum sativum 353
Leptandra virginica see *Veronicastrum virginicum*
leptandrin 369
Leptospermum scoparium 66
Lettuce see *Lactuca*
American wild see *Lactuca canadensis*
great see *Lactuca virosa*
prickly see *Lactuca serriola*
wild see *Lactuca serriola*; *L. virosa*
lettuce opium see lactucarium
Levant cotton see *Gossypium herbaceum*
Levisticum officinale 150, **303**, 379, 382, *392*
Levy, Juliette de Baïracli 239
Li Shi Zhen 19, 350, 357
lian fang (*Nelumbo nucifera*) 316
lian geng (*Nelumbo nucifera*) 316
lian qiao (*Forsythia suspensa*) 284
lian xu (*Nelumbo nucifera*) 316
lian zi xin (*Nelumbo nucifera*) 316
liatrin 303
Liatris
callilepis 151
chapmannii 303
punctata 303
scariosa 303
spicata 151, **303**
'Alba' *151*, **303**
squarrosa 303
lichen acids 282
lichens 10
Licorice see *Glycyrrhiza glabra*
American see *Glycyrrhiza lepidota*
Chinese see *Glycyrrhiza uralensis*
Indian see *Abrus precatorius*
Italian see *Glycyrrhiza glabra* var. *typica*
Manchurian see *Glycyrrhiza uralensis*
Persian see *Glycyrrhiza glabra* var. *violacea*
Russian see *Glycyrrhiza glabra* var. *glandulifera*
Spanish see *Glycyrrhiza glabra* var. *typica*
Turkish see *Glycyrrhiza glabra* var. *violacea*
wild see *Glycyrrhiza lepidota*
Licorice fern see *Polypodium glycyrrhiza*
Life-of-man see *Aralia racemosa*
Liferoot see *Senecio aureus*
light requirements 382
lignans 332, 349
Lignum vitae see *Guaiacum*

officinale
Maracaibo see *Bulnesia arborea*
Paraguay see *Bulnesia sarmienti*
Ligusticum
canbyi 303
levisticum see *Levisticum officinale*
porteri **303**
scoticum *151*, **303**
sinense 151, **303**
'Chuanxiong' 151
Ligustrum
lucidum *151*, **304**
'Excelsum Superbum' *151*, **304**
Lilac
California see *Ceanothus*
French see *Galega officinalis*
Persian see *Melia azederach*
Lilium
candidum 14-15, *14*, 35, 60, *151*, **304**
concolor 304
Lily see *Lilium*
blackberry see *Belamcanda chinensis*
flame see *Gloriosa superba*
glory see *Gloriosa*
leopard see *Belamcanda chinensis*
madonna see *Lilium candidum*
Malabar glory see *Gloriosa superba*
May see *Convallaria majalis*
Mozambique see *Gloriosa superba*
resurrection see *Kaempferia galanga*
sweet-scented water see *Nymphaea odorata*
water see *Nymphaea*
white pond see *Nymphaea odorata*
lily oil 48
Lily turf see *Ophiopogon japonica*
Lily of the valley see *Convallaria*
Lily-flowered magnolia see *Magnolia liliiflora*
Lime see *Citrus aurantiifolia; Tilia*
mock see *Aglaia odorata*
limonene 359
Linaloe see *Bursera glabrifolia*
Mexican see *Bursera glabrifolia*
linalol 239, 251, 318, 362
Linaria vulgaris *152*, **304**
Linden see *Tilia*
Lindera
benzoin *152*, **304**
glauca 304
strychnifolia 304
Lindley, John 19
Ling see *Calluna vulgaris*
ling zhi (*Ganoderma lucidum*) 286
Linnaeus, Carl 10, *10*, 160
linoleic acid 304
linolenic acid 304, 325
Linseed see *Linum usitatissimum*
Linum
bienne 304
catharticum 304
usitatissimum *152*, **304-5**, 317, 366
Lion's foot see *Alchemilla vulgaris*
liposoluble complex 335
Lippia
adoensis 305
alba 305
citriodora see *Aloysia triphylla*
dulcis 305
graveolens *152*, **305**, 319
micromera 305
palmeri 305, 319
pseudo-thea 305
Lipstick tree see *Bixa orellana*
Liquidambar
formosana 305
orientalis *152*, **305**
styraciflua 52, *152*, **305**
'Aurea' *153*, **305**
'Variegata' see *L. s.* 'Aurea'
'Worplesdon' *153*, **305**
taiwaniana 305
Liriosma ovata see *Dulacia inopiflora*
Lithospermum
erythrorhizon *153*, **305**
officinale subsp. *erythrorhizon* see *L. erythrorhyzon*
ruderale 305
Liverleaf see *Hepatica nobilis*
liverworts 10
European see *Hepatica nobilis*
Livingstone, David 356
Livre des Merveilles 45
Lobaria pulmonaria 186
l'Obel, Matthias de 153
Lobelia
cardinalis 305
chinensis *153*, **305-6**
inflata 52, 53, *153*, 236, 290, 305, **306**, 309, 328, 348, 352, 361, 363, 365, 368
radicans see *L. chinensis*
siphilitica 305
tupa 305
Lobelia
Chinese see *Lobelia chinensis*
great see *Lobelia siphilitica*
lobeline 305
Lonchocarpus 330
London Dispensatory 231
London Pharmacopoeia 226, 327
long dan cao (*Gentiana scabra*) 288
Long pepper
Indian see *Piper longum*
Javanese see *Piper retrifractum*
Longleaf pine see *Pinus palustris*
Lonicera
caprifolium 306
japonica 30, *30*, 65, *153*, 284, 289, **306**
'Aureoreticulata' *153*, **306**
'Halliana' *65*, 153
var. *repens* 153
periclymenum 306
Loofa (Loofah) see *Luffa*
Loosestrife see *Lythrum*
purple see *Lythrum salicaria*
Lophanthus rugosus see *Agastache rugosa*
Loquat see *Eriobotrya japonica*
Loranthus europaeus 370
Lotus see *Nelumbo*; *Nymphaea caerulea*; *N. lotus*
African see *Ziziphus lotus*
Egyptian see *Nymphaea lotus*
jujube see *Ziziphus lotus*
sacred see *Nelumbo nucifera*
white see *Nymphaea lotus*
Louis XIV 64
Lovage see *Levisticum*
alpine see *Ligusticum*
black see *Smyrnium olusatrum*
Canby's see *Ligusticum canbyi*
Chinese see *Ligusticum sinense*
Porter's see *Ligusticum porteri*
Scots see *Ligusticum scoticum*
sea see *Ligusticum scoticum*
Szechuan see *Ligusticum sinense*
Love parsley see *Levisticum officinale*
Love-in-a-mist see *Nigella damascena*
Low cudweed see *Gnaphalium uliginosum*
LSD see lysergic acid diethylamide
lu gen (*Phragmites australis*) 326
lu hui (*Aloe vera*) 235
Lucerne see *Medicago sativa*
Lucky bean see *Abrus precatorius*
Luffa
aegyptica see *L. cylindrica*
cylindrica 39, *154*, **306**, 383
Lunaria annua 'Alba Variegata' *34*, 35
Lungwort see *Lobaria pulmonaria*; *Pulmonaria*
luteolin glycosides 287
Lycium
barbarum *154*, **306**
chinense see *L. barbarum*
europaeum see *L. barbarum*
Lycoperdon
gemmatum see *L. perlatum*
perlatum *154*, **306-7**, 390
Lycopodium complanatum 307
Lycopus
americanus 307
europaeus 307
lucidus 307
virginicus *154*, **307**
lysergic acid diethylamide (LSD) 16, 263
Lythrum salicaria *154*, **307**

M

ma bian cao (*Verbena officinalis*) 368
ma bo (*Lycoperdon perlatum*) 306
ma chi xian (*Portulaca oleracea*) 334
ma dou ling (*Aristolochia debilis*) 242
Ma huang see *Ephedra distachya*
Ma-kou (goddess) *64*
mace 315
Mace, sweet see *Tagetes lucida*
macerations 47
Mad dog skullcap see *Scutellaria lateriflora*
Mad dog weed see *Alisma plantago-aquatica*
Madagascar 58
Madagascar cardamom see *Afromomum angustifolium*
Madagascar periwinkle see *Catharanthus roseus*
Madder see *Rubia*
Indian see *Oldenlandia umbellata*; *Rubia cordifolia*
Madonna lily see *Lilium candidum*
magnocurarine 307
Magnolia 388
acuminata 307
liliiflora *155*, **307**, 308
'Nigra' *155*, **307**
officinalis *155*, **307**, 308
quinquepeta see *M. liliiflora*
tripetala 307
virginiana *155*, **307-8**
Mahonia 248
aquifolium *155*, 270, **308**, 334
'Apollo' *155*, **308**
repens 308
mai men dong (*Ophiopogon japonicus*) 319
mai yu (*Hordeum vulgare*) 294
Maidenhair fern see *Adiantum*
Maidenhair tree see *Ginkgo*
Majorana
hortensis see *Origanum majorana*
onites see *Origanum onites*
Makhanna see *Euryale ferox*
Makulan see *Piper auritum*
Malabar glory lily see *Gloriosa superba*
Malabar kino see *Pterocarpus marsupium*
Malabar nut see *Justicia adhatoda*
Malay tea see *Psoralea corylifolia*
Male fern see *Dryopteris filix-mas*
dwarf see *Dryopteris oreades*
Mallow see *Malva*
blue see *Malva sylvestris*
common see *Malva sylvestris*
dwarf see *Malva neglecta*
high see *Malva sylvestris*
marsh see *Althaea officinalis*
musk see *Abelmoschus moschatus*; *Malva moschata*
rose see *Hibiscus*
Malva
moschata 27, 308
neglecta 236, 308
spp. *26*
sylvestris *156*, 236, **308**
'Cottenham Blue' *156*, **308**
subsp. *mauritiana* 'Bibor Felho' *156*, **308**
'Zebrina' **308**
verticillata 308
Malvaviscus arboreus 293
man jing zi (*Vitex rotundifolia*; *V. trifolia*) 370
Manaca see *Brunfelsia uniflora*
Manchurian licorice see *Glycyrrhiza uralensis*
Mandarin orange see *Citrus reticulata*
Mandragora officinarum 15, *156*, 251, **308**
Mandrake see *Mandragora*
American see *Podophyllum peltatum*
English see *Bryonia dioica*
Indian see *Podophyllum hexandrum*
Mango ginger see *Curcuma amada*
Manihot esculenta 249
Manioc see *Manihot esculenta*
Manjishta see *Rubia cordifolia*
Manna ash see *Fraxinus ornus*
Manuka see *Leptospermum scoparium*
Mao Tse-tung 64
Maoris 66
Mapá see *Hedeoma floribunda*
Mapato see *Krameria triandra*
Maracaibo lignum vitae see *Bulnesia arborea*
Marañon see *Anacardium occidentale*
Marapuama see *Dulacia inopiflora*
Margosa see *Azadirachta indica*
margosa oil 247
Marigold see *Calendula*; *Tagetes*
African see *Tagetes erecta*
Aztec see *Tagetes erecta*
bur see *Bidens*
French see *Tagetes patula*
hen-and-chickens see *Calendula officinalis* 'Prolifera'
Mexican see *Tagetes lucida*
pot see *Calendula officinalis*
trifid bur see *Bidens tripartita*
Marijuana see *Cannabis sativa* subsp. *indica*
Marjoram see *Origanum*
hop see *Origanum dictamnus*
knotted see *Origanum majorana*
pot see *Origanum onites*
Spanish wood see *Thymus mastichina*
sweet see *Origanum majorana*
wild see *Origanum vulgare*
winter see *Origanum vulgare* subsp. *hirtum*
Markham, Gervase 21
Marrubium vulgare 47, *156*, 236, 247, 278, 293, 295, 297, **308-9**, 328, 361, 363, 365, 368
Marsdenia
cundurango **309**
tinctoria 309
Marsh cudweed see *Gnaphalium uliginosum*
Marsh mallow see *Althaea officinalis*
Marsh samphire see *Salicornia*
Marsh tea see *Ledum palustre*
Marsh trefoil see *Menyanthes trifoliata*
Marsh woundwort see *Stachys palustris*
Mary, Queen of Scots 49
Massoia bark see *Cinnamomum massoia*
Masson pine see *Pinus massoniana*
Mastic thyme see *Thymus mastichina*
Mastic tree see *Boswellia sacra*; *Pistacia lentiscus*
Maté see *Ilex paraguensis*
Materia Medica of South Yunnan 354
Matico see *Piper angustifolia*
Matricaria
parthenium see *Tanacetum parthenium*
recutita *156*, **309**, 374, 377
Matrimony vine see *Lycium barbarum*
Mattioli (Mattiolus), Pierandrea 18
May see *Crataegus laevigata*
Mayapple see *Podophyllum peltatum*
May Day rituals 15, *15*
May lily see *Convallaria majalis*
Mayas 361
Mayflower see *Epigaea repens*
Maypops see *Passiflora incarnata*
Mayweed, scented see *Matricaria recutita*
Meadow cress see *Cardamine pratensis*
Meadow saffron see *Colchicum autumnale*
Meadowsweet see *Filipendula ulmaria*
Medicago sativa 61, *157*, **309**
Medical Flora 337, 364

Medicinal tea tree see *Melaleuca alternifolia*
medicine man *53*
medicines 46-7, 48
Medick see *Medicago*
Mediterranean bed 32, *32*
Medizinal-Pflanzen 59
Medlar, Japanese see *Eriobotrya japonica*
Mehnert, G. H. 291
mei gui hua (*Rosa rugosa*) 342
Melaleuca
alternifolia 66, **309-10**
cajuputi 309
leucadendron 67, *157*, 309, **310**
quinquenervia 309
spp. 280
viridiflora 309
Melanthium cochinchinensis see *Asparagus cochinchinensis*
Melegueta pepper see *Afromomum melegueta*
Melia
azadirachta see *Azadirachta indica*
azederach 157, 247, **310**
indica see *Azadirachta indica*
Melilot see *Melilotus*
Melilotus
arvensis see *M. officinalis*
caerulea 310
officinalis 11, *157*, 288, **310**
Melissa 388
officinalis 12, 33, 85, *157*, 270, 283, **310-11**, 317, 370, 374, 377, 378, 379, 385
'All Gold' *157*, **310**
'Aurea' 22, *23*, 25, *157*, **310**
'Variegata' see *M. o.* 'Aurea'
Menispermum palmatum see *Jateorhiza palmata*
Mentha 154
aquatica 158, 283, **311**, 312, 378, 379, 381
arvensis 158, 278, **311**, 312
var. *piperascens* 65, 311
var. *villosa* 311
austriaca see *M. arvensis*
canadensis see *M. arvensis* var. *villosa*
cardiaca see *M.* x *gracilis*
crispa see *M. spicata*
diemenica 311
x *gentilis* see *M.* x *gracilis*
x *gracilis 158*, **311**
'Aurea' see *M.* x *g.* 'Variegata'
'Variegata' *158*, **311**
hirsuta see *M. aquatica*
incana see *M. longifolia*
insularis see *M. suaveolens*
longifolia 158, **311**
macrostachya see *M. suaveolens*
nemorosa var. *alopecuroides* see *M.* x *villosa* var. *alopecuroides*
nigricans see *M.* x *piperita*
x *piperita* 22, 41, 49, *158*, 227, 283, 294, **311**, 314, 328, 347, 374, 377, 379, *379*, 393
'Citrata' *158*, **311**
pulegium 30, *159*, 252, 291, **311**, 312
'Cunningham Mint' *159*, **311**
requienii 30, *31*, *159*, **311**, 312, 375, 379
rubra see *M.* x *smithiana*
satureioides **311**, 312
x *smithiana 159*, **312**
spicata 22, 29, 49, 57, *159*, **312**, 378, 379, 393
'Crispa' 30, *159*, **312**
'Moroccan' **312**
spp. 379, 382, 384, 385, 388
suaveolens 159, **312**, *382*
'Variegata' 22, 27, *27*, 33, 85, *159*, **312**, 384
sylvestris see *M. longifolia*
x *villosa* var. *alopecuroides 159*, **312**
viridis see *M. spicata*
menthol 311, 335, 359
Menyanthes trifoliata 30, *160*, 240, 261, **312**, 334, 347, 372, 378, 379, 381
Mescal bean see *Sophora secundiflora*
methadone 17
methi (*Trigonella foenum-graecum*) 364
methyl chavicol 318
methyl cinnamate 318
methyl salicylate 248, 286, 358, 359
Mexican linaloe see *Bursera glabrifolia*
Mexican marigold see *Tagetes lucida*
Mexican oregano see *Lippia graveolens*; *Poliomintha longiflora*
Mexican sarsaparilla see *Smilax aristolochiaefolia*
Mexican tea see *Chenopodium ambrosioides*
Mexican yam see *Dioscorea macrostachya*
Mezereon see *Daphne mezereum*
Michaelmas daisy see *Aster* p. 245
microclimates 375
micropropagation 389
Microtaena cymosa 332
microwave-drying 392
Middle East, herbs in wild 60-1
Mignonette tree see *Lawsonia inermis*
mildew 382
Milfoil see *Achillea millefolium*
Milk bush see *Euphorbia tirucalli*
Milk thistle see *Silybum*
Milk vetch see *Astragalus*
Milkweed see *Asclepias*
Milkwort see *Polygala*
common see *Polygala vulgaris*
dwarf see *Polygala amarella*
Milky pine see *Alstonia scholaris*
Millet, foxtail see *Setaria italica*
Mimosa see *Albizia julibrissin*
Mint see *Mentha*
American see *Mentha arvensis* var. *villosa*
apple see *Mentha suaveolens*
Bowles' see *Mentha* x *villosa* var. *alopecuroides*
corn see *Mentha arvensis*
Corsican see *Mentha requienii*
field see *Mentha arvensis*
ginger see *Mentha* x *gracilis*
hoary mountain see *Pycnanthemum incanum*
horse see *Mentha longifolia*; *Monarda*
Japanese see *Mentha arvensis* var. *piperascens*
Korean see *Agastache rugosa*
mountain see *Pycnanthemum*
red raripila see *Mentha* x *smithiana*
red see *Mentha* x *gracilis*
slender see *Mentha diemenica*
spear see *Mentha spicata*
squaw see *Hedeoma pulegioides*
Virginia mountain see *Pycnanthemum virginianum*
water see *Mentha aquatica*
woolly see *Mentha suaveolens*
Mint bush see *Prostanthera*
round-leaved see *Prostanthera rotundifolia*
Mioga ginger see *Zingiber mioga*
Mishmi bitter see *Coptis chinensis*
Mistletoe see *Viscum*
mulberry see *Loranthus europaeus*
Mitchell, John 160
Mitchella repens 160, **312**
Mithridates 345
Mitsuba see *Cryptotaenia canadensis*
mo yao (*Commiphora myrrha*) 265
Mock lime see *Aglaia odorata*
Moctezuma 13
Modern Herbal 19, 99, 285, 297, 299, 307, 318, 332, 349
Mohicans 247
moist positions, herbs for 379
Mole plant see *Euphorbia lathyrus*
Momordica
charantia 160, 230, **312**
cochinchinensis 312
elateria see *Ecballium elaterium*
grosvenori 312
Monarda
austromontana 313
'Cambridge Scarlet' 160
citriodora 313
didyma 22, 25, *26*, 27, *160*, **313**, 384
fistulosa 160, **313**
menthaefolia 313
punctata 160, **313**
Monardes, Nicolas 16, 19, 315
monastery gardens 12-13
Mondo grass see *Ophiopogon japonica*
Monk's pepper see *Vitex agnus-castus*
Monkshood see *Aconitum*
azure see *Aconitum carmichaelii*
Monte Cassino, Italy 12
Mooli see *Raphanus sativus* var. *macropodus*
Moreton Bay chestnut see *Castanospermum australe*
Morinda
citrifolia 161, **313**
officinalis 313
tinctoria 313
morindin 161
Moringa
oleifera 161, **313**
peregrina 313
pterygosperma 313
Mormon tea see *Ephedra trifurca*
Morning glory see *Ipomoea*
morphine 17, 279, 322
Morus
alba 161, 288-9, **313-14**
'Pendula' *161*, **314**
nigra 38, 61, 161, 313
Mosquito plant see *Hedeoma pulegioides*; *Ocimum americanum*
Moss
bog see *Sphagnum cymbilifolium*
Iceland see *Cetraria islandica*
Irish see *Chondrus crispus*
oak see *Evernia prunastri*
peat see *Sphagnum*
sphagnum see *Sphagnum cymbilifolium*
mosses 10
Mother of Herbs see *Artemisia vulgaris*
Mother of thyme see *Thymus serpyllum*
Motherwort see *Leonurus*
Chinese see *Leonurus sibiricus*
mound layering 389
Mount Atlas daisy see *Anacyclus*
Mount Rainier National Park *52*
Mountain balm see *Eriodictyon californicum*
Mountain box see *Arctostaphylos uva-ursi*
Mountain flax see *Linum catharticum*
Mountain grape see *Mahonia aquifolium*
Mountain laurel see *Kalmia latifolia*
Mountain mint see *Pycnanthemum*
hoary see *Pycnanthemum incanum*
Virginia see *Pycnanthemum virginianum*
Mountain pepper see *Tasmannia lanceolata*
Mountain pine, dwarf see *Pinus mugo* var. *pumilio*
Mountain spinach, red see *Atriplex hortense* 'Rubra'
Mountain tobacco see *Arnica montana*
Mouse-ear hawkweed see *Hieracium pilsella*
Moutan peony see *Paeonia suffruticosa*
Mouth root see *Coptis groenlandica*
Moxa, Chinese see *Artemisia vulgaris*
Mozambique lily see *Gloriosa superba*
mu dan pi (*Paeonia suffruticosa*) 321
mu gua (*Chaenomeles speciosa*) 258
mu jing (*Vitex negundo* var. *heterophylla*) 370
mu tong (*Akebia trifoliata*) 232
mu xiang (*Saussurea lappa*) 350
mu zei (*Equisetum hyemale*) 278
mucilages 11
Mucuna
bennettii 314
deeringiana see *M. pruriens* var. *utilis*
pruriens **314**
var. *utilis* 314
prurita see *M. pruriens*
utilis see *M. pruriens* var. *utilis*
Mugwort see *Artemisia vulgaris*
Western see *Artemisia ludoviciana*
white see *Artemisia lactiflora*
Muir, John 52
Muira-puama see *Dulacia inopiflora*
Mulberry see *Morus*
dyer's see *Morinda tinctoria*
Indian see *Morinda citrifolia*
white see *Morus alba*
Mulberry mistletoe see *Loranthus europaeus*
Mulberry-leaved chrysanthemum see *Dendranthema* x *grandiflorum*
mulching 384
Mullein see *Verbascum*
dark see *Verbascum nigrum*
great see *Verbascum thapsus*
large-flowered see *Verbascum densiflorum*
orange see *Verbascum phlomoides*
Multiplier onion see *Allium cepa* Aggregatum group
Munjeet see *Rubia cordifolia*
Murray red gum see *Eucalyptus camaldulensis*
Murraya
koenigii 44, *161*, **314**
paniculata 76, 161
Musa, Antonius 355
Muscatel oil 347
Muscatel sage see *Salvia sclarea*
Musk mallow see *Abelmoschus moschatus*; *Malva moschata*
Musk okra see *Abelmoschus moschatus*
Musk root see *Ferula sumbul*
Musk seed see *Abelmoschus moschatus*
Mustard
black see *Brassica nigra*
brown see *Brassica juncea*
Chinese see *Brassica juncea*
garlic see *Alliaria petiolata*
hedge see *Sisymbrium officinale*
Indian see *Brassica juncea*
white see *Sinapis alba*
mustard oil 11, 254, 316, 346
Mustard tree see *Salvadora persica*
Muster-John-Henry see *Tagetes minuta*
mutations 384
Myddfai, Wales 18
Myrica
californica 314
cerifera 162, **314-15**, 348, 372
gale 30, *162*, 314, **315**, 379
pensylvanica 162
Myristica
argentea 162
fatua 162
fragrans 67, *67*, *162*, **315**
malabarica 162
myristicin 315
Myrobalan see *Terminalia*
bastard see *Terminalia belerica*
beleric see *Terminalia belerica*
emblic see *Phyllanthus emblica*
myrosin 250
Myroxylon
balsamum 162, **315**
var. *pereirae* see *M. pereirae*
pereirae **315**
peruiferum see *M. pereirae*
toluiferum see *M. balsamum*
Myrrh see *Commiphora myrrha*
garden see *Myrrhis odorata*
Myrrhis odorata 33, *162*, **315-16**, 379, 382, 386
Myrtle see *Myrtus*
bog see *Myrica gale*
Jew's see *Ruscus aculeatus*
wax see *Myrica*
Myrtle flag see *Acorus calamus*
Myrtus 388
communis 15, 29, 60, *163*, **316**
'Flore Pleno' *163*, **316**
'Jenny Reitenbach' see *M. c.* subsp. *tarentina*

'Microphylla' see *M. c.* subsp. *tarentina*
'Nana' see *M. c.* subsp. *tarentina*
subsp. *tarentina 163*, **316**, 381
'Tricolor' see *M. c.* 'Variegata'
'Variegata' 30, *163*, **316**, 381, 383
myths 14-15

N

Naawa see *Aspidosperma quebracho-blanco*
Naked ladies see *Colchicum autumnale*
nan gua zi (*Cucurbita maxima*) 269
nan sha shen (*Adenophora stricta*) 229
nan xing (*Arisaema*) 241
naphthoquinone 358
Napoleon Bonaparte 370
Nard see *Nardostachys grandiflora*
Nardostachys
grandiflora 164, **316**, 317
jatamansi see *N. grandiflora*
Narrow-leaved sage see *Salvia lavandulifolia*
Nash, John 372
Nasturtium
indicum see *Tropaeolum majus*
officinale 164, **316**, 378, 381, 387, 388
Nasturtium, garden see *Tropaeolum majus*
National Institute of Medical Herbalists 19
National Parks, North America 52, *52*
Native hops see *Dodonaea viscosa*
Natural History (*Historia Naturalis*) 19
Natural History of Simple Drugs 99
Neem see *Azadirachta indica*
Nelumbium speciosum see *Nelumbo nucifera*
Nelumbo
nucifera 14, 63, *164*, **316-17**, 318
'Alba Grandiflora' *164*, **316**
'Rosea Plena' *164*, **316**
Nepeta
cataria 165, **317**, 379
'Citriodora' **317**
x *faassenii* 165
glechoma see *Glechoma hederacea*
hederacea see *Glechoma hederacea*
Nerium oleander 60
neroli oil 263
Nerve root see *Cypripedium parviflorum* var. *pubescens*
Neue Kreuterbuch, 18
Nettle see *Urtica*
annual see *Urtica urens*
Roman see *Urtica pilulifera*
stinging see *Urtica dioica*
New England's Rarities Discover'd 19
New Guide to Health, or, Botanic Family Physician 19
New Herball 19, 275
New Jersey tea see *Ceanothus americanus*
New Zealand, herbs in wild 66
New Zealand flax see *Phormium tenax*
Ngai camphor see *Blumea balsamifera*
niaouli oil 309
Nicholson, G. 95, 99, 351
Nicotiana sylvestris 34, 35
nicotine 278
Nigella
damascena 165, 317
sativa 165, **317**
Night-blooming cereus see *Selenicereus grandiflorus*
Nightshade see *Atropa*; *Solanum*
deadly see *Atropa belladonna; Solanum dulcamara*
Nimba see *Azadirachta indica*
Nindi (*Ninde*) see *Aeollanthus*
Ningpo figwort see *Scrophularia ningpoensis*
Nispero see *Eriobotrya japonica*
niu bang zi (*Arctium lappa*) 241
nordihydroguaiaretic acid (NDGA) 290
norpseudoephedrine 278
North America, herbs in wild 52-3
North American cow parsnip see *Heracleum lanatum*
Northern ash see *Fraxinus bungeana*
Northern prickly ash see *Zanthoxylum americanum*
Norway spruce see *Picea abies*
nu zhen zi (*Ligustrum lucidum*) 304
nuo dao gen xu (*Oryza sativa*) 320
Nur Jehan, Empress 316
nurseries 378, *378*
Nut grass see *Cyperus rotundus*
Nutmeg see *Myristica*
Nutmeg flower see *Nigella sativa*
Nutmeg geranium see *Pelargonium* 'Fragrans'
Nux-vomica see *Strychnos nux-vomica*
Nymphaea
alba 30, 317
caerulea 14, 317
lotus 14, *165*, **317**
miniature spp. *380*
odorata 165, **317**
'Sulphurea Grandiflora' *165*, **317**
tuberosa 165, 317

O

Oak see *Quercus*
English see *Quercus robur*
golden English see *Quercus robur* 'Concordia'
holm see *Quercus ilex*
pedunculate see *Quercus robur*
upright English see *Quercus robur* f. *fastigiata*
white see *Quercus alba*
Oak moss see *Evernia prunastri*
Oak-leaved geranium see *Pelargonium quercifolium*
Oat see *Avena*
Oaxtepec 13
Ocimum
americanum 318
basilicum 29, 30, 50, *166*, **318**, 382-3, 386, 393
'African Blue' *166*, **318**
'Anise' *166*, **318**
'Cinnamon' *166*, **318**, 383
var. *citriodorum 167*, **318**
var. *crispum 167*, 318, **318**, 383
'Dark Opal' 36, *166*, **318**, 374, 383
'Genovese' *166*, **318**
'Lettuce Leaf' see *O. b.* var. *crispum*
'Licorice' see *O. b.*'Anise'
'Mini Purpurascens Wellsweep' *166*, **318**, 381
var. *minimum 167*, **318**, 381
'Purple Ruffles' 41, *167*, **318**
'Purpureum' see *O. b.* 'Dark Opal'
canum see *O. americanum*
citriodorum see *O. basilicum* var. *citriodorum*
gratissimum 167, **318**
kilimandscharicum 318
micranthum see *O. americanum*
sanctum 167, **318**
spp. 375
suave see *O. gratissimum*
tenuiflorum see *O. sanctum*
viride see *O. gratissimum*
Oenothera biennis 22, 49, 57, *167*, **318-19**, 374, 386
offsets 389
"oil of tranquility" 369
oils
medicinal 47
preserving herbs in 393
ointments 47
Okra, musk see *Abelmoschus moschatus*
Old man see *Artemisia abrotanum*
Old man saltbush see *Atriplex nummularia*
Oldenlandia
diffusa **319**
hedyotidea 319
umbellata 319
Olea europaea 60, *167*, **319**, 381
Oleander see *Nerium oleander*
climbing see *Strophanthus gratus*
Olibanum see *Boswellia sacra*
Olive see *Olea*
Oliver bark see *Cinnamomum oliveri*
omega-3 fatty acids 334
Omeiro 253
Omissions from the Materia Medica 232, 267
Onion see *Allium*
Catawissa see *Allium cepa* var. *proliferum*
common see *Allium cepa*
Egyptian see *Allium cepa* var. *proliferum*
ever-ready see *Allium cepa* Aggregatum group
multiplier see *Allium cepa* Aggregatum group
potato see *Allium cepa* Aggregatum group
sea see *Drimia maritima*
spring see *Allium fistulosum*
tree see *Allium cepa* var. *proliferum*
Welsh see *Allium fistulosum*
Ontario poplar see *Populus* x *candicans*
Opalbalsamum see *Commiphora gileadensis*
Ophelia chirata see *Swertia chirata*
Ophiopogon japonicus 167, **319**, 350
opium 16, 17, 322
lettuce see lactucarium
Opium goddess *16*
opium pipe *16*
Opium poppy see *Papaver somniferum*
Orache see *Atriplex*
Orange
bergamot see *Citrus bergamia*
bitter see *Citrus aurantium*
hardy see *Poncirus trifoliata*
Japanese bitter see *Poncirus trifoliata*
mandarin see *Citrus reticulata*
Seville see *Citrus aurantium*
Orange mullein see *Verbascum phlomoides*
Orangeroot see *Hydrastis canadensis*
Ordeal bean see *Physostigma venenosum*
Oregano see *Hedeoma floribunda*; *Origanum vulgare*; *Plectranthus amboinicus*
Greek see *Origanum onites*
Mexican see *Lippia graveolens*; *Poliomintha longiflora*
oregano oil, Spanish 362
Oregon grape see *Mahonia aquifolium*
creeping see *Mahonia repens*
Oriental bush cherry see *Prunus japonica*
Oriental sweet gum see *Liquidambar orientalis*
Origanum
dictamnus 56, *56*, 118, *168*, **319**, 320
majorana 168, **319-20**, *382*
x *majoricum* **320**
maru var. *aegypticum* 295
onites 168, **320**
'Aureum' 22, **320**
spp. 57, 349, 374, 385
syriacum 295, 319
vulgare 22, *22*, 37, *168*, 319, **320**, 379
'Acorn Bank' *169*, **320**
'Album' *168*, **320**
'Aureum' *23*, 27, *27*, 28, 30, 38, *39*, *168*, **320**
'Aureum Crispum' *168*, **320**
'Compactum' 29, 36, *169*, **320**, 380, 381
'Gold Tip' *40*, *169*, **320**
subsp. *hirtum* 319
'Humile' see *O. v.* 'Compactum'
'Nanum' **320**
'Polyphant' *169*, **320**
'White Anniversary' *169*, **320**
ornamental herbs, indoors 383
Orris see *Iris germanica* var. *florentina*
Oryza
sativa 169, **320**
subsp. *indica* 320
subsp. *japonica* 320
'Arborio' *169*, **320**
Osha see *Ligusticum porteri*
Osier see *Salix*
American red see *Cornus sericea*
purple see *Salix purpurea*
osladin 333
Osmorhiza
claytoni 315
longistylis 315
Oswego tea see *Monarda didyma*
Osyris tenuifolia 348
otto of roses 342
ou jie (*Nelumbo nucifera*) 316
ouabain 356
Oval buchu see *Agathosma crenulata*
oven-drying 392
Owé cola 264
oxalates 344
oxygen 382

P

Pacific yew see *Taxus brevifolia*
Padma see *Nelumbo nucifera*
Padua, University of 13
Paeonia
albiflora see *P. lactiflora*
lactiflora 65, *170*, **321**
'Duchesse de Nemours' *170*, **321**
moutan see *P. suffruticosa*
officinalis 170, **321**
spp. 307, 386
suffruticosa 64, 65, *170*, **321**
'Reine Elizabeth' *65*
veitchii 321
PAF (platelet activating factor) blockers 288
Pagoda tree
Japanese see *Sophora japonica*
yellow see *Sophora flavescens*
Paigle see *Primula veris*
Painted sage see *Salvia viridis*
Pale touch-me-not see *Impatiens pallida*
Palma-christi see *Ricinus communis*
Palmarosa see *Cymbopogon martinii*
palmarosa oil 229
Palmetto, saw see *Serenoa repens*
Palsywort see *Primula veris*
Pamprana see *Pausinystalia lane-poolei*
Panama bark see *Quillaja saponaria*
Panax
ginseng 50, 64, 65, 141, *170*, 264, 277, 289, **321**, 322, 333, 350, 358, 371, 372, 373
notoginseng 64, 170, 321
pseudo-ginseng **321-2**
quinquefolius 50, 52, 53, *53*, 64, 321, **322**
spp. 65, 277
zingiberensis 170
Pandanus
amaryllifolius 322
odoratissimus 66, *170*, **322**
var. *laevis* 322
tectorius see *P. odoratissimus*
Pansy, wild see *Viola tricolor*
papain 55, 255
Papaver
rhoeas 30, *31*, *171*, **322**, 374, 378
'Shirley Single Mixed' *171*, **322**
somniferum 11, 15, 17, *43*, 61, *171*, 279, 300, **322**, 350, 391, *391*
'Danebrog' *171*, **322**
subsp. *hortense* 322
'Peony-flowered Mixed' *171*, **322**
subsp. *somniferum* 322
spp. 386
papaveretum 322
Papaya see *Carica papaya*

Paper rush, Egyptian see *Cyperus papyrus*
Paperbark, weeping see *Melaleuca leucadendron*
Papoose root see *Caulophyllum thalictroides*
Paracelsus 16, 19, 46, 310
Paradisi in Sole 19, 238
Paraguay jaborandi see *Pilocarpus pinnatifolius*
Paraguay lignum vitae see *Bulnesia sarmienti*
Paraguay tea see *Ilex paraguensis*
Pardanthus chinensis see *Belamcanda chinensis*
Pareira see *Chondrodendron tomentosum*
Pareira brava see *Chondrodendron tomentosum*
Parietaria
diffusa see *P. judaica*
judaica *171*, **322**
officinalis see *P. judaica*
Parkinson, John 19, 238
Parsley see *Petroselinum crispum*
breakstone see *Aphanes arvensis*
cow see *Heracleum maximum*
French see *Petroselinum crispum* 'Italian'
Hamburg see *Petroselinum crispum* var. *tuberosum*
Italian see *Petroselinum crispum* 'Italian'
love see *Levisticum officinale*
plain-leaved see *Petroselinum crispum* 'Italian'
poison see *Conium maculatum*
turnip-rooted see *Petroselinum crispum* var. *tuberosum*
Parsley piert see *Aphanes arvensis*
Parsley grape see *Vitis vinifera* 'Ciotat'
parterres *13*
Partridge berry see *Mitchella repens*
Pasque flower see *Pulsatilla*
small see *Pulsatilla pratensis*
Passiflora incarnata 52, 53, *171*, 300, **323**, 330, 356, 367, 374
Passionflower see *Passiflora*
pastes, herb 393
Patchouli see *Pogostemon cablin*
patchouli alcohol 316
patchouli oil 332
pâte de guimauve 236
Pau d'arco see *Tabebuia impetiginosa*
Pau rosa see *Aniba roseaodora*
Paullinia
cupana *171*, **323**
sorbilis see *P. cupana*
yoco 323
Pausinystalia
lane-poolei 323
macroceras 323
tillesii 323
yohimbe 59, **323**
paving 377
Pawpaw see *Carica papaya*
American see *Asimina triloba*
Pea
pigeon see *Sophora subprostrata*
scurf see *Psoralea*
Peach see *Prunus persica*
Pear, balsam see *Momordica charantia*
Peat moss see *Sphagnum*
peat tar 355
pectin 344
Pedunculate oak see *Quercus robur*
peganine 299
Peganum harmala 61, *174*, **323**
pei lan (*Eupatorium fortunei*) 281
Pelargonium 375, 388
acetosum 324
antidysentericum 324
betulinum 323-4
capitatum *173*, 323, **324**
citronellum *172*, **324**
'Clorinda' *172*, **324**
crispum *172*, **324**, 325
'Major' *172*, **324**
'Peach Cream' *172*, **324**
'Variegatum' 30, 41, *172*, **324**
'Fair Ellen' *172*, **324**
'Fragrans' *173*, **324**
'Fragrans Variegatum' *173*, **324**
'Galway Star' *173*, **324**
graveolens 30, *173*, 229, 323, **324**
hybrids 381
'Lady Plymouth' *173*, **324**
'Mabel Grey' 32, **324**
odoratissimum *172*, **324**, 325
'Old Spice' *173*, **324**
'Prince of Orange' *173*, **324**
quercifolium **324**
radens *173*, **324**
'Radula' *173*, 323, **324**
'Radula Rosea' *173*, **324**
rapaceum 324
'Rober's Lemon Rose' 27, *173*, 323, **325**
'Royal Oak' *173*, **325**
scented 383, 385
spp. 59, 381
'Sweet Mimosa' *173*, **325**
tomentosum *173*, **325**, 379, 383
triste 324
pelletierines 338
Pellitory see *Anacyclus pyrethrum*; *Parietaria*
Dalmatian see *Tanacetum cinerariifolium*
of Spain see *Anacyclus pyrethrum*
Pellitory-of-the-wall see *Parietaria judaica*
Pemberton, John 16
Pennyroyal see *Mentha pulegium*
American see *Hedeoma pulegioides*
Australian see *Mentha satureioides*
Brisbane see *Mentha satureioides*
Pennywort, Indian see *Centella asiatica*
Peony see *Paeonia*
Chinese see *Paeonia lactiflora*
common see *Paeonia officinalis*
moutan see *Paeonia suffruticosa*
tree see *Paeonia suffruticosa*
Pepper see *Capsicum*; *Piper*
Ashanti see *Piper guineense*
bell see *Capsicum annuum* var. *annuum*
bird see *Capsicum annuum* var. *glabriusculum*
chili see *Capsicum annuum* var. *annuum*
Chinese see *Zanthoxylum planispinum*
hot see *Capsicum frutescens*
Indian long see *Piper longum*
Jaborandi see *Piper longum*
Jamaica see *Pimenta dioica*
Japanese see *Zanthoxylum piperitum*
Javanese long see *Piper retrifractum*
Melegueta see *Afromomum melegueta*
monk's see *Vitex agnus-castus*
mountain see *Tasmannia lanceolata*
Sichuan see *Zanthoxylum piperitum*
spur see *Capsicum frutescens*
sweet see *Capsicum annuum* var. *annuum*
Tabasco see *Capsicum frutescens*
tailed see *Piper cubeba*
tree see *Capsicum pubescens*
water see *Polygonum hydropiper*
West African see *Piper guineense*
Pepper tree see *Drimys*; *Tasmannia lanceolata*
Peppermint
Australian see *Eucalyptus dives*
broad-leaved see *Eucalyptus dives*
Peppermint geranium see *Pelargonium tomentosum*
Perfoliate honeysuckle see *Lonicera caprifolium*
Perforate St. John's wort see *Hypericum perforatum*
perfumery 48-9, 377
Perilla
crispa see *P. frutescens* 'Crispa'
frutescens 45, *174*, **325**, 383
'Crispa' 30, *174*, **325**, 374, 383
perillaldehyde 325
Periwinkle see *Vinca*
greater see *Vinca major*
lesser see *Vinca minor*
Madagascar see *Catharanthus roseus*
rosy see *Catharanthus roseus*
Pernambuco jaborandi see *Pilocarpus jaborandi*
Pernod, Henri 243
Persian Insect Powder 359
Persian lilac see *Melia azederach*
Persian licorice see *Glycyrrhiza glabra* var. *violacea*
Persians 49
Persicaria bistorta see *Polygonum bistorta*
Persimmon see *Diospyros virginiana*
Chinese see *Diospyros kaki*
Japanese see *Diospyros kaki*
Peruvian bark see *Cinchona pubescens*
pests 383
petha (*Benincasa hispida*) 248
petitgrain 263
Petiver, James 19
Petiveria alliacea *174*, **325**
Petroselinum
crispum 22, 36, 38, *38*, 57, *174*, 261, 322, **325**, 374, *375*, 379, 382, 386, 393
'Italian' *174*, **325**
'Moss Curled' 25, 29, 30, 36, *40*, *175*, **325**
var. *tuberosum* *43*, 174, *175*, **325**
spp. 378
Peucedanum graveolens see *Anethum graveolens*
Peumus boldus 55, *175*, **325-6**
Pfaffia paniculata 55, 321
pfaffic acid 321
pH requirements 377
Phaseolus vulgaris 'Purple Teepee' 38
Pheasant's eye, yellow see *Adonis vernalis*
Phellodendron 210, 348
amurense *175*, **326**, 351
chinense 326
phenolic acids 343
phenolic glycosides 354-5
Philadelphus 'Belle Etoile' 35
phlobaphene 300
phloroglucinol 276
Phormium tenax 66
photosynthesis 382
Phragmites
australis *175*, **326**
'Variegatus' *175*, **326**
communis see *P. australis*
Phygelius capensis 36
Phyllanthus emblica 62, 63, 360
Phyllostachys
henonis see *P. nigra* var. *henonis*
nigra *176*, **326**, 381
'Boryana' *176*, **326**
cvs 381
var. *henonis* *176*, **326**
pubescens 326
Physalis
alkekengi *176*, **326**
franchetti see *P. alkekengi*
peruviana 326
physic gardens 13
Physiomedicalism 19, 46, 52, 305
Physostigma venenosum 58, 59, *59*, **327**
physostigmine 59, 327
Phytolacca 174
acinosa *176*, **327**
americana 53, *176*, 247, 297, **327**
decandra see *P. americana*
spp. 43
pi pa ye (*Eriobotrya japonica*) 278
Picea abies 226
Pick-pocket see *Capsella bursa-pastoris*
Picraenia excelsa see *Picrasma excelsa*
Picrasma
ailanthoides 327
excelsa **327**, 353
Pigeon pea see *Sophora subprostrata*
Pigweed see *Chenopodium*
Pilewort see *Ranunculus ficaria*
Pill-bearing spurge see *Euphorbia hirta*
pilocarpine 55, 327-8
Pilocarpus
japorandi 327
microphyllus 327, **328**
pinnatifolius 327
spp. 55
trachylophus 327
Pilosella officinarum see *Hieracium pilosella*
Pimenta
acris 301, 328
dioica 55, 304, **328**
racemosa see *P. acris*
Pimento see *Pimenta dioica*
Pimpernel see *Anagallis*
blue see *Anagallis arvensis* var. *caerulea*
greater see *Pimpinella major*
scarlet see *Anagallis arvensis*
small see *Pimpinella saxifraga*
Pimpinella
anisum 57, *176*, **328**
major 176, 328
'Rosea' 176
saxifraga 176, *177*, **328**
var. *nigra* 328
pinching out 379
Pine see *Pinus*
Aleppo see *Pinus halepensis*
American ground see *Lycopodium complanatum*
Chinese red see *Pinus tabuliformis*
dwarf mountain see *Pinus mugo* var. *pumilio*
golden Scots see *Pinus sylvestris* 'Aurea'
ground see *Ajuga chamaepitys*; *Lycopodium clavatum*
horsetail see *Pinus massoniana*
longleaf see *Pinus palustris*
Masson see *Pinus massoniana*
milky see *Alstonia scholaris*
prince's see *Chimaphila*
Scots see *Pinus sylvestris*
screw see *Pandanus*
southern pitch see *Pinus palustris*
pine oil 329
Pineapple sage see *Salvia rutilans* 'Scarlet Pineapple'
Pinelli, Giovanni 177
Pinellia ternata *177*, 234, **328-9**
pinene 280, 329
Pink see *Dianthus*
Chinese see *Dianthus chinensis*
clove see *Dianthus caryophyllus*
fringed see *Dianthus superbus*
rainbow see *Dianthus chinensis*
Pink hyssop see *Hyssopus officinalis* f. *roseus*
Pinus 226
halepensis 329
subsp. *brutia* *60*
massoniana 329
mugo var. *pumilio* *177*, **329**, 381
palustris **329**
pinaster 329
spp. 13, 52
strobus 334
succinifera 329
sylvestris 56, *177*, **329**
'Aurea' *177*, **329**, 381
tabuliformis 329
Piper
angustifolia 329
auritum 329
betle *178*, 241, 329, **330**
cubeba *178*, 266, **330**
guineense 329
longum *178*, 329, **330**
methysticum 329, **330**
nigrum 63, 100, *178*, 317, 329, **330**
retrofractum 329
piperidine 329
piperidine alkaloids 305
piperitone 280
Pippali see *Piper longum*
Pipsissewa see *Chimaphila umbellata*
Piscidia
erythrina see *P. piscipula*
piscipula 55, 287, **330**
Pistachio see *Pistacia*

Pistacia
lenticus 56, *56*, *178*, **330-1**
terebinthus *178*, **330-1**
Pitch pine, southern see *Pinus palustris*
pits, growing herbs from 387
pituri (*Duboisia* spp.) 66
Plain-leaved parsley see *Petroselinum crispum* 'Italian'
planning a garden 374-7
plant chemistry 10-11
plant classification 10-11
Planta genista see *Cytisus scoparius*
Plantagenet, house of 271
Plantago
arenaria 331
asiatica *178*, **331**
'Variegata' *179*, **331**
indica 63, 331
major 56, *57*, 178, *179*, 291, **331**, 339, 368
var. *asiatica* see *P. asiatica*
'Rubrifolia' *179*, **331**, 384
ovata 331
psyllium 178, *179*, **331**
spp. 126
Plantain see *Plantago*
Asian see *Plantago asiatica*
greater see *Plantago major*
rat-tail see *Plantago major*
water see *Alisma plantago-aquatica*
planters 41
planting *378*, 379, *379*, *386*
plantlets, propagation by 389
Platycladus orientalis see *Thuja orientalis*
Platycodon 388
grandiflorus *179*, **331**
var. *apoyama* *179*, **331**
Plectranthus
amboinicus *179*, **331**, 332
barbatus 179, *180*, 331, **332**
patchouli 332
Pleurisy root see *Asclepias tuberosa*
Pliny 94, 139, 151, 182, 194, 217, 237, 238, 249, 251, 283, 297, 298, 304, 334, 342, 343, 360, 365, 368
Plum see *Prunus domestica*
Chinese see *Prunus japonica*
date see *Diospyros lotus*
Indian see *Ziziphus jujuba*
Plumbush see *Santalum lanceolatum*
podophyllin 332
podophyllotoxin 299, 332
Podophyllum
emodi 332
hexandrum 63
peltatum 53, *180*, 305, 308, **332**
Poet's jessamine, see *Jasminum officinale*
Pogostemon
cablin *180*, 230, 316, **332**, 388
comosus 332
heyneanus 332, 377
patchouli see *P. cablin*
Pohl see *Brunfelsia uniflora*
Poinsettia see *Euphorbia pulcherrima*
Poison ivy see *Rhus radicans*
Poison nut see *Strychnos nux-vomica*
Poison parsley see *Conium maculatum*
poisonous herbs 11, 43, 379
Pokeberry, Indian see *Phytolacca acinosa*
Pokeroot see *Phytolacca americana*
Pokeweed see *Phytolacca americana*
pokeweed mitogens 327
Polchresta Herba Veronica 368
Polemonium
caeruleum *180*, **332**
'Album' *180* **332**
reptans *180*, **332**
'Pink Beauty' **332**
Poliomintha longiflora 291
Polo, Marco 120
Polygala
amarella 332
senega 275, 293, 332, **333**, 369
spp. 354
tenuifolia 332, **333**
vulgaris 332
Polygonatum
multiflorum 333
odoratum *181*, **333**
'Variegatum' *181*, **333**
officinale see *P. odoratum*
Polygonum
baldschuanicum 181
bistorta 33, *33*, *181*, **333**
'Superbum' *181*, **333**
hydropiper 333
multiflorum 181, **333**
odoratum 333
polyphenols 252
Polypodium
glycyrrhiza 333
vulgare *181*, **333-4**
'Cornubiense' *182*, **334**
Polypody see *Polypodium*
polysaccharides 260
Pomegranate see *Punica granatum*
Poncirus trifoliata 262
Pond lily, white see *Nymphaea odorata*
pools, herbs for 379
Poor man's weatherglass see *Anagallis arvensis*
Poplar see *Populus*
balsam see *Populus balsamifera*
black see *Populus nigra*
Ontario see *Populus* x *candicans*
white see *Populus alba*
Poppy see *Papaver*
California see *Eschscholzia californica*
corn see *Papaver rhoeas*
field see *Papaver rhoeas*
Flanders see *Papaver rhoeas*
opium see *Papaver somniferum*
Populus 388
alba *182*, **334**
'Richardii' *182*, **334**
balsamifera 334
x *candicans* *182*, **334**
'Aurora' *182*, **334**
x *gileadensis* see *P.* x *candicans*
nigra 334
tremuloides 334
Poria cocos see *Wolfiporia cocos*
porphyrins 309
Porteranthus trifoliatus see *Gillenia trifoliata*
Porter's lovage see *Ligusticum porteri*
Portulaca
grandiflora 334
oleracea *182*, **334**
var. *aurea* *182*, **334**
'Golden' 36
var. *sativa* 182
Pot marigold see *Calendula officinalis*
Pot marjoram see *Origanum onites*
pot-bound plants *378*, 379, 381
potpourri garden 26-7, *26-7*
potagers 21, *21*, 38-9, *38-9*
potash 284
potassium bitartrate 371
potassium salts 360
Potato see *Solanum tuberosum*
Potato onion see *Allium cepa* Aggregatum group
Potentilla
anserina 334
erecta 11, *183*, 264, 300, **334**, 347
reptans 334
tormentilla see *P. erecta*
Potentwood see *Dulacia inopiflora*
Poterium officinalis see *Sanguisorba officinalis*
potherbs 44
Potter, Beatrix 259
Pouch of Pearls 321
poultices 47, *47*
powders 47
Prairie hyssop see *Pycnanthemum virginianum*
preserving 391, 392-3
Prickly ash see *Zanthoxylum*
northern see *Zanthoxylum americanum*
southern see *Zanthoxylum clavaherculis*
winged see *Zanthoxylum planispinum*
Prickly lettuce see *Lactuca serriola*
Prickly Moses see *Acacia farnesiana*
Prickly waterlily see *Euryale ferox*
Primrose see *Primula vulgaris*
evening see *Oenothera*
Primula
spp. 167, 386, 389
veris 43, *183*, 278, 290, **334-5**, 393
vulgaris 43, *183*, 214, **334-5**, 378
'Alba Plena' *183*, **335**
subsp. *sibthorpii* *183*, **335**
Prince's feather see *Amaranthus hypochondriacus*
Prince's pine see *Chimaphila*
Prinos verticillatus see *Ilex verticillata*
Privet see *Ligustrum*
Chinese see *Ligustrum lucidum*
Egyptian see *Lawsonia inermis*
glossy see *Ligustrum lucidum*
pro-vitamin A 309
procaine 16
processing herbs 391, 392-3
produce, propagation from 386-7
propagation
by seed 382, 386-7
vegetative 388-9, *388-9*
Propertius 343
prostaglandins 285
Prostanthera
cineolifera 335
rotundifolia *183*, **335**
spp. 66
protein 309
prunasin 335
Prunella vulgaris *183*, **335**
pruning 384-5
Prunus
africana 59, 335
amygdalus see *P. dulcis*
armeniaca 49, *184*, 335, **336**
'Hemskerk' *184*, **336**
avium 335
domestica *184*, **336**
'Prune d'Agen' *184*, **336**
dulcis 49, 61, *184*, 278, **336**
'Macrocarpa' **336**
japonica 335, **336**
laurocerasus *184*, **336**
'Castlewellan' *185*, **336**
'Marbled White' see *P. l.* 'Castlewellan'
'Schipkaensis' *185*, **336**
mume *185*, 335, **336**
'Beni-chidori' *185*, **336**
'Beni-shidori' see *P. m.* 'Beni-chidori'
persica *185*, **336**
serotina 11, *185*, 317, 328, 334, 335, **336**, 363
spinosa 335-6
spp. 384, 385
prussic acid 304
Pseudoevernia purpuracea 282
Psoralea
corylifolia **337**
esculenta 336
linearis see *Aspalathus linearis*
psoralene 236
Psyllium
black see *Plantago indica*
blond see *Plantago ovata*
golden see *Plantago arenaria*
Spanish see *Plantago psyllium*
Ptelea 348
trifoliata *185*, **337**
'Aurea' *185* **337**, 374
pteridophytes 10
Pterocarpus
marsupium 62, *185*, **337**
santalus 337
Pterocladia pinnata 287
pu gong ying (*Taraxacum officinale*) 360
pu huang (*Typha latifolia*) 366
Puccoon, red see *Sanguinaria canadensis*
Pudding pipe tree see *Senna fistula*
Puerari, Marc 186
Pueraria
lobata *186*, **337**
thunbergiana see *P. lobata*
Puffball see *Lycoperdon*
Pukeweed see *Lobelia inflata*
pulegone 252, 311, 317
Pulmonaria
officinalis *186*, **337**
'Cambridge Blue' *186*, **337**
'Sissinghurst White' *186*, **337**
pulque (*Agave americana*) 231
Pulsatilla
chinensis 338
patens 338
pratensis 338
vulgaris 56, *186*, 281, **338**, 367
var. *alba* *186*, **338**
var. *rubra* *186*, **338**
Pumpkin see *Cucurbita maxima*
ash see *Benincasa cerifera*
Punica
granatum 61, *187*, **338**, 387
var. *nana* *187*, **338**, 381
Purging croton see *Croton tiglium*
Purging flax see *Linum catharticum*
Purple clover see *Trifolium pratense*
Purple coneflower see *Echinacea purpurea*
Purple echinacea see *Echinacea purpurea*
Purple loosestrife see *Lythrum salicaria*
Purple osier see *Salix purpurea*
Purple sage see *Salvia officinalis*, Purpurascens Group
Purple-flowered raspberry see *Rubus odoratus*
purpurin 343
Purslane see *Portulaca*
golden see *Portulaca oleracea* var. *aurea*
tree see *Atriplex halimus*
pushkaramula (*Inula*) 296
Pussy toes see *Antennaria*
Pycnanthemum
flexuosum 338
incanum 338
muticum 338
pilosum 338
virginianum *187*, **338**
pyrethrins 359
Pyrethrum
cinerariifolium see *Tanacetum cinerariifolium*
roseum see *Tanacetum coccineum*
Pyrethrum see *Tanacetum cinerariifolium*
pyrrolizidine alkaloids 233, 249, 271, 281, 351, 351-2, 357, 365

Q

qian cao gen (*Rubia cordifolia*) 343
qian shi (*Euryale ferox*) 282
qin jiao (*Gentiana macrophylla*) 287
qing dai (*Indigofera suffruticosa*; *Polygonum tinctorium*) 297
qing hao (*Artemisia annua*) 243
qing mu xiang (*Aristolochia debilis*) 242
qing pi (*Citrus reticulata*) 263
qu mai (*Dianthus chinensis*; *D. superbus*) 273
Quack grass see *Elymus repens*
Quassia
amara 231, 327, 353
cedron see *Simaba cedron*
excelsa see *Picrasma excelsa*
Quassia
Jamaica see *Picrasma excelsa*
Japanese see *Picrasma ailanthoides*
Surinam see *Quassia amara*
quassia extract 327, 353
quassinoids 231, 353
quebrachine 245
Quebracho see *Aspidosperma quebracho-blanco*
red see *Schinopsis quebracho-colorado*
white see *Aspidosperma quebracho-blanco*
Queen Anne's lace see *Ammi majus, Daucus carota*
Queen of the meadow see *Eupatorium purpureum*; *Filipendula ulmaria*
Queen-of-the-night see *Selenicereus grandiflorus*
Queen's delight see *Stillingia sylvatica*
Quercus
alba 338
ilex *57*
infectoria 338

robur 56, *187*, 227, 291, 333, **338-9**, 365
'Atropurpurea' *187*, **338**
'Concordia' *188*, **338**
f. *fastigiata* 187, *188*, **338**
spp. 286
Quickset see *Crataegus laevigata*
Quillai see *Quillaja saponaria*
Quillaja saponaria *188*, **339**
quillajasaponin 339
Quince see *Cydonia oblonga*
flowering see *Chaenomeles*
Japanese see *Chaenomeles japonica*
quinidine 261
Quinine see *Cinchona*
Australian see *Alstonia constricta*
quinone glycosides 260
Quinsy berry see *Ribes nigrum*

R

Rabbit-eye blueberry see *Vaccinium ashei*
Radicchio chicory see *Cichorium intybus*
Radish see *Raphanus*
wild see *Raphanus raphanistrum*
Radix arthritica see *Primula veris*
Rafinesque, Constantine 337, 364
Ragwort see *Senecio jacobaea*
golden see *Senecio aureus*
tansy see *Senecio jacobaea*
Rainbow pink see *Dianthus chinensis*
rainforests 18, 54, *54*, 58, *67*
raised beds, color wheel 25, *25*
Rakkyo see *Allium chinense*
Ramanas rose see *Rosa rugosa*
Rameses II 12
Ramps see *Allium tricoccum*
Ramsons see *Allium ursinum*
Ranunculus
ficaria *188*, 291, **339**
var. *albus* *188*, **339**
'Brazen Hussy' *188*, **339**
var. *flore pleno* 30, *188*, **339**
Raphanus
raphanistrum 339
sativus *189*, 316, **339**
'Cherry Belle' 38
var. *macropodus* 339
raphinin 339
Raripila mint, red see *Mentha* x *smithiana*
Rashona see *Allium sativum*
Rasp-leaved geranium see *Pelargonium radens*
Raspberry see *Rubus idaeus*
black see *Rubus occidentalis*
Chinese see *Rubus coreanus*
purple-flowered see *Rubus odoratus*
Rat-tail plantain see *Plantago major*
Ratanhia see *Krameria triandra*
Rats-and-mice see *Cynoglossum officinale*
Rattlesnake master see *Eryngium yuccifolium*
Rattlesnake root see *Polygala senega*
Rattleweed see *Baptisia tinctoria*
Rau ram see *Polygonum odoratum*
Rauvolfia
serpentina 17, *17*, 62-3, *189*, 230, **339-40**, 369
vomitoria 58, 339
Rauwolf, Leonhart 110, 189
Rauwolfia see *Rauvolfia serpentina*
Ravensara aromatica 361
Ray, John 328
Recherches sur les superstitions en Chine *64*
Red birch see *Betula nigra*
Red bryony see *Bryonia dioica*
Red bush see *Salvia microphylla*
Red cedar see *Juniperus virginiana*
Red cinchona see *Cinchona pubescens*
Red clover see *Trifolium pratense*
"Red Data Books" 51
Red elm see *Ulmus rubra*
Red ginseng see *Salvia miltiorhiza*
Red gum see *Eucalyptus camaldulensis*
Red mountain spinach see *Atriplex hortensis* 'Rubra'
Red orache see *Atriplex hortensis* 'Rubra'
Red osier, American see *Cornus sericea*
Red pine, Chinese see *Pinus tabuliformis*
Red puccoon see *Sanguinaria canadensis*
Red pyrethrum see *Tanacetum coccineum*
Red quebracho see *Schinopsis quebracho-colorado*
Red raripila mint see *Mentha* x *smithiana*
Red River snakeroot see *Aristolochia reticulata*
Redroot see *Ceanothus americanus*
Red rose of Lancaster see *Rosa gallica* var. *officinalis*
Red sage see *Salvia officinalis*, Purpurascens Group
Red stinkwood see *Prunus africana*
Red valerian see *Centranthus ruber*
Red-flowered thyme see *Thymus serpyllum* var. *coccineus*
Red-ink plant see *Phytolacca americana*
Red-rooted gromwell see *Lithospermum erythrorhizon*
Red-topped sage see *Salvia viridis*
Redmint see *Mentha* x *gracilis*
Reed, common see *Phragmites australis*
Reedmace, great see *Typha latifolia*
Regula Monachorum 12
Rehmann, Joseph 189
Rehmannia
elata 189
glutinosa 64, *189*, **340**
Reishi see *Ganoderma lucidum*
religious rituals 14-15
remedies
growing in container 41
preparing at home 47
ren shen (*Panax ginseng*) 321
repotting 381
reserpine 17, 62, 339, 369
resins 11, 43, 391
Resurrection lily see *Kaempferia galanga*
Rh-ya 253
Rhamnus
alnifolia 340
catharticus *189*, **340**
davurica 340
frangula 56, 57, *189*, **340**
infectoria 340
purshiana 52, 53, **340**
utilis 340
Rhatany see *Krameria triandra*
Rhein-cassic acid 352
Rheum
australe 341
x *cultorum* 11
officinale 11, 267, 340-1
palmatum 11, 162, *189*, **340-1**, 373
'Atropurpureum' see *R. p.* 'Atrosanguineum'
'Atrosanguineum' *190*, **341**
var. *tanguticum* **341**
palmatum x *R. coreanum* 341
rhabarbarum 11, 341
rhaponticum see *R. rhabarbarum*
spp. 65
Rheumatism root see *Dioscorea villosa*
Rhine berries see *Rhamnus catharticus*
rhizomes 42-3, 391
Rhubarb see *Rheum*
Chinese see *Rheum palmatum*
chinghai see *Rheum palmatum*
Himalayan see *Rheum australe*
Indian see *Rheum australe*
Japanese see *Rheum palmatum* x *R. coreanum*
Rhus
aromatica 341
chinensis 341
coriaria 341
glabra *190*, **341**
'Laciniata' *190*, **341**
x *pulvinata*, Autumn Lace Group 190
radicans 338, 341
Ribbed melilot see *Melilotus officinalis*
Ribes nigrum *190*, 318, **341**, 385
Rice see *Oryza*
wild see *Zizania aquatica*
Richweed see *Collinsonia canadensis*
ricin 341-2
Ricinus
communis 43, 59, *190*, **341-2**, 379
'Carmencita' *190*, **342**, 381
'Impala' *190*, **342**
Rig Veda 18
River red gum see *Eucalyptus camaldulensis*
Rivera, Diego 13
Robinia 161
Robusta coffee see *Coffea canephora*
Rocambole see *Allium scorodoprasum*
Rock, Joseph 65
Rock hyssop see *Hyssopus officinalis* subsp. *aristatus*
Rock rose see *Cistus*
Rock samphire see *Crithmum maritimum*
Rock sweet flag see *Acorus gramineus*
Rocket see *Eruca vesicaria*
Rocky Mountain juniper see *Juniperus scopulorum*
Rocoto see *Capsicum pubescens*
Roman chamomile see *Chamaemelum nobile*
Roman coriander see *Nigella sativa*
Roman de la Rose *12*
Roman nettle see *Urtica pilulifera*
Roman wormwood see *Artemisia pontica*
Romans 12, 14, 49, 373
roof gardens, growing herbs on 380-1
Rooibos see *Aspalathus linearis*
Roosevelt, Theodore 52
roots 42, 391
storing *393*
Rorippa nasturtium-aquaticum see *Nasturtium officinale*
Rosa 388
herbs with 37
x *alba*
'Semi-plena' *34*, 35
variants 342
canina *191*, **342-3**
centifolia 342
x *centifolia* 'Muscosa' 37
'Complicata' 37
'Comte de Chambord' 37
damascena 14, 60, 61, 191, 342
eglanteria *191*, **342-3**
gallica 342
var. *officinalis* 26, 27, *191*, **342-3**
'Versicolor' 37, *37*
laevigata *181*, **342-3**
'Mme. Alfred Carrière 37
'Mme. Isaac Pereire' 37, *37*
rubiginosa see *R. eglanteria*
rubra 191
rugosa *191*, **342-3**, 389
'Alba' *191*, **342**
spp. 49, 392
Rose see *Rosa*
apothecary's see *Rosa gallica* var. *officinalis*
Cherokee see *Rosa laevigata*
dog see *Rosa canina*
guelder see *Viburnum opulus*
Japanese see *Rosa rugosa*
of Lancaster see *Rosa gallica* var. *officinalis*
Ramanas see *Rosa rugosa*
rock see *Cistus*
sage see *Turnera ulmifolia*
sun see *Cistus*
Rose geranium see *Pelargonium graveolens*
Rose mallow see *Hibiscus*
rose oil 342
rose water, distillation *60*
Rosée du soleil see *Drosera rotundifolia*
rosehips, preserving 393
rosella hemp 293
Roselle see *Hibiscus sabdariffa*
Rosemary see *Rosmarinus*
wild see *Ledum palustre*
rosewood oil 239
Rosha see *Cymbopogon martinii*
rosin 329
rosin oil 226
rosmarinic acid 343, 346
Rosmarinus 388
lavandulaceus see *R. officinalis*, Prostratus Group
officinalis 22, 27, 29, 30, 47, 49, *192*, 287, 301, **343**, 349, 377, 378, 379, 384
var. *albiflorus* *192*, **343**
'Arp' *192*, **343**
'Aureus' *192*, **343**
'Benenden Blue' *192*, **343**, 381
'Collingwood Ingram' see *R. o.* 'Benenden Blue'
'Erectus' see *R. o.* 'Miss Jessopp's Upright'
'Fastigiatus' see *R. o.* 'Miss Jessopp's Upright'
'Fota Blue' *192*, **343**
'McConnell's Blue' *192*, **343**
'Majorca Pink' *192*, **343**
'Miss Jessopp's Upright' *192*, **343**
'Pinkie' *193*, **343**
'Primley Blue' *193*, **343**
Prostratus Group 30, *193*, **343**, 376, 381
'Roseus' *193*, **343**
'Roseus-Cozart' see *R. o.* 'Majorca Pink'
'Severn Sea' *40*, *193*, **343**
'Sissinghurst Blue' *193*, **343**
'Sudbury Blue' *193*, **343**
'Tuscan Blue' *193*, **343**
'Variegatus' see *R. p.* 'Aureus'
spp. 375, 382
Rosy periwinkle see *Catharanthus roseus*
rotenoids 330
rotetone 55, 330
rou dou kou (*Myristica fragrans*) 315
rou gui (*Cinnamomum cassia*) 262
Rough horsetail see *Equisetum hyemale*
Round-headed garlic see *Allium ampeloprasum* var. *ampeloprasum*
Round-leaved mint bush see *Prostanthera rotundifolia*
Round-leaved sundew see *Drosera rotundifolia*
Roupellia grata see *Strophanthus gratus*
routine care 384-5
Roxburghia gloriosa see *Stemona tuberosa*
Royal Botanic Garden Edinburgh 60
Royal jasmine see *Jasminum grandiflorum*
ru xiang (*Boswellia sacra*) 250
Rubia
cordifolia *193*, **343**
manjith see *R. cordifolia*
tinctorum *193*, 285, **343**
rubiacin 343
Rubus
chingii 344
coreanus *194*, **344**
fruticosus *194*, 312, **343-4**
hispidus 344
idaeus *194*, **343-4**, 363
'Aureus' *194*, **344**, 374
occidentalis 344
odoratus 344
parviflorus 344
procumbens 344
spp. 385
villosus 344
Rucola see *Eruca vesicaria* subsp. *sativa*
Rue see *Ruta*
fringed see *Ruta chalapensis*
goat's see *Galega officinalis*
Syrian see *Peganum harmala*
Rum cherry, wild see *Prunus serotina*
Rumex
acetosa 29, 38, *39*, *194*, **344**,

345, 385
acetosella 344
aquatica 194, 344
crispus *194*, 241, 257, 297, **344-5**, 351, 354, 364, 370
obtusifolius 344
scutatus 25, *194*, **344-5**
'Silver Leaf' 36
'Silver Shield' *194*, **344**
Running box see *Mitchella repens*
Ruscus aculeatus *195*, **345**
Russian comfrey see *Symphytum* x *uplandicum*
Russian henbane see *Hyoscyamus albus*
Russian licorice see *Glycyrrhiza glabra* var. *glandulifera*
Russian tarragon see *Artemisia dracunculus* subsp. *dracunculoides*
Russian vine see *Polygonum baldschuanicum*
Ruta
chalapensis 345
graveolens 32, 43, *195*, 343, **345**, 372, 378, 384, 385
'Jackman's Blue' 25, 35, *35*, *195*, **345**
'Variegata' *195*, **345**, 386
rutin 280, 282, 343, 345, 347, 354
Ryntem root see *Gentiana scabra*

S

Sacred basil see *Ocimum sanctum*
Sacred lotus see *Nelumbo nucifera*
sacred plants 14
safety 43
Safflower see *Carthamus tinctorius*
saffron 268-9
false see *Carthamus tinctorius*
meadow see *Colchicum autumnale*
Saffron crocus see *Crocus sativus*
Saffron thistle see *Carthamus tinctorius*
safrole 261, 315, 349, 359
Sage see *Salvia*
apple-bearing see *Salvia pomifera*
clary see *Salvia sclarea*
common see *Salvia officinalis*
fruit-scented see *Salvia dorisiana*
Greek see *Salvia fruticosa*
Jim see *Salvia clevelandii*
muscatel see *Salvia sclarea*
narrow-leaved see *Salvia lavandulifolia*
painted see *Salvia viridis*
pineapple see *Salvia rutilans* 'Scarlet Pineapple'
purple see *Salvia officinalis*, Purpurascens Group
red see *Salvia officinalis*, Purpurascens Group
red-topped see *Salvia viridis*
Spanish see *Salvia lavandulifolia*
Texas see *Salvia coccinea*
tricolor see *Salvia officinalis*
white see *Artemisia ludoviciana*
wood see *Teucrium scorodonia*
Sage bush see *Artemisia*
Sage rose see *Turnera ulmifolia*
Sage-leaved germander see *Teucrium scorodonia*
Saigon cinnamon see *Cinnamomum loureirii*
St. Gall, Switzerland 12
St. Ignatius' bean see *Strychnos ignatii*
St. John's wort see *Hypericum*
common see *Hypericum perforatum*
perforate see *Hypericum perforatum*
salad herbs 44
Saladin of Askalon 126
salicin 17, 334, 369
Salicornia spp. 268
salicylates 11, 334, 335
salicylic acid 17, 283, 345
Salix
alba *195*, **345**, 347, 369, *385*, *388*
'Chermesina' see *S. a.* var. *vitellina* 'Britzensis'
var. *vitellina* *195*, **345**
'Britzensis' *195*, **345**
babylonica 195
cinerea 345
fragilis 345
nigra 345
pentandra 345
purpurea 345
Salmon, William 19
Salt bush see *Salvadora persica*
Saltbush, old man see *Atriplex nummularia*
Salvadora 345-6
persica 60, 61, *61*, **346**
Salvia
calycina see *S. pomifera*
clevelandii *196*, **346**, 347
coccinea *196*, **346**, 347
'Lady in Red' **346**
dorisiana *196*, **346**, 347
elegans 'Scarlet Pineapple' *196*, **346**, 347, 383
fruticosa *196*, **346**, 347
hispanica 54, 346
horminum see *S. viridis*
lavandulifolia *196*, **346**, 347
microphylla 54, 346
miltiorhiza **346**, 347
officinalis 29, *40*, 57, *196*, 227, 344, **346-7**, 348, 378, 379, *382*, 384
'Albiflora' 35, 37, *196*, **347**
'Berggarten' 32, 37, *197*, **347**
'Icterina' 22, *22*, 28, *197*, **347**
'Kew Gold' *197*, **347**
Purpurascens Group 22, *23*, 25, 27, *27*, 28, 30, 37, *197*, 346, **347**, 374, 378
'Purpurascens Variegata' **347**
'Tricolor' 30, 41, **347**, 381
pomifera *197*, 346, **347**
rutilans see *S. elegans* 'Scarlet Pineapple'
salvatrix see *S. officinalis*
sclarea 27, *197*, 346, **347**
var. *turkestanica* *197*, **347**
spp. 374, 375, 382, 383
triloba see *S. fruticosa*
viridis *197*, **347**
'Claryssa' *197*, **347**
cvs 381
Sambucus
nigra 15, *33*, 49, 188, *197*, 227, 281, 290, 314, 317, **347**, 363, 377, 379, 385, 391, 393
'Albovariegata' see *S. n.* 'Marginata'
'Argenteomarginata' see *S. n.*'Marginata'
'Aurea' *197*, **347**
cvs 385
'Guincho Purple' 30, *197*, 218, **347**
f. *laciniata* *197*, **347**
'Marginata' 33, *197*, **347**
'Purpurea' see *S. n.* 'Guincho Purple'
Samphire see *Crithmum*
marsh see *Salicornia*
rock see *Crithmum maritimum*
san huang zhe she ye (*Coptis chinensis*; *Phellodendron amurense*; *Scutellaria baicalensis*) 267, 326, 351
San qi ginseng see *Panax pseudo-ginseng*
Sand leek see *Allium scorodoprasum*
Sandalwood see *Santalum*
Australian see *Santalum spicatum*
Indian see *Santalum album*
white see *Santalum album*
sang bai pi (*Morus alba*) 314
sang shen (*Morus alba*) 314
sang ye (*Morus alba*) 314
sang zhi (*Morus alba*) 314
Sanguinaria
canadensis 49, 52, 53, *198*, 214, **347-8**
'Flore Pleno' see *S. c.* 'Plena'
'Multiplex' see *S. c.* 'Plena'
'Plena' *198*, **348**
Sanguisorba officinalis *198*, 231, **348**
sanguisorbins 348
sanguiins 348
Sanicle, American see *Heuchera americana*
santalols 348
Santalum
album 62, 63, *198*, 266, 298, **348**
fernandezianum 348
lanceolatum 66, 348
spicatum 66, 348
Santolina *375*
chamaecyparissus 22, 24, *198*, **348**, 379, 384, *385*
'Lemon Queen' *198*, **348**
var. *nana* *198*, **348**, 381
'Pretty Carol' *199*, **348**
santonin 243
santoxin 243
sap, collecting 391
Saponaria
officinalis 11, *199*, **348-9**
'Dazzler' *199*, **349**
'Rosea Plena' 199
'Rubra Plena' 30, *199*, **349**
'Variegata' see *S. o.* 'Dazzler'
saponins 11, 256, 321, 333, 335, 339, 345, 348, 354, 364, 369, 370
steroidal 63, 273, 354, 365
Saracen corn see *Fagopyrum esculentum*
Sargassum fusiforme 289, **349**
Sarothamnus scoparius see *Cytisus scoparius*
Sarpagandha see *Rauvolfia serpentina*
Sarsaparilla
Ecuadorian see *Smilax febrifuga*
Honduran see *Smilax regelii*
Mexican see *Smilax aristolochiaefolia*
wild see *Aralia nudicaulis*; *Smilax glauca*
sarsaponin tablets 354
Sassafras albidum 52, 53, *199*, 261, 328, **349**
Sassafras
black see *Cinnamomum oliveri*
California see *Umbellularia californica*
Satureja
acinos see *Acinos arvensis*
hortensis 30, *40*, *199*, **349-50**
montana 29, 199, *200*, **349**, 350, 377, 379
nepeta see *Calamintha nepeta*
repandra see *S. spicigera*
spicigera 30, 36, 199, *200*, **349-50**, 375
spp. 382
thymbra 199, *200*, **350**
Sauce alone see *Alliaria petiolata*
Saussure, Horace Benedict de 200
Saussurea
costus see *S. lappa*
lappa 62, 63, *200*, **350**
Savin see *Juniperus sabina*
Savory see *Satureja*
creeping see *Satureja spicigera*
summer see *Satureja hortensis*
thyme-leaved see *Satureja thymbra*
winter see *Satureja montana*
Saw palmetto see *Serenoa repens*
Sawai see *Strophanthus gratus*
Saxifrage
burnet see *Pimpinella saxifraga*
greater burnet see *Pimpinella major*
scale insects 383
Scallion see *Allium fistulosum*
scarification 386
Scarlet pimpernel see *Anagallis arvensis*
Scarlet willow see *Salix alba* 'Britzensis'
scent, herbs for 374
Scented mayweed see *Matricaria recutita*
Schinopsis quebracho-colorado 245
Schinus terebinthifolius 329
Schisandra
chinensis *200*, **350**
sphenanthera 350
Schisandra, southern see *Schisandra sphenanthera*
Schizonepeta tenuifolia 311, 317
scillarin 275
scilliroside 275
Sclerotium cocos see *Wolfiporia cocos*
scopolamine 276
scopoletin 369
Scopoli, Giovanni Antonio 200
Scopolia
atropoides see *S. carniolica*
carniolica *200*, 276, **350**
lurida 350
physaloides 350
tangutica 64, 350
Scotch broom see *Cytisus scoparius*
Scots lovage see *Ligusticum scoticum*
Scots pine see *Pinus sylvestris*
golden see *Pinus sylvestris* 'Aurea'
Screw pine see *Pandanus*
Scrophularia
auriculata 350
ningpoensis *201*, **350-1**
nodosa *201*, 285, 291, 350, **351**
Scurf pea see *Psoralea*
Scutellaria
altissima 201
baicalensis *201*, 246, 326, 329, **351**
barbata 351
galericulata 351
lateriflora 52, 53, *201*, 246, 268, 271, 300, 343, **351**, 355, 365, 367, 368, 377
macrantha see *S. baicalensis*
Sea fennel see *Crithmum maritimum*
Sea holly see *Eryngium maritimum*
Sea Island cotton see *Gossypium barbadensis*
Sea lovage see *Ligusticum scoticum*
Sea onion see *Drimia maritima*
seaweeds 10
sedatives, planting for 377
Sedge see *Cyperus*
Sedge root see *Cyperus rotundus*
seed heads *391*, 392
seedlings, planting out *386*
seeds 42
harvesting 391
propagation by 382, 386-7, *386*
saving 386, *387*
scarifying 386
stratifying 386
Selenicereus grandiflorus *202*, 268, **351**
self-seeding 384
prevention *384*
Selfheal see *Prunella*
Sempervivum
planting *378*
tectorum 41, *202*, **351**, 378, 379, 380, 381
cvs 381
'Royal Ruby' *202*, **351**
Seneca snakeroot see *Polygala senega*
Senecio
aureus *202*, **351-2**
jacobaea 352
vulgaris 352
Senna
alata 352
alexandrina *202*, 267, 269, 298, **352**, 359
fistula 352
laevigata 352
marilandica 53, *202*, **352**
obtusifolia 277, 352
occidentalis 352
reticulata 352
sericea 352
sieberiana 352
sophera 352
surattensis 352
Senna
Alexandrian see *Senna alexandrina*
sickle see *Senna obtusifolia*
Tinnevelly see *Senna alexandrina*
wild see *Senna marilandica*
sereh (*Cymbopogon citratus*) 270
Serenoa
repens 52, 53, *203*, 269, **352**, 365, 389
serrulata see *S. repens*
serotinin 366
Serpentary see *Aristolochia*

serpentaria
English see *Polygonum bistorta*
Serpentwood see *Rauvolfia serpentina*
African see *Rauvolfia vomitoria*
serpolet oil 362
Sesame see *Sesamum indicum*
Sesamum indicum 61, *293*, **352-3**
sesquiterpene alcohols 348
sesquiterpene lactones 359
Setaria italica 317
Seven barks see *Hydrangea arborescens*
Seville orange see *Citrus aurantium*
sha ren (*Amomium xanthioides* 237
shade, herbs for 379
Shaggy speedwell see *Agrimonia pilosa*
Shallot see *Allium cepa*. Aggregatum group
shamanism 46
shan yao (*Dioscorea opposita*) 274
shan zha (*Crataegus pinnatifida*) 268
shan zhu yu (*Cornus officinalis*) 267
shang lu (*Phytolacca acinosa*) 327
Sharplobe hepatica see *Hepatica acutiloba*
Shatavari see *Asparagus racemosus*
Shave grass see *Equisetum arvense*
she gan (*Belamcanda chinensis*) 247
Sheep's sorrel see *Rumex acetosella*
Shelter Island 13
shen jin cao (*Lycopodium clavatum*) 307
Shen Nong Canon of Herbs 19, 228-9, 233, 247, 278, 328, 331, 337, 341, 343, 348, 349, 351, 364
sheng di huang (*Rehmannia glutinosa*) 340
sheng ma (*Cimicifuga americana; C. dahurica; C. foetida*) 261
Shepherd's purse see *Capsella bursa-pastoris*
shi chang pu (*Acorus gramineus*) 228
shi di (*Diospyros kaki*) 274
shi hu (*Dendrobium nobile*) 273
shi liu pi (*Punica granatum*) 338
shi nan xing (*Arisaema*) 241
Shiso see *Perilla frutescens*
shogaols (*Zingiber officinale*) 373
shou wou teng (*Polygonum multiflorum*) 333
Shrimp plant see *Justicia brandegeana*
shrubs
specimen 381
training 385
shu di huang (*Rehmannia glutinosa*) 340
Shungiku see *Chrysanthemum coronarium*
si gua luo (*Luffa cylindrica*) 306
si jun zi tang (*Atractylodes macrocephala*; *Glycyrrhiza uralaensis*; *Panax ginseng*; *Wolfiporia cocos*) 372
Si-Ling, Empress 314
Siam benzoin see *Styrax tonkinensis*
Siamese ginger see *Alpinia galanga*
Siberian ginseng see *Eleutherococcus senticosus*
Siberian milkwort see *Polygala tenuifolia*
Sichuan aconite see *Aconitum carmichaelii*
Sichuan Journal of Chinese Herbal Medicine 372
Sichuan pepper see *Zanthoxylum piperitum*
Sicilian sumac see *Rhus coriaria*
Sickle senna see *Senna obtusifolia*
Sickle-leaved hare's ear see *Bupleurum falcatum*
Siddha medicine 62
Siegert, Dr. J. G. B. 285
sikimotoxin 296
silica 278
Silk tree see *Albizia julibrissin*
Silk-cotton tree see *Ceiba pentandra*
Silkweed see *Asclepias*
Silver birch see *Betula pendula*
Silver boxwood see *Buxus sempervirens* 'Elegantissima'
Silver fir see *Abies*
Silver hedgehog holly see *Ilex aquifolium* 'Ferox Argentea'
Silverweed see *Potentilla anserina*
Silybum marianum 32, 57, *203*, 255, **353**
silymarin 57
Simaba cedron **353**
Simaruba amara see *Quassia amara*
Simmonds, T. W. 203
Simmondsia
californica see *S. chinensis*
chinensis 49, 50, *51*, 53, *203*, **353**
simples 46
Sinapis
alba 11, 61, 63, *203*, 233, 250, 254, 305, 339, 346, **353**
juncea see *Brassica juncea*
nigra see *Brassica nigra*
Singer's plant see *Sisymbrium officinale*
sinigrin 233, 250
sirop de capillaire 229
sisal see *Agave sisalina*
Sisymbrium
alliaria see *Alliaria petiolata*
officinale 203, **354**
site 377, 378
Six-rowed barley see *Hordeum polystichum*
Skullcap see *Scutellaria*
Baikal see *Scutellaria baicalensis*
barbed see *Scutellaria barbata*
European see *Scutellaria galericulata*
mad dog see *Scutellaria lateriflora*
Virginia see *Scutellaria lateriflora*
Skunk cabbage see *Symplocarpus*
Sky god's tree see *Alstonia boonei*
Sleeping hibiscus see *Malvaviscus arboreus*
Slender mint see *Mentha diemenica*
Slippery elm see *Ulmus rubra*
Sloane, Sir Hans *54*, 290
small gardens, growing herbs in 374, *375*
Smallage see *Apium graveolens*
Smartweed see *Polygonum hydropiper*
Smilax
aristolochiaefolia 354
china 204, **354**
febrifuga 354
glabra 349, 354
glauca 53
glyciphylla 354
officinalis see *S. regelii*
ornata see *S. regelii*
regelii **354**
spp. 344
Smooth strophanthus see *Strophanthus gratus*
Smooth sumac see *Rhus glabra*
Smyrnium olusatrum 204, **354**
Snake bush see *Justicia adhatoda*
Snake gourd see *Trichosanthes kirilowii*
Snake-needle grass see *Oldenlandia diffusa*
Snakehead see *Chelone glabra*
Snakemouth see *Chelone glabra*
Snakeroot (Snake root) see *Aristolochia*
black see *Cimicifuga racemosa*
button see *Eryngium aquaticum*; *Liatris spicata*
Indian see *Rauvolfia serpentina*
Red River see *Aristolochia reticulata*
Seneca see *Polygala senega*
Texas see *Aristolochia reticulata*
Virginia see *Aristolochia serpentaria*
Snakeweed see *Polygonum bistorta*
Snowball bush see *Viburnum opulus* 'Roseum'
Soapbark tree see *Quillaja*
Soapwort see *Saponaria*
Socotra 60
Socotrine aloe see *Aloe perryi*
Socrates 265
sodium cromoglycate 17
soil 377
Solanum
capsicastrum 176
carolinense 354
dulcamara 204, **354**
'Variegatum' 43, *204*, **354**
tuberosum 354
Soldiers and sailors see *Pulmonaria officinalis*
Soldier's woundwort see *Achillea millefolium*
Solenostemon 174
Solidago
canadensis 355
odora 355
rigida 355
virgaurea 204, 290, **354-5**
Solomon, King 103
Solomon's seal see *Polygonatum*
angular see *Polygonatum odoratum*
song jie (*Pinus tabuliformis*) 329
Sophora
flavescens 273, **355**
japonica 205, **355**
'Pendula' *205*, **355**
secundiflora 205, 355
subprostrata 355
Sorrel see *Rumex*
buckler-leaf see *Rumex scutatus*
French see *Rumex scutatus*
Jamaica see *Hibiscus sabdariffa*
sheep's see *Rumex acetosella*
Sorrel leaf see *Pelargonium acetosum*
South America, herbs in wild 54-5
South-Sea Herbal 19
Southern pitch pine see *Pinus palustris*
Southern prickly ash see *Zanthoxylum clavaherculis*
Southern schisandra see *Schisandra sphenanthera*
Southernwood see *Artemisia abrotanum*
Spanish bugloss see *Alkanna tinctoria*
Spanish chestnut see *Castanea sativa*
Spanish jasmine see *Jasminum grandiflorum*
Spanish lavender see *Lavandula stoechas*
Spanish licorice see *Glycyrrhiza glabra* var. *typica*
Spanish needles see *Bidens bipinnata*
Spanish oregano oil 362
Spanish psyllium see *Plantago psyllium*
Spanish sage see *Salvia lavandulifolia*
Spanish thyme see *Plectranthus amboinicus*
Spanish wood marjoram see *Thymus mastichina*
sparteine 271
Spearmint see *Mentha spicata*
specialist nurseries 378, *378*
Species Plantarum 10
specimen trees and shrubs 381
Speckled alder see *Alnus rugosa*
Speedwell see *Veronica*
common see *Veronica officinalis*
heath see *Veronica officinalis*
shaggy see *Agrimonia pilosa*
sphagnol 355
Sphagnum
cymbilifolium 205, **355**
japonicum 355
Sphagnum moss see *Sphagnum cymbilifolium*
Spice bush see *Lindera benzoin*
spices 44-5
spider mites 383, *383*
Spikenard see *Nardostachys*
American see *Aralia racemosa*
Spinach, red mountain see *Atriplex hortense* 'Rubra'
Spindle see *Euonymus*
Spindle tree see *Euonymus europaeus*
Spiraea ulmaria see *Filipendula ulmaria*
Sponge gourd see *Luffa cylindrica*
spores, propagation by 389
sports 384
Spotted cranesbill see *Geranium maculatum*
Spring onion see *Allium fistulosum*
Spruce, Norway see *Picea abies*
Spur pepper see *Capsicum frutescens*
Spurge see *Euphorbia*
caper see *Euphorbia lathyrus*
pill-bearing see *Euphorbia hirta*
Spurge laurel see *Daphne laureola*
Squash see *Cucurbita*
winter see *Cucurbita maxima*
Squaw mint see *Hedeoma pulegioides*
Squaw root see *Caulophyllum thalictroides*
Squaw vine see *Mitchella repens*
Squaw weed see *Senecio aureus*
Squill see *Drimia maritima*
Indian see *Drimia indica*
Squirting cucumber see *Ecballium elaterium*
Stachys
betonica see *S. officinalis*
officinalis 205, **355-6**, 365, 377
'Rosea Superba' *205*, **355**
palustris 205, **355-6**
Stagbush see *Viburnum prunifolium*
Stag's horn clubmoss see *Lycopodium clavatum*
Star anise see *Illicium verum*
Star grass see *Aletris farinosa*
Starwort, yellow see *Inula britannica* var. *chinensis*
Stavesacre see *Delphinium staphisagria*
Stellaria media 47, 56, *205*, **356**, 393
Stemona
japonica 356
sessilifolia 356
tuberosa **356**
stems (stalks) 42, 391
stepping stones 377
steroidal saponins 63, 273, 354, 365
steroids 17
sterols 276
Sticklewort see *Agrimonia eupatoria*
Sticky hop bush see *Dodonaea viscosa*
Sticky Willie see *Galium aparine*
Stiff goldenrod see *Solidago rigida*
still-room books 18
Stillingia sylvatica 297, **356**
Stinging nettle see *Urtica dioica*
Stinking Roger see *Tagetes minuta*
Stinkwood, red see *Prunus africana*
Stizolobium pruriens see *Mucuna pruriens*
Stobart, Tom 268
Stoerck, Anton von 265
Stone root see *Collinsonia canadensis*
storax 357
Storax see *Liquidambar orientalis*
American see *Liquidambar styraciflua*
storing herbs 391, 392-3
Strassburg turpentine 226
stratification 386
Strawberry see *Fragaria*
wild see *Fragaria vesca*
strawberry jar 41, 380, *380*
Strong man's weed see *Petiveria alliacea*
strophanthin 356
Strophanthus
gratus 206, **356**
hispidus 356

intermedius 356
kombe 356
spp. 58, 59
strophanthus 356
Strychnine see *Strychnos nux-vomica*
Strychnos
ignatii 357
nux-vomica 54-5, 67, *206*, **357**
spp. 271
Stuart, G.A. 267
Styrax
benzoin 67, 305, **357**
hypoglauca 357
tonkinensis 357
su gen (*Perilla frutescens*) 325
su he xiang (*Liquidambar orientalis*) 305
Su Song 302, 340
su zi (*Perilla frutescens*) 325
suan zao ren (*Ziziphus jujuba*) 373
Succory see *Cichorium intybus*
suckers 384, 389
Sudanese tea see *Hibiscus sabdariffa*
sugar, preserving in 393
suk gok (*Dendrobium nobile* 273
sulfur 11, 365
sulfur glycosides 371
Suma see *Pfaffia paniculata*
Sumac see *Rhus*
Chinese see *Ailanthus altissima*; *Rhus chinensis*
Sicilian see *Rhus coriaria*
smooth see *Rhus glabra*
tanner's see *Rhus coriaria*
Sumerians 17
Summer savory see *Satureja hortensis*
sun
herbs for 379
requirements 382
Sun plant see *Portulaca grandiflora*
Sun rose see *Cistus*
Sundew see *Drosera*
round-leaved see *Drosera rotundifolia*
Sunflower see *Helianthus*
Supplement to the Extension of the Materia Medica 268
Surinam, S America *50*
Surinam quassia see *Quassia amara*
Swallow wort see *Chelidonium majus*
Swamp dewberry see *Rubus hispidus*
Sweet Annie see *Artemisia annua*
Sweet basil see *Ocimum basilicum*
Sweet bay see *Laurus nobilis*; *Magnolia virginiana*
sweet birch oil 248
Sweet briar see *Rosa eglanteria*
Sweet chervil see *Myrrhis odorata*
Sweet chestnut see *Castanea sativa*
Sweet cicely see *Myrrhis odorata*
Sweet clover, yellow see *Melilotus officinalis*
Sweet corn see *Zea mays*
Sweet everlasting see *Gnaphalium obtusifolium*
Sweet fennel see *Foeniculum vulgare* var. *azoricum*
Sweet fern see *Comptonia peregrina*
Sweet flag see *Acorus*
grass-leaved see *Acorus gramineus*
rock see *Acorus gramineus*
Sweet gale see *Myrica gale*
Sweet galingale see *Cyperus longus*
Sweet goldenrod see *Solidago odora*
Sweet grass see *Hierochloe odorata*
Sweet gum see *Liquidambar*
oriental see *Liquidambar orientalis*
Sweet mace see *Tagetes lucida*
Sweet marjoram see *Origanum majorana*
Sweet pepper see *Capsicum annuum* var. *annuum*
Sweet tea vine see *Gynostemma pentaphyllum*
Sweet vernal grass see *Anthoxanthum odoratum*
Sweet violet see *Viola odorata*
Sweet woodruff see *Galium odoratum*
Sweet wormwood see *Artemisia annua*
Sweet-scented water lily see *Nymphaea odorata*
Swertia
chirata 63, **357**
japonica 357
Sylvester Manor, Shelter Island, New York 13
Symphytum 337
officinale 47, 48, 49, *206*, 236, 249, 271, 273, 288, 351, **357-8**, 365, 372, 379, 393
peregrinum see *S.* x *uplandicum*
x *uplandicum* *206*, **358**
'Variegatum' 30, *206*, **358**
Symplocarpus foetidus 30, *206*, 328, **358**
synergistic effect 11, 46
Syrian rue see *Peganum harmala*
syrups 47, 393
Syzygium
aromaticum 67, *206*, 274, 288, 314, **358**
cumini 358
Szechuan lovage see *Ligusticum sinense*

T

Tabasco pepper see *Capsicum frutescens*
tabasher (*tabashir*) 326
Tabebuia
avellanedae see *T. impetiginosa*
heptaphylla 358
impetiginosa *207*, **358**
incana 358
insignis var. *monophylla* 358
neochrysantha 358
rosea 358
serratifolia 358
Tagetes
erecta 358
lucida *207*, **358-9**
minuta *207*, **358-9**
patula 25, *39*, 197, *207*, **358-9**
cvs 381
'Honeycomb' *207*, **359**
'Sophia Mixed' 38
spp. 54, 252
Tahiti vanilla see *Vanilla tahitensis*
Tailed pepper see *Piper cubeba*
Tale of Peter Rabbit 259
Talmud 238
Tamarack see *Larix laricina*
Tamarind see *Tamarindus*
Tamarindus indica *207*, 235, **359**
Tanacetum
balsamita *208*, **359**
var. *tomentosum* 32, *208*, **359**
cinerariifolium *208*, 237, **359**, 360, *376*
coccineum 359
densum subsp. *amani* *32*
parthenium 41, *208*, **359-60**, *376*
'Aureum' 25, 35, *208*, **360**
dwarf cvs 197
'Flore Pleno' see *T. p.* 'Plenum'
'Golden Ball' *208*, **360**
'Golden Moss' *208*, **360**, 381
'Plenum' *209*, **360**
'Snowball' *209*, **360**
'Tom Thumb White Stars' 22, *22*, 27, *209*, **360**
'White Bonnet' *209*, **360**
vulgare 27, *27*, *209*, 359, **360**, 379, 384
var. *crispum* *209*, **360**
'Isla Gold' *209*, **360**
'Silver Lace' *209*, **360**
tanbark 66
Tang Materia Medica 246, 248, 306, 362
Tangerine see *Citrus reticulata*
Tanner's sumac see *Rhus coriaria*
tannic acid 338
tannins 11, 252, 274, 288, 300, 314, 331, 334, 339, 341, 344, 348, 349, 355, 369
Tansy see *Tanacetum*
Tansy ragwort see *Senecio jacobaea*
Tao Hong Jin 233
Tao Hong-Ying 326
Tao Kuang 64
tao ren (*Prunus persica*) 336
Tar weed see *Eriodictyon californicum*
Taraktogenos kurzii see *Hydnocarpus kurzii*
Taraxacum officinale 56, *210*, 240, 281, 307, 344, 354, **360**, 369, 384, 393
Taro see *Colocasia esculenta*
Tarozaemon, Minoya 287
Tarragon see *Artemisia dracunculus*
French see *Artemisia dracunculus* var *sativa*
Russian see *Artemisia dracunculus* subsp. *dracunculoides*
Tarweed see *Grindelia camporum*
Tasmanian blue gum see *Eucalyptus globulus*
Tasmannia lanceolata 54, 275
Tatarian aster, see *Aster tataricus*
Tavoy cardamom see *Amomum xanthioides*
taxol 360
Taxus
baccata 35, 210, 360
brevifolia *210*, **360**
canadensis 360
Tea see *Camellia sinensis*
Brigham see *Ephedra trifurca*
Hottentot see *Helichrysum serpyllifolium*
Labrador see *Ledum groenlandicum*
Malay see *Psoralea corylifolia*
marsh see *Ledum palustre*
Mexican see *Chenopodium ambrosioides*
Mormon see *Ephedra trifurca*
New Jersey see *Ceanothus americanus*
Oswego see *Monarda didyma*
Paraguay see *Ilex paraguensis*
Sudanese see *Hibiscus sabdariffa*
rooibos 244
Tea tree
medicinal see *Melaleuca alternifolia*
weeping see *Melaleuca leucadendron*
tea tree oil 309
Tea vine, sweet see *Gynostemma pentaphyllum*
Tea-tree, Duke of Argyll's see *Lycium barbarum*
Teaberry see *Gaultheria procumbens*
Teak, bastard see *Pterocarpus marsupium*
teas
garden for 374
preparing 47
Teinturier grape see *Vitis vinifera* 'Purpurea'
tejpat (*Cinnamomum tamala*) 262
temperatures required 375
tender plants 375, 382-3
Tennent, John 332
Terebinth tree see *Pistacia terebinthus*
Terminalia
arjuna 62, 360
belerica 62, 63, 360
chebula 62, 63, *210*, **360-1**
spp. 63
Tetradium
officinalis see *T. ruticarpum*
ruticarpum *210*, 289, **361**
Tetrapanax papyrifera 320
Tetterwort see *Chelidonium majus*
Teucrium
chamaedrys 27, 37, *210*, **361**, 379
divaricatum 361
x *lucidrys* 24, 37, 210, 361
'Variegatum' *384*
scorodonia 361
Texas sage see *Salvia coccinea*
Texas snakeroot see *Aristolochia reticulata*
Thailand
herbs in wild 67
rainforest *67*
Thea sinensis see *Camellia sinensis*
Theatrum Botanicum 19
Theobroma 388
cacao 49, 55, *210*, **361**
theobromine 264, 296
Theophrastus 19, 167, 211, 212, 216, 276, 319, 330
Thimbleberry see *Rubus occidentalis*; *R. odoratus*; *R. parviflorus*
thinning out 385, 386
thiophene derivatives 277
thiophenes 359
Thistle
blessed see *Cnicus benedictus*; *Silybum marianum*
carline see *Carlina*
holy see *Cnicus benedictus*
milk see *Silybum*
saffron see *Carthamus tinctorius*
Thistle daisy, Chinese see *Atractylodes macrocophala*
Thlaspi bursa-pastoris see *Capsella bursa-pastoris*
Thomson, Samuel 19, 46, 52, 305
Thomsonian Materia Medica 19
Thomsonian system 314
Thor 338
Thorn apple see *Datura*
Thoroughwort see *Eupatorium fortunei*; *E. perfoliatum*
Thorow-wax see *Bupleurum*
thrips 383
Thuja
occidentalis 52, 53, *211*, **362**
'Holmstrup' *211*, **362**
'Rheingold' *211*, **362**
orientalis *211*, **362**
'Aurea Nana' *211*, **362**
thujone 243, 346, 359, 362
Thunberg, Carl 89
Thyme see *Thymus*
Azores see *Thymus caespititius*
basil see *Acinos arvensis*
broad-leaved see *Thymus pulegioides*
caraway see *Thymus herba-barona*
Cilician see *Thymus cilicicus*
conehead see *Thymus capitatus*
creeping see *Thymus praecox*; *T. serpyllum*
false see *Lippia micromera*
golden lemon see *Thymus* x *citriodorus* 'Aureus'
large see *Thymus pulegioides*
lemon see *Thymus* x *citriodorus*
mastic see *Thymus mastichina*
mother of see *Thymus serpyllum*
red-flowered see *Thymus serpyllum* var. *coccineus*
Spanish see *Plectranthus amboinicus*
upright see *Thymus vulgaris* 'Erectus'
wild see *Thymus praecox*; *T. serpyllum*
woolly see *Thymus pseudolanuginosus*
Thyme-leaved savory see *Satureja thymbra*
thymol 280, 313, 317, 318, 319, 350, 362, 363
Thymus *381*, 388
caespititius **362**
'Aureus' *212*, **362**
capitatus *212*, 319, **362**, 363
cilicicus *212*, **362**, 363
x *citriodorus* 29, 36, *212*, **362**, 363
'Anderson's Gold' see *T.* x *c.* 'Bertram Anderson'
'Archer's Gold' *36*, *212*, **362**
'Aureus' 36, *212*, **362**
'Bertram Anderson' *212*, **362**
'E. B. Anderson' see *T.* x *c.* 'Bertram Anderson'
'Golden King' **362**
'Silver Queen' *212*, **362**
herba-barona 30, *212*, **362**, 381
lanuginosus see *T. pseudolanuginosus*
mastichina **362-3**
praecox *213*, **363**
pseudolanuginosus 30, *213*,

363
pulegioides 28, *213*, **363**
serpyllum *213*, 362, **363**, 386
var. *albus* **363**
'Annie Hall' *213*, **363**
var. *coccineus* 30, *213*, **363**
'Elfin' *213*, **363**, 381
'Goldstream' **363**
subsp. *lanuginosus* see *T. pseudolanuginosus*
'Minor' **363**
'Pink Chintz' 22, 30, *31*, *213*, **363**
'Rainbow Falls' *213*, **363**
'Russetings' 30, *213*, **363**
'Snowdrift' 30
'Vey' *213*, **363**
spp. 232, 374, 375, 376, 378, 382, 384, 385
vulgaris 11, 22, 29, 41, 49, 57, *213*, 278, 283, 295, 349, 362, **363**, 378, 379, 381
'Aureus' 30
'Erectus' *213*, **363**, 381
'Silver Posie' 27, *27*, 32, *213*, **363**
'Variegatus' see *T. v.* 'Silver Posie'
zygis 362
tian hua fen (*Trichosanthes kirilowii*) 364
tian ma (*Gastrodia elata*) 286
tian men dong (*Asparagus cochinchinensis*) 245
tian nan xing (*Arisaema*) 241
tian zhu huang (*Phyllostachys*) 326
tiao dang shen (*Codonopsis tangshen*) 264
Tibet 14
Tienchi ginseng see *Panax pseudo-ginseng*
Tiger grass see *Centella asiatica*
Tiger nut, edible see *Cyperus esculentus* var. *sativus*
Tilia
americana 363
cordata 56, *214*, 347, **363**
x *europaea* 214, 363
parviflora see *T. cordata*
platyphyllos 214, 363
spp. 47, 227, 268, 288
tinctures 47
Tinnevelly senna see *Senna alexandrina*
tisanes 47
Toadflax see *Linaria*
Tobacco
devil's see *Lobelia tupa*
farmer's see *Malva verticillata*
Indian see *Lobelia inflata*
mountain see *Arnica montana*
Tohunga 66
Tollund man 106, 254
Tolu balsam see *Myroxylon balsamum*
Tonka bean see *Dipteryx odorata*
Tonquin bean see *Dipteryx odorata*
Toothache tree see *Zanthoxylum americanum*
Toothbrush tree see *Salvadora persica*
Toothed wrack see *Fucus serratus*
top-dressing 381
Torchwood see *Bursera*
Tormentil see *Potentilla erecta*
Touch-me-not, pale see *Impatiens pallida*
Trachyspermum
ammi 61, **363-4**
copticum see *T. ammi*
TRAFFIC (Trade Records Analysis of Flora and Fauna in Commerce) 51, 295
Tragacanth see *Astragalus gummifer*
Trailing arbutus see *Epigaea repens*
training 385
tranquilizing alkaloids 67
transplanting 385, *385*
"Traumatick Decoction" 231
Travels in North America 299-300
Tree artemisia see *Artemisia arborescens*
Tree basil see *Ocimum gratissimum*
Tree of heaven see *Ailanthus altissima*
Tree onion see *Allium cepa* var. *proliferum*
Tree peony see *Paeonia suffruticosa*
Tree pepper see *Capsicum pubescens*
Tree purslane see *Atriplex halimus*
Tree wormwood see *Artemisia arborescens*
trees, specimen 381
Trefoil, marsh see *Menyanthes trifoliata*
Trichosanthes
cucumeroides 364
japonica 364
kirilowii *214*, **364**
rosthornii 364
trichosanthin 364
Trifid bur marigold see *Bidens tripartita*
Trifolium
pratense 126, *214*, 241, 285, 297, 354, 356, 358, **364**, 370
'Broad Red' 214
'Gold Net' see *T. p.* 'Susan Smith'
'Susan Smith' *214*, **364**
spp. 309
Trigonella foenum-graecum 61, *214*, **364**
trigonelline 364
trikatu (*Piper longum*; *P. nigrum*; *Zingiber officinale*) 330
Trilisa odoratissima 303
Trillium
erectum 33, *33*, 52, *214*, 258, 288, 295, **364-5**, 369
f. *albiflorum* *215*, **365**
kamtschaticum 364-5
spp. 386
tschonskii 365
triphala 62, 63, 360
Tropaeolum
majus *38*, *215*, 253, **365**, 382
'Alaska' 41, *215*, **365**
'Empress of India' 25, *215*, **365**, 381
'Hermine Grashoff' *216*, **365**
'Peach Melba' *216*, **365**
Whirlybird Series 38
tropane alkaloids 55, 57, 66, 272, 276, 279, 295, 350
tropical herbs, from seed 386
True unicorn root see *Aletris farinosa*
Trumpet tree see *Tabebuia*
tu si zi (*Cuscuta japonica*) 270
tubers 43, 391
tubocurarine 17, 55, 260
Tuckahoe see *Wolfiporia cocos*
Tulipan del monte see *Malvaviscus arboreus*
Tulsi see *Ocimum sanctum*
Turkey red see alizarin
Turkey red oil 48
Turkish licorice see *Glycyrrhiza glabra* var. *violacea*
Turmeric see *Curcuma longa*
wild see *Curcuma aromatica*
Turner, William 19, 275
Turnera
diffusa var. *aphrodisiaca* **365**
ulmifolia 365
Turnip, Indian see *Arisaema triphyllum*
Turnip-rooted parsley see *Petroselinum crispum* var. *tuberosum*
turpentine 329, 330
essence of 330
oil of 226, 329
spirits of 329
Strassburg 226
Cyprus see *Pistacia terebinthus*
turpentine substitute 329
Turpeth see *Ipomoea turpeth*
Turtlehead see *Chelone*
Tuscan jasmine see *Jasminum sambac* 'Grand Duke of Tuscany'
tussie-mussie *48*
Tussilago farfara *216*, 232, 238, 288, 293, 297, 309, 328, 348, **365**, 368, 370
Tutankhamun 48, 233
"twilight sleep" 350
Twitch see *Elymus repens*
Two-rowed barley see *Hordeum distichum*
Two-toothed amaranthus see *Achyranthes bidentata*
Typha
latifolia *216*, **366**, 379
'Variegata' 30, *216*, **366**

U

Ulmus
fulva see *U. rubra*
minor var. *vulgaris* 366
rubra 53, *217*, 236, 252, 296, 317, 356, 365, **366**
Umbellularia californica *217*, **366**
Umbrella grass see *Cyperus involucratus*
Umbrella tree see *Magnolia tripetala*
Unani medicine 46, 62
under cover, growing herbs 382-3
Unicorn root
false see *Chamaelirium luteum*
true see *Aletris farinosa*
Universal Herbal 18
Upland cotton see *Gossypium hirsutum*
Uppsala University, Orangery *10*
Urginea maritima see *Drimia maritima*
Urtica
dioica 47, 56, *217*, 249, 278, 285, 365, **366-7**, 370
pilulifera 366
urens 366
Urucú see *Bixa orellana*
U.S. National Formulary 258, 266, 276, 279, 290, 291, 312, 323, 364
U.S. Pharmacopoeia 233, 247, 260, 266, 271, 274, 286, 288, 291, 293, 294, 295, 297, 298, 307, 313, 327, 335, 338, 344, 347, 351, 279, 290, 305, 334, 338, 340, 344, 355, 362
Ustilago zeae 263
Uva-ursi see *Arctostaphylos*

V

Vaccinium
ashei 217
corymbosum 217
myrtillus *217*, **367**
vitis-idaea 367
valepotriates 367
Valerian see *Valeriana*
American see *Cypripedium parviflorum*, var. *pubescens*
common see *Valeriana officinalis*
red see *Centranthus ruber*
Valeriana
jatamansi 367
mexicana 367
officinalis 33, 57, *217*, 271, 294, 300, 316, 317, 323, 330, 332, **367**, 377, 378
Van der Heyden, Herman 261
Van Deveer, Dr 351
Vanilla 367-8
planifolia 55, *217*, **368**
'Variegata' 217, *218*, **368**
pompona 368
tahitensis 368
Vanilla
Tahiti see *Vanilla tahitensis*
West Indian see *Vanilla pompona*
vanilla essence 368
Vanilla grass see *Hierochloë odorata*
Vanilla leaf see *Trilisa odoratissima*
vanilla resinoid 368
variants 43
variegated plants
light requirements 382
reversion 384
Vasak see *Justicia adhatoda*
vasicine 299
Vavilov, N. I. 60
Vavilov Centers 60
Vegetable arsenic see *Colchicum autumnale*
Vegetable mercury see *Brunfelsia uniflora*
Velvet bean see *Mucuna*
Verbascum
densiflorum 368
nigrum 368
phlomoides 368
spp. *32*
thapsus *218*, 293, 295, 365, **368**, 379
Verbena
hastata 368
officinalis *218*, 283, 301, 343, 355, **368**, 377
urticifolia 338
Verbena, lemon see *Aloysia triphylla*
Vernal grass, sweet see *Anthoxanthum odoratum*
Veronica, St. 368
Veronica officinalis *218*, **368**
Veronicastrum
virginicum *218*, 248, 360, **368-9**, 369
'Album' 35
var. *roseum* *218*, **369**
Vervain see *Verbena officinalis*
blue see *Verbena hastata*
white see *Verbena urticifolia*
Vespucci, Amerigo 54
Vetch, milk see *Astragalus*
Vetiver see *Vetiveria*
Vetiveria zizanoides *219*, **369**
Viburnum
opulus *219*, **369**
'Aureum' *219*, **369**, 374
'Fructuluteo' 219
'Roseum' *219*, **369**
'Sterile' see *V. o.* 'Roseum'
'Xanthocarpum' *219*, **369**
prunifolium 330, **369**
spp. 386
Vidari-kanda see *Ipomoea digitata*
Vietnamese coriander see *Polygonum odoratum*
Villandry, Château de 13
Vilmorin, 160
vinblastine 17
Vinca 33
major 33, 57, *220*, 288, 301, 365, **369**, 370, 379
'Maculata' *220*, **369**
'Reticulata' *220*, **369**
'Variegata' *220*, **369**
minor 369, 381
cvs 381
rosea see *Catharanthus roseus*
spp. 384
vincamine 369
vincristine 17
Vine
grape see *Vitis vinifera*
vinegars, herb 393
vino mescal 231
Viola
cornuta 'Alba' 35
diffusa 370
inconspicua 370
odorata *220*, 247, **370**
'Alba' *220*, **370**
patrinii 370
striata 370
tricolor 41, *220*, **370**, 380, 381
wittrockiana 'Universal Series' 36
yedoensis **370**
Violet see *Viola*
Chinese see *Viola yezoensis*
sweet see *Viola odorata*
Virgin Mary 14
Virginia bugleweed see *Lycopus virginicus*
Virginia mountain mint see *Pycnanthemum virginianum*
Virginia skullcap see *Scutellaria lateriflora*
Virginia snakeroot see *Aristolochia serpentaria*
Viscum
album 15, *221*, 268, 367, **370**
coloratum 370
Vishwabhesaj see *Zingiber officinale*
vitamin
A 272, 283, 325, 352, 366
B group 309, 352
C 254, 255, 262, 268, 283, 293, 309, 325, 341, 342, 344, 366
D 309
E 309, 352
K 309
P 284
Vitex
agnus-castus *221*, **370-1**
negundo *221*, 370, **371**
var. *cannabinifolia* see *V. n.* var. *heterophylla*

var. *heterophylla* *221*, 370, **371**
rotundifolia 370
trifolia 370
Vitis
spp. 385, 388
vinifera *32*, 61, *221*, **371**, 383, *383*, 387, *387*
'Apifolia' see *V. v.* 'Ciotat'
'Ciotat' *221*, **371**
'Incana' 32, **371**
'Laciniosa' see *V. v.* 'Ciotat'
'Pinot Noir' *221*, **371**
'Purpurea' *221*, **371**
'Spätburgunder' see *V. v.* 'Pinot Noir'
Voacanga
africana 59
spp. 58
volatile oils 11, 390

W

Wafer ash see *Ptelea trifoliata*
Wahoo see *Euonymus atropurpureus*
Wake robin see *Trillium erectum*
Wall germander see *Teucrium chamaedrys*
Wallace's Line 66
walls, growing herbs against 385
Walnut see *Juglans*
cut-leaved see *Juglans regia* 'Laciniata'
English see *Juglans regia*
white see *Juglans cinerea*
Warburgia salutaris 59
Wasabi see *Wasabia*
Wasabia japonica *222*, **371**
Water agrimony see *Bidens tripartita*
Water dock see *Rumex aquatica*
Water figwort see *Scrophularia auriculata*
Water horehound see *Lycopus americanus*
Water lily see *Nymphaea*
sweet-scented see *Nymphaea odorata*
Water pepper see *Polygonum hydropiper*
Water plantain see *Alisma plantago-aquatica*
Watercress see *Nasturtium*
watering 381, 384
Waterlily, prickly see *Euryale ferox*
Watermint see *Mentha aquatica*
Watson, Sereno 203
Wattle see *Acacia*
Wax gourd see *Benincasa cerifera*
Wax myrtle see *Myrica*
weeding 384
new site 377, *377*
weeds, pernicious 11, 13
Weeping forsythia see *Forsythia suspensa*
Weeping paperbark see *Melaleuca leucadendron*
Weeping tea tree see *Melaleuca leucadendron*
wei ling xian (*Clematis chinensis*) 263
Welsh onion see *Allium fistulosum*
West African pepper see *Piper guineense*
West Indian holly see *Turnera ulmifolia*
West Indian kino see *Coccoloba uvifera*
West Indian vanilla see *Vanilla pompona*
West Indian wild cinnamon see *Canella winterana*
Western mugwort see *Artemisia ludoviciana*
White birch see *Betula pubescens*
White bryony see *Bryonia dioica*
White cedar, Eastern see *Thuja occidentalis*
White cinnamon see *Canella winterana*
White deadnettle see *Lamium album*
White gourd see *Benincasa cerifera*
White horehound see *Marrubium vulgare*
White lotus see *Nymphaea lotus*
White man's foot see *Plantago major*
White mugwort see *Artemisia lactiflora*
White mulberry see *Morus alba*
White mustard see *Sinapis alba*
White oak see *Quercus alba*
White pond lily see *Nymphaea odorata*
White poplar see *Populus alba*
White quebracho see *Aspidosperma quebracho-blanco*
White sage see *Artemisia ludoviciana*
White sandalwood see *Santalum album*
White vervain see *Verbena urticificolia*
White walnut see *Juglans cinerea*
White willow see *Salix alba*
whitefly 383, *383*
Whortleberry see *Vaccinium myrtillus*
Wilde als see *Artemisia afra*
Willow see *Salix*
bay see *Salix pentandra*
black see *Salix nigra*
crack see *Salix fragilis*
golden see *Salix alba* var. *vitellina*
gray see *Salix cinerea*
scarlet see *Salix alba* 'Britzensis'
white see *Salix alba*
Willow herb see *Epilobium*
Willow-leaf bay see *Laurus nobilis* 'Angustifolia'
windowboxes 13, 40, *40*, *381*
herbs for 381
windowsills, growing herbs on 382, *382*
Winged prickly ash see *Zanthoxylum planispinum*
Winter, Captain John 275
Winter cherry see *Solanum capsicastrum*; *Withania somnifera*
Winter marjoram see *Origanum vulgare* subsp. *hirtum*
winter protection 385
Winter savory see *Satureja montana*
Winter squash see *Cucurbita maxima*
Winterberry see *Ilex verticillata*
Wintergreen see *Gaultheria procumbens*
Winter's bark see *Drimys winteri*
false see *Cinnamodendron corticosum*
witch doctors *58*
Witch hazel see *Hamamelis*
common see *Hamamelis virginiana*
witchcraft 15
Witches' pouches see *Capsella bursa-pastoris*
Withania somnifera 63, *222*, 245, **371**, 388
Witloof chicory see *Cichorium intybus*
Woad see *Isatis tinctoria*
Wolfiporia cocos 64, 246, 264, **372**
Wolfsbane see *Aconitum napellus*
wood 43, 391
Wood avens see *Geum urbanum*
Wood betony see *Stachys officinalis*
Wood marjoram, Spanish see *Thymus mastichina*
Wood sage see *Teucrium scorodonia*
Woodbine see *Lonicera periclymenum*
Woodfordia fruticosa 63, *63*
woodland herb garden 33, *33*
Woodruff see *Galium odoratum*
Woolly foxglove see *Digitalis lanata*
Woolly lavender see *Lavandula lanata*
Woolly mint see *Mentha suaveolens*
Woolly thyme see *Thymus pseudolanuginosus*
Worldwide Fund for Nature (WWF) 60
Wormseed see *Chenopodium ambrosioides*
Levant see *Artemisia cina*
Wormwood see *Artemisia absinthium*
fragrant see *Artemisia capillaris*
Roman see *Artemisia pontica*
sweet see *Artemisia annua*
tree see *Artemisia arborescens*
Woundwort
marsh see *Stachys palustris*
soldier's see *Achillea millefolium*
Wrack see *Fucus*
toothed see *Fucus serratus*
Wrinkled giant hyssop see *Agastache rugosa*
wu jia pi (*Eleutherococcus* spp.) 277
wu mei (*Prunus mume*) 336
wu tou (*Aconitum carmichaelii*) 228
wu wei zi (*Schisandra chinensis*) 350
wu zhu yu (*Tetradium ruticarpum*) 361

X

xanthine 343
Xanthium
sibiricum see *X. strumarium*
strumarium *222*, 290, **372**
xanthones 357
xi yang shen (*Panax quinquefolius*) 322
xia ku cao (*Prunella vulgaris*) 335
xiang fu (*Cyperus rotundus*) 271
xin yi (*Magnolia liliiflora*) 307
Xochimilco floating gardens 13
xuan fu hua (*Inula britannica* var. *chinensis*) 296
xuan shen (*Scrophularia ningpoensis*) 350

Y

ya dan zi (*Brucea javanica*) 250
Yam see *Dioscorea*
Chinese see *Dioscorea opposita*
cinnamon see *Dioscorea opposita*
Mexican see *Dioscorea macrostachya*
wild see *Dioscorea villosa*
yan hu suo 268
Yangshou, China *64*
Yarrow see *Achillea millefolium*
Yaw root see *Stillingia sylvatica*
yegoma (*Perilla frutescens*) 325
Yellow bedstraw see *Galium verum*
Yellow dock see *Rumex crispus*
Yellow Emperor's Classic of Internal Medicine 19
Yellow gentian, great see *Gentiana lutea*
Yellow lady's slipper see *Cypripedium parviflorum*
larger see *Cypripedium parviflorum* var. *pubescens*
smaller see *Cypripedium parviflorum* var. *parviflorum*
Yellow melilot see *Melilotus officinalis*
Yellow pagoda tree see *Sophora flavescens*
Yellow pheasant's eye see *Adonis vernalis*
Yellow starwort see *Inula britannica* var. *chinensis*
Yellow sweet clover see *Melilotus officinalis*
Yellowroot see *Hydrastis canadensis*
Yerba de la sangre see *Mahonia aquifolium*
Yerba dulce see *Lippia dulcis*
Yerba maté see *Ilex paraguensis*
Yerba santa see *Eriodictyon californicum*
Yew see *Taxus*
Canadian see *Taxus canadensis*
English see *Taxus baccata*
Pacific see *Taxus brevifolia*
yi my cao (*Leonurus sibiricus*) 302
yi tang (*Hordeum vulgare*: *Oryza sativa*) 320
yi yi ren (*Coix lacryma-jobi*) 264
yi zhi (*Alpinia ozyphylla*) 235
yin chen hao (*Artemisia capillaris*) 243
yin yang huo (*Epimedium sagittatum*) 278
Ylang-ylang see *Cananga odorata*
Yohimbe see *Pausinystalia yohimbe*
yohimbine 245, 323
Young's weeping birch see *Betula pendula* 'Youngii'
yu jin (*Curcuma aromatica*) 270
yu li ren (*Prunus japonica*) 336
yu mi xu (*Zea mays*) 372
yu xing cao (*Houttuynia cordata*) 294
yu zhu (*Polygonatum odoratum*) 333
yuan hua (*Daphne genkwa*) 272
yuan zhi (*Polygala tenuifolia*) 333

Z

Zanthoxylum
acanthopodium 372
americanum *222*, 261, 369,**372**
armatum 372
capense 372
clavaherculis 372
piperitum *222*, **372**
planispinum 372
schinifolium 372
simulans 372
spp. 327
zanthoxyloides 372
Zanzibar aloe see *Aloe perryi*
ze xie (*Alisma plantago-aquatica*) 233
Zea
mays 54, 55, *223*, 241, 299, 301, 322, **372-3**
cultivation *13*, 14
'Black Aztec' **373**
'Gigantea Quadricolor' *223*, **373**
'Gracillima Variegata' *223*, **373**, 381
'Quadricolor' see *Z. m.* 'Gigantea Quadricolor'
'Strawberry Corn' **373**
Zedoary see *Curcuma zedoaria*
zerumbone 373
zhang nao (*Cinnamomum camphora*) 262
Zhang Yuan-Su 321
Zhao Xue Min 19
zhe bei mu (*Fritillaria verticillata*) 284
zhi ke (*Citrus aurantium*) 263
zhi mu (*Anemarrhena asphodeloides*) 238
zhi shi (*Citrus aurantium*) 263
zhi zi (*Gardenia augusta*) 286
zhu li (*Phyllostachys*) 326
zhu ru (*Phyllostachys*) 326
Zhu Zhen Heng 268
zi cao (*Lithospermum erythrorhizon*) 305
zi hua di ding (*Viola yezoensis*) 370
zi su geng (*Perilla frutescens*) 325
zi su ye (*Perilla frutescens*) 325
zi su zi (*Perilla frutescens*) 325
zi wan (*Aster tataricus*) 245
zimbolee oil 314
zinc 269
Zingiber
cassumar 373
mioga 373
officinale *223*, 234, 244, 249, 270, 274, 281, 296, 298, 307, 309, 314, 329, 330, 352, 361, 372, **373**, 383, 387
spp. 299
zerumbet 373
Zizania aquatica 169
Ziziphus
jujuba *223*, 340, **373**
lotus 223
vulgaris 373
Zoom see *Paullinia cupana*
Zubrovka see *Hierochloë odorata*

Books for Further Reading

Bensky, D. and Gamble, A., *Chinese Materia Medica* (Seattle, WA, 1993)

Buchanan, R. ed., *Taylor's Guide to Herbs* (Boston, NY, 1995)

Chin, Wee Yeow and Hsuan Keng, *Chinese Medicinal Herbs* (Sebastopol, CA, 1992)

Duke, J., *A Handbook of Northeastern Indian Medicinal Plants* (Lincoln, MA, 1986)

Duke, J. and Vasquez, R., *Amazonian Ethnobotanical Dictionary* (Boca Raton, FL, 1994)

Evans, W. C., *Trease and Evans' Pharmacognosy* (London, 13th ed., 1989)

Felton, E., *Artistically Cultivated Herbs* (Santa Barbara, CA, 1990)

Fenaroli, *Handbook of Flavor Ingredients*, vols i and ii (3rd ed., Boca Raton, FL, 1995). Includes regulatory citations, FEMA numbers, and substance identities.

ed. Flora of North America Editorial Committee, *Flora of North America North of Mexico, vol. 1 – Introduction* (New York, 1993)

Flora of North America North of Mexico, vol. 2 – Pteridophytes and Gymnosperms (New York, 1993)

Foster, S. and Duke, J., *Field Guide to Eastern / Central Medicinal Plants* (Boston, MA, 1990)

Heywood, V. H., *Flowering Plants of the World* (New York, 1993)

Iwu, M., *A Handbook of African Medicinal Plants* (Boca Raton, FL, 1990)

Kartesz, J., *A Synomized Checklist of the Vascular Flora of the United States, Canada, and Greenland*, 2 vols (Portland, OR, 1994)

Kuhnlein, H. and Turner, N. J., *Traditional Plant Foods of Canadian Indigenous Peoples: Nutrition, Botany and Use* (Philadelphia, PA, 1991)

Mabberly, D. J., *The Plant-Book* (New York, 1987)

Magic and Medicine of Plants (Pleasantville, NY, 1986)

Nadkarni, Dr K., *The Indian Materia Medica* (Bombay, 1993)

Norman, J., *The Complete Book of Spices* (New York, 1991)

Plotkin, M., *Tales of a Shaman's Apprentice* (New York, 1994)

Schultes, R. E., Evans, R., and Raffauf, R. F., *The Healing Forest* (Portland, OR, 1990)

Schultes, R. E. and Raffauf, R. F., *Vine of the Soul – Medicine Men, Their Plants and Rituals in the Colombian Amazonia* (Oracle, AZ, 1992)

Tolley, E. and Mead, C., *Cooking With Herbs* (New York, 1989)

Tyler, V. E., *The Honest Herbal* (Binghamton, NY, 1993)

—, *Herbs of Choice* (Binghamton, NY, 1994)

Wilson, J., *Landscaping with Herbs* (Boston, NY, 1994)

Wrensch, R. D., *The Essence of Herbs: an Environmental Guide to Herb Gardening* (Jackson, MS., 1992)

Also recommended

HerbalGram

Published quarterly by the American Botanical Council and the Herb Research Foundation
P. O. Box 201660
Austin, TX 78720
512-331-8868

Subscriptions are $25.00 per year

Herb Gardens to Visit

Agecroft Hall, 4305 Sulgrave Rd, Richmond, VA 23221-3256. 804-353-4241. Elizabethan garden, knot garden, medicinal, culinary, and fragrant herbs.

Atlanta Botanical Garden, Piedmont Park at the Prado, Atlanta, GA 30357. 404-876-5859. A knot and herb garden with fragrance plants.

W.J. Beal Botanical Garden, Michigan State University, 412 Olds Hall, East Lansing, MI 48824-1047. 517-355-9582. A botanical collection of herbs.

Brooklyn Botanic Garden, 1000 Washington Ave., Brooklyn, NY 11225-1099. 718-622-4433. Herb gardens with a knot garden and specialty gardens.

Caprilands Herb Farm, 5354 Silver Street, Coventry, CT 06238. 203-742-7244. A charming herb farm, surrounding an eighteenth-century farm house, with a Silver Garden, Saint's Garden, etc.

Chicago Botanic Garden, Lake Cook Rd., Glencoe, IL 60022. 708-835-5440. Formal and informal herb gardens with a knot garden, and culinary, dye, and medicinal collections.

Cleveland Botanical Garden, 11030 East Boulevard, Cleveland, OH 44106. 216-721-1600. A great herb garden design, cared for by The Herb Society of America. It has a knot garden, historic roses, and dye, culinary, and fragrance gardens.

The Cloisters, Metropolitan Museum of Art Medieval Herb Garden, Fort Tryon Park, New York, NY 10040. 212-233-3700. Recreation of a medieval monastic garden.

Colonial Williamsburg, Williamsburg, VA 23185. 804-220-7645. Williamsburg has a series of gardens, many of which contain colonial herbs.

Cornell Plantations, Robison York State Herb Garden, 1 Plantation Rd., Ithaca, NY 14850-2799. 607-255-3020. A series of herb gardens, some in raised beds, with a broad range of native herbs.

Dallas Civic Garden Center, P.O. Box 26194, Dallas, TX 75226. 214-428-7476. A Shakespearean garden, rose garden, and an herb and fragrance garden with Braille labels.

Devonian Botanic Garden, University of Alberta, Edmonton, AB T6G 2E1, Canada. 403-987-3054. A herb garden with a variety of culinary, medicinal, and economic herbs.

J. Paul Getty Museum, 17985 Pacific Coast Hwy., Malibu, CA 90265-5799. 213-458-2003. Herbs appropriate to ancient Rome, set in gardens of a recreated Roman villa garden.

Hancock Shaker Village, Rt. 20, Hancock, MA 01237. 413-441-0188. Herbs that were grown, used, and sold by the Shaker community, in a farm setting.

The Herbfarm, 32804 Issaquah-Fall City Rd., Fall City, WA 98024. 206-784-2222. A series of theme gardens featuring many varieties of herbs.

Huntington Botanical Gardens, 1151 Oxford Rd., San Marino, CA 91108. 818-405-2100. An extensive collection of herbs set in a series of specialty gardens.

Longwood Gardens, P.O. Box 501, Kennett Square, PA 19348-0501. 215-388-6741. A formal herb garden, children's garden, and idea garden.

Matthaei Botanical Garden, The University of Michigan, 1800 N. Dixboro Rd., Ann Arbor, MI 48105. 313-998-7061. A traditional herb garden that includes a knot garden and broad range of herbs.

Michigan 4-H Children's Garden, 4700 South Hagadorn Rd., East Lansing, MI 48823. 517-353-6692. A series of innovative children's gardens.

Missouri Botanical Garden, P.O. Box 299, St. Louis, MO 63166. 314-577-5111. A fenced formal garden with a variety of ornamental and culinary herbs.

Montreal Botanical Garden, 4101 Sherbrooke Street East, Montreal, QC H1X 2B2, Canada. 514-872-1400. Extensive collections of economic plants and herbs in their outdoor and conservatory gardens.

The National Herb Garden, U.S. National Arboretum, 3501 New York Avenue, N.E., Washington, DC 20002. 202-245-2726. A project of The Herb Society of America. Features a knot garden, historic rose garden, and ten specialty gardens.

New York Botanical Garden, Bronx, NY 10458-5126. 212-220-8700. This garden features knot gardens done with clipped boxwood and planting beds of ornamental herbs.

Royal Botanical Gardens, 680 Plains Road West, Burlington, ON L7T 8H4, Canada. 905-527-1158. A large garden with a teaching garden for children that includes herbs and extensive collections of roses.

University of British Columbia (UBC) Botanical Garden, 6804 Southwest Marine Drive, Vancouver, BC V6T 1Z4, Canada. 604-822-9666. Recreation of a 16-century European physic garden.

University of California at Davis Arboretum, Davis, CA 95616. 916-752-2498. Medicinal plants, specialty gardens, and culinary herbs.

University of Minnesota Landscape Arboretum, 3675 Arboretum Drive, Chanhassen, MN 55317. 612-443-2460. A small knot garden, and collections of historic, medicinal, culinary, and fragrant herbs.

University of Washington Medicinal Herb Garden, University of Washington, Seattle, WA 98195. 206-543-1126. A medicinal herb garden.

VanDusen Botanical Garden, 5251 Oak Street, Vancouver, BC V6M 4H1, Canada. 604-878-9274. A 55-acre garden, including an Elizabethan maze, with over 6,500 plants from six continents.

Acknowledgments

1	4	7	10
2	5	8	11
3	6	9	12

The publishers are grateful to the following for permission to reproduce material. Photographs found in the Catalog are identified by two numbers: the page number followed by the specific number(s) of the photograph(s), separated by hyphens. The photograph number is determined by its position on the page, according to the grid shown above. Photographs found elsewhere in the book are identified by their page number, followed by their position on the page: t = top, m = middle, b = bottom, l = left, c = centre, r = right.

AKG, London 12bl (British Museum), 18l
A-Z Botanical 128/9 (Derek Shimmin), 143/6 (Jiri Loun), 146/10 (F. Collet & U. Lund), 150/4 (K. Jayaram), 180/9 (Ron Bass), 198/12 (Mike Maidment), 210/12 (Andrea Balogh)
Gillian Beckett 109/6, 222/9
Biofotos/Heather Angel 42bc, 51tr, 112/4, 125/7, 200/10
Deni Bown 25bl, 26tc, 26tr, 26bl, 27c, 27cb, 27bc, 31br, 32tc, 33cl, 33bl, 34tr, 35cr, 37bc, 37br, 38tc, 55tr (W. Tait), 58br, 70/10, 75/10, 76/3, 78/5-6, 79/10, 81/10, 83/8, 87/2-12, 88/5, 89/11, 91/5 (W. Tait), 93/5-12, 101/2-6, 102/6, 105/9, 111/6-8, 112/8-12, 113/1, 120/4-5, 121/10, 122/11, 123/4-6, 124/2, 126/2, 127/6-7-10, 128/5-7-10, 129/12, 130/5-10, 132/6-11, 135/2-8, 139/9, 141/10, 142/1, 143/10, 144/8-9, 145/11-12, 147/4, 147/6-9, 149/9, 150/6, 151/6, 152/10, 154/6, 155/4, 156/10, 157/4-11, 162/3-10-12, 164/6-8-9, 168/2, 170/3-5, 172/3, 173/3, 176/8, 178/10, 183/3, 186/5, 188/9-10, 189/5, 191/2, 194/9, 195/3-12, 196/8-12, 197/2, 197/10, 200/1, 203/6, 205/8, 206/4-11, 207/12, 209/7, 214/12, 216/10, 217/5-11, 218/12, 219/5, 220/11, 223/4, 379tr
Bridgeman 10cl, 15tc (Bibliothek Nationale, Vienna), 19br (British Library)
Pat Brindley 82/11, 194/8, 197/3, 223/7
British Museum 12tr, 14cl
R.B. Burbridge 104/12
Neil Campbell Sharp 13tr, 20tc, 118/6, 176/6, 180/8, 186/7, 374cr, 378br, 382br
Jean-loup Charmet 53cr
Bruce Coleman 7tc (Kevin Rushby), 45tr (Dr Sandro Prato), 46br (John Murray), 48bl (Michael Freeman), 50cl (Michael Freeman), 50tc (Frank Lanring), 51bl (Luiz Claudio Marigo), 52tr (John Shaw), 54tr (Luiz Claudio Marigo), 56tr (Atlantide SDF), 56cl (Michel Viard), 57tr (Norbert Schwirtz), 57br (Hans Reinhard), 58tr & 58cl (Gerald Cubitt), 62tr (Gerald Cubitt), 62br (Michael Freeman), 63cr (Dr Jaroslav Poncar), 66tr (George Bingham), 66cl (Fritz Prenzel), 67tr (John Murray), 67bl (Alain Compost), 217/12, 390bl (Hans Reinhard)
Eric Crichton 24tr, 30br, 38tr, 39tr, 39br
Tom Croat 99/6, 133/3
James Davis 50br
CM Dixon 16bl
Frank Dobson 105/4
Ente Nazionale Risi 169/9
ET Archive 12cl (Topkapi Museum), 14tr, 15tr, 45bl, 54cl
Mary Evans 64cl
John Fielding 74/4-5, 76/4, 166/11, 205/2
Steven Foster 84/8, 90/6-10, 107/4, 108/6, 154/11, 170/8, 202/10, 214/5, 217/4
M.P. Frankis 60cl, 61cb
Andrew Gagg 94/4, 113/12, 141/5, 200/3
Garden Picture Library 6tc (Linda Burgess), 20cl, 47tr (Mayer/le Scanff), 187/9 (Brian Carter), 224 (Didier Willery), 374tc (Christel Rosenfeld), 374bl (Clive Boursnell), 375tr (Neil Holmes), 375br (Lynne Brotchie), 384br (Bob Challinor)
John Glover 375tl, 376bl, 383tl
Derek Gould 34cl
Robert Harding 13bc, 43bc (Robert Frerck/Odyssey, Chicago), 49cr, 53br (SH & DH Cavanaugh), 56bl (Fiore), 65tl,
Hutchison 43br, 46bl (Felix Greene), 54bc, 55c, 60tr
Image Bank 44cr (Harald Schon)
Image Select 10tr (Anne Ronan)
Andrew Lawson 25cl
Charles Mauzy 210/5
Miranda Morris 61cla, 61cr, 61bl
National Trust Photographic Library 68 (Mike Williams)
Clive Nichols 21cr (Glazely Old Rectory), 39cr (Le Manoir Aux Quat), 376tr (Old Rectory, Shropshire), 376br, 381tr (Lucy Huntington), 381br
Oxford Scientific Films 42tc (Deni Bown), 57tc (Peter Ryley), 103/4, 165/6 (James Robinson), 165/9 (Karen Ross/Partridge Films Ltd), 171/12 (Rob Cousins), 186/4 (Jack Dermid)
Panos 59tr (Victoria Keble-Williams)
Photos Horticultural 78/7, 91/9, 109/2, 121/6, 128/1, 146/6, 147/5, 183/11, 216/3, 220/9
Pictor 387bl
Royal Botanic Garden Edinburgh 59tl (David Rae), 59br, 61br, 146/4, 160/5, 164/4 (R.M. Beath), 61br
RHS Wisley Photographic Collection 18br, 19cl, 19tr, 383br
Royal Photographic Society 15b (Robinson)
Science Photo Library 17crb (John Greim), 46tr (Jean-loup Charmet)
Harry Smith Collection 17tr, 43tr, 56br, 70/3, 99/4, 125/10, 133/1 (Ivan Tolunix), 138/2, 160/8-9, 170/10, 178/8, 179/6, 209/3, 221/9, 222/6, 223/3, 380br
South American Pictures 13cr
Derek St Romaine 100/12
Telegraph/Colorific 64tr (Patrick Morrow/Blackstar), 64bl (Michael Yamashita)
Trip 54br (A. Gasson), 60bl, 61tr (H. Rogers)
John Vander-plank, National Collection of Passiflora 171/11
Werner Forman Archive 46cl
Joan Wilder 189/6
Steve Wooster 1c, 2 & 3, 20br, 21tc, 21bl, 29cl (John Brookes), 29bl (Anthony Park), 40tr

Abbreviations

AD	Anno Domini	g	gram(s)	p(p).	page(s)
BC	Before Christ	ha	hectare	pl.	plural
c.	circa	illus.	illustrated	sing.	singular
C	centigrade	in	inch(es)	sp.	species
cm	centimeter(s)	kg	kilogram(s)	spp.	species (pl.)
cv.(s)	cultivar(s)	lb	pound(s)	sq	square
F	fahrenheit	m	meter(s)	subsp.	subspecies
f.	forma	ml	milliliter(s)	syn.	synonym
fl. oz	fluid ounce(s)	mm	millimeter(s)	var.	varietas
ft	foot, feet	oz	ounce(s)	yd	yard(s)

Author's Acknowledgments
Warmest thanks are due to the editorial team, especially to Laura Langley (Project Editor), Rachel Gibson (Project Art Editor) and Claire Folkard (Editor), who tackled the complexities with such patience and good spirit. Many thanks too, to Neil Fletcher for his friendly and expert contribution to the photography. Also to the following:

Specialist advice
Roger Hyam (taxonomy); Penelope Ody (Chinese herbs); Elizabeth Dauncey (non-Chinese herbs); Alison Denham (non-Chinese herbs); Adrian Whiteley, Royal Horticultural Society (plant descriptions); Frances Hutchison (Australia and New Zealand); Carol Church (research); Susyn Andrews, Royal Botanic Gardens, Kew (*Lavandula*); Rose Clement (*Teucrium*), Dr. Chris Page (*Cedrus*), Dr. Mark Watson (Umbelliferae), all of the Royal Botanic Garden Edinburgh; James Morley, Royal Botanic Gardens, Kew (economic botany); Sue Minter, Chelsea Physic Garden (economic plants); Susie White, Hexham Herbs (*Thymus* and *Origanum*); Ben Nash, Rio Trading Company (Amazon herbs); Harriet Gillet, IUCN (conservation); Lindsay Lardner, Wellcome Foundation, London; Henry Head (*Lavandula*); Diana Miller (*Pelargonium*); Mr M. W. Kotze, Rooibos Tea Natural Products (*Aspalathus linearis*); Peter Wilde (essential oils); Pandora Thoresby, Yorkstock Herbs, Wetherby, Yorkshire (*Rosmarinus*); Moles Seeds, Colchester, Essex (*Catharanthus* cvs.); Mario Casali, Ente Nazionale Risi, Italy (*Oryza*); Western Hybrid Seeds, California (*Capsicum* cv.).

Locations for photography
Directors and staff of the following institutions: Royal Botanic Garden Edinburgh; Royal Botanic Gardens, Kew; Royal Horticultural Society, Wisley; Royal Botanic Gardens, Peradeniya, Gampaha Botanic Garden, Ganewatta Botanic Garden, and Haputale Botanic Garden, Sri Lanka; Singapore Botanic Gardens; Kirstenbosch Botanic Garden, Cape Town, S Africa; Tropical Botanical Gardens and Research Institute, Trivandrum, India; Chelsea Physic Garden, London; Harlow Carr Botanical Gardens, Harrogate, Yorkshire; Birmingham Botanical Gardens; Glasgow Botanic Gardens; US National Arboretum, Washington DC; Kenilworth Aquatic Gardens, Washington DC; New York Botanical Garden; Arnold Arboretum, Boston; New England Wildflower Society, Massachusetts; Westonbirt Arboretum, Tetbury, Gloucestershire; University Botanic Garden, Cambridge.

Sincere thanks also to: the proprietors and staff of Hollington Nurseries, Newbury, Berkshire; The Herb Garden, Hardstoft, Derbyshire; Hill Farm Herbs, Brigstock, Northamptonshire; Hexham Herbs, Hexham, Northumberland; Norfolk Lavender, Kings Lynn; Rooibos Tea Natural Products, Clanwilliam, S Africa; Poyntzfield Herb Nursery, Ross and Cromarty; Congham Hall Hotel, Congham, Norfolk; Ryton Gardens (Henry Doubleday Research Association), Coventry; Beth Chatto Gardens, Colchester; Alex Brenton's Cottage Garden Plants, Wareham, Dorset; Chessington Nurseries, Surrey; Bridgemere Garden World, Cheshire; Holly Gate Cactus Nursery, Ashington, W Sussex; Reads Nursery, Norfolk; Cally Gardens, Gatehouse of Fleet, Scotland; Cheshire Herbs, Little Budworth, Cheshire; Salley Gardens, Nottingham; The Cottage Herbery, Tenbury Wells, Worcestershire; The Herb Farm, Reading, Berkshire; Waterperry Gardens, Oxford; Barnsley House Garden, Gloucestershire; Acorn Bank Garden, Temple Sowerby, Cumbria; Hardwick Hall, Derbysnire; Iden Croft Herbs, Staplehurst, Kent; Herb and Heather Centre, Selby, Yorkshire; Ripley Castle Gardens, Harrogate, Yorkshire; Hyde Hall Garden, Chelmsford, Essex; Arne Herbs, Chew Magna, Avon.

Additional assistance
Julian Holland (initial project development); Lesley Brown (secretarial help); Anna Walsh and Rebecca Wallen, Oxford Scientific Films (author's archive pictures); Jon and Sue Atkins, Summerfield Books (supplying books); Jenny Evans (liaison), Royal Botanic Gardens, Kew; Kate Haywood (liaison), Royal Horticultural Society, Wisley; Norma Gregory (liaison), William Tait (photography), both Royal Botanic Garden Edinburgh.

Dorling Kindersley, Inc. would also like to thank: Janet von Nostrand, President, The Herb Society of America, Inc., for her support and assistance; Kathleen Kent and Jill Hamilton for editorial assistance.

Jane Aspden, Alison Copland, Maggie O'Hanlon, and Kate Swainson for editorial work, Bob Gordon, Geoff Manders, and Ina Stradins for design work, and Dorothy Frame for the index.

Illustrators:
Karen Cochrane: p.21, p.22, p.27, p.28bl, p.29t, p.32b, p.30, p.33t, p.35t, p.36b, p.37t, p.38, p.40m, p.41tr & bl. Martine Collings: p.23, p.26, p.31, p.34–35, p.36m, p.39, p.40b, p.41tr & br. Valerie Hill: p.28br, p.29b, p.32m, p.33b, p.37m.

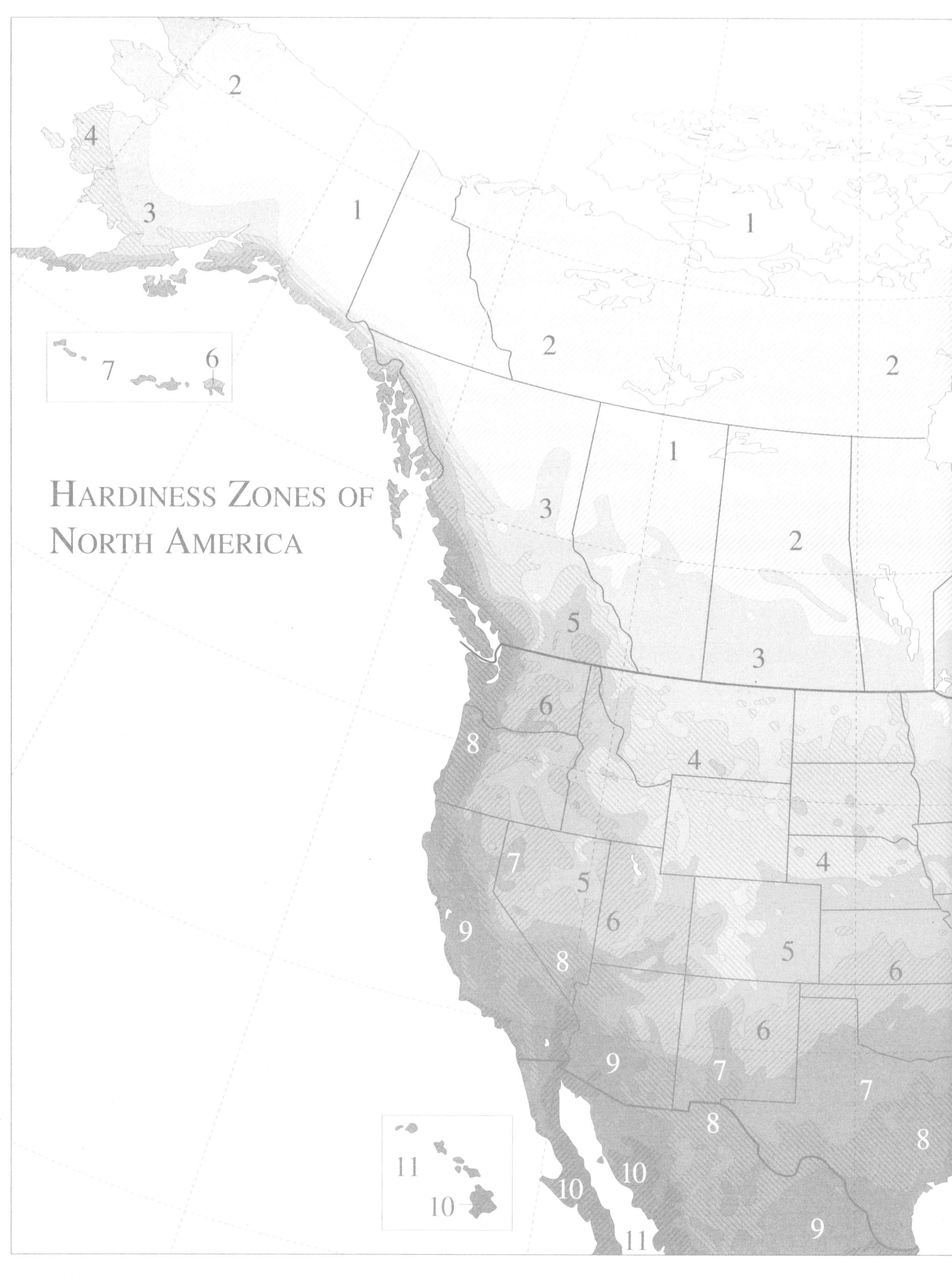
HARDINESS ZONES OF
NORTH AMERICA
1
2
3
4
5
6
7
8
9
10
11